THE GREAT
CONTEMPORARY
ISSUES

SOUTHEAST ASIA

OTHER BOOKS IN THE SERIES

THE GREAT CONTEMPORARY ISSUES

SOUTHEAST ASIA

The New York Times

ARNO PRESS

NEW YORK / 1980

DREW MIDDLETON
Introduction

GENE BROWN
Editor

Library of Congress Cataloging in Publication Data
Main Entry under title
Southeast Asia.
  (The Great Contemporary issues)
  Bibliography: p.
  Includes INdex.
  1. Asia, Southeastern — History — Addresses, essays, lectures. I. Middleton, Drew, 1913- II. Brown, Gene. III. Series: Great contemporary issues.
Ds526.6.S65   959   80-21640
ISBN 0-405-13399-5
Manufactured in the United States of America

Contents

Publisher's Note About the Series

It would take even an accomplished speed-reader, moving at full throttle, some three and a half solid hours a day to work his way through all the news The New York Times prints. The sad irony, of course, is that even such indefatigable devotion to life's carnival would scarcely assure a decent understanding of what it was really all about. For even the most dutiful reader might easily overlook an occasional long-range trend of importance, or perhaps some of the fragile, elusive relationships between events that sometimes turn out to be more significant than the events themselves.

This is why "The Great Contemporary Issues" was created—to help make sense out of some of the major forces and counterforces at large in today's world. The philosophical conviction behind the series is a simple one: that the past not only can illuminate the present but must. ("Continuity with the past," declared Oliver Wendell Holmes, "is a necessity, not a duty.") Each book in the series, therefore has as its subject some central issue of our time that needs to be viewed in the context of its antecedents if it is to be fully understood. By showing, through a substantial selection of contemporary accounts from The New York Times, the evolution of a subject and its significance, each book in the series offers a perspective that is available in no other way. For while most books on contemporary affairs specialize, for excellent reasons, in predigested facts and neatly drawn conclusions, the books in this series allow the reader to draw his own conclusions on the basis of the facts as they appeared at virtually the moment of their occurrence. This is not to argue that there is no place for events recollected in tranquility; it is simply to say that when fresh, raw truths are allowed to speak for themselves, some quite distinct values often emerge.

For this reason, most of the articles in "The Great Contemporary Issues" are reprinted in their entirety, even in those cases where portions are not central to a given book's theme. Editing has been done only rarely, and in all such cases it is clearly indicated. (Such an excision occasionally occurs, for example, in the case of a Presidential State of the Union Message, where only brief portions are germane to a particular volume, and in the case of some names, where for legal reasons or reasons of taste it is preferable not to republish specific identifications.) Similarly, typographical errors, where they occur, have been allowed to stand as originally printed.

"The Great Contemporary Issues" inevitably encompasses a substantial amount of history. In order to explore their subjects fully, some of the books go back a century or more. Yet their fundamental theme is not the past but the present. In this series the past is of significance insofar as it suggests how we got where we are today. These books, therefore, do not always treat a subject in a purely chronological way. Rather, their material is arranged to point up trends and interrelationships that the editors believe are more illuminating than a chronological listing would be.

"The Great Contemporary Issues" series will ultimately constitute an encyclopedic library of today's major issues. Long before editorial work on the first volume had even begun, some fifty specific titles had already been either scheduled for definite publication or listed as candidates. Since then, events have prompted the inclusion of a number of additional titles, and the editors are, moreover, alert not only for new issues as they emerge but also for issues whose development may call for the publication of sequel volumes. We will, of course, also welcome readers' suggestions for future topics.

Introduction

The steady expansion of American political, military and economic involvement in Southeast Asia is one of the most significant developments of the second half of this strident century. This expansion is part of a growing national awareness in the United States of the importance of Southeast Asia to all Americans; a border scuffle between Russians and Chinese on the Usuri River, a revolution in the Philippines, the failure of the rice crop in Thailand all would have a direct impact upon our national policies.

The United States fought the longest and least successful war in its history in Vietnam, now the most powerful country in Southeast Asia. The Philippines were America's first and most successful experiment in colonial rule. United States economic investment in the states of the Pacific basin exceeds that in Western Europe. Militarily America is pledged to assist in the defense of Japan, the Philippines and Thailand. The boldest diplomatic initiative of recent American history was the decision to establish friendly relations with the People's Republic of China which is deeply involved militarily and politically in the affairs of Southeast Asia.

Since Admiral Dewey fought and won the battle of Manila Bay in 1898 there has been American interest in Southeast Asia. But until 1941 America's major involvement lay in Europe. This was understandable. It was the great European powers — Britain, Germany, France, Russia — that exerted the greatest influence on world politics. Moreover throughout the first half of the century powerful economic links between the United States and Europe proliferated. Today, however, Americans look both east and west. And to many, Asia is the more intriguing. They will not be disappointed in the contents of this book. For *The New York Times* news stories present a fascinating picture of opulence and famine, heroism and betrayal, feeble democracies and rigid totalitarianism.

The sun glitters on the great dome of the Arakan Buddha's pagoda in Mandalay, Vietnamese troops burst into the streets of Saigon after more than 20 years of war. The streets and roads and rivers of Indonesia run red with the blood of slain Communists. The tide of Japanese soldiery spreads over Thailand. Malaya in the most successful anti-Communist campaign in Asia quells Communist-led rebellion. And with these scenes, are old, half-forgotten names of leaders — Sukarno and Ho Chi Minh, Ngo Dinh Diem and Bao Dai — and place names creep in and out of the headlines — Dien Bien Phu, Da Nang, Kuala Lumpur, Phnom Penh.

The sad conclusion the reader must reach is that democracy anywhere is a tender flower easily withered by the blasts of war, and the hardships of economic depression. For in the great arc of states that runs from Singapore to Manila, democracy as Americans or West Europeans know it is virtually non-existent. Yet when the imperialist powers departed in the aftermath of World War II most of the emerging states set their political courses toward the establishment of democracies. They had the best intentions and in some cases the best advice. But democracy eluded them.

In some instances the establishment of self-government meant hardship. Burma, once the rice bowl of Southeast Asia, now has to import rice. The economies of Cambodia and Vietnam are a shambles. The corruption that so offended Americans when they glimpsed it in Saigon during the war now appears endemic to the governments of the area.

The earliest clippings from *The New York Times* give us a glimpse of the last days of imperialism in the area. The British are busy in Burma eliminating slavery and in Singapore they build the lavish fortifications that are to protect the city from attack by sea — an attack that never came. The French move into what is now Vietnam in 1883 and by 1928 boast that it is a valuable colony.

The Americans are building their model colony in the Philippines after quelling a local insurrection which inspired the soldier song whose final verse runs:

"And beneath the starry flag
Civilize them with a Krag*
And return us to our own beloved home."

The Dutch and the British have divided the East Indies in 1982 without any tiresome poll of the islanders' wishes. In 1926 the Dutch kill 260 Indonesians and offer the stock excuse that the rebels were inspired by the Soviet Union.

The Japanese come later. In 1940 the invade northern

*The Krag-Jorgensen rifle.

Thailand and in July 1940 the supine government of Vichy France sanctions their invasion by treaty. The Japanese were the last and militarily the most successful imperialists in Southeast Asia. At the Rising Sun's zenith, Tokyo's writ ran from Manila to Singapore. Only the combined efforts of the United States and the British Empire ousted them. The erosion of imperialism began before World War II. In the Philippines, Malaysia, the Dutch East Indies and Burma the first tentative movements toward independence developed. Understandably these were hailed by progressives around the world who, perhaps unwisely, equated a desire for independence with an equally strong desire for the establishment in the independent states of democracy. Independence came. Democracy was different.

The Second World War sounded the knell of imperial rule in Southeast Asia. It is possible that had the war not occurred the Europeans would have been able to hang on a little longer. But not much longer. There was a ferment through Asia in the late thirties.

The United States and Britain understood sooner than the other states that the old order was finished. The British, their economy shattered by the war, already were divesting themselves of responsibility in India and, moving eastward, did the same in Burma, Malaya and Singapore.

The Philippine Republic was born in July 1946. Liberal Americans always had been a little ashamed of colonial rule in the Philippines but the democratic Administration of Harry S. Truman was not so liberal that it overlooked the strategic importance of the islands. At the time the republic was born, negotiations were under way to secure sea and air bases in the Philippines on a 99 year lease.

It was at this point in the immediate post-war years that the long Vietnamese struggle began. The original components included Ho Chi Minh, an able and intelligent Vietnamese leader, a series of stubbornly obtuse French governments who failed to realize that it was the second half of the 20th rather than the 19th century, the Soviet Union's penchant for fishing in troubled waters and aiding the Vietnamese with arms and advice and, finally, the economic and psychological exhaustion of France after five years of defeat, humiliation and painful regeneration.

The French experience in Vietnam had a powerful impact on the west's involvement in Southeast Asia. The defeat of a French army in the battle of Dien Bien Phu set alarm bells ringing in Washington. President Dwight D. Eisenhower enunciated his "domino theory" which held that once one country of the region fell to Communism, others would follow.

Great sport was made with this by opponents of American involvement in Asia. But there was much in what Eisenhower said. By 1980 Communism ruled the mainland of Southeast Asia from Vietnam's border with China around to the northeastern frontier of Thailand.

Dien Bien Phu finally convinced the French the game was up. A treaty was concluded at Geneva that divided Vietnam into a Communist "Democratic" Republic in the north and a Republic of Vietnam, allegedly democratic, in the south. The last vestiges of imperialism save for a few tiny and unimportant outposts were gone. What was Southeast Asia like?

From the economic standpoint it was rich, both actually and potentially. The imperialists had discovered oil in Burma and Indonesia, they had produced rubber in Malaya, improved agriculture in the Philippines and Vietnam. The region by any standards was far better off than the new People's Republic of China whose economy, already shattered by civil war, was under the somewhat erratic ministrations of Chairman Mao.

It is noteworthy, too, that, as these pages show, the end of the foreign rule did not mean the end of foreign investment and commercial and technical help. The British remained an economic power in Malaysia, and in Singapore. The Dutch administered the economy of the East Indies and the French plantation owners and businessmen held on in South Vietnam.

The political picture was a good deal less promising. Reports by *New York Times* correspondents throughout the area paint a sad picture of assassinations and coups, riots and rebellions.

In the Philippines for example, long held as a model of political stability, the Hukbalahap insurrection broke out and was put down with the utmost severity by the Philippine Constabulary, originally raised and trained by Americans. In Malaysia local Communists armed and advised by their Chinese colleagues launched a guerrilla war against the government. Only British intervention guided by a group of exceptionally able soldiers and civil servants brought peace to the land. The Dutch, whose withdrawal was long and agonizing, were still fighting in Indonesia in 1947 with the usual results against guerrillas; victory whenever the guerrillas offered battle but more often a long-drawn bitter little war of ambush and assassination.

The circumstances were not favorable for the growth of democratic governments and it is not surprising that few grew. Instead the prevailing political trend was toward one man rule; Sukarno in Indonesia, Ngo Dinh Diem in South Vietnam, Sihanouk in Cambodia, Lee Kuan Yew in Singapore.

Dictatorship verging on totalitarianism did not, however, quiet the turbulence and insure stability. As the fifties ended the area showed few signs of economic or political improvement.

This period also was one of growing involvement in Southeast Asia by three of the world's great powers, the United States, the Soviet Union and the People's Republic

of China. The Russians and Chinese, in pursuit of their individual national interests stoked the fires of insurrection
wherever flames burned. The Communist Pathet Lao in
Laos received nearly 2,000 plane loads of Soviet arms during one six month period. The Chinese harried Burma's
northern frontier and tested Thai defenses. The United
States began to take the first fateful footsteps toward intervention in Vietnam.

The Vietnamese, as we see, were not solely anti-French
or anti-American. They were strongly nationalist and they
hated the Chinese (who at some sacrifice had helped them
during the war) as much as they did the Americans.

The American operations in Vietnam were characterized
by a few brilliant operations on a small scale, an astigmatic
view of what was happening in Washington, and continued
political turbulence in Saigon. It is very clear that successive governments in the south failed to institute the
reforms that the Americans urged upon them, that corruption was as bad as anywhere in Asia and that South Vietnamese troops would not or could not fight for the defense
of their country. There were, in every case, exceptions but
on the whole the overview of South Vietnam that emerges
from these pages is accurate.

In the spring of 1975 the North Vietnamese launched
their final offensive.

They moved with stunning speed and success. The last
American troops had left Vietnam and the bombing of the
north had ended in 1973. The South Vietnamese army so
carefully trained and so lavishly equipped by the United
States crumbled under fierce attacks or found itself encircled by superior tacticians.

Hue, a scene of some of the most successful fighting
during the American involvement, was abandoned. The
great bases at Da Nang and Camh Ran Bay were taken.
The North Vietnamese supported by the peasants in the
countryside thrust closer to Saigon.

On April 21 President Nguyen Van Thieu resigned, denouncing the Americans as untrustworthy allies. On April
30, his successor, Duoang Van Minh announced the
south's unconditional surrender as the northern army
swept into the capital. Two weeks earlier Phnom Pen, the
capital of Cambodia, had fallen to the guerrillas of the
Khmer Rouge. The quiet of the concentration camp and
the grave settled over Indochina.

The Southeast Asia that has emerged in the five years
since the final elimination of South Vietnam, Cambodia
and Laos as independent states in many ways appears more
dangerous than that of the fifties.

The Vietnamese, "the Prussians of Asia," despite grave
economic difficulties have taken control of Cambodia and
Laos. In each country there are occasional spurts of
resistance which are methodically eliminated by the best
disciplined and equipped army in the region.

The Pol Pot regime in Cambodia, an odious tyranny
supported by the P.R.C., has been supplanted by a
somewhat more modern Communist government supported by Vietnam. Vietnamese troops have established
themselves on the Thai frontier leading that country's
shaky government to ask for more American arms aid.

Ferdinand E. Marcos after years of martial law runs the
Philippines with his relatives and friends prospering and
with few signs of any return to democracy.

Singapore and Malaysia are islands of relative stability.
The Thais, cursed with a long frontier and the hostility of
the Chinese and the Vietnamese, are in a perilous position,
one made no better by their involved internal political
situation. The East Indies are relatively quiet under the
rule of Suharto, Sukarno's successor, but there, too,
economic problems multiply.

Political turbulence and economic hardship are the bases
for further discord. No one who reads the dispatches in
this book can feel optimistic about the future of Southeast
Asia.

China and Russia are the two elements in the situation
with which the book, because of its regional limitation,
does not deal. The Soviet Union is pumping $3 million of
economic and military aid into Vietnam each day in return
for political support against China and the use of the
American-built bases at Da Nang and Cam Ranh Bay.
Russia has replaced America as the primary outside power
in Southeast Asia.

China's position is more obscure.

Peking has long aspired to the leadership of Southeast
Asia seeing the region as a sphere of interest akin to
Russia's in eastern Europe. But China today does not have
the economic resources to exploit its ambitions. Nor has
military intervention been spectacularly successful.

The People's Liberation Army invaded northern Vietnam in February 1979. Success was limited. The Chinese
had intended to "teach the Vietnamese a lesson." It was the
P.L.A. that learned the lesson that well armed troops,
holding well built defenses cannot be driven out by armies
deficient in modern weapons.

The future, mercifully, is hidden to man. We cannot
now predict the course of events in Southeast Asia. But on
the evidence of the past 35 years three assumptions seem
warranted. One is that political turbulence, intermittently
broken by small wars, will continue. A second is that the
current economic decline will continue except in
Singapore, Malaysia and, perhaps, Thailand. The third is
that Russia, China and, perhaps, the United States will be
involved in the region's tangled destinies.

— *Drew Middleton*

CHAPTER 1

Southeast Asia Colonized

Raffles Hotel in Singapore, built in 1886. W. Somerset Maugham wrote of this symbol of Britain's colonial past that it "stands for all the fables of the exotic East."

UPI

THE PHILIPPINE ISLANDS.

Facts About the Archipelago, Where Spain Again Finds Trouble.

The Philippine Islands—Islas Filipinas, as they are called in Spanish—form a large archipelago of from 1,200 to 1,400 islands in the southeast of Asia, extending from 4 degrees 40 minutes to 20 degrees north latitude, and from 116 degrees 40 minutes to 126 degrees 30 minutes east longitude, and the islands cover a land area of 115,528 square miles. Only 400 of these islands, however, are inhabited. The population is estimated at 8,000,000.

On the west and northwest, the archipelago is separated by the China Sea from China and the Indo-Chinese Peninsula; to the east is the Pacific, on the north a number of small islands stretch toward Formosa, and to the southwest is Borneo and the Celebes Sea.

The principal islands are Luzon in the north, Mindanao in the south, and Patawan, Panay, and Mindoro in the middle of the group. The islands are traversed by a chain of mountains from north to south, rising in some of them to nearly 9,000 feet.

There is a good deal of mineral wealth in the archipelago. There are two extensive coal fields, one in South Luzon and another in the western slopes of Cebu and eastern slopes of Negros, probably extending under the Straits of Tañon. There is plenty of iron ore of excellent purity in Luzon and other islands, and there are copper mines in the Province of Lepanto. Gold is found in many of the islands, but in very small quantities.

The climate varies in different islands, but the characteristics are tropical, and three seasons are known—the cold, hot, and rainy. The cold or cool season is between February and March, the hot from March to June, and then follows the wet, during which the rainfall is often very heavy. Terrific thunderstorms often take place in May and June.

The productions of the islands are mangoes, plantains, jack fruit, and other Malayan fruits; potatoes, sweet potatoes, gourds, peas, and rice, which is the staple food of the inhabitants, and of which the natives often do not raise sufficient quantities for their own use. Other products are Manila hemp, coffee, and tobacco, which is a Government monopoly.

The archipelago is said to be of volcanic origin, and several volcanoes still exist. Monte Caqua, nearly 4,000 feet in height, on the northeast promontory of Luzon, always smokes, and there is a regular volcano in Babuyan Claro. Several craters are situated in a small triangular island in Lake Bombon, or Bongbong. Earthquakes are frequent, and several very severe ones have occurred during the present century.

The islands were discovered by Magellan in 1521, and were settled by the Spaniards during the reign of Philip II., after whom they were named.

Formerly there was a large trade between these islands and China and Japan, but Spain placed so many restrictions in favor of its own trade that that was practically broken up. The exports from the islands now amount to about $16,000,000 annually, and the imports to about $15,000,000, and consist of machinery, linens, coal, iron, earthenware, hardware, woolens, and apparel.

Manila is the seat of government and the residence of the Governor General, who is appointed by the Spanish sovereign. Most of the public revenue is derived from duties on imports and exports, the tobacco monopoly, and a capitation tax.

The Governor General is invested with supreme powers, and is assisted by a junta of authorities, consisting of the Archbishop, the commander of the forces, the Admiral, and the President of the Supreme Court. Every Indian has to pay a tax of $1.17, but descendants of the first Christians of Cebu and new converts are exempt. Chinese are subject to special taxes, and Europeans and Spanish half-castes have to pay a poll tax of $2.50.

The press is under strict civil and ecclesiastical control, and all discussion of Spanish or general European politics is forbidden.

The original inhabitants of the Philippines are supposed to be the Aetas, or Negritos, so-called from their dark complexion, but they are rapidly disappearing. They were driven into the more inaccessible parts by successive invasions of Malay tribes, who now form a large proportion of the population.

There are many Chinese, and in Manila alone they number over 30,000. Of Europeans there are not over 10,000. Large numbers of Japanese have immigrated to the Philippines, and during the last Chinese-Japanese war there was talk of an invasion of the islands by the Japanese after the termination of the war.

September 3, 1896

PHILIPPINE REBELS YIELD

Chief Aguinaldo and the Insurgent Government Agree to Go to Hongkong.

MADRID JOYFUL AT THE NEWS

A Report that the Spanish Royal Family Is in Danger from an Uprising Qualified by News of the Victory.

MADRID, Dec. 16.—An extraordinary number of the Gazette, issued to-day, publishes dispatches received from Manila, capital of the Philippine Islands, saying that the insurgent chief, Aguinaldo, has ordered all his followers to submit, and that he and the entire insurgent Government will be allowed to go to Hongkong.

Marshal Primo Rivera, the Governor General of the Phillipines, has sent a dispatch to the Government, according to The Gazette, saying that in his opinion the submission of the rebels is the result of the recent Spanish victories, and that a peace has been attained, which leaves Spain's honor secure. He asks the Government's approval of the steps he has taken, and sanction for the rebel chiefs to emigrate.

Señor Segasta, the Premier, telegraphed the necessary authority in reply, with congratulations and an expression of the Queen Regent's satisfaction.

In answer to this Gen. Rivera telegraphed that the rebels had embodied their submission in a document very honorable to Spain. He added, " I ordered Gen. Teigiro to suspend operations on condition that the rebel government would start for Hongkong the same day. Lieut. Col. Primo Rivera accompanies them in conformity with their request for a personal guarantee."

At the Cabinet Council to-day Señor Gullon, the Minister for Foreign Affairs, read dispatches from Washington which, it is said, gave " general satisfaction."

December 17, 1897

WAR ALMOST CERTAIN

Expected by the Administration, Congress, and the Army and Navy.

War between this country and Spain seems inevitable according to the latest news from Washington and Madrid.

It is settled beyond question that the United States will not be turned from its purpose to free Cuba. Unless Spain shall ask a reopening of negotiations with this country for the purpose of arranging terms for Cuba's freedom, the President will send a message to Congress recommending armed intervention in Cuba, and there is no doubt that the response from Congress will be a declaration of war.

The President has not receded an iota from his determination to end the dominion of Spain in Cuba. This fact was manifest in an impressive way in the reply the President made to the representatives of six of the great powers of Europe, who called on him to express the hope that war between this country and Spain might be averted.

" The Government of the United States," said the President, " appreciates the humanitarian and disinterested character of the communication now made on behalf of the powers named and for its part is confident that equal appreciation will be shown for its own earnest and unselfish endeavors to fulfill a duty to humanity by ending a situation the indefinite prolongation of which has become insufferable."

The news from Madrid offers no suggestion of yielding by the Spanish Government. On the contrary, it indicates that Spain means to fight. Nevertheless great pressure continues to be exerted upon the Spanish Government by persons and European powers for the purpose of persuading it to make concessions to this country.

April 8, 1898

NAVAL BATTLE IMMINENT

Dewey's Squadron Sails from Hongkong to Capture the Philippine Fleet.

CHIEF AGUINALDO WITH IT

Spanish Warships Taking Up Position for Engagement—Forts Will Support Them—British Cruiser to Follow Our Ships.

LONDON, April 28.—The Hongkong correspondent of The Times, telegraphing yesterday, says:

" The American fleet, headed by the flagship Olympia, sailed at 2 o'clock this afternoon direct for Manila. The British cruiser Immortalité will follow the American squadron."

The Hongkong correspondent of The Daily Mail says:

" United States Consul General Williams, after spending the evening ashore with United States Consul Wildman, accompanied the American squadron. Thirty insurgent leaders here wanted to accompany it, but Chief Aguinaldo goes as their representative. He will take charge of the insurgent forces at Manila. Admiral Dewey has issued strict orders that no barbarous or inhuman acts are to be perpetrated by the insurgents.

" The primary object is the capture of the Spanish fleet, which Admiral Dewey thinks more important than capturing Manila. He is determined to prevent its preying upon American vessels. On reaching Manila he will demand its capitulation within half an hour of his arrival.

" His men are in the best spirits and excellent health. There have been nine desertions, including six Chinamen, one Italian, and one German, during the fleet's stay at Hongkong. Every preparation has been made. The ships are cleaned and painted for battle, and the general opinion is that the fight in these waters will result in an easy victory for America. Her ships carry 122 guns, as against 96 or thereabout in the Spanish fleet.

Manila Forts in Bad Condition.

" The co-operation of the American fleet with the rebels has been kept a strict secret. The latter await the arrival of the fleet, when Manila must soon succumb. Its defenses are in a wretched state. The Americans in the Philippines are anxious to see British rule established there, and the proposal has been favorably received here.

" The Manila press, on the contrary, says there is great enthusiasm among the population for Spain, and that an obstinate resistance will be offered to the Americans, but the papers qualify this bold allegation by referring to the 'phlegmatic character of the natives, which prevents any excited expression of opinion.' These journals say, too, that the treason of a few hundreds or a few thousands of the rebels does not affect the virtue of the race, and they haughtily add that the Philippines will prove worthy of Spain.

" The Governor of the Philippines has issued several proclamations. One requires all able-bodied Spaniards to enroll themselves for military service, and accords permission to foreigners to join. Exemption is granted to all American citizens.

A Queer Proclamation.

" One extraordinary proclamation has excited great distrust here. It asserts that ' the American people are composed of all social excrescences, who have exhausted our patience and provoked war with their perfidious machinations, their acts of treachery, and their outrages against the law of nations and international conventions.'

" The proclamation proceeds to say: ' A squadron manned by foreigners, possessing neither instruction nor discipline, comes to this archipelago with the ruffianly intention of robbing us of all that means life, honor, and liberty. The aggressors shall not profane the tombs of your fathers. They shall not gratify their lustful passions at the cost of your wives and daughters. They shall not cover you with dishonor or appropriate the property your industry has accumulated as a provision for your old age. They shall not perpetrate any of the crimes inspired by their wickedness and covetousness because your valor and patriotism will suffice to punish these miserable people, who, claiming to be civilized and cultivated, have exterminated the unhappy natives of North America instead of bringing to them the light of civilization and of progress.' "

According to a special dispatch received here yesterday from Madrid, the Spanish Minister of Marine, Admiral Bermejo, received a cipher mesage from the Spanish Admiral in command at Manila, Admiral Monteje, announcing that after taking the measures necessary to organize the naval defenses of Manila and Cavite, he was about to sail with his squadron to take up a position and await the coming of the United States fleet.

The Minister of Marine forthwith communicated with Premier Sagasta, who summoned the Minister of War, Gen. Correa, and the three Ministers held a conference.

Shortly afterward another dispatch arrived from the Captain General of the Philippine Islands, detailing the military measures he is taking to support the action of the Spanish squadron and to defend Manila, Cavite, and other places against any American attempt to land in combination with the insurgents.

Sensation in Madrid.

The news soon reached the clubs and the newspapers and created an immense sensation.

The Minister of Marine expressed the belief that the United States squadron would reach Manila in about sixty hours, and a battle, therefore, is expected in about three days.

The naval men here who are acquainted with the Philippine Islands believe the Spanish squadron will take up position near Cavite, so as to be supported by the batteries there and at Manila.

Many Spanish vessels, according to a dispatch from Manila to The Daily Telegraph, are leaving the capital of the Philippines, crowded with passengers and carrying much treasure. The dispatch says the American squadron is anticipating rich prizes.

April 28, 1898

POSTSCRIPT

4:30 A. M.

VICTORY AT MANILA

The Governor General of the Philippines Concedes a Spanish Defeat.

SHIPS BLOWN UP, SUNK, AND BURNED.

MADRID, May 1.—The following is the text of an official dispatch from the Governor General of the Philippines to the Minister of War, Lieut. Gen. Correa, received here at 8 P. M., reporting a naval engagement off Manila to-day:

" Last night, April 30, the batteries at the entrance to the fort announced the arrival of the enemy's squadron, forcing a passage under the obscurity of the night. At daybreak the enemy took up positions, opening with a strong fire against Fort Cavite and the arsenal.

" Our fleet engaged the enemy in a brilliant combat, protected by the Cavite and Manila forts. They obliged the enemy with heavy loss to manoeuvre repeatedly. At 9 o'clock the American squadron took refuge behind the foreign merchant shipping on the west side of the bay.

" Our fleet, considering the enemy's superiority, naturally suffered a severe loss. The Maria Christina is on fire, and another ship, believed to be the Don Juan de Austria, was blown up.

" There was considerable loss of life. Capt. Cadarso, commanding the Maria Christina, is among the killed. I cannot now give further details. The spirit of the army, navy, and volunteers is excellent."

Ships Sunk to Avoid Capture.

An official telegram received at a later hour from the Governor General of the Philippines says:

" Admiral Montejo has transferred his flag to the cruiser Isla de Cuba from the cruiser Reina Maria Christina. The Reina Maria Christina was completely burned, as was also the cruiser Castilla, the other ships having to retire from the combat, and some being sunk to avoid their falling into the hands of the enemy."

The official dispatch does not mention the destruction of any American vessel, although it says that the United States Squadron finally cast anchor in the bay behind the foreign merchantmen.

Another official dispatch from the Governor General of the Philippines says: " The equipping of volunteers continues. We are ready to oppose any debarkation and to defend the integrity of the country."

Report of the Spanish Naval Bureau.

The Naval Bureau at Manila sends the following report of the encounter with the United States squadron, signed " Montejo, Admiral ":

" In the middle of the night the American squadron forced the forts, and before daybreak appeared off Cavite. The night was completely dark. At half-past 7 the bow of the Reina Maria Christina took fire, and soon after the poop also was burned. At 8 o'clock, with my staff, I went on board the Isla de Cuba. The Reina Maria Christina and the Castilla were then entirely enveloped in flames.

" The other ships having been damaged retired into Baker Bay. Some had to be sunk to prevent their falling into the hands of the enemy. The losses are numerous, notably Capt. Cadarso, a priest, and nine other persons."

May 2, 1898

A PHILIPPINE REPUBLIC NOW

Aguinaldo Proclaims Its Birth on July 3 and Says He Can Take Manila Any Day.

GERMANS LANDING SUPPLIES

Floods Cover the Country for a Radius of Eighteen Miles About Manila— Gen. Monet Sent Back to the Troops He Deserted.

LONDON, July 8.—The Hongkong correspondent of The Times says:

"Gen. Aguinaldo, on July 3, proclaimed the birth of the Philippine Republic. He claims to be ready to take Manila any day. The steamer Eddie reports that the Germans are landing supplies north of Manila at nightfall, and that the rebels are still harassing the Spaniards."

The Hongkong correspondent of The Daily Mail says:

"The whole country, within a radius of eighteen miles of Manila, is flooded. Gen. Monet's arrival astonished everybody. He reported that his soldiers, whom he had deserted, were starving and surrounded by thousands of rebels. He was ordered back to Pampanga."

July 8, 1898

OUR PUPILS IN POLITICS.

We may be obliged to maintain schools of instruction in civil government in Cuba and the Philippines for many years. It will be a noble duty, and we should not shrink from it. The Cubans are but imperfectly prepared for self-government. They would get on after a fashion, no doubt, but their politics would be factional and turbulent, revolutions frequent, and the reign of law and order uncertain. The poor Filipinos are still more backward. AGUINALDO, to be sure, is full of politics. Pronunciamientos flow glibly from his pen, and his organizing mind grasps all the details of civil institutions, down to the showy golden collar and the jeweled cane. But he is a precocious child of nature. Few of his compatriots are abreast of him. A very large part of the people of the island have not now, and perhaps never will have, any capacity for governing themselves.

Nevertheless, during the period of our military control of Cuba and the Philippines we can easily put the native genius for administration to the test by admitting all who are worthy to participation in local government. Even in autocratic Russia the peasants get in their village councils no little practice in the forms and duties of government. When it was proposed to grant a Constitution based on the suffrage, it was held that the subjects of the Czar would be able at once to assume intelligently their new rights and duties. We should have little difficulty in setting up the machinery of local self-government in Cuba, where, in spite of the gleeful assertions of some opponents of the war, the natives are not all brigands or all worthless.

The natives of the Philippines will be less manageable, but if we can win their confidence and destroy the influence of the corrupt monks, the experiment will not be hopeless. The mistake of inviting either the Filipinos or the Cubans to enjoy at once the blessings of universal suffrage we shall not, of course, commit. We did make the mistake of giving the ballot to the negroes at the close of our civil war, and it has proved a costly mistake for the blacks and for the country. Blind sentiment misled us then. We abhorred slavery because it was based on the false and inhuman assumption that one race of men was of an animal inferiority to another race of men. Destroying that cruel inequality by the emancipation proclamation, we went too far and tried to make the freedmen the political and even the social equals of their late masters. The attempt has failed because the blacks were not fitted for the duties they were asked to perform, and our mistaken kindness brought great misery on them. We shall be in no danger of being carried away by sentiment now. The fundamental principle of our own institutions is that government rests upon the consent of the governed. We must apply that principle as far and as fast as we can in the possessions we have taken from pain so long as we hold them. But neither in Cuba, in the Philippines, in Puerto Rico, nor in our own Hawaii shall we be obliged by principle or consistency to fly in the face of reason and experience by putting votes into the hands of men who can make no intelligent use of them. A few years of experimenting with the natives will instruct them in the duties of freemen and ourselves in regard to their capacities.

July 27, 1898

Anti-Imperialist League Protest.

WASHINGTON, Nov. 25.—The Anti-Imperialist League, an organization originating in Massachusetts and of which ex-Gov. Boutwell is President, to-day, through its Secretary, Mr. Erving Winslow of Boston, presented to President McKinley a "protest against any extension of the sovereignty of the United States over the Philippine Islands in any event, and over any other foreign territory without the free consent of the people thereof, believing such action would be dangerous to the Republic, wasteful of its resources, in violation of Constitutional principles, and fraught with moral and physical evils to our people." The President informed Mr. Winslow of his willingness to receive from the league any plan it might offer short of surrender of the islands to Spain.

November 26, 1898

AGUINALDO IS DEFIANT

Issues a Manifesto at Manila After Gen. Otis's Proclamation.

PROTESTS AGAINST OUR SWAY

Says We Recognized Rebels as Belligerents—Urges His Followers to Stand Firm.

MANILA, Jan. 7.—Within a few hours of the proclamation issued by Gen. Otis, in behalf of President McKinley, the agents of Aguinaldo billed Manila with a manifesto which attracted considerable attention. The revolutionary President protested against Gen. Otis signing himself Military Governor of the Philippine Islands.

Aguinaldo in this manifesto declared he had never agreed, at Singapore, Hongkong, or elsewhere, to recognize the sovereignty of the Americans here, and insisted that he returned to the Philippines on an American warship solely to conquer the Spaniards and win independence. He asserted that both his proclamations of May 24 and June 12 stated this fact officially, and he claimed that Major Gen. Merritt confirmed this by a proclamation days before the Spaniards capitulated, stating clearly and definitely that the American forces came to overthrow the Spanish Government and liberate the Filipinos.

In conclusion, Aguinaldo declared that he had natives and foreigners as witnesses that the American forces recognized not only by acts that the Filipinos were belligerents but by publicly saluting the Filipino flag "as it triumphantly sailed these seas before the eyes of all nations."

Aguinaldo then solemnly protested, in the name of the Deity who empowered him to direct his brethren in the difficult task of regeneration, against the intrusion of the American Government, and reiterated that

he can produce proof that he was brought here on the understanding that the Americans promised him their co-operation to attain independence.

The revolutionary leader then called upon all his followers to work together with force, assuring them he is convinced that they will obtain absolute independence, urging them never to return "from the glorious road" on which they have "already so far advanced."

Gen. Otis attaches no importance to the manifesto. He says he feels confident that the opinion of the better classes of the Filipinos is not expressed in it, but as to whether the Filipino masses can be controlled and the Filipino Army kept in check he does not know, although he hopes for a pacific outcome of the trouble.

MADRID, Jan. 7.—Gen. Rios, in command of the Spanish troops in the Philippine Islands, cables that the hostility between the Americans and the Tagalos is increasing.

January 8, 1899

FIGHT AT MANILA WITH FILIPINOS

American Troops Attacked by Aguinaldo's Forces.

HOSTILE NATIVES WHIPPED

Driven Back by the Fire of Our Soldiers and Warships.

MANILA, Feb. 5—8:15 P. M.—The long-expected rupture between the Americans and Filipinos has come at last. The clash came at 8:45 yesterday evening, when three daring Filipinos darted past the

Nebraska regiment's pickets at Santa Mesa, but retired when challenged.

They repeated the experiment without drawing the sentries' fire. But the third time Corp. Greely challenged the Filipinos and then fired, killing one of them and wounding another. Almost immediately afterward the Filipinos' line, from Coloacan to Santa Mesa, commenced a fusillade, which was ineffectual.

The outposts of the Nebraska, Montana, and North Dakota regiments replied vigorously, and held their ground until reinforcements arrived. The Filipinos, in the mean time, concentrated at three points, Coloacan, Gagalangin, and Santa Mesa.

At about 1 o'clock this morning the Filipinos opened a hot fire from all three places simultaneously. This was supplemented by the fire of two siege guns at Balik-Balik and by an advance of their skirmishers at Poco and Pandacan. The Americans responded with a terrific fire, but owing to the darkness they were unable to determine its effect.

The Utah Light Artillery finally succeeded in silencing the native battery. The Third Artillery also did good work on the extreme left. The engagement lasted over an hour.

The United States cruiser Charleston and the gunboat Concord, stationed off Malabon, opened fire from their secondary batteries on the Filipinos' position at Coloacan and kept it up vigorously. At 2:45 there was another fusillade along the entire line, and the United States seagoing double-turreted monitor Monadnock opened fire on the enemy from off Malate.

With daylight the Americans advanced. The California and Washington regiments made a splendid charge and drove the Filipinos from the villages of Poco and Santa Mesa. The Nebraska regiment also distinguished itself, capturing several prisoners and one howitzer and a very strong position at the reservoir, which is connected with the waterworks. The Kansas and Dakota regiments compelled the enemy's right flank to retire to Coloacan.

There was intermittent firing at various points all day long.

The losses of the Filipinos cannot be estimated at present, but they are known to be considerable. The American losses are estimated at 20 men killed and 125 wounded. The Ygorates, armed with bows and arrows, made a very determined stand in the face of a hot artillery fire, and left many men dead on the field.

Several attempts were made in this city last evening to assassinate American officers.

February 6, 1899

PROCLAMATION AT MANILA

The American Commissioners Outline Plans of Government.

SELF-GOVERNMENT IS GRANTED

Supremacy Over the Islands " Must and Will Be Enforced " — Policy Heralded to the Natives.

MANILA, April 4.—The United States Philippine Commission issued a proclamation to-day reviewing the situation here and outlining the Government's policy. The proclamation contains eleven articles, declaring America's intentions, as follows:

1. The supremacy of the United States must and will be enforced throughout every part of the archipelago, and those who resist can accomplish nothing except their own ruin.

2. The amplest liberty of self-Government will be granted which is reconcilable with the just, stable, effective, and economical administration, and compatible with the sovereign rights and obligations of the United States.

3. The civil rights of the Filipinos will be guaranteed and protected, their religious freedom will be assured, and all will have equal standing before the law.

4. Honor, justice, and friendship forbid the exploitation of the people of the islands. The purpose of the American Government is the welfare and advancement of the Philippine people.

5. It guarantees an honest and effective civil service in which, to the fullest extent practicable, natives shall be employed.

6. The collection and application of taxes and other revenues will be put upon a sound, honest, and economical basis. The public funds, raised justly and collected honestly, will be applied only to defraying the proper expenses of the establishment and maintenance of the Philippine Government, and such general improvements as public interests demand. Local funds collected for local purposes shall not be diverted to other ends. With such prudent and honest fiscal administration it is believed the needs of the Government will in a short time become compatible with a considerable reduction in taxation.

7. The establishment of a pure, speedy, and effective administration of justice, by which the evils of delay, corruption, and exploitation will be effectually eradicated.

8. The construction of roads, railroads, and other means of communication and transportation, and other public works of manifest advantage to the people will be promoted.

9. Domestic and foreign trade and commerce and other industrial pursuits and the general development of the country in the interest of its inhabitants will be the constant objects of solicitude and fostering care.

10. Effective provision will be made for the establishment of elementary schools, in which the children of the people will be educated. Appropriate facilities will also be provided for higher education.

11. Reforms in all departments of the Government, all branches of the public service, and all corporations closely touching the common life of the people must be undertaken without delay and effected conformably with common right and justice, in a way to satisfy the well-founded demands and the highest sentiments and aspirations of the Philippine people.

The preamble of the proclamation of the commission recites the cession by the Peace Treaty of the Philippine Islands to the United States, refers to the appointment of the commission, assures the people of the cordial good-will and fraternal feeling of the President of the United States and the American people, and asserts the object which the United States Government, apart from the fulfillment of its solemn obligations, as assumed toward the family of nations by the acceptance of the sovereignty over the islands, is the well-being, prosperity, and happiness of the Philippine people, and their elevation and advancement to a position among the most civilized peoples of the world.

Continuing, the proclamation says: " The President believes this felicity and perfection of the Philippine people will be brought about by the cultivation of letters, science, and the liberal and practical arts, by the enlargement of intercourse with foreign nations, the expansion of industrial pursuits by trade and commerce, by the multiplication and improvement of means of internal communication, and by the development of the great natural resources of the archipelago.

" Unfortunately, these pure aims and purposes of the American Government and people have been misinterpreted to some of the inhabitants of certain islands, and in consequence the friendly American forces, without provocation or cause, have been openly attacked. Why these hostilities? What do the best Filipinos desire? Can it be more than the United States is ready to give? They say they are patriots and want liberty. The commission emphatically asserts that it is willing and anxious to establish an enlightened system of government under which the people may enjoy the largest measure of home rule and the amplest liberty consonant with the supreme ends of the government, and compatible with those obligations which the United States has assumed toward the civilized nations of the world."

The proclamation then says there can be no real conflict between American sovereignty and the rights and liberties of the Filipinos, for America is ready to furnish armies and navies and all the infinite resources of a great and powerful nation to maintain its rightful supremacy over the islands, so it is even more solicitous to spread peace and happiness among the people and guarantee them rightful freedom, to protect their just privileges and immunities, to accustom them to free self-government in ever-increasing measure, and to encourage those democratic aspirations, sentiments, and ideals which are the promise and potency of fruitful National development.

In conclusion, the proclamation announces that the commission will visit the Philippine provinces to ascertain the enlightened native opinion as to the forms of government adapted to the people, conformable with their traditions and ideals, invites the leading representative men to meet the commission, and declares the policy of the United States, in the establishment and maintenance of the Government, is to consult the wishes and secure the advice and co-operation of the people.

The belief is spreading among the residents here that the effect of the capture of Malolos, the former rebel capital, followed by the proclamation of the United States Philippine Commission, will be to convince the natives that Aguinaldo's bubble has burst.

Dr. Schurman, President of the commission, said: " The Filipinos have been asking unceasingly: ' What do you propose to do for us?' The proclamation answers the question, and it should satisfy them."

Col. Charles Denby, member of the commission and former Minister to China, remarked: ' It is the most important proclamation since the Declaration of Independence. Spanish, Tagalman, and English versions have been printed, and it is proposed to circulate them about Malolos and at all the seaports. They will be sent to the lake towns by gunboats."

April 5, 1899

PROGRESS IN THE PHILIPPINES.

WASHINGTON, April 3.—Gen. Otis has cabled to the War Department, probably with a view to correcting erroneous impressions that exist in this country as to the state of the insurrection in the Philippines, a summary of the result of the development of the campaign since the first of the calendar year. His figures go far toward offsetting the belief that exists in some quarters that since the adoption of guerrilla methods of warfare the insurgents have inflicted substantial loss upon American arms in comparison with the punishment which they have themselves received.

A significant sentence in the report differentiates insurgents and ladrones, showing that Otis has taken cognizance of the fact that a considerable number of the hostiles are not soldiers under the rules of war, and may not expect the same treatment. The report, which is dated Manila, April 3, is as follows:

"Since Jan. 1, 124 skirmishes in Philippines have been reported, mostly very slight affairs. Our casualties were 3 officers and 78 enlisted men killed, 13 officers and 151 men wounded. Insurgent and ladrone loss in killed and left on field, 1,426; captured, mostly wounded, 1,453; small arms secured, 3,051; pieces of artillery, 165; large captures of other insurgent property. A number of important insurgent officers are surrendering, and the situation is gradually becoming more pacific."

April 4, 1900

AGUINALDO IS NOW A PRISONER

MANILA, March 28.—Gen. Frederick Funston's daring project for the capture of Aguinaldo in his hiding place in the Province of Isabella, Island of Luzon, has proved completely successful.

Aguinaldo was captured there March 23.

The United States gunboat Vicksburg, Commander E. B. Barry, with Gen. Funston and Aguinaldo on board, arrived here this morning.

March 28, 1901

AGUINALDO TAKES THE OATH

Accepts the Terms of the Amnesty Proclamation.

He Will Remain in Custody for the Present—Gen. MacArthur Hopes to Accomplish Much Through Him.

Special to The New York Times.

WASHINGTON, April 2.—The War Department received to-day information from Gen. MacArthur that Aguinaldo has taken the oath of allegiance to the United States under the terms of amnesty offered by Gen. MacArthur by direction of the President. The cablegram as given out by the department is as follows:

Manila.

Adjutant General, Washington:

Since arrival at Manila Aguinaldo has been at Malacanan investigating conditions in archipelago. He has relied almost entirely upon the instructive advice of Chief Justice Arellano. As a result to-day he subscribed and swore to the declaration on Page 11 of my annual report.

MacARTHUR.

The oath referred to is as follows:

"I, ———, hereby renounce all allegiance to any and all so-called revolutionary Governments in the Philippine Islands, and recognise and accept the supreme authority of the United States of America therein; I do solemnly swear that I will bear true faith and allegiance to that Government; that I will at all times conduct myself as a faithful and law-abiding citizen of the said islands, and will not, either directly or indirectly, hold correspondence with or give intelligence to an enemy of the United States, nor will I abet, harbor, or protect such enemy; that I impose upon myself these voluntary obligations without any mental reservations or purpose of evasion, so help me God."

April 3, 1901

DUAL RULE IN PHILIPPINES

Civil Governor Taft Inaugurated at Manila.

Ceremony Enhanced by Receipt of Message of Congratulation from President McKinley—Gen. MacArthur Sails.

MANILA, July 4.—Civil government in the Philippines was auspiciously inaugurated to-day. Commissioner William H. Taft was escorted by Gens. MacArthur and Chaffee from the palace to a great temporary tribune opposite the Plaza Palacio. Standing on a projecting centre of the Tribuna, Mr. Taft, Civil Governor of the Philippine Islands, took the oath of office, which was administered by Chief Justice Arellano. Gov. Taft was then introduced by Gen. MacArthur, a salute being fired by the guns of Fort Santiago.

A feature of the inaugural address of Gov. Taft was the announcement that on Sept. 1, 1901, the Philippine Commission would be increased by the appointment of three native members. Dr. Wardo Detavera, Benito Legarda, and José Luzuriaga. Before the 1st of September departments will exist as follows, heads having been arranged thus: Interior Commissioner—Worcester; Commerce and Police Commissioner—Wright; Justice and Finance Com-

missioner—Ide; Public Instruction Commissioner—Moses.

Of the twenty-seven provinces organized, Civil Gov. Taft said the insurrection still exists in five. This will cause the continuance of the military government in these provinces. Sixteen additional provinces are reported without insurrections, but as yet they have not been organized. Four provinces are not ready for civil government.

Gov. Taft predicted that with the concentration of troops into larger garrisons it would be necessary for the people to assist the police in the preservation of order. Fleet launches will be procured, he said, which will facilitate communication among the provinces as well as aid the Postal and Revenue Departments. In connection with educational efforts, Civil Gov. Taft said that adults should be educated by an observation of American methods. He said that there was a reasonable hope that Congress would provide a tariff that would assist in the development of the Philippines instead of an application of the United States tariff. According to the Civil Governor, there is an unexpended balance in the Insular Treasury of $3,700,000 and an annual income of $10,000,000.

Gov. Taft said that any possible friction between civil and military subordinates should be discouraged. The patriotism of the leading Filipinos was commended. In conclusion Civil Gov. Taft reiterated a hope expressed by the President that in the future the inhabitants would be grateful for the American Philippine victories, and that they would be indissolubly linked in ties of affection with the common country.

The reading of President McKinley's message of congratulation was enthusiastically cheered. The entire front of the Tribuna, a block long, was decorated with flags, and several hundred officers, with their families and friends, were seated therein. Gen. MacArthur, Civil Gov. Taft, and Military Gov. Chaffee occupied the

centre, with the other Generals on their right. Rear Admiral Kempff and his staff were on their left. The United States Commissioners and the Justices of the Supreme Court were immediately in the rear with the foreign Consuls. The mass of the people stood in the park opposite. The Filipino leaders were there, but there were more Americans than Filipinos present.

The President's message is as follows:

"TAFT, Manila:

"Upon the assumption of your new duties as Civil Governor of the Philippine Islands I have great pleasure in sending congratulations to you and your associate Commissioners and my thanks for the good work already accomplished. I extend to you my full confidence and best wishes for still greater success in the larger responsibilities now devolved upon you and the assurance not only for myself, but for my countrymen, of good will for the people of the islands, and the hope that their participation in the Government which it is our purpose to develop among them may lead to their highest advancement, happiness, and prosperity.   "WILLIAM McKINLEY."

The transfer of the military authority to Gen. Chaffee was carried out in the presence of the Generals in Gen. MacArthur's office. There was no formality. Gen. MacArthur presented the new commander to the Generals and remarked:

"I bequeath to you all my troubles."

All the high civil and army officers accompanied Gen. MacArthur to the river front, where he formally embarked. Gov. Taft and Gen. Chaffee then returned to the palace and received the public.

The closing event of the celebrations of the Fourth of July was a reception in honor of Gen. MacArthur at the residence of the Civil Governor. Mrs. Taft and Mrs. Chaffee assisted in receiving the guests. The United States Army transport Meade sailed to-night for Nagasaki with Gen. MacArthur and the members of his staff on board.

July 5, 1901

FRIARS MAKE A CONTRACT

Deal Completed to Buy Their Lands for $7,239,784.

Special to The New York Times.

WASHINGTON, Dec. 23.—The settlement of the long controversy over the friars' lands in the Philippines is nearing the end. A cablegram was received at the War Department to-day from Gov. Taft saying

that an agreement had been reached to pay in bonds the sum of $7,239,784 for 391,000 acres involved in the purchase.

A conference between Secretary Root and Secretary Shaw followed at the White House, and it was decided to issue $7,000,000 of 4 per cent. bonds, redeemable after ten and within thirty years, to liquidate the payment. This is an average of $18.51 an acre for the land thus purchased. The lands were not bought in a lump, but were appraised and the sums named represent the totals. All the lands are regarded as very valuable as agricultural properties, being mainly sugar, coffee, and hemp pro-

ducers. The lands will be offered for sale early in January.

The Philippine Government will sell the lands to the natives for a reasonable price, giving the occupying tenants the preference and allowing the payments to extend over a convenient period of years. Six months will be allowed to resurvey the lands, examine and verify titles, and make all necessary arrangements for the transfer to the Government. The bonds will be paid to the Pope, and not to the orders in the Philippines. The fund will, however, remain in the islands to be used in establishing churches, schools, and charitable insti-

7

tations under the auspices of the Church.

It is expected that there will be a good deal of trouble in getting possession of some of the lands. There are several hundred friars in the islands who claim that the proceeds should be theirs, and they have resorted to various means to thwart the transfer to the Philippine Government. In some cases they have sold to fictitious stock companies, and in others have transferred to others in trust. The Pope has, however, announced his rule of action in the matter to this Government, and there is little doubt as to the ultimate success of Gov. Taft's project of securing the lands for the people who live on them, and at the same time of ridding the islands of the objectionable friars.

Over a thousand friars have departed, and there now remain very few that are received by their parishes or have any stand-

ing whatever in any part of the archipelago. Following this settlement of the controversy over the lands of the friars there will be inaugurated a policy of sending young Filipino students to the United States to be educated for the priesthood, and there will from this time forward be a growing disposition to send priests from the United States to the Philippines. Spanish priests, it is declared, will no longer be sent there by the Church of Rome.

Cardinal Gibbons, who has been consulted throughout the negotiations, will have control of the details of the new policy. The agreement for the sale of the lands is the result of conferences extending over many months between Gov. Taft and his Cabinet and Bishops Rooker, Hendricks, and Dougherty, who were sent to the islands for the purpose.

Some details concerning the issue of the bonds yet have to be worked out, but no doubt is expressed that a ready market for

them will be found in this country. During the past seven months an aggregate of $6,000,000 of 4 per cent. Philippine bonds have been issued and floated in the United States in lots of $3,000,000 each. More than half these bonds are now on deposit with the Government as security for public money. The bonds previously issued were sold on terms regarded as favorable to the Government, each lot of $3,000,000 commanding a figure above par. It is believed that the forthcoming issue also will bring a good price.

MANILA, Dec. 23.—The agreement for the sale of the friars' lands has been signed, to take effect in six months, the time allowed for surveys and examination of titles.

The bureau organized to administer the affairs of these lands will dispose of them when possible to the present tenants on long terms of payment. Three-fourths of this land is included within the populated districts, which makes it a difficult proposition for the Administration's bureau.

December 24, 1903

INDEPENDENCE PARTY WINS.

Philippine Elections Show Nationalists Are in the Lead.

MANILA, July 30.—The independence factions that united in the campaign under the name of the Nationalists appear to have won the general election held throughout the islands to-day. Complete returns from 50 out of 80 districts show that 31 Nationalists were elected, 10 Progressives, 8 Independence candidates, and 1 Catholic.

In Manila the Nationalists won by a large majority in both districts. Dominador Gomez claims the election in the First District in the city, while Justo Lakban contests the election of both Independence candidates.

It probably will be ten days or two weeks before the complete returns are received.

The people do not seem to realize the methods of the management of the election. The authorities are trying to impress the voters with the idea that the election is entirely within the control of the people.

July 31, 1907

VALUE OF PHILIPPINES.

Furnish a Good Training Ground for American Soldiers.

To the Editor of The New York Times:

Your leader for to-day is so clean-cut a piece of work, is so clear and forcibly put, that it made a distinct impression upon the writer, as doubtless upon all thinking readers of THE TIMES. The Philippines are not often enough in our thoughts, as an enormous problem, upon which our children's children will still be at work, I believe. They have been studied from many angles, but it would seem that one point of view remains without the attention which surely it deserves.

In the opinion of the writer, perhaps the one greatest reason for maintaining our hold as a nation upon this collection of savage and semi-savage peoples is the opportunity it has given us to enable our soldiers to become the real article, and not merely—regulars and volunteers alike—carpet soldiers; men who

have never seen powder burned in anger, nor heard the zip of a rifle bullet fired by a military enemy worthy of consideration as such.

Now that our Indians, through process of elimination, have become "good" and no longer are severely troublesome to outlying districts of our country, what opportunities offer for the real training of our men? Aside from the Philippines, none at all worth mentioning. And yet were we to be at war with some power, using against us an army of seasoned soldiers, they would inevitably sweep us away like chaff, costing, at least in our earlier battles, many thousands of lives and the bitter mortification of defeat. Nobody of sense can question this; and it would result from the lack, among officers and men alike, of opportunities granted them in which and whereby to become professionals instead of amateurs at war.

Let us thank God for the Philippines, therefore. In them our troops have had for years now the genuine article of

real fighting and rough living, and hardships such as are needed for their best interests, and ours, ultimately.

Regarded from a financial standpoint, the Philippines certainly have not paid. Far from it. But having put our hand to this plow we cannot without disgrace turn back. And neither should we wish to do so. We are a blessing there to the mixed multitudes of relatively unstable equilibrium. And in a wholly different way, no less are they a blessing to us, particularly the more savage tribes, as I have endeavored to point out.

It rather looks at this present moment of writing as if Mexico bids fair to contribute a similar and further blessing. At least, it behooves us to try to regard it in that light.

ROBERT H. M. DAWBARN.
New York, Nov. 17, 1913.

November 20, 1913

WILSON PROMISES TO HELP FILIPINOS GET INDEPENDENCE

Secretary Baker Reads His Letter to Delegation Making Formal Demand.

PLEDGES HIS OWN SUPPORT

Memorial from Islands Legislature Presented by Forty Prominent Citizens.

NEW CONGRESS TO DECIDE

Governor General Harrison Expresses Belief That Past Opposition Has Disappeared.

WASHINGTON, April 4.—The Philippine Islands today, through a delegation of forty prominent Filipinos headed by Manuel Quezon, President of the Filipino Senate, asked for complete independence. They presented a memorial from the Filipino Legislature to Secretary of War Baker, who not only assured them of his agreement with their views, but read to them a letter written by President Wilson to him in which the President, with foreknowledge of the visit and its purpose, expressed the hope that it would gain the desired end.

The fate of the Filipino plea rests with the next Congress.

President Wilson's letter to Secretary Baker under date of March 3 was as follows:

"Will you please express the gentlemen of the commission representing the Philippine Legislature my regret that I shall be unable to see them personally on their arrival in Washington, as well as my hope that their mission will be a source of satisfaction to them, and that it will result in bringing about the desirable ends set forth in the joint resolution of the Legislature approving the sending of the commission to the United States?

"I have been deeply gratified with the constant support and encouragement received from the Filipino people and from the Philippine Legislature in the trying period through which we are passing. The people of the United States have, with reason, taken the deepest pride in the loyalty and support of the Filipino people.

"Though unable to meet the commission, the Filipino people shall not be absent from my thoughts. Not the least important labor of the conference which now requires my attention is that of making the pathway of the weaker people of the world less perilous—a labor which should be, and doubtless is, of deep and abiding interest to the Filipino people.

"I am sorry that I cannot look into the faces of the gentlemen of this mission of the Philippine Islands and tell them all that I have in mind and heart as I think of the patient labor, with the end almost in sight, undertaken by the American and Filipino people for their permanent benefit. I know, however, that your sentiments are mine in this regard and that you will translate truly to them my own feeling."

Secretary Baker's Promise.

In receiving the Filipino delegates, Secretary Baker said:

"My first duty is to convey to you an expression of the President's regret at his absence from Washington at the time of your visit. When it was first suggested that the mission should come to the United States, the President foresaw his absence and caused me to suggest that the visit be deferred in the hope that he might be personally here when the mission came and have an opportunity to meet you and hear your views and express his own. It has turned out, however, that his engagements in Europe required his return there and so he is unable to be in Washington now to receive you. He left, before he went, a letter addressed to me which he asked me to read to you.

"We have long been fortunate in the representatives whom you have chosen to send to us. Those who are here now are all men of temperate judgment, fine aspirations, and have worthily represented the Filipino people. This larger group of men has come charged by the Legislature of the Insular Government with this mission of visiting the United States, and making known to the people of the United States the fact of the Philippine progress, the growth and development of political capacity in the islands, the spread of education, and the natural growth of aspirations for political independence. You are to make all this known to the people of the United States.

"For a long time the Philippine people had been discussing among themselves their aspirations. As soon as the United States became involved in the great enterprise of the world war, the Philippine people with fine self-restraint abandoned the discussion of that question as inopportune at the time, and threw all their energies and their resources into the common weal with the people of the United States, so that throughout the entire period of the war the relations between the people of the United States and your people have been those of cordial co-operation and confidence and growing appreciation and esteem.

"When the United States went into the Philippine Islands, it set up a military government. What has been going on is the rapid progress and development of a new civilization in the Philippine Islands; not an Americanization of the islands, but the growth of a Philippine civilization. It is normal that people should desire to be free and independent.

"The Philippine Islands are almost independent; your Legislatures govern the islands. The strongest tie between the Philippine Islands and the United States at present is this tie of affection of which I speak, rather than the political. I know that I express the feeling of the President, I certainly express my own feeling. I think I express the prevailing feeling in the United States when I say the time has substantially come, if not quite come, when the Philippine Islands can be allowed to sever the more formal political tie remaining and become an independent people, and I trust as you go about the United States and address audiences you will not hesitate to paint the picture of the past relations between the people of the United States and the Filipino, of the progress which you have made, the extent to which your islands are self-governing and the almost exclusive extent to which the officers of the executive administration are filled by the native sons of your own islands.

"I am myself in favor of Philippine independence. I trust the day is very close at hand when it can be formally accomplished and when it will no longer be necessary for your children in your public schools to write essays and make orations on the aspirations of your people, but when the theme of those essays and the theme of those orations can be one of appreciation of a fact accomplished, and all the energy of your people can be devoted to the further development of the fine civilization which is already inaugurated there.

"America is proud of the Philippine Islands, and her pride will increase, rather than cease, when they cease to be her political possession and become her political sister in the sisterhood of nations."

Francis Burton Harrison, Governor General of the Philippines, expressed sentiments identical with those voiced by Secretary Baker. The formal act granting independence, he said, was one that Congress must take up, and the Administration would present the matter to Congress at the appropriate time. From his own experience in two months' stay at home, he added, he could assure the mission that the objection to Filipino independence that seemed to prevail in the United States a few years ago had greatly diminished, if it had not virtually vanished.

The Filipino Memorial.

In presenting the formal memorial asking for complete independence, Senor Quezon said in part:

"Independence is the great national ideal of the Filipino country, and we believe this is the proper time to present the question, looking to a favorable and decisive action, because of the declared and uniform policy of America to withdraw her sovereignty over the Phillipines and to recognize our independence as soon as a stable government has been established. There now is a stable government and the fulfillment of this solemn promise you owe to yourselves, to us and to humanity at large.

"You have truly treated us as no nation ever before has treated another under its sway, and yet you—will none better than you—will understand why, even under such conditions, our people still crave independence, that they, too, may be sovereign masters of their own destinies."

The Philippines have had self-government since Oct. 16, 1916. By act of Congress, approved Aug. 29, 1916, better known as the Jones bill, the old Philippine Commission was abolished, there being substituted as the Upper House of the Legislature a Senate, composed of twenty-four members, and, instead of the Assembly, a House of Representatives of ninety members, all elected at triennial elections, excepting two Senators and nine Representatives appointed by the Governor General to represent the non-Christian provinces.

The political attitude of the present Administration was set forth in the preamble to the Jones bill, which declared "it was never the intention of the people of the United States in the incipiency of the war with Spain to make it a war of conquest or for territorial aggrandizement," that "it has always been the purpose of the people of the United States to withdraw their sovereignty over the Philippine Islands and to recognize their independence as soon as a stable government can be established therein," and that "for the speedy accomplishment of such purpose it is desirable to place in the hands of the people of the Philippines as large a control of their domestic affairs as can be given them without, in the meantime, impairing the exercise of the rights of sovereignty by the people of the United States, in order that, by the use and exercise of popular franchise and governmental powers, they may be the better prepared to fully assume the responsibilities and enjoy all the privileges of complete independence."

HOLD PHILIPPINES, WOOD REPORT SAYS

Governor General and W. Cameron Forbes Recommend "Present General Status" Continue.

FIND DISQUIETING FACTORS

People Not Yet Organized to Defend Themselves Against "Any Powerful Nation."

FOR CHANGES IN JONES LAW

Would Give Governor General "Authority Commensurate With the Responsibilities of His Position."

WASHINGTON, Nov. 29.—The Philippine Islands should remain in their "present general status" until the people there "have had time to absorb and thoroughly master the power already in their hands," former Major Gen. Leonard Wood, now Governor General, and W. Cameron Forbes, former Governor General, say in their report to President Harding, based on their six months' study of conditions in the islands.

"We are convinced," they say, "that it would be a betrayal of the Philippine people, a misfortune to the American people, a distinct step backward in the path of progress and a discreditable neglect to our national duty were we to withdraw from the islands and terminate our relationship there without giving the Filipinos the best chance possible to have an orderly and permanently stable Government.

"We feel that, with all of their many excellent qualities, the experience of the last eight years, during which they have had practical autonomy, has not been such as to justify the people of the United States in relinquishing supervision of the Government of the Philippine Islands, withdrawing their army and navy and leaving the islands a prey to any powerful nation coveting their rich soil and potential commercial advantages."

These observations of the investigators are contained in the "general conclusions" and "recommendations" made in the report, which was made public today. The complete report, covering 100 typewritten pages, will be made public later.

General Conclusions of the Inquiry.

The "general conclusions" are as follows:

"We find the people happy, peaceful and in the main prosperous and keenly appreciative of the benefits of American rule.

"We find everywhere among the Christian Filipinos the desire for independence, generally under the protection of the United States. The non-Christians and Americans are for continuance of American control.

"We find a general failure to appreciate the fact that independence under the protection of another nation is not true independence.

"We find that the Government is not reasonably free from those underlying causes which result in the destruction of government.

"We find that a reasonable proportion of officials and employes are men of good character and ability and reasonably faithful to the trust imposed upon them; but that the efficiency of the public services has fallen off and that they are now relatively inefficient due to lack of inspections and to the too rapid transfer of control to officials who have not had the necessary time for proper training.

"We find that many Filipinos have shown marked capacity for government service and that the young generation is full of promise; that the civil service laws have in the main been honestly administered, but there is a marked deterioration due to the injection of politics.

"We find there is a disquieting lack of confidence in the administration of justice, to an extent which constitutes a menace to the stability of the government.

"We find that the people are not organized economically nor from the standpoint of national defense to maintain an independent government.

"We find that the legislative chambers are conducted with dignity and decorum and are composed of representative men.

"We feel that the lack of success in certain departments should not be considered as proof of essential incapacity on the part of Filipinos, but rather as indicating lack of experience and opportunity and especially lack of inspection.

"We find that questions in regard to confirmation of appointments might at any time arise which would make a deadlock between the Governor General and the Philippine Senate."

Chief Recommendations.

These recommendations are made in the report:

"We recommend that the present general status of the Philippine Islands continue until the people have had time to absorb and thoroughly master the powers already in their hands.

"We recommend that the responsible representative of the United States, the Governor General, have authority commensurate with the responsibilities of his position. In case of failure to secure the necessary corrective action by the Philippine Legislature we recommend that Congress declare null and void legislation which has been enacted diminishing, limiting or dividing the authority granted the Governor General under act No. 240 of the Sixty-fourth Congress known as the Jones bill.

"We recommend that in case of a deadlock between the Governor General and the Philippine Senate in the confirmation of appointments that the President of the United States be authorized to make and render the final decision.

"We recommend that under no circumstances should the American Government permit to be established in the Philippine Islands a situation which would leave the United States in a position of responsibility without authority."

November 30, 1921

COOLIDGE DECLARES FILIPINOS NOT READY FOR INDEPENDENCE

Roxas Is Told by President in Letter That Time Is Not Ripe for Separation.

REASONS GIVEN IN DETAIL

Special to The New York Times.
WASHINGTON, March 5.—President Coolidge has put an end for the time being to any hope of success of the present agitation looking to granting immediate independence to the Philippine Islands. A letter written by the President and made public at the White House today makes clear that any measure of Congress proposing to grant complete self rule to the Filipinos within the near future will be disapproved by him.

The letter was addressed to Manuel Roxas, Speaker of the Philippine House of Representatives and Chairman of the Philippine mission now in Washington. While it is dated Feb. 21, Speaker Roxas said that it was not received by him until today. He declared that

"President Coolidge hasn't anything to do with it anyhow," and explained that he meant that the effort of the Philippine mission to obtain independence and bring about the removal of Governor General Wood was a matter for Congress and not for the President except in so far as it concerned some measure laid before him for approval or disapproval.

The President's letter to Señor Roxas reads:

The White House,
Washington,
Feb. 21, 1924.

My dear Mr. Roxas:
The resolutions adopted by the Senate and House of Representatives of the Philippines, touching upon the relations between the Filipino people and the Government of the United States, have been received. I have noted carefully all that you have said regarding the history of these relations. I have sought to inform myself so thoroughly as might be, as to the occasions of current irritation between the Legislature of the Philippines and the executive authority of the islands.

In your presentment you have set forth more or less definitely a series of grievances, the gravamen of which is that the present executive authority of the islands, designated by the United States Government, is in your opinion out of sympathy with the reasonable national aspirations of the Filipino people.

If I do not misinterpret your protest, you are disposed to doubt whether your people may reasonably expect, if the present executive policy shall continue, that the Government of the United States will in reasonable time justify the hopes which your people entertain of ultimate independence.

The declaration of the Commission of Independence charges the Governor General with illegal, arbitrary and undemocratic policies, in consequence of which the leaders of Filipino participation in the Government have resigned and their resignations have been accepted by the Governor General.

The Commission of Independence declares that it is necessary "to take all needful steps, and to make use of all lawful means within our power to obtain the complete vindication of the liberties of the country now violated and invaded." It proceeds: "And we declare, finally, that this event, grave and serious as it is, once more demonstrates that the immediate and absolute independence of the Philippines, which the whole country demands, is the only complete and satisfactory settlement of the Philippine problem."

Moderation of Declaration Praised.

It is occasion for satisfaction to all concerned that this declaration is couched in terms of moderation, and that it goes no farther than to invoke "all lawful means within our power." So long as such discussions as this shall be confined to the consideration of lawful means, there will be reason to anticipate mutually beneficent conclusions. It is, therefore, a matter of congratulation which I herewith extend, that you have chosen to carry on this discussion within the bounds of lawful claims and means. That you have thus declared the purpose to restrict your modes of appeal and methods of enforcing it is gratifying evidence of the progress which the Filipino people, under American auspices, have made toward a demonstrated capacity for self-government.

The extent to which the grievances which you suggest are shared by the Filipino people has been a subject of some disagreement. The American Government has information which justifies it in the confidence that a very large proportion at any rate, and possibly a majority of the substantial citizenry of the islands, does not support the claim that there are grounds for serious grievance. A considerable section of the Filipino people is, further, of the opinion that at this time any change which would weaken the tie between the Filipinos and the American nation would be a misfortune to the islands.

The world is in a state of high tension and unsettlement. The possibility of either economic or political disorders calculated to bring misfortune, if not disaster, to the Filipino people unless they are strongly supported, is not to be ignored.

It should not be overlooked that within the past two years, as a result of international arrangements negotiated by the Washington Conference on Limitation of Armament and problems of the Far East, the position of the Filipino people has been greatly improved and assured. For the stabilizing advantages which accrue to them in virtue of the assurance of peace in the Pacific, they are directly indebted to the initiative and efforts of the American Government. They can ill afford in a time of so much uncertainty in the world to underrate the value of these contributions to their security.

By reason of their assurance against attack by any power; by reason also of that financial and economic strength which inevitably accrues to them; by reason of the expanded and still expanding opportunities for industrial and economic development—because of all these considerations, the Filipino people would do well to consider most carefully the value of their intimate association with the American nation.

Time for Independence Not Ripe.

Although they have made wonderful advances in the last quarter century, the Filipino people are by no means equipped, either in wealth or experience, to undertake the heavy burden which would be imposed upon them with political independence. Their position in the world is such that without American protection there would be the unrestricted temptation to maintain an extensive and costly diplomatic service and an ineffective but costly military and naval service.

It is to be doubted whether, with the utmost exertion, the most complete solidarity among themselves, the most unqualified and devoted patriotism, it would be possible for the people of the islands to maintain an independent place in the world for an indefinite future.

In presenting these considerations, it is perhaps worth while to draw your attention to the conditions in which some other peoples find themselves by reason of lacking such guarantees and assurances as the Filipino people enjoy. The burdens of armament and of governmental expenses which many small nations are compelled to bear in these times are so great that we see everywhere the evidence of national prosperity and community progress hindered, if not destroyed, because of them.

During the World War the Filipino people were comparatively undisturbed in their ordinary pursuits, left free to continue their fine progress. But it may well be doubted whether, if they had been shorn of the protection afforded by the United States, they could have enjoyed so fortunate an experience. Much more probably they would have become involved in the great conflict and their independence and nationality would have become, as did those of many other peoples, pawns in the great world reorganization.

There could be no more unfortunate posture in which to place a people such as your own. You have set your feet firmly in the path of advancement and improvement. But you need, above all else, assured opportunity of continuing in that course without interference from the outside or turmoil within. Working out the highest destiny of even the most talented and advanced of peoples is a matter of many generations.

A fair appraisal of all these considerations and others which suggest themselves which do not require enumeration will, I am sure, justify the frank statement that the Government of the United States would not feel that it had performed its full duty by the Filipino people, or discharged all of its obligations to civilization, if it should yield at this time to your aspiration for national independence.

Our Responsibility Unsought.

The present relationship between the American nation and the Filipino people arose out of a strange and almost unparalleled turn of international affairs. A great responsibility came unsought to the American people. It was not imposed upon them because they had yielded to any designs of imperialism or of colonial expansion. The fortunes of war brought American power to your islands playing the part of an unexpected and a welcome delivery. You may be very sure that the American people have never entertained purposes of exploiting the Filipino people or their country.

There have, indeed, been different opinions among our own people as to the precisely proper relationship with the Filipinos. There was some among us, as there are some among your people, who believe that immediate independence of the Filipinos would be best for both.

I should be less than candid with you, however, if I did not say that in my judgment the strongest argument that has been used in the United States in support of immediate independence of the Philippines is not the argument that it would benefit the Filipinos, but that it would be of advantage to the United States.

Feeling as I do, and as I am convinced the great majority of Americans do regarding our obligations to the Filipino people, I have to say that I regard such arguments as unworthy. The American people will not evade or repudiate the responsibility they have assumed in this matter.

The American Government is convinced that it has the overwhelming support of the American nation in its conviction that present independence would be a misfortune and might easily become a disaster to the Filipino people. Upon that conviction, the policy of this Government is based.

Philippine Internal Affairs.

Thus far I have suggested only some of the reasons related to international concerns, which seem to me to urge strongly against independence at this time. I wish now to review for a moment some domestic concerns of the Philippine Islands which seem also to argue against present independence. The American Government has been most liberal in opening to the Filipino people the opportunities of the largest practicable participation in, and control of, their own Administratin.

It has been a matter of pride and satisfaction to us, as I am sure it must also have been to your people, that this attitude has met with so fine a response. In education, in cultural advancement, in political conceptions and institutional development, the Filipino people have demonstrated a capacity which cannot but justify high hopes for their future.

But it would be idle and insincere to suggest that they have yet proved their possession of the completely developed political capacity which is necessary to a minor nation assuming the full responsibility of maintaining itself in the family of nations. I am frankly convinced that the very mission upon which you have addressed me is itself an evidence that something is yet lacking in development of political consciousness and capability.

One who examines the grounds on which are based the protests against the present situation is forced to conclude that there has not been, thus far, a full realization of the fundamental ideals of Democratic-Republican Government. There have been evidences of a certain inability, or unwillingness, to recognize that this type of governmental organization rests upon the theory of complete separation of the legisla... , executive, and judicial functions. There have been many evidences of disposition to extend the functions of the Legislature, and thereby to curtail the proper authority of the executive.

It has been charged that the present Governor General has in some matters exceeded his proper authorities, but an examination of the facts seems rather to support the charge that the legislative branch of the Insular Government has been the real offender, through seeking to extend its own authority into some areas of what should properly be the executive realm.

Confidence in General Wood.

The Government of the United States has full confidence in the ability, good intentions, fairness and sincerity of the present Governor General. It is convinced that he has intended to act, and has acted, within the scope of his proper and constitutional authority. Thus convinced, it is determined to sustain him, and its purpose will be to encourage the broadest and most intelligent cooperation of the Filipino people in this policy.

Looking at the whole situation fairly and impartially, one cannot but feel that if the Filipino people cannot cooperate in the support and encouragement of as good administration as has been afforded under Governor General Wood, their failure will be rather a testimony of unpreparedness for the full obligations of citizenship than an evidence of patriotic eagerness to advance their country.

I am convinced that Governor General Wood has at no time been other than a hard-working, painstaking and conscientious administrator. I have found no evidence that he had exceeded his proper authority or that he has acted with any other than the purpose of best serving the real interest of the Filipino people. Thus believing, I feel that I am serving those same interests by saying frankly that it is not possible to consider the extension of a larger measure of autonomy to the Filipino people until they shall have demonstrated a readiness and capacity to cooperate fully and effectively with the American Government and authorities.

For such cooperation I earnestly appeal to every friend of the islands and their people. I feel all confidence that in the measure in which it shall be extended, the American Government will be disposed to grant in increasing degree the aspirations of your people. Nothing could more regrettably affect the relations of the two peoples than that the Filipinos should commit themselves to a program calculated to inspire the fear that possibly the governmental concessions already made have been in any measure premature.

In conclusion, let me say that I have given careful and somewhat extended consideration to the representations you have laid before me. I have sought counsel of a large number of men whom I believed able to give the best advice. Particularly I have had in mind always that the American nation could not entertain the purpose of holding any other people in a position of vassalage.

In accepting the obligations which came to them with the sovereignty of the Philippine Islands, the American people had only the wish to serve, advance and improve the condition of the Filipino people. That thought has been uppermost in every American determination concerning the islands. You may be sure that it will continue the dominating factor in the American consideration of the many problems which must inevitably grow out of such relationship as exists.

Filipino People the Gainers.

In any survey of the history of the islands in the last quarter-century, I think the conclusion inescapable that the Filipino people, not the people of the United States, have been the gainers. It is not possible to believe that the American people would wish otherwise to continue their responsibility in regard to the sovereignty and administration of the islands. It is not conceivable that they would desire, merely because they possessed the power, to continue exercising any measure of authority over a people who would better govern themselves on a basis of complete independence.

If the time comes when it is apparent that independence would be better for the people of the Philippines, from the point of view of both their domestic concerns and their status in the world, and if when that time comes the Filipino people desire complete independence, it is not possible to doubt that the American Government and people will gladly accord it.

Frankly, it is not felt that that time has come. It is felt that in the present state of world relationship the American Government owes an obligation to continue extending a protecting arm to the people of these islands. It is felt also, that quite aside from this consideration, there remain to be achieved by the Filipino people many greater advances on the road of education, culture, economic and political capacity, before they should undertake the full responsibility for their administration. The American Government will assuredly cooperate in every way to encourage and inspire the full measure of progress which still seems a necessary preliminary to independence.

Yours very truly,
CALVIN COOLIDGE.

Blow to Filipino Agitators.

President Coolidge's unqualified support of General Wood will be a severe blow to the agitators who are behind the independence movement, which is suspected of being a mere cover of an attempt to have General Wood removed from office in order that the politicians responsible for the constant political turmoil in the islands may regain the practically free hand they had until General Wood undertook to overcome the difficulties in which the insular Government had become involved through mismanagement of the Philippine National Bank and essays into unprofitable business ventures.

Two days ago the Committee on Insular Affairs of the House of Representatives paved the way for Congressional consideration of the Philippine question by agreeing to prepare a measure providing for the independence of the islands. The vote to make the report was 11 to 5, but it was explained that several members of the committee who had voted with the majority were opposed to Philippine independence and had given their assent to the motion to report an independence measure merely to bring the problem of the Philippines squarely before the House.

This forward step appears now to have been robbed of any significance it may have assumed. For Congress to undertake consideration of the independence question in the light of President Coolidge's attitude, as expressed in his letter to Speaker Roxas, would be superfluous. Even the passage of a bill or resolution providing for immediate independence would receive the President's veto. Any other course on his part would be inconsistent with the utterances contained in his letter.

Roxas Assails the President.

Mr. Roxas, the youthful head of the Filipino Independence Mission, was not polite in his comment on the expressions of President Coolidge in opposition to immediate Philippine independence. He is quoted as saying to a representative of the Foreign Affairs News Service that President Coolidge's support of General Wood "is just another political move, similar to his defense of Attorney General Daugherty and other members of the Administration who have been attacked."

In its account of its interview with Speaker Roxas the Foreign Affairs News Service says:

"Chairman Roxas stated that the reply made by 'President Coolidge was not unexpected by members of the Independence Commission and that the fight for independence would be continued with undiminished vigor.

" 'President Coolidge hasn't anything to do with it, anyway,' Roxas continued. 'Our charges against the Wood Administration were made to Congress and not to the President; and the question of Philippine independence is also properly one for the consideration of Congress. The only time President Coolidge has a direct interest in the matter is when some measure comes up to him either for his veto or approval.'

"Roxas expressed surprise that the President should have addressed a personal letter to him. He also called attention to the fact that while President Coolidge's letter bears the date of Feb. 21, it was not mailed until March 4 and was received by him today. The Filipino leader attributed this delay to a desire on the part of the President to choose an opportune time for 'checking the growing favorable sentiment in the Senate toward Philippine independence.'

"Taking up various statements made by President Coolidge in his letter, Roxas declared the Chief Executive had stated conclusions without showing how he arrived at those conclusions, and added that information furnished by the commission had shown these conclusions often not to be warranted by the facts. For example, he said, President Coolidge seemed to think that the Philippine Legislature had been the offender in the controversy with General Wood, whereas in realty the Independence Mission had demonstrated that the blame lay with the Governor General.

"Roxas said he expected to make a reply to the President's letter, but indicated that this reply would be little more than a mere acknowledgment.

"The Filipino Chairman said he believed the President's letter would have the effect of spurring the Filipinos to greater efforts for independence. And he emphasized their intention to continue the fight before Congress, where something can be accomplished.

" 'Before we left the Philippine Islands for the United States we knew, as did every Filipino, that it would be useless to hope for the Administration's support in our fight for independence,' Roxas declared, 'therefore the President's letter occasioned no surprise among the members of the commission.'

"Asked whether the President's letter would cause any demonstration in the Philippines, Mr. Roxas said: 'No. My people will not be surprised by the attitude taken by President Coolidge. They understand Mr. Coolidge must play politics in the matter, but they do have faith in the American Congress.' "

March 6, 1924

HOLD ON TO THE PHILIPPINES BUT INCREASE HOME RULE, THOMPSON URGES COOLIDGE

SEES SOVEREIGNTY REMOTE

President's Investigator Says Natives Could Not Stand Alone.

PROPOSES CIVIL CONTROL

Would Have Islands Under a Separate Bureau and Drop Wood's Army Aides.

Special to The New York Times.

WASHINGTON, Dec. 22.—Indefinite postponement of absolute independence of the Philippines, but a gradual extension of internal autonomy, were recommended by Colonel Carmi A. Thompson of Cleveland to President Coolidge in Colonel Thompson's report on his mission to the islands, which was made public today when the President transmitted it to Congress.

The President and Colonel Thompson are in accord in holding that if the islands are to have independence of American rule it is a matter for consideration in the remote future.

Colonel Thompson, who spent three months in the Philippines last Summer as a special representative of Mr. Coolidge, advises that the question of independence be taken up when the islands are sufficiently developed to maintain an independent Government and that in the meantime there be granted such further freedom in the management of internal affairs as conditions may from time to time warrant.

In transmitting Colonel Thompson's report to Congress President Coolidge explained that he had contemplated making the report the basis for more specific recommendations concerning the Philippines than were contained in his annual message of Dec. 7, but he found "that the general line of his conclusions are in such close agreement with what is already recommended that this seems unnecessary."

The President, however, told Congress that he did not agree "entirely" with all Colonel Thompson's views and recommendations, but omitted any explanation of wherein they disagreed.

Wood's Army Aides Criticized.

From the fact that Colonel Thompson makes some indirect criticism of Major Gen. Leonard Wood's administration as Governor General, and the President, in his message, reiterates his recommendation of General Wood's course, the inference was drawn that their differences of opinion concerned General Wood's conduct of Philippine affairs.

In his message today the President repeated the comment of his annual message that General Wood had administered his office with tact and ability and to the advantage of the Filipino people.

While indicating that responsibility for friction in the management of Philippine affairs "appears to be divided between the executive and legislative branches of the Government," and that General Wood's military aides have been "one of the factors which have made such cooperation difficult," Colonel Thompson concedes that "on the whole General Wood is to be commended for his efficient conduct of affairs during his Administration."

An independent Government under present economic conditions would be impossible to maintain, according to Colonel Thompson. He takes direct issue with the Filipino independence politicians, who contend that the Filipino people are homogeneous. There are many languages and dialects and the Filipinos do not have the homogeneity and solidarity necessary to a strong, democratic nation, says Colonel Thompson. Independence before there is a common language would mean an oligarchy or a splitting-up of the people in warring factions, he adds.

Colonel Thompson declares "that no leader, either in politics or business, expects independence for a long time to come" and that he learned that, with the exception of a small radical minority, "all that the Filipinos really hope for is an ultimate settlement of their relations with the United States on a basis which would eventually give them complete autonomy in internal affairs, but with the United States directing all foreign relations."

Reports Urgent Need of Revenue.

Economic conditions in the islands he found to be very bad. Business was at a standstill and much unemployed labor was emigrating to Hawaii. Restrictive laws of the Philip-

pine Legislature make it impossible to obtain capital for economic development and many existing investments are regarded as unsafe. Unless there is more revenue it is impossible for the islands to go ahead, he reports.

Colonel Thompson's view is that the present restrictive laws against any large economic development of the Philippines with outside capital should be made more liberal, but by the native Legislature.

He thinks there is great possibility for rubber development and for other agricultural enterprises if the way is opened for the use of capital.

A right step would be to put the administration of Philippine affairs under a separate department of the Government or a bureau in a civilian department instead of in the War Department as at present. Colonel Thompson suggests. He recommends

that provision be made for supplying the Governor General with civil advisers instead of making him dependent upon officers detailed from the War Department.

He opposes the proposal for separating the Moro provinces from the rest of the islands, but thinks there should be stronger American control in the Moro country in place of the present Christian Filipino control.

Colonel Thompson sees no necessity for changing the Jones act, which is the fundamental law of the islands. He believes that business conditions would be improved by applying the Federal Reserve Bank system to the islands and establishing land banks there.

December 23, 1926

COOLIDGE VETOES FILIPINO PLEBISCITE ON INDEPENDENCE

He Says It Would Be Untimely and Unconvincing and Imperil the Islands' Well-Being.

Special to The New York Times.
WASHINGTON, April 6.—President Coolidge tonight rejected the holding of any plebiscite of the people of the

Philippine Islands on the question of independence.

In a veto message addressed to Major Gen. Leonard Wood, Governor General of the Philippines, the President returned without approval an act of the Philippine Legislature proposing such a plebiscite, turning it down on the ground that the result of such a vote by the Filipino people would be unconvincing, that discussion of the question of immediate or proximate absolute independence is untimely and submitting independence to a vote of the Filipinos, unless such action were requested by the American Congress, would be disturbing to good relations.

It is the first time an American President has vetoed any act of the Philippine Legislature, and the President's message, based on close and careful consideration of the whole question of American-Filipino relations, is regarded as an able State

paper intended not only to point out clearly, and rather frankly, to the Filipinos the attitude of the American Government in opposition to immediate independence but in a manner that would carry to them a full appreciation of all that American withdrawal from the islands would involve.

The plebiscite act was submitted to the President in compliance with Section 19 of the organic law of the Philippines, which vests the President with the right of veto over acts of the native Legislature.

President Coolidge reiterated with emphasis his view that the Government of the United States would not feel that it had performed its "full duty" by the Filipinos or discharged all of its obligations to civilization if it should yield to the Philippine aspiration for national independence.

April 7, 1927

PRESIDENT ADVISES PHILIPPINES TO SHUN HASTY INDEPENDENCE

Economic Stability Must First Assure a Sound Government, He Declares.

PROBLEM 'ONE OF TIME'

Political Freedom Today Would Mean a Collapse of Insular Revenues, He Says.

Special to The New York Times.
WASHINGTON, Oct. 27.—President Hoover made it clear today that his administration was opposed to immediate independence for the Philippine Islands.

After canvassing the situation at today's biweekly Cabinet meeting, the first to be attended by Secretary Hurley since his return from a tour of the islands, the President stated that the durability of the insular government must be assured before complete independence can be effected. Economic freedom, he added, must be attained "before political independence can be successful."

The President admitted that every President of the United States since the Spanish-American War had directly or indirectly promised the independence of the Philippines, but "the problem is one of time." Independence tomorrow, without proper economic organization, would result in a "collapse of Philippine government revenues and the collapse of the economic life of the islands."

The question was the absorbing topic at the Cabinet meeting. With Secretary Hurley's return and growing indications here that the independence agitation has been revived in the islands and is likewise gaining adherents in the agricultural sections of the United States, the President added it to the growing list of problems facing his administration.

October 28, 1931

HOUSE, 274-94, OVERRIDES VETO OF PHILIPPINES BILL; SENATE WILL ACT MONDAY

HOOVER PICTURED PERIL

He Said Islands Would Face Invasion, and Asked Plebiscite.

HARE SCOFFS AT WARNING

Asserts Measure Proves Nation's Courage—Dyer Lays Opposition to Military.

OSIAS URGES HOUSE MOVE

Makes Plea for 'Justice and Freedom'—Manila Leaders Hail President's Action.

Special to THE NEW YORK TIMES.

WASHINGTON, Jan. 13.—President Hoover vetoed the Philippine independence bill today, and in less than two hours the House overrode the veto by a vote of 274 to 94, or twenty-nine more than the two-thirds majority required.

No action was taken in the Senate on the message, but it is scheduled to come up for consideration Monday, with Republican leaders already confident that the President will be sustained and Democrats

expressing little hope of rejecting the veto.

If, as expected, the Senate upholds the President's position, it will be necessary for the friends of Philippine freedom to initiate a new move in the next Congress, a program which they said tonight was already contemplated.

No doubt existed that President Hoover would disapprove the independence program, but surprise arose over the vigor of his language.

Suggesting that a plebiscite for freedom be deferred for fifteen or twenty years, he said the bill would put the people of the United States and the Philippines not on the road to "liberty and safety, but on the path leading to new and enlarged dangers to liberty and freedom itself."

Hoover Warns of "Chaos."

Emphasizing a triple responsibility by the United States to the Philippine people, the American people and the world at large, the President warned against projecting the Filipinos into "economic and social chaos, with the probability of a breakdown in government."

He said that American agriculture would receive little benefit from the plan, and that during the transition period the United States Government, with continuing moral responsibility, would daily be faced "with the likelihood of having to employ military measures to maintain order in a degenerating social and economic situation."

The President spoke strongly of danger of "peaceful infiltration or forcible entry" into the Philippines by "immense neighbor populations."

"Many of these races are more devoted to commercial activities than the population of the islands and the infiltration is constant and

fraught with friction," he stated. "Nor has the spirit of imperialism and the exploitation of peoples by other races departed from this earth."

Bill Is Held No Safeguard.

The President declared that although the United States would have an option, under the vetoed bill, to continue its military and naval bases in the Philippines after the ten-year transitional period was ended, this would give no promise of maintaining independence against pressure from outside except for an offer to attempt "neutralization," which would be a "feeble assurance" of independence.

Maintaining that the United States must undertake further steps toward the liberation of the islands, but that they should be based upon a plebiscite to be taken in fifteen or twenty years, the President declared that "on such an occasion there would be a full impress upon the Filipinos of the consequences of their act."

He asserted that they should then have freedom to form their own Constitution and government, but that the United States in the meantime should develop a larger importance to their own officials, and immigration should be restricted at once.

"We should cooperate with them to bring about their economic independence before the plebiscite by very gradual reduction of their free imports," the President added.

"The United States should plainly announce prior to the time of this plebiscite whether (a) it will make absolute and complete withdrawal from all military and naval bases, and from every moral or other commitment to maintain their independence, or (b) the conditions as to authority and rights within the islands under which we will continue that protection."

But the President's words fell on deaf ears in the House, where 191 Democrats, 82 Republicans and one Farmer-Laborite voted to reject the veto. Only one Democrat, Martin of Oregon, a retired regular army general and a graduate of West Point, voted with 93 Republicans to stand by the President.

January 14, 1933

FILIPINOS ALTER PHRASING.

Senate 'Declines' to Accept Proposed Insular Independence.

MANILA, Oct. 12 (AP).—The Philippine Senate tonight joined the House in approving a concurrent resolution declining the offer of insular independence in the form presented by the last United States Congress.

The Senate authorized a new mission to be headed by its President, Manuel Quezon, to ask assurance of the Washington administration that Congress will consider amendments before the Hawes-Cutting Act lapses Jan. 17.

The Senate changed the wording "rejects" to "declines to accept" in acting upon the independence offer. The House is expected to concur in the softened phrasing.

October 13, 1933

ROOSEVELT SIGNS PHILIPPINES BILL

Jubilant Manila Greets Law for Freedom in 1945 With Din of Bells and Whistles.

ISLANDS TO ACCEPT MAY 1

Dern Warns Against 'Unjust Taxation' by Us Now as Violation of Compact.

By The Associated Press.

WASHINGTON, March 24.—With a flourish of his pen, President Roosevelt today wrote upon the statute books a plan for the complete freedom of the Philippine Islands in 1945 or soon thereafter.

To the click of cameras and in the presence of the authors of the measure and members of the Philippine independence mission here, the President shortly after noon signed the McDuffie-Tydings independence law passed this week, and Philippine leaders announced immediately it would be accepted on May 1 by their Legislature. Blowing of whistles and ringing of bells greeted news of the action in Manila.

"This is a great day for you and for me," the President told President Manuel L. Quezon of the Philippine Senate, adding that if invited he would attend the inaugural ceremonies of the new republic ten to twelve years hence.

Senator Tydings, co-sponsor of the measure, said May 1 had been designated as acceptance date for the bill to honor the memory of Admiral Dewey, who steamed in, destroyed the Spanish fleet and took Manila Bay on that date in 1898.

Insurrection Ended in 1901.

Enactment of the measure came almost exactly thirty-three years after American troops captured General Emilio Aguinaldo to end the Filipino insurrection on March 23, 1901. General Aguinaldo now lives in comparative pensioned retirement, but still is an important figure in island politics.

Signing of the bill, which is a re-enactment with a few modifications of the Hawes-Cutting Law which passed Congress fourteen months ago, was accompanied by a warning from Secretary Dern against taxation of Philippine imports prior to independence.

"We still have obligations to these people, and trade restrictions such as proposed now in a bill before Congress would violate the spirit of this act," said the Secretary after he witnessed signing of the law.

He referred to the proposed application of a 3 cents a pound excise tax on Philippine cocoanut oil, contained in the general revenue bill now before the Senate.

Recalling he had already voiced Presidential objections to this taxation, the Secretary said:

"We ought not to spoil our fine record in the Philippines through an unjust taxation act at the last minute. An excise tax is equivalent to a tariff and we have no right to apply the tariff to these islands until they become free."

Military Withdrawal Studied.

The law provides for United States withdrawal of all military bases in the islands after independence. Secretary Dern said this would mean native soldiers of the Philippine Scouts, now used as the island's constabulary, would be mustered out of American service at that time. The 5,000 white troops stationed there would be transferred elsewhere.

The War Department already is studying problems entailed in the military withdrawal, even though it does not become effective for more than ten years.

Secretary Dern said he hoped to visit the islands in September or October.

Senator Tydings, chairman of the Senate Territories Committee, is planning a trip to Manila in May or June at the head of a joint Congressional commission to study Philippine objections to economic provisions of the new law.

Members of the Philippine independence mission expect to sail for home April 7.

Celebration in Manila.

MANILA (Sunday), March 25 (P).—President Roosevelt's signing of the Philippine Independence Bill was followed within a few minutes by the shrieking of whistles and ringing of bells as the news was flashed to Manila.

It was early Sunday morning in Manila when the bill was signed by the President at noon Saturday in Washington, but arrangements were made in advance for a noisy hailing of the proffer of separate government.

The jubilation was more evident than it was fifteen months ago when the Hawes-Cutting Independence Bill was enacted over President Hoover's veto. Then factions were divided, and it was widely sensed the Legislature would reject the freedom offer, as it did the following October.

Now, however, there is no question of prompt acceptance of the renewed offer of independence, with its provisions for relinquishment by the United States of army and navy bases in the islands.

Commonwealth to Be Hastened.

Governor General Frank Murphy told Quentin Paredes, Speaker of the House, he was ready to summon a special session of the present Legislature, which is the same that refused to accept the Hawes-Cutting measure. The Governor said he would do this when a concrete program was presented, and he believed formal action could be had within a few weeks.

Mr. Murphy expressed the opinion the Legislature might act upon the independence offer April 30 or May 1, immediately following the return here of Manuel Quezon, president of the Philippine Senate, who has been in Washington working for independence.

Indications are that Filipino leaders intend to hasten steps to set up a transition-period commonwealth government, including election of delegates to a constitutional convention which will draw up a charter for President Roosevelt's approval.

It is possible the new government, with a Filipino as Chief Executive and an American as High Commissioner, will be functioning in a little more than a year.

March 25, 1934

Times Wide World Photo.

THE PRESIDENT SIGNS PHILIPPINE INDEPENDENCE BILL.

Mr. Roosevelt, surrounded by authors of the bill, and Representatives of the island government, as he affixed his signature to the measure yesterday. Standing left to right are Senator Joseph C. O'Mahoney, Secretary of War George Dern, Senator Elpidio Quirino, Manuel Quezon, President of the Philippine Senate; Senator Millard Tydings and General C. F. Cox, Chief of the Bureau of Insular Affairs.

FILIPINOS ENDORSE NEW CHARTER, 25-1

Incomplete Count From All Sections Shows 438,847 in Favor, 11,089 Against.

NO DISORDERS AT POLLS

Leaders Elated Over Solid Support of Commonwealth—Suffragists Heartened.

MANILA, Wednesday, May 15 (Æ).—Election returns flowing in early today indicated the Filipinos, with women balloting for the first time, voted by a margin of probably 25 to 1 yesterday to ratify the Constitution of the forthcoming commonwealth government.

First returns indicated more than a million votes were cast. Bulletins from all sections of the Philippine archipelago gave an incomplete count today of 438,847 votes for the Constitution and 11,089 against it.

It was the first step toward complete independence from the United States—to be granted after ten years of preparation under the commonwealth which will be inaugurated late this year.

The plebiscite was peaceful. There were no disorders like the uprising of the Sakdalistas or immediate independence advocates, whose revolt May 2 cost sixty lives.

Many Women Cast Votes.

Women enthusiastically exercised their right to vote for the first time and in some sections cast more ballots than the men. This was taken by some women leaders as an indication that women would be able to muster the necessary 300,000 votes in a special plebiscite to be held within two years to determine whether they wish the right to vote in future elections.

The convincing demonstration of solidarity in favor of a commonwealth elated political leaders.

General Emilio Aguinaldo voted for the first time since his capture thirty-four years ago ended the insurrection he headed against the United States. His entire family accompanied him to the polls.

The influence of Sakdalista extremists, who opposed ratification of the Constitution ostensibly because it postpones independence, was little evidenced—except in the smaller number of votes in Laguna, Bulacan and Cavite Provinces. In those provinces, where the uprising was centred, Sakdal leaders had urged their followers to boycott the polls.

Igorotes Oppose Ratification.

One exception to the otherwise virtual unanimity was recorded in the sub-province of Benguet in the mountains of Northern Luzon Island, the inhabitants of which are aboriginal Igorots who have been much benefited by the American régime. Nine of the fourteen precincts gave 175 votes for ratification and 575 against it.

The plebiscite represented the first opportunity the mass of Filipinos have had in their decades of freedom to vote on whether they really want independence. The Congressional Act states that if a majority of the votes cast favors the Constitution, that "shall be deemed an expression of the will of the people * * * in favor of Philippine independence."

The next step is for the Legislature within thirty days to canvass and certify the results to Governor General Frank Murphy. He is required by the Independence Act to call an election of officers for the Commonwealth, to be held in from three to six months.

May 15, 1935

QUEZON'S ELECTION SURE IN PHILIPPINES

Senator Far Ahead of Rivals in Race for First President of New Commonwealth.

WILL TAKE OFFICE NOV. 15

Full Independence for Islands in 10 Years—Murphy to Be Resident Commissioner.

Wireless to THE NEW YORK TIMES.

MANILA, Wednesday, Sept. 18.—An overwhelming victory appeared assured for Manuel Quezon in the election of the first President of the new Philippines Commonwealth as returns came in from yesterday's polling.

The showing of the two candidates opposing Senator Quezon was distinctly disappointing to their followers. Bishop Gregorio Aglipay, head of the independent Philippines Catholic Church, apparently failed to carry more than three provinces. General Emilio Aguinaldo, leader of the revolt against the United States thirty-five years ago, is running behind Senator Quezon by more than two to one in the city of Manila, where he had expected at least to break even.

In a public statement tonight, Senator Quezon and his running-mate for the Vice Presidency, Senator Sergio Osmeña, expressed themselves as "overwhelmed" by the result. They affirmed their readiness to take up their new responsibilities at the inauguration of the Commonwealth Government on Nov. 15.

Claims of fraud, violence and coercion have begun to pour in from many election districts. But, even if all these disputes were decided against the Quezon-Osmeña party, it is not believed the election result would be upset.

Actually the voting was more peaceful than had been expected. Two persons were reported to have been killed in the town of Santa Barbara in the Province of Pangasinan and two at San José in the Province of Antique.

Indications are that the total vote will prove light because many persons were kept at home by stormy weather and perhaps by fear of violence. In addition, considerable apathy was manifest because a Quezon-Osmeña victory was a foregone conclusion.

September 18, 1935

THE FRENCH IN INDOCHINA

THE FRENCH IN ANNAM.

PARIS, Aug. 27.—A dispatch to the *Figaro* from Saigon says: "M. Harmand, the French Civil Commissioner, has gone to Hue at the special request of the Emperor of Annam, who is desirous of placing himself and the capital under French protection, as his position is most insecure. He nearly lost his life on the first day of the bombardment by the French of the forts and batteries at the mouth of the River Hue. M. Harmand is provided with most complete powers to negotiate with the Emperor, and is instructed to obtain from him a strict definition of the protectorate over Annam conferred on France by existing treaties. He is also instructed to demand that the Annamite bands encamped in Tonquin be immediately recalled."

The *Temps* has a telegram from Cochin China stating that the Emperor of Annam received M. Harmand on Aug. 23. The Emperor showed complete submission. Annam is compelled by treaty to pay the costs of the war, the French to retain the forts on the Hue River pending payment. The Annamite troops in Tonquin are to be placed at the disposal of Gen. Bouet, the French commander. A prompt settlement of the question at issue is expected.

Reinforcements to the number of 1,500 men will embark for Tonquin in about a fortnight.

LONDON, Aug. 28.—The *Standard's* correspondent at Hong Kong says it is rumored there that a revolution has broken out at Hué.

August 28, 1883

CRUEL DEEDS OF FRANCE

NO QUARTER GIVEN TO MEN, WOMEN, OR CHILDREN.

THE FRENCH FORCES ACCUSED OF UNHEARD-OF CRUELTIES IN ANNAM UNDER OFFICIAL ORDERS FROM ADMIRAL COURBET.

PARIS, Oct. 29.—Mail advices from Saigon show that the French forces in their encounters in the vicinity of Hanoi, in the early part of September, met Chinese regulars, who were well-armed and officered. After a conflict of three days, during which the French took some of the enemy's works, they withdrew, leaving Haiphong still in the hands of the enemy. Some of the troops of the King of Annam were with the enemy.

A letter from Saigon to the *France* states that unheard-of cruelties were committed near Hué on the occasion of its capture by the French sailors. Admiral Courbet directed, in an official order, that there should be no quarter given to men, women, or children. Three hundred Annamites who had taken refuge in the mouth of the bay of Thuan, were killed, all of them being shot. One hundred and fifty more who were drifting in a junk, without arms or oars, were also massacred.

The *Figaro* declares that Admiral Courbet, at the instance of Commissioner Harmand, allowed the perpetration of such acts in order to terrorize the Annamites.

The *Temps* denies that Admiral Courbet gave such orders, but admits that 1,200 of the enemy were slain at Thuan.

The *Gaulois* says that in view of the contingency of war between France and China, several French iron-clads have been ordered to be put in readiness to reinforce the French squadron in Chinese waters.

The discussion of M. Granet's interpellation of the Tonquin question was begun in the Chamber of Deputies to-day.

M. Gatineau has decided to postpone until after the Tonquin debate his motion to expel the Orleans Princes from France.

The *Journal de Paris* states that Commissioner Harmand has ordered Commandant Coronat, who was chief of Gen. Bouet's staff, to return to France.

The *Gaulois* says that four French gunboats now preparing for the Red River will be named after French officers killed in Tonquin.

October 30, 1883

FRANCE'S MANY INTERESTS.

PARIS, June 7.—The new treaty between France and Annam has been signed. By its terms the Provinces of Bin-thuan and Than-goa are restored to Annam. A customs system similar to that in force in Cochin-China is established. A French military occupation of all strategic points in Annam and Tonquin may be effected if necessary. A permanent French garrison will hold a portion of the citadel of Hué, capital of Annam. Annam accepted the treaty as proposed by France without making any modifications. By it Annam is placed under a French protectorate. The French President in Cochin-China will represent Annam in all her foreign relations, and Annam will form a customs union with Cochin-China. The Departments of Public Works, of Postal and Telegraph Service, and of Finance and Customs will form a single branch of administration under the direction of a French agent. M. Patenôtre, the French Minister to China, who has been in Hué the past few days negotiating this treaty, will return to Hong Kong on June 25.

June 9, 1884

ANAM

The fresh territorial and administrative rights which the French have just acquired in Anam from the monarch who has shown himself so subservient to their wishes mostly relate to the northernmost province, Tonquin. The towns now formally yielded to the French are in the valley or the delta of the Sang-Koi, the chief river of Tonquin, and Ha-Noi, as is well known, is the capital of the province, while Hai-Fong, also mentioned among the concessions, is its port. Ever since the French agent in Anam obtained the treaty of Hué, in which a French protectorate practically took the place of the ancient acknowledgment of subjection to the Middle Kingdom, it has been clear that the extent to which the protectorate should extend depended more on Paris than on Pekin. And although France and China shortly afterward found themselves at war, this was strictly a result of the subsequent Langson affair rather than of the original compact with Anam. The concessions now made will doubtless occasion no trouble, French control at Ha-Noi and in its neighborhood having long ago been recognized.

October 9, 1888

FRENCH INDO-CHINA A VALUABLE COLONY

More Than 50 Per Cent. of Its Imports Are Supplied by the Mother Country.

BASE FOR RAW MATERIALS

France Has in It a Potential Source for Tropical Products—Our Trade Is Growing.

French Indo-China's external trade is probably a better index to the economic development of the country than any other available, and it also reveals quite clearly the strong hold that France maintains upon the commerce of her colony, according to the American Trust Review of the Pacific.

From 1893 to 1901 the value of Indo-China's trade increased 123 per cent.; from 1901 to 1913, only 13 per cent., but from 1913 to 1925, 105 per cent., allowance being made in the last percentage for the great inflation of the franc. The following table shows the imports and exports of the colony for various years since 1900:

FRENCH INDO-CHINA'S IMPORTS AND EXPORTS, 1901-1925.

Year.	Imports.	Exports.
1901	$39,078,000	$30,771,000
1910	36,931,000	48,110,000
1913	45,318,000	55,094,000
1920	59,369,000	68,745,000
1922	68,828,000	91,191,000
1924	74,207,000	92,120,000
1925	87,661,000	117,897,000

The unification of French control on the peninsula in 1887 may or may not have been responsible in part for the great trade increase from 1893 to 1901. It probably was, says the Review. But the post-war trade increase is declared to be the result of an entirely different factor, namely, the rapidly increasing demand of Europe and America for tropical products. The colony has not taken very readily to the growing of such commodities itself, but it has increased its rice production to feed those countries that have done so, and there is some evidence, the Review points out, that the colony is becoming interested in these products. Rubber is its second most important export.

In 1925 rice constituted 64 per cent. of the country's total exports; rubber, 8 per cent.; dried fish, 4 per cent.; coal, 3 per cent.; zinc, a little over 1 per cent., and pepper, less than 1 per cent. The other exports in order of importance were: maize, lac, cement, animals and copra.

After feeding her own 20,000,000, Indo-China exported in 1926 more than 1,600,000 tons of rice. In 1901 the rice shipments aggregated only 912,434 tons. Although the country's rice production curve fluctuates greatly from year to year, it has a fairly steep general upward trend. The Dutch East Indies and the Philippines buy their Indo-Chinese rice principally through Hongkong and Singapore.

France Takes Most Rubber.

France, according to 1926 figures, took nearly all of the colony's rubber, 210,000,000 francs worth, which amounts to about a fifth or sixth of her total rubber consumption. Of the 1926 shipments of dried, salted and smoked fish, about half went to feed the Chinese population of Singapore; the rest was destined principally for Siam and China. Although Tonking coal is shipped to all French Oriental possessions, Japan is the chief market for it. Belgium takes all the zinc. Of the 292 tons of tin exported in 1926, nearly all was shipped to France. About 80 per cent. of the raw silk exports are destined for the mother country. The pepper shipments in 1926 were valued at 25,823,-000 francs and were divided more or less equally between France and Great Britain. The 1926 sticklac exports totaled 8,040,000 francs, 60 per cent. of which sent to France. Virtually all the cotton produced goes to Hongkong.

"The fact that the British entrepots of Hongkong and Singapore handle about 34 per cent. of the colony's exports and about 19 per cent. of its imports is somewhat distressing to the French—so it appears from the comments of the Le Monde Coloniale," the Review states. "Wedded to the ambition to make Indo-China an industrial centre of the Orient is the ambition to make Indo-China a trade distributing centre of the Far East. But neither Haiphong nor Saigon can hope to compete with Hongkong or Singapore in this respect until they become free ports also. It was by making Singapore a free port that the British took the entrepot trade of Southeastern Asia away from the Dutch East Indies.

"France and her colonies take about 25 per cent. of the country's exports. In normal years, the United States buys very sparingly of Indo-China. Its imports from there in 1925 were valued at $100,000. Indo-China's export trade is principally with her rice-eating neighbors.

"The products chiefly demanded by several of Indo-China's customers are as follows: By Japan, rice, coal and zinc; by China, rice, coal, dried fish and cement; by the Dutch East Indies, rice; by Singapore, dried fish, rice, rubber and swine; by the Philippines, rice and buffalos; by Belgium, zinc, rice, kapok and sticklac; by Great Britain, rice teak and lac; by Siam, dried fish and silk.

"The imports are, of course, a great deal more varied than the exports. Cotton goods, the leading item on the import list, constituted but 16 per cent. of the total 1925 import values. Petroleum constituted 6 per cent. and metal goods, machinery and silk goods, each 4 per cent. The other principal items, in order of importance, are cotton and wool, iron and steel, automobiles, wheat flour, chemical products, cigarettes and rubber goods.

Potential Cotton Source.

"Indo-China is not only a great potential cotton-growing country, but is also a potential cotton manufacturing country with vast numbers of Chinese, Japanese and Malayan cotton cloth buyers near by. However, owing to the fact that France has a monopoly on the colony's cotton market, it is not probable that the cotton manufacturing industry will be the industry to usher in the era of Indo-Chinese industrialism.

"France's rival in the Indo-Chinese automobile market is Italy and not America. It may be of interest to know that fireworks form a large item of import, all of which comes from China. The Annamese burn up an enormous amount of firecrackers and other pyrotechnics during their many fêtes. And even of more importance in terms of total import value is the ritual paper purchased from China for religious purposes. Two other items that also might be added to the list of important imports are coal tar, of which Japan

supplies 95 per cent., and soft coal, of which Japan supplies 50 per cent. Japan and Hongkong send quantities of foodstuffs to Indo-China to offset, partly, the great amounts of rice and fish that they buy from there.

"About 53 per cent. of the import trade is with the mother country. The United States' share in this trade in 1925 was but slightly over 1 per cent.—that is, $1,371,000. However, even this small amount represents a 183 per cent. increase over that of 1913, and a very much greater increase over that of 1901, when America's exports to Indo-China totaled but $58,000. At least it can be said that the American Indo-Chinese commerce is growing. The fact that America's import and export trade with Indo-China in 1920 was four or five times greater than it was in 1926 is not significant to the normal growth of that trade, for 1920 was an abnormal year in both trade and shipping. The share of the West Coast in the United States shipments to Indo-China was 76 per cent. in 1926 and 50 per cent. in 1925.

Indo-China's Imports.

"The leading articles shipped into Indo-China by various countries are as follows: By Hongkong and China, gold, cotton thread, silks, handkerchiefs, tea, beans, noodles, refined sugar and fresh vegetables; by the Dutch East Indies, refined oil products, coal, refined sugar and coffee; by British India, cotton and wool, jute sacks and cordage; by Singapore, areca nuts, refined sugar, jute, thread, wheat flour, oil, vegetables and cotton goods; by the United States, petroleum and petroleum products, canned fish and machinery; by Japan, porcelain, cotton goods, silk, cement, coal and coal tar; by Great Britain, coal

tar, sheet iron, agricultural machinery, cotton thread and cotton prints; by Switzerland, canned milk; by Belgium, pottery, steam boilers and sheet zinc; by Siam, areca nuts and pottery; by Italy, automobiles, tires, dynamos and other electrical equipment; by the Netherlands, milk, cigars and cheese, and by Germany, agricultural machinery.

"Even in the matter of ship tonnage entering Indo-China, France leads all other nations with over a 30 per cent. share in the total. The total tonnage entered in 1925 was 3,778,109, of which 1,213,484 tons belonged to France; 861,947 tons to Japan, and 729,179 tons to Great Britain. America was about sixth on the list, with 179,519 tons.

"In Indo-China France has a potential French-controlled supply of tropical raw materials, a large Colonial market, a trading base in Far Eastern commerce and a French-controlled investment field. The French are at work there setting out new plantations, opening new mines, building new roads, constructing new irrigation systems and establishing new industries. The colony promises to be to France what British Malaya and the Dutch East Indies are to Great Britain and Holland—even more perhaps if her industrial ambitions there mature.

"But to America and other countries Indo-China is a restricted field of trade and industry—no more so, however, than are the Philippines to France and other countries. There are some American products, such as have been indicated, that have a sale in the French colony, and as the country develops industrially the demand for American goods will most likely increase."

July 1, 1928

INDO-CHINA UNREST HAS FRANCE ANXIOUS

Uprisings Inspired by Secret Revolutionary Organizations Grow Increasingly Serious.

ALL ASIA SEEN AS UNEASY

Sarraut Says "It Is a Strange Time the Americans Choose to Weaken Naval Power."

Special Cable to THE NEW YORK TIMES.

PARIS, Feb. 13.—Considerable anxiety is evident in France over the abortive revolutionary movement in French Indo-China and the mutiny of Tokinez troops at Yenbay on the Red

River, ninety miles from Hanoi. It now appears that three French officers, two sergeants and five loyal Annamite soldiers were killed, while the losses of the mutinous forces in killed and wounded are reported to have been heavy.

The attack was made upon an entrenched camp at Yenbay by several hundred Tonkinese sharpshooters and sixty natives belonging to revolutionary societies. Calm has been restored throughout the country, but the presence of secret revolutionary organizations believed inspired by Moscow is regarded here as a serious menace.

Albert Sarraut, former Governor of Indo-China, writing tonight in Le Journal des Debates, says it is not surprising that the natives are in an agitated frame of mind when it is recalled that China, the Dutch Indies, British India and "the Philippines, where sedition is growing against the authority of the United States," have all given to French Indo-China a bad example.

"In view of the present vast revolutionary movement shaking the whole Asiatic world, it is a strange time the Americans have chosen to seek to weaken the naval power of those countries which are most exposed to the agitation of the masses in Asia," says M. Sarraut.

"For protection and maintenance of order in their Asiatic possessions, these powers have need of their full strength and all the vessels they possess."

In common with other competent observers, M. Sarraut believes France will be forced to develop a better means of defense in Indo-China.

PARIS, Feb. 13 (AP).—Bomb-throwing and the increased seriousness of revolutionary outbreaks in French Indo-China were announced by the French Minister of Colonies today.

Bombs were reported to have been thrown in Hanoi by a squad of bicyclists, some of whom were arrested and admitted that they sought to terrorize the population and prevent loyal troops being sent to crush the mutineers.

Twenty revolutionists have been arrested, among them one of the leaders of the movement, who died of his wounds.

February 14, 1930

NEW RELIGION SPURS INDO-CHINESE RISING

Special Cable to THE NEW YORK TIMES.

PARIS, Feb. 27.—A strange new religion described as a mixture of Taoism, Confucianism, Buddhism and Christianity is playing an important part in the present revolutionary agitation in Indo-China.

Under the mystic leadership of Le Van Trung, former adviser to the French Government and Officer of the Legion of Honor, Cao Daism, as the new cult is called, is making a strong appeal to the more intelligent portions of the population, especially natives employed in government services. From a humble beginning in 1926 with several hundred adherents, it has grown to be a flourishing religion counting 600,000 enthusiastic supporters and 3,000 priests.

By permitting converts to continue

to accept what they regard as essential in their old beliefs, Cao Daism attempts to combine the best of all the established forms of worship. The new religion is said to be strongly flavored with nationalism, and the members of the cult are taught that by the concentration of their spiritual attention upon the supreme God—Cao Dai—"the independence of Indo-China," which the gods of older religions failed to preserve, will later be restored.

French political agents whose duty it is to keep in close touch with the sentiment of the native population believe the new religion is being used in a subtle way to arouse the people to rebellion.

Latest reports from the French Far Eastern possession state that a new centre of revolutionary activity has just been discovered in Khalam, in the Province of Kienan. Loyal native forces under the command of French officers operating in the re-

gion of the Bas Delta came upon a veritable fortress in which were stored guns, munitions, uniforms and other equipment. The assistant chief of the canton was found to be the leader of the movement, which had for its purpose an attack upon the European colony in Kienan, capital town of the province of the same name.

Kienan contains the central observatory of the Indo-China naval wireless station. Seized documents indicate Communist influence.

February 28, 1930

INDO-CHINA IS RULED WITH STRONG HAND

French Are Quick to Check the Periodical Outbreaks of Annamite Nationalists.

MOST NATIVES PEACEFUL

Those Who Are Educated, However, Prefer Easy Life in the Cities to Agriculture.

By HERMANN NORDEN.

Special Correspondence, THE NEW YORK TIMES.

PARIS, May 6.—The February rebellion in French Indo-China, of which I was an eyewitness, had become a thing of the past when I sailed on April 1 from Saigon after four months zigzagging through most of the country. The outbreak, during which twelve Europeans were killed, was limited to a small area in the Red River delta, chiefly in the barracks of the tirailleurs. The Nationalist party of Annamites, where some Communist agitators found fertile ground, had been active among the native troops. Such affairs happen periodically in Indo-China and are put down as soon as they have started. In this case the Colonial infantry and the Foreign Legion—ever dreaded for their ferocity by evildoers—were rushed to the scene and two villages in Kien-an province known to be hotbeds of communistic propaganda, were bombarded by airplanes. But only a dozen casualties occurred, previous warning having been given. Without such immediate action the disorder might have spread.

While I have had occasion to see something of France's dominions in Africa and Syria, the organization in

their Asiatic colony and protectorates seems to be more elaborate than anywhere else. The government's vigilance never relaxes. There are the military, gendarmerie, militia, native police and tribal retainers, all for the preservation of order, and in the cities and larger villagers the pousse-pousse (ricksha) coolies act as detectives in the same way as the concierges in Paris. The result is that travel in the Indo-China Union, composed of Tonkin, Annam, Cochin-China, Cambodia and Laos, is safe even on the by-ways, on which I mostly made my way, either by automobile, horseback, chaloupe, pirogue or pirogue with a motor.

Savages Aid Roadbuilding.

Even within the Annamite chain of mountains peaceful penetration by means of roadbuilding progresses with the aid of the native Mois, an Annamite word for savages. The Mois are of Malay-Polynesian origin. It was only while in Upper Tonkin along the Chinese border and in Yunnan that I came into contact with marauders, pirates and opium smugglers and gun runners. Owing to the impenetrable forests the task of the military forces in the border range of mountains is a very difficult one, but from what I have seen any invasion by the Chinese is out of the question, for the frontier is guarded in the same way and by the same calibre of men as the northwest border of India is guarded by the British and with the same esprit de corps. Many of the French officers are veterans who saw service in the Riff and Druse campaigns as well as in the World War.

The economic expansion of Indo-China became evident to me when first landing at the twin city of Saigon-Cholon, a Chinese city under a French Mayor and government, which has more than doubled in population in the last few years owing to immigration from Southern China. Saigon has 100,000 and Cholon 225,000 inhabitants. Rice is king and rubber may eventually become viceroy. Coffee and tea plantations are prospering on the highlands further north. Timber abounds. The mining regions in Tonkin reminded me on a small scale of the pioneer days in our West, with prospectors trickling in and talk of this strike and another of tin, gold and other ore, and also coal.

But progress is bound to be slow until the government encourages exploitation more than it does at present. It seems to fear to have new-

comers on its hands in case of sickness on account of the climate, or in case of failure. The business is at present in the hands of a few big companies with large resources which have been paying dividends for years. From my experience the climate compares favorably with that of the rich mining regions in the Belgian Congo and other countries.

French Extend Education.

The French have brought their temperament into Asia with them. One of the results is that the French Annamite, or Annamite Frenchman, is lively, quick and alert and snappy. Many of them speak good French, or at least pigeon French. Intense education is the keynote of the French wherever they have colonies. It makes it easy for the stranger from the Occident. Whether a European education is a highly desirable thing for the native is a matter of opinion. Personally, I think the disadvantages are many. Unless such education be based upon a thorough understanding of the natives' religious belief, the basis of which in Indo-China is Animism, a cult of ancestors, it cannot penetrate the pupil's mind. Much will go over his head, and it will have the desired result in isolated cases only. Perhaps much of the unrest in the Far East today has been caused by overeducation of the native.

The same applies to legal matters. The sentences meted out to the assassins at Yenbay have to be submitted for approval to the home courts in France. Months may pass before the execution can take place. By that time the native mind has forgotten all about the crime and the effect upon the population is nil.

During my stay I traveled alone a good deal, and had to depend on Annamites. They are good and friendly people and hospitable to the stranger. But those who live up-country well off the beaten track and outside the European sphere are more dependable and genuine than those who live in the cities. The educated Annamite today has lost interest in the tilling of the soil and prefers city life, government jobs and office positions. It takes an Annamite two hours to do what a Chinese could do in an hour.

May 18, 1930

INDO-CHINESE ATTEMPT PARIS DEMONSTRATION

Fifty Students Are Routed From Presidential Palace—Twelve of Them Are Arrested.

Special Cable to THE NEW YORK TIMES.

PARIS, May 22.—Fifty Indo-Chinese students who attempted to stage a political demonstration in front of the President's residence, the Elysée Palace, today were quickly dispersed by Republican Guardsmen stationed in the palace grounds. Twelve manifestants were arrested.

The demonstration was intended as a protest against the sentences in

connection with the recent Communist outbreak in Indo-China. The students succeeded in reaching the very gate of the Elysée Palace before they met opposition, which is exceptional, as the palace is closely guarded and is just opposite the headquarters of the Sureté Générale [Secret Service] and the Ministry of the Interior.

They came in small groups, afoot and in taxicabs, and, suddenly producing a large banner inscribed "Release Our Thirty-nine Comrades Condemned to Death," began a determined march on the Elysée Palace gates. There was a brief clash with the guards, who sounded a call for help, and the demonstrators were dispersed.

May 23, 1930

FRENCH PLAN TO DRIVE REDS FROM INDO-CHINA

Minister of Colonies Pledges Relentless War on Agitators He Blames for Disorders.

PARIS, June 13.—Placing the responsibility for the current disorders in Indo-China unreservedly upon Communist agents, François Piétri, the French Minister of Colonies, in the Chamber of Deputies today declared merciless war against all agitators, whether nationals or foreigners, in the Far East.

The Minister, replying to interpellations on the government's conduct of Indo-China affairs, admitted there were faults to be overcome in the colonial administration and announced the departure of a commission of inquiry.

"There is need for the administration to establish a closer contact with the natives," he said. "There is need for our officials to speak the native language and for enlarging opportunities for the natives. There is also a serious need for reorganization of the troops there.

"For all these problems, the government has formulated a definite program. But the outstanding fact in connection with the Indo-China troubles of the past ten years is the appearance of bolshevism in our colonies. The government has decided to combat it implacably, and no agitator who falls into our hands will escape punishment."

The Minister added that he could give solemn assurance that the French sovereignty remained unshaken and would remain so if exercised with authority, combined with a measure of humanity and justice.

This discussion, which already had lasted through two Fridays, will be continued by the Chamber next week.

June 14, 1930

IN RESTLESS INDO-CHINA FRANCE FACES PROBLEM

In the Far Eastern Outpost of Her Colonial Empire the Natives Are Stirred by the Tide of Nationalism

By T. J. C. MARTYN

FRENCH INDO-CHINA is again troubled. The unrest there, attributed variously to Soviet activities and a wave of nationalist insurgency kindled by Gandhi in India on the one hand and by the Chinese civil war on the other hand, is seized upon by France as a factor necessitating a re-orientation of her naval policy. As a result, the French Minister of Colonies, François Piétri, has announced that France will create a naval base at Saigon, the principal port of Indo-China, as well as at other nerve centres of her far-flung empire.

In the five States which comprise French Indo-China trouble has been simmering for years. The World War, with its corollary of respect for the rights of small nations and minorities, had its effect on the psychology of the Orient as elsewhere. To the north of Indo-China there has been a China fighting for nationalism and freedom from foreign control. To the southwest there have been the teachings of Gandhi demanding an India for Indians. And in the Dutch East Indies Indo-China saw the beginnings of what threatened to be a serious revolt. Now the French declare that the doctrines of Moscow have torn through Indo-China with the force of a monsoon.

Why not Indo-China for the natives of Cochin-China, Annam, Laos, Cambodia and Tonking, the five States of French Indo-China? Xenophobia, fanned by Moscow and the resurgence of nationalism, drew blood from the French. Stern measures were taken and France let it be known that she was not to be stampeded by a policy of "anarchy and murder."

French Reforms.

Nevertheless the French have come to the conclusion that reforms are necessary. In a statement in the French Chamber early last Summer M. Piétri was forced to admit that "there is need for the administration to establish a closer contact with the natives."

"There is a need," he continued, "for our officials to speak the native languages and for enlarging opportunities for the natives. There is also a serious need for a reorganization of the troops there. For all these problems the government has formulated a definite program."

The temper of Indo-China may be gauged by the Tonkingese legend of the sword that came out of Petit Lac. Once upon a time a fisherman drew up a sword in his net, and a mysterious voice told him to use it in defending his country against the invading Chinese. He took it and put the Chinese to flight. Soon afterward he chanced to pass by the lake and the lake drew the sword from his side. The blade returned to the waters in the form of a dragon. Today in Tonking the legend is a symbol, and many a nationalist devoutly longs to have the sword returned to him that he may drive the French out with it.

French influence in Indo-China dates from 1787, when a treaty was signed with Cochin-China. With a foothold there, the French could hardly help extending their hold to the four neighboring kingdoms. In fact, her intervention has brought her to the verge of serious trouble at different times with China and Siam.

In due course Cochin-China became a French colony with the right to be represented by one Deputy in the French Chamber. Her status is entirely different from the other four States, which are kingdoms under a French protectorate, much the same as Morocco. Cambodia, which nestles on the southern frontier of Siam, became a French protectorate in 1863. The present King, Sisowathmonivong, reigns but does not rule, the French Resident Superieur looking after the chief affairs of government. Cambodia is rich in archaeological treasure and its ruins in Angkor are world famous.

Protectorate Over Annam.

Annam was next to accept a French protectorate, in 1886. This State, a long, narrow stretch of land skirting the China Sea, is perhaps the most progressive of the five. Her picturesque Emperor, Bao-Dai, lives, and lives well, in a palace whose interior is as magnificent as its exterior is moldy. The palace lies in a vast park behind walls studded by lattice-work in blue tiles. The road to it is called the Route Mandarin, and along it the rich Annamese go to pay court to the Emperor. The Emperor of Annam reigns, but he governs only through the French and a Chamber of Representatives.

Tonking came under the French during an altercation with China. The territory lies in the northernmost part of Indo-China, on the Chinese frontier. It is a low-lying land whose rice fields are partly submerged in red muddy water and fenced off by somber mud walls. The Tonkingese are aloof but friendly, and consider themselves vastly superior to the Annamese. Being contiguous to China they are greatly influenced by Chinese thought. Their King although a symbol of nationalism, is a cipher in the government.

Laos, which runs hundreds of miles into the north along the northern frontier of Siam, touches at its extreme north both Burma and China. It was the last of the French Indo-China States to come under a French protectorship, in 1893. In it there is a sort of restricted area, called Luang Prabang, where the King resides and does as much ruling as the French Resident Administrator lets him.

In all, Indo-China is a little larger than the State of Texas. It has a customs union applying in the various States and it is also a unit so far as finances are concerned. In all other ways, except that of the individual nationalism of its several parts, it is a disunion. French is the official language, but few natives speak it. Linguistically, Indo-China is chaos and has numberless dialects, in which Chinese, Kawi and Sanskrit largely figure.

France has done much to encourage production, especially of rubber, and has built many fine roads and official buildings. But largely the French occupation has been one of force of arms. French difficulties there serve to illustrate the extraordinary commitments which republican France has undertaken in the government of peoples who still owe nominal allegiance to kings and emperors, not only in Indo-China, but also in Northern Africa. They serve also to show how diverse and far-flung is the gigantic French Empire, second only to Britain's immense imperial realms.

October 5, 1930

France Plans to Fortify Navy Base in Indo-China

Wireless to THE NEW YORK TIMES.

PARIS, Aug. 8.—A part of the 400,000,000-franc loan recently floated, partly in Indo-China, for the defense of France's Eastern possessions will be devoted to fortifying Cam Ranh Bay in Annam, French Indo-China, for use as a naval base. This work, it is stated, will be begun in the very near future.

This project has been under consideration for many years, but recent events in the Far East have made its fulfillment seem necessary.

Cam Ranh Bay, on the South China Sea, has such a natural defense that no great expenditure will be needed to make it a safe base for the French fleet in Far Eastern waters.

August 9, 1938

THE DUTCH EAST INDIES

POSSIBILITIES IN BORNEO.

From the London Times.

To most of the British public Borneo is still a geographical term. Granting to Australia the dignity of a continent, then Borneo would class as the largest island. Its size, indeed, combined with its form, has hitherto been its greatest drawback. The other islands in the torrid zone present a great length of coast in comparison with their bulk, so that the interior is comparatively accessible. Borneo, three times as large as Great Britain, which even the ancient geographers observed to be penetrated everywhere by noble estuaries, drawing thence an augury of its ocean dominion, lies like a round bulk across the equator. It was credited with impermeable forests and swamps, thickly peopled with wild beasts and venomous creatures, and about 3,000,000 "Dyaks"—generally speaking, pirates, robbers, and murderers. Chinese and Malays had made settlements on the coast, just as the Phœnicians and Greeks had on the shores of the Mediterranean. In our nursery days, Borneo was a waste, a casualty, not to be reconciled with any intelligent or moral idea of cosmogony. But so had New-Holland been not long before. But there came rumors of its mineral and vegetable wealth.

It was only waiting for the opportunity and the man, and these came when Rajah Brooke won the dominion of Sarawak, and founded the British colony of Labuan. He proved at least the possibility of dealing with the natives on whatever terms they might prefer, whether peaceful or otherwise. In fact, he disenchanted the island, and Borneo is now a mercantile idea. As appears by the proceedings of the first general meeting of the British North Borneo Company there is now a British settlement there, in very good hands, and undergoing the usual phases of colonial growth. There is a Government, with the proper commission and instructions, now taking the place of the former Provisional Association. The company has taken over the existing staff; it has an approved flag, and a coinage already found a great convenience and expected to be a source of profit. It offers land and jungle rights on favorable terms. It is making and concluding arrangements with various Australian and Chinese companies for passenger and mercantile traffic. Indeed, it appears that Borneo need no longer fear being out of the world. It will very soon have a complete judicial system. Singapore, about 400 miles from Borneo, appears to be the nearest point of the civilized world. The island is known to abound in gutta-percha and the other substances now in increasing request for electric cables. Its mineral resources have yet to be ascertained, but there is no doubt of its wealth in coal. Last, but not least, in the enumeration of its advantages, the company enjoys the diligent attention and the great abilities of Sir Rutherford Alcock, no novice in those regions and in such undertakings.

October 22, 1882

A PARTITION OF BORNEO.

THE DIVISION OF THE ISLAND BY THE BRITISH AND THE DUTCH.

SHANGHAI, China, July 31.—A disturbance, which it was feared might lead to serious trouble between England and Holland, has this month been amicably adjusted. For several years the boundary line between the English and Dutch possessions in Borneo has caused much hard feeling among the settlers of both countries living near the disputed lines, which has on several occasions almost broken out into open fighting.

Last month a war vessel was sent by each of the two Governments and an agreement was arrived at by which the parallel of 4° 10' north should be the dividing line, the English taking all north and the Dutch all south of this parallel. By this arrangement Great Britain acquires thousands of square miles of t. s tropical timber, with large areas of fertile land already under cultivation. The Dutch obtain the larger part of the island, but the more mountainous and less valuable section, and with but few good harbors.

The concession on the part of Holland is much deplored by the Dutch settlers in the East Indies, and it is feared that they may not peaceably submit to this loss of their territory, although sanctioned by their home Government. By this agreement many of the old Dutch spice plantations, which have been successfully operated for generations, pass under English control.

August 31, 1891

COLONIES OF THE DUTCH

Successful Management of Their Densely Populated Islands.

MANY LIBERTIES ALLOWED

Thirty Thousand Hollanders in Java Dominate the 25,000,000 Native Javanese—The Dutch System.

Foreign Correspondence NEW YORK TIMES.

BRUSSELS, July 4.—In governing its new possessions in the Far East the United States has much to learn from the Dutch, who have long since solved the problem of how successfully to rule a Crown colony. It certainly is a matter for wonder that the little Dutch people should be able to maintain their authority over the 35,000,000 inhabitants of the East Indies. The question has often been asked how the 30,000 Hollanders of Java could dominate the 25,000,000 native Javanese, and how a handful of officials can govern the densest population in the world, (10,496 inhabitants per square mile.)

The secret of the successful Dutch system is to be found in the liberal régime adopted by the home Government. This régime is diametrically opposite to the colonial systems of other European powers. The absolute respect for all native customs and traditions is the secret of Holland's success in the East Indies.

In connection with the Dutch Indies, the work recently published by M. Jules Leclercq, "Un Séjour dans l'Ile de Java," is of prime importance, being the first complete work on Java published for many years. M. Leclercq gives a detailed account of his various expeditions in Java, with descriptions of the natives, their customs, and manner of living. By far the most interesting chapter of the work is, however, the one devoted to the Dutch colonial system of government. M. Leclercq begins by saying that, when, after his return from Java, he was asked by the Dutch people what he considered of most striking interest in the colony, he felt inclined to answer that the most wonderful fact, in his opinion, was that the Dutch should have been able to remain in possession of the island. And M. Leclercq is not far wrong.

When the English gave back Java to the Dutch in 1816 it is probable that they were unaware of the fact that they were giving up the finest colony in the world. As England is not in the habit of relinquishing conquered territory, it is doubtful if she would have returned Java to the Dutch—as she did after Waterloo, out of gratitude to Holland—had she known what great natural wealth the island contained.

The executive power of the Dutch Indies is placed in the hands of a Governor General, who resides at Batavia, the capital of Java. This Governor General wields practically absolute power. He is Commander in Chief of the colonial army and navy, and exercises supreme control over the various departments of the Government. He declares war and concludes treaties of peace and of commerce with the natives. He makes all appointments in the colonial army and civil service. He has the power of pardon; and no sentence of death can be carried out without his consent. One of his most important duties is the protection of the natives. He may, if he deems it advisable, expel any foreigner from Dutch territory. In fact the representative of the

the Crown is invested with absolute power and is really King of the Dutch East Indies.

There is it is true, under him an Executive Council, consisting of a Vice President and of four members, but this is merely a deliberative body, whose advice the Governor General asks, without being compelled to follow it.

HOW JAVA IS GOVERNED.

The Island of Java is divided into twenty-two provinces; at the head of each of these is a " resident " appointed by the Governor. These officials, who have been trained at Delft or at the University of Leyden, are highly educated, capable men, who have passed special examinations, drawn up by the Minister of Colonies. The real duty of these residents consists in concealing their authority, by giving the native Princes the illusion of power and the people the conviction of relative independence. Under the " residents," who are all Dutch, come the " regents," who are all natives, and often of princely birth. The natives are placed under the power of the regents.

The " residents " are considered as kind of " elder brothers " of the regents; in this capacity they give " good advice," and it is in this manner, a most pleasing one to the natives, that the island is governed.

The " regent," moreover, enjoys a number of compensations attached to his office. Everything that can dazzle the multitude is given him. He has a luxurious Asiatic Court, is better paid than the " resident," and has the right of precedence over all public officials, excepting his " elder brother." The regent is always chosen from among the nobles who governed the province before the Dutch conquest. Under him is a " voliono," a district chief, likewise a man of noble birth, chosen by the natives, under approval of the resident.

Instead of following the example of other European nations, and doing away with the language of the natives, the Dutch have found it a better policy to learn the language of their East Indian subjects. This, in Java, is a somewhat complicated matter, for there are four different races in the island, each with a language of its own—Malays, Soendanese, Javanese, and Madoerese. Many " residents " in Java are obliged to speak these four languages fluently.

But, to give the Javanese still more the illusion of their semi-independence, the Dutch, besides the native chiefs of the various provinces, have also retained the Emperor of Soerakarta. This monarch rules over a small empire, that of Vorstenlanden, the area of which is about one-fifteenth of the entire island, last vestige of the once powerful Kingdom of Mataram. The territory of Vorstenlanden is divided into two districts, governed respectively by the Emperor of Soerakarta and by his Sultan. Formerly the Vorstenlanden country formed but one province. But at the end of the last century the Emperor Hameng-Koe, unable to quell a Chinese insurrection, called upon the Dutch for assistance. Shortly after the insurrection had been put down by the Dutch troops, the Emperor's brother claimed half of the empire for himself.

The Dutch were then asked to act as arbiters between the two brothers, and settled the matter in a manner most advantageous to themselves by dividing this powerful native State into two kingdoms. Of these, the larger was given to the Emperor and the smaller to his brother. It is from these two Princes that the present Emperor and Sultan are descended. The Emperor is looked upon as the Sultan's " elder brother."

SULTAN KNEELED TO EMPEROR.

In this connection, a typical anecdote is related of the clever method of Dutch colonial government. Formerly the two sovereigns, Emperor and Sultan, had an annual interview at Gavan, near Djokjakarta. This meeting took place with great pomp, and the Sultan paid his respects to his feudal lord by removing his sandals and kneeling before him. But as this ceremony brought together a large number of natives, the Dutch thought it prudent to put an end to it.

For this purpose they persuaded the Sultan that it was beneath the dignity of a really independent Prince to kneel before any human being. Consequently, at the next annual fête, the Sultan refused to go through the traditional custom, and treated the Emperor as an equal, not a superior. Deeply offended, the Emperor smothered the insult, but that meeting put an end to the annual interviews between the two Princes. Thus the Dutch achieved their purpose.

The population of Java consists of 25,000,-000, divided as follows: 24,500,000 natives, Javanese, Madoerese, and Soendanese; 260,-000 Chinese, 50,000 Europeans, 17,000 Arabs, and 3,000 Japanese.

The foreign trade of Java is of great importance. Naturally, the principal importing country for Javanese products is Holland; then follow British India, China, and the United States. The chief exports are coffee, sugar, tobacco, indigo, spices, and swallows' nests.

The Javanese roads are, perhaps, the finest in the world. They are all highways, built by the Government at the beginning of the present century, and are divided off into two portions, one for cattle and heavy traffic, the other for ordinary traffic. The first railroad on the island was inaugurated in 1594 between Batavia and Buitenzorg. Since then several other railways have been built, from the coast to the interior of the island.

The first European conquerors of Java and the East Indian Islands were the Portuguese. In the sixteenth century they had the commercial monopoly of all the products from these islands. For many years the Dutch went to Lisbon for all the East Indian products which they required. But when Philip II., King of Spain, annexed Portugal, he decided to revenge himself upon his former Dutch subjects by closing all the ports of the peninsula to them. The Dutch then decided to go to the East Indies themselves. It was, however, necessary to find the ocean route, the secret of which the Portuguese carefully kept to themselves. After two unsuccessful attempts in 1594 and 1596, Capt. Corneliz Houtman succeeded in buying some Portuguese maps, and thus ascertained the true route around the cape. A Dutch East Indian Company was at once formed by ten merchants of Amsterdam. From that time on the trade relations between Holland and the Indies increased rapidly. Later on the Dutch Government was obliged to intervene to protect Dutch colonists from the Portuguese; and thus, in time, Java and the adjoining islands came into the possession of Holland.

Mr. Leclercq's work is illustrated with various typical scenes from Javanese life, and specimens of natives, among them the Emperor of Soerakarta.

BRADFORD COLT DE WOLF.

July 16, 1899

DUTCHMEN KILL 260 NATIVES.

Fortifications in Sunda Razed by Fire of Warships.

AMSTERDAM, July 31.—The Dutch expedition sent against the rebellious native State of Boni, in the Island of Celebes, one of the Sunda Islands in the East Indies, inflicted severe punishment on the natives, 260 of whom were killed.

The fortifications of Badjoewa, one of the chief towns, were razed by the guns of the warships.

August 1, 1905

REVOLTS IN SUMATRA BLAMED UPON SOVIET

Achines, Who Had Been Quiet 20 Years, Kill Dutch Soldiers, Fighting Only With Swords.

Copyright, 1926, by The New York Times Company.
By Wireless to THE NEW YORK TIMES.

LONDON, April 22.—The Communist propaganda, which has caused trouble in China, aggravated the unrest in India and even embittered the industrial part of England, has now, according to reports, spread to the Dutch East Indies and Sumatra.

Its success among the Achine natives in particular there is causing the Dutch authorities much anxiety and has made it necessary for them, after almost twenty years of peace, to show the strong hand once more.

The Achines of Sumatra are a race of such martial qualities that they resisted the Dutch forces for more than thirty years. Drastic military operations subdued them two decades ago, and since then civil rule has been substituted for military authority.

Communism, however, it is said, also sprang up, and the result has been a series of attacks on Dutch patrols in which a number of lives were lost.

On March 1 a Dutch patrol of twelve men was wiped out in a surprise attack and their rifles and ammunition were stolen.

On April 5 another patrol was attacked, its commander, Captain Paris, and five men being killed and eleven wounded. Nineteen rebels were killed.

Recently nine Achines were killed in an assault on a Dutch force, of which one captain and five men were wounded.

The rebels fight with their native swords, and although they are without firearms they show the greatest daring.

April 23, 1926

OPPOSE JAVA COUNCIL STEP

Europeans There Criticize Governor's Plan for a Native Majority.

Copyright, 1927, by The New York Times Company.
Special Cable to THE NEW YORK TIMES.

BATAVIA, Java, Nov. 22.—Jonkheer De Graaf, Governor-General of the Dutch East Indies, whose firmness in suppressing native uprisings in Java and Sumatra and banishing several hundred native agitators to the interior of Dutch New Guinea won the praise of European settlers, 's now being criticized for his support of the native aspirations for a greater share in the administration of the Government. De Graaf and his ministry propose to give the natives a majority in the Volksraad, the council of the Dutch East Indies which was established ten years ago.

The proportion in the Volksraad is now thirty Europeans to twenty-five natives. The Government proposes to reverse this ratio, despite the opposition of leading men of Java and Sumatra, who have asked that the advice of the present Volksraad be taken.

A petition deprecating any debate on the question under the present circumstances has been sent to Governor General De Graaf. The petition says that, whatever decision the Volksraad might take on the proposal, public discussion would only be to the advantage of the discontented Javanese and tend to widen the breach between them and the Dutch authorities.

November 23, 1927

DUTCH EAST INDIES COMPOSE AN IMMENSE COLONIAL EMPIRE

Scene of Navy Mutiny, Now Burdened by Depression, Is Densely Populated and Extremely Productive

THE recent mutiny by native members of the navy in the Dutch East Indies focuses attention on those distant colonies of the Netherlands. Salary cuts are reported to have been the cause of unrest, the first in many years.

The Dutch East Indies, officially known as Netherlands India, include several large islands and archipelagos, lying along the Equator like "a string of emeralds." Their total area is 733,681 square miles, as compared with the 13,000 square miles of the mother country. The census of 1930 showed a population of 60,731,000, while crowded Holland has only 8,032,000. Thus in regard to its colonial possessions Holland resembles Great Britain. Both are dwarfed in size and population by the colonies they govern.

The principal islands of the Dutch colonial empire are Java, Sumatra, Borneo and Celebes. The largest of these is Borneo, whose notorious "wild men" are now reported to be friendly. The most populous island is Java, which, together with its neighboring small island of Madura, is the home of more than 40,000,000 of the colony's 60,000,000 inhabitants. It is one of the most densely populated land masses in the world, 821 people living on each square mile, as compared with an average of 41.3 in the United States.

Java and coffee have become synonymous. At one time coffee was Java's most important product, but now it accounts for only about 5 per cent of the colony's exports.

Rubber now takes first place among the colony's products and sugar second. The Dutch East Indies rank second only to Cuba in exports of cane sugar. In 1930 the total sugar exports were 2,694,456 metric tons; in 1931, under the Chadbourne plan, exports of sugar from the Dutch East Indies were limited to 2,300,000 tons.

Figures on exports and imports in the last four years are given in the following table. The totals for 1932 are estimated on the basis of preliminary reports.

	Exports.	Imports.
1929	$579,954,948	$425,200,224
1930	478,977,372	370,752,942
1931	322,485,606	244,471,476
1932	220,000,000	150,000,000

The figures reveal that, while retaining a favorable balance of trade, the commerce of the Dutch East Indies has fallen off steadily till it is now considerably less than half that of 1929.

Holland's interest in the East Indies dates back to the years of budding imperialism in the seventeenth century. In 1602 the East India Company was formed and given a free rein in conquering and exploiting the islands. With the dissolution of the company in 1798 the government itself took control. Holland also has colonies in South America (Dutch Guiana) and the Caribbean (Curaçao, also known as the Dutch West Indies).

At present the Dutch East Indies are under the supervision of a Governor General appointed by the Queen. He is assisted by a Council of Seven, also appointees of the Queen, and a Volksraad or People's Council, which advises the Governor General on the budget. The People's Council has sixty members, thirty-eight elected by members of local councils and the remaining twenty-two appointed by the Governor General. In 1931 thirty of the People's Council were Indonesians, twenty-five Dutch, four Chinese and one Arabian.

Though the East Indies are spoken of, even in Holland, as "colonies," officially they have been an integral part of the kingdom since 1922.

February 12, 1933

MALAYA

KALANTAN RUBBER COUNTRY WAS DISCOVERED BY AN ODD CHANCE

UNITED STATES motor car manufacturers and drivers should have a considerable interest in the rubber colony of Kalantan, added to the British Federal States of Malay (under direct control of the British Government) through the activities of R. W. Duff. This adventurous Englishman when on the military police pursued Malay insurgents into Kalantan, opened its possibilities, and finally "outwitting the Siamese," secured concessions from the local Rajah, enabling him to practically rule the little State, to inoculate the natives against smallpox and cholera, to open mines and to plant thousands of acres with rubber trees. These administrative powers he yielded to the British Government in 1000 on condition that the Singapore-Bangkok railway be laid through his plantations. It was not so laid and Duff in a suit has just won damages and costs of £378,000 from his Government.

Singapore, south of Kalantan, had been secured to British authority by Sir Stamford Raffles in 1819. He had entered and explored it as a naturalist. In five years after he had brought Singapore under British authority he had elevated it from a village of 150 inhabitants to a city of 10,000 residents. This largely because he determined to make Singapore a "free port." It has become one of the greatest rubber marts in the world, throwing into the shade such important rubber centres as Para, in Brazil, or Kampala, in Uganda.

Kalantan River and city lie on the east side of the State, almost on the Gulf of Siam, but facing the South China Sea. They, therefore, suffer from windstorms, but for many months the climate is warm and in most parts healthful for Europeans. Visitors from Europe must, nevertheless, return to their native climate every three to five years and their children, left on the Malay Peninsula, after the fourth year must leave or deteriorate. "Sumatra" is the Malay word for wind, which accounts for the nomenclature of that tropical island.

Wild rubber trees are indigenous to Kalantan, but all over the Malay Settlements have been planted trees of the Para type and these do well, returning profitable garnerings of sap. The province also possesses coal and tin; indeed, Singapore supplies half the world with its requirements in the matter of tin. Other exports are gold, cocoanuts, copra, sugar, coffee, sago, tobacco, rice, tea, and tapioca, the cassava root flourishing in this, as in most tropical climes.

Much of Kalantan State has yet to be explored and charted, as is the case with other portions of the Malay Peninsula. The inhabitants rarely travel on foot, but follow the rivers by boat. This accounts for the large number of boat-builders on the Kalantan River. Kalantan itself has a computed population of something over 300,000 people and possesses good roads; indeed, the Malay Peninsula has something approaching 3,000 miles of roads, all fit for negotiation by motor-car drivers.

There is also a fairly speedy railroad service. A passenger can travel from Penang to Singapore (489 miles) in about twenty-four hours. The capital of Kalantan is Kota Bharu, but the future lies with the port of Kalantan on the South China Sea. Thence may be shipped the rubber product.

December 6, 1925

SINGAPORE TO BE NEW LINK IN BRITISH DEFENSE CHAIN

Far Eastern Base for Warships Commands the Trade Routes Leading to the Pacific, Now the Centre of Naval Strategy

By ALLANSON SHAW.

ONE of the consequences of the World War was the shifting of the naval strategic centre from the North Sea to the Pacific Ocean. Recognizing this, the American Government based its battle fleet in the Pacific, while the British naval authorities realized the desirability of having a Far Eastern naval base of the first rank.

The battle of Coronel, in which the British squadron was wiped out by the Germans under von Spee, caused Great Britain to cast a regretful eye upon Singapore and brought about the resolution to build a great dockyard there. The Labor Government threw the plans into the waste basket, believing that the Singapore base would be a "menace to the peace and safety of the empire," to use the words of Premier MacDonald. This decision has now been reversed by the Baldwin Government, and Singapore is destined to become another link in the chain of far-flung defenses that Britain has forged for the protection of her trade.

Covering a period of many centuries, the greatest trading nation the world has known has been the British. Its policies have been largely dictated by commercial considerations, and have reflected trade perhaps more frankly than those of any other people. An insular folk, the British people have gone abroad seeking raw materials to keep spindles revolving and mouths filled, and searching for marts in which to sell the finished fabrics.

Joint enterprises in foreign lands brought about the chartering of great trading companies, among them those that explored, for business purposes, India, the American Northwest, the Levant, the Baltic and Muscovite lands. So vast were some of these operations that their policies became almost synonymous with those of the nation. When the company became too unwieldy for its own good or that of the people with whom it was associated it was merged in the nation, as happened in the case of the British East India Company.

Pioneers of British Trade.

Fortunately, there sprang from the ranks of this sea-going people a succession of great trading pioneers, probably unequalled in the history of nations thus far; men who were traders of the highest calibre, and something more—men capable of wide vision, who saw in primitive conditions and situations the possibilities of future development. They were dreamers of practical dreams. They thought in terms of continents and centuries: and when you have men at the head of affairs able to do this, national eminence is assured. These men picked out key positions for trading and the protection of trade, and so one finds Great Britain entrenched at Quebec, Gibraltar, Suez, Singapore and many another toll-bar place on the roads of the world

Since much of the prosperity of Great Britain was derived from its Far Eastern possessions and commerce, the routes east of Suez have been of great importance, particularly in view of the comparatively recent development of Australasia. Thus the value of Singapore has become more fully appreciated, and from this appreciation has emerged the decision of the Baldwin Government to make Singapore a first-class naval base, capable of refitting and repairing capital ships.

A glance at the map of Asia will show, stretching southward from Siam and Burmah, broadly speaking, a snake-shaped land extension—the Malay Peninsula. At the tip of the serpentine head is the Island of Singapore, separated from the mainland by a strait, a scant half-mile wide at its narrowest point. At the southern extremity of the island is the town of Singapore, fronting the Strait of Malacca, and in close proximity to the Strait of Sunda.

One needs no second glance to appreciate the commercial and strategic value of the place. It stands midway between Hongkong and Calcutta; across the Strait of Malacca are Sumatra and Java to south and west; Borneo lies to the east, with the Celebes, New Guinea and Australia further east and the innumerable islands of the Malay Archipelago, with the Philippines, to the north. Traffic going east from the Arabian Sea, Indian Ocean and Bay of Bengal passes the door of Singapore, via the strait, to the seas of China and Japan and the great trading countries washed by these seas.

Critics of the projected base have asserted that either Bombay, Colombo or Trincomali would have furnished a more convenient haven for ships traveling from Suez to the Eastern Seas; but their argument is not very convincing and overlooks the closer proximity of Singapore to Australasia, which is keenly interested in the development of the naval station.

In the year of Trafalgar, 1805, a young Yorkshireman, Thomas Stanford Raffles, was in the employ of the London office of the East India Company. Family impoverishment had driven him to an "extra clerkship" in the company's employ when he was in his fourteenth year. Physically he was a delicate lad, but he had great energy and ambition, so that by the time he was 24 Raffles had raised himself from the ranks and was sent out to the Penang office of the company in a secretarial position.

He was an instinctive traveler and explorer, with broad sympathies and an astonishing gift for languages. He found the Dutch in virtual command of the Eastern Seas, but there was one spot that had been overlooked by the usually astute Hollander. It was the Island of Singapore, which was, at that time, almost entirely jungle and sparse-

ly inhabited. History intimates that the former population had been wiped out by Javanese invaders, and nature, with a hot, humid climate to help, had covered the island with luxuriant vegetation.

Purchased in 1819.

Raffles perceived its great value, and in 1819 secured its cession, by purchase from the Sultan of Johore. Raffles, himself, raised the British flag over the newly acquired territory. He died in his forty-fifth year, after a vivid life that had seen much disappointment and loss, but he had done a great stroke of business for his country within the limited time allotted to him. He did more than acquire territory; far in advance of his time he abolished forced labor in the lands under his rule, and won the censure of his company, for freeing the slaves within his jurisdiction. His statue, done by Chantry, stands in the north aisle of Westminster Abbey, tribute to a great and beneficent pioneer, who had done more than any other to assure British supremacy in the Eastern seas.

Today Singapore stands unrivaled as a trading centre in this part of Asia. There are seven miles of quays and shipyards along its waterfront, and it may be readily understood that, considering the awakening of the Far East, the advance of Japan, the slow but not less sure development of China, the great future in store for Australia, the importance of Singapore will increase rather than diminish as the years go by.

Here Great Britain has had a minor naval base since 1882, with fairly good fortifications, but conditions have changed so notably within recent years that the modernizing of the base would seem to be nothing more than ordinary business prudence and efficiency. At present Great Britain has no efficient naval base for capital ships east of Suez. If one of its large ships needs overhauling she must be sent home, a distance of 8,000 miles.

It is proposed to spend some $50,000,000, covering a term of years, in creating the new base, a sum that Japan is spending in a single year for two modern naval bases. The late Sir Percy Scott objected to the establishment of the Singapore base, contending that the battleship was obsolete and that future sea fights would be determined by undersea vessels and aircraft. It is significant that the British Admiralty, having given due weight to the experience gained in the World War, does not agree with Sir Percy's views. The Nelson and the Rodney will combine features of the present capital ship as to size with those of the aircraft carrier.

Other critics, mostly British, with economy in mind, have suggested that the modernizing of the Singapore base indicates a spirit of antagonism toward the two great Pacific powers—the United States and Japan. Probably the last people to take this view will be the reasonable folk of the two countries named, and even in Great Britain the suggestion is made rather half-heartedly, being inspired by the conviction that any kind of stick may be used to beat the undesirable dog of extravagance.

The importance of the project becomes still more apparent when one considers the situation of Singapore in relation to other geographical points of significance. It is 4,948 miles from Suez, 5,631 from Cape Town, 4,306 from Sydney, 4,991 from Auckland, 5,209 from Seattle, 2,902 from Yokohama. Standing at the end of an 8,000-mile line from England it would undoubtedly be a protection for the trade routes leading to the Pacific.

Whatever the truth about the jingoistic policies of British Governments in times past, these policies have never been characteristic of the Dominions, and it should be remembered that in the matter of the Singapore naval base Great Britain has been somewhat slow in meeting the demands of the overseas parts of the empire. There is some reason for this hesitancy, because a large part of the bill will have to be paid by British taxpayers, and in these hard times new and exceptional expenditures are viewed sternly.

In 1923 at the imperial conference held in London the mind of Australia and New Zealand, as well as of India, was vigorously expressed, spokesmen of these countries asserting that the establishment of the Singapore base was absolutely essential to the mobility of the fleet and their own protection. Prime Minister Bruce of Australia said "the heart of the British Empire has been transferred from the North Sea to the Pacific," New Zealand, Australia and the Legislative Council at Singapore have offered to pay their share of the cost of developing the base which, they believe, will insure them against aggression and promote the development of trade in the Far East and Australasia.

February 8, 1925

SIAM

FRANCE'S CRUSADE IN ASIA

ORIGIN AND GROWTH OF HER CONFLICT WITH SIAM.

Great Britain, Russia, and China Directly Intereste in the Result of the Operations on the Mekong and Menam Rivers —The Disputed Strip of Territory Between the Mekong and the Laos Mountains — Britain's Frontier Problem and France's Approaching Elections.

Obscure and remote as are the roots from which sprung France's quarrel with Siam, they confessedly furnished a colorable pretext rather than a legitimate provocation for the arbitrary attitude and belligerent acts of the European power.

For about a century there has stretched between Siam and its eastern neighbor, Annam, a tract of territory claimed by both, possessed by neither. It has been virtually a no-man's land. British geographers and mapmakers, as a rule, awarded it to Siam, while their Gallic confrères with equal tenacity attached it to Annam, or depicted it as neutral and disputed soil.

This strip of land, irregular in width because of the tortuous windings of the Mekong River, lies between that stream on the west and the Laos Mountain chain on the east. France now abruptly insists that the river is the rightful western boundary of Annam, (a State under French protection,) as far north as the twenty-third parallel. Siam expresses a willingness to leave the matter to arbitration.

Russia is supposed to be tacitly encouraging France's scheme of territorial expansion in Asia, while Great Britain has declared that it will not meddle with the question of the delimitation of frontier, provided the independence of Siam is not menaced. In this proviso there is as much virtue as in the proverbial "if."

In his London *Truth*, that cynical Englishman, Henry Labouchère, sums up the situation as follows:

"What is going on in Siam is interesting. There is a huge peninsula. West is Burmah; east is Tonquin, Annam, and Lower Cochin China, and in the middle is Siam. We annexed Burmah. The French annexed Tonquin, Annam, and Lower Cochin China. The French now, on a question of frontier, have fallen out with the King of Siam, and the entire dominion of that potentate is to them as Naboth's vineyard was to Ahab. This we regard as most criminal, not because we have any particular affection for the Siamese, but because we hold that, having annexed Burmah, Siam becomes so far within our sphere of influence as to render it undesirable that it should fall into French hands.

"This is probably true, and it will be well if Siam remains as a buffer State between us and the French in the far East. But I really cannot get up any indignation against the French; for if it is monstrous of them to want to absorb Siam, it was equally monstrous of us to absorb Burmah. As regards the entire peninsula, we are both Ahabs, and our rival lust of what belongs to neither will possibly keep both of us out of Siam, to the great advantage of the Siamese."

What menace to Britain's Indian Empire would be involved in the subjugation of Siam by France is succinctly stated by the London *Telegraph* of July 18 in these cogent words:

"For there must be no mistake about the relations of England to this sudden and dangerous situation. We could not stand by and see the Siamese Kingdom overthrown. We could not accept any acts or events which should impair its integrity or reduce it to a tributary and vassal State. Siam is the Trans-Gangetic Afghanistan, the independence of which is absolutely necessary to the security of our Burmah borders; and, besides, there is the fact that we have enormous commercial and civil interests there, and a compact of friendship and good-will with its extremely enlightened and cultivated Sovereign, King Chulalong Korn.

"The high intelligence of the French statesmen must and may be trusted to understand this; for, properly considered, it is for their interests, as well as ours, not to push to the point of despair this central State of the Buddhist world, the further frontier of which is a frontier of the British Empire. What they wish for, or dream of, upon the Upper Mekong is a matter for equitable argument and for negotiation—not for forcible proceedings, which are no longer possible in that region of Asia without violent and undesirable results. The time has passed when policies can be pushed in the dark by headstrong and ambitious subordinates, rendered reckless by frequent Ministerial changes at home. There are imperial necessities stronger than mountains and broader than rivers, which must be taken into account, and which limit modern adventure. Judicious minds on this side, aware of these necessities, without being jealous of the natural aspirations of others, will continue to rely, in the present really anxious position of affairs, upon France's high sense of honor and acute perspicacity, and will abstain from any word or deed which, in the ancient Greek phrase, might 'stir the fire with a sword.'"

Half a minute's study of any modern atlas will show that the extension of French power and influence in the peninsula must leave Britain's Indian Empire gripped as in a vice between Russia on the northwest and Russia's reputed ally on the southeast, and the utterances of the French press are not pitched at a key calculated to reassure or tranquilize England. China, too, is dissatisfied and inimical to the aggressive approaches of both Russia and France.

Thus it comes to pass that, no matter how the present difficulty may be adjusted, the most disturbing factor in European politics for a season is likely to originate on the banks of the Mekong and Menam instead of on those of the Bosporus or the Rhine.

As an illustration of the logic of the wolf in dealing with the lamb, it is interesting to trace the incidents which led to the presentation of the French ultimatum.

Intercourse between France and Siam began about the year 1680, when King Phra Nerain, by advice of Constantine Phaulcon, an adventurer, who had become a Minister to the Siamese Crown, sent an embassy to visit "Le Grand Monarque," Louis XIV. The courtesy led to an exodus of missionaries and argonauts from France to Siam, whose assumptions and intrigues ere long resulted in the death of Phaulcon, the persecution of Christians, and a total cessation of intercourse with France.

The magnitude of British conquests in Asia eclipsed and wilted French colonizing projects in the East, and it is only in comparatively recent years that France has begun to advance her flag in the Orient and in Central Africa. She feels that she needs something more distant and promising than Algeria for the exercise of her troops and fleets and the extension of her commercial enterprises.

Moreover, the elections are approaching, and the Government is not above indulging in a demonstration which helps to divert popular thought from Panama scandals and other unpleasant topics. It is a repetition, in a measure, of the policy which induced the third Napoleon to issue the order, "On to Berlin!"

In explaining to the French Chamber of Deputies the abrupt issuance of the ultimatum to Siam, the Minister of Foreign Affairs, M. Develle, delivered an argument which may be summarized as follows:

First—That France has always contended that the left bank of the River Mekong ought to be considered the limit of her Indo-Chinese possessions.

Second—That on account of France's inaction, forbearance, and seeming apathy, Siam had become emboldened "to encroach on our dependencies of Cambodia and Annam" and to withhold reparation for wrongs done to French citizens.

Third—That Siam, after evacuating the island of Khong, tried to recapture it and seized Capt. Thoreux and his troops, who had taken possession of it.

Fourth—That Inspector Grosgurin had been "the victim of a cowardly assassination in his tent by the orders of the Siamese Mandarin whom he was to conduct back so as to protect him against the population, the victims of his exactions."

Siam's version of the case is materially different. The Ministers of the Lord of the White Elephant affirm that never until very recently did France's protégé, Annam, lay claim to any lands as far west as the Mekong River, and certainly not above the eighteenth parallel. They declare that their outposts were attacked and driven away by Franco-Annamite forces, and that Inspector Grosgurin was killed in a fair fight provoked by himself. And, while not renouncing jurisdiction over the island of Khong, they point to the fact that Capt. Thoreux was liberated for the sake of peace.

Bangkok, the capital of Siam, is situated inland, twenty-seven miles from the mouth of the Menam River, a stream not navigable for vessels drawing more than thirteen feet. Under existing treaties no foreign war ship is permitted to ascend the stream more than a few miles without the express consent of the Siamese Government. Nevertheless, when hostile operations began in the disputed territory, the French gunboats Inconstante and Comète prepared to steam up to the capital, for the avowed purpose of protecting the lives and property of French residents in Bangkok.

Siamese pilots being refused to them, the gunboats proceeded up the river on the night of July 13 in the wake of the mail steamer Jean Say, and, after exchanging a brisk but almost harmless fire with the Paknam forts, resulting in damage to the Say alone, anchored in front of the capital and cleared for action. The French claim that their vessels possessed as much right to ascend the Menam as did an English gunboat which had preceded them, and at all events they plead as justification that the forts first opened fire.

Subsequent events are fresh in the minds of all newspaper readers. France's ultimatum was transmitted on July 19. It demanded heavy money indemnities, the immediate appointment of a frontier commission, and the cession of the left bank of the Mekong River up to the twenty-third parallel. Twenty-four hours were allowed for deliberation, with the possible alternative of the bombardment of the capital.

To have shelled Bangkok would not have been much of a feather in the cap of the French Republic. Apart from the lack of adequate provocation for any such summary action, the city is known to be almost defenseless. Excepting the palace, temples, monasteries, and new barracks, the buildings are constructed chiefly of wooden posts and matting walls, not fit to resist rifle bullets, much less artillery. While every able-bodied free man is supposed to be trained for fighting, and while the Siamese are courageous enough, their army could offer scant resistance to a compact force of European troops armed with modern rapid-fire rifles and Gatling guns and supported by the cannon of the war ships.

Under such circumstances a bombardment of the Siamese capital would have been manifestly barbarous—a fact which the French themselves tacitly admitted when they altered their plan of operations and proclaimed a blockade.

Of the two European powers most directly interested, neither cares the toss of a button for Siam's rights or autonomy, as such. The Paris *Temps*, which, albeit anti-Ministerial on home issues, is credited with being an inspired organ of the Foreign Office, jauntily says:

"The healthy portion of the European colony cannot have been vexed at the appearance of our ships. The Europeans inhabiting the far East hold that in dealing with Asiatic races the nations of the West must always make themselves respected, and that, in spite of differences of interest, there is a certain solidarity between us. It is with Siam as with China, and on the whole the action of our vessels and the boldness shown by them in punishing the insult to our flag cannot have displeased the colonists settled in Siam.

"As for the English officers on the Pallas outside the bar and those at anchor off Bangkok, they certainly watched with great professional interest Capt. Borie's action. They betted for or against its success, reflecting in their hearts that our men were brave fellows to undertake that perilous adventure. And we are sure that this has only increased their esteem for the French Navy. Assuredly it was an adventure, an audacious act. If the Siamese had any military training, the inconstante and the Comète would now be wrecks on the muddy banks of the Menam, and we should have to deplore a disaster.

"The Siamese admit that they opened fire. Now, from that moment we were free to do whatever we chose, and not to see this requires the passion imported by certain English journals into their judgments on all colonial affairs."

The British judgment on the situation is presented as follows by the London *Times:*

"There is no desire to meddle with any portion of the French case which does not directly concern us or our Indian fellow-subjects. No one dreams of objecting to the French claim for satisfaction on account of any loss, whether of property or of life, that may have been sustained by French subjects. We are too much accustomed to dealings with imperfectly-civilized races to call in question the propriety of exacting reparation for any proved injury. Nor does any one in this country object to the delimitation of frontiers in the Mekong Valley, even though it should result in slicing off from Siam a certain amount of territory to which she has laid claim on grounds which we have little chance of appraising with accuracy.

"But if rectification of frontiers goes the length of seriously maiming Siam and threatening her independence, the most irascible of Frenchmen must surely perceive that other nations have the same rights which France claims with so much energy in parallel cases. In the same way, without at all calling in question the French right to exact reparation for injuries, or even attempting to prescribe the mode in which she shall exact it, Great Britain, as well as any other power having treaty engagements or even commercial intercourse with Siam, must take a serious view of proceedings that may result in upsetting altogether a not too stable Government and handing over the country to the worst forms of internal disorder."

With recollections of Egypt, the Suez Canal, and the Tonquin campaign rankling in memory, Frenchmen are persuaded that "perfide Albion" is implacably hostile to every effort on the part of France to participate in that "civilizing process" which is Britain's pretext for the constant acquisition of new territory.

Englishmen, on the other hand, contemptuously allude to the "Chauvinistic spirit" of the French people, and the increasing bitterness of comment on both sides reveals a jealousy and an enmity which may have been at times disguised, but which have continued, either active or dormant, from the time of the earlier Henrys, through the Napoleonic wars, down to our own day.

It may be predicted without rashness that Siam must ere long become a ward and dependency of either France or Britain. The London *Graphic's* blunt declaration that a protectorate over Siam is necessary to restore British prestige surprises nobody who is familiar with the trend of European civilizing processes in Asia and Africa.

Two months have passed since the Bombay *Gazette* made the startling assertion that Lord Salisbury three years ago came to an understanding with M. Waddington, by which India was to occupy the Shan States between Burmah and the northeast frontier of Siam, though claimed by the latter country, while France was to have all the left bank of the Mekong. Such a statement taxes credulity and does not accord with the recent attitudes of the French and British Cabinets or newspapers. Nevertheless, England at the present moment seems to be as certain of absorbing Siam as if the Gladstone Ministry were oath bound to fulfill a compact arranged by Salisbury and Waddington.

August 6, 1893

Siam Yields to France Again.

BANGKOK, Oct. 1.—The final settlement of the questions in dispute between France and Siam was concluded to-day. The convention will be signed on Tuesday morning, and in the afternoon M. le Myre de Vilers, France's special envoy, will leave this city, probably for Saigon.

LONDON, Oct. 2.—The Times's correspondent in Bangkok says: "The draft of the new treaty is comparatively satisfactory, and embodies the ultimatum, but the convention attached is entirely unsatisfactory. The latter contains terms exceeding and contrary to the ultimatum, stipulating that France shall occupy Chantaboon after the original stipulations shall have been carried out, and until the left bank of the Mekong and the reserved zone shall have been completely evacuated and pacified. Unless France faithfully fulfills the pledges given by M. de Vilers, Chantaboon will long remain in the possession of the French.

"The proces verbal accompanying the convention reiterates that France will evacuate Chantaboon as early as possible under the agreement. Siam has agreed to all, largely owing to the King's resolve not to sacrifice the Danish officers, which demand, in view of the compliance otherwise, M. de Vilers abandoned during this morning shortly before Siam's decision was given. The French man-of-war Aspic raised steam this afternoon. The American war ship Concord arrived at the bar this morning."

October 2, 1893

ME-KONG TREATY IS SIGNED.

Liberal Party Opinion That It Is an English Knuckle Under.

PARIS, Jan. 16.—A treaty was signed yesterday by representatives of Great Britain and France settling the Me-Kong dispute, each power agreeing upon the Me-Kong River as the boundary of British and French territory from the north of Siam to the frontier of China, and that the Upper Me-Kong, in Siam, shall be the sole buffer between the territories of the two powers. The question of a buffer State was eliminated from the controversy.

LONDON, Jan. 16.—The Daily News will to-morrow say that it regards the signing of the treaty with France for the settlement of the Mekong dispute as a complete English knuckle-under.

January 17, 1896

AVERTS CONFLICT WITH SIAM.

France Signs a Treaty Delimiting the Frontier Between Siam and Cambodia.

Special Cable to THE NEW YORK TIMES.
[Copyright, 1904.]

PARIS, Feb. 14.—Any chance of complications in the Far East in consequence of the lapse Monday of the Franco-Siamese treaty has been averted by the colonial group headed by M. Francois Deloncle, Deputy for Indo-China, and brother of the unfortunate commander of the Bourgoyne.

M. Deloncle insisted that until the Franco-Siamese frontier had been delimited, Chantaboon, which is temporarily occupied by French troops, should not be evacuated. It was felt that to evacuate Chantaboon at this moment might have caused a general uprising of the yellow nations under the rule or protectorate of European powers. Great Britain's rôle in the Siamese combination being to give France a free hand, nothing is to be feared in that direction.

M. Francois Deloncle, whom I saw in the Chamber of Deputies yesterday afternoon, speaking for himself and the colonial group, expressed the fullest approval of and sympathy with America's attitude toward the Russo-Japanese war and the Far Eastern question generally.

The United States, he said, had done more to civilize the Philippines in a few months than Spain had in centuries. He hoped the United States would join hands with Europe in solving the Far Eastern problem, and his dream was the partition of Japan, France to take Formosa, the United States Northern Japan, while Russia and England would divide the rest. As Japan is certain to be overwhelmed by Russia in the long run, he foresaw this absorption of Japan by Europe as the final outcome of the struggle.

By The Associated Press.
PARIS, Feb. 13.—The danger of a conflict between France and Siam has been dissipated by the signing this evening by Foreign Minister Delcassé and the Siamese Minister to France of a treaty delimiting the frontier between Siam and Cambodia, a French protectorate in Indo-China.

This treaty secures substantial territorial and economic advantages to France and an increase of her political influence in the country. One article of the convention assures freedom in Siam to the trade of all nations.

Strained relations between France and Siam have existed for some time in consequence of the inability of the countries to agree upon the boundary line between Siam and Cambodia, and because of the hesitation of Siam to accept certain modifications of the treaty of 1902 which were demanded by France.

February 14, 1904

BRITAIN GETS PART OF SIAM.

Treaty Transferring Sovereignty Over Four States Is Ratified.

WASHINGTON, July 14.—Great Britain secures about 15,000 square miles of territory, in return for which she makes same very important concessions to Siam, by the terms of the British-Siamese treaty, which was framed on March 10 anl has just been ratified. Politically, Great Britain gives to Siam partial release from extraterritoriality on condition that Siam gives to her certain guarantees of improved courts for British subjects and the right to property and travel.

Siam agrees to build the portion in Siamese territory of a railway to connect Singapore and Bangkok on condition that England shall allow Siam a free hand in the so-called sphere of British influence, shall make to her a loan to be used in the construction of the railway, and shall pay to Siam the amount which the provinces taken over by Great Britain owe to her.

Siam transfers to Great Britain the States of Kelantan, Tringganu, Kedah, Perlis, and the adjacent islands.

July 15, 1909

AN ABSOLUTE MONARCH PAYS US A VISIT

King Prajadhipok of Siam Uses His Power With Restraint, and His People Are Contented

King Prajadhipok of Siam, accompanied by Queen Rambhai Barni, will arrive in the United States this week. This is the first time a reigning Asiatic monarch has come to America. The chief object of the King's visit is to allow him to undergo an operation on his eyes. Therefore he is traveling incognito as the Prince of Sukot'hai, so that his reception here can be unofficial. In the following article the King and his country are described; the author was formerly attached to the Siamese Government service.

By L. J. ROBBINS

KING PRAJADHIPOK of Siam —or, to give him his full title, Prabat Somdet Pra Paramindr Maha Prajadhipok Pra Pok Klao Chao Yu Hua—is a visitor of unique distinction. He is one of the last remaining absolute monarchs in the world and certainly the most important of them. King Haile Selassie of Abyssinia and Nadir Khan, the ruler off Afghanistan, have despotic power; but Abyssinia and Afghanistan are wild and primitive countries in comparison with Siam, which is almost as large as France, which has a population of nearly 12,000,-000, which was a participant in the World War on the side of the Allies and is now a respected member of the League of Nations—no longer merely the place from which come twins, cats and white elephants.

There is no limit to the authority of the King of Siam. He receives the most complete submission of the entire nation and, in theory, his lightest whim or caprice must be obeyed without hesitation. He is the head of all government institutions, and he can direct that the national revenue be spent in any way he pleases. There is a special and traditional royal language in which the pronouns indicate that the person addressing him is less than the dust beneath his feet. His absolutism is as strong today as it was in the darkest periods of tyrannical oppression in the history of Siam, when the kings found that their safety depended on exciting the abject fear of their subjects; the hereditary instinct of the race prompts it to render utter obedience without question or resentment.

But King Prajadhipok's power is not abused; on the contrary, it is wielded entirely for the good of his subjects. In fact, in both behavior and appearance, he is the complete antithesis of the tyrant of romance. He is 37 years of age, small and slight, not much over five feet in height, and has the typical Mongol-like features of the royal house of Chakkri. He was educated at Eton College in England; he served in the British and French armies; and he has traveled all over the world. Unlike his forefathers, he has only one wife, since monogamy is now definitely favored by the progressive Siamese.

Queen Rambhai Barni is the King's cousin and is still in her early twenties. She is generally admitted to be one of the most beautiful women in the East. She accompanies the King everywhere, and, like him, speaks English and French fluently. It will be interesting to see if she wears the pa-sinn which modern Siamese women have adopted from the Laos of northern Siam—an extremely graceful skirt of colored silk which quite possibly may set a new fashion when the Queen appears.

Siam is a lucky country; it is perhaps the most peaceful land in the world, completely free from international problems and complications. even "red" Chinese immigrants find that making money is easier than making trouble. The Siamese call themselves with complete justification the "T'hai," or Free People.

Yet, without disrespect to the Siamese, it can be said that Siam's survival as an independent kingdom has been largely influenced by its geographical position, "in the backwash of the China seas" between Malaya and Indo-China. At the end of the nineteenth century British power had practically ceased growing in Malaya, but the French in Indo-China felt the need for further expansion. Siam was the victim. A skirmish on the border was magnified into a diplomatic incident and full satisfaction was demanded. But England considered it desirable to maintain a buffer State between the British and the French possessions, and France was finally induced to be satisfied with a slice of Siamese territory instead of all of it. (Incidentally, this slice contains the huge ruins of Angkor, which are now being preserved against the inroads of the jungle by the admirable work of French archaeologists.) The future independence of Siam was assured by treaty. But the Siamese had re-

The All-Powerful King of Siam

ceived an unpleasant jolt and they set themselves to speed up the process of Westernization, in order to be able to command more respect from stronger powers.

The task of modernization was no easy one For many centuries Siam had fought continually with her neighbors, the Burmese and Khmers; it was divided by internal struggles and it was not until the end of the eighteenth century that it became united. All this time, and until about seventy years ago, the only Europeans who knew anything about the country were a few adventurers and missionaries. Siam deliberately tried to close her doors to the outside world and was exploited for the benefit of a privileged aristocracy.

But in the middle of the nineteenth century the King then reigning realized that the inevitable day of foreign incursion was dawning and that he was powerless to avert it. He died before he was able to effect many reforms, but his son, King Chulalongkorn—father of Prajadhipok—laid the foundations and erected a great part of the structure of an entirely new social edifice.

This was an extraordinary achievement. Slavery was abolished, a properly regulated system of taxation was instituted, government administration and a legal code along Western lines were introduced, and an educational scheme begun. Large numbers of European advisers were called in and huge engineering projects started. A regular army was founded and conscription set up, applying alike to prince and peasant. Almost overnight the ancient Constitution was transformed through the will of one man. And under his son, Prajadhipok, the huge work of transformation and reform has been carried on ceaselessly.

• • •

THE new régime has perhaps had less effect on the general conditions of life in Siam than might be expected, but it must be remembered that the Siamese are essentially a tropical people of indolent and conservative habits that are deeply rooted. The country is made up of wild, dense jungle and immensely fertile plains which produce the best rice in the world.

The bulk of the peasant population is engaged in rice cultivation. Though they now have far more personal freedom and are no longer oppressed by rapacious tax gatherers, they still exist like their forefathers, in small village settlements of palm-thatched huts. They are shy of new agricultural methods and machinery, and, in spite of the back-breaking labor involved, prefer to plant and reap by hand. The wooden plow drawn by water buffaloes is still one of the most familiar sights of the land.

• • •

COMMERCE and manufacture on an organized and extended scale are quite foreign to the Siamese temperament, and the export and import trade of the country is almost entirely in the hands of Europeans and Chinese. Every town and village has its small shopkeepers, but they are not ambitious and do not appreciate the blessings of the chain-store system.

An abrupt transition occurs between the peasants and the upper classes—the town dwellers—who are still, in practice, if not in principle, the feudal overlords of the common people. It is they who derive the chief outward benefits of Westernization. Formerly their chief diversion lay in the ceremonies and intrigues of court life, but the spread of education has given them a fresh and wide range of interests. Now most of them gravitate to Bangkok, the capital.

Bangkok, a city of well over half a million inhabitants, has a life quite apart from that of the rest of the country. It is still somewhat in the position of the tail that wagged the dog. The more obvious fruits of civilization—such as iced drinks, plumbing, electric lights, paved streets, hotels—barely exist in the up-country regions. A decentralizing process is required if the condition of the people as a whole is to be improved.

Siam, however, is in the curious position of needing a middle class. At present there are only the aristocratic and official classes and the peasantry. The social system is a sort of pyramid. There is no perpetual hereditary nobility. According to tradition, even the descendants of the King become commoners after the fifth generation; but during the descent they form the governing class. This was a wise provision in the heyday of polygamy to prevent an embarrassing excess of royalty. Formerly the kings were so prolific that all the stages of the pyramid were well populated. But now things are rather in a state of flux—a state that is emphasized by the fact that King Prajadhipok has as yet no children.

• • •

WHEN Prajadhipok came to the throne in 1926 affairs of State were in a somewhat tangled condition. He did not directly succeed his father, but was preceded by Rama VI, an elder brother, who was a man of letters rather than one of action. During Rama's reign of fifteen years the court life was very brilliant, but the economic development of Siam suffered. He instituted a number of developments but he was too much swayed by a few favorites and allowed his schemes to be carried out by incompetent and dishonest subordinates. There was a constant drain on the finances of the kingdom, and the King himself, in spite of the enormous income attached to the throne, was personally in debt to the extent of several million dollars at his death. It seemed as if Siam were resting on its oars after the initial burst of achievement.

Prajadhipok was not actually crowned until his brother had been cremated, several months after the beginning of the new reign. The people had had time to appreciate the merits of their latest ruler, who had been rather an unknown quantity owing to his long residence abroad. Consequently the coronation, which included all the traditional and colorful ceremonies of past centuries, was the occasion for much public rejoicing.

I well remember the King's first formal appearance in full regalia. All the high officials and the foreign diplomatic representatives in full dress were gathered together in a tightly packed throng in the terrific heat of one of the gilded but unventilated audience halls of the palace. Among the Europeans there was much wilting of collars.

Suddenly there was a fanfare of trumpets and a purple curtain at one end of the hall was drawn aside to reveal the King in jeweled robes, seated on a raised throne beneath the nine-tiered State umbrella, with a pointed golden crown on his head. He sat absolutely immobile, like a carved figure, while the national anthem was played, except that his dark eyes moved restlessly as he watched the crowd facing him. He was known to be ill at the time, and many present wondered if he would bear up under the strain of directing his nation through a difficult period ahead. But for four years he has worked as hard as any one in his kingdom. He faced the difficult situation that confronted him when he came into power in a most statesmanlike manner and soon gained a reputation for wisdom and progressiveness that has steadily grown.

In the first place he appointed a Supreme Council to advise him, consisting of five of the elder royal Princes who had been his father's right-hand men, together with a Privy Council of high government officials. This was an almost revolutionary step, since it involved a sort of voluntary curtailing in theory at any rate, of his ancient prerogative of absoluteness.

Then he undertook to balance the national budget by reducing expenditure. The matter was attacked at its roots. For some years past many government posts had been happy sinecures for betel-chewing old gentlemen and their hangers-on. Within a short time there was a tremendous shake-up; many officials were dismissed and useless departments abolished.

The result was an extraordinary illustration of the calmness and hereditary submissiveness of the Siamese. No resentment was shown; the victims accepted their lot with characteristic fatalism and were willing to admit that the King had done well. The policy of the King is to put the best possible men in administrative posts without favoritism (another great innovation) and, what is more important, to give them more or less unhampered powers of action.

The world depression has begun to hit Siam recently, though in such a country of easy living bread lines are not likely to appear. There has been a definite effect on the rice industry. European and Chinese shippers have been forced to buy at low prices, and by a natural but unfortunate reaction the millers have been supplying rice of inferior quality by adulterating the well-known "garden rice." As a result the fine reputation of Siamese rice abroad has been lowered. But steps are now being taken at the instigation of the King to control the millers so that the former position can be rapidly regained when the economic tide turns.

Meanwhile, large irrigation projects are being pushed forward. These are of the utmost importance, for their purpose is to avoid "bad years" for the rice crop, though this work is hampered by lack of cooperation because of ignorance on the part of the peasantry. The railways are admirably run and have a fine tradition of comfort and reliability. Roads are being built in inaccessible parts of the country where formerly only buffalo cart tracks existed. The fishing industry is being scientifically encouraged.

There are other and more startling evidences of the transformation of the land from the ancient to the modern aspect. The flying service is highly commended by all foreign aviators. Two great bridges have been thrown across the broad Menam River at Bangkok. A fashionable seaside resort has been built at Hua Hin, which may in time become an Eastern Lido. The talkies have appeared, and the King has contributed toward the cost of an elaborate sound-equipped theatre. A powerful radio station has been erected which broadcasts in Siamese, English and French.

IT was a happy omen for this new era that a white elephant was discovered in the second year of the King's reign, though now that Siamese Princes go to Oxford and Siamese girls shingle their hair, white elephants no longer receive extreme veneration, and some people are bold enough to say that an albino animal is only a freak of nature and not a supernatural manifestation.

In past centuries white elephants were believed to embody the spirits of wise princes and heroes. Then the happy discoverer had his mouth stuffed with gold as a fitting reward for a bearer of good news and the jungle was leveled to make a path for the sacred animal on its way to the capital, where it was received with elaborate ceremony and installed in the royal stables to lead a life of pampered luxury. Now any tourist to Bangkok can visit the stables and feed the white elephants on sugar cane.

For the sake of tradition and in spite of modern thought, the arrival of King Prajadhipok's white elephant, though it was only a baby and not very white, was made the occasion of a public festival. But, as a sign of the times, it was brought down from its native jungle in an upholstered railway truck.

April 19, 1931

SIAM'S ARMY ENDS ABSOLUTE MONARCHY; KING ACCEPTS CURBS

Special Cable to THE NEW YORK TIMES.

BANGKOK, Siam, June 24.—The army and navy in Bangkok, combining as a new people's party, started a successful "peaceful" revolution early this morning against the traditional absolute monarchy, which for more than sixty years has been conducted on the lines of a benevolent paternal despotism.

King Prajadhipok was absent at Huaahin when the revolutionaries—it is hinted with some high court officials to guide them—swept through the city to seize strategic points.

It was announced tonight, however, that the King had accepted a restriction of his former absolute power and had agreed to a constitutional monarchy.

The leaders of the revolution, in their early-morning rush through the city, seized as hostages Prince Paribatra, the King's brother and heir to the throne, and Prince Purachatra, the Minister of Communications. The chief of police was also seized and the law courts occupied.

It was reported that the chief of the general staff, Lieut. Gen. Phyra Siharaj Dejojai, had resisted the revolutionaries and been shot dead.

The capital is quiet tonight and it is understood that the King is returning immediately.

Hitherto the Siamese Government has been largely staffed by princes and other members of the royal house who had had the advantage of an European education. Both the

King and the heir to the throne were educated at Eton and the King left Woolwich Academy as a Lieutenant in the Royal Horse Artillery in 1914.

The absolutism against which this morning's overturn was directed has, in the opinion of many European observers, been highly advantageous to the country. Under the guise of despotism many useful reforms have been introduced, including inland air mails, radiophone to Europe and magnificent automobile roads.

The King, to meet a national financial stringency, recently made a large contribution to the public revenue from his private purse.

June 25, 1932

SIAM GETS CONSTITUTION.

Senate to Be Formed Soon—Suffrage for Women Is Reported.

BANGKOK, Siam, June 28 (Æ).— A Constitution providing for a limited monarchy, with a temporary dictatorship by the People's party, was promulgated today after it had been signed by King Prajadhipok.

The document, the outgrowth of a brief revolt last week that deprived the King of his absolute powers, provides that the dictatorship shall be replaced by suffrage when the people have been educated in the responsibilities of self-government.

A Senate is to be formed soon, half the members to be appointed by the executive of the People's party and the other half to be elected.

It was reported that the Constitution gave the voting privilege to women. All the important Princes arrested in the army and navy coup last Friday were released today, excepting Prince Puributra.

June 29, 1932

LEADER OF REVOLT IS OUSTED IN SIAM

Pradit, Instigator of 1932 Coup, Replaced by Conservative as Head of State Council.

KING FEARS COMMUNISM

BANGKOK, Siam, April 2 (Æ).— The first change in the Siamese Government since its conversion in last year's coup d'état from one of the world's few remaining absolute monarchies to a democracy was effected peacefully and without bloodshed today.

By the change, the young idealists led by Luan Pradit, instigator of the coup last June, whose tendencies have been more toward the extreme Left forces, were replaced by older men who are regarded as liberals but not Socialists or Communists.

The crisis arose when Luan Pradit presented an economic plan which the older and more conservative elements in the government regarded as a compromise between democracy and communism.

King Prajadhipok, from his seaside resort at Huahin, issued a decree which said that present members of the State Council had communistic convictions "which cannot possibly harmonize with the policy of any nation not wholly communistic." The manifesto further declared that "a situation now exists which would force any government and any country to take extraordinary measures."

In conformance with the royal decree, a new State Council was organized, headed by Phya Manopakarana and other Ministers of the old Cabinet whose tendencies are conservative.

The crisis—and today's change—were accompanied by no military display, although armed forces were placed discreetly in the Throne Hall district.

Any possibility of a counter-movement by Luan Pradit was deemed slight, for he is known as a patriot interested only in restoring the prosperity of the farmers, developing health education and similar matters.

Phya Manopakarana's actual title has not been changed, but Luan Pradit almost immediately moved from the palace and his place was taken by his successor.

April 3, 1933

REBELS OUST REGIME OF SIAM'S MONARCH

They Wire King Prajadhipok, on Vacation, They Are Loyal to Him, However.

BANKKOK, June 21 (Æ).—The government of Siam again had changed hands today as a result of a bloodless coup d'etat by the Army and Navy and civilians led by Phya Bahol, commander-in-chief who resigned his post last week.

All State councilors whom the King appointed in April resigned. Phya Bahol became Chief Executive.

The revolutionists asserted the ousted government was unconstitutional and proposed an immediate reconstitution of the assembly, with popular elections.

They sent a message to King Prajadhipok, on vacation at a seaside resort at Huahin, assuring him of their loyalty and asserting the move was aimed at observance of the constitution.

June 21, 1933

SIAM'S GOVERNMENT PUTS DOWN REVOLT

Rebels Who Attacked Bangkok Have Fled—Leader of the Uprising Arrested.

BANGKOK, Siam, Oct. 18 (Æ).— Reports both from the northern and southern centres of the insurrection that broke out last week indicated today that the government forces had triumphed over the rebels.

In the north the rebels who attacked Bangkok have fled, while in the south the revolt at Petchaburi has been suppressed.

The rebel leader and a number of others have been arrested, including high army and civilian officers.

The anxiety of the foreign communities was relieved as business returned to normalcy and rail services were resumed.

October 19, 1933

Prajadhipok of Siam Abdicates
Because Democracy Is Rejected

CRANLEIGH, Surrey, England, March 3. — King Prajadhipok of Siam abdicated at 1:45 yesterday afternoon. His abdication became effective the moment he affixed his signature to the formal act.

The document was handed to Chao Phya Sri Dharmadhibes, president of the Siamese National Assembly and head of the delegation that has been negotiating with the King, at 4:30 in the Siamese Legation in London.

The first official news of the abdication was given to a group of three newspaper men, including representatives of two British agencies and THE NEW YORK TIMES, by M. B. Smaksman, the King's private secretary, shortly after 11 o'clock this morning at Knowle house here, where the King has been living for some time the life of an English country gentleman.

Although the abdication was reported from Bangkok last night, for reasons of etiquette and diplomacy every precaution was taken to prevent any word leaking out until the official announcement to-day.

Probably never in history was the abdication of a king announced with so little formality. The King's dapper young secretary, wearing gray flannel trousers and a pullover sweater beneath his coat, received the newspaper men in his little studio, which was littered with official documents, books, typewriters and sporting guns. Two others of the royal household and one of the Scotland Yard detectives who are guarding the King were also present.

"Well, it's over now," said the secretary, standing before a roaring fire. "He is no longer King."

March 4, 1935

Japanese Mission Wins Increased Hold on Siam

By The Associated Press.

BANGKOK, Siam, May 17. — Japanese political and economic influence in Siam has received new impetus through a month's visit by a Japanese economic mission.

Warm official and business receptions for the mission are held to mark a significant phase in the increasing friendship between the two countries, which has been viewed with anxiety by Western powers, particularly Great Britain and France.

A Japanese adviser has been appointed to the Siamese Ministry of Agriculture to promote cotton cultivation in Siam and Japanese engineers have been engaged by the Bangkok municipal administration. Japanese exports to Siam more than doubled from 1933 to 1935.

May 18, 1936

SAME PLACE: Any one addressing letters henceforth to the city of Bangkok must write "Bangkok, Thailand." The ancient name of the Siamese was Thai (pronounced Tie), and the Siamese Government recently decided that Siam should be known as Thailand. The American State Department last week adhered to the Thai decision.

July 23, 1939

BURMA

EVENTS BEYOND THE SEA

ANNEXATION OF BURMAH BY GREAT BRITAIN.

THE PROCLAMATION TO BE ISSUED TO-DAY

—IRISH HOME RULE NEGOTIATIONS—

LONDON, Dec. 31.—By a proclamation which will be issued in India and England tomorrow Burmah will be formally annexed to the British Empire. The proclamation will say that the territories formerly governed by King Theebaw will no longer be under his rule, but will become a part of the dominions of the Queen of Great Britain and Ireland and Empress of India, and that the government of the country will be administered during Her Majesty's pleasure by officers appointed by the Viceroy of India.

January 1, 1886

'ROAD TO MANDALAY' LOSES WILD CHARM

Burman Tigers and Crocodiles Driven Back to Forests, Says Oil Official.

SPENT 18 YEARS THERE

After an absence of eighteen years passed in the oil fields of Burma, between Rangoon and Mandalay, P. C. Corey returned yesterday on the Orbita of the Royal Mail Line with his wife and two daughters who were born on the outskirts of the great teak forests where the bells rang with the breeze in the old pagodas.

During the time he has been in Burma, Mr. Corey said, conditions had changed. Young Burmans had studied at the University of California and returned to their native land with a dislike to work and a desire to stir up trouble.

"Through the anarchistic doctrines preached by these students," Mr. Corey continued, "there is a great deal of discontent in labor circles throughout the country instead of the contentment of the workers which existed years ago.

"In the old days the Burmese women did the work while the men sat around and smoked, and this condition still exists. The men are as lazy as ever, and talk more since they have imbibed the doctrines imported from Calcutta.

"The tigers have been driven back to the great forests beyond Mandalay by the advance of civilization, but there are still plenty of them in Burma if one wants to look for them. Personally, I never lost any tigers," Mr. Corey said.

"The crocodiles are gone from the Irrawaddy, too. I have not seen a crocodile or an alligator between Rangoon or Bhamo in Upper Burma, which is close to the borders of China and Tibet."

Mr. Corey said that the Indo-Burma Company, with which he was connected, and the Burma Oil Company produce from 12,000 to 15,000 barrels a day, and have a working agreement not to cut the prices against each other. The Standard Oil Company is not represented in Burma, he added.

The two great industries of Burma are the cultivation and export of teak and rice. The ruby mines in upper Burma are flourishing because of the scarcity and high prices of these stones. The women still smoke their big cigars, and the men smoke cigarettes, he declared.

July 10, 1923

BURMA LABOR SAYS WORKERS ARE KEPT ALMOST IN SLAVERY

FORMAL human slavery in Burma has finally been stamped out through the efforts of the British Government, represented principally by Deputy Commissioner Barnard of the Burman Frontier Service, whose freeing of 3,445 slaves at a cost of 19,000 rupees (about $7,000) was described in recent cablegrams from Allahabad, India. But there seems to be room for further improvement in the condition of the working people composing the bulk of the some 13,-000,000 inhabitants of Burma.

According to a report recently sent to the Amsterdam Bureau of the International Federation of Trade Unions by the General Secretary of the Burma Labor Association, which is affiliated with the All-India Trade Union Congress, the workers of Burma are divided roughly into three main classes: those employed in factories, workshops and steamers; those not employed by anybody, but making their living by pulling rickshaws and working as bazaar coolies, and those recruited by agents or contractors for definite periods to work as coolies on wharves and in mills and mines.

All these people are said to live in most miserable quarters. Those working in factors, &c., receive free accommodations from their employers, but these are described as hardly fit for human habitation, being barracks of corrugated iron roofing, poorly ventilated and lacking in sanitary arrangements, and so crowded that in some cases the room allowed to each person is only 5 by 4 feet. Pure water is said to be unobtainable and fatal epidemics are reported frequent.

The contract system is branded as little better than out-and-out slavery, as the workers frequently have to bribe the contractors to get work and then have to pay more bribes in order to collect wages due. Attempts at escape are punished under the contract law. The authorities are criticized for their alleged lack of care for the interests of the native workers.

The Labor Association of Burma was organized in 1920, and its General Secretary says that despite a shortage of capable leaders and numerous other handicaps it has been able to improve the lot of the workers by means of several strikes waged upon quite a big scale. The labor unions of British India have the moral and material support of the labor organizations of Great Britain, as was demonstrated during the textile strike in Bombay last Fall.

May 23, 1926

LONDON SEES RISING IN BURMA AS BASIC

Scattered Outbreaks, Laid at First to Agitators, Are Traced to Economic Depression.

Since early in April dispatches from Simla in India and from Rangoon and Mandalay in Burma have periodically related the episodes of revolts in various isolated regions of Burma, but it was not until May 17 that the Secretary of State for India, in the British House of Commons, so linked these episodes that a general revolution against British rule was revealed. Then on June 1 came a wireless dispatch to THE NEW YORK TIMES from Simla saying that "military operations on a large scale against the Burma rebels are likely to begin."

At first, it is said, the authorities at Rangoon were disposed to regard the unrest as spasmodic outbreaks inspired by the secret agents of the "Golden Crow," who proclaimed himself "King" last Autumn in the north and then disappeared in the jungles, leaving no trace, but the information on which the Secretary of State for India, W. Wedgwood Benn, based his statement of May 17 shows that the source of the revolts is not political but economic and that agriculture and labor, rather than political ambition, are involved.

Advices from Mandalay have directed the attention of the Secretary to the fact that there is not and never has been any purely political impulse in the life of the Burmese, such as there is in the life of the Indians. The Burmese, it is said, are not naturally cohesive except for entertainment and pleasure. They are generous and improvident, eat well and clothe themselves well—where, as a rule, the Indians do neither. Long ago, it is said, the Burmese lost all interest in nationalism, and the fact that the London round table last Spring contemplated giving them an autonomous administration independent of that of India and of more immediate realization, is said to have come as a surprise to most Burmese, who merely mentioned it in their native press with little comment.

The round table, however, is said to have made them self-conscious of their possibilities, and so they looked about for a formula on which they could unite. The old one, a hierarchy, favored by the Buddhist monks and said to have been the inspiration of the "Golden Crow," was not revived, and it was not until they began to feel the pressure of the closing of foreign markets and were overwhelmed with Indian cheap labor that they sought to better themselves by organizing gangs of peasants which plundered the large plantations and the settlements under their protection. Soon these gangs grew into small armies, disciplined, through the Burmese love of order and routine, and armed from the hunting outfits of their victims. When their camps have been attacked in force by the police, the Punjabis, or imported Sepoys, they have dispersed in the jungle only to reunite at another time and place.

Mr. Benn showed how their activities had been particularly pronounced in the Tharrawaddy, Insein, Henzada, Thayetmyo and Hanthawaddy districts of the central and northern parts of Burma, while in Lower Burma the beginning of the monsoon with its heavy rains had seemed to have dampened their spirits.

This was said to be the situation in the rural districts. In the towns the Burmese are said to have taken a leaf from the Indian book of concentrated revolt by loosely organized campaigns of boycott of British goods and of civil disobedience. Thus the town dwellers have abandoned the use of alcohol, tobacco, and the wearing of European dress, and killings for not observing the rules of boycott and defiance of law have been common. The chief instrument of this crime is the "dah," a curved knife about ten inches in length, which most Burmese wear concealed in their clothing.

Even the agents sent out from the C. I. D. at Allahabad, capital of the United Provinces, have been unable to fathom the mysterious manner by which the rebels learn of a meditated attack on the camps or the route of a convoy which they ambush on its way to provision some isolated post of police or troops. Mysterious, too, are the means by which camps, far distant one from another, communicate for a united assault on a plantation or village.

The military operations, announced to be preparing in the dispatch of June 1, contemplated "an irregular corps of mounted infantry recruited from British and Indian units on the spot."

June 7, 1931

BURMESE ELECTION BEWILDERS BRITISH

Wireless to THE NEW YORK TIMES.

LONDON, Nov. 15.—On the eve of the third round-table conference on Indian affairs, which meets here Thursday, official London was dismayed and completely bewildered today at the news that Burma had voted against separation from India.

Yesterday it had been reported the Separationists had a plurality of two seats.

Rangoon dispatches today announcing the result of the Burmese general election show the Anti-Separationists have won thirty-nine seats in the provincial Legislature, the Separationists twenty-nine and neutrals nine. This result runs directly counter to all British policy and expectations since the Simon report in 1930, which recommended that Burma, hitherto a province of India, should be separated with self-government and a constitution of its own.

The recent round-table conference on Burma, held in London, worked out a constitution for Burma on the assumption that the voters there would give an overwhelming decision in favor of separation. On the same assumption neither Indian round table conference made any provision for Burma in its plans. These conferences evolved outlines for an Indian Federal constitution which did not include Burma.

For the moment the British government is silently awaiting official confirmation of the election returns from Burma. If they are correct and if Burma's new Legislature stands firm against separation, Great Britain will be confronted with two disagreeable alternatives.

One is to accept the verdict and

keep Burma as a province, somehow making room for her in the new All-India Federation. This, however, would involve recasting the round-table agreements and probably would affect the third round-table conference, which is about to begin.

The second alternative, which the British are reluctant to accept, is to disregard the apparent wishes of the Burmese voters and force a self-governing constitution on them.

The government is firmly resolved, however, that, if Burma joins the All-India Federation, she will never again have a chance to break away.

There is some hope in official circles that the new Burmese Legislature will realize this truth and will vote for separation before it is too late.

Indian Propaganda Blamed.

Wireless to THE NEW YORK TIMES.

RANGOON, Nov. 15.—The Separationists were defeated in the Burmese election, they assert, by stories spread by Indians in Rangoon to the effect that Burma, if separated, would become a white man's paradise and a home for British unemployed. Stories also were said to have been circulated that taxation under a self-governing régime would be enormously increased and the Buddhist religion would be ruined.

The Anti-Separationists openly declare they do not desire to join India but want a better constitution than Great Britain offers. The Separationists are clinging to the faint hope they will still win when the Legislature takes its first vote on the separation issue.

November 16, 1932

VEXED INDIA GETS NEW CONSTITUTION

Protests Planned for Today Despite Strict Ban—Schools in Calcutta Are Closed

MINORITY CABINETS GO IN

George Sends Plea for Amity as Congress Party Balks— New Rule for Burma, Aden

Special Cable to THE NEW YORK TIMES.

DELHI, India, Thursday, April 1.—Provincial autonomy, the first stage of governmental change under the new Indian Constitution, came into force at midnight without the cooperation of the All-India Congress party, which had obtained majorities in the Legislatures of six of eleven provinces.

[The Indian Government put a strict ban on huge demonstrations planned for today and on a proposed general strike, The Associated Press reported.]

In five of the provinces—Madras, Bombay, the Central Provinces, Bihar and Orissa—minority coalition Ministries have been formed, and in the sixth, the United Provinces, one is being organized. Coalition Ministries that expect to command majorities in their Legislatures have been formed in Bengal, Sind and the Northwest Frontier, but Cabinet-making thus far has not advanced in Assam.

Message Sent by George

Under this cloud George VI, the King-Emperor, has sent a message to the Indian people expressing hope that the new opportunities afforded by the Constitution "will be used wisely and generously." To the people of Burma, which now becomes separated from India, King George says he believes the change will "enable them to find a road to ever-increasing happiness and prosperity."

Notwithstanding the refusal of the Congress party to form Ministries in the provinces where they have majorities, the inauguration of the Constitution went forward on schedule. Last night's official Gazette of India Extraordinary consisted of 800 pages containing all the orders promulgated for the inception of the Constitution, letters patent reconstituting the office of Governor General and constituting the new office of Crown Representative, and notifications of all the adaptations of laws required to meet changed circumstances in India, Burma and Aden.

Governor of Burma Named

LONDON, March 31 (British Official wireless) — King George has appointed as Governor of Burma Sir Archibald Cochrane, Knight of the Grand Cross of the Order of Saint Michael and Saint George, under the new régime there resulting from the Indian Constitution taking effect tomorrow.

Provincial autonomy henceforth obtains over two-thirds of the total area of India and affects directly a total population of more than 290,-000,000.

April 1, 1937

BURMA CURBS REBELLION

State of Emergency Decreed in Rising Against British Power

Wireless to THE NEW YORK TIMES.

RANGOON, Burma, Dec. 22.—A state of emergency has been proclaimed as a result of a rebellion against British authority. It is believed to foreshadow the possibility of large-scale arrests.

The Governor has returned from Mandalay, where he had gone to spend Christmas.

RANGOON, Burma, Dec. 22 (P).—Under tonight's state of emergency police took precautions against any repetition of last night's window smashing and attacks on motorists. They have power to break the sit-down strikes started Tuesday in a civil disobedience campaign.

One of the leaders of the patriotic front organization, which sponsored the campaign, was sentenced to two months in jail in default of his fine.

A hundred students have been injured in disorders marking the campaign against the Burmese Government.

December 23, 1938

NEW CABINET IN BURMA

U Pu Succeeds Dr. Maw, Defeated Over Recent Disorders

RANGOON, Burma, Feb. 20 (P).—A new coalition government under U Pu took office today after Parliament had defeated Dr. Baw Maw's Cabinet, Burma's first since her separation from India in April, 1937, over its allegedly lax handling of recent racial disturbances.

Dr. Maw's ban on demonstrations had failed to prevent religious-racial disorders in Rangoon Feb. 13, and Mandalay Feb. 11, where twenty-four were killed when the police fired into a mob. The demonstrations were a continuation of riots beginning July 26, 1938, when a mass meeting was conducted here against a book said to contain insults to Buddha, and lasting until last October, with a toll of 220 deaths and injuries to 926 persons.

From Mandalay the recent outbreaks spread to Rangoon, where the police resorted to tear gas to check rioting following a bomb explosion that injured two persons.

February 21, 1939

JAPAN'S NEW ORDER EXPANDED TO COVER GREATER EAST ASIA

Totalitarian-Cast Regime Sets Plans for French Indo-China and Netherlands Indies

By The Associated Press.

TOKYO, Aug. 1—The government of Premier Prince Fumimaro Konoye announced today a plan for a brand new Japanese State, based on a sweeping totalitarianism at home and dedicated to an independent foreign policy that would extend Japan's domination southward over French Indo-China and the Netherlands Indies.

In a statement of policy the government outlined a strongly centralized and unified State designed for creation of "a new order for Greater East Asia," with the yen bloc—Japan and her continental satellites whose currencies are based on the yen—as the foundation.

The government's statement coined the phrase "Greater East Asia" in naming the sphere Japan aims to dominate. Previously it had been simply "East Asia," meaning Japan, Manchoukuo and the occupied sections of China.

August 2, 1940

INDO-CHINA ALLOWS JAPANESE TO ENTER

Permits 2,000 Troops to Land at Haiphong and Move to Bases in North Province

BOMBS HERALD ARRIVAL

Killing of 15 Civilians by Tokyo Flier Called a Mistake— French Protest

HAIPHONG, French Indo-China, Friday, Sept. 27 (AP)—Two thousand Japanese troops landed in Indo-China yesterday under the powerful but silent French guns commanding the entrance to the Red River and marched across the hot countryside into Haiphong, the rail, highway and river gateway to the Northern province of Tongking and to Southwest China beyond.

Japanese planes heralded the approach of these land forces by dropping bombs on a railroad crossing, damaging several buildings and killing fifteen and wounding eighteen civilians, while the frightened population ran for shelter under the trees of the countryside.

The Japanese commander said the bombing was a mistake. Last night the French authorities announced that a strong protest of the incident had been lodged with Tokyo.

En route to the barracks provided for them by the French, the Japanese regiments—marching behind a squadron of their light tanks—exchanged with the French nothing more hostile than curt salutes.

The crack battalions of French colonial infantry moved out, their fine artillery and machine guns muzzled—another undefeated army on the road back without ever having come to grips with the advancing force. Only Haiphong's normal French garrison will be left to exercise a passive check on what many observers thought would be a progressive Japanese attempt to develop a foothold into complete control of the colony.

For yesterday's detachments of Japanese troops were but the forerunners of at least 4,000 or 5,000 more scheduled to debark this week to garrison three air bases in Northern Indo-China granted to the Japanese by the French Government at Vichy.

The Japanese came ashore six miles from this city. Some observers of the strange scene thought that its peaceful accomplishment might enable a settlement of something else that the French have called an act of force—an overland thrust into Indo-China begun last Sunday night by Japanese troops from the Japanese-occupied Chinese Province of Kwangsi. The Japanese position is that the clashes that followed this incursion are to be blamed on the "insufficient arrangements by Indo-China authorities."

The Japanese forces that entered from Kwangsi were reported to have taken Langson, eighty miles northeast of Hanoi. The French said their troops had been withdrawn there only after having been encircled by superior forces.

Japan's moves in this colony are directed, at least ostensibly, toward finding another theatre from which to attack the Chinese—this time from the south—and toward cutting off one more avenue of possible Chinese support.

September 27, 1940

Thai Army Driving Into Indo-China; French Retire, but Claim 40 Planes

By The Associated Press.

HANOI, French Indo-China, Jan. 9—French military authorities reported tonight the destruction of at least forty Thai (Siamese) war planes as brisk border fighting shifted to air and artillery battles.

French communiqués did not mention land activity, but earlier tonight a general French withdrawal of five to ten miles within the frontier of Cambodia Province was acknowledged.

French seaplanes operating from Tonle Sap [Great Lake] in Cambodia aided land planes in attacking Thai airdromes, the French reported as the undeclared war gained momentum. Simultaneously, Thai planes bombed Indo-China towns, and the French said there had been twenty-two casualties at Siemreap, near the northern end of Tonle Sap.

Sporadic artillery dueling was reported in progress across the Mekong River boundary and at various points along the Cambodian battle front. The French insisted, nevertheless, that Thailand's drive, the most ambitious in weeks of sporadic border fighting, was merely "fireworks."

While the French frontier forces "retired to new defense lines" in Cambodia, that part of Southwestern Indo-China that juts into Thailand, friction developed in Northern Indo-China between Japanese soldiers and the French at Hanoi, the capital, and at Haiphong, principal northern seaport.

So-called "unauthorized" Japanese demands for police powers at Hanoi and Haiphong have been refused. Frenchmen blamed the "excitability" of Japanese soldiers newly arrived from Canton, China, for numerous recent Japanese-French clashes.

January 10, 1941

JAPANESE TIGHTEN GRIP ON INDO-CHINA

Mediation Terms Are Said to Give Them Naval Base and an Economic Monopoly

By DOUGLAS ROBERTSON
Wireless to THE NEW YORK TIMES.

SHANGHAI, Feb. 1 — The Japanese-mediated peace imposed on French Indo-China and Thailand, while resulting in the cessation of hostilities, has deprived the authorities of Indo-China of virtually all political and economic control of their country.

That political and economic control is passing into Japanese hands, according to foreign radio advices from Haiphong, French Indo-China. These were later confirmed in responsible quarters here in Shanghai.

While the peace negotiators were signing a peace pact between French Indo-China and Thailand, Japan and Indo-China also concluded a pact, which apparently has been received with some surprise by foreign powers, especially the United States and Britain. This latter pact is reported to contain the following six articles, all decidedly in Japan's favor:

1. Japan gets a virtual monopoly on Indo-China's production of rice, rubber and coal.

2. Japanese interests will have a free hand in the exploitation of French Indo-China's natural resources, especially minerals.

3. Japanese military garrisons will be established on the border between Indo-China and China proper.

4. Japanese inspectors will be stationed in all of Indo-China's customs houses.

5. A Japanese naval base will be established at Cam Ranh Bay, while the Japanese will acquire also a defense concession at Saigon.

6. Indo-China will allow Japan the free use of all the present air bases established in French Indo-China, while new bases will be established wherever deemed necessary.

[Cam Ranh Bay is on the east coast of Annam, just south of the most easterly point that juts into the South China Sea. It is 1,200 miles north of Batavia, capital of the Netherlands Indies; 800 miles northeast of Singapore, and slightly less than that almost due west of the American position at Manila, directly across the South China Sea. The French had planned to make Cam Ranh one of the strongest bases in the world, and its natural characteristics—deep water and high surrounding hills—are ideally suited

GAINS FOR JAPAN SEEN

The right to establish military garrisons on the border of Indo-China and China (1), a naval base on Cam Ranh Bay (2) and a defense concession at Saigon (3) is reported to have been obtained by Tokyo in a treaty concluded in connection with its negotiation of a truce between Indo-China and Thailand.

to this purpose. French equipment and fortification of the base have not been completed, but its possession by the Japanese would be of great strategic importance since it offers a foothold in the South China Sea and lessens the threat to the Japanese southward supply line from flanking submarine attacks out of Hong-kong or Manila or both.]

The receipt of the news of Japan's latest move in the Far East is causing much speculation here. Some qualified foreign observers declare that the latest Japanese acquisitions are likely to produce a postponement of Japan's plans for further southward expansion.

Under this new agreement Japan will be able to acquire large quantities of much-needed rice and since the Netherlands Indies is now supplying Japan with oil to the extent of 40 per cent of her requirements, and since other stipulations in the pact allow Japan great expansion, it seems logical that Japan will pause while these projects are developed.

Also the establishment of Japanese garrisons along the border of Indo-China and China would give Japan an opportunity to strike along a new front against the Chinese Government at Chungking. It might be possible for Japan to cut off the supplies at present going into Free China over the Burma Road. It is believed here that if Japan could utilize these garrison posts on the border to cut off the Burma Road she would be willing to talk peace terms with Generalissimo Chiang Kai-shek.

This could eventually involve and almost complete troop withdrawal from Central and South China. North China, of course, would be retained under Japanese domination as a flanking protection for Manchuria in the event of a second Russo-Japanese conflict.

Foreign Observers Skeptical

Foreign observers here believe that such a move is possible, but they are rather skeptical about it. They observe that there are at least 800,000 Japanese troops at present in Central and South China and they hold that it is unlikely that the Japanese authorities are either able or willing to have these troops transported to Japan after their long terms of service in China. The possibility is discussed that Japan

may withdraw most of these troops from Central and South China and send them to Indo-China for a possible drive against Burma, Singapore or even India.

Japan's campaign in South and Central China has not resulted in any practical gains, in spite of the fact that the Chinese armies have been driven off. What gains Japan has made have been bought only at a considerable price and have proved entirely unprofitable.

Another possible line of action may be adopted by Japan, according to foreign observers here. When Ambassador Admiral Kichisaburo Nomura arrives in the United States he may propose an unconditional reopening of the Yangtze and Pearl Rivers to American trade as long as a free hand is allowed to Japan in French Indo-China.

Japan Would Retain Control

Japan has many times reiterated that she is willing to give up her extraterritorial rights in China and has urged that other powers enjoying such rights follow suit. Should Japan evacuate her troops she would nominally give up these rights, but Japan, of course, would maintain some control over various key points in the Yangtze Valley and in South China. Such a course of action would give Japan complete control of Central and South China, whether under General Chiang or under the "puppet" government of Wang Ching-wei, while it would allow her to muster her armies for future adventures.

Germany's hand in Far Eastern political intrigues and manoeuvres continues to be seen. It has been learned here that Berlin pressed Vichy to accede to the Japanese demands regarding the French Indo-China-Japan pact. However, there is little doubt that Japan would have used force to attain her end and that Indo-China was faced with two propositions, either to give in as gracefully as possible or to face a much stronger power, with possible resultant hostilities that could only end in defeat.

In this connection the presence of a Japanese naval squadron off the Indo-Chinese coast during the mediation is regarded here as a reminder for French Indo-China that unless there was complete acceptance of a Japanese-dictated pact the "mediation" would be followed by virtually immediate armed invasion.

February 2, 1941

VICHY ANNOUNCES PACT WITH JAPAN

'Common Defense' Declared Provided for Indo-China in the Agreement

TOKYO'S PHRASING USED

VICHY, France, Saturday, July 26 (AP)—The French Foreign Ministry announced at 4 A. M. today conclusion of an agreement with Japan for the "common defense" of French Indo-China.

The defense plan respected the territorial integrity of Indo-China

and French sovereignty, the French said.

Details of the military and technical accords were still being examined, it was stated.

The Foreign Office communiqué quoted a statement by the Japanese Government for most of its length, adding only two confirmatory sentences on France's part. Its issuance here was timed to correspond with a Tokyo announcement planned for noon, Japanese time.

Text of Vichy's Announcement

The Vichy statement follows:

"The Japanese Government Information Office published this morning the following declaration:

"'Since conclusion of the accord signed last August by Minister of Foreign Affairs Matsuoka and French Ambassador Arsene Henry, friendly relations have continued

to be consolidated between Japan and French Indo-China; they rapidly developed with accords which followed.

"'Complete unity of views between the two governments has been realized following friendly conversations concerning the common defense of French Indo-China.

"'The Japanese Government is firmly decided to fulfill its duties and responsibilities which fall on Japan in consequence of the divers accords existing with France, particularly in virtue of the solemn engagement taken by France concerning respect for the territorial integrity of French Indo-China and French sovereignty over that union.

"'In making the utmost effort to tighten still further the bonds of Franco-Japanese friendship it hopes to contribute to the common pros-

perity of the two nations.'

"In fact, for some time the question of Indo-China defense in the present exceptional circumstances has been the object of conversations between the French and Japanese Governments.

"In the spirit which inspired the declarations of Aug. 30, 1940, and the diplomatic acts of May 6, 1941, these conversations have just terminated.

"Accords which presently are under study here will fix the practical details of Franco-Japanese cooperation in view of the common defense of Indo-China in limits respecting the territorial integrity of French Indo-China and French sovereignty in all parts of the territory of the union."

July 26, 1941

M'ARTHUR MADE CHIEF IN FAR EAST

Former U. S. Army Head to Lead Combined Force With Rank of Lieutenant General

HIS PLANS UNDER SCRUTINY

Washington Reveals Surprise at Smallness of Filipino Army Now Available

Special to THE NEW YORK TIMES.

WASHINGTON, July 26—General Douglas A. MacArthur, who retired in 1937 at the age of 57 years, was today recalled to active service in the United States Army, and supplementing President Roosevelt's order creating a new Army component to be known as "The United States Army Forces in the Far East," received the rank of lieutenant general and command of the combined United States Army in the Philippines and the entire Filipino forces.

Under his new appointment, General MacArthur, who has been military adviser to the Philippine Commonwealth since 1935, and has ranked as a field marshal of the Philippine Army in the islands since 1937, will now outrank Major Gen. George Grunert, commander of the Army's Philippine Department. He will have the task of welding into a single efficient military unit the United States troops now in the islands and the partially trained Filipino reserves. His new appointment created a stir in military and political circles here today because of the divisions of expert opinion on his plans for defending the islands.

Was Adviser in Philippines

General MacArthur, who was the youngest Chief of Staff the United States Army has ever had, was assigned as military adviser to the Philippine Commonwealth in 1935, two years before he retired, and just after he completed five years as Chief of Staff in Washington.

His plans for raising and training a defense force for the Philippines were at first received with acclaim by President Manuel L. Quezon and many other Filipino leaders, but a year ago continuing criticism of the feasibility and effectiveness of his scheme evidently cooled Mr. Quezon's enthusiasm for the project, for the Commonwealth President then stated publicly that he did not believe an invader could be repelled even if every citizen were to be well equipped militarily and perfectly trained.

A month before President Quezon's statement the American High Commissioner to the Philippines, Francis B. Sayre, had criticized the MacArthur plan, stating that he did not believe that even the then whole military strength of the United States Army could successfully defend the islands.

In 1939, envisaging a possible Japanese attempt at an invasion, General MacArthur issued a statement at Manila saying: "The battle would have to be brought to these shores, so that the full strength of the enemy would be relatively vitiated by the vicissitudes of an overseas expedition. * * * In any event, it would cost the enemy, in my opinion, at least a half million men and upward of five billions of dollars in money to pursue such an adventure with any hope of success."

This led to a series of sharp disputes with other military men, who cited Japan's overseas expeditions to China, their successes against Chinese armies infinitely better drilled and equipped than the Filipino forces, and the fact that long before the Japanese suffered 500,-000 casualties in China they had conquered an area more than five times as large as the area of the whole Philippine Archipelago.

The MacArthur plan, adopted by the Commonwealth in 1936, envisaged a Filipino defense force of 400,000 men by 1947, each of whom would have had roughly half a year of training. The plan was to train 40,000 youths of 20 years of age every year. When the plan first went into effect it was received with enthusiasm by the Filipinos, and in the first two years there were many more than the 40,000 desired applicants, but only 40,000 were accepted each year.

Early in 1939 General MacArthur declared that the Commonwealth then had a well-trained army of 80,000 men. In view of this statement, more than two years ago, today's estimate issued here by the War Department, that the force now consists of only 75,000 men, occasioned considerable surprise.

While it is true that the initial enthusiasm for the service subsided, and that there were only about 20,000 men trained in 1939, and less in 1940 and this year, the size of the Philippine forces had been estimated in other circles as nearly 140,000 partly trained men. The Commonwealth in 1939 made the plea that money was not available to train that year's quota of 40,000. The annual budget that year was about $45,000,000, with only $1,000,-000 appropriated for extra defense purposes.

General MacArthur estimated to the Commonwealth Legislature that the entire scheme, including pay and sustenance for the men, camps, uniforms and equipment, would cost only from $8,000,000 to $10,000,000 annually for the whole ten-year period.

As Field Marshal and military adviser to the Commonwealth, General MacArthur has been receiving a salary of $25,000 a year from the Philippine Government, plus free living quarters which include most of the third floor of the spacious and luxurious Manila Hotel. He was previously stationed in the Philippines three times, as an active officer of the United States Army, and for the two years ending September, 1930, was Commander of the Philippine Department.

General MacArthur was born in Little Rock, Ark., in January, 1880, and went to the Philippines as a second lieutenant of engineers soon after graduation from West Point as the head of his class in 1903. In 1905 he was transferred to Tokyo as aide to his father, Lieut. Gen. Arthur MacArthur, who was military attaché to the American Embassy.

He sailed for France in October, 1917, and was in various American offensives, including that at St. Mihiel, that of the Meuse-Argonne and the Sedan offensive. He was Chief of Staff of the famous Rainbow Division. He commanded the Eighty-fourth Infantry Brigade of the Army of Occupation in Germany until April, 1919, when he returned to the United States.

July 27, 1941

MALAYA AND INDIES HELD VITAL TO U. S.

Singapore Stresses That We Get 85 Per Cent of Their Tin, 80 Per Cent of Rubber

JAPAN BUYS IN THAILAND

Indo-China Also Sends Large Amount of Rubber to Tokyo —French Quota in Peril

By F. TILLMAN DURDIN
Wireless to THE NEW YORK TIMES.

SINGAPORE, Oct. 11—The importance of America's stake in the rubber and tin resources of British Malaya and the Netherlands Indies is shown in figures available here, revealing that the United States is now importing roughly 80 per cent of their rubber and 85 per cent of their tin production.

British authorities here cite these facts to demonstrate how important to the United States is defense of this region.

Estimates here of the amount of rubber Japan is obtaining from Indo-China and Thailand show that nearly all Japan's requirements are being filled by these countries. Japan also is getting tin from Thailand.

Official sources here say that rubber production in Malaya and the Indies is sufficient for the Allies' requirements as long as the Pacific routes are open and shipping is available. Ninety per cent of the total world production of rubber, which was 1,400,000 tons in 1940, is controlled by Britain and her allies.

Rubber Production Increasing

British Malaya's production of rubber in 1940 was 589,655 tons, that of the Netherlands Indies 536,219 tons. In 1941 the production will be higher and of this the United States has already imported approximately 200,000 tons in the first six months from the Netherlands Indies and 300,000 tons from Malaya.

Thailand's rubber production is about 50,000 tons a year. Normally nearly all this would come to Malaya, but since April the Japanese have been buying in Thailand, so small quantities of lower-grade rubber are sent to Malaya.

Authorities here would like to keep Thai rubber in the hands of the Allies, but doubt that any move to achieve this could be successful if, as it appears, Thailand is acting under Japanese pressure and is committed to supplying Japan at least 30,000 tons a year.

Indo-China's rubber production is estimated at 70,000 tons a year. Authorities here assert that Japan has been promised 40,000 tons of this and probably will get a large share of the balance despite the fact that 15,000 tons were earmarked for France.

Japan's requirements are estimated at 45,000 to 60,000 tons a year. Between January and June Japan obtained 3,000 tons of rubber from Malaya, 10,000 tons from the Netherlands Indies and 3,000 tons from North Borneo, but exports from Malaya to Japan ceased in July and since the freezing of Japan's credit, no rubber has gone from the Netherlands Indies and North Borneo to Japan.

Because of British ownership most of Thailand's tin production is kept from Japan, though Japanese purchases in Thailand, at prices ranging up to 100 per cent above Malayan prices, have increased greatly in recent months.

Thailand's tin production is estimated at 18,000 tons a year, all but 5,000 tons of which is produced by British-owned and Australian-owned mines. In the first six months of 1941 Thai tin exports to Malaya totaled about 10,000 tons. Japan got 1,000 tons, nearly half of the total in June.

In the first half of 1941 60,000 tons of the 70,000 tons of tin exported from Malaya went to the United States. Exports of tin from here to Japan has ceased and as a result of freezing Japan is receiving no important minerals from Malaya. Iron and bauxite exports terminated last month.

October 12, 1941

JAPAN WARS ON U. S. AND BRITAIN

GUAM BOMBED; ARMY SHIP IS SUNK

U. S. Fliers Head North From Manila—Battleship Oklahoma Set Afire by Torpedo Planes at Honolulu

104 SOLDIERS KILLED AT FIELD IN HAWAII

President Fears 'Very Heavy Losses' on Oahu—Churchill Notifies Japan That a State of War Exists

By FRANK L. KLUCKHOHN
Special to THE NEW YORK TIMES.

WASHINGTON, Monday, Dec. 8—Sudden and unexpected attacks on Pearl Harbor, Honolulu, and other United States possessions in the Pacific early yesterday by the Japanese air force and navy plunged the United States and Japan into active war.

The initial attack in Hawaii, apparently launched by torpedo-carrying bombers and submarines, caused widespread damage and death. It was quickly followed by others. There were unconfirmed reports that German raiders participated in the attacks.

Guam also was assaulted from the air, as were Davao, on the island of Mindanao, and Camp John Hay, in Northern Luzon, both in the Philippines. Lieut. Gen. Douglas MacArthur, commanding the United States Army of the Far East, reported there was little damage, however.

[Japanese parachute troops had been landed in the Philippines and native Japanese had seized some communities, Royal Arch Gunnison said in a broadcast from Manila today to WOR-Mutual. He reported without detail that "in the naval war the ABCD fleets under American command appeared to be successful" against Japanese invasions.]

Japanese submarines, ranging out over the Pacific, sank an American transport carrying lumber 1,300 miles from San Francisco, and distress signals were heard from a freighter 700 miles from that city.

The War Department reported that 104 soldiers died and 300 were wounded as a result of the attack on Hickam Field, Hawaii. The National Broadcasting Company reported from Honolulu that the battleship Oklahoma was afire. [Domei, Japanese news agency, reported the Oklahoma sunk.]

Nation Placed on Full War Basis

The news of these surprise attacks fell like a bombshell on Washington. President Roosevelt immediately ordered the country and the Army and Navy onto a full war footing. He arranged at a White House conference last night to address a joint session of Congress at noon today, presumably to ask for declaration of a formal state of war.

This was disclosed after a long special Cabinet meeting, which was joined later by Congressional leaders. These leaders predicted "action" within a day.

After leaving the White House conference Attorney General Francis Biddle said that "a resolution" would be introduced in Congress tomorrow. He would not amplify or affirm that it would be for a declaration of war.

Congress probably will "act" within the day, and he will call the Senate Foreign Relations Committee for this purpose, Chairman Tom Connally announced.

[A United Press dispatch from London this morning said that Prime Minister Churchill had notified Japan that a state of war existed.]

As the reports of heavy fighting flashed into the White House, London reported semi-officially that the British Empire would carry out Prime Minister Winston Churchill's pledge to give the United States full support in case of hostilities with Japan. The President and Mr. Churchill talked by transatlantic telephone.

This was followed by a statement in London from the Netherland Government in Exile that it considered a state of war to exist between the Netherlands and Japan. Canada, Australia and Costa Rica took similar action.

Landing Made in Malaya

A Singapore communiqué disclosed that Japanese troops had landed in Northern Malaya and that Singapore had been bombed.

The President told those at last night's White House meeting that "doubtless very heavy losses" were sustained by the Navy and also by the Army on the island of Oahu [Honolulu]. It was impossible to obtain confirmation or denial of reports that the battleships Oklahoma and West Virginia had been damaged or sunk at Pearl Harbor, together with six or seven destroyers, and that 350 United States airplanes had been caught on the ground.

The White House took over control of the bulletins, and the Navy Department, therefore, said it could not discuss the matter or answer any questions how the Japanese were able to penetrate the Hawaiian defenses or appear without previous knowledge of their presence in those waters.

Administration circles forecast that the United States soon might be involved in a world-wide war, with Germany supporting Japan, an Axis partner. The German official radio tonight attacked the United States and supported Japan.

December 8, 1941

MANILA AND CAVITE BASE FALL, ARMY FIGHTS ON

JAPANESE PRESSING

Invaders Drive Hard as MacArthur Shortens Lines to the North

FORTS ON BAY HELD

Fortress of Corregidor Is Believed Headquarters —Cavite Demolished

By CHARLES HURD
Special to THE NEW YORK TIMES.

WASHINGTON, Jan. 2—The two great symbols of American development of the Philippine Islands, the city of Manila with its 600,000 population and Cavite naval base, passed today into Japanese hands as General Douglas MacArthur, commander of the United States armed forces in the Far East, tightened his lines for a final battle in the hills northwest of the city. The city and the base alike were occupied apparently without fighting but without surrender.

The city of Manila has been "open" and undefended for a week, but nonetheless ravaged by Japanese bombing planes, which particularly sought out its historical churches, hospitals and residential districts.

The naval base was left in ruins, a vacant and demolished establishment in which oil and other non-transportable supplies were destroyed. Its only American occupants consisted of wounded who could not be carried away, and hospital corps men left to care for them.

Defenders Continue Fight

While officials here did not minimize the tragedy implied in Japanese occupation of these points, it was emphasized repeatedly that the United States-Filipino forces were continuing to fight stubbornly north and northwest of Manila against Japanese attacks, even though these are "being pressed with increasing intensity."

In addition, while the Japanese hold the principal city, they have not got control of the port. The Army announced that it still held Corregidor, a Gibraltar-like island fortress guarding the entrance to Manila Bay, and other defensive positions that make the bay untenable for shipping as long as their guns command its waters.

The United States-Filipino forces are gathered largely in the mountainous region north of Manila Bay, where General MacArthur still retains a harbor for use either in event of final withdrawal or to take his forces to Corregidor. This is on Subic Bay, an indentation in the west coast of the Philippines, around which simulated war games have been played for forty years.

New Line Announced

The communiqué announcing the realignment of forces north of Manila, issued here as of 9:30 A. M. today, read in part as follows:

"The tactical situation in the vicinity of Manila necessitated a radical readjustment of the lines held by American and Philippine troops and a consolidation of defense forces north of Manila. This manoeuvre was successfully accomplished in the face of strong enemy opposition. The consequent shortening of our lines necessarily uncovered the road to Manila and made possible the Japanese entrance into the city. As it had been previously declared an open city, no close defense within the environs of the city was possible.

"The loss of Manila, while serious, has not lessened the resistance to the Japanese attacks. American and Philippine troops are occupying strong positions north of the city and are holding the fortified Island of Corregidor and the other defenses of Manila Bay effectively, preventing the use of this harbor by the enemy."

January 3, 1942

JAPANESE INVADE DUTCH INDIES AT TWO POINTS

FOE GETS ASHORE

Netherlanders Battle at Tarakan and Three Places on Celebes

PARACHUTISTS USED

By The United Press.

BATAVIA, Netherlands Indies, Jan. 11—Japanese sea-borne and parachute troops, grasping for the wealth of the Netherlands Indies, have invaded Borneo and Celebes, hurling a challenge to the Allied war effort that the Netherlanders, met by bombing Japanese warships and transports that took part in the operation and battling Japanese planes, it was announced tonight.

A strong fleet of enemy transports escorted by a cruiser forced one landing at Tarakan, island oil center off the northeast coast of Borneo. Other sea-borne invaders, aided by parachutists, landed at three places in Minahassa, the northern arm of the island of Celebes.

Netherland air, land and sea forces rushed into action. Two transports were bombed off Tarakan by Dutch planes and a "near miss" presumably damaged the cruiser. Three Japanese seaplanes were shot down there.

Celebes Demolition Effected

In Minahassa, the defenders were forced to give ground and it was announced that "several destructions were carried out according to plan."

No details of ground fighting had been received, but it was believed that the Netherland defenders were putting up a fierce battle for Tarakan, one of the most prolific sources of oil in the Indies. The garrison there had expected to receive the first Japanese attack on the islands and was prepared for it.

The colonel in command was quoted as saying recently that if the Japanese ever entered Tarakan they would find nothing but "charred oil plants and wells and dead Dutchmen." The fact that no mention was made of the destruction of oil properties there was taken as an indication that the garrison was holding its own.

The strategy behind the Japanese plan of attack appeared to be aimed directly at cutting off United States aid to the Indies.

United States convoys to Java, where the Allies have set up a supreme command under General Sir Archibald P. Wavell, normally would use the Molucca Passage, between Celebes and the Molucca Islands to the east. With Japanese planes operating from the Manado region of North Celebes, United States ships would be vulnerable to air attack in the Passage, and might even have to circumnavigate Australia for safety, adding a week to their sailing time.

U. S. Warships Operating in Area

The enemy invasion of the Netherland Indies, richest prize in the Pacific war, had been long expected. The element of surprise was virtually removed last week when a large Japanese ship concentration was reported off the Philippine island of Mindanao, 275 miles north of Celebes. The direction and intent of this force was apparent and it remained only to learn the point of attack.

Netherland sources said that United States warships were operating in Indies waters and that "it is assumed they will join in fighting off the invasion."

January 12, 1942

NETHERLANDS PLANS POST-WAR REFORMS

Imperial Conference Projected to Foster Colonial Freedom

LONDON, Jan. 28 (Netherlands Indies News Agency) — Measures to prepare the way for a Netherlands imperial conference after the war to carry out certain reforms to foster political emancipation of the overseas territories within the existing framework of the empire were announced tonight by the Netherlands Government in London.

The first step toward these empire reforms will consist of a preliminary conference before the end of the war, to which representatives of the four Netherland territories—the Netherlands, the Netherlands Indies, Surinam and Curacao—will be appointed. The second step will be the meeting of a committee to consider reports submitted by the preliminary conference and draw up specific plans for the imperial conference. The government of the Netherlands Kingdom then will act on the recommendations.

The Netherlands Indies often has declared its intention of achieving maximum autonomy within the structure of the empire and in anticipation of such a status has steadily extended the sphere of native participation in the territory's administration.

Surinam and Curacao have expressed satisfaction with the government's plan to ask each to send three representatives to the conference. This is interpreted as an appreciation by the government of the growing economic importance of the West Indies.

January 29, 1942

SINGAPORE SURRENDERS UNCONDITIONALLY

BRITISH CAPITULATE

Troops to Keep Order Until Foe Completes Occupation of Base

3 DRIVES HEM CITY

Tokyo Claims Toll of 32 Allied Vessels South of Singapore

By JAMES MacDONALD
Special Cable to THE NEW YORK TIMES.
LONDON, Feb. 15—Singapore has fallen.

The long dreaded news that the key British base of the Pacific and Indian Oceans would be captured by the Japanese—a major reverse clearly foreseen many days ago—was announced tonight by Winston Churchill, a few hours after dispatches from Vichy and Tokyo reported that Lieut. Gen. Arthur E. Percival's forces had surrendered unconditionally at 3:30 P. M. today British daylight saving time [9:50 P. M. Sunday Singapore time and 10:30 A. M. Eastern war time].

London officials naturally declined to disclose what plans had been made or were perhaps in the making for establishing a naval base elsewhere to meet the grave emergency arising from the loss of Singapore. They could not or would not divulge how many Imperial troops were taken prisoner or how many got away.

Commanders Meet

According to the official Tokyo announcement, fighting ceased along the entire front three hours after a meeting between General Percival and the Japanese Commander in Chief, Lieut. Gen. Tomoyuki Yamashita, in the Ford motor plant at the foot of Timah Hill, where the documents of surrender were signed. The terms were not disclosed here, but a Japanese Domei Agency dispatch late tonight said that under the capitulation up to 1,000 armed British soldiers would remain in Singapore City to maintain order until the Japanese Army completed occupation.

Similar terms, it is recalled, were contained in the surrender of Hong Kong on Christmas Day.

The Tokyo radio said the Japanese had constantly kept pouring in fresh troops to make up for losses from the fierce resistance of British Imperial troops.

In the final battle, three Japanese columns were said to have advanced on the city. Yesterday the central column completed occupation of the water reservoirs and a part of this column reached the northern outskirts of the city on a six-mile front. Another column bypassed the reservoirs, crossed the Kalang River and cut the road from Singapore to the civil airport. The third column reached Alexandria Road in the western part of the city.

Some Resisting, Tokyo Says

[Japanese units left the main island in barges and seized Blakang Mati, the island opposite Keppel Harbor, thereby gaining control of the sea approach to Singapore from the south, according to a Tokyo broadcast recorded by The United Press.

[Japanese troops entered Singapore City today under the terms of the surrender by the British, but a Domei dispatch said some of the defending forces and "other hostile elements" still were resisting, another Tokyo broadcast heard by The United Press stated.]

The Berlin radio, quoting the Japanese newspaper Asahi, said the largest part of the British and Australian forces "obviously" left Singapore Friday for Sumatra.

February 16, 1942

RANGOON CAPTURE CONFIRMED IN INDIA

Defending Forces Withdrawn After Destroying Whatever Foe Could Have Used

BURMA COMMAND SHIFTED

General Alexander in Charge —Japanese Are Reported to Be Pushing Westward

By RAYMOND DANIELL
Special Cable to THE NEW YORK TIMES.

LONDON, March 9—The Japanese flag flies over Rangoon tonight. This grim news was given in a communiqué from New Delhi, India, saying that British forces started to withdraw from the capital of Burma on Saturday. Before abandoning the city, which had been the principal port of entry for the Burma Road, the British destroyed everything that could have been used by the enemy.

[According to The United Press, it was believed in New Delhi that the Japanese were sweeping westward across Southern Burma.]

With the fall of Rangoon the plight of Burma grows more desperate and the threat to India increases. The gravity of Burma's peril was emphasized by Sir Reginald Dorman-Smith, its Governor, in a broadcast to officials in Burma. He urged all to have the courage to make decisions on their own without consulting higher authority.

"Do not worry about referring to any one," he said. "Act, provided that your decisions are calculated to embarrass the enemy and contribute to our war effort. I will back you, right or wrong."

It was disclosed here that Lieut. Gen. Harold R. L. G. Alexander had taken over command of the British forces in Burma from Lieut. Gen. Thomas J. Hutton two days before Rangoon was yielded.

In Command at Dunkerque

General Alexander, one of the youngest and best-known British generals, was in command during the latter stages of the evacuation of Dunkerque. He has had more experience than most Guards officers, and is regarded as one of the best choices possible for the difficult task of saving something from the wreckage of Far Eastern hopes.

Civilian officials and business men had been evacuated from Rangoon before the army, Burma's Governor informed the Secretary of State for Burma. Earlier the Japanese had announced the occupation of Rangoon and reported the destruction of the "main enemy forces" in the neighborhood. Dispatches from Burma indicated that the Japanese again had had overwhelming air superiority, although they lacked tanks. The British used tanks in an effort to stem the advance.

Although there has been much talk of the scorched-earth policy in the Far East, reports from Mandalay said that many of the fires in Rangoon had been started by saboteurs. According to these reports, important modern buildings were untouched and the telephone and power systems were working, at least until the last moment, although the poorer district had been burned out.

Although Rangoon is a grave loss for all the United Nations, as well as for Britain, all is not lost. A message from Bombay tonight said that a Japanese threat to an "important railway junction" on the road from Rangoon had been disrupted by heavy and concentrated air action.

Important Port Is Lost

But the British have lost another important Far Eastern port, Rangoon's sea-borne tonnage in peacetime amounted to 5,250,000 a year, and its river trade amounted to 750,000 tons. The port was equipped with modern machinery and docks.

By occupying Rangoon, the Japanese not only have closed the Burma Road at its main entrance but also have gained control of all the sea-borne exports of Burma the most important of which were oil, rice, timber and minerals. All the oil, three-quarters of the timber and half of the rice went to India. The loss of the oil will be severely felt, but an alternative source exists for India. India's imports of Burmese rice amounted to only about 4 per cent of her own production, so the cutting off of the Burmese supply will cause only inconvenience. Burma's most important mineral product was tungsten, most of which came from the Tavoy district, occupied by the Japanese in January.

Although the Burma Road's chief source of supply is in enemy hands, the road from Lashio to China still is open and there is said to be an accumulation of matériel at Lashio that will require several months to move. It is probable that the Japanese, by advancing along the railroad and main highway to Mandalay through the Shan States, will try to reach Lashio and seize these supplies.

The main British forces, now in danger of encirclement, will have to be dispersed to meet this threat. Exactly what forces are available to defend the rest of Burma has not been disclosed, but it is known that the Chinese have sent and are sending substantial reinforcements.

The difficulty of reinforcing Burma from India would be very great, even if India had the troops to spare. It is the hope of the British that the forces now in Upper Burma, with Chinese reinforcements will be able to prevent the invader from overrunning the country quickly and will succeed in blocking the way to Lashio until most, if not all, of the supplies awaiting shipment there can be sent to China.

March 10, 1942

MANDALAY CAPTURED, JAPANESE CLAIM

BRITISH FALL BACK

All Troops in Mandalay Area Retire, Menaced by Flanking Threat

By DAVID ANDERSON
Special Cable to THE NEW YORK TIMES.

LONDON, May 2—Mandalay, old capital of Burma, has been occupied by Japanese troops, according to a communiqué of Tokyo Imperial Headquarters broadcast today and inferentially confirmed by the British communiqué. The invaders, however, were said by Chungking to have been checked in their headlong rush over the Burma Road northeastward from Lashio. The Chinese reported inflicting heavy casualties on the foe at a point north of Hsenwi.

The Japanese announced that Mandalay fell yesterday. While this was not confirmed in authoritative quarters here, it was explained that "with Lashio already in enemy hands, it would not be worth while to suffer great losses to defend Mandalay."

[With Mandalay and Lashio, the Japanese hold all the strategic points in Northeast Burma—adjoining Free China — excepting Bhamo, which is eighty miles northwest of Hsenwi, and Myitkyini. Bhamo, at the head of navigation on the Irrawaddy River, is the terminus of an old and important Caravan route to Kunming, capital of Yunnan Province. Myitkyini, eighty miles north of Bhamo, is the terminus of a narrow-gauge railway from Mandalay.]

Mandalay had already been largely destroyed by Japanese air raids, and the tactical situation that developed in the area in the last few days made defense virtually impossible at any cost. The belief held here that the topography around Mandalay might favor its defense has been proved unreliable.

The enemy communiqué said the fall of Mandalay followed ten days of fighting in which "British and Chungking forces were annihilated in various places." Once the Japanese had advanced beyond Kyaukse, about twenty miles away, it was evident Mandalay was doomed since the enemy already was thrusting in the direction of Monywa on the west and from Hsipaw on the northeast.

A New Delhi communiqué today stated that "on the Mandalay front all British troops were being withdrawn from positions north of the Irrawaddy." The British headquarters in India added that the road and rail bridges across the Myitnge River had been successfully blown up. Two spans of the Ava Bridge also were demolished.

May 3, 1942

10,000 PRISONERS IN MANILA BAY FORTS

PHILIPPINES LOST

Wainwright a Prisoner With End of Organized Resistance on Isles

ONLY GUERRILLAS REMAIN

Japanese Gain Use of Manila Bay Harbor for Fleet and Can Release Their Forces

By CHARLES HURD
Special to The New York Times.

WASHINGTON, May 6—Organized resistance to the Japanese in the Philippine Islands ended today with the surrender of a starving force of not more than 10,000 Americans and Filipinos on Corregidor and the satellite island forts named Hughes, Drum and Frank.

Lieut. Gen. Jonathan M. Wainwright notified the War Department that "resistance of our troops has been overcome" and that "terms are being arranged covering the capitulation of the island forts in Manila Bay." This was the language of the War Department here.

A few hours earlier General Wainwright described a final six-day cannonading of the island, supplemented by aerial bombardment, in which the Japanese used many new guns to prepare the way for landing parties that yesterday crossed the three-mile strip of water separating Corregidor and Bataan Peninsula.

Surrender of the fortress closed the most tragic chapter of American participation in World War II, but this conclusion had been expected almost from the time the Japanese invaded the Philippines.

Guerrilla Warfare to Go On

There was every expectation, however, that the Japanese would face constant guerrilla warfare in their occupation of the islands. From Luzon in the north to Mindanao in the south are numerous bands of American officers and soldiers and native forces who may well support themselves indefinitely with the aid of friendly groups of natives.

No definite statement as to the total number of Americans left on the Manila Bay island forts at the time of surrender was forthcoming, but the Navy said in a communiqué that it counted on Corregidor about 175 officers and 2,100 enlisted Navy personnel and 70 officers and 1,500 men of the Marine Corps. General Wainwright had reported only that casualties had been very heavy in the last few days of fighting. [A United Press dispatch from Washington said 3,000 civilians were on Corregidor Island.]

These sailors and marines, who were ordered from Bataan by General Wainright before the peninsula forces capitulated on April 9, were serving under Captain Kenneth M. Hoeffel of the Navy and Colonel Samuel L. Howard of the Marine Corps. The fall of Corregidor removed the famous Fourth Marine Regiment from the active rolls. The regiment was removed from Shanghai two weeks before the start of the war on Dec. 7 and transferred to the Philippines.

Small Warships Destroyed

In the final hours of fighting on the beaches of Corregidor the Navy completed destruction of small warships already damaged by Japanese bombs and shells, with the result that not even a small boat was left for salvage by the invaders.

May 7, 1942

BURMA IS AT WAR WITH U. S., BRITAIN

Declaration Follows Granting of 'Independence,' According to Tokyo Broadcasts

Japan "granted independence" to occupied Burma yesterday, announced the "withdrawal of the Japanese military administration" and then transmitted "a declaration of war" by Burma against the United States and Great Britain.

The developments were made known in Japanese broadcasts recorded by the United States Foreign Broadcast Intelligence Service.

The granting of "independence" was made one year after Dr. Ba Maw was established as puppet Premier of Burma by Japanese forces at Rangoon. During the year Japanese propagandists have devoted considerable efforts to explaining "the coming independence" of the country, but on several occasions Tokyo broadcasts stated that the Shan States, richest and most militarily important section of Burma, would not be affected by any independence plan. Two of the Shan States were recently "ceded" to the puppet State of Thailand by Japan.

In yesterday's broadcasts Government monitors found no reference to the Shan States nor any definite description of "the new Burma State." One Tokyo broadcast explained the change as follows:

"Burma has now become the fifth independent country in the Greater East Asia Co-prosperity Sphere, after Japan, China, Thailand and Manchukuo."

The text of a treaty of alliance, signed yesterday in Rangoon by Renzo Sawada, Ambassador to Burma, and the Premier, indicated that Burma remained bound to the Japanese as tightly as she had been and as closely as the other "independent" areas of Manchukuo, Thailand and the so-called national government of China at Nanking.

According to the broadcasts yesterday's events began with an announcement by Lieut. Gen. Mazikazu Kawabe, commander in chief of Japanese forces in Burma, that his military administration was being withdrawn. The twenty-five members of the Independence Preparatory Committee then met and formed a National Assembly. Dr. Ba Maw was named Premier.

The next stage was the war declaration against the United States and Britain. One broadcast said:

"It is a significant detail that the declaration of war was made before the conclusion of the treaty of alliance with Japan."

On March 26, during a visit to Tokyo, Dr. Ba Maw defined the aim of his government as the "sharing of life and death with Japan in the war."

August 2, 1943

JAPANESE IN INDIES EXPECTING ATTACK

By FRANK L. KLUCKHOHN
By Wireless to The New York Times.

SOMEWHERE IN AUSTRALIA, Oct. 3—The Japanese in the Netherlands Indies are nervous about the Allied advances in New Guinea, according to information from reliable sources.

After their march southward early in 1942 the Japanese acted in the Indies like unbeatable conquerors, but now they are showing signs of deep worry.

At first in the Indies they took the attitude that the war there was over. They dissolved air raid units, eliminated the blackout and acted with a ferocity that indicated they felt they were there to stay. They hanged natives for minor "offenses."

Now the air raid precautions have been reinstituted, bomb cellars are being dug and every effort is being made to woo the natives.

But there is accumulating evidence that the Japanese have made as great a failure of their "co-prosperity sphere" in the Indies as they made a success of the conquest and that in varying degrees they are meeting widespread passive resistance on the part of native elements.

Oil Shipments Cut Down

So bad has the situation become that the Japanese have been forced to change commanders in the area, and this has not brought results.

There is every indication that lack of shipping caused by depredations of Allied submarines in Far Eastern waters, as well as the losses they have suffered in New Guinea and the Solomons, is reducing to a relatively unimportant scale enemy shipments of oil from the Indies. The same factors are

Allied soldiers marching into a landing ship tank for the attack on the New Guinea base

Associated Press

reducing tin and other exports the Japanese need.

Requiring cotton, the Japanese have made the natives withdraw considerable production from rice and tobacco, and are demanding

120 pounds of cotton for one sarong. This change in crops has created a widespread shortage of rice in Java, one of the most thickly populated areas in the world with its close to 50,000,000.

The Japanese tried to impose their medieval laws upon the natives, who were used to following their own customs under the Dutch Government. It did not work. Here, too, the Japanese are being

forced to change their policy.

In Sumatra, one of the three most important islands, many of the natives have moved from the land to the cities, and in all the islands the natives are reported to be growing just enough to take care of themselves, if that much.

Fifth Column Growing

Coco oil for lamps has been eliminated, hardships are the order of the day and there is evidence that a sizable fifth column is growing. For example, the Japanese first imposed the death sentence for listening to the radio, then sealed the parts of the sets covering wave-bands for Dutch broadcasts. Nevertheless, they now have been forced to confiscate all radios on Celebes Island, where some of the most belligerent natives live.

At first the Japanese presumed that the Eurasians—half white and half native—would welcome Japanese dominance. Then they plaintively began a campaign to convince them that 'we have no hard feelings because you are contaminated with white blood." Now the Japanese are trying to force them into line.

Briefly, on the military side the Japanese in the Indies are taking the stand of men who expect to be attacked and are deeply worried over the outcome.

They are getting relatively little from what has been regarded as one of the richest raw material areas in the world, partly because of lack of shipping, partly as a result of mismanagement, and partly because they can obtain worthwhile benefit only by world export, which is shut off by the war.

There is every reason to believe that the fifth column in the Indies is composed actively or potentially of every element of the population and that millions in the Indies want a hand in eliminating the Japanese when the time comes.

October 4, 1943

TOKYO 'FREEING' MALAYA

Reports Step Toward Home Rule in Former British Region

The Japanese extended their so-called "independence" to the former British possession of Malaya yesterday with the creation of provincial and municipal councils "entirely composed of Malayans."

The Berlin radio, as recorded by The United Press, quoted a Tokyo dispatch as saying the measure was a "further step toward the administrative independence of Malaya." Another Berlin broadcast said the Javanese Central Council would meet for the first time Oct. 15.

The Tokyo radio, in a broadcast recorded by the Federal Communications Commission, said Emperor Hirohito had appointed Shozo Murata, supreme advisor to the Japanese military administration in the Philippines, to be "ambassador extraordinary" to the Philippines.

October 6, 1943

PHILIPPINES NOW 'FREE'

Tokyo Declares End of Army Rule and Islands' 'Independence'

The Tokyo radio broadcast today an announcement that the "military administration over the Philippines has been terminated as of today" and the islands now had their "independence."

"The birth of the glorious new Philippines is now a consummated fact," the broadcast said, according to The Associated Press. It quoted an announcement from Lieut. Gen. Shigenori Kuroda Japanese commander on the islands.

The general was quoted as telling Filipinos that "I can well imagine your profound joy at obtaining independence" and advising them that "the happy event" was due largely to their "wholehearted cooperation." Japanese troops remain in full control of the islands.

The United States Foreign Broadcast Intelligence Service reported that the Japanese-controlled Manila radio had outlined plans for an elaborate "independence" celebration in the Philippines to mark the event and the inauguration of José P. Laurel as puppet president of the "republic."

October 14, 1943

Tokyo Admits Difficulty In Winning the Filipinos

Filipinos have been so "bewitched" for years by American "motion pictures and dancing" that efforts of Japanese propagandists to "banish America" from the Philippines has not been "an easy matter," a Japanese propaganda report said yesterday.

Domei, Japanese news agency, in a wireless dispatch to the controlled press in East Asia, said that "our cultural war in the Philippines is devoted mainly to destroying and removing the materialistic culture introduced by America and restoring the original cultures of the Philippines and oriental culture."

May 8, 1944

INDO-CHINA'S FOOD IS TAKEN BY JAPAN

Trading Balance in Tokyo Is Frozen So Finished Products Cannot Be Obtained

Although the Japanese have allowed occupied Indo-China to retain the technical status of a Vichy dependency, recent domestic broadcasts by the Saigon and Tokyo radios have disclosed that the invaders have looted the country to such an extent that serious shortages of food, clothing and medicine have developed, the Office of War Information said today.

Paul Baudouin, chairman of the Bank of Indo-China, was quoted by the Saigon radio as saying that Indo-China had a trading balance of more than 500,000,000 yen in Tokyo. These funds, which M. Baudouin said had been frozen by Premier Hideki Tojo's Government and cannot be used in trade with other countries, are indicative of the Japanese policy of taking Indo-China's raw materials without delivering promised finished products in return.

Before she was occupied and partitioned, following the Japanese engineered border dispute with Thailand in 1941, Indo-China traded off her raw materials on the international market for finished goods.

Her production included rice, rubber, fish, cattle, hides, coal, zinc, tin, iron, bauxite, manganese, tungsten and phosphates. She imported cotton and silk, metal goods, kerosene and motor cars.

Indo-China is still producing her pre-war commodities, all of which are taken by the Japanese for "military reasons," but her imports have been reduced by Japan's failure to deliver goods promised in several trading agreements.

Baudouin Explains Plight

Summing up Indo-China's position, M. Baudouin said:

"The position of Indo-China is today much more difficult than it was a year ago. The lack of equipment is very noticeable. The means of transportation are inadequate. The country has only one buyer, Japan.

"Japan pays with yen that Indo-China cannot use in payment for the imports she requires. The surplus of her balances with Tokyo is more than 500,000,000 yen, which is frozen, and only a few articles can be obtained from Japan in exchange.

"In reality, trade assumes a more and more one-sided character. It now consists almost exclusively of deliveries by Indo-China, and very little is received in return."

According to the Tokyo radio, representatives of Indo-China and Japan met at Hanoi on March 27 to sign a new trade agreement for 1944. While neither the Tokyo nor Saigon radio has revealed all the terms of the new agreement, it is believed that the pact extends the provisions of a 1943 accord, under which 40 per cent of Indo-China's rice crop is reported to have been consigned to Japan.

Before the signing of the new agreement, which followed a tour of investigation by a Japanese commission in Indo-China, the Tokyo radio told its Japanese listeners:

"An undisclosed number of tens of thousands of tons of rice and other grains that are the staple food of the Japanese people has been guaranteed to Japan."

The 1943 rice shipments to Japan and the signing of the new 1944 agreement took place while the Saigon radio was broadcasting stories of rice shortage and general food problems in Tongking and other areas.

Saigon Radio Stresses Need

As the negotiations for the new agreement were progressing, the Saigon radio, in a broadcast dealing with rice production, declared that "the total quantity produced continues always to be below needs."

To make up for the shortage of rice, Indo-China's chief product, the puppet Government of Admiral Jean Decoux, Governor-General of the Vichy "dependency," has urged the people to turn to the production of corn. In discussing the new food agreement, however, a Japanese spokesman on the Tokyo radio indicated that Japan has also made arrangements to appropriate this substitute staple.

Tokyo and Saigon broadcasts have disclosed that the Japanese have set up police arrangements in Indo-China to assure the delivery of rice, corn and other foods. A "department of investigation" was established several months ago in the Japanese Embassy at Hanoi. As the Japanese explained it, the purpose of the department is "to intensify mutual understanding between Japan and French Indo-China and to facilitate Indo-China's contribution."

A lack of adequate shipping space is preventing the Japanese from transporting all of Indo-China's rice crop as soon as it is harvested, but the Tokyo radio announced in March that the Mitsui Company had begun the construction of a large warehouse in Indo-China to store the rice until ships could be found to carry it to Japan.

Aside from taking rice from Indo-China while the people go without it, the Japanese have also used inflation to make rice more costly in Indo-China. The Saigon radio has been reassuring the Indo-Chinese that while they are experiencing inflation it is not so severe as in other parts of the Orient.

Difficulties Are Combatted

Food shortages have become so severe and prices so high that the Saigon radio announced recently that "various measures are being taken to cope with the difficulties brought about by economic isolation resulting from the war and the increase in the cost of living for the working class."

The Saigon radio has revealed a shortage of medical supplies as well as a scarcity of food and clothing. Although Japan has occupied Far Eastern areas producing the bulk of the world's quinine, Indo-Chinese authorities declared recently that their country was undergoing a severe quinine shortage.

May 14, 1944

SIGNS LEGISLATION TO FREE PHILIPPINES

Special to The New York Times.

WASHINGTON, June 30—President Roosevelt has approved two resolutions of Congress covering the policy of the United States toward the Philippines in the future, and in announcing this today he promised full restoration of democratic government in the islands, removal of enemy collaborationists and constructive measures for rehabilitation.

The resolutions deal with the acquisition of air and land bases in addition to naval bases and fueling stations for mutual protection, a program which meets with the approval of the Philippine authorities, and the creation of a joint economic mission on lines broad enough to include consideration of proposals for economic and financial rehabilitation of the islands.

Thus it will be possible, the President said, to proclaim independence as soon as practicable after constitutional processes and normal functions have been restored in the Philippines, while the measure concerning bases will contribute to the prevention of aggression in the Pacific.

THE ROOSEVELT STATEMENT

Roosevelt's statement was as follows:

"I have signed today two joint resolutions of Congress respecting the Philippines. The first of these resolutions lay down a policy for the granting of independence and for the acquisiton of bases adequate to provide for the mutual protection of the United States and the Philippine Islands.

"In that resolution it is declared to be the policy of 'the Congress that the United States shall drive the treacherous, invading Japanese from the Philippine Islands, restore as quickly as possible the orderly, free democratic processes of government to the Filipino people, and thereupon establish the complete independence of the Philippine Islands as a separate self-governing nation.' The measure makes it possible to proclaim independence as soon as practicable after constitutional processes and normal functions of government have been restored in the Philippines.

"It is contemplated that as soon as conditions warrant civil government will be set up under constitutional officers. It will be their duty forthwith to take emergency measures to alleviate the physical and economic hardships of the Philippine people and to prepare the Commonwealth to receive and exercise the independence which we have promised them.

Would Punish Jap Helpers

"The latter includes two tasks of great importance: Those who have collaborated with the enemy must be removed from authority and influence and the political and economic life of the country; and the democratic form of government guaranteed in the Constitution of the Philippines must be re-

stored for the benefit of the people of the islands.

"On the problem of bases, the present organic act permitted acquisition only of naval bases and fueling stations, a situation wholly inadequate to meet the conditions of modern warfare. The measure approved today will permit the acquisition of air and land bases in addition to naval bases and fueling stations.

"I have been informed that this action is most welcome to Commonwealth authorities, and that they will gladly cooperate in the establishment and maintenance of bases both as a restored Commonwealth and as an independent nation. By this we shall have an outstanding example of cooperation designed to prevent a recurrence of armed aggression and to assure the peaceful use of a great ocean by those in pursuit of peaceful ends.

"The second joint resolution signed today brings into effect the

joint economic commission first ordained in the present organic act, and enlarges its scope to include consideration of proposals for the economic and financial rehabilitation of the Philippines.

Role of People Acclaimed

"We are ever mindful of the heroic role of the Philippines and their people in the present conflict. Theirs is the only substantial area and theirs the only substantial population under the American flag to suffer lengthy invasion by the enemy. History will attest the heroic resistance of the combined armies of the United States and the Philippines in Luzon, Cebu, Iloilo and other islands of the archipelago.

"Our character as a nation will be judged for years to come by the human understanding and the physical efficiency with which we help in the immense task of rehabilitating the Philippines. The resolution creates the Philippine

Rehabilitation Commission whose functions shall be to study all aspects of the problem, and after due investigation report its recommendations to the President of the United States and the Congress, and to the President and the Congress of the Philippines."

Manuel L. Quezon, President of the Philippines, in a statement stressed that the action of Congress, now approved by the President, advanced the date of Philippine independence in case the island were liberated before July 4, 1946, and, in any event, did not postpone it beyond that date.

He quoted assurances to that effect, which he said he had received from sponsors of the legislation in Congress.

July 1, 1944

DUTCH IN MOROTAI LANDING

Civil-Affairs Officials Go Ashore With American Troops

WITH AMERICAN TROOPS, On Morotai, Sept. 16 (U.P.)—A large detachment of Netherlands Indies Civil Administration officials went ashore with American assault troops when they stormed Morotai, the Netherlands News Agency revealed today.

The administration force was the largest that had gone into any Indies place except the Hollandia area of Netherlands New Guinea, which, as the scene of the first liberation of Netherlands territory, was naturally regarded as of extreme importance, the agency pointed out.

September 17, 1944

M'ARTHUR INVADES CENTRAL PHILIPPINES

BEACHHEADS WON

Americans Seize East Coast of Leyte Isle, Are Widening Hold

By The Associated Press.

GENERAL MACARTHUR'S HEADQUARTERS in the Philippines, Friday, Oct. 20 (Army radio pool broadcast)—American

invasion of the Philippines was officially proclaimed today by Gen. Douglas MacArthur.

Two years and six months after he took sad leave of the islands and relinquished them to Japanese invaders, vowing "I shall return," he announced that his Navy and air-covered ground forces had landed in the archipelago.

[Japanese broadcasts, beginning some twenty-four hours previously, had listed at least three landings, all in the central

sector where the invaders would be in position to split the archipelago's 150,000 defenders in half.]

General MacArthur, aboard a warship, went along with the huge convoy from New Guinea, and within four hours after his forces landed began making plans to go ashore.

East Coast Seized

The special communiqué text, in part, follows:

"In a major amphibious operation we have seized the eastern coast of Leyte Island in the Philippines, 600 miles north of Morotai and 2,500 miles from Milne Bay from whence our offensive started nearly sixteen months ago.

The landings pitted the invaders against Japanese Philippine defenders, estimated at 225,000 under command of Field Marshal Juichi Terauchi.

[The Japanese exulted exactly four days ago that their alleged

43

LAND AND SEA ACTION FLARES UP IN THE FAR EAST

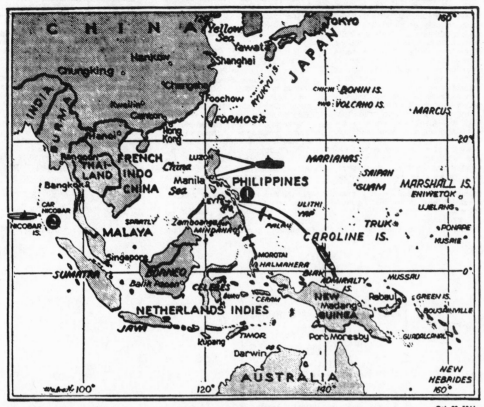

Oct. 20, 1944

The American invasion of the Philippines (1) apparently sprang from the direction of New Guinea and was covered by aerial onslaughts launched from Morotai Island and the Palau group. Carrier planes continued blows at Luzon. The Japanese reported that a carrier force had bombed and shelled Car Nicobar (2). This may well have been a diversionary effort.

naval-air victories off Formosa had set back "the impending invasion of the Philippines by at least two months." It turned out that they didn't score any naval-air victories either.]

Eyewitness accounts from the scene reported the American Navy and airforce were on hand in such mammoth strength that the Japanese Navy was nowhere in sight and the Japanese air force, knocked out at all airfields in the Philippines, offered scarcely token resistance.

Every able-bodied man who escaped from Corregidor in Manila Bay before it surrendered May 6, 1942, went along on the invasion to liberate the Filipinos and their imprisoned fellow-Americans from bondage.

One correspondent said today, "Up to now no ship has been lost."

The preparation for the invasion included the destruction of more than 1,300 planes, the sinking of eighty-six ships, damaging of 127 ships and widespread devastation of airfields and reinforcement bases since Oct. 9 in task force blasts at the Ryukyus, Formosa and the Philippines.

An Associated Press war correspondent, reporting from the scene, said the invasion convoy stretched as far as the eye could see.

Tokyo radio accounts said Suluan Island, not mentioned by General MacArthur, was invaded Tuesday (Manila time) and the Leyte operations opened Thursday, at noon at Tacloban, at 7 o'clock Thursday night at Cabalian.

October 20, 1944

OSMENA REOPENS LEYTE POSTOFFICES

Issues Currency Based on U.S. Dollar in Drive to Wipe Out Japanese Influence

ADVANCE HEADQUARTERS ON LEYTE, Oct. 28 (Delayed) (AP)—Embarking on a program to wipe out every vestige of Japanese influence, President Sergio Osmena and the Philippine Commonwealth Government reopened postoffices today and issued "victory" currency based on the American dollar, worth 2 pesos.

Mr. Osmena and his Cabinet, who landed with the American troops, have already held their first Cabinet meeting on Philippine soil. They have made rapid progress in the solution of the many problems facing the Government. "It will be my cardinal policy to see to it that the slightest vestige of Japanese influence is destroyed," said Brig. Gen. Carlos P. Romulo, secretary of the Department of Information and Public Relations. "Japanese language instruction has been abolished," he said, "and American patterns of education, used prior to the war, will be re-established."

Mr. Osmena has decided to reopen the Leyte Provincial Hospital, with free public dispensaries and a center where Filipinos can come for social services.

There has been a further reorganization of the Cabinet. The Departments of the Interior and Finance have been combined under Secretary of the Interior Ismael Mathay, who was Budget Finance Secretary. Mr. Mathay will be placed in charge of the reorganization of the provincial municipal governments in liberated territory.

Already Mr. Osmena has begun to work on one of the foremost problems—that of public and private war damage. He assigned Col. A. Melchor, now military and technical adviser, to begin gathering data on such damage for submission to the Philippines rehabilitation Commission in Washington. This commission, headed by Senator Millard Tydings, is composed of nine Americans and nine Filipinos.

"These damages will be very heavy," President Osmena said. "They not only are damages caused by the Japanese, but also by Americans in returning and when forced to destroy important installations before occupation by the Japanese."

The immediate reorganization of the Philippine Army, with guerrilla forces as a nucleus, will be started, General Romulo said. The guerrilla bands on Leyte have already been made part of the American Sixth Army.

Mr. Osmena is considering creating a board of inquiry to investigate all cases of so-called collaborationists. Thus far, General Romulo said, only about fifty persons have been arrested and some of them are not classed as collaborationists.

November 2, 1944

BURMAN DOMINION IS AGAIN PLEDGED

By Wireless to THE NEW YORK TIMES.

LONDON, Dec. 12—Leopold S. Amery, Secretary of State for India and Burma, repeated in the House of Commons today his pledge that Britain would help Burma to dominion status as soon as possible after the war. He said he believed that Burmese would welcome Britons as liberators.

"It is in that spirit we mean to return," he said. "We desire to make good what the people offered, in part owing to the lack of our own defensive foresight. Nor have the Burmese forfeited or impaired in any way their claims for our assistance toward the goal of self-government."

Mr. Amery said he looked forward to Burma's working in full independence but in friendly cooperation with India. In addition to repairing enemy damage Burma must be helped to reconstruct her economy, he said, and discussions are taking place with the Burmese Government to that end.

He denied that the Burmese people had sided with the Japanese invader.

The fact is, said Mr. Avery, that the great mass of the Burmese people have shown no hostility to the British Armies or Government. Burmese were serving in the British forces, he stressed, and the Burmese Prime Minister and a number of other Ministers had come out with the British armies and had worked with the Governor ever since.

He said he did not think the Burmese people would be deceived by the facade of independence set up by the Japanese under a one-party dictatorship.

Somerset de Chair, Conservative Member of Parliament, who initiated the debate on Burma, recounted how 150 Karens from North Burma had defended a vital point forty-eight hours at a cost of 60 per cent casualties to save part of the British Army and of Gen. Joseph W. Stilwell's forces from encirclement. Resistance by Kachin hillmen, he said, had brought on their village terrible retribution by the Japanese. Burma now has her guerrillas, whose gallantry is equal to that of the partisans in Yugoslavia, Russia, the Netherlands or anywhere else, he went on.

Mr. de Chair was chairman of the committee of young Conservatives who recently proposed a program for the gradual attainment of self government for Burma.

December 13, 1944

FILIPINO CIVILIANS MASSACRED BY FOE

Bayoneted Bodies Abound in Streets—Homes Fired and Fleeing Inmates Shot

By GEORGE E. JONES
By Wireless to THE NEW YORK TIMES.

MANILA, Feb. 13 (Delayed)—A beaten enemy is wreaking his vengeance on Manila and its people and we are obtaining a glimpse of the same wanton cruelty and pillage that the Japanese military visited upon other oriental cities.

There are established facts to support this conclusion, facts known to American soldiers and correspondents who have seen the evidence at first-hand. The evidence is not pretty to see. Yesterday American infantrymen, picking their way along the Marques de Comillas Street in the Ermita district, came across a horrible sight —approximately twenty Filipino women, with their hands tied behind their backs, lying dead in pools of their own blood. They had been bayonetted.

A few minutes later the Americans came across two Chinese with severe saber wounds in the neck.

There were also bodies of dead children.

Today in one compound south of the Pasig River advancing American troops found thirty bodies of Filipino civilians who had been shot or burned. The bodies of a woman and her suckling child were among them. They had been killed by rifles.

An officer told correspondents today that a Piper Cub artillery spotter flying over Intramuros saw Japanese using civilians as shields for their battery. The Japanese mortar opened up on the American-occupied zone in Manila, he said. When the American guns began replying to the fire the Japanese were seen to herd many civilians into the building where the mortar was located with the evident intention of forcing the Americans to cease fire or hit the helpless populace.

Examples Termed Typical

These things are typical of blazing Manila as the enemy wields fire and sword against the helpless civilians, just as he did in Nanking, Hong Kong and Singapore. Homes have been burned, while Japanese soldiers, slowly retreating before the American advance, fire rifles and machine guns into men, women and children who try to escape. There have been cases of men who have been taken away for questioning, imprisonment and, in many cases, mass execution. Japanese shells fall indiscriminately into civilian residences.

February 15, 1945

REINS IN INDO-CHINA WRESTED BY JAPAN

French Disarmed, Key Points Seized—U. S. Operates Air Base There, Tokyo Says

By The Associated Press.

LONDON, Saturday, March 10 —The Japanese wiped out the last vestige of French control over the puppet state of Indo-China early today, taking over full administration of the land after charging that French officers had tried secretly to join hands with the Allies.

Moving swiftly, the Japanese Army seized all key installations and facilities from the "resisting" French and announced that they would defend the land "single-handed," a Tokyo broadcast said.

The broadcast charged that during a conference of French Indo-China wartime military leaders in Hanoi on Feb. 20 "many of them were known to have strongly advocated immediate launching of an armed attack on Japan."

French officials were accused of "secretly cooperating with the United States air forces in the Philippines, China and India, as well as with enemy submarines" and added that American planes had dropped supplies to French forces in the colony "a number of times between Feb. 20 and Feb. 22."

Although the colony had been occupied by the Japanese since before Pearl Harbor, Tokyo has announced repeatedly that administration was left up to French officials there. This was the first outward break between them and the Japanese.

Marshal Henri-Philippe Pétain's Vichy Government was reported to be in contact with French officials in Indo-China before the Allied landings in France, but Gen. Charles de Gaulle has regarded the colony more as conquered territory and has announced that French troops will be ready to participate in a battle for its liberation.

Even after the Japanese occupation, the French were permitted to maintain a small armed force in the colony.

Admiral Jean Decoux is the French Governor General of Indo-China and Tokyo's references to him have always been friendly.

March 10, 1945

INDO-CHINA TO GAIN LIMITED AUTONOMY

De Gaulle Reveals Post-War Plan—Move Is Regarded as Anticipating Trusteeship

'FRENCH UNION' IS FORMED

By DANA ADAMS SCHMIDT
By Wireless to THE NEW YORK TIMES.

PARIS, March 23—Gen. Charles de Gaulle's Cabinet announced today that Indo-China will gain limited self-government after the war, and at the same time introduced into French statecraft a new term—"the French Union."

It described the "French Union" as being composed of France and all parts of "the imperial community." Indo-China, it said, "will have a federal government presided over by a Governor-General and composed of Ministers responsible to him. The Ministers will be chosen from among the Indo-Chinese as well as Frenchmen resident in Indo-China."

In a statement to be issued tomorrow the French Government furthermore will declare citizens of the Indo-Chinese Federation to be simultaneously citizens of the "French Union" and qualified to hold all offices within the Union. It will give Indo-Chinese access to all ranks in an Indo-Chinese army, navy and air force to be created in the future.

The basis for all future laws in Indo-China, it will proclaim, should be liberty of thought, liberty of creed, liberty of the press, liberty of assembly "and all other democratic liberties."

These announcements, observers agreed, are gestures by which General de Gaulle hopes to anticipate the unwelcome ideas of "international trusteeship of colonies" that are likely to be submitted to the San Francisco World Security Conference by liberalizing the organization of the French Empire while simultaneously drawing its parts into a relationship of organic unity with the mother country.

Colonial Era Closing

General de Gaulle will expound his concept of the "French Union" in a speech in the near future.

The final decisions, however, are to be left to the constituent assembly that will write a new French constitution after the war.

High French officials, meanwhile, explained that they have felt increasingly on the one hand that the era of colonies is drawing to a close and on the other hand that France has particular post-war moral obligations toward her colonies and protectorates because of the loyalty displayed by the native populations during the most difficult days of the war.

They cautioned against too close a comparison between the "French Union" and the "British Commonwealth," pointing out that in contrast to the territories dependent on France the British Dominions are inhabited largely by highly developed peoples of European extraction and organically are linked to the mother country only by loyalty to the crown. In the "French Union," however, it is contemplated—though not yet decided—that each dependent territory ultimately should have its own elected assembly that would in turn send representatives to an "Assembly of the Empire" to sit in Paris alongside the assemblies of metropolitan France.

Would Control Own Budget

Each colony or protectorate would be given a status commensurate with its development. Thus in Indo-China it is thought there may be three or possibly four of five colonies and protectorates sufficiently advanced to have elected assemblies. These would be represented in the "Assembly of the Indo-Chinese Federation" that would send its representatives to Paris.

The Indo-Chinese Assembly would control its own budget and have the power to legislate on economic and internal matters, but

BURMA RESISTERS SEEK BIGGER ROLE

Communists Are Prominent in Groups That Plan to Set Up Their Own Government

By TILLMAN DURDIN
By Wireless to THE NEW YORK TIMES.

CALCUTTA, India, May 17 (Delayed) — Political and military groups organized among the people to resist the Japanese are today potent factors in the politics of Burma and may become increasingly important.

Communist leadership is prominent among these resistance groups, and in many ways they closely resemble the Maquis of France, the Elas of Greece and other European resistance organizations. Among the British agents parachuted in during the last year to work with these groups behind the Japanese lines are a number who served with the Maquis.

What immediate or long-range political intentions the Burma resistance groups have are not entirely clear. However, members of the Anti-Fascist League, within which is incorporated the Burma National Army, are reported to be trying to retain the arms they received from the Japanese and British.

In the Nyaunglebin district of lower Burma British civil affairs officers discovered the anti-Fascist League had named members of a National Government for Burma, which League leaders said would take over when Britain granted independence to Burma.

Some quarters fear a repetition of recent events in Greece and Belgium. Others think the Anti-Fascist League and particularly the Burma National Army are inspired by opportunism and do not have the political breadth or patriotic fervor necessary for the genuine struggle for power on a national scale.

PARIS IS STRESSING INDO-CHINA ISSUE

By HAROLD CALLENDER
By Wireless to THE NEW YORK TIMES.

PARIS, Aug. 15—For the French Japan's capitulation marks the

the territory would remain dependent on France for decisions of foreign affairs and national defense.

The possible jurisdiction of the Assembly of the Empire in Paris has not yet been worked out.

Farthest advance of all plans for the Empire are those for Madagascar, which were expected to be made public shortly.

There are other plans, less advanced, to give the Cameroons and the Ivory Coast assemblies with limited powers. New Caledonia is

Seek Burma's Independence

Anti-Fascist League chiefs have stated that they advocate independence for Burma and that they opposed the Japanese because they believed they had a better chance of realizing their hopes under the British than under the Japanese. Some Burma National Army men frankly say they deserted the Japanese because the Japanese were losing the war.

The BNA was organized by the Japanese to fight for them and did participate in attacks on Allied troops in 1942 and for more than two years thereafter. Two months ago the BNA turned against the Japanese and began to cooperate with the British forces.

The shift was made at the time of the capture of Mandalay. Since then BNA members have attacked stragglers, sabotaged Japanese communications, taken Japanese prisoners, and served as guides and intelligence agents for the British.

The Anti-Fascist League and the BNA are almost entirely organizations of Burmese proper, people of the cities and plains as distinct from the hill tribes. The Burmese proper number about 10,000,000, the hill people about 6,000,000.

The Anti-Fascist League seems to incorporate many members of the old pre-war Thakin party, nationalist advocates of Burmese independence. The Thakins, before the war, had Communists in their ranks.

In contrast to the Burmese, virtually all the hill peoples of Burma except the Shans and some minor savage tribes fought the Japanese from the moment they entered Burma and are still fighting. Under American leadership the gallant little Kachin guerrillas of North Burma have killed 5,000 Japanese. During the North Burma campaign they operated hundreds of miles in the enemy's rear as raiders and spies and provided by radio daily reports on the strength and movements of the Japanese.

Karens Killed Many Japanese

The Karens, of the autonomous East Burma Karenni states and the most numerous of the Burma hill peoples, also have opposed the Japanese from the beginning of their invasion of Burma. Recently, led by British officers, they killed

end of an epoch that brought France low. It was a dramatic coincidence that the fall of Japanese power came the same day as the condemnation of Marshal Henri-Philippe Pétain, who symbolizes France's downfall, and that it preceded by only a few days Gen. Charles de Gaulle's long-planned visit to Washington, which

considered qualified to have its own assembly.

The existing Tunisian Assembly may be modified and steps may be taken to introduce one in Morocco. Algeria is administered as an integral part of metropolitan France. With a view to introducing some democratic machinery into the more developed areas, there is a plan to divide French West Africa into three parts and French Equatorial Africa into several parts.

March 24, 1945

nearly 2,000 Japanese. Recently Karen warriors held up movements of elements of two Japanese divisions attempting to escape from Mandalay, killing more than 1,000 and enabling the Fourteenth Army to occupy Toungoo.

The Chins also have a record of successful warfare against the Japanese and the Nagas were effective allies during the Japanese invasion of the Kohima area of Manipur last year.

The resistance groups among the hill men are not opposed to British rule. They want mainly the right to have their own simple way of life, free of encroachments by the Burmese and Chinese. Most are turning back their weapons when asked to do so.

The resistance movement against the Japanese sprang into life last year among the people of Arakan, that long segment of land flanking the Bay of Bengal and separated from Central Burma by broad mountain barriers. When the Japanese first came to Arakan political groups cooperated with the invaders and partisans attacked the retreating British.

Gradually disillusionment set in and the people of Arakan learned from Japanese brutalities and the corruption of the puppet Rangoon Government that nothing would be done by them to satisfy separatist aspirations or alleviate economic difficulties. A left-wing Buddhist monk, U Pinnyathaiha, organized the peasants in a food blockade against the Japanese and with the aid of young Communist collaborators formed partisan bands to wage guerrilla warfare.

British officers were parachuted in to work with Pinnyathaiha's forces. The British have had Burmese Communists within their propaganda and intelligence organizations, working from India, since 1942.

Maung Thein, Burmese Communist who wrote the anti-Fascist book, "What Happened in Burma," when he escaped from Burma after the Japanese invasion, has served as one of the links between British intelligence and the anti-Fascist League.

May 19, 1945

symbolizes France's rise from the abyss.

Both the downfall and the rise were results of forces outside France. Marshal Petain bet on one of those forces, General de Gaulle bet on the other. None of the V-J Day comments in the Paris press today is so striking as General de Gaulle's prophetic words of

June 18, 1940, when he alluded to "the immense industry of the United States" and said victory would be won by "the superior mechanical force." Such, he added, was the key to "the destiny of the world."

It is an historic irony that General de Gaulle, who foresaw the American role in the world sooner than most Americans did, so far misunderstood the United States that when our forces landed in France he feared our power would be used to curtail rather than to restore French sovereignty. That fear was not removed by his visit to Washington a month after that landing. It remains to be seen whether it will be removed by his second visit next week.

Causes of Apprehension

Apprehension of such tremendous power in the hands of another —even if it is a liberating power— is perhaps inevitable on the part of the French who have the second largest empire in the world but lack the means to defend it. Hence the concern about the fate of Indo-China, and the suspicions provoked by every American allusion to bases that have been so conspicuous in French comment in the press and elsewhere as Japan's sun began to set and America's power seemed immeasurably expanded.

It seems certain that General de Gaulle at the White House and Foreign Minister Georges Bidault at the State Department will speak of Indo-China, as does the whole French press. General de Gaulle today sent a message from "the mother country to the Indo-Chinese union," expressing France's "joy, solicitude and gratitude" for Indo-China's "loyalty to France" and resistance to the Japanese. He promised again that upon the recovery of Indo-China France would keep her engagements to create a free regime there.

French touchiness on the subject of Indo-China and other colonies in the weakened state of France today is kept acute by American comments like that cited today by the newspaper Combat. None of these comments, however obscure or unofficial the source, is overlooked here.

Combat says The Washington Times Herald asserted that "the United States did not conquer Japan to give back to European countries their lost colonies." Combat says the American paper then specified Hong Kong, Netherlands Indies and Indo-China. Combat remarks that regarding Indo-China, "we have something to say," and it wonders whether idealism will become "the best ambassador of business men," an allusion to what the French call American economic imperialism.

August 16, 1945

The Trials of Nationhood

President Sukarno of Indonesia built up his own image as well as his country. The real Sukarno is at the lower right of this picture.

UPI

France Holds On to the Indo-China Tiger

She would like to let go, but the pressures on Paris to continue the war are strong.

By THEODORE H. WHITE

PARIS.

THERE is an oriental expression which is almost untranslatable in French. It is "to have a tiger by the tail," a phrase used for a situation in which it is as dangerous to hold on as to let go. During the past six months this phrase, in its various French equivalents, has become an almost precise definition of a dilemma for which no man, party or leader in the whirling kaleidoscope of French politics has any working solution. This dilemma is France's bloody war in Indo-China, a war that flickers and flares over a 1,000-mile front of jungle, forest and swamp, which has already cost France 18,000 men and has finally become along with the domestic inflation it helps stoke, the root problem of French national policy.

Nor is this a dilemma which the French insist on keeping to themselves. It is a dilemma which they have become increasingly willing, or rather eager, to share with the United States. This was made plain here in discussions, following the recent signing of the Contractual Agreement with Germany, in which French officials asked American Secretary of State Acheson for a further speed-up of American aid in Indo-China.

FOR the United States the dilemma is posed in somewhat different form. The core of our Atlantic policy is to create a powerful French force in Europe, not only sufficient to defend the vast and vital expanse of France on the Continent, but confident enough to accept partnership with the Germans—thus permitting, eventually, the release of American troops from garrison in central Europe. In Asia, however, American policy is to contain the expansion of communism on the vast fringes of revolutionary China; to do this it is considered essential that the French seal the surge of turbulence on the south, in Indo-China, as we are doing in the north in Korea. If, however, France's exertions in Asia paralyze her effort to create an effective military force in Europe, what then? If, in the coming year, it becomes apparent that France cannot play her assigned role in both Asia and Europe, which is more important?

Since, to the average Frenchman, the defense of France in France is more important than the defense of a distant colony in Asia, the brutal answer is inescapable. To Americans the answer is not quite so simple. One American observer in Paris described it thus:

THEODORE H. WHITE, free-lance writer now living in Paris, acquired an extensive background on Asia as correspondent there.

"We're approaching now the same situation we faced in the spring of 1947 when things got too much for the British and they dumped Greece and Turkey in our laps. The French can barely hold with what they have here now. A major catastrophe like a full-scale revolt in North Africa, a failure of the wheat crop here at home, or the direct participation of the Chinese Communists in the Indo-China thing—if any of these happen, the French have got to face one of two alternatives: either pull out of Indo-China or go over to full wartime mobilization. If they pull out, the question is put to us."

NONE of these dramatic events is, of course, imminent. Indeed, the calendar of the seasons which determines the course of oriental warfare promises a five-month respite from disaster. In May the gushing monsoon sweeps in off the South Pacific, transforming roads into quagmires and jungles into swamps. Not until October, the usual season of attack in Indo-China, will the land dry, the roads harden and the next Communist offensive be due.

Before then the French hope to have an answer from the United States and Britain as to where they stand. Since early this year, in strictest diplomatic secrecy, the French have been trying to elicit from the American and British Governments a response to the question of how much, and what kind of aid they will get if the Chinese Communists intervene directly in the Indo-China war as they have in Korea. Neither the American Department of State nor the joint Chiefs of Staff have come to any conclusion, for this is an election year in America and the underwriting of a new war in Asia is a political, not an administrative, decision which surpasses their capacity.

While the French Government has been canvassing its Allies for support in the event of graver crisis in Asia, a curious and subtle transformation of opinion has been taking place in the Assembly, which is the Government's source of sovereignty. For the first time, prominent and powerful Frenchmen outside the Communist party and hostile to it have raised the question of whether it might not be wisest for the French to get out of Indo-China now, while the getting is good.

REASONS for the shift in French sentiment are not hard to find. Year by year, the cost and drain of oriental combat have increased while both victory and political settlement have receded into the distant future. Today, the French bear a burden in Indo-China which cannot be increased without wrecking every other objective of French policy, domestic or foreign.

The most common calculation of the strain of the Indo-China war is normally given in figures of money. Of a total national defense budget of 1,400 billion francs, the French have budgeted 435 billion francs for Indo-China, or something more than a billion dollars. Since, traditionally, the Government underestimates

WHAT INDO-CHINA HAS COST FRANCE

IN MEN	IN MONEY
Each symbol equals 20 thousand men	Each symbol equals 50 billion francs
1946 — 40,000	1946 — 27 bil.
1947 — 115,000	1947 — 53.3 bil.
1948 — 130,000	1948 — 89.7 bil.
1949 — 140,000	1949 — 130 bil.
1950 — 162,000	1950 — 201 bil.
1951 — 181,000	1951 — 308 bil.
1952 Est. — 200,000	1952 Est. — 435 bil.

Black shading represents killed, wounded and missing

Indo-China costs for its unenthusiastic Assembly (last year it underestimated them by 33 per cent, which had to be added by deficit appropriation) it is guessed that this year's cost of the Indo-China war will run between 500 and 600 billion francs.

Such figures seem small measured against America's massive defense appropriations but they take significance when measured in French terms. The $3,700,000,000 dollars that France has spent on the Indo-China war since it began is larger than all the Marshall Plan aid she received from America.

FAR more important than the cost in money is the drain of the Indo-China war on the human resources of France. France maintains in Indo-China a regular army of 206,-000 men, a figure almost double that of four years ago. Of these, 76,000 are Frenchmen from France troops, airmen, sailors. Another 19,000 are Foreign Legionnaires, including many Germans. There are 30,000 African Moslems, 17,000 French African Negroes and 60,000-odd native Annamites. Casualty figures are relatively high. Besides the 18,000 killed or captured, another 25,000 French have been invalided home with crippling wounds or debilitating tropical disease. Each year the French claim to lose as many junior officers as graduate from Saint-Cyr, the French West Point.

It is not the casualty figures in Indo-China, however, that create the drain on France's home effort of defense but the conflicting requirements in quality and caliber of manpower of the war in Asia and the remobilization in Europe. To meet her North Atlantic commitments France must form fourteen divisions this year in Europe. These divisions are made up of French conscripts and reserves who must be shaped, trained, and commanded in their eighteen months compulsory service by personnel of the regular army —particularly by leathery old non-coms and technicians who make soldiers out of recruits, and lieutenants and captains who command them at company level.

The French Army counts roughly 20,000 regular army officers. Of these, 6,723 are at present in Indo-China and an estimated 1,200 or 1,300 out of action either en route to the war (a month's journey), en route home, or enjoying the four months leave the French grant officers for recuperation after tropical service. Indo-China has thus immobilized 40 per cent of all French regular officers, predominantly junior officers of the finest combat quality, whose skills are required for whipping French

reserves into the posture of a standing army in Europe. The proportion of non-coms, technicians, squad and section leaders in Indo-China is even larger—one out of two regular army non-coms are involved in the Asian war.

THESE figures are, moreover, charged with a peculiar emotional-political content. So unpopular is the war in Indo-China that the French Assembly has never dared to alter the statutes that forbid the sending of draftees and reserve officers to any overseas war in time of peace—and the war can continue only on condition that the Assembly Deputies are not forced to draft their own voters to fight it.

The result has been twofold —a bitterness, in the regular cadres of the French Army, who believe they are fighting gallantly in defense of a cause neglected and abandoned by their compatriots at home; and an embarrassment on the part of the French Government that cannot ask for the direct military aid of the United States, which it so desperately wants. French Ministers of State, all of them seasoned politicians, realize that no American Congress will commit American draftees to defend an Indo-China for which the French Assembly refuses to draft Frenchmen.

Perhaps the most puzzling and depressing of all the facets of the Indo-China war as seen from Paris is the groping, desperate and constantly failing attempt of all French Governments to offer any plausible political solution, hope of victory, or any other perspective to their people beyond a stubborn insistence not to be driven out in defeat.

THE war in Indo-China, which began at the end of 1946, out of the yeast of Asia's

French trooper guards Chinese Communists captured in Indo-China.

nationalist and Communist ferment against all colonial empires in the Orient, has been a war which the French have attempted to fight, as their enemy has, on two fronts—the one political, the other military. The tragedy has been that Paris' understanding and response have always followed so tardily on events in Asia that they no longer met the situations which evoked them.

By the time, in 1948, that the French realized that legitimate Annamite Nationalist aspirations were being channeled into Communist strategy, and belatedly moved to separate the Nationalist rebels from the Communists by sweeping concessions, it was too late. The Communists, led by their frail and goateed chieftain, Ho Chi-Minh, had capped the rebellion with their own iron discipline and liquidated or absorbed all leadership but their own.

When the French finally realized that only a massive military effort could crush the rebels in the field it was again too late—the Communist triumph in China in 1949 had swept to the borders of Indo-China and given the rebels a base of support and source of supply which multiplied their power by a continent of allies.

What began as a negligent and not carefully thought-out police operation five years ago —one which the French Communist party then supported— has become an action that can be definitively and finally won only by mobilizing all France for a major war in the turbulent Orient. The enemy, once painted as bomb-throwing terrorist or hill-sniper lurking in night ambush, has become a modern army increasingly skillful, armed with artillery, organized in divisional groups.

WHAT has happened is that history has turned against the French. The nineteenth-century empire that France

conquered around the world with a flick of her hand and a brigade or two of adventurers has become a burden that exhausts her.

Over the course of the past three years, France has been beaten back by a jungle army from the frontiers of China to the rice delta of Tonkin.

Last January a debate in the French Assembly illuminated with a brilliant flashback in history the contrasting power of France yesterday and France today. In urging the Assembly to persevere in the Indo-China war, France's then Minister of National Defense, Georges Bidault, a one-time Professor of History, recalled to the Assembly the courage and endurance of France in the last century when, faced with another rebellion in northern Indo-China, she had persisted to victory. Bidault was followed to the rostrum next day by Pierre Mendes-France, a Radical, former Economics Minister and the leader of the Assembly factions that want to withdraw from Indo-China.

MENDES-FRANCE declared that he had made his own historical inquiries after Bidault's speech. He had found that to reconquer Indo-China after the Langson uprising in 1885 had required of France the dispatch of a punitive corps of only 500 men, a far cry from the 206,000-man army that France must maintain today. Indeed, he had found that all of Tonkin (northern Indo-China) had been seized by a French landing force of 180 men in 1873, their rifles in slings. And while France was disposing of her Asian troubles in the last century with the back of her hand, she had maintained in Europe an army of continental defense of 560,000 men. Is it worth while, asked Mendes-France inferentially, for France to strip herself dry in Europe today to maintain a tiny perimeter in Asia at such a cost, for so long a time?

It is this question that has riven French politics since the beginning of the year, or, roughly, since the death of Marshal DeLattre de Tassigny, the French commander in Indo-China, disclosed that only the brilliance and bravado of that great soldier had obscured the fact that there was no change in the dreary vista of combat.

Apart from the Communists whose dogma commits them unquestioningly to support the Cominform line of total surrender there are two main schools of thought in French politics.

The first is that of the Government. The Government is trapped by the responsibility of power. It fears two things first, that defeat and expulsion by force of arms in Asia will kindle revolt in North Africa and bring expulsion from Africa, too; second, that the American Government will, in some way, penalize it if it abandons the Indo-China war and gives the Communists a new beachhead in Southeast Asia.

The Government, therefore, is committed to continuing the war in a perspective described by its conscientious and hardworking Resident-Minister for Indo-China, Jean LeTourneau, as "to accomplish the task that France has set for herself there." This task is to create, in the heat of violent war, a friendly native nationalist Government that will assume the burden of war with the Communists and let the French withdraw gracefully once the blockhouses are fully manned by anti-Communist Annamites.

To head this native Vietnam Government the French have chosen as their instrument a nominal Emperor, His Majesty Bao Dai. Bao Dai, a man who has in the past been either acquiescent, cooperative or loyal first to the French Republic, then to Marshal Pétain and Vichy France, then to the Japanese Army of Occupation, then to Communist Ho Chi-Minh and now again to the French Republic, has failed to evoke great loyalty or cooperation from his own people.

THIS French policy that France cannot withdraw until a friendly anti-Communist Government is built to replace her rule has received, and receives, the official support of America. The United States has recognized Bao Dai as sovereign of Vietnam, sponsored a $47-million aid program of peasant welfare which has been excellently administered, and delivered some 130,000 tons of American arms directly to Indo-China ports. In addition, several hundred million American dollars are earmarked in our over-all aid to the French Government as direct subsidy in the Indo-China war.

The second school of French thought is categorically opposed to Government thinking. It believes that three years of Bao Dai have proven that no emperor set up by Frenchmen can present himself as an authentic independent attractive enough to woo Annamites away from Ho Chi-Minh, the Communist leader; and that while France pursues the experiment, each year the cost grows heavier, the number of French casualties higher. The solution, the protagonists of this school advocate, is withdrawal, now, period.

No development has given greater weight to this school in recent months than America's policy in Europe. If France is to be urged to quick union with Germany in a European army, it is essential (many Frenchmen think) that the French contingent in this army be stronger than the German contingent. This can only be achieved if the French Army professionals are brought home from Asia and posted for defense in Europe.

IN recent months this thesis, whose chief spokesman is M. Mendes-France, has been winning increasing support in the French Assembly. Its program is to publicly offer a cease-fire now to the enemy; to negotiate whatever settlement is possible; to withdraw as fast as possible for the defense of France in Europe. It is a thesis supported by most of the French Socialists, a good part of the Catholic Republicans, and by an evergrowing number of Peasant and economy-minded Deputies of the Right.

It is not yet a majority thesis, but the next galvanizing emergency of French politics may well make it so. At that point the French may loosen their grip on the tiger's tail and turn to America saying, "Here, you take it, it's your tiger now."

June 8, 1952

RUSSIAN-MADE ARMS USED IN INDO-CHINA STIR FEAR FOR AREA

Soviet Trucks and Ammunition Seized by the French in Raid Cause Washington Concern

CHINA FINISHES RAIL LINK

Attack-Free Supply Route Now Extends From Moscow to Southeast Asia Area

By The Associated Press
WASHINGTON, Nov. 24—State Department and Defense Department experts said today that Russian-made war supplies were pouring into Indo-China over a transcontinental Communist railway system protected from Allied air attack because it cut through China.

Officials said this gave new striking power to the Communist-led forces in Indo-China, and presented a new and sinister threat to Burma and to Thailand.

Informants said evidence that the Vietminh rebels were receiving Russian supplies was found in a recent raid by French and native defense forces on Phutho, a Communist supply center.

Allied raiders captured, among other items, twenty-five tons of Russian-made mortar shells and four Russian Molotova trucks with gasoline engines.

The presence of these two-and-a-half-ton trucks at the Vietminh base means that Red forces in Indo-China must now be regarded as far more mobile than ever and thus creates a new degree of danger for all Southeast Asia, officials said.

Trucks Show Supply Line Working

In the raid on Phutho many other types of weapons and ammunition were captured, including supplies of French, American, British and Japanese manufacture, as well as Chinese materials.

But interest here centered on the four Russian trucks because of their possible strategic significance. The fact that they are in Indo-China at all, responsible authorities said, means that the Red railway line and Indo-Chinese supply routes are functioning against all obstacles.

November 25, 1952

CONFLICT WIDENING IN INDO-CHINA WAR

Central and North Vietnam and Laos Are Now Battle Areas

Special to THE NEW YORK TIMES.

SAIGON, Vietnam, March 16—The area of the Indo-China war never has been so extensive as now. Pending military events concern not only North Vietnam (Tonkin), but also Laos and Central Vietnam (Annam). The armed watch covers a territory as big as one-third of France.

The clash began March 12 in Central Vietnam. After a four-day battle the French-Vietnamese troops lifted the threat to Hue—the capital of the ancient Empire of Annam. The same date two Vietminh battalions launched an attack against the post of Ductrong, which is only ten-and-a-half miles from Hue. The Vietnamese company defending the post was overrun but the defense gave supporting forces time to encircle two enemy battalions.

A GAIN IN INDO-CHINA: French-Vietnamese successes in the Hue area (1) are believed to have eased problems of defense in the north (2).

The New York Times   Mar. 17, 1953

For three days the Communist-led Vietminh forces attempted in vain to break through but the defense held and the Vietminh battalions were half destroyed.

This enemy loss greatly relieved the French, whose shock forces are limited in Central Vietnam, where they are opposed by two regular Vietminh divisions.

On the Moi plateaus and against the military base at Tourane, the rebel threat is represented by two regiments, known as "Quangnhai" regiments. They attacked Angkhe six weeks ago. In the coastal region between Hue and Donghoi the threat is from the 325th Division.

The French now can devote themselves to North Vietnam with an easier mind, because of the improvement in Central Vietnam. The small scale maneuver that was so successful in relieving Hue can be used in the defense of two other weak points in Central Vietnam, in the area around Tourane and on the Moi plateaus against the two rebel regiments still intact there.

In the northern part of Central Vietnam, the vulnerable point is the small port of Donghoi, on the borderline of Vietminh-held territory. The 325th Division still has two regiments in that area.

March 17, 1953

French, Criticized on War, Name New Indo-China Chief

By HENRY GINIGER
Special to THE NEW YORK TIMES.

PARIS, May 8—The French Cabinet, at a meeting today, named Gen. Henri Eugene Navarre as Commander in Chief of French Union Forces in Indo-China. General Navarre, who is Chief of Staff to Marshal Alphonse-Pierre Juin, Commander of the Allied Ground Forces Central Europe under Gen. Matthew B. Ridgway's North Atlantic Command, will replace Gen. Raoul Salan, who has conducted the Indo-China operations since the death of Marshal Jean de Lattre de Tassigny in January last year.

The shift in command came amid mounting criticism in press and Parliament both of the conduct of the war and of allegedly large-scale profiteering by influential groups in Indo-China and France interested in seeing the war continue.

The Cabinet also decided to tighten up the military administration in Indo-China and other parts of the French Union by concentrating all funds for land forces in those areas in the hands of the

Ministry of War. Previously the funds had been handled by several Ministries.

Criticism on War Mounts

The replacement of General Salan was made ostensibly because his tour of duty in the Far East was up. But the seemingly easy invasion of Laos by the Communist-led Vietminh has unleashed a strong attack here on the French high command for having done little on its own to halt it.

A dispatch in the afternoon paper Paris-Presse by its Indo-China correspondent, Max Harmier, declared that the French had neither the tactics nor the means to defeat the Vietminh at this time. M. Harmier, whose story was presumably cleared by the French censor at Saigon, asserted that the French had been unable fully to control the vital rice-growing delta region of North Vietnam (Tonkin), which had been Marshal de Lattre's

plan and which he had successfully carried out for a time.

M. Harmier said that by infiltration, the Vietminh had moved two divisions clandestinely into the Delta where they circulated freely and collected men, money and food for operations elsewhere. He said General Salan failed to counteract these Vietminh maneuvers. M. Harmier estimated that the French would need 100,000 more men to clear the enemy from the delta but that they could be had only by sending conscripts to Indo-China, which is not now done, or from foreign troops. Without reinforcements, he said, the French would have to abandon Indo-China, except for the delta and Saigon.

The invasion of Laos has been accompanied by an increasing number of published charges of French profiteering in currency as a result of the artificial maintenance of the exchange rate for the Indo-Chinese piaster.

The latest assertion to this effect was made by the neutralist weekly L'Observateur and the daily newspaper Franc-Tireur.

The operation, according to these papers, has consisted of buying United States dollars on the French black market for anywhere from 350 to 400 fancs for each dollar. The dollars then are sold in Indo-China for fifty piasters to the dollar. The piasters, in turn, are converted back into francs at the official, but highly overvalued,

rate of seventeen francs for a piaster with a consequent profit of as much as 150 per cent.

Rebels Profited, Papers Say

Both papers said that many dollars bought in Paris and sold in Indo-China had found their way into the hands of Vietminh agents, who have used them to buy arms with which to kill Frenchmen. They added that the French Treasury had been losing 500,000,000 francs (about $1,400,000) a day because of the spread between the official piaster rate of one-to-seventeen francs and its real value on international markets of one piaster to eight and one-half francs. Both papers talked of official complicity in these operations.

The press also has reported that a parliamentary committee that visited Indo-China had given a secret report to Premier René Mayer and President Vincent Auriol containing details both on profiteering and on mistakes that had characterized the war.

General Navarre, who inherits what could be mildly described as an unenviable situation, is 54. He was Deputy Commander of French forces in Germany before becoming Marshal Juin's aide in October, 1950.

The Cabinet communiqué announcing his appointment emphasized his close association with the Marshal as a factor in winning him the appointment to his new post.

May 9, 1953

KING WINS CONTROL OF CAMBODIA ARMY

Accord With Paris Raises Hope of Full Agreement—French to Command 3 Battalions

Special to THE NEW YORK TIMES.

PARIS, Oct. 17 — Almost complete agreement on Cambodia's military sovereignty was reached today after laborious negotiations in Pnompenh, capital of Cambodia.

As a result, optimism rose that a general accord between France and Cambodia for strengthening the French Union and defending it in Indo-China against the Communist-led Vietminh could be reached in forthcoming negotiations in Paris.

Full command over all Cambodian territory and forces was given to King Norodom Sihanouk and his Government. This transfer of sovereignty included five battalions of Cambodian troops operating directly under the French and two battalions stationed in Cambodia under mixed or French Union command.

The French, in turn, received "operational" control over three Cambodian battalions in the sector on the left bank of the Mekong River, but the legal status of this group was left to a decision to be made in Paris.

Signature of the agreement came after six weeks of talks that at several times had broken down and had produced a near rupture between the two countries. Cambodia had been more intransigent on the subject of sovereignty than the other two associate states of Indo-China, Laos and Vietnam, and had even threatened uprisings and withdrawal from the French Union.

For strategic reasons the French were eager to avoid an open break, since Cambodian territory and men were needed for an eventual defense not only of Cambodia but also of Laos to the north.

Cambodia has long been dependent on France and the United States for economic and technical help.

The military talks constituted one phase of the general talks between France and Cambodia leading to the latter's sovereignty. Transfers of sovereignty in the judicial and police fields have already been agreed upon, and talks will begin Monday on economic and financial matters.

The turn of events in Cambodia comes at an opportune moment from the French point of view, since next door in Vietnam, the largest and most important of the three states, the French Union is being seriously questioned by nationalist elements.

October 18, 1953

PARIS SIGNS TREATY MAKING LAOS FREE, BUT IN FRENCH UNION

Auriol Criticizes Nationalists of Vietnam—Assembly Will Debate Indo-China Today

By HAROLD CALLENDER
Special to THE NEW YORK TIMES.

PARIS, Oct. 22—A treaty declaring Laos to be "fully independent and sovereign" but within the French Union was signed today.

Designed as the first of three to be negotiated with the Associated States of Indo-China, the treaty was signed by President Vincent Auriol and King Sisavang Vong of Laos on the eve of tomorrow's debate on Indo-China in the National Assembly. During the debate the Government's policy in Indo-China will be attacked.

At about the same time today Premier Joseph Laniel handed to Prince Buu Loc, Vietnam's High Commissioner, a note for Bao Dai, Chief of State of Vietnam, inquiring whether the state intended to

The New York Times   Oct. 23, 1953

PACT SIGNED: France and Laos (diagonal shading) concluded a treaty on the Indo-Chinese state's independence. In Vietnam a Vietminh base at Phunhoquan (cross) fell.

remain within the French Union, the association of France and her overseas territories. Such a condition is a French prerequisite of any new agreement.

After signing the treaty, which was general in its terms and will be supplemented by conventions specifying what full independence means, M. Auriol made a speech expressing some of the indignation he felt toward the National Vietnam Congress, which proposed to reject the French Union "in its present form." The nationalist group, meeting in Saigon last week, at first refused to participate in the French Union entirely, but later modified its stand.

"Those who from irresponsibility or a bargaining spirit or ingratitude misunderstand France and the French Union are belied by the facts," said M. Auriol.

"Not only is the French Union not an obstacle to national independence; its purpose is to guarantee and defend that independence. * * * They are very imprudent who forget what they owe to the French Union and what they would lack for their defense if that union were absent."

The definition of the French Union is somewhat vague and is not made any clearer by the treaty signed today. The definition in the French Constitution, which created the union in 1946, is that the union is composed of nations and peoples uniting to increase their prosperity and insure their security.

The Constitution then proclaims: "France intends to lead these peoples for whom she has assumed responsibility to the liberty of self-administration and democratic management of their own affairs. Rejecting all systems of colonization founded on arbitrary power, she guarantees to all equal access to public office and the individual and collective exercise of the rights and liberties proclaimed or confirmed herein." These include equality of rights for all members of the union.

The Constitution does not use the words independence or sovereignty, even as describing goals. But today's treaty says that Laos reaffirms her membership in "the French Union, an association of independent and sovereign peoples, free and equal in rights and duties, in which all the associates place in common their resources to guarantee the defense of the union as a whole."

This article, taken literally, indicates that members of the union are already independent and sovereign, although the Constitution does not say this. For this reason the French Government in July proposed to "complete" the independence of the Indo-Chinese states—Vietnam, Laos and Cambodia in a series of negotiations.

October 23, 1953

LANIEL LIMITS GOAL IN INDO-CHINA WAR

Special to THE NEW YORK TIMES.

PARIS, Nov. 12—Premier Joseph Laniel told the Council of the Republic today that France was not seeking an unconditional surrender of the Communist-led enemy in Indo-China and would be happy to find "an honorable solution" to the conflict.

The Premier's statement, made during a debate in the upper house, aroused considerable comment here, since it contrasted with that made by Vice President Richard M. Nixon during his recent visit to Indo-China. Mr. Nixon told the Vietnamese and the French there that they could not lay down their arms "until victory is completely won" and warned that the United States would not approve any peace negotiation that would leave the Indo-Chinese in bondage.

M. Laniel, who is feeling heavy pressure from political forces who wish an end to the war, said his Government did not consider that the Indo-Chinese problem ought necessarily to receive a military solution.

November 13, 1953

PARATROOPS SEIZE BIG VIETMINH BASE

French Union Forces Capture Reds' Dienbienphu Center, Near Laos, in Dawn Drop

HANOI, Vietnam, Saturday, Nov. 21 (UP)—More than 1,000 French Union paratroopers dropped in a mass jump at dawn yesterday to attack a Communist stronghold 125 miles west of here.

The paratroopers jumped from a fleet of more than sixty planes that roared out of Hanoi under cover of twenty B-26's in a top secret operation. General Rene Cogny, French northern commander in Indo-China, supervised the take-off.

Little resistance was encountered at the Red stronghold, Dienbienphu, the reports said.

November 21, 1953

Indo-China Is Sliced in Two As Foe Reaches Thai Border

By TILLMAN DURDIN
Special to THE NEW YORK TIMES.

SAIGON, Vietnam, Dec. 26—Communist-led Vietminh troops have spanned the hundred-mile waist of central Indo-China and reached the Mekong River, the border with Thailand. A swift-moving vanguard of a Vietminh force that had crossed the Annamite mountain chain from Vietnam was believed to have arrived at the river today.

The French high command announced that a small French-led Laotian garrison at the Mekong town of Thakhek had been evacuated last night.

[A Reuters dispatch from Bangkok said that Thailand had rushed troops to the border after proclaiming a state of emergency in the threatened area. Thakhek is just across the Mekong River from Nakhon Phanom, strategic Thai town.]

It is assumed that the Vietminh forces have entered Thakhek, which has a population of several thousand and marks the junction of the main Laos north-south highway and the road followed by the Vietminh troops in their advance.

The Vietminh forces are now at the frontier of Thailand and have cut Indo-China in two, roughly along the Nineteenth Parallel. Many Laotians are reported here to have fled from Thakhek and its vicinity across the river into Thailand, where reinforced Thai border police forces are on guard.

The French made no attempt to defend Thakhek and the handful of men who had been stationed there left without incident. A French spokesman said that the Thakhek garrison had headed for a "regrouping zone" fixed by the French high command.

Since they overwhelmed the defending French-Laotian forces just across the Vietnam border in Laos five nights ago after a march through wild mountain country southward from the Vietnam coastal city of Vinh, the Vietminh forces have been confronted with only scattered harassing attacks. French tactics have been to concentrate forces for holding, and subsequent counter-attacking action.

Just where the French defense will be made in central Laos has not been revealed but one point that the defenders will obviously try to hold is the big Seno airfield, about sixty miles south of Thakhek. Seno, which can accommodate four-motored planes, is near the important Mekong River port of Savannakhet.

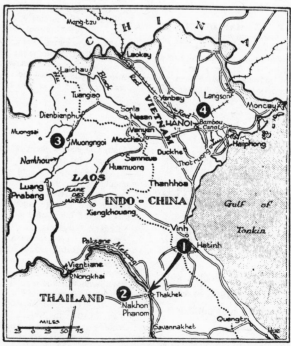

The New York Times   Dec. 27, 1953

VIETMINH BISECTS INDO-CHINA: The rebels entered abandoned Thakhek (1) and Thailand reinforced the Nakhon Phanom area (2). French-led forces joined in the Namhou valley (3) and mopped up in the Red River delta (4).

Gen. André Franchi has been appointed head of the new operational command for the central Laotian war zone. The French continued to rush reinforcements to the threatened area to strengthen defenses.

The French have known for some time that the Vietminh command was moving for an attack somewhere in central Indo-China but the size of the Vietminh thrust across Laos has come as a surprise. The Vietminh forces may have committed 20,000 men to the operation.

December 27, 1953

Vietminh's Defeat In Half-Year Seen

By The United Press.

HANOI, Vietnam, Jan. 1—Gen. Henri-Eugene Navarre told his French Union forces in Indo-China today that he fully expected victory in the long war against the Communists after six more months of hard fighting.

The French Commander in Chief hinted in his New Year's message that he would carry on and intensify his strategy of lightning strikes deep into Red territory.

Meanwhile scattered but brisk clashes occurred on the front lines.

Communist-led Vietminh troops still were massing ominously in the hills around the key French base of Dienbienphu in northwest Indo-China.

January 2, 1954

INDO-CHINA REBELS LAUNCH BIG DRIVE ON BESIEGED POST

10,000 Enemy Troops Attack French-Held Dienbienphu, on Laos-Tonkin Line

By TILLMAN DURDIN
Special to THE NEW YORK TIMES.

SAIGON, Vietnam, March 14—Communist-led Vietminh forces launched a massive assault last night against Dienbienphu in what may become a decisive battle in the Indo-Chinese war.

More than 10,000 troops hurled themselves at three different strong points on the French perimeter. The attack came after preliminary bombardment from Vietminh mortars and artillery and was met with withering fire from the French fortifications.

Savage fighting went on all night and was continuing today. A French headquarters source said tonight that the defenders had the situation "well in hand."

Vietminh losses so far were described as "very heavy." French casualties were not specified, but in view of the intensity of the combat are probably considerable.

[The Associated Press reported from Hanoi that the Vietminh troops had retreated into the hills Sunday morning, leaving behind more than 1,000 casualties. However, Reuters said the French Command reported early Monday the loss of a point outside Dienbienphu.]

The new Vietminh attack ended two months of speculation over whether Gen. Vo Nguyen Giap, the Vietminh commander, would actually throw his legions against the French airfield bastion in the Thai country 180 miles west of Hanoi.

Post Set Up in November

Established by the French last November as a barrier to the developing Vietminh drive toward northern Laos, Dienbienphu had been built by January into a position of great strength around which the Vietminh concentrated more than 30,000 troops.

When the Communist forces failed to attack Dienbienphu in January and instead sent a division into northern Laos, many military observers here believed there remained little likelihood of a major assault on the outpost.

With the division back from Laos, Vietminh forces have now at last lunged against the French strongpoint. They may fail to follow up last night's opening surge, but the general opinion here is that General Giap now is committed to an all-out effort.

The Vietminh achieved no tactical surprise at Dienbienphu. From prisoners and from the steadily closer enemy encirclement of their perimeter the French commanders at Dienbienphu had concluded by late Friday that a big attack was coming the following day.

March 15, 1954

PRESIDENT WARNS OF CHAIN DISASTER IF INDO-CHINA GOES

Says Result of Such a Loss to the Free World in Asia Would Be Incalculable

JOINT NOTICE IS PRESSED

Dulles Declares Admonition to Peiping Might Obviate Need for 'Action' Later

By ANTHONY LEVIERO
Special to The New York Times.

WASHINGTON, April 7 — President Eisenhower said today that a Communist conquest of Indo-China would set off throughout Asia a chain reaction of disaster for the free world.

The consequences would be incalculable, the President said. In his news conference he spoke calmly but gravely about the crisis of the Indo-China war.

General Eisenhower said it was too early to report on results of the United States current efforts to marshal allies for united action to cope with the crisis.

While the war and negotiations with allies were still in a delicate stage, the President declined to say whether the United States would seek United Nations action or, as a last resort, go it alone to save Indo-China.

Dulles Reviews Policy Again

Meanwhile John Foster Dulles, Secretary of State, asserted that if the free nations demonstrated their united will, "it will diminish the need for united action." He reviewed foreign policy at a meeting of Republican women.

"I believe that, in general, most of our great problems come from not making sufficiently clear in advance what the dangers are to a potential aggressor," said Mr. Dulles.

[The Peiping radio declared Thursday that Secretary of State Dulles "lied and slanderously charged that China intervened in the Indo-China war," an Associated Press dispatch from Tokyo said. The broadcast charged Mr. Dulles "attempted to use this vile method to deceive and hoodwink world public opinion, cover up the crime of active United States intervention in the Indo-China war and create a pretext for the United States to extend its intervention there."]

Most of the twenty-five minutes of General Eisenhower's news conference was devoted to questions about the Indo-China war. In his discussion the President spoke with the same sense of urgency that Secretary Dulles has been giving to the Indo-China problem in recent weeks. A few days ago the Secretary of State declared in a Congressional hearing that the overt actions of Communist China in the Indo-China war came close to the point of inviting instant and massive retaliation under this country's concept of protecting its vital interests.

Secret Talks Continue

The stress of this country's present policy was on mobilizing a ten-nation coalition for united action against the Communist forces that threatened to overcome Indo-China. Negotiations toward this goal were going on secretly with Britain, France, Australia, New Zealand, the Philippines, Thailand and the Associated States of Indo-China—Vietnam, Laos and Cambodia.

The negotiations were being pressed intensely, for the Administration was pessimistic about the possibilities of reaching a satisfactory settlement while France alone carried the main burden of the fighting.

President Eisenhower said he did not think the chances were good for negotiating a settlement with the Communists at the forthcoming conference on Far East problems in Geneva.

He reiterated this country's willingness to go as far as prudence would allow in seeking settlement of any world problem by conciliation or negotiated agreement. But he firmly said the United States would not overstep the safety line of its security by making any agreement with Communists that did not rest on a foundation of fact and deed.

President Eisenhower made in effect a geopolitical survey of the consequences of defeat.

Already about 450,000,000 persons have fallen under Communist dictatorship in Asia, and the free world cannot afford more losses of that kind, the President said.

The loss of Indo-China would lead to the loss of Burma, of Thailand, in fact of all of the great peninsula on which they are situated he said. With these countries would be lost tin, and tungsten and rubber and other materials needed by the free world, the President declared.

In the next consequence the strategic geography would go bad, he said. The whole island defense chain of Japan, Formosa and the Philippines would be turned or flanked, and this would also project the threat down into Australia and New Zealand, General Eisenhower went on.

The President noted one economic consequence. Japan must have the Indo-China region as a trading area, he said. If deprived of that trading area Japan will be compelled to turn in only one direction — the vast Communist empire of Red China or Manchuria, he added.

Thus in the span of exactly eight weeks the President was expressing a sharply revised viewpoint that took account of the possibility of intervention by the United States along with its allies if that were necessary to save Indo-China.

In seeking a special united front to deal with the threat to Indo-China the Administration was hopeful that the sheer weight of the arrangement would tend to bring about a solution by peaceful means.

On Feb. 10 President Eisenhower said that no one could be more bitterly opposed than he to getting the United States involved in a hot war in Indo-China. He also said he could conceive of no greater tragedy for this country than to get heavily involved there in an all-out war, especially with large units.

The President was asked if he agreed with Senator Joseph F. Kennedy, Democrat of Massachusetts, that Indo-China's independence should be guaranteed to justify an all-out effort there.

General Eisenhower said he always had tried to insist, in many years of talking with different Governments, on the principle that no outside country could be helpful to another if it did something that local people did not want.

President Eisenhower added that he did not know whether the Associated States of Indo-China wanted independence in the same sense that the United States was independent

But the President went on to say that the aspirations of the peoples of the Far East must be met or else in the long run there could be no answer to the unrest there.

Advance notice to "potential aggressors" that their efforts were "doomed to failure," would greatly reduce the ultimate need

The New York Times   April 8, 1954

EISENHOWER EXPLAINS DANGER TO STRATEGY: Loss of Indo-China to the Communists, the President told his news conference yesterday, would imperil the military position of the free world in the Far East (cross-hatching) and threaten its vital resources there.

for collective action or participation by governments alarmed by the grave developments in Indo-China, Mr. Dulles told the Republican women.

"With united will created it will diminish the need for united action," said Mr. Dulles. "But there should be, I hope, a willingness to have united action if the events should be such as to require that. I don't believe that things will go that far, particularly if we can create a unity of will which would make it apparent that the ambitious efforts of the Chinese Communists to dominate all of Southeast Asia and the Western Pacific are doomed to failure because it will encounter a united opposition so strong that it could not be overcome."

On Capitol Hill Roger M. Kyes, Deputy Defense Secretary, and Admiral Arthur W. Radford,

Chairman of the Joint Chiefs of Staff, met with a bipartisan group of Senate leaders.

They were the Republican leader, William F. Knowland of California, and Leverett Saltonstall, Republican of Massachusetts, chairman of the Armed Services Committee, Lyndon Johnson, Democrat of Texas, the minority leader, and Richard B. Russell of Georgia, ranking minority member of the Armed Services group.

Some time after the meeting Senator Knowland confirmed that Indo-China had been the subject of discussion. "All I can say is that it was to keep us abreast of developments," he said.

April 8, 1954

France Signs a Promise of Total Independence for Vietnam State

By LANSING WARREN

Special to The New York Times.

PARIS, April 28—France and Vietnam signed today a joint declaration of agreement for the "total independence" of Vietnam.

The declaration was intended chiefly to satisfy the United States, which has been pressing France to grant full independence to the Associated States of Indo-China in connection with the conference at Geneva.

United States diplomacy has considered that Allied support could be given more readily to independent countries than to states whose sovereignty is subject to the supervision of another nation. The way would be opened also to Vietnamese participation in a Southeast Asia defense pact.

The drafting of two treaties to which the joint declaration refers has been virtually finished. But they will not be signed until some other related accords are also completed. These are accords between France and Vietnam over juridical, military, economic and cultural affairs in Vietnam that are to be directed jointly by the French and Vietnamese Governments.

The signing today was said in French official circles to have ended the friction caused by the refusal Sunday by Bao Dai, Chief of State of Vietnam, to have the declaration signed. Marc Jacquet, Under-Secretary for the Associated States of Indo-China, left Paris tonight for Cannes to confer with Bao Dai.

It is thought that their talk would turn on the possibility that the insurgent Vietminh regime might also take a seat at Geneva when the conference on Indo-China begins. Prince Buu Loc, Vietnamese Premier, also was expected soon in Cannes to confer with Bao Dai after wide consultations in Indo-China with a view to making the Vietnamese delegation to Geneva as broadly representative as possible.

Laniel Signs for France

Premier Joseph Laniel signed the declaration for France and Nguyen Trung Vinh, Vice Premier, signed for Vietnam. The ceremonies took place in the French Premier's offices in the Hotel Matignon.

According to the document, "France, having the aim of granting Vietnam independence," and Vietnam, "resolved to maintain and consolidate its traditional friendship with the French people," proclaim their agreement "to settle their mutual relations on the basis of two fundamental treaties."

One of these treaties recognizes the total independence of Vietnam and its full and entire sovereignty. The other treaty establishes a French-Vietnamese association to be placed within the French Union. A joint direction on a basis of equality will concern military, economic and cultural affairs that mutually interest the two nations.

It is on the last points that negotiations have progressed the least and on which several disputed questions remain to be solved. One is the question of the monetary status of Vietnam, whose currency is now dependent wholly on the franc. Customs and other economic matters are still under debate. Military relations are as yet to be defined.

Until these matters have been agreed upon, the French have said, the two fundamental treaties will not be initialed.

Bao Dai has consistently protested against any French negotiations with the Communist-led Vietminh for peace. His preference has been for United States, or international, intervention in the Indo-Chinese war.

His principal objection a few days ago to the signing of the joint declaration was his contention that the unity of Vietnam had been threatened and that Vietnam could not agreed to a partition of the country or creation of a buffer state.

April 29, 1954

Bao Dai Agrees to Admit Vietminh to Geneva Parley

By TILLMAN DURDIN

Special to The New York Times.

GENEVA, April 29—Vietnam's Chief of State agreed today to the participation of Vietminh representatives in the Geneva conference on Far Eastern affairs. French and United States officials here said Bao Dai attached certain reservations to his agreement but confidence was expressed that any difficulties in this connection could be ironed out.

Bao Dai's acquiescence to the Vietminh's participation is believed to have removed one obstacle to the talks on Indo-China. The prospects for these were improved from another direction.

A personal appeal from the British Foreign Secretary, Anthony Eden, to the Governments of India, Ceylon and Pakistan increased the possibility of wide participation by Asian nations in a settlement of the Indo-China war.

Mr. Eden asked the three South Asian Commonwealth countries if they could associate themselves with whatever plan for ending the Indo-China conflict that was worked out at Geneva. In a message sent to the three governments yesterday as the Colombo conference opened in Ceylon, Mr. Eden said he "had good hopes" that some solution for the Indo-China problem would be reached here.

Seeks Widest Support

Emphasizing that it was important that any agreement reached at Geneva have the widest possible backing and support, Mr. Eden said he would be grateful if the three Governments would consider whether—at some later date or in some form or other—they might find it possible to associate themselves with such support. He mentioned the possible need for guarantees in connection with his plea for support.

Mr. Eden's message was noteworthy in that it was a personal appeal. There have been many consultations between Britain and the Asian Commonwealth countries recently regarding Indo-China and the new Pacific pact proposal, but these have all been on a government-to-government basis.

British sources here said Mr. Eden had two aims in making his new appeal. One was to keep the Colombo conference from adopting a negative attitude toward the West's participation in an Indo-China settlement and possibly rejecting out of hand Western plans. The other was to line up Asian countries themselves in the widest possible support for the West's efforts to end the Indo-China war without ceding the area to communism.

No Commitment Asked

It was pointed out that Mr. Eden's proposal was deliberately couched in broad terms and asked no particular commitments. It was designed to link Commonwealth Asian states with Western policy and counter Soviet efforts to draw Asian nations into conflict with Western moves regarding Indo-China.

In agreeing to the participation of Vietminh representatives in the Geneva conference, Bao Dai was reported to have said he wanted his acceptance expressed in such a way as not to imply recognition of the Vietminh regime as the government of Vietnam.

April 30, 1954

A Chronology of the Administration's Policy on Indo-China

Special to The New York Times.

WASHINGTON, May 3—Following is a catalogue of the Eisenhower Administration's main statements of policy on Indo-China:

APRIL 16, 1953
President Eisenhower to the American Society of Newspaper Editors in Washington

The free world * * * knows that aggressions in Korea and Southeast Asia are threats to the whole free community to be met only through united action. * * *

With all who will work in good faith toward such a peace we are ready—with renewed resolve—to strive to redeem the near-lost hopes of our day. The first great step along this way must be the conclusion of an honorable armistice in Korea.

This means the immediate cessation of hostilities and the prompt initiation of political discussions leading to the holding of free elections in a united Korea.

It should mean no less importantly an end to the direct and indirect attacks upon the security of Indo-China and Malaya. For any armistice in Korea that merely released aggressive armies to attack elsewhere would be a fraud. We seek throughout, as throughout the world, a peace that is true and total.

AUG. 4, 1953
President Eisenhower at the Governors' Conference

Now let us assume that we lost Indo-China. If Indo-China goes, several things happen right away. The peninsula, the last little bit of land hanging on down there, would be scarcely defensible. The tin and tungsten that we so greatly value from that area would cease coming, but all India would be outflanked.

Burma would be in no position for defense. * * *

So when the United States votes $400,000,000 to help that war, we are not voting a giveaway program. We are voting for the cheapest way that we can prevent the occurrence of something that would be of a most terrible significance to the United States of America, our security, our power and ability to get certain things we need from the riches of the Indonesian territory and from Southeast Asia.

AUG. 7, 1953
Report of the Korean Unified Command to the United Nations

We, the United Nations members whose military forces are participating in the Korean action, support the decision of the Commander in Chief of the United Nations Command to conclude an armistice agreement. * * *

We affirm, in the interest of world peace, that if there is a renewal of the armed attack, challenging again the principles of the United Nations, we should again be united and prompt to resist. The consequences of such a breach of the armistice would be so grave that, in all probability, it would not be possible to confine hostilities within the frontiers of Korea.

Finally, we are of the opinion that the armistice must not result in jeopardizing the restoration or the safeguarding of peace in any other part of Asia.

SEPT. 2, 1953
Secretary Dulles to the American Legion convention

Communist China has been and now is training, equipping and supplying the Communist forces in Indo-China. There is the risk that, as in Korea, Red China might send its own army into Indo-China. The Chinese regime should realize that such a second aggression could not occur without grave consequences which might not be confined to Indo-China. I say this soberly in the interest of peace and in the hope of preventing another aggression miscalculation.

FEB. 9, 1954
Secretary of Defense Wilson to a news conference

Q. Do you think a military victory can be won in Indo-China or that peace will have to be negotiated there? A.—I would think that a military victory would be perhaps both possible and probable.

FEB. 10, 1954
President Eisenhower before his news conference.

Q. Mr. President * * * there seems to be some uneasiness in Congress that sending these technicians to Indo-China will lead eventually to our involvement in a hot war there. Would you comment on that? A. (Permitting direct quotation) Well, I would just say this: no one could be more bitterly opposed to ever getting the United States involved in a hot war in that region than I am. Consequently, that every move that I authorize is calculated, so far as humans can do it, to make certain that that does not happen.

Q. Mr. President, should your

remarks on Indo-China be construed as meaning that you are determined not to become involved or, perhaps, more deeply involved in the war in Indo-China, regardless of how that war may go? A. Mr. Eisenhower replied that he was not going to try to predict the drift of world events now or the course of world events over the next months.

He would say that he could not conceive of a greater tragedy for America than to get heavily involved now in an all-out war in any of those regions, particularly with large units.
* * *

FEB. 17, 1954
President Eisenhower at his news conference

Q.—Is there any way to distinguish between aid to the anti-Communist forces in Indo-China and support of colonialism? A. —The President replied that the questioner had asked the very question that was the crux of this whole thing. There was no colonialism in this battle at all.

France, he added, had announced several times, and most emphatically last July, that she was fighting to give the three Associated States their freedom, their liberty. He believed it had been agreed they would live inside the French Union, but as free and independent states.

MARCH 10, 1954
President Eisenhower at his press and radio conference

Q.—Mr. President, Senator Stennis said yesterday that we were in danger of becoming involved in World War III in Indo-China because of the Air Force technicians there. What will we do if one of those men is captured or killed? A.—I will say this: there is going to be no involvement of America in war unless it is a result of the Constitutional process that is placed upon Congress to declare it. Now, let us have that clear. And that is the answer.

MARCH 24, 1954
President Eisenhower at his news conference

Q.—Mr. President, would you care to say anything, sir, about the conference at Geneva with reference to Indo-China and Communist China? A.—The President replied that he would say only a very few things: one, he didn't believe that it was necessary to argue the importance of all this great Southeast Asian area, and the Southwest Pacific—its importance to the United States and to the free world. All that region, was of the most transcendent importance.

Now, this fighting going on in Indo-China: no matter how it started, had very manifestly become again one of the battlegrounds of the people that want to live their own lives against this encroachment of Communist aggression.

MARCH 29, 1954
Secretary Dulles to the Overseas Press Club of America in New York

Under the conditions of today, the imposition on Southeast Asia of the political system of Communist Russia and its Chinese Communist ally, by whatever means, would be a grave threat to the whole free community. The United States feels

that that possibility should not be passively accepted, but should be met by united action. This might have serious risks, but these risks are far less than would face us a few years from now if we dare not be resolute today.

APRIL 15, 1954
Admiral W. Radford, Chairman of the Joint Chiefs of Staff, to the American Society of Newspaper Editors

The free nations cannot afford to permit a further extension of the power of militant communism in Asia. In the interests of preventing aggression, full advantage should be taken of the fact that non-Communist Asia has a considerable potential for development of defensive military forces * * * it's (Indo-China's) loss would be the prelude to the loss of all Southeast Asia and a threat to a far wider area.

APRIL 16, 1954
Vice President Nixon in a background talk to the American Society of Newspaper Editors (this was not attributed to him at first but later published).

Q. If the French pulled out of Indo-China, what should the United States do? A. The Vice president replied that there was no reason why the French could not stay on and win, but on the assumption that they did withdraw—an assumption he did not accept — Indo-China would become Communist in a month.

He added: The United States as a leader of the free world could not afford further retreat in Asia. It was hoped that the United States would not have to send troops there, but if this Government could not avoid it, the Administration must face up to the situation and dispatch forces.

Therefore, the United States must go to Geneva and take a positive stand for United Action by the free world. Otherwise it would have to take on the problem alone and try to sell it to the others * * *

This country was the only nation politically strong enough at home to take a position that would save Asia. Negotiations with the Communists to divide the territory in any form would result in Communist domination of a vital new area * * *

APRIL 20, 1954
Vice President Nixon, in Cincinnati, at the twentieth Annual University of Cincinnati Day Dinner

The aim of the United States is to hold Indo-China without war involving the United States, if we can. We have learned that if you are weak and indecisive, you invite war. You don't keep Communists out of an area by telling them you won't do anything to save it.

APRIL 21, 1954
Vice President Nixon in Des Moines, Iowa

The purpose of our policy is to avoid sending our boys to Indo-China or anywhere else to fight. We believe a strong policy has the best chance to accomplish that purpose.

APRIL 26, 1954
President Eisenhower to the United States Chamber of Commerce

I think each of us senses that when we meet, as you are meeting today, we are doing so in a time of great decisions. I think it is no longer necessary to enter into a long argument or exposition to show the importance to the United States of Indo-China and of the struggle going on there.

No matter how the struggle may have started, it has long since become one of the testing places between a free form of government and dictatorship. Its outcome is going to have the greatest significance for us, and possibly for a long time into the future. * * *

And then we turn our eyes to Geneva, and we see representatives of great—and some antagonistic—powers meeting there, trying to arrive at some situation that at least we could call a "modus vivendi." We do not hope, I think, very soon to have the type of understanding that we believe we can ultimately develop among ourselves as to great issues. But we would hope that the logic of today's situation would appeal to all peoples, so that they would see the futility of depending upon war, or the threat of war as a means of settling international difficulty. * * *

APRIL 29, 1954
President Eisenhower to his news conference

Q. Mr. President, in a recent speech you referred to the desirability of a modus vivendi in Indo-China. Could you give us anything further on your thoughts, what is in your mind, by a modus vivendi? A. The President replied that we were steering a course between two extremes, one of which, he would say, would be unattainable, and the other would be unacceptable. It wouldn't be acceptable, he thought, to see the whole anti-communistic defense of that area crumble and disappear.

On the other hand, we certainly could not hope at the present state of our relations in the world for a completely satisfactory answer with the Communists. The most you can work out is a practical way of getting along.

Q. Mr. President, I would like to go back, sir, to what you said about modus vivendi. It is a question of interpretation. I may not have caught all you said, but I caught this much; that you want to get along on a practical basis, as we are not getting along in Europe. * * *

The President replied that he didn't mean to endorse, even by indirection, any specific means of getting along. He pointed out that a completely trustworthy peace, one in which we could have confidence as between ourselves and the Communist world today, seems to be something over the horizon. We work toward it; we have not achieved it, and we would be foolish to think we could do this quickly.

On the other hand, he added, we also understand what the loss of this region would mean to us. There is fighting going on, and, of course, everybody would like to see fighting stopped, but, he was merely talking about some solution that could be—that would be acceptable to us, and would stop the bloodletting * * *

May 4, 1954

DIENBIENPHU IS LOST AFTER 55 DAYS; NO WORD OF DE CASTRIES AND HIS MEN

ASSAULT SUCCEEDS

Fort Falls After 20-Hour Fight — Last Strong Point Is Silent

Special to The New York Times.

PARIS, May 7 — The fall of Dienbienphu was announced today by Premier Joseph Laniel.

The news of the worst military defeat that the French have suffered since the Indo-China war began in December, 1946, came suddenly.

It was received with confused emotion. The heroic defense of Dienbienphu, besieged for fifty-five days, had been followed in screaming headlines since March 13, when the Vietminh launched its first attack — as if for the first time in more than seven years the public had fully realized that the country was fighting an enormously bloody and costly war.

M. Laniel told the Assembly that the heroic stronghold had been taken after twenty hours of fighting and continuous alertness for the last two months. He could not issue any information on the fate of the commander, Brig. Gen. Christian de Castries, or of the defenders or the wounded who have wasted underground for several weeks.

Final Concentration

All that he knew, the Premier said, was that the southern resistance point called Isabelle was still defended under the command of Col. André Lalande. French artillery with some tanks were concentrated at that center.

[Contact with the Isabelle outpost had been lost, according to an Associated Press dispatch from Saigon.]

"The Vietminh now are only a few meters away," were the last words heard from General de

The New York Times   May 8, 1954
The Communist-led rebels enveloped Dienbienphu (cross on map of general area) capturing strong points in the southwest (1 on detailed map), the northeast (2) and the east (3). To the south the bastion called Isabelle (4) had not been heard from.

Castries over the radio-telephone, the French Cabinet was told. The last dispatch received from the battle was that the central strong point had been submerged.

For the defenders of Dienbienphu there was French pride in their heroism and sadness for their fate. There was also some grim anger against those who had engulfed them in defeat and, if not anger, at least unkindly feelings for those responsible for French political and military policy.

Before last March the name of Dienbienphu, now solidly entrenched in French military annals, was unknown here, but not in Indo-China, where it had some importance.

The Vietminh had taken Dienbienphu, a peaceful community of 9,000 persons, who grew rice and poppy for opium, in February, 1953, and used it to help launch operations against Laos in the following April.

French Seizure Nov. 21

Last November when a Vietminh column was spotted heading northwest in the Thai country to the French base of Laichau, the French decided to evacuate Laichau and seize Dienbienphu, using parachutists from the Tonkin area.

A successful operation was launched Nov. 21 and after the Laichau garrison moved in the French began daily efforts to strengthen it by building underground fortifications, improving the airfield and setting up barbed wire.

The establishment of the Dienbienphu base had strategic and political reasons. Close to the Laotian border, it helped fend off Vietminh attacks southward into Laos and against the capital of Luang Prabang by threatening the Vietminh rear and blocking supply lines.

The fact that the Vietminh withdrew from Laos and did not attack Luang Prabang is attributed to French control of Dienbienphu. The French also wished to remain in the Thai tribal country to encourage and help the Thai guerrillas hostile to the Vietminh.

Finally, Dienbienphu, because of its geographical position, was expected to require a large Vietminh force to attack it, thus relieving pressure on French defenses in the much more vital Tonkin delta area.

This is precisely what happened. The French garrison numbered 10,000 to 12,000 men, about 5,000 of whom were Vietnamese. The French Foreign Legion, which included a strong proportion of Germans, was also an important element.

There were also colonial troops, consisting of Tunisians, Algerians and Moroccans and a battalion of Thais, totaling perhaps 800 men. The great majority of officers were French. Against this force the Vietminh concentrated four divisions or about 40,000 men. On March 13, what the French Cabinet a few days ago compared to the World War I battle of Verdun was on with a massive Vietminh attack. It was thrown back with losses to the enemy estimated at from 5,000 to 8,000 men out of action. The second attack was launched March 30 and little by little, despite heavy Vietminh casualties, the French began to be squeezed into a smaller and smaller area of resistance.

'Asphyxiation' Tactics Used

From then until last night the Vietminh bit off progressively more and more applying what was called here asphyxiation tactics. Supply air drops became more and more difficult as the area of the airfield in French hands became smaller and smaller.

Early this morning only a single 105-mm howitzer out of twelve was in condition for firing and in the central redoubt only one 55-mm gun was working. Ammunition was very low.

Comparison with Verdun was apt in some respects. In neither case was a vital military position at stake, but in both national honor was intensely involved. But every Frenchman consolingly knows a victory was won at Verdun despite the terrible loss of lives. At Dienbienphu there was nothing left at the end but the defender's courage.

A late dispatch said that General de Castries told Hanoi headquarters before the telephone went silent that he had instructed all able-bodied men to try to get to the southern resistance center of Isabelle, which was then holding out. As far as he was concerned, he was saying, "We are not giving up."

May 8, 1954

PREMIER IN SAIGON TO TAKE HIS POST

Special to The New York Times.

SAIGON, Vietnam, June 25 — Newly appointed Premier Ngo Dinh Diem arrived today and received an enthusiastic welcome from his Roman Catholic supporters. However, the great mass of the Saigon population stayed home.

The demonstration to mark the new Premier's arrival from Paris to take up his duties had been awaited with great interest as a gauge of Ngo Dinh Diem's popularity and hold over the country.

The Premier, who succeeds Prince Buu Loc, called for national unity in a ceremony at Gialong Palace. He said that he was "destined to open the way to national salvation and to bring about a revolution in all fields." He asserted that he had also returned to denounce Communist maneuvers at Geneva that sought to divide Vietnam.

He added that he would seek to eliminate the last vestiges of foreign domination. The Premier did not mention France or the French Army. Observers here thought that he would seek to play alone the role of savior of Vietnam.

However, after the ceremony,

the Premier's first act was to confer with Gen. Raoul Salan, French deputy commander. The French say that, whatever his nationalist aspirations, Ngo Dinh Diem will have to count on the French expeditionary corps to continue a nationalist war against the Communists.

Relationship to Bao Dai

Fifty-three-year-old Ngo Dinh Diem, who had been away from Vietnam for several years, is reputed to be strong minded. This has raised a question in political circles here about the Vietnamese Cabinet's future relationship with the Chief of State.

As Chief of State with power to appoint and remove Cabinet leaders, Bao Dai has been the supreme indigenous political figure on the anti-Communist side in Vietnam. Those familiar with Ngo Dinh Diem's background believe he will insist on a clearcut political understanding and a strong hand for the Premier.

Ngo Dinh Diem, who comes from an influential Catholic family in Annam, is regarded here as a man of great personal integrity who has consistently opposed foreign domination in Vietnam and also taken a fundamental stand against the Communist-led Vietminh movement.

In the past, Ngo Dinh Diem has espoused the principles of unity and independence, social reform and anti-communism. After a term in 1932-33 as Minister of the Interior in the royal cabinet at Hue, he went to Japan because of opposition to French policy.

Nevertheless, he declined a post in the Japanese-sponsored collaborationist Government here in 1945 and also refused to participate in the post-war Vietminh Government established by Ho Chi Minh.

Ngo Dinh Diem left Vietnam in 1950 and visited the United States.

June 26, 1954

INDOCHINA ARMISTICE IS SIGNED; VIETNAM SPLIT AT 17TH PARALLEL

LONG WAR ENDING

2 Accords Completed —One on Cambodia Due Later Today

By THOMAS J. HAMILTON
Special to The New York Times.

GENEVA, Wednesday, July 21 —Armistice agreements bringing the fighting in Vietnam and Laos to a halt were signed this morning by representatives of the French and Communist Vietminh forces.

A French spokesman said the armistice would take effect forty-eight hours later.

The signing ceremony, witnessed by representatives of the nine delegations participating in the Far Eastern conference here, began at 3:42 A. M. (9:42 P. M. Tuesday, Eastern daylight time). It brought to a close the eight-year struggle for Indochina.

The armistice in Cambodia will not be signed until later this morning. The Far Eastern conference will hold its final session this afternoon to complete work on the political settlement. Under it Laos and Cambodia will be neutralized and elections to create a unified government in Vietnam will be held within two years from the date of the armistice.

Pierre Mendès-France, French Premier, who had set July 20 as his deadline to obtain an armistice or resign, had missed it by a few hours. He canceled a radio speech to the French people and went to bed before the two agreements were signed at the Palais des Nations, former headquarters of the League of Nations, where conference sessions have been held since the Indochina negotiations began last May.

Rebels Get Northern Part

Under the Vietnamese agreement, Vietnam is to be divided into two parts, about equal in area and population, between the Communist-led Vietminh rebels who will hold northern Vietnam, north of a line along the Seventeenth Parallel, and the French-sponsored Government of Bao Dai.

The partition line thus is far enough north to preserve Hue, the ancient capital of Annam; Tourane, an important port and naval and air base, and the only major highway leading to Laos from the coast.

The French will not give up Hanoi and Haiphong, in the Red River delta area, in the north, for approximately a year, which will give them time to evacuate personnel of the French expeditionary force in the territory remaining to them in the delta, plus civilians fearing persecution by the Communists.

Under the armistice agreements, the Communists recognize the Governments of Laos and Cambodia. However, regrouping areas for Communist troops were authorized in Laos. The forces of the Communist "resistance government" in Laos will be concentrated in two provinces near the frontier with Vietminh territory. [Some sources identified the two provinces as Samneua and Phongsaly.]

The Cambodian delegation held

Associated Press Radiophoto

AGREE ON TRUCE: Pierre Mendès-France, French Premier, as he appeared yesterday with Pham Van Dong, Vietminh Foreign Minister, left, at French headquarters in Geneva. Behind them are Guy de la Tournelle, wearing eyeglasses, and Georges Boris, aides to French leader.

out against the provision, and prolonged sessions of the "drafting committee" of the Vietminh and Cambodian representatives were necessary before an agreement could be reached early this morning. By that time it was too late to put the armistice in final form so that it could be signed along with the Vietnamese and Laotian agreements.

These were signed by Brig. Gen. Henri Delteil, representative of Gen. Paul Ely, French Commander in Chief in Indochina, and by Col. Ta Quang Buu, the Vietminh's Vice Minister of Defense.

Gen. Walter Bedell Smith, Under Secretary of State, who returned recently to take over the chairmanship of the United States delegation, took no part in the whirlwind diplomatic activity yesterday and this morning that resulted in agreement. A spokesman had said that the United States, not being a belligerent, was not primarily concerned. However, the delegation was represented by an observer at the ceremony.

Smith Issues Statement

General Smith issued the following statement:

"The United States delegation is very pleased with the important progress that has been made tonight toward ending the bloodshed in Indochina. As soon as we have had an opportunity to examine the final texts of the agreements reached by the bel-

ligerents, the United States delegation will express its views with regard to them."

"Meanwhile, we share the fervent hopes of millions throughout the world that an important step has been taken toward a lasting peace in Southeast Asia, which will establish the right of the peoples of that area to determine their own future."

Supervision of the three armistice agreements is entrusted to supervisory commissions composed of India, Canada and Poland. Each commission will operate by majority rule, except in important issues that "might lead to a resumption of hostilities."

Unanimous decisions will be required for these, meaning that Communist Poland will have a veto. However, the agreements provide that such cases shall be reported to the nine conference participants — France, Britain, the United States, the Soviet Union, Communist China, Vietnam, Laos, Cambodia and the Vietminh—which will take it up at a meeting of Ambassadors.

The Hanoi-Haiphong area in the north, as well as four or five regroupment areas south of the partition line for the Vietminh forces, are to be evacuated over a period of 300 days. The agreement provides that prisoners of war and civil internees captured in any circumstances will be freed within thirty days from the agreement's entry into force.

While the Laotian and Cambodian Governments will remain

in control, they are to be neutralized, with their armed forces limited to those necessary for self-defense. These provisions will prevent the United States from supplying military instructors or equipment, and the two nations' only real protection will be the realization by the Communists that an armed attack may precipitate intervention by the United States.

Georges Bidault, Foreign Minister in the Government of former Premier Joseph Laniel, which fell because of its stand in the Geneva talks, had opposed any political settlement at this time. M. Mendès-France had sought to avoid fixing a date for Vietnamese elections, fearing that if they were held soon the Vietminh would gain control of the entire country.

The Communists, who had insisted originally that elections be held within six months, finally agreed that they be within two years. They will be supervised by India, Canada and Poland.

Reds to Stay in Laos

Moreover, the Communists will not evacuate all of Laos, although it had been the Western contention that the Communist forces in both Laos and Cambodia were Vietnamese rebel invaders and that both nations should be preserved intact.

The three key figures in the final stage of the conference—Premier Mendès-France, Anthony Eden, British Foreign Secretary, and Vyacheslav M. Molotov, So-

viet Foreign Minister, met last night to discuss the situation. Shortly before midnight they called in Tep Phan, Cambodian Foreign Minister, and Pham Van Dong, Deputy Premier and acting Foreign Minister of the Vietminh, in hopes of reaching an agreement on Cambodia's objections to the "pockets" in its territory for Communist troops.

General Smith has been confined by an attack of lumbago, which was better yesterday. He stayed in his hotel while Mr. Eden, M. Mendès-France and Mr. Molotov—and to a lesser extent Chou En-lai, Premier of Communist China, and Pham Van Dong—engaged in whirlwind diplomatic activity.

Throughout the day's busy exchanges, General Smith was studying the tentative texts of the various agreements, which were understood to be nine in all. He had told the conference on his return that if it reached agreements that the United States could "respect," the United States, in accordance with the United Nations Charter, would issue a unilateral statement that it would not seek to overturn them by force. A United States spokesman's only further comment was that if his Government found it could not "respect" the agreements, it might dissociate itself from them.

July 21, 1954

Nearly 165,000 Casualties

Special to The New York Times.

HANOI, July 22.— Casualties suffered by the French-Vietnamese forces in Indochina from 1945 to May 31, 1954, included 34,242 killed. The data show 10,725 others died, 48,370 were missing and 71,560 wounded. The total is 164,897. The figures were provided on request here today by the French Military Information Service. Vietminh losses in the

period are estimated at 120,000 to 150,000, but no details are available on these insurgent casualties.

The French Union casualties, including officers were: Killed, 17,909; died, 5,633; missing, 20,-918; wounded, 43,308.

All Vietnamese casualties, including those of men serving in the French Union Expeditionary Corps: Killed, 16,333; died, 5,092; missing, 27,452; wounded, 36,252.

Casualties among French Union officers included 1,202 killed, 286 died, 779 missing and 3,101 wounded.

Vietnamese officer casualties, including those of officers serving in the French Union Expeditionary Corps were listed as 175 killed, 44 died, 141 missing and 359 wounded.

July 23, 1954

POST-WAR THAILAND

Gun Kills Siam's Young King; Palace Death Held Accident

Ananda Mahidol, 20, Ruled Ancient Country Since 1935—Was Set to Fly to U. S. —Brother, 18, Named Successor

By The Associated Press.

BANGKOK, Siam, Monday, June 10—Ananda Mahidol, 20-year-old King of Siam, was found dead of a bullet wound yesterday in the royal palace, and twelve hours later the Siamese Legislature

named his brother, Prince Phumiphon Aduldet, 18, as the new king.

The Siamese police director general told an emergency session of the Legislature last night that the king's death was accidental and

that the bullet went through the center of his forehead.

Ananda, whose death occurred almost on the eve of a projected trip to the United States, had been indisposed for the last two days. He arose at 6 A. M. yesterday and took some medicine. Nothing was known of his actions from then until his body was found by a servant in the bedroom of the Barompinan Palace about 9 A. M.

The historic night session of the Legislature unanimously selected Phumiphon Aduldet as the new king, rising together to signalize his election with a "Cha Yo, Cha Yo, Cha Yo"—the Siamese hurrah.

Phumiphon Aduldet was born in Boston while his father, the late

Prince Mahidol of Songkhla, was studying at Harvard University. He was a constant companion of his elder brother and attended school with him in Switzerland.

The Legislature also appointed a three-man Council of Regency to guide the new king in matters of state. Pride Panymyong, who was reappointed Premier three days ago, told the Legislature he would recommend a Premier to the regency, but legislative sources said there was little doubt that Mr. Panymyong would receive the post.

The entire nation was stunned by the news of Ananda Mahidol's death. The young king had gained great popularity since his return from Switzerland last Dec. 5.

[In Berne, Switzerland, Paul Rey, director of the school where the King studied, said the monarch's retinue had been worried before Ananda's departure from Switzerland over the possibility of assassination. Asked about reports that the King was depressed because he was unable to marry a fellow student, M. Rey said Ananda had "gone with" one or two girls but had not had a serious romance.]

Ananda, a fancier of firearms, always kept a weapon near him and often practiced firing in the palace grounds. Several weeks ago a thief stole his favorite Luger automatic and the King was disturbed.

The King's young mother, Queen Phraratanani Sri Sangwan, was prostrate with grief.

Around the palace great crowds gathered in silent sorrow as the news spread.

Most of Bangkok was unaware of the death of the quiet, studious ruler until the Government broadcast the news at 7 P. M. Immediately a wail went up from a crowd gathered in the square before the publicity building, near the royal palace.

Ananda, who ascended the throne eleven years ago, had planned to fly this week to the United States and remain there about a week before flying to Switzerland, where he planned to resume his studies. His mother and a royal suite of twenty had been expected to accompany him.

Diffident, bespectacled and boyish, Ananda was often described as a reluctant monarch who found his greatest pleasure in playing his saxophone and driving his American jeep about the palace grounds.

A month ago King Ananda signed a new Constitution. It provided for a Senate and a House of Representatives, both elected by the people. On June 1 he opened the first wholly elected Siamese Parliament.

At that time, in accordance with a Constitutional requirement, Premier Panymyong and members of the Cabinet resigned, continuing to serve, however, while the Parliament considered the selection of a new Premier.

Ananda was proclaimed King March 2, 1935, under a regency, on the abdication of his uncle, King Prajadhipok, but he spent little time in his own land. Born in Germany on Sept. 20, 1925, he was taken to Siam at the age of 2. He studied there and went to Switzerland in 1933. He was educated in Lausanne, and most of his last twelve years were spent in Switzerland, except for a brief visit home in 1938. Prajadhipok died in 1941.

During Ananda's minority a Council of Regency ruled Siam. It was made up of Prince Aditya, a nephew of Prajadhipok; Chao Phya Bijayendra Yodhin, a former army general, and Chao Phya Yomaraj, former Minister of the Interior, who died in 1938.

The ancient absolute monarchy of Siam, which lasted from 1350 to 1932, was overthrown in a bloodless revolution three years before Ananda ascended the throne, but the Siamese revered him.

Ananda's recently expressed desire to return to Switzerland was opposed by the elder members of the royal family and powerful politicians. They wished to bring in tutors for him, arguing that his presence in the country heightened morale.

Last Friday, however, the Government announced that the King and his royal party would leave the following Thursday in an Air Transport Command C-54 plane. United States diplomatic attachés in Bangkok were to have accompanied him.

Ananda's personal life in Siam was passed largely within the palace walls. None of the informal social expeditions that popularized monarchs in the Western world were permitted to him. His mother was said to have exerted a strong influence on the young ruler of 18,000,000 subjects.

Since his return to Siam from Switzerland last December the King obediently followed the dictates of pomp and ceremony, and it seemed to have heightened his popularity. The King attended many functions and always conducted himself strictly as a monarch.

Siam's bloodless revolution on June 24, 1932, was led by army officers and Government officials. Three days later Prajadhipok signed a temporary Constitution, which was replaced the following December by a permanent one.

Under that system the King appointed a State Council of Ministers composed of a President and fourteen to twenty-four other Ministers. It provided for a one-house assembly of people's representatives.

The change from the absolute to constitutional monarchy was attributed generally to the infiltration of Western ideas because of the custom of sending Princes and sons of prominent families to Europe and the United States for their education.

Modern trends were evident in Bangkok even before the war. Hollywood movies, airliners linking the country with Europe, heavy motor-car traffic, well-constructed buildings and flourishing commercial life in the cities were signs of the times for the Siamese.

The King died at a time that may be critical in his country's history. The country has applied for membership in the United Nations, and recently charged the French had invaded Siam from Indo-China in areas ceded by the Vichy Government to Siam during the war. The Siamese hoped to present this case to the United Nations Security Council.

Siam was invaded by the Japanese on Dec. 7, 1941, while the King was in Switzerland. A puppet Government declared war on Britain and the United States in January, 1942, but the Americans considered the declaration to have been made under duress and did not recognize a state of war with Siam.

Last January Britain and the United States announced formal recognition of the new Siamese Government.

The ancient name of Siam was restored officially in September, 1945. From 1939 until 1945 the name of Thailand had been used.

June 10, 1946

SIAM'S KING SLAIN, INVESTIGATORS SAY

American Physician and 13 of 20-Man Board Find Ananda Probably Assassinated

BANGKOK, Siam, July 1 (U.P.)—An American physician and thirteen other members of a twenty-man medical investigation board said in a formal report tonight that King Ananda of Siam probably was assassinated. The American, Dr. Cort, said: "It looks like murder."

Although the first Government report attributed the 20-year-old monarch's death to an accident, the medical board asserted this was the least likely of three possibilities. If he was not assassinated, the King was a suicide, the board reported.

The suicide theory was expounded earlier today by Nai Chit Singhaseni, chief attendant of Ananda, who told the inquiry commission that he was the first to reach the King's bed after the fatal shot was heard on June 9.

The board investigated the mysterious circumstances under which the King died and made a thorough post-mortem examination, the report said. The investigators disagreed over the cause of death, but the majority held it probably was caused by an assassin's bullet.

All twenty members of the board, including an American, two Britons and one British Indian physician, agreed that the fatal bullet entered the front of Ananda's head from a gun held about seven and one-half inches from his forehead. They also agreed that no trace of poison was found.

A record crowd pushed into the inquiry room to hear the witnesses. Siamese, stirred by the King's death and suspicious of the official version that he was killed accidentally, had clamored for the hearing.

July 2, 1946

Siamese Cabinet Ready to Return 4 Disputed Areas to Indo-China

BANGKOK, Siam, Oct. 14 (AP)—A five-year border dispute between France and Siam appeared settled today with the announcement that the Siamese Cabinet had agreed to return four disputed frontier areas to French Indo-China.

Parliament recessed tonight without endorsing the Cabinet's agreement and tempers flared in Bangkok over the proposed surrender of territory.

In four hours of hot debate, the Opposition claimed that the Government was trying to pass off responsibility, to which the Government replied that the territorial agreement needed parliamentary ratification.

Representatives of the border provinces including Government party members, opposed acceptance of the proposal.

At tomorrow morning's debate the Government was expected to get a vote of endorsement but there remained some possibility of a Government defeat.

Premier Thamrong Nawasuwat announced the Cabinet's action and said that it was backed by both major political parties. A special emergency meeting of Parliament was called this afternoon to ratify the action.

Scene of Fighting

The disputed territory, obtained by Siam in 1941 under a Japanese-negotiated treaty with Vichy France, has been the scene of

Oct. 15, 1946

Siam's Cabinet has agreed to hand back to French Indo-China the territory around Luang Prabang (1) and around Battambang, Siemreap and Sisophon (2). These areas were transferred to Siam by the Vichy regime.

fighting between Siamese and French colonial troops.

The four areas in question total approximately 20,000 square miles, some of it jungle territory bordering the Mekong River. The areas are Battambang, Siemreap and Sisophon, in Cambodia, and Luang Prabang in Laos. [Siemreap is the district in which the famous ruins of Angkor are situated.]

The post-war French Government has refused to recognize the Japanese-sponsored treaty, and the French colonial administration has maintained that "a technical state of war" exists between Siam and Indo-China.

Siam had contended that the areas were historically Siamese, and were ceded to French empire builders under duress in 1907. The little kingdom appealed to the United Nations Security Council last July to mediate the dispute, and accused the French of wanton aggression. France proposed that the dispute be placed before the International Court of Justice at the Hague.

October 15, 1946

JAPAN'S EX-PUPPET AT HELM OF SIAM AFTER ARMED COUP

Songgram Ousts Government in Bloodless Move but Faces Possible Counter-Attack

PREMIER AND AIDES ESCAPE

By The United Press.

BANGKOK, Siam, Nov. 9—A group of Siamese military officers led by Field Marshal Luang Pibul Songgram, wartime puppet dictator under the Japanese, seized control of Bangkok early today and announced that the Government of

Premier Luang Dhamrong Nawasawat had been overthrown.

The rebels struck at 2 A. M. and met no serious opposition. The capital remained calm. A spokesman said the revolt was directed at widespread Government corruption and that a new constitution would be drawn up.

An announcement by the rebel group said that Government leaders had fled the capital and that Marshal Songgram had been named supreme commander of armed forces following the successful coup d'état.

The two members of the Regency Council, Prince Dibabha Aditya and Gen. Chao Phya Bijayendra Yodhin, are under the rebels' control, the announcement said. Siam's 19-year-old King, Phumibol Aduldet, who succeeded his brother, Ananda Mahidol, after the latter was found shot dead in his palace on June 9, 1946, is a student in Switzerland.

Tanks lumbered through Bangkok's streets on patrol as the coup

became known. Armored cars and anti-aircraft guns were set up about the Ministry of Defense Building, where leaders of the rebel group set up headquarters.

There were no signs of fighting, but events indicated that escaped Government leaders were massing loyal troops in the countryside and might attempt to retake the capital.

The rebel group announced in a 9:30 A. M. communiqué that Gen. Abul Dejarat, Commander in Chief of the Army in King Phumibol's Government, was among the leaders who fled. The communiqué said General Dejarat was mobilizing troops loyal to him at "certain stations" to suppress the coup.

A later communiqué, however, said that an agreement had been reached with General Dejarat under which bloodshed would be avoided.

November 10, 1947

SIAM'S 'STRONG MAN' IS PICKED AS PREMIER

BANGKOK, Siam, April 8 (AP)—Field Marshal Pibul Songgram, Siam's "strong man," was expected today to emerge as the head of a new Siamese Government.

The former dictator and ex-Premier, who led Siam into wartime alliance with Japan, was asked by the Supreme State Council to form a new Government following the resignation yesterday of Premier Khuang Aphaiwong, who acted under military pressure.

The Khuang Cabinet agreed unanimously to boycot the Pibul

Songgram government, although several members, including Khuang himself, were asked to take portfolios.

Pibul Songgram directed the military and monarchial coup last November that ousted Premier Thamrong Nawasawat and put to flight from the country the wartime resistance leader against the Japanese, Pridi Phanomyong.

After the bloodless November coup, the monarchists gained the upper hand and Aphaiwong's Democratic party won a majority in Parliament over Pibul Songgram's Tharmatipat party in the January elections.

April 9, 1948

SIAM IS THAILAND AGAIN

Premier Issues Decree Changing Name of That Country

BANGKOK, Thailand, May 11 (UP)—Premier Phibun Songgram issued a proclamation today changing the country's name from Siam to Thailand.

The name was changed to Thailand before World War II, but recognition of this name by world powers was withdrawn after the country had joined Japan in declaring war on Great Britain and the United States.

Premier Songgram was the wartime puppet dictator under the Japanese. He seized control of the postwar government in November, 1947.

A royal proclamation today declared that the "state of emergency" in this politically turbulent country ended.

In recent weeks the government has announced suppression of a plot against it and the arrest of a number of Premier Songgram's political opponents.

May 12, 1949

Thais Report Arms Aid Of $10,000,000 by U. S.

By The Associated Press.

BANGKOK, Thailand, April 11—Thailand is to receive $10,-000,000 worth of United States military aid to resist communism, Premier Pibul Songgram announced today.

So far as was known here, this is the first grant under a new United States policy of arming Asian nations willing to stand up against the Communists. Thailand has lined up with the West in the "cold war."

The Premier made his announcement at a meeting of the Cabinet. The Cabinet at once issued an expression of thanks, saying that the allocation showed that the United States was "a true friend at all times."

[There was no immediate comment from the State Department in Washington on the report of the grant.]

The Premier said the military aid would include arms and equipment, such as bulldozers.

The arms and supplies will come from the $75,000,000 China area fund set up by Congress.

April 12, 1950

RULER OF THAILAND CROWNED IN RITUAL

Coronation of Phumiphon as King Rama IX Marked by Oriental Splendor

BANGKOK, Thailand, May 5 (AP)—A slight, bespectacled young man who was born in Boston and educated in Switzerland crowned himself King of Thailand today in ceremonies of traditional oriental splendor.

The measured boom of a 101-gun salute, the fanfare of trumpets and the tinkling of stringed instruments made known to the waiting populace that Phumiphon Aduldet had become King Rama IX, continuing in unbroken succession the Chakri dynasty that began in 1782.

The date, chosen with care in advance by the royal astrologers, was one week before the King's twenty-third birthday.

The glittering ritual began with a bath, the King laying himself in waters brought especially from every quarter of the kingdom.

Then, as he changed into resplendent coronation dress, the astrologers worshipped his guiding stars before an altar of twenty-two flickering candles, one for each of his years.

Holding a silver joss-stick and a golden candle, Phumiphon ascended an eight-pointed throne, facing the east. The chief astrologer proclaimed the moment auspicious, and the Brahman high priest handed the King a nine-tiered crown.

Ninth in his line, Phumiphon lifted the crown to his head and assumed his formal name of Rama. He read a royal edict elevating his bride of one week, the Princess Sirikit Bitiyakorn, to the status of Queen.

Later the King led a procession to the Temple of the Emerald Buddha, where he paid homage and, in the presence of the old Prince Regent Rangsit, declared himself defender of the faith.

The coronation was the climax of a triple occasion of state for which the King came home from Switzerland March 24. On March 29 he cremated the body of his brother, King Ananda Mahidol, who was mysteriously shot to death in 1946. On April 28 he was married to the 17-year-old Sirikit; and today he donned his crown.

The King and Queen intend to return to Europe shortly to complete his schooling. They will come back to live in Thailand in about two years.

May 6, 1950

THAILAND TO SHIFT VIETNAM REFUGEES

Fearful of Fifth Column Threat, Government Plans to Resettle 50,000 Who Fled Indo-China

By TILLMAN DURDIN
Special to The New York Times.

BANGKOK, Thailand, Nov. 28—Fifty thousand Vietnamese refugees have become a major problem for Thailand as Communist-led Vietminh and allied groups step up their drives for power in Indo-China.

The refugees fled from Indo-China areas to this country during the past few years of warfare in their homeland. They now represent a difficult fifth-column threat for Thailand at a time when the kingdom's northeastern frontiers are becoming increasingly menaced by the upsurge of Communist activity in Indo-China.

Thailand welcomed the Vietnamese refugees when they moved into this country, mostly in 1946. The majority came from Laos, where they feared reprisals after the "Free Laos" Government' closely linked with Ho Chi Minh's Viet-minh, was eliminated by the new Franco-Laotian agreement.

Vietnamese now are scattered in many parts of Thailand. Many were originally pro-Vietminh and have remained so. A recent Ministry of Interior statement complained that many Vietnamese solicit funds "for political undertakings against French Indo-China."

It also was declared that some of the refugees had accumulated arms while most had failed to obtain identity papers and to repay loans given them to help them set up in businesses.

Other informed sources say some Vietnamese secretly operate small arms factories. The Vietnamese in Thailand are believed to be one of the sources of arms for the Vietminh.

Officials point out that only a minority of the refugees have been seriously subversive. Most have become good settlers who contribute appreciably to the Thailand economy and work harder than their more easy-going Thai neighbors.

It has been decided, however, that in order to enforce better control of the refugees they must all be concentrated in the five provinces adjoining the Cambodian and Laotian frontiers in which they first settled. The decision of the Thai Government has drawn strong objections not only from Vietnamese but also from French, Cambodian and Laotian authorities.

The latter are alarmed at the prospect of 50,000 Vietnamese settled next to the Laotian and Cambodian borders where they can be used by Vietminh and pro-Vietminh groups within Indo-China as contributors of supplies and recruits for military service.

Although the Ministry has announced its intention of going ahead with the concentration plan, the program already has been delayed several times. The heavy expense and difficulty of rounding up the refugees may yet cause revision of the plan.

November 29, 1950

Premier Pibul Ousted in Thailand, Only to Head Successor Regime

Premier Pibul Songgram
Associated Press

Old Cabinet Is Overthrown as Failing to Suppress Reds and Fight Inflation

BANGKOK, Thailand, Friday,
Nov. 30 (UP)—A group of generals
and admirals overthrew Premier
Pibul Songgram yesterday, only to
restore him to power a few hours
later at the head of a new anti-
Communist regime.

Leaders of the Thai army, navy,
air and police forces announced
yesterday that Premier Pibul — a
field marshal and postwar "strong
man" of Thailand—had been deposed because he had "failed to
suppress communism and corruption."

An official broadcast early today
said that the "provisional national
executive council" formed to replace Premier Pibul had appointed
a reshuffled cabinet with the field
marshal at its head.

Cabinet Members Listed

Ministers in the new cabinet are:
Premier and Defense—Pibul Song-
gram.
Vice Premier and Communications
—Lieut. Gen. Sawat Sawatdikiart.
Interior—Maj. Gen. Banyat Pheha-
satin.
Foreign Affairs—Barakarn Bancha.
Finance—Vichi Tradhakarn.
Agriculture—Maj. Gen. Tao Dari-
bhanyudhakit.
Commerce—Air Vice Marshal Muni
Mahasantana.
Education—Nakorn Promyothi.
Justice—Sunkit Nimnachint.
Without Portfolio, — Payun Cama-
montri, Sima Winwirit, Luen
Pongsophon.

The Interim Executive Council
previously had appointed Police
Lieut. Gen. Phao Sriyanon "national peace preservation officer." It
was not clear whether he still held
this post, or what his precise
duties were. The police organization is the nation's largest armed
force.

It was the second time in less
than six months that military
rebels had risen against the Premier, who seized power in Novem-

ber, 1947. Late in June, the Premier was kidnapped by navy men.
The Army, the Air Force and the
police remained loyal, however,
and the revolt was crushed after
fighting in which at least sixty-
eight persons were killed and 1,100
wounded.

Regime Held Ineffective

In announcing the overthrow of
the Pibul regime yesterday, the
Executive Council said the Premier had been ousted and Parliament dissolved because the Pibul
Government had failed to deal effectively with the problems of inflation, official corruption and
communism.

"With these facts in mind, action was taken by members of the
armed forces, the police force, promoters of the 1932 coup and others
who realized that the present conditions could not be tolerated," the
announcement said.

The Council then added that it
would govern under the 1932 Constitution, drafted by Premier Pridi
Banomyong—Premier Pibul's predecessor—but never put in force,
uphold Thailand's constitutional
monarchy, fight communism, respect the rights of foreigners and
uphold the United Nations Charter.

November 30, 1951

FROM EAST INDIES TO INDONESIA

DUTCH RUSH PLANS TO REVIVE EMPIRE

Many Problems Cause Anxiety, but Foreign Aid Is Expected to Speed Reconstruction

By DAVID ANDERSON
By Wireless to The New York Times.

THE HAGUE, Aug. 30 — Rush
plans for the return of their rich
colonial empire in the Netherlands
Indies are causing anxiety here, according to Pieter A. Kerstens, Commissioner to the Home Government,
who will leave soon for the Far
East. The sudden collapse of Japan

caught the Dutch unaware and
they are busy gathering their scattered resources and wits.

In many respects it could have
been much worse. Mr. Kerstens, a
member of the London Government
during the war, said he was convinced that little physical destruction had been done by the enemy.
Exports of sugar, tea, oil and rubber can be expected within a few
months, though an accurate check
on the spot will have to be made
before any estimate can be given
of dates for the resumption of former production.

Recovery of the Indies will be
far quicker and easier to bring
about than that of the Netherlands, Mr. Kerstens believes. Here
in Europe extensive sabotage of
transport and industrial plants by
the Germans has resulted in a mass
of intricate problems, whereas the
wealth in the Far East is largely
agricultural and presumably it re-

mains in a workable state.

Foreign capital, a major part of
it American, must be realized for
redevelopment of the Indies. Financing of all eastern undertakings
will be under close Government
supervision, as too will expenditures to be made by various companies concerned. Netherland Government control of private enterprise in the Indies will consist in
the main of priority control for the
allocation of funds and it is a certainty because authorities here feel
the credit worthiness of the Netherlands is too important to be left
to chance.

The Government is prepared to
contribute to the cost of rehabilitating the Indies, as well as guaranteeing loans floated abroad. One
of the heaviest charges against
this country will be an outlay needed to replace 1,500,000 tons of shipping that once served the Indies.
Direct participation of foreign

capital in the Netherland possessions abroad is officially welcomed.
However, many quarters in The
Hague and Amsterdam view with
dismay the joint British and Australian "occupation of the empire."
It is felt this may have a bearing
on outside interest in the colonies.

What the Dutch want, of course,
is to employ their own military
force of 20,000 men, which has
been denied them, since Australian
and British troops are on the spot.
Joint administration, Mr. Kerstens
admitted, "won't be easy. Indeed,
the whole thing is difficult enough
in any event."

The fear that Japanese domination of Java, Sumatra and Borneo
may have bred a wish for "Asia
for Asiatics" does not appear to be
founded in fact, he continued. A
visit to liberated areas of the
Indies some months ago convinced

his that the natives are as friendly as ever toward Dutch rule and quite content to accept it once more.

The Japanese have lost more face than has the white man in the Far East, he argued, adding that Gen. Douglas MacArthur's handling of the surrender negotiations thus far has been masterly, particularly in the instance that Emperor Hirohito had to deliver his unprecedented radio appeal.

Nevertheless, Netherland policy in the Indies Empire is going to accelerate moves toward self-government—social, economic and education phases are to be far more liberal than heretofore and carried forward with greater speed.

Mr. Kerstens spoke of discarding the old class system.. There will be complete equality between Europeans and natives, he said. The Japanese-inspired Committee for Independence in Java was de-

scribed as a delayed-action bomb from which the fuse will be removed by the Dutch. There is nothing new in the present policy, it was emphasized, beyond an intention to pursue it consistently and in its most liberal interpretation.

The pressing need is trained manpower in the Indies—that and shipping space for materials essential to the recovery of the colonies. The Japanese removed machinery

from sugar mills in Java, leaving five mills out of sixty in working order, and, even worse, they messed up the carefully calculated method of producing rice crops to feed the dense population. The enemy used the fields for cotton and vegetable oils, with the result that there is a prospective food shortage that may be grave.

August 31, 1945

DUTCH SHIP TROOPS IN BRITAIN TO INDIES

LONDON, Oct. 5 (U.P.)—A Netherlands military source said today that 3,500 Netherland troops trained in Great Britain had been transported in three weeks to the Netherlands Indies, where Indonesian independence groups have been active, and 4,000 more were scheduled to leave next week.

"We hope to transport a much

larger number soon," said Colonel van der Harst of the Netherlands Expeditionary Forces.

Numbers of Indonesians, many of them in Holland throughout the German occupation, have arrived here en route to the Indies by plane this week-end, it was reported. They were said to include eight leaders of an independence movement that has been active in the Netherlands almost continuously since 1921. It was understood they would be attached to the Netherlands Army Civil Affairs Depart-

ment and would wear Netherland military uniforms.

Johan H. A. Logemann, Netherlands Minister of Overseas Territories, announced recently that the Government would ask these members of the Indonesian independence movement to act as intermediaries with Nationalist leaders in the Indies. Mr. Logemann said the Netherlands Government would reject any suggestion of negotiating with Soe Karno, Nationalist leader.

October 6, 1945

VAN MOOK WILLING TO DISCUSS INDIES

Lieutenant Governor Insists, However, That Disorders in Java Cease First

By Wireless to THE NEW YORK TIMES.

BATAVIA, Java, Oct. 15—Two Dutch women were shot this morning in the center of Batavia by

Indonesians. One was killed and the other seriously wounded.

In clashes near Chilitan Airfield, about ten miles southeast of Batavia, which is being guarded by Dutch troops, two Dutch soldiers were ambushed and killed. Indonesians fired machine-guns from trees. Skirmishing was still in progress this afternoon.

Except for these two incidents the lull in Batavia continued today.

In response to requests for a statement on the policy of the Netherlands Government in the present situation in Java, Dr.

Hurbertus J. Van Mook, the Lieutenant Governor of the Netherlands Indies told correspondents this morning that the Government was ready, indeed eager, to open discussions with the Indonesian leaders on the basis of Queen Wilhelmina's speech in 1942.

Bars Parley During Disorders

He added, however, that the Government would not negotiate as long as the lives of 100,000 interned men, women and children were in the hands of the Nationalists who might be tempted to regard them as hostages or bargaining counters, or not so long as many representative of Indonesians

not in Soekarno's "government" were afraid to come forward and meet the Dutch.

He said that a measure of order and stability would have to be restored before the negotiations could be initiated.

Asked whether he would be willing to meet Soekarno or other members of the Soekarno faction, Dr. Van Mook said that he would have no objection to meeting any representatives of the Indonesian people, but as things were at present he could see no basis for discussion.

October 16, 1945

INDONESIAN ISSUES APPEAL TO FORCE

Soekarno Says Javanese Must Be Ready to Fight—Tells of 'Council of Defense'

By The United Press.

BATAVIA, Java, June 8—"President" Soekarno of the unrecognized Indonesian Republic called upon his followers throughout Java to mobilize against the Dutch in a radio address today in which he hinted ominously at an imminent breakdown in negotiations.

Mr. Soekarno disclosed that the Indonesian Government had formed a "council of defense" that included "Premier" Sutan Sjahrir

and representatives of the Government, army and people.

He insisted that negotiations with the Dutch were still continuing, but nevertheless proclaimed a "state of emergency" throughout Java and added:

"The Dutch have now unsheathed their sword on the Indonesians. We must rise to defend ourselves. A crisis unprecedented in Indonesian history is now confronting the people . . . the outlook is gloomy."

It was feared that Mr. Soekarno's broadcast portended a renewal of the bloody fighting that met the British when they occupied the island after Japan's surrender. Britain now has turned over virtually all Java garrisons to Dutch forces.

"Our country is in danger," said the Soekarno broadcast. "We must mobilize our total power and bring preparations for national de-

fense to a stage of perfection.

"In order to force their unreasonable proposals on the Indonesians, the Dutch are increasing their military strength and attacking us more severely each day.

"If the Dutch will not recognize the sovereignty of our country and attempt to force their will on us, we will have to answer them with force."

This call to the colors was issued fifteen days after "Premier" Sjahrir announced the Indonesian rejection of the latest Dutch proposals for settlement of Indonesian independence demands.

"Made in Japan"

The Dutch proposals were presented after a two-day debate in the Netherlands Parliament in The Hague early in May. The lenient policy of the Government in Indonesia was strongly criticized then and the unrecognized Indonesian Republic was described as a "made-in-Japan product of force, murder and robbery."

Following the Indonesian rejection the Indonesian Cabinet held a series of urgent meetings at Jogja-

karta last week which Mr. Sjahrir said were designed to "strengthen and consolidate the Government and prepare it for any emergency."

Meanwhile Allied planes dropped leaflets throughout Java warning Japanese deserters that the death penalty would be imposed on them if they failed to surrender by June 15 either to the Allies or to the Indonesian Republican Army.

The order was signed by the commander of the Japanese Sixteenth Army. The number of Japanese deserters in Indonesia is not accurately known, but it is believed to run into the thousands.

The plight of thousands of Chinese in the Tangerang area, who have been murderously attacked by Indonesian extremists, was reported eased today. They were being herded into barricaded areas west of Tangerang, where they could be protected from the "People's Army" by regular Republican Army troops.

June 9, 1946

DUTCH EMPIRE PACT DROPS COLONIALISM

Indonesian Accord Preserves Queen's Authority Over Self-Ruled Republic

By ROBERT TRUMBULL
Special to THE NEW YORK TIMES.

BATAVIA, Java, Nov. 13—The agreement reached between the Dutch and the Indonesians in Cheribon last night was a masterpiece of compromise that dissolves Dutch colonialism in the East Indies yet preserves the Queens' empire intact. Such is the feeling of the Dutch negotiators, who returned here today.

The plan adopted for the recognition of the Indonesian Republic will be "initialed" by the Commission General from The Hague on Friday and formally signed within three weeks, when the Commission General will have completed a flying round-trip to Holland to explain the pact to the Government.

Indonesian objections to remaining under the sovereignty of the House of Orange fell last night before persuasive assurances by the Dutch that the Queen's role was merely nominal. It remains for President Soekarno of the Indonesian Republic to sell this new point of view to the fervent nationalists. This, M. Soekarno promised the commission that he would do "with the full power of my personality," according to a source in intimate contact with the negotiations.

Within Constitution

The de facto recognition of the Indonesian Republic, including Java, Sumatra and the smaller island of Madura—a foregone conclusion for weeks— will be formalized by the commission's signature

NEW SET-UP FOR DUTCH OVERSEAS POSSESSIONS IS SHAPED

Nov. 14. 1946

Under an agreement between the Dutch and the Indonesians, recognition of the Indonesian Republic, embracing Java, Sumatra and Madura, will be formalized in a few weeks. Then in about two years a United States of Indonesia will be formed, comprising the Indonesian Republic and the autonomous States of Borneo and the Great East. The Great East is to include Bali, Celebes, Netherland New Guinea, the Moluccas and the Lesser Sundas. The United States of Indonesia is to be linked with the motherland in a Netherlands-Indonesia Union.

late this month or early in December. This act requires no change in Holland's Constitution, by which Indonesia is now an integral part of the kingdom.

However, the establishment of the United States of Indonesia, including the Indonesian Republic and the autonomous states of Borneo and the Great East (Bali, Celebes, Dutch New Guinea, the Moluccas and the Lesser Sundas) and the linking of this federation to the Netherlands in the Netherlands-Indonesia Union in equal partnership under the Queen require a constitutional revision by the Netherlands States General. The alteration of the Dutch Constitution and the intricate legalities involved in forming the U. S. I. will take time. Jan. 1, 1949, has been set as the target date for making the alliance a formal reality. Holland will then sponsor the U. S. I. in the United Nations.

Meanwhile, the Netherlands retains sovereignty over the islands not included in the Republic, but promises to take measures assuring the Indonesian Republic—Java, Sumatra and Madura—of international recognition as a free nation.

Dutch Retain Voice

The basic compromise allows the Indonesians to choose officers of the U. S. I., who will govern all internal policies, but it makes the Queen the nominal head of the joint Dutch-Indonesian body that will run the affairs of the Netherlands-Indonesia Union. Matters of mutual Dutch-Indonesian interest — which significantly include economic considerations—will be handled by negotiation between the U. S. I. and the N. I. U.

Foreign business interests with heavy investments in Indonesia are particularly interested in the agreement guaranteeing that foreign enterprises will not be taxed more heavily than Indonesian industries. This affects the Americans and British as well as the Dutch. The Dutch also obtained for themselves a special assurance of equal treatment with the Indonesians and of common civil rights.

The statutes governing the Netherlands-Indonesia Union will establish various joint bodies to decide in the name of the Crown all matters of common interest, including defense, foreign affairs and currency. Until Jan. 1, 1949, there will be close collaboration on such items and the Dutch will begin absorbing Indonesians into their foreign service.

Long Negotiations Seen

Protracted negotiations between the Indonesian Republic and the two non-republican states will now ensue. Neutral observers foresee a long period of tension and mutual distrust fomented by numerous extremists on both sides. The Republican Government of President Sukarno and Premier Sutan Sjahrir, which accepted this compromise with the Dutch, has a rocky road ahead.

While the economic position of the Dutch in these islands will be little impaired by the new political status, the personal situation of the colonial-minded Dutch will not be to their liking. Now they must accept Indonesians as equals and in many cases must reconcile themselves to working under Indonesians. One Hollander of the highest prominence in both business and politics believed that foreign firms operating here would have to place Indonesian administrators alongside European bosses in order to obtain the cooperation of Indonesian workers. All matters affecting labor, he believed, must be entrusted entirely to Indonesian managers. Such innovations will doubtless cause many petty dissatisfactions.

November 14, 1946

INDONESIAN ACCORD NOT FULLY REACHED

Relations Between the Dutch and Republic Deteriorates Despite Formal Pact

By ROBERT TRUMBULL
Special to THE NEW YORK TIMES.

SINGAPORE, May 17—Relations between the Netherlands and the Indonesian Republic, as reflected in Indonesian broadcasts, communiqués and private comments from both sides, appear to

have deteriorated seriously in the seven weeks that have passed since the signing of the Cheribon Agreement in Batavia.

These seven weeks have been a period notable for the appearance of new points of disagreement rather than the hoped-for implementation of the Cheribon accord.

Dutch business interests accepted the Cheribon formula grudgingly, on the promise that the economic rehabilitation of the Netherlands East Indies would swiftly follow. Lack of progress toward the promised return of the Java and Sumatra plantations to their pre-war operators has confirmed the opponents of the Cheribon pact in their skepticism and has even augmented their numbers.

On the Indonesian side there has been disillusionment, since the ex-

treme Indonesian interpretation of the Cheribon pact proved to be at variance with the more conservative Dutch conception. Extremist political pressure from within the republic has prevented moderates, like Premier Sutan Sjharir, from carrying out their honest intention of finding quick and orderly formulas in consultation with the Dutch.

Republican officials have informed the Dutch that non-Indonesian estate owners or lessors may return now to their pre-war holdings in the interior. At the same time, according to authoritative Dutch informants here, the Indonesian leaders are forced to acknowledge that they cannot guarantee the safety of the Dutch in the interior.

Apparently the Republican Cab-

inet is willing to transfer the plantations, in accordance with the Cheribon treaty, but the acquiescence of the Indonesians now actually in possession of the estates is another matter. Thus the present impasse arises.

Two points to be settled with reference to the interior properties concern payment to the pre-war owners or lessors for produce exported by Indonesians and compensation to Indonesians for maintaining the plantations during the interim. It is understood that the latter consideration has occupied most of the recent economic discussions and that the debate is deadlocked because of the inability of the Dutch to examine personally the actual conditions of the estates.

Meanwhile, the Dutch naval blockade of the Indonesian ports

—its purpose being to prevent export of rubber and other produce from non-Indonesian properties and the import of military materials—continues to be a source of irritation to the Republic. The Dutch look with extreme disapproval upon the Republic's dealing with Chinese shippers from Malaya who according to Dutch sources are "bleeding the rich country dry."

Another point brought up by Indonesian spokesman here is the desire of the Indonesians now occupying the estates to deal directly with the pre-war owners and lessors. This is apparently in opposition to efforts by both the Indonesian and Dutch negotiating committees to settle the economic questions in joint conference.

Open Rupture Suggested

Dutch activities in military and political fields are a subject of intense dissatisfaction among Indonesian political circles, which seem to have access to the official Republican radio. Listening to the propaganda from the Republican capital of Jogjakarta, one would think that relations between the Dutch and Indonesians were approaching open rupture.

There was certain to be a protest from the Republican side after the Chief of the Netherlands General Staff, Gen. J. J. Kruls, announced this week the imminent arrival in Java of the Dutch Second Division, thus materially increasing Dutch strength in the Indies. The Dutch declare that these are not reinforcements but replacements for veterans of the Netherlands East Indies Army who will be released or returned to Holland.

It is clear that there will always be military incidents with recriminations until the armed forces on both sides are actually reduced. There is little immediate prospect of that.

New States Cause Conflict

The establishment, with Dutch aid, of the autonomous states of East Indonesia and West Borneo is viewed by the Indonesians as a clear violation of the Cheribon pact, since the Republic was not consulted. Here there is an irreconcilable variation in the interpretation of the Cheribon treaty's terms.

It is clear to any observer that the Indonesians want all of the Netherlands East Indies included in the Republic, and it is equally clear that the Dutch are opposed to this. It is certain that the two new non-Republic autonomous territories are to be the scene of internal political conflict.

The Dutch intend to stand by the clause in the Cheribon pact that guarantees the right of all peoples in the Indies to decide their own political relationship both to the Netherlands and to the Indonesian Republic. In every case where such a determination is exercised contrary to the interest of the Republican expansionists, there will be irritations such as now arise over East Indonesia and West Borneo.

The economic rehabilitation of the Indies, as envisioned by the drafters of the Cheribon accord, would remove much opposition to the present terms of settlement in Holland. Delay, such as is now seen, is the most serious of all threats to stability in the East Indies.

The moderates, represented by Premier Sjharir and Acting Governor General Hubertus J. van Mook, are impeded in their attempts for a solution by the impatience of the Dutch industrialists on the one hand and political quibbling within the Republic, on the other. Hot-headed military groups on both sides constantly aggravate the difficulties of negotiation.

May 18, 1947

DUTCH TROOPS TAKE KEY POINTS IN JAVA AS TRUCE CRUMBLES

Republic's Offices in Batavia and Some Leaders Seized Without Any Bloodshed

GUNFIRE STARTS NEAR CITY

By The Associated Press.

BATAVIA, Java, Monday, July 21 — Dutch military operations against the Republic of Indonesia were launched with startling abruptness at midnight last night, but not until daylight neared was any sound of gunfire heard in Batavia.

Acting Governor-General Hubertus J. van Mook, announcing the failure of months of negotiation, said that Dutch troops had begun "police action" on undisclosed fronts.

Gunfire in the direction of the Bekassi River perimeter indicated that there was a clash about eight miles east of the city and there were two flurries of shooting near the British Cricket Club on the south edge of Batavia. A Dutch officer reported the first casualty, an Indonesian who tried to escape from a Dutch patrol in the Pengangsaan district.

Indonesian Republic establishments and a number of Republican leaders in Batavia were seized without bloodshed and without the firing of a shot. They were under heavy guard and sentries were posted at numerous spots throughout the city, but there was no disorder.

"Everything has gone remarkably smoothly," another Dutch officer said.

Won't Contest Batavia

An Indonesian leader said last night before the Dutch operations began that the Republic had no intention of contesting complete Dutch military control of Batavia.

Dr. van Mook announced that special Dutch units had struck unexpectedly at key points where sabotage under the promised Indonesian scorched earth policy had been feared.

July 21, 1947

INDONESIANS BURN SOME JAVA CITIES AS DUTCH ADVANCE

Their Radio Announces Policy of Scorched Earth, but It Is Minimized in Batavia

TWIN DRIVES GO FORWARD

By The Associated Press.

BATAVIA, Java, Thursday, July 24—Indonesian Republicans began a systematic application of a scorched earth policy yesterday as Dutch armor and infantry threatened the Indonesian capital of Jogjakarta with a two-way drive.

Dutch troops driving in from three sides have captured the important north Java coast port of Cheribon, semi-official dispatches from the Cheribon area said today.

The reports said that Dutch forces moved into the city, 130 miles east of Batavia, this afternoon. Cheribon's Indonesian defenders offered no resistance and bridges in the area were captured intact, the dispatches added.

The port city was reported captured by troops who pushed halfway across Java from Bandung It is in the heart of the rich northwest Java rice-growing area.

Four Republican towns were put to the torch by the Republicans, an Indonesian communiqué announced. Salatiga, important objective south of Semarang, was burning when Dutch forces, driving from Semarang toward Jogjakarta, entered the town. Salatiga lies forty-six miles by road across mountainous terrain from Jogjakarta.

Other Towns Burned

The retreating Republicans also set fire to Lawang, twelve miles north of Malang, in east central Java, toward which other Dutch forces were advancing and to Sumedang and Chichalengka, twenty miles east of Bandung, in western Java.

[The Indonesian radio also announced demolition and burning of the major cities of Magelang and Surakarta, The United Press reported.]

July 24, 1947

Indonesians Give Truce Order; Ask for Commission to Supervise

By The Associated Press

BATAVIA, Java, Tuesday, Aug. 5—The Republic of Indonesia issued a cease-fire order to its troops last night, paralleling a similar Dutch order on Sunday.

The orders, giving the United Nations Security Council its greatest victory for peace, became effective at midnight.

Indonesian President Soekarno, in a brief radio speech, ordered the whole Indonesian population to halt hostilities against the Dutch. He addressed Republican troops as Commander in Chief and also told the civil population to cease guerrilla and scorched earth tactics.

The commands to stop fighting found Dutch forces at Salatiga, Java, in a position which their staff officers declared would have enabled them to capture Jogjakarta, the Republican capital, within two or three days. Skirmishes were under way at many points throughout the East Indies yesterday as the deadline for the truce approached.

Earlier, Republican Premier

Amir Sjahriffoedin said the cease-fire order was being issued "without any reservations at all." He quickly added that the Republic would demand appointment of an international commission by the United Nations to supervise the cease-fire orders.

Mr. Sjahriffoedin told the United Nations that the Dutch had delayed transmission of the Security Council message, making it difficult to achieve cessation of hostilities on short notice.

The Premier's demand for an international commission was interpreted as meaning that the Republic did not favor the tendered United States offer of mediation, which the Dutch have accepted.

Mr. Sjahriffoedin said that the commission should see that carrying out the cease-fire orders included release of imprisoned Indonesian youths, restoration of Republican officials to their positions, return of troops on both sides to the demarcation lines existing at the time hostilities started (July 20), cessation of

hostile propaganda, and cessation of attempts to sponsor any separationist movement which would break areas away from the Republic.

He said it was understood that "all this cannot be done at once, but we stick to these demands."

He said the Dutch had issued their cease-fire "with qualifications," since they had declared they intended to continue "clearing actions."

[A Netherlands Government spokesman at The Hague said that, if the Indonesian troops did not respect the cease-fire order, the Dutch would defend themselves vigorously. He expressed the fear that a situation would arise similar to that which followed the truce of October, 1946, with "skirmishes to and fro and infinite negotiations."]

The Dutch order Sunday was issued by Dr. Hubertus J. van Mook, acting Governor General in the Indies. Before the deadline was reached, however, a Dutch Army spokesman announced that Dutch forces had landed on Madura, the island off the east coast of Java. Under the Cheribon Agreement, the island, which has a population of more than 1,000,000, was to be included in the Indonesian Republic.

A previous announcement by the Dutch Army had said that the inhabitants were in a starving condition as a result of being cut off from Java and that Netherlands forces had taken "safety measures

on the island" at the request of the population.

Commenting on this communiqué, the spokesman said that "naturally we must have Dutch units there, or such measures could not be carried out." The Army said large shipments of rice were being sent to Madura.

Resistance Claim Denied

An Indonesian Army communiqué last night declared that heavy fighting occurred when Netherlands forces landed on Madura, but the Dutch said this was "a fantasy." The Dutch said their landing was small-scale and met no resistance.

A Dutch fighter plane carried to the airfield of Jogjakarta, the Republican capital, the original copy of the United Nations' note calling for an end to the Indonesian hostilities. The copy was dropped in a weighted container. The Batavia radio advised Jogjakarta of the fighter's mission and asked the Republicans not to fire on it.

The Republican communiqué said the field was attacked by Dutch fighters shortly after the courier plane dropped the message and expressed belief the courier pilot had carried out reconnaissance, since specific objectives were the targets.

Total Dutch casualties for the two weeks of fighting were announced officially yesterday as 60 killed, 131 wounded and 17 missing.

August 5, 1947

Dutch Sign Truce With Indonesia, Keep Interim Rule of Rich Areas

By The Associated Press.

BATAVIA, Java, Jan. 17—The Netherlands and the Indonesian Republic signed today a truce that in effect gives the Dutch at least temporary control of the most productive areas of Java and Sumatra, rich in oil and rubber.

With the signing, the United Nations Good Offices Committee gained its initial objective: termination of the warfare that broke out in the East Indies last summer. The committee, which has been engaged in negotiations for eleven weeks, faces the task of assisting the Dutch and Indonesians to reach a final political settlement.

The truce was signed aboard the United States Navy transport Renville, anchored off Batavia. Identical orders to Dutch and Republican troops in Java, Sumatra and Madura to cease fire and stand fast are to be fully effective forty-eight hours after the signing.

Raden Abdul Kadir Widjojoatmodjo, head of the Netherlands

delegation, and Amir Sjarifudin, Premier of the Indonesian Republic, signed the agreement. Their signatures were witnessed by the committee members, Dr. Frank P. Graham of the United States, Richard C. Kirby of Australia and Paul van Zeeland of Belgium.

Mr. Widjojoatmodjo and Dr. Sjarifudan also signed a statement of twelve principles agreed upon as the basis of future political discussions. The delegation heads received from the committee six additional principles, which are expected to be formally accepted Monday.

The political principles give the republic the status of a sovereign and independent state in the projected United States of Indonesia. Provision also is made for plebiscites in Java, Sumatra and Madura within six months to a year after the final political agreement is reached. In the plebiscite areas residents will decide whether they wish to join the republic or form a separate state.

The truce agreement provides for the establishment of a demili-

tarization zone between the forward positions of the Dutch and Indonesian forces. It is based on the line proclaimed Aug. 29 by Hubertus J. van Mook, Acting Dutch Governor General of the Indies.

This line gives the Dutch most of eastern, western and north central Java, the east plantation coast and the southern oil fields of Sumatra and western Sumatra around Padang. It gives the republic south central Java and Sumatra's mountainous back country.

Final boundaries between Dutch and Republican territory are not specified in the truce.

Dr. Sjarifudin told those who witnessed the signing that the republic would carry out the agreement to the best of its ability even if Republican circles were "disappointed that the truce finally agreed upon departs so far from what we hoped for."

Mr. Widjojoatmodjo described the truce as "the initial victory for reason and common sense." Dr. Graham said the agreement "by common consent surely will take its name from the Renville." Much of the negotiating was done aboard the vessel.

Neutral military advisers of the United Nations committee are to investigate whether Republican troops are still resisting inside Dutch positions. Any found to be doing so are to withdraw under supervision of these advisers.

On each side of a demarcation

line law and order will be maintained by the civil police force of the party having jurisdiction there. One party's police are not to cross into the other's demilitarized territory without a military adviser of the committee. Military personnel may be used temporarily by either side as civil police, but must be under civil control.

All prisoners taken by each side are to be released. Trade is to be resumed between Dutch and Republican areas and is to be restricted only as both parties agree, with committee assistance if necessary.

The truce will remain effective indefinitely unless the Netherlands or the Republic informs the committee that it considers that the other party has committed a violation.

Bloody fighting between Netherlands and Republican forces began July 20, when the Dutch Army began what it called "police action" against the Indonesians. On Aug. 1 the United Nations Security Council called for both sides to issue cease-fire orders effective three days later. The orders were issued, but sporadic fighting continued, each side blaming the other. Subsequently the committee was established to implement the cease-fire order.

January 18, 1948

ABSOLUTE POWERS GIVEN IN INDONESIA

Republic's Parliament Moves to Cope With Threat as Reds Proclaim Revolution

Dispatch of The Times, London.

BATAVIA, Java, Sept. 20—The Indonesian Republic's Provisional Parliament at a special session today granted unlimited power for a period of three months to President Soekarno to cope with the situation arising from a Communist coup in East Java Province and the city of Madiun.

All Left Wing newspapers have been banned by a Government decree. Headquarters at Jogjakarta of the army unit of the Communist Youth Movement, Pesindo, and of the Federation of Trade Unions have been seized by Government forces. Several hundred persons are reported to have been arrested in the Republican capital, including Communist leaders.

The Right Wing Masjumi party and the center party, P. N. ., have formed a national independence front "to safeguard the Republic."

Little is known about the situation at Madiun, third largest city in the Indonesian Republic, except what is heard over the Madiun radio.

At Surakarta, fifty miles west of Madiun, where fighting apparently went on during the week-end, the Republicans took firm measures to quell the Communist revolt, the Republican news agency Antara reported.

The newly appointed commander in the Surakarta area, Col. Gatot Soebrotö issued an ultimatum ordering that shooting cease before noon today. He also ordered the commanders of army units to appear before him before noon tomorrow. Any commander disobeying these orders will be regarded as an insurgent and most severely punished.

September 21, 1948

Java Republicans Retake Madiun From Reds; Other Towns Fall in Sweep, Muso in Flight

BATAVIA, Java, Sept. 30 (AP)—Indonesian Republican troops have recaptured Madiun, the Communist capital, and are moving against the Communists south of the city, a Government spokesman said today.

Col. Gatot Subroto, military governor of Madiun, announced the fall of the Communist stronghold in a broadcast over the Jogjakarta radio. He said that the towns of Wonogiri, Ngawi and Magetan also had been taken and that Government forces now were sweeping toward Ponorogo, twenty miles south of Madiun.

[Muso, the Moscow-trained Communist leader, and his lieutenants fled as Republican troops approached Madiun, The United Press reported.]

Wonogiri is fifteen miles south of Surakarta, Magetan is twelve miles west of Madiun and Ngawi is twelve miles northwest of Madiun. Other goals are Purwodadi, thirty miles north of Surakarta, and Pajitan, near the island's southern coast.

In an order of the day, the military governor said that only the unconditional surrender of the Communists would be accepted. Captured snipers were ordered treated as guerrillas, without the status of prisoners of war.

The Madiun radio, now back in Government hands, charged that the Communists had murdered religious leaders, teachers, non-Communist political leaders and civil servants before leaving the adjacent village of Gereng, which fell on Tuesday.

Madiun, the third largest city in Republican territory, was retaken after an eight-day campaign.

Directed by Communist Leader Muso, recently returned from Moscow, the rebels overthrew the Madiun Government on Sept. 19 and set up a Soviet regime. The next day the then-Communist controlled Madiun radio called for the complete overthrow of the Indonesian Government which has headquarters in Jogjakarta.

The Indonesian Parliament gave President Sukarno emergency powers and Government troops began moving toward the central Java city. On Sept. 23, Government reports said a three-pronged offensive was under way toward the Communist stronghold. The Government has reported gradual gains since.

October 1, 1948

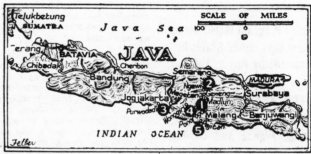

The New York Times   Oct. 1, 1948

Government forces announced the recapture of Madiun (1), main stronghold of the Communist insurrectionists, and near-by Magetan before moving on Ponorogo. Also reported retaken were Ngawi (2) and Wonogiri (4). Other objectives of the advancing Republican forces are Purwodadi (3) and Pajitan (5).

DUTCH TAKE CHIEFS AND JAVA CAPITAL; U. N. BODY IS CALLED

PARATROOPS SWOOP

By The Associated Press.

BATAVIA, Java, Dec. 19—Dutch parachute and airborne troops seized Jogjakarta today and immediately interned the top leaders of the young Indonesian Republic.

A Netherlands communiqué said that Dr. Soekarno, President of the Republic; Premier Mohammed Hatta, Foreign Minister Hadji Agus Salim, Gen. Soerderimen, Army head, and Sutan Sjahrir, a former Premier, were taken into custody.

[An emergency meeting of the United Nations Security Council has been called for Monday morning in Paris to consider the Indonesian situation. The meeting was requested by the United States delegate.]

The capture of Jogjakarta deprived the Republic of its capital in the first hours of renewed warfare in the East Indies.

The Dutch also announced that their units had advanced across old truce lines at several places in Java and Sumatra. Thus far the poorly equipped Republican Army appears to have put up little resistance. There was no word from either side that the Republicans were employing the scorched earth tactics that they have threatened.

One Fire in Capital

Jogjakarta, 225 miles southeast of Batavia, was occupied by the Dutch at 3:30 P. M. (3:30 A. M. E.S.T.), the bulletin said. Only one fire was observed there. The Indonesian Republicans said earlier that the city had been bombed.

The city is the largest in Republican territory. It now has an estimated population of 1,000,000, because of the great influx of Indonesians from rural areas in Republican Java.

As the seat of the Republican Government, Jogjakarta has been the spiritual center of the nationalist movement in the Indies. According to the Dutch it also has been the center of far-reaching terrorist activities in Dutch areas of the islands.

Dutch paratroopers opened the way for the swift capture of Jogjakarta by dropping down on the Maguwo airfield, five miles east of the city. There was no resistance there, the communiqué said, and the field was in shape to receive airborne reinforcements at once.

At the end of the day, Dutch Army headquarters said six Dutch soldiers had been killed and eight wounded in all operations. Three Dutch were wounded during the taking of Jogjakarta.

Lieut. Gen. S. H. Spoor, the Netherlands Commander-in-chief, watched the paráchute drop from his plane. After the paratroopers flashed an "all clear" signal from below General Spoor flew to Semarang, forty-five miles north of Jogjakarta, to inspect the embarkation of the airborne force.

The Jogjakarta operation was supported by a Dutch advance eastward in Central Java. Dutch troops along the Batavia-Jogjakarta trunk railway advanced fifteen miles from the area of Gombong to positions beyond Kebumen.

That force passed through Karanganjar, which the communiqué said was a few miles east of the old truce line. It is now within fifty miles of Jogjakarta.

Another Netherlands column moving through Eastern Java reached the rail town of Kepanjen, ten miles south of Malang.

Dutch marines, supported by units of the Netherlands Navy, landed on the north coast of East Java shortly after midnight, the communiqué said. It added that the landing "progressed according to plan."

December 20, 1948

U. N. APPROVES PLAN FOR FREE INDONESIA; SEEKS END TO FIGHT

Council Program Would Set Up Sovereign United States in Islands by July 1, 1950

DUTCH ATTACK PROPOSAL

Russia, France and Ukraine Abstain on Most Points as 4-Power Resolution Is Voted

By A. M. ROSENTHAL
Special to THE NEW YORK TIMES.

LAKE SUCCESS, Jan. 28—The United Nations Security Council voted approval today of a step-by-step plan that would transfer sovereignty of the rich islands of Indonesia (Netherlands East Indies) from the Dutch to a new United States of Indonesia by July, 1950.

Every paragraph of the long Indonesian settlement plan—denounced in blistering phrases by the Netherlands—was voted by the Council. The tally usually was 8 to 0, with Russia, France and the Ukraine abstaining, and the Council skipped the formality of an over-all vote on the resolution, which had been introduced jointly by the United States, Cuba, Norway and China.

Before the final vote, the Council turned down a strong Russian amendment that would have ordered the Netherlands to withdraw all troops at once from Republican territories. The Soviet Union, the Ukraine, Egypt and Cuba supported the move—which was in line with the recent New Delhi conference of Asiatic and African nations—but the abstentions of the seven other Council members were enough to kill it under the rules.

The resolution adopted by the Council dealt with two major problems: Stopping fighting in Indonesia and setting up the Republic again as a going concern, and organizing the eventual freedom of all the islands in a federated union.

Under the four-power proposal, the Netherlands and the Republic are called on to stop all military activity — regular and guerrilla. The Hague is asked to free imprisoned Republican leaders and turn over to them the city and environs of Jogjakarta as the administrative center of the Republic.

Looking to the future, the resolution sets up a three-nation commission on Indonesia composed of Australia, representing the Republic, Belgium,' representing the Netherlands, and the United States, as a neutral. The commission would supervise this three-point program for Indies independence:
(1) Establishment of an interim Government by March 15, 1949.
(2) Elections for an Indonesian Constituent Assembly by Oct. 1, 1949.
(3) Transfer of sovereignty for the Netherlands to the United States of Indonesia by July 1, 1950—and preferably earlier.

Voting on the resolution was not only paragraph by paragraph but sometimes line by line and phrase by phrase. The job took well over an hour, but final approval of the motion was shadowed by the harsh Dutch attack that came before and after the balloting.

Dutch Delegate Reads Statement

Dr. Jan Herman van Royen, Netherlands delegate, reading carefully from a twenty-two-page prepared speech, charged that the resolution amounted to imposing a United Nations "guardianship" over his country. He warned that no country could "concede" to the "sacrifices" demanded by the resolution, and told the delegates bluntly that they would be responsible for creating an "almost unbridgeable gap" in the entire Indonesian situation.

Point by point, Dr. van Royen ripped into the resolution. He said that returning Jogjakarta to the Republic might result in more disorder, that power was given to the commission to interfere in Netherlands domestic affairs, that the Council itself was taking upon itself the right to decide the fate of Indonesia in spite of Netherlands sovereignty.

The Netherlands delegate said that The Hague would accept the resolution only so far as it was compatible with its responsibility for maintaining law and order in Indonesia. But during his speech and in a press conference after the meeting Dr. van Royen attacked almost every provision in the resolution as leading to just the opposite—lawlessness and disorder.

Spokesmen for the Republic, meanwhile, said that they would have to reserve final comment until the Netherlands freed all Republican leaders. Until that time, they said, it was impossible to know "the collective opinion" of the Republican Government.

January 29, 1949

Dutch Summon Round Table To Speed Accord on Indies

Would Release Political Prisoners, Form Free, Sovereign Federation Well in Advance of U. N. Timetable

Special to THE NEW YORK TIMES

THE HAGUE, The Netherlands, Feb. 26—Decisions to transfer sovereignty over Indonesia at a date earlier than that laid down in the United Nations Security Council's resolution, to set free immediately Republican leaders and to convene a round-table conference for the furtherance of effective discussions were announced today by the Dutch Government.

The statement, which summed up the results of last week's talks between the Cabinet and the High Representative of the Crown in Indonesia, Dr. Louis J. M. Beel, said that the Netherlands Government had "decided to endeavor to effectuate this transfer of sovereignty considerably earlier than at the date of July 1, 1950, which, in accordance with the previous plans of the Netherlands Government, has been laid down in the resolution of the Security Council of Jan. 28, 1949, as the ultimate date for the transfer of sovereignty."

[In Washington the Netherlands Ambassador, Dr. van Kleffens, indicated that the plan could be put into effect by about the middle of June, but the United Press reported from Batavia that both Indonesian Republican and United Nations sources had greeted it with a "marked lack of enthusiasm."]

The statement, however, emphasized that the achievement of this endeavor required the sincere cooperation of all parties and that the Dutch were of the opinion "that the common purpose eagerly aimed at justifies the confidence that all parties will show their readiness to cooperate."

The Republican leaders are to be released in conformity with the Security Council's resolution. The Dutch will "consult with them concerning their wishes as to their future residence and the arrangements which will have to be made in this respect," the statement declared.

February 27, 1949

Indonesian Leaders Agree To Set Up a United Republic

By Reuters.

JOGJAKARTA, Java, July 23—Republican and Federalist leaders in Indonesia announced at the end of their two-day conference here today that they had reached an agreement on the creation of a United States of Indonesia, to be known as the Republic of Indonesia Serikat (United).

The number of units in the new republic, and the area of each unit, will be determined before the transfer of sovereignty, but the territory will be as envisaged under the Renville agreement, the leaders said.

The Renville agreement recognizes the existence of East and West Java, East and South Sumatra, and Madura as autonomous units.

The new republic will be governed by a constitutional president acting on the advice of a prime minister and cabinet.

The agreement envisages a period of transition, after sovereignty has been transferred, during which preparations will be made for framing a new constitution and for general elections.

During this period a provisional government and a provisional parliament will be set up to insure stability.

Actual composition of the provisional government, as well as financial and economic arrangements between the various units of the federation, will be determined when both delegations resume discussions in Batavia next Saturday.

It was agreed that all persons living in the Netherlands Indies or the Indonesian Republic, including Chinese, Arabs and Europeans, should have the right to new Indonesian citizenship if they wished.

July 24, 1949

DOCUMENT SIGNED FREEING INDONESIA

Transfer of Dutch Sovereignty Sets Up Union Headed by Queen Juliana

PARLIAMENTS MUST AGREE

Cooperation Is Established in Military, Financial, Economic, Cultural and Social Fields

By SYDNEY GRUSON
Special to THE NEW YORK TIMES.

THE HAGUE, the Netherlands, Nov. 2—In a klieg-lighted ceremony in the ancient Knights' Hall of the Parliament building a Dutch Cabinet Minister today signed the document transferring sovereignty over Indonesia "unconditionally and irrevocably" to the United States of Indonesia.

Although the formal transfer will not take place for some weeks —the document specified that it would not be later than Dec. 30— everyone in the hall for the closing plenary session of the round-table conference considered that a new era for Indonesia had begun.

The Cabinet Minister was J. H. van Maarseveen who heads the Ministry for Overseas Territories. His signature also pledged the Netherlands which has ruled the Pacific archipelago for more than three centuries, to recognize the new country as an "independent and sovereign state."

The document was accepted for the United States of Indonesia by Republican Premier Mohammed Hatta and Sultan Hamid II of Pontianak, leader of the Federalist delegation. The signatures of these three men meant that approval not only of the draft Charter of the transfer of sovereignty but also of other agreements had been reached during the conference.

Queen to Head Union

These included the Statute binding the two countries in a Union headed by Queen Juliana of the Netherlands, and arrangements for cooperation in military, economic, financial, social and cultural affairs. The Queen will formally transfer sovereignty in Amsterdam next month when all these agreements have been ratified by the Indonesian and Dutch Parliaments.

The draft Charter had two articles, the first transferring sovereignty and the second excluding Dutch New Guinea from the terms of transfer. In reference to the decision to postpone the settlement of New Guinea's future for one year, Dr. Hatta said that Indonesian happiness over "this historical moment" had been "somewhat tempered because everything could not be solved now."

There were only the faintest touches of nostalgia for the past centuries in the speeches of Mr. van Maarseveen and Dutch Premier Willem Drees, chairman of the conference. Presenting the cultural agreement, Mr. van Maarseveen said, "the often-heard thesis that East and West will never be able to understand each other was rejected by those who cooperated in drawing up this accord."

"Beautiful Future" Foreseen

A "beautiful future" for two peoples, each independent and sovereign but understanding and aiding one another, now could "begin to flourish out of uncertainties and difficulties" of the past, Mr. van Maarseveen added.

It was left to Sultan Hamid in presenting the military committee's report to sound the warning that the documents meant nothing if mutual understanding, preparedness to make sacrifices and restraint were not present in the implementation of the various agreements. If fruitful cooperation were possible in the military field, particularly regarding the withdrawal of Dutch troops, the rest would flow easily, he said.

A covering resolution for the agreements was signed for the United Nations Conciliation Commission by Raymond Herremans, Belgian chairman of the week. The commission's contribution to the success of the conference was praised by all speakers. Replying for the commission, M. Herremans said the conference agreements were proof that the "most inextricable disputes can be solved by conciliation with individual aims achieved and mutual benefits assured."

Dutch Investments Guaranteed

THE HAGUE, Nov. 2 (UP)—The federated "Republic of the United States of Indonesia" includes Java, Sumatra and a string of thousands of other tiny islands. The new nation will be linked to the Netherlands through a loose Dutch-Indonesian union headed by Queen Juliana.

Rich Dutch investments in the archipelago, with its abundant material resources, thus are guaranteed. The Dutch, however, must withdraw all army, navy and air force units within a year after the agreement becomes effective.

The Dutch agreed to promote membership of the new republic in the United Nations.

Future relations between the Netherlands and the new state were set down in a "Union Statute." It provides that "the two partners undertake to base their form of government on the principles of democracy and to aim at an independent judiciary."

Arbitration Court Set Up

A Court of Arbitration, consisting of three Dutch and three Indonesian judges, will rule on any legal disputes arising from the statute.

The two nations also agreed to name high commissioners with the diplomatic rank of ambassador to "further the interests of the partners with each other's territory."

The new republic, in a concession to Dutch land and industry owners, pledged itself to recognize privately owned property. Indonesian left-wing leaders have demanded that all key industries be nationalized.

November 3, 1949

Indonesian States Elect Sukarno As First President of New Regime

By The Associated Press.

JOGJAKARTA, Java, Dec. 16— Dr. Sukarno was elected today the first President of the United States of Indonesia—the independent nation for which he fought for more than twenty years.

It took only fifteen minutes for electors from all sixteen states of the East Indian islands to choose him unanimously. He will be sworn in tomorrow. He will formally take over when the new country comes into being as an equal partner of the Netherlands under the Dutch Crown on Dec. 27.

Dr. Sukarno has been President since 1945 of the Indonesian Republic, a Jogjakarta-seated Government controlling parts of Java and Sumatra, two of the main islands. It is to have a major voice in affairs of the new nation.

Only a year ago, Dr. Sukarno was a prisoner of the Dutch. Parachute troopers had captured Jogjakarta and carried him off into exile under a decree issued from the Dutch Governor-General's palace in Batavia. Now the Republican leader is moving into the Dutch palace.

Like many Indonesians, Dr. Sukarno has no first name. A Moslem, he sips wine socially but sparingly. He speaks Dutch well, while his German, French and English are clear, though hesitant. He likes to quote from Lincoln and Washington and to compare Indonesia's struggle for freedom to the American Revolution.

Looking younger than his forty-nine years, the new President talks easily, but hedges on controversial subjects. He is both a social reformer and an opportunist. To further the cause of Indonesian nationalism, he has been known to take help where he can get it, even from the Japanese.

Conservatives, who had regarded him as an extreme radical, now must rely on him to keep Indonesia from falling into the hands of more rabid revolutionists.

A radical national movement was fostered in 1927 by Dr. Sukarno. He was jailed, then released in 1932, but kept up his agitation. The Dutch put up with it for two years, then exiled him to a remote island in the Flores and later held him in Sumatra. When the Japanese swept across Indonesia in 1942, Dr. Sukarno was freed.

Behind the Japanese flag, he revived Indonesian nationalism. He cooperated with the Japanese, preaching their doctrine of "Asia for the Asiatics."

After the Japanese capitulation, Dr. Su Karno and his followers declared their independence of the Dutch. He became President of the Indonesian Republic Aug. 17, 1945.

Four years of a bloody, bitter struggle between the Indonesians and the Dutch followed.

A United Nations committee stepped in. While it brought brief cessation of hostilities, agreements were scrapped and military violations on both sides continued.

A year ago the Dutch opened a full scale miltary action, capturing Republican leaders and all their territory but the northern tip of Sumatra. The United Nations Security Council called for a halt in the fighting and for Dutch withdrawal from captured areas.

The Republicans, in the hills, continued guerrilla warfare. The Dutch finally softened their policy to the point of reversing it. There followed a round-table conference at The Hague that arranged for transfer of the sovereignty.

December 17, 1949

INDONESIA BECOMES NATION IN CEREMONY IN THE NETHERLANDS

---

347 Years of Dutch Rule End— Queen Juliana Makes Plea to Both Countries to Cooperate

---

HATTA ACCEPTS TRANSFER

Crowds in Java City Celebrate Their Freedom Peacefully— 7 New Nations Since War

---

By SYDNEY GRUSON
Special to THE NEW YORK TIMES.

AMSTERDAM, The Netherlands, Dec. 27—The Netherlands' long-held sovereignty over Indonesia was formally transferred to the new republic today in a brief ceremony during which Queen Juliana appealed to both Dutch and Indonesians to "cooperate loyally" in the new relationship between the two countries.

Dr. Mohammed Hatta, Premier of the newly formed United States of Indonesia and long a leader in the struggle for independence, accepted the transfer on behalf of his country. He echoed the Queen's hope that the resulting union of two free and equal partners would bring happiness to both peoples.

The Queen signed the act of transfer at 10:22 A. M., ending three and a half centuries of Dutch rule over the rich Pacific islands that have been wracked by warfare between the Dutch and Indonesians in the last four years.

Dressed in black velvet with a collar of emeralds glistening at her neck, Queen Juliana in the only formal speech of the ceremony said that the Netherlands relinquishment of sovereignty, its assumption by the new state and the union represented "one of most deeply moving events of the times, piercing as it were to the very roots of our existence."

Take Stations Side by Side

"No longer do we stand partially opposed to one another," the Queen said. "We have now taken our stations side by side however much we may be bruised and torn carrying scars of rancor and regret."

She added that the entire Dutch nation concurred "with the principle of transfer of sovereignty," emphasizing the word "principle" as if to take note of some Dutch objection to the method and time of transfer. She reiterated the Netherlands' desire to assist Indonesia whenever assistance was requested.

Only about 300 persons, mainly Dutch notables, Government officials and some members of the diplomatic corps, witnessed the thirty-two-minute ceremony in the marble Burgherzall (Hall of Citizens) of the Royal Palace, which was built in the seventeenth century as a town hall shortly after acquisition of the East Indies ushered in the Netherlands' golden age.

It was a sober ceremony conducted so matter-of-factly as to detract somewhat from the significance of the occasion. The seven Indonesian delegates, the Dutch Cabinet and other officials were seated along both sides of a red felt-covered table, and the Queen, after being escorted into the hall by two of her Ministers, was seated between Premier Hatta and Dutch Premier Willem Drees. Her husband, Prince Bernhard, sat opposite her.

Leaders Sign Protocol

The ceremony began with reading of a protocol covering results of the recent round-table conference where the Dutch agreed to grant Indonesia immediate independence. The protocol was signed by the two Governments' leaders.

Then the Queen signed an Act of Confirmation in which she gave her assent to "the new order of law" between the two countries and a few minutes later the act transferring sovereignty.

This was countersigned by the Dutch Cabinet and all seven Indonesian delegates signed a declaration of acceptance, which was made part of the act.

After the Queen spoke the national anthems of the two countries were played, but participants in the ceremony had been cautioned not to sing by a note on the official program. Faint echoes of singing filtered into the palace from a few voices raised among the crowd outside.

JAKARTA (Batavia), Java, Dec. 27 (AP)—The 77,000,000 people of Indonesia snapped their colonial bond with the Netherlands today and took their place as a new nation in Communist-threatened southeast Asia.

Throughout the chain of islands stretching nearly 3,000 miles between the Pacific and Indian Oceans, Indonesians tonight peacefully celebrated their first hours of freedom after 347 years of Dutch rule.

Thousands of the red-and-white banners of the new United States of Indonesia draped the Dutch brick buildings and Chinese shops along the streets of Jakarta (the former Indonesian name for Batavia has been restored), thronged by crowds shouting "Merdeka" (freedom).

Street cars clanging along the canal-lined streets were jammed with cheering youngsters and every street corner was clamorous with Javanese gong and tom-tom music from loudspeakers.

The one tie that remains be-

A NEW NATION: THE UNITED STATES OF INDONESIA

The New York Times   Dec. 28, 1949.

1—REPUBLIC OF INDONESIA	5—STATE OF MADURA	9—AUTONOMOUS AREA OF S. E. BORNEO	13—STATE OF BILLITON
2—STATE OF SOUTH SUMATRA	6—STATE OF EAST JAVA	10—AUTONOMOUS AREA OF BANJAR	14—STATE OF BANGKA
3—BANTAM, UNDER PROV. FED. GOVT.	7—STATE OF EAST INDONESIA	11—STATE OF GREAT DAYAK	15—STATE OF RIOUW
4—STATE OF PASUNDAN (WEST JAVA)	8—AUTONOMOUS AREA OF EAST BORNEO	12—AUTONOMOUS AREA OF WEST BORNEO	16—STATE OF EAST SUMATRA

tween the Netherlands and Indonesia is the Dutch crown. They are partners in a union under that crown, but each is free to go her own way. The arrangement resembles that of the British Commonwealth nations.

Seventh New State Since War

The new state is the seventh new and independent nation to be formed since the war. Others are the Philippines, India, Pakistan, Ceylon, Burma and Israel. In addition, Korea gained independence from the Japanese, then split into sections along lines of the Russian and United States occupation zones.

Most of the Indonesian islands were under martial law, a hangover from the turbulent years of guerrilla warfare.

Lieut. Col. Daan Jahja, military governor of Jakarta, warned that "irresponsible elements" would be dealt with severely. Officials had feared Communists might seek to make trouble.

Freedom came in brief, colorful ceremonies held almost simultaneously in Amsterdam and in the glistening white palace of Dutch governors in Jakarta.

The stifling heat of a tropical evening was stirred by beating fans as Dutch High Commissioner A. H. J. Lovink and Indonesian Deputy Premier Sultan Hemangku Buwono signed the protocol of transfer here.

Conciliatory Address Made

Sultan Buwono made a conciliatory address on behalf of the Indonesians. He said that this day "incorporated the spirit of Christmas," a spirit which he prayed would bring "inward and outward peace for the Netherlands people, the Indonesian people and for other nations all over the world."

"During the period of battle just now ended, courage and self-reliance have been born in the soul of our people," he declared, but added the new nation would need the help of other nations, "particularly the Netherlands which is skilled, experienced and imbued with a sincere wish to help our people."

The ceremony here was witnessed by twenty-two delegations representing foreign nations. H. Merle Cochran, a member of the three-nation United Nations commission whose good office were instrumental in settlement of the Indonesian conflict, failed to arrive in time to attend the ceremonies. Mr. Cochran is expected to be the first United States Ambassador to the new nation.

Simultaneously the Republic of Indonesia at Jogjakarta signed away its sovereignty and became one of the sixteen states in the new federal republic. Tomorrow President Soekarno, who headed the republic, and who leads the new nation, will fly here for a triumphant parade and a speech.

December 28, 1949

Amboinese Secede From Indonesia In New Federation's Fourth Revolt

By The Associated Press.

JAKARTA, Indonesia, April 26 —Amboinese authorities declared the South Moluccas independent today. A radio message to Macassar told of this, the fourth revolt in four months within the United States of Indonesia.

The Moluccas, once renowned Spice Islands now in a commercial backwash, dot the sea between Celebes and New Guinea. Amboina is the name of both one district and the capital. They were included in the State of East Indonesia.

Military sources in Jakarta said Indonesian troops of the Netherlands Indies Army joined the rebellion. A battalion is garrisoned at Amboina. These are among troops who have been awaiting demobilization or transfer to the United States of Indonesia's Federal Army since the Netherlands gave Indonesia independence last December. The Federal Government has no soldiers in the Moluccas.

Observers in Jakarta said it may take weeks to quell the uprising because of probable backing by the people of the area.

The independence declaration said the South Moluccas — Amboina, Banda, the Kai Islands, Ceram and Aru—no longer felt secure within the East Indonesian State and were cutting their ties with the United States of Indonesia.

The revolt, like the others, appeared to stem from efforts by Premier Mohamed Hatta's Central Government to junk the Federal structure and make a single state of all the islands based on the Indonesian Republic, which led the fight for independence.

This move was in the background of the short-lived West Java rebellion of Capt. R. R. P. (Turk) Westerling, a previous flare-up among Dutch-trained Indonesian troops in Amboina and seizure of Macassar, the East Indonesian capital, by Indonesians newly transferred from the Dutch to United States of Indonesia Army service. All were put down.

Neutral sources here said the Molucca Separatists were led by Dr. Soumokil, former Attorney General of East Indonesia. Other leaders were reported to be the acting chief of the previous administration on Amboina, a man named Manahutu, and a South Moluccas councilman named Wairisal. (Few Indonesians have more than one name.)

The Amboinese include a large proportion of Christians. Most Indonesians of the other islands are Moslems.

April 27, 1950

Federal Indonesia Government and Republic Agree to Establishment of Over-All Regime

JAKARTA, Indonesia, May 19 (AP)—The Federal Government of the United States of Indonesia and the original Republic of Indonesia —the largest state within the federal regime—agreed today on the formation of an over-all government in the former Dutch East Indies.

The decision to set up a single new government came as reports, seeping through central government censorship, told of new serious fighting in Macassar, capital of the recalcitrant state of East Indonesia. There Indonesian soldiers clashed with troops of the K. N. I. L., the Indonesian corps of the Dutch armed forces.

Under the agreement for a unitary regime, a joint committee representing the United States of Indonesia and the Republic of Indonesia will lay the groundwork for the new government "in the shortest possible time," according to a joint communique of both Governments.

It was agreed also that President Sukarno of the United States of Indonesia, former president of the republic, would head the new state.

The procedure calls for the dissolution of the present federal regime, the continuance of the West European-type of Cabinet, abolition of the Senate and the creation of a Parliament made up of members of the Republic and United States of India representative bodies.

The new unitary state will be temporary and its constitution provisional until a final constitution is drawn up by an assembly elected by the people on the basis of one member for every 3,000 residents, plus representatives of racial minorities.

The present United States of Indonesia constitution calls for a final constituent assembly by the end of 1950. The constitution of the new state will be a revision of the United States of Indonesia constitution with essentials of the republic's constitution. It will be based on socialistic principles envisioned in the original proclamation of independence of Aug. 17, 1945.

The formation of the new Government will mark the end of the system of states set up by the Dutch during the last five years in areas outside the Indonesian Republic.

Republicans, who dominated the new nation, were determined that the other states—formerly derided as Dutch puppets—should go. The struggle to bring them into the fold produced political chaos and actual warfare since Indonesia gained her independence.

Since the United States of Indonesia was created last December, the original sixteen states have dwindled to the present three—the republic, East Sumatra and East Indonesia—leaving the autonomous area of West Borneo as the only area in the islands outside the Federal set-up.

May 20, 1950

INDONESIA SHIFTS NAME

President Proclaims Republic to Replace Federation

JAKARTA, Indonesia, Aug. 15 (UP)—Indonesian President Sukarno today abolished the federated "United States of Indonesia" and proclaimed the unified "Republic of Indonesia" to take its place.

President Sukarno said Jogjakarta would be the capital of the new state and that he would continue as President.

After reading the proclamation to the Federal Parliament, the President flew to Jogjakarta to dissolve Premier Mohammed Hatta's Government of the "Republic of Indonesia," previously a member state in the federated republic.

Premier Hatta is scheduled to surrender the mandate tonight. President Sukarno then will have supreme powers until a new Cabinet is formed.

August 16, 1950

SUKARNO GIVES DUTCH NEW GUINEA WARNING

JAKARTA, Indonesia, Aug. 17 (AP)—President Sukarno declared today the Dutch would have a fight on their hands if they did not yield control of West New Guinea to Indonesia by the end of 1950.

The Dutch-Indonesian agreement that gave Indonesia independence last Dec. 27, in a joint union under Queen Juliana's Crown, provided that West New Guinea would remain in the Crown's control for a year. In that period the Dutch were to study the political and economic factors of the area with a view to granting it sovereignty as a part of Indonesia.

President Sukarno declared that the Netherlands was maintaining "colonial control" of West New Guinea.

The President spoke from the Palace steps before a crowd of thousands observing the fifth anniversary of the Indonesian proclamation of independence.

Red and white flags of the republic flew in the capital. Chinese Communist flags also appeared. Indonesia has recognized Red China. The military governor of Jakarta prohibited the Chinese population from flying Nationalist China's emblem.

"According to our Constitution," President Sukarno said, "West New Guinea is also Indonesian territory—not tomorrow, not the day after tomorrow, but now, at this very moment. Dutch de facto authority over West New Guinea is recognized for this year only.

"If a settlement by negotiation cannot be arrived at within this year, a major conflict will arise on the issue of who will be in power in that island from then onward."

The President charged that, "morally, the Netherlands Government is responsible" for bloody outbreaks this year against Jakarta's rule.

August 18, 1950

Dutch Turn Down Indonesia's Proposal For Control Over Western New Guinea

Special to THE NEW YORK TIMES.

THE HAGUE, the Netherlands, Dec. 8—The Netherlands flatly rejected today an Indonesian demand for sovereignty over Western New Guinea.

A note to this effect was handed to the Indonesian delegation in reply to its proposal yesterday that the territory be transferred to the Indonesian flag within six months, subject to the working out of agreements to safeguard Dutch interests.

As a result of the Dutch reply, the Indonesian delegation asked that the conference on the status of the territory be recessed until Monday, while it asked Jakarta for instructions.

Indonesian leaders expressed the belief tonight that their delegation would be ordered home. It has booked plane passage for Tuesday.

As reasons for refusing to give up their rule, the Dutch cited their responsibilities to the people of New Guinea and to the United Nations, and referred to the tense international situation.

The document said that the Netherlands intended to maintain sovereignty until the New Guinea natives had been brought to such a stage of development that they could make their own choice. It denied that the Netherlands had colonial designs on the area.

Dutch Foreign Minister Dirk U. Stikker was said by Indonesian sources to have expressed fear that Australia would take over all of New Guinea rather than allow Indonesia a foothold. He was represented as having given his personal view that with the prospect that the Far Eastern hostilities might turn into a naval campaign, the United States might prefer to see the status quo maintained in an area where it had bases during the second World War.

When a version of Dr. Stikker's remarks was published in the Dutch press this morning, the United States Embassy said it was "greatly surprised," in view of the "well-known" American standpoint, that the New Guinea question should be decided through bilateral negotiations without outside intervention.

December 9, 1950

Indonesia to Nationalize Banks and Big Estates

By The United Press.

JAKATA, Indonesia, Monday, May 28—The new Government of Premier Sukiman Wirjosandjojo announced a broad Socialist program today, including nationalization of important enterprises, banks and large estates, many of which are foreign owned.

In its first policy statement, presented to Parliament this morning, the Government also announced that the main planks of its foreign policy would be neutrality in the West-East "cold war," the reconsideration of existing relations with the Netherlands, and the continued claim to sovereignty over Dutch New Guinea.

May 28, 1951

DUTCH WIN FRIENDS IN INDONESIAN ROLE

Many Still in Important Posts in Government and Hold Control of Economy

By TILLMAN DURDIN

Special to THE NEW YORK TIMES.

JAKARTA, Indonesia, Nov. 13—Despite their disagreement over the control of West New Guinea and a number of other matters, everyday working relations between the Netherlands and Indonesia and the nationals of the two countries have improved considerably since Indonesia gained her independence from the Netherlands twenty-two months ago.

Roughly 100,000 Dutchmen and their families continue to live in Indonesia, approximately the population of pre-war days. There has been a big exodus of the Dutch, but newcomers have largely replaced those who have departed.

The Dutch in Indonesia are engaged in business or work for the Indonesian Government. With the passage of time, their existence has become steadily more normal, their contacts with Indonesians increasingly relaxed.

Most Dutchmen here realize there is no turning the clock back and that the Netherlands would gain the most by helping the new state and promoting Dutch-Indonesian friendship and collaboration.

The Dutch stake in Indonesia remains enormous. The pre-war Dutch investments and property in Indonesia had a value of several billion dollars. The East Indies were estimated to have contributed 15 per cent of the Netherland's national income.

The Dutch suffered heavy property losses during the revolution. Since independence there have been some additional losses, but the big proportion of Dutch interests and enterprises still exist. The Dutch still have the paramount position in Indonesian economy.

Dutch Produce Most Exports

The Dutch estates still produce most of Indonesia's exports of rubber, coffee, tea, chinchona and sisal. The Dutch have nearly a one-third interest in Indonesia's rich tin mines and still dominate in the fields of banking and importing and exporting. A Dutch firm still has a monopoly of Indonesian coastwise and inter-island shipping. They also hold a half interest in Indonesia's domestic air transport monopoly.

A large proportion of Indonesia's exports go through Dutch hands and figure in Dutch payments operations in Europe.

There were 16,000 Dutch officials in Indonesia in the pre-war days. There are now 6,000 Dutch in the Indonesian Government in advisory capacities.

A Dutch military mission of nearly 1,000 officers and men is engaged in helping train and organize the new Indonesian army, air force and navy.

Dutch business men are not putting new capital into Indonesia. Many feel that Indonesia plans to reduce the present Dutch economic holdings and take over themselves in one way or another. The Dutch utilities, for example, are due for nationalization. Indonesia has already ordered ships that will be used, at the start, in limiting, if not eliminating, the paramount position of the Dutch in domestic shipping.

Dutch leaders here, however, feel that, barring a serious outbreak of anti-Dutch feeling in connection with New Guinea or some other issue, the Dutch will always retain considerable participation in Indonesian life.

November 14, 1951

LEFT NATIONALIST INDONESIA PREMIER

Wilopo of P. N. I. Heads New Multi-Party Cabinet After 5-Week Crisis Over U. S. Aid

JAKARTA, Indonesia, April 1 (AP)—A new Indonesian Premier was proclaimed tonight, ending a five-week crisis brought on by the previous regime's dispute over acceptance of United States aid under the Mutual Security Administration program. The new Premier is Dr. Wilopo, a nationalist P. N. I. leader of leftist leanings.

President Sukarno announced the new Government headed by Dr. Wilopo, who served as Economics Minister in the previous Cabinet of Premier Suekiman. For the present, at least, Dr. Wilopo is to be his own Foreign Minister.

It was Dr. Suekiman's Foreign Minister, Achmad Subarjo, who touched off the crisis when he agreed in an exchange of letters with United States Ambassador H. Merle Cochrane to accept United States aid. His action brought heavy fire from most members of Parliament, who believed this strategic island nation should retain its position as an independent in East-West quarrels.

Dr. Suekiman quit Feb. 23.

The new Government's platform differs little from its predecessor's. It stands for continuation of an "independent" foreign policy, insistence upon winning West New Guinea from the Dutch and pro-United States aid agreement.

The Moslem Masjumi and P. N. I.—Indonesia's two main political groups—each hold four seats in Dr. Wilopo's Cabinet. Two have been allotted to the small, well-organized Socialist party. The Defense Ministry has been given to the nonparty Sultan Hamengku Buwono of Jogjakarta. The other seats were distributed among nonpolitical and minor groups. The Cabinet is to be sworn in Thursday.

April 2, 1952

INDONESIA LIFTS SIEGE

Ten-Year-Old Emergency Decree Revoked Except for 4 Areas

Special to THE NEW YORK TIMES.

JAKARTA, Indonesia, July 30—President Sukarno issued a decree today lifting the ten-year-old state of war and siege for the whole of Indonesia. The decree said that the Presidential decision was motivated by the general overall restoration of normal law and order throughout the most of the country.

However, four regions will continue under indirect military control: Java where fanatical Islamic bands still roam the western part of the island; South Celebes, where the Government today is actively localizing a rebellion among former guerrillas who deserted the National Army; Ambon and Ceram, two East Indonesian islands where peaceful conditions are now being restored following the revolt of former Dutch-commanded troops, and the Riau archipelago near Singapore, a smuggler's lair which the Navy will continue to patrol.

July 31, 1952

INDONESIA IN AID PACT

Free Military Help Omitted From Agreement With U. S.

WASHINGTON, Jan. 12 (AP) — The United States and Indonesia concluded today a new aid agreement that omits free military assistance.

The agreement went into effect with an exchange of notes with Ambassador Merle Cochran and Foreign Minister Mukarto. It takes the place of a controverted former agreement that led to the fall of the Indonesian Cabinet last year.

Critics of the Indonesian Government assailed its routine pledge of mutual aid and cooperation, on the ground that this compromised Indonesia's neutrality policy in the East-West cold war.

The new agreement covers only economic and technical assistance, which is expected to range up to more than $5,000,000 in this fiscal year.

Altogether, the United States supplied about $5,000,000 worth of arms and military equipment to bolster Indonesian internal security. By the new agreement, the Indonesian Government agreed to pay for any military equipment it may obtain from the United States in the future.

January 13, 1953

LEFT-WING CABINET FORMS IN JAKARTA

Moslems and Socialists Are Left Out of Government Led by Envoy to U. S.

Special to THE NEW YORK TIMES.

JAKARTA, Indonesia, July 30—The formation of a predominantly Leftist Government was announced tonight by President Sukarno. Indonesia had been without a Government for fifty-eight days.

The new cabinet is headed by Dr. Ali Sastroamidjojo, now Indonesia's Ambassador in Washington, who is a moderate Nationalist party leader. For the most part, however, the remainder of the Cabinet is composed of the Nationalist party's radical wing and Marxist-minded politicians.

A formation of a Government had been assigned by the President to Dr. Wongsonegoro, Chairman of the Greater Indonesia party, a Nationalist splinter group, who becomes First Deputy Premier. He succeeded after five other political leaders had failed.

The coalition led by former Premier Wilopo fell July 3 before the combined Parliamentary pressure of the Nationalists and the Communists.

Cabinet Has Majority

The new Cabinet will command 114 of the 212 votes in Parliament plus about 25 more from the Communists and their various fronts.

Significantly, the Cabinet conspicuously omits Indonesia's dominant anti-Communist Moslem party, which has been the target for a series of Nationalist and Communist-front demonstrations during the past month. The Moslem party has been accused of being a cloak for Darul Islam, a Moslem terrorist organization that is seeking to establish an Islamic state.

This is the first time since the transfer of sovereignty from the Dutch in 1949, that the Cabinet has no Moslem members.

Also conspicuously absent from the new Cabinet is former Premier Sutan Sjahrir's Socialist party, which also has been under months-long Nationalist and Communist-front attacks from alleged implication in the affair of Oct. 17 when the Army bluffed a coup in a public demand for the dissolution of Parliament and speedy elections.

Reds Regain Influence

Today's action swings the pendulum in favor of the Communists after their earlier severe setback during the crisis when other Nationalist party leaders failed to put together a Cabinet.

July 31, 1953

TIES OF INDONESIA TO DUTCH SEVERED

Pacts to End Union Signed— West New Guinea Still an Unsolved Problem

Special to The New York Times.

THE HAGUE, the Netherlands, Aug. 10—Indonesia and the Netherlands, after more than four years of uneasy partnership, signed agreements tonight to dissolve their union.

Foreign Minister Sunarjo of Indonesia and Co-Foreign Minister Joseph M. A. H. Luns of the Netherlands signed a protocol and letters establishing a new basis for what both sides hopefully termed friendly relations.

These instruments remove the last vestiges of Indonesia's 1949 agreement to recognize the Netherlands' crown as the head of a union. In reality, what began as a partnership of "free will, equality and complete independence" never developed into more than a hollow vessel on which Indonesia drummed this steady complaint: sovereignty was not consistent with union.

In final speeches marking the successful conclusion of their six-week conference, the two foreign ministers referred bluntly to the surviving major dispute between the two nations. Both nations claim sovereignty over West New Guinea, but while the Netherlands has effective possession over the primitive territory, Indonesia points to the 1949 agreement providing that the future of the land be settled by negotiation within a year.

Dr. Luns noted that his Government had informed Indonesia last April that the status of New Guinea could not be discussed "in the negotiations concerning the Netherlands-Indonesian relations, because there exists on this point a difference of opinion that cannot be bridged."

Dr. Sunarjo replied by calling the Dutch action "one-sided."

Of the complex of bilateral agreements reached when Indonesia won her sovereignty in 1949, those concerning cultural, political and military cooperation were scrapped today.

The Dutch had been most anxious about maintaining the essential provisions in the 1949 financial agreement, and succeeded in doing so.

Both countries agreed to cancel a clause that provides for consultation and cooperation in economic and financial matters, except for a vital part dealing with the transfers of funds from Indonesia to the Netherlands.

Dr. Luns expressed the hope that two subjects treated outside the framework of the conference—"the treatment of the Dutchmen retained in Indonesia and the problem of the Amboinese temporarily residing in this country"—were headed toward a settlement. Dr. Sunarjo echoed his colleague's optimism.

[The Amboinese problem is that of returning to their homeland on the Island of Amboinesia thousands of soldiers and their families who received sanctuary in the Netherlands after revolting against the Indonesian Government. Before Indonesian independence they had fought with the Dutch.]

August 11, 1954

MALAYA: FEDERATION AND FREEDOM

Oct. 11, 1945

Britain plans to fuse the Malay States and the Straits Settlements into a "Malayan Union" and constitute Singapore as an entirely separate colony.

Malaya Union Planned by Britain; Singapore to Be a Separate Colony

Promise of the New Status Is Reply to Nationalist Demands —Better Reward for Workers Pledged by Colonial Office

By Wireless to THE NEW YORK TIMES.

LONDON, Oct. 10—A new constitutional status for British Malaya that will create a Malayan Union consisting of the Straits Settlements and the Malay States is planned by the British Government. This was announced in the House of Commons today by George Hall, Colonial Secretary, and it is clearly intended to be Britain's answer to the nationalist aspirations that are causing much ferment in that part of the world.

Singapore, in view of its special military and economic situation, will be constituted as a separate colony.

A new Malayan citizenship will be established, said Mr. Hall, for those born in the Malayan Union or those who acquire citizenship by long residence.

"However, the British character and British citizenship attaching to all the present settlements will not be affected by the constitutional measures we have in mind," he went on. "The people of the settlements of Penang and Malacca will lose none of their rights as British citizens and it is as British settlements with their own appropriate institutions of local government no less than those in the States that Penang and Malacca will form part of the Malayan Union."

It will be necessary to make fresh agreements with the sultans of the various Federated Malay States and unfederated Malay States, Mr. Hall continued, "which will enable His Majesty to possess and exercise full jurisdiction" and after that is done "it is intended by Order in Council to constitute the Malayan Union."

"No one must rely upon past privilege or regard Malaya simply as a source of material wealth," he concluded, "and, while it is to the advantage of all the world and not only Malaya that the production of her mineral and agricultural resources should be restored and developed by industry and research, it is right that the Malayan people should be assured of their full share in the rewards of their industry."

October 11, 1945

'Chartered Company' Rule Is Ended in North Borneo

By Wireless to THE NEW YORK TIMES.

SINGAPORE, July 15—British North Borneo said good-by to its old government under the Chartered Company today when it was formally proclaimed a crown colony in a ceremony at Jesselton. Malcolm MacDonald, Governor General of British Territories in Southeast Asia, was present.

Labuan Island also entered a new chapter in its history, becoming a part of the colony of North Borneo. Labuan began as a separate colony with its own governor, in Victorian times, and was part of the Straits Settlements before the war.

George Hall, Colonial Secretary, noted in a message that the British North Borneo Company was the last of the great chartered corporations entrusted not only with the economic development of vast colonial territories but with the political government of vast colonial territories. He said that the company had played the same romantic pioneering part as had the East India Company and the Hudson's Bay Company.

July 16, 1946

UNREST IN MALAYA A THORN TO BRITISH

Civil Regime, Unable in First Year to Return to Normal, Plans New Measures

By ROBERT TRUMBULL
Special to THE NEW YORK TIMES.

SINGAPORE, April 3—Lawlessness, political disaffection and economic dislocation are the legacies of war in Malaya. The British Government, which this week marked the first anniversary of the resumption of civil administration, has had little success in restoring conditions to normal.

It is widely believed that the Communists are responsible in large measure for the long-drawn-out wave of strikes in vital services and industries that have hampered rehabilitation. The entire Malay Peninsula is beset by labor unrest, which often is accompanied by violence. Inflated prices and low wages are partly to blame.

Colonial Secretary P. A. B. McKerron in his report this week referred obliquely to "certain anti-social and subversive elements whose interest is that unrest and lack of confidence should continue to prevail." He declared the Government in the coming year would take action on this problem.

Significantly, the Government recently affirmed its intention to enforce the pre-war "Banishment Act," by which alien undesirables can be expelled from Malaya. Thus far the expulsion penalty has not been applied.

In Kuala Lumpur, capital of the Malayan Union, a court this week fined the leader of a Malayan youth organization for showing pamphlets advocating revolution by force to attain the aims of the Malay nationalists.

The Malays have not been making a great deal of noise politically since the Government offered its proposed constitution for the Malayan Federation that is to replace the present Malayan Union established at the end of the war. There is vocal opposition to the movement, which attacks the constitutional proposals as prejudicial to the legitimate aspirations of the Malay people, but the most vociferous protests come from Chinese business men.

The Chinese charge that the new constitution gives insufficient representation on legislative bodies to the Chinese, who form the largest single racial segment in Malay's 5,000,000 population. They desire that the entire question be re-examined by a royal commission.

Numerous powerful groups are opposed to the proposed separation of Singapore island, which alone of the present political subdivisions in Malaya would remain a crown colony outside the Malayan Federation.

Organized banditry, kidnapping and extortion are rife throughout Malaya. The Singapore Government is recruiting extra police to reduce waterfront pilfering, which has amounted to millions of dollars. Householders must hire night watchmen to guard their homes and chauffeurs to watch their cars.

The cost of living, which reportedly is second highest in Asia —after Shanghai—appears to be beyond the Government's ability to remedy.

April 4, 1947

MALAY SULTANS SIGN PACTS OF FEDERATION

KUALA LUMPUR, Malay States, Jan. 21 (P)—The rulers of nine Malayan States signed pacts with Britain today marking the creation of the Federation of Malaya for the almost 5,000,000 residents of the peninsula. Only the Crown Colony of Singapore remains under British rule outside the Federation.

Sir Edward Gent, Governor and Commander in Chief of the Malayan Union, will issue an Order in Council on Feb. 1 to put the Federation on a going basis. After that date Britain will waive jurisdiction over everything in the 50,000 square miles of Malaya except foreign affairs, defense and appeals to the Privy Council.

Under the new set-up Sir Edward will become High Commissioner and a British Resident Commissioner in each state will have only advisory powers.

The rulers who affixed their signatures were the Sultans of Kelantan, Kedah, Pahang, Selangor, Perak, Trengganu, the Rajah of Perlis and His Highness the Yang Di-Pertuan Besar, the ruling chief of Negri Sembilan.

Later a special plane flew to Johore at the extreme south of the Malay Peninsula to obtain the signature of the Sultan of Johore, whose illness prevented him from attending the ceremony.

The chief representative body of the Federation will be a seventy-five-member Assembly. Each state will also have its own Legislature.

January 22, 1948

Malaya Declares Emergency

SINGAPORE, June 18 (P)—A state of emergency was declared throughout Malaya today in an effort to halt a wave of terrorism allegedly caused by Communists.

The emergency proclamation was made by Sir Edward Gent, High Commissioner for Malaya. It affects all nine states of the Malay federation.

The police received broad powers under the decree, and were authorized to recruit British army officers in Malaya whose terms have expired. [On Wednesday it was announced in London that Sir Edward had proclaimed preventive measures in the areas then affected.]

Four murders during the past twenty-four hours brought to twenty-four the total number of persons killed since the trouble began seven weeks ago. Two cases of arson were reported since yesterday.

One of the latest killings was that of Chong Fee Nam, who was shot to death last night at his home on the Dublin estate owned by the Malayan Rubber Company,

a subsidiary of United States Rubber.

In Johore a gang raided the Yong Peng Union rubber estate, burning four rubber smokehouses, the European manager's bungalow, and outbuildings. A Chinese foreman was shot to death at Senai.

In Kelanttan state four Malays were reported to have murdered a Moslem priest.

Several houses were burned on the Kiapa Bali rubber estate in Perak.

States of emergency already had been declared in Perak and Johore

where violence had reached a peak.

Maj. Gen. D. A. L. Wade, General Officer Commanding the Malaya District, went to Perak to visit trouble spots.

Thus far in the disturbances five British subjects have been killed.

Reservists in the Malay Regiment are being called up to help the police. One official said the reservists were being put into service in Perak state, where three Europeans were killed on Wednesday.

June 19, 1948

BRITISH OPEN DRIVE ON REDS IN MALAYA

Army, Navy, Air Force Thrown Into Assault to Foil What Is Called Plot to Seize Power

By The Associated Press.

SINGAPORE, July 7—Britain has thrown Army, Navy and Air Force units into a military campaign to smash a Communist attempt to seize power in Malaya.

Malcolm MacDonald, Commissioner General for the United Kingdom in Southeast Asia, made this announcement tonight in a speech prepared for broadcast throughout Malaya.

"The present terrorist outbreak in the Federation, which may at any time spread to Singapore, is part of a deliberate plan by Malayan Communists to stage a violent revolution and capture the Government by force," he said.

Mr. MacDonald said that captured documents and grilling of prisoners verified this "sober statement of fact."

[In London, The United Press reported, Colonial Undersecretary David Rees-Williams told the House of Commons that the situation in Malaya was slightly better. He listed fifty-two murders, twenty-seven attempted murders, eleven cases of arson and thirty-one robberies with assault or intimidation during May and June. Mr. Rees-Williams said that 221 persons were arrested and seven were shot dead "in the course of operations." He dodged a direct question whether he would send military reinforcements to Malaya.]

An RAF spokesman at Kuala Lumpur said that dive-bombing Spitfires fired rockets late Tuesday into a suspected Communist guerrilla camp in Northern Perak State. Ground troops later found the jungle camp abandoned. The occupants left signs of a hasty flight.

Communist guerrillas attacked a small Javanese settlement near Kuala Kansar, in northwest Malaya, killing three Javanese. Yen Long, a Chinese rubber estate owner, was murdered in Jahore, apparently by a Communist gunman. A Malayan regiment soldier killed a suspect in Selangor State when the man tried to run during a raid.

The terrorist campaign started nine weeks ago. Dispatches from north Malaya said that terrorists killed five more Chinese yesterday.

Mr. MacDonald said that British and Gurkha troops, with the police, had launched a military campaign in Johore, Perak and Pahang states.

"It has not yet had time to develop full power," he said.

Whole Peninsula Scouted

RAF planes are scouting the whole Malayan mainland and eastern seaboard hunting Communist guerrilla hideouts. Royal Navy ships are patrolling the coasts to prevent gun running and reinforcements, which might come from Chinese Communists in Siam or South China.

The Commissioner said that the 9,500 police on duty in the Malayan Federation would be increased by about 3,000. Another 300 will be added to the 2,700 on duty in Singapore.

British Army forces in action or preparing to strike include some of the most famous regiments such as

79

the Royal Artillery, the King's Own Yorkshire Light Infantry, the Devon Regiment, the Seaforth Highlanders, the Gurkhas' Malay Regiment and the Royal Air Force Regiment of Malaya.

Some few reinforcements have been requested. Generally the Government believes that sufficient forces are on the spot to rout the Communists. Mr. MacDonald said that London had indicated that requests for more troops would be met swiftly.

Mr. MacDonald said that additional forces would be raised inside Malaya. These will be volunteers knowing the wild terrain and able to meet the guerrilla Reds on equal terms as jungle fighters.

Mr. MacDonald indicated indirectly that the Malaya-Siam border would be closed during operations, saying:

"Success will require among other things effective closing of the land frontier against clandestine insurgent reinforcements." The only land frontier Malaya has is with Siam.

The Commissioner listed three groups of Communists. One group is made up of small killer gangs instructed to kill European planters, anti-Communist Chinese and friendly Asian laborers. Their purpose is to disrupt tin and rubber production and frighten large numbers of workers from their jobs.

Strike From Jungle Hideouts

A second group is the large guerrilla bands striking from jungle hideouts. The third group is Communist "agitators who are the real directors of the present terror."

Mr. MacDonald made no estimate of the number of Communist guerrillas. Informed Singapore sources have estimated that at least 5,000 are in the jungle bands and that another 1,000 are in the killer groups.

Mr. MacDonald said thousands of guards would be posted on rubber plantations and tin mines to protect workers. He said that 3,000 to 4,000 Gurkha troops would relieve Malayan police in the cities and that the police, more familiar with the jungles, would go to the estates. Other British and Gurkha troops will strike offensively.

Planters and miners will be armed. Special constabulary forces will be sworn in. Mr. MacDonald said that under the emergency powers, more than 1,000 suspects had been arrested, "throwing out of gear" the enemy plans.

He said that future trials of terrorists would be held secretly and that the results would not be published. The reason is to prevent terrorists from murdering witnesses. He said that trials would be speeded so that only days would elapse between a terrorist's "capture to the time of his death." He pledged that emergency powers would not be misused and would be revoked when the stress ended.

"There will be no security in Malaya until the Communists are smashed," Mr. MacDonald said. He declared that Britain would continue the campaign until the Reds were routed.

July 8, 1948

BRITAIN IS WARNED ON LOSS OF MALAYA

Opposition Demands Priority in 'War' on Guerrillas— Reinforcements Pledged

Special to The New York Times.

LONDON, April 6—Britain was warned in the House of Commons today that the most serious consequences would ensue from loss of the "war against the Communist-led guerrilla bands in Malaya."

"I beg the Government," said Col. Oliver Stanley, one of the principal Opposition leaders, "to regard this whole question of Malaya as priority number one, not only in foreign and defense policy but in our economic policy, because all will come crashing to the ground if we lose this war in Malaya."

Alluding to the fact that Malaya, with her rubber and tin, is the sterling area's chief dollar earner, Capt. L. D. Gammans, a Conservative party expert on colonial affairs and a former colonial official, declared that it was not much good talking about closing the sterling area's dollar gap if Malaya were lost.

The concern expressed in the House of Lords yesterday that nearly 100,000 troops and police had been unable to suppress 3,000 Chinese and Malayan bandits, was echoed in the House of Commons debate.

Captain Gammans asserted that the present type of military and police action had failed and that in the "anti-bandit month," just held, seventy-seven members of the security forces had been killed as against thirty-eight bandits.

"Is there any wonder, now that the Communist regime in Peking [Peiping] is recognized [by the British Government] that the Chinese in Malaya look over their shoulders and wonder who is going to control Malaya in a few years?" Captain Gammans asked.

The Colonial Secretary, James Griffiths, acknowledged that the situation in Malaya was serious and that bandit attacks recently had increased. He said that plans for continuation beyond the "anti-bandit month" were being put into operation. These plans included the development of an auxiliary police force to relieve the regular forces for operational duty, reinforcement of the army units in Malaya by 2,000 Gurkhas from Hong Kong and the dispatch of additional aircraft, including heavy bomber squadrons from Britain.

Since the beginning of the campaign in June, 1948, the Colonial Secretary said, a total of 2,148 bandits had been killed or captured or had surrendered, against 1,280 police, soldiers and civilians killed.

Besides conducting military operations against the Communists, Mr. Griffiths said that the British "must show there is a better way" than communism by meeting "reasonable demands" for a better standard of life.

Colonel Stanley said, however, that it was a farce to pretend that the standard of life could be raised overnight. He and others demanded more vigorous action against the bandits.

April 7, 1950

CHINESE HELD KEY IN MALAYA REVOLT

They Are Not Participating Extensively in Campaign Against Guerrillas

By TILLMAN DURDIN
Special to The New York Times.

KUALA LUMPUR, Malaya, April 17—In the fight against the Communist revolt in Malaya, the biggest factor in the situation is that the Communist question is the Chinese question.

The insurgents themselves are nearly all Chinese, and their activity largely depends on the amount of voluntary or involuntary support they can obtain from the Malayan Chinese. The Chinese constitute nearly half the population of the federation of Malaya, and the colony in Singapore dominates most of the local business activity.

The 2,500,000 Moslem Malays who make up the other large racial group are almost unanimously anti-Communist. Among the Communist rebels there are only scattering Malays. Fifty-eight thousand Malays are among the police force of 72,000 men combating the Communists, compared to 3,400 Chinese.

The great majority of the Malayan Chinese are opposed in principle to the Communist uprising. Many Chinese leaders and the main Chinese organizations are on record in support of the Government's campaign of suppression. Most Malayan Chinese here enjoy a better livelihood and more freedom than they would have in China, and the Chinese community as a whole has no serious grievances that are not on the way to being rectified by peaceful evolutionary measures. The grievances that do exist are not generally associated with the Communist program.

However, the fact remains that the Chinese are not participating extensively in the anti-guerrilla campaign. One reason for this is the traditional Chinese indifference to Government and civic responsibility, and the attitude accentuated in Malaya by the fact that the Chinese until recently have taken little part in the administration of the country.

Another reason is the fear among many Chinese that communism after all may win in all Southeast Asia. There is a widespread disposition to sit on the fence and avoid trouble with the terrorists at this stage for Communist terrorism is a daily menace to tens of thousands Malayan Chinese.

Chinese cooperation is vital to the Red guerrillas. Among the Chinese rural squatter villages of laborers and gardeners, the rebels can conceal themselves to get food and recruits. From Chinese merchants and rubber planters they can get supplies of money.

Failure to cooperate with the guerrillas means death for several Chinese somewhere in Malaya almost every day. Whole families have been slaughtered in reprisal for members aiding the Government or refusing to help the bandits.

Far more Chinese have been killed in the Malayan struggle than persons of any other national origin. Emergency regulations provide severe penalties for anyone giving money or otherwise assisting the insurgents, but in the circumstances the sheer fear of reprisals impels many Chinese to serve the Communists. Few Chinese are armed, but the Government has been unable to extend its security net widely enough to guard Chinese individuals and communities from guerrilla attacks and pressures.

The authorities are trying to increase the protection for the Chinese and thus persuade them to resist the terrorists more resolutely. Steps are also being taken to enlist a larger number in the police and other anti-guerrilla groups. Upon the success of such measures the outcome of the Malayan struggle will largely depend.

April 18, 1950

FEAR GRIPS MALAYA UNDER RED TERROR

Rubber Estates Are Virtual Fortresses — Guerrillas' Tactics Baffle British

Special to THE NEW YORK TIMES.

SINGAPORE, Nov. 14—Malaya, producer of half the world's rubber, most of which goes to the United States, is today a land of fear.

Although the planters are receiving the highest prices in history for their raw rubber, this is possible only under virtual siege conditions.

Thousands of well-armed Communists—the Malayan People's Liberation Army, they call themselves—are based deep in the jungles, from which they are waging a hit-and-run war that has baffled a British army numbering in the tens of thousands, supported by squadrons of heavy bombers, rocket-firing Spitfires and a rigid coastal patrol.

Every rubber estate is a virtual fortress. The planter's bungalow is ringed with barbed wire, trenches and machine-gun posts, and floodlighted throughout the night. Squads of armed guards maintain a twenty-four-hour patrol. The planter himself never leaves his house without a pistol strapped to his hip and perhaps a submachine gun in the crook of his arm.

Passenger cars are sheeted with bullet-proof steel, and a housewife driving to the nearest town to shop and market takes with her a car full of guards bristling with guns and grenades.

Even so, more than sixty British planters have already been killed by the Communists who ambush roads and pathways, snipe at estate buildings and often attack in force overwhelming fortifications and guards to burn and kill and disappear back into the surrounding jungle.

Officially, there are no Communists in Malaya. Contemptuous reference is made only to "bandits" or "terrorists"—despite the fact that they wear distinctive uniforms and distribute unmistakable Communist propaganda.

Yet, after two and a half years of large-scale military operations, frustrated authorities acknowledge that "banditry" in Malaya is still a long way from being liquidated.

An average of three Communists are killed, captured or wounded daily. For this, the cost of military operations alone is more than 300,-000 Singapore dollars ($100,000 U. S.) a day.

Organization of Army

The organization of the Malayan People's Liberation Army closely resembles its Chinese counterpart in earlier days. It includes:

1. A well-armed force of regulars forming a hard core of highly trained fighting men whose principal purpose is to prepare themselves for a hoped-for general uprising or a Communist invasion from the north.
2. A civilian underground auxiliary known as the Armed Labor Group whose job it is to feed and supply the troops, transmit intelligence and render military aid when required.
3. Hit-and-run guerrillas operating in small units who keep the pot boiling with road ambushes, arson, sniping and train derailments.

While the regular troops are estimated at no more than about 5,000, the Armed Labor Group, guerrillas and passive sympathizers number more than 500,000.

The regulars are based deep in the jungle. They are organized in regiments of approximately 1,000 men, each with a semi-autonomous district and a headquarters of its own. In an emergency, when pressed too hard by the British forces, the regiment will split into companies of 150 men, or platoons of forty to sixty.

The regulars are ably led. They are armed with the very latest weapons — mostly British — and train constantly. For practical experience, each unit is expected to carry out at least one military operation a month.

Members of the Armed Labor Group are difficult to identify. Their ranks are filled with farmers, shopkeepers, artisans and laborers, all apparently peaceful citizens with identity cards.

The principal duties of the Armed Labor Group are to collect funds and food—forcibly, if necessary—for the regular troops and to provide a courier service.

Will-o-the-Wisp Tactics

The guerrillas engage in general will-o-the-wisp harassment to dissipate the British forces and treasure. A pair of them will rake a passing train with machine-gun fire. A road bridge is blown up in the night. A police post is grenaded. An interurban bus is stopped, the passengers are relieved of their identity cards and the bus itself is set on fire.

Directing all this is the Central Executive Committee of the Malayan Communist party.

Communist propaganda today insists that the policies and actions of the Malayan People's Liberation Army are guided solely by democratic principles. An interesting definition of these "democratic principles" was revealed in a recently captured document on the subject of "democratic discipline." In one passage, it is carefully explained why leaders and working committees must often be appointed from above instead of elected by the membership of a political or military group. The election system had been fairly tried, it alleges.

"But many comrades do not fully understand the significance of the voting system," the document says. "Too often unsuitable persons are entrusted with leadership. Consequently, such elections cannot be approved and must be ignored inasmuch as our comrades have wrongly used the democratic right. Voting must be carried out correctly, or else there is no democracy."

November 25, 1950

MALAYA RESETTLES 290,000 SQUATTERS

Relocation Is Part of Program to Cut Off Supply Sources for Red Jungle Bandits

By HENRY R. LIEBERMAN
Special to THE NEW YORK TIMES.

KUALA LUMPUR, Malaya, Aug. 18—More than 290,000 squatters, who formerly occupied scattered huts and worked isolated agricultural plots throughout the Malayan countryside, have been resettled by British authorities here in a systematic attempt to cut off the sources of supply, support and recruitment of the Communist-led guerrillas.

About 160,000 remain to be resettled under the "Briggs plan," which calls for concentrating squatters in compact settlements that can be guarded more easily by the Malayan police. There are 280 settlements — some representing new "towns" of as many as 17,000 residents, with barbed-wire fences surrounding shopping areas as well as the transplanted huts.

Thus far the Malayan Government, which derives most of its income from export taxes on rubber and tin, has spent about 60,-000,000 Straits dollars (20,000,000 United States dollars) on the resettlement program. Additional welfare funds have been provided by the Malayan Chinese Association, organized in September, 1949, to "promote racial harmony, maintain law and order and promote the interests of the Chinese."

Most Squatters Are Chinese

Like the guerrillas of the Communist-led Malayan Races Liberation Army, most of the resettled squatters are Chinese. During the Japanese war thousands of Chinese living in towns moved into rural areas, setting up shacks in jungle clearings, on old mining lands and in pockets adjacent to communication lines.

Although some eventually obtained "temporary occupation licenses" British officials say the squatters have no legal claim to land they occupy. Little was done about them, however, until after the Malayan Communists returned to the jungle in 1948 and launched their present armed insurrection.

Resettlement on a large scale did not begin in fact until last summer following the arrival here of Lieut. Gen. Sir Harold Briggs (retired) as civilian director of "bandit suppression" operations. Outlining objectives of resettlement program Sir Harold said in an interview:

"All these 450,000 squatters were beyond the realm of administration and were dominated by the bandits. They were compelled to provide food and money and even recruits. They were exposed to Communist propaganda.

"The Communists organized the Min Yuen [people's movement] cells among them and they went around threatening people telling lorry companies, for example, that their lorries would be burned if they did not pay or drop off food. As we could not take the administration to the people, we had to bring the people to the administration."

Not all the Chinese Reds are being relocated in the resettlement communities. What the British call the "bad eggs" are taken to detention camps and divided into three categories: "whites," "blacks" and "grays" with the blacks being deported to China at the first opportunity.

Since 1948, 11,000—including dependents—have been deported by ship and about 8,000 now are under detention here. A deportation ship leaves for Canton once every two weeks.

Besides concerning itself with the resettlement of the squatters as an immediate security problem, the "Briggs plan" also envisages using the resettlement camps as bases for social development.

Many of the resettled squatters have received new land. Each community elects its own village committee and raises its own "home guard." Moreover, in laying out new camp sites the Survey Office makes provisions for the building of new roads, sewage systems and schools.

When this correspondent recently visited the wire-enclosed resettlement area at Kulai in Johore State, the relocated squatters were electing their own health, education, sanitation and security officers by secret ballot.

The residents there were free to come and go through the gate until 6 P. M. when a "road curfew" went into effect. Behind the wire, the residents had to be in their huts by 9:30 P. M.

Once a squatter gets notice to move, a truck provided by the local resettlement office transports his family and their dismantled hut into the resettlement area. Family members draw a small allowance while setting up their house on the new plot they themselves have leveled.

There is considerable grumbling when a squatter family is uprooted but the grumbling seems to wane once the family gets settled.

Despite rigid food control measures, British officials concede that some food is still being smuggled out to the guerrillas from the settlement areas. They maintain, however, that the resettlement program has hurt the guerrillas considerably by reducing their food supply and at the same time making the Chinese squatters more willing to provide information because they have a feeling of greater security.

August 19, 1951

British Chief in Malaya Slain; Draws Red Fire, Saves Wife

High Commissioner Gurney Walks Toward Assassins as They Fight Escort

By The United Press.

SINGAPORE, Oct. 6—Sir Henry Gurney, British High Commissioner for Malaya, walked to his death in a Communist ambush today, sacrificing himself to save his wife's life.

Communist-led machine gunners attacked the three-car convoy, in which the 53-year-old High Commissioner and Lady Gurney were traveling as it was rounding a tricky S-curve on the Bentong highway, sixty miles north of the Malayan capital at Kuala Lumpur.

Sir Henry's Malayan driver was killed by the first volley, and two tires on his official Rolls-Royce were punctured by bullets, forcing it to stop.

The High Commissioner, already wounded, pushed his wife to the floor of the limousine and stepped down from the car. He staggered away down the road, deliberately drawing fire away from the car, until he fell dead.

The Communist bandits lurked near the scene for twenty minutes, dueling with members of Sir Henry's police escort and shooting at anything else that moved, but Lady Gurney escaped injury. D. J. Staples, Sir Henry's private secretary, and a number of the escorting police were wounded.

Michael Hogan, Acting High Commissioner, and Mohammed Rashid, a 23-year-old Malayan policeman wounded in the ambush, told the heroic story of Sir Henry's last moments in a radio broadcast

Sir Henry Gurney
Associated Press

tonight. Mr. Rashid's account was relayed from a bed in the Kuala Lumpur general hospital, where he was being treated for bullet wounds in both legs.

He said that police reinforcements who arrived on the scene about twenty minutes after the start of the attack found Lady Gurney still lying on the floor of the official limousine. She was the only person in the car who had not been hit in the brief skirmish.

Sir Henry's body lay face down in the grass at the roadside, some distance from the car. Mr. Rashid told how the High Commissioner had stepped out of the Rolls-Royce and walked away, defying the hail of bullets until he fell.

The Gurneys, escorted by a police radio car and an armed truck, were on the way from Kuala Lumpur to the Government resort at Fraser's Hill for the week-end.

The Malaya radio said the ambush occurred shortly after 1 P.M. just outside Kuala Kubu Bahru in northeastern Selangor State, a few miles from the turn-off for Fraser's Hill.

Security police and British troops of the West Kent Regiment fanned out into the near-by hills to seek the assassins, but tonight they had found no traces of the fleeing bandits.

Lady Gurney remained with her husband's body, leaving the scene only when an army truck arrived to carry his remains to Kuala Kubu Bahru. Funeral services will be held in Kuala Lumpur at 10 A. M. Monday.

Malcolm Macdonald, British Commissioner General for Southeast Asia, canceled a scheduled tour of North Borneo when he heard of the killing. He is expected to arrive here tomorrow.

Lady Gurney received cabled condolences from King George VI, and Queen Elizabeth, Prime Minister Attlee, Colonial Secretary James Griffiths and Sir Franklin Gimson, Governor of Singapore.

It was the second attempt in recent years to kill Sir Henry. He was in Jerusalem's King David Hotel when it was dynamited by Zionist terrorists in 1946, but escaped uninjured.

It also was the second time since World War II that a high British official had been assassinated in Southeast Asia. Governor Duncan Stewart of Sarawak was shot dead by Malay fanatics in 1949.

Sir Henry was a veteran of thirty years' service in the British Colonial Office. He went to work for the government agency in Africa's Kenya Colony in 1921, after having served the army during World War I, and held increasingly important posts in Jamaica, East and West Africa and Palestine over the years.

Instituted Draconian Laws

SINGAPORE, Oct. 6 (AP)—Sir Henry Gurney was an initiator of many Draconian measures to reach his goal of stamping out terrorism by the end of 1951. His death was preceded by twenty-four hours by the announcement of a plan to starve out Communist bands.

Lieutenant Gen. Sir Harold R. Briggs, director of military operations, explained "Operation Starvation" in a film shown in all Singapore theatres.

The plan calls for rigid control of all sales of rice, tinned foods, medicines and clothing, movement of all trucks by prescribed routes and a close check of their cargoes to prevent supplies from being smuggled or dropped off to the Communists.

British forces have lost 318 killed and 465 wounded since the jungle war emergency was proclaimed June 1, 1948. Altogether 2,812 civilians, police and soldiers have been killed by the Reds in that time, 2,363 wounded and 896 listed as missing.

The Communists are reckoned to have lost 2,376 in killed, 1,129 wounded, 823 captured and 593 surrendered.

But the hard core of guerrillas, mostly Chinese, is still estimated at between 3,000 and 5,000—about the same as a year ago. The Communists have had no difficulty making up their losses with new recruits and conscripts.

Sir Henry came here Oct. 6, 1948, after the end of the mandate ended his job in Palestine in May. He began a vigorous effort to stamp out terrorism.

Thousands of squatters were rounded up from the jungle fringe and settled in barbed wire-encircled settlements to deprive the Communists of support. Some villages were ordered razed as a measure of collective punishment for cooperating with the Communists.

Sir Henry was educated at Winchester and Oxford and saw service in the first World War.

One of Sir Henry's last public acts was to escort Governor Thomas E. Dewey to Kuala Lumpur last July for a first hand inspection of conditions under which rubber growers are carrying on from behind barricaded plantations.

October 7, 1951

New Labor Party Formed in Malaya As Political Tempo Is Stepped Up

Multiracial Group, 2d Organization Created Within Week, Aims at Independence and Democratic Control of Resources

By TILLMAN DURDIN
Special to The New York Times.

SINGAPORE, June 27—An All-Malayan Labor party, the second new political party to be created in Malaya within a week, came into being yesterday in the Federation capital of Kuala Lumpur.

The party announced its intention to work for Malayan independence and social justice "through cooperative ownership and democratic control of the economic resources of the community."

Its formation followed an announcement last week-end that the powerful Malayan Chinese Association, which hitherto had operated mainly as a welfare organization would transform itself into a full-fledged political body and would contest elections both in Singapore and the Federation of Malaya. Sir Cheng Lock-tan, association leader, stands for Malayan independence, but within the British Commonwealth as a dominion.

The new party decided against a proposal that it designate dominion status as the aim for Malaya. It adopted the view that Malayans should decide, after having gained independence, whether they wished to stay in the Commonwealth.

Indian Among Delegates

A multiracial group with delegations from Singapore, Selangor, Perak and Penang, and including Chinese, Indians, Malayans and Ceylonese, organized the new Labor party. Mohammed Sopiee, a Malay, was elected chairman. Singapore's delegation included Peter M. Williams, an Indian, who was jailed by the Singapore police last week for having advocated peace with, and legal recognition of, the Malayan Communist party if the party agreed to operate on a legal basis. He was released after he had pledged to cease advocating such a procedure and had disavowed his sympathy for communism.

The Labor party platform includes opposition to conscription for a defense force, favoring instead recruitment on a voluntary basis. The Federation Government is now applying compulsory measures in creating armed forces to fight the Communist rebellion.

A resolution approved by the new party favored liberalization of citizenship laws in the Federation. It urged that Chinese and other immigrants, who had either been born in Malaya or had lived in the area for ten years, could become citizens. Another resolution advocated the right to land ownership for all who tilled the soil.

Limited Scope for Test

The Labor party, as other Malayan parties, will have only a limited scope for testing its popularity at the polls. The separate colony of Singapore votes for the party elected colonial legislature and city council.

In the Federation of Malaya, no state or national elections are held but the beginning of a system of popular government has been made with elections at local levels. State and federal elections are envisioned for some indefinite future date.

The new party is the fourth of importance to have been formed on a Malaya-wide basis. Paralleling the Chinese Association is a party called the United Malay National Organization. In addition, there is the Independence for Malaya party, which has aimed at bringing Malayans and Chinese together on an independence program, but which has not gained wide support.

With the formation of the Labor group, Malaya will experience a revival of the political labor movement, once dominted by the Communist party. Legal labor activity in both the trade union and political fields was dissipated when the Communists went into revolt in 1948. But it has been slowly rebuilt on a non-Communist basis with official British encouragement and guidance.

Meanwhile, controversy continues over turning the Chinese Association into a political party, with opponents condemning the move as likely to promote communal rivalries. Dato Onn Bin Jafar, leader of the Independence for Malaya party, which Sir Cheng helped to promote, has denounced the changed status of the association.

Sir Cheng has answered critics by declaring that the association, while guarding the interests of the Chinese, will not oppose the welfare of other racial groups. He has said that his group may back non-Chinese candidates in electoral campaigns and will cooperate with other racial communities.

June 28, 1952

BRITISH NOW COURT CHINESE IN MALAYA

They Constitute Almost Half of Population and Are Seen as Key to Communist Issue

By TILLMAN DURDIN
Special to THE NEW YORK TIMES.

KUALA LUMPUR, Malaya, July 22—British policy is giving increasing attention to the welfare and the aspirations of Chinese inhabitants of the Federation of Malaya. The new attitude is a departure from the traditional approach which put the emphasis on safeguarding the rights and interests of the indigenous Malay population.

The new policy is a reflection of the importance of position the Chinese have come to occupy in the scheme of things in Malaya. It underlines recognition of the fact that the Chinese have become a large and permanent element in the population and play a vital role in the Malayan struggle against Communism.

Chinese inhabitants of the Federation of Malaya exceed 2,000,000 compared with 2,600,000 Malays and 600,000 Indians and Pakistanis. A generation ago most of the Chinese in Malaya had not been born here but had come from China as immigrants. A large proportion still regarded China as home and planned eventually to return there.

Today the situation is different. Two-thirds of the present day Chinese inhabitants of the Federation were born in the area. Because they were born in Malaya or have lived here for a long time and because of Communist rule in China a vast majority of Federation Chinese now look upon Malaya as their permanent home and are developing the attachment of citizens or potential citizens.

Most Important Group in Malaya

Through their industriousness as businessmen, laborers and artisans, the Chinese have become economically the most important racial group in the Federation.

The Communists of Malaya are for the most part Chinese. Chinese also are some of the most effective anti-Communists in the Federation. Despite wide participation in the anti-Communist struggle of the Moslem Malays and other communities of Malaya, it has become evident defeat of the Communists will require the cooperation of a large proportion of the Chinese population.

Thus, the new British policy represents an effort to give the Chinese a bigger share in the political and official affairs of the Federation, improve Chinese educational opportunities and promote the economic security of the poorer Chinese in rural areas who have been one of the main supports of Communist rebel activities. The aim of the new policy is to win the Chinese away from the appeal of the Communists by increasing the sta e, the responsibilities and the opportunities of the Chinese in non-Communist Malaya.

The Malay States are in the process of passing new laws which will give the right to full citizenship for most of the Chinese in the Federation who, heretofore, have not had such a right. More Chinese are being taken into career positions with the Federation Government.

State grants to Chinese schools have lately been doubled. Long term occupation rights to rural lands at a nominal cost is being given Chinese villagers resettled in the recent wholesale shifting of rural inhabitants to remove them from contact with the Communist guerillas.

A regular military force is being formed for the Federation in which the Chinese will for the first time be able to participate. The British police and civil officials in the Federation now are being required to learn Chinese dialects in addition to the Malay which formerly was the only native language most of them had to know.

Meanwhile, the Malays are watching the new policy with some concern.

July 23, 1952

Malay Red Chiefs Flee to Indonesia

By Reuters.

KUALA LUMPUR, Malaya, Feb. 8—British security forces chalked up a major victory today in their six-year war against the Malayan Communist terrorists. They disclosed that the Malayan Communist party's high command had fled the country.

The party headquarters has moved to the Indonesian island of Sumatra, an official source said tonight. Direction of the estimated 6,000 jungle terrorists operating in Malaya probably will be carried on from across the Strait of Malacca. Sumatra's chain of coastal islands is within fourteen miles of Malaya at the closest point, so liaison could be conducted by boat.

The British source said the transfer had been preceded by the dispatch of Communist cadres to attempt the establishment of an "Indonesian front" similar to the organization tried but never successfully developed in Malaya and neighboring Thailand. In Indonesia, the Communists may be able to benefit by the presence of a Chinese Communist Embassy.

Intensified operations by the British security forces here have put the terrorists increasingly on the run and hampered the distribution of propaganda tracts.

Security headquarters revealed yesterday that Communist casualty and surrender figures for January were the highest in sixteen months. Ninety-nine terrorists were killed, five were captured and thirty-nine surrendered.

Heavier pressure also has been put on the terrorists by recent cooperation between Malay and Thai units along the northern border of the Malay Federation. Following the flight of many terrorists into Thailand, that country established a state of emergency in its southern provinces and opened the border for units from Malaya pursuing the Communists. Last week it was reported that a special Thai police unit had been dispatched to the area to operate jointly with a large force of Malayan policemen.

Traffic between the rubber plantations and tin mines, which are the foundation of the Malayan economy, has been made comparatively safe by the latest security operations. Nevertheless, a recent flare-up of Communist attacks claimed a number of British, Chinese and Malayan victims.

February 9, 1954

SINGAPORE STAYS RICH ON COMMERCE

SINGAPORE, Aug. 7 (AP)—The thriving city of Singapore seems to be getting more prosperous all the time and it is wide open to foreign investors.

That applies, too, to the Federation of Malaya.

Both the Malayan Federal Government and that of this British Crown Colony make it easy for foreign businesses to establish and operate here.

There is no nationalization of any industry or business. There are no choking restrictions against aliens or big taxes to pay.

Foreign businesses operate on the same basis as the British in this colony, or Malayan or others in the Federation of Malaya. All businesses must register and pay a nominal licensing tax. Outside of that, they are permitted to export reasonable amounts of profit and have to pay tax only on income.

That tax can be called reasonable, when compared with high levies in Britain or the United States. The rate of tax chargeable on the income of companies is 30 per cent.

Income Tax Exemptions

Individuals, unmarried, have an income tax exemption of Malayan $3,000 (United States $1,000) annually. A married man has an exemption of $5,000, with added exemptions for children.

As in many countries of Southeast Asia, it is the Chinese who control the lifelines of commerce in Singapore and much of the Federation of Malaya. With nothing to worry about except income tax, their businesses seem to mushroom overnight.

The more than 800,000 Chinese out of Singapore's population of more than 1,000,000 are probably.

over-all, the richest to be found anywhere in Asia.

There is no discrimination against any aliens coming to establish businesses in Singapore and Malaya, so long as none of them can be regarded as "security risks." For Malaya still is fighting a war against Communist terrorists.

Thus, any Communist Chinese or Russian might find it difficult to get a permit to enter Singapore or Malaya to establish a business.

Remittances to Red China

Chinese doing business here are

permitted to send monthly remittances to relatives in Red China. These totaled $12,549,348 Malayan in the federation alone in 1953.

British, French, United States citizens, Dutch, Chinese, Indians and Scandinavians are the leading investors in Singapore and Malaya.

Because of the liberal tax policy of the Singapore and Malayan Governments, hardly a week passes without notice of some new European or United States company or agency opening a business.

Rubber and tin still play the

top role in the economy of Singapore and Malaya, even though prices for both have tumbled sharply within the last three years.

Rubber, in mid-February, 1951, when the United States still was a heavy buyer, hit a record price of $2.38 Malayan a pound. Tin shot up to $784 Malayan a picul, or one-sixteenth of a ton. Now rubber sells around 70 cents a pound and tin around $380 Malayan a picul.

But, even with the United States imports of rubber and tin sharply reduced, just about everybody in the rubber and tin

business seems to be doing well.

Hundreds of new homes, apartment buildings, new clubs, swimming pools, recreation centers, and the increasing stream of new United States-made automobiles on the streets of Singapore all attest to one thing: prosperity.

August 8, 1954

LEFT WING SCORES IN SINGAPORE VOTE

Two of Its Factions Gain Edge Over Conservatives Under New Constitution

---

Special to The New York Times.

SINGAPORE, Sunday, April 3 —Two left-wing parties gained a slight lead over the conservative factions in the elections held under Singapore's new constitution yesterday. For the first time the voters selected a majority of the members of a legislative assembly.

The Labor Front, with ten seats, emerged as the biggest party in the new Assembly of thirty-two members, twenty-five of whom were elected yesterday and seven of whom will be named by the Governor. The People's Action party, a far-left group, won three seats and one independent left-oriented candidate won his contest.

The most striking result of the elections was the defeat of the Progressive party, a conservative

group that has held a majority of the elected seats in Singapore's legislatures since 1947. The Progressives won only four seats in the new Assembly.

Another recently formed business party, the Democrats, split the conservative vote and gained three seats. A Malay-Chinese Alliance party won three seats and independents gained three.

A Surprising Success

The Labor Front's success was a surprise and something of a shock to British leaders here who had hoped the moderate Progressives would take over the reins of government under a Constitution that for the first time provides for a Cabinet responsible to a legislature with an elected majority.

The Labor Front is pledged to seek, among other leftist projects, repeal of the Emergency Regulations under which the colony has fought Communist subversion for the last seven years. There is no certainty, however, that the Labor Front will be able to form a Cabinet.

Lee Kuan Yew, youthful attorney and head of the People's Action party, said last night that his group would refuse to participate in a coalition with the Labor Front.

This will force the Labor

Front to seek allies among the other parties, all of whom are conservative and would be likely to refuse cooperation. There is a possibility, however, that the Alliance party and one or more independents might be willing to join in a Cabinet with the Labor Front.

Under the new Constitution a Cabinet of nine will govern Singapore and have full authority except in the fields of foreign affairs and finance, which remain in British hands. The Governor retains veto powers for use if a critical matter arises.

The Governor will name three Cabinet members, the Financial Secretary, the Chief Secretary and the Attorney General, but these ministers must vote with the Government. Ministers from elected Assemblymen will head the Departments of Education, Health, Communications, Lands and Housing, Commerce and Industry and Labor and Social Welfare.

Chance of New Election

If the Labor Front fails to form a Cabinet new elections will have to be held. The Front leader, the only white man to win a seat in the Assembly, is a 39-year-old Briton named David Marshall who is destined to

be Singapore's first Chief Minister if his party succeeds in organizing a government.

Yesterday's voting went off without trouble. The Communist-inspired students called off planned demonstrations when the police plainly showed they were prepared to use force to break them up.

A majority of the 300,000 voters and most of the seventy-nine candidates were Chinese in a territory where Chinese make up 80 per cent of the inhabitants.

For the first time in Singapore elections the voters were registered automatically and this ruling enfranchised more than 200,000 new Chinese voters as contrasted with only 75,000, mostly middle-class individuals who voted in previous elections. The defeat of the conservative parties is laid to this development.

Indians, Malays, Ceylonese, Britons and Eurasians in this colorful multiracial island colony trooped to the polls. Several Indians and two Malays were elected.

April 3, 1955

MALAYA ALLIANCE ELECTION VICTOR

Coalition Party of Malays Chinese and Indians Wins First National Poll

---

By TILLMAN DURDIN
Special to The New York Times.

KUALA LUMPUR, Malaya, Thursday, July 28—The Alliance party won yesterday the first national elections ever held in the Federation of Malaya.

Returns up to 7 o'clock this morning gave the Alliance, a coalition of Malays, Chinese and Indians, victories in thirty-two out of thirty-three constituencies that had reported by that time.

It seemed likely the Alliance would gain all but a few of the fifty-two seats that have been allotted for elected members in the ninety-eight-member Federal Legislative Council. In most cases Alliance victories were by big majorities and in some constituencies Opposition candidates polled so few votes that deposits were forfeited.

The chief rival party, the Negara (Country) party, made a poor showing almost everywhere.

Sir Onn Bin Ja'afar, 60-year-old Malay leader and head of the Negara party, lost his own district of Johore Bahru to his opponent of the Alliance, Suleiman Bin Dato Abdulrahman.

On the other hand, the Alliance chief, Tengku Abdul Rahman, won in his constituency of Sungei Muda, in the state of Kedah, by an overwhelming margin over his independent opponent, Syed Jan Aljeffri.

The only seat lost to the Alliance among the constituencies reporting results up to 7 o'clock was for the Krian district of the state of Perak. In this constituency of Moslem Malay rice farmers, Haji Ahmaj Tuan Hussain of the pan-Malayan Islamic party won. The party made its appeal primarily on the ground of the Moslem religion and Malay interests.

Leftist Party Defeated

The only Left-Wing party in the elections, the Labor party, lost all the four seats it contested.

Voting was generally quiet and orderly. Wide-scale precautions had been taken against possible attempts of Communist terrorist rebels to disrupt the voting, but no trouble was reported anywhere.

The Alliance is a cooperative grouping of the United Malay National Organization, the Ma-

layan Chinese Association and the Malayan Indian Congress. Its primary aim is political cooperation between the Malays and Chinese, the two biggest ethnic groups in Malaya.

The Negara party is chiefly a proponent of Malay interests and its candidates and agents indulged in anti-Chinese attacks during the election campaign. The Alliance victory augurs well for harmony among the ethnic groups.

The Alliance stands for independence within the British Commonwealth for the Federation of Malaya within four years and a fully elected Legislative Council before that time. Yesterday's vote was for a small majority of the seats in the council, with the remainder to be filled by appointments of the British High Commissioner.

July 28, 1955

Malayan Dominion Status Is Slated by August, 1957

The New York Times   Feb. 9, 1956
Dominion status for Malaya's federated states is nearer

By KENNETT LOVE
Special to The New York Times.

LONDON, Feb. 8—British and Malayan representatives signed an agreement today to make "every effort" toward Malayan independence within the British Commonwealth by August, 1957. The agreement provided for the transfer to Malayan ministers in the immediate future of control over internal defense and security, finance, and commerce and industry. It gave the Malayan Chief Minister a greater voice in the Government at the outset of the transitional period from colonial to independent dominion status. Terms were laid down for the appointment of a commission to begin work as soon as possible on drafting a constitution for an independent Federation of Malaya.

Recommendations were made to place Malayan commissions in full authority over government services July 1, 1957.

Implementation of the report is to begin as soon as it has been approved by the rulers of the nine princely states in the Malayan Federation and by the British Government. Such approval is said to be a formality.

The federation is composed of the princely states of Johore, Negri Sembilan, Pahang, Selangor, Perak, Kedah, Perlis, Kelantan and Trengganu, and the two British settlements of Penang and Malacca.

Singapore, which is not in the federation, will be the subject of similar talks in April, when a delegation from that crown colony will arrive in London.

Among the provisions in the Malayan agreement are that the British advisers to the princely rulers shall be withdrawn within a year and that Britain shall continue to give Malaya economic and military aid against the Communist rebels. Military matters are to be covered by a mutual defense treaty after Malaya becomes independent.

Tengku (Prince) Abdul Rahman, Chief Minister of Malaya, said the agreement "heralds the birth of a new nation." At the same time, he added, it strengthens Malaya's ties to Britain.

The Tengku, who today observed his fifty-third birthday, headed the nationalist political alliance of Malays and Malayan Chinese and Indians that won an overwhelming victory in the colony's first elections last year. As leader of the Malayan elements in the Colonial Government and the partly appointed Legislature, the Chief Minister led an eight-man delegation that began negotiating with colonial officials here Jan. 18.

He recalled that Britain's relations with Malaya began in the eighteenth century when the East India Company leased the Island of Penang from his ancestor, the Sultan of Kedah.

The Tengku renewed his vow to mobilize the entire population in what he said would be not only a "shooting war" against the Communists, but also a "psychological, political and economic war."

Answering expected criticism of his agreement to let British forces remain in Malaya, Tengku Rahman said that Malayan forces alone could not fulfill their responsibilities toward the Commonwealth and the world.

He recalled the promise made in December by the Communist leader, Chin Peng, to lay down his arms if the Tengku obtained control of internal defense and security.

"I have now obtained that measure of control," he said, "and it only remains to be seen whether the Communist terrorists will honor their words."

Alan Lennox-Boyd, Colonial Secretary, who signed the agreement with the Tengku, said it was not to be regarded as "a victory for either side." "It is a recognition of Malaya's new status and of our common interests," he added.

February 9, 1956

Singapore Signs Self-Rule Pact; Voices 'Shock' at Election Curb

By LEONARD INGALLS
Special to The New York Times.

LONDON, April 11—Terms of an agreement between Britain and Singapore granting internal self-government to the Crown Colony became known today with the signing of the document.

Singapore is to be self-governing at a date to be set Jan. 1.

When a new constitution outlined in the agreement goes into effect, the small island at the southern tip of the Malay Peninsula will be known as the state of Singapore. However, it is to remain within the British Commonwealth, and Britain is to retain strong measures of control.

Lim Yew Hock, Chief Minister of Singapore, expressed "considerable shock" tonight at a last-minute condition laid down by the British.

This was that persons known to have engaged in subversive activity must be barred from election to the new state's first legislative assembly. Britain insisted, over vigorous objections by Singapore, that there could be no new constitution unless it included this provision.

"It was a considerable shock to be told by the Colonial Secretary of the decision to disallow detainees * * * from contesting the first elections," Mr. Lim declared. He commented at the airport before leaving for home.

The Chief Minister, who is expected to become the new state's first Prime Minister, said the British demand affected about ten persons—"some of them may be Communists, some of them may be fellow-travelers."

"We can fight them, and we feel that it is wrong to bar them from contesting the election," he added.

At the signing ceremony, Mr. Lim said that, except for the new provision, the proposed constitution was "entirely satisfactory." He termed the provision "a departure from the normal democratic practice."

The proposed constitution also provides that Britain is to have two representatives of high authority in the new state.

One will be a Malayan head of state, replacing the present governor as the representative of Queen Elizabeth. The other will be a United Kingdom commissioner who, in extreme circumstances, would have the authority to assume the government of Singapore.

However, the proposed constitution represents a big step for Singapore toward control of its affairs. Negotiations toward this goal have been proceeding with intermittent constitutional improvements for the colony since the end of World War II, when Singapore was part of the Straits Settlements.

The discussions that led to the agreement signed today began last year. They were resumed four weeks ago by delegations led by Mr. Lim and by Alan Lennox-Boyd, Colonial Secretary of Britain.

Britain is to continue to have jurisdiction over Singapore's defense and external affairs.

She also will have a strong voice in the maintenance of internal security on the island. The British insisted on this because of Communist influences that had led to trouble in Singapore in recent years.

An internal security council is to be set up composed of three Singapore representatives, three British representatives and a member from the Government of the neighboring Federation of Malaya. The federation is to become a fully independent member of the British Commonwealth in August.

The United Kingdom commissioner will be council chairman.

Commenting on this provision, Mr. Lim said the agreement of the Malayan Federation to participate in the council gave hope that "the dream of a united Malaya will soon come true."

The British retain the right to suspend the constitution of Singapore if they feel that conditions have deteriorated in the new state to the extent that Britain could not carry out her responsibilities for Singapore's foreign affairs or defense.

The same would apply if Singapore contravened the constitution. It would be in these circumstances that the United Kingdom commissioner would take over the government.

In addition to the internal security council, there also is to be an intergovernmental committee headed by the United Kingdom commissioner as chairman.

This committee is to be formed because Singapore will enjoy certain rights to conduct her own cultural and trade relations with other states and these rights may overlap Britain's responsibilities for foreign relations and defense.

The new constitution provides also for an enlarged legislative assembly of fifty-one elected members. It includes safeguards for the rights of minorities, establishes citizenship requirements and voting rights and outlines Malayanization of the judiciary and civil service.

April 12, 1957

Ruler for Independent Malaya Is Elected to Serve for 5 Years

Sir Abdul Rahman Will Have the Status of Monarch— Sultan to Be Deputy

Special to The New York Times.

SINGAPORE, Aug. 3—The ruler of Negri Sembilan State, Sir Abdul Rahman, was elected today for a five-year term as the first supreme head of independent Malaya. The state will attain independence Aug. 31.

The method of appointment of the paramount ruler—in Malay the Yang di-Pertuan Agong—is unusual for modern constitutional monarchies. Sir Abdul will be designated "His Majesty."

Malaya will be the only free nation in the Commonwealth other than Britain to have its own monarch.

The Sultan of Selangor, Sir Alam Shah, was chosen as deputy to the supreme head of the state.

Sir Abdul was elected by a conference of rulers. When Malaya gains independence, he will be supreme commander of the armed forces of the federation. It will be his duty to appoint a Prime Minister, guided by the Cabinet.

He will be one of the highest paid men in Asia, receiving a privy purse equivalent to $5,000 a month tax free.

Sir Abdul, who is not related to the present Chief Minister, Tengku (Prince) Abdul Rahman, is 62 years of age. He ascended his state throne in 1933. He was called to the English bar at London's Inner Temple in 1928. Upon his return to Malaya he was appointed to some minor posts. He was a district officer in Perak state when elected Yang di-Pertuan Besar, or head chieftain, of Negri Sembilan state upon his father's death.

August 4, 1957

BURMA: INDEPENDENCE AND CIVIL WAR

British Bare Burma Terror Reign; Land, Sea Forces Fight Bandits

By SYDNEY GRUSON
By Wireless to THE NEW YORK TIMES.

LONDON, June 7 — Something akin to a state of war has broken out in Burma, with British land and naval forces in action against guerrilla bands armed with mortars and automatic rifles and apparently in control of large sections of the country.

A brief debate in the House of Commons today disclosed conditions that had been generally unknown here, but whose seriousness Arthur Henderson, Under-Secretary of State for India, did not attempt to minimize. Mr. Henderson said that "combined operations" had been launched against the armed bandits in recent months. But the situation, he added, remained "serious."

Before Mr. Henderson wound up the debate for the Government, members of the House had painted a picture of Burma torn by robbery, murder and violence, with the Government's authority operating only in and near the large towns and villages and the effects of Japanese-stirred nationalism still echoing loudly against British attempts to restore their rule.

Sir Basil Neven-Spence, Conservative, told the House that in March—excluding Rangoon—there were 246 murders, 558 robberies with attempted murder, 785 robberies and 347 cases of cattle theft.

All the speakers agreed that for the most part peasants were the victims of this violence.

As a result of the debate it was brought out that terror-stricken peasants have refused to cultivate Burma's rice fields while the country itself, and practically all of the Far East, cried out for grains.

Sir Basil questioned the Government's policy of suppressing the news of terrorism with Burma, where, he said, Government, propaganda was "conspicuous by its absence." On the other hand, he added, "tub-thumping seditionists" were building up anti-British feeling and spreading stories that the "British and Americans are fighting the Russians and that we are losing."

Laborite Tom Driberg advised the Government to hand over the administration of the country to the Burmese themselves as quickly as possible so as to kill the idea held by nationalist leaders that the present British rule was the "reinstitution on a big scale of the prewar capitalist enterprise which exploited the people of Burma."

Mr. Henderson was not overly optimistic about the chances of restoring a degree of normality quickly. He said it was hoped to establish a Burmese Ministry by the time of the elections there in April. In the meantime, he added, weapons were being made available for village defense and the "considerable use" was being made of the military forces because of the shortage of experienced police officials.

He disclosed that the Government had issued a "general warning" against "unlawful meetings and the making of seditious speeches." Apparently in reference to Mr. Driberg's advice that the Government consult with the leaders of the People's Voluntary Organization, which Mr. Driberg described as "a kind of unarmed home guard," Mr. Henderson declared:

"We will not tolerate anything in the nature of a private army. We know from experience in other countries how dangerous they are."

Demonstration in Rangoon

RANGOON, Burma, June 7 (Reuter)—A mass demonstration of 50,000 Burmese marched through Rangoon's main streets today shouting slogans such as "We want complete independence," "We don't want a Governor" and "Withdraw the occupation force."

The demonstration, which was staged by the Burmese Anti-Fascist League and led by Maj. Gen. Aung Sang, former leader of the "Patriotic Burmese Force," was in protest against what were described as the Government's "repressive measures," including a recent incident at Tanbabin, forty miles from Rangoon, where police fired on demonstrators.

Recent interviews with Sir Reginald Dorman-Smith, Governor of Burma, had yielded no result, General Aung Sang said.

June 8, 1946

ATTLEE ANNOUNCES FREE BURMA SET-UP

Parliament Gets Details of the Accord—Churchill Terms It 'Dismal Transaction'

By HERBERT L. MATTHEWS
Special to THE NEW YORK TIMES.

LONDON, Jan. 28—The settlement with the Burmese leaders, granting Burma the right to elect a Constituent Assembly and have an interim government with great powers on the way to speedy independence, was announced to Parliament today.

Winston Churchill promptly hit back in the House of Commons by calling it "this dismal transac-

tion." But the Government's majority will see this, like the similar Indian settlement, through Parliament.

The general terms of the settlement were set forth in a London dispatch to THE NEW YORK TIMES yesterday. They were agreed to by U Aung San, the most important Burmese political leader, and all but two members of the Burman delegation—Thakin Ba Sein and U Saw.

A Government command paper gives the terms of the agreement on the "methods by which the people of Burma may achieve their independence, either within or without the Commonwealth, as soon as possible."

It calls for the election of a Constituent Assembly in April. During the transition period the Executive Council will constitute an Interim Government "conducted generally in the same manner as the Interim Government of India at the present time."

Burma will have a High Commissioner in London and will ap-

point other diplomatic representatives. U Aung San told this correspondent yesterday that one of the first would be a Minister to Washington.

Inquiry Set on Hill Peoples

With regard to the frontier areas in the North, where the primitive hill people live, it was agreed that the objective is early unification, but only with the free consent of the frontier inhabitants. A committee of inquiry is to be set up to get their views.

There is a financial annex to the agreement in which the British Government agrees to make a further contribution to Burma's budgetary deficit, and, what is more important, the British interest-free loan of £80,000,000 upon which Burma is now living is going to be turned into an outright grant.

It was this that gave point to Mr. Churchill's question:

"Does this statement mean that we pay and we go, or only that we go?"

"The statement does not mean that we go," replied Prime Minister Attlee who had presented the

command paper to the House. "It means that the people of Burma have the right to decide in future whether they should stay in the commonwealth or go outside."

Mr. Churchill and Mr. Attlee went on arguing about it without convincing each other.

Meanwhile, the Burmese leaders have been preparing to leave and the scene will now shift to Rangoon where U Aung San will have to put over this agreement with the political extremists, including his own followers, who have been demanding, among other things, a British assurance of independence within a year.

The chances of Burma's being free in a year are very slim, it is conceded here. However, the British are convinced that Thakin Ba Sein, U Saw and the Communists will not be able to cause much trouble.

January 29, 1947

3 LEADERS IN BURMA SAY VOTE WAS UNFAIR

Special to THE NEW YORK TIMES.
RANGOON, Burma, April 11—Leaders of the three parties forming the Independence First Alliance, which boycotted Wednesday's elections to the Constituent Assembly, today condemned the elections as unfair.

U Saw of the Myochit party charged many had been forced to withdraw as candidates on threats from the People's Freedom League and that armed Burmans had threatened violence to any who failed to vote for the league.

Dr. Ba Maw, head of the Maha Bama party, said that in modern Burma "worship of the gun has become a fetish." He alleged that 10 to 15 per cent of the votes cast in Rangoon were fraudulent.

Thakin Ba Sein of the Dobama Asiayone said:

"You may not have seen intimidation at the polling booths but there was plenty of it. Never before in Burma has there been such a thing as an uncontested seat, but in this election there were 102."

April 12, 1947

BURMA FOR INDEPENDENCE

Votes to Be Sovereign Republic —Hopes British Go in Year

RANGOON, Burma, June 17 (AP) — The Constituent Assembly adopted unanimously today a resolution stating that Burma's constitutional set-up would be that of an independent, sovereign republic to be known as the "Union of Burma."

[A Burmese delegation headed by Thakin Nu, president of the Constituent Assembly, will leave for London, probably on Thursday, for discussions with the British Government, Reuters said it had learned.]

U Aung San, deputy chairman of the Governor's Executive Council, presented the independence resolution and concluded a two-day debate by expressing again the hope that the British would transfer powers in a cordial atmosphere.

"We must get independence within one year," he said.

June 18, 1947

KILLERS MOW DOWN PREMIER OF BURMA AND FIVE TOP AIDES

Aung San Is Slain as Assassins Spray Executive Council With Sten Gun Bullets

By HERBERT L. MATTHEWS
Special to THE NEW YORK TIMES.

LONDON, July 19—Six of the top leaders of Burma's Interim Government were assassinated and two were wounded this morning as the Executive Council was holding session in Rangoon, it was announced by the Burma Office here.

Among those killed was U Aung San, leader of the Anti-Fascist Peoples Freedom League, de facto Premier in the Interim Government and the most powerful figure in Burmese politics.

[In Seoul, Korea, Lyuh Woonheung, popular Leftist, but anti-Communist leader, was assassinated by a gunman who climbed upon the back of his car.]

The mass assassination in Rangoon was carried out by three men of a band of six. The assassins, carrying Sten guns, forced their

way into the Executive Council Chamber and sprayed it with bullets. Then they fled.

Rangoon is cut off tonight. The only communication that has reached the public was broadcast by the British Governor, Sir Hubert Rance, who denounced "this dastardly act."

The Governor announced that a new Executive Council had been formed. It will be headed by Thakin Nu, vice president of the Freedom League, President of the Constituent Assembly and right-hand man of U Aung San.

July 20, 1947

Burma Police Seize U Saw In Gun Battle, Kill Three

Former Premier and Nineteen Associates Held as Suspects in Assassination —Order Restored in Rangoon

By The Associated Press.

RANGOON, Burma, July 20—Burmese police have killed three followers of former Premier U Saw and arrested him and nineteen lieutenants in a raid in connection with the machine gun massacre of seven Burmese Council Ministers, including U Aung San, the de facto Premier, the Government announced today.

The police struck at U Saw's home last night.

A barrage of gunfire marked the arrests.

U Saw, impassive, thick-set leader of the Myochit party who was once detained by the British as a Japanese collaborator, was brought under heavy escort to the Rangoon central jail.

A curfew was imposed on the city from 7 P. M. until 5 A. M. nightly, until further notice.

Burmese newspapers said that nearly fifty persons had been arrested as an aftermath of the assassinations. Those reported held included Thakin Ba Sein, leader of the Dobama Asiayone party. [Arrests have reached a total of 178, Reuters reported.]

Ba Sein and U Saw were the only members of a six-man Burmese delegation to London who had refused to sign the British-Burma agreement on Burmese independence, on the ground that it did not go far enough.

A new Ministry was sworn swiftly into office to succeed the nine-man Executive Council, which was virtually wiped out in a spray of bullets yesterday morning, while meeting in the Government House.

Six of the Ministers died instantly or succumbed within a few hours in hospitals. A seventh, the Sawbwa of Mong Pawn, died this morning. Two attachés also were shot to death by the gang of five gunmen, who later fled unscathed in a jeep.

July 21, 1947

Burma Independence Pact Signed; Nation to End British Ties Jan. 6

By MALLORY BROWNE
Special to THE NEW YORK TIMES.

LONDON, Oct. 17—Burma will become an independent nation completely outside the British Commonwealth under the terms of a treaty signed in London today by Prime Minister Attlee and Premier Thakin Nu of Burma.

Provisions for the maintenance of close relations between Britain and Burma are contained in the agreement. The terms of the pact will be made public Oct. 24 when the British Government will submit to Parliament a Burma Independence Bill to authorize the transfers of power.

The treaty covers matters of defense and military establishments, finances, citizenship, contracts and other questions arising out of the transfer of full sovereignty to the Burmese people. The actual transfer—that is, the effective date of the treaty—is expected to be Jan. 6, 1948.

[The Burmese Cabinet at Rangoon on Thursday night set Jan. 6, 1948, for the date of the independence of the Republic of the Union of Burma, Reuters said.]

Foreign Secretary Ernest Bevin and other members of the British Cabinet were present at the ceremony of the signing at 10 Downing Street. Premier Thakin Nu was accompanied by several Burmese Government officials, including Defense Minister Bo Let Yar, Finance Minister U Tin Tut and Minister for Industry and Labor Mahn Win Maung.

Describing the occasion as "unique," Mr. Attlee emphasized that the treaty had been concluded "in anticipation of a transfer of sovereignty which has not resulted from the exercise or the threat of force."

Mr. Attlee expressed regret that Burma would cease to be a member of the British Commonwealth of Nations, but this had been a matter for the decision of the Burmese people.

Thakin Nu in a brief speech recalled that relations between Britain and Burma "were in the past not as happy as they are today." He expressed the conviction that the treaty arrangements would "form a firm and solid basis for Angle-Burmese friendship."

At a news conference later, Thakin Nu stated that his Government intended to negotiate treaties of alliance with India and Pakistan and to apply for membership in the United Nations and to study the matter of megotiations with China, the United States and the Soviet Union.

As indication of Burma's recovery, the Premier said his Government hoped to arrange a "token" shipment of 10,000 tons of rice to Britain. He estimated that this year Burma would have 1,500,000 tons of rice available for export, chiefly to India. By 1951, the surplus for export was expected to be about 3,500,000 tons, or about the per-war volume of rice exports.

October 18, 1947

BURMESE REGIME SEIZES REDS' AIDES

100 Leaders of the People's Volunteer Organization Are Arrested in Rangoon

By TILLMAN DURDIN
Special to THE NEW YORK TIMES.

RANGOON, Burma, Aug. 1—The difficulties of Premier Thakin Nu's Socialist Government have been accentuated by an open breach with the People's Volunteer Organization. More than 100 PVO leaders have been arrested in Rangoon in the last three days.

The Government said the arrests were made after it had become evident that PVO members were leaving cities to join the Communist rebellion in a wide area of Lower Burma.

The PVO is a modified successor of the guerrilla forces of the Anti-Fascist People's Freedom League. Under the leadership of the late Gen. Aung San the guerrillas cooperated with the Allies when the League turned against the Japanese in 1944 to help win the war in Burma.

Since the end of the war repeated attempts have been made to get the PVO disarmed. Some arms have been turned in, but many PVO members still have guns.

The Communists' guerrilla warfare is disrupting communications in several key areas. Some observers believe the Government will gain by moving against the PVO because the lines of conflict between the pro-Communist and the anti-Communist groups have been more sharply drawn.

The coalition Thakin Nu Government, backed by what remains of the People's Freedom League, says it follows the teachings of Marx and Lenin.

The Communists were in the League but broke away over differences regarding the independence treaty with Britain, the foreign policy and tactics in enforcing Socialist measures.

Premier Thakin Nu favors bringing socialism through gradual constitutional processes; the Communists seek immediate revolution and control of the Government. The present Government wishes to remain on good terms with Britain and the United States while having friendly relations with Russia. The Communists want to swing Burma completely into the Soviet bloc.

The cabinet, going ahead with nationalization, has taken over several big British concerns with promises of compensation later. A land reform program calls for the reduction of land rents and the allotment of plots to tenants. The reform is expected to result in the redistribution of farm land.

Some observers expect a political settlement with the Communists because they cannot be eradicated by the Burmese Government's forces. The rebellion started last spring, after the Communist Southeast Asia Conference at Calcutta.

August 2, 1948

REVOLT CONFIRMED IN BURMESE HILLS

RANGOON, Burma, Aug. 26 (Æ) —Sama Duwa Sinwa Nawng, Minister for the Kachins, today confirmed reports that an insurrection had broken out in the Kerenni Hill tracts, seventy miles northeast of Toungoo. In a letter to Sao Shwe Thaik, Burma Union President, he said: "The Karenni people are trying to wrest power from the Burma Union Government by armed force."

Previous reports said rebels had attacked the Mawchi mines in the Karenni Hill tracts yesterday and had captured a mine official. Three Burmese newspapers reported today that martial law had been declared in Karenni. The War Office here did not deny the reports but said it was awaiting confirmation from the Karenni states.

There was little rebel activity during the last twenty-four hours, according to today's communiqué, which mentioned only one major incident.

The incident occurred in Kalaukchaik, across the Hlaing River from Rangoon, as rebels attacked a police station, where they obtained fifteen guns. Traveling upstream in sampans towed by motor launches, the rebels encountered home guards and suffered ten casualties. Troops also were sent to Monyo, west of the Irrawaddy River, where the town reportedly was threatened by a rebel band.

August 27, 1948

BURMA FEUDS HELD HEADACHE OF WEST

Natives Are Little Concerned With Internal Turmoil, but World Requires Output

TRADE PICTURE SHOCKING

Dominant View Is Marxist, but Communist Organizers Are Said Not to Exceed 50

By ROBERT TRUMBULL
By Air Mail to THE NEW YORK TIMES

RANGOON, Burma, Jan. 5—Out of the utter confusion that is Burma after one year of independence, one impression comes clearly: none of the continual fusing and fissioning of Burma's amorphous politics, her economic prostration, her four-pronged civil war, or the tide of communism is primarily Burma's headache.

These matters concern the West, which wants to stop communism, and needs Burma's natural riches, especially her rice for hungry Asia.

Assassination and strife bother the Burmese little, for these have been customary, even traditional, in their history. Communism is not a bogey in a country where, to quote not one but several observers of different nationalities, "a British Socialist would be regarded as an extreme Right Winger."

The average Burmese, well-fed and with food to spare in his un-der-populated country, needs no oil, tin, lead or zinc, or not so much as the industrial West needs it. As for gold, he plasters that in slabs a quarter of an inch thick all over the 339-foot spire of the 2,500-year-old Shwe Dagon Pagoda in Rangoon, the Mecca of Buddhism, where it will stay as long as Buddhism survives.

When rice is low, unrest is high in Asia. Burma before the war produced 40 per cent of the world's export rice, and is back to 75 or 80 per cent of that figure now. This is rice the Burmese do not need; the West needs it, to keep the crowded, hungry other Asians content.

A brief visit to Burma and a number of interviews lead one to suspect that this is the basis of Burma's astonishing ego, her resentment of foreign prying, her desire to be let alone to sort out her own problems in her own way while her incredibly youthful leadership gains maturity.

The Burmese feels that there will come a settling-down after the growing pains, and that then his country will make important contributions besides rice to the well-being of the world.

Prevailing Philosophy Marxism

The prevailing philosophy is Marxism, often of a naïve and sophomoric kind. Highly qualified observers admit, unanimously, that Burma is fertile ground for Communist expansion. But it is the studied opinion of valued sources that "there are not more than fifty real Communist organizers in Burma, and they control only a few districts."

A link is said to exist between Burmese Communists and the party in India, and therefore, perhaps tenuously, with Moscow. The southward sweep of Communism in China is viewed with concern by Western diplomats, and contact may exist in that direction now. There are no known Moscow-trained Communists in Burma.

As to the situation at the moment, the Government says that the Communist risings in Burma are "all but suppressed." Others, with a less interested point of view, say that the Communists are powerful still in central and lower Burma.

Everyone says that all politicians of Burma are more or less Communist, and radically so. However, in the fantastic mushrooming of dissidents since Burma became independent, there have come out two Communist groups: the White Flags, who favor change by constitutional means and compensation to vested interests whose properties are nationalized; and the Red Flags, described as extreme terrorists, anxious for immediate social overturn.

Aside from abhorrence of violent methods, the Government's main difference with both Communist parties—as explained by an official Government spokesman—is that the Government wants friendly relations with all other powers, while the various Communists are for alignment with the Soviet bloc alone.

Burma has somewhat the internal make-up of India, on a much lesser scale. The main groupings, linguistically and racially, are the Burmese, Karens (famous in the West for their "long-necked women" of the sideshows), the Shans (racially the same as Siamese), the Kachins of the north and the hill-dwelling Chins.

Numerous Petty States

Like India, Burma has the complicating factor of numerous petty royal states within the Union, ruled by chiefs known as Sawbwas. Some Sawbwas have joined the Government.

Besides the Communists, in their two forms, there are divisions and sub-divisions of parties, some of whom shoot at each other. And often it is hard to separate these activities from the operations of the dacoits, Burma's notorious robber caste. The Red Flag Communists, too, often blend with bandits in the Arakan area.

In Arakan there is a group that agitates for an autonomous state. Adding to the complexity are the Arakan Moslems who want to join adjacent East Pakistan.

The complications cited—except the Communists—are rather secondary now to the Karen problem. These people are a militant race, much favored by the British in the armed forces, and predominantly Christians of United States Baptist persuasion. They ask independence for their State of Karenni, plus certain other Karen territories.

The Burmese suspect the Karens of enlisting foreign support, partly because they are Christianized, because they were with the British from the beginning in World War II, and because politically they want American and British advisers to help develop their country. They are more conservative in politics than other groups.

The commercial picture, which is the practical reason for Western concern with this new country, is shocking.

Before the war Burma produced all her own petroleum requirements and 52 per cent of India's needs (but she imported fuel oil from Iraq because the Burmese product was too rich in valuable exportable paraffin to be burned). A single mine, the Mawchi, was the world's largest single producer of tungsten and the third largest in tin. Another mine, the Bawdwin, was first in both silver and lead and it also produced zinc.

Burmese output in all these fields is negligible today, mostly because of the internal unrest and partly because uncertainty about the Government's nationalization policy restricts development of the immense foreign-owned properties, such as the mines mentioned and the Burma Oil Company (British).

January 14, 1949

BURMA'S CIVIL WAR FACES STALEMATE

By HENRY R. LIEBERMAN
Special to THE NEW YORK TIMES

RANGOON, Burma, July 24—A strategic stalemate now prevails in the complicated civil war that has ravaged Burma from the birth of her independence, Jan. 4, 1948.

Premier Thakin Nu's National government holds the main towns and lines of communication, but multiple insurgent groups and dacoits (bandits) are still disrupting transportation and raising havoc in many rural areas.

The mining of tracks, ambushing of trains and looting of freight cars are frequent incidents on Burma's war damaged railways. Notwithstanding an improvement in inland waterway communications, river boats traveling in convoy are subject to snipers' fire both in the Irrawaddy delta and territory to the north.

Under the present circumstances the insurgents, however divided, are not regarded as strong enough on their own to constitute an immediate military threat to the government. Such disappointment as is registered by western observers here seems to be based primarily on their view that the Government is making less progress in restoring law and order than it made a year ago.

One influential Burman is of the opinion that this attitude is too pessimistic. "Previous Government successes caused the insurgents to split up into small guerrilla bands," he said. "It is obviously more difficult to eliminate these bands than it was to deal with the main bodies of insurgents in earlier clashes."

Thakin Nu's young government is the offshoot of a coalition of the Anti-Fascist People's Freedom League established by the late General Aung San toward the close of the Japanese war. When the

89

war ended this coalition included Communists, Socialists and the armed People's Volunteer Organization (P. V. O.) But the Communists subsequently broke away and attracted some members of the Volunteer Organization to their side.

What remained of the anti-Fascist league showed surprising staying power in dealing with a sequence of disasters between the spring of 1948 and the fall of 1949: The Communists' insurrection in March, 1948, a separate Karen revolt, mutinies among Karen elements in the national army and strikes by government workers in Rangoon were some of the disturbances.

As various insurgent groups seized a number of major cities and some territory around Rangoon, it appeared for a time as if the capital itself might fall. During the dry season, from October, 1949, to June, 1950, the government recovered the lost cities and reopened most main lines of communication.

This campaign led to some improvement in the general economic situation.

Between 15,000 and 20,000 insurgents of various hues are now warring on the government, it is estimated. Almost as many dacoits supplement them in freebooting, nonpolitical banditry. Among insurgent groups operating here are:

1. The Burma Communist party or White Flag Communists headed by Thakin Than Tun, who was First Secretary General of the Anti-Fascist People's Freedom League. This pro-Stalinist group, which has received the propaganda approval of the Chinese Communists, disposes between 5,000 and 10,000 troops.

2. The Communist party, Burma, or Red Flag Communists headed by the ultra-radical Thakin Soe who split with Thakin Than Tun in 1946. This group, usually represented as "Trotskyist," has an estimated strength of only a few hundred.

3. The Karen National Defense Organization which has been pushing demands for a separate Karen state larger than the government feels it is in a position to grant. At one time this Karen organization provided the main military threat to the government, but suffered serious reverses in the government counter-offensive that led to the death of its leader, Saw Ba U Gyi, in August, 1950. Present strength of this group is estimated about 5,000.

4. White Band members of the People's Volunteer Organization, representing a part of the group established by Aung San to encompass anti-Japanese guerrillas. Their present strength is estimated at about 2,000.

With the decline of the Karen revolt, the White Flag Communists have come to the fore as the molder of a People's Democratic Front that is seeking to unite the feuding insurgent factions into a single revolutionary movement.

July 25, 1951

Karens in Burma Defy Government And Continue War With Chinese Aid

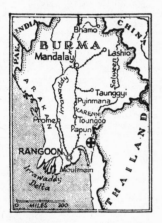

The New York Times Jan. 17, 1953

BURMA HEADACHE: The Karen rebellion continues. Its forces, with headquarters at Papun (cross), still control several hundred miles of territory along the Thai border, and claim a greater area.

Refugee Nationalist Army Is Reported Helping Rebels With Advice and Arms

By TILLMAN DURDIN
Special to THE NEW YORK TIMES.

RANGOON, Burma, Jan. 14—The Karen rebellion continues to be a major headache for the Burmese Government. Some progress, both politically and militarily, has been made during the past year in suppressing the Karen insurrectionists but diehard elements among them continue their resistance and seem determined to fight on indefinitely.

The rebel Karen forces still control stretches of territory extending several hundred miles along the rugged, malaria-ridden border of Thailand and maintain a loose fluctuating domination over numerous pockets in the rice-growing Irrawaddy delta.

Many insurgent Karens have surrendered to Government troops, or simply ceased fighting, during 1952, but it is estimated several thousand—some sources say between 5,000 and 10,000—armed Karens still are in revolt.

The Karens are a racial minority that has sought an autonomous state within a union of Burma. They ask a much greater area for their state than the Burmese Government has been willing to concede.

Karen resistance to the Burmese Government has been strengthened lately by the development of co-operation with Chinese Nationalist troops in Burma. The Nationalists, who retreated from Communist China in 1950, have been in East Burma ever since. During the past year they have been collaborating with the Karens, giving military advice and training some Karen officers in their base area in Kengtung.

It is widely believed here that the Nationalists also have supplied arms to the Karens.

The Nationalists, among other things, appear to be seeking food and trafficking in opium and other products across the Thai border.

The Government has a liberal policy for Karens who surrender. Their insurgency usually is forgiven and they even are permitted to keep their guns if these are needed to protect their villages from attacks by Karens still in revolt.

January 17, 1953

THE PHILIPPINES: AN AMERICAN SHOWCASE

ARMED FILIPINOS A THREAT TO ORDER

Many Guerrillas Who Fought Japanese Now Turn Hate Against Estate Owners

By Wireless to THE NEW YORK TIMES.

MANILA, Oct. 29 — Informed estimates of the number of men illegally retaining arms furnished to them as guerrillas in the Philippines run as high as 200,000. The guerrillas are distributed in large and small bands throughout the provinces of the extensive archipelago. The potential threat to law and order is obvious, not only in the figures but in the concern that the Philippine Government is now showing.

The secreting of arms—a pastime to which rural Filipinos have always been partial—became an organized business in the dark days after the fall of Bataan and Corregidor, when escaped American and Filipino soldiers formed the guerrilla section of the United States Army Forces in the Far East.

At the same time, there were thousands of "irregular guerrillas" who obtained weapons in various ways, often stealing them from the Japanese. And there were the Hukbalahaps, which now constitute a vast organization of mystery and dread.

A Hukbalahap — usually abbreviated to "the Huks," is a contraction of Hukbo Bayan Sa Lahap Sa Hapon, which, translated literally, means "Army of the People for Fighting Japan."

Fight the Japanese, they did, but, with the end of the war, the Huks are said by many here to be a ready-made army of unrest. Tales filter into Manila from the provinces of Communist-led Huk raids on the great haciendas in Pancho Villa style.

That there is an active Communist party in the Philippines is not doubted, and many say that the Huks are the militant wing of the party. They are said to stand for the break-up of the widespread system of tenant farming through which the economic concepts inherited from the Spanish dons have been kept alive and thriving in the Commonwealth.

In this connection, there also are rumors of strong Falangist cells existing among the Spanish element—that is, Spaniards whose roots are in Spain rather than in the Philippines. Many of these men are said to be planning to return to Spain when passage is available. According to the anti-Falangists here, it is certain that no Spanish Republicans are eager to go to Generalissimo Franco's country.

Manila newspapers occasionally publish stories—usually brought from the provinces by traveling Filipino officials or business men—that indicate some unrest exists. Apparently, some of these indications have reached the White House.

All Philippine public issues, from collaborationism to agrarian reform, appear to be clouded by contradictions and confused by self-seekers. It is almost impossible for an observer to obtain the truth in any reasonable time because almost everyone that one talks to intimates that everyone but the speaker is a liar.

The nearest thing to a general opinion, however, is this: The Philippines today are a powder keg. The Hukbalahaps and other "unrecognized guerrillas" roam the land with rifles on their shoulders and ideas for Government reform in their heads and with hatred of the landed aristocracy in their hearts.

Thus far, agrarian dissatisfaction has taken the form of mere isolated banditry. The danger is inherent, especially where the Hukbalapas are concerned. The power of this already immense organization—centrally governed and with tentacles throughout the Commonwealth—is greatly feared. Considering the present economic circumstances of the country, it is not difficult to conceive of casual highwaymen and ranch raiders becoming revolutionaries.

October 30, 1945

INVESTMENT BY U. S. IS INVITED BY ROXAS

Capital Welcome and Needed in Philippines, He Says, to Avert 'Economic Vacuum'

By WALTER H. WAGGONER
Special to THE NEW YORK TIMES.

WASHINGTON, May 11—Manuel A. Roxas, President-elect of the Philippines, today extended a hearty invitation for American investment in the Philippines' postwar economy. He contended that if United States capital did not "rush into this economic vacuum," other investors would fill the need and possibly involve his Government in uncomfortable relations with other countries.

Sketching briefly the nature of the Philippines' desperate economic situation as a result of war and Japanese occupation, Mr. Roxas told a news conference, in response to a question, that he would "welcome American capital." He borrowed from Paul V. McNutt, American High Commissioner in the Philippines, the term "Economic Vacuum" to describe the plight of the country and warned that "unless American capital rushes in to fill that space, other capital will be drawn in and perhaps involve us unfortunately with other countries."

Appearing with Mr. McNutt at the joint conference, Mr. Roxas appealed for the loan now being considered for the Philippines Republic. The money is necessary, he said, not only to help the Government meet current essential expenditures, but also to speed the liquidation of war damage claims.

He predicted that the country would need financial aid probably for another five years. Revenues are "very small," he went on, approximating about 40,000,000 pesos compared with expenditures for purely governmental activities of about 269,000,000 pesos. The Philippines faces a deficit at the end of the year of about $100,000,000 which will not be reduced until the Islands are able to rebuild their productive capacity, he explained.

The President-elect also praised the United States for its Philippines trade program, which, he observed, contrasts with the nation's general trade policy.

"Indeed we are grateful for the wisdom and generosity you have shown in providing trade relations which are, as President Truman said, alien to the over-all international trade policy of the United States. You have provided preferential trade relations with the Philippines, although elsewhere in the world you are trying to break down the system of trade preference," stated Mr. Roxas.

"We recognize, and recognize clearly, that your Congress approved such a formula precisely because it was the only feasible formula for the earliest possible revival of a skeleton economy in the Philippines, whereas today we have virtually no productive economy, except for local consumption."

Danger of Contradiction

He said that his Government had realized, too, that Congress took this action in spite of the danger that "some might point out the anomaly of your seeking to eliminate trade preference as a world system while you, yourself, established trade preference with the Philippines."

The United States, only "substantial and permanent" market for the Philippines' coconut products, sugar, cigars and tobacco, provides also, Mr. Roxas stressed, the only "economic sustenance" for the national existence of the islands.

"On the other hand," he continued, "the Philippines are a prime market for your products, too. As a matter of fact, your exports to the Philippines will far exceed in value Philippine exports to the United States for a good number of years. We hope, and I think you hope, too, that this trend will be arrested and reversed."

Mr. McNutt declared that his only interest in his assignment as High Commissioner, which will end when the Philippines attains its independence, was to see "a free, democratic, liberal and prosperous Philippines, a perpetual monument to American pioneering and American policy in the Orient."

May 12, 1946

Philippine Republic Is Born As U. S. Rule Ends in Glory

Roxas, Lowering American Flag, Promises Continued Unity—MacArthur Acclaims Filipino Struggle—Truman Pledges Aid

By H. FORD WILKINS
By Wireless to THE NEW YORK TIMES.

MANILA, Thursday, July 4—The Stars and Stripes were gently lowered at 10 o'clock this morning before a huge assembly of dignitaries and citizens as the Philippine national emblem, red, white and blue with sun and three stars, took its place, signaling the transfer of sovereignty to the independent Philippines.

Simultaneously sirens wailed out in Manila and church bells rang all over the Philippines, marking the moment the Philippine Republic was born.

President Manuel Roxas, the last of four distinguished speakers in the four-hour ceremony, said that the United States flag "has been lowered from the flagstaffs of this land not in defeat, not in surrender, not by compulsion, but by the voluntary act of the sovereign American nation."

"In the hearts of millions of Filipinos the Stars and Stripes flies more triumphantly than ever before" he continued. "We mark here today a forward thrust of the frontiers of freedom."

Filipinos generally observed Independence Day more as a solemn occasion than one for spontaneous rejoicing at having attained a goal they had sought during the forty-eight years of American sovereignty.

The same note sounded all through long addresses by Senator Millard Tydings, Democrat, of Maryland; Gen. Douglas MacArthur, former High Commissioner Paul V. McNutt, who automatically became United States Ambassador to the new republic.

President Truman also sent a special message in which he pledged continued United States aid.

The independence ceremonies took place on Manila's broad green Luneta overlooking Manila Bay crowded with ships of all nations and visiting naval units.

The grandstand, accommodating 1,500, was erected directly in front, partly obscuring the monument of Jose Rizal, Philippine patriot who was shot by the Spaniards on that spot half a century ago. The speakers' rostrum, built like a vessel's prow, symbolized the newly-launched Ship of State.

The customary Fourth of July use of firecrackers never caught on extensively here although the day had been observed since the American occupation as a holiday, so aside from the cheering and applause and a gun-salute the ceremony was markedly quiet and at moments solemn.

Ambassador McNutt, as President Truman's representative, read the Presidential proclamation of Philippine independence. After having recounted the progress of Filipinos under United States rule Mr. McNutt said he never had been prouder of being an American. Mr. Truman promised "we will continue so to conduct our relations here as to maintain and multiply the bonds between our two peoples."

Truman Proclamation Read

One more sobering influence was the note of finality sounded in Mr. Truman's proclamation, which said: "The United States of America hereby withdraws and surrenders all rights, possession, supervision, jurisdiction and control of sovereignty now existing and exercised by the United States of America in and over the territory and people of the Philippines and on behalf of the United States I do hereby recognize the independence of the Philippines as a separate self-governing nation and acknowledge the authority and control over the same by the Government instituted by the people thereof under the Constitution now in force."

Mr. McNutt ended: "A nation is

born. Long live the Republic of the Philippines! May God bless and prosper the Filipino people and keep them safe and free."

Then the flag-raising ceremony took place, accompanied by the United States and Philippine national anthems and twenty-one gun salute. Mr. Roxas and Elpidio Quirino took the oaths of office as President and Vice President of the republic.

President Roxas and Mr. McNutt stepped forward and signed a formal state agreement for the establishment and promotion of diplomatic relations between the United States and the new republic. Then they reviewed an hour-long military and civic parade.

Both Senator Tydings and General MacArthur received ovations. Mr. Tydings, who has been intimately associated with Philippine affairs in the Senate for a number of years, said: "We look forward to the hour when a representative of the Republic of the Phillipines will sit with the United States representative at the council table of nations and there we two shall continue our great work in these larger fields."

General MacArthur, too, struck an international note when he said: "Let history record this event in the sweep of democracy through the earth as foretelling the end of the mastery of peoples by the power of force alone—the end of empire as a political chain which binds the unwilling weak to the unyielding strong."

General MacArthur had flown from Tokyo to attend the ceremonies. His military career was intimately associated with the Philippines and he often has expressed an abiding regard for the Filipino people.

It remained for President Roxas to sound a note of broadest internationalism and a pledge on the part of the newly-formed republic to join in the United Nations' endeavors.

"We cannot build on the principles of isolation," he said. "The affairs of Trieste must be our concern. Today we, too, have an interest in the Mediterranean. The Poles and Czechs are our neighbors, their fate concerns us as intimately as the destiny of China. The world today is becoming one.

"Today the concept of independence is overshadowed by the dynamic growth of international interdependence. On all fronts the doctrine of absolute sovereignty is yielding ground. Heavier grows the pressure of the world's anxiety for peace and security directed against the principle of total sovereignty. We have by our membership in the United Nations already surrendered some of our sovereignty.

"If called to help the enforcement of peace we must supply that help. We, as other nations, have granted the right to the United Nations to utilize our land and our resources, if required for purposes of international security."

President Roxas paid high tribute to American friendship, which he called "the greatest ornament of our independence." He said, "any doubts which may still linger in some quarters of the earth as to the benign intentions of America should be resolved by what she so nobly and unselfishly accomplished here."

"Subtract the influence of the United States from the rest of the world and the answer is chaos," he declared.

July 4, 1946

ROXAS DEFENDS USE OF FOREIGN CAPITAL

Warns Filipinos Against Any 'Supernationalism' While Analyzing Their Ills

By H. FORD WILKINS
Special to THE NEW YORK TIMES.

MANILA, Sept. 28—President Manuel A. Roxas took his countrymen strenuously to task today for manifesting, as a newly independent people, signs of a "supernationalism" in their fear of sovereign encroachment by a foreign State or by business interests. Although Mr. Roxas did not designate American interests, it was plain that that was what he meant.

"Foreign capital must be invited here to help us in our great tasks," he said. "We should have confidence in our own Governmental skills, our own powers of regulation, our own ability to safeguard our national interests. We should have no fear of foreign capital. We can well afford to pay it its due reward and retain for our own nation the benefits of development and employment brought to us."

Addressing the alumni of his Alma Mater, the University of the Philippines, Mr. Roxas brought into the open the nationalistic tendencies that have been seriously worrying Americans here in recent months. The most recent manifestation was the closeness of the Congressional vote on the plebiscite to amend the Constitution to provide equal rights for Americans in accord with the Philippine Trade Act. The debate over this amendment brought out seriously expressed fears that Americans would override Philippine sovereignty and make independence a national joke.

Opening of Campaign

Many persons interpreted this plain-spoken admonition by Mr. Roxas as the opening gun of a national campaign to put across the plebiscite supporting the trade act. The date for this plebiscite has not been set, but it will probably be next February or March.

Mr. Roxas assumed the role of physician to this physically and spiritually ailing nation. He undertook to diagnose what was wrong with the Philippines. He concluded that what was really wrong with it was fear.

"Why are we afraid?" he asked. "Because we are suffering from an inferiority complex that we are too proud to admit. And we call it nationalism."

"Physical ruin is only a small part of what the war has wrought here," he continued. "We must face the truth that the dry rot of enemy occupation has eaten deep into our moral fiber. The virtue of honesty, having little immediate survival value under the Japanese rule, has gone much out of use.

Many of our people have come to accept easy advantage, bribery, evasion, untruth, graft and even corruption. Thievery is rampant. The easy-way life attracts many of us. We become callous to death and violence. A two-line item in our newspapers disposes of our reaction to murder.

"A large part of our younger generation eschews the sterner virtues. It looks lightly upon sobriety, chastity, obedience, truth and arduous toil. The family, once the bedrock of our society, is loosed from its moorings.

"Our unique culture, formed by the meeting here of three great currents in civilization — Latin, Anglo-Saxon and that of the East —is in danger of becoming mongrelized and disintegrated.

"These are the symptoms of our national ailment and I judge them to be serious indeed, holding all the perils of disaster."

But Mr. Roxas said that he was not discouraged over the ability to overcome these ills. He said that the Filipinos had enough common sense, nobility and plain courage innate in the people "to halt the inroads that expediency and cynicism are making in our national character."

The President mentioned Japan and Germany as nations that had gone down to ruin because of a type of supernationalism that he declined to admit. He cited the United States as a nation that had opened its gates as a struggling young republic to the brains and ingenuity of other nationals.

"I should like to indicate the economic blindness of the view, often expressed here, that so long as we have resources we need not worry; that it does not matter if they are undeveloped; that the matter of primary importance is keeping them exclusively for ourselves. This is economic nonsense. It is the philosophy of the miser who hoards his money and denies it even to himself.

"Our generation has every right to exploit and enjoy these resources. Let us do it ourselves if we can; if we cannot, let us do it with the help of others. Mine is not the view of defeatism; it is the challenging one, practical and proven."

In his prepared speech Mr. Roxas had mentioned American military bases here, but he skipped this part in delivery. In the manuscript, indicating that it was not easy to reach an accord in the current discussions on military bases, he attacked the local critics "who would gain political advantage by inflammatory denunciation" of the Philippines' turning over land for American military installations. Then he wrote:

"Most nations are spending from one-third to two-thirds of their national budgets for defense. We support an army of 12,000 men, mostly in training, at a cost of less than one-tenth of our budget. We are fortunate that we can devote the greater part of our substance to the pursuits of peace."

September 29, 1946

FINDS MARINES ROUGH

Philippine Representative Says U. S. Is Ready to End Abuses

MANILA, Nov. 17 (Æ) — The Presidential Palace today published a report by Representative Ramon Magsaysay supporting Filipino charges of manhandling by United States Marine guards at Olongapo naval base but stating that "these were isolated cases, not following any set pattern."

The Representative, who conducted an investigation, said he had found three Filipino civilians who said they had been handled roughly by the marines but that they had not brought their complaints to the attention of American authorities.

He said there also were some instances of holding arrested persons without charge beyond the six-hour limit set by Philippine law and some bullying by "ill-mannered M. P.'s," but that "these were exceptions and not the rule." Señor Magsaysay's report stressed American "readiness to correct abuses when the facts are brought to the commandant's attention."

November 18, 1946

FILIPINOS APPROVE PARITY ENACTMENT

Equal Privilege for Americans Backed About Six to One— Grenade Victim Dies

By FORD WILKINS
Special to THE NEW YORK TIMES.

MANILA, Wednesday, March 12 —An estimated 1,500,000 Filipino electors in a national plebiscite yesterday effectively endorsed a constitutional amendment required by the Philippine Trade Act by a majority that is predicted to be about six to one. This is on the basis of incomplete returns. There will not be a full tally for another week.

The nation-wide balloting was without incident and was orderly. No violence was reported either to the Government or to the newspapers following Monday night's attempted assassination of President Manuel A. Roxas.

The Manila Daily Bulletin reported returns from the capital and the Provinces, some complete and some partial. These gave ratios ranging from three-to-one to thirty-five-to-one in favor of the amendment to give equal rights to Americans in the development of the nation's natural resources and the operation of its public utilities. The Constitution had to be amended because it specified that 60 per cent of all corporate businesses must be owned by Filipinos.

The indicated smallness of the total vote tempered the satisfaction of President Roxas with the outcome. Less than half of the nation's 3,000,000 registered voters cast ballots, according to newspaper estimates.

Silent Protest Seen

There were indications, especially in some Manila precincts, of a deliberate quiet conspiracy against voting. Its purpose was to express silent disapproval of what many consider the onerous terms of the Philippine Trade Act.

More "no" votes were cast in Manila than elsewhere. The national capital is conceded to be more inclined toward economic nationalism than are other sections.

In 513 of the 546 Manila precincts the count was 41,415 favoring the amendment and 15,114 against it.

Other large cities gave larger favorable majorities. Cebu, home of former President Sergio Osmeña, accepted parity by ten to one while early scattered reports from rural areas indicated about the same ratio as Cebu.

There were no indications that the attempted Presidential assassination had any bearing on the vote one way or the other.

Manila police, meanwhile, failed to establish any connection between the confessed grenade thrower, Julio Guillen, 50-year-old barber shop owner, and any subversive organization. Closely questioned, Guillen re-enacted the bomb-throwing episode for police and camera men, steadfastly maintaining that he conceived and executed the attempted slaying alone.

He repeated that he would try it again if he had an opportunity. He said he was disgusted with the President's economic policies and failure to live up to campaign promises.

March 12, 1947

U. S. Signs Philippine Pact; Obtains Bases for 99 Years

By The Associated Press.

MANILA, March 14—In the festive atmosphere of a farewell ball for Ambassador Paul V. McNutt, the United States and the Philippines tonight signed a ninety-nine-year agreement for American military and naval bases in these islands.

Mr. McNutt signed for the United States and President Manuel A. Roxas for the Philippines in Malacanan Palace. Mr. McNutt plans to leave by air tomorrow morning, via India and Paris, for Washington, where he will resign the Ambassadorship.

The agreement provides that in the interests of international security any of the bases may be made available to the Security Council of the United Nations.

No Bases in Cities

The Philippine Government issued a statement saying the United States had met "in every respect the request of the Philippine Government that no permanent bases, and especially no operating bases, be established in centers of population. There will be no bases in the city of Manila or its immediate environs."

Mr. McNutt read a statement from Acting Secretary of State Dean Acheson that "the United States proposes to retain in the Philippines only such armed forces as are required to man bases and to constitute a small military mission. Troops now in the Philippines not required for these purposes will be shifted to other areas to continue support of the occupation of Japan."

The Philippines retain the right to exercise jurisdiction over all offenses committed outside bases unless in the performance of specific military duty or in cases involving only Americans.

March 15, 1947

President Manuel A. Roxas

The New York Times, 1946

PRESIDENT ROXAS IS DEAD IN MANILA

First Head of the Philippine Republic Stricken at Clark Field After Amity Speech

By FORD WILKINS
Special to THE NEW YORK TIMES.

MANILA, Friday, April 16— President Manuel A. Roxas of the Philippine Republic died of a heart attack last night at Clark Field, Pampagna, the largest American military base in the Philippines, where he had gone yesterday morning on an official inspection trip with Government officials. His age was 56.

President Roxas was stricken just after finishing an address to officers of the Thirteenth Air Force in which he excoriated world aggression and promised if war came the Philippines would fight side by side with America.

The hour of his death was officially given as 10 P. M. yesterday, but official confirmation was withheld until early this morning. Malacanan Palace announced "with deepest regret, the untimely demise of his excellency, Manuel Roxas."

The announcement said he died of heart failure at the residence of Maj. Gen. E. L. Eubank, commanding general of the Thirteenth Air Force, who was his host during the inspection ceremonies.

Vice President Elpidio Quirino, who succeeds Mr. Roxas as Chief Executive, was informed by radio of the President's tragic death. Mr. Quirino was aboard the Philippine Coast Guard cutter Anemone in southern waters on an official trip. He had been in poor health recently, suffering from what physicians said was high blood pressure. He resumed his official duties recently as Secretary of Foreign Affairs, a post he held concurrently with the Vice Presidency.

Next in the line of succession to the Philippine Presidency is José Avelino, Senate president.

Early this morning a special train filled with Government officials and close friends of President Roxas proceeded to Clark Field to bring the body back to Malacanan Palace.

The shock of the President's death had not reached the nation yet and will not for several hours as this is written. But it was visible in the tragic faces of those who learned the sad news at Malacanan early this morning. The President's death is regarded as the greatest tragedy that could have befallen this young republic, with so much depending on his leadership during the critical period of growth.

April 16, 1948

Quezon City, Not Manila, Now Capital of Philippines

By The Associated Press.

MANILA, July 17 — Quezon City, namesake and dream capital of the late President Manuel Quezon, replaced Manila today as the official capital of the Philippines. President Elpidio Quirino signed the act effecting the change.

More than a year of construction must precede the Government's actual move to the fashionable, but incompletely developed suburb ten miles northeast of Manila. However, President Quirino said:

"From now on, Manila will be our show window and Quezon City will be our workshop in so far as our Government is concerned."

Quezon City, once a country estate of the Puason family in Rizal Province, was chosen in 1937 by President Quezon as the site of a new capital. He called it New Manila, but the Commonwealth Legislature changed it to Quezon City in his honor. The Government shift is expected to help relieve dangerous congestion in Manila, which now has a population of nearly 2,000,000.

July 18, 1948

FEAR OF HUKS CUTS LUZON FOOD OUTPUT

Peasants Flee Their Villages as Drive on Rebels Exposes Them to Double Danger

By TILLMAN DURDIN

Special to The New York Times.

MANILA, June 19—Rebel activity in central Luzon, heartland of the Hukbalahap movement, has caused widespread displacement of rural inhabitants, accentuating hardships, reducing food production and increasing the evil of absentee landlordism.

Harassed and endangered by Huk demands for food and concealment on the one hand, and menaced by Government drives against Huk supporters on the other, peasants have left their homes in outlying villages by the tens of thousands to seek security in the bigger towns and cities. At the same time the big landowners, fearful of death at the hands of the Huks, have left their rural estates to hired overseers and sought refuge in the provincial capitals or Manila.

During a tour the writer has just concluded of "Huklandia" in central Luzon, Gov. Juan Chioco of Nueva Ecija said that in his province more than 100,000 peasants out of a total provincial population of 460,000 had moved from urban barrios [villages] to the bigger population centers. He reported that of 400 barrios in the province roughly half had been evacuated.

Many Villages Abandoned

Conditions in Nueva Ecija are the worst in central Luzon, but in other provinces abandoned barrios are also numerous. The result is acute congestion in the towns and cities and an augmented Government relief problem.

Most peasants are continuing to cultivate their lands in daytime, making treks of five to ten miles to reach their fields. Along the roads of Nueva Ecija at dawn and dusk thousands of farm families can be seen plodding between their lands and the distant refugee shelters.

Governor Chioco estimated that in his province tillers had ceased to farm 150,000 acres. Some of these fields already are choked by tough, tall cogon grass. He calculated that agricultural production in some regions was off 20 per cent as a result of the Huk troubles.

The landlords who have left their haciendas now rely on managers. These men often increase the dissatisfaction of the tenants, who have a hard life even in normal circumstances, by cutting in on the crop percentages of both tenant and landlord.

Peasants Bar Return

On some estates, left by their owners at the height of the Huk troubles in 1947, peasants have refused to accept the return of either the owners or their managers. In these instances, the tillers are in virtual control of the estates, although in most such situations, when the crops are harvested, they hand over a small percentage to the owner or his agent.

One of the main objectives of the Huk suppression troops now is to induce the peasants to return to their home barrios. More than 5,000 armed regulars of the Army and Constabulary are now engaged in an anti-Huk drive in central Luzon, and many of these are spread out in small units in the outlying villages in an attempt to give the inhabitants confidence so they will resume their normal lives.

In an effort to reduce fears of reprisals from the Government side if the peasants have dealings with the Huks, villagers are now being told that they will not be harmed for giving supplies to the Huks if they will tip off Government men as soon as possible about the movements of the rebels.

In many areas barrio dwellers are heeding the Government and returning home. In others the peasants are still reluctant to go back, and a high degree of pacification will be necessary to lure them to their homes.

June 20, 1950

PAST ABUSES HURT PUSH AGAINST HUKS

Constabulary's III - Treatment of Filipinos Has Left Army With Difficult Problem

By TILLMAN DURDIN

Special to The New York Times

MANILA, June 20—Past abuses of authority by regular and irregular pacification forces have complicated the problem of Hukbalahap suppression in Central Luzon. Today, anti-Huk fighters with a new policy of seeking public goodwill are having to combat fears and aversions among the people created by the harsh, ill-controlled methods formerly employed.

The particular target of popular resentment in the past has been the constabulary or national gendarmerie. Until the Army was thrown into the anti-Huk campaign three months ago the constabulary was the main force fighting the Huks.

The constabulary seemingly attempted to deal by force alone with people caught in the inescapable tentacles of the Huk movement. There was indiscriminate shooting of village dwellers who had relations with the Huks—relations that the unarmed rural peoples often were in no position to resist—and reprisals such as burning of homes and villages for suspected collaboration with the Huks.

Constabulary units stationed in the villages were sometimes guilty of exacting from villagers "protection favors" in the form of food or labor service. Thus peasants were forced to give to the Huks with one hand and to the constabulary with the other.

Road "check points" became spots for abuse. Travelers were shaken down for portions of whatever they happened to have in their possession or allowed to pass without trouble for a small fee.

Because it accepted favors from big landowners and well-to-do politicians, the constabulary tended to identify itself with vested interests and to work at cross purposes with the mass of poorer people among whom the Huks sought support.

On a tour of Central Luzon last week this writer found one constabulary unit handsomely billeted in a comfortable clubhouse with a swimming pool in a big sugar hacienda as part of its mission to protect the estate from Huks.

Gov. Juan Chioco of Huk-plagued Nueva Ecija Province told this correspondent that in the past the people had been more afraid of the constabulary than of the Huks. "People's rights were openly violated," he said. "Houses were broken into and people searched without warrants and sometimes shot. Court action against the constabulary is difficult because witnesses are intimidated."

The Governor said there had been a big improvement in relations between the pacification forces and the people of his province since the Army had come in. A similar improvement was reported in Tarlac Province by an American Roman Catholic priest who said the constabulary had maintained a "regime of fear."

In several Central Luzon provinces large numbers of temporary police and civil guards have been as much of a bane among the people as the constabulary and like the latter indulged in illegal exactions and much irresponsible shooting.

Convinced that rural peoples must be drawn into the anti-Huk campaign by close cooperation with military forces, the Government has been making an effort lately to enforce better performance from its armed agents. The Army, with its more democratic, tolerant approach, is making progress in winning support in the villages.

June 22, 1950

U.S. OFFERS MANILA $250,000,000 IN AID, BUT ASKS REFORMS

Truman Releases Bell Report, Backs Its Recommendations for Overhauling Economy

CLOSE SUPERVISION ASKED

Loans and Grants Over 5-Year Period Can Bar Collapse of Philippines, Mission Says

By WALTER H. WAGGONER
Special to The New York Times.

WASHINGTON, Oct. 28—The United States today offered the Philippine Republic up to $250,000,000 in closely supervised loans and grants over a period of five years on condition that basic economic, fiscal and land reforms would be undertaken by that nearly bankrupt island country.

The recommendations had the personal endorsement of President Truman, who forwarded to President Elpidio Quirino an exhaustive study of the Philippine economy by a mission of experts sent to Manila by the White House last July.

The mission, headed by Daniel W. Bell, a banker and former Under Secretary of the Treasury. spent two months in the country and returned with the conclusion that the Quirino Government was in such a critical situation that nly the most far-reaching program of reform and self-help, supported by technical and economic assistance from this country, could save the Philippines from total collapse.

Persons looking for a bitter attack on the Manila Government or its officials were due for a disappointment. The whole purpose of the study was to point out deficient, outmoded, or anachronistic practices of Government policies,

particularly with respect to economic, fiscal and land-holding systems. But the manner was forthright rather than harsh.

Early in the report one paragraph calls attention to the failure of certain officials to apply necessary corrective measures even though they knew what should be done. The statement is also made that "inefficiency and corruption in the Government service is widespread."

Members of the the mission made no effort in a news conference this morning to soften that charge of corruption. Mr. Bell explained that the roots of the corruption and graft lay in the chaos and misery of the immediate postwar period, when the Filipinos had to use their wits at the sacrifice of their principles to get along.

Other members agreed that corruption and graft, however "widespread," were by no means the cause of the present critical condition of the Philippine economy.

He said he was confident that the Philippine Government could, through such remedies as the mission proposed, get back on its feet. He added, also, that he believed the United States has an obligation to help the island republic.

Defining the "basic economic problem" as inefficient production and very low incomes," the Bell mission gave top priority among its several recommendations to a demand that the inflationary threat be met by substantially increasing tax revenues. This should be done primarily by tapping to a greater extent the high incomes of business men and large landholders, the report stated.

Recommendations Summarized

Other recommendations of the mission were:
1. The whole agricultural economy of the island should be overhauled. This would include not only steps to increase food production and farm workers' incomes through improving crops and methods of cultivation but also through reforms in land transfer and tenure practices, and the extension of credit at low rates to the poor and perennially debt-ridden small farmer.
2. The economy of the country should be diversified by the introduction of new industries, encouraged by public and private lending agencies and the development of better transportation and power facilities.
3. Non - essential and dollar - consuming imports should be discouraged through the imposition

of a special emergency tax of 25 per cent on all imports except important foods and fertilizers. This would call for revision of the present trade treaty with the United States, and the Bell mission proposed that the agreemen be re-examined for that purpose.
4. Social reforms should include ambitious programs for improving public health, urban housing and educational services and enactment of legislation assuring workers the right to organize trade unions for protecting their own economic interests.
5. Public administration should be reorganized to "insure honesty and efficiency," and this could be accomplished by placing the civil service system on a merit basis, raising civil service salaries to a "decent" level, and the employment of foreign technicians.

Those recommendations — demanding sweeping changes in the economy of the country, the techniques of management and the mental attitudes of many Philippine leaders—plus the acceptance of a United States technical mission to help carry them out, are the only conditions on which this Government would agree to make $250,000,000 available over a period of five years, the report stated.

The financial help would be in the form of both loans and outright grants, but the mission did not specify the proportion of the two. Members said also that the extent to which Congress would have to authorize or appropriate the funds had not yet been determined.

Edward M. Bernstein, on leave from the International Monetary Fund and chief economist of the mission, emphasized that the proposals were not intended to make a utopia of the Philippines but only to help the country solve its worst problems and meet the present crisis.

One of the objectives of the proposed reform program is to combat the attractions of the Communists, who lead the rebellious and threatening Hukbalahap movement. Asked whether the program would "cut the ground out from under the Huks," Mr. Bell cautiously replied that it was designed to improve the economic situation that the Communists exploited but would probably not bring about the sudden collapse of the rebel movement.

One of the chief concerns of the study mission was the status of the agricultural economy, which gives employment to about 75 per cent of gainfully employed Fili-

pinos and supports about 80 per cent of the population.

In addition to the disparity between the sub-standard wages of farm workers, many of whom are paid as little as one peso (50 cents a day), and the great profits of the big landholders, the report cited the failure of the Government to recognize agriculture as the major Philippine resource.

Farming contributes about 56 per cent of the island's gross national product, but is assisted by only about one-fourth of 1 per cent of the budget, the report pointed out.

"The Philippine farmer is between two grindstones," the mission found. "On top is the landlord, who often exacts an unjust share of the crop in spite of ineffective legal restrictions to the contrary. Beneath is the deplorably low productivity of the land he works.

"The farmer cannot see any avenue of escape. He has no credit except at usurer's rates. There is no counsel to whom he can turn with confidence. He is resistant to change for fear of losing the meager livelihood he and his family possess. The incentive to greater production dies aborning when what he regards as an unjust share of the harvest of his work goes to the landlord."

Better Techniques Urged

The mission proposed several ways to remove the "grindstones." It asked, generally, that improved farming techniques be put to use in order to increase the income from the island's chief source of wealth.

Of a more revolutionary character were its proposals for making more land available to the Philippine farmer through encouragement of homesteading on Government land, and the division and redistribution of large private land-holdings.

The latter would be accomplished through Government purchase of large estates at "a fair value" for resale in small holdings to the actual farm workers.

President Truman forwarded the Bell report to President Quirino with a letter stressing the history of friendly relations between the two governments.

"Our two nations have been the closest of friends over a period of more than half a century," he wrote. "Our relations have been marked by a spirit of straightforwardness and candor in our dealings with each other. I earnestly hope that we can continue in this same spirit."

Mr. Truman said he was making public the report to dispel rumors and speculation that would serve only to "confuse our joint efforts."

October 29, 1950

Philippines Signs E.C.A. Accord

MANILA, April 27 (AP)—President Elpidio Quirino and United States Ambassador Myron M. Cowen signed today an agreement for administering Economic Cooperation Administration aid in the Philippines. The terms are similar to those under which Marshall Plan aid was administered in Europe. The United States will send interim aid of $15,000,000 pending approval by the United States Congress of a larger program to extend several years.

April 28, 1951

U. S. and Philippines Sign Treaty for Mutual Defense

Special to THE NEW YORK TIMES.

WASHINGTON, Aug. 30—With Presidents Truman and Elpidio Quirino solemnly pledging that their countries "would always be friends," the United States and the Philippines entered into a mutual defense treaty today.

The ceremonies took place in the Inter-departmental Auditorium, where Secretary of State Dean Acheson and Brig. Gen. Carlos P. Romulo, Philippine Secretary of Foreign Affairs, signed the pact (the text of which was published in THE NEW YORK TIMES Aug. 17).

General Romulo said the present treaty was the first of a series of agreements that would lead to the "speedy conclusion of a Pacific security pact in order to overcome the growing menace of totalitarian aggression."

In his message President Quirino declared: "We have no aggressive aims against anyone. Our purpose is rather to give notice that a potential aggressor must henceforth take due account of our common purpose and united will to act in self-defense."

President Quirino conveyed the "deepest sentiments of good will and friendship" from his people and concluded, "I bring to witness at this signing, Mr. President, the faith in democracy of the Filipino people and the courage to defend it with all our strength."

Symbol of Close Ties

In response, President Truman said that "the signing of this treaty symbolizes the close ties that bind the people of the Philippines and the United States."

"We have demonstrated that two peoples, however different they may be in background and experience, can work together for their common welfare if they have the same belief in democracy and the same faith in freedom," Mr. Truman added.

The President concluded by saying that the people of the United States were happy to join with the Philippines in "this mutual expression of our united will to go forward in the cause of peace and freedom."

At that point Mr. Truman, in an addition to his prepared speech, turned to President Quirino and said: "I return to you, President Quirino, the pledge that we shall always be friends."

Secretary Acheson, after having welcomed the Philippine delegation said that the defense treaty "is the natural outgrowth of the relationship of over half a century between the Philippines and the United States."

Mr. Acheson also assailed the outlawed terrorist Hukbalahap organization. "The Hukbalahap movement, servile to an ideology which is repellent to all Filipino traditions and interests, has been doing everything within its power to destroy the Filipino nation and place it under a foreign and oppressive yoke," he asserted.

General Romulo raised some speculation when he stated, "this obligation covers any act of aggression, whether proceeding from a new source or arising from a repetition of aggression." Observers here questioned whether General Romulo, in the phrase "repetition of aggression" was making reference to Japan at whose draft peace treaty discussions the Philippine delegation will sit next week.

In addition to Secretaries Acheson and Romulo, the treaty was signed by the following: Ambassador John Foster Dulles, consultant to the State Department; Joaquin M. Elizalde, Philippine Ambassador to the United States; Senator Tom Connally, Democrat of Texas, chairman of the Senate Committee on Foreign Relations; Vicente Francisco, chairman of the Philippine Senate Committee on Foreign Relations; Senator Alexander Wiley, Republican of Wisconsin, ranking minority member of Senate Foreign Relations Committee, and Diosdado Macapagal, chairman of the Philippine House Committee on Foreign Affairs.

After the ceremony, President Truman was host to President Quirino and the United States and Philippine delegations at a lunch in Blair House, the President's temporary residence.

August 31, 1951

Magsaysay Election Victory In Philippines Is Conceded

By TILLMAN DURDIN
Special to THE NEW YORK TIMES.

MANILA, Thursday, Nov. 12—President Elpidio Quirino conceded victory in the Philippines Presidential election to Ramon Magsaysay, leader of the Nationalist-Democratic coalition, at noon today. In his statement Mr. Quirino said:

"The people's verdict should be accepted for the sake of national unity. I have nothing but good wishes for the country and my successor."

Mr. Quirino said that in this year's elections the people had evidently expected a change of administration.

"My most fervent prayer at this hour is that the change is for the better," he added.

Additional unofficial returns from Tuesday's elections, received early today, showed that Mr. Magsaysay was leading Mr. Quirino by better than two to one.

The tabulations of the Philippines News Service gave the Nationalist-Democratic coalition candidate 1,688,172 votes, compared with 708,398 for the incumbent President.

The total number of votes cast is now being estimated at something more than 4,000,000 out of 5,500,000 registrants. Thus, roughly half of the estimated total of the ballots has been counted.

[In the Vice Presidential race, according to The United Press, the latest figures gave Mr. Magsaysay's running mate, Carlos P. Garcia, 1,423,000 to 783,889 for José Yulo of the Liberal party.]

Official Count Shows Trend

Unofficial press tabulations of the election returns began to be supported last night by the first announcement of official counts through the Commission on Elections. The commission reported 431,848 votes for Mr. Magsaysay and 176,182 for Mr. Quirino on the basis of canvassed results from more than 200 cities and towns.

Press compilations showed that the entire Senate slate of the Nationalist-Democrats was winning along with Mr. Magsaysay and most of the coalition's candidates for the House of Representatives. It appears likely, therefore, that the Nationalist-Democrats not only will improve the majority they already have in the Senate but will wrest control of the House as well from the Liberals.

Last night individual Liberal Congressional candidates were conceding victory to their opponents but Mr. Quirino yesterday refused to admit defeat. An announcement from the Presidential Palace said it was then hoped that the count of votes in the provinces would counterbalance the big Nationalist-Democratic majorities in the cities and towns and give the President a margin for re-election.

It was pointed out, moreover, that the election picture, so far, was based mainly on the unofficial recording of ballots and that only official returns could be considered as final.

The Senate president, Eulogio Rodriguez, a leading Nationalist-Democrat, yesterday sent telegrams to all party provincial chairmen urging them to continue vigilant surveillance of the vote canvassing and the handling of ballot boxes to guard against possible attempts to tamper with the ballots.

In his statement Mr. Rodriguez credited the successful election to the persons and groups who had worked to insure a free and honest vote.

Delayed information reaching here reported several more dead and injured in election-day violence in the provinces. Fifty-five persons, described as the gunmen of Cavite's Liberal Governor Dominador Camerino, have been arrested for questioning in connection with the election-day killing of six persons and the wounding of three in Cavite. The armed forces of Chief of Staff, Maj. Gen. Calixto Duque, has ordered a continued alert for the nation's military services.

There is a growing sense of pride and satisfaction among the Filipinos over the fact that Tuesday's elections went off well in general despite the violence, intimidations and attempts at fraud in some places.

Rodrigo Perez, one of the election commissioners, declared that this year's elections were the best conducted national polling since the Japanese war.

In his statement Mr. Quirino said that the conduct of Tuesday's elections "stands as incontrovertible proof that democracy is secure in our country and an assurance that we firmly hold aloft its bright torch in our part of the world."

The Liberal Vice Presidential candidate, José Yulo, was running ahead of Mr. Quirino in the total of votes but was losing in his home province of Negros Occidental. For a while yesterday one Liberal Senate candidate, José Figueras, had a lead over his Nationalist-Democrat opponent, Ruperto Kangleon, but later returns canceled it out.

So far only three Liberal candidates for the House seemed sure of victory. Manila appeared likely to give Mr. Magsaysay a majority of 136,000 votes, the largest for any candidate in the city's history.

November 12, 1953

PHILIPPINES HELD TO BE TEST OF U. S.

Asian People Associate New Republic With Washington —Reds Call It Puppet

By ROBERT ALDEN
Special to The New York Times.

MANILA, March 17 — More than any other country in this part of the world, the Philippines is identified with the United States in the minds of the people of Asia. Therefore the young Philippine republic has become in a sense a showcase for the United States.

What this means is that if the Philippines makes good progress in development, that reflects favorably on the United States. If it does not, the United States receives a large measure of the blame.

Free Elections Held

One factor is that the Philippines have held free elections.

There is much, of course, that is lacking between the promise of the forward-looking reforms of the Government of President Ramon Magsaysay and actual execution of his program.

But here the people have hope. Communist propaganda tries to picture the Philippine Government as an exploited puppet of the United States. Filipinos, however, wish to demonstrate to their neighbors that they are in a free and independent republic and that they are improving conditions within their country.

To this end they have invited from time to time visitors from near-by countries. A group of fifty Indonesian officers who came here to study at an army service school, for example, are said to have been quite surprised at the achievements in self-government in this country. They had expected to find an exploited satellite of the United States, as portrayed by Communist propaganda. In its stead they found something quite different.

and the Communist threat for the present has been reduced to a minimum.

The Philippines is only an infant republic—eight years old. United States observers feel that a new republic is bound to stumble from time to time.

The problems in the Philippines have been tough, there have been shortcomings here in handling them and at least in part, according to Filipinos, there have been shortcomings of the United States in preparing them for democracy.

The United States made great advances in improving health conditions in the country and in expanding educational facilities.

The United States, of course, also laid the groundwork for democracy: training Filipinos to take over the management of their country, teaching them the institutions of democracy, teaching them of their right to speak freely and write freely.

At the same time the United States did nothing to break down the feudal system of landowning that was inherited when the country was taken over by the United States from Spain just before the turn of the century.

Even when elections took place here before the Philippines was proclaimed free, the large landowners had themselves elected to the legislature by their tenants, and there they were able to perpetuate their power.

They are still being elected to the legislature, and now the Government is having difficulty instituting the greatly needed economic and social reforms that the United States failed to bring about when it governed the country.

But the feeling of the common people here toward the United States is still most warm and friendly. Today as then it is possible for an American to wander anywhere through these islands and be received in a friendly, open-handed fashion by the Filipinos. Although the Communists would have it otherwise, the Filipinos and Americans still get along very well together.

March 18, 1955

PHILIPPINES FACES ECONOMIC HAZARD

Pace of Population Growth Exceeds That of Output, but Balance Is Sought

Special to The New York Times.

MANILA, March 25 — The gravest economic problem facing the Philippine Islands today is caused by a rapidly expanding population. Each year there are a half million more persons to feed.

In the last twenty years the population of the country, which now stands at a little more than 21,000,000, has increased by 48 per cent. That means that, to hold the standard of living at a level, production, industrial and agricultural, must have increased by 48 per cent during the twenty-year period.

That is a sizable increase and, because available statistics here are not apt to be too accurate, it is difficult to determine to what extent this acceleration has been accomplished.

Certainly during the war years and the years that followed, production could not keep pace and great hardship resulted.

By 1953 the country, with the help of a special United States war rehabilitation program and other economic aid, could point to some progress. Production was 25 per cent over the 1937 level. But population had increased by 38.4 per cent in the same period.

Now the situation is said to be better with an additional production increase in the last year matching the population increase. But there is a constant pressure on the economy here to keep expanding or the country will suffer a drop in its standard of living.

That standard of living is none too high, although in the context of Asia it is not markedly low. The vast majority of people in the Philippines lives at the bare subsistence level. People do not starve. There are enough coconuts and bananas growing on the trees. They do, however, often suffer from malnutrition.

As a hangover from the days before the turn of the century, when Spain ruled this country, there are vast estates on which many peasants work as tenant farmers. Wealth is concentrated in the hands of a small number and a middle class population has not, as yet, grown to any appreciable extent.

More than 70 per cent of the people depend on agriculture, fishing and forestry for support. Rice and corn are raised for domestic consumption, while sugar, coconut products and Manila hemp are the principal exports. Other exports, such as lumber, pineapple, iron and chromite ores, are of considerably less importance.

As for imports, to survive the Philippines must bring in certain food items — including grains, dairy products and canned fish. The other major imports are textiles, machinery, iron and steel products, tires, automobile parts (the cars are assembled in the Philippines) and petroleum products.

When the balance sheet of overseas trade is added up the Philippines is found to be chronically in the red.

The duty-free period of trade between the United States and the Philippines is coming to an end. Under a scale that must be approved by the respective legislative bodies of the two countries, all favored treatment will be closed out by 1974.

Although population pressure and the unfavorable balance of trade make for knotty economic problems, the economic prospect need not be a dark one, in the view of observers here.

Only about 65 per cent of the arable land is under cultivation.

Guidance, rather than dollar allotments, seems to be the principal need of the Philippine economy at this stage of its development.

April 10, 1955

PHILIPPINE CROWD HAILS MAGSAYSAY

President's Visit to a Town Attests to His Popularity —People Air Problems

By ROBERT ALDEN
Special to The New York Times.

SILAY, the Philippines, July 27
President Ramón Magsaysay has enormous popularity with the Filipino people. That popu-that seems to have no bounds.

During an informal visit, the people from the little towns of the island of Negros Occidental came rushing from their homes to surround him and shake his hand and shout greetings until they were hoarse.

The crowd contained old men and women, children and workers from the sugar cane fields in this sugar-rich island, women with babies in their arms and young girls in their neat blue school uniform.

No one had to organize this demonstration. No one had to organize it because it was heartfelt.

As President Magsaysay drove to the edge of this town, the swarm of people blocked the road. He got out from the automobile and walked right into the thickest part of the crowd.

The President shook hands with hundreds of persons. He patted children. A tearful old woman told Mr. Magsaysay that her blind son required treatment in Manila but that she could not afford the trip. Mr. Magsaysay promised the woman that the boy would be taken to Manila that afternoon in the President's plane.

Shirt Remains Intact

It took President Magsaysay a half hour to walk a hundred yards through the crowd. When it was done the President drank some coconut milk.

"Well, at least I didn't lose my shirt here," he said. In a previous visit to another town his shirt had been torn from his back by a crowd.

It is not hard to explain President Magsaysay's popularity. An hour after his welcome here, when he mounted a rostrum in the village square of Silay, women wept openly as he told them of an old woman who had informed him of her poverty and her nine children.

"I have not nine children," the President said. "I have 20,-000,000 children. And when they suffer, I will suffer. When they die, I will die."

No grievance seems too small for the President's personal attention. By the time the President had reached the midpoint in his speech his aide's notebook was choked with various memoranda:

There was the name of a woman involved in a land dispute with a neighbor, the name of a boy who needed treatment for meningitis and tuberculosis.

There was a note on a complaint by a school group on a Japanese burlesque show in a neighboring town and a request by a farmer for a dirt road into his village.

"The Government is to serve the people," Mr. Magsaysay told the crowd. "The public servant is to serve you. If you know of any public servant who is dishonest, who will not help you when you come to him for help, who is more interested in his personal comfort than in doing his job, send me a telegram and let me know about him.

"You are my eyes and ears. Working together we can get good clean government."

President Magsaysay recalled how only a few years ago this island was controlled by politicians with a private police force.

"The people were afraid to speak out," he said. "But now they are not afraid. You can go to the polls and vote as you please and no one will hurt you."

As he finished his speech, the crowd closed in on the President.

Those who accompany the President say it is this way through all the islands of the Philippines. Even his political opponents acknowledge that there is no challenging the President's popularity.

August 12, 1956

MAGSAYSAY DEAD WITH 24 IN PLANE; GARCIA SUCCESSOR

Philippine Officials Suspect Sabotage—Crash Scene a Cebu Mountain

PRESIDENT'S BODY FOUND

U. S. Air Force Helicopters to Fly It Out—New Leader on Way From Australia

By The Associated Press.

MANILA, Monday, March 18 —President Ramon Magsaysay's charred, burned body was found today by rescuers in the wreckage of his plane on Cebu Island.

The popular President's body was identified by his brother, Jesus, who flew to the scene in a helicopter.

This blasted a lingering hope

Associated Press Radiophoto

BEFORE ILL-FATED FLIGHT: President Ramon Magsaysay of the Philippines in the city of Cebu on Saturday. This is believed to be the last photograph taken of him before his death. Twenty-four others died in the plane, which was on way from Cebu to Manila.

THE TRIALS OF NATIONHOOD

on the part of Mr. Magsaysay's family and staff in Manila that he might have survived the crash yesterday on a Cebu mountain of his twin-motored plane soon after its take-off on a night flight back to Manila from Cebu City.

The crash also killed twenty-four others in the party. One passenger on the ill-fated plane, a Filipino newspaper man, survived. He was brought out by farmers.

Guard Put at Wreckage

A tight guard was thrown around the wreckage of the plane in a mountain ravine about thirty miles northwest of Cebu City. Security officers were checking the possibility of sabotage.

President Magsaysay as Defense Secretary had broken the back of the Communist Hukbalahap rebel movement in the island republic. Officials said they did not rule out the possibility of Communist sabotage; some strongly suspected it.

Among the other victims of the crash was Brig. Gen. Benito Ebuen, commanding general of the Philippine Air Force.

A sorrowing Philippine people awaited the arrival of Vice President Carlos P. Garcia, who will be sworn in as the young republic's new Chief Executive. He succeeded immediately upon Mr. Magsaysay's death.

Mr. Garcia was flying from Australia, where he had attended last week's conference of the Council of the Southeast Asia Treaty Organization. He will serve until a President is chosen in the regular elections in November.

November Election Outlook

Mr. Magsaysay, who won the Presidency by a landslide in 1953, was a candidate for re-election and had been considered an overwhelming favorite. He was firmly and actively pro-United States as well as anti-Communist in his views. His opponent, Senator Claro M. Recto, is regarded as anti-American and neutralist.

March 18, 1957

CHAPTER 3

Communist, Neutralist or Pro-West?

Nguyen Cao Ky (left) and Nguyen Van Thieu, Vice President and President of South Vietnam. They were not smiling when their regime collapsed in 1975.

UPI

ASIAN AID TREATY SIGNED AT MANILA; DEFENSE LINE SET

By TILLMAN DURDIN
Special to The New York Times.

MANILA, Wednesday, Sept. 8 —A defense treaty for Southeast Asia and the Southwest Pacific was signed here this afternoon.

The security arrangement was worked out in a three-day conference attended by representatives of the United States, Britain, France, Pakistan, Thailand, Australia, New Zealand and the Philippines.

The last important problem involved in completing the pact that binds the signers to resist aggression in the prescribed area was settled in a conference session this morning.

A compromise was reached with Britain, Australia and New Zealand over the question of including somewhere in the treaty a declaration on the right of peoples to independence and self-determination.

The morning session was not terminated until 1:15 P. M., more than four hours after it had begun. A round of clapping was heard from the closed conference hall before the delegates emerged smiling and remarked, "It's all over."

It is understood that purely technical details of drafting took a great deal of time after basic agreement had been reached on outstanding questions.

Issues Resolved Tuesday

All other major obstacles to the conclusion of the treaty were resolved at two intensive, three-hour closed sessions of the treaty conference delegates yesterday morning and afternoon. Difficulties were reported to have developed on a number of points.

But compromises were reached and most details were settled for a pact that will not differ greatly from the treaty proposals the United States submitted as a working draft to experts of the eight powers who assembled to produce a composite document here last week.

It was decided that the area of the treaty would be the general area of Southeast Asia, including the entire territories of the Asian members of the pact and the Southwest Pacific, not including the Pacific area north of Lat. 21 degrees 30 minutes N. This line excludes Hong Kong and Formosa.

Conference sources said one of the main treaty problems was solved yesterday when the United States compromised on its insistence that the pact be exclusively an anti-Communist one.

It was agreed that an American declaration, stating that as far as the United States was concerned the pact applied only to Communist aggression, would become a part of the treaty. In return, John Foster Dulles, United States Secretary of State, conceded the omission of the word Communist in the reference to aggression in the operative article of the treaty.

Pakistan, Britain, Australia, France and New Zealand in particular are said to have registered strong objection to an exclusive anti-Communist provision in the treaty.

Another problem that produced considerable controversy among the treaty drafters was adjusted when the United States and Thailand, advocates of having the operative article of the treaty specifically state that Cambodia, Laos and South Vietnam would be protected, agreed to a French proposal that mention of the three states be made in a protocol.

The protocol, included as a part of the treaty document, extends to the three states the anti-aggression provisions of the treaty and makes them eligible for economic aid under the pact.

The French and British are reported to have taken the view that the Geneva agreements settling the Indochina war made mention of Cambodia, Laos and South Vietnam in the operative article of the Southeast Asia treaty inadvisable.

In the discussion today on the right of self-determination, the Marquess of Reading, British Minister of State for Foreign Affairs and his country's chief delegate to the conference, argued strongly against terminology that might be susceptible to use by the Malayan Communists for propaganda.

The Philippines agreed to drop her demand for an article on the question and to accept a modified statement in the preamble.

Richard G. Casey, Australian Minister for External Affairs, announced at this morning's session that he had referred to his Government articles in the treaty dealing with enforcement and treaty machinery. He said the articles had met with his Government's approval.

Advocacy of North Atlantic Treaty-type terminology for the Southeast Asia pact by the Philippines and Thailand was dropped after Mr. Dulles assertedly had maintained that a proposed clause in the Southeast Asia treaty providing for action against aggression according to constitutional processes was not weaker than the Atlantic pact provisions.

An article on economic assistance and self-help agreed upon yesterday is said to have left the programs and instrumentalities discretionary. It was agreed that a treaty council would meet from time to time to engage in military planning and consult on implementation of the pact.

Manila, Singapore, Bangkok and an Australian city were offered as sites for the first meeting of the treaty council. Upon the suggestion of Mr. Dulles, it was decided to settle questions of time and place through diplomatic channels.

What Treaty Contains

MANILA, Wednesday, Sept. 8 (AP)—This is what the Southeast Asia security treaty is expected to look like when it is signed today by eight nations:

Preamble: Reaffirms faith in the United Nations Charter; desires to promote stability and well being in the treaty area, strengthen peace and uphold democratic principles; promote economic development; declares signers stand united against aggression and members will coordinate their efforts for collective defense. (May also contain recognition of the right of all nations in Southeast Asia to self determination.)

Article I calls for settling international disputes by peaceful means under the United Nations Charter.

Article II says member nations by self help and mutual aid will maintain a capacity "to resist armed attack and to prevent and overcome subversive activity directed from without."

Article III proposes cooperation among members "to promote economic stability and social well being."

Article IV agrees that each party will meet the "common danger" of armed attack in the treaty area or against any member "in accordance with its constitutional process"; in case of aggression members will "consult immediately in order to agree to measures which should be taken for common defense"; aid will be sent to an attacked nation only on request.

Article V establishes a council able to meet at any time.

Article VI says the treaty does not affect the rights of members under the United Nations Charter, nor does it conflict with other existing treaties.

Article VII provides that members by unanimous consent can invite other nations to join the pact.

Article VIII defines the treaty area as all Southeast Asia and the western Pacific (but not Formosa).

Article IX provides for depositing ratification articles with the Philippines.

Article X says the treaty will remain in force indefinitely, with any party able to withdraw by giving one year's notice.

Article XI says that English is the official language of the treaty.

September 8, 1954

CONFEREES ADOPT PACIFIC CHARTER

Companion Document to Pact Upholds Peoples' Rights in Southeast Asia

By ROBERT TRUMBULL
Special to The New York Times.

MANILA, Wednesday, Sept. 8 —The eight nations who signed the Southeast Asia collective defense treaty today also adopted a Pacific Charter upholding the "principle of equal rights and self-determination of peoples" in Southeast Asia and the Southwest Pacific region.

The document was signed by the foreign ministers of the United States, Britain, Australia, New Zealand, the Philippines, Thailand and Pakistan. Guy de la Chambre, French Minister for Relations with the Indochina States, initialed the Charter pending the approval of Paris.

There had been dispute over whether the principles this charter contains should be an operative article in the Southeast Asia defense pact or be included in the defense treaty today also adopted a Pacific Charter upholding the preamble. As a compromise the Pacific agreement, which had been initiated by the Philippines, was made a separate but companion document to the defense treaty. One paragraph of the preamble to the defense treaty summarizes the principles that are elaborated in the charter.

The charter binds the participating nations to "earnestly strive by every peaceful means to promote self-government and to secure the independence of all countries whose peoples desire it and are able to undertake its responsibilities."

The signatories assert they are prepared to "continue taking effective practical measures" to achieve the charter's purposes, in effect an emphatic reiteration of adherence to the United Nations Charter as it relates to dependent peoples.

The charter was adopted along with the defense treaty to provide a clear understanding among doubtful Asians and others as to the intentions of the five Western adherents to the Southeast Asia treaty.

The signatories agree to "continue to cooperate in the economic, social and cultural fields in order to promote higher living standards, economic progress and well-being" in Southeast Asia and the Southwest Pacific area.

The final paragraph of the

twenty-one line document links the charter with the Southeast Asia collective defense treaty by serving warning that the adhering powers "are determined to prevent or counter by appropriate means any attempt in the treaty area to subvert freedom or to destroy sovereignty or territorial integrity."

Informal interpretations clearly define this paragraph as a warning to communism that the charter signatories are now pledged to bring non-self-governing territories toward full freedom in an orderly fashion.

These objectives, which the Asian delegates especially desired to have spelled out, are stated to have the purpose of establishing "a firm basis for common action to maintain peace and security" in the region.

September 8, 1954

INDOCHINA: THE AMERICAN YEARS

EISENHOWER RELUCTANTLY ACCEPTS INDOCHINA ACCORD, BUT WARNS REDS; U. S. ALOOF FROM 8-NATION PLEDGE

NO CHOICE IS SEEN

President Asserts U. S. Will Not Be Bound by Armistice Terms

By WILLIAM S. WHITE
Special to The New York Times.

WASHINGTON, July 21—President Eisenhower made it clear today that the United States accepted the settlement in Indochina in the spirit of making the best of a bad bargain.

There was simply no visible alternative, he said in substance.

The President declared at his news conference that the agreement by which Vietnam is to be partitioned between Communist and non-Communist areas contained features "which we do not like."

The United States will accept no primary responsibility for the armistice, he said. It will neither be bound by the armistice's decisions nor attempt to overturn them by force, since the overriding United States obligation is to remain loyal to the principles of the United Nations, the President added.

He warned the Communists that further aggression "would be viewed by us as a matter of grave concern."

Speaking of the world generally, the President declared his belief that, while the Communists would go on trying to bite off areas here and there by subversion, they were not likely to challenge the whole free world in a war of exhaustion.

He declined to describe the armistice in the angry terms equivalent to "appeasement" and "surrender" that were applied to it in Congress. When one is up against it to find an alternative and cannot find one, he is not going to criticize what others did, the President observed.

John Foster Dulles, Secretary of State, took the same position in an appearance before the Foreign Affairs Committee of the House of Representatives in a closed session during the afternoon.

An authorized summary of the meeting said Mr. Dulles had observed that the United States "regretted" many aspects of the solution and "disassociated itself in the sense of declining to join the conference declaration."

The President's attitude was one neither of minimizing the gravity of the free world's setback nor of unrelieved gloom.

His manner, more clearly than his words, suggested that, while the United States found it hard to stomach what had occurred, there was no point now in recriminations.

The thing to do now, he said in effect, is to press on with all vigor with plans for collective security so that there will be no further free world disasters in Asia—to deal with the future rather than the past.

It was plain tonight that the United States had reached more than one fork in the road.

For one example it was officially disclosed that military aid shipments now en route to Indochina would be halted and diverted to United States or Allied ports for re-routing later, possibly to the Southeast Asian defensive alliance now being sought.

For another, the Administration seemed to be confronting a rising storm within the Republican party. The assertion of Senator William F. Knowland of California, the Senate Republican leader, that the settlement was "one of the great Communist victories of this decade" forecast much trouble for Secretary of State Dulles in Congress.

From the very outset Mr. Knowland's group had been critical of Mr. Dulles for ever having agreed to put Indochina on the agenda of the Geneva conference.

They do not, in private at least, accept the President's thesis that the outcome of the Geneva conference was not in any important sense any real responsibility of the United States.

The President, for his part, opened his press conference by reading off a carefully prepared statement in which he made the point that at all events there had been an end to the bloodshed in Indochina.

He recalled that the United States had not been a belligerent and thus was not a party to the conclusions reached.

He underlined the point that the interest of the United States in free Indochina had in no way lessened.

To illustrate this continuing concern, he disclosed that this country would send an Ambassador or Minister to both Laos and Cambodia and would maintain its mission in Saigon, in the non-Communist part of Vietnam.

A reporter noted that in Congress men were "branding the Geneva settlement as appeasement."

"Do you think there are any elements of appeasement in the cease-fire agreement?" the President was asked.

Well, he replied, he hesitated to use such words, as he had often told the reporters. He found that so many words meant so many different things to different people. But he would say this much: This agreement, in certain of its features, is not satisfactory to us. It is not what we would have liked to have had.

But the President did not know, when he was put up against it at this moment to find an alternative, to say what we would or could do. If the President had no better plan he was not going to criticize what others had done.

Asked about earlier reports that the French had asked in vain for a United States air strike in aid of the besieged city of Dienbienphu in Indochina, the President replied it was possible the Administration would issue a White Paper of explanation on the whole subject.

There is perhaps a need to get it all into focus he said. For example, when you say "No" to a request, the mere reporting of that fact alone might suggest you had a harsh and unsympathetic attitude, he said.

But when you know the whole long weary route of negotiations that has gone before you will find that the "No" is merely consistent with what you have been doing and trying to do for months.

July 22, 1954

Ho Chi Minh Vows to 'Free' Southern Region of Vietnam

By The Associated Press

TOKYO, July 25—Ho Chi Minh, the Vietminh leader, has pledged to "liberate" the southern part of Vietnam, the Peiping radio said today in a Chinese-language broadcast. The broadcast said the following statement was made by Ho Chi Minh on July 22:

"At the Geneva conference we gained a great victory with the full assistance of the Soviet Union and China. We must continue our utmost efforts during the peace to win the unification, independence and democracy of the whole nation [Vietnam].

"During the cease-fire we must adjust our military zones as the first step toward our final goal. The demarcation of the military zones, however, is just a provisional measure to be taken to restore the peace and realize the unification of the nation by means of general elections.

103

"The demarcation line does not mean the political and territorial border line. North, Central and South Vietnam are unseparable parts of our nation's territory. We assure the people of each region that they will be liberated.

"The people of South Vietnam are those who dared to spearhead the 'patriotic war'. I assure those people that without fail we will struggle shoulder to shoulder to win peace, unification, independence and democracy for the whole of Vietnam.

"The struggle is long and difficult. All the people and soldiers from north and south must unite to achieve a final victory."

Earlier the Peiping radio carried a broadcast of the order of the day of Vo Nguyen Giap, the Vietminh military commander, to the effect that South Vietnam was only temporarily in French hands.

By the terms of the Geneva cease-fire agreement, Vietnam was divided near the Seventeenth Parallel into a northern zone, controlled by the Vietminh and a southern zone, under the jurisdiction of the French-supported Vietnamese Government.

The demarcation line dividing Vietnam is to remain in effect pending general elections in 1956 that are to bring about the unification of the country.

July 26, 1954

U. S. Hopes Arms Sent to French Will Be Left for Vietnam's Army

Native Forces Estimated at 260,000 Men at End of Fighting—Equipment Would Allow Doubling of That Strength

By DANA ADAMS SCHMIDT
Special to The New York Times.

WASHINGTON, Aug. 18—The United States expects the French to leave behind for the Vietnamese Army the military equipment the United States supplied for the Indochina war, United States officials said today.

With this equipment, the officials estimated, the Vietnamese Army, which numbered about 260,000 when fighting ended, could be expanded to twice that size. The cease-fire agreement, while prohibiting import of additional weapons into Vietnam, placed no limitation on the size of the Vietnamese Army.

Foreign Operations Administration figures showed that up to March 31 this year the United States had delivered $800,000,000 worth of military supplies to the French in Indochina. While much of this has been worn out, destroyed in combat or destroyed by the French themselves because it could not be evacuated from North Vietnam, United States officials reported that the French had stockpiled large amounts in safe areas.

Washington officials dealing with this question assume that France intends to evacuate her Expeditionary Corps progressively during the two years leading up to elections in North and South Vietnam. But the French Government has not officially declared its intentions.

Plans to equip and expand the Vietnamese Army by this means are one phase of a program to exert the full material and moral influence of the United States to "win the peace" in Vietnam now being formulated by a committee composed of State Department, Defense Department, Foreign Operations Administration and United States Information Services officials.

Chairman of the committee is Ambassador Robert M. McClintock, whose appointment as Ambassador to Cambodia was confirmed by the Senate yesterday.

The first phase in the program is to transport and help care for every North Vietnamese who wants to be evacuated to South Vietnam. The United States Navy, which began moving refugees from Haiphong to Saigon on Monday, is prepared to transport 100,000 persons a month, officials said.

The Vietnamese Government has estimated that the refugees will number 700,000, but reports from United States officials on the spot indicate the number will probably be under 500,000.

It was noted at the State Department that no indication of any desire whatsoever of Vietnamese to flee from South to North Vietnam had been reported.

The Vietnamese Government has undertaken to feed the refugees. It has obtained from the United States Army 2,000 tents housing twenty persons each and plans to purchase another 2,000 to help shelter the refugees.

United States voluntary agencies have also stepped into the picture. The war relief service of the National Catholic Welfare Fund has dispatched a supply of dried milk and plans programs of child feeding, medical care and clothing distribution to the refugees.

The Cooperative for American Remittances to Everywhere, Inc.

(C. A. R. E.) will this week dispatch 10,000 food packages and 2,500 packages of cotton goods.

The Vietnamese Government has informed the Foreign Operations Administration that it could resettle 500,000 refugees at an estimated cost of $33,000,000. The principal area for resettlement chosen is in sparsely populated plateau country between Saigon and Hue.

Meanwhile, the United States is planning as an initial move to double its existing health, education and public works programs in South Vietnam. On the assumption that travel will now be safe, it intends to send its field representatives into remote areas hitherto controlled by the Vietminh.

The United States officials are working on the assumption that what the United States does to assist refugee movement and resettlement and to build up South Vietnam generally will have a direct bearing on whether the country can be saved from the Communists during the next two years.

For this purpose all the funds needed will be available out of the $700,000,000 earmarked for Southeast Asia and the Western Pacific in the foreign aid program.

August 21, 1954

PREMIER REVISES VIETNAM CABINET

Seeks to Strengthen Regime by Including Commanders of Armies of 2 Sects

By TILLMAN DURDIN
Special to The New York Times.

SAIGON, Vietnam, Sept. 24—Premier Ngo Dinh Diem announced today a Cabinet reshuffle that brought into his Government representatives of the Hoa Hao and Cao Dai religious sects, and a number of new independents.

The Premier at the same time outlined a comprehensive program of social and economic reform.

Gen. Tran Van Soai, commander of the Hoa Hao military formations, and Gen. Nguyen Thanh Phuong, chief of the Cao Dai forces, were added to the Government as Ministers of State and members of the Committee of National Defense. In addition, Hoa Hao appointees were named Ministers of Economics and Agriculture, and Cao Dai members were designated as Ministers of Information and Social Action. Premier Ngo Dinh Diem retained the interior portfolio for himself, but named one deputy each from the Hoa Hao and Cao Dai groups.

Sects Are Described

The Hoa Hao, a reformed Buddhist sect, says it has more than a million adherents, mainly in southwest Cochin China. The Hoa Hao military forces total between 20,000 and 30,000 men.

The Cao Dai consists of followers of a religion that combines Christianity, Buddhism, Taoism, Confucianism and Hinduism. It numbers about 1,500,000 adherents and is concentrated mostly in northwest Cochin China. The Cao Dai military forces are estimated to total 20,000 men.

Dr. Tran Van Do retains the foreign affairs portfolio in the reorganized Cabinet. Tran Huu Phuong was named Minister of Finance. Nguyen Van Thoai was shifted from finance to reconstruction. He will head the ministry through which United States aid will be administered. Dr. Tran Van Do, Tran Huu Phuong and Nguyen Van Thoai, as directors of key Cabinet positions, are independents and close collaborators of the Premier.

Ngo Dinh Diem has broadened the representation of his Government by today's reorganization. Just how much he has strengthened it is hard to say.

In national politics, the Hoa Hao and Cao Dai sects have manifested shifting loyalties. Only a few weeks ago they were bitterly denouncing Ngo Dinh Diem and making common cause with the Premeir's enemies.

Dispute With Army Chief

Premier Ngo Dinh Diem, one of the leading Roman Catholics of Vietnam, still must deal with the question of opposition from the armed forces Chief of Staff, Gen. Nguyen Van Hinh. Another serious problem for the Premier is his lack of control of the National Police, now in the hands of the Binh Xuyen organization.

The Premier declared General Nguyen Van Hinh to be in a state of rebellion against the Government and ordered him to leave the country. Ngo Dinh Diem says the order has been approved by Chief of State Bao Dai. The Chief of Staff has refused to leave.

The reorganization of the Cabinet may bring a sharpening of the conflict between the Premier and his supporters on the one side, and General Nguyen Van Hinh and the Binh Xuyen on the other.

It is believed Bao Dai's inclination is to support General Nguyen Van Hinh and the Binh Xuyen. The Chief of State is on the French Riviera.

Gen. Nguyen Van Xuan, onetime gang leader who heads the Binh Xuyen, was appointed last week by Ngo Dinh Diem to be Vice Premier and Minister of National Defense. He turned in his resignation today, saying the steps being taken by the Premier were intensifying the dissension. In the reorganized Cabinet, his defense portfolio went to Ho Thong Minh.

General Nguyen Van Xuan demanded either a complete new organization of the Cabinet or the nomination by Bao Dai of a new Premier.

September 25, 1954

EISENHOWER ASKS VIETNAM REFORM

In Letter to Saigon Premier, President Links Aid Pledge to Stable Regime There

By TILLMAN DURDIN
Special to The New York Times.

SAIGON, Vietnam, Oct. 24—In a letter to Premier Ngo Dinh Diem, President Eisenhower has expressed the hope that "indispensable reforms" would be carried out by South Vietnam in connection with the receipt of United States aid.

The President also voiced the wish that this aid plus Vietnamese efforts would contribute effectively to the building of an independent Vietnam with a strong government.

A French text of the letter was published today by the official Vietnamese news agency.

President Eisenhower wrote that the United States was prepared to grant direct aid to South Vietnam instead of through the French Government as heretofore.

He added that the United States Ambassador here had been instructed to study with Ngo Dinh Diem a program of United States assistance. The President asserted, however, that consideration would be given to how United States aid could be helpful, provided the Vietnamese Government was disposed to strengthen the sum total of the effort it would put forth in case aid was given.

Senator Mansfield's Report

President Eisenhower's letter on aid followed the publication here last week of a report by Senator Mike Mansfield, Democrat of Montana, on the political situation in Vietnam. The Senator found Ngo Dinh Diem's Government hamstrung by a political opposition that included Gen. Nguyen Van Hinh, Army Chief of Staff; Gen. Le Van Vien, chief of an armed band known as the Binh Xuyen, and Gen. Nguyen Văn Xuan, a retired French Army man.

Senator Mansfield expressed doubt over the advisability of aid being given if Ngo Dinh Diem was overthrown.

October 25, 1954

BAO DAI REMOVES HEAD OF HIS ARMY

Acts to End Feud Between Gen. Nguyen Van Hinh and Premier of South Vietnam

Special to The New York Times.

PARIS, Nov. 29—General Nguyen Van Hinh, Chief of Staff of the Vietnamese Army, was dismissed from his post here today by Bao Dai, Vietnam's Chief of State.

Bao Dai thus confirmed in the strongest possible manner his support of the Government of Premier Ngo Dinh Diem, whose conflict with General Nguyen Van Hinh had produced a crisis of authority in the part of Vietnam preserved from the Communists by the accords ending the Indochina fighting signed in Geneva last July.

The buttressing of the weak civilian authority over the Army in Saigon was in line with the attitude taken by the United States, which had asserted its support of Premier Ngo Dinh Diem and had expressed the hope that opposing forces could reconcile their differences in the interest of a strong and stable political front against the spread of communism.

The most recent public expression of Washington's attitude was given on Nov. 17 by Gen. J. Lawton Collins, special ambassador to Vietnam, who said in Saigon that United States aid would go to the Ngo Dinh Diem Government to permit it "to save the country."

November 30, 1954

VIETNAM PREMIER CLINGS TO POWER AS RIVAL FLEES; GIVES BAO DAI NEW CHANCE

COUP IS A FIASCO

Bao Dai Takes Milder Stand After His Man Fails to Win Army

By A. M. ROSENTHAL
Special to The New York Times.

SAIGON, Vietnam, Monday, May 2—Premier Ngo Dinh Diem is in control of South Vietnam's army after a struggle with Chief of State Bao Dai's backers.

It was a fifteen-hour struggle in which the weapons were not guns but personal loyalties and political strength.

The Premier's opponent in the fight for the army was Inspector General Nguyen Van Vy named by Bao Dai to take military command. At midnight Saturday the general was a prisoner in the Premier's palace. At 9 A. M. yesterday, he announced that the army was his and that there was no government in Saigon. And at 3 P. M. he fled the city.

Last night the Premier cabled to Bao Dai, who lives on the French Riviera, that the army was loyal to the Government and that the general's coup had failed. The Premier warned Bao Dai that unless the Chief of State stopped his war-by-cablegram against the Government, the whole country would go up in revolution.

[The Chief of State Sunday told the Premier in a cablegram sent from Cannes that he was interested in avoiding a civil war. Bao Dai also said he sought a government with a broader base. The message was mild and was viewed as a backdown by Bao Dai.]

Premier 'Studying' Demands

Meanwhile, the Premier applied the brakes to a revolutionary committee of his backers. The committee on Saturday night had moved into the Government Palace and announced that Bao Dai was deposed. The Premier said he was "studying" the revolutionists' demands that he form a new government without allegiance to Bao Dai.

It was obvious the Premier was letting Bao Dai know that if the Chief of State tried to oust him he would not bow but would go along with the revolutionary committee.

"We are giving Bao Dai one more chance to come to his senses," said Ngo Dinh Nhu, the Premier's brother and adviser.

May 2, 1955

DIEM REJECTS BID TO ELECTION TALK

Declines Red North's Offer to Discuss Vietnam Unity —Sees Bar to Free Vote

By The Associated Press.

SAIGON, Vietnam, Aug. 10 —Premier Ngo Dinh Diem rejected today an offer from Communist North Vietnam to discuss general elections to reunite the country.

Premier Diem's note said his Government favored "essentially free elections," but "nothing constructive * * * can be done as long as the Communist regime in the north does not permit each Vietnamese citizen to enjoy the democratic liberties and the fundamental rights of man."

Under the armistice, elections are scheduled for not later than July, 1956. A preparatory meeting was to have been held last month, but Premier Diem delayed until today replying to North Vietnam's proposal.

The United States, Britain and France had recommended that Premier Diem meet with Ho Chi Minh's Red regime so as not to imperil Indochina's uneasy truce.

Premier Diem's supporters say he is not bound by the armistice conditions because he did not sign the Geneva accord.

On July 20 North Vietnam's Foreign Minister, Pham Van Dong, asked Premier Diem to name the date and select a city on Vietnamese territory for the election conference.

A week earlier Premier Diem made it plain he would not even talk about elections as long as the Communist Government in the north resorted to what he called terrorism and totalitarian methods.

Thus, a year after the nine-nation meeting at Geneva ended the Indochina war, the uneasy peace again is menaced.

A Canadian member of the Armistice Control Commission said: "The south can do as she pleases. She did not sign the accords. But is she prepared to face up to the consequences? The Vietminh [North Vietnam] may decide to settle the question by war."

Official declarations have indicated that Premier Diem's Government wants the United Nations and not the Indian-Polish-Canadian armistice commission to supervise the voting.

August 11, 1955

CAMBODIA SEVERS TIES WITH FRANCE

Declares Her Independence —Prince Norodom Takes the Post of Premier

PNOMPENH, Cambodia, Sept. 25 (UP)—The Indochinese Kingdom of Cambodia formally declared her independence from France today after nearly 100 years of association. Prince Norodom Sihanouk was named Premier.

The Cambodian National Congress, in its first action, severed the kingdom's last formal ties with France by striking from its Constitution all mention of association with the French Union.

It then asked the 33-year-old Prince, who abdicated from the throne last March, to become Premier. He agreed to take the post for at least three months.

The Congress is composed entirely of Deputies of Norodom's Socialist Peoples Community, which the new Premier led to victory in the first nation-wide elections early this month. It met for the first time today.

The Congressmen voted to replace the words "Cambodia, autonomous state belonging to the French Union as an associated state" with "Cambodia, a sovereign and independent state."

In 1863 France signed a protectorate agreement with Cambodia and saved it from Siamese domination.

The Congress was opened by King Norodom Suramarit, father of the new Premier, in the royal palace.

Members of the Government and the entire diplomatic corps attended the session while 40,000 Cambodians massed outside the palace.

The decision to sever formal relations with France came as no surprise.

September 26, 1955

DIEM WINS POLL IN SOUTH VIETNAM, OUSTING BAO DAI

Premier's Victory Confronts Big 4 at Geneva With Task of Implementing Truce

By HENRY R. LIEBERMAN

Special to The New York Times.

SAIGON, Oct. 23—Premier Ngo Dinh Diem replaced Bao Dai as South Vietnam's Chief of State today in a ballot-box revolution aimed at establishing a new republic.

It was the first national vote ever taken in South Vietnam. The vote involved a referendum on whether or not the people wanted Bao Dai removed and Mr. Diem to become Chief of State "with the task of organizing a republic."

Twenty-four hours or more may elapse before the official result is announced. By midnight tonight, however, the only question in Government quarters here was just how big Mr. Diem's victory vote would be. Vietnamese officials predicted Mr. Diem would get 80 to 90 per cent of the ballots.

The announced returns from Dalat, Bao Dai's former summer capital, gave Mr. Diem 98.7 per cent of 26,623 votes cast there. An unofficial tally showed Mr. Diem had 98.2 per cent of the 45,750 votes cast in the first of six Saigon-Cholon districts to report.

Some Ballots Invalid

In this district 519 ballots and at Dalat 231 ballots were declared invalid. The referendum was preceded by rumors here Communists had been instructed to deface their ballots.

Bao Dai, who has been in France for more than a year, was installed by the French as Vietnamese Chief of State in 1949. He recently "dismissed" Mr. Diem as Premier, but the latter continued anyway with his plans for today's referendum.

Tens of thousands of South Vietnamese went to the polls in warm, clear weather to choose between Mr. Diem and the absent Bao Dai.

The results of the referendum confront the Big Four foreign ministers meeting later this week at Geneva with a fait accompli regarding the 1954 Geneva armistice agreement. The agreement, which split Vietnam in two at the Seventeenth Parallel, was signed by French and North Vietnamese representatives.

The declaration also projected general elections for all of Vietnam in July, 1956. But South Vietnam did not sign the Geneva agreement and Mr. Diem has shown no disposition to accept it.

If there are to be general elections next year, the North Vietnamese Government will presumably have to deal with Mr. Diem instead of with the French. For days now the Hanoi radio has been denouncing the South Vietnamese referendum as a "farce and swindle" designed to "sabotage the Geneva agreement" and "stifle the fighting spirit of the Vietnamese people."

Today's referendum has been interpreted by foreign observers as a preliminary step intended to activate the political life of South Vietnam. It is officially represented as a forerunner of moves to elect a National Assembly in the South and evolve a new Constitution.

A total of 5,335,688 men and women over the age of 18 were eligible to vote in the referendum.

Minor incidents were reported of Communist sympathizers trying to make speeches at polling places. But they were silenced quickly by small numbers of troops and white-uniformed policemen stationed at the voting centers to keep order.

In Cholon, Saigon's twin Chinese-populated city, the shopkeepers hung out the flag of the Chinese Nationalists along with the South Vietnamese banner.

The ballots, which were about six by six inches in size, consisted essentially of two pictures. One was a reddish-tinted photo of a smiling Mr. Diem among the people and the other was a greenish-tinted photo of a sullen-looking Bao Dai in court dress.

After having made their choice in curtained booths, the voters tore off the picture of the man they favored, put it in an envelope and placed the envelope in a sealed ballot box.

The 54-year-old Mr. Diem, a devout Roman Catholic and stubborn nationalist, began his political career as an official at the royal court in Hue. He was named Premier by Bao Dai in 1954 just as Vietnam was about to be partitioned at Geneva.

The 42-year-old Bao Dai, who abdicated as Emperor of Annam in 1945 and was restored by the French as Chief of State four years later, has been losing political influence here for some time.

October 24, 1955

VIETNAMESE LAW TO BE SET FORTH

Nation Will Promulgate Its Constitution Tomorrow— Ban on Communism Set

By BERNARD KALB
Special to The New York Times.

SAIGON, Vietnam, Oct. 24— The Republic of Vietnam will celebrate its first anniversary Friday by promulgating a Constitution that gives the President broad powers and outlaws communism.

After months of drafting and redrafting ,the preamble and ten chapters of the Constitution were completed last week-end by the 123-man Constituent Assembly.

From one end of Saigon to the other the Vietnamese—men in their working clothes and women in their conical straw hats and pajama-like dresses—were prettying up their capital.

Paint brushes have been applied throughout the city, Vietnamese flags have been put out and the tree-lined streets were being scrubbed clean.

Many important officials from neighboring Southeast - Asian countries have been invited to watch the year-old republic make history. and the President, Ngo Dinh Diem, and the residents of the capital want Saigon to look its best.

Authority to Be Divided

The Constitution provides for a division of authority with separate executive, legislative and judicial branches. But of the three, the executive branch is endowed with the bulk of the power, a fact that Vietnamese officials freely admit was planned that way.

A true democracy is a fine thing, these officials say. but it is an extravagance that South Vietnam can not afford at this critical time in its infancy. They note that the northern half of Indochina is Communist, that the Communist potential for subversion in South Vietnam is still re ıl, and that South Vietnam now is living, not in a state of peace, but in a state of tension.

Some legal experts in the West may question the advisability of parts of the Constitution, they add, but they insist that they are doing the best they can by democracy without introducing a constitutional apparatus that would allow the Communists to operate under the cover of the law.

Faith in President Is Cited

President Diem, they say, is the man who created a going republic out of the chaos left both by the French and by almost a decade of civil war. The broad constitutional powers given to the President, they say, represent an act of faith in him.

The Constitution, drawn up by a pro-Diem Assembly with numerous suggestions from the President himself, contains the following provisions:

¶The President and the National Assembly shall be elected by universal secret ballot; the President's term shall be for five years, the Assemblymen's term for three years; the President shall be eligible for two more terms.

¶The Assembly can pass laws over a Presidential veto if a three-quarters majority of the Assembly is obtained.

¶"All activities having as their object the direct or indirect diffusion or implementation of the Communist doctrine in whatever form shall be contrary to the principles embodied in the Constitution."

¶A constitutional court shall be established to ascertain the constitutionality of laws. Proposals for amendments to the Constitution may be made by either the President or a two-thirds of the Deputies in the Assembly.

¶The President, with the consent of the Assembly, may organize a national referendum, presumably when there is disagreement between the Executive and legislative branches.

¶Every citizen has the right to freedom of thought, of speech, and "within the limits set by law, of meeting and association."

October 25, 1956

Communist Rulers Of North Vietnam Promise Reforms

HONG KONG, Nov. 2 (AP)— North Vietnam's Communist rulers, apparently fearful of repercussions from the anti-Red revolts in Eastern Europe, promised today a sweeping liberalization of their regime. A statement broadcast by the Hanoi radio said the Communist north's first elections would be held in 1957, " enabling the people further to participate in management of the state and control of the administration."

The broadcast said an extraordinary meeting of the Council of ministers presided over by President Ho Chi Minh also decided:

¶"To readjust and develop the democratic organs of the people."

¶To give new powers to the present puppet National Assembly, appointed ten years ago.

¶"To insure the people's democratic rights and strengthen the basis of democratic legality."

¶To pass new laws guaranteeing greater freedom of movement and speech.

¶To improve living conditions of workers through "a more reasonable wage system."

Relation to Red China

The Government that rules 12,500,000 people in the northern half of war-divided Vietnam admitted "grave mistakes and present difficulties."

North Vietnam was the first Asian Communist nation to act since the rebellion against Communism in Hungary and against Soviet control in Poland.

Communist China, while showing its approval of the East European independence movement, has announced no steps to loosen the tight grip the Peiping regime holds on its 600,000,000 population.

The Hanoi announcement indicated for the first time the extent and seriousness of the dissatisfaction that exists against Communist leadership in the North.

Vietnam was divided into a Communist North and Free South by the armistice of 1954. The North has often been reported in economic difficulties since then.

The Reds admitted yesterday their much-publicized agrarian reform program was on the rocks and blamed two leaders, Ho Viet Thang and Le Van Luong. Both were dismissed.

Ousting of 3 Red Leaders

The first indications of trouble in Communist North Vietnam came last Monday. The Hanoi radio reported that three Communist party leaders had been disciplined and punished for mistakes in the conduct of agricultural policy.

Truong Chinh, General Secretary of the Vietnam Lao Dong party, resigned and was replaced by Ho Chi Minh. Ho Viet Thang, who had been in charge of the party's agricultural program, was dismissed from the Central Committee and reduced to the status of an ordinary party member. Le Van Luong was expelled from the party's Politburo and Secretariat and relieved also of his post as head of the party's Central Organization Committee.

November 3, 1956

South Vietnam Head Escapes as Gunman Fires at Him at Fair

By FOSTER HAILEY
Special to The New York Times.

BANMETHUOT, South Vietnam, Feb. 22—An attempt was made to assassinate President Ngo Dinh Diem this morning as he was presiding at the opening of an exposition here. He was not injured.

The assailant fired from not farther than ten feet away with an automatic pistol of Austrian make. The Presidential party was nearing the exposition center after a ribbon-cutting ceremony.

A bullet ripped through the back of the coat of a Vietnamese reporter and struck the Minister of Agricultural Reform in the right arm and side. penetrating the right lung.

Assailant Not Identified

The name of the attacker was not immediately revealed by the police. One report was that he had identified himself as being from Communist North Vietnam. The country was divided by the armistice of 1954.

The assailant's face was bleeding from blows struck by policemen, Presidential aides and bystanders. He seemed to be not badly hurt.

The pistol shot was so muffled and the prisoner and the wounded minister were taken out of the area so quickly that many in the crowd were unaware that anything unusual had happened.

February 23, 1957

Red Gains in Laos and Cambodia Said to Threaten South Vietnam

Saigon Observers Skeptical of Neighbors' Anti-Communist Protestations— Continued Subversion Feared

By GREG MacGREGOR
Special to The New York Times.

SAIGON, Vietnam, Feb. 6— Cambodia and Laos have done little to quiet apprehension here over Communist activities in Southeast Asia, observers said today.

The coalition leadership of Laos, which combines the Communist-supported Pathet Lao and the royalist government, was accepted as a strategic loss for the anti-Communist forces of Asia. Southern Vietnamese held little hope for a completely nationalist Laos to the exclusion of Communist influences.

Political observers here pre- dicted that a substantial number of Communist candidates would be elected in the coming elections in Laos.

In Cambodia, recent anti-Communist protestations by Premier Norodom Sihanouk were largely discounted. His remarks were written off as the "unpredictable comments of a mercurial personality."

Underground Is Active

South Vietnamese officials concede privately that the Communist underground here is still a threat. The exact size of the movement is doubtful. Estimates of the number of Com- munists in Saigon range from 15,000 to 70,000. The city's population is 2,000,000.

Communist activities in the rural areas also worry the South Vietnamese Administration. The current resettlement program of coastal farmers and fishermen in the northern plateau section is evidence of the government's concern for this hitherto almost unpopulated section.

At the cost of more than half of the agricultural aid funds allotted by the United States, President Ngo Dinh Diem has endorsed the program, under which about 30,000 persons will be moved into areas considered "dangerous."

By the end of last month 10,000 persons had been resettled in this so-called invasion-route section and free land as well as substantial Government support were guaranteed to families who remained.

New Lands More Fertile

While emphasizing the point that the peasants would be better off in the new and more fertile virgin lands, officials also said that prosperous and satisfied settlers would be less likely to yield to Communist enticements. A home guard in the new villages is to deal with any Communist subversion.

Although many of South Vietnam's 10,000,000 farmers need assistance badly, more than half of the available funds have been diverted for the use in resettlement programs involving only about 100,000. This, according to agrarian experts, points up the priority given to projects that are intended to discourage subversion.

When bombs were hurled here late last year against a United States Information Service library, the Government was quick to place blame on Communist agents. Numerous arrests were made but police officials conceded today that they were powerless to uncover agents from the Communist underground. The bombings have remained unsolved.

Administration leaders say the only means of combating subversion here is with a healthy economy and satisfied population.

February 7, 1958

Envoy to Cambodia Is Recalled For Report on Communist China

Ambassador Strom Is Summoned Home to Discuss Meaning of Pnompenh's Recognition of Peiping

By E. W. KENWORTHY
Special to The New York Times.

WASHINGTON, July 24— The United States has called home its Ambassador to Cambodia for a report on Cambodia's recognition of Communist China.

On July 18 the Peiping radio announced that Prince Sihanouk, Cambodian Premier, had sent a letter to Premier Chou En-lai notifying him that the Cambodian Government had decided to recognize the Peiping regime.

Lincoln White, State Department press officer, said today, "We are asking Ambassador Carl W. Strom to return to Washington to report to us personally on the significance of what has occurred."

Mr. White said that the State Department was "very much surprised" at Cambodia's action, especially in view of the sentiments expressed by Prince Sihanouk in an article in the current issue of Foreign Affairs.

Prince Sihanouk wrote:

"A prince and former king must be well aware that the first concern of the Communists is to get rid of the king and natural élite of any country they succeed in laying hands on."

This, the Prince added, was sufficient reason to deter him from any "flirtation" with the Communists.

Commenting on the Cambodian action, Mr. White said:

"While we, of course, do not question the right of the sovereign Government of Cambodia to take any steps which it considers to be in the national interests of its people, we regard this action as regrettable.

"All free Asian nations are threatened by the Chinese Communists who have employed force and the threat of force in their foreign policies. They are engaged in subversive activities throughout Southeast Asia."

One possible reason advanced today for the action was that Premier Sihanouk might be trying to play off Peiping against Washington to get more aid from both.

In the fiscal year ended June 30, Cambodia got about $30,-000,000 in economic aid from the United States. In June, 1956, Communist China announced that over the next two or three years it would grant the equivalent of $22,400,000 in aid to Cambodia.

July 25, 1958

RED ACTIVITIES UP IN SOUTH VIETNAM

Rise in Sabotage and Deaths Viewed by Some as Drive to Undermine Republic

By TILLMAN DURDIN
Special to The New York Times.

SAIGON, Vietnam, April 12 —The Communist underground in South Vietnam has stepped up its activities in recent months.

Some observers here believe this may represent a Communist shift to a concerted campaign to undermine the South Vietnamese republic. Others think it is too early to draw such a conclusion because every spring there is some increase in dissident activity.

Communist sabotage and assassinations have been more evident lately. Propaganda of Communist North Vietnam against the south has been intense.

Communist activity in South Vietnam is especially apparent in western Cochin China along the Cambodian frontier, at the southern tip of Cochin China and in the forested region north of Saigon that stretches to Cambodia.

Other dissident elements also exist in these areas, fugitive remnants of the Binh Xuyen, Cao Dai and Hoa Hao groups that rebelled against President Ngo Dinh Diem in 1955. It is difficult to differentiate between actions of 'Communist and non-Communist agents.

Reds Left Agents Behind

The Communists left underground agents in the south after the redisposition of forces between North and South Vietnam that followed the 1954 Geneva settlement of the Indochina war. Until recently, these agents and subsequent recruits seemed mainly to pursue a policy of political infiltration and propaganda.

There is evidence, however, that Communist cadres have slowly built up in the south, aided by infiltrations from the north across the highlands of

The New York Times   April 13, 1959
Rising activity by Reds is reported from Cochin China (diagonal shading).

central Vietnam, southwestern Laos and northeastern Cambodia.

The Communists have been helped by Cambodia's neutral

policy and the bad feeling between South Vietnam and Cambodia.

Communist assassins have been choosing for targets provincial officials who are especially zealous and effective. Sometimes the assassins have chosen private persons known as strong supporters of President Ngo's Government.

Communist agents have particularly sought to hamper South Vietnam's land-reform program. They have destroyed farm machinery and threatened some farmers for accepting land under the reform program.

There is concern but not alarm here about the Communist activity. To combat it, training and expansion of the Civil Guard are being pushed and army troops are combing areas known to have Communist hide-outs.

Enactment of a law that would give military tribunals jurisdiction over crimes involving political sabotage and terrorism is being considered. The aim would be to insure quick and stern punishment.

April 13, 1959

TWO U.S. SOLDIERS SLAIN IN VIETNAM

Red Terrorists Kill Major and Sergeant—Captain Hit in Attack During Movie

Special to The New York Times.

BIENHOA, Vietnam, July 9— Increasing Communist terrorism in South Vietnam was emphasized sharply here last night when two United States soldiers, a major and a master sergeant, were killed and a captain was wounded by the Vietminh.

All three were part of the eight-man United States Military Assistance Advisory Group attached to the South Vietnamese Army at Bienhoa, twenty miles northeast of Saigon.

[The Associated Press identified the men killed as Maj. Dale R. Buis of Imperial Beach, Calif., and M/Sgt. Chester M. Ovnand of Copperas Cove, Tex., and the wounded officer as Capt.

Howard B. Boston of Blairsburg, Iowa.]

Reds Attacked in 1957

According to diplomatic sources, this was the first time the Communist Vietminh has carried out a successful assassination mission against Americans.

Bombings of an advisory group bus and a United States Information Service library in 1957 by the Vietminh resulted in thirteen wounded, but no one was killed.

July 10, 1959

LAOS AGAIN A COMMUNIST TARGET

By TILLMAN DURDIN
Special to The New York Times.

VIENTIANE, Laos, Aug. 8— In Laos communism is an illicit import from Vietnam. With the Communist half of Vietnam this little landlocked kingdom has 600 miles of mountainous, poorly guarded, badly marked frontier. Across the monsoondrenched northern stretches of this frontier Communist Vietnam this week acted to spark a recrudescence of Communist insurrection in Laos.

Military units composed of soldiers from the Meo and Thai minorities of Vietnam thrust into three Laotian provinces, Phongsaly, Luang Prabang and Samneua and linked up with kinsmen of the same ethnic groups in Laos.

Infiltrators Renew An Old Battle

The Laotian tribesmen were Communist activists originally spawned in the Communist Vietnamese invasions of Laos during the Indochina war. They had been quiet since 1957, when the Laotian Government reached a settlement with the Communist Pathet Lao rebels, then in control of most of Phongsaly, Samneua and other areas in Laos.

Hard to Gauge

Because of poor communications from these remote and sparsely populated areas, the scope of the uprisings is difficult to gauge. They appear to involve several thousand men with arms and other supplies which Laotian officials believe came from Vietnam. In clashes at Laotian army outposts the invaders and rebels captured no major towns, but there were scores of casualties.

The Communist flare-up places Laos in a serious new domestic and international crisis.

Crisis of any sort seems out of place in this peaceful, tropical land remote from the main stream of modern life. Laos has less than two million people in an area as big as Kansas. Half the population is easy-going Buddhist lowlanders called Laos; the other half is made up of more than twenty different

kinds of mountain dwelling, mostly primitive, anamist tribesmen.

There is poverty, but no grave economic unrest, in predominantly agricultural Laos. The country is one of the most underdeveloped on earth. It has few roads, no railways, no known natural resources of great importance. Its government is struggling to create a modern state with scanty financial means and a dire lack of trained men. The United States is spending $25,000,000 annually to bolster the weak Laotian state. More than half this sum is allocated to financing the kingdom's poorly-trained, badly organized 25,000-man army.

Scanty Means

Aside from rivalries between the leading families there were no series conflicting forces among Laotians until the Vietnamese brought communism

109

into the land. During the Indochina war against the French from 1946 to 1954 Laos became an independent nation again after sixty years as a French protectorate. It had been for the most part on the side of the French against the Vietnamese Communists and nationalists. The Communists, however, made headway among some of the mountain peoples along the Vietnamese frontiers, capitalizing on the hillmen's resentment of the Lao lowlanders' domination of the country and Government.

It was by way of the hill areas of Laos that the Vietnamese Communist forces launched their big drives against the French in 1953-54. Vietnamese columns coursed through the Northern provinces to the gates of the royal capital of Luangprabang and other contingents advanced across the narrow waist of Laos, threatening Tahkhek Savannakhet on the Mekong River.

Under the Geneva agreements that ended the Indochina war the Vietnamese invaders retreated into North Vietnam while their Laotian collaborators—mostly hillmen but with some lawlanders—regrouped in the Northern provinces of Phongsaly and Samneua. After

LAOS—THE TROUBLED AREAS

Areas of fighting

Population . . 12,000,000
Area (sq. mi.) 60,000

Population . . 1,700,000
Area (sq. mi.) . . . 69,000

desultory fighting Laotian dissidents who styled themselves "Pathet Lao" (Land of Lao) in 1957 accepted peace on the basis of formation of a neutralist coalition Government including insurgent leaders, a promise of new elections and a plan for integration of rebel civil and military personnel into national

life and the army. The soldiers of the 7,500-man Pathet Lao army were disbanded except for 1,500 men who were to be integrated into the national forces.

After the Elections

The 1957 agreement was in main carried out, and after the elections the international com-

mission composed of representatives of India, Poland and Canada that had assisted in negotiating and implementing the pact was disbanded. The Laotian Government took the view that it had fulfilled the terms of the Geneva accords, which had prescribed the general lines of the settlement that was achieved, and that the commismission had no further role to play in Laos.

The Communist-front Neo Lao Hak Yat party formed by Pathet Lao elements caused such concern among non-Communist political groups by polling a heavy vote in the elections that an anti-Communist united front was formed. The National Assembly voted Premier Phoui Sananikone emergency powers to deal with the Communist problem and to push a program of national development and rural rehabilitation.

Excluded from the Government, faced with the growing effectiveness of government policies, the Communists have now resorted again to insurrection and to getting support as before from Vietnam. Rebel activity again is concentrated among the hill peoples where the Communists have their following.

August 9, 1959

U. S.-FRENCH UNITS TO TRAIN LAOTIANS

Americans to Teach Use of Arms—Joint Program to Start This Month

By TILLMAN DURDIN
Special to The New York Times.

VIENTIANE, Laos, Aug. 9—French and United States specialists will begin a new joint training program for the Laotian Army this month. The American role in the program will be to give instruction on the use and maintenance of weapons and other equipment. The French will deal with tactics.

The new program will associate Americans for the first time with the training of Laotian combat forces. The limiting of Americans to nontactical activities is in conformity with the primacy accorded to the French under terms of the French-Laotian mutual defense pact and the Geneva agreements of 1954.

The Geneva accords ending the Indochina war authorized

France to maintain a military training mission in Laos and to retain an air base at Seno, 200 miles southeast of here.

The number of Americans participating in the program, including administrative personnel, will total 107. French and American training specialists will operate as twelve sixteen-man teams, with eight Americans and eight Frenchmen on each team.

The teams will set up field training centers in different parts of the country. Key Laotian military personnel will receive intensive seven-week courses at these centers and then return to their units to impart what they have learned to the rank-and-file Laotian forces.

France's military commitments in Algeria and Europe have made it impossible for the French military mission to fulfill its role of training the Laotian Army. The Geneva agreements authorized a French training mission of 3,500 men for Laos.

Own Soldiers Inexperienced

The mission actually has only a few hundred. These are occupied either in administering the mission or in posts within the Laotian forces and are not engaged in training.

As a result, the Laotian

Army and Air Force of 25,000 men are poorly trained and organized. Organized hurriedly during the final years of the Indochina war, the Laotian forces have never had proper instruction. Laos has lacked experienced military men of her own to do the job.

The United States supplies and pays the salaries and other costs of Laotian military contingents. In some respects the quality of the Laotian forces has been deteriorating in recent years. French and American officials here hope the new one-year program will produce cadres that can reshape Laotian units and improve their effectiveness.

The new French-American training teams will be under the over-all command of Gen. Jean d'Arrivere, who is in charge of the French military mission here. Most of the Americans to participate in the new training program have already arrived.

The Laotian Army is equipped with only light weapons and is organized to operate in small mobile units. It could not hope to resist an attack by a strong enemy force. Its mission is to combat internal dissidence and wage guerrilla-type warfare in case of invasion.

August 10, 1959

Army Rules in Laos As Premier Resigns

By The Associated Press.

VIENTIANE, Laos, Dec. 31 —Laos was placed under army control today following the resignation of Premier Phoui Sananikone.

King Savang Vathana twice rejected Mr. Phoui's resignation, then sent him a sharply worded letter accepting it.

"It is apparent that, in the face of the powerlessness of the Government to control an explosive situation, it is not morally possible for us to leave the nation in uncertainty of the future," the King told his reluctant Premier.

An official at the Premier's office said "the security of the country has been immediately placed under control of the army until a new Cabinet is formed." He added:

"Please don't dramatize the situation. It's a coup d'état Laotian style and not on the South American level. It's all en famille. No bloodshed."

Vientiane was enjoying the usual calm of the siesta hour as the Government radio broadcast the King's letter.

The King was believed to be backing an anti-Communist reform group, the Right-wing Committee for Defense of the National Interest, which includes top military commanders.

Three armored cars were drawn up beside the Royal Palace in Vientiane. The Premier's office said they were there for "protection" and had apparently been summoned by the King's chamberlain. The King had come to Vientiane from the royal capital at Luang Prabang for a meeting of the National Assembly.

The conflict between the army officers and Mr. Phoui developed when they accused him of adopting an appeasement policy toward the Communists and jeopardizing the electoral system.

The officers had called on the King to name a nonparty cabinet, including themselves, to prepare for new elections in April, 1960.

Mr. Phoui had accused some of them of seeking dictatorial powers. A Cabinet minister close to Mr. Phoui said the Premier felt menaced "politically and physically."

Mr. Phoui first sent his resignation to the King Monday, after the death of Deputy Premier Katay Don Sasorith. When it was rejected, he sent a second offer to quit.

Mr. Katay was the strong man in the Cabinet as president of the ruling Rally of the Laos People party, which controls thirty-six seats in the fifty-nine-member National Assembly. Mr. Phoui, the party vice president, has the allegiance of only about a fourth of the members.

Earlier this month Mr. Phoui defied a challenge from the officers' committee, which held seven posts in the Cabinet at the height of the fighting against the pro-Communist rebels. These ministers resigned Dec. 15 after Mr. Phoui had switched to a neutralist international policy. The Premier rode out that crisis with the support of Mr. Katay.

Mr. Phoui announced then that the Government and Assembly intended to stay in power until the April elections, even though their terms expired last Friday. The Assembly supported him.

January 1, 1960

PEASANTS SHIFTED BY SOUTH VIETNAM

Saigon Acts to Detect Reds by Regrouping Populace Into New Rural Towns

By TILLMAN DURDIN
Special to The New York Times.

SAIGON, Vietnam, April 28 —In a move to combat growing Communist sabotage and political and terrorist activity in South Vietnam, the Government has begun a large-scale regrouping of the rural population.

Peasant families are being moved from scattered hamlets of farm houses into newly created rural towns called agrovilles. Each agroville, with a population of about 10,000, will be the residential center for farmers of near-by lands.

The Government hopes to be able to maintain such close surveillance by the police in the agrovilles that Communist agents among the residents can be detected and apprehended.

The growing violence represents a new aggressive attitude toward the South by Communist North Vietnam. During the last six months the North may have infiltrated as many as 2,000 new agents into South Vietnam.

Seeks State of Defense

In the conception of President Ngo Dinh Diem, the agrovilles will put the South Vietnam countryside in a state of permanent preparedness against the Communist efforts.

Each agroville will be built around a big central market square. The homes will be constructed in groups of nine, with each home possessing a garden plot, the Government said. Defensive bamboo fences, hedges and canals will surround the area.

At night, when the Communist terrorists are most active, the town will be in a state of alert. All who enter or leave will be checked.

For each town the Government is building a library, schools and playgrounds, in addition to the central market. Electricity will be provided. Merchants will get loans to erect shops, but the householders will have to construct their own homes, streets and other facilities.

Only one agroville, at Vithanh, in the ricelands about 100 miles southwest of Saigon, is completed and in full operation. Seventeen others are under construction. Scores more are planned.

Even to regroup only the rural population in the parts of South Vietnam where Communist activity is the most extensive would mean the resettling of hundreds of thousands of peasants.

Officials here are confining themselves now to saying that the creation of agrovilles will go as far and as fast as possible.

Considerable resistance to the new towns has been reported among the peasants, who must not only leave their countryside but also expend much labor in the construction.

But Government officials maintain that the Vithanh agroville has proved to be a success because Communist activity has been sharply reduced in that area.

Authoritative sources in Saigon estimate that there are 3,000 to 5,000 armed Communist terrorists in the South. These agents assassinate rural officials, raid local defense posts, burn bridges and harass communications.

The terrorists often kill indiscriminately to spread fear as well as to induce people to give them protection and not to cooperate with the Government.

During some weeks since the first of the year deaths in the South from terrorists have averaged ten a day. In their biggest coup this year a Communist band surprised an army post northwest of Saigon in January, killed thirty-four soldiers and made off with a large amount of arms and ammunition.

The Communists have made some roads and inland waterways unsafe at night but have so far caused no major disruption of economic or social life. Production and commercial activities go on without interruption and the South's highways are crowded with daily traffic.

April 29, 1960

DICTATORIAL RULE IN SAIGON CHARGED

By TILLMAN DURDIN
Special to The New York Times.

SAIGON, Vietnam, April 30— Eighteen well-known Vietnamese asked President Ngo Dinh Diem today to liberalize his regime and to permit them to function as an opposition political group.

The eighteen men sent a petition to the President charging his Government with denying elementary civil liberties, carrying on "one-party" rule and copying "dictatorial Communist methods." The petition said continual arrests had filled prisons to overflowing and asserted that a swollen Government bureaucracy was corrupt and inefficient.

The eighteen signers of the petition included ten who were ministers in former Vietnamese Governments. Tran Van Van, a former Minister of the Economy and Planning, and Phan Khac Suu, a former Minister of Agriculture and Labor, handed out copies of the petition at a news conference this morning.

They described themselves as promoters of the petition and of a national front to be constituted by the signatories.

Other signers include Dr. Tran Van Do, Foreign Minister for the Vietnamese Government at the time of the Geneva Conference that divided the country in 1954 and brother of South Vietnam's present Ambassador in Washington; Dr. Phan Huy Quat, former Minister of National Defense; Le Quang Luat, former Minister of Information; Dr. Phan Huu Chuong, former Minister of Public Health, and Tran Van Tuyen, a former Minister of Information.

Mr. Van denied that presentation of the petition had any connection with events in South Korea, where popular uprisings toppled the Government of President Syngman Rhee last week. Consideration of the petition began five months ago, he declared.

He stated that he and Mr. Suu had sought a personal meeting with President Diem to present the petition but had received no reply and consequently had sent the petition by messenger.

"We hope the President will

allow an open Opposition to help him find the way to alter government policies." Mr. Van said. "We follow the same line as the President with this difference, that we would like to have a regime without corruption—with more liberty and efficiency."

Mr. Van declared that all members of the new national front opposed communism and that the Government itself could oppose communism better if it were more efficient and less corrupt. He said the national front would attempt to register as a political group, but

if it were refused would still seek to carry on open political activity by legal and peaceful means.

The Diem Government keeps tight control of the press and of all Opposition groups. Even political organizations that are clearly non-Communist have a difficult time.

One leading opponent of the Government, Dr. Li Chung Dam, head of a group called the Democratic bloc, defeated his Government-backed rival in last year's National Assembly election but was disqualified from taking his seat by a technical-

ity. At present there is no significant opposition to the Government in the Assembly.

Government sources confirmed today that the petition had been received, but voiced no reaction. There were indications, however, that the document had caused no great concern.

Foreign observers said the signers of the petition are well known but do not have a larger political following. Most of them were members of the Vietnamese Governments before full independence was obtained in 1954 and therefore have a colonialist taint in the eyes of the public.

The petition said that people

around the President had kept knowledge of the "bitter and harsh truth" from him. It asserted there was a danger that the truth would explode "in soaring waves of hatred and **resentment of a terribly suffering people standing up to break the chains that restrain them."**

It charged that the Government had suppressed freedom and silenced the press and public opinion. It

May 1, 1960

TOP REBELS JAILED IN SOUTH VIETNAM

Ngo Regime Crushes Coup Attempt—All Insurgent Troops Surrender

By JACQUES NEVARD
Special to The New York Times.
SAIGON, Vietnam, Nov. 12—
The attempt by a brigade of paratroopers to oust President

Ngo Dinh Diem by a military coup ended in complete failure tonight.

By nightfall all paratrooper units had surrendered and had pledged to cooperate with the Government, the capital had been occupied by troops of the Fifth and Seventh Infantry Divisions and the President was master of the situation.

Four leaders of the abortive coup were in custody.

Lieut. Col. Vuong Van Dong, chairman of the Revolutionary Committee, and his military superior, Col. Nguyen Chanh Thi, a committee member, seized a light plane at the Saigon air-

port this afternoon and attempted to escape.

However, they were forced to land in central South Vietnam by fighter planes and they have been arrested.

Two civilian members of the committee were arrested here. They were Dr. Phan Quang Dan, who was the political counselor of the group, and Tran Van Van, who was identified last May as one of eighteen leaders of an opposition group formed here.

The President announced he would grant a complete pardon to all troops of the parachute brigade except its two leaders.

The coup attempt had been

aimed at ousting Ngo Dinh Diem and members of his family from the Government. Rebel leaders said they sought to strengthen South Vietnam's fight against Communist subversion and terrorism and to establish greater civil liberties.

These plans evaporated when their attempted coup collapsed a little more than twenty-four hours after it began. The number of casualties in fighting yesterday and today had not been determined but responsible sources estimated that at least 100 had been killed and many more wounded.

November 13, 1960

DIVIDED LAOS A KEY TO S.E. ASIA

Communist Progress Is a Threat To Other Nations in Region

By TILLMAN DURDIN

The little kindom of Laos, never a very solid entity, has split into so many regional and political fragments recently that there is no longer any single dominant faction in the country.

The process of disintegration has divided the forces that were formerly united in combating the Communists, leaving the rebels, with their several thousand guerrilla troops and a widespread network of political cadres and sympathizers, in a highly advantageous position. Indeed, they may already be the strongest single element in the kingdom. Their progress poses the most serious threat to the anti-Communist position in Southeast Asia since the compromise between Communist and Western forces that ended the Indochina war in 1954.

Stratigic Position

If Laos were to become Communist, Communist-bloc territory would be added along the borders of Thailand, South Vietnam and Cambodia. Communist North Vietnamese would have a new and easier means of infiltrating anti-Communist South Vietnam, already gravely endangered by the terrorist and

THE STRATEGIC POSITION OF LAOS

sabotage activities of several thousand northern agents.

The balance of power shift that a Communist takeover of Laos would represent would be certain to damage the morale of anti-Communist forces in Southeast Asian countries and produce a parallel boost in confidence for the Communists and their allies.

In Laos the non-Communist political groups and leaders, the bureaucracy and the 29,000-man national army formerly associated with the national Government have now broken into four different factions.

One is centered at Vientiane. Here Captain Kong Le, the intense little paratrooper who started the fragmentation process with his takeover of the capital on Aug. 9, still controls the city, commands several thousand troops personally loyal to him in the Vientiane area and has a wide but undetermined amount of influence and control among other troops of the national army.

Also in Vientiane is a government under Prince Souvanna Phouma, set up as a consequence of the Kong Le coup and committed to the program Kong Le rebelled to achieve—peace with the Communist-led Pathet

Lao rebels and a more neutralist international policy for Laos

Components of the Vientiane faction are far from united. Prince Souvanna, the suave French-speaking aristocrat who is recognized by the United States, Russia and other powers as heading the legal Government of the country, is not pro-Communist and would like to concede less than Captain Kong Le in making peace with the Pathet Lao faction. He would also like to make less of a shift away from Laos' present reliance on the United States than the captain.

Military Dispute

The high command of the national army under General Ouane Rathikone is still in Vientiane, and Captain Kong Le has been appointed General Rathikone's deputy. However, the captain and the general do not always see eye to eye, and the general is a long-time friend of General Phoumi Nosavan, leader of dissidents in revolt at Savannakhet against the Vientiane Government. How much of the army General Rathikone now actually controls doubtless not even he knows.

Titular head of the third faction, at Savannakhet, is Prince Boun Oum, the portly, heavy-drinking senior member of a family that once ruled the formerly separate south Laotian principality of Champassak. The real power in Savannakhet, however, is in the hands of General Nosavan, who is opposed to making peace with the Communists and would like to see Captain Kong Le court-martialed.

A third faction has just begun to crystallize at the little royal city of Luang Prabang, capital of a northern province of the same name. Luang Prabang is the family seat of King Savang Vatthana, whose ancestors for centuries were rulers of a kingdom centered at Luang Prabang and often in conflict with Champassak and another principality at Vientiane. National army units in the province are the power nucleus of the Luang Prabang faction, which is anti-Communist but has not been getting along with the Savannakhet faction.

The Communists lead the fourth faction, which, however, also includes disgruntled non-Communists incorporated into Communist-led military forces called Pathet Lao and the Neo Lao Hak Xat (Patriotic Front) political party.

The struggle between opposing groups in Laos is, at the moment, in an indeterminate stage. Prince Souvanna is negotiating in Vientiane with Pathet Lao representatives on the basis of incorporating the Communist-led elements militarily and politically into the national community. The Pathet Lao agents are asking more than Prince Souvanna wants to give, but the immediate points at issue have not been revealed. Prince Souvanna has also been trying to make peace with the Savannakhet faction,

October 23, 1960

Laos Chief Flees Country; Fears a Clash in Vientiane

By United Press International.

PNOMPENH, Cambodia, Dec. 9—Premier Souvanna Phouma of strife-torn Laos fled here by plane tonight with his family and a group of Government Ministers from Vientiane.

The Premier fled as Communist-led Pathet Lao forces from northern Laos and Right-Wing, pro-Western revolutionary troops from the southern part of the country converged on Vientiane for a showdown.

[Two battalions of Right-Wing troops reached Vientiane Friday night and laid siege to the city, The Associated Press reported.]

Premier Souvanna Phouma said here that he feared Vientiane was in danger of becoming the scene of violent combat between forces of the Pathet Lao movement and Government troops, which proclaimed loyalty to his neutralist regime, but were threatening to fight among themselves.

Earlier in the day, it was reported that paratroopers loyal to the Premier and backed by armed jeeps and tanks had foiled an attempted Rightist coup against his Government.

Premier Souvanna Phouma and his party arrived here aboard an Air Laos plane. A second Air Laos plane, with only the crew aboard, arrived about the same time.

December 10, 1960

PRO-WEST FORCES TAKE VIENTIANE

New Premier Enters Laos Capital as Fighting Ends

Because of communications difficulties, the following dispatch was filed jointly by correspondents in Vientiane.

VIENTIANE, Laos, Dec. 16—Prince Boun Oum, the new Premier of Laos, and the rightist pro-Western general, Phoumi Nosavan, drove into Vientiane at dusk today and announced the liberation of this shattered administrative capital.

At the same time, Capt. Peng, a cheerful Laotian tank officer, was busy cleaning from hold-out positions at the Vientiane airport the stubborn remnants of Capt. Kong Le's pro-Communist paratroops and guerrillas of the Communist-led Pathet Lao movement.

The seventy-six-hour battle for Vientiane ended at 5 P. M. local time [5 A. M., Friday, Eastern Standard Time].

December 17, 1960

Laos Proclaims Neutrality; King Suggests an Inquiry

Asks Mission by Burma, Cambodia and Malaya to Note Aim of Peace

By The Associated Press.

VIENTIANE, Laos, Feb. 19—King Savang Vathana proclaimed today that war-torn Laos was a neutral land seeking peace and he asked that three neutral neighbors send in investigators to confirm it.

He said Premier Prince Boun Oum's Government aimed to adopt a policy of nonalignment.

[The United States welcomed the King's program as "constructive and promising."]

"We hope that our very close neighbors, the Kingdom of Cambodia, the Union of Burma, and the Federation of Malaya, whose impartiality in the sphere of foreign affairs and whose devotion to the cause of universal peace are recognized and respected by all countries, will form a commission, which would come to Laos in order to establish that this country threatens no one and aspires solely to peace," the King said.

"This commission would have as its mission the denouncing of all foreign intervention—direct or indirect, open or camouflaged—which would result in the imperiling of the kingdom's independence, integrity and neutrality."

The 54-year-old monarch thus opened the way for a new international approach to an issue on an issue on which big powers of which big powers of the East and West have dead-locked. The issue is the mechanics of inquiry and pacification to end a six-year conflict.

King Savang Vathana spoke in French at his Vientiane residence before the pro-Western Premier, Cabinet ministers and foreign diplomats. He asked that his declaration be brought before all members of the United Nations through Secretary General Dag Hammarskjold.

Ignoring a Communist contention that Prince Souvanna Phouma is the legal Premier, the King said Premier Boun Oum's regime was the only recognized Government, "properly invested by the National Assembly in accordance with con-

The New York Times
King Savang Vathana

stitutional rules and which we ourselves designated by royal ordinance."

Prince Souvanna Phouma, deposed in the battle of Vientiane last December, is a refugee in Cambodia.

The King, wearing a dark tunic and traditional Laotian trousers, read his message through gold-rimmed glasses.

"Raising our voice above individual and party quarrels," he said, "we declare that Laos entertains no feeling of hostility whatsoever toward any country in the world, but on the contrary, aspires to live in an atmosphere of friendship, understanding and peace."

Refugees in Cambodia

The King said Laos would honor international agreements into which she had "freely entered." Presumably this includes the continued acceptance of millions in United States funds that finance the Laotian army.

The King said this jungle nation of 2,000,000 people had not known peace or security for more than twenty years. Laos was occupied by the Japanese in World War II and then went through the southeast Asian upheaval that led to the Indochina War.

Under the Geneva settlement of 1954, a three-nation truce commission operated for about four years in Laos. Reactivation of the commission, made up of India, Canada and Poland, was proposed by the West in the current crisis, but the Communist powers lean toward a new international conference as the first step.

Move Welcomed by U. S.

By DANA ADAMS SCHMIDT

Special to The New York Times.

WASHINGTON, Feb. 19—The United States welcomed as "constructive and promising" today the move by the King of Laos to establish his country's neutrality and end all forms of intervention by East and West.

The move by King Savang Vathana, who rarely takes public positions, followed consultations in Washington between Winthrop G. Brown, United States Ambassador, and President Kennedy and subsequent talks between the Ambassador and the King.

It appears to be an attempt to break the East-West impasse over proposals to bring about a settlement of the Laotian conflict.

The commission proposed by the King would perform some of the functions of the Indian-Polish - Canadian international control commission, whose operations were suspended in 1958 and which India and Britain have been trying to revive.

A Cambodian proposal for a fourteen - nation conference aroused no enthusiasm in Washington or London. A possibility favored by Britain is the reconvening of the participants in the 1954 Geneva conference.

Diplomats here saw evidence in the warm United States welcome of a distinct shift in policy since the first days of January, when United States forces in the Pacific and strategic air units were alerted for possible action.

The shift, amounting to a decision not to be drawn into a Laotian jungle war, appears to have been made about Jan. 6.

It appears to have been based on the reluctance of Britain, France and other United States allies to go along with a hard line and doubts as to the practicability of waging a campaign in landlocked Laos.

The King's statement, according to diplomats here, sets forth a line that could have been endorsed by Prince Souvanna Phouma, a neutralist, and that implied concessions by the West as well as the East.

Laos, the King said, will join no military alliance and will not have on its territory "either foreign forces or military bases." This, the diplomats said, may mean the end of the base at Seno that France was permitted to retain under the Geneva agreements.

The King appealed to all countries to refrain from intervention "even in the form of aid, if the latter has not been sanctioned" by agreement with the Laotian Government.

Lincoln White, State Department press officer, said the United States would respect the wishes the King had enunciated.

"All of Laos' friends, including the United States," Mr. White said, "have given and will give the Lao authorities every encouragement to work out their difficult problems around this concept of true neutrality.

"The United States, for its part, welcomes the position taken by the King and gives assurances that it will respect the wishes enunciated by his majesty on behalf of the Lao people."

February 20, 1961

MAJOR OFFENSIVE BY LAOS LEFTISTS GAINS KEY POINTS

Pathet Lao Troops Seize Strongholds on Highway —Cut Rightist Defense

VIENTIANE REMAINS CALM

By The Associated Press.

VIENTIANE, Laos, March 11 —Assault troops of the pro-Communist Pathet Lao movement burst through Government defenses in central Laos today, severing the main highway link between this administrative capital and the royal capital of Luang Prabang.

The attackers fanned out to exploit the break-through at the strategic road junction of Sala Pou Koun, a Government military source said, and captured Muong Kassy, a stronghold twenty-two miles to the south.

Government troops fled in two directions, he said, giving the rebels their biggest victory since January and a stranglehold on the Queen Astrid Highway forty miles south of Luang Prabang and less than 100 miles north of Vientiane.

Troops Defend Third Point

At the last report, Government defenders, supported by heavy artillery, were making a stand on high ground surrounding Sala Pou Keng, eight miles north of the road junction and the third key point in Government defense plans for the highway.

Vientiane sources said the outcome of the battle would be in doubt for several days. They said systematic destruction of the highway had made it useless to the advancing rebels.

The Government made no announcement of the battle or casualties. The rebel radio reported that about 300 Government troops had been killed or wounded and "one battalion completely wiped out" during the month-long skirmishing that preceded the attack yesterday by nine battalions of the Pathet Lao movement.

Rebels' Claims Reported

The rebels were quoted by Hsinhua, official Chinese Communist press agency, as having asserted that four Government armored cars, a tank and many trucks had been destroyed and that three United States-supplied planes had been shot down or damaged.

Rumors of the rebel advance flew through Vientiane, but the city remained quiet.

Government sources said the Leftist success was a result of a massive airlift of supplies to the rebels in recent weeks by Soviet-built transport planes. They also said Soviet trucks had been used to rush fresh rebel troops into the fighting.

March 12, 1961

PRO-REDS ACCEPT LAOS CEASE-FIRE; ASK TRUCE TALKS

Later Attack by Rebel Unit Fails to Dim Hopes That All Fighting Will Stop

KONG LE HALTS TROOPS

Souvanna Phouma Proposes Political Parley to Set Up a Coalition Regime

By The Associated Press.

VIENTIANE, Laos, May 3—Pro-Communist Laotian rebels proclaimed a cease-fire effective at 8 A. M. today. A later attack by the rebels on a key town in the narrow southern waist of Laos failed to dim hopes here that all fighting would soon stop.

The tendency was to attribute this morning's assault, in battalion size, at Pha Lane to a failure in communications. Western military experts have predicted that there might be some incidents and fighting even after a formal cease-fire.

The cease-fire order to Pathet Lao forces and their rebel allies was broadcast over the North Vietnamese radio.

It was coupled with an appeal to the Western-backed Laotian Government of Prince Boun Oum to negotiate an armistice followed by a peace conference.

Vientiane Ceases Attacks

The Government forces were ordered last week not to fire unless fired upon.

It was disclosed tonight that Prince Souvanna Phouma, the neutralist who is recognized by the Communists as legal Premier of Laos, had called on all parties in the civil war to gather for a political conference Friday at Ban Namone, the site of the military truce talks. The establishment of a coalition government would be discussed at the meeting.

Hsinhua, the Chinese Communist press agency, said the call for the conference was broadcast by the rebel Voice of Laos.

Prince Souvanna Phouma said the discussions would concern "first of all the question of a coalition government and that of Laos' representation at the Geneva conference."

Neither the fighting at Pha Lane, fifty miles east of Savannakhet, nor a rebel attack last night on Hin Heup, fifty miles north of Vientiane, clouded hope that both sides were inching toward a halt in the long conflict. An armistice could pave the way to a political solution to be weighed by fourteen nations at a conference in Geneva scheduled to begin May 12.

May 4, 1961

Red Guerrillas War On South Vietnam

By ROBERT TRUMBULL
Special to The New York Times.

SAIGON, Vietnam, March 15—South Vietnam is embroiled in a war with Communists in which the casualties are far greater than in the more publicized hostilities in Laos.

Official figures for losses to the Communists have not been made public. However, local authorities estimated that 200 to 500 loyal villagers and others were killed every month in the operations of the Viet Cong, a guerrilla organization directed by Communists. A few months ago the estimate was 800.

President Ngo Dinh Diem's Government asserts that the losses inflicted on the Viet Cong exceed the casualties among the loyal population. Nevertheless, the number of pro-Communist guerrillas is believed to have tripled in the last three years to the present estimated total of 9,000.

The Viet Cong is now thought to be regrouping after several months of severe losses to the South Vietnamese armed forces. However, the authorities expect its disruptive activities to be stepped up during the Presidential election campaign, which opened officially today.

President Ngo Dinh Diem and Vice President Nguyen Ngoc Tho are expected to win re-election easily against two sets of relatively unknown opponents in the balloting on April 9. But it is expected that the Viet Cong will attempt to force a heavy opposition vote, or mass abstention from the election, by intimidation tactics.

The ultimate aim of the Viet Cong is reunification of Vietnam under the Communist Government of President Ho Chi Minh in Hanoi, which holds the region north of the Seventeenth Parallel. The pro-Communist guerrillas are attempting to further this plan by causing a complete breakdown of authority in rural areas of the south.

The Communists have had considerable success in cutting the contact between President Ngo Dinh Diem's Government and the people in the rich delta area south of Saigon. Their activities have hampered almost every effort of the Saigon Administration to improve the life of peasants and villagers.

Loyal local officials are assassinated. Schools are forced to close. Farmers are punished for accepting Government crop loans.

Health Officers Killed

Householders are urged to prevent anti-malaria teams from doing their work. Village health officers are killed or kidnapped. Technicians are frightened away from their posts, and persons who attend Government-sponsored civic meetings are threatened.

South of Saigon, for example, the intimidation of teachers has left more than 25,000 school children without classes to attend. In the same general area, sixty medical aid stations have been destroyed by the Viet Cong. Road communications were disrupted by the damaging or destruction of 284 bridges last year.

Telephone poles are taken down and used to form roadblocks. Canal surveyors are kidnapped and their boats stolen. Rail lines are torn up. All sorts of equipment, including generators, well-drilling rigs and medical supplies, are stolen by the Communists.

The effect of all this activity has been to advertise the Government's inability to provide security where the Viet Cong operates. At the same time the Administration is prevented from carrying out improvement programs whose implementation should win more popularity for the Saigon regime.

The Government's success in improving the level of living along numerous lines is credited with preventing more widespread subversion by the Viet Cong through propaganda. But as long as the military problem remains, the scope of the Government effort is limited.

It is acknowledged here that President Ngo Dinh Diem's army of 150,000 is insufficient to wipe out the guerrillas and at the same time guard 1,200 miles of border against infiltration or possible attack from the north or from pro-Communist guerrilla bases in neighboring Cambodia and Laos.

However, the army and a civil guard numbering more than 50,000 are undergoing intensive training in anti-guerrilla tactics. In recent weeks the President has ordered his forces to take the offensive against pro-Communist concentrations.

March 16, 1961

Ngo Sweeps Vote In South Vietnam; Reds Suffer Blow

By ROBERT TRUMBULL
Special to The New York Times.

SAIGON, Vietnam, Monday, April 10—President Ngo Dinh Diem and Vice President Nguyen Ngoc Tho were returned to office with about 78 per cent of the total vote, according to complete unofficial returns from South Vietnam's first Presidential election yesterday.

Early returns indicated that about 90 per cent of more than 7,000,000 registered voters cast ballots.

The result was taken as a resounding defeat for Communist agitators, who had urged abstention from voting to show disapproval of the strongly centralized Ngo regime.

Mr. Ngo and his running mate led their opponents by a decisive percentage in the voting in Saigon, the country's largest constituency, and the two northern districts of Dalat and Tuyen Duc.

The Saigon electorate gave the Ngo ticket 354,732 votes to 51,098 for Nguyen Dinh Quat and Nguyen Thanh Phuong and 146,518 for Ho Nhat Tan and Nguyen The Truyen.

Mr. Quat is a wealthy 44-year-old rubber planter. Mr. Tan, 75, is a practitioner of Chinese medicine. Hardly anyone had expected these candidates to offer a serious challenge to Mr. Ngo, who was first chosen as head of state in a referendum against the former Emperor Bao Dai in 1955.

The violence expected from Communists seeking to unseat Mr. Ngo did not materialize except in isolated minor incidents. One provincial administrative officer was ambushed by a band presumed to have been Communist guerrillas but escaped unhurt. One grenade explosion was reported, but no one was injured.

The overwhelming vote for Mr. Ngo was generally attributed to three factors.

First, he controls the government machinery, which is a determining force in an Asian country whose people have been conditioned throughout its history to respect power. Second, he unquestionably is the best-known personage in the nation. Finally, under his rule South Vietnam has experienced considerable prosperity, as exemplified by the fact that the conical hats worn by many of the women voters were covered with cellophane over the traditional raw straw. Many electors in or near the capital went to the polls on Italian-made motor scooters instead of on bicycles or afoot.

April 10, 1961

FULBRIGHT HINTS U. S. WEIGHS USE OF TROOPS IN ASIA

Senator Indicates President Is Studying Intervention in Vietnam and Thailand

MORE AID WILL BE SENT

Rusk Says Saigon Is to Get Increased Arms Help to Counteract Red Threat

Special to The New York Times.

WASHINGTON, May 4—Senator J. W. Fulbright strongly indicated tonight that the Kennedy Administration was considering the possibility of direct military intervention to counteract Communist threats in South Vietnam and Thailand.

The Arkansas Democrat, who is chairman of the Senate Foreign Relations Committee, said he would support the moves in South Vietnam and Thailand if they were considered necessary and if the nations concerned wished them.

The Senator had opposed the United States' role in the Cuban exile landings last month and had also registered his opposition to any United States intervention in the fighting in Laos.

Reds in Terror Campaign

Earlier today Secretary of State Dean Rusk said that South Vietnam would get new assistance from the United States to help it resist the Communists, who are conducting a terrorist campaign in many parts of the country.

Mr. Rusk also left the implication that an increase in economic assistance would be forthcoming. He said that situations like the one in South Vietnam "cannot be dealt with solely in military terms."

It was disclosed early this week that the United States was working out with President Ngo Dinh Diem of South Vietnam the details of a $41,000,000 program of new military and economic aid.

The announcement by Senator Fulbright, made in the White House lobby after a long discussion with President Kennedy scheduled at the Senator's request, came as a surprise.

Distinction Is Drawn

Noting his opposition to intervention in Laos, Mr. Fulbright said the primary distinction between the situation there and that in South Vietnam and Thailand, in his view, was that those countries were willing to defend themselves while the Laotians were indifferent and unwilling to shoot "even if you gave them a gun."

The Senator emphasized that he was not willing to make the United States the primary defensive factor in Southeast Asia over a long period. He said it was up to Japan and India to play a role. If they did not, he added, "it would be just too bad."

May 5, 1961

VIETNAM CONFLICT FEEDS ON UNREST

Drive on Ngo Viewed as Echo of War Against French

By ROBERT TRUMBULL
Special to The New York Times.

SAIGON, Vietnam, May 27—As the Communist-led drive to overthrow President Ngo Dinh Diem's pro-Western Government gains steadily in power, the conflict in South Vietnam is taking on a more complex character than that of simple guerrilla warfare.

The Viet Cong (Vietnamese Communist) movement, which took an average of 500 lives a month last year, is thought by some authorities here to be capable of developing into the same kind of broadly based popular uprising that the French were unable to defeat in nine years of bitter fighting.

Considering all the factors underlying the Viet Cong rebellion, it is doubted in thoughtful quarters that the situation can be saved with only the same military tools that failed the French in a similar predicament.

The political and social character of this war has been conveyed to President Ngo. It was clear also to Vice President Johnson when he visited here earlier this month.

President Ngo's efforts to undermine the Viet Cong leadership with social and economic improvements have been largely vitiated in decisive areas by the insurgents' disruptive activities. There are many places where it is unsafe for Government officials to go.

In other areas, the popular dissatisfactions upon which the Viet Cong feeds have been intensified by the summary actions of some officials. An example was the enforced labor levied by local functionaries to build the rural community settlements called "agrovilles."

The tight controls exercised by the Government, such as press censorship, are regarded in various quarters as having also aided the insurgents. But President Ngo considers such measures necessary in what he describes as a "war situation."

Apart from the Communist agitation, the underlying factors in the conflict here boil down to a question whether most of the people are for the Government or for those who would tear it down. The answer to this question is ominously unclear.

In many distressing aspects, the Viet Cong rebellion appears to be really a continuation of the colonial war against the

116

French. The people fighting President Ngo are the same who fought the French, and in their own view they are in arms for essentially similar reasons.

Country dwellers find themselves under the authority, in many cases, of officials who in the past were known as French collaborators. The army, it has been conceded, often finds it necessary to use the same unpleasant methods that the French employed against members of the populace here and in Algeria.

And the image of the vile foreigner, through clever Communist propaganda, has been transferred successfully from the French to the Americans. Many Vietnamese villagers, according to the best authority, believe that not only the Ngo Government and the army but even the country's commercial life down to small shops are controlled by Americans for the aggrandizement of the United States in Asia.

Meanwhile, although the economic condition of South Vietnam has improved amazingly under President Ngo's rule, many peasants remain in poverty. Moreover, they remain in a degree of ignorance that the Communists exploit to debase them even further.

One of the most significant considerations in all this, according to a view widely held here, is that only a relatively few of the insurgents are Communists. It is said that an overwhelming majority of the dissidents are non-Communist villagers who feel abused by local authorities in one way or another and therefore hold a grudge against the regime.

The principal appeal of the Viet Cong to the peasant lies in the guerrilla organization's identification with the resistance against the French. For ten years the "resistance" stood for democracy and social justice. The label has not worn off in the five years under President Ngo.

Vietnamese officials feel that the situation is serious, even desperate, but not hopeless. The answer to the Viet Cong power, they say, lies in an effective information program accompanying an extension of economic development and political reforms, along with an expanded military effort.

May 28, 1961

SOUTH VIETNAMESE REPORTED IN LAOS

Commandos Said to Combat Infiltrators From North Along Jungle Trails

By The Associated Press.

SAIGON, Vietnam, Aug. 12—South Vietnamese troop units are reported to be operating in southern Laos to cut the flow of Communist supplies and guerrilla reinforcements moving down from Communist North Vietnam.

There are also strong indications that small United States-trained special units of South Vietnamese troops are operating inside North Vietnam.

Some observers feel these could be the beginning steps in a program to turn the tables against the Communists, who have sent a steady flow of guns and men for almost seven years to bolster rebel forces in South Vietnam.

Government officials here deny that any South Vietnamese troops are operating ouside the nation's borders. United States officials also have denials or no comment.

But highly reliable sources report that special South Vietnamese troops have taken up strategic positions and are patrolling the route the Communists use through southwest Laos—known in Saigon as "the Ho Chi Minh" trail.

This pathway of subversion is named for the North Vietnamese President, Ho Chi Minh. It begins far to the north and moves down through the unguarded mountains of Laos, skirting the well-patrolled border between Communist North Vietnam and South Vietnam.

Along this route, the Communists have been able to move men and guns in relative safety into central South Vietnam.

High South Vietnamese officials say there has been a sharp upswing of Communist activity recently in the thinly populated central mountain and highland regions of the nation.

According to one source, intelligence reports show that during the month of July alone the Communist Viet Cong rebels infiltrated 528 agents across this border region.

Government reports say that in Pleiku Province of the high-lands during an eleven-day period in late July Government forces killed 297 Viet Cong guerrillas, captured eighty-two others and destroyed a number of rebel supply dumps.

Thirty Viet Cong rebels were killed and about fifty more wounded in a major clash Aug. 1 in Xuyen Province, at the tip of South Vietnam, the Government said today. It was the biggest single engagement reported since army troops killed more than 167 guerrillas July 16 southwest of Saigon.

These figures indicate Government successes against the rebels, but they also are a measure of the growing problem.

So far, informed sources say, the numbers of South Vietnamese troops operating in Laos are small. "Dozens rather than hundreds," one source said.

Presumably they are highly trained, mobile units. More than 6,000 of these commando-type troops have been trained under United States guidance for hard-hitting thrusts at Viet Cong units around the country. They operate at company-size level or smaller.

It would be assumed that any such operation in Laos would have the consent and gratitude of the Laotian Government of Prince Boun Oum in Vientiane, which is fighting its own battles with Communist rebels. What might happen after a change of the Laotian Government is another question.

A much more sensitive question here is the report of units operating in North Vietnam itself.

Recently there have been indications that operations there have taken on a character besides the normal intelligence gathering activities that have been carried on for years. The operations would still be quite small, however.

Some veteran observers say logical spots for any anti-Communist operations would be in North Vietnam's vast mountain areas inhabited by independent minded Meos, Black Thais and other tribal groups opposed to Communist rule. These are scattered throughout the northern hinterlands.

August 13, 1961

U.S. to Help Saigon Fight Reds With More Experts and Planes

By E. W. KENWORTHY
Special to The New York Times.

WASHINGTON, Nov. 16—President Kennedy has decided on the measures that the United States is prepared to take to strengthen South Vietnam against attack by Communists.

The measures, which received final approval yesterday at a meeting of the National Security Council, closely follow the recommendations made by Gen. Maxwell D. Taylor, the President's military adviser. General Taylor returned Nov. 3 from a three-week mission to Southeast Asia.

The United States' plans do not include the dispatching of combat units at this time. They call for sending several hundred specialists in guerrilla warfare, logistics, communications, engineering and intelligence to train the forces of President Ngo Dinh Diem. The plans also call for fairly large-scale shipments of aircraft and other special equipment.

Officials emphasized that President Kennedy and the National Security Council had not foreclosed the possibility of sending ground and air combat units if the situation deteriorated drastically. The President, it was said, does not wish to bind himself to a "never-position."

However, the President and General Taylor are agreed, according to reliable informants here, that the South Vietnamese Government is capable of meeting and turning back the Communists' threat provided it speeds the training of its regular forces, solves the problem of mobility, develops a reliable intelligence system and adopts reforms in its military staff structure to free it from political interference.

The measures contemplated by the United States, it was emphasized, depend for their success on Vietnamese cooperation. Discussions are going forward with President Ngo Dinh Diem and his advisers.

U. S. Told Envoys of Plan

Earlier this week, Secretary of State Dean Rusk detailed the United States proposals to the British and French Ambassadors here. It was understood that neither the British nor the French voiced any objections. However, it was said that the French lack of enthusiasm for a larger American involvement was not disguised.

It is the present intention of the White House, officials said, to put the measures into effect while making them public only in general terms.

Dispatches from Saigon have indicated that some of the measures are already being effected. But officials said the arrival of some fighter-bombers and transports should be considered part of a "constant acceleration of effort" that had been going on since Vice President Johnson returned from his Asian trip last May. Few of the measures proposed by General Taylor, they said, have yet got under way.

General Taylor found that most of the Vietnamese regular forces were held at fixed positions key towns, bridges, and highways. The problem, he said, is to increase the flexibility of the defending forces by enlarging the mobile reserve and provide it with helicopters and C-47's so that it could be transported quickly to areas infested with Communist guerrillas.

November 17, 1961

117

G.I.'S IN WAR ZONE IN SOUTH VIETNAM

Join Tactical Operations To Shoot if Fired On

By JACK RAYMOND
Special to The New York Times.

WASHINGTON, Dec. 19— United States military men in South Vietnam were understood today to be operating in battle areas with South Vietnamese forces that are fighting Communist guerrillas.

Although the Americans, who are in uniform, are not engaged in actual combat operations, they are authorized to shoot back if fired upon.

About 2,000 Americans in uniform are in South Vietnam, instead of the officially reported 685 members of the military advisory group.

These soldiers, under new arrangements with the South Vietnamese Government, are taking part in tactical operations in battle areas. The operations include support roles in transport and communications.

Officials here are aware that the American soldiers may be subject to attack by Communist guerrillas, who are known as the Viet Cong.

December 20, 1961

SAIGON BUILDS UP FOR DRIVE ON FOE

Hopes New Techniques Will Turn Tide Against Reds

By ROBERT TRUMBULL
Special to The New York Times.

HONG KONG, Dec. 31— Aided by a build-up in United States military support, South Vietnam is preparing a strong counter-offensive against Communist guerrilla forces threatening President Ngo Dinh Diem's pro-Western Government.

Numerous techniques hitherto unseen in South Vietnam's jungle warfare are being inaugurated or are about to be used to help turn the tide of battle against the Viet Cong, as the Vietnamese Communist guerrillas are called.

One of these techniques is "defoliation" from the air, a chemical means of stripping leaves from the foliage that hides Viet Cong movements in thickly wooded areas. Known Viet Cong bases will be surrounded by bare stretches where the guerrillas will find it difficult to move undetected from their hideouts, which are often underground.

Many United States Army war dogs also will be employed to flush out the enemy. Some of these highly trained animals are already being used and have demonstrated their talent in tracking down men who easily elude human searchers.

Swift movement of troops by helicopters operated by United States Army personnel is another technique to be stressed. American officers hope that with the deployment of big helicopters in conjunction with better intelligence and better communications, it often will be possible to surround Communist attackers and cut off their lines of retreat.

On the other hand, helicopters are vulnerable to ground fire. Americans in Saigon expect casualties to rise considerably.

The Saigon Government has embarked upon an intensive program to regroup large numbers of the vulnerable rural population into "strategic hamlets" and other resettlement centers that can be defended easily.

Activity in North

One of the most important elements of the South Vietnamese counter-offensive involves guerrilla activity against North Vietnam, giving the Communists north of the Seventeenth Parallel a taste of their own medicine.

Organizing such guerrilla activity behind enemy lines is a function of the United States Army Special Forces, which for some months have been quietly moving experts in guerrilla warfare into Vietnam.

Another important element in South Vietnam's expanding defenses is the pledge made by President Ngo Dinh Diem to recast the command structure of his army. The President has agreed to give more authority to his field commanders and to refrain from personal intervention in tactical operations, which has caused confusion and damaged the army's efficiency in the past.

Authoritative circles have indicated the likelihood of a greater role for American officers in the South Vietnamese military establishment. This is considered necessary to heighten the effectiveness of the increasing United States participation.

January 1, 1962

South Vietnam and Guerrillas Vie for Loyalty of Tribesmen

President and Red Opponents Seek Support of 500,000 Natives of Highlands

By HOMER BIGART
Special to The New York Times.

PLEIKU, Vietnam, Jan. 29— Here in the western highlands of South Vietnam, the regime of President Ngo Dinh Diem and its Communist opponents are in a desperate race to win the loyalty of about a half million tribesmen.

These tribesmen, pleasant, easy-going descendants of the ancient Champa Empire are of Malayo-Polynesian stock. They fear and distrust the Government and the insurgents.

All the tribesmen ask is to be left alone. But they occupy strategic land near the frontiers of Cambodia and Laos.

The French called these tribesmen Montagnards (mountain people) and won their favor by reserving an area for them and forbidding settlement by the Vietnamese there. However, the South Vietnamese regime resettled thousands of Vietnamese on tribal lands without any compensation to the Montagnards.

Exploiting this program of President Ngo Dinh Diem's Government, the Communists are promising autonomy for the tribes once the "American Diem imperialist clique" is driven from the highlands. The Communists have proposed for the highlanders a modified North Vietnamese flag — with the same yellow star on a red field, but with the bottom half of the field blue for the Montagnards.

In Pleiku Province, the Government is using the present lull in the fighting to regroup the tribesmen. This regroupment brings together several tribal hamlets into large strategic villages.

This plan is designed to isolate the Montagnards from the Communists and to deprive the Communists of food and information. The plan generally is hated by the Montagnards, who complain that they are unaccustomed to living in big villages miles from their old rice paddies and fields.

The regrouping was necessary, in the Government's view, because some tribes were heavily infiltrated by the Communists. Some tribes supplied food to the guerrillas and helped to fortify roads.

Two weeks ago Hiao, a Jarai tribal village twenty miles southwest of Cheo Reo, was punished by South Vietnamese troops. The village sentiment was largely pro-Communist and most of the young men had fled to the woods to join the guerrillas.

The Government troops rounded up the remaining tribesmen, ordered them to get their blankets and rice pots and then marched them to Cheo Reo to await resettlement. Before withdrawing, the troops burned the empty village.

Yesterday, the Rev. Charles Long of Charlotte, N. C., a representative of the Christian Missionary Alliance, drove this correspondent to Trol Deng, a Jarai village near the Cambodian frontier. It was an attractive place surrounded by banana and papaya trees, but it was being abandoned on orders of the Government.

Half naked Jarai women smoking pipes were carrying bamboo huts section by section across a hill to a wide, ugly clearing where the wind whipped up eddies of red dust. Mr. Long said the villagers were torn between obeying the Government or the Communists.

The Communists ordered the villagers to hide in the woods. The Communists told the Jarai that the Government regrouping was designed to make them a suitable target for bombing and strafing. For one day, the villagers did follow the Communist orders, but the Government troops found them and sent them back.

East of Pleiku in the Ankhe district only six villages of Bahnar tribesmen had any contact with the Government. Of 32,000 Bahnar tribesmen in the area, only 2,000 were under Government control.

Mr. Long and other American missionaries saw hopeful signs of changing the Government attitude. In Saigon, President Ngo Dinh Diem and the Coordinating Secretary of State, Nguyen Dinh Thuan, are aware of the necessity to woo the Montagnards.

January 30, 1962

PENTAGON SETS UP VIETNAM COMMAND UNDER A GENERAL

Move Designed to Prevent Red Take-Over—Tactical and Advisory Aid Split

By E. W. KENWORTHY
Special to The New York Times.

WASHINGTON, Feb. 8 — The United States established a new military command in Communist-threatened South Vietnam today and named a four-star general to head it.

Although there were organizational reasons for creating the command, a primary purpose was to manifest the determination of the United States to prevent a Communist take-over.

The new military headquarters, established with the concurrence of the Government of President Ngo Dinh Diem, is called "United States Military Assistance Command, Vietnam."

Its commander will be Gen. Paul Donal Harkins, who was promoted from lieutenant general to four-star rank on the decision of President Kennedy and the Joint Chiefs of Staff to emphasize the importance attached to his command. General Harkins had been Deputy Commander in Chief and Chief of Staff, U. S. Army, Pacific.

Advisory Group to Continue

The new command will include the present Military Assistance Advisory Group, which will continue under the command of Lieut. Gen. Lionel C. McGarr.

There are military advisory organizations in most countries to which the United States is supplying military aid under mutual security agreements. However, the new command in Saigon is unusual. Only once before — in Greece during the late Nineteen Forties—has a United States military aid mission been commanded by a full general.

The decision to create the new command was motivated by military, political and psychological considerations.

Traditionally military assistance groups have advised and trained local military forces. They have not taken on operational functions.

Political Purpose Served

Under the stepped-up program of aid to South Vietnam, however, United States forces are manning helicopters and small transport planes and participating in coastal and river patrols by small, fast craft. It was decided that the operational functions should be placed under a separate command.

There was a political reason for the division. The military advisory groups, because they have been limited to training, have achieved a status and identification throughout the world. It was thought best to maintain this status lest the Communists be given any ground for charging that military advisory groups were engaged in direct military operations.

The United States wished to make plain that South Vietnam was a special situation and that United States forces were taking part in operations because of the constant attacks by the Communist guerrilla forces known as the Viet Cong.

Finally, the command was established, as a Pentagon spokesman said today, to demonstrate that "we're drawing a line here" and "this is a war we can't afford to lose."

Pentagon officials have declined to give the number of Americans in uniform now in South Vietnam because the United States has not officially reported to the International Control Commission the increase in recent months over the 685 members of the advisory group authorized under the Geneva accords.

February 9, 1962

M'NAMARA WARNS SOVIET TO BEWARE OF LIMITED WARS

Finds U. S. Ready to Fight 'Twilight Zone' Battles in Struggling Countries

By AUSTIN C. WEHRWEIN
Special to The New York Times.

CHICAGO, Feb. 17 — Secretary of Defense Robert S. McNamara warned the Soviet Union tonight that the United States and its allies were preparing to challenge Communist "subversion and covert aggression."

Asserting that there had been a shift in military thinking, he said that the United States was training men both to fight and to teach fighting to the people of free but still struggling nations.

Mr. McNamara's speech was delivered before a dinner of the fellows of the American Bar Foundation, the research agency of the American Bar Association. The foundation's annual midyear meeting is being held through next Tuesday at the Edgewater Beach Hotel.

Read at White House

The Pentagon announced that the speech had been read "at the White House" and by Secretary of State Dean Rusk. Mr. McNamara's aides described the speech as a major statement of policy, the first the Secretary has made in this field, and a rationale for United States involvement in South Vietnam.

Tomorrow Mr. McNamara flies to Hawaii, where military and diplomatic officials connected with the Vietnam operation will confer.

The Defense Secretary said that the United States was ready to fight in a "twilight zone" between combat and political subversion.

The tactics of the Communists include sniping, ambushing, raiding, terror, extortion and assassination, he said.

Favors Limited Response

He asserted that such tactics called for a response not with big weapons and large forces, but with companies, squads and individual soldiers. The Army, Navy and Air Force are training men to fight this kind of battle, he said.

"You cannot," the Secretary observed, "carry out a land reform program if the local peasant leaders are being systematically murdered."

February 18, 1962

U.S. PILOTS AIDING COMBAT IN VIETNAM

WASHINGTON, March 9 (AP) — United States officials said today that American pilots were engaged in combat missions with South Vietnamese pilots in training them to fight Communist guerrillas.

There have been reports from South Vietnam that Americans had taken part in bombing and strafing attacks against the Communists.

No immediate clarification was available from the State Department as to whether this conformed with United States policy as enunciated by President Kennedy — that Americans in Vietnam are assigned for training, not combat, but are under orders to fire back if shot at.

Officials emphasized that the American pilots were always accompanied by South Vietnamese pilots on the combat missions.

The purpose of such flights by the Americans is to train the Vietnamese so they can carry out combat missions in the future on their own, it was stated.

March 10, 1962

PEASANTS RESIST SHIFT BY VIETNAM

Many Are Still Suspicious of Resettlement Program

By HOMER BIGART
Special to The New York Times.

SAIGON, Vietnam, April 19 —Vietnamese peasants in Binh Duong Province remain fearful of Government plans to resettle them.

During the last three days 142 more families have been removed, voluntarily or forcibly, from several isolated settlements in the forests north of Bencat. Their houses have been burned by Government troops.

But first the peasant were allowed to pile movable belongings on oxcarts supplied by the Government. They have been promised compensation and new land at the village of Ben Dong So, where the Government says they must live.

Ben Dong So is four miles north of Bentuong, the first settlement of Operation Sunrise, which seeks to isolate peasants from the Communist guerrillas in this area and break the Communist-controlled arc running from Cambodia to the South China Sea through nine provinces above Saigon.

Failure to spread sufficiently information on the reasons for the removals has been blamed for the passive resistance encountered by Vietnamese troops when they surrounded the settlements.

Young Men in Forests

An old man told a Vietnamese officer: "We heard many good things about the resettlement, but we did not believe them."

Some Vietnamese officers have expressed little faith in the persuasiveness of printed leaflets. More credence would be achieved, they said, if photographs were dropped showing happy peasants in front of their new homes.

The Americans learned that few if any leaflets explaining the benefits of the resettlement had been dropped in the immediate area of the round-up because the Vietnamese Government wanted to achieve a "surprise." It was feared that families might bolt into woods if they suspected troops coming and that leaflets might forewarn them.

Reds Plan Sabotage

The guerrillas are now engaged in a plan to sabotage American efforts to install $1,000,000 worth of transistorized radios in 2,000 villages.

These villages have had no means of quick communication to call for help when attacked by Communist guerrillas.

Last month the United States operations mission began installing radios in near-by Gindinh Province. The sets cost $500 each, but the mission decided to take the risk of their falling into the hands of the Communist rebels.

So far none of the sixty-seven radios installed in Gindinh villages or in the extreme southern province of An Xuyen have been captured or destroyed. But United States technicians have been ambushed en route to the villages.

Because of the hazards of the operation and the desire for faster transportation, the operations mission asked the United States military advisory force for the use of helicopters.

"If we could move by helicopter, we could install 300 radios monthly," said Frank E. Walton, chief of the operations mission's public safety division.

He said the mission hoped to have all the sets installed by Nov. 1.

The program for village radios was conceived a year ago by Arthur Z. Gardiner, director of United States assistance operations here.

April 20, 1962

U.S. SHIPS AND 1,800 MARINES ON WAY TO INDOCHINA AREA; LAOS DECREES EMERGENCY

KENNEDY REACTS

Seeks to Counter Red Gain in Laos—Still Hopes for Coalition

By MAX FRANKEL
Special to The New York Times.

WASHINGTON, May 12— President Kennedy ordered today that United States naval, air and land forces, including a battle group of 1,800 marines, move toward the Indochinese peninsula.

The President's reaction to a major military victory by pro-Communist forces in Laos promises to be a major new phase in the attempt to save the country from Communist control.

The President was described by associates as taking an extremely serious view of the situation in Laos. They said the military movements were not just a traditional "show of force" but an effort to get into position for more direct action should it be required.

Some of the United States Marine forces are believed to be headed for Thailand, whose border has been reached by pro-Communist forces in Laos. The Pathet Lao movement broke an uneasy cease-fire this week and seized control of most of northern Laos.

United Press International Telephoto

ON WAY TO CONFERENCE ON CRISIS: Secretary of State Rusk, left, Under Secretary of State George W. Ball, center, and Assistant Secretary of State W. Averell Harriman arrive at White House to meet with President Kennedy on Southeast Asia crisis.

Administration leaders, after two emergency meetings today, were described as still reluctant to send United States troops into Laos. At the same time, no one is yet willing to rule out the possibility of such intervention.

The decision, it was said, hinges not only on actions on the pro-Communist side but on the policy followed by the leaders of the Right-wing Royal Laotian Army.

Washington had no way of knowing tonight how much farther the pro-Communist forces would press their offensive. They already control about two-thirds of Laos and have triumphed in the last week in the northern regions between Thailand and Communist China.

The army has been written off here as a virtually useless military force. Its commanders are being referred to as totally unreliable.

The dispatch of a carrier task force of the Seventh Fleet and the Marine battle group toward the Gulf of Siam was ordered after the President held the first of his two meetings with members of the Cabinet

The New York Times   May 13, 1962
As the Laotian situation deteriorated, Washington sent a Seventh Fleet task force to the Gulf of Siam (cross).

The New York Times   May 13, 1962
Pro-Red forces took over Houei Sai (1) and claimed the capture of Tanoun (2).

and the Joint Chiefs of Staff.

The hope remains that this display of the United States' interest in resisting Communist pressures on Southeast Asia may still make possible the formation of a neutralist coalition government for Laos.

Such a government would consist of representatives of the Right-wing, neutralist and pro-Communist forces. Efforts to form such a government under Prince Souvanna Phouma over the last six months have been unsuccessful primarily because of the Right Wing's refusal to cede the key Interior and Defense Ministries to the neutralists.

May 13, 1962

COALITION REGIME IS FORMED IN LAOS; NEUTRALITY IS AIM

Souvanna Phouma Will Be Premier and Defense Chief —Boun Oum to Retire

KEY PROBLEMS REMAIN

Freezing of Troop Positions and Demobilization of Rebels Still Unsettled

By The Associated Press.

KHANG KHAY, Laos. June 11—The three feuding princes of Laos finally put together today a coalition Cabinet intended to bring peace and neutrality to this jungle kingdom. All three appeared pleased at the end of six months of wrangling over the composition of the government.

Prince Souvanna Phouma, the 61-year-old neutralist who is to head the new Government. announced the agreement.

The accord represented the achievement of a major goal of the fourteen-nation conference that opened deliberations in Geneva thirteen months ago on the Laotian crisis. Formation of a coalition regime had been energetically pressed by the United States. But big obstacles to success remain.

A major problem is the demobilization of rebel neutralist troops and guerrillas of the pro-Communist Pathet Lao movement or their merger with the armed forces of the royal Laotian Government.

Big Army Not Needed

As a neutral state, with her frontiers presumably guaranteed by the world powers, Laos would not need a big army.

An agreement is still to be reached on the freezing of positions of the opposing forces to supplement the oft-violated cease-fire of May, 1961.

The agreement on the Cabinet came at a meeting of Prince Souvanna Phouma with his half-brother, Prince Souphanouvong, 50-year-old leader of the Pathet Lao, and Prince Boun Oum, 50-year-old Premier of the royal Government in Vientiane, at this rebel stronghold on the Plaine des Jarres.

Prince Boun Oum, a southern Laotian Rightist of pro-Western sympathies. decided to retire from governmental affairs.

"I am happy." he said, "and **I want to thank all those who helped to achieve the formation of the coalition Cabinet.**"

However, his Deputy Premier and Defense Minister, Gen. Phoumi Nosavan, who has been criticized by United States diplomats recently for his opposition to some aspects of the coalition, is staying on as a Deputy Premier. General Phoumi Nosavan will also become Minister of Finance.

Prince Souvanna Phouma, in addition to serving as Premier, will take over the Defense Ministry. Another neutralist, Pheng Phongsavan, will head the Interior Ministry, which controls the police.

General Phoumi Nosavan's foot-dragging, a factor in suspension by the United States last February of $3,000,000 in monthly economic aid to the royal Government. was based on a call for ironclad assurances that the defense and interior ministries would not fall into the hands of pro-Communist leaders.

Prince Souphanouvong, who likes to be addressed as "Your Royal Highness" despite his Marxist bent, is to become a Deputy Premier and Economics Minister.

The Foreign Ministry goes to Quinim Pholsena, a neutralist who has made some bitterly anti-American statements.

Of the nineteen men named for the Cabinet, eleven are neutrals, four are members of the present royal Government and four are from the Pathet Lao movement.

Among the neutrals, seven belong to the Premier-designate's rebel faction and four are classified as "Vientiane neutrals." The latter have tended to go along with Prince Boun Oum's Government on most Laotian issues.

Accords reached in Geneva provide for withdrawal of all foreign troops from Laos to help insure the country's neutrality in world affairs. The troops include about 300 American advisers to the royal armed forces and 5,000 or more Communist North Vietnamese.

June 12, 1962

ACCORDS ON LAOS SIGNED IN GENEVA

Khrushchev and Kennedy Hail Neutrality Pacts

By SYDNEY GRUSON
Special to The New York Times.

GENEVA, July 23—In a casual twenty-five-minute ceremony, the representatives of fourteen countries signed agreements today guaranteeing the neutrality and independence of Laos.

The ceremony in the green and gold council chamber of the Palais des Nations, European headquarters of the United Nations, ended the fifteen-month conference designed to take the Southeastern Asian kingdom out of the power struggle between West and East.

Foreign Minister Andrei A. Gromyko of the Soviet Union presided over the ceremony. Secretary of State Dean Rusk and W. Averell Harriman, Assistant Secretary for Far Eastern Affairs, signed for the United States.

There were two documents. All fourteen members of the conference signed the protocol setting out the terms of reference for the International Control Commission that will oversee the withdrawal of foreign troops and other measures to

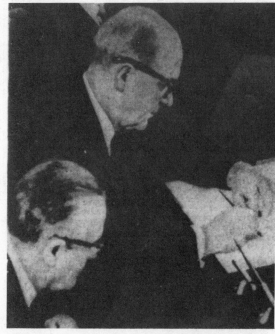
Associated Press Radiophotos

Secretary of State Rusk signs for the United States. W. Averell Harriman, left, Assistant Secretary of State for Far Eastern Affairs, also signed documents of the pact.

establish Laotian neutrality.

The second document, signed by all except Laos, was a pledge to respect the kingdom's new status. This document incorporated the agreement among the three rival Laotian factions to cooperate in a Government of national unity under the neutralist Premier, Prince Souvanna Phouma.

Premier Khrushchev of the Soviet Union and Prime Minister Macmillan of Britain sent congratulatory messages to this morning's final gathering. Their countries had served as co-chairmen of the conference.

Mr. Macmillan expressed his assurance that the agreements "will afford the people of Laos the chance to pursue their own peace and prosperity to which all parties in Laos are devoted."

"The conference has been able to show the world that difficult international problems can be solved by discussion and mutual compromise," he said.

This point was also made by Premier Khrushchev, who described the agreements as "of signal international importance" in removing a "dangerous hotbed of war" in Southeast Asia.

The first to sign today was the Laotian Foreign Minister, Quinim Pholsena. Then came the representatives of Poland, South Vietnam, Thailand, the United States, Burma, Cambodia, Canada, Communist China, North Vietnam, France, India, Britain and the Soviet Union.

At one point in the signing ceremony, as the delegates chatted across the table, the voice of the Earl of Home, Britain's Foreign Secretary, came clearly through a microphone accidentally left on.

"I always think the decorations on the walls of this place are rather depressing," he said.

The sepia and gold murals by José-Maria Sert, the Spanish artist, depict justice, strength, peace, law and intelligence.

An agitated aide rushed over to Lord Home, pointed at the press gallery and whispered something. The microphone went dead.

At 10:50 A. M., Central European time, Mr. Gromyko signed for the Soviet Union and this agreements went into effect.

July 24, 1962

SUBVERSION LAID TO NORTH VIETNAM

Indians and Canadians on Truce Group Condemn Aggression in South

Special to The New York Times.

SAIGON, Vietnam, May 25—The Canadian and Indian members of the International Control Commission have found Communist North Vietnam guilty of subversion and covert aggression against South Vietnam, reliable sources said today.

This was reported here after the Hanoi radio in North Vietnam had broadcast sections of an impending report by the commission on its investigation of violations of the cease-fire agreement reached at Geneva in 1954.

According to the sources, the Indian chairman of the three-nation commission, Gopalaswami Parthasarathy, found North Vietnam guilty of stirring up Communist rebels in South Vietnam. The Canadians supported the finding.

The Polish delegation to the commission rejected the charge.

Hanoi Assails Indian

The Indian chairman will also charge that the United States violated the 1954 Geneva agreement by a massive build-up of support for the South Vietnamese military forces.

But in a letter with the report he is said to view the United States moves as a reaction to subversion by North Vietnam. Also, the United States was not a signatory of the Geneva agreement.

May 26, 1962

SAIGON REPORTED AVOIDING CLASHES

U.S. Advisers Find Tendency to Let Reds Escape

By DAVID HALBERSTAM
Special to The New York Times.

SAIGON, Vietnam, Feb. 28— Commanders of South Vietnam's military forces in the Mekong River delta have developed a tendency to avoid contact with large concentrations of Vietcong guerrillas. In addition, United States military officials

feel that escape routes for the Communists have been left open so that military operations could be evaded.

The Americans are also deeply concerned by the tendency of Vietnamese commanders to launch operations where intelligence has shown Communist strength to be minimal.

This has taken place in much of the rice-growing region of the delta where two Vietnamese divisions are deployed and some areas north of Saigon where the Vietnamese Fifth Division is stationed.

In the view of some observers, this may account in part for the widely varying judgments on

the progress of war given by Americans in the field and Americans in Saigon.

Field observers feel the Saigon officials have tended to concentrate on the number of Government launched operations and the number of enemy killed. They usually find that enemy casualties are considerably greater than those of the Government. But the men in the field are aware not only of where Government forces are operating but also where they are not operating and this may be the crucial difference.

In the view of American observers, there was already an inclination to shun major clashes in 1962, but they feel it has sharply increased since the bat-

tle of Ap Bac on Jan. 2, when a cornered battalion of Vietcong regulars inflicted heavy losses on superior numbers of Vietnamese troops brought in by helicopter.

The tendency is depressing to the American for two reasons. First, it is a negative sign at the end of the first year of the American buildup on the important question of Vietnamese aggressiveness. Second, while Vietnamese regulars, in the view of most Americans, have generally improved during the last year, so have the Vietcong.

At present these detachments of Communists are operating at company strength or more, and if the war is not carried to them soon there will be serious consequences.

March 1, 1963

MEMO ON COVERAGE OF WAR ADMITTED

WASHINGTON, May 7 (AP) —The White House acknowledged today the existence of a memorandum on news coverage of the warfare in South Vietnam but said it was designed to promote coverage rather than to curb it.

The memorandum, obtained by a House subcommittee, was reported to have been sent by Secretary of State Dean Rusk to the American Embassy in Saigon about a year ago.

Informants said over the

weekend that it laid down guidelines for restricting movements of American correspondents and made two main points: that American reporters should be kept away from areas where United States troops were doing all or almost all the fighting, and that they should be kept away from any area that would disclose the extent of President Ngo Dinh Dien's failure to command the complete loyalty of the South Vietnamese.

Asked about the memorandum, Assistant White House Press Secretary Andrew T. Hatcher said "There was such a memo."

May 8, 1963

7 Reported Dead In Riots Over South Vietnam Order

SAIGON, Vietnam, May 9 (Reuters)—Seven persons including five children, were killed when riot police and troops broke up a demonstration by 9,000 people in Hue yesterday, reliable sources said today.

Reports from Hue, 400 miles north of here, said the troops and police threw grenades to disperse the crowd. But a South Vietnamese Government spokesman here said the casualties were caused by a grenade thrown from the crowd. The Government said the police used firearms and hoses.

The demonstrators were protesting against a Government order forbidding the flying of flags and processions on Buddha's birthday, which is also the anniversary of Communist victory over the French at Dienbienphu in 1954. The anniversary is a major holiday for the Communists.

May 10, 1963

Monk Suicide by Fire In Anti-Diem Protest

SAIGON, Vietnam, Tuesday, June 11 (AP)—An elderly Buddhist monk surrounded by 300 other monks calmly put a match to his gasoline-drenched yellow robes at a main street intersection here today and burned to death before thousands of watching Vietnamese.

The victim, Quang Duc, was protesting alleged persecution of Buddhists by President Ngo Dinh Diem's Government.

Nuns and monks around him carried banners reading: "A Buddhist priest burns himself for five requests."

The demonstration was the latest in a wave of Buddhist protests against the Government. The Buddhists demand guarantees of religious freedom and social justice.

June 11, 1963

Vietnam's 'Untidy' War

Washington Is Unhappy With Saigon, But Thinks That Support Is Necessary

By MAX FRANKEL
Special to The New York Times

WASHINGTON, July 2 — Once in a while Washington remembers that there is a war on in South Vietnam. It remembered last week when President

Kennedy chose Henry Cabot Lodge to be Ambassador to Saigon. It remembered the week before when President Ngo Dinh Diem's dispute with

News Analysis

Buddhists almost provoked the Administration to denounce him. But for long stretches, the war against Communist-led guerrillas in Vietnam fades from memory here, not because no one cares, but because the men who care most decided long ago to discuss it as little as possible.

It is not only a "dirty, untidy, disagreeable" war, as Secretary of State Dean Rusk once called it. It is a politically embarrassing war in which the United States finds itself allied

with the authoritarian South Vietnamese regime, whose methods it doubts and whose popularity it questions.

At least 12,000 American soldiers are involved in the war, fighting alongside 200,000 South Vietnamese troops against a hard-core force of 25,000 guerrillas and their peasant supporters. But it is not the kind of war in which success can be reckoned on the battlefield alone. Every military triumph must be balanced by social and political progress. The results have rarely been better than mixed.

Statements of military victory are often counteracted by statements of defeat the next day or by political turmoil the next week. Proposals for reform by the Saigon Government are generally disputed by non-Communist opponents in the cities or by peasant defections in the hills.

No Choice, U.S. Says

When they are pressed hard enough, officials here say that the battle has "turned an important corner," that progress is "steady but slow," that the Saigon Government has finally gained "control" of more than half its territory, that millions of peasants now feel safe from Communists, that it may be possible soon to bring back some United States troops and that, in any case, there is no alternative.

To hold Southeast Asia against pressure by North Vietnam and Communist China, the Administration says, it must hold South Vietnam. And to hold South Vietnam, it must "sink or swim with Diem."

Preferably, therefore, offi-cial Washington wants to say nothing on what is obviously a tender subject. When the Administration's displeasure over Saigon's mistreatment of Buddhists was reported recently, newsmen were denounced as saboteurs of the war effort and their sources were investigated like subversives.

Explaining his anger, one official remarked: "What do you want us to do? We're in a box. We don't like that Government but it's the only one around. We can't fight a war and a revolution at the same time, so lay off."

But though the Washington press corps is often kept out of reach of the facts of the war, serious questions and criticism continue to appear in the dispatches of almost all American newsmen in Vietnam, in the reports of legislative inquiries and in the commentaries of nongovernmental observers.

Four Senators who visited Saigon at President Kennedy's request six months ago, including the majority leader, Mike Mansfield of Montana, found the Saigon regime less stable and more removed from "popularly responsible and responsive government" than seven years ago.

The senators and other critics contend that the weekly death and injury of American soldiers and the expenditure of more than $1,000,000 a day for Vietnam justify much greater pressure for political, military and social reforms by president Ngo Dinh Diem.

As Prof. Hans Morgenthau of Chicago University's center for the Study of American Foreign and Military Policy put it a year ago, "The domestic political status quo is the greatest single impediment to successful military defense, short of commitment in men and material on the part of the United States out of all proportion to the American interests at stake."

To all this the Administration responds that it is as firm as it can be in Saigon without destroying the cooperation necessary to conduct the war. It concedes that President Ngo Dinh Diem has often treated his own intellectuals and officers as more dangerous than the guerrillas, that he resists the decentralization of authority and that he has not done nearly enough to win the loyalists of his largely rural population.

But every reluctant comment here ends on the same note: that there is no alternative, no intention to seek one, no change of policy and no further comment.

When he takes over as Ambassador in the fall, Mr. Lodge may find some tolerance here for a slightly stiffer tone in dealing with the Saigon regime. But that, officials add, is largely a matter of personal ambassadorial style. They find no fault with the performance of the present Ambassador, Frederick E. Nolting Jr., who is said to have placed heavy emphasis on the need to cooperate with Mr. Ngo Dinh Diem.

All they want, officials indicate, is to get on quietly with the war.

July 3, 1963

CRISIS IN SOUTH VIETNAM DEEPENS AS DIEM'S FORCES RAID PAGODAS;

BUDDHISTS SEIZED

Police Hurl Tear Gas and Grenades During Saigon Attacks

By United Press International

SAIGON, Vietnam, Wednesday, Aug. 21 — Hundreds of heavily armed policemen and soldiers, firing pistols and using tear-gas bombs and hand grenades, swarmed into the Xa Loi pagoda early today and arrested more than 100 Buddhist monks.

The big pagoda has been the scene of frequent clashes between Buddhists, demonstrating against what they call religious persecution by the Government, and Government troops.

Policemen and soldiers also stormed into three other pagodas in Saigon, but the Xa Loi pagoda is the main cathedral of the Buddhists, who have been embroiled in a religious and political crisis with the Government.

Grenade explosions were heard and tear-gas smoke could be seen rising from inside the walls of the main pagoda.

Outspoken Opponent

On Sunday more than 15,000 Buddhists held an all-day sit-down hunger strike in front of the pagoda to protest the policies of President Ngo Dinh Diem and of his sister-in-law, Mrs. Ngo Dinh Nhu, both Roman Catholics.

Mrs. Nhu, one of the most outspoken opponents of the Buddhists, has accused them of treason, murder and Communist tactics and has ridiculed the Buddhist suicides by fire.

Violence has also been reported in Hue and other Buddhist centers. Martial law was imposed yesterday in the coastal city of Danang after demonstrators clashed with soldiers during a Buddhist mass march.

Danang, about 380 miles northeast of Saigon, is headquarters for the Vietnamese First Army Corps and is a ma-jor military base on the northeast coast.

Regime Cites Protests

The Government press agency said officials imposed martial law after a Vietnamese soldier was wounded and a Government vehicle damaged during protests Sunday by about 1,000 demonstrators.

A Buddhist protest letter to President Ngo Dinh Diem said that 36 demonstrators were injured, 18 seriously, and that 200 Buddhists were arrested in Danang. It said eight priests and nuns were among those seriously injured.

Tinh Khiet, Vietnam's supreme Buddhist priest, charged that Government troops were too harsh in putting down the demonstrations.

Other sources in Saigon reported that the demonstrators in Danang numbered about 3,000. They said the trouble began when a Vietnamese Army captain and two soldiers riding in a jeep became entangled in a long procession of demonstrators.

A dispute broke out between the soldiers and the demonstra-tors, the sources said, and one of the soldiers fired three shots into the crowd, wounding two demonstrators slightly.

The sources said the crowd turned on the captain, beating him, pummeled the soldier who fired the shots, and burned the jeep.

In Hue, a group of professors who resigned from the University of Hue last week in protest against Government policies called on the nation's intellectuals to support them.

In an open letter, signed by 41 of the 47 who resigned, the professors reaffirmed their determination not to return until the Buddhest crisis was settled.

The resignations were specifically in protest against the dismissal of the university's Roman Catholic rector, the Rev. Cao Van Luan. The reason given for his dismissal was that he had failed to prevent students from joining in Buddhist demonstrations.

August 21, 1963

VIETNAM'S ARMY ABSOLVED BY U.S. IN PAGODA RAIDS

State Department Hints It Blames Nhu—Encourages Military to Intervene

---

POLICE CALLED 'BRUTAL'

By TAD SZULC
Special to The New York Times

WASHINGTON, Aug. 26 — The United States formally and pointedly absolved South Vietnamese military leaders today of responsibility in last week's attacks on Buddhist temples.

The State Department said the military chiefs were "not aware of plans to attack the pagodas, much less the brutal manner in which they were carried out."

A statement underlined the Administration's emerging policy: to encourage army commanders to intervene in Vietnamese politics.

The hope appeared to be that the military leaders, portrayed before world opinion as the victims of a betrayal by President Ngo Dinh Diem and by his brother Ngo Dinh Nhu, would force a change in the regime.

Nhu Is Singled Out

Mr. Nhu, head of the secret police and a dominant figure in Saigon, was singled out indirectly but clearly for blame. The State Department indicated that he was responsible for a crisis that was increasingly hampering the war against the Communist guerrillas of the Vietcong.

Although Washington's stand now reflects early accounts of the crisis, it opposes the view that prevailed for several days.

The Government's intelligence reports convinced it for a time that the army was at fault.

In issuing the Administration version of last week's events, the State Department's spokesman, Richard I. Phillips, said:

"Current information makes it clear that these attacks on the pagodas, and the widespread arrests of Buddhist monks and nuns in Saigon, were carried out by the police, supported by small groups of Special Forces troops not under the command of the Vietnamese armed forces."

He Controls Police

Mr. Nhu controls the police and the palace units of the Special Forces mentioned by Mr. Phillips.

According to Mr. Phillips, United States representatives are maintaining general contacts with military commanders.

August 27, 1963

REBELS IN VIETNAM OUST DIEM, REPORT HIM AND NHU SUICIDES; SHARPER FIGHT ON REDS VOWED

PALACE BESIEGED

Army, Air Force and Marines Combine to Oust President

By HEDRICK SMITH
Special to The New York Times

WASHINGTON, Saturday, Nov. 2—The South Vietnamese Government of President Ngo Dinh Diem has fallen in a swift military coup d'état.

The insurgents reported over the Saigon radio this morning that Ngo Dinh Diem and his powerful brother Ngo Dinh Nhu had committed suicide.

High officials here confirmed that President Ngo Dinh Diem surrendered to the rebels at 6:05 this morning, Saigon time (5:05 P.M. Friday, New York time), and that the brothers were arrested. There was no official confirmation of the suicide report, which was relayed by the United States Embassy in Saigon.

All indications were that the military committee that staged the coup was firmly anti-Communist and pro-Western. It was viewed as eager to eliminate the repressive features of the Ngo Dinh Diem Government, which had so frustrated the United States recently.

The insurrectionists pledged

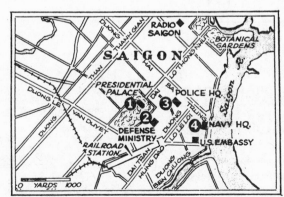

The New York Times   Nov. 2, 1963
Heavy fighting was reported at the Presidential Palace (1) in Saigon. Anti-Government forces seized the Defense Ministry (2) and police and navy headquarters (3 and 4).

to intensify the country's struggle against the Communist guerrillas—the cause that the United States feared might suffer from Ngo Dinh Diem's loss of popular support.

According to the Saigon radio, the brothers escaped the rebel forces after their surrender and sought asylum in a church. Then, the radio added, they were recaptured. The time of their suicide was given as 10:45 this morning (9:45 P.M., Friday, New York time).

Officials said that Vice President Nguyen Ngoc Tho, a Buddhist highly regarded in Washington, was expected to become Premier of a caretaker civilian government.

Discrimination Was Issue

Vu Van Mau, who resigned as South Vietnam's Foreign Minister last August, was also expected to play a prominent role.

His resignation protested the Government's Aug. 21 destruction of Buddhist pagodas, which intensified the religious crisis that led to the coup.

Since last May South Vietnam's Buddhists had been charging the Government of the Roman Catholic Ngo family with religious discrimination.

The military leaders were reported to have assured Ambassador Henry Cabot Lodge that they intended to turn over control of the Government to responsible civilian officials.

This made it likely that the United States would extend diplomatic recognition to the new Government within the next few days.

The end of the smoothly organized uprising was announced by the Voice of the Armed Forces in a broadcast from Saigon at 6:25 A.M. today, Saigon time (5:25 P.M. Friday, Eastern standard time).

The broadcast said that rebel forces had seized the Presidential Palace and that President Ngo Dinh Diem had "surrendered unconditionally" at 6:05 A.M. Saigon time.

High officials here, who had discounted earlier reports of President Ngo Dinh Diem's surrender as premature, confirmed that this time the claim of the rebels was correct.

In its early stages the revolt moved like clockwork. Elements of the Vietnamese army, air force and marines seized virtually every key point in Saigon but the presidential palace, where fighting raged late into Friday night.

The primary resistance came from some units of the Vietnamese navy, which fired at insurgent air force planes strafing loyal military headquarters, and from loyal Special Forces and Palace Guard troops.

The palace was the last outpost of the President and his brother. Late into last night they were defended by about 1,500 troops. Then, just before dawn, the State Department reported, there was a brief lull in the fighting.

As dawn broke the insurgents launched the decisive attack on the palace.

November 2, 1963

CAMBODIA BREAKS U.S. MILITARY TIES

Economic Relations Also, Severed—Rebel Asserts C.I.A. Supplied Arms

By The Associated Press

PNOMPENH, Cambodia, Wednesday, Nov. 20—Prince Norodom Sihanouk, the ruler of Cambodia, severed yesterday all economic and military ties with the United States.

The Prince charged that United States aid was being used to undermine him.

His decision to sever the ties, announced in a fiery speech before an emergency session of his political party at a Pnompenh stadium, was unanimously approved.

He told the wildly cheering stadium rally that American equipment had been used by rebel Cambodians operating from South Vietnam.

[The Prince presented a captured rebel who asserted that the United States Central Intelligence Agency had supplied arms and funds to the Khmer Serai, the Free Cambodia rebel movement, Reuters reported.]

Diplomatic Tie Remains

The Cambodian ruler said that while he would stop receiving any form of American assistance, he planned to maintain diplomatic ties with the United States.

There are about 300 Americans in official capacities in this nation of six million, including about 65 officers and men of the United States armed forces.

The Prince had at the rally two prisoners who said they had conducted activities against the Cambodian Government in a fortified hamlet in neighboring South Vietnam under control of United States military advisers.

They said Radio Free Cambodia transmitters had been set up in such villages. One prisoner said he had been supplied with a transmitter by United States officials.

U. S. Denies Role

Prince Norodom Sihanouk has charged that these secret stations have waged a campaign against him with the blessings of United States officials. Last week he announced his intention to end the annual United States military and economic aid programs unless the United States used its influence to halt hostile broadcasts by Cambodian rebel groups from South Vietnam and Thailand.

United States officials repeatedly have disclaimed responsibility for the broadcasts. They believe they came from within Cambodia herself.

November 20, 1963

CAMBODIAN HAILS PEKING AS FRIEND

Sihanouk Reports Offer of Aid Against Aggression

PNOMPENH, Cambodia, Nov. 22 (Reuters)—Prince Norodom Sihanouk said today that "Cambodia's best friend" was Communist China.

The Prince disclosed at a news conference that he had received a note from the Chinese Government promising full military, political and diplomatic support in case of "aggression" from South Vietnam or from Thailand.

He asserted, however, that Cambodia would not turn Communist if there was no aggression, adding that "our neutrality is not at stake."

Cambodia could turn Communist if the other Communist countries allowed her to be free like Yugoslavia, Prince Sihanouk added, "but I don't want to be a satellite."

'People's Republic' Is Aim

Prince Sihanouk severed his country's economic and military ties with the United States Tuesday. He has said he intends to create a "people's republic" to bridge the widening gulf between rich and poor. He plans to prevent what he considers a bloody revolution through austerity moves under "Buddhist national socialism."

The Prince said Cambodia would retain her French advisers after American civilian and military advisers left. He suggested that if the United States wished, it could continue to aid Cambodia through France.

He strongly denied that Cambodia would become a Chinese satellite and he termed Peking "the explanation and cause of our survival" because of a "balance of menaces" between China and hostile Vietnamese and Thai troops who want to "kill" Cambodia.

At his news conference the Prince said: "Financial reasons oblige us to cancel some Cambodian embassies abroad. But we will keep embassies in Communist countries since they protect us."

He added: "Paris will be kept. Washington also — but it will be closed in case of aggression against Cambodia by South Vietnam or Thailand."

November 23, 1963

VIETNAM JUNTA OUSTED BY MILITARY DISSIDENTS WHO FEAR 'NEUTRALISM'

4 GENERALS HELD

Tanks Surround Home of Minh in a Swift, Bloodless Revolt

By HEDRICK SMITH
Special to The New York Times

SAIGON, South Vietnam, Thursday, Jan. 30—Power was seized from South Vietnam's ruling junta today in a swift-moving, bloodless coup d'état.

At least four top members of the junta were reported under arrest.

The fate of Maj. Gen. Duong Van Minh, head of the junta that deposed President Ngo Dinh Diem Nov. 1 and 2, was uncertain. Troops and tanks surrounded his home.

The coup was led by Maj. Gen. Nguyen Khanh, commander of the Vietnamese Army's I Corps.

Paratroopers in camouflage uniforms and steel helmets took up key positions throughout Saigon in support of the coup. Not a shot was heard in or around the capital.

The leaders who were said to have been arrested were Maj. Gen. Tran Van Don, the Commander in Chief; Maj. Gen. Le Van Kim, chief of the General Staff; Maj. Gen. Mai Huu Xuan, head of the national police, and Maj. Gen. Ton That Dinh, Minister of the Interior.

Minh Reported Detained

General Minh was reported to be under house arrest, but officers in charge of troops at his home would not disclose his whereabouts. First reports said the general had not been formally arrested.

Later in the morning General Minh was seen being driven to the junta's headquarters under armed guard.

With General Khanh in the leadership of the coup were Col. Cao Van Vien and Col. Nguyen Chanh Thi, paratroop officers. They were reported to be backed by the commanding officers of the three other corps in the Vietnamese army.

Colonel Thi led an attempt at a paratroop coup against the Diem regime in November, 1960. When that move failed he fled to Cambodia, where he remained until last November, when General Minh and his associates toppled the Diem government.

Leader Assures Americans

Reliable informants in Saigon said General Khanh had told Americans that the coup was intended to save South Vietnam from a neutral settlement like the one imposed in Laos in 1954.

General Khanh, it was reported, told the Americans that the four detained junta members had been working with French agents to force the country into neutralism.

The plot, he said, was to have coincided with France's recognition of Communist China, which was announced Tuesday. Since last August President de Gaulle has been indicating that he favors the unification of North and South Vietnam under a neutral government.

During the coup the United States Embassy here was placed on full alert. At dawn, traffic moved normally and children were seen on their way to school. Workers leaving for their jobs seemed unaware of the change in the Government.

After paratroopers occupied key points in the capital, General Khanh moved into the headquarters of the General Staff, where the junta had offices. The building was quickly ringed with troopers, tanks and armored cars.

The general was reliably said to be in full control of the operation. He apparently had the support of three other army corps commanders.

General Khanh also arrested Lieut. Col. Nguyen Lan, a Vietnamese who once served as an intelligence officer in the French Army. He is reported to have entered the country secretly.

Military sources said Vietnamese soldiers from the Fifth Division at Bien Hoa, 15 miles north of the capital, established roadblocks during the night along a main highway. They were armed with heavy machine guns and recoilless rifles.

At Mytho, about 40 miles south of Saigon, 30 armored cars and two battalions, comprising 700 troops, were reliably reported to have blocked the southern highway to the capital. They were said to be from the Seventh Division.

General Khanh, 36 years old, is generally considered pro-American. He was educated in the United States and in France. He did not participate in the November coup, apparently because his I Corps command was on the North Vietnamese border, far removed from Saigon, where the action occurred.

January 30, 1964

U.S. PUTS A JET WATCH OVER LAOS; INFORMS U.N. IT WILL BACK ASIANS SEEKING HELP AGAINST SUBVERSION

Planes Scouting Reds Because Truce Unit Cannot Function

By HEDRICK SMITH
Special to The New York Times

WASHINGTON, May 21 — The Government disclosed today that unarmed United States jet planes piloted by Americans had been flying reconnaissance missions over the Plaine des Jarres, in central Laos, to gather information on Communist forces.

A State Department spokesman said the missions had been undertaken at the request of the Government of Laos because of "the current inability of the International Control Commission to obtain adequate information" on recent attacks on neutralist and right-wing forces in Laos.

The commission, made up of representatives of India, Canada and Poland, is assigned to supervise the numerous truces in the fighting between pro-Communist Pathet Lao and anti-Communist forces in Laos.

U. S. Provides Bombs

Coupled with the disclosure of the reconnaissance flights was a report by qualified sources that the United States had provided bombs being used by the Laotian Air Force for raids against Pathet Lao and purported North Vietnamese forces.

These sources indicated that the bombs were supplied some time ago at the request of the Laotian Government under the July, 1962, Geneva agreements between East and West. Under these accords Laos was to be unified and neutralized, with a government to consist of neutralist, rightist and pro-Communist factions.

The current raids were the first in which the bombs were used.

The announcement of the reconnaissance flights was the first official acknowledgment since the signing of the Geneva accords that the United States was taking a military role in Laos.

Planes Fired On, Peking Says

The disclosure came in the wake of reports from Tokyo quoting the Peking radio to the effect that Pathet Lao troops had fired on American planes over Laos. Officials here could not confirm that any planes had been fired on.

[The United States jets were fired upon over Khang Kay and Phongsavan, the Peking radio said, according to United Press International.]

The State Department's acknowledgment of the flights was viewed by observers here as having more importance than the military value of the flights themselves.

It was interpreted as part of a carefully developed plan by the Johnson Administration to demonstrate that it was prepared to go beyond traditional diplomatic gestures of showing its concern over military attacks against the neutralist forces.

The announcement was also viewed as a parallel move to a speech in the United Nations

Security Council today by Adlai E. Stevenson, the United States delegate, in which he denounced aggression in Laos and South Vietnam.

Officials did not disclose where the reconnaissance flights originated but they left the impression that the planes flew from and landed outside Laos, presumably using neighboring Thailand. The type of planes being used was also not disclosed.

The officials turned aside suggestions that the reconnaissance flights might be a violation of the 1962 accords by noting that they make no mention of reconnaissance flights.

Washington also argued that continued violations of the accords by the Pathet Lao and North Vietnamese forces and their refusal to permit the In-

ternational Control Commission to inspect their areas made the flights necessary to preserve the accords.

It was repeatedly emphasized that the United States considered that the agreements were still in force and that the reconnaissance flights would certainly not cause them to be scrapped.

The agreements, signed by the United States and 13 other powers, including North Vietnam and Communist China, forbid "the introduction of foreign regular and irregular troops, foreign paramilitary formations and foreign military personnel into Laos."

May 22, 1964

LAOTIAN ECONOMY IS A WAR VICTIM

Feeble at Best, It Suffers Effects of Long Fighting

By EMERSON CHAPIN
Special to The New York Times

VIENTIANE, Laos, June 2—The continual outbreaks of war in Laos have caused havoc in her economy, which is so primitive that most transactions are still conducted by barter.

Insecurity, war damage and the uprooting of large numbers of people over the last two decades have blocked economic development and heightened the kingdom's dependence on foreign assistance, largely from the United States.

"This country will need aid for at least 20 years," an American official commented.

Maintenance of large armed forces is a heavy burden for a state whose annual gross national product, or total of all goods and services, is only about $170 million. This amounts to only $70 per person. But like other data in Laos, these figures are only estimates.

"Laos has no actual statistics and no professional people," an official said.

If the civil strife could be ended for good, the attainment of self-sufficiency would not be difficult, American economic advisers believe.

They feel that food production could be increased rapidly, the labor shortage resolved by return of soldiers and waste curtailed.

But any real economic development is a distant dream. Underpopulated Laos is most deficient in the key requisite—human resources.

With only one high school that includes a 12th grade, there are only 75 high school graduates a year. And few of them can be sent abroad for college because they are needed at home.

Laos has about 2.5 million people in a rugged and heavily forested area slightly larger than Britain. She has no railroads and only a primitive road system. Almost all manufactured products must be imported because only the most rudimentary industries exist.

The war between the pro-Communist Pathet Lao and the neutralists and rightists has driven hundreds of thousands of Laotians from their homes in

recent months. Harried United States refugee officials lament that a whole season's resettlement work can be wiped out in a few days by shifting patterns of military activity.

"We have about 185,000 refugees on our hands now," one official said. In addition to food, the refugees must be supplied with clothing, cooking utensils and shelter.

The United States is airdropping 50 tons of rice daily to Laotians isolated by the military action. Agricultural experts on the aid staff here have plans to double rice output in three to five years through improved seed and better land utilization. At present 65,000 tons of rice are imported yearly to make up for war depredations.

Tests have indicated the feasibility of increasing vegetable production in the Vientiane area by 80 per cent.

Of key importance to Laos is educational development. The United States aid program emphasizes textbooks, primary schooling and teacher training. Most trainees are taken from the sixth-grade to 10th-grade levels. "That's the only way to get the thing going," an American remarked.

More than half the members of the big United States aid staff here are stationed outside Vientiane, the unkempt, steamy capital beside the Mekong River. They live in 18 provincial centers, sometimes in tents or straw houses, administering the agricultural, economic, military and development-aid programs.

Providing incentives to a primitive people is the major problem. Since the assurance of outlets for produce is essential, American experts who are trying to increase production emphasize the need for roads.

Laotian exports bring in no more than $3 million yearly, leaving a trade deficit of about $27 million. The budget amounts to about $75 million, with revenues, chiefly from customs duties, meeting only a fraction of that amount.

The deficits are met largely by United States assistance amounting to about $45 million a year. The French also provide substantial help.

Many Laotian officials engaged in petty bickering and in maneuvering for position appear unconcerned at the country's critical situation.

June 4, 1964

U.S. JET ATTACK ON LEFTIST BASE IN LAOS REPORTED

By HEDRICK SMITH
Special to The New York Times

WASHINGTON, June 9—United States Navy jets have attacked a Communist gun position in north-central Laos in retaliation for ground fire that downed two American jets over

the weekend, reliable sources said today.

The Peking radio, in a Chinese-language broadcast, asserted that six American jet fighters had dropped 12 bombs and fired two rockets at Phongsavang, a town held by the Communist-led Pathet Lao, and had flown over Khang Khay, the Pathet Lao headquarters. Both are on the eastern edge of the Plaine des Jarres.

The broadcast also said that Pathet Lao batteries had hit and damaged two of the jets.

[In Vientiane Premier Souvanna Phouma said United

States "reconnaissance flights will end June 10, 1964," according to Reuters. The Premier was also reported to have said that he had not agreed to United States fighter escorts for the unarmed reconnaissance planes. United States officials said the sending of escorts had had the approval of the Laotian Government.]

The Washington sources said the attack, which was made at dawn, was a result of high-level discussions in the Administration yesterday. The President and his principal advisers were reported to have decided to

destroy one Communist gun emplacement to underline the United States' determination to stand firm in Laos.

The decision was also interpreted as an effort to recoup prestige in the wake of the downing of the jets.

No details of the raid were disclosed. The State and Defense Departments clamped a tight lid of secrecy on the activities of the Navy reconnaissance and fighter planes operating over central Laos. Officials refused to comment on reports that an attack had been carried out.

June 10, 1964

Sabotage Raids on North Confirmed by Saigon Aide

By PETER GROSE
Special to The New York Times

SAIGON, South Vietnam, July 22—The commander of South Vietnam's Air Force confirmed today that "combat teams" had been sent on sabotage missions inside Communist North Vietnam and that Vietnamese pilots were being trained for possible larger-scale attacks.

Teams have entered North Vietnam by "air, sea and land," Air Commodore Nguyen Cao Ky said at a news conference.

He indicated that clandestine missions had been dispatched at intervals for at least three years. This confirmed, in effect, charges of such penetration broadcast by the Hanoi radio.

From evidence so far made known unofficially, these raids have had virtually no success. More than 80 per cent of undercover teams were reported to have been apprehended before they had made any progress in their sabotage missions.

More Teams Being Trained

More infiltration teams are undergoing training, Commodore Ky said. He also said that Vietnamese pilots were being trained to fly jets on bombing attacks. Thirty Vietnamese have qualified as jet fliers, he added.

"We are ready," Commodore Ky said. "We could go this afternoon. I cannot assure that all of North Vietnam would be destroyed, but Hanoi would certainly be destroyed."

His statements disturbed the commander of the United States Second Air Division, Maj. Gen. Joseph H. Moore, who attended the news conference. At one point, General Moore tried to suggest that Commodore Ky did not have a complete command of English and might be misinterpreting questions. At another time, the general said that newsmen were twisting Commodore Ky's statements.

United States policy has been to restrain South Vietnamese leaders in their evident enthusiasm for an extension of the war to the North. The reasoning has been that such actions would divert energies from the task of defeating the Communist insurgency in South Vietnam.

Commodore Ky's insistence on acknowledging past sabotage missions and readiness to undertake more and bigger attacks in the future reflected the stand taken by Premier Nguyen Khanh in a speech delivered Sunday.

Addressing a mass meeting, General Khanh said his government, and by implication the American Government, could no longer "remain indifferent before the firm determination of all the people who are considering the push northward."

There is no evidence that American personnel participated in raids by the combat teams Commodore Ky mentioned.

There is widespread belief, however, that some American fliers might have assisted in ferrying these units to North Vietnam.

Commodore Went on Raid

SAIGON, July 22 (AP)—Commodore Ky disclosed today that he had personally piloted a plane over North Vietnam and that the raids were continuing.

A United States official, who declined to be identified, said that he understood Commodore Ky's flight was made three years ago, which by now was "ancient history."

The Commodore's disclosures came as United States advisers expressed growing concern about successful Communist ambushes in South Vietnam.

United States spokesman said that Communist military activity reached the highest level of the year last week, with a total of 920 sections, ranging from one-man forays to attacks in force. At the same time the United States casualty rate reached a weekly record — four killed and 27 wounded. Since December, 1961, 158 Americans have been killed in combat here.

July 23, 1964

RED PT BOATS FIRE AT U.S. DESTROYER ON VIETNAM DUTY

Maddox and Four Aircraft Shoot Back After Assault 30 Miles Off Coast

ATTACKERS DRIVEN OFF

American Units Undamaged —Rusk Says 'Other Side Got a Sting Out of This'

By ARNOLD H. LUBASCH
Special to The New York Times

WASHINGTON, Aug. 2 — Three North Vietnamese PT boats fired torpedoes and 37-mm. shells at a United States destroyer in international waters about 30 miles off North Vietnam today.

The destroyer and four United States aircraft fired back, damaged them and drove them off.

The incident was announced here in an official statement by the Defense Department. It said that neither the destroyer

The U.S.S. Maddox was attacked in the Gulf of Tonkin (1). North Vietnam said U.S. planes raided a border area (2).

nor the aircraft sustained casualties or damage.

The statement said that the

destroyer, the 3,300-ton Maddox, was on a routine patrol when an unprovoked attack

took place in the Gulf of Tonkin.

At first Government officials were cautious in commenting that the attacking boats presumably came from North Vietnam, but Secretary of State Dean Rusk said in New York tonight that the attackers were North Vietnamese.

"The other side got a sting out of this," the Secretary said. "If they do it again, they'll get another sting."

Reports received here, apparently based on close air surveillance of the attacking boats, indicated there was no doubt that they were from North Vietnam.

President Johnson was informed immediately and received reports from top Government officials at a 45-minute White House meeting. He issued no statement.

Not Regarded as Crisis

Government officials said later that the attack was not regarded as a major crisis. They said the United States Seventh Fleet had been patrolling the area for some time, would continue its patrols and had sufficient strength on hand.

Adm. U. S. Grant Sharp Jr., Commander in Chief in the Pacific, was advised of the incident by radio as he flew back to his Pearl Harbor headquarters from a visit to South Vietnam.

August 3, 1964

U.S. PLANES ATTACK NORTH VIETNAM BASES; PRESIDENT ORDERS 'LIMITED' RETALIATION AFTER COMMUNISTS' PT BOATS RENEW RAIDS

FORCES ENLARGED

Stevenson to Appeal for Action by U.N. on 'Open Aggression'

By TOM WICKER
Special to The New York Times

WASHINGTON, Aug. 4—President Johnson has ordered retaliatory action against gunboats and "certain supporting facilities in North Vietnam" after renewed attacks against American destroyers in the Gulf of Tonkin.

In a television address tonight, Mr. Johnson said air attacks on the North Vietnamese ships and facilities were taking place as he spoke, shortly after 11:30 P.M.

State Department sources said the attacks were being carried out with conventional weapons on a number of shore bases in North Vietnam, with the objective of destroying them and the 30 to 40 gunboats they served.

The aim, they explained, was to destroy North Vietnam's gunboat capability. They said more air strikes might come later, if needed. Carrier-based aircraft were used in tonight's strike.

2 Boats Believed Sunk

Administration officials also announced that substantial additional units, primarily air and sea forces, were being sent to Southeast Asia.

This "positive reply," as the President called it, followed a naval battle in which a number of North Vietnamese PT boats attacked two United States destroyers with torpe-

does. Two of the boats were believed to have been sunk. The United States forces suffered no damage and no loss of lives.

Mr. Johnson termed the North Vietnamese attacks "open aggression on the high seas."

Washington's response is "limited and fitting," the President said, and his Administration seeks no general extension of the guerrilla war in South Vietnam.

Goldwater Approves

"We Americans know," he said, "although others appear to forget, the risks of spreading conflict."

Mr. Johnson said Secretary of State Dean Rusk had been instructed to make this American attitude clear to all nations. He added that Adlai E. Stevenson, chief United States delegate, would raise the matter imme-

diately in the United Nations Security Council. [The Council was expected to meet at 10:30 A.M. Wednesday.]

The President said he had informed his Republican Presidential rival, Senator Barry Goldwater, of his action and had received his endorsement.

Congressional leaders of both parties, the President went on, have assured him of speedy and overwhelming passage of a resolution "making clear that our Government is united in its determination to take all necessary measures in support of freedom and defense of peace in Southeast Asia."

Mike Mansfield of Montana, the Senate majority leader, said the Congressional resolution Mr. Johnson had requested would be introduced "sometime in the morning."

August 5, 1964

CONGRESS BACKS PRESIDENT ON SOUTHEAST ASIA MOVES;

RESOLUTION WINS

Senate Vote Is 88 to 2 After House Adopts Measure, 416-0

By E. W. KENWORTHY
Special to The New York Times

WASHINGTON, Aug. 7—The House of Representatives and the Senate approved today the resolution requested by President Johnson to strengthen his hand in dealing with Communist aggression in Southeast Asia.

After a 40-minute debate, the House passed the resolution, 416 to 0. Shortly afterward the Senate approved it, 88 to 2. Senate debate, which began

yesterday afternoon, lasted nine hours.

The resolution gives prior Congressional approval of "all necessary measures" that the President may take "to repel any armed attack" against United States forces and "to prevent further aggression."

The resolution, the text of which was printed in The New York Times Thursday, also gives advance sanction for "all necessary steps" taken by the President to help any nation covered by the Southeast Asia collective defense treaty that requests assistance "in defense of its freedom."

Johnson Hails Action

President Johnson said the Congressional action was "a demonstration to all the world of the unity of all Americans."

"The votes prove our determination to defend our forces, to

prevent aggression and to work firmly and steadily for peace and security in the area," he said.

"I am sure the American people join me in expressing the deepest appreciation to the leaders and members of both parties in both houses of Congress for their patriotic, resolute and rapid action."

The debates in both houses, but particularly in the Senate, made clear, however, that the near-unanimous vote did not reflect a unanimity of opinion on the necessity or advisability of the resolution.

Except for Senators Wayne L. Morse, Democrat of Oregon, and Ernest Gruening, Democrat of Alaska, who cast the votes against the resolution, members in both houses uniformly praised the President for the retaliatory action he had ordered against North Vietnamese tor-

pedo boats and their bases after the second torpedo boat attack on United States destroyers in the Gulf of Tonkin.

There was also general agreement that Congress could not reject the President's requested resolution without giving an impression of disunity and non-support that did not, in fact, exist.

There was no support for the thesis on which Senators Morse and Gruening based their opposition—that the resolution was "unconstitutional" because it was "a predated declaration of war power" reserved to Congress.

Nevertheless, many members said the President did not need the resolution because he had the power as Commander in Chief to order United States forces to repel attacks.

Several members thought the language of the resolution was unnecessarily broad and they were apprehensive that it would be interpreted as giving Congressional support for direct participation by United States troops in the war in South Vietnam.

August 8, 1964

Vietnam Outlook Bleaker A Year After Diem's Fall

By PETER GROSE
Special to The New York Times

SAIGON, South Vietnam, Nov. 1—One year after the overthrow of the Ngo Dinh Diem regime, the war with the Communist guerrillas has reached a stage more desperate for South Vietnam than ever.

The deterioration is both military and political, and it has touched all aspects of the life of a weary people. An immense effort, in men, money and ideas from the United States has not sufficed to break the momentum of a Communist revolution.

Observers trace some of the present decay directly to the collapse of the central Government last Nov. 1, when a coup d'état ended President Diem's nine-year iron rule over the newly independent state of South Vietnam, and brought his death at the hands of the rebels.

But a more significant deterioration dates from months before the coup, when the Diem Government had become so ineffective as to make its claims to authority and popular support appear specious.

Regime Was Authoritarian

The coup came after months of unrest marked by anti-Government demonstrations by Buddhists and an increasing authoritarianism directed by the President's brother, Ngo Dinh Nhu, also killed in the revolt.

With President Diem at the helm, articulate Vietnamese and Americans concluded that the war could not be won. Without him, they felt, there would be a possibility of success.

A year later that possibility has diminished. There is still no effective Government authority. What little there had been in Mr. Diem's last months has all but vanished, and the decay already under way has accelerated.

Detailed field reports from American and Vietnamese sources, as well as spot checks in key provinces by correspondents of The New York Times, have established that none of the country's 45 provinces can claim an improvement in the Government's position with respect to the Vietcong.

South Vietnam is a country of 65,000 square miles—about the size of the state of Washington. The Hanoi radio said recently that the Communists controlled two-thirds of South Vietnam's territory. Saigon says that about 60 per cent of the population of 15 million is under Government control.

Both claims seem exaggerated. Neither can be proved, for the criteria for control are elusive. Most of the countryside is disputed territory.

Intensified military operations have produced bigger and more frequent clashes with large Vietcong units—battalions and companies—but the results in territory secured or people brought under Government control have been negligible.

In fact, Communist insurgents are spreading terror now in areas of the countryside and in cities that they could not penetrate before. Officials find themselves unable to visit districts that the Government once controlled.

Bold Raid on U.S. Base Underlines Gains

The United States effort in South Vietnam was itself the target of a bold Communist attack on the anniversary of Mr. Diem's downfall. Mortar shelling of the top-security airport of Bienhoa, with the loss of four American lives and the destruction of five American B-57 jet bombers, was vivid evidence of the increasing vulnerability of United States forces as the Communists acquire access to more areas of the country.

The attack on the Bienhoa base was startling in its swiftness and accuracy, but tight Vietcong control over territory near this major United States installation has been proved before. In August, when an American B-57 crashed 10 miles from the base, armed rescue parties were unable to fight their way to the scene of the crash, which was in a Vietcong stronghold.

Loyal officials in hamlets and villages are being assassinated or kidnapped at the rate of 80 to 100 a month, according to official statistics.

Strategic Hamlets Seen As Symbol of Futility

Torn barbed wire hanging limply from twisted fence posts and the bare dirt floors of razed homes are all that remain of once prized strategic hamlets in parts of the Mekong Delta.

Strategic hamlets are centers to which people in rural areas were moved for their protection and in hope of winning loyalty to the Government. Built and fortified with the aid of millions of American dollars, they symbolized the seemingly vain hope that people could be induced to fight for a Government with which they felt no identity.

What was considered an essentially local insurgency a year or so ago has now become a broad-scale war. The United States has never made a declaration of war here, but it cannot withdraw without a grievous loss of power and prestige.

Few dispute the contention that the struggling South Vietnamese Government owes its existence to United States financial aid and the presence of more than 22,000 American soldiers serving with the South Vietnamese Army, advising when they are asked, shooting when they are attacked.

On occasion the United States has entered into direct aerial combat with North Vietnam. A dozen other countries have sent aid and personnel to bolster the South Vietnamese Government.

Outside help has accumulated for the other side, too. This year 8,000 to 10,000 trained and strongly motivated Communist guerrillas infiltrated into South Vietnam, according to cautious intelligence estimates.

Infiltration Quadrupled Over Earlier Years

This is an increase of four or five fold over previous years. The infiltrators are dispatched by the Communist regime in North Vietnam, which seeks to complete the conquest of Vietnam, half achieved in 1954. In that year Vietnam was divided into a Communist North and non-Communist South in a settlement that ended the eight-year war with France.

"From last November to now, it's been one year lost," a senior American general said. Other officials considered even that admission too mild.

The United States military build-up that started early in 1962 has reduced the gap in military effectiveness between the resourceful Communist army and the Government forces, but not enough, in the view of American strategists here, to produce anything but a military stalemate.

Despite a combat death toll of nearly 15,000, the strength of the Vietcong's main force has risen from about 23,000 a year ago to more than 30,000 now, according to intelligence statistics. These are fulltime soldiers, but an additional 80,000 part-time guerrillas are available for harassment and terrorism.

Government forces have risen in number from less than 200,000 at the end of last year to more than 225,000 now, according to manpower figures.

Whereas the Vietcong were armed with crude home-made weapons a year ago and could not cope with moving helicopters, ground fire at aircraft has now become accurate and weaponly advanced.

The Vietcong now possess 75-mm. recoilless rifles in far larger numbers than last year. Equally deadly is the 81-mm. mortar, now being used increasingly. This was the weapon used in the Bienhoa air base attack.

The ratio of Vietcong killed to Government forces killed in combat is one test of military effectiveness. It has declined during the last year from often three to one in favor of the Government to nearly one to one in some recent weeks.

With no visible battlelines, with an enemy more dangerous within supposedly loyal ranks than when viewed through a gunsight, it is hard to measure progress or decline in the war. But it is clear that in much of the country, notably the central lowlands where the deterioration since Diem has been most pronounced, territory and population have been lost to the Vietcong.

The Phuoc Chau pacification effort in the northern part of the country seemed to be succeeding during the summer, but then the Vietcong attacked and the land once reclaimed by the Government was lost.

In the Mekong Delta, where the bulk of the country's population lives, the deterioration of security conditions that President Diem tried to conceal has continued, with only isolated and short-lived reversals of the Vietcong tide.

A high-priority United States campaign to extend Government control in Long An Province about 12 miles south of Saigon was undercut in its preliminary phases in February by the removal of key Vietnamese officials for political reasons.

Less publicized pacification measures in Dinh Tuong Province in the heart of the delta achieved more success, until once again political upheavals in the capital last August and September robbed the program of its momentum.

It is this interplay of war and politics that has proved so frustrating to the United States.

3d Regime Since Diem Now Beginning

The country is now embarking on its third government since the Diem period ended. The junta that overthrew the Ngo family rule held on only until January, when Nguyen Khanh, an ambitious and young major general, seized power.

He held it successfully for six months, but when he moved to consolidate all power in his own hands in August, urban agitation forced him to step down.

During the spring and early summer the dissatisfied religious and political elements in the country were relatively quiescent. But their agitation in the streets of Saigon and other cities turned the last days of August into what an American general called an "agony" from which anti-Communist forces barely recovered.

After that it took two months for a successor regime to emerge.

To the amiable but frail Phan Khac Suu, the new chief of state, falls the responsibility of forging a new Government administration, virtually from top to bottom. He is working against the relentless pressure of a highly organized insurgent machine.

131

500 Officials Kidnapped In 9-Month Period

Between January and October this year nearly 500 Government officials were kidnapped by Vietcong terrorists in the villages, roughly comparable to American townships, and in the hamlets, the clusters of homes where peasants live. Almost the same number were assassinated.

Intelligence analysts suspect that many of the kidnapped officials are put through indoctrination courses and possibly sent back to insurgent areas to administer them for the Vietcong.

There seems to be a pattern and purpose in what at first glance looks like random terrorism. The majority of the victims are individuals who have been most effective against the insurgents. But in some cases they have been men hated by the local population, and the insurgents have received credit for eliminating unpopular personalities.

Observers were stunned by the cruelty of a Vietcong attack against civilian houses in the district capital of Cai Be last July 19. At least 40 civilians, dependents of the local paramilitary troops, were killed.

Only later did it become known in Saigon that these dependents came from far away and had been foisted on the hamlet. They were unpopular with the residents, who were relieved to be rid of them.

Early this year terrorism—including harassment and kidnappings—replaced attacks by armed units against Government concentrations as the main Vietcong effort. In the most recent statistics available, overt attacks accounted for only 2.3 per cent of all Vietcong incidents, whereas acts of terror occurred on 80 per cent of the occasions in which the Vietcong struck in Government areas.

Analysts of Vietcong tactics have noted the careful phases through which the insurgents extend their territorial control. Isolated terrorism and assassinations are an early phase, an apparent prelude to fuller military control.

Last year's focal points of terrorism against Government officials were in Binh Duong, Long An, Go Cong, and Hau Nghia Provinces — now areas where the Vietcong have largely replaced the Government as the effective local authority.

Killings and kidnappings are now reported concentrated in the central lowlands, where last year President Diem's control was firm, and in the provinces of Bien Hoa and Phuoc Tuy, between Saigon and the seacoast.

Roads Safe a Year Ago Now Endangered

Roads, including main arterial highways that civilians could travel a year ago, are now the scene of ambushes and minings. Many roads in the delta, some only a few miles from Saigon, are more or less permanently cut off by Vietcong roadblocks or trenches dug across the right of way.

The provincial capital of An Loc, center of a rubber growing area, now receives its food supplies over a circuitous detour of several hundred miles because the main road to Saigon has been cut.

One of the principal difficulties in the countryside is unstable and inadequate administration. Government attempts to fill war vacancies in the provincial administrations falter from a shortage of trained manpower and a general reluctance of the few qualified men to be exposed to the risks of a hostile countryside.

Doctors return from lengthy training overseas but choose to set up their practices in the comfort of Saigon rather than risk death in a province, even though there may not be a single civilian physician to care for the peasants.

4 of 70 New Graduates Killed by Terrorists

Training of young men as administrators is a long process, but the years of preparation can be quickly nullified. Of 70 graduates of the American-supported National Institute of Administration who took up field assignments 10 months ago, four have already been murdered by terrorists.

Saigon, moreover, has contributed its share to the upheavals in the countryside administration. With every change in the central Government, local representatives have been shifted, often before they have learned how to carry out reforms.

After the fall of President Diem, about 7,500 civil servants were abruptly dismissed on the ground that they were too closely associated with the old regime.

Most of the provisions in the country have had at least three province chiefs in the last year although, as one province chief said, it takes six months to learn the job.

Because province chiefs are almost invariably military officers, their terms are closely linked to changes of fortune in the army. Since the attempted coup of Sept. 13 against General Khanh, 13 province chiefs have been replaced.

Leadership Changes Tell On Troops' Morale

Lack of continuity of leadership was fatal to pacification efforts in Long An and Dinh Tuong Provinces, but it also tells on the morale of the fighting units.

One officer in Quangnai Province, dutifully trying to show his loyalty to the Government, first hung a photograph of Maj. Gen. Duong Van Minh, head of the November junta, in his barracks. He replaced it in early February with a picture of General Khanh. Finally, he settled for a pin-up of Marilyn Monroe.

Alienation of the armed forces from the new civilian Government is a serious concern of American officials, who are trying to return the country's energies to the war effort.

Long An Province directly

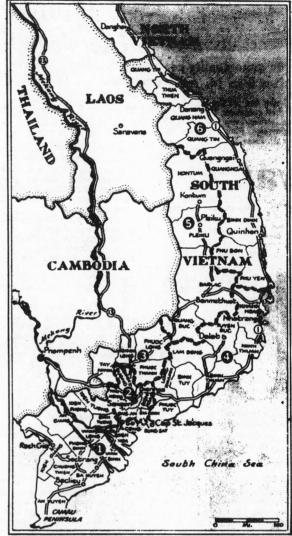

The New York Times   Nov. 2, 1964

VIETNAM A YEAR AFTER COUP: The Government's war on the Vietcong is believed to be at its most desperate stage. In the Mekong Delta (1), there is gradual deterioration of the military situation. Around Saigon (2), despite intense effort, guerrillas have made inroads. To the north (3) of the capital, Communist guerrillas roam freely, as they have since 1954. Coastal provinces (4) are comparatively peaceful despite an increase in assassinations. In the highlands (5) counterinsurgency work hangs in the balance because of tribes' dissatisfaction with Saigon. The central area (6) shows the most severe deterioration.

south of Saigon symbolizes the despair of the pacification effort in South Vietnam in the last year.

A year ago a Vietnamese who visited the hamlet of Thanh Tan dressed as a peasant found it a large and relatively serene place.

A neat bridge formed the entrance in the double rings of barbed wire fences surrounding the cluster of more than 1,000 homes. About 140 militiamen made up the defense force.

Last week that visitor returned to Thanh Tan. The bridge, he reported, had been blown up by the Vietcong only a week earlier. The outer fence had been torn down to use the wire to strengthen the inner fence.

Patrols Became Wary Of Venturing Out

The area between the two rings, where more than 200 houses had stood, had been abandoned, and hamlet patrols no longer dared to leave the inner perimeter after dark.

Only 29 militiamen were left to defend the hamlet, and they said they had no hope that the district or province capitals would send reinforcements. The sound of artillery and automatic weapons was heard nearby throughout the night, and Vietcong troops fishing in adjacent canals were clearly visible from inside the hamlet fence.

Long An received the highest priority for American assistance of any province in South Vietnam during much of the last year.

Here is a breakdown of the general regions of South Vietnam, with an assessment of their security based on information drawn from numerous sources:

The Mekong Delta: This is roughly the area south of Saigon, the country's agricultural center where about 50 per cent of the population is concentrated. It was the focus of greatest concern in the last weeks of the Diem regime and deterioration has continued, though gradually.

The sharpest decline has occurred in the coastal province of Kien Giang, opening new infiltration routes by sea for arms and supplies.

About 10,000 soldiers in the Vietcong's main force are believed to be based in four delta provinces along the Cambodian frontier. From there they can fan out across the whole region, confident of their rear base area.

Of one province in the delta, however, an official said: "If they were all as safe as that one, the war would be won." This is the province of An Giang, home of the Hoa Hao religious sect. The sect has what amounts to a private army to prevent any intruders—Communist or otherwise—from disturbing the peace.

Nearby provinces have been virtually given up by the Government. An Xuyen covering the southernmost tip of Vietnam, the forbidding Camau peninsula; Kien Tuong, the swampy plain where none but Vietcong troops would choose to live; the southern part of Chuong Thien, bordering on Camau and formed relatively recently from the most insecure districts of neighboring provinces.

The environs of Saigon: roughly a circle of 30 miles around the capital, center of the most intense American effort at pacification now, for both psychological and military reasons.

Provinces Near the Capital Still Red Strongholds

The provinces immediately north of Saigon: long considered impenetrable base areas. No improvement occurred in the last year. In one of the provinces, Tay Ninh, the Vietcong are believed to have established their main military and political headquarters.

Coastal provinces from Bienhoa and Phuoc Tuy to the resort of Nhatrang: remains the most peaceful section of South Vietnam despite an increase in assassinations and an increasing reluctance of foreigners

and Vietnamese to drive along the roads to the resorts of Cap St. Jacques and Dalat.

Highland provinces form Quang Duc to Kontum: homeland of the montagnards, an ethnic minority long suppressed by the Vietnamese. Here the political situation of the montagnards, dramatized by an attempted revolt in September, gives the Vietcong an opportunity for political gain and security for infiltration routes.

A three-year program of United States Special Forces counterinsurgency teams is hanging in balance here, not because of military failures but because of political conflict between the mountain peoples and the Vietnamese Government.

The central area from the 17th-Parallel border with North Vietnam to Phu Yen province, including the important towns of Hue and Danang: This is the scene of most alarming deterioration in South Vietnam in the last year.

Traditionally, this was a strong base for the Vietnamese Communist movement, but a ruthless Government apparatus directed by Mr. Diem's brother, Ngo Dinh Can, kept Vietcong organization ineffective and underground.

Mr. Can was executed with great fanfare in Saigon last May, but from almost the first week after Mr. Diem's downfall the Vietcong have intensi-

fied their activity in Quangngai and Binh Dinh Provinces.

Quangngai has a population of about 650,000, including nearly 95,000 families with relatives in North Vietnam. Because of this, infiltrators can often settle down with relatives or friends and bide their time for action.

Throughout 1963 and early this year the Vietcong were building their forces for a shift in strength from the mountains of the province to the coast. The shift apparently began two or three months ago.

Increased infiltration and Vietcong activity in four provinces above Quangngai raise fear once again that Communists might try to cut the country in two from the mountains to the sea, preventing ground movement from the delta to Hue.

Thus, three years after the United States dramatically enlarged its commitment to South Vietnam, Communist pressures and the weakness of the Government have once again brought the country to the brink of collapse.

Once again many American and Vietnamese officials are thinking of new, enlarged commitments—this time to carry the conflict beyond the frontiers of South Vietnam.

November 2, 1964

U.S. AIDES SILENT ON '62 LAOS PACT AFTER AIR STRIKES

Nonintervention Treaty Held Useful Though Some Feel It Is No Longer Binding

By JOHN W. FINNEY
Special to The New York Times

WASHINGTON, Jan. 15 — The State Department declined today to say whether the United States still felt bound by the Geneva accord prohibiting foreign military intervention in Laos.

The department's silence reflected the difficulty of the position in which the country finds itself as a signer of the 14-nation accord, which was reached in July, 1962.

The principal objective of the agreement was to guarantee the neutrality and independence of Laos.

On one hand, the Administration does not wish to renounce the agreement openly. In fact, it hopes the accord may provide an avenue for removing Laos from the East-West struggle in Southeast Asia.

Confronted, however, with the rising Communist insur-

gency in Southeast Asia, the Administration wants to take military actions in Laos that are not sanctioned by the agreement.

The Administration's dilemma, imposed by conflicting legal obligations and military objectives, has been heightened by the increasing activity of United States warplanes over Laos on reconnaissance and attack missions that have been going on quietly for about six months.

On Wednesday a squadron of American fighter bombers wrecked a bridge on a Communist supply route near the central Laotian town of Ban Ban.

Officials acknowledge privately that there is no legal basis under the 1962 accord for carrying out such missions in Laos.

Thus far, officials insisted today, the United States air strikes have been limited to Communist supply routes in Laos. The officials were emphatic in denying that the United States had participated, even indirectly, in air strikes against North Vietnam.

After a closed-door briefing of the Senate Foreign Relations Committee, Secretary of State Dean Rusk said that no United States air strikes had been carried out against North Vietnam. Senator John J. Sparkman of Alabama, acting chairman of the committee, said, "We can

plainly say we are not escalating the war."

The State Department also denied reports from Saigon that the United States had been providing air and naval cover for South Vietnamese attacks on military targets in North Vietnam. State Department spokesmen said, "There has been no U.S. involvement in such reported actions."

Officials did not deny, however, that South Vietnamese forces had been carrying out occasional air and naval raids against North Vietnamese targets near the border. Such raids were understood to involve only small penetrations into North Vietnamese territory.

Thus far the Administration has been reluctant to extend United States air operations into North Vietnam, partly because of concern over the instability of the South Vietnamese Government and partly because of uncertainty over the reaction of Communist China. But the Administration wants South Vietnam to step up its air strikes against North Vietnam.

The principal difficulty, according to officials, is in training South Vietnamese crews to a point at which they could strike without American assistance.

In the case of Laos, however, officials made it clear that the

United States intended to continue air strikes against Communist supply routes.

The principal purpose of these raids is to slow the flow of supplies to the Pathet Lao forces in Laos. But they are related indirectly to the American strategy in South Vietnam.

A shift of thinking is apparently taking place within the Administration; instead of taking a separate view of the struggles in Vietnam and Laos, the Administration is tending to view the two as interdependent.

By conducting air strikes in Laos, therefore, the Administration can emphasize its firmness in South Vietnam.

The legal justification offered by officials for reconnaissance missions in Laos was that these flights have been requested by the Laotian Government.

The Geneva accord permits the Laotian Government to request outside military assistance, but this is limited to the supply of military equipment and does not include military activities. In fact, one provision specifically prohibits the introduction of "foreign troops or military personnel in any form whatsoever."

Privately, officials argued that the Communists had virtually nullified the accord by introducing troops, by breaking the cease-fire and by using Laos to introduce supplies and men into South Vietnam. The legal justification, therefore, is that since the accord has been violated by the Communists, the United States is no longer bound by it.

January 16, 1964

133

U.S. JETS ATTACK NORTH VIETNAM IN REPRISAL FOR VIETCONG RAIDS;

By TOM WICKER
Special to The New York Times

WASHINGTON, Feb. 7 — United States aircraft struck at North Vietnam early today in response to what President Johnson called "provocations ordered and directed by the Hanoi regime."

Mr. Johnson made it clear, however, that the air strike was a limited response rather than a signal for a general expansion of the guerrilla warfare in South Vietnam.

In what appeared to be the most threatening crisis in Southeast Asia since the Gulf of Tonkin clash last August, Washington replied to severe Vietcong attacks.

The guerrillas had struck without warning against major American installations at Pleiku in the central plateau of South Vietnam, at an airstrip in Tuyhoa and at villages near Nhatrang.

49 Aircraft in Action

At the President's order, **49** carrier-based fighter planes bombed and strafed barracks and staging areas of the Vietcong guerrillas in the vicinity of Donghoi, just north of the border between North and South Vietnam.

The raid occurred swiftly about 2 P.M. Sunday, Vietnamese time (1 A.M., Eastern standard time). Secretary of Defense Robert S. McNamara said one American plane had gone down in the South China Sea. The Hanoi radio in the North Vietnamese capital said four aircraft had been knocked out.

EXPLAINS TACTICAL PROBLEMS: Secretary of Defense Robert S. McNamara during news conference yesterday. He shows point in North Vietnam where attacks on the South (arrows) are believed to have started, as well as situation of carriers off the coast.

Today, amid tension, President Johnson ordered the evacuation of about 1,800 dependents of United States military and civilian personnel stationed in South Vietnam.

He also ordered into the Danang area of South Vietnam an air-defense battalion equipped with Hawk ground-to-air missiles.

In the Vietcong attack at Pleiku, 8 Americans were killed and 108 wounded, but first reports did not indicate American casualties in the two other attacks.

Tension in Washington was heightened, and the United States response appeared conditioned to some extent by the Hanoi visit of Premier Aleksei N. Kosygin of the Soviet Union. Mr. Kosygin said in a speech to a Hanoi group that Moscow would assist North Vietnam against any nation that encroached on its territory.

Administration officials insisted that the air attack had been carried out without regard to Mr. Kosygin's visit to Hanoi and would have been staged even if he had not been there.

In a White House statement announcing the retaliatory attack, Mr. Johnson repeated the pledge, given at the time of the Tonkin incident, that "we seek no wider war."

But the President cautioned that "whether or not this course can be maintained lies with the North Vietnamese aggressors."

The response to the Vietcong attacks, he said, "was carefully limited to military areas which are supplying men and arms for attacks in South Vietnam." Thus, he said, "the response is appropriate and fitting."

February 8, 1965

HANOI AGGRESSION DETAILED BY U.S. IN WHITE PAPER

By JOHN W. FINNEY
Special to The New York Times

WASHINGTON, Feb. 27 — The United States issued today a detailed, documented indictment charging North Vietnam with flagrant and increasing aggression against South Vietnam.

The charge was accompanied by a warning that the United States might be compelled to abandon its present policy of "restraint" and to expand the war in Vietnam if the Communist aggression from the North did not cease.

The indictment was contained in a 64-page white paper of more than 14,000 words made public by the State Department. It was predominantly a compilation of intelligence information on North Vietnamese activities.

The document was titled "Aggression From the North—the Record of North Vietnam's Campaign to Conquer South Vietnam." It contains what it describes as "massive evidence"

establishing "beyond question that North Vietnam is carrying out a carefully conceived plan of aggression against the South."

The Principal Conclusions

From the evidence presented these principal conclusions emerged:

¶The infiltration of soldiers from North Vietnam is increasing to the point that personnel trained in the North now provide the "backbone" of the Vietcong in South Vietnam.

¶Increasing quantities of weapons produced in Communist China and other Communist countries are being smuggled into South Vietnam.

¶The directing political and military force behind the Vietcong movement is the Government of North Vietnam.

State Department officials described the white paper as an "information document" designed to describe the United States position in the Vietnamese crisis. They insisted that it did not deal with questions of policy.

The white paper declared that the United States believed that the evidence of Hanoi's aggression "should be presented to its own citizens and to the world."

February 28, 1965

160 U.S. AND SAIGON PLANES BOMB 2 BASES IN NORTH IN RECORD RAID; CONTINUING STRIKES ARE EXPECTED

U.S. PLANES LEAVE ON RAID: F-100 Supersaber jets taking off yesterday at base in Danang for the attack on North Vietnam. Standing at the left is a helicopter.

Associated Press Radiophoto

6 AIRCRAFT LOST

But 5 Pilots Are Saved —Targets Are Part of Military Complex

By JACK LANGGUTH
Special to The New York Times

SAIGON, South Vietnam, March 2—More than 100 United States jet aircraft bombed a North Vietnamese munitions depot today and also provided air cover for 60 South Vietnamese bombers striking at a Communist naval base.

The naval base, at Quanghke, although farther north in North Vietnam than any target hit within the last month, was part of a military complex in the southern third of the country.

The raids on Quanghke and the munitions depot at Xombang were the first that did not follow immediately upon an attack by Vietcong guerrillas in South Vietnam against American installations.

[President Johnson said that six planes had been shot down during the missions but that five of the pilots had been rescued, United Press International reported. It also said North Vietnam's Hanoi radio had asserted that, in addition to the six aircraft downed, "many others" were damaged.]

The missions were carried out by the largest number of planes yet used in one day against targets in North Vietnam. In the single strike of Feb. 11 the number involved was also given as more than 160, but United States Air Force officials said today's total was greater.

The pilots of the downed planes, one of whom was a Vietnamese, were picked up by United States Navy aircraft.

The attacks followed by a day a declaration by Premier Phan Huy Quat that there could be no peace until "the Communists end the war they have provoked and stop their infiltration." The Premier spoke out as talk of peace through negotiations was increasing in Saigon.

The strikes also followed an unrelated disclosure earlier in the day that three United States jets accidentally bombed South Vietnamese Government forces last Sunday, killing four soldiers and wounding 15.

The step-up in the war indicated by the raids was further underlined by reports that a United States Marine unit would be landed on the coast of South Vietnam later this week to provide security for the air base at Danang.

According to Col. Hal L. Price of Orlando, Fla., the director of operations for the Second Air Division in Saigon, the targets were hit at about 3:45 P.M. and the last planes had returned to Danang by 6 o'clock.

The Quangkhe naval base, bombed by the South Vietnamese planes, is about 65 miles north of the 17th Parallel, which forms the border between North and South Vietnam. The Xombang munitions depot is about 10 miles inside North Vietnam.

Colonel Price said the missions had been "without doubt very successful." The targets were "really well beat up," he added, estimating that 70 to 80 per cent of both had been destroyed.

About 70 tons of bombs were dropped on Quangkhe, the colonel said, and more than 120 tons at Xombang. He described the bombs as "conventional general-purpose ordnance," weighing from 250 to 750 pounds.

Pilots reported ground fire that they termed "light and not accurate" despite the aircraft that were lost.

Colonel Price suggested that the absence of heavy air defenses indicated "that the element of surprise is still there."

In addition to the supply and administrative buildings bombed at Quangkhe, the South Vietnamese A-1H Skyraiders sank three to five small vessels at the port, Colonel Price said.

They were accompanied by United States jet fighters for suppression of antiaircraft fire. F-100's, F-105's and B-57's made the raid at Xombang without Vietnamese participation.

A spokesman for the American mission denied that the strikes, the fourth and fifth in the last month, represented a change in United States policy.

He said that the bombing raids of Feb. 7, 8 and 11 had not been specifically provoked by Communist bombing and mortar attacks on American barracks at Pleiku and Quinhon.

Seeking to avoid the impression that the United States only responded to assaults on Americans, Ambassador Maxwell D. Taylor has said several times recently that the bombing raids were replies to "the continuous aggressive acts" by Hanoi.

A joint statement issued today by South Vietnam and the United States mission cited the discovery of a North Vienamese arms ships last Feb. 16 in Vungro Bay as "conclusive new evidence of Hanoi's aggression."

The statement also mentioned "two examples of recent terrorism" by the Vietcong that it said had been taken from a long list of Communist actions. The most recent, it said, occurred Feb. 22.

A United States spokesman declined to say when the mimeographed text had been prepared but it had clearly been ready for some time.

Informed American sources said the missions had been scheduled for last Friday but delayed because of bad weather.

Attached to the statement was a second page dated March 2, 1965. It asked "newsmen having knowledge of aircraft taking off on strikes against North Vietnam or of such strikes actually in progress voluntarily to refrain from filing such information or discussing it over communications facilities until the aircraft have returned."

The request, made in the name of Barry Zorthian, the United States Embassy's minister-counselor for public affairs, indicated that further strikes were planned. But the American mission spokesman declined all comment on further military actions.

March 3, 1965

U.S. FLIERS USING NAPALM IN RAIDS

Air Strikes in North Vietnam Aided by Fire Bombs

By JACK RAYMOND
Special to The New York Times

WASHINGTON, March 19 — The United States, apparently in a change of policy, is using napalm bombs in aerial strikes against North Vietnam.

Such bombs contain a sticky jelly substance that slows the rate of burning and increases the area of intense damage. They were used with devastating effect in World War II and the Korean War.

Emphasizing that napalm bombs are considered "conventional ordnance," officials said today that commanders had the authority to use or not to use them, depending on military requirements.

Reports from Saigon disclosed that napalm bombs were used Monday and again today in United States raids against North Vietnam.

Civilian Targets Avoided

These bombs were not used previously in the air attacks on North Vietnam, although they had been used in aerial strikes against the Vietcong Communist guerrillas in South Vietnam.

Officials have emphasized that in all the raids on North Vietnam great care has been exercised to select only military targets that were not clear civilian population centers.

Napalm has an awesome effect on personnel. When hurled into buildings it not only burns them but consumes oxygen so rapidly that the people inside may be asphyxiated even when untouched by flame.

Arthur Sylvester, Assistant Secretary of Defense for Public Affairs, said in reply to an inquiry that napalm bombs were not used until now against North Vietnam because commanders "had not considered it necessary."

He said authority for use of the bombs in the hostilities in Vietnam rested with Pacific Command Headquarters in Honolulu and commanders in Saigon.

The Pentagon, he said, was not called upon to authorize their use specifically in the latest raids, nor was it notified in advance. That they had been used was reported to Washington along with other details, he said.

Defensive Fire Reduced

Mr. Sylvester said that, according to military reports, napalm was used in the latest raids as "suppressive action" to reduce antiaircraft fire.

In the pinpoint bombing and strafing raids against North Vietnam's military targets, he said, the United States planes swooped in low. But several planes were lost in the initial raids against North Vietnam even though the defending force had only relatively small-caliber antiaircraft weapons.

Military officials in South Vietnam therefore decided that they would send in rocket-firing planes equipped with napalm to clear the way for the attack forces. This was done by the Air Force in the raid against Phuqui Monday and by the Navy planes of the Seventh Fleet in today's attack in the Phuvan-Vinhson area.

While emphasizing that napalm bombs were considered to be conventional ordnance, officials reiterated earlier statements that no thought was being given to the possibility of using nuclear weapons of any kind in the Vietnamese hostilities.

March 20, 1965

U.S. REVEALS USE OF NONLETHAL GAS AGAINST VIETCONG

Chemical Causing Nausea Is One Type Employed by Saigon Forces

SCATTERED BY COPTERS

Officials Defend Weapon as Humane Form of War— Cite Its Aid in Riots

By MAX FRANKEL
Special to The New York Times

WASHINGTON, March 22— The United States disclosed today that it was giving the South Vietnamese some temporarily disabling "types of tear gas" for combat use against the Vietcong.

The gases, at least some of which induce extreme nausea, have been employed a "few" times, officials said. South Vietnamese soldiers were reported to have "operated" the gas dispensers aboard United States helicopters.

One source said he believed the gases had been used twice, once in December and once in January, in areas where rebels had mingled with civilian populations to avoid bombing attacks.

As far as is known, this was the first time that the United States was involved in the combat use of gas since World War I.

Effect Is Temporary

The blister gases widely used in World War I had a delayed rate of action, destroying tissue and injuring blood vessels several hours after contact. They sometimes led to death. The gases used in Vietnam apparently have an immediate but temporary disabling effect that wears off after several hours.

Officials, obviously sensitive to the propaganda problems posed by the disclosure, insisted that the use of "nauseous gases" was "not contrary to international law and practice."

The United States is not a party to any valid international agreement outlawing the use of gas, but it has shared a general abhorrence of "inhuman" forms of warfare. A spokesman said the State Department did not consider the gases used in Vietnam to be the kind barred from warfare by law or consensus.

Officials here, as well as in Vietnam, suggested that gases that had "only temporary effects" were more humane in certain situations than indiscriminate artillery fire or bombardment. The State Department said the gases in question were "similar to types of tear gas employed in riot control all over the world."

However, the Administration did not reveal the chemical characteristics of the gases used in Vietnam. One spokesman said they were not the simple forms of tear gas that produce only eye, skin and respiratory irritations, but rather tear gases mixed with nauseating agents.

According to reference works, vomiting gas in undiluted forms

Associated Press Cablephoto
CARRYING GAS MASK: A South Vietnamese soldier wearing a case containing the mask on his left hip.

can produce, in progressive order, irritation of the eyes and mucous membranes, viscous discharge from the nose, sneezing, coughing, severe headache, acute pains and tightness of the chest, nausea and vomiting. Reports from Vietnam said one of the gases used there had caused extreme nausea and another had acted as a cathartic.

The official view that the use of such gases was permissible under codes of warfare was challenged by Senator Wayne Morse, Democrat of Oregon, an international lawyer and vigorous critic of the Administration's Vietnam policies.

He said he was sure that gases inducing nausea were among those that the United States, as well as other nations, had in the past described as "justly condemned by the general opinion of the civilized world."

"It is interesting to see," Mr. Morse said, "how easy it is, once we depart from the principles of international law, to violate more and more of them."

A number of other officials here doubted the wisdom of introducing a controversial weapon in Vietnam, whether or not it was "legal." The United States Information Agency said its news outlets were reporting the story "straight" by quoting Administration statements.

The use of gas in Vietnam was first reported by unspecified officials sources in Saigon and then quickly confirmed by an American spokesman there. His statement was also distributed by the Defense Department. It said:

"In tactical situations in which the Vietcong intermingle with or take refuge among non-combatants, rather than use artillery or aerial bombardment, Vietnamese troops have used a type of tear gas. It is a non-lethal gas which disables temporarily, making the enemy incapable of fighting. Its use in such situations is no different than the use of disabling gases in riot control."

The State Department then added the information that "tear gas in standard form, as well as tear gas inducing nausea, has been supplied by the United States and used by Vietnamese forces in a few instances—for example, to meet riots and in technical situations where the Vietcong have mingled with innocent people."

Apparently this meant that "standard" tear gas had been used for riots while gas "inducing nausea" had been used in combat operations.

March 23, 1965

CAMBODIA BREAKS TIE WITH THE U.S.

Prince Cites Border Attack and a Magazine Article— Move May Bar Talks

By SEYMOUR TOPPING
Special to The New York Times

HONG KONG, May 3—Prince Norodom Sihanouk, Chief of State of Cambodia, announced today that his Government had severed diplomatic ties with the United States.

Relations between Cambodia and the United States have deteriorated steadily during the last two years while Prince Sihanouk guided his Indo-chinese kingdom closer to Communist China.

Diplomatic observers said the rupture of relations seemed to exclude the possibility that an international conference could be convened soon to guarantee the neutrality and borders of Cambodia. The major powers have considered using such a conference as a forum for at least informal talks on a settlement of the war in Vietnam.

Prince Sihanouk, in a broadcast to his people, said the decision to break off diplomatic relations had been taken because of an attack on two Cambodian border villages on April 28 by four Skyraider fighter planes of the South Vietnam Air Force.

Western military attachés who were taken from Pnompenh, the Cambodian capital, to the villages were told that a 13-year-old boy was killed in the attack and three other civilians wounded.

The Prince recalled that he had warned United States officials that he would break off relations if another Cambodian life was lost in the recurring incidents on the South Vietnamese border. "Our warnings were not heeded," he said.

The United States, as military ally of South Vietnam and supplier of military equipment, had been held responsible by the Prince for the border clashes. The South Vietnam Government has explained some of the incidents as resulting from military action taken during pursuit of Vietcong forces that, it charged, have used Cambodia as a sanctuary for hit-and-run raids across the poorly defined jungle border.

Another immediate cause of the break in ties cited by the Prince was an article that appeared in the April 5 issue of Newsweek magazine.

Quoting what it described as sources in Pnompenh, the Newsweek article asserted that Queen Mother Kossamak, mother of Prince Sihanouk, was "money-mad and reportedly runs a number of concessions in town, plus a string of bordellos at the edge of the city."

A mob of 20,000 Cambodians, mostly students, rioted before the United States Embassy last Wednesday in protest against the article. Four days later the Pnompenh Government, citing the article, barred from the country almost all journalists and photographers of the "so-called free world."

Prince Sihanouk has been especially sensitive to adverse comment about Cambodia in the foreign press. He has maintained a secretariat that monitors publications abroad and replies to remarks held unfair to his country.

May 4, 1965

U.S. DENIES SHIFT ON TROOP POLICY IN VIETNAM WAR

But White House Confirms Potential Combat Role for American Ground Units

DEFENSE TASK STRESSED

Vietcong Say Stand Enables Them to Seek Volunteers From Friendly Lands

By JOHN W. FINNEY
Special to The New York Times

WASHINGTON, June 9—The White House confirmed today that United States ground troops in South Vietnam had been authorized to enter into combat to support Vietnamese forces against Communist attacks.

It insisted, however, that there had been no change in the primary mission of American combat troops: to protect important bases in South Vietnam.

In a statement issued through the White House press office the Administration sought to counter the impression that the United States was embarking upon an expanded combat role in the war against the Vietcong.

[The Vietcong said that the combat role of United States troops entitled them to call for volunteers from North Vietnam and other friendly countries, according to the Chinese Communist press agency. The American policy was termed a blatant violation of the 1954 Geneva accords on Vietnam. Page 2]

Why the White House felt compelled to issue a statement that, in essence, duplicated one issued yesterday by the State Department remained unclear. The apparent reason was that the White House was disturbed by the conclusion, drawn from yesterday's statement on a wide scale, that the Administration was deepening the commitment in Vietnam by undertaking open combat against the guerrillas.

June 10, 1965

Vietnam Shifts Since '63

Following is a chronology of the major government upheavals in South Vietnam beginning with the ouster of President Ngo Dinh Diem:

1963

Nov. 1-2—Military junta led by Maj. Gen. Duong Van Minh deposed and executed President Ngo Dinh Diem, the country's controversial and autocratic leader since 1954.

1964

Jan. 30—General Minh was deposed in a swift, bloodless coup d'état led by Maj. Gen. Nguyen Khanh.

Aug. 16—General Khanh, by now a lieutenant general, was named President by the Military Revolutionary Council, which promulgated a constitution giving him wide emergency powers. The move touched off rioting by Buddhist groups.

Aug. 27—The Revolutionary Council named a triumvirate to head the Government, with Generals Khanh, Minh and Tran Thien Khiem in charge.

Aug. 29—General Khanh resigned; Dr. Nguyen Xuan Oanh became acting Premier.

Sept. 5—General Khanh returned as Premier.

Sept. 13—A bloodless coup led by Brig. Gen. Lam Van Phat was foiled by a group of young generals who became known as the Young Turks. They were loyal to General Khanh.

Oct. 30 — Saigon's Mayor,

137

Tran Van Huong, was appointed Premier, restoring a facade of civilian government.

Dec. 20 — The Young Turk generals dissolved the High National Council, a 17-man group serving as provisional legislature.

1965

Jan. 9 — The armed forces announced the restoration of full power to the civilian Government of Mr. Huong.

Jan. 27—Premier Huong was deposed; Dr. Oanh became Acting Premier.

Feb. 16 — Dr. Phan Huy Quat, a former Foreign Minister, replaced Dr. Oanh as Premier, but General Khanh retained actual power. A 20-man advisory legislative council was named.

Feb. 19 — Col. Pham Ngoc Thao and a group of military men staged a coup, charging that General Khanh was a dictator.

Feb. 20—General Khanh reasserted control as his troops returned to city.

Feb. 21 Military leaders who had backed General Khanh now

voted "no confidence" in him, and soon afterward he was sent abroad as an ambassador at large. Dr. Quat and Chief of State Phan Khac Suu remained in office under military control.

May 6 — The Armed Forces Council returned "full power" to Dr. Quat's civilian Government, announcing that it had "shown that it can be trusted."

May 21—Dr. Quat announced that a pro-Communist coup against his Government had been crushed.

May 27 — Roman Catholic charges of religious discrimina-

tion and Dr. Suu's refusal to approve Premier Quat's proposed Cabinet changes touched off a political crisis.

June 9 — Dr. Quat asked South Vietnamese military leaders to mediate the dispute with Dr. Suu.

June 12 — A Government spokesman announced that Dr. Quat had decided to "hand back the reins of government to the military."

June 13, 1965

27 HEAVY BOMBERS FROM GUAM HIT VIETCONG FORCE IN SOUTH VIETNAM;

2 B-52'S ARE LOST

By JOHN W. FINNEY
Special to The New York Times

WASHINGTON, June 17— Twenty-seven B-52's based on Guam carried out today—early Friday in Vietnam—the first attack by these heavy bombers in the war in Vietnam, the Defense Department announced tonight.

Thirty planes started out on the raid against a Vietcong concentration north of Bencat in Binhduong province, 30 miles north of Saigon. One B-52 went down about 100 miles northwest of Luzon Island in the Philippines after a collision with another B-52.

There was radio silence during the flight, and the fall of the second plane was not observed, so its fate was not known. But it was missing and was believed to have fallen into the sea.

One survivor from the first plane was rescued and others were sighted, the Pentagon said. The B-52's usually have crews of six men.

A third plane reached the target area but because of mechanical difficulties was unable to release its bomb load.

First Combat Use

The attack by the big, jet-powered bombers was the first mass bombing raid in Vietnam on World War II tactics. The action also marked the first use of the planes in combat.

[The Pentagon reported early Friday that the two B-52's that had collided on the way to Vietnam crashed; 27 of the bombers returned to the Guam base, and the plane that had mechanical

Heavy U.S. Bombers and MIG's in Action in Vietnam

The New York Times ⠀⠀⠀⠀⠀⠀⠀⠀⠀⠀⠀⠀⠀⠀ June 18, 1965

U.S. heavy bombers from Guam (A) flew to Vietnam (B) and struck at Vietcong forces near Bencat (1). Other U.S. planes downed two MIG's 40 miles south of Hanoi (2).

usually uninhabited area five miles from the nearest village.

In explaining the switch to the B-52 bombers, an announcement issued jointly by the United States and the South Vietnamese Government said the B-52's had been used because of "their greater effectiveness" compared with the tactical aircraft used until now.

"B-52's were selected for this mission because their bomb-carrying capacity and equipment make them the aircraft best suited to carry out such an attack most accurately and safely," the Defense Department said.

Because of the heavy forest canopy in the area, the Pentagon said, it had not been possible to pinpoint Vietcong targets. If the Vietcong forces were to be destroyed, it said, "it could only be by an area attack uni-

trouble was diverted to Clark Air Base in the Philippines, The Associated Press said.]

There was no immediate information on the effectiveness of the B-52 attack, which was carried out at the request of the Vietnamese Government.

In the bombing raids in Vietnam up to now, the United States has used tactical fighter-bombers, which can carry only limited bomb loads and therefore have to resort to precision bombing of targets.

The B-52's in the raid carried out a "pattern bombing" attack using high-explosive bombs. In patern bombing, the bombs are dropped to blanket an area.

The target of the big planes was a heavily forested area of about 1 by 2 miles. According to intelligence information, Vietcong guerrillas had been concentrating in the area, apparently preparing for a surprise attack against the nearby South Vietnamese villages.

The Pentagon declined to disclose the total tonnage of the bombs dropped, except to say it was "a very heavy load" of 750-pound and 1,000-pound bombs.

The B-52, America's largest bomber, was first placed in service in 1952. It has a bomb capacity of more than 30,000 pounds and can carry 51 of the 750-pound bombs.

If the planes were fully loaded, as presumably they were, the bomb load dropped was probably about 500 tons.

The round trip from Guam for the bombers was about 4,300 miles. They were refueled in flight by tanker planes. The collision apparently occurred during the refueling operations off the Philippines.

The fact that the planes refueled in the air indicated that they carried full bomb loads, for refueling presumably would not have been required at such range with a light load.

The Pentagon emphasized that the target was an isolated,

formly distributed and rapidly executed."

Attacked in Daylight

The bombing was carried out in daylight, with the last bomb dropped at 7:18 A.M., Friday, Saigon time (7:18 P.M. Thursday, Eastern Daylight time). Precise delievry of the bombs was assured by the assistance of electronic systems ordinarily employed by the strategic bombers, the statement said.

The weather over the target during the high-level bombing raid was described as good by the Pentagon. There were scattered clouds at 3,000 and 10,000 feet. Visibility was 10 miles.

The B-52, powered by eight big jet engines, has a maximum speed over 650 miles an hour with a range of over 10,000 miles. Its ceiling is above 50,000 feet.

By comparison, the B-29 Superfortress, the biggest bomber of orld II, had a top speed of about 360 miles an hour. Its range was 6,500 miles, its ceiling close to 32,000 feet. It carried up to 20,000 pounds of bombs.

The military objective of the attack was to disperse as well as destroy the Vietcong forces. The announcement said that South Vietnamese ground troops were continuing attacks against the Vietcong forces in the area.

The wing of B-52's was reassigned to Guam early this year in the belief that they might be needed as the Vietcong mounted their offensive during the current monsoon season.

From the wording of the Pentagon announcement, it was evident that such mass bombing attacks probably would be conducted in the future to destroy concentrations of Vietcong troops before they can attack.

In recent months, the Pentagon noted, it has become evident that the Vietcong have been using a new tactic of concentrating forces in uninhabited areas covered by heavy forest canopies prior to attacking a

South Vietnamese town.

The Vietcong followed this practice, it was pointed out, prior to the attacks 10 days ago in Quangngai province in central South Vietnam and last week in Dongxoai.

In recent days, the Pentagon said, reliable intelligence pointed to a new grouping of Vietcong forces in an uninhabited, heavily forested area of Binhduong province. The Vietcong forces, the statement said, evidently were preparing to open a surprise attack in the next day or two against one or more South Vietnamese villages or district towns.

June 18, 1965

Ky New Saigon Premier; Pledges Full Mobilization

Special to The New York Times

SAIGON, South Vietnam, Saturday, June 19—Air Vice Marshal Nguyen Cao Ky formally assumed office today as Premier of South Vietnam and declared that he would mobilize all able-bodied men to spur the war against the Vietcong.

Marshal Ky, 34-year-old commander of the South Vietnam Air Force, asserted that the country would be considered in a "state of war" and that all measures would be taken to assure unity, austerity and heavy penalties against war profiteering.

In a ceremony at the stately white Dienhong Mansion, Marshal Ky presented his Central Executive Council, or War Cabinet. It consists of 17 members, including 14 civilians and three military men.

Marshal Ky will serve as chairman, or Premier, of the council, with direct control over the administrative machinery of the country. The council will be subordinate to the 10-man military National Leadership Committee headed by Maj. Gen. Nguyen Van Thieu, which this week had named Marshal Ky

to take the Premiership.

Taylor Accepts the Action

The United States mission here under Ambassador Maxwell D. Taylor, which had resisted the appointment of Marshal Ky, has bowed to the decision of ruling military committee. American officials hope that the Marshal, who has been regarded as too inexperienced and volatile in temperament, will be subject to the moderating influence of General Thieu and Maj. Gen. Pham Xuan Chieu, who will serve as Secretary General of the National Leadership Committee.

The militant Buddhist faction and other political groups in the country, which would have preferred civilian Government, are still restive but apparently are willing to accept the appointment of Marshal Ky for the time being.

Thich Tri Quang, the religious leader of the United Buddhist Church, has threatened to agitate against the military Government if its policies prove unfavorable to his faction. In his broadcasted speech accepting the premiership, Marshal Ky did not minimize the seriousness of the crisis before the country.

"The country is in danger," the Marshal asserted. He said that the war against the Communists was going badly and he complained of political instability, lack of security, economic disorder and war profiteering.

Marshal Ky spoke before his Ministers and the Leadership Committee, of which he is also a member. He has said he would give up his command of the Air Force.

As a sign of the new austerity, all of his Ministers were dressed in white civilian shirts without ties.

The War Cabinet includes Brig. Gen. Nguyen Huu Co, commander of the Army's II Corps area, who becomes Commissioner General of the War Ministries. These include Defense, Interior and the Ministry of Psychological Warfare and Information. General Co, who will give up command of the II Corps area, will also serve as Defense Minister.

In his speech, Marshal Ky said that all ablebodied men would be required to take military training. Not all of these would be drafted, he asserted. Some will act as part-time militia to support the regular fighting troops. The new training program would also provide for ideological indoctrinations.

The Cabinet includes eight ministers of the Cabinet of Premier Phan Huy Quat, which resigned last Friday under the attack of Roman Catholics and southern political factions. The Leadership Committee formally took charge of the country Monday. Among Dr. Quat's ministers held over is Foreign Minister Tran Van Do.

General Chieu, the Secretary General, read out publicly the new charter or Constitution of the nation, which replaces the Charter of Oct. 20, 1964, and gives no date as to when power might be restored to civilian authority.

Ky a Flamboyant Airman

SAIGON, Saturday, June 19 (AP)—Marshal Ky, taking office today, is the youngest Premier in the history of the Vietnamese Republic. A flamboyant, mustached airman, he has personally led his planes on air strikes against North Vietnam.

Marshal Ky has been air force commander since a month after the coup against the Diem regime. The air force, with United States aid, has grown steadily under his leadership.

Marshal Ky received part of his military training in the United States. He was sent to the Air Command and Staff School at Maxwell Field, Ala., in July, 1958, and returned to Saigon in January, 1959.

June 19, 1965

Brutality Is Rising on Both Sides in South Vietnam

By JACK LANGGUTH
Special to The New York Times

SAIGON, South Vietnam, July 6—Harsh and brutal measures have increased on both sides as the intensity of the war in South Vietnam has risen.

Much publicity has been given to the recent execution of a Vietcong terrorist in the Saigon market place, the subsequent killing by the Communists of a United States soldier and the mining of a riverside restaurant. But there are hundreds of other examples that are seldom reported.

For years the Communist insurgents have used terrorism as a principal tool in their campaign to subvert the Government. Thousands of Government functionaries have been assassinated throughout Vietnam in the last five years.

In the aftermath of the attack last week at the Danang air base, patrols found the body

of a village woman floating in the river with her feet cut off.

Also last week, two civilians were kidnapped and buried alive near Loinong in the Mekong Delta, and five women were kidnapped in Haungia Province. A child was killed and two others were wounded by intentional Vietcong gunfire in Binhdinh Providnce.

Similar incidents have also been staged by Government supporters.

Sometimes, however, the United States advisory command has been able to exert a tempering influence. Terrorism by the country's secret police disappeared with the overthrow of President Ngo Dinh Diem late in 1963.

On the other hand, Americans have urged for years that Communist prisoners, and particularly deserters from the Vietcong, be treated better by the Government. This was based on the expectation that word of good treatment would circulate among the people and spur defections.

The Vietnamese officials at prison camps have only occasionally shown themselves impressed by the American argument.

During the Phubon battle last week, at least five Communist prisoners were shot because the capturing Government troops felt they could not guard them properly.

At another place a day later, a Western newsman watched while a Government guard stepped forward without warning and beat a 15-year-old youth accused of aiding the Vietcong.

A Fall From a Helicopter

With a greater United States participation in the war, brutality has begun to occur among the American troops as well.

One American helicopter crewman returned to his base in the central highlands last week without a fierce young prisoner entrusted to him. He told friends that he had become infuriated by the youth and had pushed him out of the helicopter at about 1,000 feet.

When a superior warned him that he would be court-martialed, the crewman changed his story. He said that the prisoner had attacked him and had fallen accidentally.

What has concerned some United States commanders more than such isolated actions, however, has been the decision during the last six months to bomb heavily throughout South Vietnam.

"I don't like to hit a village," said one American pilot in his mid-20's, who has flown more than 100 missions. "You know you're hitting women and children, too. But you've got to decide that your cause is noble and that the work has to be done."

The South Vietnamese Government has set up an elaborate communication system to prevent planes from hitting their own troops. The system is also supposed to prevent the bombing of uninvolved villagers. But as the Communists have extended their control over much of the countryside distinctions have become more difficult.

If the Vietcong retreat to a village, the bombers generally follow, although any assistance given by the villagers to the Communists may have been extracted by force.

A year ago, the United States mission turned the phrase "winning the hearts and minds of the people" into a cliché through repetition. The phrase is seldom heard now.

Similarly, well-documented reports reaching Saigon indicate that the Communists have started to bear down on the hamlets and villages they occupy.

They are increasing taxes and food demands while showing less concern with the behavior of their troops toward the civilian inhabitants.

In Saigon, commanders who acknowledge the problem also note the bombing that accompanied the liberation of France in World War II.

"It was a friendly population there," one senior officer said, "but some of them died. War is no good for anyone."

July 7, 1965

Saigon: The Tragic Paradox of Vietnam

By JAMES RESTON

SAIGON, Aug. 28 — The American military build-up in Vietnam is beginning to rattle the windows. You don't need official figures to feel what's happening. The sky over Saigon is alive with noisy aerial boxcars, stuttering helicopters and flashing Skyhawk fighter-bombers. The airports, the bars and the restaurants are now all a little high—not to mention the G.I.'s on leave—and even the fancy hotels are beginning to smell like a men's locker room.

When Uncle Sam moves in, somebody has to move over. The concentrated power of America is staggering, and this may prove to be the most significant paradox of the war. For this power is now hitting not only the Vietcong, but the civil population of South Vietnam, and the critical question is which of these two will endure the punishment.

Military Transformation

There seems to be no dissent here—even among the diplomats of allied countries that have been critical of American policy in the last six months—that the application of American power in this country since last February has transformed the military situation.

Between last August and last February, the Vietcong ranged through the central lowlands virtually at will. The South Vietnamese Army could not, or at least did not stop them. Over 100,000 refugees were driven into the coastal city of Quinhon alone, and the disintegration within the South Vietnamese Army and Government was alarming.

Recognizing this, the United States took three decisions that have stabilized the military situation. It extended the war into North Vietnam. It increased its forces here to over 125,000, and it sanctioned the use of American air, artillery and naval strikes against the Vietcong in South Vietnam.

War in the Hamlets

This last decision to search for and destroy the enemy anywhere in South Vietnam is regarded here as the most effective and least understood of the three decisions. The Vietcong, which used to raid the countryside and then bivouac in the hamlets, are now being hounded from the air and attacked in the hamlets.

The people in the South Vietnam hamlets now know that if they dig tunnels for the Vietcong and give them food and refuge, they are likely to be shelled or bombed, and this has undoubtedly complicated the enemy's problem, but it has raised a new problem on our side. For it has caused great suffering and destruction among the civilian population.

This country is now beginning to take a frightful beating from the air. Yesterday's U.S. communiqué, for example, listed 57 Air Force strikes in a single day in the southernmost area of South Vietnam, and 95 strikes elsewhere in South Vietnam by Navy fighter-bombers from the aircraft carrier U.S.S. Coral Sea. The Navy said it dropped more than 65 tons of bombs and estimated that it killed five Vietcong, destroyed 102 structures and damaged 65.

In the Mekong Delta in the south, the Navy also reported that the destroyer U.S.S. De-Haven fired over 355 rounds of 5-inch ammunition at Vietcong assembly areas on shore. "Spotters estimated very good effect on the targets," the communiqué said. "Six buildings were destroyed with very good shrapnel effect over a very large area."

The only difficulty with this is that the Vietcong do not usually have isolated training and supply centers apart from the South Vietnamese, but operate among the people where the shrapnel has "very good effect" on Communists and non-Communists alike.

American Dilemma

This is the devilish dilemma of the present American strategy in the South. We are chasing guerrillas with bombs and it is apparently having much more effect on the Vietcong than anybody thought possible, but in the process, we are attacking and often destroying the areas we want to pacify.

It is now estimated that there are between five hundred thousand and six hundred thousand refugees in this country. Most of them are living in shacks and pens that would make the slums of Harlem look like the LBJ ranch. And by the end of the year U.S. air power will be more than doubled.

This country normally produces a rice surplus, but this year the United States has already had to commit itself to bring in 100,000 tons of rice to make up for the lost production of peasants driven off the land.

Multiple Trap

There has been some ominous muttering about this American bombing policy in South Vietnam by Thich Tri Quang, the powerful Buddhist bonze from Hué, but otherwise the tragedy has been accepted with remarkable calm, maybe because people here expect the white man to bring "trouble."

Nevertheless, this is a problem that will get worse as more bombers are added. War has a way of trapping everybody concerned. The United States is trapped between accepting the Vietcong attacks or striking back and hitting the South Vietnamese in the process. In a way the Vietcong is trapped between the power of the U.S. and China.

But above all, the people of Vietnam are trapped in a power struggle beyond their understanding or control. Maybe nothing can be done about it, but somewhere in a corner of the mind, their tragedy must be remembered. For we could win the war and lose the people, and that would be the final irony of the story.

August 29, 1965

Air Strikes Hit Vietcong—And South Vietnam Civilians

By CHARLES MOHR

Special to The New York Times

SAIGON, Sept. 4—In Kien Hoa Province south of Saigon, on Aug. 16, United States aircraft accidentally bombed a Buddhist pagoda and a Catholic church.

The Buddhists could not have been surprised, although two of them were terribly burned by napalm, because it was the third time their pagoda had been bombed in 1965. A temple of the Cao Dai religious sect in the same area has been bombed twice this year.

In another delta province there is a woman who has both arms burned off by napalm and her eyelids so badly burned that she cannot close them. When it is time for her to sleep her family puts a blanket over her head.

The woman had two of her children killed in the air strike which maimed her last April and she saw five other children die. She was quite dispassionate when she told an American "more children were killed because the children do not have so much experience and do not know how to lie down behind the paddy dikes."

These incidents must be balanced against some place names that ring with the bloody history of this summer's monsoon offensive by the Vietcong guerrillas—Song Be, Dong Xoai, Route 19. In those major battles it was air power that saved hundreds of lives of Government troops and perhaps saved the Government from collapse.

Although the daily air raids against North Vietnam have received most of the public attention, the ever increasing ferocity of aerial bombardment in South Vietnam may have a much greater ultimate effect on the outcome of the guerrilla war here. Few Americans appreciate what their nation is doing in South Vietnam with airpower.

What Statistics Say

The statistics give some meager measure of the effort.

The U.S. Air Force says that during August it destroyed 5,349 "structures" or buildings and damaged 2,400 others. Thousands of more huts and buildings were knocked out by naval and marine air attacks. Although the exact figure is classified, the Air Force, Navy, Marines and South Vietnamese Air Force is now flying more than 11,000 sorties a month in contrast to about 2,000 in January.

The Air Force has not publicly released the figure, but it believes it has accounted for more than 15,000 "confirmed" kills since the first of the year.

"We are flying more sorties in this country than we did in Korea," an Air Force combat officer said.

But the statistics do not reflect the policy dilemma and the growing, although still muted, controversy over "in-country air strikes."

Many of the American military commanders here are known to feel that air power has done an outstanding job in disrupting the growing strength of the Vietcong and in saving the day during the critical months of spring and early summer.

But another American official says, "Nothing is doing more to lose the war for us here than the indiscriminate use of air power."

Maddeningly, both opinions may be correct at the same time.

There is no criticism of traditional "close air support"—air strikes staged to assist ground troops who are engaged in combat with the enemy. In this role, fighter-bombers have done magnificent work and earned the fervent admiration of the ground troops. They have also saved many American and Vietnamese lives from an armed, determined enemy.

The real question involves the growing use of air to harass and interdict suspected Vietcong troop concentrations, buildings and transport. This amounts to strategic bombing with fighters against targets which are strategic only in the relative terms of a guerrilla war (somewhat like the Russians bombing Johnson City, Tex.).

But this is strategic bombing in a friendly, allied country. Since the Vietcong doctrine is to insinuate themselves among the population and the population is largely powerless to prevent their presence, no one here seriously doubts that significant numbers of innocent civilians are dying every day in South Vietnam.

If the humanitarian and moral problem can be forgotten, there remains a most serious political problem.

It used to be an accepted principle that guerrilla war cannot be won without winning "the hearts and minds of the people" although some American officials will now bluntly say that "this is no longer relevant." To many American soldiers and officials here the principle still stands and they are agonizingly worried that while the U.S. is disrupting the Vietcong it may also be digging its political grave in Vietnam with 750-pound bombs.

Already more than 5 per cent of the population has fled into refugee camps. Although it is popular among Washington officials to say that the refugees are fleeing from Vietcong terrorism, some officials on the scene are quite willing to concede or even to volunteer that the majority are flee-

ing from the insecurity of the countryside and that air strikes are the largest single cause of that insecurity.

One army officer with considerable experience cringes when he reads the communiques listing dozens of "Vietcong sampans" sunk by bombs. He asks: "Don't they know the sampan is the bicycle of the Delta? You cannot just go around sinking sampans in this country."

'Target Selection'

No weapon is intrinsically bad in war (napalm is one of the very best), so a sophisticated understanding of the problem depends on some knowledge of the process called "target selection."

Distressingly, the whole air strike process follows a circular path which begins and ends with "agent reports" or the words of pro-Government Vietnamese intelligence agents operating in areas either controlled by or disputed by the Vietcong.

The agents report the presence of, say, a Vietcong platoon in an area. Hours or a day later the Vietnamese province chief may approve an air strike—a period which does not include the time it took the agent to walk or to bicycle to a Government headquarters. Some Americans believe that most agents are unreliable and most field advisers think that many often are.

The air strike itself is directed and controlled by forward air controllers called "FAC's," flying low in single-engine Cessna airplanes, and they are unquestionably very skillful in marking targets and telling pilots where to drop their bombs.

They are not infallible, however. The Catholic church struck in Kien Hoa last month was not only outside the strike zone but had been specifically pointed out to the FAC, sources said.

When the strike is over the forward air controllers can do a good job of reporting on buildings destroyed or burning, but it is much more difficult for them to count bodies, especially those of real guerrillas holed up in shelters. Thus final strike evaluation depends in great measure on a report by the same "agent" who helped to originate the strike in the first place.

Aerial photography and classified electronic machines also play a role in target selection. Moreover, scores of "free strike zones" have been declared around South Vietnam. One Air Force officer estimates they cover about 5 per cent of the nation's area. In these zones, which are longtime Vietcong strongholds or enemy-infested wilderness, pilots can bomb at will and often use them to drop unex-

pended ordnance with which they do not want to land.

Many Are Bothered

That all of this is not a perfectly precise process bothers many people, including some Air Force officers.

Responsible sources said this week that no single command question is receiving so much concentrated attention at U.S. Headquarters here as the question of how to apply American power effectively but selectively.

What is not so clear, however, is whether answers to the problem will be found. One factor is that attitudes vary widely among military men here.

Col. John Groom, deputy, of the Tactical Air Control Center, which controls air strikes, said, "The question is—how do we know that man on the ground is a Vietcong? It all depends on working with really good intelligence and we are doing our best. We do not make any preplanned strikes without the approval of the Vietnamese province chief."

Groom's humane thoughtfulness is apparent to a questioner. But another Air Force officer says, "Yes, we get the province chief's approval to get in and hit targets."

One officer will say, "It is not only wrong but silly to kill civilians or to hit any target which does not have military value, and that certainly does not apply to a civilian hamlet."

But another field-grade officer will say, "The Vietcong are not hard to find. The problem is that they hole up in these people-targets. I think we are going to have to give up our inhibitions about hitting people-type targets. The people will have to learn that if they are going to cohabit with the Vietcong they will get bombed."

Divergent Views

It is possible to hear one senior officer say over an evening drink, "We know that the application of sheer violence will never win this war and that we must give top priority to winning the allegiance of the people."

But it is also possible to hear another senior officer conclude a conversation by saying, "I think it's a myth that this is a new and different kind of war. It seems like a pretty straightforward war to me."

There are many reasons to believe, according to the most qualified sources, that air power has done more to hurt the Vietcong in this critical year than any other factor. But the wrong application of air power could in the end turn a majority of the population against the Government and make a war which cannot be lost impossible to win either, other observers say.

The problem does not become easier the closer one gets to it. A civilian observer recently flew in an O-1 observation plane to watch two air strikes from a close-up grandstand seat. One left an apparently empty patch of jungle smoking from napalm. "There is no way to know whether we accomplished anything except through agent reports," said a pilot.

The other strike involved four Navy planes which slammed a typical elongated delta hamlet with its houses strung out along a canal near Phuong Hiep in the Mekong rice bowl. Rockets flashed as they struck in a path hundreds of yards long and the deadly surf of napalm splashed through the village. There were also big general purpose bombs.

"I wonder if any civilians were killed?" a pilot was asked. "Who the hell knows?" was the answer.

September 5, 1965

U.S. Vietnam Force Told To Protect Civilian Lives

Care in Attacks Ordered

By CHARLES MOHR

Special to The New York Times.

SAIGON, Sept. 17—United States forces in Vietnam have been ordered to take special and continuing measures to decrease the number of civilians killed by American air strikes and military operations, reliable sources revealed today.

In an order to all commands issued Sept. 7, the United States commander, Gen. William C. Westmoreland admonished his subordinates that the use of unnecessary force would embitter the population and drive them into the arms of the Vietcong guerrillas.

American troops in Vietnam must exercise a restraint not normally required of soldiers on a battlefield General Westmoreland's order said.

He listed bombing and artillery "prestrikes" of helicopter landing zones in populated areas, "reconnaissance by fire" into hamlets and poorly planned harassing and interdictory artillery fire as specific examples of things to be avoided.

Planning Scored

A "prestrike" is a bombardment made before a landing and meant to suppress enemy fire in the landing zone and to disperse the enemy. Reconnaissance by fire is the shooting into a suspicious area in the hope of drawing fire which will reveal the enemy location. Harassing and interdictory fire is artillery fired not at known or confirmed targets but into areas where it may hamper enemy movements.

Some American officials in Vietnam have long felt that some undiscriminating air strikes, unobserved artillery fire and such incidents as the burning of huts would hamper eventual victory in the war by increasing peasant sympathy for the Communist guerrillas.

General Westmoreland's order was preceded by intensive consultations on the psychological aspects of the war by the entire American Mission in Vietnam which includes Embassy and other civilian officials. However, sources said that General Westmoreland had strengthened the recommendations of the others and made clear his own interest in the problem.

As outlined by the sources General Westmoreland's order and a message to his own military superiors on the subjects is a succinct primer of the laws of guerrilla warfare.

He said it is mandatory that special precautions be taken by commanders to avoid unnecessary loss of civilian life. He called for tight control of air strikes, including the all-important problem of selecting targets to bomb on the basis of intelligence agent reports. He said that all commanders in Vietnam must be made acutely aware of their very great responsibilities to avoid needless death and destruction, which, he said, would only have a detrimental effect on the course of the war.

The war, General Westmoreland said, seesaws back and forth over the Vietnamese countryside and the hapless Vietnamese peasant is often unable to have any control over whether his village is occupied by Vietcong guerrillas. This appeared to be an answer to those military thinkers here who say that villagers must be shown that it is dangerous to "allow" the Vietcong to enter their areas.

The use of what General Westmoreland called unnecessary force will make pacification of the country more difficult and costly, his order said.

He said American military combat commanders must strike a balance between the force necessary to accomplish their immediate objective and the high importance of reducing civilian casualties.

Specifically General Westmoreland ordered his military subordinates to:

¶Consider both the military and the psychological aspects of every operation they are planning.

¶Give their troops an indoctrination briefing on the importance of saving civilian lives before each mission.

¶Develop a "civic action" plan as part of each military operation. Civic action is Vietnam jargon for action meant to help and to win the allegiance of civilian populations.

¶Redraw the boundaries of so-called free strike zones to avoid all populated areas except acknowledged Vietcong base areas. Free strike zones are areas, comprising perhaps 5 per cent of the area of South Vietnam, where bombers may drop their bombs anywhere without any prior permission.

¶Vietnamese liaison officers should be attacked to United States military operations and the Vietnamese Army should be encouraged to join American battles so the war did not appear to be a battle between the United States and the Vietnamese people.

September 18, 1965

Air Raid Fatal to 48 Laid to Saigon Error

By CHARLES MOHR

Special to The New York Times

SAIGON, South Vietnam, Oct. 31 — A map-reading error by South Vietnamese military officers caused American planes to bomb a friendly village yesterday, a United States spokesman reported today.

A Vietnamese officer transposed the first two numerals of a grid coordinate, or map-reading code, thus directing two United States fighter-bombers to the village of Deduc rather than to a Vietcong guerrilla concentration six miles farther west, the spokesman said.

The planes, A-1E propeller-driven Skyraiders, killed 48 South Vietnamese civilians and wounded 55 with 260-pound fragmentation bombs

The New York Times Nov. 1, 1965
The village of Deduc (1) was bombed in error. B-52's pounded a Vietcong camp in the Mekong delta (2).

and white-phosphorus fire bombs. American military men in Saigon are shocked and chagrined by the incident, although it did not result from an American error.

"Think how those pilots must feel," said a senior officer.

Deduc, the bombed village, is near the South China Sea, a little more than 300 miles northeast of Saigon. On American maps, its grid-coordinate location—indicated by crisscrossing lines—is BR878984.

The "BR" designates a map zone 100,000 meters square, or 62.2 miles square. The first three digits designate a point 87,800 meters east of the zone's western edge, and the last three digits a point 98,400 meters north of the zone's southern edge.

Yesterday, according to the information made available here, a Vietnamese infantry unit drew fire from an area with the map-coordinate location BR788984 and called for air support.

Figure Passed to U.S.

Somewhere in the South Vietnamese chain of command, the first two numerals of the coordinate were reversed, and an erroneous location was passed on to an American air liaison officer. He diverted two Skyraiders that were flying cover over units of the United States First Cavalry Division (Airmobile).

Military regulations require that all American air strikes in South Vietnam be directed by a "forward air controller," flying in a single-engine plane much like the pleasure craft that crowd American airports.

The air controller marks the target with smoke rockets or smoke grenades and tells the bomber pilots how to hit the assigned target accurately.

In this case, the controller had already been over the Deduc area and was familiar with it. He questioned the order to bomb because Deduc was close to an important government town, Bongson, and did not appear hostile.

His radioed request for clarification was passed by an American air liaison officer to South Vietnam's 22d Division. According to a United States spokesman, this officer reaffirmed the map coordinates and again asked for the strike.

The bombing was then carried out. According to a traveler from the area, the pilots were surprised that the villagers did not run or take cover when they approached, as is usually the case in a pro-Vietcong village.

B-52'S SAID TO HIT FOE'S LAOS ROUTE

Secret Series of U.S. Raids to Cut Off Aid to Vietcong Is Called a Week Old

By United Press International

SAIGON, South Vietnam, Saturday, Dec. 18 — Giant B-52 bombers from Guam have secretly struck at improved Vietcong infiltration routes in neighboring Laos, military sources disclosed early today. The first in a series of raids was conducted more than a week ago, the sources said.

The B-52 jets, which have

A United States Embassy spokesman said Ambassador Henry Cabot Lodge was "deeply saddened by this tragic accident" and planned to express his regrets to Premier Nguyen Cao Ky.

A military spokesman said Gen. William C. Westmoreland, the United States commander in Vietnam, wanted it known "how

been used for some time inside Vietnam, hit such military targets as all-weather supply routes and way stations for North Vietnamese military units seeping through Laos to aid the Vietcong in the South.

Network Is Improved

Under an agreement between the United States and Prince Souvanna Phouma, the Laotian neutralist Premier, smaller United States Air Force and Navy planes have been attacking Communist positions in the southern Laotian panhandle since early this year.

The decision to use America's mightiest bombers in the attacks was prompted by a stepped-up use of the Laotian corridor by the Vietcong, military sources said.

North Vietnam is said to have improved the infiltration network—known as the Ho Chi

deeply he personally regrets the incident."

Although the latest error was apparently South Vietnamese, according to spokesmen, such mistakes have also been made by Americans. Several weeks ago, for example, American armed helicopters fired bullets and rockets at a friendly village near Kontum because of

Minh trail—to a point where as many as 4,500 men and 2,500 tons of supplies might soon move south each month.

American military officials became especially concerned when they noted that the North Vietnamese had taken heavy road-building and earth-moving equipment into areas of Laos bordering on the South Vietnamese province of Kontum and Quangnam, where all-weather infiltration roads are being constructed.

The construction was said to defy deterrence by smaller tactical warplanes.

As soon as darkness shields them from attacks, the Vietcong repair the roads— usually in a matter of hours.

United States air operations against Vietcong targets in Laos have been kept secret to the extent that American military personnel are used only with greatest reluctance on

a map-reading error.

In addition, a number of officials suggest that from time to time villages are struck intentionally but in the erroneous belief that they are sheltering Vietcong troops.

November 1, 1965

helicopter rescue missions.

Many officials have maintained that major American action in Laos would wreck any semblance of Laotian neutrality, agreed upon by the 14-nation Geneva convention of 1962.

For that reason the rescue of American pilots downed in Laos is handled by a band of hired civilian pilots working for an organization known as Air America, described as a private concern.

Military sources said the United States would not officially announce the B-52 bombing raids against Laotian targets, as it had in the case of strikes by smaller tactical aircraft. The United States Defense Department has, however, officially announced the loss of planes shot down over the country.

December 18, 1965

U.S. TO LET FORCES GO INTO CAMBODIA IN 'SELF-DEFENSE'

By R. W. APPLE Jr.
Special to The New York Times

SAIGON, South Vietnam, Dec. 20 — United States field commanders have been authorized to pursue enemy troops into Cambodia in some circumstances, authoritative sources said today.

The commanders also have been given permission to call in artillery barrages and tactical air strikes on enemy positions across the border if necessary. This could be done without consulting higher headquarters in Saigon, Honolulu or Washington.

According to the sources, actions of this sort will be permitted only in cases of "clear self-defense" — that is, only when the responsible officers feel that a failure to give chase would jeopardize the lives of American troops.

[In Peking, Premier Chou En-lai said the United States might extend the war in Vietnam to the whole of Indochina and to China. Page 9.]

Pursuit in self-defense, as explained by the sources, would come into play only when an

American unit was locked in combat with a Communist force that was falling back across the border and still fighting actively as it did so.

Wider Confrontation Due

The decisions of the United States to build more airfields in Thailand, to intensify the bombing of Laos, and now to penetrate into Cambodia suggest that American officials are edging closer to a commitment to resolute confrontation of the enemy throughout Southeast Asia.

"It's obvious that we are getting into a gray area," one source said. "It's not easy for a man in the heat of battle to weigh dispassionately whether he's chasing an enemy in self-defense or because he has a chance to destroy him."

If American troops or fighter-bombers crossed into Cambodia, that country's head of state, Prince Norodom Sihanouk, would almost certainly raise the most serious objections. Diplomatic sources here said the Prince had not yet been told of the new American policy.

Prince Sihanouk, who has followed in recent months a policy of nonalignment with strongly anti-American overtones, is regarded warily by American diplomats here. For this reason they refuse to discuss the Cambodian situation in public.

American military officials

are convinced that North Vietnamese regulars are using Cambodia as a staging area and a sanctuary despite Prince Sihanouk's vehement denials. Some officials concede that the Cambodian Government may not be aware of the extent of such activity in their country.

The problem was brought into focus by the battle of Iadrang Valley last month, in which the First Cavalry Division, (Airmobile) fought the North Vietnamese within 10 miles of the border. The division's officers began asking why they were forced to pull up short when they neared Cambodia.

Ultimately, the problem came under reconsideration in Washington and the Johnson Administration authorized the policy of pursuit in self-defense.

The sources who made known the new United States doctrine took great pains to distinguish it from the doctrine of "hot pursuit," which permits one military force to follow another that it has been fighting back into the territory from which the second force came.

Many officers feel that, now that the orders to avoid Cambodia in all events have been eliminated, the first test is likely to be at hand soon. The Highlands provinces of Kontum, Pleiku and Darlac, adjacent to Cambodia, have been the scene of intense fighting since midsummer, and as many as six North Vietnamese regiments are believed to be operating in that general area.

At present, the United States has no intention of using B-52

strategic bombers in Cambodia, even in support of American troops who might be engaged there under the new policy. The sources said the big bombers would not be "an appropriate weapon" in such a situation.

The Stratofortresses from Guam began blasting infiltration routes in southeastern Laos for the first time last week. It is not been made known how many missions they have flown or how often they are to be sent over Laos.

One source suggested, however, that they would be used at least one or twice a week.

The question of pursuit into Cambodia—like the problem of what targets to bomb in North Vietnam and how to cut off the infiltration routes through Laos—is a part of the major strategic problem underlying the war in Vietnam: Should the allies continue to apply limited tactics in an effort to wear down the foe, or should they extend the conflict into Indochina at large in the hope of winning a decisive military victory?

Many political scientists and diplomats have argued for years that it is futile to attempt a solution of the problem by isolating the situation in Vietnam from those in neighboring countries. But the sensitivity of the governments of Thailand, Laos and Cambodia has made it difficult to embody this attitude in a workable United States policy.

December 21, 1965

143

RAIDS ON NORTH VIETNAM RESUMED BY U.S. PLANES AS 37-DAY PAUSE IS ENDED

Saigon Reports Strike by Navy and Air Force Bombers

By CHARLES MOHR

Special to The New York Times

SAIGON, Monday, Jan. 31—United States war planes resumed bombing attacks on North Vietnam today.

The bombing raids on that Communist country had been suspended for 37 days from 6 P.M. on Christmas Eve, Dec. 24, until today as one step to encourage Hanoi to negotiate a peaceful settlement of the Vietnam war.

Today's raids apparently signaled the end of the so-called Washington peace offensive and marked a return to a hard military line toward the North Vietnamese.

Embassy Announcement

Barry Zorthian, Minister Counselor of Information for

The New York Times   Jan. 31, 1966

North Vietnamese troops are among those fighting Americans near Anthai (1). Marines landed in Quang-ngai Province (2) and may join fighting around Anthai.

the United States Embassy here, summoned reporters to a press briefing at 3 P.M. (2 A.M., Monday, New York time) and read the following announcement:

"The Prime Minister of the Republic of Vietnam (South Vietnam) and the American Ambassador to Vietnam announce that United States aircraft today attacked targets in designated areas of North Vietnam."

Mr. Zorthian added that the raids today had already been completed and that full details would be made available later at the regular daily military briefing.

He turned aside other questions.

It was not stated whether the planes that struck North Vietnam today followed the same rules of engagement which had governed airstrikes before the long pause. These prohibited pilots from striking the population centers of Hanoi or Haiphong.

Efforts at Negotiation

The United States has twice ordered cessation of bombing in the North to encourage negotiations. The first pause was for a period of five days last May.

Air raids against North Vietnam began almost a year ago, on Feb. 7, 1965 after Vietcong guerrillas raided an American compound at Pleiku and caused a number of American deaths.

It was noted that the resumption of bombing came at a time when military activity in general was being elevated by the United States. A series of large scale military operations, involving United States Army and Marine Corps troops along the Central Vietnam coast, amounted to a general offensive in that area.

Other large scale operations were also under way near Saigon.

Until they were suspended United States air raids on North Vietnam were staged on a daily basis except when bad weather infrequently made all air action impossible.

January 31, 1966

HUMPHREY TO VISIT SAIGON TO STUDY REFORM EFFORTS DECIDED UPON IN HONOLULU

By TOM WICKER

Special to The New York Times

HONOLULU, Feb. 8—The United States and South Vietnamese Governments issued today a Declaration of Honolulu that appeared to place new emphasis on winning the war through a combination of military action and expanded civic reform programs.

At the same time, President Johnson announced that he was sending Vice President Humphrey to Saigon. Officials said Mr. Humphrey's mission would be to see South Vietnamese reform programs in action so that he could pull together the Johnson Administration's efforts to increase their effectiveness.

After a final meeting with Vietnamese leaders this morning, Mr. Johnson left at midday for Los Angeles for a talk in transit with Mr. Humphrey.

Determination Pledged

The Vice President, whose first stop is Honolulu, will fly to Saigon tomorrow with Lieut. Gen. Nguyen Van Thieu, South

Vietnamese chief of state, and Air Vice Marshal Nguyen Cao Ky, the Premier.

In the declaration the Vietnamese leaders joined with President Johnson in pledging "their determination in defense against aggression, their dedication to the hopes of all the people of South Vietnam and their commitment to the search for a just and stable peace."

Specifically, Marshal Ky and General Thieu stated:

"It is a military war, a war for the hearts of the people. We cannot win one without winning the other. But the war for the hearts of the people is more than military tactic. It is a moral principle. For this we shall strive as we fight to bring about a true social revolution."

In the same declaration, the United States Government

pledged that its purpose in Vietnam was to prevent Communist aggression and that to that end it would give "full support" to political and social reforms and "special support" in helping stabilize the economy, increase food production, stamp out disease and enlarge education.

There was scarcely a word in the declaration or in a communiqué that accompanied it to suggest an expanded war, intensified bombing of North Vietnam or other increased military activities.

In the communiqué, the two Governments stated only "full agreement upon a policy of growing military effectiveness and of still closer cooperation between the military forces of Vietnam and those of the United States."

Both Governments also noted "with regret the total absence of a present interest in peace on the part of the Government of North Vietnam," but agreed upon "continued diplomatic efforts for peace."

In a section of the declaration setting forth "the purposes of the Government of the United States," it was stated that "the United States Government and the Government of Vietnam will continue in the future, as they have in the past, to press the quest for a peaceful settlement in every form."

Despite the "harsh and negative response" received so far, the declaration said, both Governments remain determined that "no path to peace shall be unexplored" and that "the peace offensive of the United States Government and the Government of South Vietnam will continue until peace is secured."

Action by 1967 Hoped For

Marshal Ky said at a news conference that he hoped the political evolution of a constitutional government could be completed next year.

Several specific reforms were set forth in the communiqué as immediate targets. They included rural construction "efforts of particular strength and intensity in areas of high priority"; directing these efforts "to meet the people's need for larger output, more efficient production, improved credit, handicrafts and light industry, and rural electrification"; moving new and more productive strains of rice, corn and vegetable seeds from the laboratory to the farmers' fields; speeding land reform and increasing efforts to train health personnel and improve medical logistics.

The Secretary of Health, Education and Welfare, John W. Gardner, will make a later trip to Saigon to inspect the health effort, and other programs to build schools, train teachers and provide textbooks.

A special effort will also be made, the communiqué said, to care for refugees and to provide schools for refugee children.

The communiqué pledged "further concrete steps" to combat inflation.

To further the rural construction program, both Governments said, particular emphasis will be put on building democracy in rural areas—"an effort as important as the military battle itself"—and on concentrating resources in regions that could be protected against Vietcong attack.

All these steps have long been urged by those who have contended that the only way to defeat Communist insurgency was to attack the social, economic and political defects that caused it even while the military struggle was continuing.

High United States officials here conceded, for instance, that not even an aerial assault on North Vietnam at four times the intensity of that now being carried out could win the war in the South.

Government officials said the purpose of Vice President Humphrey's trip to South Vietnam, which they estimated might last two or three days, would be to "continue the momentum" toward the social and economic reforms discussed here. They said President Johnson wanted a top-level official who might later be put in charge of marshaling American assistance for the reform programs.

The details of the rest of Mr. Humphrey's tour were not made public in Honolulu because the Administration was waiting for diplomatic clearance from the six other countries in "Southeast Asia and the subcontinent" that Bill D. Moyers, the White House press secretary, said were involved.

Mr. Humphrey will be accompanied to Saigon by the Secretary of Agriculture, Orville L. Freeman; Ambassador at Large N. Averell Harriman; McGeorge Bundy, the President's special assistant for national security affairs; Leonard Marks Jr., director of the United States Information Agency; Jack Valenti, a special assistant to the President, and Lloyd N. Hand, the State Department's chief of protocol.

February 9, 1966

B-52'S MAKE RAID ON NORTH VIETNAM

Big Bombers, in Their First Attack Outside South, Hit Approaches to a Pass

Special to The New York Times

SAIGON, Tuesday, April 12— United States B-52 strategic bombers were used in attacks on North Vietnam for the first time early today.

A military spokesman said that the Guam-based heavy bombers raided the approaches to Mugia Pass, within a mile of the Laotian border. The number of planes used was not disclosed.

Mugia Pass is the main road between eastern Laos and North Vietnam for the infiltration of men and equipment into Laos and subsequently into South Vietnam.

The area is lightly populated. Apparently the heavy bombers were attempting to close the road with a saturation bombing attack.

The pass is about 70 miles northwest of the 17th Parallel, the dividing line between North and South Vietnam, and about 200 miles south of Hanoi.

The raid this morning was approved by Washington on a "one-time basis," an informed source said, adding that there was no present authorization to make future raids with the heavy Air Force bombers.

However, he remarked, "once you open up something like this there is no reason not to press on.'"

April 12, 1966

The Generals' Retreat

As Saigon Junta Yields to Buddhists, Some Shining Hopes Are Shattered

By CHARLES MOHR
Special to The New York Times

SAIGON, April 14—The generals who rule South Vietnam were in full retreat today.

Among the baggage they were leaving behind on a littered political battlefield was some shining American hopes. These included the hope that the Government of Air Vice Marshal Nguyen Cao Ky would

News Analysis

accomplish a true social revolution in South Vietnam, secure the countryside militarily and hand power back to the people in a careful and gradual manner stretching over almost two years.

The ruling National Leadership Committee agreed to hold elections for a constitution-writing assembly in three to five months, and many observers did not believe that Premier Ky could hold on much past that election. Other observers doubt that he can last even that long since the powerful Unified Buddhist Church has already begun to call for his almost immediate resignation.

It was slightly more than two months ago that Premier Ky and President Johnson left their Honolulu conference in an atmosphere of exultation. How could Marshal Ky's political position have deteriorated so rapidly?

That position was inherently a weak one; the Premier had virtually no popular support. But this had not had time to show up in the few months he held office before arriving in Honolulu on Feb. 6.

Publicity Called Harmful

The publicity that Premier Ky received from the Honolulu meeting, much of it picturing him as being "embraced" by President Johnson, is widely regarded as having been harmful to him.

This weakened Marshal Ky for attacks from clever Buddhist monks only too willing to exploit a streak of natural xenophobia in the proud Vietnamese people.

It also helped to bring to a climax the long-simmering feud between the 35-year-old Premier and Lieut. Gen. Nguyen Chanh Thi, a fellow member of the 11-general junta and overlord of the five northern provinces.

Generals Ky and Thi were the officers with the best social and

145

political instincts in the directory and the most ability to lead a complex military and political struggle against the Communists. However, both are often described as vain, erratic and impetuous. General Thi deeply resented the publicity Marshal Ky had received.

One United States official reports that the mere fact that the news magazine Time put Marshal Ky's picture on its cover was a considerable factor in the ultimate deterioration of the political situation because it put General Thi in a foul mood.

'What a Crazy Crisis'

"What a crazy crisis this has been," the official sighed.

Marshal Ky's decision to dismiss General Thi, which he took March 10, was at first painted by both United States and South Vietnamese officials as a long-thought-out one, based primarily on a desire to strengthen the central Government's control over regional commands. As now reconstructed, the sequence of events seems somewhat different.

Earlier in March the Premier made a visit to the I Army Corps area, which General Thi commanded. The general, in a bad mood because of Honolulu, helped to humiliate Marshal Ky at a public meeting, berating the Government as inept. Then General Thi's civilian deputy for political affairs did the same thing in even more insulting terms.

On the following Wednesday, March 9, Marshal Ky informed United States Embassy officials that he was planning to purge General Thi on the following day and that he had the votes in the junta to do it. More

important, he told the United States officials that he had taken "careful soundings" among Buddhist and other leaders and that he had concluded that the general's supposed political strength in the northern provinces was a myth.

The embassy officials had little time to do their own checking but, at least until Marshal Ky's action began to go dramatically sour, they left the impression that they agreed with his assessment and applauded the move against General Thi.

The same officials had previously said that the junta was a delicately balanced mechanism and that the generals realized that they could not afford to fight among themselves.

The moment General Thi was pushed out, the delicate mechanism began to go haywire. Almost all his military and civil appointees began to tolerate and then to foster an anti-Ky campaign. The area has since been out of the central Government's control.

An Academic Question

Whether the Buddhist leaders had promised Premier Ky they would not oppose General Thi's ouster became totally academic. They did not protest the ouster; they merely used it to charge that the Ky Government was too busy engaging in purges to govern—actually, it was the only such quarrel since the junta took power last June—and to demand an elected government.

The Premier might still have been able to survive and carry out his original plan of a gradual evolution to democracy by late 1967, but there followed a

train of events that bled away his strength. They can be told as a series of "ifs."

If the Deputy Premier, Lieut. Gen. Nguyen Huu Co, had not pointed a gun at General Thi's chest on the night of March 10 to prevent him from boarding a plane to return to Danang, General Thi might have been more willing to accept his fate. Instead, he was furious.

Reversal of a Decision

If Marshal Ky had not overruled General Co the following week and sent General Thi back to Danang, the generals newly appointed to command the I Corps and the First Division might have been able to keep their troops loyal to Saigon.

If on the first day that public officials in Danang and Hue turned the radio stations over to anti-Government students and supported general strikes, Premier Ky had sent loyal troops to the area and removed the officials, he might have regained control there without bloodshed.

Above all, if he had never held a news conference on April 3, he might still have saved the situation. On that occasion, to the apparent amazement of his fellow generals, Premier Ky announced that Danang was in the hands of "Communists," that he was sending troops to "liberate" it and that he would shoot

the anti-Government Mayor, Dr. Nguyen Van Man.

The plan to move troops to Danang had been agreed upon; to have done so quietly and firmly might have had a good effect on the demonstrators. Marshal Ky's strong words were interpreted not as a sign of "strength" but as a silly faux pas.

The Buddhists in Saigon went streaming into the streets in full-scale demonstrations, meant more to "exploit the mistake than to protest" the threat. Until then demonstrations in Saigon had been feeble.

By pointing a gun at the head of Danang and Hue, Marshal Ky made impossible any really plausible resolution of the near-rebellion there. After 48 hours he called off the effort, leaving all of his political enemies neither harmed nor chastened.

Buddhist Demands Adopted

However, his decision precluded the awful possibility of Vietnamese troops killing each other and civilians. By this time all the options were almost equally bad.

Finally, Marshal Ky and the other generals called an appointed national political convention in Saigon this week to suggest the means by which the junta could more rapidly surrender power without seeming to give in to the ever-increasing pressure from the Buddhists.

When the Buddhists boycotted the meeting, it seemed possible that it could be used as a counterforce to help the Government resist the Buddhist demands. Instead, the convention adopted all of the Buddhists' demands, especially for a constituent assembly that could turn itself into a national legislature and for an amnesty for all anti-Government forces.

The Buddhists promptly elevated their demands to include the early resignation of Marshal Ky or a drastic reshuffle of the Government.

April 15, 1966

Vietnam Is a Proving Ground for New Weapons

By HANSON BALDWIN

Two of the finest fighters in the world— one U.S., and one of Soviet design—clashed in the skies above North Vietnam last week in a war that has become, in limited scope, a proving ground of new military technology.

The aerial battles between the U.S. McDonnell F4C fighter aircraft, which holds many speed and altitude records, and the Soviet MIG-21, a maneuverable supersonic fighter, matched in battle some of the latest U.S. and Russian weapons for the first time since Korea and the 1958 Taiwan Straits air clashes between the Chinese Nationalists and Communists.

The results at the weekend were inconclusive, though the indications were that although the Russians produce extremely maneuverable flying machines, U.S. planes are superior as fighting machines. But the clashes, in addition to invoking the specter of escalation, demonstrated what the services have long known—that as far as military technology is concerned, the "battle is the payoff."

Vietnam, in a different way and to some extent a more limited de-

gree, has become, like the Spanish civil war of 1936-39, a proving ground for new weapons, new tactics, new ideas. Both sides—but the United States in particular—have utilized modern military technology in fighting a limited war.

In a way, Vietnam has provided two proving grounds for new weapons, rather than a single one. In South Vietnam, in what is called in Saigon the "in-country" war, development efforts have been concentrated upon types of weapons best utilized in jungles and rice paddies and best calculated to meet the peculiar needs of what was been variously described by former Soviet Premier Khrushchev as "wars of national liberation," and by the late President Kennedy as "counter insurgency" warfare. In the "out-country" war over and around North Vietnam, both sides have utilized some of the same type weapons that might be utilized in a modern all-out nuclear war— the latest jet fighters, fighter-bombers and bombers, air-to-air and anti-aircraft missiles, sophisticated radars, robot and other reconnaissance planes, aircraft carriers and specialized aircraft fitted

to jam the enemy's electronics systems.

The array and variety of new or modified weapons used in combat for the first time in Vietnam are so many as to preclude even a complete catalogue.

Airmobile Divisions

In the "in-country" war in the South, probably the most important single development is the extensive use of helicopters to provide tactical mobility for the ground forces. The organization of a new type of division—the airmobile division— has been built around the helicopter as a replacement for the traditional Army truck and jeep, and, at least in Vietnam, the helicopter has proved its worth completely as a vehicle for tactical mobility, one which has demonstrated a remarkably low combat loss rate. The performance of the helicopter has generated intense enthusiasm in the Army, though the experience of Vietnam cannot be applied, without major modification, to a war against an enemy supported by modern air power and heavy anti-aircraft weapons.

On the water—and that strange

mixture of environment, half-land, half - water which characterizes much of the coastal areas of South Vietnam—the Navy and Marines have had to develop new types of shallow-water coastal patrol and river craft for coastal surveillance and what the Marines call "Riverine warfare." Most of these are adaptations of existing commercial types; one of the latest is a plastic-hulled river patrol boat (its hull, unlike wooden hulls, is immune to the teredos or marine boring worms which so quickly destroy wood in warm seas), with water-jet (propellerless) quiet-running engines, and a draft measured in inches. An application of this same type is the air-propelled boat, used across the swampy grasslands. Later this year, the Navy may test other new types, including hydrofoils, a powerful patrol gunboat with both gas turbines and diesels, and the air-cushion vehicles which ride above land or water on a few inches of trapped air.

In the land war all sorts of new weapons, gadgets or ideas have either been tried and approved, or tested and discarded. The Claymore mine, an electrically con-

146

trolled, directional mine which when detonated spews out a broadsword of steel pellets mowing down everything in its path, was developed by the U.S. Engineers and the Infantry some years ago but has received its first test of war in Vietnam. It forms some of the principal defenses of every U.S. camp or position in Vietnam. Unfortunately the Vietcong have learned how to make it in their jungle factories in far cruder—but effective—form. A new lightweight, rapid-fire high-velocity small caliber rifle, the M-16, firing a bullet of about .223 caliber, has proved extremely popular in Vietnam with American troops, and forecasts the probable future trend in firearms. The 40 mm. grenade launcher, on the ground, or mounted on trucks or helicopters, is also widely praised.

Detection Devices

All sorts of intrusion or warning devices have been tried to provide visual or sound warning of attempted sneak attacks, and even a bullet detector for helicopter pilots has been tested—though so far its sole result has been to make the pilots nervous.

In the air the oldest, modified, compete with the newest products of technology. The old C-47 workhorse has become in Vietnam a weird sort of fighter. It has been equipped with ten barrelled "miniguns" of 7.62 caliber, with a rate of fire of 6,000 rounds a minute, and it is used in emergencies to deliver heavy fire against Vietcong ground forces. Many antipersonnel weapons of various types have also been tried with air dispensers—from bomblets and darts to a modern variety of cannister.

Perhaps some of the most significant developments both in the "incountry" and "out-country" wars in Vietnam are in the field of intelligence collection. All kinds of new sensors and collection devices, from tape recorders and ground radars, to aircraft-mounted cameras, infrared instruments, sidelooking radar and other gadgets have been prodigally employed to detect a single Vietcong in a rice paddy, a supply train under the jungled canopy of the Ho Chi Minh trail or SAM-2 missile sites in Notrh Vietnam. The science of air reconnaissance which had lagged somewhat in the United States between wars is now under tremendously rapid development. With this has gone a spurt in counterelectronics warfare. RB-66 aircraft or other types specially fitted with proper instruments, have had a lot to do with the success of our planes in evading enemy ground missiles. At the same time the Russians have learned a good bit about what is wrong wtih their anti-aircraft missiles and what

they can do to make improve them.

Aircraft armament — particularly those types used against ground targets—have experienced the stern test of combat and some of them have been found wanting. We have, as yet, no sure-fire bridge busting missile, and both an anti-radar missile and the Navy's Bullpup have proven to have some major weaknesses. The air clashes have not yet been frequent enough to provide a real test of comparative air-to-air armament but it is certain that if the MIGS intervene in full force, as many observers believe they will do, the U.S. and Russian armory of aircraft missile and cannon will face the final test of any kind of military equipment

May 1, 1966

BUDDHIST PROTEST BEING INTENSIFIED; SUICIDE TOLL AT 5

Girl in Hue Dies in Hospital After New Self-Immolation —Saigon Girl Also Dead

---

TWO MONKS MAKE PLEA

Moderate and Militant Both Ask an End of Sacrifices Aimed at Ouster of Ky

---

Special to The New York Times
SAIGON, Tuesday, May 31—The toll of Buddhist suicides by fire in the drive against the Ky regime rose to five today as two young girs burned themselves to death.

It appeared that the wave of horror and fanaticism would outstrip that of 1963, when South Vietnamese Buddhists first used suicides as a political weapon in a campaign that helped to bring down the regime of President Ngo Dinh Diem.

Now the object is the overthrow of the military Government led by Premier Nguyen Cao Ky and Chief of State Nguyen Van Thieu.

The toll reached five this morning when a 17-year-old girl, tentatively identified as Nguyen Thi Van, poured gasoline over herself and set it alight on a street in Hue, 400 miles northeast of Saigon. Reports from Hue said that she died in a hospital of severe burns.

Girl Leaves Letters

Last night in Saigon a 19-year-old Buddhist nun spread a mat of rise straw on a curb, folded her legs in the lotus position of her faith and set herself afire. The nun was at first identified after the burning as a young man, but this morning official Buddhist sources identified the victim as Nguyen Thi Kim Chau, whose religious name was Thich Nu Vien Ngoc.

The sources said she was a native of Hue and the daughter of an officer in the Vietnamese Marine Corps, which helped quell the rebellion in Danang recently and thus aroused new Buddhist ire.

The girl left letters to President Johnson and others protesting against the rule of the military junta, monks asserted.

Her action followed by less than six hours a formal statement by Thich Tam Chau, chairman of the Institute of Secular Affairs of the Unified Buddhist Church, asking all Buddhists "to stop immediately their intentions to immolate themselves by fire or to indulge in self-destruction."

[In Hue, Thich Tri Trang, the powerful monk leading the Buddhist movement in South Vietnam's northern provinces, called for an end to self-sacrifice, The Associated Press reported.]

Early yesterday in the mountain resort town of Dalat, a monk, Thich Quang Thien, 30, burned himself to death. Sunday a nun immolated herself in Hue and another Buddhist killed herself Sunday night on the grounds of the secular institute.

The Unified Buddhist Church was still divided on the struggle against the Ky Government, and on tactics, although the division had narrowed in public.

In a news conference yesterday Thich Tam Chau, the leading "moderate," joined more militant Buddhist leaders in calling for the resignation of Air Force Vice Marshal Ky and Lieutenant General Thieu.

However, many political observers believed that Thich Tam Chau still hoped to effect a compromise between the junta and the Buddhists and had not wholly endorsed the militant line of Thich Tri Quang.

Tich Tri Quang, secretary general of the Religious Affairs Institute of the church and Vietnamese Buddhism's leading political tactician, is in the rebel-held city of Hue, where he has taken an increasingly intransigent line against Marshal Ky and has accused Americans of responsibility for Buddhist deaths.

The degree of responsibility of major Buddhist leaders for such immolations was difficult to fix.

May 31, 1966

Ky Feels Junta Is 'Over Hump' in Crisis

Troops Control All Hue

By R. W. APPLE Jr.
Special to The New York Times
HUE, South Vietnam, Sunday, June 19 — Government troops swept unopposed this morning into the last section of the city controlled by Buddhist dissidents.

Loyal marines, paratroopers and combat policemen occupied the Dieu De Pagoda and the area around it early yesterday and later pushed into the old walled city. This morning they moved into the residential neighborhood surrounding the Tu Dam Pagoda.

The effort of the ruling military junta to reassert its authority in Hue thus appeared to have succeeded. The four-day campaign ended on the first anniversary of the junta's seizure of national leadership.

Less Costly Than Danang

The government triumph in Hue proved far less costly than its armed pacification of Danang last month, which cost dozens and perhaps hundreds of lives. In Hue, the Buddhists simply chose not to fight, and no blood was spilled yesterday or today.

Brig. Gen. Pham Xuan Nhuan, who had sided with the Buddhists in their dispute with the regime of Premier Nguyen Cao Ky, was dismissed as commander of the Vietnamese First Infantry Division. He was succeeded by Col. Ngo Quang Truong, deputy commander of the airborne division.

General Nhuan's troops stood aside when the United States Consulate in Hue was burned earlier this month.

June 19, 1966

U.S., EXTENDING BOMBING, RAIDS HANOI AND HAIPHONG OUTSKIRTS; CITES REDS' DISPERSAL OF FUEL

DESCRIBING THE TARGETS: Defense Secretary Robert S. McNamara uses maps of Haiphong and Hanoi as he tells reporters about U.S. strikes against oil facilities. Arrows, which have been added to photograph, show raided areas.

United Press International Telephoto

HEAVY LOSS SEEN

Oil-Storage Capacity Is Reduced by 50%, Pilots Indicate

By CHARLES MOHR
Special to The New York Times

SAIGON, South Vietnam, June 29—United States bombers struck close to the heart of Hanoi and Haiphong today in raids that military informants said had damaged the gasoline and oil supplies of North Vietnam severely.

The raids marked a change from restrictions that had kept American planes well away from the two major cities since they began hitting the North in February, 1965. It also marked an important escalation of the United States effort against the North Vietnamese-backed guerrillas in South Vietnam.

Whether the restrictions will now be further altered to allow raids on manufacturing plants, military airfields and other targets around Hanoi and Haiphong was unclear, but some informed sources believed that such targets would soon be hit. The decision, like that to carry out today's raids, must be made in Washington.

Air Force Joins Attack

Navy A-4 and A-6 jet fighter-bombers attacked a large tank farm for petroleum products at the very edge of Haiphong, two miles northwest of the center of the city.

The complex, which represents 40 per cent of the fuel-storage capacity of North Vietnam and 95 per cent of the facilities for unloading tanker ships, was 80 per cent destroyed, according to preliminary damage reports by returning pilots.

Air Force F-105 jet fighter-bombers struck another large tank farm 3½ miles from the center of Hanoi that contained 20 per cent of the nation's storage facilities. The pilots estimated that they had destroyed 90 per cent of the target area.

Haiphong, the port for Hanoi, is about 60 miles from the capital.

In a Single Stroke

If the assessments are correct, the raids, in a single stroke, destroyed 50 per cent of North Vietnam's fuel-storage capacity as well as most of its ability to unload petroleum products from ships efficiently and expeditiously.

Another petroleum facility at Doson, 12 miles southeast of Haiphong, was also bombed, but there was no damage assessment.

The United States command made it clear that it had staged the raids because previously restricted air action had failed to deal with the major problem of North Vietnamese infiltration of troops and supplies to the Vietcong.

The Hanoi radio claimed seven United States planes shot down, three near Haiphong and four near Hanoi. Such reports have been exaggerated and there was no reason to doubt the accuracy of an American statement that only one plane, an F-105, had been lost.

The nearest previous strike in relation to Haiphong was a bridge five miles away bombed on April 19. The target nearest to Hanoi was a missile site 15 miles away hit on the preceding day.

Four major air raids on nine petroleum storage areas in other regions of North Vietnam have been carried out since June 21.

Military sources said that more than half of North Vietnam's supply of oil and gasoline and lubricants—estimated at two to four months' supply—had presumably been destroyed.

"I'm sure this has crippled their effort for some time," a military spokesman said.

An official military statement said: "The destruction of these facilities will make infiltration of men and supplies into South Vietnam more costly and difficult."

Dense Clouds of Smoke

The raids, which sent dense black smoke billowing 20,000 feet over Haiphong and 35,000 feet over Hanoi, represented an important change in American policy although efforts were made to minimize this aspect of the situation.

The official statement said: "The strike is consistent with our continuing policy of bombing only military targets in North Vietnam. The petroleum facilities in Hanoi and Haiphong have become vital in supporting the mounting North Vietnamese aggression against the South and therefore are prime military targets."

The United States had hesitated to strike the targets, informed sources said, because of fears that such raids might evoke active Chinese Communist intervention, might risk hitting Soviet and other Communist-bloc or neutral ships in the Haiphong harbor or might inflict extensive civilian casualties.

A military spokesman said everything would indicate that no significant number of civilian casualties had been inflicted.

Officially, the spokesmen said they had no information on whether tanker ships had been struck in the Haiphong harbor. Other sources said it was unlikely because of the target limits imposed on the pilots.

Four MIG's Encountered

At first the military spokesmen reported that no opposition by MIG fighter planes or Soviet-built surface-to-air missiles had been encountered, but it was learned later that four MIG fighters had attacked the Air Force F-105's and that one MIG was believed to have been shot down.

No American planes were struck by or lost to the MIG's, but the F-105 was shot down by heavy antiaircraft fire encountered over Hanoi, the spokesmen said. The Navy pilots met only light flak, it was reported.

It was also learned that at least one surface-to-air missile had been fired at the Navy plane but missed.

June 30, 1966

MILLION REFUGEES LISTED BY SAIGON

6% of Population Uprooted in South Vietnam in Last 2 Years, Figures Show

By ERIC PACE
Special to The New York Times

SAIGON, South Vietnam, July 4 — Government statistics made public today indicated that more than a million South Vietnamese fled from their homes in the last two years.

As the war has grown, the figures show, 6 per cent of the country's population of 16 million has been uprooted. This is about 100,000 more than the number of refugees who poured into the country after the partition of 1954.

Finding homes for the refugees of the nineteen-fifties was one of the main accomplishments of the late Ngo Dinh Diem when he was President. But the Government of Premier Nguyen Cao Ky is having a harder time resettling those seeking sanctuary from bombings, ground fighting and the Vietcong.

As of June 30, the Ky regime's special department for refugees reported 500,732 refugees were housed in temporary quarters, ranging from sampans to austere camps. An additional 140,-502 have returned to their home villages, and 360,574 have obtained new homes.

"The majority of the refugees are women and children, who are therefore handicapped in their quest for work," the Ky Government's chief commissioner for refugees, Dr. Nguyen Phuc Que, has observed.

'Caught in the Middle'

"These are people caught in the middle," an official of the Agency for Industrial Development said. They are "people whose husbands, sons and fathers have been killed or drafted into the Saigon Government armed forces or the Vietcong."

Most of today's refugees flee simply to escape the fighting. Though B-52 raids are generally in sparsely settled country, air strikes have destroyed civilian housing, and bigger military operations by both sides since early 1965 have made large areas temporarily uninhabitable.

Thus 12,000 residents of Binhdinh province, by American count, fled during Operation Masher, later named Whitewing, a' vast sweep involving more than a division of United States and South Vietnamese troops.

A United States Army Civic Action Team joined civilian officials in feeding, sheltering and giving medical treatment to the refugees during 10 days of fighting, when the guns fell silent, 9,000 Vietnamese returned to their villages—most of which are now again under Vietcong control—while 3,000 others preferred to stay as refugees under the Government's wing.

Officials of the development agency, who accept Dr. Que's statistics, said they knew of no refugees who had moved from Government territory into that of the Vietcong. They maintained that Vietcong oppression and a mounting feeling that the Saigon Government will win the war had fed the refugee flow.

It is the Agency for International Development, which distributed $21-million worth of aid, that provides the greater part of the relief funds for refugees. Last year the agency distributed $31-million worth of aid, in items ranging from aluminum roofing to bulgur wheat, which the Vietnamese do not like as much as rice, although it is nutritionally better for them.

The Ky Government has budgeted more than $16-million for refugee aid this year, although some American field workers contend that much of this, as well as much American aid, is siphoned off by corrupt local officials.

Nonetheless, the United States is encouraging private organizations to help the refugees, much as it welcomes token military units from other countries to help fight the war.

July 5, 1966

THIEU CALLS VOTE A BLOW TO HANOI

Chief of State Says Turnout Will Give Enemy Pause

By CHARLES MOHR
Special to The New York Times

SAIGON, South Vietnam, Sept. 12—The large turnout of registered voters in South Vietnam's national election yesterday will force North Vietnam "to have second thoughts" about the war and "to adopt a wiser attitude," the South Vietnamese chief of state said tonight.

According to figures issued by the Government today, 4,274,812 of the nation's 5,289,652 registered voters cast ballots. That was 80.8 per cent.

The voters chose 117 people, 10 of them military officers, to sit in a new constituent assembly charged with drawing up a democratic constitution that may lead to civilian government next year.

The chief of state, Lieut. Gen. Nguyen Van Thieu, said in a formal report tonight on the elections that the turnout showed that the people had belief and confidence in the military Government and that "final victory is growing near."

Premier Nguyen Cao Ky, wearing black flight suit and a lavender scarf, said during the Government program the success of the election "certainly announces the beginning of the end" for the Communist Vietcong movement.

Warns of Obstacles

Air Vice Marshal Ky warned, however, that "we have not yet achieved final victory" and that "many obstacles" lay ahead for South Vietnam.

South Vietnamese officials were clearly delighted with the turnout in the election. Although the United States Embassy avoided any immediate comment, American officials were pleased, too.

The Vietcong guerrillas threw almost none of their 112,000-man main-force regulars into direct attacks against voters. There was, however, a significant increase of terror incidents, apparently aimed at intimidation.

The Vietcong and North Vietnam appeared to have made a political blunder by denouncing the elections in advance and urging that the people "smash" them.

The Hanoi radio and the Liberation Radio of the Vietcong called the elections fraudulent today and denied that they had any meaning, according to reports of broadcast monitorings.

Hanoi said the people had been forced to go to the polls by the "armed puppet police" and the Americans. The Vietcong radio said the voter turnout figures had been "concocted" and asserted that the Vietcong controlled 10 million of the population, estimated at 16 million.

Although the percentage of registered voters who turned out was high, it was not a surprise to some observers. The Government had vigorously prepared for the event in areas that it controlled.

No evidence of election irregularities or of dishonestly inflated figures came to light, and diplomatic observers doubted there were any significant irregularities. Candidates generally thought the elections had been run fairly and well.

A small percentage of ballots cast were invalid and some of them may have been cast by citizens deliberately registering a protest against the Government and the election. The militant Unified Buddhist Church had called for a boycott of the voting, as had the Vietcong.

Invalid Votes in Hue

In the city of Hue, which has been a center of anti-Government dissent, 11 per cent of the ballots were invalid, an informed source said. In Saigon the total was 6.5 per cent. In the nation as a whole, a Government source said, only a little more than 2 per cent of the ballots were "spoiled."

Voter turnout ranged from about 65 per cent in populous, hard-to-control Saigon to a high of 97.5 per cent in the sparsely populated mountain province of Phubon. Fewer than 19,000 voters were registered in Phubon.

The constituent assembly that emerged appeared, on the whole, to be a strongly anti-Communist body unlikely to favor any compromise with the Vietcong. The candidates had been screened beforehand to eliminate those with known Communist or neutralist sympathies.

At the same time, it was not very likely the assembly would prove to be a tool of the military Government. Some of the prominent members have spent long terms in jail for activities against the authoritarian regime of the late President Ngo Dinh Diem and strongly favor democratic, civilian government.

With only 10 active-duty military officers elected, a bloc representing the ruling military junta's interest did not seem to have materialized.

But if the junta can put together a bloc of 40 members responsive to its wishes, from whatever sources, it will have effective control of the new assembly. That is because of a junta decree that enables the junta to veto any objectionable part of the draft constitution unless the junta's veto is overridden by a two-thirds vote.

According to the junta's own rules, the new assembly must be convened on or before Sept. 27. It then has a maximum of six months to prepare and adopt a draft constitution.

The old Constitution of the Diem regime was abrogated by the generals who overthrew him and the nation is now without a formal constitution.

A new national charter should be in force within seven months under these rules, but Marshal Ky recently said he thought the Assembly could finish its work within three months and that a national election for executive and legislative branches could take place by March.

Among the best known candidates elected was Dr. Phan Quang Dan, a Harvard-trained physician who once achieved the feat of winning election to President Diem's rigged National Assembly against Mr. Diem's wishes. Forced out of his seat, Dr. Dan later spent three years in jail on charges of complicity in an attempted coup d'état.

Other prominent winners were:

¶Phan Khac Suu, 61 years old, the last civilian chief of state in the succession of unstable governments in 1964 and 1965.

¶Tran Van Van, 58, a businessman who has been critical of the concept of military government but is chairman of the figurehead civilian advisory

149

body known as the "People's and Armed Forces Council."

¶Dr. Dang Van Sung who unlike almost all of the other candidates was openly critical of military government and its "failures." He is a strongly

anti-Communist newspaper publisher.

The Unified Buddhist Church, which last spring appeared to have an excellent chance of winning the largest single bloc of seats, did not participate openly in the election.

A handful of persons in the past associated with the Unified Church and still probably friendly to its moderate faction, at least, did win office despite the church's boycott.

One political party that showed some organized strength

was the Vietnamese Kuomingtang or Nationalist party, which won seven of the 17 seats at stake in the five northernmost provinces. The party is strongly anti-Communist.

September 13, 1966

A VISITOR TO HANOI INSPECTS DAMAGE LAID TO U.S. RAIDS

A Purposeful and Energetic Mood in Embattled Capital Found by a Times Man

2 RECENT ATTACKS CITED

Witnesses Certain American Bombs Dropped Inside City Dec. 13 and 14

The writer of the following dispatch is an assistant managing editor of The New York Times, who reached Hanoi Friday.

By HARRISON E. SALISBURY
Special to The New York Times

HANOI, North Vietnam, Dec. 24—Late in the afternoon of this drizzly Christmas Eve the bicycle throngs on the roads leading into Hanoi increased.

Riding sidesaddle behind husbands were hundreds of slender young Hanoi wives returning to the city from evacuation to spend Christmas with their families. Hundreds of mothers had small children perched on the backs of bicycles—children being returned to the city for reunions during the Christmas cease-fire.

In Hanoi's Catholic churches mass was celebrated, and here and there in the small foreign quarter there were more elaborate holiday observances. Five Canadian members of the International Control Commission had a fat Christmas goose brought in specially for them from Vientiane, Laos, on the I.C.C. flight into Hanoi yesterday.

Visitors Have a Party

And in Hanoi's rambling, old high-ceilinged Thongnhat (Reunification) Hotel (formerly the Metropole), there was a special Christmas party for a handful of foreign visitors who chanced to be here.

But this random evidence of Christmas spirit did not convey the mood of North Vietnam's capital, at least not as it seemed to an unexpected observer from the United States.

The mood of Hanoi seemed much more that of a wartime city going about its business briskly, energetically, purposefully. Streets are lined with cylindrical one-man air-raid shelters set in the ground at 10-foot intervals.

The shelters are formed of prestressed concrete with concrete lids left ajar for quick occupancy—and they are reported to have been occupied quite a bit in recent days with the sudden burst of United States air raids. There is damage, attributed by officials here to the raids, as close as 200 yards from this hotel.

Hanoi was laid out by French architects with broad boulevards over which arch leafy trees, and with squares, public gardens and pleasant lakes. Today it seems a bit like a mixture of the Moscow and Algiers of World War II. There are khaki and uniforms everywhere and hardly a truck moves without its green boughs of camouflage. Even pretty girls camouflage their bicycles and conical straw hats.

Christmas Eve found residents in several parts of Hanoi still picking over the wreckage of homes said to have been damaged in the United States raids of Dec. 13 and 14. United States officials have contended that no attacks in built-up or residential Hanoi have been authorized or carried out. They have also suggested that Hanoi residential damage in the two raids could have been caused by defensive surface-to-air missiles that misfired or fell short.

[Although American authorities have said that they were satisfied no bombs fell inside Hanoi and that only military targets were attacked, the State Department said Thursday that "the possibility of an accident" could not be ruled out. A spokesman said that if the bombing had caused civilian injury or damage, the United States regretted it.]

This correspondent is no ballistics specialist, but inspection of several damaged sites and talks with witnesses make it clear that Hanoi residents certainly believe they were bombed by United States planes, that they certainly observed United States planes

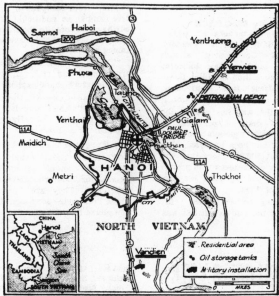

The New York Times   Dec. 25, 1966

HANOI VISITED: Areas near the western approaches (cross) of the Paul Doumer Bridge were damaged during American air attacks on targets shown by underlining.

overhead and that damage certainly occurred right in the center of town.

Large, Sprawling City

Hanoi is a very large, sprawling city. The city proper has a population of 600,000, and the surrounding metropolitan area brings the total to 1,100,000.

The built-up, densely populated urban area extends for a substantial distance in all directions beyond the heavy-lined city boundaries shown on a map by the State Department and published in The New York Times of Dec. 17. [The map appears on this page.]

For instance, the Yenvien rail yard, which was listed as one of the targets in the raids Dec. 14 and 15, is in a built-up area that continues south west to the Red River with no visible breaks in residential quarters. Much the same is true of the Vandien truck park south of the city, which was another listed target.

Oil tanks between Yenvien and Gialam, listed as another target, are in a similarly populated region. It is unlikely that any bombing attack on such targets could be carried out without civilian damage and casualties.

The location of two of the damaged areas inspected today suggests that the western approaches to the Paul Doumer Bridge may have been aimed for.

Both damaged areas lie in

the Hoankiem quarter of Hanoi. Other administrative quarters of the city are Badinh, Haiba and Dongda. All have suffered some damage.

The first area inspected was Pho Nguyen Thiap Street, about a three-minute drive from the hotel and 100 yards from the central market. Thirteen houses were destroyed—one-story brick and stucco structures for the most part. The Phuc Lan Buddhist pagoda in the same street was badly damaged.

Five persons were reported killed and 11 injured, and 39 families were said to be homeless.

Says Bomb Exploded

Tuan Ngoc Trac, a medical assistant who lived at 46 Pho Nguyen Thiep Street, said he was just going to the clinic where he works when an air alert sounded, indicating planes 25 kilometers (about 15 miles) from Hanoi. He had stepped to the street with his medical bag in his hand when he heard a plane and flung himself to the ground.

He said that the next instant a bomb exploded just over a row of houses, collapsing nine on the other side of the street. Tuan Ngoc Trac displayed an American leaflet, which he said he had found in the street, warning Hanoi residents not to remain in the vicinity of military objectives.

The North Vietnamese say that almost simultaneously—also about 3 P.M. Dec. 13—about 300 thatch and brick homes and

150

huts along the Red River embankment, possibly a quarter of a mile from Pho Nguyen Thiep Street and equally distant from the Thongnhat Hotel, were hit. The principal damage was again done by a burst just above the houses, but there were also three ground craters caused either by rocket bursts or small bombs.

This area, 200 by 70 yards, was leveled by blast and fire. Four persons were reported killed and 10 injured, most of the residents having been at work or in a large well-constructed shelter.

Another damage site inspected was in the Badinh quarter, which is Hanoi's diplomatic section. There, on Khuc Hao Street, lies the rear of the very large Chinese Embassy compound, backing on the Rumanian Em-

bassy. Minor damage was done to the roofs of the Chinese and Rumanian Embassies by what was said to have looked like rocket fire. Both embassies produced fragments, which they said had come from United States rocket bursts.

House Is Inspected

Also examined was a house on Hue Lane in the Haiba quarter. It was reported hit Dec. 2, with the death of one person and the wounding of seven others, including two children.

Contrary to the impression given by United States communiqués, on-the-spot inspection indicates that American bombing has been inflicting considerable civilian casualties in Hanoi and its environs for some time past.

The North Vietnamese cite as

an instance the village of Phuxa, a market gardening suburb possibly four miles from the city center. The village of 24 houses was reported attacked at 12:17 P.M. Aug. 13 by a United States pilot trying to bomb a Red River dike. The village was destroyed and 24 people were killed and 23 wounded. The pilot was shot down.

A crater 25 feet deep was reported blasted in the dike, but it was said to have been filled within three hours. The village has now been completely rebuilt, and has a small museum of mementos of the attack. In the museum is the casing of a United States fragmentation bomb, which bears the legend, "Loaded 7 66." A month after that date it was said to have fallen on Phuxa village, releasing 300 iron spheres, each about the size

of a baseball and each loaded with 300 steel pellets about the size and shape of bicycle bearings. Those missiles are reported to have caused most of the Phuxa casualties.

It is the reality of such casualties and such apparent byproducts of the United States bombing policy that lend an atmosphere of grimness and foreboding to Hanoi's Christmas cease-fire. It is fair to say that, based on evidence of their own eyes, Hanoi residents do not find much credibility in United States bombing communiqués.

December 25, 1966

Corruption Is Taking Up to 40% Of U.S. Assistance in Vietnam

By The Associated Press

SAIGON, South Vietnam, Nov. 12—Among the traditional byproducts of war are theft, bribery, black marketing, currency manipulation and waste.

In the Vietnamese conflict, these corrosive influences on the morale and economy of a nation have developed on a scale far vaster than should be expected for the size of the war.

A two-month study has found that unquestionably hundreds of millions of United States dollars have gone, or are going, down the drain.

Estimates vary: $500-million, $750-million, $1-billion.

Despite several Congressional investigations and many other studies, no official measure of such losses has emerged.

However, close observers of the Vietnam scene have made estimates ranging up to 40 per cent of United States assistance funds and goods.

On just economic imports and post-exchange supplies for United States servicemen, the loss is most often put at 20 per cent.

A figure of 5 per cent is usually cited as the probably loss in straight military-aid items.

Based on the $715-million annual economic aid and surplus food programs and a PX supply inflow of nearly $150-million a year, a 20 per cent loss in those areas would mean nearly $175-million in the fiscal year that ended June 30. This is nearly half a million dollars a day.

A 5 per cent loss on military aid would come to a huge sum.

In the last 10 years, the United states has spent more than $5-billion in direct economic and military aid to South Vietnam. This does not include the bil-

lions now being spent on the massive American involvement in the fighting.

In the last fiscal year, United States aid to keep the South Vietnamese Army in the field and to support the civilian economy came to about $1.2-billion.

Discussed by President

The losses have reached such levels that the problem was reported by several sources to have been the subject of a private meeting between President Johnson and Premier Nguyen Cao Ky of South Vietnam, with top United States aid officials attending the President's visit last month.

At the conference, according to reports, it was pointed out that one insurance company had received $4-million in loss claims for economic aid items alone in a 120-day period. There were suggestions that a huge ring was at work, with connections extending to Singapore, Burma and other Asiatic points.

In Washington, an official of the Agency for International Development discounted the idea of a ring, insisting that the evidence pointed instead to a multitude of small, independent operators.

What happens to some of the stolen goods can be seen around Saigon. A stolen generator lights a night club. Irrigation pumps intended for farmers are in use at privately owned car wash stations. American beer is on sale in many bars and night clubs.

May Never Know Cost

The United States probably will never know how much has been stolen, how much has been misused.

Until recently, record keeping was haphazard or nonexistent. Audits now getting under way are concerned with the present and the future, not with the past.

In the case of military aid to South Vietnam, there has not

been an audit since 1960. Since then $2-billion has been spent on training and equipment for the South Vietnamese Army, Navy and Air Force.

In rice imports paid for by the United States, there are no real American controls. There are indications that much of the food, lumber, medicines and fertilizers provided by the United States go to enrich provincial and district officials and help supply the Vietcong.

A United States aid official said:

"The only way to plug the leaks would be to post an American at the side of virtually every South Vietnamese official or businessman involved — an obvious impracticality, an impossibility."

In the second week of October, the biggest convoy of the war moved several hundred truck loads of rice to the rubber-growing provinces near the Cambodian border and hauled 2,500 tons of rubber back to Saigon.

Four battalions of infantrymen from the United States First Division spent a week in the jungles along bitterly contested Highway 13, risking ambush and sniper fire, mines and mortars, to protect the long line of more than 700 trucks.

The rice was to feed the thousands of people living on the plantations, and the return cargo brought nearly a third of the area's annual rubber production to the Saigon docks, 80 miles away, without a cent of "taxes" being levied by the Vietcong.

But French planters said that officers of the South Vietnamese forces had exacted a tribute equal to about $10,000.

When told by a reporter of the extortion, a high American officer sighed and spoke of the "realities" the United States had to face in conducting the war in Vietnam.

A construction boss at one of the big bases being built by a combine of American companies with Vietnamese labor, said:

"Pilferage and diversion go on at all echelons of the Vietnamese social structure—it is not limited to the peasantry.

"The larger stuff, like bulldozers and generators, we usually get back sooner or later,

but the great percentage of unaccountable materials and supplies would take an army to protect."

Another construction man, James A. Lilly, general manager of the American construction consortium, blamed the United States military for some of the headaches.

"The military," he said, "has flatly refused to assume security obligations.

"Our 30-odd construction sites are patrolled by a security force of 1,200 Vietnamese armed with nothing more than an armband. We are not allowed to shoot at looters.

"A G.I. can drive up to a supply yard in his six-by-six truck, wave a carbine at the Vietnamese guards, order them to open the gates and load up with everything he wants."

The consortium is Vietnam's largest employer. It has dotted the land with huge warehouses, jet airstrips, deep water ports and other facilities that are nothing short of overnight miracles.

It is called RMK, for Raymond International of Delaware, Inc.; Morrison-Knudsen Company of Asia, Inc.; Brown & Root, Inc., and J. A. Jones Construction Company.

Navy and Pentagon officials supervising the contracts, which will reach $800-million, about $200-million above estimates, say that the consortium has not kited costs.

Officials say the increase is a result of Pentagon errors in estimating the costs.

Losses from pilferage and theft at construction sites, is put at $5-million.

United States servicemen support and sustain the black market in PX goods and troop commodities. Some construction workers have been sent home for currency manipulation and smuggling. So have other United States civilians.

A Navy Captain, Archie C. Kuntze, once called "the military mayor of Saigon," was reassigned to the United States in July after a board of inquiry began looking into allegations of personal misconduct.

Last week he was brought to trial in California, and accused, among other things, of black

151

marketeering and currency manipulation.

By this fall, there were at least 400 servicemen and civilians facing official action for profiteering or black-market operations. RMK says it has sent "upwards of 30" of its American workers home for currency manipulation.

There is no way of assessing how much American aid, military or economic, winds up in the hands of the Vietcong.

Supplies for Viet Cong

At Bahao, 50 miles from Saigon, the United States 196th Light Infantry Brigade recently captured a Viet Cong camp. There they found a store of United States supplies, including a million and a quarter pounds of rice, 440 gallons of gasoline, 600 gallons of cooking oil, 88 shovels, 750 pounds of salt.

The bags of rice, enough to feed a Vietcong division for two months, still bore the names of the American exporters.

To handle the huge flow of stolen goods, the Ankhanh Peninsula, across the river from downtown Saigon, has become a warehousing and transshipment area for the black market.

Customs men never go there, nor do the police.

The government of Premier Ky has promised repeatedly to move on war profiteers and black marketers. So far, the crackdown has manifested itself only in the public execution of a Chinese businessman for black marketing and bribery, and in the setting up of a special office to deal with corruption.

The United States Defense Department is instituting some measures to reduce the looting.

Container ships bring materials and goods in containers too big and too securely built to be looted with ease.

Truck loads of crated goods are wrapped in steel bands to prevent easy looting on the road.

In some storage areas, dogs now are on patrol.

November 13, 1966

VIETCONG VILLAGE TO BE BULLDOZED

3,800 People in Hostile Town to Be Resettled

Special to the New York Times

BENSUC, South Vietnam. Jan. 8—For years this quiet, ill-kept village hugging an elbow of the Saigon River 30 miles northwest of the capital has been a haven for the Vietcong.

One pacification program after another has failed here and since a Government military post was abandoned more than a year ago, Bensuc has been considered a "hostile" village. It has been an embarrassing problem for Saigon.

This morning 600 allied soldiers — mostly Americans — descended on the village and began "solving" the problem.

Within two weeks the more than 3,800 residents of Bensuc will be living in a new refugee settlement 20 miles to the southeast and it is likely that the tattered huts and small shops here will be flattered by bulldozers.

Long a Meeting Point

The village of Bensuc, which for so long served as a meeting place for Vietcong political cadres and as a supply point for insurgent troops in two provinces, will be swept from the face of the earth.

"This is probably the only military or political solution for this place," said an American colonel.

Allied officers in Bensuc acknowledged that the residents might be reluctant to leave their property and the revered graves of their ancestors, but they said that new land would be given to them along with frame, tin-roofed homes that will be "a lot better than what they have now."

Vietcong villages are typically found in disrepair, but Bensuc is an extreme example. There is no evidence that any new buildings have been put up in months. The old ones are crumbling and chronic illness is widespread.

'Do What They're Told'

Firmly supporting the resettlement, the colonel said: "I imagine there will be a lot of wailing and gnashing of teeth, but they'll do what they're told."

Sixty helicopters landed the troops in seven clearings within the village walls this morning so a human net could be quickly drawn around the residents and the soldiers could avoid the maze of booby traps around Bensuc.

Shortly afterward, a helicopter equipped with loudspeakers began broadcasting this message:

"Attention people of Bensuc! You are surrounded by Republic of South Vietnam and allied forces. Do not run away or you will be shot as V.C. Stay in your homes and wait for further instructions from the air and on the ground. You will not be hurt if you follow instructions."

Then came a second message telling men, women and children: "Go immediately to the schoolhouse. Anyone who does not go to the schoolhouse will be considered a V.C. and treated accordingly."

Most Follow Instructions

Most of the residents, considered to be passive Vietcong, followed the instructions. Forty-one did not and during the day they were tracked down and killed. There was little question that the men fleeing on bicycles, crawling through rice paddies and thrashing in the murky river were Vietcong. Some carried rifles, others wore packs. Three were discovered at the mouth of a cave with an assortment of surgical instruments and commercially produced drugs.

At the schoolhouse the people were separated into groups according to age and sex, interrogated, given a warm meal and were seen by an army doctor. One hundred males 15 to 45 years old, unable to prove their identity, were taken away as Vietcong suspects. Eleven men were judged on the spot to be Vietcong.

Belongings Go With Them

The villagers were allowed to file home this evening, but tomorrow they will be ordered back to the school, their homes will be searched and in a day or so more the troops will begin loading them into barges for the trip downstream. Part of their houses, their furniture and their livestock will go with them.

"It takes time and it's troublesome, but I think you find a little less resentment if you take everything they've got and move it with them," said Brig. Gen. James F. Hollingworth, an assistant commander of the United States First Infantry Division.

The move into the village was the opening part of an allied operation called Cedar Falls. More than 15,000 soldiers are being deployed in what the military describes as the most thorough search ever of the 60 square miles of the Thanhdien Forest and the thick jungle that the Americans call the Iron Triangle.

Intelligence officers believe there may be no more than 100 enemy soldiers in the 60 square miles. But they hope to find a tunnel the length of the seven-mile-long triangle and to disrupt operations at the headquarters of Vietcong Military Region 4. The headquarters, which controls Vietcong operations in and around Saigon, has been traced to the triangle.

The allied goal at Bensuc was to deny the Vietcong a strategic base and to capture important political figures. At least three of the 11 taken today appear to be prime suspects. The allies also believe that they will be able to win the allegiance of the people once they have been removed from the Vietcong sphere.

January 11, 1967

FOE'S SANCTUARY HIT BY FIRE BOMBS

B-52's Attempt to Defoliate Zone D Forest Believed Hiding Vietcong Camps

By JONATHAN RANDAL
Special to The New York Times

SAIGON, South Vietnam, Thursday, Jan. 19 — United States Air Force B-52 bombers dropped tons of incendiary bombs yesterday on War Zone D, a Vietcong sanctuary, in an attempt to burn away dense foliage hiding suspected enemy camps and infiltration routes.

Ten waves of the big bombers dropped magnesium incendiary bombs in radar-controlled parallel patterns over a 28-square-mile patch of the thickly forested area 30 miles northeast of Saigon.

"It looked just like the Fourth of July," said an American military spokesman who watched the air strikes from a helicopter near the target area.

Black Clouds of Smoke

Black clouds of smoke billowing 15,000 feet into the air were

The New York Times   Jan. 19, 1967
United States B-52's dropped incendiary bombs on Zone D (underlined) to burn off foliage over enemy regions.

seen by a civilian pilot flying near the forest, which is scarred by brown swatches, the results of defoliant chemicals sprayed in the past.

The spokesmen declined to es-

timate the effectiveness of the fire bombs on the 200-foot trees.

"It looked like a forest fire, except you couldn't see many flames," the civilian pilot said, indicating that the bombs may have set afire some of the forest under the top canopy.

The incendiary bomb strike was the second of the Vietnam war. The first took place in the Central Highlands in August.

Informed sources said further incendiary bomb raids might be necessary to burn away all the layers of foliage in Zone D.

The bombs were dropped from 30,000 feet. At 8,000 feet they burst out of their canisters and ignited before tumbling into the forest.

Today, a few miles southwest of the bombing raid, American troops killed seven Vietcong in Operation Cedar Falls in the "Iron Triangle" while suffering light casualties themselves, mostly inflicted by mines and booby traps.

Along with 19 Vietcong bodies found in a mass grave, today's Vietcong toll raised to 508 the number of enemy killed in the biggest American operation of the war.

Since it began on Jan. 8, the operation has involved 28 battalions in systematically destroying enemy bunker and tunnel systems and base camps. A battalion has 300 to 500 men.

January 19, 1967

CIVILIANS' LOSSES TOP SAIGON ARMY'S

Survey Implies 1,250 Died of War Injuries in a Month

By NEIL SHEEHAN
Special to The New York Times

WASHINGTON, Jan. 31— A statistical survey in hospitals in South Vietnam during December indicates that the war caused more civilian than military casualties among the South Vietnamese.

To meet this and other critical medical problems in South Vietnam, the United States has doubled its medical aid program there from $21-million in the 1966 fiscal year to $49.6-million for the current fiscal year, which ends June 30.

The survey, conducted by the United States civilian mission in South Vietnam, informed sources said, showed that of 33,475 civilian patients admitted to all Government hospitals there during December, 7.5 per

cent, or 2,510, were wounded as a result of the war.

2 Wounded for Each Killed

During the same period, according to official reports, 815 South Vietnamese soldiers were killed in battle. For the last six months the South Vietnamese Government has refused to disclose the number of soldiers hospitalized with battle wounds, but over the last six years it has averaged two wounded for each man killed in action.

Presumably, then, the number of South Vietnamese soldiers hospitalized with battle wounds in December totaled 1,600 to 1,700.

Because of administrative chaos and the control of large areas of the country by the Vietcong, no statistics are available on the number of civilians killed by the fighting during the month. But if the same military ratio of two wounded to one dead is applied, a minimum figure of 1,250 civilian dead for the month is reached.

The civilian patients covered by the survey did not encompass all civilian victims for the month since the survey includ-

ed only those who reached hospitals.

Conditions in South Vietnam make it clear that many others never reach a hospital because of primitive transportation and disruptions of the war. These victims either die without treatment or obtain help at South Vietnamese military outposts or Vietcong field hospitals and dispensaries.

The survey made no attempt to determine who was responsible for wounding the civilians. The wounded included victims of mines and bullets and South Vietnamese and American air attacks. But the majority, it is likely, were wounded by South Vietnamese artillery and air bombardments.

Since the huge American military build-up began in the summer of 1965, the United States has made a sustained effort to improve South Vietnam's primitive medical facilities.

Thirty-nine medical teams are now working at hospitals in provincial capitals and at dispensaries in smaller district capitals. Twenty-five of the teams are composed of American physicians, nurses and technicians while the rest are from the Philippines, South Korea, Spain, Iran, Switzerland and Taiwan.

United States Army, Marine

Corps and Air Force doctors and other medical people also treat civilians in the villages when possible.

In October 55,000 Vietnamese were immunized for bubonic plague, 92,000 for cholera and 38,000 for smallpox.

Most to Buy Supplies

The $49.9-million available for medical aid in this fiscal year is more than nine times the amount spent for this purpose in the fiscal year of 1965.

The bulk of the funds this year, $29.8-million, will be spent for drugs and medical equipment and $10.3-million will be spent to build new facilities and renovate old ones.

To increase South Vietnam's potential to improve its facilities, $2-million will go for new classrooms and laboratories and for teacher training at the medical and dental departments of the University of Saigon.

An American medical professor has joined the faculty there and four others are to follow soon. By 1970 it is hoped that South Vietnam will be capable of producing 200 physicians and 50 dentists a year.

There are only 1,000 South Vietnamese doctors for a population of 16.5 million. Of these 700 have been drafted.

February 1, 1967

U.S. Tactics in Vietnam

Once-Scorned French Principles Used, But Superior Means Make Difference

By JONATHAN RANDAL
Special to The New York Times

SAIGON, South Vietnam, Feb. 17—Principles laid down by the French Army in the Indochina and Algerian campaigns are gradually but almost imperceptibly coming into use in United States military tactics in Vietnam.

In the past the American military have been critical of French tactics. It was in part because of this attitude that the United States took over the training of the South Vietnamese Army from the French following the end of the Indochina war and the partition of Vietnam in 1954.

News Analysis

That army, trained along conventional lines in keeping with the then fresh experience of the Korean conflict, proved incapable of dealing with guerrilla warfare perfected by the Vietcong from the model tested by the Vietminh against the French.

Today the French tactical imprint is visible in Vietnam from one end of the tactical spectrum to the other.

In the midfifties, the French pioneered the use of helicopters both as troop carriers and armed gunships in Algeria. Indeed, when the United States Army half a decade later began experimenting with helicopters with the formation of the 11th Air Assault Division—the precursor of the First Cavalry Division (Airmobile) — it drew heavily on French expertise.

Small Outposts Used

At the other end of the tactical scale, squads of American marines are assigned to small outposts in South Vietnamese villages, serving with South Vietnamese militiamen as cadre "stiffeners."

Their armament belies the commonly held belief of overpowering American firepower. A typical post is equipped with a radio, a machine gun, a few mortars but no vehicles. The men do their extensive joint night-and-day patrolling on foot.

These mixed units recall hundreds of similar outposts the French used in the Algerian and Indochina conflicts, and indeed some are quartered around old French bunkers. They represent a concept once criticized by American commanders as overly static.

More than 60 of these units are spread out in the areas the marines are trying to pacify in the northern part of South Vietnam. As they did for the French, they provide intelligence at the hamlet level, improve the training of the militia and free companies and battalions for other missions.

This tactic has been restricted so far to the marine sector, where 90 per cent of the populace lives within 15 miles of the South China Sea, thus making population control efforts in pacification possible.

Other instances of similar tactics first used by the French and now by the Americans include armed river patrol squadrons to search and board sampans and supply fire support for land operations.

Tribesmen from the highlands are used as irregular troops with American cadres much as they were by the French 20 years ago.

American civic action teams designed to win the confidence of the people in South Vietnam are remarkably similar to the "special administrative sections" the French organized in Algeria after having learned the techniques from the Vietminh, often in prisoner-of-war camps.

Free fire zones, areas where artillery and air strikes can be used at will, exist in South Vietnam now as they did in Algeria. In Algeria, the French forcibly moved rural Moslems from their homes and considered anyone inside such an area to be an enemy.

Americans have tried to refrain from wholesale application of such tactics on the theory that more points are lost than made in uprooting a population deeply attached to its home and ancestral graves. However, last month, in Operation Cedar Falls, more than 6,000 villagers were moved out of the Vietcong sanctuary known as War Zone D near Saigon and taken to refugee centers.

Of course, the enormous disproportion between the means available to the French 20 years ago in all of Indochina—Laos, Cambodia and both Vietnams—are dwarfed by the American presence today.

A single statistic gives an indication of the difference. The French had 13 helicopters in Indochina in 1954. Today there are more than 2,000.

French Tied Up by Vietminh

Moveover, the French were, in general, powerless against Vietminh tactics that tied up their remaining mobile reserves. By comparison, the United States has been able to launch three major operations simultaneously.

Still, if the French experience has any conclusive validity today, it is not encouraging.

In Algeria, the 450,000-man French Army, supplemented by thousands of mobile gendarmes and Moslem militiamen, managed to dot the country with a grid system of static positions while the 50,000-man general reserve troops smashed large enemy units.

Despite the lessons the French Army learned in losing in Indochina and later applied in Algeria, it failed because it was never able to practice successfully Mao Tse-tung's maxim: "The people are the sea in which the guerrillas swim."

The French won the Algerian war militarily, but like the Indochina conflict before and the Vietnam war now, Algeria was not just a military struggle.

If such grid system tactics as the French employed in Algeria and the marines are using to some degree here were adopted for all Vietnam, one senior American officer in Saigon estimated that "we would need 1.5 million men."

February 18, 1967

NEW BLOWS AT ENEMY: Some rivers were mined, and U.S. warships had orders to shell targets located between Thanhhoa (1) and buffer zone (2).

U.S. PLANES DROP MINES IN RIVERS IN NORTH VIETNAM

MOVE IS 'LIMITED'

It Is Called No Peril to Deep-Water Ships— Shelling Stepped Up

By R. W. APPLE Jr.
Special to The New York Times

SAIGON, South Vietnam, Monday, Feb. 27—The United States has begun dropping mines into rivers in North Vietnam, the American command disclosed this morning.

A terse announcement said that "a limited number of air-delivered non-floating" mines had been placed in rivers in the southern part of North Vietnam. The mines, the announcement indicated, are designed to stop the movement of sampans and junks.

"This action poses no danger to deep-water maritime traffic," the command asserted.

Yesterday, the United States command said American cruisers and destroyers, which began shelling supply routes in North Vietnam earlier in the day, had been ordered to fire on the routes on a continuing basis and to move within several hundred yards of the beach when necessary.

Issue of 3-Mile Limit

That would violate the three-mile limit, which under international law reserves jurisdiction over coastal waters to the nations to which they are adjacent.

[Officials in Washington said neither the mining of rivers in North Vietnam nor the naval shelling of supply routes in the North represented an escalation of the war. The steps were explained as supplemental moves to curb the southward flow of enemy supplies.

[In Danang, South Vietnam, an American spokesman said the Vietcong killed 11 Americans and at least 30 Vietnamese in a mortar and rocket attack on the American base, The Associated Press reported. Page 3].

Presumably, the mining involves nonfloating devices because they would not be carried down the rivers into the Gulf of Tonkin, where they might collide with ocean-going freighters. But conceivably if the freighters attempted to move into estuaries to discharge their cargoes, they could be blown up.

Ports to Be Avoided

A military spokesman said, however, that the United States did not intend to mine the mouths of rivers or harbors adjacent to key deepwater ports such as Haiphong, Honggai and Campha. Most other ports are incapable of taking ocean-going vessels.

The mining, the spokesman said, began this morning.

Advocates of a tougher American policy toward North Vietnam have urged for many months that the Haiphong harbor be mined to prevent its use by Soviet, Chinese and other vessels carrying war material. President Johnson has still not authorized such measures, American sources said, for fear of creating a grave diplomatic crisis.

Ships of Great Britain and other allies of the United States call regularly at Haiphong to deliver all types of cargo.

February 27, 1967

Civilian Dead Put at 95 In Raid in South Vietnam

200 Hurt in Blow Near Laos—U.S. Calls Planes Presumably 'Allied'

By The Associated Press

SAIGON, South Vietnam, Saturday, March 4—Ninety-five South Vietnamese civilians are reported to have been killed and 200 wounded when two jet planes knifed in from Laotian territory Thursday night and bombed and strafed Langvei, a village near the border.

The rising death toll was announced this morning by a South Vietnamese military spokesman as an urgent inquiry was started to determine which planes had carried out the raid. A spokesman for the United States Command said the attack was presumably made by "allied" aircraft.

United States ordnance teams were combing the fire-scarred village for bomb fragments that might disclose the identity of the planes.

Americans hospitalized about 150 of the most seriously injured victims and flew blankets, food and clothing to survivors of the village, in the northwestern border area.

If the attack was a mistaken American bombing, it was the worst such mistake of the war. If it was the work of enemy pilots, it would have been their first such strike into South Vietnam.

The two jets, which a United States special forces officer reported were delta-winged, spread destruction and death with three combat passes over Langvei about five hours after ground fire had downed a United States helicopter in the area.

Several American jet planes have the swept wings that would fit the description by the officer, Capt. John J. Duffy of San Diego, Calif. North Vietnam's Soviet-designed MIGs also are delta-winged, but they are of relatively short range.

The raid destroyed about 100 bamboo and thatch houses in cutting a 400-yard swath through Langvei, home to about 2,000 people, largely mountain tribesmen.

The toll of victims considerably surpassed that in the accidental bombing last Aug. 9 of a government village in Phuoc-dinh Province in the Mekong Delta. That set a record of 63 civilians killed and 83 wounded.

Langvei is a mile from the border of Laos, which is controlled in that area by Communists, and 15 miles below the demilitarized zone between North and South Vietnam.

It is thus on the western side of a sector where 10,000 United States Marines and two South Vietnamese divisions have been battling intermittently against infiltrators.

March 4, 1967

The New York Times   March 4, 1967

U.S. troops hunted through ruins in Langvei (cross) for civilian dead and wounded.

DOWNTOWN HANOI RAIDED FIRST TIME BY U.S. BOMBERS

North's Major Power Plant, Mile From City's Center, Is Target of Navy Jets

FOUR MIG-17'S DOWNED

By R. W. APPLE Jr.

Special to The New York Times

SAIGON, South Vietnam, Saturday, May 20 — United States pilots bombed downtown Hanoi yesterday for the first time. Five planes were lost, an American military spokesman said.

[The North Vietnamese press agency said 10 American planes had been downed and five pilots captured, United Press International reported. It said two of the pilots had been displayed at a news conference within hours of their capture. Page 2.]

Navy fighter-bombers, using air-to-air missiles, shot down four enemy MIG-17 jets during battles high above the capital, the military spokesman said. A fifth was reported damaged.

Hoalac Airfield Bombed

Jets from the carrier Bon Homme Richard in the Gulf of Tonkin struck early in the afternoon at a 32,000-kilowatt power plant, the largest in North Vietnam.

In another raid, Air Force Thunderchief jet from the 355th Tactical Fighter Wing in Thailand dropped 750-pound bombs on the MIG airfield at Hoalac, 20 miles west of Hanoi.

The Hoalac strip was reported to have been put out of operation last week after repeated strikes. The new raid, the spokesman explained, was intended "to keep the air field unusable."

Other planes of the 355th struck an area just south of the field, where aerial photographs had shown three MIG-17 jets hidden under camouflage. Two nearby structures were said to have been destroyed, but there was no word on whether the planes had been hit.

The spokesman added that all the downed planes had been carrier-based Navy craft.

3 Bases Still Untouched

For more than two months, American planes have been blasting objectives that were previously ruled off limits by the White House—MIG bases, targets within Haiphong and targets on the outskirts of Hanoi.

The major targets remaining untouched are the Haiphong docks and three large fighter-bomber bases.

In the past, the closest strike to the North Vietnamese capital was a raid on the railroad repair shops two miles northeast of the city, on April 28.

According to the spokesman, the power plant, which supplies about 20 per cent of North Vietnam's electricity, is 1.1 miles from the center of the city, as measured from the Cuanam market. It is within the city limits and the built-up area of Hanoi.

May 20, 1967

155

U.S. CASUALTIES EXCEED SAIGON'S

Figures Since May 1 Indicate That Burden of Fighting in Vietnam Has Shifted

Special to The New York Times

SAIGON, South Vietnam, July 17—Official statistics indicate that the burden of fighting the Vietcong and North Vietnamese has passed decisively to American troops.

A study of casualty lists since Jan. 1 shows that while more South Vietnamese soldiers than Americans were killed in the first weeks of the year, the situation has been reversed. South Vietnam has more than 650,000 men under arms and the United States commitment here totals about 465,000 men.

[In the war, 16 Vietcong were reported to have been killed in a 10-hour battle with United States marines near Danang. Page 3.]

Since the first of May, 2,427 Americans have been killed, compared with 2,010 South Vietnamese. Since June 4, when the Saigon Government began announcing figures on those wounded in action, 5,838 Americans have been wounded as compared with 2,231 South Vietnamese.

Total for Year Is Given

So far this year 5,562 South Vietnamese and 4,996 Americans have been killed, but unless there is an unexpected reversal of the trend, year-end statistics will show American losses higher.

Last year, the Saigon Government's losses were more than twice as high as those of the United States. The announced totals were 11,193 South Vietnamese killed in action, compared with 5,024 Americans.

As of July 1, the number of American servicemen killed since Jan. 1, 1961, was 11,534 and the wounded totaled 69,850.

In the opinion of analysts in Saigon, the statistics demonstrate a continued tendency on the part of South Vietnamese commanders to avoid battle whenever possible, despite a determined effort by Gen. William C. Westmoreland's command to instill better, more aggressive leadership.

During the last six months, about half the 120 maneuver battalions of South Vietnamese have been detached from offensive operations and assigned to pacification efforts. The change has unquestionably reduced South Vietnamese losses.

The casualty figures also reflect the intense pressure of the North Vietnamese along the demilitarized zone, where most positions are held by American marines. United States casualties in recent months have been heaviest there.

Secretary of Defense Robert S. McNamara said during his visit to the combat zone last week that South Vietnamese troops would have to prove themselves in hand-to-hand fighting, and would have to be substantially augmented, before the United States would be willing to increase its troop deployment here by significant numbers.

Mr. McNamara's comments were apparently dictated, at least in part, by Administration unhappiness over the performance of the Vietnamese.

July 18, 1967

THIEU AND KY ARE VICTORS IN SOUTH VIETNAM BALLOT; 83% OF ELECTORATE VOTES

TWO GENERALS WIN

Their Goal Was 40% but They Get Only 27% of Total

By R. W. APPLE Jr.
Special to The New York Times

SAIGON, South Vietnam, Monday, Sept. 4—Lieut. Gen. Nguyen Van Thieu, the candidate of the armed forces, won a four-year term as President of South Vietnam yesterday in the country's momentous national election.

General Thieu, the incumbent chief of state, and his vice-presidential running mate, Premier Nguyen Cao Ky, built their victory on two strongpoints — the 700,000-man army and the minority groups whose support they had sought: hill tribes, Roman Catholic refugees, ethnic Cambodians and Chinese, and religious splinter sects.

But the military candidates, in a field of 11 slates, fell far short of the 40 per cent of the vote that their supporters had hoped for. With the count nearing completion, the generals had only 27 per cent of the vote, even though they outpolled their closest rival by better than two to one.

Lawyer Finishes Second

In a major surprise, Truong Dinh Dzu, a wealthy Saigon lawyer, finished in second place, running well ahead of both Tran Van Huong, a former Premier, and Phan Khac Suu, the Speaker of the Constituent Assembly. Mr. Suu, although his campaign had appeared to gain momentum in the last week, was a badly beaten fourth.

At 2:30 P.M. today (2:30 A.M. New York time), with 90 per cent of the vote counted, a New York Times tabulation showed:

Nguyen Van Thieu . 1,398,581
Truong Dinh Dzu 651,745
Tran Van Huong . . 428,680
Phan Khac Suu 425,341

A total of 4,868,266 persons —51 per cent of the 8.5 million persons of voting age and 83 per cent of the 5,853,384 registered voters—marched to the polls on a brilliant, cloudless Sunday.

About 2,650,000 persons of voting age were not registered, most of them because they live in Vietcong-controlled or contested areas. Parts of nearly every province, including some places within 15 miles of Saigon, were on the list of nonvoting localities.

The turnout exceeded the expectations of the Government. It was slightly larger than the participation in last year's Constituent Assembly elections, when 80.8 per cent voted.

The military ticket ran strongly in virtually every section of the country, with the exception of the area around Hue in central Vietnam, where Mr. Suu dominated the field. The generals did particularly well in the Mekong River delta, the presumed center of Mr. Huong's organizational strength.

Mr. Dzu, 50 years old, campaigned on a peace platform and strongly criticized the Government. Paradoxically, his strong run appeared to have hurt the chances of the civilian nominees by splintering the anti-Government vote.

Speaking at an impromptu news conference, Mr. Dzu said he had done so well because "90 per cent of the people want peace." He charged the Government with fraud, and promised to form a "committee for democracy" to protest the election results.

General Thieu promised during the campaign to propose a pause in the American bombing of North Vietnam of one week or longer in the hope of starting peace negotiations, but said he doubted that his proposal would bear much fruit.

Despite a series of Vietcong attacks and shellings that took the lives of at least 26 Vietnamese, the voting was interrupted at only 3 of the 8,824 polling places. To insure the voters' safety, United States and South Vietnamese forces mounted one of the largest security operations ever undertaken here.

September 4, 1967

U.S. Aides Say Foe's Strength And Morale Are Declining Fast

By TOM BUCKLEY
Special to The New York Times

SAIGON, South Vietnam, Nov. 11 -- United States military officials said today that the "fighting efficiency" of the Vietcong and North Vietnamese troops had "progressively declined" in the last six months.

During this period, it was said, 40,000 enemy troops were killed in action. These men have not been replaced, the officials said, and the result is a drop from 285,000 to 242,000 in the estimated strength of the Vietcong and the North Vietnamese in the South.

The morale of these forces, confined to inhospitable mountains and jungle and often on the verge of starvation, was described as sinking fast.

At the same time, it was acknowledged that the enemy's declining fortunes had not yet sharply shown themselves in a falling off of the quality of leadership or in an increasing number of desertions or captures.

One United States official said that there was evidence that enemy troops were being forced into battle with machine guns at their backs. One division was said to have set up drumhead courts-martial for the first time to deal with an increasing number of cases of shirking and cowardice.

"We have, gentlemen, 600 documents that attest to this decline in morale," he said, referring to papers that have been taken from enemy soldiers or found in caches.

These assertions were made at a 3-hour-and-20-minute briefing for newsmen at American military headquarters. It was held at about the same time that President Johnson was touring military bases in the United States.

The Hanoi Government was described as having taken complete control of the guerrilla movement and was said to be drafting men in their late 30's. Many boys in their early teens have already been taken for service in the South, the officials said.

Of the 163 enemy battalions fighting in the South, the number of those no longer fit for combat because of losses was said to have increased from 31 to 76 in the last 12 months.

Rate of Defectors Cited

The number of North Vietnamese fighting in the South, last publicly estimated by the American command at around 55,000, is thought to have increased dramatically, but intelligence officials have not yet arrived at a new estimate. However, it was said that several nominally Vietcong formations, including the Ninth Division, which was locked in combat with the United States First Division at the beginning of the month northwest of Saigon, is now more than 50 per cent North Vietnamese.

The number of defectors, which early in the year seemed certain to double the 1966 figures, has leveled off in recent months to a monthly average of 2,083 for the year so far, as opposed to 1,385 for last year.

In some recent weeks, moreover, the figure has been lower than for the corresponding period in 1966.

Adding to the difficulties of the enemy, the officials stated, was the fact that 10 or 12 of every 100 men who started "down the trail" from North Vietnam through Laos to the fighting fronts was killed by bombs, died of disease or deserted before they arrived.

The effectiveness of the United States campaign was said to have required the shipping of two bags of rice from Hanoi to get one to the men in the field.

Commenting on the outbreak of fighting in the last three weeks along the Cambodian border, the United States military officials indicated that the North Vietnamese and the Vietcong had been forced by recent reverses into essentially foolish actions "to show they're not losing the war."

The enemy, it was said, regarded the control of the Vietnamese population as its primary objective, and in recent months had seen it slide from its grasp.

Graphs were displayed containing figures arrived at by new computerized calculations. These showed that two-thirds of the 17 million people of South Vietnam now lived in areas securely held by the Saigon Government, one-sixth in disputed areas and one-sixth under the control of the insurgents.

Describing the present military situation, the official said he expected the fighting between the North Vietnamese First Division and units of the United States Fourth Division and 173d Airborne Brigade in the Central Highlands near Dakto to continue, perhaps for several weeks.

"That one is not yet over," he said. "This may be one of the live fronts."

The area around Khesanh, just below the western end of the demilitarized zone, where the Marines fought a savage and ultimately successful battle in late March and April for three hills overlooking the town, was described as "ominously quiet."

"Historically, the enemy likes to operate against Khesanh at this time of year," the official said.

The official said that the build-up of American forces from "fire brigade" size to about 425,000 men was completed only about a year ago. The force presently numbers 463,000 and President Johnson has authorized an increase to 525,000 by next June.

"During the coming year we should be able to progressively apply pressure," the official stated. "I anticipate that it will accelerate, will build up."

North Vietnamese units were thought likely, he added, to return to the demilitarized zone in strength before Christmas. Action fell off dramatically there last month after a bombardment of Marine positions in September around Conthien and Giolinh that totaled 10,000 rounds.

In general in reviewing operations of the last six months —the rainy season in the South and the dry season in the North —the officials painted a highly successful picture.

From captured documents, intelligence officers were said to have pieced together elaborate enemy plans for the period, including an offensive from the demilitarized zone and the capture of Quangtri city. These plans were balked by quick American and South Vietnamese countermeasures.

November 12, 1967

Vietcong Attack 7 Cities; Allies Call Off Tet Truce

Rockets Destroy 6 U.S. Planes at Danang— Prisoners Freed

By TOM BUCKLEY
Special to The New York Times

SAIGON, South Vietnam, Tuesday, Jan. 30—Vietcong raiders drove into the center of seven major Vietnamese cities early today, burning Government buildings, freeing prisoners from provincial jails and blasting military installations and airfields with rockets and mortars.

The surprise thrusts, which were accompanied by scores of attacks on smaller centers, came only hours after the allied forces canceled their 36-hour cease-fire for the lunar new year in the five northern provinces because of the massive South Vietnamese build-up there. Today was the first day of the new year.

As word of the attacks flooded into American headquarters this morning, the high command abruptly called off the cease-fire for the rest of South Vietnam as well in the name of President Thieu, who was reported not immediately available to sign the proclamation.

[American sources in Saigon said the bombing pause over the heart of North Vietnam was not affected, Reuters reported.]

The heaviest attack took place at Danang, the second largest city in the country and the base area for military operations along the demilitarized zone.

The guerrillas smashed the giant airbase at the southern edge of the city with rockets and mortars, destroying four F-4 Phantoms and two A-6 Intruders on the ground.

Other units fought their way through to the headquarters of the Vietnamese Army First Corps, about half a mile from the field. Pitched battles were reported still in progress on the streets of the city late this morning with hurriedly mobilized detachments of marines, military police and Vietnamese rangers engaging the enemy.

Other Targets Listed

The other raids in the unprecedented show of Vietcong strength were carried out against Nhatrang and Quinhon, on the coast 190 and 290 miles northeast of Saigon, respectively, and against the cities of Banmethuot, Pleiku and Kontum in the Central Highlands.

Fighting was said to be still going on in all of these cities at noon today, with American troops being rushed in to reinforce South Vietnamese forces. The attack on Danang closed the airfield, halting a large

157

The New York Times   Jan. 30, 1968

Truce in South Vietnam was canceled after attacks on major centers (underlined).

percentage of the air strikes that were to have been flown against North Vietnamese positions around the marine bastion of Khesanh today and choking off, at least temporarily, the flow of supplies, which must be delivered by air.

Khesanh Airstrip Hit

Only scattered contacts and light shelling was reported in the Khesanh area, 14 miles south of the demilitarized zone and seven miles east of the Laotian border, where the American command is all but certain that a major North Vietnamese blow will fall in the next few days.

But reports from the fortress this morning said that the vital 3,500-foot airstrip had been temporarily closed by four large rocket craters, which were being filled in.

American sources seemed dismayed by the success of the closely coordinated attacks. They apparently caught the Vietnamese army and militia forces, which have primary responsibility for guarding the cities, off guard while they were celebrating the arrival at midnight of the Year of the Monkey.

The first attack started at midnight precisely at Quinhon. Others came at 12:35 A.M. at Nhatrang and an hour or two later in the other cities, with the start of the attack at Danang put at about 3:30 A.M. The roar of rockets and mortars blotted out the snapping of the millions of firecrackers with which the Vietnamese celebrate the most important holiday of their year.

At Nhatrang, the headquarters of the American First Field Force and the Fifth Special Forces Group, the enemy was said to have occupied the province headquarters and many other installations.

At Pleiku, 250 miles northeast of Saigon and the main air base and supply area for operations in the Dakto region, the provincial prison was raided. Hundreds of Vietcong prisoners were reported freed.

At Kontum, the base area of a Vietnamese army task force was reported overrun.

The closest attack to Saigon came at Banmethuot, 150 miles to the north. Starting at 1:35 A.M., the Vietcong mortared the headquarters of the Vietnamese Army's 23d Division and swept into the city, occupying the offices of Darlac Province.

The other sizable city attacked was Hoian, the capital of Quangnam Province. It is about 15 miles south of Danang.

In addition, the Vietcong attacked a major helicopter base of the First Cavalry Division (Airmobile) in the Bongson plain, about 40 miles north of Quinhon.

The announcement yesterday that the truce would be partially canceled was made by the Vietnamese Government less than an hour before the scheduled start of the cease-fire at 6 P.M. in Saigon.

At the time it was announced that air strikes would continue without interruption against enemy supply routes south of the North Vietnamese city of Vinh, about 150 miles north of the border.

The announcement said the truce could not be observed in the northern provinces "without serious risk to the lives of the defending South Vietnamese and American forces."

The "extensive build-up" around the marine stronghold at Khesanh, in neighboring Laos and in nearby North Vietnam established conclusively, the statement said, that "North Vietnamese forces are engaged in a major offensive against the northern areas of South Vietnam."

Underscoring the seriousness with which the military situation is viewed, an American military spokesman said that a fourth North Vietnamese division had been identified in the area below the demilitarized zone, bringing the estimated enemy infantry strength there to 32,000 to 40,000 men. In addition, there are rocket, artillery, engineer and other supporting units, totaling possibly 10,000 men.

"This isn't infiltration anymore," the spokesman said. "It is an invasion."

Two divisions, the 325C and 304th, had previously been identified around the Marine stronghold which is seven miles northwest of the Laotian border and 14 miles south of the demilitarized zone.

The 324B division holds the eastern end of the front, near the allied Conthien and Giolinh strongpoints. The new division, the 320th, which like the 304th had previously been stationed in central North Vietnam, was reported to be maneuvering near Camp Carroll, the Marines' major military base, about 18 miles northeast of Khesanh.

To meet this threat American forces in Quangtri and northern Thuathien Provinces have been sharply increased in the last 10 days.

Informed sources did not rule out the possibility of raids by American troops in southern areas of North Vietnam and in eastern Laos as a counterstroke to cut supply lines.

January 30, 1968

FOE INVADES U.S. SAIGON EMBASSY; RAIDERS WIPED OUT AFTER 6 HOURS; VIETCONG WIDEN ATTACK ON CITIES

AMBASSADOR SAFE

By TOM BUCKLEY
Special to The New York Times

SAIGON, South Vietnam, Wednesday, Jan. 31—A 17-man Vietcong squad seized parts of the United States Embassy in the center of Saigon and held them for six hours early today.

The Vietcong, wearing South Vietnamese Army uniforms, held off American military policemen firing machine guns and rocket launchers. Finally the invaders were routed by squads of American paratroopers who landed by helicopter on the roof of the building.

[Ambassador Ellsworth Bunker was taken from his residence about five blocks from the embassy to what was described as a secure area, The Associated Press reported. He returned to the embassy at 11 A.M., about two hours after the last enemy resistance was wiped out. Others of the embassy staff were also said to be safe. The American flag was raised in front of the embassy at 11:45 A.M., almost five hours later than normal.]

The daring raid was the most dramatic of scores of attacks launched by enemy commando units that carried the Vietcong's Lunar New Year offensive to the capital.

Fighting was continuing in Saigon at 2 P.M. local time (1 A.M., New York time.) A Vietcong squad, armed with a captured American machine gun and rocket launchers, was firing from among the concrete beams and pillars of a half-completed hotel across the street from the Presidential Palace.

Only scattered reports of American losses were available

The U.S. Embassy compound in Saigon, which was invaded by Vietcong, in a photo taken recently as a copter landed on-roof. Building was designed to resist minor attacks.

by midafternoon. The total was perhaps 40 men killed and twice as many wounded. The guerrillas forces were believed to number no more than 500.

Elsewhere in the country, heavy fighting was reported in the capitals of the five provinces of the I Corps area, the northernmost section of the country, and in several district towns there and in the Central Highlands cities of Banmethuot, Pleiku and Kontum.

Targets Widespread

The raiders in Saigon, besides attacking the embassy, fought their way onto the grounds of the Presidential Palace.

Waves of helicopters raked them with rockets and machine-gun fire.

The palace houses the executive offices of President Nguyen Van Thieu and Vice President Nguyen Cao Ky. The United States Embassy said the President was safe at an undisclosed place. The whereabouts of the Vice President was said to be unknown.

As the fighting raged, this correspondent was pinned down for 15 minutes behind a military police jeep as tracer bullets arched a few feet overhead.

The bodies of at least two American military policemen, lay perhaps 50 yards away. Vietcong and civilian dead also sprawled on the sidewalk.

Heavy fighting was also reported near the runway at Tansonnhut Airport, where an enemy company of about 100 men was making a suicide stand against a larger force of Vietnamese troops and American military policemen. The field was closed to all but emergency flights.

A handful of commandos held out in the building housing the Saigon radio, only a few blocks from the embassy. Part of the structure was burning.

The attacks began at 3 A.M. today. Eleven hours later, only fragmentary reports could be obtained of many of the guerrilla assults that turned Saigon, a relatively placid island in a widening sea of war for the past tow and a half years, into a battle ground.

Three American officers billets were attacked, as was the Philippine Embassy, the headquarters of the Vietnamese Navy, the Vietnamese Joint General Staff compound adjoining the airport, and the Gialong Palace, which houses government offices.

The embassy attacked capped a night of terror unmatched since the overthrow of President Ngo Dinh Diem on Nov. 1, 1963.

Beginning at 3 A.M. with mortar fire and a rocket barrage, guerrillas also struck three American billets for officers, the Tansonnhut air base

on the edge of the city, the compound of the South Vietnamese General Staff adjoining the airport, the Philippine Embassy, South Vietnamese Navy headquarters and the studios of the Saigon radio.

While early reports said the Vietcong had taken over the main embassy building, or chancery, Marine officers denied that this had occurred. The raiders rampaged through the consular section, still housed in prefabricated buildings on the ground, and through the lower floors of a villa occupied by Col. George Jacobson, the mission coordinator.

Gen. William C. Westmoreland, the American commander in Vietnam, visited the embassy grounds a few minutes after the American troops had taken control. He said: "The enemy's well-laid plans went afoul. All the enemy in the compound have been killed."

Heavy fighting was reported elsewhere in the country.

Fighting was reported throughout the former imperial capital, Hue. The Vietcong continued the attack begun yesterday in Hoian, with two battalions dug in around the provincial hospital and in an adjoining Vietnamese army compound. Six companies of Korean marines were reported moving to the attack.

The attacks occurred on the second day of Tet, the Lunar New Year.

Despite public warnings by

the Saigon police that a terrorist assault could be expected last night in the aftermath of the enemy's attacks on major cities, the raids seemed to have caught both the Americans and the South Vietnamese by surprise.

An American military-police battalion and the Saigon city police found themselves outgunned.

Not until the arrival of the first helicopters at the embassy were any infantry troops, American or South Vietnamese, seen in the center of the city. There were no tanks or heavy weapons to meet the enemy.

Safety Was Key Aim

The embassy compound, covering four acres, opened last September. The primary consideration in its construction was security—even down to the helicopter landing pad installed atop the Chancery, the compound's main structure, so Ambassador Bunker would not have to travel through crowds that might sometimes be hostile.

While Saigon was being attacked, reports of raids elsewhere were flooding into the American mission. Targets included the Bienhoa airbase and the headquarters of the American II Field Force at Longbinh, northeast of the city.

Danang, the second-largest city in South Vietnam, came under heavy attack, a day after it was rocked by rocket and mortar barrages.

The South Vietnamese police had warned yesterday afternoon that attacks by guerrilla "suicide squads" were expected. American civilians had been told to remain indoors. Servicemen were already under orders to remain indoors to leave the streets clear for the celebration of Tet.

The downtown streets were quiet and deserted when the first mortar rounds exploded on the block-square grounds of the Presidential Palace.

New Assaults Reported

Small-arms fire crackled in a dozen places. As the cannonade continued, allied helicopter gunships swung overhead, sweeping enormous lights over the area.

The fresh wave of attacks was viewed by some officers as the start of a general offensive, intended to force the United States to the bargaining table or make it face the likelihood of a greatly expanded and more costly war.

The new raids came as coherent reports of yesterday's sweeping raids became available.

Ground attacks, following mortar and rocket barrages had struck eight major cities—Danang, Nhatrang, Quinhon, Kontum, Hoian, Pleiku, Banmethuot and Tuyhoa—between midnight and 4 A.M.

Then, instead of slipping away in the darkness, enemy

The New York Times   Jan. 31, 1968

The U.S. Embassy is marked at left. The names of other centers raided by the Vietcong are underlined at right.

formations continued to hold positions in all of them except Danang and Tuyhoa, with fighting reported continuing this morning.

In the case of Kontum and Banmethuot, new assaults from outside the city were reported.

At Danang, South Vietnamese rangers and United States marines, supported by waves of helicopter gunships, pursued the retreating enemy through the southern outskirts of the city.

North Vietnamese snipers roamed the streets of Nhatrang 24 hours after attacking an American compound. Lieut. Gen. William R. Rosson, commander of the I Field Force,

and Lieut. Gen. Myung Shin Chae, commander of South Korean ground forces, had narrowly escaped the raid.

The situation remained unclear in Tuyhoa, the capital of Phuyen Province on the central coast, and Banmethuot, the capital of Darlac Province in the Central Highlands, where the enemy also mounted apparently successful assaults.

In all the raids, the enemy displayed coordination and offensive strength without precedent in the war.

While South Vietnamese military and governmental installations bore the brunt of the attacks, the American command disclosed that several Ameri-

can installations had also been hit. These included an Army airfield nine miles north of Camranh Bay, the vast supply base that had been visited twice by President Johnson. It was regarded as the most secure area in the country.

While casualty reports were incomplete and often contradictory, it appeared that American forces had escaped fairly lightly, with fewer than 50 men killed and perhaps 100 men wounded.

South Vietnamese losses were probably heavier.

Although the enemy units generally achieved surprise, they took heavy casualties in the prolonged fighting that followed.

The figure may reach a total of more than 500 enemy dead. Informed sources in Saigon regarded this as a bargain price for the enemy to have paid for the enormous blow scored against Government prestige.

In response to the wave of attacks, the South Vietnamese Government canceled the 36-hour cease-fire it had ordered throughout the country for the Lunar New Yorr.

American forces at Khesanh and elsewhere along the demilitarized zone, in the Dakto region and in the border areas northwest of Saigon, had gone on full alert as soon as word of the attacks in the rear areas was received. But there was no attempt by the North Vietnamese units opposing them to stage coordinated assaults.

An especially heavy enemy attack was directed at Danang,

in Quangnam Province, 370 miles northeast of Saigon.

Gene Roberts, chief of the New York Times bureau in Saigon, reported from Danang that four Phantom jets and two Marine Corps Intruder jets, all-weather aircraft equipped with radar navigation systems, had been destroyed in a rocket barrage.

At Pleiku, the major air base and supply terminal for the Central Highlands, at least 50 buildings were reported afire by Army officials early in the morning. Hundreds of refugees were said to be roaming the streets.

At Kontum, a province capital 50 miles north of Pleiku on Highway 14, a Vietcong force estimated at two battalions, striking about 3 A.M., fired mortars at the airfield, seized the post office and other Government buildings and attacked the Soviet Vietnamese Army's headquarters.

At Nhatrang, the brunt of an attack by a North Vietnamese and a Vietcong battalion apparently fell on two adjoining American compounds, one housing senior officers and the other a military-police company and a sector headquarters near the center of the city.

An interim report on casualties said that 12 Americans had been killed and 10 wounded, 7 Vietnamese soldiers killed and 23 irregulars wounded in the ambush. Sixty of the enemy were said to have died in the assault and 15 to have been taken prisoner.

January 31, 1968

Offensive Is Said to Pinpoint Enemy's Strengths

Despite U.S. Stress on Toll, Vietcong Gains Are Seen in Morale and Prestige

By TOM BUCKLEY

Special to The New York Times

SAIGON, South Vietnam, Feb. 1 — "Well, they can't stand many more days like that," an American general said yesterday, glancing up from an early report that said the Vietcong had lost more than 700 men on the first day of the latest wave of attacks throughout South Vietnam.

The enemy death toll for three days was tabulated at 5,800 men, as against 535 allied dead. If correct, the figure on enemy losses would equal the toll usually claimed for three

weeks of fighting. [On Friday morning the announced death tolls were 10,593 of the enemy, 281 Americans and 632 South Vietnamese.]

Whatever price the guerrillas paid, the results were viewed in Saigon as incalculable in several respects: the effect on the Vietnamese civilians who may be regarded as loyal to the South Vietnamese Government; the stiffening of morale in Hanoi and guerrilla strongholds in the South; the reflection on American assertions that large sections of the country are "pacified," and the degree of belief with which such estimates are received around the world.

The Vietcong attacks have hit nearly every important province capital in the country, scores of district capitals and many airfields, hellicopter landing zones and military installations.

Surprise Is Achieved

In almost every case, the attackers appeared to have reached the centers of the cities and to have remained there, repulsing American and South Vietnamese troops for hours or days.

The apparent success of the first night's attacks in surprising the South Vietnamese troops, who have the primary responsibility for guarding the cities, is to some degree understandable in view of the gusto with which the arrival of the Lunar New Year is celebrated and the fact that a truce was in effect in three of the four corps areas.

What is difficult to understand is how the second night's attacks, including the one on Saigon, where an alert had been issued the previous afternoon, also succeeded.

Among the points that the

attacks may have demonstrated are these:

¶Despite official statistics to the contrary, no part of the country is secure either from terrorist bombs or from organized military operations.

¶Even local guerrilla battalions, as distinct from the main force, still possess highly efficient communications, leadership and coordination. Despite the prevalence of Government informers and security agents, the battalions are able to carry out their preparations in secrecy. They have an arsenal of excellent weapons.

¶Most important, after years of fighting and tens of thousands of casualties, the Vietcong can still find thousands of men who are ready not only to strike at night and slip away but also to undertake missions in which death is the only possible outcome.

As a result, only a relative

Fourth Infantry Division assigned to the area — some 12,000 men — were patrolling the ridges and jungle to the west within 15 miles of the Cambodian border.

Lieut. Gen. Fred C. Weyand, commander of the II Field Force, which operates in the area, said that certain of these units had been moved back when the enemy threat became apparent, but he declined to go into details.

Major units of the First and 25th Divisions and the 199th Light Infantry Brigade, which until November had been within 15 or 20 miles of Saigon, were drawn 60 to 90 miles north of the capital by a series of North Vietnamese and Vietcong attacks.

In Saigon itself, the nerve center of American military, diplomatic and civilian aid activities, almost the only American forces on duty when the blow came at 3 A.M. yesterday were 300 military policemen, at least half of them assigned to individual guard posts.

These men performed well, by all accounts, in the fighting that followed. They possessed only rifles and light machine guns, which they were unaccustomed to using in combat, and they lacked armored vehicles and heavier weapons that could have made short work of the guerrillas.

The reserve battalions of South Vietnamese paratroops handful of American troops could be brought in quickly to reinforce the hard-pressed South Vietnamese policemen and militiamen, few of them as well armed as the attackers.

By and large, the South Vietnamese armed forces have not clearly demonstrated such an extreme dedication to duty. And the tactics of the American forces are calculated to keep casualties at a minimum.

Some observers feel that the attacks may put into doubt the wisdom of the American military policy of sending tens of thousands of the most effective combat troops into the empty border regions to hunt, almost always unsuccessfully, for North Vietnamese units while leaving the defense of populated areas to the South Vietnamese Army, militia and police.

All eyes were fixed on Khesanh, the marine outpost on the Laotian border, when the blow fell against every capital in the northern provinces of South Vietnam. Some 5,000 marines were in the fortress, still waiting for an attack by two divisions or more of North Vietnamese reported to be in the hills, and a large, powerful and highly mobile force was rushed into positions from which the fortress could quickly be reinforced.

Some Units Moved Back

While enemy units fought their way to the center of Pleiku, the two brigades of the and marines near the center of the city seemed slow to react. It was understood that despite the alert in the city, only 50 per cent of them—the same figure as with the national police—had been in their barracks. The rest were out on holiday leave.

American forces from Bienhoa and Longbinh, themselves under Vietcong attack, were unable to help until 8:30 A.M., when a platoon of paratroops landed on the roof of the embassy.

These men, as far as could be determined, were the only American reinforcements who arrived in the city throughout the day and into the night, when the Vietcong struck again at two police stations and blew up a power plant in the Cholon section.

Effect of Embassy Raid

The Vietcong's choice of the new American Embassy as a major target appeared to indicate an attempt at humiliation. To the extent that the guerrillas blasted their way through the stone wall and fought from the compound for six hours, the attempt succeeded.

Whether the guerrillas entered the building itself seems of relatively little importance to anyone except members of the mission and the State Department. Despite the rush of official denials, statements from witnesses indicate that the guerrillas did temporarily take part of the main building's first floor.

"I don't know why they did it," an American officer said this morning. "They didn't achieve anything militarily. It was obviously just a propaganda thing."

More important than allied casualties, in the view of many officials, is the effect among the four million people — nearly 25 per cent of the South Vietnamese — who have enjoyed high degree of security in this war-torn country for more than two years.

The reasoning may be incorrect, motivated by a sudden rush of fear, but it can be speculated that many people in scores of cities and towns are less certain now than they were two days ago that the allies are winning the war.

For the Americans and the South Vietnamese, the problem is to try, in the popular phrase here, "to get the ducks back back in a row," to pick up the pieces, to make another effort to reorganize the South Vietnamese Army and to win back the ground that has been lost.

February 2, 1968

Survivors Hunt Dead of Bentre, Turned to Rubble in Allied Raids

By BERNARD WEINRAUB
Special to The New York Times

BENTRE, South Vietnam, Feb. 7—On this warm, languid day in Bentre, children picked through the smoldering rubble in the market place, American soldiers patrolled shattered streets, South Vietnamese troops scoured empty blocks for bodies and Mrs. Dieu Thi Sam sat stunned in the bombed wreckage of her home and wept.

She pointed to the sky. "The first bomb landed on the next house," she said in Vietnamese. "I ran down the street and began to cry. My house exploded. I keep crying. I cannot stop."

In this provincial capital in the Mekong delta, 30 miles south of Saigon, nearly 1,000 South Vietnamese are believed to be dead after one of the bitterest battles of the week's Vietcong offensive.

'Still Digging Them Out'

"We're still not too sure of the casualties," said one American officer in the steamy military compound facing the Bentre Canal. "We figure 1,000 dead and 1,500 wounded. We're still digging them out."

Four hamlets thought to be controlled by the Vietcong have been razed by allied bombing and artillery attacks and fire from armed helicopters. Near the canal, still fringed with pines and mango trees, is an area of the town where a zigzag row of bricks is the only remnant of two-story and three-story houses.

"The VC had people all over this town," said Maj. Phillip Cannella, the operations officer for the Military Assistance Command in Bentre. "Christ, they were everywhere."

As the capital of Kienhoa Province, this town of 50,000 has long been a stronghold of the Vietcong. Among South Vietnamese, Bentre is sometimes considered a Vietcong rest and recreation area where guerrillas prepare for moves throughout the delta and Saigon.

Regiment Sweeps In

The Vietcong attack on Bentre began last Wednesday shortly after 1 A.M. Firing recoilless rifles, 82-mm. mortars and rockets, a reinforced Vietcong regiment of 2,500 men swept into the capital from the south and east, hitting the Bentre airstrip and moving swiftly toward a four-block square in the heart of town, the headquarters of the Government provincial chief and the American and South Vietnamese military forces.

"They had apparently infiltrated into most of the town," an American officer said today. "They were probably living with the people. It was Tet and there were plenty of strangers in town."

Because of Tet—the Lunar New Year—the protection of Bentre was limited. The two South Vietnamese battalions guarding the perimeter had a total of only 500 men, half the normal number. The other soldiers were on a holiday.

The 40-man United States military compound, under heavy ground attack, called for support. Five patrol boats with .50-caliber machine guns steamed south along the canal, opening fire on the Vietcong, who were staging their heaviest ground attacks at the South Vietnamese military headquarters.

"In those first 24 hours," an American military official said, "We can credit those Navy PBR's with keeping them off. If it weren't for them, we wouldn't be here." PBR's are river patrol boats.

For nearly 40 hours, American officers say, the Vietcong controlled the town except for the four blocks near the canal.

By Thursday afternoon, bombing raids and fire by helicopter gunships and artillery were ordered for sections of the town. "We were calling artillery and gunships just yards away from our own positions," one officer said.

Two Companies Land

As stucco and brick and straw homes collapsed under the bombing, two companies of the United States Ninth Infantry Division landed in the center of the city and were immediately attacked.

Within the square and at a nearby bridge, the American troops and the Vietcong fought bitterly through the night. Two more Ninth Division

161

companies were brought in by helicopter.

By dawn Friday, the fighting subsided. The Vietcong lost as many as 400 men, according to officers here. The number of Americans who died remains unclear, but may be 20 to 30 men.

At the 350-bed hospital, the maimed and wounded filled the beds and floors and aisles.

The market place is rubble and near the gutted homes nearby women in shawls sit in the noon heat and mourn with loud groans.

Major Describes Move

BENTRE, Feb. 7 (AP)—"It became necessary to destroy the town to save it," a United States major said today.

He was talking about the decision by allied commanders to bomb and shell the town regardless of civilian casualties, to rout the Vietcong.

February 8, 1968

HALF SAIGON ARMY ON LEAVE FOR TET

SAIGON, South Vietnam, Feb. 8 (AP) — Approximately half of the South Vietnamese Army was on Tet New Year's leave when the Communists launched their countrywide offensive against major cities last week, qualified sources said today.

These sources declared the South Vietnamese Joint General Staff had authorized leaves up to 50 per cent for the time around the lunar new year holiday Jan. 30. The holiday is the most important one on the calendar for Vietnamese and, by tradition, a time for visits to families.

In addition, the Vietcong had proclaimed a week-long cease-fire extending before and after the three or four days on which the Vietnamese celebrate Tet. Allied commanders have said they had advance intelligence of planned Communist attacks during the Tet holidays, despite the declared truce.

Because of this intelligence, the Tet leaves were canceled in a few South Vietnamese units, notably the Rangers and the marines and the 23d Infantry Division based at Banmethuot in the central highlands.

February 9, 1968

Death Holds Hue In a Quiet Agony

By BERNARD WEINRAUB

Special to The New York Times

HUE, South Vietnam, Feb. 29 —Death grips this shattered city of marble temples and tombs.

It is everywhere—in mass graves of South Vietnamese soldiers on the south bank of the Huong River, in the open holes where the bodies of North Vietnamese sprawl, in the women who sit and grieve with birdlike cries beside the graves near the city's main hospital, in the young pregnant woman in a purple sweater who wept hysterically this afternoon on the bridge that spans the river.

"Oh, no, oh, no," she whispered to a young man who held her arm.

The man turned to another Vietnamese who stood with an American. "The war," he said with a shrug. "A bullet in her husband's head."

Some Bitter Fighting

In the aftermath of one of the most bitter battles of the war, which left 129 American marines dead and 810 wounded, the ancient city appeared in the throes of a quiet agony.

"Hue has nothing now, nothing," a 24-year-old medical student, Nguyen Van Chu, said in Hue Civilian Hospital.

"It is not only the loss of our buildings and monuments," he said, "it is the loss of our spirit. It is gone."

In more than three weeks of battle, savage house-to-house fighting and allied bombing attacks to destroy the North Vietnamese, 1,000 civilians were killed. And that figure may rise considerably as American and South Vietnamese pick through the rubble. In addition, 3,000 civilians were wounded, many severely.

Stunning Losses

As South Vietnam's second most important city—and the intellectual capital of the country—Hue has suffered other stunning losses.

More than half of the city is destroyed or damaged, according to American officials. Some of these buildings were elaborately carved stone and marble relics, churches and monuments and homes. The city government itself is in chaos, with only 500 civil servants at work instead of the usual 2,000. The bodies of some of the missing civil servants were reported found today in a mass grave, about 500 yards from the Citadel wall surrounding the northern sector of Hue. City employes were believed to have been a key target of the North Vietnamese.

Anger Has Surfaced

In the slow struggle to return to normal, a residue of anger has come to the surface —an anger at the enemy, an anger, in some cases, at the allied troops and an anger at the South Vietnamese officials.

Several Americans say that Vietnamese officials are barely coping with such immediate problems as the city's refugees, who have reached a peak of 60,000, the threat of plague, the lack of sanitation, even burial of the dead.

"Everything you worked for just collapsed in this place and they're not doing a damn thing to start moving again," complained one young American official.

At Hue Civilian Hospital, two exuberant American doctors have virtually taken over. The young Public Health Service physicians, who are based in Danang but moved north during the fighting, are Dr. Gilbert Herod of Indianapolis and Dr. Allen H. Pribble of Covington, Ky.

"You know, the Vietnamese are not known for being altruists," said Dr. Pribble. "That seems to be especially true of their doctors."

Walking into a bare ward, the 27-year-old doctor sat down and sighed. "It's astonishing," he said. "The patients have not been fed regularly, we're short of rice, and we found one Vietnamese doctor who filched 39 bags of rice for his own use. I'm trying to get rid of him.

"As soon as the fighting began, all the Vietnamese doctors here moved into the university refugee center and they holed up in a single room with their families. They took all their medical supplies with them.

"The wounded were brought to the university refugee center and would go to the emergency room and the doctors would not come out," he said. "The only people who did anything were the Catholic sisters who did what they could—if it was a partial amputation they would finish it. They would clean out the wounds, too.

"In the midst of all this unbelievable chaos and filth, the doctors just stayed in their rooms with their wives, and families and medical supplies."

Dr. Pribble, a thin, bespectacled physician who has worked in Vietnam for more than a year, said:

"Their whole little world was torn down and they just withdrew. Instead of giving when they were most needed they gave up. They totally insulated themselves. Astonishing."

The staff of the 1,200-bed hospital now includes nearly a dozen medical students who are working as physicians. "Everything's sort of basic and rudimentary," Dr. Herod said.

"When some of the patients finally arrive here, it's too late, just too late," he added.

"Most of the wounds we're getting now are similar in that they have a lot of dead tissue and they're very likely to get tetanus or gangrene.

Gangrene Before Arrival

"That man lying over there," said Dr. Herod, pointing to a body whose face was covered with a piece of jagged cardboard, "he had gangrene two days before he got here. We took off his arm and a leg, but. . . .'

Possibly the most delicate and often-discussed topic during the last two days has been the looting by South Vietnamese soldiers as well as by some American marines. Vietnamese soldiers carrying radios, tape recorders, clothing, umbrellas, linoleum flooring and mattresses are seen walking along the banks of the Huong.

The booty of the United States marines was generally limited to whisky and wine. The bulk of the looting seemed to be by South Vietnamese Army men.

To American officials here, who are openly annoyed at the brazen looting by South Vietnamese soldiers, the theft of packs of rice and meat in this hungry city was only one more disappointment of many over the last months.

"I get the feeling we're starting all over again," said an American official, "and I don't have the energy or the spirit or, I suppose the faith, anymore to make things work."

Inside the Hue Citadel, however, an American civilian in fatigues was approached by a scholarly-looking South Vietnamese soldier. "Thank you for saving my city," he told the startled American.

For most of the city's residents the question of blame appeared virtually meaningless.

"My Hue is gone," said Vinh Chanh, a 21-year-old medical student. "I loved my city, but, all, gone."

___

Loss of Hue Not Reported

HANOI, North Vietnam, Feb. 29 (Agence France-Presse)— Hanoi's newspapers have not yet informed their readers of the recapture of Hue by American and South Vietnamese forces, but everyone knows about it. The name of the city, which was in headlines daily during the battle, has simply disappeared from the press.

March 1, 1968

In Hue, Graves Disclose Executions by the Enemy

The following dispatch is by Stewart Harris, a correspondent of The Times of London.

HUE, South Vietnam—North Vietnam's army and the Vietcong executed many South Vietnamese, some Americans and a few other foreigners during the fighting last month at Hue.

I am sure of this after spending several days in Hue investigating allegations of killings and torture. I am not convinced about the torture, although men who saw many bodies and seem balanced in their judgment are so convinced.

Frank Jakes, an American official in charge of psychological operations, said that he could get no conclusive evidence of torture, noting that no bodies had been medically examined.

In the green valley of Namhoa, about 10 miles southwest of Hue, I was with Warrant Officer Ostara, an Australian adviser with the South Vietnam Army, who has been here for four years, speaks a little Vietnamese and knows the village of Namhoa very well.

Two Bodies Found

We were standing on the sloping sides of a recently dug hole. In the bottom were rush mats over sheets of plastic. Mr. Ostara drew them back, revealing the bodies of two Vietnamese with their arms tied behind their backs just above the elbows. They had been shot through the back of their heads.

The day before, 27 women from the village walked out three miles carrying mattocks to dig for their missing husbands and sons, having heard about this patch of disturbed earth near the roadside. Mr. Ostara was with them as they worked. They left the unrecognized bodies for others to look at.

Driving back to the village, Mr. Ostara said that the enemy had come through on the way to Hue. They had taken 27 men. Some were leaders and some were younger, strong enough to be porters or even auxiliary soldiers.

Graves are still being discovered. On the previous afternoon, Mr. Jakes took me to Longtho, about three miles west of Hue on the south side of the Huong River.

We came upon a woman wailing and throwing herself about between two coffins. In them were her two sons, who had been at high school and had gone with or been taken by the enemy on Feb. 29. Their bodies were taken from a grave discovered two miles away the previous day.

Another family was gathered beside two more coffins. They wore the traditional white headbands for mourning. One body was that of a 20-year-old youth whose sister said that he had disappeared on Feb. 15.

Another body was brought in, slung between two bamboo poles. Down the road, in a shattered house, was the body of the hamlet chief, the father of six little children.

Earlier that afternoon I had talked with Bob Kelly, the senior provincial adviser in Thuathein, who has been in Vietnam for many years and speaks the language fluently.

"I have heard of no confirmed instances of torture," Mr. Kelly said. "Men were simply condemned by drumhead courts and executed as enemies of the people. These were the leaders, often quite small men. Others were executed when their usefulness ceased, or when they didn't cooperate they were shot for their trouble."

"Some of my staff were badly mutilated, but I am inclined to believe this was done after they were killed. Their hands were tied and they were shot behind the head. I helped to dig one body out, but I have been told by Vietnamese whom I respect that some people were buried alive."

Lieut. Gregory Sharp, an American adviser with the South Vietnamese 21st Ranger Battalion, said that his men came across about 25 new graves in a cemetery five miles east of Hue on March 14.

From half a dozen of the graves, the heads were sticking up out of the sandy soil.

"They had been buried alive, I think," Lieutenant Sharp said. "There were sort of scratches in the sand in one place, as if someone had clawed his way out, but then he may have been playing possum. I don't really know."

At Quantangan, three Australian warrant officers saw seven men in one of three graves they had found. The seven, they said, had been shot one after the other, through the back of the head, hands tied.

Inspected Sites

Soon after arriving in Hue, I went in a jeep with three South Vietnamese officers to inspect sites where the bodies of executed men were said to have been found.

We went first to Giahoi High School in District 2, east of the Citadel. Here, 22 new graves had been found, each containing three to seven bodies. It is still a horrifying place. The officers told me that victims had been tied and, again, that most had been shot through the head. But some had been buried alive, they added.

Estimates of the number of people executed in the Hue area vary. The most conservative was given by the police chief, Doan Cong Lap, who said the figure was about 200. Other civilian casualty figures he gave were: killed, 3,776; wounded, 1,909; captured or taken away, 1,041.

There are about 40,000 Roman Catholic Vietnamese in Hue. What happened to them? Information comes from several people who would be safer if they were anonymous.

Catholic Resisted Foe

About three-quarters of the Catholics in Hue live in Phucam, on the southern outskirts of the city. They resisted strongly when the enemy came in and some were executed. Four South Vietnamese priests were taken away and three foreign priests were killed.

Two French priests were given permission by the Vietcong to return to Phucam and help the sisters—and then were shot on the way back. But this might have been an error. Another French priest, a Benedictine, was executed, perhaps because he was chaplain to the Americans.

One thing is abundantly clear: the Vietcong and North Vietnamese put into practice, with their usual efficiency, the traditional Communist policy of punishing by execution selected leaders who support their enemies, the Government of South Vietnam and its American allies. They also executed American allies. They also executed American civilian advisers.

In Hue, as elsewhere, they were unable, on the whole, to capture and execute the mor important officials, because these men are careful to protect themselves in heavily fortified compounds, defended by soldiers and the police. In Hue, as elsewhere, the more defenseless people were the victims—the village and hamlet chiefs, the teachers and the policemen.

According to the police chief, Doan Cong Lap, the Government has 477 Vietcong and North Vietnamese soldiers in custody.

"What about suspects?" he was asked. "What about officials and civilians who should have supported the Government and either went over to the enemy or went into hiding until they saw the Government would win? How many of these have you taken?"

After three visits to the police chief and one to the new provincial chief, Colonel Than, the figure was given: "Nearly 300."

They also said that none of these people had been executed and that none had been brought to trial. Colonel Khoa, the provincial chief until two weeks ago, had been given temporary power to execute summarily any traitor holding a senior position. Moreover, six weeks ago the South Vietnamese promised to set up immediately a military tribunal in Hue. Yet no one has been tried.

Colonel Khoa disappeared for several days, and then reappeared with a tale about shooting, with his guards, 11 Vietcong. Yet his house must be one of very few in Hue that is not damaged.

According to Chief Lap, the only men likely to be executed are two who have been members of the Vietcong for a long time and a third man whose name he could not remember

March 28, 1968

163

CAMBODIA REVOLT IS SAID TO EXPAND

Forces Led by Communists Reported in More Areas

By HEDRICK SMITH
Special to The New York Times

WASHINGTON, March 13 — The Communist-led rebellion in Cambodia is reported to have increased in intensity and to have spread to new areas.

In recent days, Prince Norodom Sihanouk, the Cambodian Chief of State, has stepped up his public attacks against the rebels, broadening earlier charges that they were receiving help from Asian Communist countries.

According to Western analysts who follow Cambodian affairs, the Government-controlled Cambodian press prints reports almost every day of skirmishes, raids, bomb incidents, minings and shootings in the western provinces along the border with Thailand, especially in the province of Battambang.

Experienced Western diplomatic observers estimate that a thousand or more men may now be involved in the rebellion, including three former Deputies in the Cambodian National Assembly.

In recent speeches and published correspondence, Prince Sihanouk has been more outspoken than previously in charging that Communist countries are supporting the rebellion in an effort to overthrow his neutralist regime. He has also issued a veiled public threat to seek American aid to combat the rebellion.

Secretary of State Dean Rusk, testifying before the Senate Foreign Relations Committee this week, cited the Cambodian situation to support his contention that Asian Communists had "an appetite for aggression" extending beyond South Vietnam. He cited a letter from Prince Sihanouk to the French newspaper Le Monde in which the Cambodian leader asserted that "it is perfectly clear that Asian Communism does not permit us any longer to stay neutral" and uninvolved in the war in Vietnam.

"Not being able to make of us—who do not intend to die for Hanoi or Peking, any more than for Washington—allies supporting it unconditionally, Asian Communism strives to overthrow our regime from within," the Prince concluded.

Hanoi Victory Predicted

He also charged that Cambodian rebels had received propaganda materials, arms and equipment through the Thai Patriotic Front, the rebel group in Thailand that he described as subservient to Communist China.

Western diplomats regard the Prince's recent charges as more pointed than any made since the rebellion flared in the open in early 1967. But they note that he faces a dilemma, desiring to suppress Cambodia's internal rebellion but eager at the same time to avoid angering North Vietnam, Communist China and the Vietcong.

Traditionally, not only has he been more friendly to these countries than to the United States and its Southeast Asian allies, but he has also expressed the view that Hanoi and the Vietcong will ultimately prevail in the Vietnam war.

The rebellion first flared in Battambang Province, about 150 miles northwest of the capital of Pnompenh and a stronghold of the North Vietnamese Communists during the first Indochina war against French rule in the nineteen-fifties.

In the last two months, knowledgeable analysts have seen indications that the rebellion has been spreading southward into the provinces of Kompong Speu, Koh Kong and Kampot, along Cambodia's western frontier and touching the border of Thailand. Prince Sihanouk has in the last two weeks installed a new military governor in Kampot Province.

Both Prince Sihanouk and the Cambodian press have spoken of Cambodian Government successes in skirmishes with the rebels. But Western observers note that not only have the number of reported skirmishes increased but also that the Government's reports on the size of rebel bands now run up to 50 men in an ambush.

March 14, 1968

Americans' Impact on Vietnam Is Profound

By BERNARD WEINRAUB
Special to The New York Times

SAIGON, South Vietnam, June 27—Ten years ago fewer than 1,000 American servicemen were stationed in Vietnam, and their presence was scarcely noticed.

Today, 530,000 American troops and 12,000 civilians are swarming through this tortured country, and their presence is affecting the very roots of South Vietnamese life.

To a growing number of South Vietnamese officials and intellectuals, "la présence Américaine" is corrosive. Two weeks ago, the Information Minister, Ton That Thien, in a monograph written for presentation in Honolulu, termed the American influence "devastating, disintegrating, explosive."

To American officials here, the impact is positive. At the most basic level, the officials say, the massive American presence is thwarting the Communists from taking over. Beyond this, the officials add, the Americans are successfully pressing South Vietnam toward democracy, toward a viable economy and toward change in the rigid social structure and the bureaucratic morass.

What is the American impact in Vietnam? The visible part of it is everywhere. The streets of Saigon, once a slumbering, tropical capital, are clogged with jeeps, motor scooters, buses, Lambrettas and cars. In 30,000 to 40,000 homes and in village squares throughout the country, South Vietnamese families watch in fascination "The Addams Family," and "Perry Mason" on armed forces television. In college classrooms students read John Updike and J. D. Salinger. In coffee shops, young men who work for United States agencies and girls in miniskirts sip Coca-Cola and complain that the Americans have taken over.

The American presence has also contributed to a tangle of more profound changes that remain, with a war on, contradictory and complex. Students, teachers, Government employees and businessmen insist, for example, that the influx of American soldiers, civilians and dollars is tearing the family apart and creating social havoc.

The Vietnamese family and its home were a cornerstone in the society through a thousand years of Chinese domination and nearly a hundred years of French rule. Many Vietnamese feel that the cornerstone has crumbled.

"An impossible situation has been created," said an American-educated lawyer. "The poor families come to Saigon from the countryside because of the war. The father has few skills, so he becomes a day laborer or drives a pedicab. Before he was respected by the children. He knew about the farm. He knew about the land. Now he knows nothing.

"The young boys wash cars for the Americans or shine shoes or sell papers or work as pickpockets," the lawyer went on. "They may earn 500 or 600 piasters. [$5 or $6] a day. Their fathers earn 200 piasters a day. Here is a 10-year-old boy earning three times as much as his father. It is unheard of."

Beyond the impact of Americans and American dollars, of course, there is the over-all, shattering impact of the war itself. Virtually every young farmer or peasant is forced to join the Government forces or the Vietcong; more than a million people have become refugees; the disruption of farms and villages has led an additional two million to flee to the cities. Most of them are expected to remain there after the war.

This traumatic break for many farmers — and the social problems that await them in the cities — has stirred anger among many Vietnamese, especially since thousands of families in rural areas are physically moved out of their farms by allied troops to create free-strike zones.

'Want to Die There'

"The Vietnamese never wants to leave his village," said a professor at Saigon University. "They want to be born there and they want to die there.

"That is not easy for you Americans to understand, since you can move from village to village in your country," he went on. "But here it is very painful for a Vietnamese to leave his village, and when they are forced to move they hate you. It is as simple as that — they hate you."

To most American officials, the changes in the family are partly the tragic result of the war, partly the natural impact of Western culture on an Asian country.

"This country is going from a kind of Victorianism to a plastic imitation of the teeny-bopper in the matter of a few years," said a junior American official. Another declared:

"It's easy to blame everything wrong here on the Americans — the Vietnamese love doing it. But, look, this society was damned rotten when we got here and what we're getting now is an exaggeration of the rottenness, the corruption, the national hangups."

The American influence has touched religion, culture and, on a broad scale, the rigidly, defined class systems of Vietnam.

Buddhist and Roman Catholic leaders insist that the American impact on religion is minimal, but several American officials indicated that both the Buddhists and the Catholics were undergoing some difficulty in attracting young Vietnamese to churches and pagodas.

The membership of both churches appears relatively stable and unchanging. Of the approximately 16.5 million South Vietnamese, about 11 million are believed to be Buddhists, but only 4 million are thought to be practicing followers. The rest are ancestor-worshipping farmers and peasants.

The powerful Catholic Church is believed to have more than a million and a half members.

Influence on Young Monks

In the Mekong Delta, an American volunteer who has worked in Vietnam more than two years observed of the younger Buddhists:

"I don't know if it's our influence or not, but a lot of the younger people say they're very glad their parents pray four or five times a day at the altar, but they don't have the time to do it. They're too busy. It's like that here."

The American influence is especially marked in a small but growing number of young monks who have studied in the United States.

"I am especially impressed with the American way of life — at least what it is supposed to be," said one of the young monks, Nguyen Tanh, who majored in philosophy at Yale. "I am not impressed with its reality here."

"I see a very strong impact on intellectual life, on literary style," he said, leaning forward and speaking softly. "The rising generation read Hemingway, Faulkner, Salinger much more than the French. They have a great influence here.

"We like your writers and their attitude toward living, toward writing, toward thinking," he went on. "In particular, your American writers live in a very intense way. They live their thoughts and ideas. They are men of action. This means something to us."

Culturally, the American influx appears to have had an uneven impact. Traditional Vietnamese lacquerware and art—which most Americans find poorly made — remain untouched. Several paintings bear strong resemblances to Monet and Matisse, but there are virtually no American influences such as pop art.

Ironically the strongest American cultural influence

The New York Times

American goods are prominently displayed in shops along the streets of Saigon. South Vietnamese youngsters, some of them of draft age, ride through the city on motorbikes.

has touched folk singing in the antiwar ballads of the most famous college singer in Vietnam, Trinh Cong Son.

The broadest social—and, by extension, cultural—impact of the Americans has fallen on the powerful middle class, who exclusively ran the Government's bureaucracy, taught in primary schools and colleges and served as lawyers, doctors and businessmen. This socially conscious class, to all indications, had little link to or sympathy for the peasants, or even the army.

American officials say privately that the disruption within this entrenched class is welcome. Middle-class Vietnamese are naturally bitter. Especially at their decline in status.

"A university professor may earn 18,000 piasters a month [$150], while a bar girl can earn 100,000 piasters [$850], said 58-year-old Ho Huu Tuong, a lower-house representative who was a prominent intellectual in the nineteen forties.

"The intelligentsia are the disinherited, the lost, because of the American impact. We have lost our position."

"Money has become the idol," said Mr. Thien, the Information Minister. "Money, money, money."

The theme is echoed by poorer Vietnamese—the pedicab drivers, the small businessmen, the maids, the cooks — but for them the problem of status is irrelevant and the flow of American dollars is hardly unwelcome. "How can I hate the Americans?" asked a grinning woman who sells black-market cigarettes at a stand on Tu Do, in the heart of Saigon. "They have so much money in their pockets."

Taxation a Problem

At the official level, only enormous American assistance —$600-million this fiscal year —keeps Vietnam afloat. The figure is exclusive of American military expenditures of more than $2-billion a month.

Seeking to streamline—and

possibly even uproot—the tangled economic structure, American advisers are struggling at the outset to work out a fair system of taxation, a central problem here. Only 6 per cent of last year's budget was met by direct taxes on income and business profits in comparison with about 80 per cent in the United States.

This results in Government reliance on levies on foodstuffs, tobacco, alcohol, matches and other items that fall with heavy weight on the poor. And, through bribes and bureaucracy, the rich often pay no taxes at all.

"There's no records system here, no highly developed banking system, less than 200 lawyers in the country and nothing equivalent to accountants," said an American official. "And, of course, we have the security problem. It's not easy."

Working with a U.S. Internal Revenue Service team, the South Vietnamese Government

165

has begun reorganizing its tax administration under one directorate instead of four. In the last year the team has also spurred a witholding tax system on salaried employes and companies, and an auditor-training program.

The earliest results of the I.R.S. efforts are faintly optimistic. In the first five months of 1968, despite the major enemy offensive in January and February, tax collections rose 5 per cent over the first five months of 1967.

Taxes Fall on Poor

But although internal tax collections may increase by as much as 2 billion piasters this year, the bulk of the taxes, once again, will fall on the poor.

"The infrastructure of this economy we haven't touched yet," said a prominent American official.

Possibly the most intensive—but still uncertain—economic effort in Vietnam remains in the rural areas, where 65 per cent of the population earn their livelihood. The thrust of the American effort has focused on rice production.

With American supervision, a massive program has started in the countryside with an experimental "miracle rice" termed IR-8. The hybrid rice seed, developed in the Philippines in 1962, yields double or even triple the amount of rice produced in a paddy field.

By 1971, officials say, South Vietnam is expected to emerge self-sufficient in rice production. A measure of the impact of the war—and Vietnam's dependence on the United States —is that in 1964-65 Vietnam was self-sufficient in rice. This year, the United States shipped 700,000 tons of rice into the country, or 70 per cent of the rice consumed in Saigon.

One of the key problems in the experimental rice program is that it involves teaching Vietnamese farmers advanced methods of production such as water management and the use of new fertilizers and pesticides.

An even more basic problem was raised by Gen. William C. Westmoreland, the former American commander here, who asked agriculture officials at a meeting in May: "Do the Vietnamese like the rice?" There have been indications that the Vietnamese farmers find it less than tasteful.

The effort to spur rice production is coupled with an aid-to-agriculture drive, which, even if only half as successful as the United States mission insists, will have an impact in Vietnam. Tons of improved seed, fertilizer, insecticides and other supplies are distributed in farming areas. Everything from improved-breed pigs to watermelons are produced for the first time under American supervision.

For some American officials, however, the positive impact of these programs is partly negated by the South Vietnamese

Associated Press

A FRIENDSHIP GESTURE: A marine chaplain demonstrates toys being distributed to village youngsters in pacification program. Often, children are forced to work or steal to support themselves and families; some boys manage to earn more than their fathers.

Government's failure to act on land reform, which the United States has pressed for. Since 1962, land distribution in South Vietnam has been at a virtual standstill and the bulk of the land remains in the hands of absentee landlords.

To most observers here, the American impact on politics — on personalities — is, at once, powerful and delicately fragile. The United States mission has succeeded in helping to set up the forms of democracy here for the first time. Beyond this, however, there are contradictions.

Although the Government is hailed as democratic, there is little opposition. Newspaper censorship has been lifted, but no reports even vaguely supporting the idea of a coalition government are printed. Due process of law is practiced, but the Government jailed the peace candidate, Truong Dinh Dzu, and the Buddhist leader, Thich Tri Quang, and held them in "protective custody" for months.

Legislature Created

Surprisingly, American officials here feel that the major political impact of the United States was its role in the creation and election of the two legislative bodies. The 60-member Senate was elected last September with a disproportionate Catholic majority that has given the body a conservative tinge. The lower house, with 137 members, appears to be somewhat less conservative.

Both bodies—as well as the Constitution—were forged with considerable American help. "Yes, they may not have accomplished too much in the last six months, but the point is a lot of these people are young, they're cantankerous, and for the first time they're feeling their oats," said a prominent American official. There have been several instances of legislative resistance, sometimes successful, to measures proposed by the regime.

"There is an energy now, a drive, especially in the lower house, that's exciting and quite new in Vietnam," said another American official. "A kind of instant democracy has been created here with plenty of problems. They have got a hell of a lot to learn, but they seem to be doing it."

A handful of American officials are convinced that the possible emergence of young politicians is welcome and far-reaching.

"Frankly, I would call the present regime transitory," said

one knowledgeable American. "But I think you'll find new alliances now—students, young people, Catholics, even the young military," he went on.

He and others suggested that the eight to nine-month training of more than 2,200 officers over the last two years in the United States—as well as the training of thousands of soldiers in Vietnam—could have a progressive influence not only on the army but also on the Government.

But so far the political impact of the Americans remains cloudy. Some Vietnamese feel that the Americans publicly support the merging of the nearly 50 registered political parties into a viable Opposition, but privately seek to keep the groups fragmented, since President Nguyen Van Thieu's power and popularity are not entirely secure.

Ambivalence Detected

Some Americans feel that despite the surface trapping of an American-style democracy, the Saigon Government remains ambivalent about corruption, nepotism and the need for revolutionary reform.

American officials in the Mekong Delta, south of Saigon, annoyed and disappointed recently when the Government had accepted the resignation—for reasons that are unclear—of Lieut. Gen. Nguyen Duc Thang, the IV Corps commander. A charismatic and able officer, his aggressiveness found much favor among Americans here.

General Thang is considered allied to Vice President Nguyen Cao Ky. There was one report that President Thieu wanted to remove the general because his impressive performance in the delta was creating a "national hero."

If the substance of Vietnamese politics undergoes slow change, the style has shifted rapidly. President Thieu's speeches, once rambling and dull, are now terse. Television appearances are common, and tend to be sprinkled with such words as "image" and "task force."

"A few years ago Vice President Ky would fly to a city wearing his flight suit, make a speech and never shake hands or mingle with the crowd," said an American official. "If he did shake hands, he'd always leave his gloves on."

Now he doesn't wear his flight suit, and after a speech he always moves into the crowd, talks, listens and kids around," the official went on. "He takes off his gloves, too."

There is a general feeling that Mr. Thieu, Mr. Ky or any other Vietnamese leader would have enormous political difficulties, even if they agreed to every possible reform that the Americans have urged.

For the heart of the Government or "system" is an unwieldy, Kafkaesque bureaucracy that hampers progress at every turn. And in that area, the American impact has been minimal.

Paperwork, documents, stamps, bored officials, bribes are everywhere. Officials work four-hour days.

"It will take us at least a generation to change the system," said one of the highest American officials at the United States mission. "Maybe more than a generation."

Possibly the clearest explanation of the cumbersome and often callous bureaucracy is made in a recently published book, "Government and Revolution in Vietnam," by Dennis J. Duncanson, a former counselor for aid in the British Embassy in Saigon. He wrote:

"The common effect of both [China and France] upon the mind of Vietnam has been to discourage a practical approach to the responsibilities, and the art of Government."

The United States, seeking to break the bureaucratic stranglehold on the Government, has placed American advisers into virtually every South Vietnamese official agency. The United States has also supported a National Institute of Administration, which graduated 200 students last year. Most, however, have been placed in the army.

Basic education, which is supported this year by more than $10-million in American funds, remains especially hard hit by by the war and, essentially, a middle-class privilege.

Dropouts Increasing

Just last week, the education Minister, Nguyen Van Tho, said that the number of Vietnamese children who had not finished five year elementary school education had been growing "tremendously."

The lack of progress in some programs — the progress in others — appears, at this point, complicated by a curiously shifting relationship between many Americans and South Vietnamese. This changing relationship is underscored by Mr. Thien's remarks about the American impact.

"Something has changed over the past few months," said an American official. "There's a hell of a lot of anger now. It may have been caused by the Tet offensive or the American election campaign or the Paris talks. It may be a combination of all three. They're angry at us, though, and resentful of a lot of our efforts here."

"The roles have never been defined and we spend half our time worrying about whether or not we're offending their feelings," said an American who has worked in Vietnam more than two years.

'Guests In This Country'

A South Vietnamese publisher told an American recently: "You are our guests in this country and Vietnamese have been very friendly to you. Do not outlive our hospitality."

An American voluntary-agency worker said: "We have 350 men dying each week here and they say we're only guests and we should be only treated like guests. Come on now!"

Certainly to many Americans here, meetings and chats and lunches with many Vietnamese end in anger and growing frustration.

"Smugness of so many of them is appalling," said a junior American official. "If we were not at war it would be funny."

But a student in La Pagode, a coffee shop on Tu Do, observed: "Americans must fight for us so we can live in peace."

Had the student volunteered to join the army? "No, I must study, I am a student," he replied.

July 6, 1968

Search-and-Destroy Missions Gaining Flexibility

By GENE ROBERTS
Special to The New York Times

SAIGON, South Vietnam, Sept. 9—As American troops streamed into South Vietnam in 1966 and 1967, the peak build-up years, they moved out into the field in massive search-and-destroy operations.

Almost immediately critics said this was the wrong way to fight a war in a country with dense tropical jungle, rugged mountains, vast swamps and abundant escape routes to neighboring countries.

Today, the military is doing more searching and destroying than ever, but doing it—many officers say—with more flexibility and with less "thrashing about in the jungles."

The trend now is away from prolonged and massive infantry sweeps and toward searching with electronic devices and more small reconnaissance patrols.

Improved methods of detection, according to several generals, has meant that American bombers are becoming more effective in mountainous areas and jungles and thus, making it less imperative for battalions

Small Patrols and Electronic Devices Now Being Used to Rout Enemy in Vietnam

of infantrymen to go into these areas.

In less rugged terrain, the generals are increasingly breaking down their search-and-destroy missions into two operations. Small groups of men and helicopters go out in search of the enemy.

Once the enemy is found, troops are ferried in by helicopter in what officers call the pile-on technique.

The changes in tactics, field commanders say, are not a result of criticism or of new faces in the high command in Saigon. They are made possible, they say, by accumulated experience, increased mobility and improved technology, and also because the enemy has changed his tactics.

"The enemy hasn't stayed in his jungle base camps as much this year. He's moving in closer to the cities," Keith L. Ware, commander of the First Infantry Division said. "When he was spending most of his time in the jungle, he was as hard to find as a needle in a haystack. That's why you used to see more large, mutibattalion search-and-destroy sweeps.

Even when the enemy is in jungle base camps, the tendency now is to let the B-52's from Guam and Thailand try to do the job with bombloads that range as high as 27 tons a plane.

The generals occasionally send several battalions into the jungle once the enemy has been located, but there is increasing confidence that B-52's can do the job if the enemy can be pinpointed.

Maj. Gen. Ellis B. Williamson, now commander of the 25th Infantry Division, said:

"When I was out here before, we'd go into the jungles behind a B-52 strike and we'd find a dead snake or a dead monkey, but not much else." General Williamson commanded the first American brigade to arrive in South Vientam in 1965.

"Now we are finding evidence of successful strikes," he said at division headquarters at Cuchi. "The reason they are more effective is that we're getting better at telling the bombers where the enemy is."

"I don't want to oversell this, because we've got a long way to go in finding the enemy," the general went on. "But we are so much better than we used to be, it's hard not to be pleased. When I was here before, one of my soldiers used to say that B-52 strikes were the world's most expensive way of turning trees into matchsticks."

Special Sensing Equipment

Helicopters and airplanes that are outfitted with devices that detect heat from engines, body odors given off by humans and movements of large numbers of men and equipment are in heavy demand by field commanders, although some complain that they have yet to receive enough of the equipment, and that some of it is fragile and subject to frequent breakdowns.

When the equipment is available and working it often is used to check intelligence reports.

If, for example, agents say

167

they have seen enemy troops moving in a specific area, the sensing devices are flown over the jungle to try to pinpoint the location.

Some commanders use long-range foot patrols to double check the intelligence and sensor reports before calling in the bombers.

While many commanders will call in bombers on the basis of information from sensors, many are still reluctant to order a pile-on solely on the basis on sensors.

Maj. Gen. O. M. Barsanti, who commanded the 101st Airborne Division (Air Mobile) until he was returned to the United States recently, used dozens of small patrols to ferret out the enemy and set in motion what he called a cordon and pile-on operation.

"I'd send out maybe 50 little patrols and just let them wiggle around," General Barsanti said just before he left South Vietnam. "Then, if the enemy shot at some of those guys, I'd grab every soldier I could lay my hands on — cooks, clerks, and everybody—and throw me a tight cordon around the area.

"The idea was that once we found the enemy we didn't let him get away. We wouldn't try to kill or capture just part of the unit, we wanted to get every single man in there."

The officer generally ac-knowledged as having perfected the cordon and pile-on is Col. Henry Emerson of Milford, Pa., who commanded a brigade of the Ninth Infantry Division until he was hospitalized recently from burns suffered when his helicopter was shot down.

Combination of Methods

Colonel Emerson used not only infantry patrols but also detectors and radar to find the enemy. Then he often pounded the area with tear gas in an effort to drive the enemy into the open.

When the enemy's presence was confirmed, the colonel surrounded the area and called in bombers and artillery, fol-lowed by an infantry sweep. In one operation last month, his men killed 130 of the enemy.

The secret to an effective cordon and pile-on, Colonel Emerson said, is speed and mobility.

"If you want to get the enemy before he gets away then you've got to surround him fast," the colonel said. "And the fastest way is usually by helicopter."

"Everyone is employing cordon and pile-on now," said General Ware. "You reinforce as rapidly as you can to prevent him from fading away from you and to defeat him as rapidly as possible."

September 10, 1968

CAMBODIA ADMITS SANCTUARY ROLE

U.S. Quotes Sihanouk Report of Reds' Occupying Areas Next to South Vietnam

By BERNARD GWERTZMAN
Special to The New York Times

WASHINGTON, Oct. 4 — United States officials say that Cambodia has conceded indirectly what American military commanders have been saying for years: that North Vietnam and the Vietcong have been using Cambodian territory for attacks against South Vietnam.

According to monitored reports received here, top Cambodian officials have charged publicly that Vietnamese Communist forces are occupying parts of three Cambodian provinces that border on South Vietnam. This is believed by United States officials to be the first time Cambodia has made that admission.

A recent speech by Prince Norodom Sihanouk, the Cambodian Chief of State, and a report by Sosthene Fernandez, the Cambodian Secretary of State for National Security, were quoted by the United States officials. Prince Sihanouk told his nation that Cambodia was having trouble with Vietnamese Communists who were disregarding their pledges to recognize the integrity of the country's frontiers.

"The problem is a follows: Though having accepted recognition of our frontiers, the Vietnamese Reds have sent their troops to [the provinces of] Ratanakiri and Mondulkiri," he said.

The Prince said that "many of them have come to live on our territory."

"How will this affair affect us in the future?" he asked. "I do not dare solve this problem, so I bring it to the attention of the people and all high personages so that you may ponder it."

Report by Fernandez

Ratanakiri and Mondulkiri are sparsely inhabited provinces that the United States military command has said are used as supply routes into South Vietnam. A third province, Svayrieng, was mentioned in a report made by Mr. Fernandez on Thursday.

He said that in Svayrieng province—known as the "Duckbill" because it juts into South Vietnamese territory close to Saigon — "despite efforts of the provincial authorities to repel them, armed Vietnamese are continuing to install themselves on Khmer [Cambodian] territory near the frontier."

"These Vietnamese are becoming increasingly hostile to the local people and authorities." the report said.

Mr. Fernandez's report was broadcast by the Pnompenh radio and monitored by American sources.

Cambodia has consistently denied American allegations about the use of her territory by North Vietnamese and Vietcong forces. On occasion, Prince Sihanouk has said that the Vietcong might have intruded briefly, but that they always left promptly when asked to do so by

The New York Times   Oct. 5, 1968
Cambodian provinces where Vietcong troops and North Vietnamese are said to be operating are shown black.

Cambodian authorities.

State Department officials, studying these new reports, believe they reflect Prince Sihanouk's growing concern over stepped-up activity within his country by "Khmer Reds" as well as over the increased use of Cambodian territory by the Vietnamese troops, thereby endangering Cambodia's hard-sought neutrality.

There has been no indication that Prince Sihanouk is looking to the United States for help. In fact, he has criticized those Cambodian officials who think the country should seek American assistance.

But ever since the spring of 1967, when the Prince first mentioned the Khmer Reds' activity in the western province of Battambang, Cambodia's relations with Communist China and North Vietnam have cooled.

Prince Sihanouk has asserted that the Khmer Reds were being financed by Thai Communists living in Peking and by Hanoi.

Letter to Le Monde

In March of this year, Prince Sihanouk wrote to Le Monde, the Paris newspaper, and complained that "it is perfectly clear that Asian Communism does not permit us any longer to stay neutral and withdrawn from the conflict between the Chinese-Vietnamese and the Americans."

"Not being able to make of us—who do not intend to die for Hanoi or Peking any more than for Washington — allies supporting it unconditionally, Asian Communism strives to overthrow our regime from within," the Prince said.

In his speeches around the countryside, he has increased his attacks on the Communists, prompted, in part, by the invasion of Czechoslovakia.

He criticized some local Communists who said Cambodia "can have national, independent Communism."

"Communist Czechoslovakia tried to become independent but has been denied and has been told: 'You have no right to independence, and you are not entitled to shape your domestic policy according to your domestic policy according to your desire,'" he said.

October 5, 1968

ATTACKS ON NORTH VIETNAM HALT TODAY

PEACE CALLED AIM

Saigon and N.L.F. Can Join in the Enlarged Paris Discussions

By NEIL SHEEHAN
Special to The New York Times
WASHINGTON, Oct. 31—President Johnson announced tonight that he was ordering a complete halt to all American air, naval and artillery bombardment of North Vietnam as of 8 A.M. Friday, Eastern stand-ard time (9 P.M., Vietnam time).

"I have reached this decision on the basis of the develop-ments in the Paris talks," the President said, "and I have reached it in the belief that this action can lead to progress to-ward a peaceful settlement of the Vietnamese war."

"What we now expect—what we have a right to expect," the President said in a television boradcast, "are prompt, pro-ductive, serious and intensive negotiations in an atmosphere that is conducive to progress."

Face Shows Fatigue

His face showed fatigue as he made the announcement cul-minating weeks of secret nego-tiations.

Mr. Johnson did not an-nounce any reciprocal military commitments from North Viet-nam, which he has often said he must have in order to halt the air and naval bombardment that began on Feb. 7, 1965.

Washington officials said the bombing of infiltration trails in Laos would continue and that there was no prohibition against reconnaissance flights over North Vietnam.

'Reason to Believe' Foe

Senior Administration sources said the United States had "rea-son to believe" North Vietnam would not escalate the war in South Vietnam as a result of the bombing cessation.

They said Hanoi "clearly un-derstood" that Mr. Johnson would resume the bombing if it attacked South Vietnamese population centers or took mili-tary advantage of the demili-tarized zone.

On its side, North Vietnam had apparently not obtained the unconditional bombing halt it has consistently demanded.

Mr. Johnson said that in ex-change for the bombing halt Hanoi had agreed to accept participation of the South Viet-namese Government at the Paris talks and the United States had in turn accepted the Paris talks and the United States had in turn accepted the participation of the South Viet-nam National Liberation Front, the Vietcong guerrillas.

November 1, 1968

EXPANDED VIETNAM TALKS BEGIN IN PARIS TOMORROW; ROUND TABLE AGREED UPON

DEADLOCK ENDED

Washington and Hanoi Concur on Seating After 10 Weeks

By PAUL HOFMANN
Special to The New York Times
PARIS, Jan. 16—An agree-ment was announced here to-day for the opening of the ex-panded talks on the Vietnam war. The first session is to be held Saturday at 10:30 A.M. (4:30 A.M., New York time).

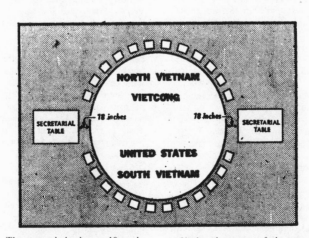

The accord broke a 10-week deadlock on procedural matters that had blocked negotiations on substantive issues by the participants in the conflict.

Under the terms of the agree-ment, representatives of the United States, South Vietnam, North Vietnam and the National Liberation Front or Vietcong, will sit at a circular table with-out nameplates, flags or mark-ings.

Two rectangular tables, meas-uring about 3 feet by 4½ feet, will be placed 18 inches from the circular table at opposite sides.

Shape of Table an Issue

The seating arrangements were the main stumbling block to the expanded talks.

The Saigon regime and Wash-ington contended that the round-table proposal would give the Front the same status as South Vietnam and insisted on some device to indicate the existence of only two sides. This would buttress their con-tention that the Vietcong guer-rillas were only agents of North Vietnam.

Today's agreement provided a seating formula elastic enough for the allies to speak of two sides and for the enemy to speak of a four-sided affair. This ambiguity permits all par-ticipants to claim victory(in the protocol dispute.

Saturday's meeting will take up—and possibly dispose of—the question of procedures to be followed in substantive four-way negotiations on the war.

W. Averell Harriman, the departing head of the United States delegation, and other American officials here said they hoped that the procedural matters could be taken care of quickly. This could lead to negotiations on troop with-drawals, reduction in the level of fighting, a cease-fire, the status of the demilitarized zone at the border between North and South Vietnam and con-trols along South Vietnam's borders with Laos and Cam-bodia.

Negotiations may also deal with the political future of South Vietnam and, perhaps, reunification of the South and North.

Eventually, a larger con-ference may provide interna-tional guarantees for any agreements.

Among the procedural ques-tions to be discussed at the broadened talks Saturday is a name for the conference.

The Saigon regime speaks of a "Meeting on Vietnam" in Paris, Hanoi and the Vietcong term the parley the "Paris Conference on Vietnam," and the United States uses officially such names as "Vietnam Peace Talks," or "Vietnam Confer-ence."

January 17, 1969

U.S. Center in Vietnam Seeking To Comfort Wronged Civilians

DONGTAM, South Vietnam, Jan. 19 (UPI)—The United States command has begun a modest operation of apology to some of the thousands of Viet-namese who have been em-bittered and humiliated by in-terrogation and harassment.

The operation is conducted from what is called the In-nocent Civilian Center.

There, the numbers affected are kept on file. Through last week, 738 "innocent civilians" had been treated as special guests before their release from custody as suspected members of the Vietcong.

Established last June at the United States Ninth Infantry Division base at Dongtam, 37 miles southwest of Saigon, the motel-like center is the divi-sion's way of admitting that a mistake has been made.

A Sensitive Period

One of the most sensitive contacts between soldier and civilian in the Vietnam war comes during the interrogation following cordon operations in populous areas. Depending on how it was handled, this con-tact can either dispel or rein-force Vietcong horror 'tales about how Americans treat civilians.

"When I first started work-ing in the civic action pro-gram" an Army officer said, "the Vietcong used to tell the civilians I ate babies. Many of them believed it."

With this in mind, the Ninth Infantry established its Inno-cent Civilian Center.

"We treat them as guests," said Maj. Don Stiles, 35 years old, of Terrell, Tex. "The cen-ter is the last step in their re-turn home, and we want to make sure we don't leave a bad taste in their mouths."

While transportation is being arranged to return the cleared Vietcong suspects to their homes, a South Vietnamese in-terpreter explains to them that they were detained because it was otherwise impossible to tell who belonged to the Vietcong. He says that the Americans are sorry about the inconvenience, and tries to criticize the enemy subtly.

Movies Every Night

The civilians—mostly old men and women—stay at the 50-bed facility from a few hours to two days, or until transporta-tion home is available. They are fed and given a health kit with soap and toothpaste. Medical attention is provided. Movies are shown every night.

"Most of them are as scared as hell when they're brought in for questioning," Major Stiles said. "They have been told some pretty bad stories by the Vietcong about how we sup-posedly treat civilians.

"So everything we can do to prove the Vietcong liars pays off" he continued. "Some of the civilians already have given us valuable intelligence infor-mation."

January 20, 1969

22 DIE IN SAIGON IN ROCKET ATTACK; SCORES WOUNDED

Slum Neighborhood Heavily Shelled — Vietcong Radio Says Tempo Will Rise

---

CAPITAL HIT 4TH TIME

At Least 7 Missiles Fired— Shooting at Premier Laid to Guerrilla Agent

---

Special to The New York Times

SAIGON, South Vietnam, Thursday, March 6—The heav-iest and most damaging rocket attack of the year hit Saigon early this morning, killing at least 22 civilians and wounding scores.

Military sources said that the number of deaths might reach 35 when final police and hospital reports were received.

The enemy fired at least seven rockets into the capital. Most of them landed in a dense-ly populated slum neighborhood on the city's fringes.

The bombardment came less than 24 hours after President Nixon said that the United States "will not tolerate a con-tinuation of this kind of at-tack without some response that will be appropriate."

[The Vietcong radio said in a broadcast heard in Hong Kong that the offensive would not stop and that the tempo of ground fighting would in-crease. Guerrilla forces must keep up their fighting spirit for weeks to come, the broad-cast added, according to Agence France-Presse.]

Offensive Began Feb. 23

The attack this morning was the fourth on the capital since the enemy offensive began Feb. 23.

In another aspect of the of-fensive, a spokesman for Pre-mier Tran Van Huong said that he was the target of a Vietcong assassination plot yesterday.

The police arrested four men but had not identified them as Vietcong agents.

The most damaging explo-sion today occured in a densely populated block of houses not far from the city's docks. Eleven bodies were carried out through the narrow footpaths that thread between the houses. Military sources said the rock-ets all came from the east, as did the three earlier attacks of the offensive.

At the scene of the explo-sions, firemen uncovered the body of an old woman's hus-band and carried it out of the wreckage. After her first cry of grief, the woman followed silently behind the litter, her head bowed and her palms pressed together at her fore-head in a Buddhist prayer.

A Halting Argument

Nearby, a man started a tear-ful, halting argument with his dead sister's husband. He be-labored his brother-in-law with not being in the house at the time of the blast and with fail-ing to protect his family.

Early reports showed that the enemy fired about 35 mor-tar and rocket barrages through-

The New York Times   March 6, 1969

out the country last night. Most of the targets were al-lied military installations, United States Army sources said. Over-all damage and casualties in the other attacks were reported to have been light.

In other action in South Vietnam, American infantry forces fought North Vietnamese regulars early yesterday morn-ing 10 hours after ending an all-day fight with the same enemy force.

The fight took place 5 miles northeast of Trangbang and 29 miles northwest of Saigon, in an area beset by enemy troops.

The infantrymen fought the green-uniformed North Vietnamese battalion until dusk Tuesday, and camped on the battlefield for the night. At 4:45 A.M. their camp was struck by mortar fire and then attacked by the North Vietnamese infantry and the weary American troops got up to fight again.

Helicopter gunships and artillery from nearby allied bases backed up the infantrymen until the enemy retreated at dawn.

In a search of the battlefield afterward, the Americans found the bodies of 66 enemy soldiers, and a number of weapons. An American report said that 3 United States soldiers died in the attack and 11 had been wounded.

A total of 84 bodies of North Vietnamese soldiers were left on the field after Tuesday's fight, and the United States force lost 3 killed and 19 wounded, an American military communiqué said.

The South Vietnamese national police reported that 249 Vietnamese civilians had been killed in terrorist incidents, which include shellings, during the first week of the offensive. In addition, 660 were wounded and 86 were kidnapped.

The report added that since the first of the year, 1,009 civilians were killed by terrorists, 2,708 were wounded and 1,885 abducted.

In the attack on the Premier, the spokesman for his office said this morning that a man arrested after the shooting in central Saigon confessed to the police that he was a member of the Vietcong.

The man led the police to a house in Saigon where they found three Chinese-made automatic pistols and about six pounds of plastic explosive, the spokesman added.

Several pistol shots were fired at the 66-year-old Premier as he was being driven home to lunch, and a pedicab carrying an explosive charge—possibly a mine with a directed charge—was wheeled toward his car.

None of the shots hit Mr. Huong or his car and the explosive failed to detonate.

Security police who normally escort Mr. Huong in four jeeps returned the fire of the assassins and swarmed after them.

At the scene of the incident —a tree-shaded boulevard adjacent to the Premier's office and two blocks from the United States Embassy — the police said that they had arrested four men. A spokesman for the Premier said that one of them, the man who later confessed to the police, was wearing the uniform of the South Vietnamese Army.

Mr. Huong was attacked only a day after the fatal shooting of Dr. Tran Anh, the acting dean of the University of Saigon's faculty of medicine, on a sidewalk a few blocks from his home in Cholon, the Chinese quarter of Saigon.

Dr. Anh had been a close friend of Dr. Le Minh Tri, the Minister of Education who died after a hand grenade exploded in his sedan in downtown Saigon two months ago.

Dr. Anh and Dr. Tri shared progressive and pro-American views on education that sometimes found opposition on the French-founded campuses of South Vietnam. Both had received anonymous letters that threatened their lives.

March 6, 1969

NIXON TO REDUCE VIETNAM FORCE, PULLING OUT 25,000 G.I.'S BY AUG. 31;

A MIDWAY ACCORD

Leaders Agree First Cutbacks Will Begin Within 30 Days

By HEDRICK SMITH
Special to The New York Times

MIDWAY ISLAND, June 8—President Nixon met with President Nguyen Van Thieu of South Vietnam today and announced that 25,000 American soldiers would be withdrawn from Vietnam before the end of August.

After the first two hours of five hours of talks on this Pacific island, Mr. Nixon emerged to declare that the Presidents had agreed that troop withdrawals would begin within 30 days.

And with Mr. Thieu standing at his side, Mr. Nixon held out the hope of further reductions in the 540,000-man American force when this first phase was completed.

Replacements Available

He said that the equivalent of a combat division could leave Vietnam because of progress in the training and equipping of South Vietnam's Army.

Both President Nixon and President Thieu underscored the point that the American forces being withdrawn would be replaced in the field by South Vietnamese forces.

Mr. Nixon termed the withdrawal a "significant step forward" toward a lasting peace in Vietnam. At the end of the five-hour conference, Mr. Thieu said that the step was "good news for the American people that Vietnamese forces replace United States combat forces."

Both in announcing the troop withdrawal and in presenting a joint statement to the press at the end of their meeting, the two leaders sought to emphasize their solidarity.

Differences Not Mentioned

Their joint communiqué made no allusion to differences in approach to the Paris negotiations, and President Thieu remarked afterward that it was "not true" that he had come to Midway to thresh out differences with the new American Administration. But little

Associated Press
MEET AT MIDWAY: President Nixon and President Nguyen Van Thieu of South Vietnam after their arrival.

was noted in the public statements of either man that might quiet Saigon's fears about the ultimate intentions of the United States leadership.

Although the announcement of the troop withdrawal was aimed at placating domestic critics of the war and putting pressure on North Vietnam and the Vietcong to negotiate more seriously in Paris by seeking to demonstrate South Vietnam's growing strength, Mr. Nixon mentioned neither American war critics nor the enemy.

As if pleading for more patience from the American pub-

June 9, 1969

NIXON PLANS CUT IN MILITARY ROLE FOR U.S. IN ASIA

By ROBERT B. SEMPLE Jr.
Special to The New York Times

MANILA, Saturday, July 26—President Nixon declared yesterday that the United States would not be enticed into future wars like the one in Vietnam and would redesign and reduce its military commitments throughout non-Communist Asia.

Mr. Nixon promised, however, that the United States would continue to play a sizable role in the Pacific and would not forsake its treaty commitments.

This was the essence of views put forward by the President in an informal news conference before he set forth from Guam on the diplomatic leg of his global journey

President Exhilarated

The President, who seemed exhilarated by the successful moon venture of Apollo 11, arrived here today for the first foreign stop of a tour taking him to Indonesia, Thailand, India, Pakistan, Rumania and, briefly, Britain.

During his short stop in Guam, Mr. Nixon set forth in considerable detail the purposes of his week-and-a-half trip and disclosed major points he would be making to the Asian leaders. He spoke for publication but asked that his words not be directly quoted.

The President defined his Asian policy in more specific and forceful terms than at any time since taking office. Some of his views had been expressed earlier in articles and in the political campaign last fall, but he went further today in emphasizing his intention of limiting United States commitments.

New Aid Is Hinted

Specifically, he said he might order a reduction of military operations in South Vietnam if that would help the negotiations to end the war.

The President also hinted that new forms of economic aid to the Asian nations might soon be forthcoming, but — perhaps mindful of growing ill will toward foreign aid at home and the constraints that inflation has placed on new Government spending—he carefully avoided promising an increase in aid.

The President spent the major part of his news conference, held at the naval officers' club in Guam, on questions relating to Vietnam and Asia, demonstrating that despite all the early publicity devoted to visit he will pay to Rumania Aug. 2, he himself was placing highest priority on the Asian part of the journey. Yet in the course of his unusually relaxed and unusually long session—it last 52 minutes, compared with his average news-conference length of 30 minutes—Mr. Nixon also made these points:

¶He remains willing to participate in a top-level meeting with the Soviet Union to talk about the Vietnam war, the Middle Eastern crisis and the arms race, but only if such a meeting were to be preceded by lower-level consultations and held out some promise of success.

¶While he most wishes for a summit meeting to enlist the Soviet Union in the search for an end of the war, he doubts that Moscow would work for a settlement, even if it wants one, in so public and highly visible a forum.

¶There is no basis for what he called speculation that his visit to Rumania would be an affront to either the Soviet Union or Communist China; instead, it is designed to develop communication with Eastern European nations.

¶Recent charges by some Senators that the United States had struck a secret defense agreement with Thailand are without foundation.

Mr. Nixon acknowledged at the outset his consuming interest in the future of Asia after the end of the war in Vietnam. He said further that the Asians were equally interested in whether the United States would continue to play a significant role in their area or whether, like the French, British and Dutch, it would withdraw from the Pacific and play a minor part.

He conceded that many Americans were extremely frustrated by the Vietnam war and, in their frustration, wished for a substantial reduction of Amer-

ica's Pacific commitments. He indicated by his tone that he understood these frustrations and to a certain extent sympathized with them.

But he argued that the United States could not withdraw from its Asian commitments, first because withdrawal might well pave the way for other wars; and second, because the United States itself is a Pacific power with a major stake in Asian stability.

In answering subsequent questions, however, Mr. Nixon sought more clearly to define the future dimensions of that commitment. He asserted, for example, that except when Asian nations were threatened by a nuclear power such as Communist China, the United States would insist that both internal subversion and external aggression be dealt with increasingly by the Asians themselves.

Collective Security Urged

He said it was foolish to believe that the non-Communist Asian nations could soon devise collective security arrangements enabling them to defend themselves against Communism. Collective security now is a weak reed to lean on, he said, and it will take five to 10 years for the non-Communist Asian nations to devise adequate collective security arrangements among themselves.

This blunt assessment of the prospects for collective security prompted a question on what the United States would do in the event of another Vietnam situation in the five to 10 years in which the Asian nations would be struggling to devise mechanisms for self-protection. The President replied that such incidents would have to be judged case by case.

But he will consider each case very carefully, he asserted, with an eye to avoiding what he called creeping involvements that eventually submerge a great nation, as, he said, the Vietnam conflict has submerged the United States in emotional discord and economic strain.

To illustrate his point, the President recalled a line from his election campaign that he said he had used in every speech, drawing loud applause each time. He said the statement had been made to him by Mohammad Ayub Khan, former President of Pakistan, in 1964.

"The role of the United States in Vietnam or the Philippines, or Thailand, or any of these other countries which have internal subversion," the

statement went, "is to help them fight the war but not fight the war for them."

Mr. Nixon then declared, in answer to a question, that military assistance of all kinds, including the commitment of United States troops, would be reduced. He did not say how large such reductions would be, or how soon they would be carried out.

To compensate in part for the reduced military assistance, Mr. Nixon indicated that the United States would soon be suggesting initiatives on the economic side designed to add fresh momentum to what he said was the developing economic strength of non-Communist Asia. He promised that United States aid would be adequate to meet the challenge of Asian economic problems.

The President professed to see several hopeful signs that non-Communist Asia had recently become stronger, including rapid economic development. He rattled off an impressive list of statistics showing the economic growth of South Korea, Japan, Thailand, Indonesia, India and Pakistan.

Another sign, he said, was the dwindling capacity of Communist China to foment internal insurgencies in other countries. Early in the news conference, Mr. Nixon declared that China was the single biggest threat to stability in Asia, but later he expressed a conviction that the appeal of the Communist philosophy had dwindled in some Asian countries in the last 16 years. He cited Pakistan, India, Indonesia and Japan as examples.

The President returned to the same themes on his arrival at the Manila International Airport, where he was greeted by President and Mrs. Ferdinand E. Marcos and a large delegation of Filipino officials.

"I want to convey throughout the trip," he said, "the great sense of respect and affection which the people of the United States feel for their Asian neighbors and the readiness of my country to support the efforts of Asian nations to improve the life of their peoples. I will also offer the view that peace and progress in Asia must be shaped and protected primarily by Asian hands and that the contribution which my country can make to that process should come as a supplement to Asian energies and in response to Asian leadership."

July 26, 1969

Laos

A Forgotten War in a Land Cursed by Geography

The writer of the following dispatch is chief correspondent for Southeast Asia and recently visited Laos.

HONG KONG—The situation in Laos has been bad for years. But the problem had one virtue—bad as it was, it didn't seem to get worse.

Recently, however, even that one virtue has seemed to fade. The situation has deteriorated to the point that it might compound the already difficult United States position in Southeast Asia.

Last year and early this year, the combined North Vietnamese and indigenous Communist Pathet Lao forces cleared out virtually all of the pro-Government Meo hill-tribe guerrilla positions in northeast Laos which had harassed the Communists for many years and which had protected clandestine American helicopter and fixed-wing airplane "landing sites" in the remote mountains. Then, this summer, strong North Vietnamese-Pathet Lao forces overran Muongsuoi near the strategic Plain of Jars and scattered the pro-Government neutralist" army battalions headquartered there.

Finally, the week before last, the North Vietnamese Government charged that the United States had "invaded" Laos with 12,000 troops and had started a separate war there. The charge was untrue, but the motives behind it may be grave. The North Vietnamese may have made the accusation to justify further military moves by what the Communists call the "patriotic" forces in Laos.

Laos was ostensibly "neutralized" by international agreement in 1962 and slightly more than 600 American Special Forces troops and other combat troops who had been advising the right-wing Vientiane regime's army formally withdrew through a checkpoint manned by the International Commission. The much larger North Vietnamese force that had assisted the Pathet Lao sent only a token handful of 41 persons through an I.C.C. checkpoint, but most of the rest did withdrew via other routes.

Souvanna's Position

Prince Souvanna Phouma, a neutralist who has always believed that the unwarlike La-

POINTS OF INTENSIFIED CONFLICT

Communist forces seized town dominating crossroads.

North Vietnamese and Pathet Lao routed pro-government tribes.

The Pathet Lao has stabilized its positions in this strategic area.

To protect Thailand, U. S. wants Mekong clear of Communists.

North Vietnam needs control of supply route to South Vietnam.

Rising tension in strategically located Laos is compounding U.S. problems in Southeast Asia.

otians could solve their own problems if the world left them alone, assumed leadership of a coalition. In the tripartite Cabinet, Mr. Souvanna's neutralists had 11 seats to four each for the Pathet Lao and the rightists.

Laos was not betrayed so much by a bad treaty as by geography. North Vietnam needed a secure infiltration corridor in eastern Laos—the Ho Chi Minh trail—for the buildup in South Vietnam that was to come, and a secure buffer in northeast Laos against its western border. The United States needed to keep the Mekong River valley in non-Communist hands to protect Thailand.

The first major violations of the 1962 agreement came in

1963 when Communist forces began to try to subvert the neutralist military forces still on the Plain of Jars and finally drove them westward to Muongsuoi. By 1964, the civil war had resumed—in its desultory fashion — and at Prince Souvanna's request, the United States had made its first air strikes against Communist positions.

The North Vietnamese violations of the 1962 neutralization agreement have been massive in terms of manpower—more than 40,000 North Vietnamese soldiers are now estimated to be in Laos. The United States violations were requested by the Souvanna Government and were a response; but they were unquestionably violations. In terms of firepower, they have been massive, too, and military men have said that American air raids have been "critical" in preserving the Laotian Government's position.

The United States has never stationed any combat units in Laos, except at clandestine helicopter pads associated with the air war over North Vietnam; but it has permitted raids on the Ho Chi Minh trail by American-led special operations groups from Vietnam and the parachute insertion of elite behind-the-lines trail watchers. It has also stationed 70 "military attachés" in Laos to advise the Royal Army, and civilian American pilots fly the hazardous supply missions to isolated Laotian outposts.

All of this was tolerable because neither side seemed to want a showdown in Laos. The civil war followed an annual ritual. Each wet season the Government forces would "nibble" at Communist positions, taking advantage of the Communist lack of airpower and loss of ground mobility caused by the rains. Each dry season the Communists would throw the Government forces out of the positions they had taken—and then stop. This wet season, however, they did not stop but took Muongsuoi and moved to consolidate their positions in many areas.

Potentially Ominous

There is yet no clear sign that the Communists plan to try to capture cities or the Mekong Valley, but the situation is potentially more ominous than it has been for years. The accusation of a 12,000-man American "invasion" may have been a new ploy in a persistent Communist attempt to get the bombing of "liberated Laos" stopped. Or it may only be another move to discredit Prince Souvanna as a "neutralist" and kill hopes that the coalition can be restored when the Vietnam war ends and thus diminishes Laos's most important curse—its geography and strategic importance.

—CHARLES MOHR

August 10, 1969

SUPPORT BY U.S. ALTERS LAOS WAR

Territory Is No Longer Goal in Hit-and-Run Conflict

By T. D. ALLMAN
Special to The New York Times

VIENTIANE, Laos, Sept. 30— As a result of a general increase in United States bombing and logistical support in Laos, following Communist gains earlier this year, many factors governing the Laotian conflict have been altered.

What was essentially a conventional war for control of territory has become a hit-and-run war of attrition.

The main United States targets now, according to sources in both the Laotian Government and the Pathet Lao rebels, are the rebel economy and social fabric.

The restraints on the United States in bombing Laotian targets have been significantly relaxed over the last six months.

The daily total of United States bombing sorties has risen to the hundreds with United States jets often refueling over Laos rather than returning to their Thai or South Vietnamese bases as they continue their round-the-clock search for targets.

According to Laotian sources, the object now "is to hit the enemy wherever he is" and to allow no sanctuary.

Until early this spring, when North Vietnamese troops began a series of advances in northeast Laos, the Laotian war was a strictly limited contest between Laotian forces, backed by the United States and the Pathet Lao, supported by the North Vietnamese. There was a relatively large but static number of North Vietnamese troops in Laos, according to United States intelligence estimates, totaling about 48,000 men. Intensive but selective United States bombing of Pathet Lao territory was aimed at North Vietnamese supply routes — both to South Vietnam and to the Laotian front—and at concentrations of enemy troops. Civilian population centers and farmland were largely spared.

Supply and Training Mission

Americans were involved in the supply training and logistic support for the Royal Laotian armed forces, but the United States effort, like the North Vietnamese effort, was directed toward helping a Laotian ally hold or regain relatively small parcels of territory.

This almost classic limited war, however, created serious problems for the United States and the Laotian Government this year. The Communists, within the limited-war contact, were able to deal the Government of Prince Souvanna Phouma several serious defeats.

Since both sides concede that territorial control would have a bearing on the makeup of a postwar Laotian coalition government, the rebel gains increased the likelihood that the United States and the Laotian Government might ultimately be forced to make political concessions as part of an eventual Laotian peace settlement.

The war has also become increasingly a war for control of populations rather than control of territory. With United States bombers able to destroy, almost at will, any given town, bridge, road or concentration of enemy soldiers or civilians, control of specific territory has become increasingly less important.

Refugees from the Plaine des Jarres area say that during recent months most open spaces have been evacuated. Both civilians and soldiers have retreated into the forests or hills and frequently spend most of the daylight hours in caves or tunnels. Refugees said they could only plow their fields at night because they were unsafe during the day.

"So long as the United States bombing continues at its new level," a European diplomat said here this week, "so-called Communist territory is little but a shooting range. They find it difficult to move troops and supplies, agricultural production drops, the civilian populations become upset. They lose their tax and labor base. That is why the Pathet Lao continue to make a cessation of United States bombing the prerequisite of any peace talks."

The bombing has contributed directly to the production of refugees, many of whom have been evacuated from Communist-held territory, usually in United States aircraft. The Laotian war, according to Government figures, so far has produced more than 600,000 refugees, or about a quarter of the population of the kingdom.

Refugees invariably cite two main reasons for their willingness to leave their homes and resettle in new areas: the bombing and the fact that the Pathet Lao rebels force every able-bodied man and woman to work as much as a month a year carrying supplies and arms toward the front.

The bombing, by creating refugees, deprives the Communists of their chief source of food and transport. The population of the Pathet Lao zone has been declining for several years and the Pathet Lao find it increasingly difficult to fight a "people's war" with fewer and fewer people. The exodus from territory being bombed has served to increase Pathet Lao dependency on the North Vietnamese.

October 1, 1969

HO CHI MINH DEAD AT 79;

HAS HEART ATTACK

He Won Independence for Nation and Led War Against U.S.

By TILLMAN DURDIN
Special to The New York Times

HONG KONG, Thursday, Sept. 4—President Ho Chi Minh of North Vietnam died yesterday morning in Hanoi at the age of 79.

A Hanoi radio report at 7 A.M. this morning announced that he succumbed at 9:47 A.M. Hanoi time yesterday "after a very sudden, serious heart attack."

The radio disclosed only at 4 A.M. yesterday that President Ho had been gravely ill for several weeks and was under emergency treatment day and night by "a collective of professors and medical doctors.".

There was no explanation for the delay of almost 24 hours in announcing the President's death.

White House Silent

Under the North Vietnamese Constitution, the Vice President take over if the President dies or is incapacitated, pending a

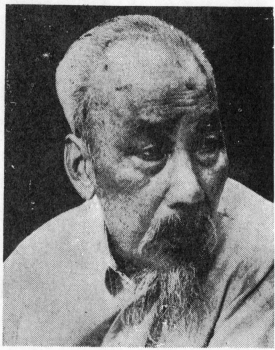

Camera Press-Pix

Ho Chi Minh

new election. The Vice President is an obscure figure, Ton Duc Thang, 81.

[In San Clemente, Calif., the Western White House said that President Nixon would have no comment on Mr. Ho's death.]

The Hanoi announcement, in the form of a communiqué issued in the name of the Central Committee of the Vietnam Workers (Communist) party,

the Standing Committee of the National Assembly and the Council of Ministers, said:

"We feel boundless grief in informing the entire party and the entire Vietnamese people that Comrade Ho Chi Minh, President of the Central Committee of the Vietnam Workers party and President of the Democratic Republic of Vietnam, passed away at 9:47, Sept. 3, 1969, after a very sudden,

serious heart attack at the age of 79.

"Everybody has done his best, determined to cure the President at all costs. But due to his advanced age President Ho Chi Minh has departed from us." After the first announcement of Mr. Ho's death, the Hanoi radio was being organized "with the most solemn rites of our country" and that a period of mourning from today until next Wednesday had been fixed.

A further special communiqué recapitulated the account of the death and described Mr. Ho as "the great, beloved leader of our Vietnamese working class and nation who all his life devotedly served the revolution, the people and the fatherland."

A thin, gaunt and stooped bachelor with a mustache and wispy beard, Mr. Ho was the prime mover of revolution in Vietnam for almost half a century and enjoyed enormous prestige even among anti-Communist Vietnamese.

He was titular head of the North Vietnamese Government and President as well of the Central Committee of the party, and though ill health in recent years impaired his functioning, he was the symbol of unity and continued struggle over South Vietnam.

Called for Sacrifices

Observers do not believe he had been making the day-to-day decisions for the Vietnamese Communists for the last year or two, but he frequently visited troops and made numerous declarations exhorting all Vietnamese to the maximum effort and sacrifice in the war.

September 4, 1969

Ho Chi Minh Was Noted for Success in Blending Nationalism and Communism

By ALDEN WHITMAN

Among 20th-century statesmen, Ho Chi Minh was remarkable both for the tenacity and patience with which he pursued his goal of Vietnamese independence and for his success in blending Communism with nationalism.

From his youth Ho espoused freedom for the French colony of Vietnam. He persevered through years when his chances of attaining his objective were so minuscule as to seem ridiculous. Ultimately, he organized the defeat of the French in 1954 in the historic battle of Dienbienphu. This battle, a triumph

of guerrilla strategy, came nine years after he was named President of the Democratic Republic of Vietnam.

After the supposed temporary division of Vietnam at the 17th parallel by the Geneva Agreement of 1954 and after that division became hardened by United States support of Ngo

Dinh Diem in the South, Ho led his countrymen in the North against the onslaughts of American military might. In the war, Ho's capital of Hanoi, among other cities, was repeatedly bombed by American planes.

At the same time Ho was an inspiration for the National Liberation Front, or Vietcong, which operated in South Vietnam in the long, bloody and costly conflict against the Saigon regime and its American allies.

In the war, in which the United States became increasingly involved, especially after 1964, Ho maintained an exquisite balance in his relations with the Soviet Union and the People's Republic of China. These Communist countries, at ideological sword's points, were Ho's principal suppliers of foodstuffs and war goods. It was a measure of his diplomacy that he kept on friendly terms with each.

Small and Frail

To the 19 million people north of the 17th parallel and to other millions below it, the small, frail, ivorylike figure of Ho, with its long ascetic face, straggly goatee, sunken cheeks and luminous eyes, was that of a patriarch, the George Washington of his nation. Although his name was not attached to public squares, buildings, factories, airports or monuments, his magnetism was undoubted, as was the affection that the average citizen had for him.

He was universally called "Uncle Ho," a sobriquet also used in the North Vietnamese press. Before the exigencies of war confined him to official duties, Ho regularly visited villages and towns. Simply clad, he was especially fond of dropping into schools and chatting with the children. Westerners who knew him were convinced that, whatever his guile in larger political matters, there was no pose in his expressions of feeling for the common people.

Indeed, Ho's personal popularity was such that it was generally conceded, even by many of his political foes, that Vietnam would have been unified under his leadership had the countrywide elections pledged at Geneva taken place. As it was, major segments of South Vietnam were effectively controlled by the National Liberation Front despite the presence of hundreds of thousands of American troops.

Intelligent, resourceful and dedicated, though ruthless, Ho created a favorable impression on many of those who dealt with him. One such was Harry Ashmore of the Center for the Study of Democratic Institutions and former editor of The Arkansas Gazette.

Mr. Ashmore and the late William C. Baggs, editor of The Miami News, were among the last Americans to talk with Ho at length when they visited Hanoi in early 1967.

"Ho was a courtly, urbane, highly sophisticated man with a gentle manner and without personal venom," Mr. Ashmore recalled in a recent interview. At the meeting Ho was dressed in his characteristic high-necked

white pajama type of garment, called a cu-nao, and he wore open-toed rubber sandals. He chain-smoked cigarettes, American-made Salems.

Adept in English

Their hour-long conversation started out in Vietnamese with an interpreter, Mr. Ashmore said, but soon shifted to English. Ho astonished Mr. Ashmore by his adeptness in English, which was one of several languages—the principal others were Chinese, French, German and Russian—in which he was fluent.

At one point Ho reminded Mr. Ashmore and Mr. Baggs that he had once been in the United States. "I think I know the American people," Ho said, "and I don't understand how they can support their involvement in this war. Is the Statue of Liberty standing on her head?"

This was a rhetorical question that Ho also posed to other Americans in an effort to point up what to his mind was an inconsistency: a colonial people who had gained independence in a revolution were fighting to suppress the independence of another colonial people.

Ho's knowledge of American history was keen, and he put it to advantage in the summer of 1945 when he was writing the

Declaration of Independence of the Democratic Republic of Vietnam. He remembered the contents of the American Declaration of Independence, but not its precise wording. From an American military mission then working with him he tried in vain to obtain a copy of the document, and when none could supply it Ho paraphrased it out of his recollections.

Thus his Declaration begins, "All men are created equal; they are endowed by their Creator with certain inalienable Rights; among these are Life, Liberty, and the pursuit of Happiness." After explaining that this meant that "all the peoples on the earth are equal from birth, all the peoples have a right to live, to be happy and free," Ho went on to enumerate, in the manner of the American Declaration, the grievances of his people and to proclaim their independence.

'Likable and Friendly'

Apart from Americans, Ho struck a spark with many others who came in contact with him over the years. "Extraordinarily likable and friendly" was the description of Jawaharlal Nehru, the Indian leader. Paul Mus, the French Orientalist who conducted delicate talks with Ho in 1946 and 1947, found him an "intransigent and incorruptible revolutionary, à la Saint Just."

Marc Riboud—Magnum

With Mr. Dong, whom he called his "favorite nephew," in garden of the former palace of French Governors, Hanoi.

A French naval commander who observed the slender Vietnamese for the three weeks he was a ship's passenger concluded that Ho was an "intelligent and charming man who is also a passionate idealist entirely devoted to the cause he has espoused" and a person with "naïve faith in the politico-social slogans of our times and, generally, in everything that is printed."

Ho was an enormously pragmatic Communist, a doer rather than a theoretician. His speeches and articles were brought together in a four-volume "Selected Works of Ho Chi Minh" issued in Hanoi between 1960 and 1962. The late Bernard B. Fall, an American authority on Vietnam, published a collection of these in English in 1967 under the title "Ho Chi Minh on Revolution." They are simply and clearly worded documents, most of them agitational or polemical in nature and hardly likely to add to the body of Marxist doctrine.

Like Mao Tse-tung, a fellow Communist leader, Ho composed poetry, some of it considered quite affecting. One of his poems, written when he was a prisoner of the Chinese Nationalists in 1942-43, is

called "Autumn Night" and reads in translation by Aileen Palmer:

In front of the gate, the guard stands with his rifle.
Above, untidy clouds are carrying away the moon.
The bedbugs are swarming around like army tanks on maneuvers,
While the mosquitoes form squadrons, attacking like fighter planes.
My heart travels a thousand li toward my native land.
My dream intertwines with sadness like a skein of a thousand threads.
Innocent, I have now endured a whole year in prison.
Using my tears for ink, I turn my thoughts into verses.

Ho's rise to power and world eminence was not a fully documented story. On the contrary, its details at some crucial points are imprecise. This led at one time to the suspicion that there were two Hos, a notion that was discounted by the French Sûreté when it compared photographs of the early and the late Ho.

One explanation for the confusion is that Ho used about a dozen aliases, of which Ho Ch[i]

Minh (which can be translated as Ho, the Shedder of Light) was but one. Another was Ho's own reluctance to disclose biographical information. "You know, I am an old man, and an old man likes to hold on to his little mysteries," he told Mr. Fall. With a twinkle, he continued, "Wait until I'm dead. Then you can write about me all you want."

Nonetheless, Mr. Fall reported, before he left Hanoi he received a brief, unsigned summary of Ho's life "obviously delivered on the old man's instructions."

Despite Ho's apparent self-effacement, he did have a touch of personal vanity. Mr. Fall recalled having shown the Vietnamese leader a sketch of him by Mrs. Fall. "Yes, that is very good. That looks very much like me," Ho exclaimed. He took a bouquet of flowers from a nearby table and, handing it to Mr. Fall, said:

"Tell her for me that the drawing is very good and give her the bouquet and kiss her on both cheeks for me."

Although there is some uncertainty over Ho's birth date, the most reliable evidence indicates he was born May 19, 1890, in Kimlien, a village in Nghe-An Province in central Vietnam. Many sources give his true name as Nguyen Ai Quoc, or Nguyen the Patriot. However, Wilfred Burchett, an Australian-born correspondent who knew Ho well, believes (and it is now generally accepted) that Ho's birth name was Nguyen Tat Thanh.

He was said to be the youngest of three children. His father was only slightly better off than the rice peasants of the area, but he was apparently a man of some determination, for by rote learning he passed examinations that gave him a job in the imperial administration just when the French rule was beginning.

An ardent nationalist, Ho's father refused to learn French, the language of the conquerors of his country, and joined anti-French secret societies. Young Ho got his first underground experience as his father's messenger in the anti-French network. Shortly, the father lost his Government job and became a healer, dispensing traditional Oriental potions.

Ho's mother was believed to have been of peasant origin, but he never spoke of her.

Attended Lycée

Ho received his basic education from his father and from the village school, going on to a few years of high school at the Lycée Quoc-Hoc in the old imperial capital of Hue. This institution, founded by the father of Ngo Dinh Diem, was designed to perpetuate Vietnamese national traditions. It had a distinguished roster of graduates that included Vo Nguyen Giap, the brilliant guerrilla general, and Pham Van Dong, the current Premier of North Vietnam.

Ho left the school in 1910 without a diploma and taught briefly at a private institution in a South Annam fishing town. It was while he was there, according to now accepted sources, that he decided to go to Europe. As a step toward that goal, he went to a trade school in Saigon in the summer of 1911 where he learned the duties of a kitchen boy and pastry cook's helper, skills in demand by Europeans of that day.

His training gave Ho a gourmet's palate, which he liked to indulge, and an ability to whip up a tasty dish, which he delighted to do when he could.

For the immediate moment, though, his training enabled him to sign aboard the Latouche-Treville as a kitchen boy, a job so menial that he worked under the alias Ba. In his travels, he visited Marseilles and ports in Africa and North America. Explaining the crucial significance of these voyages for Ho's education as a revolutionary, Mr. Fall wrote in "The Two Vietnams":

"His contacts with the white colonizers on their home grounds shattered any of his illusions as to their 'superiority,' and his association with sailors from Brittany, Cornwall and the Frisian Islands — as illiterate and superstitious as the most backward Vietnamese rice farmer — did the rest.

"Ho still likes to tell the story of the arrival of his ship at an African port where, he claims, natives were compelled to jump into the shark-infested waters to secure the moorings of the vessel and were killed by the sharks under the indifferent eyes of passengers and crew.

"But his contacts with Europe also brought him the revelation of his own personal worth and dignity; when he went ashore in Europe in a Western suit, whites, for the first time in his life, addressed him as 'monsieur,' instead of using the deprecating 'tu,' reserved in France for children but used in Indochina by Frenchmen when addressing natives, no matter how educated."

In his years at sea, Ho read widely — Shakespeare, Tolstoy, Marx, Zola. He was even then, according to later accounts, an ascetic and something of a puritan, who was offended when prostitutes clambered aboard his ship in Marseilles. "Why don't the French civilize their own people before they pretend to civilize us?" he is said to have remarked.

(Ho, incidentally, is believed to have been a bachelor, although the record on this point is far from clear.)

With the advent of World War I, Ho went to live in London, where he worked as a snow shoveler and as a cook's helper under Escoffier, the master chef, at the Carlton Hotel. Escoffier, it is said, promoted Ho to a job in the pastry kitchen and wanted to teach him the art of cuisine. However that may be, the 24-year-old Vietnamese was more interested in politics. He joined the Overseas Workers Association, composed mostly of Asians, and agitated, among other things, for Irish independence.

Sometime during the war, Ho gave up the Carlton's kitchen for the sea and journeyed to the United States. He is believed to have lived in Harlem for a while. Ho himself often referred to his American visit, although he was hazy about the details. According to his close associate, Pham Van Dong, what impressed Ho in the United States were "the barbarities and ugliness of American capitalism, the Ku Klux Klan mobs, the lynching of Negroes."

Out of Ho's American experiences came a pamphlet, issued in Moscow in 1924, called "La Race Noire" ("The Black Race"), which assailed racial practices in America and Europe.

About 1918 Ho returned to France and lived in a tiny flat in the Montmartre section of Paris, eking out a living by retouching photos under the name of Nguyen Ai Quoc.

At the Versailles Peace Conference of 1919 Ho emerged as a self-appointed spokesman for his native land. Seeing in Woodrow Wilson's proposal for self-determination of the peoples the possibility of Vietnam's independence, Ho, dressed in a hired black suit and bowler hat, traveled to the Palace of Versailles to present his case. He was, of course, not received, although he offered a program for Vietnam. Its proposals did not include independence, but basic freedoms and equality between the French rulers and the native population.

Whatever hopes Ho may have held for French liberation of Vietnam were destroyed in his mind by the failure of the Versailles Conference to settle colonial issues. His faith was now transferred to Socialist action. Indeed, his first recorded speech was at a congress of the French Socialist party in 1920, and it was a plea not for world revolution but "against the imperialists who have committed abhorrent crimes on my native land." He bid the party "act practically to support the oppressed natives."

Immediately afterward Ho became, fatefully, a founding member of the French Communist party because he considered that the Socialists were equivocating on the colonial issue whereas the Communists were willing to promote national liberation.

Associated Press

In a happy mood at a Hanoi rally. Jawaharlal Nehru, the Indian leader, described him as "likable and friendly."

U.S. Army

With Vo Nguyen Giap, later to become his Defense Minister. The year was 1945, after Japan surrendered to Allies.

"I don't understand a thing about strategy, tactics and all the other big words you use," he told the delegates, "but I understand well one single thing: The Third International concerns itself a great deal with the colonial question. Its delegates promise to help the oppressed colonial peoples to regain their liberty and independence. The adherents of the Second International have not said a word about the fate of the colonial areas."

Edited Weekly Paper

With his decision to join the Communists, Ho's career took a marked turn. For one thing, he became the French party's resident expert on colonial affairs and edited Le Paria (The Outcast), the weekly paper of the Intercolonial Union, which he was instrumental in founding in 1921. This group was a conglomeration of restless Algerian, Senegalese, West Indian and Asian exiles in Paris who were united by a fervid nationalism and, to a lesser extent, by a common commitment to Communism.

For another thing, the fragile-looking Ho became an orator of sorts, traveling about France to speak to throngs of Vietnamese soldiers and war workers who were awaiting repatriation.

In addition, Ho gravitated to Moscow, then the nerve center of world Communism. He went there first in 1922 for the

Fourth Comintern Congress, where he met Lenin and became a member of the Comintern's Southeast Asia Bureau. By all accounts, Ho was vocal and energetic, meeting all the reigning Communists and helping to organize the Krestintern, or Peasant International, for revolutionary work among colonial peoples.

After a brief sojourn in France, Ho was back in Moscow, his base for many years thereafter. He attended the University of the Toilers of the East, receiving formal training in Marxism and the techniques of agitation and propaganda.

Following his studies in Moscow, Ho was dispatched to Canton, China, in 1925 as an interpreter for Michael Borodin, one of the leaders of the Soviet mission to help Chiang Kai-shek, then in Communist favor as an heir of Sun Yat-sen. Once in Canton, Ho set about to spread the spirit of revolution in the Far East. He organized Vietnamese refugees into the Vietnam Revolutionary Youth Association and set up the League of Oppressed Peoples of Asia, which soon became the South Seas Communist party, the forerunner of various national Communist groups, including Ho's own Indochinese Communist party of 1930.

For two years, until July, 1927, when Chiang turned on

his Communist allies, Ho sent apt Vietnamese to Chiang's military school at Whampoa while conducting a crash training course in political agitation for his compatriots.

Fled to Moscow

After the Chiang-Communist break, Ho fled to Moscow by way of the Gobi. His life immediately thereafter is not clear, but it is believed that he lived in Berlin for a time and traveled in Belgium, Switzerland and Italy, using a variety of aliases and passports.

After 1928 Ho turned up in eastern Thailand, disguised as a shaven-headed Buddhist monk. He traveled among Vietnamese exiles and organized political groups and published newspapers that were smuggled over the border into Vietnam.

In 1930, on advice from the Comintern, Ho was instrumental in settling the vexatious disputes that had arisen among Communists in Indochina and in organizing the Indochinese Communist party, which later became the Vietnamese Communist party and, still later, the Vietnamese Workers party.

In that same year a peasant rebellion erupted in Vietnam, which the Communists backed. On its suppression by the French, Ho was sentenced to death in absentia. At the time he was in a British jail in Hong Kong, having been arrested there in 1931 for subversive activities.

The French sought his extradition, but Ho argued that he was a political refugee and not subject to extradition. The case, which was handled in London by Sir Stafford Cripps in a plea to the Privy Council, was decided for Ho. He was released, and fled Hong Kong in disguise (this time as a Chinese merchant) and made his way back to Moscow.

There he attended Communist schools — the Institute for National and Colonial Questions and the celebrated Lenin School. He was, however, back in China in 1938, now as a communications operator with Mao Tse-tung's renowned Eighth Route Army. Subsequently, he found his way south and entered Vietnam in 1940 for the first time in 30 years.

A Master Stroke

The timing was a master stroke, for the Japanese, virtually unopposed, had taken effective control of the Indochinese Peninsula and the French administrators, most of them Vichy adherents, agreed to cooperate with the Japanese. With great daring and imagination, Ho took advantage of World War II to piece together a coalition of Vietnamese nationalists and Communists into what was called the Vietminh, or Independence Front.

The Vietminh created a 10,000-man guerrilla force, "Men in Black," that battled the Japanese in the jungles with notable success.

Ho's actions projected him onto the world scene as the leading Vietnamese nationalist and as an ally of the United States against the Japanese. "I was a Communist," he said then, "but I am no longer one. I am a member of the Vietnamese family, nothing else."

In 1942 Ho was sent to Kunming, reportedly at the request of his American military aides. He was arrested there by Chiang Kai-shek's men and jailed until September, 1943, when he was released, it has been said, by American request.

On his release, according to Mr. Fall, Ho cooperated with a Chinese Nationalist general in forming a wide Vietnamese freedom group. One result of this was that in 1944 Ho accepted a portfolio in the Provisional Republican Government of Vietnam. That Government was largely a paper affair, but it permitted Ho to court vigorously the American Office of Strategic Services. Thus when Ho's Vietminh took over Hanoi in 1945, senior American military officials were in his entourage. It was in this period that he took the name of Ho Chi Minh.

Independence Proclaimed

With the end of World War II, Ho proclaimed the independence of Vietnam, but it took nine years for his declaration to become an effective fact. First, under the Big Three Agreement at Potsdam, the Chinese Nationalists occupied Hanoi and the northern sector of Vietnam. Second, the French (in British ships) arrived to reclaim Saigon and the southern segment of the country. And third, Ho's nationalist coalition was strained under pressure of these events.

Forming a new guerrilla force around the Vietminh, Ho and his colleagues, according to most accounts, dealt summarily with dissidents unwilling to fight in Ho's fashion for independence. Assassinations were frequently reported. Meantime, as the Chinese withdrew from the north and the French advanced from the south, Ho negotiated with the French to save his nationalist regime.

In a compromise that Ho worked out in Paris in 1946, he agreed to let the Democratic Republic of Vietnam become a part of the French Union as a free state within the Indochina federation. The French recognized Ho as chief of state and promised a plebiscite in the South on the question of a unified Vietnam under Ho.

By the start of 1947, the agreement had broken down, and Ho's men were fighting the French Army. The Vietminh guerrillas held the jungles and the villages, the French the cities. For seven years the war raged as Ho's forces gathered strength, squeezing the French more and more. For most of this time, Ho was diplomatically isolated, for he was not recognized by Communist China or the Soviet Union until his victory over the French was virtually assured.

In an effort to shore up their political forces, the French resurrected Bao Dai, the puppet of the Japanese who held title as Emperor. Corrupt and pleasure-loving, he soon moved with his mistresses to France, leaving a weak and splintered regime in Saigon.

This, of course, proved no support for the French Army, which was also sapped by General Giap's guerrilla tactics. Finally, on May 8, 1954, the French forces were decisively defeated at Dienbienphu. The Indochina war ended officially in July at a cost to the French of 172,000 casualties and to the Vietminh of perhaps three times that many.

The cease-fire accord was signed in Geneva July 21, 1954, and it represented far less than Ho's hopes. But by that time the United States was involved in Vietnam on the French side through $800-million a year in economic aid.

Fear of Communist expansion in Asia dominated Washington, with Vice President Richard M. Nixon saying, "If, to avoid further Communist expansion in Asia, we must take the risk of putting our boys in, I think the Executive Branch has to do it."

The Geneva Accord, however, divided Vietnam at the 17th parallel, creating a North and a South Vietnam. It removed the French administration from the peninsula and provided for all-Vietnam elections in 1956 as a means of unifying the country.

Although a party to the Geneva Accord, the United States declined to sign it. South Vietnam, also a nonsignatory, refused to hold the elections. Meantime, the United States built up its military mission in Saigon and its support of the regime of President Ngo Dinh Diem as a counter to continued guerrilla activity of the National Liberation Front, which became pronounced after 1956.

The front, technically independent of Ho Chi Minh in the North, increased its sway into

the nineteen-sixties. It supplied itself from captured American arms and from materiel that came through from the North. Beginning in 1964, thousands of American troops were poured into South Vietnam to battle the Vietcong and then to bomb North Vietnam.

The halt of American bombing in 1968 finally led to the peace negotiations in Paris, but in the meantime the fighting in South Vietnam continued.

Throughout, Ho was confident of victory. In 1962, when the war was still a localized conflict between the South Vietnamese forces and 11,000 American advisers on the one hand and a smaller guerrilla force on the other, he told a French visitor:

"It took us eight years of bitter fighting to defeat you French, and you knew the country and had some old friendships here. Now the South Vietnamese regime is well-armed and helped by the Americans.

"The Americans are much stronger than the French, though they know us less well.

So it perhaps may take 10 years to do it, but our heroic compatriots in the South will defeat them in the end."

Ho was still confident in early 1967, when he talked with Mr. Ashmore and Mr. Baggs. "We have been fighting for our independence for more than 25 years," he told them, "and of course we cherish peace, but we will never surrender our independence to purchase a peace with the United States or any party."

At the close of his conversation, he clenched his right fist and said emotionally, "You must know of our resolution. Not even your nuclear weapons would force us to surrender after so long and violent a struggle for the independence of our country."

Of his own death he appeared unemotional. He had been urged to give up cigarettes, but he persisted in smoking. "When you are as old as I am," he remarked, "you do not worry about the harm of cigarettes."

September 4, 1969

Vietnamese Say G. I.'s Slew 567 in Town

By HENRY KAMM
Special to The New York Times

TRUONGAN, South Vietnam, Nov. 16 — A group of South Vietnamese villagers reported today that a small American infantry unit killed 567 unarmed men, women and children as it swept through their hamlet on March 16, 1968.

They survived, they said, because they had been buried under the bodies of their neighbors.

The villagers told their story in the presence of American officers at their new settlement, which lies in contested territory less than a mile from the ruins of their former home.

The officers refused to comment pending the outcome of an Army investigation into charges of murder against First Lieut. William Laws Calley Jr., 26 years old, of Miami.

A squad leader in the lieutenant's platoon, S. Sgt. David Mitchell, 29, of St. Francisville, La., has also been charged in the case, with assault with intent to murder.

[In Washington, a spokesman for the Army said that it would have no comment, in accordance with American Bar Association

standards on pretrial discussion.

[Capt. James L. F. Bowdish, attorney for Sergeant Mitchell, said in Houston that estimates of 400 to 600 dead went "far beyond" any figures he had heard.

[George W. Latimer, Lieutenant Calley's lawyer, said in San Antonio that he was "shocked" by the report, according to United Press International. "I only know what is in official records," he said. "My client had nothing to do with the killing of any civilians."]

A former soldier now studying at Claremont Men's College in California, Ronald L. Ridenhour, said yesterday that he had prompted the Army investigation by writing letters to Government officials after hearing several accounts of the alleged atrocity while stationed in Vietnam.

The site of the villagers' former home, about nine miles northeast of the provincial capital of Quangngai, is a desolate-looking place now.

Viewed from a helicopter, the ruins of houses along a well-used dirt road testify that a community once stood there.

The New York Times   Nov. 17, 1969

The provincial Governor, Col. Ton That Khien, said today in an interview that the killings had occurred, but he added that the number of dead was perhaps exaggerated.

A responsible Vietnamese official close to the case said that those slain probably numbered between 450 and 500.

Villagers' Account

As told by one of the villagers, Do Hoai, in the presence and with the assent of a num-

ber of others, this is what happened:

A heavy artillery barrage awakened the villagers around 6 A.M. It lasted for an hour, then American soldiers entered the village, meeting no opposition. They ordered all inhabitants out of their homes.

Although the area had been largely under Vietcong control, the villagers had engaged in no hostile action against the Americans and bore no arms.

The Americans forced the villagers to gather in one place in each of the three clusters of houses that formed part of the village of Songmy. The settlements bore the names of Tucong, Dinhhong and Myhoi.

The three death sites were about 200 yards apart.

When the houses had been cleared, the troops dynamited those made of brick and set fire to the wooden structures. They did not speak to the villagers and were not accompanied by an interpreter who could have explained their actions.

Then the Vietnamese were gunned down where they stood. About 20 soldiers performed the executions at each of the three places, using their individual weapons, presumably M-16 rifles.

In the interview, Colonel Khien said that the killings had probably been carried out by fewer soldiers than Mr. Hoai reported, but said he did not know the exact number.

179

Mr. Hoai, 40, a rice farmer like most of the villagers in this green and marshy area between the central highlands and the South China Sea, said that those who escaped the slaughter, as he and his wife did, had hidden under the bodies of victims until the Americans left. The whole incident, he said, took about 15 minutes.

Mr. Hoai said that his mother, his older brother and the brother's three children had been killed.

A gaunt old woman, wearing the black pajamas and flat conic of Vietnamese peasants, interrupted to say that her 19-year-old son had also been killed.

A number of people in the crowd during the conversation at the edge of the new settlement said that Mr. Hoai's account was correct.

Witnesses Questioned

Mr. Hoai, informed that the United States Army might prosecute Lieutenant Calley for murder, said that he stood ready to go to the United States to testify at a court-martial.

Earlier today, an investigator of the Army's Criminal Investigation detachment visited the Americal Division, which conducted the operation during which the incident occurred. He questioned witnesses and left accompanied by two surviving village officials.

Mr. Hoai and the other villagers said that they had arrived at the death toll of 567 by subtracting the number of survivors—132 according to them—from the total known population of the hamlet.

They said they thought that all survivors had been found in three new locations.

The Provincial Governor said that the dead had been buried by survivors within three days of the killings and no body count had been made.

Another Vietnamese official said that the village chief had turned over to him a list of the dead, but the official refused to disclose their total number.

Colonel Khien, who is 40 years old and considered friendly to Americans, said that he had been notified of the killings within a week but at first had assumed that they had been the result of an artillery barrage and therefore a sad but unavoidable act of war.

The colonel said that the operation had taken place in the Americans' stipulated zone and that therefore no Vietnamese clearance had been required for the shelling and infantry advance.

Later, he said, the Vietcong distributed a propaganda leaflet about the incident. For that reason, he said, full silence was observed to avoid providing support for enemy propaganda. When he realized three

months later that the case was more serious, Colonel Khien said, the scene of action was no longer accessible because of Vietcong mortar fire and he could do no more than interrogate about 30 survivors. They gave him identical accounts of the killings, he said.

Praises Division's Work

The Provincial Governor said that as far as he knew President Thieu had not been informed of the slayings and no official complaint had been lodged with the American command. The senior province adviser for Quangngai, C. Edward Dillery, also declined comment on the accusation.

The Governor declared that he admired the pacification work done in this province by the American division and considered the killings an unfortunate exception. On the whole, he said, American troops were more solicitous of Vietnamese lives than his own troops are.

While declining to comment on what action the American Army should take to assertain Lieutenant Calley's role, Colonel Khien said that if one of his officers were suspected of killing women and children he would have to face a military court.

The colonel said that he doubted Mr. Hoai's assertion that all of the villagers had been unarmed. While most of those killed were probably not

Communists, he said, there were Vietcong cadres in the village who may have used arms against the Americans.

Another responsible Vietnamese official, who declined to be identified because he feared the propaganda use that the enemy might make of the case, ruled out the possibility that the American soldiers might have killed the villagers because they had previously shown hostility to the Americans.

He said that the village had never before been entered by American troops.

Earlier, the village was identified mistakenly as Mylair, the name of six different hamlets in the vicinity.

Comments by Lawyer

Captain Bowdish, questioning estimates of the toll in the village, had this to say:

"There's a lot about this case that's unknown not only to me but to the people who are investigating it.

"I don't have many of the facts yet. I don't know how many people were killed or why.

"Sergeant Mitchell is charged with assaulting 30 people. I don't know what else went on in the village. From what I gather the platoon was pretty spread out as it went through the village and things may have taken place in one spot that were not seen in other parts."

November 17, 1969

A 'Real Tight' Company And Its Test at Songmy

By PETER KIHSS

It was on March 1, 1968, that Company C was ordered to search the village complex of Songmy in South Vietnam and ran into sniper fire that left several men wounded, former Sgt. Charles A. West recalls.

Two or three times afterward, patrols went near the village, which they called Pinkville, and "harassed it with gunfire," he said. Each time, he added, they were shot at and men were wounded, while others fell to mines and booby traps. All told, he said, 22 or 23 were wounded, four fatally.

"We were really mad about this," said Mr. West, who is now a 23-year-old mechanic in

Chicago. "We had been out in the field a lot. We were a real tight company, and some of those who were killed were really good guys. And when we had to attack Pinkville, we went in with no replacements for the men who were wounded or killed."

That was how one man remembered the company's state of mind on March 16, 1968 — the day of the alleged killing of large numbers of civilians at Songmy. Army investigators have charged a lieutenant with premeditated murder of 109 civilians and a sergeant with assault with intent to kill 30. Twenty-four other former members of Company C are subjects

of continuing inquiry.

At least three former servicemen have said publicly that they themselves killed a total of 46 persons, offering varying explanations in what has become a major national controversy.

From official statements and from interviews by reporters for The New York Times and other news media, the following picture, with some conflicting testimony, has emerged so far:

The time was one of the bloodiest periods of the Vietnam war. Before dawn, Jan. 31, 1968, enemy forces had unleashed the savage Lunar New Year, or Tet, attacks on Saigon and more than a score of other cities and bases.

Hue, the old imperial capital, had been largely destroyed amid mass executions by the enemy in 26 days of house-to-house fighting before it was recaptured. South Vietnam's government on March 14, 1968,

said the Hue toll alone had been 3,776 civilian dead, aside from military casualties.

Rarely have American deaths exceeded 500 a week in Vietnam. But American combat losses for the week ended March 2 were 542 killed, 2,191 wounded; for the week ended March 9, 509 killed and 2,766 wounded; for the week ended March 16, 336 killed and 1,916 wounded.

One Tet attack hit Quangngai, a city of 35,000 population. Six miles to the northeast is the Songmy village complex. Within that complex are six hamlets named Mylai, which on March 16, 1968, had 699 inhabitants, according to those who have survived.

Mylai 4 had three clusters of homes — some of bambo, mud and straw; a few of brick—along a dirt road on a green and marshy lowland near the South China Sea. Most of the villagers were rice farmers.

Secretary of the Army Stanley R. Resor said last week

that "Mylai 4 hamlet is located in an area which is now and has been for several years under Vietcong control" — traditional home of the 48th Local Force Battalion, one of the enemy's best.

Company C was one of four rifle companies of about 165 men each in the First Battalion, 20th Infantry, 11th Light Infantry Brigade—an American brigade formed July 1, 1966, at Schofield Barracks in Hawaii.

On Dec. 5, 1967, the brigade, 5,000 strong, shipped out for Vietnam. It set up headquarters in Ducpho, southeast down the coast from Quangnagai city.

Task Force Formed

On Jan. 1, 1968, it activated Task Force Barker—three rifle companies and an artillery battery under the command of Lieut. Col. Frank A. Barker Jr. They were Company C, regulars and draftees; Company B, Fourth Battalion, Third Infantry; and Company A, Third Battalion, First Infantry.

They operated from Landing Zone Dottie, 40 miles north of Ducpho, where the men lived in underground bunkers. Their operation area was 10 by 15 miles, northeast of Quangngai city.

The mission was to "search and clear" Vietcong and North Vietnamese infiltration. It was not headline drama—daily patrols in squad, platoon or company strength.

Enemy soldiers quickly disappeared when American infantry neared the hamlets. The Americans watched buddies being blown up by land mines or booby traps. They saw comrades skewered on bamboo stakes in elephant pits. They stepped on "punji"—bamboo sticks sharpened and tipped with excrement.

They grew angry at the civilians not only for hiding the Vietcong by night but also for not warning of traps. The civilians were terrified lest the returning Vietcong kill any informants.

Task Force Barker sent out a unit just about daily. One company "fought its way out of a V.C. ambush, leaving 80 enemy dead," three weeks before the March 16 clash, according to Pacific Stars and Stripes.

Lead members of Company C walked into three booby traps south of Lacson, not far from Songmy, on Feb. 25. Six men were critically wounded. Working to help them in an exploit that won him the Silver Star, Capt. Ernest L. Medina, the company commander, was felled by a fourth mine. One who died that day was Bobby Wilson, 19, remembered as a "damn good buddy."

Things worsened in March. "In the last week or so, we'd lost about half our company

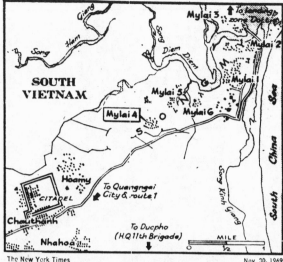

The New York Times   Nov. 30, 1969

SITE OF INCIDENT: Songmy village complex, with six hamlets each called Mylai. Alleged killing of civilians occurred at Mylai 4. Cluster of dots indicates homes. Road is dirt one. Other lines indicate ditches and canals.

to snipers and mine fields," former Pfc. Charles Gruver, 24, now a construction worker in Tulsa, Okla., recalled.

Losses to Snipers

Former Specialist 4th Cl. Varnado Simpson, 22, of Jackson, Miss., said that three or four men were lost to heavy sniper fire at the edge of Songmy "a couple of days" before March 16.

The Songmy area was a "free-fire zone." In such a zone, the local authorities warn inhabitants that anyone moving outdoors after certain hours will be assumed to be hostile —and a target.

Before the March 16 assault, Captain Medina briefed Company C. Secretary Resor says a high-priority inquiry is continuing into the extent to which the men's later actions were "pursuant to orders from their company commander or higher headquarters."

Since last December, Captain Medina had been assigned to Fort Benning, Ga., and he and his lawyer have declined comment. His men's versions of his briefing or briefings conflict.

Captain Medina was born Aug. 22, 1936, in Springer, N. M. His mother died when he was an infant, and his grandparents reared him in Montrose, Colo., a ranching and farming community on the western slope of the Rocky Mountains.

When he was 17 or 18, he joined the National Guard. He rose to staff sergeant, and then in April, 1956, he chose an Army career. A graduate of Officer Candidate School, he has been a captain since Dec. 1, 1966.

Former Pfc. Leon Stevenson

of Sidney, Mont., remembered a briefing in the morning just before they went into Songmy. He said that the captain drew a sketch on the ground to indicate where each platoon would go.

Mr. Stevenson, 19 at the time, quoted the captain as saying a battalion of North Vietnamese or Vietcong was supposed to be working out of the village. Then the captain read the "regular field order."

Night Briefing Recalled

James R. Bergthold, 22, of Niagara Falls, N. Y., and Richard Pendleton, 22, of Richmond, Calif., remembered Captain Medina briefing them the night before and warning of Vietcong in the area.

Mr. Bergthold said, in an interview copyrighted by The Niagara Falls Gazette, "The captain told us—we weren't given any orders to shoot— that if we saw anyone they might be carrying weapons, so be careful."

Mr. Pendleton recalled for The Richmond (Calif.) Independent, "He told us there were Vietcong in the village and we should 'kill them before they kill us.'"

On the other hand, former Sergeant West, in Chicago, said that Captain Medina had read an order just before the attack to "destroy Pinkville and everything in it." He said the village was "considered heavily armed and held by the Vietcong and that the North Vietnamese were believed to be in underground tunnels."

Sgt. Michael A. Bernhardt of Franklin Square, L. I., now assigned to a basic training company at Fort Dix, N. J., was

then a private and an automatic rifleman.

'No Innocent Civilians'

He said the company commander had told the men "the village and the occupants were to be destroyed," asserting that "they were all V. C. and there were no innocent civilians in the area."

Former Specialist Simpson, in Jackson, Miss., said Captain Medina briefed the company the afternoon before, instructing the men to "kill or burn down anything in sight," destroying all people, houses, livestock, chickens, cats and dogs.

Paul David Meadlo, 22, of West Terre Haute, Ind., in a Columbia Broadcasting System radio interview, recalled the captain as instructing the men "to search and to make sure that there weren't no N.V.A. [North Vietnamese Army] in the village," and to expect a fight when they got there.

Artillery Bombardment

On the morning of March 16, Army Secretary Resor has reported, Company C had "a three-minute artillery preparation on its landing zone which is thought to have produced few, if any casualties." Such bombardment is designed to destroy booby traps where helicopters will land the troops.

Company C—about 105 men, by the Resor report—landed west of the Mylai 4 hamlet. The First Platoon, under Lieut. William L. Calley Jr., advanced into the cluster of homes. Company A set up a block to the south.

"Contact with the enemy force" occurred at 7:50 A.M., according to a report sent that night to Washington. At 9:10 A.M., another company was inserted about two miles east-northeast of the original contact point, the message said. The companies, it went on, moved toward each other with "sporadic contacts" with the enemy all day. They had support from "Army artillery and helicopter gunships."

Recalls Long Barrage

The villagers, it was asserted by Do Hoai, a 40-year-old Vietnamese rice farmer, were awakened about 6 A.M. by a heavy, hour-long artillery barrage. American soldiers, he said, then entered without opposition, ordering all inhabitants out of their homes.

An account in Pacific Stars and Stripes reported 128 enemy killed during the day, as did military messages. This counted six killed by helicopter guns and 14 killed by Captain Medina's company "minutes after landing," when "two M-1 rifles, a carbine, a short-wave radio and enemy documents" were seized.

An attack on the village, this report went on, "accounted for

181

69 enemy dead, some of which were attributed to supporting artillery fire." Another platoon under Second Lieut. Thomas Willingham was said to have run into enemy fire when airlifted into a southern beach area and to have killed 30 there and eight more in "an enemy underground complex."

Mr. Meadlo's version, in his WCBS broadcast and other interviews, is different. He said he went in on the first wave of four helicopters, five soldiers in each. An "older man," he related, was noticed in a shelter, and S. Sgt. David Mitchell, squad leader, "hollered back and said 'Shott him,' " which Mr. Meadlo said was then done.

Has Bronze Star

Sergeant Mitchell, 29, of St. Francisville, La., a nine-year veteran of the Army, holds the Bronze Star for his Vietnam service. He is charged by the Army with assault with intent to murder 30 civilians in Mylai. His Army counsel, Capt. James L. F. Bowdish, has said the sergeant ought to plead not guilty.

Mr. Meadlo asserted he was next helping guard a group of 40 or 45 persons when Lieutenant Calley declared, "I want them dead."

Lieutenant Calley, now assigned to Fort Benning, is awaiting court-martial on charges of murder of 109 persons, including a 2-year-old child. His civilian lawyer, George W. Latimer, of Salt Lake City, said last Nov. 16, "My client had nothing to do with the killing of any civilians."

Wounded in Combat

The 5-foot-3-inch-tall lieutenant, who weighs 130 pounds, was born June 8, 1943, in Miami and used to be a draft-deferred railroad worker. In July, 1966, he enlisted in the regular Army. He went through officer training and joined Company C in September, 1967.

He holds the Purple Heart for a combat wound, and had been recommended for the Bronze Star with an oak leaf cluster for an action not currently being made known by the Army.

Mr. Meadlo's version is that Lieutenant Calley "started shooting" at the group gathered in the village center, "and he told me to start shooting."

Mr. Meadlo said he himself then sprayed four clips of 17 rounds each from his M-16 rifle and "I might have killed 10 or 15" men, women and children.

Another group of 70 to 75 villagers was then collected beside a ditch and "we started shooting them," Mr. Meadlo said. He told a reporter later "I must have killed about a third" of this group, to make his own personal total 35 to 40. He did so, he said, "because I felt like I was ordered to do

it" and had "lost buddies" before.

Former Specialist Simpson said he landed with the second platoon. A Vietcong soldier in black and green pajamas, carrying a weapon, ran in front of the troops into a hut, he said, and a woman followed, running despite an order to halt.

On what Mr. Simpson said was his platoon lieutenant's order, "I shot her as she was running into the door," a United Press International dispatch quoted him. He added, "When I turned her over, there was a baby, a little boy about 2 years old, I guess, under her"—and both were dead.

Mr. Simpson said he killed about 10 persons. He said he considered he was obeying orders. Most Vietcong, he said, had probably left, but the company still underwent sporadic sniper fire.

"When the attack started," former Sergeant West said, "it could not be stopped by anyone. We were mad, and we had been told that the enemy was there, and we were going in there to give them a fight for what they had done to our dead buddies. Then some of the Yannigans in the company began to kill civilians after we captured the village."

"As we entered, we drew fire from some of the huts, and then a lot of the guys sort of went crazy," former Private Gruver told The Associated Press. One soldier, he said, went behind a tree and "deliberately shot himself in the foot" to avoid taking part.

Former Private Bergthold, in The Niagara Falls Gazette, was quoted as saying he killed one old man "just to put him out of his misery."

Sergeant Bernhardt said he believed "most of the men" carried out slayings and "only a few of us refused," including himself.

Congressmen See Film

Former Sgt. Ronald L. Haeberle, 28, of Cleveland, then a combat photographer, took the pictures shown last week to members of Congress. In a copyrighted interview in The Cleveland Plain Dealer, Mr. Haeberle declared the killings were done "recklessly, wantonly and without any provocation."

The Army has honored a helicopter pilot, Chief Warrant Officer Hugh C. Thompson Jr., 27, of Decatur, Ga., with a Silver Star medal. The citation said he twice landed his helicopter that day—once to extricate 15 children trying to hide in a bunker and then to rescue a wounded child in disregard of his own safety.

Of the 600 to 700 persons in the village, about 150 were spared when an order from headquarters stopped the kill-

ing, Mr. Simpson said. This, he said, followed what a radio operator told him was a message of intervention by a helicopter pilot—still not publicly identified.

The villagers, through Mr. Hoai, the farmer, have said 132 survivors have been found in three new locations, so that they held the death toll to have been 567 civilians. They asserted the villagers were first ordered out of their homes, which the troops then dynamited and set afire.

Colonel Questions Men

Then, they said, executions took place in three groups about 200 yards apart, performed by about 20 soldiers at each group in about 15 minutes. Mr. Hoai said he and others survived under bodies of victims.

A Vietnamese Communist propaganda pamphlet last year listed an American raid of March 16, 1968, on Songmy village among other alleged atrocities. It asserted that 502 persons had been killed, including more than 170 children, and attributed the raid to "troops of the U. S. Third Brigade, 82nd Airborne Division."

Overhead in a helicopter on March 16 at one time was Col. Oran K. Henderson, who had been deputy commander of the 11th Brigade and who took over full command only the day before from Brig. Gen. Andy A. Lipscomb.

Colonel Henderson saw two groups of bodies—about five or six persons. He also received a helicopter pilot's report that a soldier had killed a civilian.

Next day Colonel Henderson caught up with Company C. He gathered 30 or 40 men, and told them approximately the following:

From initial reports he had, some civilians might have been killed, perhaps promiscuously. This overshadowed to a degree any success they had in the operation. It concerned him as brigade commander. He did not expect his soldiers to kill civilians.

He asked whether anyone in the group had observed shooting or killing of civilians. Reportedly there was a general murmur: "No, no." He pointed his finger at random at three or four men, and asked each of them. "No, sir," came the answer, loud and clear.

Company C and Task Force Barker kept up their search-and-clear mission until the force was inactivated in June.

A week or ten days later, Colonel Barker lost his life. Another aircraft had been shot down. As it plunged to earth it crashed into his flying helicopter.

November 30, 1969

CAMBODIA ORDERS TROOPS OF HANOI AND VIETCONG OUT

Disorders in Pnompenh Go Into Third Day—Role of Military in Riots Seen

SUNDAY DEADLINE IS SET

By The Associated Press

BANGKOK, Thailand, March 13—The Cambodian Government said today that it had asked Vietcong and North Vietnamese trooops to get out of Cambodia before dawn Sunday.

The request came while bands of angry Cambodians rampaged through Pnompenh, the Cambodian capital, for the third day in a row, attacking Vietnamese shops and houses, according to reports reaching Bangkok.

Diplomats in Pnompenh said it would be physically impossible for the Vietcong and the North Vietnamese to remove their troops by Sunday.

[In a dispatch from Hong Kong on Saturday, Reuters reported that North Vietnam had pledged that it would continue to respect the independence of Cambodia.]

Ruler Is Abroad

The Cambodian decisions were reported by the official press agency while Prince Norodom Sihanouk, the Chief of State, was vacationing abroad.

[Prince Sihanouk, leaving Paris, said he would stop off in Moscow and Peking to ask for curbs on the Vietcong and the North Vietnamese in Cambodia. When he reached Moscow he was extended a full-scale welcome.

[In Vientiane, Laos, informed sources arriving from Cambodia said the rioting against the Vietcong there was believed to have been insti- gated by the military to induce Prince Sihanouk to show greater firmness.]

Protests Began Sunday

Demonstrations against the presence of large Vietcong forces and North Vietnamese army units along the Cambodian-South Vietnamese frontier began Sunday in the Cambodian border province of Svay Rieng.

They spread Wednesday into Pnompenh, where thousands of rioters attacked the Vietcong and North Vietnamese embassies, burning cars and hurling papers out of the windows.

A Cambodian army spokesman said there had been 164 skirmishes between Cambodian troops or police and Vietcong units since the beginning of 1969.

Although estimates vary, it is believed that as many as 60,000 Vietcong and North Vietnamese troops are in Cambodia — many in frontier base camps from which they launch attacks into South Vietnam.

The official press agency in Pnompenh reported that the Government had told the intruders they must leave not later than Sunday.

It said the request was made in a note delivered by the Government to the Vietcong and North Vietnamese embassies. The note expressed regrets for the attacks on the embassies, the news agency said, but added the demonstrators expressed the exasperation of the people against the infiltration and occupation of Cambodian territory.

The anti-Vietnamese demonstrations were reportedly tapering off in Pnompenh today but they were spreading to rural areas and the situation remained "fluid."

Sources in Bangkok said the Cambodian bands swarming through the Vietnamese section of Pnompenh did not distinguish between pro-Communists and anti-Communists and even looted several Roman Catholic churches.

There are estimated to be 500,000 Vietnamese residing in Cambodia, which has a total population of 6.3 million. Some 55,000 of the Vietnamese are Roman Catholics.

March 14, 1970

SIHANOUK REPORTED OUT IN A COUP BY HIS PREMIER; CAMBODIA AIRPORTS SHUT

PRINCE IS ABROAD

By HENRY KAMM
Special to The New York Times

BANGKOK, Thailand, March 18—Prince Norodom Sihanouk, Chief of State of Cambodia, was overthrown today in his absence, the Pnompenh radio announced.

The Southeast Asian country was cut off from the world, except for the broadcasts. The nation's two commercial airports were closed to all traffic.

Power has apparently been seized by Lieut. Gen. Lon Nol, the Premier and Defense Minister, and the First Deputy Premier, Prince Sisowath Sirik Matak, a cousin of Prince Sihanouk.

Cheng Heng, President of the National Assembly, has been designated as interim Chief of State, pending elections, the radio announced. Informed Pnompenh sources considered him a figure of negligible political stature.

Leaves Moscow

When the announcement of his overthrow was made Prince Sihanouk, who is 47, was in Moscow where he had arrived from Paris five days ago, and was preparing to depart for Peking.

[Prince Sihanouk arrived in Peking Thursday morning from Moscow. In the Soviet capital, the Prince acted as if he were still Chief of State but spoke of the possibility of forming a government in exile.]

The announcement came after a week of anti-Communist rioting, reportedly officially inspired, in which the embassies

183

of North Vietnam and the Vietcong were sacked. These events moved Cambodia close to open hostility with the Vietnamese Communists, who are operating in large number on the Cambodian side of the long frontier with South Vietnam.

Last Friday, the Cambodian Government asked North Vietnamese and Vietcong troops to leave the country by dawn Sunday. Meetings on the demand have been held subsequently in Pnompenh, but no progress has been reported. [Reuters reported that, following the coup, the National Assembly had adjourned after failing to agree on measures to rid the country of Communist forces.]

Prince Sihanouk, a neutralist whose policies swerved often between right and left in an effort to strike a balance, is known to have struggled for a year against the hard anti-Communist position of General Lon Nol and Prince Sirik Matak.

According to informed sources, that struggle precipitated Prince Sihanouk's downfall, but was not its principal cause.

What brought him down, the sources said, was his cult of personality, his expensive striving for grandeur, the stagnation of Cambodia's economy, the corruption of leading personalities and the bureaucracy and widespread smuggling and trading in contraband goods.

No reports of violence attendant on today's events have reached the outside world.

The broadcasts are being received here imperfectly, on powerful monitoring equipment. Cable and telephone connections are not functioning.

Cambodia's two commercial airports, Pnompenh and Siemreap, were closed shortly after noon today without prior warning. The war in South Vietnam and Laos, and political strains with Cambodia's other neighbor, Thailand, have effectively cut off access to Cambodia by road.

Neighboring countries learned of the events in Pnompenh from a French-language broadcast that said:

"Following the political crisis provoked by Prince Norodom Sihanouk in the past days, the National Assembly and the Royal Council in joint session, in accordance with the constitution of the Kingdom, unanimously withdrew their confidence from Prince Norodom Sihanouk. From this day, 18 March 1970 at 1300 hours [1 A. M. Wednesday, New York time], Prince Norodom Sihanouk ceases to be the Chief of State of Cambodia and will be replaced by Cheng Heng, the President of the National Assembly, who will assume the function of the Chief of State until the election of a new Chief of State in accordance with the text of the nation's Constitution"

The New York Times   March 19, 1970

NEW TURMOIL IN SOUTHEAST ASIA: The overthrow of Cambodia's leader, Prince Sihanouk, was announced in a broadcast from Pnompenh (1). In Laos, fall of Sam Thong (2) to Communist forces was followed by a partial evacuation of nearby Long Tieng. In Thailand, tribesmen were moved from areas (3) because of Communist activity.

Prince Sihanouk had left Pnompenh on Jan. 6 for the announced purpose of taking a cure in Grasse, France, for obesity and a blood disorder. He set out on the return journey, with scheduled stops in Moscow and Peking, after the rioting broke out.

The first indication of events more serious than the rioting and the challenge last Friday by Cambodia to the Vietnamese Communists to withdraw their troops came today with the sudden closing of Pnompenh Airport.

Plane Turns Back

A Union of Burma Airways commercial flight left here for Pnompenh at 11:30 A.M. after receiving clearance for the 50-minute flight from the Saigon Control Tower, which directs traffic for the Cambodian capital. On board, the stewardess could be heard to announce that the landing was imminent.

But then the pilot's voice came over the public-address system to announce that Pnompenh Airport was closed and he was turning the jet black toward Bangkok.

No reason was given, the pilot said. The mystery persisted until shortly before 3 P.M. The Pnompenh station then came on the air to announce that a Cambodian Government communiqué was being read to a special session of the National Assembly.

In the statement, the Government accused the Vietnamese Communists of spreading false rumors, bribing Cambodian officials and distributing anti-Government leaflets, all in an effort to set Cambodians against Cambodians.

In view of this, and for reasons that were not stated, the Government announced that it was relieving the Pnompenh police chief of his functions

and would take "extreme measures" to restore calm.

Although the Pnompenh radio usually goes off the air at 3 o'clock, it stayed on after the announcement, broadcasting light music.

At 5:07 P.M., the music was interrupted for the communiqué containing the decisive announcement of Prince Sihanouk's overthrow.

Prince Sihanouk abdicated the throne of Cambodia in 1955, because, he said, the monarch was the prisoner of a rigid system and could not serve his people as effectively as he wished. He became Chief of State.

Throne Is Vacant

His father, King Norodom Suramarit, succeeded him. Since his death in 1960, his widow, Prince Sihanouk's mother, Queen Kossamak Nearireath, has represented the monarchy while the throne remains vacant.

Mr. Cheng Heng went on the air after Prince Sihanouk's ouster was announced to declare his acceptance of the title of Acting Chief of State.

He was elected President of the National Assembly in 1968 and re-elected last year. He is a wealthy lawyer and former Agriculture Minister.

In the view of the sources recently in Pnompenh Prince Sihanouk in his last year as Chief of State had shown a pronounced shift to the right toward the position of his political adversaries. He had become increasingly harder in his pronouncements against the Communists and had noticeably diminished his tendency to balance anti-Communist statements with strident attacks on "American imperialism."

Military Discontented

Nevertheless, the increasing pressure of the North Vietnamese and Vietcong largely because of their increasing need to find sanctuary in territory safer from American firepower than South Vietnam, heightened the political struggle in Cambodia by causing discontent with Prince Sihanouk's policies within the military, the sources said.

The soldiers were described as exasperated by apparent differences in the Chief of State's words and his actions. They charged that though the Prince condemned the Vietnamese Communists as the enemy in speeches, he forced the Cambodian military to release all Vietcong they captured.

They saw a contradiction between his complaints that the Vietcong were obtaining much of their food through illegal purchases from Cambodian farmers and his recognition last year of the Vietcong's so-called provisional revolutionary government and his subsequent signing of a trade agreement with it.

The military were said to resent what they considered Prince Sihanouk's ambiguous policy of ordering the armed forces to intervene against American attacks on Vietnamese Communist military targets on Cambodian soil. Cambodian gunfire was reported to have brought down an American fighter - bomber attacking a Vietnamese anti-aircraft position in Cambodia last November. The result was a heavy American attack on the Cambodian installation that killed 27 Cambodians.

These sentiments were said to have contributed to turning General Lon Nol from a loyal follower of the Prince into a determined opponent. The general's control of the small military forces—about 35,000 in a nation of 7 million—is said to be complete.

Investments Assailed

Prince Sirik Matak's opposition was said to have been rooted more in his disapproval of what he considered his cousin's flamboyant megalomania, Prince Sihanouk's insistence on nationalization of Cambodia's few industries, wastefullness in the use of limited investment capital and tolerance of widespread corruption.

Prince Sirik Matak, according to the sources, was leader of a body of opinion that believed that Prince Sihanouk was condemning Cambodia to economic disaster by ill-planned investments. Among these were his plan to build a port city named

after himself — Sihanoukville — in which less than one ship a day docked in 1969, as well as plants for the manufacture of tires, jute sacks, textiles and distilleries that produced no revenues for the state but were said to enrich those whom Prince Sihanouk named as directors.

Other investments cited were large hotels in places that do not need them; state-run nightclubs with taxi-dancers, and two movie houses, one for the international film festivals in which the Prince's own productions have on both occasions won the first prize, and one for the showing of the Prince's films to the public.

Prince Sirik Matak and General Lon Nol were reported to have agreed by last summer that the only way to return Cambodia to order was to limit the Chief of State's exercise of power. The issue was at the center of the 27th Congress last June of the Sangkum, the political movement founded by Prince Sihanouk to group all political factions under one organization, with himself on top.

When, subsequently, Premier Pen Nouth stepped down because of long illness and General Lon Nol was asked by the Chief of State to form a cabinet, the general replied that he would form a government only as Premier and not as merely a secretary to Prince Sihanouk.

A special congress was named by Prince Sihanouk and instructed to form a government.

General Lon Nol, the overwhelming choice, rejected the office at first and accepted only after the Chief of State met his conditions.

They were, principally, that he would have the right to choose his ministers and that they would report to him, not to Prince Sihanouk.

Almost A Coup

The Chief of State accepted and the Cabinet took office last Aug. 12. This acceptance by Prince Sihanouk of a government with powers not dependent on his whims was considered by some observers a bloodless coup. The Premier and Prince Sirik Matak issued decrees in the early days of their government to solidify this "coup."

The Premier ordered all Government communications and letters to be addressed to the Premier's office rather than to the Chief of State. The Deputy Premier, who made the country's economy his special field, ended the practice of having certain taxes, such as those on motorcycles and scooters, paid into the Chief of State's treasury rather than the Government's.

During the 28th Congress of the Sangkum, in the last days of last year, Prince Sirik Matak weakened the Chief of State's position by forcing the closing of the Pnompenh Casino over Prince Sihanouk's opposition. A few days later, Prince Sihanouk, reportedly under heavy pressure, left for France, with

Prince Sirik Matak, in all but in name, in charge of Cambodia.

Action Against Communists

Last month, General Lon Nol, who had been in France, returned, and open measures against the Vietnamese Communists in Cambodia followed.

The sources said that one of the most significant anti-Communist moves was cooperation between the South Vietnamese and Cambodian armed forces in fighting the Vietcong in the border areas. This is effected, according to the sources, by Cambodian officers' intentionally discussing on "insecure" telephone lines known to be overheard by the South Vietnamese the disposition of enemy troops.

The sacking of the North Vietnamese and Vietcong embassies in Pnompenh last Wednesday followed, and, in the view of the sources, Prince Sihanouk's ouster was the goal that the Prince's opponents had pursued since last summer.

In Paris the day after the embassies were sacked, Prince Sihanouk said that he believed a coup against him was a possibility, and he suggested that General Lon Nol might lead it.

March 19, 1970

U.S. Now Declares Forces May Cross Cambodian Border

Special to The New York Times

KEY BISCAYNE, Fla., March 28—The White House said today for the first time that American troops, depending on the judgment of their field commanders, were permitted to cross the Cambodian border in response to enemy threats.

The White House press secretary, Ronald L. Ziegler, who made the disclosure under questioning from newsmen,

said this did not mean a widening of the Vietnam war. It merely represents, he said, a restatement of rules promulgated by the Pentagon and already in force along the border.

When asked this evening whether American ground troops had actually entered Cambodia, Mr. Ziegler said, "I'm not aware of it." Asked whether American gunships had flown into Cambodia in recent days, the press secretary said, "I can't confirm that either."

March 29, 1970

Drive Against Vietnamese At High Pitch in Cambodia

By HENRY KAMM
Special to The New York Times

PNOMPENH, Cambodia, April 13—An officially inspired campaign of hatred against Vietnamese has reached fever pitch throughout Cambodia. It has resulted in detentions, in disappearances and, in at least one known case, in mass killings that witnesses attributed to Cambodian soldiers.

In the course of the last week or 10 days the campaign against Vietnamese residents has seriously diminished the open sympathy with which many diplomats and other foreigners initially viewed the leadership that overthrew Prince Norodom Sihanouk on March 18.

None of the leading figures of the new regime have said a word, in their flood of statements and communiqués, that might inhibit those who take the official propaganda campaign as a declaration of an open season on Vietnamese.

A standard line of argument appears to have developed among Government officials and private citizens in response to those who intercede on behalf of the frightened Vietnamese.

The Cambodians insist that foreigners simply do not understand the depth of Vietnamese Communist penetration among Vietnamese in Cambodia. They also stress the traditional enmity between the Cambodian and Vietnamese peoples and say that outsiders fail to see the issue in its historical context.

It is often asserted that the Vietnamese have been equally cruel to Cambodians and would do the same in the Cambodians' position.

Vietnamese residents of Cambodia are estimated to number 400,000 in a population of seven million. How many remain at liberty is impossible to tell. In the border provinces, where North Vietnamese and Vietcong forces moved supplies and men and found sanctuary while Prince Sihanouk was in power —his successors have been trying to get rid of them—most of the Vietnamese are believed to be under detention.

The biggest concentration is in the capital, where they live in well-defined sections, particularly along the banks of the Mekong, Bassac and Tonle Sap rivers. Reliable informants reported today that in some sections one member of each family was seized yesterday, apparently as a hostage.

Many Vietnamese, including those who have acquired Cambodian citizenship at considerable expense, have reportedly been dismissed from their jobs and would find it difficult to get new ones. Mothers are keeping their children indoors, even beyond the 6 P.M.-to-6 A.M. curfew imposed last week on all Vietnamese. Women no longer wear their distinctive national costume, the ao dai.

In a dentention center near a bridge over the Bassac, frightened Vietnamese told reporters that detainees have been disappearing. Perhaps, they said, the detainees are being taken for interrogation, but no one knows.

The episode of mass killing occurred in the village of Prasot, which later fell to Vietnamese Communist invaders. More than a hundred men, women and children were gunned down Thursday night in the courtyard of an agricultural cooperative where they were being detained.

Information of the killings has not become public but they are not denied. The province Governor, Hem Keth Sana, when questioned yesterday in Svayrieng, the nearest town, said the deaths had been a result of a "murderous" attack in which the Vietcong used the detainees as a screen. But survivors told other Vietnamese at the scene that Cambodian troops alone were responsible.

The Prasot incident became known because the village lies on the principal Pnompenh-to-Saigon highway and was at the center of fighting between Cambodian and Vietnamese Communist forces last week. Consequently many reporters visited the region. If similar slayings occurred in centers off the principal highways, they might never have come to public attention.

Officials have categorically forbidden reporters to visit detention centers, and those who slip in have been expelled immediately—on at least one occasion at pistol point.

Some foreigners have suggested to influential Cambodians with whom they have contacts that Premier Lon Nol or the First Deputy Premier, Prince Sisowath Sirik Matak, men who are generally considered moderate, might find occasion to say in their public statements that many Vietnamese residents of Cambodia and naturalize Cambodians of Vietnamese stock have taken no part in Vietcong activities.

But the foreigners report that they have run into a wall of incomprehension.

Representatives of private international groups who have discussed the issue with Cambodian officials have acted in the awareness that there is no diplomatic representation of Vietnam in Cambodia.

Diplomats and other observers have been struck by a belief, apparently sincerely held by responsible Cambodians, that the new leadership will always be in full control of the feelings unleashed by the hate campaign and that no violence will be done to the innocent.

Some foreigners long resident in Cambodia believe that the leaders have made a calculated decision to exploit extreme national feeling to capture the support of their people.

April 14, 1970

'Waste Them'

The terrifying jungles of Vietnam shield from view many atrocities on both sides of the unseen battle lines. But certain disdainful phrases rise above the smoke of "free-fire zones" to reveal the brutalizing meaning of the war.

Then somebody said, "What do we do with them?"

A G.I. answered, "Waste them."

Suddenly there was a burst of automatic fire from many guns. Only a small child survived.

Somebody then carefully shot him, too.

In the May issue of Harper's Magazine, a report appears on "My Lai 4" from a forthcoming book by Seymour M. Hersh on the massacre and its aftermath. It is a horror story, part of which already has emerged in the Pentagon report and in the daily press. Those implicated are standing trial by court-martial.

Regardless of the outcome of a trial that must be fair and based on the evidence, the language of war stands condemned. Waste them. The phrase itself is an atrocity. It tells why the war must come to an end.

April 15, 1970

KEY ROLE IS SEEN FOR KHMER ROUGE

U.S. Aides Assess Strength of Guerrillas in Cambodia

By TAD SZULC
Special to The New York Times

WASHINGTON, April 18— The Khmers Rouges, the Cambodian equivalent of the South Vietnamese Vietcong guerrillas, may become an important political element in Cambodia, in the opinion of United States Government experts on Indochina.

But this opinion is balanced by the fact that in the northeast area of Cambodia, where Khmer Rouge activity is said to be heaviest, the total strength of the bands has been put at only 450 men.

The Pnompenh authorities apply the generic name of Khmer Rouge—Khmer is the Cambodian word for their nation and rouge is French for red—to all the Communist insurgent bands that operate throughout the country. Since last autumn, the bands have been reported to be engaged in a major organizational effort.

Groups termed Khmer Rouge have fought sporadically against the Cambodian army since mid-1967, and were the targets of occasional denunciations by Prince Norodom Sihanouk, the deposed Chief of State. But until Prince Sihanouk's fall on March 18 these groups had been regarded as a minor nuisance.

Until the coup, in the judgment of United States Specialists, the Khmers Rouges confined itself to harassment of the army and to an effort to keep alive the spirit of Communism in Cambodia. At no time, it is believed here, did Khmers Rouges ever undertake operations designed to threaten the position of Prince Sihanouk and his neutralist Government.

Rose Is Increasing

Since the coup, however, the Khmers Rouges have been reported to be, increasingly, a part of the operational pattern of the North Vietnamese and Vietcong troops as the latter fight to preserve in Cambodia their sanctuaries from the war in Vietnam.

Their principal contribution to the Communist cause at this juncture is believed to be their knowledge of the country and of the Khmer language, both vital at a time when the Vietnamese find themselves in ethnic clashes with Cambodians.

The Khmer Rouge is probably the least known of the Communist movement in Indochina — unlike the Vietcong and the Pathet Lao in Laos, it has no radio stations or newspapers—but, gradually, information about the movement is seeping to the West.

The bands of Khmers Rouges run "into the thousands," according to a United States source. But the bands are still operating in separate regions and they have been divided into what the Cambodian Government calls the "reds" and the "blues," depending on organizational origins.

The two principal regions of Khmer Rouge activities are the northeastern provinces of Cambodia, adjoining the Laotian border, and the western province of Battambang where the town of Moung is situated.

The leaders of the Khmers Rouges have been identified as three former National Assembly deputies: Hu Nim, Khieu Samphan and Ho Youn. The first two are the best known and are believed to be with their forces in Battambang.

Hu Nim, believed to be in his late thirties, was a highly popular young deputy of the Communist People's party when he was first elected in 1958. He vanished in 1967, when the Khmer Rouge movement reportedly began organizing itself seriously along guerrilla lines, and is now thought to be in the southwest of Battambang in the general area of Kampot.

Khieu Samphan and Hou Youn, also in their thirties, were also elected to the National Assembly in 1958. Khieu Samphan was re-elected in 1966 and he, too is said to have vanished a year later.

In the northeast region, corresponding to Cambodia's first military region, the Khmers Rouges are reportedly led by Tou Samouth, who is described as the president of the "clandestine Khmer Communist party." His chief military adviser is an officer named Sovanna and his political counselor is Nai Saran, said to be a Communist party veteran.

Officials say that a Cambodian liberation front exists in the northeast of the country, at least in theory, but it has thus far functioned on the local level.

Most of the information available on the Khmer Rouge concerns the northeast area. Last November, a detailed report on the organization in the first military region was prepared by Lieut. Gen. Lon Nol, then Chief of Staff of the army as well as the premier.

General Lon Nol estimated that the Khmers Rouges in this area totaled about 450 men and that they operated in four separate zones from well equipped bases. He has found that the Chan Than, Meak Sarij, Keo Sophan and Reach Son bands had been "more rationally" organized than before.

April 19, 1970

Roots of Cambodian - Vietnamese Enmity Old and Deep

By GLORIA EMERSON
Special to The New York Times

HONG KONG, April 18— The recent massacres of Vietnamese civilians by Cambodians is a new dark chapter in a history of bitterness and feuding between the two peoples whose ancient, tangled roots go deep.

The leaders of Cambodia—both Prince Norodom Sihanouk and the men who overthrew him a month ago—have encouraged the hostility and revived the fears that the Vietnamese want, and will grab, Cambodian land.

The "eternal imperalism" of Vietnam under "all regimes" was a favorite battle cry of Prince Sihanouk, and Cambodia made this charge at the General Assembly of the United Nations on Jan. 22, 1965. Prince Sihanouk also charged South Vietnam with genocide of the Khmer, or Cambodian, people.

Although the new leaders in Pnompenh, including Prince Sisowath Sirik Matak, the First Deputy Premier, have privately denied that they are conducting a brutal campaign against all Vietnamese in Cambodia not just the Vietcong, indications of such a campaign are everywhere.

Memories Are Long

"Vietcong! Eaters of Cambodian Territory," is one sign that reflects the historical quarrel that Cambodians, with their long memories, do not choose to forget.

The decline of the Khmer empire, which at its height included vast areas that are now part of Vietnam, Laos, Thailand and the northern portion of the Malay pensinula, began in the 14th century partly because of Vietnamese encroachment from the east.

By the early 17th century, the Vietnamese, under the Nguyen dynasty, had moved into the Mekong delta region of Cambodia, settling in almost all of what is now South Vietnam. Thailand was the other aggressive, hungry neighbor of Cambodia who tried to claim suzerainty, and who in 1603 succeeded in seating a Cambodian king wholly under Thai domination.

For the next 260 years, the Thais and the Vietnamese struggled for control of Cambodia, each taking large areas of Cambodian land, the Thais in the west and the Vietnamese in the east. In 1946, Thailand, then known as Siam, and Annam, part of present-day Vietnam, joined forces to seat a Cambodian King, Ang Duong, the founder of the dynasty to which Prince Sihanouk belongs.

King Turned to French

Caught between the demands of two Asian powers King Ang Duong turned to the French for help. It was an appropriate choice since the French were then engaged in a war against Annam. Cambodia became a French protectorate in 1864, with one new master—France

187

—who could at least restrain or rebuff Thailand and Annam. Cambodian intellectuals still express gratitude to France for saving their country from being devoured.

The independence of Cambodia, largely engineered by Prince Sihanouk, was won in 1954. Relations with the Vietnamese had deteriorated since the French in the Elysée agreement of March, 1949, awarded the rich province of Cochin China—where nearly half a million Khmers lived—to Vietnam, rejecting Cambodian claim. Cambodian suspicions that the Vietnamese hungered for the open and sparsely populated plains of the Mekong-Tonle Sap basin in Cambodia also increased the frictions.

In Pnompenh, the new leadership has worked hard in the last month to arouse the population to hate the Vietcong, who operate in South Vietnam from sanctuaries in Cambodia. But this campaign apparently touched a deeper nerve and roused a deeper fury than the leaders might have wished.

The Cambodians had been told to hate and they did. The impression of many observers in Pnompenh is that since Cambodians, who seem to have a very vague grasp of the war in Vietnam, do not differentiate between Vietnamese Communists and those Vietnamese fighting the Communists, this hate was certain to have dangerous consequences.

"The Cambodian's greatest anxiety is that he will be unable to perceive the nature of the situation in which he is involved at the moment, and hence not know how to act or what to expect of others," David J. Steinberg and his collaborators wrote in "Cambodia," a book published for the Government by the Human Re-

lations Area Files, a nonprofit research corporation affiliated with Yale University.

The Cambodian "is therefore particularly sensitive to cues which will tell him what kind of situation he is in and what he must and must not do," the authors added.

If this assessment is accurate, it may help explain why it was possible for the hundreds of thousands of Cambodians who once worshiped Prince Sihanouk as a deity and leader to joyfully join in the national denunciation of him. It might also account in part for the massacres of the Vietnamese, hundreds of whom have been killed in recent days.

Conversations with Cambodians in Pnompenh this month as to why thhey hated the Vietnamese elicited only vague replies. A 52-year-old shopkeeper — whose Buddhist reverence for life and whose gentleness could not be disputed—said:

"They are bad for they steal from us."

"What do they steal?" he was asked.

He could not say.

A small, broad country of 67,000 square miles—about the size of the State of Washington — Cambodia has about seven million people. The Khmer make up 90 per cent of the total population. The Khmer has a darker skin than the Vietnamese — although it may range from light brown to a deep tan—bigger bone structure, a longer body and slightly flatter nose.

The most important minority groups are the Chinese and the Vietnamese who, no matter how many years they have lived in Cambodia, are always considered foreigners.

The Vietnamese—whose numbers have been estimated at 600,000 — are believed to be rarely fluent in the Khmer lan-

guage, which is unrelated to their own, and to have never integrated into Cambodian life. Nearly half of the Vietnamese are in Pnompenh, the capital, where they work as skilled artisans, small merchants, administrative clerks or servants. In the countryside they are rice farmers and plantation laborers or fishermen along the banks of the Mekong or its natural reservoir, the Tonle Sap.

"The Vietnamese in Cambodia are commercially ambitious and push themselves forward in a way that irks most Khmer," Mr. Steinberg and his collaborators wrote, "Chinese in Cambodia, too, disrespect the Vietnamese who always look to them for leftover scraps of business. While the Khmer have more or less accepted commercial exploitation by the Chinese—apparently feeling that it is somewhat natural—they find the same treatment by the Vietnamese highly objectionable."

According to the book, the Vietnamese are viewed by the Khmers as "malcontent, insolent without justification, hysterical—and even more obnoxious to Cambodians—boisterous."

Several European residents of Pnompenh, who employ Vietnamese as clerks in their offices, as drivers or as servants, said recently that in their opinion Vietnamese were more intelligent and more dependable than Cambodians.

"The Cambodian is a primitive creature still—he is gentle and lackadaisical and very likable," a French businessman said recently. "But when the Cambodian is aroused and is truly angry he is the most frightening and vicious of all men."

April 19, 1970

NIXON SENDS COMBAT FORCES TO CAMBODIA TO DRIVE COMMUNISTS FROM STAGING ZONE

By ROBERT B. SEMPLE Jr.
Special to The New York Times.

WASHINGTON, April 30—In a sharp departure from the previous conduct of war in Southeast Asia, President Nixon an-

nounced tonight that he was sending United States combat troops into Cambodia for the first time.

Even as the President was addressing the nation on tele-

vision, several thousand American soldiers were moving across the border from South Vietnam to Cambodia to attack what Mr. Nixon described as "the headquarters for the entire

Communist military operation in South Vietnam."

The area was described by sources here as the Fishhook area of Cambodia, some 50 miles northwest of Saigon.

White House sources said they expected tonight's operation to be concluded in six to eight weeks. They said its primary objective was not to kill enemy soldiers but to destroy their supplies and drive them from their sanctuaries.

Aimed at Staging Areas

"Our purpose is not to occupy the areas," the President declared. "Once enemy forces are driven out of these sanctuaries and their military supplies destroyed, we will withdraw."

The President described the action as "not an invasion of Cambodia" but a necessary extension of the Vietnam war designed to eliminate a major Communist staging and communications area. Thus it is intended to protect the lives of American troops and shorten the war, he asserted.

The President further described the action as "indispensable" for the continued success of his program of Vietnamization — under which he has been withdrawing American ground combat troops as the burden of fighting is gradually shifted to the South Vietnamese.

The President's rhetoric was tough—probably the toughest of his tenure in office—and was reminiscent of some of the speeches of Lyndon B. Johnson during the last years of his term as President.

Nixon Appears Grim

The President appeared grim as he delivered his address while sitting at his desk in the Oval Office of the White House. Occasionally he used a nearby map to point out the Communist-held sanctuaries, which were shaded in red. But no gesture could match the solemnity of his words.

He portrayed his decision as a difficult one taken without regard to his political future, which he said was "nothing compared to the lives" of American soldiers.

Discussing this future, Mr. Nixon said: "I would rather be a one-term President and do what I believe is right than to be a two-term President at the cost of seeing America become a second-rate power and to see this nation accept the first defeat in its proud 190-year history."

He added that he regarded the recent actions of the North Vietnamese as a test of American credibility requring firm response.

"This action puts the leaders of North Vietnam on notice," he said, "that we will be patient in working for peace, we will be conciliatory at the conference table, but, we will not be humiliated. We will not be defeated. We will not allow American men by the thousands to be killed by an enemy from privileged sanctuaries."

"We live in an age of anarchy, both abroad and at home," the President declared. "We see mindless attacks on all the great institutions which have been created by free civilizations in the last 500 years. Here in the United States, great universities have been systematically destroyed. Small nations all over the world find themselves under attack.

Aid Asked by Cambodians

Somewhat surprisingly, the President spoke hardly at all about the request made by the Cambodian Premier, Lieut. Gen. Lon Nol, for extensive arms and supplies—perhaps to reinforce his efforts to portray the new action in Cambodia as a tactical incident related to the Vietnam war rather than a full-fledged act of support for the Cambodian Government.

Mr. Nixon said, however, that, with other nations, the United States would try to provide small arms and equipment to the Cambodian army.

Pentagon sources said tonight that shipments would include small arms and automatic weapons, but no artillery or aircraft.

The President did not set forth any legal basis for his action, except to say that "I shall meet my responsibility as Commander in Chief of our Armed Forces to take the action I consider necessary to defend the security of our American men."

Nor did he seek to explain how the introduction of American troops into Cambodia was consistent with the doctrine that he enunciated at Guam last July—that in future he would rely on Asians to fight their own wars.

Mr. Nixon placed the responsibility for the failure of the Paris peace talks squarely on the North Vietnamese. He said they had rejected every American overture, public and private.

White House sources expressed hope, however, that tonight's action—far from deterring future negotiations—might well convince Hanoi of the Administration's resolve to weaken the enemy militarily and thus hasten the beginning of serious negotiations.

The section of Cambodia to which the American units have been sent is a sparsely populated, heavily wooded area in which enemy troops have built numerous complexes of bunkers and storage pits. It is known to military men as the Fishhook because of the configuration of the border at that point.

Area Used for Many Years

North Vietnamese and Vietcong soldiers have been operating there for years, darting across the border for raids against allied positions, then falling back to recuperate, resupply and retrain. Major command headquarters are thought to be situated in the area.

Past allied operations against similar base areas on the South Vietnamese side of the border have not always been notably successful.

Mr. Nixon's speech was virtually certain to cause new turmoil on Capitol Hill and among critics of the war throughout the country. Many Senators had already expressed dismay at yesterday's announcement by the Defense Department that American advisers had accompanied South Vietnamese troops on attacks into the Parrot's Beak section of Cambodia, about 35 miles from Saigon.

The Administration has acknowledged in the past that American commanders have permission to fire across the border at retreating enemy troops, and South Vietnamese troops have crossed the line on a number of occasions in recent days.

But it has never been clear whether American combat troops have crossed the border on the ground. The American military command in Saigon has never admitted such crossings.

Faced with the situation posed by what he said were "stepped-up" enemy guerrilla actions over the last two

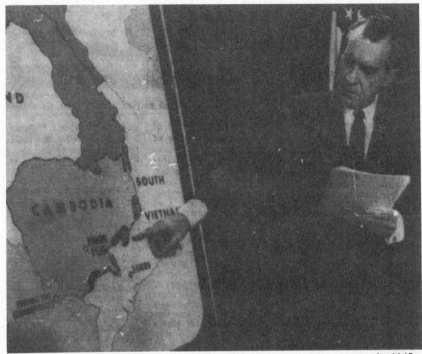

Associated Press

The President points to Fishhook area of Cambodia. Dark areas are enemy strongholds.

weeks, and with the Cambodian capital, Pnompenh, under increasing threats from Vietnamese Communist forces, the President said he had considered three options.

Policy of Inaction Rejected

The first was to "do nothing." Mr. Nixon said this would have "gravely threatened" the lives of Americans remaining in Vietnam after the next troop withdrawal.

The second, he said, was to provide "massive" military aid to Cambodia. He said that large amounts of aid could not be rapidly and effectively used by the small Cambodian Army.

The third choice, he said, was to "go to the heart of the trouble" — to clean out the sanctuaries that serve as bases for attacks on both Cambodian and American and South Vietnamese forces in South Vietnam.

Mr. Nixon's address came as Washington was still trying to digest the Defense Department's announcement yesterday that the United States had agreed to provide combat advisers, tactical air support and other forms of assistance to South Vietnamese troops attacking Communist bases in Cambodia.

The South Vietnamese offensive, involving thousands of troops, began yesterday morning and provoked widespread surprise, anger and frustration on Capitol Hill, mixed with quick expressions of support from some of the President's Congressional allies.

Many legislators, particularly Senators with a long history of opposition to the Vietnam war, saw the Cambodian action as a dangerous expansion of the conflict.

Informed sources reported that more than 1,200 telegrams arrived at the White House last night after the announcement of the South Vietnamese push into Cambodia, with United States support — an unusually large number on an issue on which the President himself had not yet made a public statement.

There was no indication of the tenor of these message but a recent Gallup Poll indicated that public approval of Mr. Nixon's Vietnam policies had dropped from a high of 65 per cent in January to 48 per cent in early April. Therefore tonight's address was regarded in the White House as having considerable political as well as diplomatic significance.

After the Defense Department announcement yesterday, Senator John Sherman Cooper, Republican of Kentucky, and Senator Frank Church, Democrat of Idaho, began drafting legislation that would preclude use of any funds appropriated by Congress for military assistance or operations in Cambodia. This would be attached as an amendment to a military sales bill now before the Senate Foreign Relations Committee.

Some of the critics of yesterday's move—including Senator Mike Mansfield of Montana, the

Senate majority leader — were among a dozen or so Congressional leaders from both parties who gathered at the White House at 8 P.M., one hour before the President was scheduled to go on the air, for an advance briefing from Mr. Nixon in the Cabinet room adjacent to the Oval Room, the President's office. Members of the Cabinet also attended.

During the briefing, Mr. Nixon was said to have summarized the speech and to have set forth the Administration's rationale for the decision to authorize American participation in the South Vietnamese offensive against areas that have served as sanctuaries for Communist forces on the Cambodian side of the border.

The main justification for the move offered yesterday and again this morning, in public statements and private conversations, was that North Vietnamese and Vietcong troops operating from Cambodia had the lives of American servicemen in South Vietnam and, posed an "increasing threat" to more broadly, to the Vietnamization program.

The offensive, Daniel Z. Henkin, Assistant Secretary of Defense for Public Affairs, declared at a briefing yesterday, "is a necessary and effective measure to save American and other free-world lives and to strengthen the Vietnamization program."

Top Aides Visit Capitol

In private, officials conceded that Mr. Nixon had deliberately

chosen to widen the conflict—temporarily, they said—in an effort to bring it to an end more quickly.

This was essentially the approach taken by Administration officials who circulated on Capitol Hill today explaining the Administration's point of view. Both the Under Secretary of State, Elliot L. Richardson, and the Deputy Secretary of Defense, David Packard, were dispatched to the Capitol to brief Republican Senators on Mr. Nixon's reasoning.

It was emphasized that the joint South Vietnamese-United States operation on Cambodian territory should not be construed as Mr. Nixon's answer to the request made by Premier Lon Nol of Cambodia for military aid.

This distinction has been drawn carefully and emphatically in nearly every utterance on the Cambodian situation by Ronald L. Ziegler, the White House press secretary. This apparently reflects an effort to persuade newsmen that the operation in Cambodia is no more than an extension of the Vietnam operation and does not represent a commitment of United States manpower to the Government of Cambodia.

May 1, 1970

U.S. SAYS BIG RAIDS IN NORTH ARE OVER

Officials Stress That There May Be Smaller Strikes if Flights Are Periled

By WILLIAM BEECHER
Special to The New York Times

WASHINGTON, May 4—The Defense Department announced today it had "terminated" large-scale air raids mounted in recent days against three areas of North Vietnam.

But Pentagon officials stressed that smaller air strikes might be conducted in

the future if American reconnaissance flights over North Vietnam were attacked.

For the first time, the Pentagon acknowledged that the raids north of the demilitarized zone over the weekend had been larger in scope than any since the bombing halt in November, 1968, and that so-called "logistics support" facilities for air defense had been struck in addition to antiaircraft gun and missile sites.

3 Areas Attacked

The Defense Department said that from 50 to more than 100 planes had been employed in each of the strikes near Barthelemy Pass, Bankarai Pass and in another area immediately north of the demilitarized zone. Barthelemy Pass, about 240 miles north of the demilitarized zone, is believed to be the far-

thest point north raided by American aircraft since November, 1968.

All three areas, officials said, are key conduits for the flow of men and matériel to enemy military units throughout Indochina, and especially in South Vietnam.

But the official statements left unresolved the question of whether supply depots, unrelated to air defense sites, had also been targets. When pressed on this question at a news briefing today Daniel Z. Henkin, Assistant Secretary of Defense for Public Affairs, said repeatedly: "The targets were antiaircraft facilities and associated logistics support."

Mr. Henkin characterized the raids as "reinforced protective reaction strikes." He insisted that only three had been contemplated, and that since those

The New York Times   May 5, 1970

had been successfully carried out no further such raids were contemplated.

Laird Recalls Notice

"But I want to tell you

again," he added, "that we are, of course, prepared as necessary to continue to protect our unarmed reconnaissance pilots." Emerging from a congressional hearing room, Defense Secretary Melvin R. Laird told reporters that at the time of the bombing halt, North Vietnam had put on notice that the United States insisted on the right to conduct aerial surveillance of enemy build-ups in the North would protect its aircraft Air strikes, he said, will resume if North Vietnam attacks any of our aircraft flying reconnaissance missions."

Mr. Henkin conceded that the air raids had been authorized in Washington. Ronald L. Ziegler, White House press secretary, said that President Nixon had been aware of the strikes and "approved the over-all policy of protective reaction."

In the 18 months since the bombing halt, American commanders in the field have had authority, officials said, to attack air defense sites that fired on American reconnaissance planes. The commanders were not required to get specific Washington approval for "air suppression" missions against offending anti-aircraft installations.

60 Raids Reported

The Pentagon said that during this period 60 missions, counting the most recent ones, had been carried out.

Pentagon spokesmen said that nine jets and one helicopter had been downed over North Vietnam since November, 1968. An additional plane was downed in last week's raids. They conceded that there had been no recent increase in the downing of American reconnaissance planes over the North. No American aircraft had been destroyed in the three months preceding last weekend's air strikes.

But officials stressed that North Vietnam had been increasing its build-up of antiaircraft sites in recent months.

Mr. Henkin insisted that in his view the recent raids represented "no change in policy." But, he added, "I will not quarrel that these attacks may have been larger than in the past."

Other sources said that anywhere from a half-dozen to two-dozen aircraft had normally been involved in so-called suppression or protective reaction missions in the past.

Over the weekend, The New York Times quoted a reliable Administration source to the effect that the recent raids were directed in part at supply depots and "logistics lines."

One source was quoted as having said that "in the past, we couldn't touch" these supplies until they crossed the border into Laos.

"That was hard to take," the source continued." The enemy had built up an awful lot of surface-to-air missiles and anti-aircraft along the northern reaches of the Ho Chi Minh Trail, waiting for us to come in."

The source said that President Nixon had approved the large-scale raids on supply bases and air defenses after his television address last Thursday, in which he announced that American troops would take part in an attack on enemy sanctuaries in Cambodia.

The "logistics support" associated with air defenses that Mr. Henkin cited apparently refers to such things as stocks of antiaircraft ammunition and missiles, radar, power generators and other facilities required to operate the antiaircraft sites.

Mr. Ziegler insisted that the recent raids did not constitute "a resumption of the bombing of the North."

May 5, 1970

Academic Experts In U.S. on Vietnam Almost Nonexistent

Despite nearly a decade of costly United States involvement with Vietnam and her people, American scholarly expertise on Vietnam, particularly North Vietnam, is almost nonexistent.

There is no scholar in the United States who devotes a major portion of his time to studying current affairs in North Vietnam, a survey by The New York Times discovered. And there is no scholar specializing in Vietnamese studies with a tenured professorship at any American university.

Fewer than 30 students in the country are studying Vietnamese. By comparison, three times that number study Thai and more than 600 graduate students are studying Chinese.

Error in Judgment Seen

Prof. John K. Fairbank, director of Harvard University's East Asian Research Center and the man generally considered the founder of modern Chinese studies in the United States, calls the academic situation a "scandal."

"It is fantastic that with our educational resources and our Government's commitment in Vietnam, we are so backward," he said.

"It has meant misjudgment of the enemy, a very serious problem. If we had known about the Vietnamese the way we knew about Britain, we would have known that a few months of bombing would not make them give up."

Professor Fairbank cites as a major reason for the lack of Vietnamese studies the academic community's distaste for Vietnam because of the war. "Academics are fed up with the whole subject of Vietnam," he said. "They would like to abolish Vietnam if they could. So students are not interested in going and studying about it."

Interviews with university officials tend to confirm this impression. While there have been some instances where students signed petitions demanding programs in Vietnamese studies, as at the University of California at Berkeley, these requests have been few in number and have had little influence.

Despite the student protest last year at Berkeley, for example, the university's Center for South and Southeast Asia Studies still does not offer instruction in Vietnamese.

The difficulty and time required to master Vietnamese present another obstacle to the development of Vietnamese studies. "It takes at least two or three years to learn to read Vietnamese, and then if you want to really understand Vietnamese you must also learn Chinese," Alexander Woodside,

a young Vietnam historian at Harvard, explained.

"Furthermore, most students want to be able to go to the country they are studying about and do research there, and for Vietnam that is largely out of the question."

Mr. Woodside also said that decreasing Government assistance for foreign-area studies and the uncertain state of the economy have made it very difficult to fund new programs in Vietnam studies.

Until last year, when the Agency for International Development made a grant of $1-million to Southern Illinois University and the Ford Foundation provided $300,000 to Harvard, no grants specifically earmarked for Vietnamese studies had ever been made.

Harvard is reportedly having difficulty raising the matching funds required by the terms of the Ford grant, because of lack of interest among university officials and alumni. "There are just too many other subjects that are considered more important," Professor Fairbank said in a recent interview.

Six schools offer courses in the Vietnamese language: Southern Illinois, Yale, Cornell, the University of Hawaii, Johns Hopkins, and the American University in Washington, D.C. Cornell's program in Vietnamese language, history and politics, which is widely believed to be the best in the country, has produced only three doctoral degrees since 1960.

Only one school in the country, Yale, offers Cambodian. Last semester two students were enrolled.

June 8, 1970

Cambodia Incursion by U.S. Appears to Unite Foe

By JAMES P. STERBA
Special to The New York Times

SAIGON, South Vietnam, June 27—As American soldiers near the end of their two-month incursion into suspected North Vietnamese and Vietcong sanctuaries in Cambodia and return to South Vietnam, the course of the war in Southeast Asia appears vastly more complicated and uncertain than before the incursion began.

Underscoring the complexity and uncertainty is the belief, shared by many intelligence sources here, that events in Cambodia have brought Communist elements in Indochina not only closer together than ever before, but also closer to China.

This survey of the situation throughout Indochina is based on reports from correspondents of The New York Times throughout the area. It is also based on extensive travels by correspondents within the battle areas, particularly since April 30, when President Nixon announced the decision to send United States troops into Cambodia, and to remove them by June 30.

With that deadline at hand, this is now the general military situation in Indochina:

¶The Communists appear to be on the offensive in Cambodia and in southern Laos to extend the Ho Chi Minh Trail, the traditional supply line from North Vietnam through Laos to South Vietnam. This extension would aid Communist forces that previously depended on shipments of supplies from the Cambodian port of Kompong Som or Sihanoukville. These offensives were under way before the United States incursion.

¶The South Vietnamese for once have carried war into someone else's territory, and South Vietnamese leaders pledge to maintain a military presence in Cambodia.

¶In Laos, the monsoon rains have dampened the seesaw battle north of Vientiane.

¶In North Vietnam, no preparations for major military moves are apparent to allied analysts in Saigon, although some of these analysts see clear signs that Hanoi will mount a major effort to move supplies down the Ho Chi Minh Trail during the wet season, which lasts until late October.

¶In northern South Vietnam, the military line-up on both sides and the level of conflict appear to be no different from previous years. In the southern half of South Vietnam the level of violence is said to be lower than three months ago, but only because substantial numbers of contesting forces have moved west into Cambodia.

In a newspaper interview in 1961, Prince Norodom Sihanouk, then the Chief of State of Cambodia, said:

"Between Laos and South Vietnam, Cambodia is like a stack of hay placed between two other stacks already set on fire. We want to survive in a merciless world."

Nine years and six months later, Cambodia was clearly burning.

For at least a decade, Vietnamese Communists have made use of Cambodia. In the last five years they have established sanctuaries and supply routes there for Vietcong and North Vietnamese troops fighting in the southern half of South Vietnam. It was less than a month after Prince Sihanouk fell from power on March 18, that South Vietnamese troops began raiding the suspected Communist sanctuaries.

and that the North Vietnamese and Vietcong in those sanctuaries began their expansion west into the Cambodian interior.

The war in Cambodia was well under way in the last days in April when thousands of South Vietnamese troops crossed the border in what was described as a search-and-clear operation. They were followed three days later by thousands of American troops.

Thus began the military alteration of Cambodia. It was still going on this week. Early in the week, more than 25,000 South Vietnamese soldiers were operating in Cambodia, but that number was expected to dwindle as the United States deadline approached. How many South Vietnamese would remain in Cambodia was not clear.

Also fighting against the Communist-led troops is a marginal Cambodian army that recently has grown from about 30,000 to about 150,000 troops, under an intensive drive for volunteers.

Facing the South Vietnamese and Cambodian soldiers are a force of 1,000 to 3,000 Khmer Rouge, or Cambodian Communists, and a force of North Vietnamese and Vietcong, whose strength is put at any level from 30,000 to 60,000.

By this week the Cambodian Army occupied less than one-third of the country's 69,000 square miles, mostly cities and towns. A Government military spokesman announced in Pnompenh today that Government forces had withdrawn from the northeastern province of Ratanakiri. Previously Cambodia had withdrawn her forces from

the three other eastern provinces — Stung Treng, Mondulkiri and Kratie. The withdrawals appear to be part of the Government's strategy of concentrating its trained troops in the Pnompenh area.

North Vietnamese troops firmly controlled one-third of the country this week and could roam at will through most of the remaining third.

Aid Seen as Vital

By late this week, the military situation in Cambodia was deteriorating rapidly for the Government, headed by Lieut. Gen. Lon Nol, that overthrew Prince Sihanouk. Whether this deterioration can be reversed appears to depend entirely on how much aid is sent to Pnompenh and how fast and well the Cambodian Army can be properly trained. According to reports from Pnompenh, the survival of the Lon Nol Government depends almost entirely on how much military help it gets from the United States, South Vietnam and, perhaps, Thailand.

It was reported from Pnompenh today that authoritative military sources had disclosed that United States planes would provide close air support for Cambodian troops engaged in major battles anywhere in the country.

Support from Thailand, which has been pledged by Thai leaders, but little has been forthcoming. A dispatch from Washington today reported that American officials had said that Thailand was unwilling to commit troops to Cambodia without a firm guarantee that the United States would underwrite the cost of their operations.

Associated Press

American soldiers at Firebase Bronco, 17 miles inside Cambodia, providing artillery support as U.S. forces were being withdrawn. Tomorrow is American pullout deadline.

Few knowledgeable military and civilian officials in Pnompenh said they believed the Communists were strong enough to take over all of Cambodia in the near future. But most of these officials said they believed that the Communists were off to a very good start toward that goal, regardless of whether they wanted to attain it.

American and South Vietnamese military men have proclaimed the success of their operations in Cambodia, but the success was being judged in terms of the short-ranged tactical advantage that the allies had gained in South Vietnam and not in terms of the long-range outlook for Cambodia. It also appears from the most recent remarks of President Nguyen Van Thieu and his military leaders that continued South Vietnamese operations in Cambodia will be designed with the primary objective of defending South Vietnam, not Cambodia.

Advantages Are Cited

The allies say that they have captured about 30 or 40 per cent of the enemy's supplies stored in border sanctuaries. They say also that the Cambodian operations have gained time for the allies in the southern half of South Vietnam; how much depends on how long it takes the North Vietnamese and Vietcong troops to restore administrative and supply networks apparently disrupted when the allies crossed the border.

Estimates of this time range from three months to a year, during which the allies expect to continue the withdrawal of Americans from South Vietnam, to proceed with "Vietnamization" programs, and to carry out an offensive against enemy forces in South Vietnam who are believed to be isolated and directionless.

The extent to which they can do all these things depends not only on the success of the operations in Cambodia, but also on the dimensions of the support the allies will be required to give or decide to give the Cambodians.

The Cambodia incursions have given the South Vietnamese troops needed boosts in morale and confidence, as well as experience in conducting large-scale maneuvers of armor, such as those conducted in World War II, while facing fairly limited opposition. They are rarely if ever called to this kind of action in their own country.

How well they will sustain morale and confidence when they return to their defensive role in South Vietnam remains to be seen.

Saigon Has Upper Hand

In any event, for the moment the military advantage in South Vietnam appears to be on the side of Saigon and its million-man armed force. It is fighting against an enemy apparatus

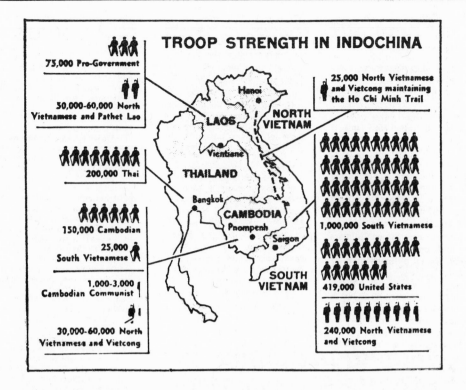

TROOP STRENGTH IN INDOCHINA

75,000 Pro-Government

50,000-60,000 North Vietnamese and Pathet Lao

200,000 Thai

150,000 Cambodian

25,000 South Vietnamese

1,000-3,000 Cambodian Communist

30,000-60,000 North Vietnamese and Vietcong

25,000 North Vietnamese and Vietcong maintaining the Ho Chi Minh Trail

1,000,000 South Vietnamese

419,000 United States

240,000 North Vietnamese and Vietcong

HANOI • / LAOS / NORTH VIETNAM / Vientiane / THAILAND / Bangkok • / CAMBODIA / Pnompenh • / Saigon • / SOUTH VIETNAM

that allied analysts continue to estimate at 240,000 men, although the reliability of that figure is open to question.

In terms of area, the situation is brightest in the Mekong delta, south of Saigon, and in the provinces around Saigon that make up the III Corps tactical zone. In these areas, where nearly two-thirds of South Vietnam's 18 million people live, the Government's presence continues to spread, and the Vietcong influence is said to be rapidly fading. The operations in Cambodia have helped that process.

In the northern half of South Vietnam, the picture is different. Largely unaffected by events in Cambodia, enemy forces remain strong and well supplied and the control of the population continues to be a seesaw struggle; both sides claim great gains.

Allied analysts cite a large body of evidence, including speeches by Hanoi leaders and instructions in captured documents, which they say show an evolution in North Vietnam's strategy. They say the shift has been from an emphasis on large-unit operations to gain a "decisive victory" toward an emphasis on small-unit guerrilla operations, terrorism and political subversion in a "protracted conflict" to gain "ultimate victory" sometime in the future.

Some analysts say they expect pitched battles between main units to become less frequent and to play only a minor and diversionary role.

For the time being, however, the war in South Vietnam is a combination of struggles in which Saigon appears, for the moment, to have the advantage.

But this advantage is being undermined by an economy that is collapsing as its foundation of American dollars withers with the withdrawal of American troops.

As of this week, there were 419,000 American soldiers in South Vietnam, including those on their way back from Cambodia. President Nixon has said that by the spring of next year, 260,000 American soldiers will remain in South Vietnam, operating in what allied officials say will be an "increasingly supportive and defensive role."

Implications for Laos

The clearest immediate implications of the Cambodian situation for Laos involve the Ho Chi Minh Trail, which is Hanoi's only link now with its forces in South Vietnam and Cambodia. Until now, the trail has been used to supply Communist forces in the northern and central portions of South Vietnam with men and munitions and to supply forces in the southern half of South Vietnam with replacements.

The North Vietnamese in Laos moved quickly after the fall of Prince Sihanouk to extend this overland supply route farther south. On April 30, they captured Attopeu, the southernmost Government stronghold in Laos. It had been surrounded by North Vietnamese troops for months and could have been taken by the Communists, according to military men, any time they wanted it.

The fall of Attopeu opened an access route to forces farther south by way of the Se Kong, a tributary of the Mekong River. They converge in Cambodia to form an all-weather route to the south. On June 9, the Communists overran Saravane, farther to the north

in Laos, leaving the only semblance of Government resistance in the southern panhandle of Laos at Pakse, along the Mekong River to the west, and roughly between Saravane and Attopeu.

The extent of any new drive the enemy might make along the trail is not now clear. According to analysts in Saigon, nothing much out of the ordinary for this time of year is apparent.

The movement of men down the trail, starting late last October, continued at a rate estimated at 10,000 a month until January, when it was said to have dwindled considerably. It has been termed light since then. The fall of Prince Sihanouk and the allied operations in Cambodia do not appear to have affected Hanoi's strategy in this area.

Hanoi made what allied officials call a record effort to move supplies down the trail during the dry season, citing the appearance of 1,000 trucks a day.

This movement slackened before the fall of Prince Sihanouk and remains at an average of about 100 trucks a day, according to these officials.

Usually the North Vietnamese make a concerted effort during the dry season to move enough supplies down the trail to last their forces in the northern half of South Vietnam through the wet season, June to October, when roads are washed out by daily rains. After this effort, substantial numbers of administrative workers turn to other jobs or move back into North Vietnam for the duration of wet season. So far this year, American sources have said, the administrative apparatus, estimated to number 25,000 men, has remained in place.

This information, taken together with captured documents and prisoner interrogations, leads allied officials to believe that a major resupply effort is planned during the wet season. By this week, however, it had not materialized.

Foe Controlled Half Laos

Elsewhere in Laos, a force estimated at 35,000 to 45,000 North Vietnamese soldiers is helping 15,000 soldiers of the Pathet Lao battle about 60,000 Royal Government troops and about 15,000 Meo hill tribesmen organize and financed by the United States Central Intelligence Agency.

The Communist-led soldiers controlled more than half the country before they began their expansion in the south. Most of the sparsely populated mountainous area from the Plaine des Jarres north and west is controlled by the Pathet Lao

and North Vietnamese. In the far northwest, about 10,000 Chinese are at work on a road-building project. They had completed about 100 miles of it from southeastern Yunnan Province in China almost to the Mekong River, when the expansion began.

Of a population of three million, the Government in Vientiane controlled more than half, most of whom inhabited the thickly populated Mekong valley lowlands.

Prince Souphanouvong, the leader of the Pathet Lao faction, has demanded that his half brother Prince Souvanna Phouma, the Laotian Premier, ask the Americans to stop bombing of Ho Chi Minh Trail as part of a settlement to end the fighting. So far, Prince Souvanna Phouma has refused to ask, and the United States has reportedly told him the bombing would not stop even if he did ask.

Lately, Souvanna Phouma

has been under some pressure from the rightists in his Government as a result of the recent gains by the Communists in the south. The Americans, aware of the rightist opposition, have told the Laotians, as one diplomat put it recently, "no Souvanna, no money."

"No matter what happens," said one well-placed American source in Vientiane, "the United States could not conceivably send in American troops."

The Laotians appear to be convinced of this, and are hoping for more American money.

There have been rumors in both Saigon and Vientiane that South Vietnamese forces might be planning forays into Laos. Knowledgable Americans and Laotians feel this might provoke strong counter-measures by the North Vietnamese.

The Laotian Government has given the new Cambodian Government a gift of 500 old French rifles — without ammunition.

Thailand is expected to play a role in the Indochina fighting sooner or later, simply because of her geography. Elements of her 200,000-man army stationed along the 400-mile border with Cambodia had been placed on full alert by this week, according to the Premier, Thanom Kittikachorn.

The Premier told the Thai Parliament that Thailand would send her troops to Cambodia if necessary, but that for the moment such a move was not necessary.

Besides the army, Thailand has a 25,000-man air force and a 15,000-man navy, but the leaders have expressed constant worry over what they say is increasing Communist infiltration. Thai officials assert since the war spread to Cambodia, the Communist have infiltrated all of their border provinces with Cambodia.

June 29, 1970

Cambodian Economy Is Badly Hurt by War

By SYDNEY H. SCHANBERG
Special to The New York Times

PNOMPENH, Cambodia, July 4—Tourism and the rubber industry are ruined, rice export has been badly hurt and the Cambodian householder is now paying more than twice as much as he used to for the charcoal with which he cooks his food.

These are some of the increasingly damaging effects that the three-month-old war with the Vietnamese Communists is having on Cambodia's fragile economy.

With the Communists seemingly able to harass and cut some of the major roads at will, the marketing of goods in this farm-based country has become a sometime thing, and it is never possible to predict what will get through to Pnompenh, the capital and largest population center.

When shrimp cocktail is scratched off the menus of the city's French restaurants, for example, it means that the road from Kompong Som (formerly Sihanoukville), Cambodia's only deepwater port, was impassable that day.

Cambodian officials remain calmly optimistic, as they do about the war, and some foreign economic experts contend that the situation is "not beyond hope." But the problem is serious and getting more so.

Every development project

in the country has been shut down, most notably the $61-million Prek Thnot dam-irrigation project, which was under construction and was the country's hope for bringing to life the dry, poor rice region southwest of Pnompenh.

Only one of the many agricultural experimental stations in the country is still in operation—an Israeli project that is barely keeping going.

Small Industries in Trouble

The only industries Cambodia has ever known—small factories and processing plants, many of which are in and around Pnompenh — are in deep trouble. Either the raw materials they import, such as plastics, are not arriving, or their labor force has virtually disappeared.

Cambodian men are all going into the army and the ethnic Vietnamese, who used to hold most of the skilled jobs have either already fled to South Vietnam or are living in Pnompenh's refugee camps, waiting to be taken there.

There used to be 100,000 Vietnamese in Pnompenh; there are only about 1,000 left.

"Their hope was to industrialize more," said one foreign economic expert, "and now that's been knocked on the head for the duration of the

war." Perhaps one reason there is no sense of crisis or emergency in the Cambodian Government is that this is a country where no one will actually starve. Ninety per cent of Cambodia's seven million people work on the land, and most of them can live off what they grow.

Rubber and rice together account for three - quarters or more of Cambodia's exports and foreign exchange earnings.

All of the rubber plantations are in the war zone and have been shut down. Many have been destroyed in the fighting, some by allied bombing. For all of them, it would take a year or maybe two to get them working again.

The only rubber that was exported this year was in stock before the fighting started; it was nearly 70 per cent less than the normal crop.

As for rice, the problem is not growing it, but marketing it—with the roads and railways dangerous. Rice exports, as a result, will be 50 per cent less than the original forecast.

The estimate for all exports now is about $46-million for 1970 less than half the previously expected total—and even this figure may be optimistic.

Cambodia's foreign currency reserves, which have been steadily falling in the last several years, are now only $60-million, and experts here estimate that this will last only until some time next year.

All these statistics point to only one thing—the economy is not generating any money either for individuals or the Government, and the latter may soon be broke.

The Cambodian budget last year was $165-million, and one-third of it was for defense. That was when the army had only 35,000 men. It has now

swollen to nearly 100,000, although half have no arms and many in the other half are poorly armed.

Foreign economists here believe the only thing that will keep the Combodian economy going is "a substantial transfusion" of foreign funds—loans and investment—to get the rubber plantations working again and to give the Government enough foreign exchange to buy what it needs for the war effort.

There have been reports of tentative feelers put out to the International Monetary Fund and the Asian Development Bank, but so far no foreign aid of the size required has even been hinted at.

Inflation has already begun here, but it is not yet critical.

Most of the price increases have been slight, such as on vegetables, meat, poultry and fish. The cost of rice, because there is still enough to meet the domestic demand, has remained fairly stable.

Some items, however, have shot up alarmingly.

Potatoes, which come largely from South Vietnam and have always been expensive here, have jumped from 25 cents a pound to $1.

Charcoal, an essential item for cooking in all Cambodian households, has climbed from about 2 cents a pound to 5. The reason is that most of the charcoal comes from territory that the North Vietnamese and Vietcong now control.

Actually, Pnompenh needs more food these days because its population, once 600,000, has suddenly grown to 800,000 because of an influx of Cambodian refugees from battle zones—and this despite the drop in the ethnic Vietnamese.

July 5, 1970

Americans Find Brutality In South Vietnamese Jail

By GLORIA EMERSON
Special to The New York Times

SAIGON, South Vietnam, July 6 — An American who visited South Vietnam's largest civilian prison last Thursday reported here today on what he described as the inhuman conditions and intimidation existing there.

Don Luce, who is gathering information in Vietnam for the Division of Interchurch Aid of the World Council of Churches, said that 500 of the 9,900 prisoners believed to be on the island known as Con Son were confined in small stone compartments, and that many of the prisoners were unable to stand. The prisoners, he said, suffer from malnutrition, physical abuse and filthy conditions.

Mr. Luce was able to visit the island, which is 140 miles southeast of Saigon, because he accompanied Representative Augustus F. Hawkins, a Democrat from the Watts area in Los Angeles, and Representative William R. Anderson, Democrat of Tennessee. The group was accompanied by a Congressional aide, Thomas Harkin, who photographed the worst of the prisons.

The legislators were in South Vietnam as part of a 12-man House committee that made a fact-finding tour on the United States' involvement in Asia.

Access to the prison is denied to newsmen. South Vietnamese officials generally deny that conditions are extremely harsh on the island, which is often referred to by its French name, Polo Condor.

The small stone compartments, known to the Vietnamese as tiger cages, were not voluntarily shown to the American visitors. The purpose of the trip had been to see if they existed.

Attempts to prevent the inspection were made by the warden, Col. Nguyen Van Ve. Mr. Luce also asserts that when the legislators asked to see six specific prisoners—four students, the editor of a French-language daily newspaper closed by the Government and another man — the colonel became angry. Mr. Luce had supplied the prisoners' names to the legislators.

After insisting that a telegram be sent to the Ministry of the Interior in Saigon asking permission for the group to see the six prisoners, Colonel Ve, according to Mr. Luce, said in Vietnamese to his own aide: "Do not worry about getting an answer—the important thing is to send it."

The warden did not know that Mr. Luce, who has been in South Vietnam for more than 11 years, speaks Vietnamese fluently.

According to Mr. Luce, Frank E. Walton, the American who heads the Public Safety Directorate — an advisory program in South Vietnam under the wing of Civil Operations-Revolutionary Development Support, known as CORDS — backed the warden in his attempts to block the visitors.

"Walton suggested we visit the curio shop," Mr. Luce continued. "He was angry to see me with the Congressmen and said, 'I thought this trip was aboveboard — Luce has misrepresented everything in Vietnam.'"

Mr. Luce, who is 35 years old and came here in 1958 as a volunteer social - service worker, has been an outspoken critic of United States involvement in Vietnam and of the Saigon Government.

Mr. Luce, who had been told of a hidden entry to the tiger cages, saw a tiny gate. Representative Hawkins asked Colonel Ve to have the door opened after the warden had said it was not possible. A guard, hearing the warden's voice, opened the door and the Americans went inside with the warden at their heels.

"We looked down from a catwalk through large openings—one for each cell," Mr. Luce related. "These were the tiger cages which are not supposed to exist anymore."

He said that in the presence of Colonel Ve the Americans visited two buildings composed of what he described as airless, hot, filthy stone compartments. In the building for men, according to Mr. Luce, three or four prisoners are in each compartment, which seemed not quite 5 feet across and 9 feet long.

"It was high enough for the prisoners to stand up but none of the men did," he related. "They dragged themselves to the spot where they could look up and speak to us. The men claimed they were beaten, that they were very hungry because they were only given rice that had sand and pebbles in it."

The prisoners also pleaded for water, Mr. Luce said, and cried out that they were sick and had no medicine.

Above each compartment, Mr. Luce related, was a bucket of powdery white lime that Colonel Ve said was used for whitewashing the walls but that the prisoners said was thrown down on them when they asked for food.

The women prisoners, who numbered about 250, told Mr. Luce, he said, that they were moved from mainland prisons seven months ago. They had the same complaints, he added, and also said there was no water for washing.

He said there appeared to be 60 or 70 compartments in each of the two buildings, with five women in a compartment.

When the group came out of the tiger camps after an hour and 15 minutes, Mr. Luce said, they met Mr. Walton, who rebuked them for "intruding" into a Vietnamese prison.

A fact sheet distributed in Saigon by Mr. Walton's agency over his signature quotes him as describing the "Con Son National Correction Center" as follows:

"In the opinion of correction advisors with lengthy U.S. penology experience, Con Son is not a 'Devil's Island,' but on the contrary is a correctional institution worthy of higher ratings than some prisons in the United States."

The center was established by the French in 1862 and its name stands for a fearful ordeal. The French, it is said, built the tiger cages.

July 7, 1970

U.S. Said to Offer A New Justification For Raids in North

By HEDRICK SMITH
Special to The New York Times

WASHINGTON, Nov. 30 — High Administration officials privately acknowledge that the United States is establishing and reinforcing a new rationale for American air strikes against North Vietnam.

The attack by a single American F-105 fighter-bomber yesterday against a North Vietnamese missile site was the first such mission since Secretary of Defense Melvin R. Laird warned on Nov. 21 that American pilots operating over Laos would resort to "protective reaction" against North Vietnamese missile sites that threatened them from across the Vietnamese-Laotian border.

Until yesterday, with one exception, all previous American air attacks on the North have been officially justified on the ground that they constituted retaliation for what were viewed as North Vietnamese violations of the 1968 understanding that ended the John-son Administration's bombing of the North.

The single exception occurred last Sept. 5, but it received little notice and no high-level policy defense. The American command in Saigon reported on Sept. 5 that an American F-105 operating over Laos had fired on a North Vietnamese missile site 21 miles southwest of Donghoi and about five miles east of the Laotian border. A spokesman said the F-105 had struck the missile site after detecting enemy radar preparing for a missile firing.

Pentagon officials contend that in both incidents—yesterday's and the one on Sept. 5—American pilots were exercising the "inherent right of self-defense."

Secretary Laird asserted at a news conference today that the "pilot has the right—and as long as I'm Secretary of Defense I'm not going to send pilots up there [without it]—to use this electronic missile to go in on the site that has them locked in [on radar]."

But officials acknowledged that this was different from claiming the right to protect reconnaissance missions over North Vietnam. And high officials concede that on Nov. 21, Secretary Laird was deliberately warning Hanoi that there would now be a new policy of striking North Vietnamese missile sites along the Laotian border when they threatened American planes operating over Laos.

The Defense Department asserts that it has become convinced of the need for such a policy because of what is described as a build-up of North Vietnamese missile sites along the Laotian-North Vietnamese border.

The initial comments of Pentagon officials left the impression that on Nov. 21 some American planes had attacked North Vietnamese missile sites because of alleged interference with American operations over Laos.

10 Miles From Border

But today, officials said this was not the case. They said that all the attacks had been undertaken at least 10 miles from the border, east of the mountain passes leading into Laos.

Mr. Laird made an unexpected appearance today at the regular Pentagon news briefing to defend himself against charges by Senator J. W. Fulbright that Mr. Laird had misrepresented the extent of American bombing of North Vietnam on Nov. 21.

Mr. Fulbright, chairman of the Senate Foreign Relations Committee, charged in a television interview that in testifying last Tuesday Mr. Laird had not mentioned an air strike carried out near Hanoi in conjunction with the raid on the prisoner-of-war camp at Sontay.

Answers Questions

Mr. Laird suggested that the fault lay not with him but with members of the Foreign Relations Committee, who had failed to question him closely enough.

"I've been as forthright as

one could possibly in answering all questions," Mr. Laird said. "Perhaps members of the committee were not asked. That is not my responsibility. Now, I answer questions, but I only answer the questions that are asked."

The Defense Secretary declared that early on Tuesday, at a closed hearing of the Senate Armed Services Committee, he had acknowledged that American planes had fired 12 to 14 Shrike missiles against North Vietnamese missile sites. Today, he said he had been in error and that only 11 Shrikes had been fired.

On Nov. 21, Mr. Laird dismissed as erroneous charges by Hanoi that an American prisoner-of-war camp had been bombed. Two days later, when the Sontay raid was first disclosed, Mr. Laird stood by as Brig. Gen. Leroy J. Manor told

reporters that there was "a minimum amount of firing" during the raid.

Mr. Laird's comments today were his first public acknowledgment that Shrike missiles had been fired at ground installations. Last week, Mr. Laird conceded that he had not even intended to make the Sontay raid public.

Just as in the case of American pilots flying along the Laotian-North Vietnamese border, Mr. Laird said, American pilots flying cover for the Sontay raiders "had the authority to use those [Shrike] missiles if the radar was locked in on them—just like the F-105 did yesterday when it was locked in by enemy radar."

December 1, 1970

Sprays in Vietnam Said to Level Fifth Of Mangrove Area

By WALTER SULLIVAN
Special to The New York Times

CHICAGO, Dec. 29—A study of defoliation in Vietnam, undertaken for the American Association for the Advancement of Science, has shown a catastrophic effect on some parts of the country.

At least a fifth of the 1.2 million acres of mangrove forest in South Vietnam have been "utterly destroyed," the study

found. Furthermore, some unknown factor has prevented any vegetation from returning to those areas.

Photographs were shown in which parts of the delta region between Saigon and the sea look as if they had been devastated by nuclear attack.

However, the search for evidence of birth defects from the spraying of such chemicals on one-seventh of South Vietnam has so far been inconclusive.

December 30, 1970

U.S. IS NOW FLYING COPTER MISSIONS FOR LAOS TROOPS

By The Associated Press

SAIGON, South Vietnam, Jan. 19—A further enlargement of the United States air role in Indochina was reported here today as official sources said American helicopter gunships were flying combat missions in Laos in direct support of Laotian ground troops.

The informants said Army, Air Force and Marine helicopter gunships had been supporting the Laotian troops for some time and had been attacking enemy troops and supplies along the Ho Chi Minh Trail through southeastern Laos.

Disclosure of this helicopter activity in Laos followed reports yesterday that United States helicopter gunships were attacking enemy forces in Cambodia in support of an allied drive to reopen a major Cambodian supply route.

January 20, 1971

SAIGON UNITS DRIVE INTO LAOS TO STRIKE ENEMY SUPPLY LINE

By ALVIN SHUSTER
Special to The New York Times

SAIGON, South Vietnam, Monday, Feb. 8—Thousands of South Vietnamese troops, supported by American planes and artillery, crossed the border into Laos this morning to strike at the Ho Chi Minh Trail network in hopes of crippling Hanoi's main artery for supplying the Indochina war.

President Nguyen Van Thieu, announcing the operation in a statement this morning, called the attack an "act of legitimate self-defense" and added that it should be "limited in time as well as in space." He asserted that South Vietnam "does not have any territorial ambition whatsoever."

The United States military command emphasized in a

statement that no United States ground combat troops and no United States advisers would go into Laos with the South Vietnamese forces. It said the United States would provide artillery support, fired from South Vietnam, and virtually unlimited air power—helicopter gunships, planes, logistics and medical evacuation missions.

U.S. Prepared Way

The attack was launched from South Vietnam's northernmost province of Quangtri and possibly other points at 7 A.M. today (6 P.M., Sunday, New York time).

American helicopters flew the South Vietnamese troops across the border while South Vietnamese armored columns and infantrymen moved across the border on Route 9, cleared last week up to the border by some of the 9,000 American troops involved in the operation along with about 20,000 South Vietnamese soldiers.

Correspondents attempting to cross the border with the South Vietnamese on Route 9 were stopped by American military policemen.

February 8, 1971

By United Press International

CAMBODIAN CHIEF SUFFERS A STROKE

By United Press International

PNOMPENH, Cambodia, Feb. 10 — Premier Lon Nol suffered a stroke Monday that paralyzed half his body, reliable sources close to the Cambodian Government said today. An official statement said he had been ordered to stop all activities for medical reasons.

Premier Lon Nol, 58 years old, is a general in the army and also serves as Cambodia's Defense Minister in charge of operations against Communist invaders.

He came to power last March after the National Assembly ousted Prince Norodom Sihanouk as Chief of State, charging that he had allowed Communist forces to infiltrate Cambodia and set up bases along the South Vietnamese border.

February 11, 1971

Calley Concedes Killings; Says He Acted on Orders

By HOMER BIGART
Special to The New York Times

FORT BENNING, Ga., Feb. 23—First Lieut. William L. Calley Jr. admitted from the witness stand today that he shot some civilian prisoners who had been herded into a ditch in the South Vietnamese hamlet of Mylai 4 three years ago, but he said he was acting under orders.

The lieutenant, who said he had no regrets, testified he told one soldier to kill a group of civilians because "that was my order, sir—that was the order of the day, sir."

"They were all enemy," he contended. "They were all to be destroyed."

The 27-year-old officer, on trial for the murder of at least 102 South Vietnamese men, women and children, said he had been acting under repeated orders from his company commander, Capt. Ernest L. Medina.

While admitting that he participated in the mass slaying at the ditch, Lieutenant Calley denied that he joined in another group slaying of men, women and children along a trail.

He is facing a court-martial on four counts of premeditated murder—two counts involving the mass killings and two counts of individual slayings. one involving a child who allegedly attempted to escape from the ditch and the other involving an old man in white

robes who might have been a Buddhist monk.

Lieutenant Calley conceded that he had shot the child. He saw a head bobbing in a rice paddy, he said, and he fired and it turned out to be "just a boy" who, he said he learned later, was a fugitive from the ditch. But he did not, as Government witnesses testified, throw the boy back into the ditch before shooting him, the lieutenant said.

He denied killing the white-robed old man. All he did, he testified, was to butt-stroke him. He hit the victim on the head with the butt of his rifle after an "interrogation," he explained.

The old man collapsed at the edge of the ditch, still alive, Lieutenant Calley testified. "Somebody's foot" propelled him into the ditch along with the others, Lieutenant Calley said.

Lieutenant Calley said he could not have killed as many as 102 persons. He said he could not recall changing his rifle's magazine during the action and that he still had left some rounds of his original magazine, which had contained 18 rounds.

Government witnesses have said they saw Lieutenant Calley

change magazines as he fired into the ditch.

Would Clear Minefields

Lieutenant Calley said he had wanted to spare some of the inhabitants of Mylai, but only to have them walk across enemy minefields that he had been told to expect on the eastern side of Mylai.

George W. Latimer, the chief defense counsel, asked if the use of Vietnamese to clear minefields was a standard practice.

"It was understood," Lieutenant Calley replied, "we'd have civilians in front of us to clear the minefields."

Under cross-examination by Capt. Aubrey M. Daniel 3d, Lieutenant Calley said that as his men entered the village he told one of his sergeants "to hang onto some of the Vietnamese" for mine sweeping.

He said he had been given these "instructions" by Captain Medina.

But in the end, he testified, he and his troops had to kill all the civilians because they "could not be moved fast enough" and Captain Medina was on the radio bawling him out for slowing up the action.

Second Day on Stand

In his second day on the witness stand, Lieutenant Calley remained a very tense witness. The military judge, Col. Reid W. Kennedy, called the mid-morning recess five minutes earlier than usual to let him regain composure.

At the end of the direct examination, he seemed to regain confidence briefly. His answers were firm as Mr. Latimer led him quickly through questions that lay at the heart of the defense strategy.

"No sir, I didn't," Lieutenant Calley replied to such questions

such as "Did you ever form an intent, specifically or generally, to waste [kill] any Vietnamese man, woman or child?" and, "Did you at any time consciously conceive the wasting of any man woman or child Vietnamese?"

Lieutenant Calley said he wanted only to "waste and destroy the enemy, sir."

The defense has relied heavily on testimony of psychiatrists who swore that Lieutenant Calley, because of his limited educational background and because of the stress of combat in Vietnam, was suffering a mental impairment and could not have premeditated the killings.

As for the mass slaying of about 30 Vietnamese, mostly women and children, on the trail, Lieutenant Calley said he had never been at that scene.

He had been placed there by at least four witnesses, including Pvt. Paul Meadlo, who testified that Lieutenant Calley ordered him to "take care" of the civilians, then upbraided him later for not "wasting" them, and finally joined Private Meadlo in gunning down the group.

Today Lieutenant Calley conceded that he encountered Private Meadlo with some Vietnamese civilians and told him merely to get the civilians moving out of the village so they could be used later to clear minefields.

Later he again encountered Private Meadlo with the civilians in "basically the same place, standing in a rice paddy," he said.

"What did you say to him? asked Captain Daniel in cross-examination.

"Told him if he couldn't move the people to waste 'em," Lieutenant Calley replied.

He said he walked away from the scene, convinced that Private Meadlo would obey his orders to kill the group.

The testimony continued:

Q. Did you hear firing from that area? A. Not specifically from Meadlo, that I know of, sir.

Q. You didn't look back? A. No, sir.

Q. Were you curious as to whether he would obey this order? A. No, sir.

Q. You didn't care whether he would obey that order either? A. I felt that he would.

Q. Why did you feel he would obey that order if he hadn't obeyed the previous order to move out? A. I felt

Meadlo was a very good troop. I had no reason to doubt that he would.

5 Occasions Cited

Lieutenant Calley testified earlier that Captain Medina told him on five separate occasions that the orders were to kill all inhabitants of Myali. Captain Medina relayed these orders at two briefings on the eve of the action, once on the morning of the incident, and twice by radio during the sweep through the village, Lieutenant Calley said.

"Did he classify in his briefing as to whether the enemy would include women and children?" Mr. Latimer asked.

"He didn't break it down,"

Lieutenant Calley replied. "We had been talking about it from the time we got here, that men, women and children were enemy soldiers."

Lieutenant Calley said that during the enemy's Tet offensive of early 1968 the American commanders in Vietnam were demanding reports of victories, reports often bolstered by inflated body counts of enemy dead.

"It was very important we tell the people back home we were killing more of the enemy than they were killing us," Lieutenant Calley said. "You just made a body count off the top of your head. Anything went into the body count: V.C., buffalo, pigs, cows. Something

was dead, you put it into your body count, sir."

Besides shooting the boy and shooting at the people in the ditch, Lieutenant Calley told the military court that he had fired at a Vietnamese male running from the village and that he had shot and presumably killed two other Vietnamese males inside a house.

One of these Vietnamese, standing in a fireplace, was dressed in a green uniform and looked as though he had just come down the chimney, Lieutenant Calley said. The other was dressed in black and was going out the window, he said.

February 24, 1971

Hopes Thin for the Millions Adrift Across Indochina

By HENRY KAMM
Special to The New York Times

SAIGON, South Vietnam, April 20—Uprooted, sometimes by those who are called friends and sometimes by those called enemies, millions of living victims of the war are adrift in Indochina.

They wash up here or there, sometimes for a brief respite, often for a long stay without a future. Then they move on, mostly to another place where they do not want to stay.

In a region where 30 years of war have made a mockery of numbers, it is a fair estimate that of the 27 million people thought to live in South Vietnam, Cambodia and Laos, at least a fourth have been uprooted at least once. About half of that number remain in places that they cannot consider home.

In all three countries tens of thousands are still being made homeless by a war from which the United States may be disengaging but to which the people of South Vietnam, Cambodia and Laos see no end.

The United States finances everything done on behalf of the uprooted in South Vietnam and Laos and will presumably do the same in Cambodia. A Senate subcommittee headed by Edward M. Kennedy has earned the respect of American officials for focusing attention on how the United States exercises its responsibilities for displaced persons. The subcom-

mittee will hold hearings on the issue tomorrow and Thursday, and William E. Colby, who is in charge of the American side of the pacification effort in South Vietnam will be the principal witness.

●

"They are not fleeing the enemy and not fleeing the allies," said Keo Viphakone, the overburdened man in charge of the insoluble refugee problem of Laos. "They are fleeing the soldiers."

In tropical lands where food grows swiftly, the refugees often go hungry because they do not even stay long enough to raise their own or because they are crowded so densely into inhospitable places where not enough can be provided.

"We are preventing them from dying," a missionary in Pnompenh said, summing up the extent of what is being done for the displaced persons of Cambodia. And—it is clear after seven weeks of travel through Indochina, visits to refugee sites and interviews with scores of displaced persons and officials charged with their care — the missionary might have been talking of those in the two other countries as well.

In the general absence of security as long as the war continues, refugees can be resettled elsewhere or returned to their native regions only at the risk of a renewal of hostilities that will again cast them adrift.

The New York Times/Nancy Moran

Laotians from island in Mekong on way to refugee camp

The greatest number of refugees is in South Vietnam, where a conservative estimate is five million displaced persons in a population of 17 million. As early as 1954, when Vietnam

was partitioned, nearly a million Vietnamese fled south rather than live under the Communists in the North.

Of the three million people thought to live in Laos, the

number of those displaced at least once is put at 750,000.

Cambodia, which lived in relative peace until last year, has not been at war long enough yet to compile even approximate statistics. But 200,000 ethnic Vietnamese have been evacuated to South Vietnam, the population of Pnompenh is thought to have risen from 600,000 to more than a million and there are refugees all over the countryside.

No figures are available on displaced persons in the Communist-controlled regions of the three countries, where regular attacks from the air have turned many inhabitants into cave dwellers. The bulk of the bombing is conducted by the United States, but the South Vietnamese, Laotian and Cambodian Air Forces are no more sparing of the lives of their countrymen.

The air war, along with other weapons in the vast arsenal that the United States has brought to Indochina, is generally accepted as a major cause of the mass displacements. That view is shared by most American refugee officials interviewed, but because of the touchiness of the subject most ask that their names be withheld.

There is another side to the problem. When the Communists enter a village and impress its men, even temporarily, to fight for them or to serve for a month or two carrying the goods of war on their backs, the village has the choice of doing their bidding—and becoming the target of American or South Vietnamese air strikes, artillery barrages or ground attacks—or facing Communist retaliation for refusal.

In the "revolutionary warfare" the Communists practice, they also spread terror to demoralize civilian populations in contested areas; not only do they employ threats and propaganda but they also carry out mortar and rocket attacks on civilian targets.

Such tactics have often caused entire villages to move voluntarily to areas more firmly under Government control, particularly since they are assured of safety from the allied air attacks that are a constant threat in areas not clearly on the Government side.

The South Vietnamese Minister of Social Welfare, Dr. Tran Nguon Phieu, noted in an interview that the United States introduced saturation bombing and shelling to save human lives, expending ammunition rather than men. Dr. Phieu, a man of tact, did not add that the lives being saved were American, perhaps at the expense of those of Vietnamese.

"Our kind of war has destroyed all the accommodations that once existed," an American official said. "The scale and scope of our operations preclude any live-and-let-live. With our air power and our artillery

we have made it a massive war all the time."

At least until recently the Americans appeared to have abandoned the tactic of large military drives that were termed "refugee-generating"—that is, entailing forcible relocation of the civilian population of an area, often without warning and preparation.

But since last year the practice has been renewed by the South Vietnamese command. Some American civil officials accuse the United States of failure to exercise the responsibility that American power confers on it in Vietnam to halt the practice.

•

"The place is called Pleikotu, and there are more than 2,000," said the foreign volunteer nurse who has been driving there daily although the road is sometimes mined by the Vietcong. "They were brought there in Vietnamese helicopters on Dec. 16. Of the 300 who have died, I think about 80 per cent were children.

"But I found only two dead today, when usually there are five or six. They die of malnutrition because all they have to eat is rice, roots and leaves.

"They're not angry. They are so beaten down they don't have any reaction. They are all alone out there."

Pleikotu is 15 miles from Pleiku, a provincial capital, regional military headquarters and the seat of a major American civil and military establishment. In the warehouse of the provincial social-welfare authorities there are large quantities of dried fish and powdered milk.

The official United States attitude is that the Americans' role is strictly advisory. "All we can do is keep the province chief's nose to the grindstone," a senior official in Pleiku said.

That attitude enrages others in CORDS, the mixed civilian-military Civil Operations and Rural Development Support organization, which is headed by Mr. Colby. In turn, the critics are termed bleeding hearts by those who accept the official line. The response to the criticism is that, however much one may sympathize with the tribesmen's plight, advisers should advise only and let the Vietnamese make the decisions.

Irving D. Hamberger, refugee adviser for the provinces of Darlac and Quangduc, accused Washington in an interview of so impressing the American advisers with the need for establishing good rapport with their Vietnamese counterparts that their advisers are encouraged to support actions that they believe to be immoral.

Mr. Hamberger, a taut and energetic former real-estate developer from Arizona, recalled

with anger hearing a colleague say, "We must be pragmatic, not moral." Mr. Hamberger is planning to leave Government service next month because of his deep dissatisfaction with the American stand on refugees.

•

About 300 people, mainly children and women, camp alongside the military airstrip at Banmethuot waiting for a plane. They have waited for a month, and no one has told them that no one intends to send a plane.

They are mountain tribesmen from Cambodia who left their homes last May and June to cross into Quaduc at a time when South Vietnam offered more peace than Cambodia. There are about 8,000 of them, and the Government in Saigon allotted money to feed them.

Local indifference has kept all but a fraction of the money from being spent on feeding the refugees. Hungry and neglected, they stowed away on planes that had brought ammunition to a military base near their camp. They thought they might get to Pnompenh, but they landed at Banmethuot, where no one wanted them.

They camp at the side of the airstrip. Some live in a shack, others in big United States Air Force packing crates, others in covered holes in the ground.

They have nothing to do but wait for a plane and hope for food. What food they get, mainly from American supplies, they divide among the families.

A sack of dried fish was divided first, little fish by little fish. Then the bigger fish were cut into small pieces that were added to each pile of little fish until the sack was empty. Each person accepted what he got without argument or complaint. They smiled.

"When is the plane coming, sir?" they asked in pidgin French.

The uprooting of Montagnards, as all the members of the many hill tribes of Indochina are called, has been a particular sore point in the record of forced relocations in Laos as well as South Vietnam. Even in times of peace the hill tribesmen have all the problems of ethnic minorities in countries governed by the people of the plain. The effect of war is the more traumatic.

The hill tribesmen have won the particular affection of

The New York Times   April 21, 1971
Only refugees in the non-Communist areas of the three nations are included in the totals, which are conservative.

Americans working with them in Laos and South Vietnam, not only for fighting well despite heavy losses in mercenary units organized by the United States but also for appearing more open and friendly than the more sophisticated Vietnamese.

Even Americans not passionately committed to the montagnard cause, as well as many Vietnamese, agree that the attitude of most Vietnamese officials toward the relocation of montagnards is indifference at best. Those more involved accuse the Vietnamese of chasing the tribesmen from their traditional lands to exploit them themselves.

●

"The Vietcong attack us, the Americans bomb us and the Vietnamese rob us," a montagnard nurse said as she rocked her infant son, whom she had tied to her body.

Over strong objection by CORDS, relocation of montagnard hamlets was resumed last summer under orders of Maj. Gen. Ngo Dzu, commander of Military Region II. Fifty-one thousand had been moved by last month, with 30,000 more due to be uprooted.

On American insistence that, with mounting Congressional interest in refugee questions, such moves might endanger American support of other programs, General Dzu suspended the relocations. "But the relocations will eventually be carried out," a senior American official said. "All we can do is try to see that they are done right."

Buon M'bre is a resettlement site for the people of six hamlets of the Rhade hill tribe near Banmethuot. Close to 900 people live in an agglomeration of temporary shelters in a cleared site off Highway 14. It has not been attacked by daylight.

The Vietcong visited their old hamlets about twice a month, lectured to the people and forced them several times to turn over a can of rice per family. Government troops also came now and then, accused them of dealing with the enemy and sometimes took away men for questioning.

Last September, just before the rice harvest, troops came to tell them they would be evacuated to more secure lands. They were lucky because there was enough transport to allow them to carry their possessions. They worried about their rice, but the soldiers assured them that security would be provided at harvest time so that they could go to reap it.

They did, but the Communists attacked the soldiers and both the soldiers and the villagers were afraid to stay. Most of the rice was lost.

The land provided for the villagers will be cleared soon and

they will plant. But it is far from sufficient for the people of Buon M'bre and it is seven months until the next harvest.

The Government gave them small amounts of food in the early stages. To buy their rice now the whole village, men and women—a boy is a man at the age of 12—work as day laborers for the Vietnamese who own most of the land around the camp. They earn 200 piasters a day, or 70 cents, except the younger ones, who get 150 piasters.

They supplement their diets with roots and leaves, digging deep for roots they do not like.

To show the people of Buon M'bre that the Government cannot give them security, the village was severely attacked in December, and six soldiers and seven members of their families were killed. The Vietcong kidnapped three teen-age girls and beat up a number of men.

About 70 per cent of the hamlets in which the montagnards of Vietnam, estimated at close to a million, live have already been uprooted, according to Gerald C. Hickey, an American anthropologist who is regarded as the leading expert on the hill people of Indochina.

"If these poorly implemented resettlements continue, there is a strong possibility that the montagnards will be left a poverty-stricken population living on the fringes of Vietnamese society," Dr. Hickey said in an interview.

His views are shared by most of the Americans concerned with civil affairs. The Minister of Social Welfare, Dr. Phieu, expressed sympathy with the montagnards but said that the generals did not often communicate their plans to him.

●

The Banxon area in the hill country north of the Laotian capital of Vientiane is the center of life for the Meo mountain tribesmen and other northern hill tribes. The United States feeds about 120,000 of them by airdrop, helicopter and plane delivery and by handing food over to those who come on foot into the valley.

The Communist soldiers of North Vietnam and the Pathet Lao left thinly defended Banxon alone until last March 6. Early that morning they broke in.

A woman sat keening softly in the wreckage of a shack near the airstrip. She pointed to a slim bundle at her feet. "Only one, only one," she said, and raised her hand with the index finger pointing upward.

The bundle was her daughter, her only child, killed a few hours earlier by a grenade fragment. The Americans who

work there called the child the watermelon girl, because of what she sold, smiling at them and joking. She was 12.

Nearby lay the body of the only enemy soldier killed in the attack. He was a Meo, some people said, but others thought that he was a Lao or a Vietnamese. He seemed little older than the watermelon girl.

The mountain people of northern Laos have been on the move since the early nineteen-sixties, retreating while fighting the North Vietnamese invaders. Most have had no time to stop and grow their rice in years, and they have depended on the United States for most of their necessities. In return, they have fought.

But there are few mountains left and life in the larger communities of the plain fills them with apprehension. American and Laotian friends of the tribesmen fear that the attacks on their civilian centers are a final warning that the depleted tribes must be led out of the enemy's way and given a better chance of survival.

The continuing forcible relocation of montagnards in Vietnam is only the most striking case of Saigon's turning its back on its stated policy of bringing security to the people rather than uprooting people to take them to security.

The policy was first proclaimed in the pacification plan for 1969, following years of what Dr. Phieu called "dumping people like baggage." It was observed until the middle of last year, when General Dzu resumed the relocation of montagnards.

This month similar operations were revived in Quangngai Province, a strongly contested area of central Vietnam and the scene of much earlier dislocation of people. American pressure managed to hold up temporarily an operation that may remove about 12,000 people, but the operation has now received the required authorization, ex post facto, and is proceeding.

An operation undertaken earlier this month slightly south of Quangnai City has already removed 650 people from

a Vietcong-controlled valley.

The operation was ordered by Maj. Gen. Nguyen Van Toan, commander of the Second Division, and was strongly supported by his senior American adviser, Col. Stephen Day. But Maj. Ben G. Crosby 3d, who as district senior adviser is part of the civilian-military province advisory team, strongly voiced his team's objections in a conversation with the colonel.

The major said the principal reason for the operation was to "upgrade" the rating of Quangngai Province on the hamlet evaluation scale, an American computerized classification of all populated places in South Vietnam as to security. The ratings run from "A" to "E" in descending order of security and end with "V," a hamlet controlled by the enemy.

Major Crosby discomfited the

colonel by declaring that he thought the principal motive for the removal of the people from their homes and fields was to eliminate the V hamlets of the Songve Valley.

The area will be under Communist control, the major said, and the people will be away from their fields with not enough forces in the region after the operation has been completed to guarantee their security.

"I don't like this kind of operation," Major Crosby said. "It's like punching a pillow."

●

"When we force them to leave the insecure areas we can control them better," said Vu Duc Chinh, a lieutenant colonel in charge of pacification and civil affairs of Military Region I in Danang, speaking of forced relocations.

"I have never yet seen a relocation that improves security in any significant way," said an American refugee official with long experience in the region about which Colonel Chinh was talking.

"The rural population remains basically uncommitted. Their primary concern is their status quo. If they have land and draw from it their subsistence, and if they can look from one growing season to the next and see survival, they do not want to move."

Among American refugee and pacification officials, from the top of the pyramid in Saigon to those at the district level, the conviction is nearly universal that the hamlet ratings are the chief villain in the return of the "refugee-generating" operations.

A high rating on the scale, designed as a "management tool" to help officials in judging the security situations, has become the goal.

Pressure for upgrading ratings, whether to reflect actual gains in security or not, originates in Washington, ranking officials said. It is then passed on by the United States mission here, anxious to show success, to the Saigon authorities, who are eager to please Washington, particularly if it can be done by bookkeeping devices.

The pressure was heightened, reliable American sources said, when President Nguyen Van Thieu quietly passed the word throughout his administration last spring that by the spring of this year he wanted all D and E hamlets brought to higher ratings.

The withdrawal of American troops, which spreads troops and security more thin, is believed to be another factor in Saigon's renewal of efforts to concentrate the population.

●

Nguyen Thieu, deputy ham-

let chief of Culac, said he did not know that his native area was known as the Street Without Joy. It was named by the French soldiers of the first war of Indochina, who found that the region of sand dunes north of Hue was more suited to the Communists than to their own forces.

He said he was glad to be back, now that security had improved. This is home, said Dang Cuoc, a 67-year-old shop-keeper.

And Col. Ngo Van Loi, province chief of Quangngai, who came from Hanoi when the Communists took over, said. "All Vietnamese want to go home eventually.

"You too, colonel?"

"Yes," he said, after a moment. "Me too."

The people of Culac returned to their village in July, 1969, after having been made refugees by the fighting in March 1967.

The Government's Return to the Village Program has helped 900,000 South Vietnamese to rebuild their lives in or near the places from which they were driven. It is the fundamental aim of most Vietnamese who have not made a new life in a city, for their ties to the native soil are strong and durable.

The return is voluntary and is usually decided on by the village elders after inspection of the site and assurances of reasonable security.

Those who resettle are entitled to a food allowance of 3,600 piasters ($13) a person and 10 sheets of tin roofing

and a 7,500-piaster ($27) construction allowance a family. Since most are not familiar with their entitlements, it is believed that many have gotten less than their due.

Even critics of the Vietnamese and American attitudes toward refugees agree that Return to Village has worked well and is consistent with the desires of the people. They hope that the increase in secure areas that has made possible the growth of the program is due more to a real increase in Government strength than to a tactical decision by the Communists to maintain a lull in fighting until the Americans withdraw.

●

There are more houses in Culac now than before the peo-

ple were driven out, the shop-keeper on the Street Without Joy said, but the village was nicer then.

"There were green fences," he related, *"and good gardens, trees and flowers. Perhaps years and years later people will make Culac nice again."*

"I do not know when," the shopkeeper continued. *"Even the Government does not know."*

"Peace depends on the Governments of Saigon and America," the deputy hamlet chief said. *"About the Government in Hanoi we do not know at all."*

April 21, 1971

Vietnam Archive: Pentagon Study Traces 3 Decades of Growing U. S. Involvement

By NEIL SHEEHAN

A massive study of how the United States went to war in Indochina, conducted by the Pentagon three years ago, demonstrates that four administrations progressively developed a sense of commitment to a non-Communist Vietnam, a readiness to fight the North to protect the South, and an ultimate frustration with this effort—to a much greater extent than their public statements acknowledged at the time.

The 3,000-page analysis, to which 4,000 pages of official documents are appended, was commissioned by Secretary of Defense Robert S. McNamara and covers the American involvement in Southeast Asia from World War II to mid-1968—the start of the peace talks in Paris after President Lyndon B. Johnson had set a limit on further military commitments and revealed his intention to retire. Most of the study and many of the appended documents have been obtained by The New York Times and will be described and presented in a series of articles beginning today.

Though far from a complete history, even at 2.5 million words, the study forms a great archive of government decision-making on Indochina over three decades. The study led its 30 to 40 authors and researchers to many broad

conclusions and specific findings, including the following:

¶That the Truman Administration's decision to give military aid to France in her colonial war against the Communist-led Vietminh "directly involved" the United States in Vietnam and "set" the course of American policy.

¶That the Eisenhower Administration's decision to rescue a fledgling South Vietnam from a Communist takeover and attempt to undermine the new Communist regime of North Vietnam gave the Administration a "direct role in the ultimate breakdown of the Geneva settlement" for Indochina in 1954.

¶That the Kennedy Administration, though ultimately spared from major escalation decisions by the death of its leader, transformed a policy of "limited-risk gamble," which it inherited, into a "broad commitment" that left President Johnson with a choice between more war and withdrawal.

¶That the Johnson Administration, though the President was reluctant and hesitant to take the final decisions, intensified the covert warfare against North Vietnam and began planning in the spring of 1964 to wage overt war, a full year before it publicly revealed the depth of its involvement and its fear of defeat.

¶That this campaign of growing clandestine military pressure through 1964 and the expanding program of bombing North Vietnam in 1965 were begun despite the judgment of the Government's intelligence community that the measures would not cause Hanoi to cease its support of the Vietcong insurgency in the South, and that the bombing was deemed militarily ineffective within a few months.

¶That these four succeeding administrations built up the American political, military and psychological stakes in Indochina, often more deeply than they realized at the time, with large-scale military equipment to the French in 1950; with acts of sabotage and terror warfare against North Vietnam beginning in 1954; with moves that encouraged and abetted the overthrow of President Ngo Dinh Diem of South Vietnam in 1963; with plans, pledges and threats of further action that sprang to life in the Tonkin Gulf clashes in August, 1964; with the careful preparation of public opinion for the years of open warfare that were to follow; and with the calculation in 1965, as the planes and troops were openly committed to sustained combat, that neither accommodation inside South Vietnam nor early negotiations with North Vietnam would achieve the desired result.

June 13, 1971

SAIGON'S SOLDIERS ATTACKING G.I.'S

Number of Incidents Rise— Robbery Often Motive

By GLORIA EMERSON
Special to The New York Times

SAIGON, South Vietnam, July 3—Growing concern is reported in some areas of South Vietnam over a perceptible increase in hostile actions by men in the South Vietnamese armed forces toward the American military.

Robbery is often said to be the motive.

"Incidents involving assaults on United States forces personnel by ARVN [Army of the Republic of South Vietnam] have been increasing in frequency over the past few months," said the daily bulletin for June 9 issued by the Headquarters of the Third Regional Assistance Command.

This is the American military headquarters in Military Region III, which includes Saigon.

Army spokesmen said they could not supply any details on the assaults.

The American military is acutely sensitive about such problems because it often feels that even discussing them would not only reflect poorly on the United States armed forces' ability to control and protect their own men but also might reflect on the ability and competence of the South Vietnamese police.

Valuables Often Stolen

In most large cities in South Vietnam, it is commonplace for Americans—military and civilian—to worry about the possibility that their watches might be snatched off their wrists when they are crossing streets or stopping in vehicles at a traffic light. Vietnamese boys on motorcycles and children who cluster around pedestrians grab watches that have expansion metal wrist bands, as well as handbags and cameras.

In Bienhoa, a city just outside Saigon, where about 250 Americans work for American agencies, a memorandum dated June 16 warns of a "recent upswing in the number of thefts of watches or other jewelry in vehicles in the area."

"Inasmuch as these persons [the Vietnamese] generally travel in groups, appear to be very bold, and in some cases violent, it is recommended that protective measures be taken to prevent thefts by staying alert," the memorandum said.

It was signed by an official for Civil Operations and Rural Development Support, which heads the pacification program. But, in an interview, the official said there was really not much of a problem.

Trouble in Cantho

The potential for trouble between Vietnamese and American soldiers is greatest in a Mekong Delta city such as Cantho, which is not off limits to the estimated 7,000 servicemen, or to South Vietnamese Ranger units stationed in the area.

Between May 21 and June 20, according to the military police, G.I. complaints of larceny involving goods over $50 numbered 203, and under $50 totaled 28.

The military police blotter for April, 1971, showed 14 single "aggravated assaults"—meaning with intent to inflict grievous harm—and a single "simple assault."

Ten of the aggravated assaults were by Vietnamese men—some listed as unknown—on American servicemen. When interviewed by a Vietnamese civilian some Vietnamese Rangers admitted they knew of, or had participated, in acts to rob Americans.

"It's a daily happening," a South Vietnamese Ranger sergeant said. "There are hundreds of different causes. One of them is the hatred between the poor —us—and the rich—them. You see they are soldiers but they have big radios, cameras, much money for drinks—and girls. The girls don't even want to talk to us and even the cyclo drivers don't want to take us because they wait for the Americans."

Low morale among the Rangers, who come back to their base in Cantho after operations, is one reason given for the incidents. Some say that it is this more than a specific hatred for Americans that prompts them to steal or harass the foreigners. One Vietnamese said it was a form of entertainment for the Rangers.

July 4, 1971

C.I.A. Says It Maintains Army in Laos

By JOHN W. FINNEY
Special to The New York Times

WASHINGTON, Aug. 2—The Nixon Administration acknowledged today, through a Senate subcommittee staff report, that the Central Intelligence Agency was maintaining a 30,000-man "irregular" force now fighting throughout most of Laos.

Many news articles in recent years have described C.I.A. sponsorship of an irregular army in Laos. However, the subcommittee report represented the first time that the agency publicly and officially confirmed its military activities in Laos. The report indicated that the use of the irregular units in Laos was more widespread than had been indicated in the news accounts.

The force has become "the main cutting edge" of the Royal Laotian Army, according to the report, and has been supplemented by Thai "volunteers" recruited and paid by the C.I.A.

The agency's involvement in a secret war in Laos was finally confirmed officially in a staff report prepared for the Senate Foreign Relations subcommittee on foreign commitments by James G. Lowenstein and Richard M. Moose, two former Foreign Service officers who made an inspection trip to Laos in April. A version of their report, once classified top secret, was made public today after clearance by the C.I.A. as well as the State and Defense Departments.

Publication of the detailed 23-page report marks the formal acknowledgment of the secret war that the United States has been conducting in Laos ever since the breakdown of the 1962 Geneva accords, which were supposed to re-establish the neutrality of that country.

August 3, 1971

SAIGON REPORTS THIEU CAPTURING 90% OF THE VOTES

By ALVIN SHUSTER
Special to The New York Times

SAIGON, South Vietnam, Monday, Oct. 4 — President Nguyen Van Thieu won a new four-year term yesterday in a one-candidate election marked by scattered protests, terrorism, intensified enemy shelling and the largest reported voter turnout in recent Vietnamese history.

Returns from the Government's Election Information Center showed that only a small fraction of the voters voted against Mr. Thieu by mutilating or throwing away their ballots before dropping the envelopes into the ballot boxes. These conditions were set by Mr. Thieu in the absence of any other presidential candidates.

Support Strong in Delta

Official figures from most cities and provinces suggested that more than 90 per cent of the voters cast regular ballots regarded by the President as "votes of confidence." One of the largest demonstrations of support—99.6 per cent—came in the delta province of Baclieu, where the President's cousin is province chief.

Even in areas of proven opposition strength, official returns showed a large turnout and a large percentage of confidence votes.

President Thieu, who voted in the morning in downtown Saigon, had said that he would resign if more than 50 per cent of the ballots were cast invalid. This was no longer an issue in view of the reported returns.

More than 87 per cent of South Vietnam's seven million eligible voters cast ballots despite enemy shellings of about a dozen cities and hamlets, including attacks on Saigon and four provincial capitals. The attack on Saigon, the first in 10 months, killed 3 and wounded 5.

The reported turnout was greater than the figures for the lower house elections in August, which was 79 per cent, the Senate races last fall, 65 per cent, and the presidential election in 1967, 83 per cent. President Thieu won his first term in that election over 10 other candidates.

Among those who refused to vote today in line with the boycott demanded by various anti-Government groups were Gen. Duong Van Minh and Vice President Nguyen Cao Ky, the two potential challengers who pulled out of the race in mid-August, charging Mr. Thieu with election-rigging.

Mr. Ky, who attacked the President as a dictator and called for his downfall, will remain Vice President until Oct. 31, when Mr. Thieu and his new Vice President, Tran Van Huong, the 70-year-old former Premier, will be inaugurated.

An opposition group centered around Mr. Ky, the People's Force Against Dictatorship, called on the United States in a statement this morning to end its support of Mr. Thieu because of the 'one-man farce" and added that the Vietnamese people do not recognize the constitutionality of the voting.

President Thieu, who won with 35 per cent of the vote four years ago, had wanted to limit his opponents this time so that he could become a majority President. But now, many observers feel, his victory in an unopposed election has undercut his legitimacy for the next four years.

October 4, 1971

U.S. Again Relying Heavily on Airpower

Johnson First Launched Big Raids on North in '65

By NEIL SHEEHAN
Special to The New York Times

WASHINGTON, Dec. 27—Nearly seven years after President Lyndon B. Johnson began sustained bombing of North Vietnam in an effort to save the South, another American President is relying heavily on airpower to achieve his objectives in Indochina.

Five times this year, including the current and most intense raids by hundreds of planes, President Nixon has ordered what are officially called "reinforced protective reaction strikes" against antiaircraft installations, fuel depots and supply dumps in North Vietnam.

A senior Pentagon official acknowledged today that the raids constituted "a limited, selective resumption of the bombing," and Defense Secretary Melvin R. Laird warned that more such raids might be ordered in the future with the over-all purpose of protecting American troops in South Vietnam.

Rolling Thunder — as Mr. Johnson's air war on the North was code-named — began on March 2, 1965, with the hope that the punishing effect of the bombing raids would persuade the Hanoi leaders to order the Vietcong guerrillas in South to halt their insurrection against the Saigon Government.

Intimidation Effort

It had been held as doctrine by a number of American policy-makers since John F. Kennedy took office in 1961, that the threat of bombing, or bombing itself, would intimidate the North Vietnamese into halting the Vietcong activity.

However, in April, 1965, within a month of Rolling Thunder's start, the Johnson Administration found itself preparing to send American combat troops into the South to prevent a military victory by the Vietcong.

As United States infantrymen moved into South Vietnam that summer, the bombing campaign against the North was transformed into a long-range effort to choke off the flow of men and supplies that Hanoi began sending down the Ho Chi Minh Trail network through Laos to match the American build-up.

The hope of some day coercing Hanoi into a settlement remained, but the immediate objective of airpower was that of enabling American troops to win a military victory on the ground in the South by crippling the flow of reinforcements from the North.

Two years later, in August of 1967, Mr. Johnson's Secretary of Defense, Robert S. McNamara, told the Senate Armed Services Committee that airpower had failed. The Ho Chi Minh Trail was now an extensive network of jungle roads, and the bombing was not stopping the thousands of trucks that hauled men and supplies to the South each dry season.

President Johnson, nevertheless, escalated the bombing of the North that fall and winter —with no noticeable improvement.

In February, 1968, the enemy launched the Tet, or Lunar New Year, offensive. Vietcong and North Vietnamese Army troops simultaneously attacked 36 South Vietnamese cities and towns. Mounting American casualties and the psychological shock of the Tet attack indicated that the strategy of winning a victory on the ground in the South with American troops could not succeed.

On March 31, 1968, Mr. Johnson restricted the bombing of the North to the 20th Parrallel in a successful effort to open peace negotiations in Paris. On Oct. 31, he ordered a complete halt in the bombing, a condition set by Hanoi for substantive discussions between North Vietnam and the Vietcong on one side and the United States and the Saigon Government on the other.

The New York Times/Dec. 28, 1971

Heavy U.S. air strikes in North were reportedly concentrated in Thanhhoa, Nghean and Quangbinh provinces.

In turn, there was an understanding, officially denied but tacitly acknowledged by Hanoi, that its forces would not shell major cities in the South, take military advantage of the demilitarized zone, which straddles the border between North and South Vietnam, or fire upon unarmed American reconnaissance planes monitoring military activities in the North.

Mr. Nixon took office in January, 1969. The American force in Vietnam reached its peak of 543,000 men in April and negotiations continued in Paris. The planes that had been striking the North had been shifted to the Ho Chi Minh Trail network in Laos.

The new President adopted a strategy known as Vietnamization. American ground troops would be gradually withdrawn to ease criticism by the American public while the South Vietnamese Army and Government were strengthened so they could stand on their own against the North Vietnamese Army and the Vietcong.

By increments, Mr. Nixon has cut American troops in the South to a level of about 158,000 men, with an announced target of 139,000 by Feb. 1.

In the process, however, he has become more and more reliant on airpower — which can be applied without heavy American casualties and attendant political attacks at home — to sustain not only the South Vietnamese Government, but also the pro-American governments in Cambodia and Laos.

Whether the great weight of American airpower will succeed in sustaining the Saigon Government against a determined enemy offensive in the South is unknown, because the enemy has undertaken no major ground actions there since Mr. Nixon took office.

In Cambodia and Laos, however, the use of American airpower has not tipped the balance.

Despite fierce air support, Laotian troops and Thai and tribal mercenaries directed by the Central Intelligence Agency have been crumbling in the face of a North Vietnamese offensive in northeast Laos.

In Cambodia, on the southern flank of South Vietnam, the military situation has also become critical. Again, despite intense American air support, Cambodian troops were routed earlier this month in a series of battles with the North Vietnamese north of Pnompenh.

December 28, 1971

Saigon: Withdrawal Pains

By CRAIG R. WHITNEY

SAIGON, South Vietnam— For the Americans in Vietnam, 1971 was the year that American troop strength began to show the effects of withdrawal — down from 337,000 to fewer than 160,000 at the end of the year.

For the Vietnamese, this "Vietnamization" has meant fewer jobs, less money, and growing uncertainty about their economic future, which the United States will still have to underwrite at the rate of $700-million a year for the next several years.

The South Vietnamese economy has been almost entirely dependent on American money for years. It has been totally altered by that fact and by the war, which has driven millions of farmers in this traditionally agrarian society away from the countryside and into the overcrowded urban centers. Now that jobs provided to them by the American presence are going, many of them do not know what to do.

A wave of thievery has swept across the big cities. Cars are being stolen and property left by the Americans is being looted. As one French-speaking driver said after his American employer's auto was stolen, "It's just what happened when the French were leaving."

The reaction to the pullout, which by no means includes all Vietnamese, is perhaps an understandable one. It was intensified in the last weeks of the year by a set of unpopular, but necessary, economic reforms announced by the Government after the uncontested October Presidential election that put Nguyen Van Thieu into office for another four years.

The reforms were put into effect at a time when it was still uncertain whether the United States Congress would approve the latest transfusion of $700-million, which the Administration had requested as economic aid — including $150-million specifically to offset the effects of the troop withdrawals.

Initially, the reforms provided for a devaluation of nearly 50 per cent in the rate of exchange (up from 275 to 400 or 410 piasters to $1) applying to financing private imports and exports. This is expected to discourage imports and encourage exports.

The rate remains the same as it had been before for the millions of dollars in commodity imports brought in under the United States aid program.

The immediate effect of the reforms was a sharp and perhaps temporary rise in the price of rice and other essential foods, and a strong sense of uneasiness. Although many Vietnamese working for foreigners and certain categories of civil servants and soldiers got raises to offset the price rises, many others did not receive any compensation and they are afraid of what will happen to them.

Inflation, of course, is an old problem for the Vietnamese, since the Government has paid for many of its expenses by simply printing piaster notes. Perhaps the worst period of inflation was from June, 1969, to June, 1970, when prices rose by about 50 per cent. Last year, things had settled down, and prices rose only about 10 per cent before the economic reforms.

Nobody is more aware than the Vietnamese Government that it must find sources of money to replace those that are drying up as the Americans leave.

The most pressing necessity for it now is to find a way to increase exports to offset all the imports, which outnumber them now by about 100 to 1. The greatest hope of doing this lies in the possibility that oil beds lying offshore will turn out to be exploitable commercial ventures.

About 18 companies, some of them American, have put in bids to the Government to explore blocks of territory, but the Government has not yet granted any concessions. Actual exploration of the oil beds appears in doubt as long as South Vietnam's economic and military future remains as shaky as it is.

The Government is also trying to encourage foreign investment and has reformed and rationalized tariff structures to entice foreign business. Ford and American Motors officials have made plans to assemble light trucks and jeeps here for the Vietnamese market. One French concern, Citroën, already does so with a small light vehicle, La Dalat.

But South Vietnam is by no means experiencing a boom. As things now stand, unemployment is expected to rise again this year as the Americans continue pulling out and begin closing down some of their vast civilian agencies too.

January 24, 1972

LON NOL TIGHTENS RULE IN CAMBODIA

By Reuters

PNOMPENH, Cambodia, March 10—Lon Nol, Cambodia's ailing Premier, took supreme power as head of state tonight and nullified the nearly completed republican constitution.

He announced the move on national radio and promised to continue the war against the Communists until he could establish peace through victory.

Earlier tonight, Cheng Heng announced his resignation as head of state in a nationwide broadcast in which he called on the army and the people to support Lon Nol. "I cannot be any longer chief of state," he said. "Lon Nol can be leader. So I give my position to Lon Nol."

Plans Left in Doubt

Lon Nol, who is 58 years old, said that the special convention of former deputies drawing up the new constitution for Cambodia had made alterations in it since it had been handed on by the Cabinet. The nature of these alterations was not immediately made clear, but they were obviously displeasing to Lon Nol.

He announced that because of them he would not carry on with plans to promulgate the new constitution and install a presidential regime.

March 11, 1972

Truck Traffic Is Heavy Southward From Hanoi

By SEYMOUR M. HERSH
Special to The New York Times

HANOI, North Vietnam, March 17 — The Ho Chi Minh Trail starts in Hanoi. Every day hundreds of heavily laden trucks leave the capital to begin the drive of more than 300 miles through Laos and into South Vietnam.

A visitor, riding south in a jeep, was passed by more than 80 trucks during a four-hour, 100-mile drive along Highway 1, the main north-south road. The heavy-duty Soviet-built and Chinese-built trucks were driven fast, almost recklessly, along the highway, which was crowded as always with bicycles, water buffaloes, small lorries, other trucks, jeeps and swarms of people.

Officials said the vehicles were heading for Laos, and those going onto the trail were easy to identify; each had one headlight and was carefully camouflaged with branches and leaves piled on hood and roof. Perhaps one in four was loaded with 55 gallon oil drums. Many others were carrying wooden cases of what seemed to be small-arms ammunition.

The drivers were regular army men, and life along the road had some touches of uniformity. There were restaurant stops where dozens of soldiers could be seen eating meals—

for which they had to pay—beside their vehicles. Only one passenger, a soldier, was visible on the trucks headed south. Most were tightly sealed.

Trains Laden With People

Only a few artillery pieces were being hauled, and no tanks or armored personnel carriers were sighted. Larger equipment may begin the journey south by railroad, but most of the trains that regularly rolled beside the highway were full of passengers. Only occasional freight trains were sighted; they invariably included half a dozen or more heavily camouflaged tank cars.

The other main road in North Vietnam, Highway 5, stretches about 60 miles from Hanoi to the harbor city of Haiphong. Although many trucks full of war matériel were seen on it, there were some distinct contrasts. None, not even those with one headlight, were camouflaged, and most of the drivers seemed to be civilians.

Both highways were heavily bombed during the air raids on the Hanoi-Haiphong area that ended in 1968; they have not been attacked in that region since.

Occasionally, large trucks carrying what the officials said

were Soviet-made surface-to-air missiles could be seen parked along Highway 5. It was explained that the missile sites were regularly moved at night, after American reconnaissance flights were believed to be over for the day.

A Considerable Project

The missiles were covered but their unmistakable fins jutted out. The complex radar equipment used to guide the heat-seeking missiles was also being moved, a maneuver that—if conducted throughout the North every night — would involve a considerable number of vehicles, technicians and workers.

Military bases appear to be impossible for foreigners to find. None were encountered in more than 400 miles of travel, much of it along back roads. None of the Western diplomats stationed in Hanoi could recall seeing one. A North Vietnamese official said that the army bases were shifted regularly.

Soldiers could be seen constantly along the highways and in the cities. A group of sailors was conducting what seemed to be a forced march along a country road near Halong Bay, on the northeastern coast. The sailors, moving in crisp formation, had fresh uniforms, boots and back packs and shiny Chinese-made automatic rifles.

In the effort to counteract the air raids, dirt trails large enough to accommodate a truck were scratched out on each side of the highway wherever possible.

A Country Well Dug In

In general the country is well dug in. When factories were destroyed, the North Vietnamese simply picked up the pieces and moved them into nearby caves or grottoes.

An underground machine shop stands in a grotto in a small hill only a few miles from the much-bombed Hamrong Bridge in Thanhhoa Province, about 100 miles south of Hanoi. The plant, destroyed early in the air war, was reassembled in three sections by early 1967.

The section visited employed more than 30 workers in three around-the-clock shifts, turning out spare parts for trucks, generators and perhaps tanks. The employes lead an eerie subterranean life, with their work area lighted by less than a dozen weak bulbs. Most of the available power was being consumed by the seven lathes, presses and polishers.

Six of the heavy tools had been supplied by the Soviet Union and North Korea, the plant manager said, but he proudly pointed out a lathe manufactured in North Vietnam.

The plant, which, according to the manager, had to produce enough parts to repair 20 engines and 10 generators in January alone, consists of two narrow corridors, one about 30 feet and the other twice as long, crammed with raw materials, machine tools and workers.

April 1, 1972

SOUTH VIETNAMESE QUIT QUANGTRI

PROVINCE IS LOST

Victory Foe's Biggest Since Month-Old Invasion Began

By SYDNEY H. SCHANBERG
Special to The New York Times

HUE, South Vietnam, Tuesday, May 2—The South Vietnamese abandoned Quangtri, their northernmost province capital, yesterday, giving the advancing North Vietnamese their biggest prize so far in their month-old invasion.

The city, the first province capital to be lost since the offensive began March 30, was

abandoned by Government forces yesterday afternoon after three days of shelling during which the enemy moved troops and tanks to the edge of the city.

The loss of Quangtri city gave the North Vietnamese control of the entire northern province of the same name.

B-52's Covered Retreat

About 80 American advisers, the commander of the South Vietnamese Third Division and his staff were evacuated in the afternoon in four big rescue helicopters that flew through heavy enemy ground fire to get the men out.

United States B-52's reportedly bombed areas as close as one mile to the northeast of Quangtri city between noon yesterday and 6 A.M. today in efforts first to beat off the

enemy attack and then to cover the retreat of the Government forces. One of the 14 missions was nine miles south of Quangtri.

Meanwhile, South Vietnamese units retreated southward toward the even more important city of Hue, Vietnam's ancient imperial capital, in Thuathien Province. They were accompanied by 10 American advisers who had decided to stay with them.

Steady Push by Foe

Hue, with a population that has swollen to more than 300,000 by fleeing refugees, is now directly threatened. The North Vietnamese have reportedly moved to within less than 15 miles of the city on the west and about 25 miles on the north.

May 2, 1972

205

ALLIED PROGRAM FAILS A KEY TEST

Vietnamization Hope Dashed in Coastal Province as Foe Overruns 3 Districts

By CRAIG R. WHITNEY
Special to The New York Times

QUINHON, South Vietnam, May 1—In Binhdinh Province, here on the coast of Central Vietnam, three county-size districts with a combined population of 200,000 have fallen to Communist attacks in two weeks with little real resistance.

Several years' work on pacification programs has been lost and Vietnamization has failed one of its most crucial tests. And the failure is readily conceded by both South Vietnamese and American officials in Quinhon, the provincial capital.

A regiment of South Vietnam's army, reduced to a quarter of its 3,000-man strength largely through desertions, is under attack near here. Few American advisers or South Vietnamese officials believe that it will pull through.

The unit—the 40th Regiment, fighting at a nearby landing zone named English—has reportedly failed every test it has faced in the last two weeks.

Since the fall of the Hoaian district on April 19, said a high-ranking South Vietnamese official who asked that his name not be disclosed, "the 40th Regiment has only 25 per cent of its strength—30 per cent were casualties and 40 per cent or so deserted."

"We lost Hoainhon after that because the local militia troops were demoralized," the official said.

"They thought the regular army had let them down," he went on. "We couldn't hold Hoainhon because the soldiers deserted, they left their posts during the night and didn't fight when the attacks came in the day." Bongson, the capital of the Hoainhon district, fell last Saturday.

"The North Vietnamese are highly motivated—they know what they are doing," the official continued.

Priest Tells of Escape

What has been lost in Binhdinh Province? Perhaps the people of the province will tell. More than a fifth of them are now under Communist control, and local Vietcong agents are

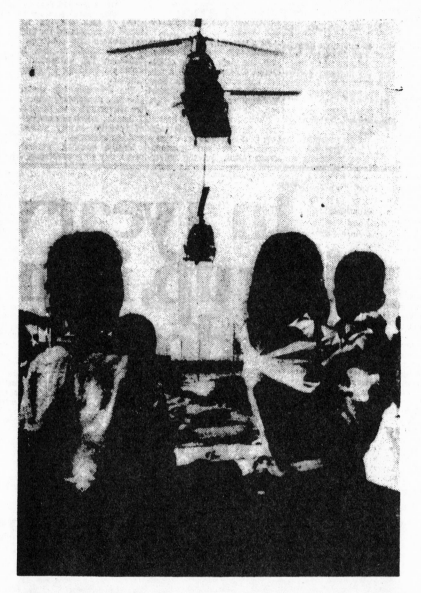

KONTUM: Young South Vietnamese awaiting evacuation look on as a big twin-rotor Chinook helicopter carries a smaller copter from the Central Highlands city for repair.

said to be preventing all the able-bodied young men from fleeing south and leaving as some of their women and children have done.

"I was stopped 10 times on the road between Bongson and Quinhon," said a young Roman Catholic priest who had walked 30 miles south. "The Communists told all the young men they must work to upset President Thieu and establish a new government of neutrality. I told them I was leading the people away because they did not want to be bombed by the Americans."

A few air strikes were called in on the northern part of Bongson and also in Hoaian after those places were abandoned, but American advisers say they took such action only in areas where they knew there would be few civilians left.

One of these advisers said that he had left Bongson after the 40th Regiment's commander and the Hoainhon district chief took their refrigerators, got in a jeep and fled, leaving their regular and militia troops behind to fend for themselves. Many of the soldiers gave up the fight and took to the hills.

"That whole district now is Communist-controlled," said

the American. "If we were to sweep them out of there tomorrow, I doubt that we could

get the people to tell us who among them had helped the other side. Those people will never feel safe with the Government again."

Many of the people of the captured districts—the third is Tamquan—have stayed there, or have gone back after fleeing the fighting. The region is on the coastal plain and the rice crop will soon be ready for harvest.

"There's usually a 25 per cent surplus of rice in Hoainhon," one of the advisers said. "You know who'll get it now."

Maj. George H. Watkins Jr., one of the Americans, was among the last to leave Bongson, a town of 40,000, before it fell Saturday afternoon.

He said that the morale of the militiamen and home guards had been "broken." They felt, he went on, that the 40th Regiment "had let them down by just not fighting at Hoaian district the week before."

The regiment did indeed give up Hoaian without a fight, according to the American advisers who were there, and they gave up Bongson with little resistance on Saturday, despite an abundance of American air power overhead.

"Hell, I had airplanes stacked up two and three rows high," said Major Watkins. "I couldn't use it as fast as it was coming in."

Air Power Alone Is Inadequate

Seldom before in all the analysis, claims and counterclaims in the rhetoric of Vietnamization has it been so clearly demonstrated that without effective fighting troops on the ground, air power is impotent. "The most effective weapon you have is the guy on the ground with his M-16 rifle," another adviser said.

A South Vietnamese official here, who may lose his job in the purge that is following on the heels of the Government debacle in Binhdinh, put it this way:

"The Americans were sincere, they tried to help the Vietnam-

ese armed forces, and from A to Z they brought equipment here," he said. "But one thing the Americans cannot bring here is leadership—they cannot bring that in from their arsenal."

"When the Communists were here before, from 1945 to 1954," he continued, "the people didn't have much to eat or good clothes on their backs but morally they were happy, because the Communists brought justice to this land for 10 years, not the corruption we have here now."

How the people of northern Binhdinh Province will react to the re-establishment of a Government presence depends on whether the 40th Regiment holds out. Its position, at Land-

ing Zone English, was the headquarters of the American 173d Airborne Brigade before it pulled out last year. There are now rumors in the Vietnamese press that 2,000 United States Marines have landed in northern Binhdinh to pull the fat out of the fire as they did in 1965, when Communist control was also spreading in the province.

The rumor is not true and it does not seem likely that the Americans will come to the rescue this time. For the moment, the only sizable American installations are here in Quinhon in the southern and most populated part of the province. And the American advisers have been pulled out of landing Zone English.

May 2, 1972

NIXON ORDERS ENEMY'S PORTS MINED; SAYS MATERIEL WILL BE DENIED HANOI UNTIL IT FREES P.O.W.'S AND HALTS WAR

SPEAKS TO NATION

He Gives the Ships of Other Countries 3 Days to Leave

By ROBERT B. SEMPLE Jr.
Special to The New York Times

WASHINGTON, May 8 — President Nixon announced tonight that he had ordered the mining of all North Vietnamese ports and other measures to prevent the flow of arms and other military supplies to the enemy.

Mr. Nixon told a nationwide television and radio audience that his orders were being executed as he spoke.

From the President's somber and stern speech and from explanations by other Administration officials, the following picture of the American action emerged:

¶All major North Vietnamese

ports would be mined, ships of other countries in the harbors, most of which are Russian, would have three "daylight periods" in which to leave. After that the mines will become active and ships coming or going will move at their own peril.

¶United States naval vessels will not search or seize ships of other countries entering or leaving North Vietnamese ports, thus avoiding a direct confrontation with the Russians.

¶American and South Vietnamese ___ and planes would take "appropriate measures" to stop North Vietnam from unloading matériel on beaches from unmined waters.

¶United States and South Vietnamese forces would interdict, presumably by bombing, the movement of matériel in North Vietnam over rail lines originating in China.

There was much confusion tonight about whether the United States and South Vietnam had proclaimed a blockade. The President did not use the word and Pentagon spokes-

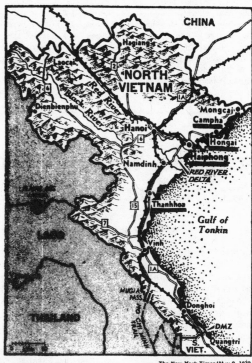

The New York Times/May 9, 1972

NEW TARGETS: Ports (underlined), rail lines from China

men denied that a blockade existed in the technical sense. But some observers felt that the practical effect on North Vietnam of the President's actions would be the same as a blockade.

[In Saigon, the United States command announced Tuesday that Navy planes had completed the initial phases of the mining operations in North Vietnamese harbors ordered by President Nixon.]

Two Basic Conditions

Mr. Nixon said the mining, the attacks on the rail lines within North Vietnam, and the efforts to interdict the movement of supplies by water would cease the moment the enemy agreed to two basic conditions: the return of American prisoners of war, and an internationally supervised cease-fire.

"Then," he said, "we will stop all acts of force throughout Indochina and proceed with the complete withdrawal of all forces within four months."

The White House would not say tonight whether, in these words, Mr. Nixon was in effect making the North Vietnamese a new peace proposal.

But observers here noted that he mentioned no political requirements for American withdrawal. Until now he has always insisted on some form of free presidential elections in South Vietnam to be organized under the terms of his proposal of Jan. 25 by an independent commission composed of all of South Vietnam's political elements.

Minutes after Mr. Nixon's speech, the State Department released the text of a letter from the United States representative at the United Nations, George Bush, to the Security Council, outlining the President's actions and the Administration's reasons for them. Mr. Bush's letter cited Article 51 of the United Nations Charter and called the President's actions "measures of collective self-defense" by the United States and South Vietnam.

The actions Mr. Nixon announced tonight seemed to stun much of official Washington,

but reaction from the public was not clear. Immediately after the speech, the White House switchboard was jammed with calls and it remained impenetrable for most of the evening.

Mr. Nixon seemed more pessimistic in his assessment of the military situation tonight than in any recent speech. He said the South Vietnamese had fought bravely, but conceded that "the Communist offensive has now reached the point where it gravely threatens the lives of 60,000 American troops who are still in Vietnam."

He did not, for once, talk about the progress of his program of Vietnamization, under which he hoped and presumably still hopes to turn over the fighting to the South Vietnamese. Accordingly, some here implied from his remarks a concession that the South Vietnamese were weaker, or the North Vietnamese stronger, than he had earlier suggested to the country.

May 9, 1972

Thieu Orders Martial Law; Ousts an Area Commander

By CRAIG R. WHITNEY
Special to The New York Times

SAIGON, South Vietnam, May 10—President Nguyen Van Thieu imposed martial law on South Vietnam tonight.

The announcement of the measure on the Government radio did not include any details about how martial law would be put into effect. It followed a Presidential declaration of emergency last night and appeared to be part of a long-delayed attempt by the Government to instill a sense of urgency in the people of the cities and towns that have not been directly affected by the heavy fighting of the last month.

In another action, the President dismissed his military commander in the Central Highlands, Lieut. Gen. Ngo Dzu, replacing him with Maj. Gen. Nguyen Van Toan. Some diplomats here viewed this too as essentially a move to heighten public awareness of the critical situation, since they consider General Toan to be less competent than General Dzu.

Most Americans in Saigon believe that the most effective military measures now being taken are by the United States Air Force and Navy planes that are bombing North Vietnam and mining the enemy's harbors and their approaches.

The last time President Thieu declared martial law was on Jan. 31, 1968, at the time of the Communists' countrywide Tet offensive, when there were 510,000 American servicemen here. The introduction of martial law, in a country already largely governed by the military, carries with it the suspension of restraints on police powers of arrest and detention and the possibility of news censorship.

May 11, 1972

Cambodia Seems Adrift After 2 Years as Republic

By CRAIG R. WHITNEY
Special to The New York Times

PNOMPENH, Cambodia, June 5—From a start full of hope two years ago, Cambodia has sunk into a deep malaise, without confidence in her leadership, institutions, or ability to decide her own future, in the assessment of a wide range of Cambodians and foreign diplomats.

The malaise has been months in developing, but has had a chance to take root in the last two months, during which the Government of President Lon Nol has been virtually paralyzed by its attempts to legitimize itself as a popularly elected presidential regime.

Yesterday the country held its first presidential election. Marshal Lon Nol was ahead in preliminary results today with 58 per cent of the vote, while his closest contender, In Tam, had 24 per cent, and the marshal will almost certainly turn out to be the winner when the final results of the light voting are proclaimed by the Government in a few days.

Marshal Lon Nol proclaimed himself President March 13 after dissolving what remained of the Cambodian legislature, with Mr. In Tam at its head, and bowed to student pressure to eliminate his friend and closest adviser, Lieut. Gen. Sisowath Sirik Matak, from the Government.

The next legislative elections will not take place for three months.

The beginning of the worst part of the decline in Cambodia's morale seems to date from the disastrous rout of Cambodian troops trying to clear Route 6 north of Phnompenh in December. Since that operation, called Tchenla 2, the Cambodian Army has made no new offensive sweeps except unsuccessful ones around the temples of Angkor.

In recent weeks the Cambodians have, almost without a fight, given up most of the territory east of the Mekong River that North Vietnamese and Vietcong troops are using as a staging area for the offensive in South Vietnam.

American Official Gloomy

A high American official, speaking of the United States' $200-million military aid program in Cambodia, shrugged his shoulders as if in despair and said: "I don't see any vigorous prosecution of the war in the cards. Tchenla 2 caused a certain lack of confidence on the part of Lon Nol and the army and the Communists' use of tanks and large amounts of heavy ammunition in their offensive has just indicated to the Khmer that they are no match for the North Vietnamese.

It was also the failure of Tchenla 2 that caused the exacerbation of political strains, but that had been growing quietly ever since March, 1970, when Marshal Lon Nol enjoyed seemingly unanimous backing at the beginning of the republic. The trend since then has been one of centralized rule in his weak hands, but with growing frustration and, with the elections of the weekend, open opposition by some who supported the President in the beginning.

Marshal Lon Nol's principal opponent in the election, Mr. In Tam, was president of the Cambodian National Assembly at the time of the overthrow of Prince Norodom Sihanouk and was one of the three principal figures of the new republic in 1970—along with the President and his close friend, General Sirik Matak.

What has happened to Mr. In Tam and to General Sirik Matak shows, in some ways, the deterioration of the regime. In the summer of 1971, Mr. In Tam became Minister of the Interior, but asked to resign and was dismissed last September as his differences with the marshal grew. He became president of the renamed Constituent Assembly in November after Marshal Lon Nol took away the legislature's law-making powers and told it to proceed with the drafting of a constitution.

But in March, after student demonstrations against General Sirik Matak, who was Lon Nol's premier and, in effect, the man who had ruled Cambodia since the marshal's stroke more than a year ago, the President bowed to these outside pressures, took General Sirik Matak out of the Government and abolished the Constituent Assembly.

Within 10 days, he had his subordinates draft a constitution to his liking, establishing a presidential form of government with a Cabinet answerable to him and to the two-house legislature, and submitted it to a nationwide referendum, which approved it April 30.

Since March, the Government has been headed by the only man Lon Nol could get to accept the job, Son Ngoc Thanh, a shadowy figure who was on the side of the anti-Sihanouk forces at the beginning of the republic but whose allegiance is now believed to be mostly to the forms and trappings of the republican Government.

"The Government has been virtually paralyzed for the past two months while Lon Nol has been trying to secure his political future," a senior diplomat said. "I would hope he'd start to govern again rather quickly after the elections."

Indeed, in the last few days in Pnompenh there have been devoted almost entirely to political activities. A giant parade of military vehicles filled with soldiers bearing placards has circled the city almost every morning, blaring Marshal Lon Nol's political propaganda and DC-3 aircraft have dropped thousands of little pictures of the marshal—similar to those printed on the ballots—all over the city.

During the voting yesterday, Mr. In Tam charged that the Government was making it difficult for his supporters to vote for him, and that his poll-watchers had not been permitted in some of the places where military people, who strongly support Marshall Lon Nol, were voting. Today, he said he would contest the re-

sults as "fraudulent and anti-democratic."

The third candidate, Keo Ann, was the dean of the Faculty of law of Pnompenh, whose students led the fight against General Sirik Matak in the spring, but he did not campaign prominently and was expected to get less than 5 per cent of the vote.

Not Entirely Bleak

In the preliminary results, Mr. Keo Ann did better than expected and the two opposition candidates together had almost 42 per cent.

American officials here point out that the situation is not entirely bleak, and say that a series of monetary reforms and changes in Government policy have staved off a serious rice shortage that seemed to be inevitable last fall. In fact, only 20,000 tons of rice was imported and only 10,000 tons had to be used, according to American economists.

The Nixon Administration has asked Congress for $75-million in economic aid to Cambodia for the fiscal year beginning July 1, twice this fiscal year's amount.

But the Cambodian budget is at a large deficit because of the war, and unrest is growing among low-paid civil servants and salaried workers whose pay has not kept up with inflation. In the last few weeks, for example, there have been a series of strikes for higher wages in Government ministries —something inconceivable in the early days of the republic.

The unrest within the Government and in political movements outside it has been matched by a growth in the ranks of the Cambodian Communists, who are fighting against the Government forces alongside the North Vietnamese and Vietcong in the occupied parts of the country.

The number of members of Khmer Rouge, the Cambodian Communist force, is now estimated at at least 30,000. "There has been a growth, a development of the movement, which, we think, has serious longer-

term meaning for the country," an American diplomat said. "But the Government seems to resist the notion that the way to stand up to them is to fight them hard."

All the Cambodian factions seem to realize that, ever since Tchenla 2, it is futile to talk of chasing the North Vietnamese out of the country and that peace will not come to Cambodia before it comes to Vietnam—in the framework of an internationally guaranteed settlement.

The outlook for the future, according to diplomats here, is that the Cambodian forces will offer only token resistance to the Vietnamese Communists, reoccupying lost territory only when the enemy abandons it, and leaving again—as the Cambodian Army has done in the last two months in Svayrieng and Preyveng provinces near the Vietnamese border—when the North Vietnamese want that territory. It is already a kind of de facto truce.

American officials who last summer talked of harassing the Communist forces in Vietnam from two sides are now, in more chastened tones, saying as one did the other day: "All we've been able to do is to give the Khmer a better chance at whatever conference table comes along some day. I think they will await a general resolution of the Vietnam war and then bring about a reconciliation here and return to their traditional, lethargic ways."

In the meantime, though, it is clear that the unanimity of support that the Lon Nol Government once enjoyed among the beleaguered Cambodian population, caught in a war not of its own making, is gone, and that the Government's momentum in establishing a new way of life in the parts of the country it controls has been irrevocably lost.

June 6, 1972

Saigon Intellectuals See Morale Collapse

By MALCOLM W. BROWNE
Special to The New York Times

SAIGON, South Vietnam, July 4—A feeling is growing within South Vietnam's small educated élite that national morale has so collapsed that only a total revolution in the whole social structure offers hope of redemption.

Such a revolution, some of them say privately, would be possible only under a strongly authoritarian government of the type in power in Hanoi. Harsh austerity, rigid enforcement of laws and compulsion to cooperate in rebuilding are viewed as vital.

Many contend that although world interest in South Vietnamese morale centers mainly on the war, the real importance of the national mood in its effect on future reconstruction of the country.

"Sociologically, China has a lot in common with Vietnam, including traditional loyalty to family with very little interest in communities larger than that," a teacher said.

"Before 1949," he pointed out, "the Chinese also had a mixture of wretched poverty and luxuriant corruption. Their warlords, whose power was

like that of feudal princes, were something like our province chiefs.

"Now America has decided that the Chinese Communist system has worked in China, and yet they still throw up their arms in horror when it is suggested it might work here, too," he said.

The teacher, like most other South Vietnamese willing to discuss the subject, asked that care be taken not to identify him. A passing remark indicating any sympathy with Communist idea in this country is sufficient for summary deportation to the penal colony on Conson Island.

The views of educated Vietnamese, in common with those of the rest of the population, are unlikely to have any measurable effect on the administration of President Nguyen Van Thieu. There is general agreement that so long as the United States backs Mr. Thieu and the war effort, his political position is unassailable.

But traditionally, the leadership and administration of both North Vietnam and South Vietnam, in common with China, have been based on the ancient mandarin principle that the primary qualification for governing is education.

In South Vietnam, this has meant that leaders have generally emerged from the professional ranks of doctors, poets, archivists and so forth, and as a class, they have tended to dominate the national administration no matter what government is in power.

In a series of interviews, general agreement was expressed by scores of persons considering themselves members of South Vietnam's intelligentsia that their society is desperately sick.

"It's not simply a matter of paying the police a few hundred piasters to overlook a traffic violation, or even of the large-scale war profiteering and black-market operations," a leading Saigon journalist said. "There's corruption all over Asia and the rest of the backward world.

"With us its much more serious. Now we have reached the stage at which human pity has mostly left us. We steal some poor soldier's watch for a few extra piasters. Our commanders drive over their own troops in their desperation to escape battles. We are ready to sell our wives to afford a television set."

"We have come to despise ourselves and our nationality," he continued, "and the more revulsion we feel, the more we excuse ourselves on ground that you cannot survive in such a system without participating in it."

A university professor looked contemptuously from the window of his drab office at a typical Saigon traffic jam and said:

"There you see Vietnamese society in microcosm. No police or stoplights, no one to tell them what to do, so they just try to jam their way ahead, making things even worse. No pedestrian could get past that —he would be run over without hesitation."

Sees Lack of Responsibility

"I have lived in London and Paris and New York," he continued, "so I know what traffic jams are in those cities. But even when they are bad, there remains a certain individual responsibility that tells drivers there that you must sometimes back up to let another car through if you ever want to move yourself. Here that never happens."

The lack of individual cooperation in any community enterprise larger than a family's is strikingly evident in the nation's politics, armed forces, and even business.

A Japanese businessman who left here recently after several years said:

"Our company is giving up on Vietnam to concentrate on Taiwan," he said. "We have never been able to solve the problem of organizing an effective Vietnamese middle level of management. Vietnamese just don't seem able to keep large groups organized, and in a factory that is essential."

Many South Vietnamese share this criticism.

Ton That Thien, a former Cabinet Minister and now head of the sociology department at Saigon's Van Hanh University, said:

"I'm afraid this country needs a taste of the whip. I don't mean it needs physical brutality, but it does need a strong hand to take absolute charge and make the Vietnamese people do the things they must to survive."

In common with many other South Vietnamese, Mr. Thien blames the Americans for many problems.

"The United States should have done one of two things," he said. "One would have been to really take charge of Vietnam and run it directly as a colony, at least for a time. They could have forced new skills and new attitudes on us that would have made survival a possibility. The French at least built a civil service they left us."

"Failing that, he continued, "the United States should have left us to work out our own problems."

"But Washington did neither of those two things," he said. "They have preserved the fiction of Vietnamese sovereignty by avoiding taking direct control of anything. Instead, they run Vietnam more or less behind the scenes, tampering with every aspect of our national life. Worst of all, they send us amateurs instead of colonial professionals, and by the time they learn something here they are ready to leave and be replaced by a new batch."

Mr. Thien does not believe anti-American feeling in South Vietnam would have been any stronger than it is now if America had openly and completely taken over the administration.

In any case, he remains a committed anti-Communist, and believes that once America removes its advisers and "political manipulators" from South Vietnam the nation will regain the moral integrity required both to rebuild the society and defeat the Communists.

Other South Vietnamese believe that no matter what happens now, reconstruction will be possible only under Communism.

A former scholar from Hue, who said he and his family would probably be jailed or killed if the Communists come to power, said:

"We have no leaders worthy of the name at present, nor will there be any, as things stand now.

"Our childish political parties have no following and within them there is only petty bickering, never statesmanship.

The public has no use for any of them, because every time some politician has shown signs of real strength, whatever Government in power has always managed to buy him off.

"Our impression is that a man becomes a politician solely to obtain leverage to force a way into the very Government he said he was opposing," he continued. "Too many of our best people refuse to try to become leaders, because they know that in the last analysis the American Embassy is the arbiter of all political events here."

"So now we are a social jungle, a vicious anarchy of indifference, greed and fear," he said.

"I hope the Communists win this war," he continued, "certainly not for myself, but for the nation. The Communists are Vietnamese too, and therefore subject to all our vices. The difference is that they are locked into a rigid system that extends from the top to the poorest farmer—a system that means no political freedom, but one in which crimes against society are punished by death.

"The Communists have both the strength and the will to restore Vietnam to the human condition."

Most educated South Vietnamese temper their criticism of the United States with expressions of gratitude for goodwill and expenditure of blood and treasure. They usually acknowledge that while the United States has made mistakes in South Vietnam, most of the social problems are of their own doing.

But a handful speak vengefully, even while denouncing the Communists.

One said: "You have exported the diseases of your own society to us, and now they are an epidemic here. It warms my heart to know, from what I read in the newspapers, that some of our diseases have infected you, too."

July 5, 1972

Mass Executions by Enemy Reported in South Vietnam

By JOSEPH B. TREASTER
Special to The New York Times

SAIGON, South Vietnam, Aug. 3 — Allied intelligence officials say that Communist political officers have publicly executed hundreds of Saigon Government officials and imprisoned thousands during their occupation of Binhdinh Province, on the central coast of South Vietnam.

The allied officials say that they have confirmed the deaths of about 250 persons through eyewitness reports and have additional information that leads them strongly to believe that the total number of dead is about 500.

People who have escaped have pinpointed three large prison camps in the rugged Anlao valley of central South Vietnam, which are said to hold about 6,000 persons, the officials say.

The main victims of the enemy were said to be hamlet and village chiefs and their deputies, pacification workers, policemen and militiamen. But teachers, doctors, nurses and minor administrative staff workers, as well as some soldiers, were among those reported imprisoned.

Lengthy interviews with people who lived in northern Binh-

dinh during the nearly three months of unchallenged Communist occupation generally corroborated the findings of the intelligence officials.

The reported executions in Binhdinh appear to be the most sizable deliberate assault on individuals connected with the Saigon Government since the massacres in Hue during the 1968 Lunar New Year offensive when, according to allied officials and independent journalists, more than 2,600 people were killed.

Some American officials see the reported executions in Binhdinh as a sample of the kind of "bloodbath" that President Nixon has predicted if the Communists succeeded in taking over South Vietnam by force.

Such violence, these officials say, especially would be expected if a Communist victory were "sudden and decisive."

Other American officials, however, say that history would suggest that a sudden and decisive victory "just isn't in the cards for either side."

These officials feel that if the North Vietnamese Communists were eventually to gain control of South Vietnam through a gradual political settlement, they might well adopt a conciliatory attitude toward their former opponents in hopes of uniting the country.

But those who most firmly subscribe to the "bloodbath theory" are convinced that any kind of enemy take-over would result in the execution of many officials in the Government in Saigon.

August 4, 1972

SAIGON TORTURE IN JAILS REPORTED

Documents and Interviews Indicate Wide Abuse of Political Prisoners

By SYDNEY H. SCHANBERG
Special to The New York Times

SAIGON, South Vietnam, Aug. 12—Documents smuggled out of South Vietnamese prisons and extensive interviews with former prisoners paint a picture of widespread torture of people jailed by the Saigon Government since the North Vietnamese offensive started four and a half months ago.

Here is a sampling of the prisoners' accounts:

¶"Nguyen Thi Yen was beaten unconscious with a wooden rod. Later, when she revived, she was forced to stand naked before about 10 torturers, who burned her breasts with lighted cigarettes."

¶"Trinh Dinh Ban was beaten so badly in the face that the swelling shut and infected his eyes. The police drove needles through his fingertips and battered him on the chest and soles of his feet until he was unable to move."

¶"Vo Thi Bach Tuyet was beaten and hung by her feet under a blazing light. Later, they put her in a tiny room half flooded with water and let mice and insects run over her body."

Stories Are Typical

These particular accounts are said to describe the torture of three student leaders still being held in South Vietnamese jails on suspicion of being Communist sympathizers. The accounts in these documents and many others obtained by this correspondent were purportedly written by prisoners —and in some cases by sympathetic guards — and then smuggled out.

The three accounts are typical of the stories told in the other documents and in the interviews about the treatment of the thousands of students, workers, peasants, women and children arrested by the national police and military authorities in the "pre-emptive sweeps" made in the search for Communist sympathizers and agents since the North Vietnamese Army began its offensive.

Some of the documents reached this correspondent through friends of prisoners or critics of the Government to whom the papers had been passed. Some of the interviews were also arranged this way. Additional information was gathered on the basis of other leads.

There is no way to verify the accounts of torture first hand, for the Saigon Government refuses to allow journalists to visit its prisons, which it calls "re-education centers." A formal written request was denied.

All of those interviewed said their names could not be used because they feared police reprisals.

As with the smuggled documents, it is impossible to corroborate the accounts given by former prisoners in interviews. But although one cannot establish after the fact that the welts and scars visible on their bodies were inflicted by the police, the widespread reports bear out the prisoners' version.

Government officials and pro-Government legislators defend the recent repressive measures by arguing that the survival of South Vietnam is at stake. Critics reply that only the Government of President Nguyen Van Thieu, not South Vietnam, is at stake.

'A Flexible View'

"Necessity requires us to accept a flexible view of the law," said one official. "You wouldn't wait until the Vietcong agent pointed his gun at your back before you handcuffed him, would you? Legal aspects do not count when there is a question of survival involved."

The victims obviously feel differently. Here, for example, is part of an account given by a woman who was interrogated intensively but not beaten in a police detention center in Saigon and then released:

"When you were being interrogated, you could hear the screams of people being tortured. Sometimes they showed you the torture going on, to try to frighten you into saying what they wanted you to say.

"Two women in my cell were pregnant. One was beaten badly. Another woman was beaten mostly on the knees, which became infected.

"One high school student tried to kill herself by cutting both wrists on the metal water taps in the washroom, but she failed. They had tortured her by putting some kind of thick rubber band around her head to squeeze it. It made her eyes swell out and gave her unbearable headaches.

"One girl was so badly tortured that the police left her in a corridor outside the interrogation room for a day— so that other prisoners would not see her condition."

This was a typical story of those interviewed. Some said that water had been forced down their mouths until they nearly drowned. Others told of electric prods used on sensitive parts of the body, of fingernails pulled out and of fingers mashed.

Several of the informants said they had discovered, while in prison, a sardonic saying favored by the police—"Khong, danh cho co." — "If they are innocent, beat them until they become guilty."

The accounts of the informants indicated that the worst torturing took place while prisoners were being interrogated in police centers — before they were transferred to prisons such as Con Son and Chi Hoa. Con Son is South Vietnam's biggest civilian penitentiary, situated on Con Son, an island 140 miles southeast of Saigon. Chi Hoa, the country's second largest prison, is in Saigon.

The informants said that most of the torture and interrogation had taken place between 10 P.M. and 3 A.M. They said some of the prisoners, under torture or fearing torture, agreed to become police agents to win their release.

Some of the documents purportedly smuggled out of the prisons gave the names of five persons who had been tortured to death recently in jail, and said this was only a part list. The documents listed Buu Chi and Nguyen Duy Hien, students from the Hue area who were said to have died in Con Son. Also listed were Ta Xuan Thanh, Dinh Van Ut and Bui Duong of Saigon, who were said to have died in Chi Hoa.

It is impossible to tell, without Government cooperation, how many thousands have been arrested since the North Vietnamese offensive began. Most foreign diplomats think the figure is well over 10,000. One American source said that slightly over 15,000 people had been jailed and about 5,000 released later. But whatever the exact figures, it is clear that thousands remain in prison and that arrests continue.

The bulk of the arrests have been in the Mekong Delta south of Saigon and in the extreme north. Many students were seized in Hue, some of them reportedly while working in refugee centers.

Little Distinction Indicated

It is also impossible to tell how many of those arrested really have Communist connections and how many are simply opposed to the Government of President Thieu, because the police seem to make little distinction. There is a third category of prisoners as well — people who were apparently seized at random and who committed no crime. They just happened to have been in the wrong place.

August 13, 1972

SAIGON DECREES END OF ELECTIONS ON HAMLET LEVEL

By CRAIG R. WHITNEY
Special to The New York Times

SAIGON, South Vietnam, Sept. 6—The South Vietnamese Government, by executive decree, has abolished popular democratic election of officials at the most basic level—in the country's 10,775 hamlets.

Under the new system, which is going into effect now and will be complete within two months, nearly all the country's administrative officials — from the province chiefs down to the hamlet level—will be appointed.

The decree ends six years of popular election at the grassroots level of the hamlets. It was issued, without publicity, on Aug. 22 by Premier Tran Thien Khiem. It orders the 44 province chiefs, who are military men appointed by President Nguyen Van Thieu, to reorganize local government and appoint all hamlet officials and finish the job in two months.

Aides to Be Appointed

The new system calls for either two or three officials in each hamlet, depending on its population. They are the average Vietnamese citizen's closest contact with his government— the men he complains to, goes to when he needs help, or hears from when the Government wants to enforce its laws.

At the next highest level, the village—villages in Vietnam are administrative groupings of hamlets, not villages in the American or European sense of the word — village chiefs and their staffs have been elected by provision of the South Vietnamese Constitution. But now, according to the Premier's decree, their deputies and staffs will no longer be elected. They, too, will be appointed by the province chiefs.

September 7, 1972

WHITE HOUSE SAYS RAIDING IN THE NORTH WILL GO ON UNTIL THERE IS AN ACCORD

A NEW TARGET LIST

Full-Scale Attacks and Mining Revived After Lull of Two Months

By WILLIAM BEECHER
Special to The New York Times

WASHINGTON, Dec. 18 — The Nixon Administration announced a resumption of full-scale bombing and mining of North Vietnam today, and the White House warned that such raids "will continue until such time as a settlement is arrived at."

Administration officials said that President Nixon, in ordering actions against military objectives in the Hanoi and Haiphong areas, had directed the Air Force and Navy to strike targets not bombed before.

[United States officials in Saigon said hundreds of planes, including B-52's, resumed attacks above the 20th Parallel in North Vietnam, carrying out the heaviest raids of the war in the Hanoi-Haiphong region. The Associated Press reported.]

Ronald L. Ziegler, the White House press secretary, voiced the threat of continuing attacks north of the 20th Parallel, after a halt of nearly two months, while insisting that their renewal was consistent with the policy enunciated by Mr. Nixon on May 8 in announcing his decision to mine the ports and bomb more extensively.

He said then that the actions would cease when American prisoners were released and an internationally supervised cease-fire was in force.

Threat of New Offensive

Mr. Ziegler also linked the latest action to the threat of another North Vietnamese offensive. "The road to peace is wide open," he said. "We want a rapid settlement to this conflict." But, he added, "we are not going to allow the peace talks to be used as a cover for another offensive."

Some military analysts, puzzled, said they knew of no signs of a major offensive.

According to the Administration officials, the principal purpose of the President's action was to insure that the North Vietnamese leaders would comprehend the extent of his anger over what the officials say he regards as an 11th-hour reneging on peace terms that were believed to be settled.

Senior planners said the latest military moves were part of a concerted political, diplomatic and military campaign designed to force North Vietnam into a more conciliatory position at the bargaining table.

Bids to Soviet and China

The first step came Saturday when Henry A. Kissinger, the President's national security adviser and chief Vietnam negotiator, held a news conference to deflate his optimistic projections of an early truce and to attribute much of the blame to North Vietnam.

Representations are being made with the Soviet Union, China and other nations to get them to use their influence on Hanoi, the officials said.

The broadened air campaign, including the attacks on targets never hit before, is the latest element of this effort, it was said.

The officials explained that the decision on expanded air activity was made tentatively by the President shortly before Mr. Kissinger returned Wednesday from the most recent round of private talks. They had been in frequent communication by cable.

The final decision was made after Mr. Kissinger's return, the sources said, upon discussions throughout the Government.

The decision on the mines, well-placed officials said was forced in part because there had been no mine-laying north of the 20th Parallel since Oct. 23, when air action there was halted.

The mines in such ports as Haiphong were set to deactivate late last week. If new mines had not been laid, and if no cease-fire agreement had been achieved, the officials said, North Vietnam might soon have realized that its principal port, Haiphong, was clear for freighter traffic.

Also, intelligence sources said North Vietnamese officials directed an evacuation of women and children from Hanoi on Dec. 4, the day the most recent round of private talks began in Paris. The sources said they presumed that the officials realized in advance that a tougher negotiating stance might result in a renewal of the bombing.

The first official confirmation of the lifting of the restrictions on air activity came this morning from Secretary of Defense Melvin R. Laird. He had invited photographers to

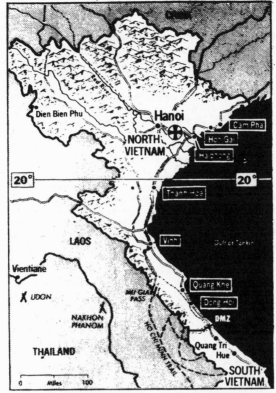

The New York Times/Dec. 19, 1972

U.S. planes resumed bombing of Hanoi-Haiphong area (cross) and mining of key ports north of 20th Parallel. Sowing of mines south of line had not been halted. (Mined ports are shown with names outlined in white.)

his office to take pictures of him and his designated replacement, Elliot L. Richardson, who

had appeared at the Pentagon for one of several transition briefings.

Hanoi Broadcasts Noted

Several reporters pressed Mr. Laird to comment on unconfirmed reports broadcast by Hanoi that bombing and mining north of the 20th Parallel had resumed.

After attempting to avoid the question, Mr. Laird said: "Air operations are being conducted throughout North Vietnam at the present time." He declined to discuss the matter further, saying it might jeopardize pilots' lives.

Later Mr. Ziegler expanded somewhat on the subject, saying, "The President will continue to order any action he deems necessary by air or by sea to prevent any build-up he sees in the South."

"Neither side can gain from prolonging the war," he added, "and neither side can gain from prolonging peace talks."

As for the new targets, military officials, citing reasons of pilot safety, declined to specify what might be hit.

Since the suspension of the bombing, the Administration officials said, North Vietnam has repaired its two main rail links to China, restored 40 per cent of its destroyed electric generating capacity and repaired or built bypasses for most main bridges.

Presumably such targets will be hit again, and that, an official remarked, would come as no surprise to North Vietnam.

December 19, 1972

U.S. LISTS TARGETS OF HEAVY ATTACKS IN NORTH VIETNAM

By JOSEPH B. TREASTER
Special to The New York Times

SAIGON, South Vietnam, Thursday, Dec. 28 — The United States military command, breaking a nine-day silence on damage inflicted in the intensive American air attacks against North Vietnam, listed nearly three dozen airfields, rail yards, power plants, supply depots and communications centers yesterday among the facilities that have been bombed.

Many of the targets were in the populous area of Hanoi and Haiphong.

Although the report ran 10 pages, it listed only military targets and did not include the Gia Lam International Airport, the Bach Mai Hospital and other civilian places in Hanoi that diplomats, journalists and the North Vietnamese had previously reported damaged.

'Only Military Targets'

Maj. Gilbert L. Whiteman, a spokesman for the command, would not comment on the bombing of the airport and the hospital or respond to any questions concerning civilian casualties from the B-52 aircraft, which lay down a carpet of bombs a mile and a half long and half a mile wide.

"We have targeted and continue to target only military targets," he said.

December 28, 1972

One-Third of Army In Cambodia Found To Be Nonexistent

By SYDNEY H. SCHANBERG
Special to The New York Times

PHNOM PENH, Cambodia, Dec. 27—The Cambodian Government acknowledged today that, because of corruption by military commanders and other "irregularities," it has "at times" paid salaries to as many as 100,000 nonexistent soldiers.

The Government said that it had sometimes met payrolls of 300,000 troops even though it has now found that the actual

number of men in the army is about 200,000. These "phantom" troops—a creation of false payrolls submitted by unit commanders — represent the most widespread form of corruption in Cambodia and have become the focus of bitter popular complaint.

A private in the Cambodian Army receives about $20 a month, so 100,000 "phantom" privates would put $2-million a month into the pockets of commanders. Virtually all of this money comes through United States aid, which will total about $300-million this year.

December 28, 1972

NEW THIEU DECREE CURBS OPPOSITION

Regulations for Parties Said To Eliminate Almost All Groups but President's

By FOX BUTTERFIELD

Special to The New York Times

SAIGON, South Vietnam, Dec. 28—Acting on the last day before the expiration of his special decree powers, President Nguyen Van Thieu last night quietly signed a law that South Vietnamese political leaders say will eliminate virtually all political parties except Mr. Thieu's new Democratic party.

The complex law requires, among other things, that each of South Vietnam's present 24 parties immediately create a vast new village-based political organization and win at least 20 per cent of the vote in any national election or be "automatically dissolved."

Opposition Leader Complains

Although Mr. Thieu had long been expected to seek some legislation regulating the country's fractious parties — which are often little more than conglomerates of personal interests—the toughness of the law caught both Saigon's politicians and the United States Embassy by surprise. There was no official announcement of the law; it was disclosed only in this evening's issue of the newspaper Tin Song, which often gives voice to the views of the Presidential Palace.

Deputy Tran Van Tuyen, a widely respected leader of the opposition party, Vietnam Quoc Dan Dang, said on hearing of the bill today, "It will drive the people underground and into the Communist side. Only Thieu's Democracy party can meet the criteria."

December 29, 1972

VIETNAM ACCORD IS REACHED; CEASE-FIRE BEGINS SATURDAY; P.O.W.'S TO BE FREE IN 60 DAYS

TROOPS TO LEAVE

On TV, Nixon Asserts 'Peace With Honor' Is Aim of Pact

By BERNARD GWERTZMAN

Special to The New York Times

WASHINGTON, Jan. 23— President Nixon said tonight that Henry A. Kissinger and North Vietnam's chief negotiator, Le Duc Tho, had initialed an agreement in Paris today "to end the war and bring peace with honor in Vietnam and Southeast Asia."

In a televised report to the nation, a few hours after Mr. Kissinger returned to Washington, Mr. Nixon said a cease-fire in Vietnam would go into effect on Saturday at 7 P.M., Eastern standard time.

Simultaneous announcements were made in Hanoi and Saigon.

Mr. Nixon said that under the terms of the accord—which will be formally signed on Saturday—all American prisoners of war would be released and the remaining 23,700-man American force in South Vietnam would be withdrawn within 60 days.

Wider Peace Indicated

He referred to "peace" in Southeast Asia, suggesting that the accord extended to Laos and Cambodia, which have also been engaged in the war. But there was no direct mention of those two nations today, and it is not known if the cease-fire extends to them as well.

Obviously pleased by the long-awaited development, ending the longest war in American history, Mr. Nixon said the Hanoi-Washington agreement "meets the goals" and has the "full support" of President Nguyen Van Thieu of South Vietnam.

Earlier Mr. Thieu had expressed strong reservations about the draft agreement worked out by Mr. Kissinger and Mr. Tho in October.

Tonight Mr. Nixon sketched only the outline of the accord. The full text of the agreement and accompanying protocols will be issued tomorrow by joint agreement with Hanoi, he said.

It was not possible, for instance, to determine from Mr. Nixon's 10-minute address what changes had been made in the agreement since October.

In his brief description of the accord, Mr. Nixon said that the cease-fire would be "internationally supervised," a refer-

C.B.S. News

President Nixon during his White House speech.

ence to the projected force of Canadians, Hungarians, Indonesians and Poles who will supervise the truce. But he did not say how large the force would be. The United States has wanted a highly mobile force of about 5,000 men. The North Vietnamese have suggested a substantially smaller force.

Mr. Nixon also said nothing about the controversial problem of the demilitarized zone that straddles the border between North and South Vietnam. Saigon has wanted this line reaffirmed to make sure, legally, that there are two Vietnams, and Hanoi had resisted this. All the President said on the subject was that the people of South Vietnam "have been guaranteed the right to determine their own future without outside interference."

Captive Issue Avoided

Nothing was said either about the release of the thousands of prisoners in Saigon's jails, many of whom were jailed on suspicion that they were Vietcong agents. At one point in the negotiations, Hanoi was seeking to make the release of American prisoners conditional on the release of Saigon's captives.

Some of these questions may be answered tomorrow when Mr. Kissinger holds a news conference at 11 A.M. It will be televised by the major networks.

Last fall, the President insisted that he would agree only to a "peace with honor," and tonight he insisted that the accord met "the goals that we considered essential for peace with honor."

Apparently in an effort to ease possible apprehensions in Saigon, Mr. Nixon pledged that the United States would continue to recognize Mr. Thieu's Government "as the sole legitimate Government of South Vietnam."

He also pledged—"within the terms of the agreement"—to continue to supply assistance to South Vietnam and to "support efforts for the people of South Vietnam to settle their problems peacefully among themselves."

The actual agreement is understood to provide machinery for the eventual reconciliation of the Saigon Government with the Vietcong. But officials here have expressed doubts in recent days that the two rivals for power would be able to resolve their hostility.

Calling on all involved parties to adhere to the agreement "scrupulously," Mr. Nixon also alluded to the Soviet Union and China, saying, "We shall also expect other interested nations to help insure that the agreement is carried out and peace is maintained."

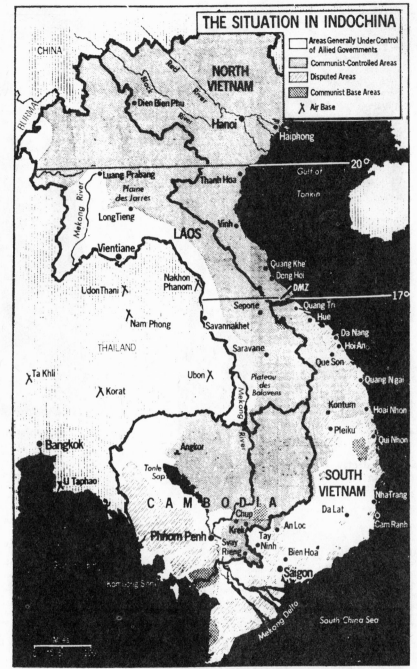

The New York Times/Daniel Brownstein/Jan. 24, 1973

Map shows approximate areas held by Communist and Government forces in South Vietnam, Laos and Cambodia. While Communists control large regions, population concentrations are mostly in Government-dominated areas.

It is expected that Secretary of State William P. Rogers will sign the agreement in Paris on Saturday at the former Hotel Majestic, along with the Foreign Ministers of North Vietnam, South Vietnam and the Provisional Revolutionary Government, or Vietcong.

Mr. Nixon ended his speech with words to the various parties to the accord, their allies, and to the American people.

Cooperation in Future

To the South Vietnamese, who in the end listened to American entreaties and did not balk at the accord, he said, "We look forward to working with you in the future." He added that the United States and South Vietnam would be "friends in peace as we have been allies in war."

To the North Vietnamese, he said, "As we have ended the war through negotiations, let us now build a peace of reconciliation."

He said that the United States would make "a major effort" to help achieve that goal, but he stressed that Hanoi would have to reciprocate. Previously, Mr. Nixon has talked about a $7.5-billion program to rehabilitate North Vietnam and South Vietnam over a five-year period. Of that total, $2.5-billion would be earmarked for Hanoi.

Making a firm call for support from Moscow and Peking, Mr. Nixon said: "To the other major powers that have been involved, even indirectly, now is the time for mutual restraint so that the peace we have achieved can last."

In Saigon yesterday, a pedicab driver read the latest issue of Dien Tin (Telegraph News), which featured on its front page a picture of a dove.

United Press International

Associated Press

Le Duc Tho of North Vietnam with Henry A. Kissinger after their meeting in Paris yesterday morning.

U.S. Aid Believed Limited

Under the terms of the accord, it is believed, the United States is limited in the amount of military aid it can supply Saigon. But American officials have warned that if the Russians and the Chinese continue to supply Hanoi with extensive military equipment the balance of power could be upset.

Mr. Nixon said nothing about a key controversial item in the negotiations—the presence of 145,000 North Vietnamese in South Vietnam. But previously, Mr. Kissinger had said that the United States would not ask Hanoi to pull these forces back because they would be needed to protect the Vietcong enclaves permitted under the accord.

To the American people, he explained his silence of recent months about the situation in Vietnam. He said that if he had discussed the efforts to achieve an agreement, "it would have seriously harmed and possibly destroyed the chances for peace."

He ended his speech with some words about Lyndon B. Johnson. who died yesterday on the eve of the settlement.

He said that no one would have welcomed this peace more than he.

Earlier, on Mr. Kissinger's return from Paris, the President set in motion a series of evening conferences before his televised report to the nation.

Mr. Nixon first met with his Cabinet officers to give them a report on the Vietnam situation, then conferred with the top Congressional leaders from both parties.

The White House said that Mr. Nixon had invited to that session the Senate majority leader, Mike Mansfield of Montana; the Senate Republican leader, Hugh Scott of Pennsylvania; the House Speaker, Carl Alpert of Oklahoma; the House Republican leader, Gerald R. Ford of Michigan, and the House Democratic leader. Thomas P. O'Neill Jr. of Massachusetts.

Throughout the day, despite the reports from Saigon and Paris about the initialing of the agreement, the White House refrained from any substantive comment.

Ronald L. Ziegler, the White House press secretary, met briefly with newsmen at about 1 P.M., after having spent much of the morning at a meeting with Mr. Nixon and White House aides.

Mr. Ziegler limited himself to announcing that Mr. Nixon would address the nation on the "status of the Vietnam negotiations," and that he would hold meeting wih the Cabinet officers and Congressional leaders tonight. In addition, Mr. Ziegler said a larger session with members of Congress would be held tomorrow morning at the White House.

The substantive talks on a Vietnam settlement began in January, 1969, in the former Hotel Majestic in Paris, the same place Mr. Kissinger and Mr. Tho held their session today.

Meetings Around Paris

The negotiations that produced the actual agreement, however, took place in villas in and around Paris between Mr. Kissinger and Mr. Tho, beginning in August, 1969.

The holding of those negotiations remained a closely guarded secret until last Jan. 26 when Mr. Nixon disclosed them in a speech accusing Hanoi of delaying tactics.

After North Vietnam's offensive in South Vietnam last spring, the secret talks resumed.

A decisive breakthrough was achieved early in October when the United States and North Vietnam agreed to a nine-point draft agreement whose outline was made public by Hanoi on Oct. 26, and was confirmed by Mr. Kissinger that same day in his "peace is at hand" news conference.

Hanoi had originally insisted that the draft be signed by Oct. 31, but Mr. Nixon asked for further meetings to tighten the terms of the agreement and to meet some of South Vietnam's objections.

The talks resumed in Paris on Nov. 20 and recessed on Nov. 25. When they began again on Dec. 4, Hanoi objected to the proposals made by the United States in the previous round, and made counterproposals that Mr. Kissinger later called "frivolous." Those talks broke down on Dec. 13.

Reportedly angry over Hanoi's tactics, Mr. Nixon ordered the war's heaviest bombing of Hanoi and Haiphong — from Dec. 18 to 29. The raids, which included strikes by B-52 bombers, were called off north of the 20th Parallel on Dec. 29 with the announcement by the White House that Hanoi had agreed to resume "serious" talks.

Apparent Accord on Jan. 13

The negotiations opened on Jan. 8 and concluded with an apparent agreement on Jan. 13. Two days later all bombing, mining and shelling of North Vietnam ceased, and on Jan. 18 — last Thursday — it was announced that Mr. Kissinger and Mr. Tho would meet again "for the purpose of concluding the text of an agreement."

Gen. Alexander M. Haig Jr., who until this month was Mr. Kissinger's chief deputy, returned to Washington on Sunday after a mission to Saigon to persuade President Thieu to add his agreement to the accord worked out by Hanoi and Washington.

Mr. Haig was with Mr. Nixon early this morning when first reports of the conclusion of Mr. Kissinger's Paris meeting were received here.

January 24, 1973

PACT TO END WAR IN LAOS, INCLUDING POLITICAL PLAN, IS SIGNED BY THE 2 SIDES

20-YEAR CONFLICT

Cease-Fire Expected to Go Into Effect at Noon Tomorrow

By MALCOLM W. BROWNE
Special to The New York Times

VIENTIANE, Laos, Wednesday, Feb. 21—The Laotian Government and the Communist-led Pathet Lao signed a peace agreement today, ending 20 years of war and establishing an interim coalition government to be made up of equal numbers from both sides.

The accord was signed this morning by the Government's chief negotiator, Pheng Phongsavan and the Pathet Lao leader, Phoumi Vongvichit. The signing took place at the residence of Premier Souvanna Phouma in the presence of the Premier and the diplomatic corps as well as members of the two negotiating teams.

[In Phom Penh, the Cambodian Government said negotiations were under way to set up a united front that could handle contacts with the Communists. In Saigon, South Vietnamese military authorities said the level of fighting had risen sharply again after a one-day decline.

Stresses Dependency

As champagne corks popped, Prince Souvanna Phouma made a brief speech, in which he pointedly told the assembled diplomats that Laos was "among the most backward nations in the world" and was heavily dependent on the great powers represented by the diplomats.

The accord provides that a cease-fire will go into effect throughout Laos at noon tomorrow (midnight Wednesday New York time).

After the signing, Mr. Pheng gave a brief news conference outside the Premier's residence. He outlined the main points of the accord, which included the following:

¶The accord creates two commissions with equal numbers from each side to deal separately with military and political questions.

¶Prisoners will be exchanged in the same period of time allowed foreign troops to be withdrawn from Laos, which will be 60 days from today.

¶Thirty days from today, a government of national union will come into being made up of equal numbers of representatives of the Government and the Pathet Lao. This government will be headed by a neutralist Premier. Presumably, it will be Prince Souvanna Phouma. No provision has been made for a deputy premier.

¶The military commission will be responsible for maintaining the cease-fire and overseeing the withdrawal of foreign troops and the exchange of prisoners.

¶The International Control Commission, established in 1962 and made up of India, Canada and Poland, will continue to have authority to oversee the cease-fire.

A Change in Names

The name of the Vientiane Government, which was a major sticking point in negotiations, is to be the "Government at Vientiane." The Pathet Lao had demanded previously that the present Government be called simply "the administration of Vientiane."

The composition of the future government has been specified only in terms of equal parts, and the number of ministers involved has not been decided.

The accord calls for general elections throughout Laos after political settlement is reached, but does not say when these elections will be held.

The accord was signed in five copies in the Lao language, one copy being transmitted to King Savang Vatthana, and one for the national archives. All copies were signed by both representatives.

After the signing, Pathet Lao officials seemed jubilant, and most Government officials seemed deeply depressed. There were rumors that serious trouble was brewing and could come to a head in the next few days from a coalition of right-wing neutralists and rightists who opposed the accord.

In any case, the agreement leaves the Pathet Lao in a far stronger position than it has ever been before in previous attempts at coalition Government, and there was wide speculation from anti-Communist officials that the agreement is tantamount to a Communist take-over.

The accord stipulates, among other things, that the administrative capital of Vientiane and the royal capital at Luang Prabang are herewith neutralized in terms to their being associated with one side or the other. The provisional capital will be Vientiane, although it seemed unlikely that the Pathet Lao capital at Sam Neua would end its activities any time soon.

The first text of any kind on the agreement itself was released in French early this afternoon by the Pathet Lao, and no text was available from the Vientiane Government.

The Pathet Lao text was seven pages long and covered general principles.

It called on the United States and Thailand to respect the sovereignty of Laos.

But did not mention the North Vietnamese troops in the country, currently estimated to tumbe about 60,000.

The accord prohibits any mopping up action or other hostile military activity by either side, or the future introduction of any kind of military troops, regular or irregular.

The future general election will be to create a new legislative assembly, which is described as the "definitive" legislature responsible for forming a permanent government.

The accord includes fourteen articles.

The Pathet Lao spokesman, Sot Petrasy, said in an interview last night that American bombing of Laos would be halted at the time of the cease-fire, although he declined to say whether he had received direct assurance from an American official that this would take place.

February 21, 1973

Indochina–the Heavy Toll

Military Casualties	Killed	Wounded
United States	45,948	303,640
South Vietnam	184,546	495,931
Communist	927,124	unavailable

Civilian Casualties		
South Vietnam	451,000	935,000

Refugees	
South Vietnam	over 6.5 million
Cambodia	over 2 million
Laos	over 1 million
North Vietnam	unavailable

U.S. Expenditures since 1965, start of buildup	$109.5-billion

Sources: U.S. Department of Defense, U.S. Agency for International Development, U.S. Senate Subcommittee on Refugees and Escapees, Cambodian Government.

April 1, 1973

Chronology of the War in Vietnam and Its Historical Antecedents From 1940

Following is a chronology of the Vietnam war and its historical antecedents:

1940

Japanese occupy Indochina, which had been under French domination since last half of 19th century, but permit French colonial authorities to govern.

1945

March—Japanese end French rule in Vietnam and allow Emperor Bao Dai to proclaim independence of Vietnam.

August — Japanese occupation of Vietnam collapses after Japan surrenders to United States. The Vietminh, led by Ho Chi Minh, take control of Vietnam. Emperor Bao Dai abdicates.

September—Ho Chi Minh proclaims Vietnam a democratic republic. He appeals to the United States for support but gets no reply. French Army returns and launches campaign to reconquer Vietnam.

1946

December—Ho Chi Minh calls on Vietnamese people to expel French, saying Vietnam is prepared to fight for 10 years.

1947

May — Anti-Communists organize Front of National Union in Saigon, calling upon Bao Dai to return to Vietnam from France to head anti-Communist government.

1948

June—Bao Dai signs agreement with French providing

Emperor Bao Dai with Gen. Alphonse Juin of France.

for formation of Vietnamese government.

1949

June — Bao Dai becomes chief of state of French-sponsored Vietnamese Government,

but Vietminh continue to hold large areas.

1950

May — United States announces it will help France in Indochina and a U.S. economic mission arrives in Saigon.

July — American military mission arrives in Vietnam.

September-October — French suffer serious military setbacks in northern Vietnam.

1951

January-March — French forces reach 391,000 men in Vietnam. Opposition to war in Indochina grows in France.

1952

October—Bao Dai, his political support evaporating, withdraws from Vietnamese scene.

1953

December — Vietminh offensive cuts Vietnam in two.

1954

February — Big Four nations agree to convene conference in Geneva aimed at seeking resolution of Indochinese and Korean situations.

March-April—The crucial battle for Dien Bien Phu takes place.

April — Geneva Conference begins.

May—Dien Bien Phu falls to the Vietminh, shattering French military power in Vietnam.

June — Ngo Dinh Diem becomes head of government in Saigon. French begin evacuating southern areas of Red River Delta. Col. Edward G. Lansdale of American C.I.A. arrives in Saigon as head of team of agents to engage in "paramilitary operations" and "political-

Gen. Vo Nguyen Giap led Vietminh to victory over the French in 1954.

psychological warfare" against North Vietnam.

July—The Geneva agreement ending the fighting in Vietnam is signed. Vietnam is divided roughly along the 17th Parallel, with the northern part recognized as the domain of the Communist regime under Ho Chi Minh, and the southern part placed under control of those representing State of Vietnam. Agreement includes a free option for all Vietnamese to select the zone in which they wish to live, removal of all foreign forces except French troops, which are permitted to remain in the South, and a ban on reprisals against Vietnamese for their wartime activities.

August—U.S. intelligence estimates indicate chances for a strong regime in South Vietnam are poor. National Security Council finds Geneva accords a "disaster" producing a "major forward stride of Communism." President Eisenhower approves council recommendation for direct economic and military aid to South Vietnam, thereby establishing U.S. policy in area.

October—Lansdale team engages in "delayed sabotage" of Hanoi railroad, contaminates oil supply for city's buses, recruits and trains two teams of Vietnamese agents. As the Vietminh occupy Hanoi and take control in North, the French increase their pressure against Premier Diem, whom they consider anti-French, in South. President Eisenhower decides to provide aid directly to South Vietnam rather than channel it through the French.

December — Gen. J. Lawton Collins, special envoy for President Eisenhower, urges removal or replacement of Diem or "re-evaluation of our plans" for aid to area. Secretary of State Dulles says he has "no other choice but to continue our aid to Vietnam and support of Diem."

1955

January — United States decides to provide aid directly to South Vietnam rather than through the French. Diem's position continues to grow stronger.

May — Draft statement by U.S. National Security Council suggests that Diem, in complying with Geneva accords providing for elections to unify Vietnam, demand free elections, by secret ballot and with strict supervision. Main points of draft statement are conveyed to Diem.

June—Government in North Vietnam demands discussions, in accord with Geneva provisions, to prepare for election in 1956.

July — Diem, noting South Vietnam did not sign Geneva agreement, says it will not take part in elections unless they

are conducted freely in North as well as South.

October—South Vietnam is declared a republic, with Diem as President.

1956

July—Month in which elections to unify Vietnam were to have been held passes without incident.

October—Republic of South

Ngo Dinh Diem, Premier of South Vietnam in 1954, became President in 1955. He was slain in 1963.

Vietnam, having moved clearly in direction of long-term independence as an entity separate from North, adopts a Constitution. U.S. sends 350 more military men to Saigon.

1957

May—Diem visits United States. President Eisenhower vows continued aid to South Vietnam.

1959

July—Two U.S. military advisers killed in terrorist attack on Bien Hoa military base, becoming the first Americans to die in Vietnam fighting.

1960

May—U.S. announces it is increasing military advisers in Vietnam to 685.

November—South Vietnam accuses North Vietnam of direct aggression, asserting North Vietnamese troops infiltrated through Laos. Attempted coup against Diem is crushed. U.S. intelligence estimates predict rising "dissatisfaction and discontent" with Diem Government.

December—U.S. military personnel in South Vietnam now total 900. National Front for the Liberation of South Vietnam is established by Vietcong, and draws prompt support from Hanoi.

1961

May—Vice President Lyndon B. Johnson visits South Vietnam and pledges additional aid.

September—President Kennedy warns in speech at United Nations that South Vietnam is under attack.

October—Gen. Maxwell D.

Taylor and Walt W. Rostow visit South Vietnam to evaluate situation. White House agrees to finance increase of 30,000 men in South Vietnamese Army and Joint Chiefs of Staff estimate 40,000 U.S. servicemen will be needed to "clean up the Vietcong threat."

October-November — Taylor recommends a Mekong Delta "relief task force" of 6,000 to 8,000 men, including combat troops. He discounts risk of "major Asian war," asserting that North Vietnam is "extremely vulnerable to conventional bombing." President Kennedy decides to send additional military advisers and equipment.

December — U.S. military forces in South Vietnam total 3,200.

1962

February—More U.S. troops arrive, bringing total to 4,000. Two South Vietnamese Air Force officers bomb and strafe the presidential palace in Saigon in attempt to assassinate Diem.

March—U.S. force in South Vietnam rises to 5,400.

May—Secretary of Defense Robert S. McNamara visits Vietnam, says U.S. aid will level off and expresses doubt that U.S. military forces will increase.

December — U. S. military forces in South Vietnam total 11,300 men.

1963

May — Defense Department spokesman says "corner has definitely been turned toward victory" over Vietcong. Riots erupt in Hue after South Vietnamese Government refuses to permit processions on Buddha's birthday.

June — More Buddhist demonstrations break out in Hue and elsewhere. Government imposes martial law and uses troops to halt rioting. Buddhist monk burns himself to death in Saigon to dramatize Bud-

dhist protest against repressive government policy.

August — Another Buddhist monk immolates himself. Government forces raid a Saigon pagoda and arrest hundreds of monks. President Diem declares nationwide martial law. Students demonstrate in Saigon and hundreds are arrested.

September — President Kennedy warns that South Vietnamese Government has "gotten out of touch with people" and threatens to cut aid unless reforms are instituted. United States Ambassador, Henry Cabot Lodge, tells Diem that Ngo Dinh Nhu, head of South Vietnamese secret police and a strong influence on Diem, must be removed from power. Diem lifts martial law, eliminates curfew and ends censorship.

October — United States troops in Vietnam number 16,732.

November—A military coup, which has tacit support of the United States, overthrows President Diem. He and Nhu are assassinated and a military junta headed by Gen. Duong Van Minh takes control of Government, promising to pursue the war with vigor.

December—U. S. begins to withdraw 1,000 troops from South Vietnam amid assurances that America will back South Vietnam's war effort as long as aid is sought.

1964

January—Military junta is overthrown by Gen. Nguyen Khanh, who names Minh chief of state and himself Premier.

March-April—U. S. officials consider escalation of the war to conform with Administration conviction that Hanoi controls Vietcong. Secretary of State Dean Rusk urges that extent of Hanoi's involvement should be "proven to the satisfaction of our own public, of our allies and of the neutralists." Joint Chiefs drew up list of 94 potential targets for bombing in North Vietnam.

Ho Chi Minh visiting Paris in 1946. At left is Pham Van Dong, who is now the Premier of North Vietnam; at right is Marius Motet, France's Overseas Minister.

May—Khanh calls on U.S. to attack North Vietnam. Mc-Namara does not "rule out" possibility of bombing but says it must be "supplementary to and not a substitute for" a successful campaign against Vietcong in the South. William P. Bundy sends President Johnson a 30-day scenario for graduated military pressure against North that would culminate in full-scale bombing attacks. He includes draft for a joint Congressional resolution that would authorize "whatever is necessary" with respect to Vietnam.

June—Top U.S. officials meet in Honolulu to review war. They conclude that U.S. must increase aid to South Vietnam. Lodge urges "selective bombing campaign" against military targets in North and questions need for Congressional resolution, which Rusk, McNamara and John McCone of C.I.A. support. President Johnson resists pressure for a Congressional resolution and decides to step up war effort. Gen. William Westmoreland takes command of U.S. forces in Vietnam, Ambassador Lodge resigns and is replaced by Gen. Taylor.

July—South Vietnamese naval commandos raid two North Vietnamese islands in Gulf of Tonkin.

August—The American destroyer Maddox, on intelligence patrol in Gulf of Tonkin, is attacked by North Vietnamese torpedo boats. Two days later, both the Maddox and another destroyer, the Turner Joy, are similarly attacked. President Johnson orders immediate retaliatory bombing of North Vietnamese gunboats and support facilities. Next day, President Johnson asks Congress to approve joint resolution pledging full support for U.S. forces in South Vietnam "to promote the maintenance of international peace and security in Southeast Asia." Measure, known as Tonkin Gulf Resolution, is approved by Congress, opening way for major escalation of U.S. involvement in Vietnam

A Buddhist monk dies by fire in Saigon, 1963, in protest against Diem.

war. Vote in House is 416 to 0 and in Senate 88 to 2.

November—Vietcong carry out mortar attack on Bien Hoa air base. Joint Chiefs urge "strong response," including air strikes against North Vietnam. Ambassador Taylor calls for bombing of "selected" targets. President declines.

December—President Johnson approves plan for air attacks on North Vietnam: reprisal air strikes for 30 days, then graduated air warfare against North backed by possible deployment of ground combat troops.

1965

February — Vietcong attack U.S. military advisers' compound at Pleiku; 8 Americans are killed, 109 wounded. President Johnson responds swiftly: 49 U.S. jets raid Dong Hoi in North Vietnam. Vietcong attack U.S. barracks at Qui Nhon, killing 23 Americans and wounding 21. U.S. launches another air attack on North Vietnam and Operation Rolling Thunder—code name for a sustained air war—is ordered.

March—Marine Corps sends two battalions to Da Nang. U.S. forces in South Vietnam now total 27,000.

April — President Johnson says U.S. is prepared to begin talks to end war. He proposes a $1-billion aid program for Southeast Asia. Hanoi rejects offer, proposes its own peace plan. At the same time, Presi-

dent Johnson approves increase of 18,000 to 20,000 men in "military support forces" and "change of mission" for Marines "to permit their more active use." At Honolulu conference, U.S. officials agree to urge increase to 82,000 U.S. troops in Vietnam, but Under Secretary of State George W. Ball proposes that U.S. "cut its losses" and withdraw.

May—More U.S. troops arrive in Vietnam, bringing total to 46,500. U.S. halts bombing of North to sound out Hanoi on peace conditions. Six days later, bombing is resumed. Vietcong begin "summer offensive."

June—Military strength rises sharply, reaching more than 74,000, and U.S. troops participate in first major "search and destroy" mission. Nguyen Cao Ky becomes Premier and Gen. Nguyen Van Thieu is named Chief of State. U.S. planes conduct raids north of Hanoi.

July—Gen. Taylor resigns as Ambassador and is replaced by former Ambassador Lodge.

October - November — Mass demonstrations against the war begin in the United States. Washington says U.S. has 148,-300 troops in Vietnam. Two Americans burn themselves to death in protest against war. Big protest march on Washington is held.

December—U.S. and Vietcong agree on 30-hour Christmas truce. U.S. suspends bombing of North, sends high-level officials to world capitals to discuss possibilities of negotiated settlement.

1966

January—Ho Chi Minh says Hanoi's peace plan must be accepted by U.S. if war is to end. A week later, President Johnson announces resumption of bombing after 37-day pause.

March — McNamara recommends U.S. bombing of oil and

Nguyen Cao Ky became Premier in 1965.

lubricant supplies in North Vietnam. Taylor proposes mining of Haiphong harbor. Protests erupt in South Vietnam demanding civilian government.

April — United States begins using B-52 bombers for raids on North Vietnam. McNamara says troop strength totals 245,000 plus 50,000 Naval personnel in area.

May — Political turmoil in South Vietnam continues, with Buddhists and students demonstrating.

June—Raids on oil installations in Haiphong and Hanoi area begin. Lodge begins series of secret meetings with Polish and Italian envoys in Saigon to explore possibilities of initiating peace negotiations. Johnson calls for unconditional peace talks.

July — Thieu proposes invasion of North Vietnam and calls for increased bombing of North. Defense Department says U.S. troop strength will be increased to 375,000 by end of 1966 and to 425,000 by spring of 1967. Joint Chiefs approve request from Westmoreland for total of 542,588 troops by end of 1967.

September—U.S. study group report to McNamara says Operation Rolling Thunder "had no measurable direct effect" on Hanoi's capabilities in South Vietnam. Study group recommends construction of electronic barrier across demilitarized zone.

October — McNamara, after visit to Vietnam, tells President Johnson in memorandum that "pacification has if anything gone backward" and that bombing has not "significantly affected infiltration or cracked the morale of Hanoi." But Joint Chiefs say military situation has "improved substantially" in last year and they urge no cutback in bombings. President Johnson says U.S. will not suspend bombing until Hanoi reduces its military activity in South Vietnam.

November — McNamara authorizes 469,000 troops in South Vietnam by end of June, 1968 — substantially below requests by military officers. He tells President there is "no evidence" that added troops "would substantially change the situation" and says bombing is having "no significant impact" on war.

December — Talks begin in Warsaw between U.S. and Polish officials growing out of discussions between Lodge and a Polish representative in Saigon. But they collapse after U.S. bombs Hanoi in mid-December. In effort to salvage talks, U.S. agrees not to bomb within 10 miles of North Vietnamese capital. At year's end, U.S. troop strength reaches 389,000; combat deaths total 6,644; the number of wounded is 37,738.

1967

May—U.S. and South Vietnamese forces move into demilitarized zone for first time. U.S. bombs Hanoi power plant one mile north of city center.

August — President Johnson announces increase in ceiling on troops in Vietnam to 525,000 and says he plans to send 40,-000 to 50,000 more. He also ap-

Gen. William C. Westmoreland, at left, with Robert S. McNamara.

proves new bombing targets in North. At Senate Foreign Relations Committee hearings, Nicholas deB. Katzenbach, the Under Secretary of State, says Tonkin Gulf Resolution gave President authority to use U.S. forces without formal declaration of war. McNamara tells Senate Preparedness Subcommittee North Vietnam cannot be "bombed to the negotiating table" but the committee, in a report, urges President to intensify air war.

September — Vietcong say their political objectives are to overthrow Saigon regime and establish a "national union democratic government" composed of Communists and other groups. Thieu is elected President and a peace candidate, Truong Dinh Dzu, runs second. President Johnson declares U.S. will end bombing of North Vietnam "when this will lead promptly to productive discussions."

November — President Johnson says he would be willing to meet with North Vietnamese leaders on neutral ship in neutral waters. North Vietnam rejects proposal. Westmoreland, on visit to Washington, says he has "never been more encouraged in my four years in Vietnam." U.S. bombers raid Haiphong shipyards.

1968

January—Hanoi radio broadcasts statement by Foreign Minister, Nguyen Duy Trinh, saying North Vietnam "will hold talks with the United States on relevant questions" if U.S. "unconditionally" halts bombing of North. U.S. resumes bombing after New Year truce. Communists begin Tet (Lunar New Year) offensive with attacks on major cities in South.

February—Rusk says Communist attacks on cities show Hanoi's lack of interest in negotiation. President Johnson says North Vietnam is no more ready to negotiate than it was three years earlier. Secretary General Thant of United Nations declares he is "reasonably assured" that if U.S. halts bombing, Hanoi will come to conference table in good faith.

March—Senator Eugene McCarthy, an antiwar candidate, wins Democratic Presidential primary in New Hampshire. Senator Robert F. Kennedy says he will seek Presidential nomination because Vietnam policies will change only when administration changes. President Johnson announces a halt in all air and naval bombardment of North Vietnam except in the area around DMZ. He also declares he will not run for re-election. Massacre occurs at village of My Lai; U.S. soldiers kill a reported 347 men, women and children.

April—North Vietnam offers to meet with U.S. "with a view to determining with the American side the unconditional cessation of the U.S. bombing raids and all other acts of war" so that peace talks may start.

May—U.S. and North Vietnam begin formal peace talks in Paris.

October — President Johnson announces that U.S. will cease "all air, naval and artillery bombardment of North Vietnam" as of Nov. 1.

November—In Paris, North Vietnam announces that a meeting of representatives of North Vietnam, South Vietnam, Vietcong and U.S. will take place Nov. 6. But Thieu says his Government will not attend until North Vietnam agrees not to include Vietcong as a separate delegation. Richard M. Nixon is elected President of U.S. After weeks of discussion, U.S. says the allied side in Paris talks will consist of separate U.S. and South Vietnamese delegations and other side "for practical

Dean Rusk, Secretary of State in the Kennedy and Johnson administrations.

purposes" will be considered a single delegation. South Vietnam agrees to attend talks.

1969

January — President-elect Nixon appoints Lodge as chief U.S. negotiator at Paris talks, replacing W. Averell Harriman. Talks bog down for weeks over shape of the conference table, but question is finally resolved and substantive discussions begin.

February—Communist forces launch a general offensive in South Vietnam.

March — President Nixon warns that U.S. "will not tolerate" continued enemy attacks and he warns North Vietnamese that appropriate reactions should be expected. Defense Department says U.S. forces in Vietnam total 541,500 —the peak level of U.S. involvement in Vietnam.

June—President Nixon meets with Thieu on Midway Island and Mr. Nixon announces that 25,000 American troops will be withdrawn from South Vietnam by end of August.

July—President Nixon enunciates the "Nixon doctrine," declaring that in future U.S. will avoid involvements like Vietnam by limiting its support to economic and military aid rather than active combat participation.

September—Ho Chi Minh dies in North Vietnam. President Nixon announces another troop withdrawal, this time 35,000 men.

November — The moratorium against the war draws huge crowds to Washington to demand an end of fighting and

rapid withdrawal of U.S. troops. Lodge resigns as chief delegate to Paris talks.

December — President Nixon announces third withdrawal of troops, this time amounting to 50,000 men by April, 1970.

1970

January—President Nixon, in State of the Union address, declares that end of Vietnam war is a major goal of U.S. policy.

Walt W. Rostow, at left, and McGeorge Bundy.

U.S. command in Saigon announces bombing of anti-aircraft missile base 90 miles inside North Vietnam.

February—Defense Secretary Melvin R. Laird says "Vietnamization" program is working and withdrawal of troops can continue despite stalemate at Paris.

March — Prince Norodom Sihanouk is overthrown as Cambodian Chief of State in coup directed by Marshal Lon Nol.

April—U.S. troop strength in Vietnam stands at 429,900. President Nixon announces plans to withdraw 150,000 more troops in coming year. On April 30 he sends U.S. combat troops into Cambodia to destroy Vietcong sanctuaries and supplies.

May — U.S. planes bomb North Vietnamese supply dumps and other targets. Two days later Defense Department announces end of "large-scale" air raids in North. It warns that small raids may be conducted if U.S. reconnaissance planes are attacked.

June—President Nixon calls Cambodia operation successful and announces resumption of withdrawal of American troops from Vietnam. Senate repeals Tonkin Gulf Resolution, and approves Cooper-Church amendment barring future military operations in Cambodia or aid to Lon Nol without Congressional approval.

November — U.S. troops make surprise raid on Son Tay, 23 miles from Hanoi, in unsuccessful attempt to rescue prisoners of war.

1971

April — President Nixon announces 100,000-man reduction in U.S. strength in Vietnam, lowering ceiling to 184,000.

June — North Vietnam presents nine-point peace proposal to Henry A. Kissinger in secret meeting in Paris. Plan calls for withdrawal of all U.S. forces, end of U.S. support for Thieu Government, formation of a government of "national con-

"cord" and a cease-fire to follow agreement on political and withdrawal issues.

October—Thieu is re-elected President of South Vietnam in one-man race. Kissinger presents revised American peace plan in continuing secret Paris meetings. The proposals call for withdrawal of U.S. forces within six months of agreement, release of prisoners of war and free elections.

November—President Nixon announces further troop withdrawal, cutting level to 139,000.

1972

January — President Nixon announces new troop withdrawal, saying he will pull out 70,000 more troops by May 1. He also reveals the holding of secret talks in Paris between Kissinger and North Vietnamese, discloses U.S. peace proposals and declares that North Vietnam refuses to continue the secret talks.

March — U.S. breaks off the formal Paris peace talks, declaring that Communists refuse to negotiate seriously. North Vietnamese troops begin major offensive in South Vietnam, crossing DMZ in force with armor and artillery.

April — U.S. bombers strike near Hanoi and Haiphong, ending four-year de-escalation of air war against major North Vietnamese targets. Ten days later U.S. announces it will resume Paris talks. President Nixon says 20,000 more troops will be brought home by July 1.

May—Quang Tri falls to the North Vietnamese, giving them control of South Vietnam's northernmost province. U.S. and South Vietnamese call off formal Paris peace talks indefinitely. In a nationwide address, President Nixon announces that he has ordered mining of Haiphong and six other major North Vietnamese ports as well as a blockade of supplies for North Vietnam. At the same time, he offers to withdraw all U.S. troops within four months after American prisoners have been released and agreement has been reached on an internationally supervised cease-fire. U.S. turns over Cam Ranh Bay base, its largest in South Vietnam, to the South Vietnamese; but Pentagon dispatches a seventh aircraft carrier to join 60 U.S. ships in Gulf of Tonkin.

June — Maj. Gen. John D. Lavelle confirms that he ordered unauthorized raids on North Vietnamese air bases, missiles and artillery between January and March. U.S. ground combat role terminated in Vietnam, leaving force of fewer than 60,000 advisers, technicians and helicopter crews. President Nixon says U.S. forces will be reduced to 39,000 by Sept. 1.

July — Paris peace talks resume. As private talks also resume, North Vietnamese say Kissinger has brought no basic change in U.S. policy.

August — President Nixon says U.S. forces will be reduced to 27,000 men by Dec. 1.

September — South Vietnamese marines recapture Quang Tri. Thieu says he is determined to reject all forms of coalition government for South Vietnam. Three American prisoners of war are freed by North Vietnam. Reports circulate that Kissinger and North Vietnamese are close to an agreement in secret talks.

October — Kissinger holds four-day secret session with North Vietnamese in Paris, then flies to Saigon for talks with Thieu. Thieu denounces peace plan as unacceptable but concedes that cease-fire may come soon. Hanoi radio says U. S. and North Vietnamese have reached agreement on cease-fire but accuses the U. S. of backing off. Kissinger says in response that "peace is at hand" but denies Hanoi's contention that U. S. had agreed to sign a nine-point draft agreement by Oct. 31.

November—Hanoi agrees to more peace talks. Reports from Saigon indicate both U. S. and North Vietnamese continue to move supplies into South Vietnam in anticipation of a cease-fire. President Nixon is re-elected. Kissinger returns to

A G.I. in Hue, 1968

Paris for seven sessions with Le Duc Tho, Hanoi's chief negotiator.

December — Mr. Nixon announces Kissinger will remain as his foreign policy adviser in second term. After eight more sessions with Tho in Paris, Kissinger returns to Washington and charges Hanoi is procrastinating. He says talks have failed to produce a "just and fair agreement." Hanoi charges that U.S. tried to reopen issues forcing it to recognize sovereignty of the Saigon Government. Mr. Nixon orders renewal of bombing attacks above the

20th Parallel in North Vietnam, including round-the-clock B-52 raids in Hanoi-Haiphong area. Amid charges from many quarters that American planes are bombing civilian targets. Communists say they will not negotiate until bombing ceases. After 12 days of raids, in which U. S. says it lost 15 B-52's and 93 airmen killed, captured or missing, Mr. Nixon orders halt in bombing above the 20th Parallel.

1973

January—Kissinger and Tho confer for total of 35 hours over six days in Paris. Citing "progress." Mr. Nixon halts bombing, mining and shelling of North Vietnam. Kissinger and Tho then hold one more session and initial agreement for Vietnam cease-fire. Secretary of State Rogers and Foreign Ministers of South Vietnam. North Vietnam and Vietcong's Provisional Revolutionary Government sign accord only hours before suspension of hostilities at 7 P.M. yesterday.

January 28, 1973

THAILAND: A ROLE FOR THE U.S.

THAILAND SLATED AS ASIAN BASTION

U. S. to Bolster Nation's Role as Base Against Reds— Lists Training Plans

Special to The New York Times.

WASHINGTON, July 13—A program to make Thailand a base for defense against Communist aggression in Southeast Asia was announced today.

The Department of Defense said that it had approved "a new and additional military assistance program." It included "accelerated development of junior officers, noncommissioned officers and technical personnel," provision of "weapons, equipment and technical training assistance," and construction of a $3,000,000 military highway through central Thailand.

Gen. Srisdi Dhanarajata, Commander in Chief of the Thai

Army and Deputy Minister of Defense, said that the number of officers and noncommissioned officers in training would be doubled. Expansion will begin "almost immediately," he said.

In addition to the Army, Navy and Air Force officers now turned out in five-year training programs, a new corps of officers is to be trained on an emergency basis in eight to twelve months so that new divisions can be activated.

Staff Talks Completed

The general's remarks were translated by Pote Sarasin, Ambassador of Thailand, at a press conference marking the conclusion of two weeks of staff talks here. The Thai mission of twelve, including officers of the Air Force and Navy, will return to Bangkok tomorrow.

The deteriorating military situation in Indochina hastened expansion of the Thai forces, the general explained. The United States Military Assistance Advisory Group, which now numbers more than 200 men, will be enlarged. The number of Thai officers being trained in the United

States, now 503, will be increased.

The general reported that some Thais had already been trained as jet pilots, that a squadron of twenty-five jet aircraft would be formed, and that construction of airfields would be hastened.

General Dhanarajata said that at meetings with Admiral Arthur W. Radford, chairman of the Joint Chiefs of Staff, possible lines of enemy attack and of defense had been discussed.

In reply to questions, he added that he had not discussed what the United States would do to help Thailand in case she was attacked, but that "this will undoubtedly be discussed when we decide on the terms of the Southeast Asian alliance which is to be negotiated."

Ambassador Sarasin remarked that it was important to strengthen the Thai forces so that they could contribute to such an alliance.

While unwilling to disclose the exact strength of the Thai armed forces, the officers acknowledged that estimates that Thailand could now put 100,000 men in the field were reasonable and added that about 100,000 men were being trained each year and added to the reserve.

The Statesman's Yearbook for 1953 says that the Thai Army consists of twenty-eight infantry battalions, four cavalry regiments, ten groups of artillery, five battalions of signals, one anti-aircraft regiment, one tank regiment and one transport battalion.

United States assistance in expanding the Thai forces is directed by Maj. Gen. W. N. Gillmore, who was director of the Joint Airborne Troop Board of the Defense Department before he was sent to Thailand in August, 1953.

The military highway to be constructed will extend 297 miles from Saraburi in central Thailand eastward to the railway junction of Nakhon Ratchasima and then northward to Ban Phai, twenty-five miles south of Khonkaen.

Extending to the eastern part of Thailand, which has been most exposed to Communist infiltration, the highway will also support the objectives of the United States technical assistance program. Excluding the new highway program, the United States has spent $28,000,000 on technical assistance for Thailand since 1949.

July 14, 1954

ANTI-RED TEAMS STIMULATE THAIS

Government Project Evokes Wide Range of Questions on 'Whats' and 'Whys'

By ROBERT ALDEN

Special to The New York Times.

BANGKOK, Thailand, May 14 —"If I can't rattle off the seven bad things about communism, will I be called a Communist myself?" a Thai villager asked.

"If the communist should occupy our country, would they permit us to drink and enjoy ourselves as we do now?" he went on.

For almost two years the Thai Government, with the support of the United States, has carried on an ambitious anti-Communist indoctrination program, and these were typical questions evoked by it. Instruction teams have reached into almost every corner of the country.

It is estimated that 3,000,000 of Thailand's 20,000,000 population have seen the anti-Communist presentation. Forty-five thousand villagers are among those who have been reached.

As explained in the lectures to the Thai people, the seven bad things about communism are that it would do away with their religion (Buddhism), their King, their family life, their personal freedom, their ownership of land, their education and their national independence.

By the flickering light of smoky coconut lamps entertainers have danced and sung songs with an anti-Communist flavor until the early hours of the morning. Motion pictures have been shown nightly in places where films have never been seen. Pamphlets by the ton have been distributed.

Most Thai peasants had never even heard about communism until the teams came along. For that reason, while most observers approve of the program, some do not.

This minority opinion holds that in the quick education process curiosity has been aroused, one that will stay alive and generate more.

The people's stimulation by the traveling teams is shown by the lively question period that usually comes at the end of a visit to a village.

Many of the questions were revealing. They will be studied carefully before further programs of this type are instituted.

"If in communism there is nothing good, why is it necessary to distribute pamphlets about it? Why not distribute something good instead?" one man asked.

"The free nations are in greater numbers than the Communists. Why is it that communism keeps expanding day after day? What is the weakness of the free nations and of democracy?" another wanted to know.

"We are a free people of a free nation—what inferiority do we feel that we fear communism so much?" a third asked.

The people were quick to equate their personal grievances with the danger of communism. Along this time, one man asked:

"Don't our present high taxes leave us easy prey for Communist infiltration?"

May 18, 1956

THAI ARMY SEIZES CONTROL IN COUP; PREMIER MISSING

Bloodless Overturn Follows Pibul's Refusal to Resign as Government Chief

TWO AIDES SURRENDER

Bangkok Under Martial Law —Revolt Laid to Rivalry of Army and Police

Special to The New York Times.

BANGKOK, Thailand, Tuesday, Sept. 17—The Army seized control of the Government of Premier Pibul Songgram in a bloodless coup early today.

Field Marshal Sarit Thanarat, Army Commander in Chief, announced the take-over in a radio speech. He said he had acted in response to demands of the people.

Troops quietly occupied Bangkok shortly after midnight and declared martial law. Navy and Air Force units supporting Marshal Sarit took over key installations.

All main objectives were reported captured by 1 o'clock this morning.

The take-over came after Premier Pibul had rejected a demand for his resignation by fifty-eight Army men who are members of Parliament.

Appeal to Premier

In his radio speech Marshal Sarit called on Premier Pibul, Gen. Phao Sriyanond, former police chief, and Admiral Yuddhasat Kosol, Navy commander, to present themselves to military headquarters.

[The Army radio later announced that General Phao and Admiral Yuddhasat had given themselves up, news agencies reported.]

The whereabouts of the Premier is unknown.

Army officers called at the United States Embassy carrying Marshal Sarit's "best wishes" and assured Ambassador Max Waldo Bishop that Thailand's foreign policy would be unchanged.

Under Premier Pibul's regime Thailand has pursued pro-Western policies and maintained membership in the Southeast Asian defense alliance. A military conference of the alliance is scheduled in Bangkok for Thursday.

Army Gets Its Orders

Shortly after midnight the military radio began broadcasting the following announcement at five-minute intervals:

"Owing to the fact that the country is now very disorderly and tends to come close to disaster, the Army is compelled to keep peace and order for the nation's sake. Let all be in peace. Army troops are now taking control of some of the more important objectives."

The crisis affecting Premier Pibul's regime has been simmering toward the boiling point for some time. It has involved long-standing rivalry between Marshal Sarit, the Army commander, and General Phao, the former police chief.

In the background were a series of moves by Premier Pibul aimed at getting Cabinet ministers to sever business ties and choose between political and Government careers. General Phao recently resigned as Interior Minister and subsequently as police chief, while Marshal Sarit resigned earlier as Defense Minister without giving up the Army command.

Last week the fifty-eight ranking military officers led by Marshal Sarit demanded that Premier Pibul resign and permit the National Assembly to choose a new Government. According to authoritative Army sources, Marshal Sarit repeated the demand yesterday.

The Army group was reported to have told Premier Pibul that the resignation of General Phao was not enough. The Premier called their action "tantamount to revolution" and refused the demands.

Later Premier Pibul hurried off to a meeting with King Phumiphon Aduldet, who had summoned him to an audience at 11 A. M.

After the audience, the King called a conference of the Privy Council. On leaving the palace, Premier Pibul refused to tell reporters what he had discussed with the King, but asserted: "I will not resign!"

Last night the premier declared again at a meeting of the ruling Seri-Mananghasila party that he would not resign. He added that he would leave the decision to the National Assembly.

Thus, he served notice that

The New York Times   Sept. 17, 1957
Thai troops hold strategic areas in Bangkok (cross).

the military could stage a coup to remove him or take their chances on constitutional means. The party voted to support Premier Pibul and expressed confidence that it still held a majority in the Assembly.

Lieut. Gen. Praphat Charusathien, commander of the First Army Division based in Bangkok and one of the strongest members of the Sarit group, said Premier Pibul had told the group yesterday that while he regarded their action as rebellious, he chose to consider it a "family quarrel."

General Praphat said the military group insisted on the Premier's resignation and said that it "must be very soon."

September 17, 1957

THAI VOTE IS COMPLETE

Middle-of-Road Group Won 45 of 160 Seats at Stake

BANGKOK, Thailand, Dec. 27 (Reuters)—Final returns announced today for the Thailand general election show that the middle-of-the-road Unionist party—since merged in the army's National Socialist party—won forty-five seats.

Of the 160 seats contested, the Right-wing Democrats won thirty-nine. Left-wing parties captured fifteen seats, compared with twenty-two at the last election.

Independents won sixty-one, most of them from the Seri Manangasila party of the former Premier, Field Marshal Pibul Songgram. Ousted by the army last September, he now is in voluntary exile in Japan.

Lieut. Gen. Thanom Kitkhachon, Thailand's Defense Minister, is the Premier-designate. He said today he would ask Nai Pote Sarasin, Provisional Premier since September, to stay on and advise his government.

December 28, 1957

Army Chief Seizes Thai Power Again

Special to The New York Times.

BANGKOK, Thailand, Oct. 20 —Field Marshal Sarit Thanarat seized power in Thailand tonight in a silent, bloodless coup in the name of the people and with the agreement of the ousted Government.

His new Revolutionary party declared martial law, scrapped the Constitution and announced that it would rule the country from army headquarters.

The coup was announced six hours after Prime Minister Thanom Kittikachorn had handed the resignation of his Cabinet to King Phumiphol Aduldet.

Marshal Sarit, Supreme Commander of the armed forces, had led a coup thirteen months ago that ousted the Government of Field Marshal Pibul Songgram. On Jan. 1 he established Premier Thanom, an army lieutenant general, in office.

It was unclear what behind-the-scenes maneuvering had led to today's action. The earlier coup had sent into exile Marshal Pibul and General Phao Sriyanond, the former Minister of Interior and national police chief. General Phao had been considered Marshal Sarit's most formidable rival.

Marshal Sarit, 59 years old, returned here secretly from England early Sunday. He has not appeared in public.

The Thailand radio announced tonight that he headed the Revolutionary party, comprised of army, navy, air force, police and civilian officials, "in the name of the people."

The announcement said the coup was necessary because of the threat of communism and "tension building up within and without the country."

The new party pledged that it would not make any changes in existing institutions "except where necessary for the safety of the nation." It pledged loyalty to the King and said "now the King and his family, embassies and consulates are protected."

The announcement ordered all ministry under secretaries to receive instructions in new "political ideals."

All armed forces were placed on a full alert this afternoon. Military units were warned against moving without orders from Marshal Sarit.

In a cold drizzle, troops took up positions at strategic positions in Bangkok. Most were armed with rifles or machine guns. A few tanks were called in.

Observers here conjectured that Marshal Sarit, who had been in England and the United States most of this year for medical treatment, had been unable to rule through Premier Thanom.

The Premier reportedly had been unable to control some of the more ambitious men within the military group that seized power last year.

In the last few days there had been talk of revising the Constitution to strengthen the executive. Today it was reported that Marshal Sarit was planning to dissolve the National Assembly.

October 21, 1958

THAILAND DEFENSE IS PLEDGED BY U.S.

Rusk Says Action Will Be Taken Without SEATO Vote if Reds Attack

By E. W. KENWORTHY
Special to The New York Times.

WASHINGTON, March 6 — The United States pledged today to defend Thailand against direct Communist aggression without waiting for "prior agreement" on action by the Southeast Asia Treaty Organization.

This pledge was contained in a joint statement by Secretary of State Dean Rusk and Foreign Minister Thanat Khoman of Thailand. Mr. Thanat has been conferring with officials of the Departments of State and Defense for the last five days.

Mr. Rusk, the communiqué said, assured Mr. Thanat that the United States regarded its obligation to defend Thailand as "individual as well as collective." Therefore, the communiqué said, this obligation "does not depend upon the prior agreement of all other parties to the treaty."

The other members of SEATO are Britain, France, the Philippines, Pakistan, Thailand, Australia and New Zealand.

Rule of Unanimity Adopted

At the first meeting of the SEATO Council in Bangkok in February, 1955, a rule of unanimity was adopted. Thailand has been concerned that she might find herself defenseless in the event of Communist attack if action by the treaty organization depended upon unanimous agreement of the other seven members.

Field Marshal Sarit Thanarat, the Premier of Thailand, has been fearful of a Communist take-over in neighboring Laos since last spring. At that time the Pathet Lao movement, which is led by Prince Souphanouvong, a pro-Communist, mounted an offensive against Premier Boun Oum's troops and overran much of northern Laos.

Premier Sarit has been dubious about the plan backed by the United States to prevent Laos from becoming a battleground in the East-West struggle. That plan calls for setting up a government headed by Prince Souvanna Phouma, a neutralist. The government would include supporters of both Prince Boun Oum and Prince Souphanouvong.

Field Marshal Sarit has feared that a neutral Laos might soon succumb to Communist domination and that Thailand would then be open first to infiltration and eventually to attack.

The Thai Government has been apprehensive whether, in this eventuality, it could count on SEATO help under the rule of unanimity. Last spring Britain and France were reluctant to intervene in Laos.

State Department officials said today that the United States pledge of independent action had reassured Foreign Minister Thanat. The extent of this reassurance, they said, was indicated by the fact that the communique said agreement was reached on the necessity of "a free, independent and truly neutral Laos."

The communique said also that the United States regarded its treaty commitment and foreign aid agreements as providing a basis for any needed help in meeting "indirect aggression."

The United States also promised to accelerate arms deliveries as much as possible. Up to last June 30, Thailand had received $632,600,000 in military aid and $341,600,000 in economic assistance.

March 7, 1962

U.S. ORDERS 4,000 TROOPS TO THAILAND

UNIT LANDS TODAY

By E. W. KENWORTHY
Special to The New York Times.

WASHINGTON, May 15— President Kennedy moved today to back up his diplomatic efforts to preserve the independence of Laos by ordering 4,000 more United States troops to be stationed in neighboring Thailand. There are now 1,000 American soldiers in Thailand.

In a statement issued at noon, the President said he was dispatching troops to Thailand because of the recent attacks by Communist forces on Royal Laotian troops in northwest Laos and because of "the subsequent movement of Communist military units toward the border of Thailand."

On the diplomatic side, Secretary of State Dean Rusk met for thirty-five minutes this afternoon with the Soviet Ambassador, Anatoly F. Dobrynin.

Truce Is Emphasized

Afterward, Lincoln White, State Department spokesman, said that the two sides had emphasized the need to maintain a cease-fire and to establish the neutral coalition government for Laos agreed to by President Kennedy and Premier Khrushchev in Vienna last June.

Mr. Dobrynin told Mr. Rusk that there had been no change in the Soviet position on a neutral Laos.

Mr. Rusk, it is understood, raised the question of a cease-fire. Mr. Dobrynin was understood to have said that the Soviet Union also wanted to maintain a cease-fire. According to informants here, the question of whether the pro-Communist Pathet Lao forces should retreat to positions held before their attack on Nam Tha on May 6 was not discussed.

In the military deployment, a Marine battalion consisting of 1,800 men will debark at the Bangkok Naval Base at 7 A. M. Thursday (6 P. M. Wednesday, Eastern daylight time).

The Marine contingent will augment an Army battle group of 1,000 men who were held in Thailand after having participated in an exercise of the Southeast Asia Treaty Organization two weeks ago.

Immediately after the President's statement, the Department of Defense announced that the total forces to be established in Thailand, including Marine and Air Force tactical air units, would reach 5,000 men.

May 16, 1962

Last of U.S. Marines To Leave Thailand

By CABELL PHILLIPS
Special to The New York Times.

WASHINGTON, July 27— The Pentagon announced late today that the last members of the Marine Corps unit in Thailand were being withdrawn.

The 2,800 Marines were a part of the 5,000-man United States combat group sent into Thailand at the request of the Thai Government in May to avert a threatened flow of Communist infiltrators across the borders of neighboring Laos.

Approximately 1,000 men were withdrawn on July 1. With the withdrawal of the remaining 1,800 ordered today, the United States force in Thailand now consists of approximately 2,200 Army troops and about 1,000 Air Force men.

The Pentagon in its brief announcement gave no reason for the latest withdrawal. However, the action came close upon the signing of a fourteen-nation agreement in Geneva guaranteeing the neutrality of Laos under a coalition Government. The withdrawal would appear to be an expression of the United States confidence in the good intentions of the new Laotian Government.

The announcement came also while Premier Souvanna Phouma, head of the new Laos coalition, was conferring in Washington with President Kennedy.

The first group of Marines was called back to their ships and stations just as the Geneva conference was getting under way.

The decision to send United States forces into Thailand, which has been friendly to the West, came after the Communist-supported Pathet Lao guerrilla forces in neighboring Laos extended their military operations close to the Thai border. They were sent at the request of Premier Sarit Thanarat.

However, the threat of a Pathet Lao invasion, or of stepped-up infiltrations across the border, did not materialize. The presence of United States fighting men, stationed along the Mekong River, which separates the two countries, is believed to have been partially responsible for this.

The presence of an American military force in Thailand did, however, excite diplomatic and propaganda protests in Communist oriented areas throughout Asia, and in the Soviet Union. Premier Khrushchev denounced the action on several occasions as one that could lead to war. He compared the situation in Southeast Asia with that of Korea prior to the outbreak of hostilities there in 1950.

President Kennedy and Secretary of State Dean Rusk have said repeatedly that the move was entirely defensive "to help insure the territorial integrity" of Thailand.

Today's statement by the Pentagon made no mention of plans concerning the army and air force units still stationed in Thailand. The text of the statement follows:

"The remaining United States marines stationed at Udorn, Thailand, are being redeployed to their ships and stations.

"On July 1 withdrawal of 1,000 marines was announced. At that time it was indicated that additional redeployment of marine units might take place should conditions warrant this step.

"These movements have been discussed with the Thai Government."

July 28, 1962

PREMIER SARIT, 55, DIES IN THAILAND

Special to The New York Times

BANGKOK, Thailand, Dec. 8 — Premier Sarit Thanarat, a strong friend of the United States and an implacable foe of Communism, died today at the age of 55.

Deputy Premier Thanom Kittikachorn became acting Premier. He ordered all military forces in the country to remain on the alert.

General Thanom, who also is Defense Minister, was elected Premier in 1958. He resigned late that year in favor of Field Marshal Sarit after a bloodless coup d'état.

Premier Sarit died in Bangkok's military hospital after "cerebral complications" that developed during treatment for an inflamed lung and kidney and for a heart ailment. He fell ill Nov. 8.

Among the physicians attending Premier Sarit at the time of his death was Lieut. Gen. Leonard D. Heaton, the United States Army Surgeon General. General Heaton operated on the Premier for a liver ailment at Walter Reed Hospital in Washington in 1957.

All of Thailand's high-ranking military commanders were at the hospital when the Premier died. The Premier was said to have died in his wife's arms.

General Thanom notified King Phumiphol Aduldet of Premier Sarit's death. The general announced that he would assume

225

control of the Government until the National Assembly recommended to the King that he or someone else be named Premier. He did not set a date for the Assembly to meet.

The new Premier called his first Cabinet meeting at the hospital an hour and a half after Marshal Sarit died. He announced that the King had decreed that extraordinary honors be paid to the late Premier.

Marshal Sarit's body will be placed in a golden urn, an honor accorded to senior members of the royal family. The official mourning rites will be equal to those accorded the regent.

The flag was ordered to be flown at half-staff for seven days and official entertainment and advertising and entertainment on radio and television will be banned for three days.

The Premier's body will be moved tomorrow to Wat Benjamabhopit, a marble temple, where the traditional Buddhist bathing ceremony for the dead will be held. The Premier's family and friends will pour water over an extended hand of the body.

Thailand, the former Siam, lies on the northern and western shores of the Gulf of Siam. The country is bounded on the south by Malaya, on the west by Burma and on the northeast and east by Laos. Cambodia lies to the southeast.

Thailand is a country of special concern to the Western world because of her strategic position in Southeast Asia and because of her nearness to countries that have been undergoing political upheavals and have been targets of Communist pressures.

Sarit Thanarat, who was to win Thailand's highest honors and to hold the power of life or death over Thai citizens, was born in humble surroundings in Dej Ananta and Chandradip Thanarat. His ancestors came from Cambodia's western provinces.

His early training was traditional—in a temple school, Wat Maharn. In 1910 he entered Thailand's West Point, the Chula Chom Klao Cadet School, from which he was graduated in 1929.

Bold, forthright, earthy, fond of liquor and women, he was well liked by his followers and rose to be captain in command of a combat unit that fought the Japanese in World War II. He ended the war as a major in command of occupying forces in a province of Burma.

A determined anti-Communist and a strong royalist, he made his first political move in 1947 when he crashed through the gates of a palace in which the left-wing Premier, Pridi Phanamyong, was holding out. His move restored Field Marshal Pibul Songgram to power. Mr. Pridi fled to Communist China, where he is still in exile. Captain Sarit became a general.

Another man who played an important part in the 1947 coup was Phao Sriyanond, Mr. Sarit's long-time friend, drinking companion and classmate. These two joined Premier Pibul in a triumvirate that the Premier controlled by playing one of the generals against the other for 10 years.

General Phao's driving ambition and the fear that his ruthless methods inspired in the people led to riots and the eventual overthrow of the Pibul regime and General Phao by General Sarit in a bloodless coup on Sept. 16, 1957.

Seriously ill of cyrrhosis of the liver, Premier Sarit put his power in the hands of a trusted lieutenant, Gen. Thanom Kittikachorn, and flew to Washington for an operation at Walter Reed hospital.

During an interim three-month premiership held by Pote Sarasin, Secretary General of the Southeast Asia Treaty Organization, General Thanom was elected Premier.

General Sarit slipped quietly back into Bangkok from his convalescence in England and, on Oct. 10, 1958, brought his tanks into the capital. With the consent of Premier Thanom he seized power.

He banned opium smoking and trading, marking the event at midnight of July 1, 1958, by a huge bonfire of thousands of opium pipes on the Royal Cre-

mation Ground in front of the Royal Palace.

His courage and his determination to win a respectable name for Thailand in the family of nations was illustrated in 1961, when he led his Government and people to accept an extremely unpopular decision by the International Court of Justice. The ruling required Thailand to cede an ancient temple on the Thailand-Cambodia frontier to Cambodia.

He came into power in a growing but disorganized nation riddled with corruption. Communism was making dangerous inroads against a government apparently powerless to stop it.

Today, six years later, there are more than 1,000 new small industries in the country, the economy has boomed, the standard of living is rising and there is political stability.

He leaves two sons from a first marriage, both of whom are army officers. Premier Sarit was divorced from his first wife after World War II. He married again in October, 1947.

a remote Mekong River village.

The future Premier, Supreme Commander of all the Armed Forces, Minister of Development and Director General of the National Police was born at Nakorn Phanom on the Thailand-Laos frontier on June 16, 1908.

He was the son of Maj. Luang

December 9, 1963

A Silent Partner For U.S. in Asia

By PETER BRAESTRUP
Special to The New York Times

BANGKOK, Thailand, Aug. 20 —Thailand's role as a partner of the United States, Ambassador Graham A. Martin suggested recently, "is not sufficiently understood back in America."

Thus, as Prime Minister Thanom Kittakachorn listened, came a rare public hint at Thailand's silent but vital role as host to 25,000 American servicemen, most of them supporting the unsung "aerial second front" against North Vietnam and the Ho Chi Minh trail, Hanoi's main infiltration route to South Vietnam.

Thailand cooperated with the Americans, Field Marshal Thanom declared, "because our intentions are the same." The smiling 55-year-old leader of Thailand's military-civilian regime and the American envoy spoke at the opening last week of the biggest air base constructed by the United States here

to date—at Satthip, on the Gulf of Siam.

Official statements on the future use of the new 11,500-foot runway were vague, but informants said privately that it could handle any U.S. military aircraft now flying—including the big B-52 bombers based at faraway Guam and used to hit targets in South Vietnam. But KC-135 jet tankers likely will be the base's first major tenants. They will refuel in flight the U.S. fighter-bombers bound for targets across the Mekong River from five bases already built in Thailand's upcountry.

Old Suspicions

"We've brought in a lot of gear," observed a high-ranking American officer, "and we want to bring in more."

A sixth combat airfield is being built; others are being expanded to accommodate new squadrons of

F-105 and F-4-C jets. In short, the U. S. Air Force's hammering at North Vietnam from Thailand has yet to reach its peak.

Despite traditional Thai suspicion of "fareng" (foreigners), the Kittakachorn regime has bet on Washington's continued willingness to help meet the human and political costs of containing Communism in Southeast Asia. But never colonized, enjoying the blessings of a rice-rich kingdom the size of France, neither the 30-million Thais nor their self-appointed political leaders rejoice over being militarily dependent on distant America.

"So far," Thai Foreign Minister Thanat Khoman said with regret in his voice recently, "we have relied on outside power to save us from being submerged."

No intimate of Lyndon Johnson's gets more irritated by the U. S. Senate's "doves" than do Mr. Thanat's associates who scorn what they term "liberal naivete" about Asians and Asian Communists. Yet, even as they publicly condemn Hanoi and Peking, the Thai Cabinet officials, in an Oriental fashion that baffles many Westerners here, ignore or deny the fact that American aircraft at-

tack North Vietnam from what are juridically Royal Thai Air Force bases. Why?

Government Moves In

"Hanoi has never admitted violating the Geneva accords by sending thousands of troops into Laos and South Vietnam since 1962," suggested a European diplomat. "Perhaps the Thais see no gain and some loss of diplomatic maneuverability if they publicly admit their own role in the Vietnam war."

Already assailed by Peking Radio as an "imperialist lackey," the Kittakachorn regime may also find its role and the bombing difficult to explain to remote Thai villagers whose contact with the Government, let alone foreign policy, is limited. "They would not understand," said Interior Minister Prapath Charusathian.

While it counts on American help in warding off any overt aggression from the north, the Bangkok Government is slowly coming to grips with the spreading but still low-level Communist subversion in parts of six provinces of the long-neglected northeast. To American aid advisers, it is the Vietnam of 1958-59 all over again. They note the lack of Government "presence" at village level, the northeasterners' resentment of petty extortion and high-handedness by local police, and the "don't bother me" attitude of distant Bangkok bureaucrats.

But, to their credit, both the Bangkok officials and American aid planners have begun to focus on the grass roots, even if Thai spokesmen tend to emphasize the sporadic Communist terrorism.

In the Government's favor, as Americans see it, are certain economic and social factors. Unlike Vietnam, there is no pressing need for land reform since most villagers already till their own rice paddies. The weak oft-suppressed Thai Communist party, unlike the Vietcong, has never been popularly identified with a nationalist struggle against foreign rule.

If Prime Minister Thanom is nominally head of a standard military "junta," he in fact heads a **conservative, Army-backed coalition of generals and civilian technicians, ruling a bureaucracy that may be corrupt and self-serving, but is less than intolerable.**

How quickly this regime's abler, more dedicated men can shake off bad old Thai political habits and provide a response to the Communists may well decide Thailand's long-run future. There is new talk of the long-promised constitution and of elections. But as the young American pilots head north daily in their camouflaged jets, it is down in the rice paddies, the teak forests and the peasant shacks on stilts that the United States' silent ally faces its most immediate struggle with the Communists.

August 21, 1966

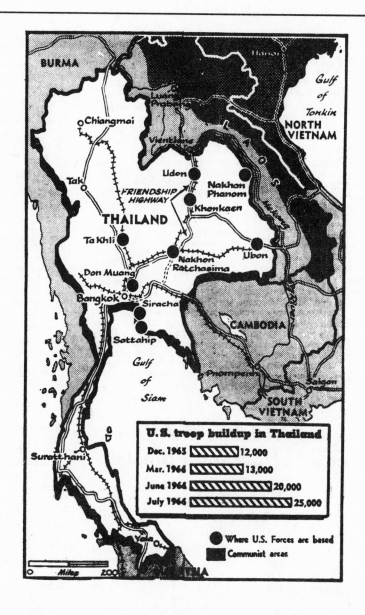

U.S. troop buildup in Thailand

Dec. 1965	12,000
Mar. 1966	13,000
June 1966	20,000
July 1966	25,000

● Where U.S. Forces are based
■ Communist areas

THAILAND COURTS CHINESE MINORITY

Assimilation Program Avoids Violence Found Elsewhere

Special to The New York Times

BANGKOK, Thailand, July 10 —Thailand has stepped up her program to assimilate the Chinese minority, swinging back and forth between "a carrot and a stick" in her approach, but avoiding the violence that has erupted in Burma, Indonesia and Malaysia.

In May the Thai Government lifted a 20-year-old ban on Chinese-language instruction in secondary schools.

The stick had been applied over the last seven months, as Bangkok barred Chinese radio broadcasts,

tive action against covert activities of about 700 Chinese associations in Thailand and was reported to have subtly persuaded the Chinese Nationalist embassy to discontinue Chinese-language classes that had been held on embassy soil for three years.

Bend With the Wind

The three million ethnic Chinese, who make up 10 per cent of the population of Thailand, have managed to survive and prosper through encouraged assimilation, bending with the winds of Thai nationalism while preserving ancestral traditions in the home, in the shop and in commercial, charitable and social associations.

"To the extent that an anti-Chinese attitude exists, it is primarily an expression of pro-Thai nationalism," a Western observer said. "The Thais understand the Chinese better than any other Southeast Asian nation and the Government's policy of assimilation is relatively more enlightened."

The common Buddhist religion, the easy-going tolerance of the Thai people, a comparative lack of prejudice against intermarriage and a Chinese immigrant quota restricted to 200 annually have eased the process.

Prof. G. William Skinner, American author of two classic studies of Thai Chinese, says there are virtually no third-generation Chinese in the country, only Thais with Chinese parents.

Thai officials remain sensitive to a conspicuous Chinese presence, but their chief security concern is with 400,000 Chinese aliens. Last month Premier Thanom Kittikachorn warned overseas Chinese to avoid involvement in the Communist terrorist movement. He noted that arrangements were being completed for deportation of 500 Chinese without citizenship who had been arrested for various reasons.

Fear of Chinese schools is also founded on security as well as on nationalism. A

clandestine Chinese school in Betong, in South Thailand, is regarded as a source of support for 500 Chinese terrorists on the Thai-Malaysian jungle border.

In the north, remnants of the old Chinese Nationalist army run a school in Mae Salong, which attracts Chinese from several provinces and, according to the Thais, promotes the idea of dual citizenship. Mae Salong is in the northernmost corner of Thailand, just west of the border point of Mae Sai.

As a result, only 200 Chinese elementary and night schools, offering 10 hours of language instruction a week may function under Thai law. Home tutorial classes preserve the heritage for those with the time and money.

The declining level of Chinese-language education is reflected in the gradual loss in circulation of the four Chinese-language newspapers in Bangkok.

July 11, 1967

Thailand Extends Martial-Law Area In Terrorist Threat

By The Associated Press

BANGKOK, Thailand, Dec. 1—The Government imposed martial law today on five southern and central provinces—including one close to Bangkok—in an effort to thwart what is considered to be a growing Communist terrorist movement.

The decision showed the Government's concern about infiltrators in the region close to Bangkok, which until a few months ago was thought to be relatively free of terrorists.

Several hundred Chinese guerrillas have been operating in the southern provinces since their rebellion was crushed in Malaya in 1960.

A decree gives the Government sweeping powers to arrest and hold suspects and to relocate villages to cut off support for the guerrillas. Martial law has been in force for several years in seven provinces of northeast Thailand, where guerrillas have concentrated their efforts. The Government last month moved a battalion of the First Army Division into the Kuiburi district of Prachuapkhirikhan Province, 150 miles south of Bangkok on the Ithmus that links Thailand and Malaysia. The country narrows down to a width of 10 miles in places, with Burma on one side and the Gulf of Thailand on the other.

There has been speculation that terrorists, thought to number 300 in Prachuapkhirikhan Province, might blow up railroad and highway bridges.

Terrorists have struck Government forces hard in Prachuapkh irikhan Province in recent months. In August a police convoy was ambushed and five policemen were killed. A month later, a few miles away, terrorists attacked a second patrol, killing all 10 officers and men.

The provinces put under full

The New York Times   Dec. 2, 1967

Thai regime imposed martial law in central (1) and southern (2) regions. The northeast (cross hatching) had been under martial law.

military control ore Prachuapkhirikhan, Petchburi and Rejburi in the south and Kanchanaburi and Supanburi in the central plain. Rejburi, Kanchanaburi and Supanburi are within 60 miles of Bangkok.

The Government's decision indicates that the battle against terrorists is not going as well as had been reported. Terrorists in the country are estimated to number 2,000. They are known to be active in 17 of Thailand's 71 provinces.

The official Peking publication Jenminh Jih Pao said today that guerrillas in Thailand had achieved "brilliant results" in the last two years.

"The Thai people's forces have won one victory after another," the publication said in an article broadcast by the Peking Radio and monitored here. "At present they are active in the northeastern, southern central and northern parts over large areas in 28 out of the 71 provinces."

December 2, 1967

Peking-Inspired Thai Rebellion Believed to Have Been Blunted

By SYDNEY GRUSON
Special to The New York Times

BANGKOK, Thailand, Feb. 3 —Communist China's two-year drive to raise a full-scale insurgency against the Thai Government is believed here to have been blunted.

This is the hopeful conclusion of Thai and United States officials involved in the struggle in the rugged jungle and hill country of the northeastern provinces bordering Laos, where a third of Thailand's 33 million people live.

No one believes that China and North Vietnam, which also trains the Thai insurgents, have given up. But the success of the counterinsurgency program has created hope that enough time has been won to avert another conflict like that in Vietnam.

The nature of the struggle could change, officials say, if the Thai Communists were "massively reinforced" from China or North Vietnam. They add that they see no sign of this. In the meantime, the counterinsurgency is being stepped up with the considerable help of American money and men.

Americans are engaged with Thais in a wide variety of training, educational, security and development projects, but they are not engaged in combat against the insurgents. Both sides want it to continue this way, although there is said to be some American military pressure for a direct voice in the actual counterinsurgency operations.

February 4, 1968

New Constitution Goes Into Effect in Thailand

Special to The New York Times

BANGKOK, Thailand, Saturday, June 22—Thailand promulgated her long-awaited Constitution yesterday and began her latest attempt at building a working democracy after almost 10 years of military rule.

In a ceremony that combined the trappings of religion, royalty and politics, King Phumiphol Aduldet symbolically presented the document to the people to the sound of temple gongs, conch shells and a 21-gun salute, while Thai Air Force planes droned overhead, strewing the area with rice and flowers.

The country has had seven

Students Clash With Police in First Political Demonstration in More Than a Decade

successful military coups and 15 governments in its turbulent 35-year history as a limited monarchy. It has been ruled by relatively restrained martial law since Oct. 20, 1958, when the late Field Marshal Sarit Thanarat seized power and banned labor unions and political parties. The next year he promised to provide a constitution and established a constituent assembly to write one.

The new Constitution provides the Thai people with elected representatives to appeal to and establishes a forum for dissent. However, it falls considerably short of genuine representational government. The Cabinet, for instance, does not have to submit its programs to a vote of confidence in Parliament.

Today, more than 1,000 students clashed with the police in the country's first political demonstration in 11 years. According to student leaders, the demonstrations were in protest against the Government's decision to retain martial law under the new Constitution.

The action started in Bangkok's central public park, where three politicians were arrested for haranguing gatherings in defiance of a law against public assembly.

Simultaneous with the arrests, about 2,000 students marched to the park from nearby Thammasat University, bearing anti-Government signs and shouting slogans. Fifty abreast, they clogged the city's vast boulevard on the march from the park to the National Assembly building, where the new Parliament will sit.

The present Government, which will probably stay in power until elections are held, within 240 days, stated that previous laws against public assembly were not in conflict with the new Constitution and would remain in force.

Political Parties Emerge

The emerging politicians are the most visible evidence of a political awakening that is sweeping Bangkok's old electoral machinery, newspaper offices and educated private citizens after the nine-year moratorium.

More than 10 political parties have emerged recently and the Thai press is becoming outspoken on issues it would hardly have dared discuss a few months ago.

The King, who had been unobtrusively pressing for the Constitution during its long delay, told the group of Thai officials and foreign diplomats in the National Assembly hall yesterday that the Thai people "should act by their rights so that the good of democracy might be gained."

Thaw Bunyakat, the retiring Speaker of the interim National Assembly, however, cautioned the Assembly that "the Constitution is stronger on paper, with rights to censure the administration, to originate money bills and to kill bills it does not like."

Observers point out, however, that the Assembly can be easily manipulated since no one party is powerful enough to get a majority coalition. Also, they say, few men of ability will stand for election to the Assembly since it does not lead directly to power.

Seni Pramote, leader of the most powerful opposition party, said in an interview that he was a candidate, but "only running to preserve the form" and that he regarded his party as a "suicide squad."

Few observers except those in the United States Embassy attribute to the present Government many altruistic motives on the promulgation of the Constitution, although most are quick to recognize the benefits it might have as a safety valve.

A Thai publisher, however, attributed the reason for the Constitution to the present regime's desire to remain benevolent. "It seems to be a tradition here," he said. "I don't know why, but we are lucky."

The country's top leaders appear content to rest on past achievements in justifying their continuance in power.

Premier Thanom Kittikachorn, who has accepted the leadership of the Government party, said in a final news conference before the promulgation: "In the administration, we are concentrating on national development to make our economy progressive in order to make the people contented and happy. This is the original policy of this Government and there will be no change in it."

The country's strongman, Deputy Premier Gen. Praphas Charusathien, raised the question of defense: "What would happen if we allowed the establishment of a weak government or a government that is unaware of the facts concerning national defense, or that is less experienced than the present Government?"

June 22, 1968

U.S. PAYS THAILAND 50-MILLION A YEAR FOR VIETNAM AID

Terms of Secret Agreement of 1967 on Troop Subsidy Disclosed in Senate

By JOHN W. FINNEY
Special to The New York Times

WASHINGTON, June 7—Senate testimony disclosed today that under the secret agreement entered into in 1967, the United States has been paying Thailand $50-million a year for sending a combat division to South Vietnam.

To encourage Thailand to assign the 11,000-man unit, the United States also agreed to increase its military assistance by $30-million for two years and to supply Thailand with a battery of Hawk antiaircraft missiles.

The broad outilnes of the arrangement were made public in testimony of State and Defense Department officials published by the subcommittee on United States security agreements and commitments abroad of the Senate Foreign Relations Committee.

20-Year Involvement Traced

The testimony, taken last November and made public after State Department censorship, traces the deepening American military involvement in Thailand in the last 20 years and, in turn, the increasing commitments and assistance demanded by Thailand.

While there have been recurring reports of American assistance to the Thai force in Vietnam, they have never been confirmed, until the publication of the Senate testimony, by the State Department. Furthermore, the newspaper reports have been denied by the Thai Government.

In a statement issued last Dec. 16 following one of the reports, the Thai Foreign Ministry asserted there "has been no payment from the United States to induce Thailand to send its armed forces to help South Vietnam defend itself against Communist aggression."

The effect of the testimony is also to challenge a recent statement by Premier Thanom Kittikachorn of Thailand as well as to raise questions about what American assistance will be provided to the "volunteers" from Thailand now being sent to assist the new military Government in Cambodia. In announcing last week that Thailand was preparing to send volunteers of Cambodian ethnic origin to asst Cambodian troops against the Communist forces, Mr. Thanom was quoted by the Bangkok radio as having said: "Unlike the volunteers for Vietnam whose expenses are paid by Thailand, the volunteers for Cambodia will be armed and equipped from aid supplied by the United States."

June 8, 1970

SUKARNO'S INDONESIA

INDONESIAN REDS CAUSING CONCERN

Showdown With Opposing Groups Seen in Steady Rise of Membership

By TILLMAN DURDIN
Special to The New York Times

JAKARTA, Indonesia, Dec. 5—The growth of the Indonesian Communist party during the last year is causing concern. The degree of anxiety varies, but there is general agreement the Communist build-up has reached threatening proportions.

In reaction, revitalized Islamic, Christian and Socialist parties are expanding too, indicating a showdown sooner or later.

Two years ago Indonesian Communist party membership had dropped to about 7,000. Today the party claims 500,000 members and candidate members and a membership in front groups of 2,800,000, including 2,000,000 in labor organizations and 200,000 in a peasants' organization.

Jakarta has three Communist daily newspapers and the party runs bookstores and publishes a widely circulated selection of magazines, books and pamphlets. It appears to have plenty of money, of which a considerable proportion is believed to come from Chinese or other foreign Communist sources. Central party offices moved this year into a big new headquarters building not far from the Chinese Embassy.

New National Front Tactic

Communist expansion has been generated by the National Front tactic of political penetration pursued since 1952. From that time the party has emphasized legal and parliamentary activities, eschewed provocative revolutionary moves and pushed infiltration into an association with nationalist groups.

The new tactics have paid off since the Government of Ali Sastroamidjojo, Nationalist party leader, came into office in October, 1953. Although not officially represented in the Cabinet the Communist party has given it unqualified Parliamentary support and lately Communist bloc votes have represented the margin of the Government's majority in the Assembly.

Certain jingo elements in the Nationalist party are friendly to the Communists and a number

229

of Ministers in the Government have cooperated during their careers in Communist causes. Premier Ali denies his regime has favored the Communists, but the respectability and influence gained by the Communists from their key role in supporting the Government have obviously facilitated their growth.

Reds Laud President

President Sukarno, sponsor and supporter of the present Cabinet, has lately added to Communist prestige by making speeches favoring "progressive" policies for Indonesia and pointing to China and the Soviet Union as countries where great construction is in evidence based upon "progressive" mass appeal. He denounced groups seeking to turn out the present Government as being in the pay of foreigners.

The Communists formerly denounced President Sukarno as an "imperialist tool," but during the last year have had good things to say about him. Lately the Peiping radio has lauded the President.

D. N. Aidit, secretary general of the party, recently announced that the party endorsed the five principles put forward in the early days of the revolution as the basis for the Indonesian republic. The principles are divine omnipotence, nationality, humanity, democracy and social justice.

The Communists have come a long way since 1948 when they attempted a revolt against the moderate revolutionary government and were defeated. Musso and other Communist leaders were captured and executed.

December 6, 1954

ASIA-AFRICA UNITY HAILED AS PARLEY OPENS IN BANDUNG

---

29 Nations' Delegates Hear They Can Aid World Peace and Human Well-Being

---

7-POINT AGENDA OFFERED

Broad Program, if Accepted Might Prevent Discussion of Israel and Formosa

---

By TILLMAN DURDIN
Special to The New York Times.

BANDUNG, Indonesia, Monday, April 18—President Sukarno of Indonesia hailed the new force represented by the nations of Asia and Africa in a speech opening the twenty-nine-power Asian-African conference here today.

He said he saw the conference as an opportunity for the resurgent countries of the two continents to make a new contribution to world peace, freedom and the well-being of peoples.

The Indonesian leader said the peoples of the world lived in fear that "the dogs of war" would be unchained again. He added that the nations in Asia and Africa whose peoples had for many generations been "the voiceless ones in the world" could not avoid finding solutions for the problems of "the life and death of humanity itself."

[President Sukarno called for the ending of nuclear arms experiments, news agency reports from Bandung said. He gave the conference two slogans, "Live and let live" and "Unity in diversity."]

Dr. Sukarno gave an address of welcome to an excited gathering of nearly 2,000 conference delegates and guests in a resplendent newly reconstructed auditorium bright with the varied costumes of persons from widely different nations and cultures. The conference is being held in this resort city in the mountains of Java. Bandung is seventy-five miles southeast of Jakarta.

Members of the diplomatic corps in Jakarta and selected Indonesian Government officials and members of Parliament were among the multi-national assemblage.

The Prime Ministers of India, Indonesia, Ceylon, Burma and Pakistan, which had sponsored the conference, welcomed the other delegation chiefs in front of the auditorium.

English will be the basic language of the conference, but it is the understanding that French, Chinese and possibly other languages may be used if the speakers provide their own English translators. President Sukarno's speech was given in English.

[At a later session, The United Press, reported, Premier Ali Sastroamidjojo of Indonesia was elected chairman of the conference. He was nominated by Premier Gamal Abdel Nasser of Egypt. The nomination was seconded by

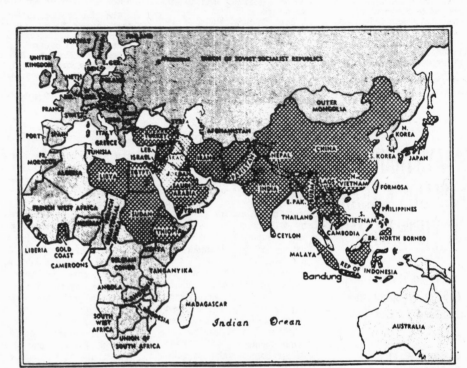

The New York Times   April 18, 1955
Cross-hatching indicates the countries participating in the conference at Bandung, Indonesia

Associated Press
President Sukarno of Indonesia, who hailed the new force of Asian and African countries at the conference.

Premier Chou En-lai of Communist China, Brig Gen. Carlos P. Romulo of the Philippines and Walid Saleh of Jordan.]

President Sukarno said the nations of Asia and Africa "are no longer the tools of others and the playthings of forces they cannot influence."

He denounced colonialism and racialism. Noting that there were countries that still were not free, he said colonialism in modern dress was in the form of economic control, intellectual control and actual physical control by small alien communities within a nation.

He referred to the American Revolution as marking the first successful struggle against colonialism. He said a new war would imperil the independence of nations that had cast off the yoke of colonialism.

Voice of Reason Seen

The Asian and African nations can inject the voice of reason into world affairs, he declared, adding: "We can mobilize all the spiritual, all the moral, all the political strength of Asia and Africa on the side of peace."

In this context he cited the part played last year by the host nations, known as the Colombo

230

powers, in ending the Indochina war.

The Indonesian leader expressed a fervent wish for the success of the conference and said his country was proud to be its host. He said the conference must give guidance to mankind and evidence that a new Asia and a new Africa had been born.

The President talked of mobilizing "moral violence" among the nations of Asia and Africa

to demonstrate that they could show the minority in the West the way to peace.

He called colonialism an evil thing that must be eradicated, but said, "It does not give up its loot easily."

The Indonesian leader said the world lived in fear of the hydrogen bomb and of ideologies. He said the latter might be more dangerous since it led men to act foolishly, thoughtlessly and dangerously.

President Sukarno conceded the diversity among Asian and African nations, but said that out of many religions and cultures and stages of development unity could be created.

President Sukarno enjoined the conference delegates not to be bitter about the past but to keep their eyes firmly on the future. He added that the highest purposes of man was his own liberation from "the physical,

spiritual and intellectual bonds which have for too long stunted the development of humanity's majority." His injunction was: "Let us remember, sisters and brothers, that for the sake of all that, we Asians and Africans must be united."

April 18, 1955

INDONESIAN ISLES STILL SEEK UNITY

Government Hopes a National Patriotism Will Eventually Replace Local Interests

By ROBERT ALDEN
Special to The New York Times.

JAKARTA, Indonesia, May 28 —When this young republic won independence six years ago there were joined together 80,000,000 people living on more than 2,000 islands stretched over an expanse of sea as great in area as the United States.

Those people speak a multitude of languages and make up a number of racial stocks, some antagonistic to one another.

Since the founding of the republic there has been fighting of one kind or another in one place or another. There are armed revolts now in northern Sumatra, parts of Java, in the southern half of the Celebes and in the Moluccas.

Some of those in revolt are bandits at the head of private armies who are robbing and plundering for their own advantage.

Most of them seek through violent means to set up an Islamic state in Indonesia, which is the most populous Moslem country in the world.

Those who rebelled in the Moluccas opposed what they said was a Government dominated by the Javanese.

The New York Times   June 8, 1955

DOMESTIC STRIFE PERSISTS: Indonesians are fighting among themselves in northern Sumatra (1), Java (2), southern Celebes (3) and the Moluccas Islands (4).

On many of the islands of the republic there is a similar kind of resentment of Javanese rule. The inhabitants feel they are not getting a fair return from Jakarta for the goods and products they send from their home islands.

The Government says that in time the private armies and bandits will be quelled and that national feeling will eventually replace the insular patriotism that now predominates in many areas.

The Government views more seriously the matter of the lack of trained technicians in the country.

There are 150 graduate Indonesian engineers to serve the needs of 80,000,000 persons.

A foreign technical adviser who is working closely with the Indonesian Government to make the transition from a colonial to a national economy said:

"In each department there are perhaps one or two really qualified persons with whom you can

work effectively. But they are simply not able to do everything.

An Indonesian Cabinet Minister charged the Americans with impatience.

"Don't try to envisage our country in your own image," he said. "We are not in a helter skelter hurry like your people. No one starves in this country. No one freezes. There are always bananas on the trees and there is always a sun in the sky.

"Things here will not be accomplished overnight but then our people are not used to having things accomplished overnight. Give us time and we will train the men and we will do the job."

In the meantime, however, in almost any field that is examined there is glaring inefficiency—understandable, perhaps, but discouraging to those who have Indonesia's best interests at heart.

For example, although the seas around the archipelago are teeming with fish, the people of the islands get only half the

protein they need to enjoy normal health.

The fisherman bringing his catch to the wharf at Jakarta is paid two and a half cents a pound for his haul. By the time the fish reaches the public through a monopolistic and archaic auction to wholesalers, the price has risen to 26 cents a pound.

As for fish production itself, its inefficiency is marked. One well-trained fishing crew operating an eighty-foot boat in the Indian Ocean off Java could bring in a daily catch equaling the catch of all the Javanese fishing industry put together.

A man with capital to invest knows that he can gain a 200 or 300 per cent profit overnight by importing goods. He obtains his import license by either bribing someone or buying it from a middleman.

The same investor, however, will not be willing to invest his capital in real estate development because of the rigid rent controls that are in force. As a result the development of new housing is almost nonexistent.

There are entries on the credit side of the ledger.

Through rigid control the Government has been able to reduce substantially the value of goods imported into the country, a favorable development as far as the economy of the country is concerned.

In addition, the Government has been able to increase the production of rice to such an extent that the country has to import only a small quantity of that essential food commodity.

June 8, 1955

INDONESIA FORMS 12-PARTY CABINET

Harahap, Leader of Moslems, Is Premier — Nationalists and Reds In Opposition

Special to The New York Times.

JAKARTA, Indonesia, Aug. 11 —A youthful political leader representing the strongest Moslem party in the country formed a new coalition Government for Indonesia today.

The new Premier is Burhanuddin Harahap of the stanchly anti-

party. At 38 years of age he is the youngest Premier in the history of the Indonesian Republic.

The Harahap Government, accepted by Vice President Mohammed Hatta, has wide diversification of political support. However, it will do without the votes of the Nationalist party, which has held the Premiership for the last two years, and the Communists, who supported the outgoing Nationalist Government.

The new Cabinet is pledged to continue Indonesia in a neutral course in world affairs based on "an independent and active policy toward peace." Particular emphasis will be stressed on political cooperation between Asian and African nations.

Domestically, Mr. Harahap promised to hold the first national Moslem Masjumi

tion-wide election in the history of the country Sept. 29 as scheduled.

He also pledged to reestablish the confidence of the army in particular and the community in general in their new government.

That confidence had been severely shaken when the cabinet of Dr. Ali Sastroamidjojo was toppled from office two and one half weeks ago when the Army defied the Government over the choice of a chief of staff. Since that time there has been much talk of corruption and scandal within the Government of Dr. Ali and the army has arrested one former government official.

In setting up a political program for himself Mr. Harahap promised to uproot corruption in the Government. He also assumed the defense portfolio so

he could deal directly with the Army.

Other matters with which the new Premier said he would concern himself were inflation, the decentralization of government power and the continuance of "the struggle for the return of West Irian [Netherlands New Guinea] into the territory of the Republic of Indonesia."

The twenty-three-seat Cabinet has representatives from twelve political parties. These parties hold 134 of the 232 seats in Parliament.

It is expected that the Opposition, led by the Nationalists and Communists, will be able to muster ninety-nine votes in comparison with 141 for the Government.

August 12, 1955

Indonesia Voids Debts to Dutch; Suez Seizure Seen as Stimulus

By Reuters.

JAKARTA, Indonesia, Aug. 4 — Indonesia repudiated today more than $1,000,000,000 in debts to the Netherlands and then announced that "in fact, the Netherlands is in debt to Indonesia."

Observers here speculated over whether the move, involving 4,081,000,000 Dutch guilders (about $1,065,141,000), had been precipitated by Egypt's seizure of the Suez Canal Company.

They pointed out that it followed a week in which leading Indonesian newspapers had hailed the Egyptian Government's act in nationalizing the canal as an example of what Indonesian leaders might do about their own troubles with The Hague.

Seven months ago Jakarta severed its last economic tie with the Netherlands, from which Indonesia, then a Dutch colony, broke away seven years ago to become an independent state associated with the Netherlands on a voluntary and equal basis.

Today's announcement stated that the Government had assumed more than 4,000,000,000 guilders in debt from the Netherlands East Indies administration when it left office in 1948.

Of the present debt, Indonesia said she would honor only 420,-000,000 guilders (about $109,-620,000) in "third-party" obligations incurred by the former Netherlands East Indies Administration with the United States, Canada and Australia.

From the remaining 3,661,000,-000 guilders, the Indonesian Government said it was subtracting 3,000,000,000 guilders because it was money "used in the war against the Republic of Indonesia," and an additional 420,-000,000 to offset the third-party debts. The 241,000,000-guilder balance would be wiped out.

August 5, 1956

INDONESIANS SIGN SOVIET LOAN PACT

$100,000,000 Technical and Economic Accord Includes Nuclear Cooperation

Special to The New York Times.

JAKARTA, Indonesia, Sept. 15 —The details of a Soviet offer of $100,000,000 in economic and technical aid to Indonesia were made public today.

The Soviet offer includes an agreement to cooperate on peace-uses of atomic energy, with Moscow proposing to train Indonesian technicians in nuclear research, medical and technical fields.

The agreement followed months of negotiations and the signing of an earlier trade pact Aug. 12. It represents a signal success for the Soviet Union's attempts to win friends in Southeast Asia.

Under the agreement the Soviet will grant $100,000,000 credit in the form of capital goods, machinery and heavy industrial equipment. Indonesia will repay the Soviet Union in twelve annual installments, starting after the initial three-year period, either in United States dollars, pounds sterling or raw materials.

Parts Purchases Foreseen

Moscow deliberately offered a low 2.5 per cent interest rate for the opportunity to introduce little known Soviet machinery and equipment into the potentially rich market of Southeast Asia. A Government source said Indonesia eventually would have to purchase spare parts and replacements from the Soviet for many years to come.

The aid will provide impetus to the Government's Five-Year Plan but so far no specific projects have been mentioned.

Indonesia's chief delegate to the talks, Dr. Subandiro, said the Government planned to build a cement factory outside Java. Indonesia is building a cement works at Gresik in Java with a bank loan from Washington totaling $100,000,000.

But it is well known the Government is giving priority to the Umbilin coal mines in central Sumatra, nickel mines at Lake Towuti, the asphalt industry on Butin Island, hydroelectric power stations at Malili in the Celebes, and coal mines at Muara in southeast Borneo.

Under the pact Soviet technicians will be sent here to review each project as it comes up. A United States official stated earlier that Soviet aid agreements invariably entailed large projects and complex equipment calling for numerous Soviet technicians to operate them.

Meanwhile, the United States has not yet announced its aid to Indonesia this year. Earlier Washington press reports mentioning $35,000,000 have not been confirmed.

The United States has granted a total of $41,000,000 technical assistance so far. The total for fiscal 1956 is $11,100,000 technical cooperation, including two special programs for malaria control and public administration. In addition, Indonesia is now midway through a two-year program granting her $96,000,-000 for surplus United States commodities.

September 16, 1956

MOUNTING POLITICAL UNREST DISTURBS INDONESIAN REGIME

By BERNARD KALB
Special to The New York Times.

JAKARTA, Indonesia, Feb. 2 —From President Sukarno down. Indonesia is desperately searching these days for the answer that has been missing for eleven uneasy years. The speed with which it is found will make a tremendous difference to the future of the country, an archipelago of 3,000 islands and 82,-000,000 persons and widespread "dissatisfaction." The "dissatisfaction" is Premier Ali Sastroamidjojo's word—he used it several times before Parliament last week in defending his Cabinet's record—but a lot of Indonesians regard it as a superb understatement of the facts.

What is this question that has plagued Indonesia since she proclaimed her independence from the Dutch in 1945 and took her destiny into her own inexperienced hands—this question that the country's political brain power is now trying to solve in the face of anti-Cabinet defiance in Sumatra and of similar rumblings in other parts of the archipelago?

TROUBLE SPOTS IN THE INDONESIAN ISLANDS

Estimated Population
Java..........55,000,000
Sumatra.......13,000,000
Celebes........6,000,000
Borneo.........3,000,000
Other Islands...5,000,000
Total: 82,000,000

U.S. and Indonesia drawn to same scale

Darul Islam, armed Moslem extremist group, is fighting at tip of Sumatra (1) for creation of Moslem state. Provincial governments of Central and South Sumatra (2) have defied Jakarta regime. Darul Islam, with rebels and bandits, is fighting also in parts of Java (3) and Celebes (4). Remnants of separatist movement hold out on Ceram (5).

From Mr. Sukarno in Merdeka Palace to the peasant in the rice terraces the people know the question the country must answer is how to strike workable relationship between the Central Government in Jakarta and the various ethnic and island groups of far-flung Indonesia. Put in a more specific way, it is how to form a stable, energetic and respected Government which will, among other things, carry out a program for promoting economic development and granting regional autonomy to the satisfaction of the people.

Cabinet Under Fire

It is a big order, all right, and fifteen Cabinets have been in and out of office in the last eleven years trying to find the magic formula. Today Cabinet number 16—Premier Ali's own coalition group—is being accused of having failed and consequently is fighting a tough battle for survival after only ten months of trying.

It is against that challenging background that the Sumatra events "suddenly" happened. Actually all that happened was that on Dec. 20 Indonesia's biggest money-making island—it is a storehouse of petroleum, rubber and other natural resources —brought its "cold war" with Jakarta out into the world's

headlines. Alarming words like "rebellion," "insurrection" and "mutiny" were freely used to describe the sequence of events but actually not a single shot has been reported fired.

What Sumatra did fire was a salvo of decision mixed with impatience. Fed up with the goings on in Jakarta and weary of waiting for the carrying out of the promises to the Central Government Sumatra decided to look after its own future and seized the administrative power. North Sumatra's military commander did the same thing two days later but he called it quits when he apparently realized that a majority of his troops were more loyal to the President than to him. He then fled. And South Sumatra pretty much followed suit by deciding to use its own fat revenues for local development rather than remit them to Jakarta.

Sumatra's Complaint

Through all those acts of defiance Sumatra apparently never forgot the elementary fact in the economic geography of Indonesia, a fact which is part of explanation of controversy between Jakarta and Sumatra. Sumatra's rich resources earn well over half of the country's foreign exchange but the island is said to receive less than half

of its receipts for its own development.

Time for Decision

With Indonesia's existing lack of unity hit by even more disunity and with the word "disintegration" being used more frequently than ever the leaders here realized that the critical moment—always expected—had perhaps at last arrived. The time for decision was staring them ominously in the face and possible answers to Indonesia's big question began coming from all sides.

President Sukarno came up with a plan for a powerful top-level advisory council which he believes would put Indonesia on the road to results—and some people believe it would bring the country one big step closer to the President's dream of "guided democracy." He has not yet made all details public—all he has done so far is confirm that he is planning the form of such a council—but he has taken pains to make it clear that the idea behind it was "to save democracy," that "in no way will it be a dictatorship." His aides said the purpose was to reduce political-party strife and give Indonesia a breathing spell from the current state of affairs.

Premier Ali thought he had the answer too. He went before

the Parliament's first session of the new year last week and promised to speed the implementation of his Cabinet's original program which calls for such things as a five-year development plan and conferring wide autonomy on the clamoring islands. He also said that Government missions would negotiate with the headstrong provinces of Sumatra in an effort "to meet the wishes" of those regions.

Move by Moslem Party

Meantime the country's biggest Moslem party, the Masjumi, which had earlier repudiated Premier Ali by pulling out its five ministers from his Cabinet suggested an answer of its own. It called for the formation of a Cabinet led by Dr. Mohammad Hatta who quit as Vice President on Dec. 1, reportedly over long-standing disagreements in policy with President Sukarno. Efforts have since been made to patch up the differences between the two leaders who jointly proclaimed the nation's independence. There are many Indonesians who believe that any approach short of restoration of that duumvirate would fail to meet the country's big problems.

February 3, 1957

SUKARNO OFFERS 'NEW STYLE' RULE, INCLUDING REDS

Indonesian President Terms Democracy of the West 'Wrong' for Country

By BERNARD KALB
Special to The New York Times.

JAKARTA, Indonesia, Feb. 21 —President Sukarno called on Indonesia tonight to abandon the Western democratic system.

The "new style" of government he advocated would include all major political parties, including the powerful Communist party.

In taking the wraps off the plan for a new governmental system, which he has termed a "conception," the President said democracy "imported" from the West was "wrong" for Indonesia. He went on to propose establishment of a new type of administration, accenting "gotong rojong"—an Indonesian term for "mutual help."

The plans the President offered the country, which has

been plagued with crises ever since she proclaimed her independence from the Dutch in 1945, had two main elements:

1. Creation of a Cabinet that would contain not a political grouping of parties, as at present, but all major parties elected in the 1955 general elections. The Communists ran fourth, winning more than 6,000,000 votes, but have been excluded from the Cabinet.

2. Establishment of a national council, led by President Sukarno, which would give "advice," required or not, to the Cabinet. Members of the council would represent a cross-section of Indonesian society.

People abroad might say such a Government was the wrong kind, the President said. But he indicated strongly he was not too concerned about that because of his conviction it was the way to make Indonesia a successful republic.

The President was apparently aware he would have to fight for his proposal to include the Communists in his Cabinet. He tried to blunt some of the expected attacks.

Stresses Red Votes

In the first place, he said, he believes all major parties have the right to sit in the Cabinet. He then challenged anti-Com-

munists by reminding them of the number of votes the Communist party polled in 1955. Can 6,000,000 votes be "ignored," he asked.

The President said he did not want to take sides; all he wanted was national unity; all he was doing was expressing the will of the people.

There are some people who charge he wants to take the Government to the Left, he continued. He then invoked Lincoln's biblical reference that "a house divided against itself cannot stand."

Once before, when the present Cabinet was formed by Premier Ali Sastroamidjojo early last year, Dr. Sukarno called for Communist participation in the Government. But he lost. The big Moslem parties that fought him then have not changed their stand.

The President, an effective orator, spoke for an hour without notes or a prepared text. He reviewed the last eleven years of Indonesia's political history. The report was an unhappy one.

He said Indonesia had been unable to find lasting stability. Difficulties had arisen because political parties had wrongly interpreted the idea of "opposition" within the framework of the Western democratic system, he said.

The idea of "opposition" in

Jakarta, he said, seems to mean opposing everything, the result being that no cabinet can long stay in power because of political crises. This has convinced him, he continued, that the Western system is "wrong" for Indonesia.

The President urged Indonesia's 82,000,000 people to return to their original idea that Indonesia is a big family, united, not divided, living in a big house together.

If his conception were accepted, he said, there would be no opposition, but brotherly discussion instead. A difference of opinion does not mean "opposition," he added.

Under his idea, he went on, the Cabinet would reflect the Parliament while the national council would reflect the society. Then, he said, "all of us will shake hands."

Dr. Sukarno's address was broadcast throughout the nation. Radio receivers were set up in cities and towns throughout the vast archipelago.

Indonesian ships at sea were urged to give crews an opportunity to listen to the broadcast. Many motion-picture houses were closed here so that people could stay at home or visit clubs to hear the address.

Several thousand persons, many carrying Communist signs, stood outside the palace and cheered Sukarno's references to the Communist party.

February 22, 1957

233

Revolts Causing Chaos in Indonesia, Jakarta Premier Tells Unity Parley

By BERNARD KALB
Special to The New York Times.

JAKÁRTA, Indonesia, Sept. 10 — Behind closed doors Indonesian civil and military leaders met here today to try to find a formula to solve the "present chaotic situation" in the archipelago republic.

The description of the country's predicament was made today by Premier Djuanda in his address at the opening session of a three-day meeting. More than a hundred officials attended the session.

The parley has brought together leaders of the central Government on Java and those of far-flung outer provinces who began defying the Jakarta Government last December in a bid for increased self-rule. The resultant crisis has become one of the worst the nation has faced in the twelve years since it proclaimed its independence from the Netherlands.

A theme that ran throughout the Premier's speech was that the conference should not get bogged down in "seeking the guilty ones and the right ones."

The Premier, who is not affiliated with any political party, heads the emergency Cabinet hand-picked by President Sukarno last April. He appealed for discussion "with an open heart in a brotherly atmosphere" and he went on to reassure the conference:

"The central Government does not intend to dictate anything."

The two basic problems under discussion, the Premier declared, are "the abnormal general situation" and "the armed forces, in which there is a dangerous split."

The gist of Premier Djuandas' speech was relayed to reporters by designated spokesmen of the parley. Accredited correspondents were permitted to attend only the formal opening of the session.

The conference participants represent twenty-one provinces and districts sprawled over 3,000 miles of the South Pacific. They are scheduled to hold two meetings daily — one in the morning and another in the evening. The hot afternoons are set aside for either consultations or sleep.

In the conference hall Premier Djuanda was flanked by President Sukarno and Dr. Mohammed Hatta, who quit as Vice President last December. Together Dr. Sukarno and Dr. Hatta proclaimed Indonesia's independence in 1940. That proclamation was made at the site where the unity parley is being held.

In recent years Dr. Sukarno and Dr. Hatta have drifted apart on basic policies. Only the other day the English-language Times of Indonesia described them as being "poles apart" on such issues as Dr. Sukarno's controversial plan for "guided democracy" for Indonesia.

Dr. Hatta is regarded by the anti-Communist, defiant outer regions as the guardian of their interests. These regions have been critical of Dr. Sukarno for advocating inclusion of Communists in a "mutual help" form of government.

Today, in separate speeches, Dr. Sukarno and Dr. Hatta called for a revival of the spirit of the country's declaration of independence.

September 11, 1957

SUKARNO, HATTA JOIN IN A PLEDGE

Vow to Uphold '45 Freedom Declaration—Indonesian Split Said to Narrow

By BERNARD KALB
Special to The New York Times

JAKARTA, Indonesia, Sept 14—President Sukarno and Dr. Mohammed Hatta, who quit as Vice President last December, joined tonight in a pledge to uphold Indonesia's proclamation of independence.

The two men, who have been at odds over the President's recent moves toward a "guided democracy," had signed that proclamation twelve years ago.

Their names, written today at the bottom of a large sheet of paper bearing the joint statement, restored at least outwardly the Sukarno-Hatta symbol that almost all sections of the sharply-divided nation had been clamoring for since Dr. Hatta resigned.

The signing was a highlight of the closing session of a five-day conference on national unity. Civil and military leaders of the central Government and the outer provinces had gathered to seek a way to reunite the Jakarta regime and the defiant outer regions that had been pressing for more provincial autonomy.

Reunion Theme of Talks

The overriding theme of the conference has been the view that the Sukarno-Hatta working relationship must be re-established. Many speakers, especially those from the defiant outer regions, which regard Dr. Hatta as a guardian of the interests of the entire nation, said reuniting the two leaders was the key to solving the problems gripping the nation.

Delegates from both the central Government and from defiant Central Sumatra said tonight that no formula had been reached that would bring Dr. Hatta back into the regime.

Yet these same delegates were in agreement that the conference was a "success." They said the joint statement was a "starting point" on which to rebuild the Sukarno-Hatta partnership.

Some delegates expressed belief that the conference might produce a turning point after nine months of provincial defiance of Jakarta. It was last December that Central Sumatra repudiated the authority of the central Government in a bid for increased economic and administrative autonomy. That touched off similar defiance in other areas of the far-flung archipelago.

Joint Statement to Nation

The document around which so much hope was built is only a few paragraphs long. The President, standing where he and Dr. Hatta jointly had proclaimed Indonesia's independence from the Dutch Aug. 17, 1945, read the joint statement tonight to the nation.

Both the President and Dr. Hatta told reporters later that they thought the results of the conference were "good."

In its final sessions today, the conference of more than 100 delegates approved proposals dealing with autonomy, reconstruction and development, and intensification of the drive against corruption.

Premier Djuanda declared that the decisions of the conferees would be used as a directive for the Government in future policy. Committees including representatives of both the central Government and provinces will be established to implement these decisions, he added.

September 15, 1957

Sukarno Escapes Assassin, But Grenades Kill 7 Others

Scores Hurt in Bombing as Indonesia President Leaves a School

By TILLMAN DURDIN
Special to The New York Times.

JAKARTA, Indonesia, Nov. 30—President Sukarno narrowly escaped assassination tonight when hand grenades were thrown at him.

The attempt on his life was made at the public school in the center of the city that his children attend. The President and his family had gone there for an observance of the school's third anniversary.

Seven persons, two of them policemen, were killed and scores of others were wounded. There was no immediate clue to the identity of the assailants, who threw the bombs from a moving automobile as the President was getting into his car to depart.

Jittery witnesses stated that four hand grenades had been thrown by the would-be assassins. One exploded close to President Sukarno. The area was immediately cordoned off by policemen.

The Presidential Palace issued a terse announcement, which was broadcast over the official radio network, saying that the President and his family were "in good health." Security officials were caught by surprise by the incident and refused to make any comment.

The assassination attempt occurred at 9 P. M. local time as most of Jakarta's citizens were out for week-end fun.

These developments coincided with the diminution of prospects for a settlement of differences between the central Government and the military-dominated autonomous provinces on the outer Indonesian islands.

A resolution pushed by delegates from the outer islands calling for a key executive role in the national Government for Dr. Mohammed Hatta was permitted to lapse at the National Reconstruction Conference that has been going on here all week.

The resolution asked that Dr. Hatta, a former Vice President and one of the founders of the Indonesian Republic, take charge of a new cabinet either as President Sukarno's deputy or as Premier.

One of the aims of the proposal's advocates was clearly to revise the present Sukarno-sponsored Government set-up, in which association with the powerful Communist party is a basic ingredient and to lessen Communist influence.

The President's insistence on a Government role for the Communists is one of the reasons why the outer provinces maintain an autonomous stand.

234

The outer provinces also want the central Government to recognize their right to more home rule and to a large proportion of their own earnings from exports. At present the local regimes in Sumatra, the Celebes and the Moluccas are conducting foreign trade pretty much on their own despite Jakarta's disapproval.

Dr. Hatta, who recently returned from a tour of Communist China, is presiding at the Reconstruction Conference. He himself dropped consideration of the resolution today when it became evident that it would split the conference.

Lieutenant Colonel Barlian, administrator of South Sumatra, left the conference today to return to his province. The colonel, who was the most important of the autonomous administrators to attend the conference, was a strong advocate at the meeting of the move to get Dr. Hatta into the Government.

Lieut. Col. Achmad Hussein, administrator of Central Sumatra, had refused to attend. He has been one of the most resolute defenders of provincial autonomy.

The conference will continue, but will discuss economic questions rather than a political settlement. Colonel Barlian maintained that it was impossible to agree on economic problems without a prior settlement of political issues.

December 1, 1957

JAKARTA SEIZES DUTCH ESTATES; SETS NEW POLICY

By TILLMAN DURDIN
Special to The New York Times.

JAKARTA, Indonesia, Dec. 9 —The Government assumed control today of the multi-million-dollar Dutch plantation properties in Indonesia.

The move was announced in a communiqué issued by Premier Djuanda. The take-over also included Dutch properties partly Indonesian-owned and all factories, experimental estates, laboratories and transport equipment belonging to the agricultural enterprises.

The Premier's announcement marked a decisive shift in the handling of the movement against Dutch economic interests. It reflected the Government's intention to take over Dutch enterprises in a planned and comprehensive fashion rather than through sporadic take-overs by workers' groups, such as took place during the last week.

Cause Is West New Guinea

The anti-Dutch campaign stems from Dutch control of West New Guinea, which Indonesia claims. The campaign began after the United Nations failed to adopt a resolution calling on the Netherlands and Indonesia to try to negotiate a settlement.

The Indonesian Government's action is believed to have forestalled a large-scale movement among workers to take over Dutch agricultural estates. Such a movement was foreshadowed by the occupation of a number of plantations in the Bandung area over the week-end.

Premier Djuanda's announcement followed a similar action in Jakarta this morning. Worker groups that had taken over the city's three large Dutch banks Saturday and declared them the property of the Republic of Indonesia were removed from control. The establishments were returned to operation by their Dutch managers under the joint supervision of the military and the Bank of Indonesia, the central bank.

December 10, 1957

DOUBT ON SUKARNO VOICED BY DULLES

Secretary Says U. S. Would Like a Jakarta Regime Reflecting Public Will

Special to The New York Times.

WASHINGTON, Feb. 11—Secretary of State Dulles said today that the United States would like to see in Indonesia "a government which is constitutional and which reflects the real interest and desires of the people."

Mr. Dulles intimated at his news conference that the United States did not regard the Government of President Sukarno and Premier Djuanda as entirely meeting this prescription. He said:

"As you know, there is a kind of 'guided democracy' trend there now which is an evolution which may not quite conform with the provisional constitution and apparently does not entirely satisfy large segments of the population."

Significance Is Twofold

In the view of diplomats in Washington, Mr. Dulles' statement took on considerable significance for two reasons: First, because the State Department has been most reticent about commenting on the Indonesian situation, and second, because the statement came on the heels of an ultimatum delivered to President Sukarno by anti-Government leaders in Central Sumatra.

Yesterday Lieut. Col. Ahmad Hussein, chief administrator of Central Sumatra, speaking on behalf of a revolutionary council, gave President Sukarno and Premier Djuanda five days to form a new Cabinet free of pro-Communist influence.

[In Jakarta, the Government rejected the ultimatum and dishonorably discharged four army colonels who lead the rebel movement.]

Hatta Role Demanded

The rebel council asked that the new Cabinet be formed by Dr. Mohammed Hatta, a former Vice President who resigned over differences with President Sukarno in October, 1956, and Sultan Hamengku Buwono of Jogjakarta, who is now in the United States.

The council said that if the ultimatum was not met it would renounce its loyalty to the Jakarta Government and would feel free to determine its next actions.

Opposition to the Sukarno Government has centered in Central Sumatra. The political and military leaders have opposed the Sukarno concept of guided democracy as promulgated by the President last Feb. 21.

After proclaiming this concept, President Sukarno set up an "extra-Parliamentary cabinet of experts," chosen not as representatives of political parties but for their "proficiency" in various fields.

He also set up a national council, with advisory powers only, on which were represented all the various groupings in Indonesian society. A few Communists and several pro-Communists are on the national council. The Communist party in Indonesia has supported the Sukarno Government.

Commenting on the situation, Mr. Dulles said: "I think that there has been a growing feeling among the Moslems, particularly in the islands other than Java * * * of concern at growing Communist influence in the Government of Java and in the feeling that the economic resources of these outer islands, like Sumatra, are being exploited contrary to the best interests of the entire Indonesian people."

The working out of these problems is primarily an internal problem for the Indonesian people, Mr. Dulles said. But he added that "we doubt very much that the people of Indonesia will ever want a Communist-type or a Communist-dominated government."

The text of the news conference as it related to Indonesia appeared to have been edited slightly by Mr. Dulles before it was released. But there appeared to be no substantial change in the Secretary's remarks or meaning.

February 12, 1958

Leaders of Indonesian Rebel Group

Pan-Asia

Sjafruddin Prawiranegara   Lieut. Col. Achmad Husein

The New York Times   Feb. 16, 1958

A rebel government proclaimed in Padang (1) is directed against Jakarta (2). The black line delimits Indonesia.

INDONESIA REBELS PROCLAIM REGIME, DEFYING JAKARTA

Revolutionary Council Sets Up a Rival Cabinet With Claim to Full Rule

SUMATRAN GROUP ACTS

Anti-Red Leaders Follow Up Ultimatum—Independent Foreign Policy Stated

By TILLMAN DURDIN
Special to The New York Times.

PADANG, Indonesia, Feb. 15 —A new revolutionary Government for Indonesia was proclaimed here tonight.

Dr. Sjafruddin Prawiranegara, 47-year-old Moslem party leader, was named Premier in a multiparty Cabinet of men from Java, Sumatra and Celebes.

The new Government was designated by a revolutionary council set up recently in this Sumatran city in opposition to the Cabinet of Premier Djuanda in Jakarta and to the actions and policies of President Sukarno.

The announcement was made by Lieut. Col. Achmad Husein, military chief of Central Sumatra and one of four high officers whom the Jakarta Government ordered to be dishonorably discharged from the army last Tuesday.

Ultimatum Rejected

The proclamation of the revolutionary regime came at the expiration of a five-day ultimatum from the council here for resignation of the Djuanda Cabinet and abandonment of President Sukarno's program of "guided democracy."

The ultimatum was rejected by the central Government and no statement has come from President Sukarno that would indicate his acceptance of it.

He is due back in Jakarta tomorrow from Japan.

A statement by Dr. Sjafruddin said the new Government would pursue an independent foreign policy and not be drawn into one of the "conflicting world blocs."

However, the basis of the new regime is strongly anti-Communist. Its members, all Moslem or Christian leaders, have repeatedly emphasized their anti-Communist views and asserted that Communist influence in the Jakarta regime was one of the main reasons for their opposition to the central Government.

February 16, 1958

INDONESIA FACING MANY PROBLEMS

By TILLMAN DURDIN
Special to The New York Times.

TOKYO, July 15—Conditions in Indonesia today are somewhat more stable than they were several months ago. Armed resistance to the Government, however, continues in many parts of the country and the economic, political and military problems facing the regime are formidable indeed.

Despite widespread sympathy in most parts of the country for the rebel views and their program, the Government has scored a limited triumph against the insurrection that broke out in Sumatra and the Celebes last February.

The insurgents, who are opposed to communism and to President Sukarno's "guided democracy" which gave the Communists a voice in the Government, sought a foreign policy more friendly to the West. They demanded an end to Jakarta's police state methods, the resto-

Economy Strained by Rebellion

ration of civil liberties and a new Cabinet organized under the auspices of former Vice President Mohammed Hatta and the Sultan of Jogjakarta.

Their tactics and leadership, however, were poor. Key sympathizers they had expected would join them, such as Colonel Barlian, military ruler of South Sumatra, and high personalities in Atjen, South Celebes, West Java and the Moluccas failed to turn against the Government when the chips were down. Soldiers of the national army in Central Sumatra refused to fight their comrades of the national army from Jakarta, leaving the main centers of the area open to Jakarta invasion forces.

Naive Conceptions

Indeed, the rebel leaders had

naïvely conceived of winning their objectives primarily through a campaign of propaganda, maneuver and financial pressure. They had banked heavily on cutting Jakarta off from its huge Sumatran oil revenues, an expectation that did not materialize because of Colonel Barlian's failure to turn over to the rebel side and consolidate rebel control of the oil fields.

Jakarta's action in rejecting a compromise and launching an all-out military attack was a surprise to the rebels. This came after Dr. Hatta had been unsuccessful in his efforts to mediate in Jakarta and after he and the Sultan had weakened the cause by declining to throw in their lot with the insurgents.

The insurrectionists made a cardinal error in setting up a rival government. Most observers now agree that the rebels would have fared much better if they had simply acted as armed

political oppositionists. When the rebels pretended to be a national government themselves the Jakarta officials were forced to take measures to suppress

PRESIDENT

Sukarno

the uprising in order to protect their own positions and to maintain their claim to exercise nation-wide authority. The prospect of civil war thus created frightened the country and lost the rebels the support of many Indonesians who did not want the opposition to Jakarta to take such an extreme form.

The insurgents had built much of their hope on unsophisticated and unfounded expectations of United States and other foreign aid, which was not forthcoming. Their obvious anticipation of help from the West contributed to the qualms among Indonesians wary of outside interference and fearful of their country becoming an East-West battleground if Jakarta was forced by Western aid to the rebels into turning to the Communist bloc for full-scale military assistance.

Alienated Followers

The violence of the rebel diatribes against President Sukarno alienated many Indonesians, especially on Java where the President's popularity is high. Most of the Indonesian Army under youthful Major Gen. Abdul Haris Nasution, Chief of Staff, remained loyal to the general, to the Government and to Sukarno, and when the Jakarta army, navy and air forces moved against the rebel centers they had a preponderance of men and equipment.

In short, the rebels did not stir the fervent national support and readiness to act and to sacrifice that was necessary for their success. Because of their disunity, mistakes and vacillations they were unable to capitalize fully on the extensive support that did exist for them.

In Central Sumatra, frontal resistance to the Government attack was negligible. In North Celebes, the Menadonese put up a tougher fight. Government troops now hold three successive rebel capitals, Padang, Bukittinggi and Menado and most other main towns in the rebel areas. The rebellion, however, is not finished.

None of the dissident leaders has been captured or has surrendered. Sjafruddin Prawiranegara, former rebel Premier in Central Sumatra, Colonel Joop Warouw, his successor in North Celebes, have all taken to the hills along with their chief collaborators and bands of loyal partisans. They are waging a spreading, effective guerrilla resistance to the Government forces and still control large areas of West Sumatra, in the Medan region and in Central and Northern Celebes.

This year's Indonesian rebellion adds new areas of conflict and disruption to others that have afflicted Indonesia for years. In West and Central Java, Darul Islam (Moslem state) bands dominate many mountain districts, regularly

THREE STEPS IN CRUSHING THE INDONESIAN REVOLT

2 April: Government occupies rebel areas.

3 June: Government takes last rebel capital.

1 Feb.: Rebel government is proclaimed.

■ Furthest extent of rebel control

Last February's rebel proclamation formalized what had been a smoldering revolt.

raid villages, roads and even big towns. Similar activity is carried on by allied guerrillas in Central and South Celebes and in Atjeh and on Ceram in the Moluccas a few hundred men fighting for what is called the Republic of the South Moluccas tie down several thousand Government soldiers.

The sum total of all the dissident fighting and sabotage in the Indonesian islands is a severe drain on the country's economy and the finances of the Government. The republic's 250,000-man army is scattered among scores of troubled regions, straining to protect at least the main population centers and communications routes.

Military Costs

The soaring cost of military operations will push this year's Jakarta budget deficit to an estimated 9,000,000,000 rupiah, the equivalent of $890,000,000 at the basic official rate of exchange, $300,000,000 at the foreign import rate.

The Jakarta leaders who control the Government recently acted to cope with the country's towering problems by making changes in the cabinet and laying down lines of policy in both the domestic and international sphere. Sumatra-Celebes rebels have so far lost their military contests with Government troops but the ideas they represent have made headway and have been reflected in Jakarta's moves and outlook.

The cry of alarm raised by the rebels over the growing power of the Indonesian Communists, for example, has found an echo in the Nationalist and other non-Communist parties and caused new efforts to check Communist influence. Even

President Sukarno is believed by some Western observers to have cooled in his desire to have the Communists as collaborators.

There is a general belief among the non-Communists that the Communists have profited by being on the band wagon against the rebellion and that the Communist party—which has been crowding the Nationalists for position as the country's biggest organized political group—is a real threat to win over all other parties in next year's general elections if effective counter-action is not taken.

Improving Relations

In keeping with this trend in the domestic sphere, Jakarta leaders have also made efforts to improve their relations with the United States and other Western nations. Jakarta officials are convinced the United States, through Formosa and the Philippines and Britain, through Singapore, indirectly aided the rebels. In April and May this brought a sharp swing by the Jakarta Government toward Moscow and there's now an effort to turn back toward the West to avoid too close ties with the Communist bloc. Among many key Jakarta officials, this reflects a basic preference for dealing with the West and a fresh realization of Indonesia's position in the Western sphere of influence.

Thus, recent Government changes made by President Sukarno dissolved the Ministry of People's Mobilization headed by A. M. Hanafie, generally regarded as a Communist agent. He was left in the Cabinet as a Minister Without Portfolio, but no longer has a Government

agency or Government money to work with.

Another change that strengthened the non-Communist complexion of the Cabinet was the addition of Colonel Suprayogi as a Minister to represent General Nasution. The general and most of his officers, many of them trained in the United States, are regarded as opponents of the Communists.

As a further appeal to the sentiments that gave rise to the Sumatra-Celebes rebellion, Premier Djuanda has announced the Government's determination to increase administrative economy and the financial allocations of the outer island provinces. Toward the rebel leaders the policy is still one of no leniency and an all-out effort to capture them and try them as outlaws. It is hoped, however, that the new Government measures and soft treatment for rank-and-file participants in the rebellion will eventually draw away the following of the rebel leaders.

Hope for Aid

To bolster it through the difficult times ahead the Government hopes for new foreign credits and other economic aid, particularly from the United States, and United States approval of large-scale military equipment purchases. Its foreign policy is still predicated on non-alignment with either the Communist bloc or the West, but the outlook is for at least more cooperative relationships between Jakarta and the West than there has been.

If United States and other foreign help on a considerable scale materializes—admittedly a very large if—the Indonesian Government would seem to have a chance of surviving its present trials and making headway with a pacification program.

Much will depend on President Sukarno, whose past encouragement of the Communists and playing off parties and individuals against each other has had a big part in promoting political instability in Indonesia and the recent rebellion. The President is still the dominant personality in Indonesia. He does not run the Government, is not a dictator, but the present Cabinet, with its recent changes, is his creation. He can determine how far it will go in countering Communist influence and how much effort it will make to cooperate with the West.

July 20, 1958

SUKARNO RESUMES DICTATOR'S POWER OVER INDONESIANS

President, Acting to 'Save' Country, Reinstates the Constitution of 1945

ARMY BACKING DECREE

By BERNARD KALB
Special to The New York Times.

JAKARTA, Indonesia, July 5—President Sukarno issued a decree today reinstating the controversial 1945 Constitution, dissolving the Constituent Assembly and throwing out the present provisional 1950 Constitution.

In one of the most sweeping actions of his revolutionary career President Sukarno, in a seven-minute speech from the steps of the Presidential Freedom Palace here, thus revived the 1945 charter under which he has virtually unrestricted powers.

His action, supported by the army, paves the way for an overhauling of the Parliamentary form of government, as practiced under the discarded 1950 Constitution, and a regime of "guided democracy" in Indonesia.

Djuanda Cabinet Resigns

The 1945 Constitution concentrates tremendous powers in the President. The President has the power to appoint and discharge ministers and is invested with legislative authority with the sanction of Parliament. He is accountable, in effect, only to the Consultative Assembly, which convenes at least once every five years.

Issuance of the decree was followed by an announcement that Premier Djuanda's Cabinet, handpicked by President Sukarno in April, 1957, would resign tomorrow. [A dispatch by United Press International early Monday reported the Cabinet's resignation.]

It will undoubtedly be asked to serve in a caretaker capacity until a Presidential Cabinet, the eighteenth government in Indonesia's fourteen-year history, is sworn in, probably this week, according to informed sources.

Sukarno Is Somber

It was an unsmiling President Sukarno who read the decree in the presence of the nation's leaders and the diplomatic corps.

The President declared he acted with the "support of the majority of the Indonesian people and impelled by our own conviction." It was the "only way possible to save the state," he asserted.

President Sukarno, who returned last Monday from a nine-and-a-half-week global goodwill tour, thus resorted to the decree to upset a setback he had suffered at the hands of the Constituent Assembly last month.

The 1945 charter, championed by President Sukarno and backed by a coalition led by nationalists and Communists, failed by forty-nine votes to win the two-thirds majority required for approval. Leading the successful opposition in the Assembly, which had about 500 members, was a hastily formed Moslem bloc that demanded amendments written into the Constitution endowing it with an Islamic overtone.

July 6, 1959

INDONESIA BEGINS ALIEN TRADE BAN

Peiping Envoy Fails in Effort to Halt Decree Aimed at Chinese Merchants

By BERNARD KALB
Special to The New York Times.

JAKARTA, Indonesia, Friday, Jan. 1—A decree aimed at breaking the Chinese stranglehold on Indonesia's rural economy went into effect last midnight.

All aliens are banned from engaging in retail trade in rural areas throughout Indonesia. It is estimated that 300,000 of Indonesia's Chinese population of about 2,500,000 are affected.

The decree, issued by President Sukarno with the strong backing of Indonesian nationalists, is causing one of the greatest economic upheavals in the history of the archipelago.

Rural trade has been in Chinese hands for generations. The Chinese, during the more than three centuries of Dutch rule, built themselves into a wealthy middle class

President Sukarno's decree paves the way for Indonesian cooperatives to take over rural retail trade.

Khrushchev to Visit Jakarta

During the day the Foreign Ministry announced that Premier Khrushchev of the Soviet Union will visit Indonesia in February. He is coming, at a date still to be set, at President Sukarno's invitation and to repay visits by Mr. Sukarno to Moscow in 1956 and last year.

The announcement said that both Indonesia and the Soviet Union were convinced Mr. Khrushchev's visit would constitute "an important development in strengthening the friendship and cooperation between the two countries.

Observers noted the coincidence of the announcement with Indonesia's dispute with Communist China over the future of Chinese aliens in this country.

The Chinese Communist Ambassador, Huang Chen, whose embassy had been officially accused of trying to sabotage the decree's implementation, met with Foreign Minister Subandrio yesterday.

After two hours and ten minutes of talks, the Peiping diplomat strode from the Foreign Ministry building, refusing to comment. Dr. Subandrio, however, disclosed some details of their meeting.

Indonesia, he said, made clear to Mr. Huang that she would not compromise on the implementation of the decree. Communist China did not ask for a postponement, he added.

In an allusion to Peiping's bitter denunciations of the ban on alien merchants, Dr. Subandrio said he had told Mr. Huang that Indonesia had "some concern" about Communist China's "inclinations" toward Indonesia.

Mr. Huang, in turn, was quoted by the Foreign Minister as having said that Peiping feared Indonesia's neutralist foreign policy was changing.

Dr. Subandrio said he had told the Chinese Communist Ambassador that uncommitted Indonesia wanted to be friends with all countries, but not at the expense of her national interests and self-respect.

January 1, 1960

SUKARNO DECREE SILENCES CRITICS

Ending of Parliament Takes Forum From Opposition— Leader's Power Grows

By BERNARD KALB

Special to The New York Times.

JAKARTA, Indonesia, March 6—President Sukarno's suspension of Parliament yesterday means that a new era of rule by decree, without opposition from any elected body, has been introduced in troubled Indonesia.

This era will last until a People's Congress, composed of members of a new Parliament and hand-picked representatives of various organizations and regional groups, is created in conformance with the 1945 Constitution, which was reinstated last year. No date has been set for the formation of the Congress.

By suspending the 257-member Parliament, elected in 1955 in the nation's first general balloting, President Sukarno removed the last remnant of Western-style parliamentary democracy and cleared the way for the establishment of total "guided democracy."

"Guided democracy" is Mr. Sukarno's term for the system of government he is setting up in Indonesia. The system concentrates virtually dictatorial powers in the hands of the President.

Decline to Comment

A sense of mourning for Parliament has pervaded various political circles in this capital. But some politicians, afraid to antagonize the authorities, declined to make any adverse public comment on the issue.

In a move aimed at silencing any criticism of the Presidential suspension decree, the Jakarta military garrison warned the domestic press against publishing "editorial misrepresentations."

The decree is believed to have been prompted by the Government's fear that Parliament would reject the controversial 1960 budget this week. But the Government also is said to have been unhappy over the constant criticism of Presidential decrees voiced by both Right-Wing and Communist factions in Parliament.

The immediate significance of the suspension is that political parties have lost their most important forum for discussing national issues. Hardest hit are the Communists, the best organized political force. They used Parliament extensively as a respectable stage from which to voice their propaganda.

With Parliament out of the way, the sweeping powers held by President Sukarno have been emphasized.

Established in July

The only major governmental bodies left are the thirty-seven-member Cabinet, the forty-five-member Supreme Advisory Council and the seventy-seven-member National Planning Council. The President's hold over these bodies is evidenced by the fact that he selected all their members.

These bodies were established last July after President Sukarno, with the army's backing, reinstated the 1945 Constitution, which stripped Parliament of its right to overthrow the Government.

Despite the suspension of Parliament, observers contend it would be a mistake to say that President Sukarno is in a position to exercise one-man rule.

They say that the President's freedom of action is subject to pressures from the country's two best organized forces, the anti-Communist army command and the Communist party.

March 7, 1960

INDONESIA INSTALLS PARLIAMENT OF 283

Special to The New York Times.

JAKARTA, Indonesia, June 25—President Sukarno today installed his hand-picked Parliament despite sharp opposition from various anti-Communist, Moslem and other political forces in Indonesia. Almost all of the 283 appointed members turned up for the ceremony, thus dashing the hopes of a sizable boycott.

The President made a brief speech during which he read the text of the new edict dealing with Parliament. He made it clear he enjoyed absolute power over this new body. He has the power to appoint and dismiss members and lay down rules under which the Parliament will function.

The President instructed members to reach decisions by means of consultations in preference to trying to reach "a simple majority plus one vote." If the Parliament could not reach a decision through consultations, the President emphasized, the leadership of Parliament should bring the issue to him for a decision.

President Sukarno disbanded the popularly elected parliament in March.

The ceremony at the State Palace went off without a hitch.

However, printed handbills were pasted on walls in different parts of Jakarta saying, "We Students Condemn the Mutual Help Parliament as Comparable to Modern Slavery," "New Parliament Is Same as Establishment Dictatorship," "We Students Demand Justice—New Parliament Violates 1945 Constitution."

June 26, 1960

Indonesia Cuts Ties With Netherlands

By United Press International.

JAKARTA, Indonesia, Aug. 17—Indonesia severed all diplomatic ties today with the Netherlands over the disputed Netherlands New Guinea territory.

President Sukarno made his announcement in his annual Independence Day speech. Today was the fifteenth anniversary of Indonesia's proclamation of independence from the Netherlands.

The President's decision was taken with the approval of the supreme Advisory Council, the major policy-making body under his new guided democracy system of government.

The announcement came as a complete surprise. Mr. Sukarno inserted the declaration in the prepared speech that he was delivering.

The break-off of relations with Indonesia's former colonial ruler was the climax of an eleven-year dispute over the Dutch-controlled 160,000 square miles of Netherlands New Guinea.

The Dutch, Mr. Sukarno said, have been getting "increasingly stubborn" in recent months.

"They even sent their (aircraft carrier) Karl Doorman," to Netherlands New Guinea, he added.

Once the President had announced the severance of relations with the Dutch the crowd that had surrounded the palace broke into wild cheering.

When the cheering abated Mr. Sukarno shouted, "Indonesia will intensify her policy of formation of power and the use of power" toward the Dutch in an effort to "liberate West Irian," the name Indonesia uses for Netherlands New Guinea.

Tension High Recently

Tension has existed between the Netherlands and Indonesia because of the dispatch recently of Dutch reinforcements, accompanied by an aircraft carrier, to Netherlands New Guinea.

Although the Netherlands had taken the precaution of sending the ship around Australia to avoid Indonesian waters, the Indonesian press charged that the Dutch were trying to provoke Indonesia into violent reaction. The Netherlands has insisted that the reinforcements were merely overdue replacements.

Last May hundreds of students stormed the Dutch diplomatic compound in Jakarta in protest against the reinforcements.

Indonesia has demanded that the Netherlands give up Netherlands New Guinea and has been claiming sovereignty over the colony.

August 17, 1960

Sukarno Sets Mobilization For Attack on New Guinea

Special to The New York Times.

JAKARTA, Indonesia, Tuesday, Dec. 19—President Sukarno ordered total mobilization of the Indonesian people today to take over Netherlands New Guinea. The President said: "I order the Indonesian people to wreck Dutch efforts to set up a Papuan puppet state."

He told his people to "fly the red and white [Indonesian] flag over the West Irian territory." The Indonesians call the Netherlands-ruled region West Irian.

[President Sukarno was reported to have informed President Kennedy that Indonesia will be compelled to use force to settle her dispute with the Netherlands over Netherlands New Guinea unless what he called Dutch provocation was halted immediately.]

President Sukarno announced that he had ordered his 500,000-man armed forces to be prepared to invade Netherlands New Guinea at any moment.

The Indonesian leader spoke in Jogjakarta, south central Java, at a mass rally commemorating the thirteenth anniversary of the Dutch capture of this city, which was the revolutionary capital of Indonesia.

The crowd at the rally was estimated at a total of 1,000,000 people. The speech was broadcast on a nation-wide hook-up.

December 19, 1961

2 Indonesian Craft Sunk By Dutch Off New Guinea

By The Associated Press.

HOLLANDIA, Netherlands New Guinea, Tuesday, Jan. 16—The Netherlands Navy announced today that Dutch destroyers had intercepted three Indonesian torpedo boats off the southern coast of New Guinea, sunk two of them and driven off a third.

Dutch naval authorities here declared that the craft had been speeding toward the coast of Netherlands New Guinea as an invasion vanguard. A naval spokesman said the boats were intercepted in Dutch territorial waters near Etna Bay yesterday.

[Indonesia confirmed the sinking of one boat but denied that the naval force that had been attacked was the vanguard of an attempt to invade Netherlands New Guinea. A military commander accused the Netherlands of a "deliberate attack" in international waters. U Thant, Acting Secretary General of the United Nations, urged a peaceful resolution of the territorial dispute.]

Indonesians Accused

A first official report here said the Dutch vessels had opened fire on the Indonesian craft after they ignored warning shots. The Netherlands Defense Ministry later said the Indonesians had been the first to fire, shooting at a Dutch patrol plane.

The Dutch radio said seventy Indonesian survivors of the clash had been picked up by the Netherlands Navy. Naval sources declared the number of men involved was proof that a landing attempt was planned since a torpedo boat's normal complement would not number more than twenty or thirty men.

No mention was made of any Dutch casualties or damage to ships. The number of Dutch warships in the engagement was not disclosed.

Aside from skirmishes with Indonesian infiltrators, yesterday's battle was the first armed clash since President Sukarno of Indonesia warned last month that he would take Netherlands New Guinea by force unless the Dutch Government handed over the territory. Despite his threats, however, the general belief has been that Mr. Sukarno would not attempt an invasion until later this year if no settlement were reached.

January 16, 1962

The New York Times   Jan. 16, 1962

NAVAL CLASH: Indonesian torpedo boats believed to be operating from the island of Amboina (1) were attacked by Dutch vessels off Etna Bay (2), in New Guinea.

Sukarno Reported Unhurt In Assassination Attempt

Special to The New York Times.

WASHINGTON, May 13—President Sukarno of Indonesia was reported today to have escaped an assassin's bullets. The State Department said that reports on two monitored broadcasts of the Jakarta domestic radio had told of the assassination attempt. Three high Indonesian officials were said to have been injured.

Lieut. Col. Sabur of Mr. Sukarno's palace guard announced that one man had opened fire on Government leaders at a prayer gathering in Jakarta's Ikada Square at 7:50 A. M. Monday, Indonesian time.

The shots were said to have injured five persons, including Zainul Arifin, the Speaker of Parliament, the Vice Speaker of Parliament and the chief of the state police.

Guard Officers Injured

The two other injured persons were described as officers of the President's guard.

The assassin was reported under arrest.

The Government broadcast attributed the attempt to a group called Darul Islam, a fanatic sect that has had a running quarrel with President Sukarno in recent years.

It said that state security forces had learned earlier of a plan by the leader of the Darul Islam group, identified as Kartosuwirjo, to have nine of his men arrange for the assassination of President Sukarno.

Two separate broadcasts said the attempt on the life of the President had been unsuccessful. Mr. Sukarno, who will be 61 years old on June 6, was elected President of Indonesia on Dec. 16, 1949.

May 14, 1962

DUTCH SIGN PACT GIVING INDONESIA NEW GUINEA RULE

U.N. TO SUPERVISE

Will Take Over Region Until Its Transfer to Jakarta May 1

By THOMAS J. HAMILTON
Special to The New York Times.

UNITED NATIONS, N. Y., Aug. 15 — An agreement to transfer to Indonesia the administration of Netherlands New Guinea was signed here tonight.

The United Nations will take over the administration of the territory Oct. 1 for an interim period. The United Nations will transfer the responsibility to Indonesia next May 1.

The agreement was signed at 6:20 P. M. by representatives of Indonesia and the Netherlands.

Under the agreement Indonesia will make arrangements for an "act of self-determination" or plebiscite, by the end of 1969, with United Nations participation. The 700,000 inhabitants, mainly Papuans, will be given a choice of remaining with Indonesia or severing ties with Indonesia.

Pledge on the Plebiscite

Nothing was mentioned about what would happen if a majority voted against continuing under Indonesian rule. Indonesia and the Netherlands pledged themselves to "abide by the results."

U Thant, Acting Secretary General, congratulated the two governments on the settlement of the dispute. Relations between the countries have been strained since the Netherlands granted independence to Indonesia in 1949.

The New York Times   Aug. 16, 1962
Netherlands New Guinea (diagonal shading) will be transferred to control by Indonesia by next May 1.

Mr. Thant said it was "good augury" that an accompanying exchange of letters between the two Governments had provided for the resumption of diplomatic relations between the Hague and Jakarta. Relations were broken off Aug. 17, 1960, when Indonesia threatened to seize all remaining Dutch possessions in Indonesia if the Dutch continued to be stubborn about Netherlands New Guinea.

The principal negotiators, Foreign Minister Subandrio of Indonesia and Dr. J. H. van Roijen, Dutch Ambassador to Washington, expressed the hope that the settlement of the dispute would lead to friendly relations between their Governments.

Dr. van Roijen emphasized that the Netherlands had been influenced by concern for the Papuans. He said that history's verdict on the agreement would depend on how it was carried out "in practice."

Dr. Subandrio declared that with the signing of the agreement the unity of Indonesia had been restored. Indonesia's "struggle for independence had been completed," he said.

The two representatives joined Mr. Thant in thanking Ellsworth Bunker, a former United States Ambassador, who drew up the plan on which the agreement was based.

August 16, 1962

DUTCH RESUMING INDONESIAN ROLE

Subandrio to Visit the Hague Soon—Technicians Active

Special to The New York Times
JAKARTA, Indonesia, March 26—It is quite usual these days to hear Dutch spoken all around the tiled terrace of the Hotel Indonesia's sumptuous swimming pool.

A year ago this would have caused considerable comment. Today, the hotel is a gathering place for a steadily increasing corps of sunburned Dutch businessmen who have come back to their former colony to see what can be promoted or salvaged from the rich holdings they once enjoyed here.

Dutch influence and goodwill in Indonesia declined rapidly during the first years after independence in 1949. They disappeared altogether in 1958, when President Sukarno confiscated Dutch holdings and expelled all Dutch citizens during the dispute over Netherlands New Guinea.

Indonesia now holds this territory, and that point of contention has been removed. Indonesia now desperately needs new markets to replace those lost when trade with Malaysia was ended.

The Dutch became interested, when that situation developed, in taking whatever advantage of it they could.

After a cautious beginning, the commercial return of the Dutch is gaining momentum, and may soon be accelerated further.

So far the Dutch Government's role has been largely played behind the scenes. On May 6 last year C. D. Barkman arrived in Jakarta to serve as chargé d'affaires at the new **Dutch Embassy. Ambassadors have not been exchanged.**

Since then Mr. Barkman, a patient, friendly man, has worked to re-establish the contacts the Dutch once had with the Indonesian Government.

Dr. Subandrio, deputy Premier and Foreign Minister, will arrive in The Hague next Wednesday on the first visit by an official of cabinet rank since 1958.

He is expected to discuss number of matters with Dutch leaders. These will include possible Government-backed commercial credits for Indonesia, an exchange of students and cultural groups, and perhaps a state visit by President Sukarno.

One subject that may not be on the agenda, but will certainly be heavily present in the background, is the question of compensation for Dutch holdings seized by Indonesia.

Unofficial estimates place the total value of these holdings at somewhere near $550 million. The Dutch in Indonesia carefully avoid discussing these claims. Mr. Barkman will not even venture an opinion on their value.

Dutch technicians have been in Indonesia surveying prospects for reclaiming huge areas of land in South Borneo and Sumatra.

Dutch businessmen have arranged to resume shipments of Indonesian tin for smelting in Holland. This ore used to go to Singapore and Penang, before the crisis over Malaysia began.

An American company has been using Dutch experts to buy Sumatran rubber for direct shipment to the United States.

The Netherlands Bank and the Bank of Indonesia have reached an agreement for an exchange of credits.

"Once the West Irian (Netherlands New Guinea) matter was ended, we suddenly found a lot of positive factors coming to the fore," a Dutch official in Jakarta said today.

March 29, 1964

INDONESIA FACING
A CRISIS ON FOOD;
MILLIONS HUNGRY

Rations on Java Reported
Insufficient for Health—
Rice Harvest Delayed

By SETH S. KING
Special to The New York Times

SEMARANG, Indonesia, March 26 — During the next six weeks, President Sukarno will have to pass through one of the most dangerous periods he has faced since he became leader of Indonesia 14 years ago.

Until the country's rice crop is harvested in early May, food supplies in this normally bountiful land will remain dangerously low.

Estimates are that more than two million Indonesians, most of them on this island of Java, now do not have enough to eat to remain healthy.

In several areas of Java and in a few scattered pockets in Bali there are people today who are lying down in the streets and dying of starvation. Hundreds have been hospitalized from the effects of lack of food.

Relief Effort Ineffective

The Sukarno Government has not been able to mount effective relief operations to prevent the widespread hunger. In these scattered areas people are dying while there is more than enough food in adjoining valleys barely 20 miles distant.

Families of impoverished villagers, hungry and in rags, have been making their way into the cities of Jakarta, Semarang, Jogjakarta and Surabaja to beg on the streets and sleep on the sidewalks.

Yet a traveler touring Bali and crossing the lush rice-producing areas along the 475 miles of roadway between Surabaja and Jakarta could see no evidence this week that Indonesia faced a major food shortage.

A long dry season and hordes of rats reduced last year's rice crop in Indonesia by at least 10 per cent.

The Rains Late Again

The rains have been late again this year. As a result the 1964 crop in the major rice-growing areas will be at least two months late and again at least 10 per cent below normal.

About two million children have been added in the year, presenting two million more mouths to feed and bringing the country's estimated population to 103 million.

President Sukarno's campaign to crush the new Federation of Malaysia has cut off most of the shipping that normally brought rice imports from Burma and Thailand through Singapore. Indonesia's credits abroad both for chartered shipping and for rice have been virtually exhausted. So have the country's foreign currency reserves with which to buy for cash abroad.

The Sukarno Government has already purchased 40,000 tons of rice from the United States this year under the surplus food program. No more rice or corn will be available until a new agreement is negotiated; and Secretary of State Dean Rusk has stated that such an agreement will not be considered until the Malaysian controversy is settled.

The difficulties caused by these factors are as severe and as potentially dangerous as any that Mr. Sukarno and the Indonesian people have confronted since the Dutch were forced out in 1949.

Indonesia's Communist party, with its two million members and about eight million sympathizers, is reported to have stepped up its organizing and propaganda efforts in villages and towns in recent months.

So far, however, the Communist leadership has concentrated on supporting President Sukarno in his anti-Malaysia campaign and on criticizing certain Government officials for their failure to provide for the people. This criticism never includes the President himself.

The Communists have also continued their demands that members of the party be named to cabinet posts, a step Mr. Sukarno has been promising to take for several years. But there have been no indications that the party is preparing to try to force a change in the Government or in its position with President Sukarno.

Armed Forces Vigilant

The armed forces, believed to be the only organized and effective element capable of countering the Communists, have continued their unpublicized vigilance against Communist expansion.

But many Western observers, particularly the Americans, who have looked to Indonesia's armed forces as an antidote to the Communists, have been disappointed by the army's recent lack of initiative in using its transport and manpower to help people in the critical areas.

The capacity of the Indonesian people to tolerate hunger, inconvenience and their Government's bungling and corruption seems limitless. Life in Indonesian villages has not changed much in 40 years. As long as the gods do not destroy the rice crops or lay waste the fruit, corn, sweet potatoes and cassava root, the peasants remain self-sufficient and placid.

But for the people of the cities, rice has become a form of currency, replacing in value the rupiah whose purchasing power has plummeted in the last three years. All civil servants, members of the armed forces, employes of the nationalized industries and of private concerns receive monthly rice rations in addition to their salaries.

The prices of virtually everything sold in Indonesia except the state-subsidized petroleum products are five to 10 times higher than two years ago. The price of rice in Jakarta has risen in six months from 60 rupiahs a kilogram to 300 rupiahs. Many governmental and private employes eat only part of their rice ration and sell the rest of it in the open market.

The Malaysia Issue

The trouble facing President Sukarno from these internal pressures and the almost total lack of support abroad for his "Crush Malaysia" campaign has convinced well-informed sources here that the President would like to find a way to back off, at least for the time being, from the Malaysia issue.

But this issue has become Mr. Sukarno's chief vehicle for stirring up the Indonesians and exhorting them to struggle "to complete the revolution."

Volunteers among the youth of Indonesia were being marshalled this week to "combat the forces of colonialism and imperialism." Volunteers were also being asked in undefined terms to help in combating the shortage of food.

The Communist party and the armed forces have, separately, taken the lead in supporting the stand against Malaysia. Pressures from these two opposing elements have, in the opinion of observers, reduced Mr. Sukarno's field of maneuver and may be expected to make it more difficult for him to compromise significantly on the Malaysia question.

From observations during a tour across Bali and Java it appeared that the Indonesians had accepted President Sukarno's animosity toward Malaysia. There seemed to be a resigned willingness to give vocal support to the campaign. But this support had to be superimposed on a preoccupation with hunger, with the steadily deteriorating Government services and with the skyrocketing cost of living.

A Union Leader's View

In Surabaja, a trade union leader said the other day:

"I am sure that in America or in Europe the people would rise up if conditions were as bad as they are here.

"But we are different here in Indonesia, we have a national feeling. We want to give our Government a chance. We want our own revolution against the old order to succeed."

The labor leader was seated in a small, crudely furnished office in downtown Surabaja. Outside, the people of Indonesia's second largest city and what was once the greatest port in the Indies east of Singapore, were flooding into the streets to begin the half holiday that Moslem Indonesia observes Fridays.

Around them the effects of

the economic difficulties were were evident.

The city's wide streets were scarred by holes. Garbage was piled up in front of many dwellings. Along the banks of the stagnant canals, the bamboo shacks of squatters were jammed in cluttered rows.

In recent weeks Surabaja's population of 1.5 million has been swollen by hundreds of villagers who have made their way into the city in the hope of finding food.

Supplies have continued to find their way into Surabaja and food can be bought in the central market or from any one of hundreds of food vendors whose carts line the streets. But prices have shot up far beyond earnings.

Adding to the problems is a rapid deterioration of the city's services. Domestic cooking gas has been cut off entirely. One out of every three days, Surabaja residents have no electricity. Low water reserves from

the drought have curtailed the operation of hydroelectric plants.

Under a contract financed by a loan from the United States Export-Import Bank, the Westinghouse Corporation is building a huge new power plant in Surabaja for the Indonesian Government. When this plant is completed, it will supply the electricity needs for Surabaja as well as for the rest of Eastern Java. But work on the plant is now months behind schedule.

A main cause of the delay is

difficulty in getting materials and equipment to the plant site from the United States. In several instances, it has taken as much as six weeks for goods brought to Surabaja to reach the site, a distance of about 600 yards from where the ships are unloaded.

March 29, 1964

Indonesians Resign Formally From U.N.

By FARNSWORTH FOWLE
Special to The New York Times

UNITED NATIONS, N. Y., Jan. 21 — Indonesia formally withdrew from the United Nations tonight, leaving the organization with 114 members.

The formal letter from Foreign Minister Subandrio was handed to the Secretary General, U Thant, in his office by Lambertus N. Palar, Indonesia's chief delegate.

The letter expressed the hope that "our decision may become the catalyst to reform and retool the United Nations in spirit and in deed, lest the present atmosphere of complacency shown by the neocolonial powers may undermine the lofty spirit of the United Nations."

Indonesia, the first nation to quit the world organization since it was formed two decades ago, objects to Malaysia's recent election to the Security Council as a nonpermanent member.

Dr. Subandrio said this was "just the further proof of this international body being manipulated by colonial and neocolonial powers."

The Foreign Minister acknowledged Secretary General Thant's plea to reconsider. But he said Indonesia's adherence to the principles of international cooperation "can be implemented outside as well as inside the United Nations' body."

He specified that Indonesia was also withdrawing "from specialized agencies like the Food and Agriculture Organization, United Nations Children's Fund and United Nations Educational, Scientific and Cultural Organization."

He asked to have the Indonesian mission maintain its official status until March 1, "which will also be the case

with your United Nations office in Jakarta."

A spokesman for the United Nations said the Indonesian message was being studied. He said there was no comment on whether the United Nations considered Indonesia a member or nonmember.

Mr. Palar said this morning on returning from consultations in Jakarta, "I have come back to close the office."

President Sukarno announced Dec. 31 that Indonesia would withdraw if Malaysia, which he does not recognize, took the nonpermanent seat on the Security Council to which it had just been elected.

Mr. Palar announced here on Jan. 2 that Indonesia no longer considered herself a member. But the United Nations Charter does not specify any procedure for giving up membership, and the Secretary General's office took the position that a formal notice had to be given in writing.

Indonesia's flag still flew this afternoon from its staff in front

of the General Assembly Building, and the Indonesia name plate marked an empty row of seats in the Assembly.

The United Nations office in Jakarta is headed by V. K. Pavicic of Yugoslavia.

Indonesia had indicated previously that she would remain in the World Health Organization. The Subandrio letter indicated that this decision stood. But it left open the question of Indonesia's continued membership in the Special Fund and related technical assistance programs.

A United Nations spokesman said Jan. 4 that Indonesia was scheduled to receive $2.6 million in 1965 and 1966 under the expanded program of technical assistance, plus $500,000 in regular programs from the United Nations and its related agencies.

January 22, 1965

MOSLEMS ON JAVA CLASH WITH REDS

By NEIL SHEEHAN
Special to The New York Times

SURABAYA, Indonesia, March 16 — A struggle for power between the Communist party and an informal alliance of Moslem and nationalist parties in East Java is growing in violence. Beatings, knifings, burning of homes and mob clashes have become almost daily occurrences throughout the province.

The conflict has intensified since June, when a Communist peasant organization, on the pretext of enforcing land reform and crop-sharing laws through extralegal means, be-

gan seizing land from Moslem and nationalist farmers and distributing it among landless Communist peasants. Village officials and farmers who resist are being beaten up by mobs of Communist youths or otherwise intimidated.

The Moslem and nationalist parties, whose strength lies among the landowning peasantry, reacted slowly at first, but gradually began retaliating with mob attacks of their own, beating up village and district Communist leaders, and in many cases burning down their homes.

In the Kanigoro area west of here, the homes of about 20 Communist leaders have been burned by mobs of Moslems. Although reports of deaths are difficult to confirm, reliable sources believe that five to 25 Communist leaders have been killed by Moslems in clashes throughout the province. A number of others have been

seriously wounded.

The struggle against the Communists grew into something of a religious crusade for the Moslems after a Communist mob invaded a mosque in Kanigoro in mid-January and one Communist allegedly put his foot on a Koran, a sacrilegious act to Moslems.

Some lower-level Communist leaders have also been attacking Islam at district and village meetings.

Last month a leading Moslem newspaper in the province printed a front-page cartoon portraying the Communist party as a wolf hypocritically singing a song about national unity while it tramples on a Koran.

Unsigned leaflets were clandestinely distributed in Surabaya and elsewhere last week calling on Moslems to wage a holy war against the Communists. A significant percentage of the 23 million inhabitants of

east Java are Moslems.

The conflict is potentially so explosive that some observers here believe that rioting of Communist and Moslem mobs could become more serious if something is not done to ease the tension.

An atmosphere of fear and intimidation prevails even in Surabaya, where the provincial Moslem, nationalist and Communist leaders now travel with bodyguards.

In the town of Banyuwangi, near the eastern tip of Java, where the conflict is particularly bitter, Moslem mobs prevented a new pro-Communist district chief from taking office early in January and smashed chairs set up for the inauguration.

The district chief still has not been installed because the provincial authorities fear renewed violence.

March 17, 1965

SUKARNO MOVES FARTHER LEFT

By NEIL SHEEHAN
Special to The New York Times

JAKARTA, Indonesia, May 29— The 45th anniversary celebrations last week of the Indonesian Communist party, the third largest in the world outside the Soviet Union and China, were the most lavish

ever held by a political party in Indonesia.

In his speech to a Communist rally Sunday at Jakarta Stadium, President Sukarno called the Communist party "my brother and my friend."

The Indonesian leader has said

this in the past, but this time his words carried considerable weight and could not be passed off as the political niceties expected on such an occasion.

For President Sukarno is pushing Indonesia's internal political development steadily to the left,

gradually enlarging the role of the Communist party and eroding elements in the country that oppose this trend.

Complexities

Although this policy has frequently been obscured by complexi-

243

ties which baffle any observer of Indonesian politics, Mr. Sukarno's internal political moves over the last 10 months have now emerged into a pattern which demonstrates a growing community of interest between himself and the Communist party.

A first indication of the direction in which he was moving came in his independence day speech last August. He indirectly denounced those who were trying to impede the growth of the Communist power as "hypocrites" and accused them of attempting to sabotage his policies. President Sukarno had made such statements in the past, but never with quite as much emphasis.

Prior to last August there were two pro-Communist ministers in the Cabinet. Dipa N. Aidit, the Communist party chairman, and M. H. Lukman, the party's first deputy chairman, had also been given ministerial rank, but they had no functions.

Last August, Mr. Sukarno gave the Ministry of Labor to another pro-Communist and brought Mr. Njoto, a polite, self-taught intellectual who is second deputy chairman of the Communist party, into the Cabinet as a minister of state attached to the praesidium, an important body which helps to develop and execute policy.

Opposition Disguised

Alarmed at the road Mr. Sukarno was taking, those elements in the Government and the armed forces who have the most to lose from Communist ascendancy launched an anti-Communist campaign in the hope of building up enough public pressure to force the President to retreat.

Since no one in this country can afford to oppose Mr. Sukarno openly, the campaign was camouflaged in a welter of slogans and vague concepts. The group even attempted to take advantage of Mr. Sukarno's vast prestige for ends quite different from his own by calling their movement the Body for the Promotion of Sukarnoism.

Adam Malik, a former Minister

of Trade; Dr. Chaerul Saleh, Third Deputy Premier, and other members of Murba, a small but influential party of Government officials, reportedly were the principal directors of this campaign. These men began their careers as Titoist Communists, but were later considered among the leading capitalists in Indonesia because of their hold over trade and state-owned industries and enterprises.

They were supported by right-wing Moslem and Nationalist politicians and by a number of high-ranking officers in the army and navy.

The campaign was carried on chiefly through about 60 Moslem, Nationalist and Murba-supported newspapers. Beginning in September, the Communist party was subjected to mounting editorial attacks. It was accused of plotting to seize power, of being anti-Moslem and of disrupting national unity by seizing land under the pretext of enforcing the land-reform law.

By November, the campaign threatened to swell into a broad anti-Communist front, but the President was gradually able to bring it under control with the aid of Dr. Subandrio, the Foreign Minister and First Deputy Premier, and the Communist party itself. Dr. Subandrio has with the tacit but evident consent of the President developed an informal working alliance with the Communists.

Power Plays

In December, President Sukarno banned the Body for the Promotion of Sukarnoism and the following month outlawed Murba and placed its party chairman, Mr. Sukarni, former Ambassador to Peking, under arrest. Twenty-one newspapers involved in the movement were later suppressed and at the end of March the President moved against Dr. Saleh and Mr. Malik.

Dr. Saleh was deprived of most of his Ministry of Basic Industry and Mining. A pro-Communist was named Minister of Mining and a

professional diplomat who is reported to be under the influence of Foreign Minister Subandrio was made Minister of Industry. Mr. Malik was completely stripped of his Trade Ministry and was named Minister for Guided Economy, a largely honorific post.

Throughout this period, with the Communists breaking ground for him, Mr. Sukarno also relentlessly reduced the United States' presence and influence in Indonesia. He seized control of rubber plantations and other businesses owned by American interests and the foreign oil companies here.

Since this last Cabinet reshuffle, President Sukarno has stepped up the pace of his movement to the left, perhaps in preparation for more Cabinet changes over the next few months that will bring additional Communists or pro-Communists into the Government.

In early April, he announced a new economic policy of greatly increased socialization and state control and hinted broadly that it might imitate Communist economic methods. He then seized control of the remaining foreign-owned enterprises here.

Generals Admonished

He also urged the Nationalist and Moslem political parties to expel right-wing elements from their ranks. He quietly warned the generals not to oppose him and to cease their "deviations" from the Indonesian revolution.

Events move slowly in Indonesia and purges have not yet actually begun. Throughout May, however, a preparatory campaign has gradually unfurled, with left-wing nationalist leaders who support Mr. Sukarno's policies chanting a chorus of demands for the elimination of "subversive elements."

The President, it is felt, does not want to destroy the Nationalist and Moslem parties but simply to purge them and remold them into his own image of extreme nationalism and Marxism.

Experienced observers here also believe that the Communist party

is at present the one element in Indonesia which most closely appeal to Mr. Sukarno's temperament and his view of the world. Its militancy, its discipline and organization and its ability to mobilize the masses strike a response in the President's love of turmoil and revolution for their own sake.

This affinity has been noticeable in the more pronounced ideological tone of the Indonesian President's recent speeches. In a talk at a meeting of Nationalist party workers in April, he told them that Indonesia was now "in the national democratic stage" of his revolution and their duty was "to crush imperialism, to stamp out colonialism, to overturn neo-colonialism, to smash feudalism and to pulverize the foreign-capital monopolies" in order "to create Socialism" in Indonesia.

President Sukarno's socialist doctrine is called Marhaenism — Marhaen is a common Indonesian name but it has been officially defined as "Marxism adapted to the circumstances and historical development of Indonesia."

Mr. Sukarno has never viewed Communism and nationalism as irreconcilable forces and he sees no reason why they cannot be welded together. The militant nationalism that the Indonesian Communist party has espoused since the early 1950's has also convinced him, it is believed, that the party is now basically an Indonesian Communist party and is no longer controlled by either Moscow or Peking.

It is not clear how far Mr. Sukarno intends to pursue his present leftward course, but he shows no signs of retreating and he is making no secret of his intention some day to build his own version of socialism in Indonesia. He has gone slowly, however, because he is not a dictator in the conventional Western sense. He has to contend with a number of powerful and conflicting forces and constantly to maneuver and compromise.

May 30, 1965

SUKARNO'S STYLE: HOSTILITY TO U.S.

Ties to Indonesia Fragile as Independence Day Nears

By NEIL SHEEHAN
Special to The New York Times

JAKARTA, Indonesia, Aug. 15—In his traditional Independence Day speech last Aug. 17, President Sukarno announced that Indonesia would spend the following year "living dangerously."

On Tuesday Mr. Sukarno will make another Independence Day address, marking the 20th anniversary of the collapse of

Japanese authority in the Netherlands East Indies and the establishment of a provisional republican Government under Mr. Sukarno that led a four-year revolt against the return of Dutch colonial rule.

As he prepared for the address, it appeared that one of the major aspects of the "dangerous" style of living—a virulent hostility toward the United States—has brought Washington's relations with Jakarta perilously close to the breaking point.

To the dismay of American diplomats, Mr. Sukarno over the last year has drastically reduced the United States' presence and influence in Indonesia and has firmly aligned his country with Communist China on a foreign policy course that directly conflicts with United

States interests in Southeast Asia.

Even before last year's Independence Day speech, the President demonstrated what he had in mind by allowing the Indonesian Communist party to enforce a boycott on American films. After the speech, however, the campaign to shrink the United States presence here, spearheaded by the Communist party but aided and abetted by Mr. Sukarno, moved forward much more deliberately.

In late August, the United States Information Service library in the central Java city of Jogjakarta was seized by the Indonesian Government.

Study Trips Barred

The following month, after a Congressional resolution urging

that the United States cease training Indonesian military and police officers because of Jakarta's confrontation policy against the neighboring Federation of Malaysia, the Indonesian Government barred the sending of Indonesians to the United States for study on grants from the United States Government or American foundations.

The training of Indonesian scholars, technicians and military and police officers in the United States had formed a key part of the United States aid program and had been a major source of American influence in Indonesia.

Simultaneously, the Indonesian press and other information media opened a barrage of anti-American propaganda, much of it racist in tone, which has steadily increased in intensity. United States policies in the Congo and Vietnam were bitterly attacked and Americans were portrayed as "vicious imperialists" who delighted in killing members of the yellow, brown and black races.

Anti - American demonstrations became almost as common as traffic accidents. Petty harrassment against the operations of the United States Government and American companies was not neglected.

Communist-led mob attacks eventually forced U.S.I.S. libraries in Jakarta and Surabaya in East Java to close, and by the end of March the information service was forced to cease

operations here. All foreign oil companies were taken over.

Bunker Mission Unsuccessful

Ellsworth Bunker, a high-level United States diplomat. arrived March 31 as a special representative of President Johnson to try to improve relations. But as one American official later remarked, "We were not singing the same tune."

Marshall Green. the new United States Ambassador to Indonesia, also attempted conciliation when he presented his credentials last month, as had his predecessor, Howard P. Jones. who departed in May.

But Mr. Green's efforts were met with a short but strong speech by Mr. Sukarno denouncing United States policy in Vietnam and American support for Malaysia. A "Go home, Green" demonstration followed.

The widespread private feeling among American officials that the two countries are heading for a break in diplomatic relations has been strengthened by the reception accorded to Ambassador Green and by recent hints by Mr. Sukarno that he is contemplating such a step. The President believes that the United States will eventually be forced to withdraw from Vietnam and that

the psychological and political shockwaves that this will set off will cause a collapse of the Western position in Southeast Asia.

He has aligned his foreign policy with that of Communist China and Peking's Asian allies in an attempt to bring this about. Singapore's separation from Malaysia last week, Western diplomats believe, has served to bolster Mr. Sukarno's belief that such a foreign policy is a correct one and will in all likelihood, result in further hostility toward the United States.

August 16, 1965

MALAYSIA STRUGGLES FOR SURVIVAL

SINGAPORE VOTING WON BY LEFTISTS

People's Action Party Routs Anti-Reds—To Form First Regime of New State

---

By BERNARD KALB
Special to The New York Times.

SINGAPORE, Sunday, May 31—The left-wing People's Action party scored a landslide victory yesterday in elections for a new Assembly that will take over local rule from the British here.

The winning party has pledged that it will pave the way for a "future Socialist society."

The Legislative Assembly of the new State of Singapore will consist of fifty-one members elected for five-year terms.

The final returns gave the People's Action party forty-three seats. It was the only party to run candidates in all constituencies.

The anti-Communist Singa-

pore People's Alliance, led by outgoing Chief Minister Lim Yew Hock, won four seats. The alliance of the United Malays National Organization and the Malayan Chinese Association won three seats. One independent was elected.

To Form New Regime

By winning a majority the People's Action party gained the right to form Singapore's first government with full internal powers. Its victory had been widely forecast.

Under the new Constitution, the British, who have their biggest military establishment in the East on this island, retain absolute powers over Singapore's defense and foreign affairs. They could suspend the Constitution if they believed it necessary.

Among the People's Action candidates elected was the party's fiery secretary general, Lee Kuan Yew. It is taken as virtual certainty that Mr. Lee, a Cambridge-educated lawyer, will become Prime Minister.

In a statement this morning Mr. Lee declared:

"The people's choice is clear and decisive. It is a victory of right over wrong, clean over

dirty, righteousness over evil."

With the People's Action party celebrating its victory attention is shifting to the party's pre-election announcement that it would refuse to form a new Government until about seven of its top leaders, arrested after the 1956 riots under an anti-subversive ordinance, were freed.

The party has said that the British Governor, Sir William Goode, had the power to order the release of these detainees. It had seemed confident that a triumph at the polls would persuade the Governor to free them.

Informal talks are expected to take place later today between Sir William and People's Action leaders about forming a government. The leaders are expected to raise the issue of the detainees then.

About 90 per cent of the registered electorate of almost 600,000 are reported to have voted. Voting was compulsory. The balloting was orderly.

Among the People's Action leaders in jail is Lim Chin Siong, who had been elected to the Assembly in 1955. He is widely regarded by local Chinese who get their political inspiration from Peiping as a man who speaks for them.

Mr. Lee warned last week that the party would not tolerate any attempts either inside or outside the party to subvert it into a Communist party. This was interpreted by some observers as aimed at Mr. Lim, among others.

The Peoples Action party's opponents had charged that a vote for the party was a "vote for slavery." Some business circles worried whether the People's Action victory would result in radical changes that would hurt Singapore's economic and political future.

The victorious party dismissed these charges saying that it was non-Communist and championed on "independent, democratic, non - Communist, Socialist Malaya." To the People's Action party this means a national state composed of the Federation of Malaya and Singapore.

The party has a "five-year plan" calling for the development of industries and agriculture and improving social welfare.

It draws its support primarily from youth and labor groups, the Chinese speaking population and left-wing extremists. It was helped by the fact that its opponents were badly divided.

May 31, 1959

SINGAPORE REGIME SCORES IMMORALITY

SINGAPORE, June 8 (Reuters)—The three-day-old government of Prime Minister Lee Kuan Yew moved today to wipe out public immorality in this traditionally wide-open island state.

Acting under a new Constitution granting internal self-rule

to this Far Eastern British bastion, the left-wing People's Action party Government banned eight publications and a stage show. All of them were termed "pornographic."

The Government served notice of its determination to raise moral standards and foster "a unified Malayan culture" in this predominantly Chinese center.

The Government move followed the arrival here today of Armand Gaspard, an observer from the International Press Institute, to look into charges

that the People's Action party threatened press freedom.

The Straits Times and other English-language papers charged that Mr. Lee had threatened their freedom in a pre-election speech warning the press not to impede relations between Singapore and Malaya.

A major aim of the party is to bring about a union of Singapore with neighboring Malaya.

June 9, 1959

Malaya, Born in War on Reds, Celebrates Her Jungle Victory

12-Year Emergency Declared Over—Fighting Goes on at the Thai Frontier

Special to The New York Times.

KUALA LUMPUR, Malaya, July 30 — Malaya's twelve year Communist war is over. The formal state of emergency proclaimed by the British administration in June, 1948, is being lifted at midnight and the Federation of Malaya, independent since 1957, will tomorrow celebrate victory over the red guerrilla army and the Communist underground.

Five hundred Communist fighters are still in the jungle, but nearly all are in the north in the Thai frontier area.

Chin Peng, secretary general of the Malayan Communist Party, is among the handful of top Communists believed to be living in jungle headquarters a few miles the other side of the frontier.

Malaya's Red war has cost 11,000 lives. The known Communist dead total 6,710. Nearly 2,500 civilians were killed by the guerrillas most of these victims were Chinese; but at least ninety-nine British planters were killed in terrorist attacks on the rubber estates.

Toll of Malaya's Forces

Also 810 civilians who were kidnapped by terrorist bands were probably slain.

The army, police and Home Guard lost 1,865 officers and men killed and more than 2,500 wounded.

At the peak of the war eight years ago twentyfive battalions

The New York Times   July 29, 1960

The Thai armed forces are battling Communists in the Malaya border area (cross).

of British troops were engaged. The police, then a para-military force. had been expanded to 90,000 men and the Home Guard, formed to defend the villages, was 350,000 strong.

The Communist guerrillas at no time numbered more than 11,500 men and women.

Out of the jungle warfare after mid-1948 grew the new Malayan nation. The British hastened the pace of political progress, and were able to hand power over to a popular and pro-Western Government, which is anti-Communist for its own good reasons even though it has remained outside the Southeast Asia Treaty Organization.

The Malays, strongly anti-Communist, have strongly manned the police force under Britain rule and joined the army in thousands. One result was that when the Federation of Malaya became independent in 1957, a small but battle-blooded Malayan army was in existence.

British and other Common

July 31, 1960

ACCORD REACHED ON MALAY UNION

Agreement Signed in London on a Federation for Wide Area of Southeast Asia

By LAWRENCE FELLOWS
Special to The New York Times.

LONDON, July 31—Britain announced tonight that agreement had been reached on the establishment of a Federation of Malaysia. It will embrace Malaya and all that remains of the British Empire in Southeast Asia.

Besides Malaya, the federation will consist of Singapore, Sarawak, Brunei and North Borneo. The federation will extend in a 1,600-mile arc around the South China Sea from the border of Thailand to the Philippine archipelago.

The documents of agreement were signed in a brief ceremony tonight by Prime Minister Macmillan of Britain and Tunku Abdul Rahman, the Prime Minister of Malaya.

Britain and Malaya Talk

The new federation is expected to benefit economically from the union of the commerce and industry of Singapore with the natural resources, mainly rubber, tin and crude oil, in Malaya and the other territories. Politically, the federation is viewed as a counter-force to Chinese Communist influence in the area and any possible expansion moves by Indonesia on Borneo. Indonesia holds part of Borneo.

Britain negotiated the agreement on behalf of all the parties but Malaya, which is an independent member of the Commonwealth.

Singapore, at the southern tip of the Malay Peninsula, is a semi-colonial territory in that it is self-governing except for defense and external affairs other than trade and cultural relations.

Schedule Not Revealed

The Sultanate of Brunei, one of the three North Borneo territories, is a British protectorate. Sarawak and North Borneo, the other two, are British colonies.

Little interest was shown in London in the suggestion made last Friday by President Diosdado Macapagal of the Philippines that the federation plan be dropped in favor of a looser confederation that would include the Philippines.

While no official comment was available here, it was believed President Macapagal would be told his proposal could

The New York Times   Aug. 1, 1962

Malaysia will be formed of Malaya (1), Singapore (2), Sarawak (3), Brunei (4) and North Borneo (5).

not be considered at this stage, but that it might be discussed after the federation is in being.

Neither the schedule for establishing the Federation of Malaysia nor any of the precise terms of the agreement were made public tonight. These, it was said, will be given in the House of Commons tomorrow by Duncan Sandys, Britain's Secretary of State for Commonwealth Relations and Colonial Secretary.

It was understood, however, that the agreement provided that the federation would be in operation in a year. This had been the goal of Tunku Abdul Rahman, a strong anti-Communist and the most outspoken advocate of the federation plan.

It was also reported that guarantees have been written into the agreement giving Britain continuing unrestricted use of her army, naval and air bases in the twenty square miles of Singapore.

As a member of the Southeast Asia Treaty Organization (SEATO), Britain is committed to collective action with the United States and other members of that organization in the event of Communist aggression in Southeast Asia.

Without the assurance of full control over the Singapore bases, the treaty organization's only foothold on the Southeast Asian mainland would have been in Thailand. Malaya is not a member of SEATO.

Another part of the agreement, it was reported, provides an explicit guarantee of the rights of the minority ethnic groups in the projected federation's population of 10,000,000.

The Chinese and Indians in the population have been suspicious of greater Malayan control.

Tunku Abdul Rahman, who has been in London since July 16 to attend the final stages of negotiation, proposed the larger federation on May 27, 1961, when discussions between Malaya and Britain were centered on a merger of Malaya and Singapore.

Malaya has 3,500,000 Malays, 2,500,000 Chinese and 850,000 Indians. Singapore has 1,125,000 Chinese and 200,000 Malayans.

The Malayan leader was said to be concerned about the large proportion of Chinese that would be in the union if it included only Malaya and Singapore.

His fears were said to be based on the steady growth of communism in Singapore and on the prospect that Chinese chauvinism would advance this trend further.

In the three border territories that he proposed be added to the union, only a quarter of the 1,125,000 inhabitants are Chinese.

The Malayan Prime Minister has agreed to the continued existence of the Singapore Legislature. To insure Singapore against Malay domination, Lee Kuan Yew, Prime Minister of Singapore, was also promised that Singapore could continue to administer its own education and labor policies.

Singapore would also have fifteen seats in the federal House of Representatives, one-eighth of the total. Singapore will have about one-sixth of the population of the federation.

Malaya has been an independent member of the Commonwealth since 1957, when Britain yielded her jurisdiction over the Malay States and the settlements of Penang and Malacca, which then became states of the Federation of Malaya.

August 1, 1962

THANT SAYS STUDY BACKS MALAYSIA

Asserts U.N. Mission Found Support of Federation

By SAM POPE BREWER
Special to The New York Times

UNITED NATIONS, N.Y., Sept. 14—The Secretary General, U Thant, has reported after investigation that "a sizable majority" of the people in the British colonies of North Borneo and Sarawak wish to join the Federation of Malaya. The new country is to be formed Monday.

His conclusions were given yesterday to the Governments of Indonesia, Malaya and Philippines in a 2,000-word document made public today. They were based on an on-site survey by a nine-man team whose 43,000-word report also was made available today.

There have been hints that Indonesia and the Philippines might contest the validity of the report, partly because the "ascertainment" was carried out in only nine days and partly because their own observers were late in arriving on the scene. They have said nothing publicly here yet.

Indonesia and the Philippines have been resisting the formation of Malaysia, which is to consist of Malaya, Singapore, North Borneo and Sarawak. The Indonesians consider the new federation a creature of British "neo-colonialism."

The Philippines are unfriendly to the idea because of their long-standing claim to North Borneo.

Both Asian countries agreed, however, to ask a United Nations mission to assess opinion on Malaysia among the people of North Borneo and Sarawak. They insisted that they be permitted to send observers to check on the work of the United Nations team.

A 'Difficult Task'

Mr. Thant said that his mission, headed by Laurence V. Michelmore with George Janecek as deputy, "accomplished a sensitive and difficult task in a relatively short period but at the same time in a thorough and wholly adequate manner."

He expressed conviction that "while more time might have enabled the mission to obtain more copious documentation and other evidence, it would not have affected the conclusions to any significant extent."

Mr. Thant complained of "misunderstanding and confusion and even resentment" in Indonesia and the Philippines because the date for formation of Malaysia had been set by its prospective members and Britain before his findings were known.

The investigation was requested Aug. 5 by Indonesia, Malaya and the Philippines after a meeting in Manila. Malaya strongly favors the formation of Malaysia.

Mr. Thant accepted the task of assessing opinion in North Borneo and Sarawak. His condition was that his conclusions be final and not subject to ratification by any of the interested parties. In his conclusions he pointed out that "there was no reference to a referendum or plebiscite in the request which was addressed to me."

He said his mission carried out its work by "consultations with the population, through the elected representatives of the people, leaders of political parties and other groups and organizations and with all persons who were willing to express their views."

Every effort was made, the Secretary General said, to ascertain the wishes of those who were detained or in exile for political reasons. In its report the mission mentioned hundreds of interviews with persons of all shades of opinion.

The conclusion was that there would have been no significant difference in recent elections if all exiles and those in detention had been able to vote in elections.

September 15, 1963

MALAYSIA'S BIRTH MARKED IN 4 LANDS

Southeast Asian Federation Asks Peace but Confronts Boycott by 2 Neighbors

By SETH S. KING
Special to The New York Times

KUALA LUMPUR, Malaysia, Monday, Sept. 16—The country of Malaysia came into being this morning with the raising of her new flag and the release of 101 white pigeons.

In a ceremony in the huge Merdeka (Freedom) Stadium, the federation of Malaya, Singapore, Sarawak and Sabah—formerly North Borneo—was completed.

Similar ceremonies were held in the three other states.

In Southeast Asia, where the British flag once flew over vast territories, Britain now retains only the colony of Hong Kong, a few islands in the Indian Ocean, and Brunei, a protectorate.

Malaysia, an anti-Communist, pro-Western grouping of 10 million people, is one of the smaller countries, in population, in this part of the world. Her armed forces are small.

Britain Pledged to Defense

But Britain, which will retain bases in Singapore and Malacca, is bound by treaty to defend Malaysia. Australia and New Zealand are also committed to come to Malaysia's aid if needed.

The releasing of the 101 pigeons—101 is considered to be an auspicious number by Malaysians—was a gesture to emphasize Malaysia's desire for peace with her neighbors, some of whom are hostile to the federation.

Indonesia, for instance, announced yesterday that she could not approve of the federation until the United Nations made certain unspecified "corrections."

Last weekend, more special forces of the Indonesian Army were flown into Kalimantan (Indonesian Borneo) to reinforce units along the Sarawak border, across which there were raids this summer by Indonesian-based "rebels."

The Philippines, which still claims North Borneo, has withheld her judgment on the federation. Neither the Indonesian nor the Philippine Ambassador was present this morning with the other diplomats and special representatives who witnessed the inaugural ceremonies.

Both left Kuala Lumpur last night for "consultations" at home.

September 16, 1963

MALAYSIA IS CAUGHT IN POWER STRUGGLE

Pressures on the New Nation Are Emphasized by The Ferocious Attacks That Greeted Its Birth

By ROBERT TRUMBULL

Special to The New York Times

HONG KONG, Sept. 21—Malaysia, the new Southeast Asian state born this week, faces a grim childhood as the object of external political contention exacerbated by Great Power rivalries and disparate internal forces pulling to Right and Left.

The new country's birth has been greeted by ferocious mob attacks on rival embassies in two capitals and hostile demonstrations in a third. These manifestations were accompanied by breaks in diplomatic relations between Malaysia and the two countries with which the new country had expected to have the closest ties, Indonesia and the Philippines.

For the immediate future, Malaysia will probably continue to be harried by guerrilla incursions from Indonesia along the new state's boundary with that country in Borneo. However, Indonesian adventurism is expected to stop short of measures that would invite war, for this would bring in British and Australian forces, pledged to defend Malaysia.

The formation of Malaysia has been bitterly opposed by Indonesia and the Philippines for localized reasons.

Also the emergence of the pro-Western federation is regarded by Communist governments as an intolerable extension of anti-Communist influence in a fluid area.

Controversial Start

The Western powers at the same time have welcomed Malaysia as a new and powerful bastion against the spread of Communism into the rich and strategic arc of Southeast Asia. These variant points of view have expanded the area of confrontation between the world's warring ideologies and have made Malaysia a political battlefield from the beginning.

What kind of country is Malaysia, that she should be the subject of such uproar in capitals far and near?

Malaysia is a place of primary economic and strategic importance. The capture of this area by the Japanese in World

MALAYSIA CRISIS AND THE THREE LEADERS INVOLVED

3 Malaysia has retaliated by breaking relations with Indonesia and Philippines.

2 Filipinos oppose the Federation because they claim North Borneo.

1 Indonesia charges Federation is a device to continue British colonial rule.

Allied with the West ● British base ⊗ U. S. base

Black Star, European, The New York Times.

Sukarno, 62, of Indonesia.　　Abdul Rahman, 60, of Malaysia　　Diosdado Macapagal, 52, of the Philippines.

War II was one reason why Americans were urged to donate their kitchen utensils to the war effort and couldn't get new tires for their cars.

It is also a fabled land of enchanting vistas and little known tropical peoples, home of the headhunting Sea Dyaks and the "wild man from Borneo" of circus fame.

As diplomats have noted, Malaysia is not really a new state but rather a new name given to the former federation of Malaya upon the addition to that sovereign member of the British Commonwealth of Nations of three satellite territories that had been British dependencies until Sept. 16 — as the eleven states of Malaya proper had also been until Merdeka (Freedom) Day on August 21, 1957.

Issue of Colonialism

This evolution of the freedom process in dependent territories has erased Western colonialism from Asia, except for the tiny British colony of Hong Kong and the even smaller Portuguese enclave of Macao on the South China coast and Portugal's half of the minuscule island of Timor in the Indonesian Archipelago.

However, neutralist Indonesia and the Communist powers have assailed Malaysia as a disguised "neo colonialist" venture prolonging Britain's presence in Southeast Asia. British military forces are to remain in Malaysia under treaty arrangement.

The new territories added to Malaya to form Malaysia are Singapore, an island at the tip of the Malay Peninsula containing a city of 1,750,000 people, mostly Chinese, and the world's fifth ranking seaport; Sabah or North Borneo, which the Philippine Republic also claims in part, and the adjacent Borneo colony of Sarawak, famed as the domain of the British Brooke family of White Rajahs from 1841 until this protectorate was ceded outright to the British Crown in 1946.

The two Borneo territories together have an area of 79,500 square miles, about the size of the state of Nebraska with Connecticut added. Much of this sprawling expanse is covered by virgin jungle and forest so thick that from an airplane window it looks like an unbroken green meadow without tracks or habitation.

But these lands are rich. They produce rubber, timber, oil, bauxite, limestone, coal, copra, tobacco, pepper, hemp, rice, fish and a little gold.

This is Malaysia's raw frontier. The Malay Peninsula itself has the most stable economy in Asia next to that of Japan. It produces a third of the world's tin and much of the world's topgrade rubber, and gives its 7,000,000 inhabitants the extraordinary (for Asia) annual income of $275 a head.

Need for Land

Most importantly, in the eyes of Communist China's hundreds of millions, under-populated Sabah and Sarawak offer the possibility of profitable settlement by a land-hungry people whose own undeveloped frontiers are climatically inhospitable and barren .

Fabulous Borneo has beckoned foreign adventurers since China opened trade with the local sultanates in the seventh century. Significant later arrivals included Magellan's fleet, the first Rajah Brooke and a British

Yardley in The Baltimore Sun
"Feeding instincts of Asian fish."

Englehardt in The St. Louis Post-Dispatch
"Baptism of fire."

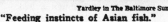

trader named Alfred Dent. Dent and an Australian, Baron Overbeck, obtained lands from the Filipino Sultan of Sulu that became British North Borneo (now Sabah). The Philippine claim to North Borneo today hinges on the validity of this deal.

Only about 1,200,000 people live in this rich and under-populated land. Most of them are animistic tribal folk like the Ibans or Sea Dyaks, whose long houses on the river banks are still decorated inside with grisly chandeliers of shrunken, smoke-blackened human heads.

Malays and Chinese

Apart from a handful of British and other Western settlers and administrators, the now indigenous population consists of Moslem Malays — whose language is spoken as a *lingua franca*—and a third of a million Chinese. The industrious Chinese, representing a fourth of the total population, hold the same overwhelmingly dominant commercial position over the natives here that they do in other tropical lands

Resentment of the prosperous, better-educated Chinese by the less advanced mass of Malays, who are outnumbered by the Chinese in Malaysia as a whole; bitterness by the Chinese against the Malays, who enjoy political preference by law; suspicion of both Chinese and Malays by the indigenous peoples and Indians; a fanatic extremist Malay Moslem element that despises everybody else; and the constant ideological struggle between Left and Right that cuts across all racial and religious groupings—these are the internal elements that imperil stable government in

Malaysia even without the interference of outsiders.

Above these clashing forces are the pro-Communist Chinese, who have a powerful political base in industrialized Singapore, and a growing anti-Government guerrilla movement in Sarawak supported by the Government of Indonesia, which is out to wreck Malaysia at any cost.

President Sukarno of Indonesia has advanced a whole complex of objections to Malaysia. He distrusts encirclement by the Western powers that want Indonesia on their side in the cold war. He is said to fear that Northern Borneo and his own borders on that island will be open to Chinese Communist penetration with a weak government in Kuala Lumpur as his neighbor; and it is suggested that he desires eventually either to incorporate Northern Borneo into Indonesia or to hold that strategic territory under Jakarta's political hegemony.

The Philippine Government has followed Dr. Sukarno's anti-Malaysian line in pursuing Manila's claim to North Borneo, or Sabah, and also out of some vaguely expressed concern that Philippine security is somehow compromised by making the near territory of Borneo part of a country that has a large Chinese population heavily infiltrated by Communists.

Savage Attack

Dr. Sukarno's deliberate unleashing of hysterical nationalism behind his aims led to the savage gutting of the British Embassy in Jakarta and almost equally ferocious attack on the Malaysian Embassy. Sympathetic demonstrations of lesser intensity were held against the British and Malaysian Embassies in Manila. A mob in Kuala Lumpur stormed the Indonesian Embassy there in retaliation. Malaysia broke off diplomatic relations with her two neighbor countries.

Many analysts, comparing

Dr. Sukarno's actions with his chauvinistic speeches flaunting Indonesia's superior military power among Southeast Asian countries (with hardware supplied mainly by the Soviet Union), have concluded that the Indonesian leader's eventual aim is to establish Jakarta's politi-

cal leadership in the entire region. This is one way he could realize a dream to make Indonesia a power of worldwide consequence.

September 22, 1963

MALAYAN REGIME WINS HEAVY VOTE

Abdul Rahman Hails Victory as Blow at Indonesia

By SETH S. KING
Special to The New York Times

KUALA LUMPUR, Malaysia, Sunday, April 26—Prime Minister Abdul Rahman's Alliance

party won a smashing victory in Malaya's elections today, taking 87 of 104 seats Malaya was allotted in the Malaysian Parliament.

With only two constituencies remaining to be counted, Prince Abdul Rahman has won a clear majority in the new Federation's lawmaking body.

The People's Action party of Singapore's Prime Minister, Lee Kuan Yew, captured only one seat, failing to win the foothold it had expected.

Prince Abdul Rahman hailed his party's victory as a mandate

to continue resisting Indonesia's efforts to "crush" Malaysia—efforts that have taken the form of guerrilla warfare on the Borneo borders of Malaysia's states of Sarawak and Sabah.

"I pray that Malaysia will continue to flourish and prosper in peace. To hell with Sukarno!" said the Prince, with a reference to Indonesia's President.

April 26, 1964

MALAYSIA UNREST RISES

Recent Racial Violence in Singapore Reflects the Internal Weaknesses Sukarno Seeks to Exploit

By SETH S. KING
Special to The New York Times

KUALA LUMPUR, Malaysia, Aug. 6—During the past two weeks, Chinese and Malay leaders in Singapore have been tirelessly trudging through the communities of their island state pleading for new cooperation between their races.

An uneasy quiet has settled over Singapore after last month's bitter fighting between Malay and Chinese residents.

But the absence of more violence has meant only a restless armistice. The scars left by the outbreaks are deep and still dangerously sensitive.

Three days ago, during one of his many tours through the city, Prime Minister Lee Kuan Yew said: "We must decide whether we want Malaysia. If we do we cannot afford a second collision because it will wreck the whole of it."

At the height of the troubles Mr. Lee sadly told an acquaintance:

"Singapore cannot legally secede from Malaysia; but it could become ungovernable."

The dynamic young Singapore-born Chinese had just lived through five days of tension and bitter communal fighting between his city-state's Chinese

majority and the Malay minority.

During those five days the other leaders of Malaysia held their breath and waited to see whether the fighting would envelop the rest of the federation.

There has been no final judgment on what touched off the riots. But their underlying cause was not questioned: Like oil and water, the new federation's Malays and Chinese have so far been unmixable.

Long-Standing Quarrel

The conditions for trouble have existed for more than a century, since the Chinese, with the blessings of the British Colonial Office, began moving in on top of the indigenous Malays.

In those 100 years there has been virtually no blending of the two peoples. They remain divided in religion, in culture and, more significantly, in economic and educational levels.

The Chinese, with their greater drive and financial cohesion, dominate Malaysia's economy. In the federation as a whole the Malays, by virtue of their slight edge in total numbers and with the general consent of Chinese businessmen, control the central Government here in Kuala Lumpur.

Each community is afraid the

other will contrive to overwhelm it. Increasing numbers of young Malays are dissatisfied with their lack of business or professional opportunities, while young Chinese are equally resentful that their talents are not being used by the Government of Malaysia.

The violence demonstrated once again how deeply the two communities distrust each other and how far Malaysia's multiracial population is from genuine unity.

Indonesia has been unable, after nearly a year, to make any significant inroads into Malaysia with the guerrilla and economic war that Jakarta is waging against the new federation.

But if Singapore's trouble spreads to other parts of Malaysia, where the climate for unrest is almost as great, this failure may not matter. The Indonesians seem now to believe that Malaysia will fall apart anyway if they will just hang on and continue their efforts to split the racial communities.

No one has expected Malaysia's early childhood to be an easy one. It has even seemed that the external pressures of Indonesia's "confrontation" helped in forcing the federation to-

Little in The Nashville Tennessean
"Hanging—"

gether in its first year.

But now the frictions of Malaysia's growing up are beginning to be felt not only in Malaysia but in Jakarta and Peking, in London and in Washington.

Indonesia has been quick to assert, especially for the benefit of the colonially sensitive countries of Africa and Asia, that the Singapore riots proved Malaysia was forced upon the people by the British.

Effects of Violence

Peking knows that its relations with Malaysia's Chinese will improve in direct proportion to the fear they have of being dominated by the Malays or surrendered by them to fellow Malays in Indonesia.

To Britain, whose thin red line of troops is Malaysia's only protection against Indonesia, the riots increased concern that fighting inside the country might become more serious than that from outside.

And to Washington it seemed for a few days that once again a Southeast Asian country was stumbling just as the United States was making a first small move toward helping it.

The effects of the violence on Malaysia's internal politics was considered just as great. The atmosphere of tension that preceded the fighting was heightened by new differences between leaders of the United Malay National Organization, the core of the coalition that governs Malaysia, and the People's Progressive party, led by Lee Kuan Yew.

Four weeks ago, while the Prime Minister, Prince Abdul Rahman, was out of the country, the more strident U.M.N.O. leaders journeyed to Singapore. There they urged the city's Malays, who make up only a sixth of the population, to boycott Mr. Lee and look to Kuala Lumpur to take care of them.

A week later Mr. Lee met with leaders of the Malay community and heard their complaints. Some he promised to answer. But he told the Malayans that free competition, not special privileges, was the only way they could hope to better themselves.

During last April's Malayan general election Mr. Lee attempted to establish his People's Progressive party as a party in Malaya. The party won only one seat, but it now has an elected foothold in Malaya.

In that April campaign Mr. Lee, who led the fight to bring Singapore into Malaysia, supported Prince Abdul Rahman's party and ran against the right-wing Chinese and leftist Socialist Front.

The People's Progressives are again organizing in Malaya. But few doubt that in the next general election in 1969 Mr. Lee will oppose the United Malayan Nationals with all his strength, which by then might be considerable.

August 9, 1964

SINGAPORE ENDS TIE OF FEDERATION WITH MALAYSIA

Prince Rahaman and Premier Lee Announce Severing of Two-Year Bond

---

BRITAIN TO KEEP BASES

Island State's Chinese and Malays of Mainland Going Own Ways as Nations

---

By Reuters

SINGAPORE, Monday, Aug. 9—The island city of Singapore today pulled out of the two-year-old Federation of Malaysia and became an independent and sovereign state.

An official announcement said an agreement to this effect was signed on Saturday by the Malaysia Prime Minister, Prince Abdul Rahman, Singapore's Premier Lee Kuan Yew, and ministers from Malaysia and Singapore.

Since her founding, Malaysia has been racked by tension between the Chinese, the largest racial community in Singapore and in the federation as a whole and the Malays, who control the Federal Government and are the second largest ethnic group in the country.

The defense of the country against the continual threat by President Sukarno of neighboring Indonesia, who has charged Malaysia was a British colonial creation to encircle Indonesia, has been a cause of tension.

Defended by British

Singapore linked up with the other former British dependencies of Malaya, Sarawak and North Borneo (now Sabah) to form the Malaysian federation on Sept. 16, 1963. Britain will keep her Singapore bases in the new accord.

Britain and the Commonwealth member nations of Australia and New Zealand have provided forces by treaty for Malaysia's and Singapore's defense against Indonesian guerrillas.

Premier Lee called attention to this factor in a press conference after the announcement of his country's secession.

Mr. Lee's first comment to foreign correspondents was that Singapore's separation was not the end but merely the beginning.

The Premier said he had already sent messages to world leaders, including the British, Australian and New Zealand Prime Ministers and the leaders of India, Egypt and Cambodia. [The Indonesian Consul General in Hong Kong said his country had "expected" the Singapore developments.]

The eight-article agreement announcing Singapore's withdrawal from the Federation said:

"Fresh arrangements should be made for the order and good Government of the territories comprised in Malaysia by the separation of Singapore and Malaysia.

"Singapore shall become an independent and sovereign state and nation, separate from and independent of Malaysia, and so recognized by the Government of Malaysia."

The agreement said that the Malaysian and Singapore Governments would enter into a treaty on external defense and mutual assistance.

They would establish a Joint Defense Council and the Malaysian Government would give Singapore assistance as may be considered reasonable and adequate for external defense.

Singapore will give the Malaysian Government the right to continue to maintain the bases and other facilities used by its military forces in Singapore and will allow Malaysia to use these bases and facilities as the Malaysian Government may consider necessary, the agreement said.

Each party would undertake

The New York Times Aug. 9, 1965

Singapore (cross) withdrew as part of Malaysia.

not to enter into any treaty or agreement with a foreign country which might be detrimental to the independence and defense of the territory of the other party.

British Bases to Continue

Britain will be able to continue using her extensive military bases in Singapore despite the island's withdrawal from the Malaysian federation, according to the text of a bill printed in the Singapore Government Gazette.

The bill was expected to be passed in the Singapore Parliament today. It states that Singapore will permit Britain to make use of these bases and facilities as long as Britain considers them necessary to defend Singapore and Malaysia, for Commonwealth defense and for the preservation of peace in Southeast Asia.

The Malaysian Federation has been engaged in an undeclared war with Indonesia, whose President Sukarno has repeatedly vowed to crush the state.

The formation of the Federation of Malaysia was actually postponed from Sept. 1 to Sept. 16, 1963 while Prince Abdul Rahman and the British, Philippine and Japanese Governments and the United Nations tried, unsuccessfully, to obtain President Sukarno's acceptance of the new country. The Malaysian Borneo states of Sarawak and Sabah, bordering Indonesia Kalimantan, have been sensitive frontiers.

British and other Commonwealth troops have been aiding Malaysian security forces to counter landings by Indonesian infiltrators.

Last month, Malaysian authorities reported having intercepted junks carrying Indonesians intending to blow up Singapore harbor.

Singapore, an island off the southern extremity of the Malay Peninsula, became an internally self-governing state within the British Commonwealth in 1958. The island port was founded by Sir Stamford Raffles in 1819.

Singapore is predominantly Chinese and in May this year a dispute flared between the parties led by Mr. Lee—himself of Chinese origin—and Prince Rahman over the preferential treatment given by statute to the Federation's indigenous Malays.

Malays make up 40 per cent of the Federation's total population — slightly less than the Chinese. In Singapore there are an estimated 254,000 Malays with 1,350,000 Chinese.

In the Malaysian capital of Kuala Lumpur, Prime Minister Rahman told the opening session of the Parliament this morning that the announcement of Singapore's secession was the "most painful and heartbreaking" in his leadership of the nation.

Prince Rahman said that since the formation of Malaysia two years ago and particularly in the last 12 months, the Central Government had had many differences with the Singapore Government.

"There is no other solution except the course of action I am going to take," Prince Rahman said.

"We feel that the only solution is to allow Singapore to break away from the Federation and go its own way and leave us in the rest of Malaysia alone."

People in Singapore gathered around radio sets in coffee shops and other public places this morning to listen to the government announcements and government announcements.

In the Geylong-Serai area, predominantly Malay, there was intensive police patrolling.

Geylong-Serai, which is four miles from the center of the city, was the scene of racial riots last year in which more than 20 people were killed and several hundred injured.

August 9, 1965

Indonesia-Malaysia Pact Signed; Borneo States Will Vote on Tie

JAKARTA, Indonesia, Thursday, Aug. 11 (Reuters)—Indonesia and Malaysia signed a peace agreement here today, formally ending the undeclared war of the last three and a half years.

The treaty, which brought about normal relations between the two countries after hostilities that claimed at least 500 lives, was signed by the Indonesian Foreign Minister, Adam Malik, and Malaysia's Deputy Premier, Prince Abdul Razak.

The pact said the Malaysian Government agreed to give the people of Sarawak and Sabah on the island of Borneo a chance to reaffirm as soon as possible their position in the Malaysian federation through independent and democratic general elections.

Diplomatic relations are to be established at once and diplomatic representations be set up as soon as possible under the agreement.

Policy of Hostility Ended

When the Malaysian federation was established on Sept. 16, 1963, Indonesia refused to grant it diplomatic recognition. President Sukarno of Indonesia charged that Malaysia, uniting the former British possessions of Malay, the two Borneo territories and, until 1965, Singapore, was a neocolonialist creation designed to perpetuate British influence in the area.

Mr. Sukarno then initiated a policy of "confrontation," which led to armed clashes not only in Borneo but also on the Malayan peninsula when Indonesian soldiers attempted landings.

Jakarta's policy underwent a profound change, however, after the army became predominate in Indonesian affairs following a Communist-led attempted coup d'état last October, which the army put down.

The present Government, in which Mr. Sukarno still holds the Presidency but Lieut. Gen. Suharto holds the power, has sought an accommodation with Malaysia as part of a broad program to return the country to economic stability.

August 11, 1966

---

2 ALLIES PROMISE MALAYSIA TROOPS

Australia and New Zealand Will Keep Forces There and in Singapore After '71

By ROBERT TRUMBULL
Special to The New York Times

WELLINGTON, New Zealand, Feb. 25—In a major policy decision affecting Southeast Asia and the Pacific area, Australia and New Zealand announced tonight that they would maintain military forces in Malaysia and Singapore after the withdrawal of British defenses there in 1971.

The commitment by the two Governments, though relatively small in terms of the weapons and manpower to be deployed, is viewed in Wellington and Canberra as far-reaching and new in the defense concepts for the region.

"It is obvious that a fundamental change in the framework of our operations in Southeast Asia is taking place," Prime Minister Keith J. Holyoake of New Zealand declared in a speech announcing the decision to the Parliament here.

The decision "has great significance for New Zealand's future policy and role" in the area, he added.

Prime Minister John G. Gorton of Australia, disclosing the plan to the Parliament in Canberra, added that his Government favored augmenting military measures with efforts to promote "a nonaggression pact or pacts" among Southeast Asian countries to advance regional stability.

In the background of the two announcements, which were made at approximately the same time in the two capitals, was the reliance of both countries upon the protection guaranteed by the United States through the Anzus—Australia, New Zealand, United States—Treaty.

A possible American involvement in Canberra's thinking on Southeast Asian defense was strongly hinted by Mr. Gorton.

The Prime Minister declared that Australia would seek the support of "outside powers" if a situation arose in which Malaysia and Singapore needed help beyond Australia's resources.

Also implicit in the new Australian and New Zealand posture was the confidence here and in Canberra, encouraged by London, that Britain will retain a military obligation to Malaysia and Singapore even after the departure of British forces from the scene.

The New York Times   Feb. 26, 1969
Australia and New Zealand will keep military forces in Malaysia and Singapore.

More detailed agreements for a multilateral defense of Malaysia and Singapore, involving Britain, are expected to be adopted at a meeting of the five states in Canberra June 19 and 20.

The British Government, under financial strain, has decided to reduce sharply its commitments "East of Suez" and will withdraw its military forces in Southeast Asia by the end of 1971. But London has indicated that an attack upon the weak Southeast Asian states could result in the swift deployment of British forces from halfway around the world by air. The feasibility of such a reaction has been tested in demonstration flights.

"We are not attempting, and we cannot attempt, to do what Britain has done," Mr. Holyoake declared, adding that his Government was "ready to accept a military role consistent with our size and resources."

The two Prime Ministers pledged their Governments to retain forces in Malaysia and Singapore at least equal to those now stationed there. These consist of two infantry companies from New Zealand and a battalion of ground troops from Australia, two Australian air force jet fighter squadrons, some New Zealand support aircraft and a few light naval vessels from each country.

Under the arrangement outlined, the Australian and New Zealand infantry will form a joint "Anzuk" force based in Singapore but with elements rotating to Malaysia. Where the air and naval components will be stationed permanently was left for later decision.

February 26, 1969

At Least 20 Killed, Many Hurt In Racial Clashes in Malaysia

By Reuters
KUALA LUMPUR, Malaysia, Wednesday, May 14 (Reuters)—At least 20 persons were killed and 60 injured in violent racial riots between Chinese and Malays in Kuala Lumpur last night and today. Unconfirmed reports put the death toll at 50.

The army was called out last night, and as dawn broke troops and policemen appeared in control. But they were still chasing groups of rioters in some areas despite a 24-hour curfew imposed on the capital and on Selangor state, in which Kuala Lumpur is situated.

The crisis was touched off yesterday when the Malaysian Chinese Association announced it would no longer participate in the coalition Cabinet of Prime Minister Abdul Rahman. This meant that there would be no Chinese in the Government for the first time since the Federation of Malaysia was formed in 1963.

The Malaysian Chinese Association is one of three components of the ruling Alliance party, whose majority was cut in general elections last Saturday. The Chinese group had lost heavily in the elections.

The Alliance's other components — the United Malays National Organization and the Malaysian Indian Congress — represent the country's Malays and Indians, respectively.

About one-third of the population of 10 million is Chinese and a little more than half is Malay. There are numerous other smaller racial groups, including a million Indians.

Rumors that there would be trouble yesterday grew after jeering supporters of largely Chinese opposition parties marched through Malay areas Monday night.

There were reports that Malay supporters of the United

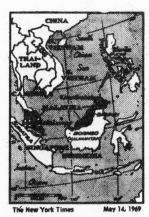

The New York Times   May 14, 1969

Malays National Organization intended to stage a demonstration calling for more guarantees of Malay rights.

Curfew Not Effective

Policemen and soldiers were attacked in various sections of the capital. They were reported to have orders to shoot if necessary.

The Prime Minister made a television and radio appeal for calm and said he was prepared to declare a state of emergency throughout the country if necessary. Mr. Rahman blamed opposition groups for the violence. He suggested setting up multiracial committees to try and restore order.

Fighting last night appeared to be concentrated in the Malay areas of Kuala Lumpur. Witnesses said cars and buses were overturned and set ablaze.

The last racial clashes in Malaysia occurred on the island of Penang and in northeast Malaya at the end of November, 1967.

Singapore, whose population of two million is predominantly Chinese, joined with three former British colonies — Malaya, Sabah and Sarawak — to form the Federation of Malaysia in 1963. It withdrew in 1965.

May 14, 1969

BURMESE NEUTRALITY

BURMA TO REFUSE U. S. AID AFTER JUNE

Action Follows Protests in U. N. on Chiang Guerrillas—

By The Associated Press.

RANGOON, Burma, March 28 —The Burmese Government, involved in guerrilla warfare with Chinese troops who claim allegiance to Generalissimo Chiang Kai-shek, announced tonight it was dropping United States aid next June 30.

Burma has received $12,000,000 in United States aid since June, 1950, and the total will reach $31,-000,000 by next June under present appropriations.

Neither the Burmese Foreign Office nor the United States Embassy officials would comment on the move. The Foreign Office said a note was delivered to United States Ambassador William Sebald on March 17. The note, signed by Burmese Foreign Minister Sao Hkun Hkio, said:

"I am to request, under Article 5 of the Economic Cooperation Agreement between our two Governments, that the Government of the United States will take note that we do not desire the aid program to continue beyond June, 1953."

Grateful for Assistance

The note expressed appreciation and gratitude for materials and services received by the Burmese Government under the Economic Cooperation Administration, "which have been of great help in implementing rehabilitation programs." It added:

"The Government of Burma wishes to make it clear that this action is not intended in any way to cast a reflection on existing programs nor on the activities of E. C. A. personnel in Burma."

There has been some rise in anti-American feeling here recently. The chief issue in Burma today is the presence of 12,000 Nationalist Chinese guerrillas within her borders. Burma charged in a note to the United Nations this week that these survivors of the war against Communist China are aggressors against Burma. Help was asked to oust them.

Despite United States protestations of innocence, the Burmese charge that the irregulars are supplied with United States weapons. And they dislike the American policy of equipping Generalissimo Chiang's forces on Formosa.

March 29, 1953

CHINESE BACK PLAN ON BURMA OUSTER

4-Nation Parley Reaches Full Accord on the Evacuation —Ratification Awaited

By TILLMAN DURDIN
Special to THE NEW YORK TIMES.

BANGKOK, Thailand, June 22— Full agreement between the representatives of the United States, Thailand, Nationalist China and Burma on procedures for evacuating Nationalist Chinese troops from Burma was announced here today by Edwin F. Stanton, United States Ambassador.

Delegates from the four countries have been meeting here for the last four weeks to consider ways and means of transferring to Formosa the Nationalist forces that retreated into Burma in 1950 from Yunnan in the face of the Communist Chinese occupation of Southwest China.

The evacuation plan as announced here today provides for Chinese troops in northern Burma to concentrate by designated routes at Myitkyina and Lashio and to be flown from airstrips at these points into Thailand for transport to Formosa.

The main Chinese forces, which are in eastern Burma around Monghsat, would march into a safety zone in the Thai-Burmese border at Tachilek and from there would cross into Thailand overland for transport to Formosa.

Small bands in the far south of Burma would be moved to the nearest transport point and thence by air to either Bangkok or Chi-engmai, before departing for Formosa.

In announcing the results of the conference, Ambassador Stanton said the evacuation plan still had to be formally approved by the Governments concerned, but this was expected without delay.

Mr. Stanton called the plan the "first essential step" in getting the Nationalists removed from Burma in accordance with United Nations April resolution that resulted from the Burmese appeal against the presence of the Chinese.

He praised the "goodwill, industry and conscientiousness" displayed by the delegates and said he had been particularly impressed by the sincerity and spirit of cooperation demonstrated by Col. Aung Gyi, chief Burmese representative and Col. I Fu-teh, chief Chinese representative.

June 23, 1953

Burma Forms New State As Karen Rebels Dwindle

The New York Times   June 2, 1954

RANGOON, Burma, June 1 (Reuters) — Dwindling resistance among Burma's Karen rebels today brought about the formal proclamation of a new state covering about 1,800 square miles of northern Tenasserim in East Burma.

President Ba U of Burma transferred local administrative powers to the government of the new state of Karen [cross on map], which had been on paper since the 1947 constitution, at a ceremony here.

Until now, guerrilla activity in the East Burma region where most of the Karens live had prevented the state government taking over three sub-districts responsible to the central administration.

The remaining guerrillas, which are said to number 3,000, are mainly concentrated around the Karen capital of Papun, which eventually is expected to become the capital of the new state. The area is held by scattered bands of Karens operating against the Government with Communist guerrillas.

June 2, 1954

RED GAINS ALARM BURMESE REGIME

Communists Increase Seats From 12 to 42 in Vote

By ROBERT ALDEN
Special to The New York Times.

RANGOON, Burma, May 3— The Communists have more than tripled their representation in Parliament, and the Government of Burma is alarmed.

With returns from last week's elections still coming in, the Communists have won forty-two seats.

The Communist National United Front has emerged as the leading party of opposition to U Nu's Anti-Fascist Peoples Freedom League.

While the league still remains firmly in control of the Government, the Communists' representation is the most formidable parliamentary Opposition in Burma's eight-year history as n independent nation.

Premier Nu yesterday ascribed the Communist success mainly to outright intimidation of voters.

Premier Nu also explained that in the villages there was some dislike of local league leaders who had a high-handed manner in dealing with the people.

He denied that the Communists had gained so many parliamentary seats because communism was becoming increasingly popular or because the people did not like the national program of the Socialist-oriented league.

Whatever the reason, the Communists received 30 per cent of the vote in the 127 districts where they ran candidates.

In the previous Parliament, the Communists held only twelve seats. Observers here had expected them to lose rather than gain seats in the new Parliament.

May 4, 1956

BURMESE TROOPS FACE RED CHINESE TO HALT INVASION

Clashes With Peiping Forces Reported—Negotiations for Withdrawal Under Way

By The Associated Press.

RANGOON, Burma, July 31— Military sources said tonight Chinese Communist troops had occupied about 1,000 square miles of Burma's northern territory after clashes with Burmese forces. Some casualties were reported.

Burma's Government said it was "seriously concerned" about the border area developments. A Foreign Office statement, confirming reports that Red Chinese troops had established outposts in northeast Burma, said the Government had brought the matter to the attention of the Chinese Communist Government in Peiping.

"Negotiations are now in progress with a view to the withdrawal of these Chinese troops to the Chinese side of the border," the Foreign Office said.

August 1, 1956

Burmese Premier Says Chinese Will Withdraw

RANGOON, Burma, Oct. 2 (UP)—Communist China has agreed to withdraw its troops from Burma, U Ba Swe, Burmese Premier, said today.

He announced that Chinese forces that had infiltrated the ill-defined border area of northern Burma in the last two years would be withdrawn to the border line defined in 1941. The demarcation was made in a treaty between the British authorities in Burma and the Chiang Kai-chek regime in China.

Burma's premier told newsmen there had been "a definite improvement" in the border situation since Burma and China had started negotiations on the problem. He said Burmese forces recently searched the border area of Burma's Kachin state and found no Chinese troops.

U Nu, former Burmese Premier, will make a private visit to China later this month and Chinese Premier Chou En-lai is scheduled to come here in December to discuss the border issue.

October 3, 1956

ARMY TAKES OVER POWER IN BURMA TO THWART REDS

Commander Accepts Bid of Premier to Govern Nation —Elections Postponed

By The Associated Press.

RANGOON, Burma, Sept. 26 —The army seized power to-night in Burma. Gen. Ne Win, Commander in Chief of the armed forces, was asked by Premier Nu to head a new Government and he agreed.

The bloodless coup apparently was designed to prevent Burma's shaky Government from drifting into Communist hands.

Premier Nu announced the action and said Gen. Ne Win had agreed to hold general elections before April 30.

Appealing to the people to support the general, U Nu said in a nation-wide broadcast:

"We intended to hold general elections in November this year, but we came to realize that the general elections to be held in November could not be free and fair. I invited Gen. Ne Win to make arrangements essential for holding such free elections within six months. I am glad to say Ne Win has accepted my invitation."

Nu to Resign Oct. 28

In a letter to the general, U Nu said he would advise President Win Maung to summon Parliament to meet Oct. 28, at which time U Nu would resign and Gen. Ne Win would be named Premier.

In his reply, the general promised to follow a neutralist policy in foreign affairs.

The army apparently took over without incident.

The well-organized operation put troops in control of all the

Act Against Reds

Premier Nu

major cities and towns in this Southeast Asian republic, which has a 1,500-mile border with Communist China.

The army said it was acting to preserve democracy and law and order. It said it wanted to end the political strife that had produced most of the growing pains in Burma since the British granted independence ten years ago.

Army leaders said a political group had been building up secret arms stocks to wipe out all opposition and take over the country. Army intelligence leaders said the Communists were preparing to help the plotters, who were not named.

Obviously unhappy with the political intrigue that has split the party of Premier Nu, a neutralist, into pro-Western and neutralist camps, army leaders reportedly had issued an ultimatum to both factions.

They were said to have warned the party, the Anti-Fascist People's Freedom League, that they would not stand by and let any political group take power by force. But they also promised that the army would relinquish power to any Government that could keep Burma stable and guarantee the nation's security.

These were the political events behind the coup:

Early in the year a split developed in the People's Freedom League between U Nu's backers and those of former Deputy Premiers Ba Swe and Kyan Nyein. Both are Socialists like U Nu, but bitter anti-Communists.

In June, U Nu released two Communist members of Parliament from jail so he could have their votes for a confidence motion that he won by eight votes. The anti-Communist dissidents then voted to expel U Nu from the party, but the expulsion did not stick.

In July the Communists announced the end of their ten-year-old jungle war against the Government. Their People's Comrade party was legalized Aug. 15.

Two days later the party proclaimed that its goal was a revolution leading to "the creation of a Communist world."

The split in his own party deepened, and U Nu canceled the Aug. 28 session of Parliament with a view toward calling elections in the fall or winter. No party appeared strong enough, however, to gain a firm enough majority for stable government.

Despite the Communists' vow to lay down their arms, the rebellion continued to hold the nation in a state of near-civil war. For the last two days an uneasy tension hung over the capital amid rumors of a planned army coup. The rumors gathered strength as the army, in a lightning move late last night, took over key points in the city, including Rangoon's Mingaladon Airport.

Soldiers in full battle dress rapidly spread through the city and suburbs. In downtown Rangoon, the army, military police and civil police searched all vehicles for arms.

The army took over the police building in Insein, twelve miles from here, with its powerful radio transmitters.

Gen. Ne Win, 48 years old, is a stanch anti-Communist. He has been quoted as insisting that "we must fight the Reds tooth and nail."

He visited the United States last year for medical treatment. While in Washington, he conferred with military and defense officials.

As Commander in Chief, he has headed an army of 60,000 to 80,000 men. He was Deputy Premier in 1950.

The New York Times   Sept. 27, 1958

Burma (cross hatching), where Army seized power from shaky Government.

Plagued by Strife

Since it became independent of Britain in 1948, Burma has been plagued by internal strife. The most important revolt was by the Communists. Fortunately for the Government, however, they were split into two factions that could not unite.

Other dissident groups, such as the Shans and the Kachins in the hills of the east and north, did not want alien control of Burma. But they did want their traditional identities respected by the Burmans.

Burma is made up of a number of diverse areas. The Government has tried to pull them together into one effective state without violating the spirit of self-determination and local autonomy.

In 1957, eight different insurrections were in progress. Murder, robbery and rape were commonplace. Highways, railroads and river transport were not safe.

Last July there were reports that the majority of jungle insurgent groups were willing to accept amnesty terms.

The strength of the insurgents, including Communists, was estimated at about 10,000. The Burmese Army was said to number 75,000 troops.

Burma lies on the eastern side of the Bay of Bengal. It borders on India, China, East Pakistan, Laos and Thailand. It is almost as large as Texas and has a population of 20,000,000.

September 27, 1958

BURMA SHAKEN UP BY REFORM DRIVE

Ne Win Regime, Acting Fast, Is Cleaning Up Public Life —Red Fronts Curbed

By TILLMAN DURDIN
Special to The New York Times.

RANGOON, Burma, March 7

—Reform has swept over Burma with dramatic swiftness under the new regime of Gen. Ne Win, commander of the armed forces. Many foreign residents here say they have never seen anything like it in this slow-moving part of the world.

Sparked by the general's drive and a "let's do it now" attitude of a group of army colonels, the military-civilian administration has wrought changes few would have thought possible when the Government took power last October.

Rangoon and other cities

have been cleaned and repainted. Their residents have been jolted into a new spirit of industriousness and civic duty. A crackdown on official corruption has been carried out and arrests have ranged as high as a former Minister of Agriculture.

Scores of agents and collaborators of the Communists and other rebel groups who formerly managed to operate above ground with impunity have been picked up. A Communist-front Rangoon newspaper has been closed and its operators have

been jailed.

Palm-fringed little Coco Island, off the south coast, has been turned into a prison camp. More than 200 offenders against national security laws, including several Assembly Deputies and scores of members of the Communist-oriented National United Front, are being kept there under indefinite detention.

Fresh Spirit Injected

A fresh spirit has been injected into military operations against Communist, Karen and other rebel bands. Inspired by

255

new confidence, villagers are cooperating more boldly with the army with the result that zones of security are steadily expanding.

Railway services have been reorganized and a new overnight express runs between Rangoon and Mandalay in defiance of guerrilla raids.

A drastic clean-up has been carried out in business, with scores of companies blacklisted for long-standing failure to repay political patronage loans

from Government agencies. Hundreds of other small concerns that were fronts for speculation in import licenses have been closed.

Indian and Chinese traders who have transgressed foreign exchange and other economic controls have been peremptorily deported. Decrees against high profits and hoarding have reduced the cost of living 25 per cent since November.

In Rangoon new buildings are going up, streets are being

paved, shrubbery cut and slovenly squatters' shacks cleared. New parks are being opened, bus services improved and war ruins torn down.

Almost Everyone Pleased

The startling changes seem to please almost everyone. However, the new regime is heading into rough, uncertain weather in some aspects of its activities.

General Ne Win was named Premier in October after he had

led the army in a bloodless seizure of power.

Since he was not an Assembly Deputy, his tenure was limited by constitution provision that no one not a member of Parliament could be a minister of government for longer than six months.

March 8, 1959

BURMA TELLS U. S. SHE WILL ACCEPT $37,000,000 GIFT

Reverses Six-Year Refusal to Take Grants—Highway and College Aid Planned

---

SHIFT LINKED TO TIBET

By DANA ADAMS SCHMIDT
Special to The New York Times.

WASHINGTON, July 6— The United States announced today that it was willing to give Burma—and Burma was willing

to receive—up to $37,000,000 in economic assistance in the next four years.

This meant Burma had reversed her six-year-long refusal to accept aid as a gift from the United States. She asked the United States to suspend all aid in 1953 after it had been charged that Chinese Nationalist guerrillas in northern Burma had received American support.

Both the State Department and the Burmese Embassy here declined to say today that the reversal represented a change in Burma's neutralist foreign policy.

Aid Requested in April

United States officials noted, however, that the Burmese Government had requested the aid last April, just after Communist China began a drastic repression of the uprising in Tibet. The ferocity of Communist

China's measures against the Tibetans has turned sentiment against Peiping in much of Asia.

The Premier of Burma, Gen. Ne Win, seized power last September in a bloodless coup aimed at thwarting Communists and preventing violence between rival factions of the Anti-Fascist People's Freedom League, which had been the ruling party.

He succeeded U Nu, who was Premier when Burma asked suspension of United States aid.

The State Department said the United States grant would be used to build a highway from Rangoon, the nation's major port, to central Burma and dormitory-classroom facilities at the University of Rangoon.

July 7, 1959

RED CHINESE SIGN PACT WITH BURMA

Nonaggression Treaty and Accord on Border Dispute Are Concluded Jointly

---

Special to The New York Times.

HONG KONG, Jan. 28—Communist China and Burma signed a treaty of friendship and mutual nonaggression and a border agreement today.

The ceremony took place in Peiping. Premier Chou En-lai signed for China and Premier Ne Win for Burma. The Chinese head of state, Liu Shao-chi, attended.

Reporting this tonight, the

Chinese news agency Hsinhua also released the text of a joint communiqué.

The communiqué said Mr. Chou and General Ne Win, who has been visiting China since last Sunday, held a "free and frank discussion on matters of common concern to the two countries."

Also taking part in the talks were the foreign ministers of the two countries, Marshal Chen Yi of China and U Chan Tung Aung of Burma.

The communiqué said the treaty and the border agreement would be published on General Ne Win's return to Burma. He is leaving tomorrow.

The communique said the "two Premiers reviewed with satisfaction the remarkable advance made in recent years in friendly relations between China and Burma."

It said the "Premiers pledged that the two Governments will

ceaselessly strengthen friendly cooperation between their two countries and continue to make joint contributions to the promotion of solidarity among Asian and African countries and safeguarding of Asian and world peace."

Burma has long wanted to see her border with China clearly defined. Observers here said it appeared that Burma had obtained a border agreement in exchange for the nonaggression treaty.

This would represent a turnabout in Burmese policy. Early last year a Burmese Government source said privately that China had offered concessions on the border question in return for a nonaggression pact, but that Burma had rejected this.

The reason for this change appears to be General Ne Win's desire to settle the question before he steps down next month, when an election will return the

country's political leaders to power.

The main border areas in dispute are three villages and two pockets of land.

One of the pockets is the Namwan tract leased in perpetuity from China by the British when they ruled Burma. The other is in the Wa area. China claims three villages and has suggested a trade of the Namwan tract for the Wa enclave.

Burma has been less interested in dickering over these areas than in getting a defined border, which would leave Chinese troops with no excuse for their frequent incursions into Burma.

Speaking at a farewell banquet tonight General Ne Win hailed the agreement as a "tribute to the statesmanship of both our Governments."

January 29, 1960

ARMY'S INFLUENCE A BURMA PROBLEM

By TILLMAN DURDIN
Special to The New York Times.

RANGOON, Burma, Feb. 10 — One big problem that the

civil government will face when it takes over in Burma in April is that of adjusting its relations with the military forces.

The armed services have penetrated widely into the administrative and economic affairs of the country since Gen. Ne Win, commander of the armed forces, took over the Government fif-

teen months ago. It was to hand over control to a civil government that elections were held Saturday.

Some thirty military officers have held important positions in the civil administration and have largely controlled all important governmental activities. They have run the port and city

of Rangoon, Burma's railways, the marketing board that collects and sells Burma's huge rice crop and the agency that handles production and marketing of teak and other timbers.

Many Tasks Unfinished

In many instances the military administrators have reorganized civil departments to improve efficiency. Some of them are known to regard their jobs as unfinished. They would like to continue in charge until they have carried out the programs now under way.

Rangoon's city manager, Col. Tun Sein, for example, has plans to shift tens of thousands of persons from squatters' shacks in the city to the suburbs. He has already moved 160,000 from the congested slum areas. The colonel has also undertaken the rehabilitation of the port of Rangoon and he would like to complete that job.

U Nu, former Premier who will form the new Government, must decide whether to collaborate with the military administrators or face a disagreement that could make his position difficult.

One of his most difficult decisions will concern the business operations of the Defense Services Institute. The institute formerly provided commodities and services to members of the armed forces but in the last fifteen months it has undertaken large-scale enterprises.

It runs retail shops, provides banking and shipping services, operates a bus company, a radio assembly plant and a construction company, manages hotels and imports coal. These enterprises have had the advantage of such Government favors as import licenses, credit facilities and contracts for Government business.

Private business men complain they are unable to compete with the institute's enterprises.

Other economic problems face U Nu. For four months Gen. Ne Win has turned down all foreign assistance projects on the ground that his caretaker Government should not get involved in foreign-financed endeavors that would extend into the life of the new Government.

As a result more than $1,000,-000 in United Nations aid projects and proposals from other agencies are being held up.

A recent regulation by the Ne Win Government bars foreign nationals from acting as importing agents of foreign products. This threatens to put some of the few remaining British concerns in Burma out of business.

Gen. Ne Win is reported to want to get his officers back to military affairs. This may simplify the new Government's problem.

February 11, 1960

ARMY SUSPENDS BURMA CHARTER

Ne Win Invokes Martial Law —Some Officials Freed

RANGOON, Burma, March 3 (UPI) — Gen. Ne Win, who seized power early yesterday in a coup d'état aimed at halting Burma's apparent drift toward the Left, suspended the Constitution today and dissolved Parliament, putting the nation under military rule.

There was no formal declaration of martial law. However, General Ne Win's actions gave his seventeen-man Revolutionary Council and his cabinet of high-ranking officers the freedom to act as they saw fit.

There was no sign of opposition against General Ne Win, a stanchly anti-Communist career soldier who forced Premier Nu out of office once before. Many political leaders applauded the general's actions and the public generally voiced support.

General Ne Win seized power in a pre-dawn coup. One person was killed when his troops surrounded the homes of U Nu and other leaders and arrested them

A total of fifty-two officials were arrested yesterday but seven were released today. Army headquarters said the other officials were being held "in a secure place and being well looked after."

March 4, 1962

15 DEAD IN BURMA IN STUDENTS' RIOT

Special to The New York Times.

RANGOON, Burma, July 8— Burmese troops fired on rioting students at the Rangoon University campus last night, killing fifteen persons and wounding twenty-seven.

The students were protesting what they termed "oppressive" new dormitory regulations. The casualties included students and onlookers.

Today military authorities blew up the Students Union building. The Government closed the university and ordered all students to go home.

Officials said the riot had been provoked by political agitators, especially a Communist underground, that had used the Student Union building to maintain contact with pro-Communist students.

Gen. Ne Win, chairman of the Revolutionary Council, which took power in Burma after a military coup d'état in March, said in a broadcast that his Government was determined to end disorder in Burma.

July 9, 1962

DISTRUST OF WEST GROWS IN BURMA

Ne Win Seeks to Eliminate All Foreign Influences

RANGOON, Burma, April 18 (AP)—The friendly face that neutralist Burma once turned toward the West is reflecting doubt and suspicion now.

The Burmese strong man, Premier Ne Win, is systematically seeking to eliminate all foreign influences within the country, but the West is being hurt the most.

General Ne Win's most recent move was to ban all foreign embassies from showing propaganda films outside Rangoon. The distribution of foreign - language publications printed outside Burma also has been forbidden.

Earlier this year, General Ne Win virtually eliminated foreign business interests through a nationalization program.

Burma has a 1,200-mile frontier with Communist China which, diplomats here say, compels her to tread a careful neutralist path in foreign affairs.

But the diplomats fear that the Premier, trying hard to unite his country after 14 stormy years of independence, may use the bogy of an imperialistic West to bring this about. He feels he can afford to upset the West but not China

Submarine Sighting Reported

A few days ago General Ne Win said that a foreign submarine had been seen off Burma's Mergui Archipelago in the Andaman Sea, and suggested that this was an attempt by a foreign power to undermine Burma's position. There was amusement here at the importance General Ne Win placed on this alleged happening, but everyone knew the charge was leveled at the West.

Burma tended to be oriented toward the West after Britain granted her independence in 1948. However, with the rise of the Southeast Asian Treaty Organization, which has its headquarters in neighboring Thailand, Burmese leaders have tended to become more suspicious of foreigners.

The Chinese Communists have been playing a careful role with Burma over the years, culminating in the signing of a border agreement beneficial to Burma in 1961.

April 19, 1963

BURMA IS CURBING REDS' INFLUENCE

Political Steps Accompany New Antiguerrilla Drive

RANGOON, Burma, Sept. 19 (AP)—Burma's military Government is moving to diminish Communist influence. With Communist China on the other side of the northeastern border, General Ne Win apparently intends to keep the Communist presence under firm control.

In the past it was mostly Western influence that suffered.

Two big American philanthropic organizations — the Ford and Asia Foundations—were forced to leave. Activities of the United States Information Service were suspended, and an $84 million American-financed highway project was scrapped. Travel by state-sponsored scholars to Western countries slowed to a trickle, and Western correspondents were virtually barred.

The pendulum seems to have swung the other way with these developments:

¶The Government has begun intensive military operations against Communist guerrillas in a determined drive to end a violent 15-year-old war.

¶A long manifesto has been issued, emphatically denying that General Ne Win's socialist-oriented regime is pro-Communist.

¶The editor of a widely circulated leftist daily, The Mirror, was arrested and his newspaper taken over by the Government.

¶Another left-wing paper, Botataung, which had editorially cheered the Government's widespread nationalization of trade and industry, was also placed under Government control.

On the military front, Communists have been kept on the run by repeated Government thrusts that have carried the fight to the Communist high command's threshold in the hills of central Burma.

The Government is known to be accepting United States military aid, although the details have not been disclosed.

Chinese Communists in Burma can no longer depend on loans from Chinese banks, which have been nationalized with Western financial houses.

Most Chinese loans were channeled into expanding influence over the country's economy.

Communist-run schools are no longer permitted to offer indoctrination courses but must follow a rigid curriculum set down by education officials.

General Ne Win has clearly embarked on a delicate balancing act between East and West, aimed at keeping Burma out of Southeast Asia's power struggle.

Deteriorating domestic conditions seem to have stiffened the Government's resolve to isolate Burma from international affairs while her leaders focus on domestic reforms.

September 20, 1964

Burma Makes Her Neutralism Stick

By HARRISON E. SALISBURY

Four years ago, when General Ne Win seized power in Rangoon, expropriated all businesses, curtailed U.S. aid, ended tourism and barred American reporters, Washington tabbed him as a dangerous neutralist and potential Communist stooge.

This week he has been feted in Washington, conferred privately with President Johnson and has been hailed as creating a model Asian state, independent in its foreign policy and dedicated to the true interests of the Burman people.

The contrast between the American attitude today and that in 1962 when General Ne Win and his military associates ousted Premier U Nu could hardly be more complete.

Equally Dramatic

On the Burmese side, there has been an equally dramatic change.

In his first months and years in power, General Ne Win pursued a course so studiously and calculatedly neutral that he permitted neither himself nor his country even the most cursory contacts with the great powers locked in the East-West conflict. The American Ambassador went for months without being received by Ne Win.

What lies behind these radical shifts?

The short answer is: mutual reappraisal and a determination by both sides to understand the other's position and policy.

On the American side, there has come about a slow but frank recognition that when General Ne Win says he is neutral he really means it. He is neutral to all sides, not neutral leaning in one direction as was long feared.

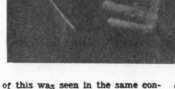

VISITOR: Burma's General Ne Win (right) is greeted by U.N.'s U Thant, a countryman, on arrival in U.S. last week. Ne Win later visited President Johnson.

When Ne Win embarked on across-the-board expropriation of private business, banking, commerce, trade and industry, the State Department feared this was a preliminary toward creating a quasi-Communist state in Burma. It was thought that by cutting back U.S. aid programs, Ne Win was opening the way to bringing in Chinese or Russian influence or both. His suppression of democratic processes, his censorship of the once lively Burmese press, his ban on foreign correspondents, his abrupt end to foreign tourism—all of this was seen in the same context.

Ne Win, it was contended in Washington, had started Burma on a path toward closer and closer association with China and the Communists. His policies might well lead to a military threat along the whole flank of the expanding American position in Southeast Asia. Thailand seemed particularly exposed.

Today, those American fears have been largely dissolved by the realization that Ne Win's draconian economic measures and fervent neutralism have as their primary objective the protection of Burma against a joint internal and external threat, stemming from the Communists and the Chinese.

Rightly or wrongly, it is now conceded, Ne Win felt that Burma faced a possible coalition of forces involving the powerful Burmese Communist movement, allied with the Chinese Communists; a large Chinese minority in Burma which had a stranglehold on much of Burma's trade and banking, particularly at the village level; several border tribes, stimulated by the Chinese Communists; plus possible intervention of China itself.

To reduce this Chinese and Communist threat — without exposing Burma to charges from Peking of discrimination or partisanship—Ne Win eliminated all foreign business, cut down all foreign aid, banned all foreign visitors.

To reinforce his complete disengagement from all the great powers, Ne Win himself saw practically no foreign envoys, made no foreign trips.

Now, however, he has begun to move about the world. Last year he went to Moscow and Peking. He has been to Europe and he has paid private visits to England. His

trip to the United States squares the diplomatic balance between the East and West.

It marks another initiative as well. The economic consequences of Ne Win's egalitarian venture into state socialism, largely administered by honest army and air force officers with little or no business experience, have been disastrous. "Things are a mess," Ne Win bluntly told his associates recently.

With his neutrality established and acknowledged by both East and West, General Ne Win feels he can shop around a bit for methods and techniques which might ease Burma's economic and social problems.

He firmly believes that foreign

aid debilitates the recipient. Burma must learn to manage its own affairs, run its own business, put its own house in order. But, perhaps within the framework of his puritan philosophy, he may find some notions — possibly in the United States or possibly in a Communist country — which will help ease Burma's problems. He is willing to look and to talk.

There is another circumstance which is strong in General Ne Win's consciousness — the Vietnam war and its possible consequences in Asia. An ardent anti-Communist, a man who has devoted much of his life to guerrilla warfare, particularly against Communists, he has strong opinions about such questions and a realistic apprecia-

tion of the consequences of escalation and proliferation.

On the American side, there is a growing interest in this Crowellian Asian who has been willing to sacrifice his country's easier comforts for the sake of Burmese independence and Burmese security. Washington has begun to see Ne Win as one of the firmer rocks on the shaky Asian landscape. The old doctrine that "if you're not with us you're against us" no longer seems so important in the realization that stability, rather than windy partisanship, is the most priceless of assets on the precarious soil of the Asian continent.

September 11, 1966

RANGOON PLACED UNDER ARMY RULE

Order Follows Slaying of Chinese Aide in Embassy

By The Associated Press

RANGOON, Burma, June 28 —General Ne Win, Chairman of Burma's Revolutionary Council, imposed martial law on parts of Rangoon tonight after a staff member of Communist China's

Embassy was reported to have been stabbed to death by two Burmese.

The Burma Broadcasting Service said that the assailants had climbed over a back wall of the embassy, killed the Chinese staff member and wounded another. Embassy personnel captured one of the killers and handed him over to Burmese authorities, it said. The other escaped.

General Ne Win placed the capital under military authority and declared martial law in four key districts.

Chinese students touched off the riots Monday. They seized Burmese teachers as hostages, defied a Government ban against the wearing of Mao Tsetung badges and beat up newsmen.

Burmese officials said that Chinese Embassy personnel had openly distributed Mao badges and the red book of the Communist leader's quotations.

Troops opened fire and dispersed a mob of demonstrators outside the embassy earlier today after more than 1,000 had broken through a barbed wire barricade and stormed the em-

bassy's 10-foot walls.

Witnesses said that three casualties had been carried from the scene.

The demonstrators returned and were met by army and navy troops who barricaded the embassy entrance.

Demonstrators destroyed virtually every Chinese-owned shop and house in Rangoon yesterday. More than 100 casualties were reported.

June 29, 1966

U.S. Arms Aid to Burma Nears $80-Million

By HENRY KAMM
Special to The New York Times

RANGOON, Burma, Aug. 23 —Under an unpublicized military aid program in Southeast Asia, the United States has provided nearly $80-million in arms and other military goods and services to Burma since 1958.

The program, which is expected to come to an end within a year, has been referred to in American official communications as a "multiyear token-pay credit-sales program."

The zeal of Gen. Ne Win, head of state and government, to safeguard Burma's neutrality had made the military assistance discreet long before President Nixon established the "low profile" as the official shape of the American presence in Southeast Asia.

Even Diplomats Uninformed

The Burmese attitude also accounts for the comparative lack of publicity for the aid,

about which even the tightly knit and self-enclosed diplomatic community appears remarkably uninformed.

The program is run at this end by a so-called military-equipment delivery team — believed to be only one of its kind—that has headquarters in an unmarked villa on the capital's outskirts.

The team, headed by Col. Kevin Carrigan, and slightly smaller than its allotted strength of 22 officers and enlisted men, comes under the Commander in Chief, Pacific, and is locally supervised by Ambassador Arthur W. Hummel Jr. Colonel Carrigan appears on the diplomatic list as a military attaché.

The team, which does not advise the Burmese on the use of the material it delivers, operates quietly but not with total secrecy. Its villa is distinguishable from its neighbors only by the 20 cars and pickup trucks in the yard. A taxi driver identified it as "the American ammunitions office."

Unlike American groups in countries receiving straightforward military assistance, the team is not allowed to inspect equipment in use.

Army Battles Insurgents

The equipment, including jet trainers, transport planes and helicopters, is designed to help Burma's army of 145,000 men fight the various Peking-supported Communist and nationalist tribal insurgencies that have plagued the country since independence from Britain in 1948. Foreign observers believe that the United States is the largest supplier of equipment.

The aid is being provided under an executive agreement concluded through an exchange of notes on June 24, 1958. The spending limit — $85.5-million, according to official sources— was set in the Administration of President Dwight D. Eisenhower in 1958 and was not subject to specific Congressional approval.

August 25, 1970

Burma's Army Fights China-Backed Rebels

The New York Times   Aug. 31, 1970

Burmese rebels have fought the army in last few months around towns in the northeast indicated by underlines.

By HENRY KAMM
Special to The New York Times

RANGOON, Burma, Aug. 23 —Rebel forces sponsored by the Chinese Communists have made a border region of north-eastern Burma a major battle-ground, inflicting heavy casualties on Government forces in three battles since May.

While Government forces have been largely successful in bringing under control Communist and Karen nationalist rebels in central and southern Burma, the new front in the northeast is presenting Government forces with increasing difficulties.

Military observers believe that Peking mounted the threat in the northeast specifically to divert the Government's attention from its troubles in the Pegu Yoma Mountains and in the Irrawaddy River Delta.

The Burmese high command refused, however, to send reinforcements to the northeast. As a result, forces there took heavy casualties.

The Government instead concentrated on winding up its campaign last year in central Burma and the south. Effective control has been restored there for the first time since independence in 1948.

The southern and central rebels, who used to harass Burma's vital transportation lines — roads, rivers and railroads — running north to south, have been reduced from thousands operating efficiently under the direction of the clandestine Burmese Communist party to hundreds hardly daring to come out of hiding in the jungle.

Official sources assert that rebel activity is low elsewhere in the country. Since independence a number of non-Burmese tribesmen — ethnic Burmese make up 70 per cent of the population — have been in permanent revolt, each group independent of the other, against the central Government's efforts to make Burma a unitary state. It has been easy for China and the Burmese Communist party, which is solidly pro-Chinese, to take advantage of these rebellions in south and central Burma to weaken Rangoon's hold over the country.

In March, the Chinese-sponsored rebels forced the Burmese Army to abandon the border town of Kyukok. The Government announced that it had withdrawn the troops because to defend the town would have meant firing into another country, China.

This is as close as Gen. Ne Win's Government has come to accusing China openly of serving as a sanctuary for the insurgents.

The last clash in the northeast took place on Aug. 15, according to official sources. More than 200 Government soldiers met a rebel force estimated at 1,000 between Namhkam and Kutkai.

The sources said that casualties had been heavy on both sides and that a number of Government soldiers were missing.

August 31, 1970

THE PHILIPPINES: FROM DEMOCRACY TO DICTATORSHIP

RIVAL SEES GARCIA PHILIPPINE VICTOR

Manahan, in Third Place, Concedes—Yulo Party Says Results Are Falsified

By TILLMAN DURDIN
Special to The New York Times.

MANILA, Friday, Nov. 15— Manuel Manahan, third-place candidate in the race for the Philippine Presidency, conceded defeat here last night.

The nominee of the new Progressive party of the Philippines sent best wishes to President Carlos P. Garcia, who has a big lead in the five-man contest. Mr. Manahan thus indicated his belief that Mr. Garcia, nominee of the Nationalist party, had won in Tuesday's election.

Mr. Garcia, who moved up from the Vice Presidency when President Ramón Magsaysay was killed last March in a plane crash, seemed certain today to win a full four-year term as President. With an unofficial vote count of 1,219,190 up to early this morning, he was more than 300,000 votes ahead of his nearest rival, José Yulo of the Liberal party, who had 856,252.

November 15, 1957

U. S. SIGNS ACCORD WITH PHILIPPINES

Settles Dispute on Control of Offending Servicemen —13 Bases Yielded

By FORD WILKINS
Special to The New York Times.

MANILA, Oct. 12—The United States signed a memorandum of agreement with the Philippines today settling most of the problems involved in revision of the military bases treaty between the two countries.

The memorandum was signed by Charles E. Bohlen, United States Ambassador, following two and a half years of discussion on revision of the treaty with the Philippines.

Mr. Bohlen will leave Manila Thursday for Washington, with a brief stop-over in Japan. He is terminating his ambassadorial assignment begun in June, 1957, to take a new State Department post as a special adviser to Secretary of State Christian A. Herter on Soviet affairs.

Before his Manila assignment, Mr. Bohlen was Ambassador to Moscow.

Personnel Issue Settled

Ambassador Bohlen and Felixberto M. Serrano, Philippines Secretary of Foreign Affairs, reached substantial agreement even on the sticky question of legal jurisdiction over American personnel on military duty. The Philippines had insisted on the right to try offending personnel under certain conditions in her own courts. Under the agreement reached, final arrangements will be worked out by Mr. Bohlen's successor as Ambassador here.

The accord signed today commits the United States to consult with the Philippines before setting up long-range missile sites on the American bases in the Philippines. The United States also agreed to consult on operational use of the bases outside of specifications in the mutual defense treaty and the Manila pact of 1954, which established the Southeast Asia Treaty Organization.

The United States had already agreed to shorten the leasehold on the bases from ninety-nine years to twenty-five years from now, with renewal provisions, and to return to the Philippines thirteen unused bases set up in World War II.

Certain delimitations in area of the four remaining major bases were also agreed upon, including relinquishment of control over Olongapo, a civilian community formerly enclosed in the Subic naval reservation.

The military bases issue has been a major bone of contention since before Mr. Bohlen's arrival here. The issue was aggravated by the insistence by advocates of Philippine nationalism on making a public issue of the negotiations, with strong emotional undertones whipped up by a segment of the Manila press.

The problem made Mr. Bohlen's term as ambassador a challenging assignment.

The Ambassador was heard to say many times that his task in the Philippines was in certain ways more difficult than anything he had encountered in the Soviet Union. However, he leaves here with sincere respect among Filipinos for his personal ability.

Diplomatic associates and independent observers quietly expressed admiration and regard for him during the round of social events preceding his departure.

October 13, 1959

Philippines Says It Was War, Not Insurrection

Special to The New York Times.

WASHINGTON, Nov. 18—The Philippines Government has unearthed a 62-year-old bone of contention to pick with the United States.

Involved is the designation of the United States-Philippines conflict of 1899-1902 as the Philippine Insurrection. The Philippines contends that this was not an insurrection and should be called the Philippine-American War.

The Philippines Ambassador, Carlos P. Romulo, set forth his Government's position in a note to Secretary of State Christian A. Herter dated Nov. 4.

The key to the dispute is whether the Philippines had already won independence from Spain when the United States claimed the islands under the 1898 treaty with Spain that ended the Spanish-American War.

Ambassador Romulo argued that the Philippine revolt of 1896-98 had already wrested control of the country from Spanish rule.

November 19, 1960

LIBERALS APPEAR FILIPINO VICTORS

Macapagal Holds Big Lead —Running Mate Ahead, Too

By JACQUES NEVARD
Special to The New York Times.

MANILA, Thursday, Nov. 16 —Diosdado Macapagal appeared today to have been elected the fifth President of the Philippines on the basis of a nearly complete but unofficial count of votes cast in Tuesday's national elections.

Results showed nation-wide rejection of the Nationalist party administration of President Carlos P. Garcia.

In an almost complete sweep of major national offices by the resurgent Liberal party, Mr. Macapagal's running mate, Emmanuel Pelaez, held what appeared to be a winning margin over his two rival vice-presidential candidates. Other members of the reform ticket seemed certain of six and possibly seven of the eight Senate seats being contested.

Unofficial returns today showed Mr. Macapagal with 3,009,891 votes to 2,363,402 for Mr. Garcia. Only about 1,500,-000 ballots remained to be counted and it appeared unlikely that the incumbent could overcome Mr. Macapagal's lead of more than 640,000 votes.

Pelaez Margin Slimmer

Mr. Pelaez held a slimmer margin. Thus far he has 2,003,-646 votes compared with 1,806,-768 for Sergio Osmena Jr., an independent candidate, and 1,461,819 for Gil J. Puyat, a Nationalist. It was held unlikely that Mr. Pelaez would be upset by votes still to be counted.

However, neither Mr. Garcia nor any other major Nationalist party candidate had yet conceded.

Most local newspapers and radio-television networks, however, even those that had supported the Nationalists, were satisfied that the unofficial tallying system the networks had set up to speed the counting of votes gave a clear mandate to Mr. Macapagal.

The Liberal party candidate, a 50-year-old lawyer and economist, has been Vice President under Mr. Garcia for the last four years. Philippine voters may split their ballots for president and vice president.

Democratic Process Hailed

The victory by opposition candidates against the rich and powerfully entrenched Nationalist party is seen here as a testimonial to the healthy state of democracy in the Philippines. Political commentators said this morning that this former United States possession was almost the only country in Southeast Asia in which voters could change the regime without a revolution or a coup d'état.

At least thirty-eight persons died and many more were injured during the campaign. But in almost every case violence appeared to be the result of a local feud that spilled over into politics rather than the result of a policy of political terror.

Mr. Macapagal is expected to keep the Philippines firmly in the Western camp and to maintain the nation's cordial relations with the United States.

A major effect of his election is likely to be felt in domestic affairs. He has pledged to work toward lowering prices, increasing employment and attracting capital from abroad.

November 16, 1961

261

MACAPAGAL DRIVE AROUSES CONCERN

'Moral Regeneration' Plan Worries Business Men

Special to The New York Times.

MANILA, Aug. 29—The month-old "moral regeneration" drive of President Diosdado Macapagal has evoked admiration in the countryside. However, big business and people concerned about civil rights are apprehensive.

Mr. Macapagal's campaign against "undesirable aliens" and Filipinos who have amassed wealth through corruption and illegal methods is stirring the imagination of the masses outside Manila and has momentarily stilled their protests against the rising costs of basic commodities.

However, residents of the Philippine capital have remained skeptical of Mr. Macapagal's bold efforts to rid the Philippines of graft and corruption. Outspoken inhabitants of Manila feel that the Administration should concentrate its efforts on keeping prices down, stabilizing the economy and nursing the shaky peso back to health.

Since Mr. Macapagal started his massive purges after ousting an American business man, Harry S. Stonehill, from the Philippines, people in the provinces have praised the President for his unorthodox anti-graft and moral regeneration campaign.

The people, long accustomed to aliens and Philippine-vested interests having their way with politicians, greeted Mr. Macapagal's purges with demands for more. With only a vague concept of civil liberties, they have ignored the protests of the Opposition that the country was heading toward a dictatorship.

While it is too early to assess the impact of Mr. Macapagal's purges, there are indications that it is affecting business.

Alien business men have fled the country, taking with them millions of dollars that they might otherwise have invested in profitable ventures here. Philippine business men fear that their "heads may roll."

The result has been a decline in trading, a drop in the stock market and a reduction in investments.

The Administration appears to be aware of these developments. It has begun an intensive public relations drive to allay the fears of business men. Administration press officers have been assuring business men that those with nothing to hide need have no fear.

Since the Administration's drive got under way Aug. 10, action has been taken against five aliens, eight naturalized Philippine citizens of Chinese extraction and three native-born Filipinos.

Two close associates of the President, former Executive Secretary Amelito R. Mutuc, now Philippine Ambassador-designate to the United States, and former acting Finance Secretary Fernando E. V. Sison, were not spared.

To convince the people of the sincerity of his moral regeneration drive, Mr. Macapagal accepted the standing resignations of these close associates, saying:

"Like Caesar's wife, my Cabinet officials must all be upright and above suspicion."

When charges were made that Mr. Macapagal was concentrating on members of the opposition Nacionalista party, the President acted swiftly against former Speaker Jose Yulo.

Mr. Macapagal said that Mr. Yulo, one of the "Old Guard" of the ruling Liberal party, had acquired land illegally. He ordered the Government to prosecute Mr. Yulo, recover the land and subdivide it among needy Filipino farmers.

September 9, 1962

Filipinos – East or West?

They Look Asian but Speak English And Strive to Coin a National Image

By ROBERT TRUMBULL
Special to The New York Times.

MANILA. March 8 — As hosts to a United Nations economic conference with representatives of 43 countries present, the Filipinos are busy this week trying to create an international image for themselves.

They have charmed their guests with spirited music, dancing, exotic food and the joyous Filipino personality, but it is still hard to say just what the image is or should be. The visitors often ask: To which world do the Filipinos really belong, East or West?

The Talk of Manila

As they begin to take a more prominent role in matters of considerable international importance in this part of the world, the Filipinos are becoming more sensitive to the national ambivalence between Orient and Occident, between America and Spain. They look Asian, but they speak English—with American slang terms and a Spanish accent.

So to other Asians, Filipinos seem like Americans. To Americans they seem more like Spaniards than anything else. What are they to themselves? This is what the Filipinos are trying to find out.

On the postage stamps now in use, the name of the country has been changed from the Spanish-sounding "Philippines," to the more Filipino-looking "Pilipinas." The first P is often pronounced as if it were "F" through a local dialectical peculiarity on the same order as the Japanese difficulty with "L" and "R." But however you spell it or pronounce it, the name still says that the country once belonged to a Spanish king called Philip.

So some Filipino scholars are searching for a good name for the country in a local language. But there are many local languages in this country of about 7,000 islands and the common tongue is still American English, although Spanish is strong as a means of communication among a dwindling older generation.

When the United States gave the Filipinos their independence in 1946, Tagalog became the so-called national language. But Tagalog is spoken only in the neighborhood of Manila, so there was unhappiness elsewhere.

Then the Government began to call Tagalog "Pilipino," to erase the regional odium. Only this week, though, the Secretary of Education admitted in the House of Representatives that there really isn't any such language as "Pilipino," — it's still Tagalog, he said.

It is still unclear what is going to be done about the linguistic problem. But English is still used for official purposes.

Filipino politicians like to assert their nationalism by criticizing the United States, the colonial ruler after the defeat of Spain in the Spanish-American war in 1898. There is usually something happening in Washington with which a Filipino can take issue. Right now it is the American backing of Malaysia, a proposed federation of Malaya, Singapore and the remaining British territories in Borneo.

The Filipinos oppose Malaysia because the Manila Government contends that the British Crown colony of North Borneo, once the domain of a Filipino sultan, should revert to the Philippines if the British leave, instead of to Malaya or some other country.

By arguing with Washington in all the Latin heat they can engender from a Spanish heritage, Filipinos think they are proving that they are not unduly influenced by the former American connection. Yet it is said that making an anti-American speech is one of the surest ways to lose an election here, and this seems to be borne out by the record. But once a candidate is elected, he is virtually required, people say, to make an anti-American speech at the first opportunity.

In spite of this, there is possibly no other foreign country in the world — and certainly not in Asia — where Americans feel and look as much at home as they do here.

Americans lounging in hotel lobbies, bars, clubs and wherever people gather look as if they really belong here. Many Americans in Manila wear the practical and becoming "barong Tagalog," a lightweight shirt worn outside the trousers with no tie or jacket, which is as acceptable as a white dinner jacket at a formal affair.

Unlike Americans who attempt the national dress in other countries, they manage somehow not to look as if they were committing the fatal fault of trying to flatter the people.

March 9, 1963

Red Filipino Terrorists Employ Vietcong Tactics

By ROBERT TRUMBULL
Special to The New York Times

MANILA, Jan. 9—Communist terrorism in the Philippine countryside is growing ominously, according to official appraisals. The increase in violent subversive activity has prompted the Government to move 2,000 troops into Pampanga Province, principal stronghold of the successors to the Hukbalahap organization.

In assassinations of local officials and other terrorist operations, the tactics of the resurgent Philippine Communists closely resemble the methods of the Vietcong in South Vietnam, but on a much smaller scale.

At the same time, officials say, Marxists are heavily infiltrating intellectual student and labor circles in Manila. Authorities in Pampanga province have listed 32 assassinations, including those of two city mayors, in the last year. Tarlac province, another center of Communist activity, has ascribed to Communist the murders of 18 village heads in the same period.

Some officials in Manila ascribe much of the violence attributed to Communists as mere banditry. But others assert that the Government takes this line because it is reluctant to recognize that there is a Communist resurgence. To do so, they say, might be interpreted in this election year as proof that President Diosdado Macapagal's administration has failed to improve depressing economic and

The New York Times   Jan. 10, 1965
The Philippines is moving against rebel units in the diagonally shaded region.

social conditions on which the Marxists thrive.

The Hukbalahap guerrilla organization formed during World War II—its name was a contraction for the Filipino words meaning People's Anti-Japanese Army—has been reconstituted. Now it is known as the Hukbong Mapagpalaya Nang Bayan, or People's Liberation Army. In popular usage, its members are still called Huks.

The Huks are described as a military arm of the Philippine Communist party. According to the Government, they number 14,000 and are armed with 9,000

rifles, machine guns and other firearms operating principally in the Pampanga, Tarlac, Pangasinan, Zambales, Bataan and Nueva Ecija Provinces of Central Luzon Island.

Like the Vietcong, they have so terrorized the peasants in their main operating areas that they have little fear of informers reporting their activity to the Government. In the affected villages, it is accepted that the fate of the informer is death. One authority on Communist activity said that the Huks controlled at least 80 villages in Central Luzon. Like the Vietcong, again, the Huks collect taxes from the villagers and constitute an effective clandestine government.

But, unlike the Vietcong and other Asian Communists, the Huks are believed to lack any direct link with external Communist parties.

Ideologically and in their field tactics, the Huks work along lines laid down by Mao Tse-tung, the chairman of the Chinese Communist party, and Gen. Vo Nguyen Giap of North Vietnam. Distrust of the Chinese is widespread in the Philippines, however, so the Huks have carefully avoided any identification with Peking.

The Soviet Union is said to be "too far away" for close ties. In addition, the Huks are said to feel that the Philippine political climate requires them to preserve the appearance of an entirely indigenous nationalist movement.

Nevertheless, Philippine Com-

munist ranks are known to be split along the lines that have been drawn in most Marxist movements over the ideological conflict between Moscow and Peking.

Here the division is identified in linguistic terms. The "Pampanga faction," whose leaders speak the language of that province, are said to be dedicated wholly to subversion of the peasants. The "Tagalog group," which takes its name from the country's official language, advocates a stronger effort to capture power in parliament.

The original Huk rebellion was put down by 1952 under the late President Ramon Magsaysay. The last known secretary general of the Communist party, Jesús Lava, was arrested in Manila last May. But the organization has survived.

From captured documents authorities know that the Huks have listed special "targets" for infiltration. These, in order of Communist precedence, are the peasants organized labor, white-collar employes, students and youth, small shopkeepers and venders professionals and intellectuals, and finally the army.

"The only course open to the revoutionary movement in the present or the future is violent overthrow," says a document captured from the Huks last May. "This should not preclude legal and other forms of activity that can facilitate the attainment of the ultimate objective."

January 10, 1965

Macapagal Apparently Defeated By Marcos in Philippines Vote

By SEYMOUR TOPPING
Special to The New York Times

MANILA, Friday, Nov. 12—Senator Ferdinand E. Marcos claimed victory last night in the Philippines presidential election as his lead over the incumbent President, Diosdado Macapagal, increased to a seemingly unbeatable 665,000 votes.

Mr. Marcos, the Nationalist party's candidate, outlined his program at a news conference and told his Liberal party opponents that "there shall be no vindictiveness" despite the turbulent election campaign.

With more than 65 per cent of the vote reported, Senator Marcos's lead already exceeds the margin of 650,000 by which President Macapagal defeated Carlos Garcia in 1961.

Liberal party leaders privately were conceding Senator Marcos's election, although a statement by President Macapagal

last night described Senator Marcos's claims as "quite premature."

Senator Marcos said there would be "no serious changes" in foreign policy. But he added that he would adopt a more flexible attitude toward the question of sending combat troops to Vietnam.

Upon assuming office, the Senator said, he will ask Congress for authority to send troops to Vietnam if this becomes necessary and it will help to compel North Vietnam to open peace talks. He said this categorically, but his remarks were later qualified in a summary issued by his press office.

Senator Marcos's party earlier had blocked approval of a Macapagal proposal that a combat engineer battalion and security force to total 2,000 men, be as-

United Press International
FAR BEHIND: President Diosdado Macapagal of the Philippines is 665,000 votes behind his opponent.

signed to Vietnam. The Nationalists, who have taken a more independent stand than the Liberals in relations with the United States, have argued that the present commitment of medical teams is adequate.

Senator Marcos, who is president of the Senate, said he did not contemplate at present any change in the agreement for the maintenance of the large United States naval and air bases in the Philippines.

The Senator indicated he was concerned about the fiscal status of the Government and especially the heavy expenditures made recently by the Macapagal Administration. There was speculation in informed quarters that the new Administration might seek additional United States credits.

At midnight the vote in the presidential race, as tabulated by the Philippine News Service, was as follows:

Senator Marcos had 2,888,748 votes to 2,223,315 for President Macapagal. The Vice-Presidential race was much closer with only 77,278 votes separating the two major candidates. Senator Fernando Lopes of the Nationalist party was leading with 2,647,978 votes to 2,570,700 votes for Senator Gerardo Roxas, the Liberal candidate.

November 12, 1965

Philippines Seeks New Identity

Old U.S. Military and Economic Ties Are Being Questioned

By SEYMOUR TOPPING
Special to The New York Times

MANILA, Nov. 20 — In its search for a new Asian identity, the Philippine Republic is drifting away from the United States.

The old economic and military ties with the United States are being questioned, in the schools, in the press, by the rising industrialist class and by politicians sensitive to the changing sentiment in the country.

Manila is a capital placarded with advertisements of American products. Its streets are crowded with American cars, and its radio and television stations blare American pop music.

But its books, newspapers and magazines, the lectures of its professors and speeches of its politicians are full of talk about Filipino Asian nationalism. This is a contradiction of Filipino life, and it is the confusion of a society in transition.

A generation of Filipinos is coming of age, a generation that has no experience of wartime comradeship with United States or of the prewar era of political tutelage.

"We want to fuse what we have inherited from you Americans and Spanish colonialists with our own ethnic Malayan roots and form an independent personality that will be respected in Asia." a University of Philippines senior said.

Agitation against American military bases and business interests is led by a group of influential left-wing university professors and writers, some of whom are linked to the clandestine apparatus of the outlawed Communist party. A resurgence of Communist activity is expected if Senator Ferdinand E. Marcos, the President-elect, who takes office Dec. 30, fails to cope with the country's enormous economic and social problems.

Strange alliances have also developed between some of the

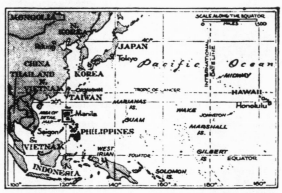

The Philippines (shown in black), strategically situated off Southeast Asia, is experiencing a rise of nationalism.

wealthiest Filipino industrialist families and the intellectual left wing, with the common aim of ousting competing American business from its privileged place in the Philippines. American companies have invested $465 million in the Philippines, and their economic interests are fostered by the Laurel-Langley agreement, which grants American businessmen parity with Filipinos in most sectors of the economy until 1974.

In the countryside, where more than 70 per cent of the 32 million Filipinos live, traditional attachments for Americans persist despite the ferment among the urban groups.

"Hello, Joe," is still the gay cry of Filipino children when Americans pass by.

"You can't win an election by being anti-American," an ultra-nationalist Senator of the Nationalist party of President-elect Marcos remarked.

U. S. Officials Worried

While the United States has begun to accommodate itself to the upsurge of nationalism in the Philippines, officials find the anti-American aspect of the ferment worrying, particularly at this time. United States naval and air bases in the Philippines have taken on greater importance because of the war in Vietnam, and their operations have been greatly expanded. The security of the bases is vital.

Clark Field, a 300-square-mile base on which 50,000 people live and work, provides the principal logistical support for the Air Force in Vietnam. The naval base at Subic Bay is the chief supply and repair depot for the Seventh Fleet.

The loss or impairment of

The New York Times   Nov. 21, 1965
Key U.S. bases are at Subic Bay (1) and Clark Field (2).

the efficiency of these bases would compel the forces engaged in Vietnam to draw logistical support from bases twice as far away in Japan and Guam—and beyond from Pearl Harbor in Hawaii.

President-elect Marcos says he contemplates no change at this time in the status of the bases which, he points out, are needed for the defense of the Philippines and the United States. However, he adds, conditions in a changing world should not be discounted, and he will be constantly listening to counsel from his advisers.

United States officials are not entirely sure that Senator Marcos will be as cooperative as the outgoing President, Diosdado P. Macapagal in backing the Vietnam war effort.

The problem arises since the United States must consult before employing the bases for purposes outside the scope of the mutual defense pact and the Southeast Asia Treaty Organization.

President Macapagal acceded readily when clearance was asked for such special operations as refueling in air by Clark Field tanker planes of B-52 bombers shuttling between Guam and their targets in Vietnam.

United States officials are hopeful that continued close cooperation can be arranged.

The Marcos Administration may need Washington's help in extricating the country from its financial crisis.

The President-elect is a strong-willed independent thinker who has not outlined his plans, but already some Manila columnists are warning him on the Vietnam issue that it would be risky to interpret his election as a mandate to sell out Philippine interests in exchange for economic aid from the United States.

Among Filipinos, there is a great sense of ideological commitment to the struggle in Vietnam.

Filipino medical and psychological warfare teams have been sent to Vietnam, and Senator Marcos has said he would drop his opposition to the Macapagal proposal for a Vietnam combat force of 2,000 men if such a move would help end the war.

In general, however, the attitude of Filipinos to the Vietnam war effort ranges from a feeling that the United States will do the job, to disinterest and active opposition from the left wing.

Senator Marcos has been urged by leftists among his advisers and an ultranationalist minority within his party to limit military cooperation with the United States.

The United States spend about $25 million a year in support of the Philippine armed forces and maintains a training mission in the country, but Washington has not succeeded in persuading Manila to join in an acceptable defense plan.

It was understood that Washington had suggested to the Philippines that it leave its external defense to the United States and organize its 15,000-man army into highly mobile lightly equipped batalion combat teams for internal security. This has evoked a nationalist outcry that the United States is denying the Philippines the means of self-defense and is attempting to perpetuate control over the country.

The Philippine Army has opted instead for a divisional-type organization and has asked for more heavy equipment. Because of an inadequate defense budget, much of the equipment and the small Air Force are not properly maintained and are often in disuse.

November 21, 1965

Marcos, Easy Election Winner, Faces Key Problems in 2d Term

By TILLMAN DURDIN
Special to The New York Times

MANILA, Nov. 12—A massive accumulation of problems faced Ferdinand E. Marcos today as he became the first Philippine President to win a second four-year term.

Projections of the returns in yesterday's Presidential election showed Mr. Marcos with 4,534,352 votes to 2,662,251 for his opponent, Senator Sergio Osmeña Jr. Mr. Marcos's Nationalist party also appeared headed for an overwhelming victory in the Congressional elections. Final official returns are not expected for several weeks.

One of the problems Mr. Marcos faces is the refusal of Senator Osmeña to concede defeat. There is a prospect that Mr. Osmeña and leaders of his Liberal party may contest the validity of the elections on the ground that the Liberal party vote was reduced by fraud, violence, vote-buying and other improprieties attributed to the Nationalists.

Marcos Making Plans

But Mr. Marcos made clear he considered himself confirmed in office and began to plan his next four years. Protests over the voting results often occur after Philippine elections, and the complaints of Senator Osmeña and his supporters will probably be dropped eventually.

The country relaxed today from the tensions of the election campaign which, despite its sporadic violence and intense factionalism, caused no major social disruptions and seemed to prove that democracy, Philippine-style, was still a viable system.

Meanwhile, aides of Mr. Marcos let it be known that he was already setting priorities for dealing with critical matters. The President said in a post-election statement early this morning that these issues would make the next four years the most important period since this tropical republic of 38,000,000 gained independence from the United States 23 years ago.

One of Mr. Marcos's aims is to reduce the Philippines' dependence on the United States and promote closer relations with neighboring Asian nations.

In his new term, the President must deal with a grave financial crisis now facing the country as a result of the near-exhaustion of foreign exchange reserves and inflationary overspending internally.

Negotiations With U.S. Due

Also urgently necessary will be the early adoption of a basic position, so far lacking, on what sort of relations with the United States the Government wants. This will be necessary before it enters into negotiations early next year with Washington on the status of American bases here, the defense treaty with the United States and the current mutually preferential trade arrangements.

At a little longer range, the Marcos Government's attitudes and arrangements for a constitutional convention scheduled for 1971 must be fixed. The convention will seek to determine whether the present system of government needs to be changed.

Senator Osmeña said tonight he had not yet decided whether to enter a formal protest over the election results as they shape up on the basis of the incomplete and unofficial returns available today. He said this would depend on investigations of the scope of alleged irregularities.

November 13, 1969

---

2 Slain as 2,000 Filipinos Storm Presidential Palace

By TAKASHI OKA
Special to The New York Times

MANILA, Saturday, Jan. 31 —Some 2,000 students and young people, hoisting revolutionary placards and upside-down Philippine flags, tried last night to storm into the grounds of Malacanang, the presidential palace, and battled with policemen into the morning.

Two students were killed by gunfire and 102 were wounded. The police arrested about 100 young people.

Seven vehicles, including two fire trucks and a bus, were burned in what was termed the worst peacetime rioting in the memory of Manila citizens.

Policemen and soldiers, responding to rocks, slingshots and gasoline bombs used by the demonstrators, fired rifles and tear-gas grenades and employed rifle butts, fire hoses, nightsticks and heavy batons and protected themselves with wicker shields.

The rioting was an outgrowth of protests over the voting last Nov. 11 in which President Ferdinand E. Marcos was overwhelmingly re-elected despite his critics' charges of fraud.

Five days ago student groups —many of which consider the President a symbol of a ruling élite—met to demand reforms in the constitutional convention planned for next year. Their rally erupted into violence, in which some 300 students and 70 policemen were injured, and charges of police brutality resulted. The new demonstrations were intended to press those allegations.

The charges of wholesale vote-buying, intimidation and fraud during the election remain to be proved but even some of the President's loyal supporters admit that his margin of victory—nearly two million votes—was embarrassingly large.

Under the present Constitution no President can serve more than two consecutive four-year terms. Many students fear that Mr. Marcos will try to get the constitutional convention to open the way to a third term.

They have been agitating to get Mr. Marcos to declare categorically that he will not run for another term and they seek the agreement of both major parties—the governing Nationalists and the opposition Liberals—that the constitutional convention will be free of partisan politics.

The day began peacefully. Numerous student groups, including large contingents from the state-run University of the Philippines and the Philippine College of Commerce as well as from several Roman Catholic institutions, scheduled protest meetings in front of Congress and the palace.

By early afternoon the crowd had swelled to approximately 30,000, mainly near the Congress building. A sizable group gathered in Freedom Park, a small triangular plot across from the elegant ironwork grille of Malacanang's main gate that is used as a public forum.

Speeches and Ice Cream

At 4:15 P.M. President Marcos invited about 20 moderate student leaders to discuss their demands. He and Nationalist leaders agreed at the meeting that the constitutional convention would be nonpartisan and nonsectarian.

On the third-term issue, the President said, "I am not interested in a third term"—a disavowal not as categorical as the students would have liked.

As the discussion went on for nearly three hours students waiting outside whiled away the time with short, humorous, biting and occasionally denunciatory speeches, relayed by loudspeaker to an appreciative throng. Vendors of ice cream and cold drinks circulated.

As time went on, the students grew restive. Some tried rattling the front gates.

"We have pledged this will be a peaceful demonstration," a professor at the Philippine College of Commerce pleaded over the microphone. "We are on trial here. Let us show how orderly we can be."

Policemen were nowhere in sight. Mayor Antonio Villegas of Manila, a political opponent of the President, had been angered by charges of police brutality during the Monday riot and had ordered the police not to interfere with the students this time.

There was a detail of presidential guards inside the palace grounds.

After darkness fell students who had been demonstrating in front of Congress began reaching the palace grounds, crowding those already there. Among the new arrivals were militants belonging to Patriotic Youth, who hoisted red flags and placards such as "Power to the People."

While some student leaders continued to plead for nonviolence, the Patriotic Youth group shouted revolutionary slogans around a bonfire built of placards and other rubbish. Some denounced the student leaders inside as traitors.

Emerging from their conference with the President, they left secretly. Then the loudspeaker failed the assembly broke into two groups and the violence began with stones hurled at street lamps.

Use of Arms Reported

Demonstrators with arms were not in evidence, but Gen. Vicente Raval, chief of the Philippine Constabulary, said some had carbines and automatic rifles.

After being repulsed by forces at the palace, the demonstrators fought running battles, retreating slowly to the vicinity of the University of the East about 10 blocks away.

Political observers fear the battle will widen the gap between the revolution-minded younger generation and the conservative, landowning political and business élite, which has run the country since independence was granted by the United States in 1946.

Mr. Marcos issued a statement condemning the attack on the palace and saying: "While the Government supports the right of any group to demonstrate, it shall not tolerate violence."

The President hinted that Mayor Villegas might be suspended for refusing to discharge his duty in maintaining peace and order."

January 31, 1970

HUK LEADER SLAIN BY TWO INFORMERS

Philippine Rebel Dies Month After Capture of Top Aide

Special to The New York Times

MANILA, Oct. 16—Pedro Taruc, commander of the Hukbalahap guerrillas in the Philippines, was shot to death this afternoon by two civilian informers who led an army unit to his house not far from the United States' Clark Air Force Base, 50 miles northwest of here.

Mr. Taruc's death came a month after the Army had captured Fautino del Mundo, also known as Captain Sumulong, his second in command. The captain faces trial on charges of murder and rebellion.

The slaying of Mr. Taruc in Angeles City, Pampanga Province, is the most spectacular report in years in the Government's quarter-century campaign against the Huks.

The elusive Communist-led insurgents, whose activities have recently increased, have been one of the most persistent problems of the administration of President Ferdinand E. Marcos. He has been striving to suppress them for the last four years with only indifferent success.

October 17, 1970

GRENADES KILL 10 AT MANILA RALLY

8 Liberal Election Rivals of Marcus Are Injured

Special to The New York Times

MANILA, Aug. 21—Terrorists hurled explosives at a rally of the opposition Liberal party tonight, killnig 10 persons and wounding 66. Among the wounded were all eight of the party's senatorial candidates in the November elections, in which they are scheduled to face the candidates of President Ferdinand Marcos' Nationalist partv.

The police said later that pieces of grenades had been found and President Marcos, calling the incident a "heinous crime," said every effort would be made to apprehend those responsible.

Among those injured were Senator Sergio Osmeña Jr., son of the late President, and his nephew, Representative John Osmeña, a senatorial candidate; Senator Genaro Magsaysay, brother of the late President Ramon Magsaysay and Senator Gerardo Roxas, son of the late President Manuel Roxas.

Rally Was on TV

Two explosions occurred at close intervals at 9:13 P.M. before some 10,000 people at Plaza Miranda, where the rally was held. Thousands of others saw it on television.

In searious condition at city hospitals were Senator Osmeña, with wounds of the back and chest; Senator Jovito Salonga, who is favored to top November's returns, and Representative Ramon Bagatsing, the opposition candidate for mayor of Manila.

Other members of the Liberal party senatorial slate who were injured were Senator Eva Estrada Kalaw, Representatives Ramon Mitra and Salipada Pendatun and former Representatives Eddie Ilarde and Melanio Singson.

Three members of the Manila Council running for re-election also were injured, as were the wives of Senatorial and city candidates on the stage with their husbands at the time of the explosion. Mrs. Judy Araneta Roxas, wife of Senator Roxas, was injured in both legs.

Five Dead in Heap

Five members of the audience, including a 10-year-old cigarette vender, were found dead in a heap just below the microphones. The other dead included two newspaper photographers.

A fireworks display, in front of the stage, began just after 9 o'clock. Witnesses said that as the fireworks were going off, two explosions were heard from the stage and some 50 people there spilled out of their rattan seats to the floor.

Police said they found grenade pins and levers indicating that two hand grenades had been detonated — an old pineapple-shaped grendade and a new model O16. Police believe that only grenades were exploded, but several witnesses said there was a bigger explosion from under the stage.

Gerardo Tamayo, Manila's Police Chief, said his men had found three witnesses who said they had seen two persons approach the stage and toss two objects, moments before the explosions.

August 22, 1971

Marcos Suspends Rights of Suspects In Rebellion Cases

Special to The New York Times

MANILA, Aug. 25 — President Ferdinand E. Marcos, acting today to stem what he called "an armed insurrection" following the bombing Saturday night of a Liberal party rally here, suspended the right of habeas corpus for all those accused of rebellion or insurrection.

The insurrection, he said, enjoys the "active moral and material support of a foreign power," which he did not identify. The President said that nine suspected Communist conspirators had been rounded up in the last 40 hours on suspicion of seeking the overthrow of the Government. They have disclosed the identities of their leaders, who will be arrested shortly, he said.

Mr. Marcos said over radio and television that in suspending the constitutional guarantee against detention without charge, he was acting in the interest of public safety against a Communist conspiracy.

Ten persons were killed and 74, including the entire Liberal slate and eight candidates running for the Senate against candidates of Mr. Marcos's Nationalist party, were injured in the bombing. Two Liberal leaders, Senators Jovito Salonga and Sergio Osmeña Jr., are still listed in critical condition.

The President's action drew mixed reactions. Some legislators and Cabinet members urged the public to remain calm since the suspension of habeas corpus rights applied only to crimes of rebellion. The Liberal party said it would challenge the suspension in court on constitutional grounds.

Radical student groups held rallies protesting the suspension and the arrests of four members of the Maoist youth group called Kabataang Makabayan, or Patriotic Youth. The group's secretary general, Luzvimindo David, was arrested yesterday and three provincial members of the group have since been held for questioning since.

Also in custody are Dr. Nemesio Prudente, head of the Philippine College of Commerce, two of his subordinates and two political commentators.

Mr. Marcos said in his address that "This is a time of national emergency." For the first time in the nation's history, he said, "eight candidates for national office, several other candidates for various lower offices, several high officials of a political party, media men and scores of plain men, women and children had become the victims of a mass assassination attempt while attending a political rally."

August 24, 1971

Cotabato, Philippine Farm Province, Reaps Harvest of Violence and Death

By HENRY KAMM
Special to The New York Times

COTABATO, the Philippines, Sept. 9—This country takes a perverse pride in a reputation for violence that often turns out to be merely verbal, but Cotabato Province is genuinely violent, and no one here is proud of it.

Since last October, more than 1,000 men, women and children have been killed in warfare instigated by Moslem and Christian outlaws, according to Gov. Simeon Datumanong. Well-informed local sources estimate that the number of unrecorded slayings nearly equals that total.

Leading Government and military officials here and in Manila have said that the situation has been "stabilized." But six killings were reported by the Philippine Constabulary yesterday and the current issue of the weekly Mindanao News Bulletin reported 27 deaths in four days last week.

This capital city of the province is said to be calm, but a 19-year-old youth, stabbed to death without provocation on the central plaza before the 9 P.M. curfew siren sounded last Monday, was thought to have been killed merely because of his shoulder-long hair. The killer, a passing Moslem who escaped, thought the youth belonged to the Christian outlaws. In fact, the victim was a casual visitor from another province.

Feudalism and Politics

Many reasons for the violence were offered in three days of conversations here and in the lush countryside ravaged by poverty, murder and arson. Observers place responsibility on the nearly feudal status of the bulk of the Moslem population and on unscrupulous politicians of all faiths and parties.

Mindanao was predominantly Moslem when World War II ended. The newly-independent republic proposed

The New York Times   Sept. 10, 1971

that the island become a land of opportunity for settlers from the crowded and war-torn islands in the north.

They came, and they settled on public land to which no one held title. Often the permission of the local datu, or chieftain of the Moslem clan, was required. The datus, drawing on an authority that is both religious and communal, remained more powerful than any organ of Government.

After the settlers made their fields produce, a practice of extortion became widespread, and still obtains. Guided, often pressed, by their datus, Moslems present claims for payment for the use of the land of their ancestors. They exact payment in kind as well as in cash, often rustling cattle for ransom.

The Christians pay, to avoid trouble, but resentments are deep and often spill over to individual cases of violence, as happened even before the present outbreak.

They Deliver the Vote

The datu system has made its leaders excellent deliverers of bloc votes and prized allies to politicians of national stature. The politicians, in return, have allowed the datus unhampered authority.

In an interview at his opulent, modern, neo-Moorish villa, the leading datu of Cotabato, Congressman Salipada Pendatun, said that "for the good of my people," he would ally himself with either major party.

Now a senatorial candidate of the opposition Liberal party, he has also been a National party leader. His opposite number in Lanao del Norte Province, Congressman Ali Dimaporo, is now a stalwart supporter of President Ferdinand E. Marcos. Mr. Dimaporo, a Nationalist, had been a Liberal.

The governors and congressmen of Cotabato, since independence, have been Moslem. This is cited by critics of the datu system in rebutting arguments that nothing has been done to establish title to Moslem peasants' land. They accuse the Moslem leaders of failing to use their power for their people.

Traces Violence to 1968

With the population of the province at 1.3 million, and Christians now in a slight majority, the datus' hold on leading posts in both parties has been challenged. Most public figures here say the changing political picture is the prime cause of the rise in violence.

Governor Datumanong, highly regarded for his moderation but not for his independence from the leading datu, Mr. Pendatun, said that organized violence began with the forming of a secessionist Mindanao independence movement in 1968.

In response to the movement, the Governor said, Christians began to form outlaw groups known as "ilagas," or rats, to strike at the Moslems. They are widely believed to have the support of anti-Datu politicians.

"You cannot reason with the Christians," a Roman Catholic missionary said. "When they are on the warpath, they kill any Moslem they see—yes, women and children too."

"We preach against the ilagas," said the Auxiliary Bishop of Cotabato, Msgr. Antonino Nepomuceno. "We preach 'Love your neighbor,' but we can't preach 'Lie down to get killed'."

In the violence over the last year, the victims have been equally divided between the faiths. The governor said that at least 60,000 people had been driven from their homes and nearly 3,000 houses, most of them belonging to Moslems, burned to the ground.

When the ilagas and their Moslem equivalents, called blackshirts, become active near a village, Christians and Moslems alike flee, often together.

The Hatred Remains

But there is palpable hatred among the people along the dirt road to the outlying district of Buldun. They returned to their villages after the fighting last month to find hardly a house spared by arson, their belongings plundered and their rice and corn burned.

Their anger is directed at the army and the ilagas, who, they say, make common cause in burning and pillaging.

But the district mayor, Bangon Aratuc, has changed sides. Until the fighting, he was suspected of being a Moslem fanatic, a sponsor of armed extremists and a loyal follower of Mr. Pendatun.

Then Mr. Aratuc was summoned to Manila to negotiate a cease-fire with the opposing party's leader, President Marcos. The President allotted him 125,000 pesos ($20,161) in public works funds and made other pledges of support.

"The attitude of the President is good," Mayor Aratuc said in an interview in his house, which had been plundered. "I promised him to become a Nationalist."

He is planning to run for re-election on Nov. 8 under his changed colors. Indicating the depth of his conversion, the mayor denied that the army or the ilagas pillaged his people. "It was bad Moslem elements from this municipality," he said. "Moslem ilagas."

September 10, 1971

267

Philippine Communist Movement Reported Growing

By TILLMAN DURDIN
Special to The New York Times

MANILA, Sept. 4—Though still on a small scale, Communist activity in the Philippines has grown to the level where it produces incidents of violence every few days somewhere in the country.

Over the last weekend, six soldiers, including a lieutenant, were killed when their unit was ambushed by armed men of the Communist New Peoples Army in a remote part of rural Isabela Province in northern Luzon.

Almost at the same time in mountainous Camarines Sur, a province at the southern end of Luzon, the Communists were the losers in an armed clash in which seven guerrillas died in a fight with a constabulary unit.

During the preceding week bomb explosions in public places in Manila, which the police say were the work of Communist terrorists, kept the city on edge. The Defense Ministry says that a terrorist unit of 19 men is operating in the capital, intent on assassinating public figures.

Events such as these have become commonplace and reflect the development of a revitalized Communist movement that is plainly gaining ground but does not yet appear to threaten large - scale revolutionary upheaval.

President Ferdinand Marcos characterizes the movement as serious but under control.

However, he said in an interview that his military commanders took a grave view of the situation and warned him that at the rate it is developing the Communist movement could "overwhelm" Philippine armed forces in two years if they are not appreciably strengthened.

Mr. Marcos indicated that he shared this view and emphasized that the republic's relatively small military establishment—618,000 men in the army, 26,000 in the Constabulary, 8,000 in the air force and 8,000 in the navy—was already under severe strain in coping not only with Communist guerrillas in many places but also with Moslem-Christian clashes in Mindanao and problems of lawlessness and violence in other areas.

"It is surprising but true," he stated, "that in almost every battle with the Communists we are outnumbered until we can reinforce. We are spread very thin. The Constabulary, for example, has to look out for the security of 1,000 villages and 62 cities in 67 provinces."

The president said in areas where they operate, the Communists are eroding the will to resist of local authorities by political assassinations.

Mr. Marcos pointed to a similar erosion in urban areas and throughout society, encouraged by what he termed an attitude of complacency and lack of support for strong measures by the nation's media.

He said in rural areas, farmers, timber operators, landowners and businessmen and in the cities businessmen and even government officials, out of fear, contributed funds to the "invisible government" of the Communists.

He deplored the failure of the Philippine Congress to approve requests he has made for more money to strengthen the armed forces. He said society seemingly would not tolerate the measures necessary to check the Communist menace now, "so the danger is we will wait until they take over a part of the country and it becomes a regular war, causing high casualties and great destruction."

The Communist effort is casting an ever bigger shadow in the Philippines today than the movement whose guerrillas—popularly called the Huks—have operated in central Luzon for years.

Offshoots of the old - line Moscow - oriented Communist party, the Huks have degenerated into extortionist and terrorist bands and lost influence to the new Communist party of the Philippines, which looks to the Chinese for ideology and support.

The youthful, vigorous party got going in 1969 under José Maria Sison, a one-time Manila University professor of political science who at 33 now leads his movement from a relatively secure base in the thick jungles of Isabela Province.

Tough, dour and aloof, Mr. Sison had a long history as a Communist activist before he and his associates set up the

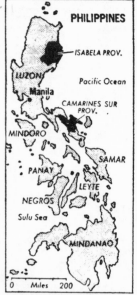

The New York Times/Sept. 9, 1972
Provinces on Luzon where clashes with Communists have occurred are shown on the map in black.

new Maoist party. He was in Indonesia as a protégé of the Indonesian Communist leader, D. N. Aidit, before the party was liquidated in the mid-1960's.

Mr. Sison has been to China at least twice. His party propagates completely Maoist, pro-China policy lines and follows Maoist precepts in waging guerrilla warfare.

Weaknesses are evident, however, in the movement. Disagreements are reported over how closely it should align itself with the Chinese and how radical it should be at this stage.

Communist China's dealings with the United States and Japan have disturbed some of the more revolutionary members. Others, heeding a traditional anti-Chinese sentiment in the country, have never been keen on close China ties.

All in all, however, the rejuvenated Communist movement seems sure to become a bigger and bigger factor in the Philippine equation if it can keep its discipline and momentum.

September 9, 1972

Manila Sets Martial Law After Attack on Minister

Special to The New York Times

MANILA, Saturday, Sept. 23 —Martial law was imposed throughout the Philippines at 2 A.M. today.

The emergency action followed by six hours an attempt on the life of the nation's Defense Secretary. It also came in the wake of a series of bomb explosions that have been set off in the Manila area in recent weeks.

Gen. Fidel Ramos, chief of staff of the Philippine constabulary, said in a telephone interview that orders had been issued to military commanders in the provinces to take over the powers of government from elected mayors and governors.

Newspapers Closed

Newspaper offices were closed as were radio stations. For the first hours, foreign news agencies and other media were for the most part unaffected.

[Agence France-Presse reported later, however, that the Philippine Government had ordered a 24-hour suspension of all out-going news traffic. Earlier the Associated Press reported that the police had closed its office in the building of The Manila Times, forcing the agency to resort to commercial communications.]

The proclamation of martial law, the first since the Philippines obtained independence from the United States in 1946, was believed to be a temporary measure to cope with what Government leaders have described as renewed Communist subversion and terrorist activity.

According to General Ramos, the martial law proclamation was dated Sept. 21 but was put into effect only today.

President Ferdinand E. Marcos said on Sept. 12 that he might be forced to declare martial law to combat increased Communist terrorist attacks. He said at the time that the heads of the Defense Department felt it would be easier to prevent further incidents if they were given greater powers.

These incidents came against a background of widespread unrest and disillusionment in the country over a high rate of unemployment and social injustice.

The assassination attempt against Juan Ponce Enrile, the Defense Secretary, was said to have occurred shortly after 8 P.M. yesterday as he was being driven home from his office.

September 23, 1972

Mass Arrests and Curfew Announced in Philippines

MANILA, Sept. 23—President Ferdinand E. Marcos followed up his declaration of martial law in the Philippines today by announcing the mass arrest of what he said were Communist conspirators plotting to overthrow the Government. He also announced plans for economic reforms.

In a nationwide radio and television address Mr. Marcos imposed a curfew from midnight to 4 A.M. daily and announced controls on newspapers, radio stations and foreign correspondents. He banned travel of Filipinos abroad except those on official missions and barred rallies and demonstrations.

[At the United Nations Carlos P. Romulo, the Philippine Foreign Secretary, said that President Marcos had told him in a phone call that the situation was calm and that some persons were being held to protect them from possible harm from insurgents.]

The President said that civil authorities would remain in power and that all national and local government officials would continue to function.

"This is not a military take-

Ferdinand E. Marcos

over," the President said.

"I have proclaimed martial law in accordance with the powers vested in the President by the Constitution of the Philippines," Mr. Marcos said.

"I as your duly elected President use this power, which may be implemented by military authorities, to protect the Republic of the Philippines and our democracy, which is endangered

The Manila Chronicle

José W. Diokno, at left, and Benigno S. Aquino Jr. are among the opposition leaders who have been arrested.

by the peril of violent overthrow of the duly constituted Government."

"We will eliminate the threat of violent overthrow of Government and we must now reform our political, economic and social institutions," President Marcos declared.

"We are falling back and have fallen back to our last line of defense. The limit has been reached because we have been placed against the wall."

There was no immediate indication how many persons had been arrested. Friends and relatives of those detained said those arrested included at least three senators, several journalists and a number of delegates to the constitutional convention.

Earlier today in predawn raids, Government troops closed all radio and television stations and newspaper offices in greater Manila. One commercial television station and three radio networks were reopened later to broadcast the President's announcement.

The presidential press office said that henceforth all foreign news agencies and correspondents of foreign publications and networks must clear their dispatches with the press office.

In his address, Mr. Marcos announced a cleanup of "corrupt and sterile government officials," a proclamation of land reform throughout the Philippine archipelago, establishment of a military commission to try and punish military offenders and a ban on the carrying of firearms by civilians and unauthorized persons, with violation punishable by death.

September 24, 1972

Wife of President of Philippines Is Stabbed and Her Assailant Slain

By TILLMAN DURDIN
Special to The New York Times

MANILA, Dec. 7 — A man in a dark suit drew a foot-long dagger and stabbed the wife of President Ferdinand E. Marcos today as she was presiding at a ceremony.

Wounds on her hands and arms required 75 stitches but Mrs. Marcos was not gravely injured. Her assailant was shot to death on the spot.

[Government investigators Friday identified the assailant as Carlito Dimaali of Cuenca, about 60 miles southwest of Manila, United Press International reported.]

The attack came as Mrs. Marcos was presenting awards to winners of a national beautification and cleanliness contest. Two other participants in the ceremony, Congressman José Aspiras and Linda Amor Robles, secretary of the beautification campaign, grappled with the attacker and were injured.

Mr. Aspiras had a deep head wound and Miss Robles a deep wound in the back. The secretary, a 22-year-old employe of the Education Department, was carried from the scene, the Nayong Filipino, a group of structures set up near the international airport to show traditional Filipino architectural styles.

Mrs. Marcos, 42, the former Imelda Romualdez, was taken by helicopter to the Makate Medical Center, where she was reported in "safe" condition. Doctors said she might leave in a few days.

However, authorities said that Dr. Robert Chase of Stanford University, California, an expert in hand surgery, had been called in for consultation and was flying to Manila.

The Philippines Secretary of Information, Francisco S. Tatad, said in a statement tonight that the attack could have been part of a right-wing conspiracy aimed at killing both the President and the First Lady.

Mr. Tatad said that the assailant could have had accomplices on the scene "because he was able to go on stage without interference. There was a cover. He was not acting alone."

He said that an hour before the incident, which occurred at 4:30 P.M., someone had phoned the palace to inquire whether Mr. Marcos would appear at the Nayong Filipino. The President sometimes pays surprise visits to ceremonies over which his wife presides.

Television cameras caught the whole episode at the exhibit, where Mrs. Marcos, at the end of the ceremony, was handing out awards to the delegation from Cotabato City.

A slim, middle-aged man about 5-foot-2, in a dark suit, mounted the stage and moved in. He drew the dagger from a sheath concealed in his left sleeve and lunged at Mrs Marcos.

He was apparently aiming at her chest but Mrs. Marcos stooped, moved sideways and parried the blow with her hands and arms. The man's momentum carried him forward. He appeared to be making two more thrusts with the knife.

The TV tape, replayed often, showed him recovering, wheeling and charging back at the First Lady, who had fallen. The assailant flailed out at those seeking to seize him, including Mr. Aspiras and Miss Robles.

There were no security guards around Mrs. Marcos when she was attacked. They arrived only after the attacker had been downed by other participants in the awards ceremony. One guard killed the man with two bullets in the back.

Authorities at the hospital said that Mrs. Marcos, at one time a beauty queen, had cuts on her hands and deep cuts on her arms and that tendons in her arms had been severed.

Mrs. Marcos is a highly popular First Lady who makes many public appearances, travels around the country constantly and has traveled abroad a great deal since her husband was elected six years ago.

She is particularly highly regarded by the peasants and has represented the President at most public ceremonies held since he decreed martial law in September.

President Nixon telephoned the palace to offer his sympathy to the Marcoses.

It was at the international airport here that, on Nov. 27, 1970, an attempt was made to stab Pope Paul VI, who was passing through at the end of a tour of Asia, Australia and the Philippines. Benjamin Mendoza y Amor, a Bolivian painter, has been sentenced to two to four years as the assailant.

December 8, 1972

Marcos Is Amassing Heavy 'Yes' Vote

By TILLMAN DURDIN
Special to The New York Times

MANILA, Saturday, July 28—Early returns from a referendum on whether Ferdinand E. Marcos should continue as President of the Philippines beyond this year indicate that a huge "yes" vote is being amassed.

The voting, which is continuing today, began yesterday after Government and local officials, the controlled press, radio and television, military leaders and others had joined in a nationwide campaign to induce the 22 million voters to say "yes."

A big turnout was reported around the country yesterday. Spurring the turnout was the threat of imprisonment of one to six months for registered neighborhood group members who fail to vote without good excuse.

Heavy Approval Seen

The proposition put to the voters in the referendum is:

"Under the present Constitution, the President, if he so desires, can continue in office beyond 1973. Do you want President Marcos to continue beyond 1973 and finish the reforms he has initiated under martial law?"

Flores Bayot, one of the members of the Commission on Elections, predicted that 90 to 95 per cent of the voters would say "yes."

Early today voting returns

showed 204,988 had voted "yes" and 39,911 "no."

As the voting began yesterday, the Commission on Elections announced that it was the consensus of the neighborhood groups that the President name a council to help him formulate and carry out Government policies and programs.

The commission said it had established the consensus from telegrams, resolutions and reports from leaders of the neighborhood groups.

Since the leaders of the neighborhood groups have always agreed to what President Marcos wants, it can be assumed he plans to set up a legislative council.

The commission also announced that the local leaders did not want the President to convene the interim National Assembly provided for in the new Constitution but favored instead an appointed legislative council with powers to act in he place of the assembly.

All Filipinos 15 years old and older were eligible to vote. Those failing to register were subject to fines equivalent to about $3.

The voters were asked to write comments on the Government on paper provided at the polls and to drop them in the ballot boxes along with their vote. But visits to many voting centers showed that few comment sheets were being used.

At a number of centers there were no supplies of the sheets. At centers where the sheets were available most voters turned them down when offered. Often they were not offered.

"They say, 'Oh, what's the use?'" one supervisor remarked.

At another center the supervisor said: "They say 'I have already voted yes so why write anything more?'"

One man who did put a comment sheet in the ballot box said afterward that he had simply written "100,000 unemployed."

July 28, 1973

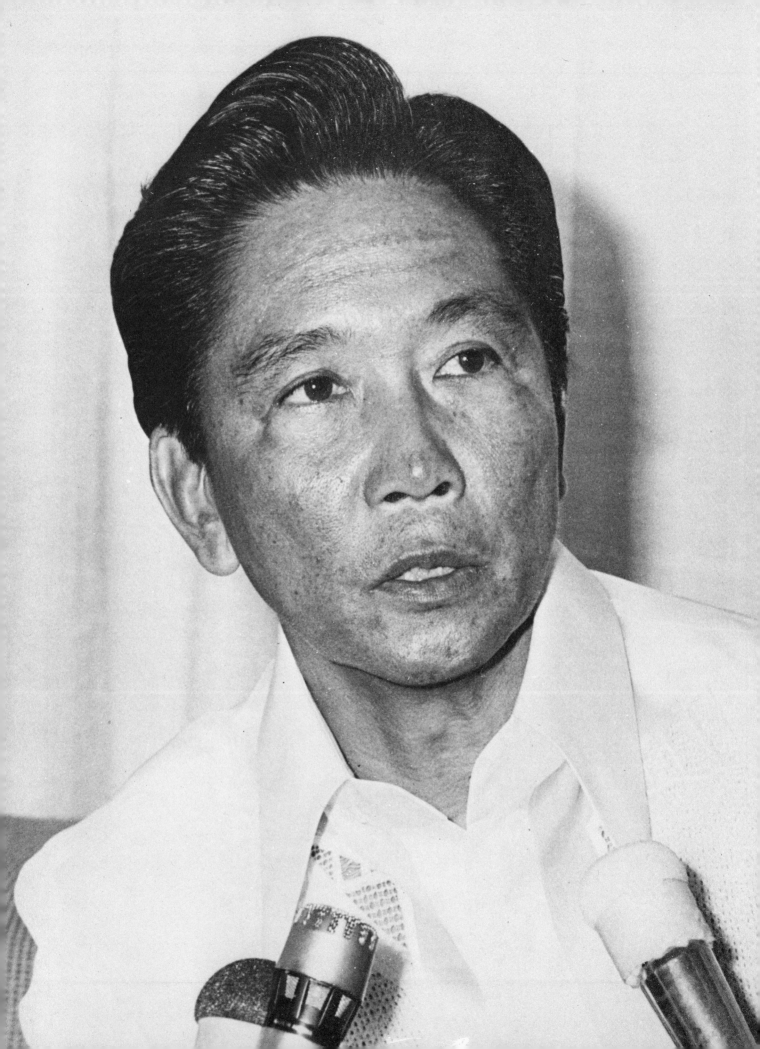

CHAPTER 4

Communism, Nationalism and Economic Development

President Ferdinand Marcos of the Philippines. Although he was chosen president in a free election in 1965 and reelected in 1969, he declared martial law in 1972 and has maintained an iron grip on the country ever since.

UPI

Asia-Pacific Council Is Formed; Nine Members Split on Vietnam

By ROBERT TRUMBULL
Special to The New York Times

SEOUL, South Korea, June 1 —A new association of non-Communist Asian and Pacific states was formed today but was unable to agree on the wording of a joint statement on the conflict in South Vietnam, one of the nine member nations.

The other members are Japan, South Korea, Nationalist China, Thailand, Malaysia, the Philippines, Australia and New Zealand. Laos is an observer.

Most of the members are represented here by their foreign ministers. New Zealand and Malaysia, however, sent other Cabinet members.

According to conference sources, Japan and Malaysia refused to accept a strong stand put forward by Australia in support of the Saigon Government and insisted on milder wording.

The second day of the three-day conference at Walker Hill, a resort complex on the outskirts of Seoul, ended without agreement on the reference to Vietnam in the joint communiqué to be issued tomorrow.

Equivocal Statement Due

A delegate from a British Commonwealth country said that the mention of Vietnam would be "a bit waffly," or equivocal, to avoid giving an ideological tone to the new organization that might prevent other non-Communist but non-aligned countries of the area, such as India, from joining.

There was full agreement, it was reported, on a statement in the communiqué condemning nuclear testing in the Asia-Pacific area. This is aimed at Communist China, which recently conducted its third nuclear explosion, and at France, which is planning a test in the southern Pacific.

The reference to nuclear tests will also avoid the strong language of the usual exchanges between Communist and anti-Communist antagonists, it was reported.

The Japanese and Malaysian delegates were reported to have contended that "provocative" wording would contribute to tensions in the Asia-Pacific area.

However, the spokesmen for all of the countries had dealt firmly with the Communist challenge, based in Peking, in their formal speeches at the opening session yesterday. The announced purpose of the conference is to strengthen the countries under a non-Communist system, by mutual cooperation.

The nine countries decided on the form of the new association, to be known as the Asian and Pacific Cooperation Council, or something similar, so that it can be called ASPAC—"an attractive name with a masculine sound," said Thanat Khoman, the Foreign Minister of Thailand.

It was agreed that the nine members should meet again on the ministerial level about a year from now in Bangkok, Thailand, and annually after that in the capitals of the other countries in turn.

Meanwhile, the Ambassadors to Thailand from the member states will form a standing committee to handle the organization's affairs under the chairmanship of the Thai Foreign Minister, whose Government will furnish a secretariat.

The committee headquarters will rotate from year to year as the successive meeting places are designated.

Strengthened Policies Seen

"Although the organization initially will be purely for economic cooperation, it cannot avoid strengthening the policies of these non-Communist and anti-Communist countries," an Asian delegation chief declared.

The standing committee, which may meet once a month in Bangkok, will have before it a number of proposals for economic cooperation. These include a plan presented by Foreign Minister Wei Tao-ming of Nationalist China and Foreign Secretary Narciso Ramos of the Philippines for a regional bank to handle the development of rice and other commodities, and a Thai suggestion for an international pool of technicians.

The organization grew out of a proposal by Lee Tong Won, the South Korean Foreign Minister. Japan participated on condition that the grouping avoid a military or ideological character, a concession by the Tokyo Government to pacifist and left-wing pressure at home.

June 16, 1966

ASIAN NATIONS FORM NEW ECONOMIC BLOC

Special to The New York Times

BANGKOK, Thailand, Aug. 8 —The Association of Southeast Asian Nations was founded today in Bangkok's Foreign Ministry with the signing of a seven-point declaration.

Ministers from Indonesia, Singapore, the Philippines, Malaysia and Thailand signed the document after two days of golf talks at Bangsaen, a seaside resort.

The declaration was vague about concrete aims and projects for the economic and cultural grouping. Deputy Prime Minister Abdul Razak of Malaysia said: "First you must have an organization and machinery, then you can consider specific projects."

August 9, 1967

SEATO, 23 YEARS OLD, PULLS DOWN ITS FLAGS

Asian Alliance, Brainchild of Dulles, Seen as Behind the Times, Though Some Term Action Premature

By DAVID A. ANDELMAN
Special to The New York Times

BANGKOK, Thailand, June 30—The Southeast Asia Treaty Organization, one of the last vestiges of the cold war in Asia, dissolved itself today. There was only a brief flash as the colors of the remaining member countries were lowered at dusk to mark its end, as contrasted with the enthusiasm amid which it was born nearly 23 years ago as a bulwark against the further spread of Communism in Asia.

Many believe its end, which was foreshadowed by the recommendation by the Thais and Filipinos in May 1975 that it be phased out, was premature. "Why should they have been so hasty in dissolving it?" asked Sunthorn Hongladarom, the fourth and last Secretary General, in an interview last week. "The two organizations, SEATO and the Association of Southeast Asian Nations, should have carried on in parallel for awhile. Later, when it was safe, the two could have converged or merged."

Thailand and the Philippines, two of the five members of the Southeast Asian grouping, which is known as ASEAN, were members of SEATO, which, formed after the Korean War, also included Pakistan, Australia and New Zealand, with the United States, Britain and France as guarantors. Pakistan withdrew five years ago after losing Bangladesh, and France withdrew a year later though it remained a signatory of the defense treaty.

End of Its Usefulness Discerned

Most of the new generation of defense and security officials who run the countries of Southeast Asia believe that SEATO had outlived its usefulness—that it was based on the idea of an Asian war that will never be fought. Three of the five countries in the region were never members—Singapore and Malaysia, being British colonies when it was formed, with their defense guaranteed by the mother country, and Indonesia, being in the process of adjusting to its new freedom under President Sukarno, who

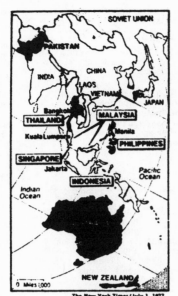

The New York Times/July 1, 1977

The five nations shown in black were original SEATO members along with the U.S., France and Britain. Thailand and the Philippines also are in Association of Southeast Asian Nations with Malaysia, Singapore and Indonesia.

followed an independent course.

The organization was an integral part of the cold war diplomacy of John Foster Dulles when he was President Dwight D. Eisenhower's Secretary of State. An understanding the United States attached to the treaty observed that it applied "only to Communist aggression."

Though SEATO was invoked only once,

in a minor incident, it built a vast structure over the years, with scores of projects, some only peripherally related to its defense function: a medical laboratory; a leading research facility in tropical medicine; the Asian Institute of Technology, which evolved from a graduate school of engineering; a regional meteorological telecommunications project; a hill tribes research center, and cultural programs and economic assistance. Some of these institutions will continue under bilateral arrangements, principally involving assistance from the United States.

Thais Acquire Headquarters

The headquarters building has been sold to the Thai Government as offices for the Foreign Ministry.

Discussing the organization's demise. Secretary General Sunthorn commented: "There was always a limit to what the Southeast Asian members could do to help one another without the backing of the major powers who were also members. These same limitations would certainly carry over to ASEAN."

The leaders of Malaysia, Singapore and Indonesia, disagreeing with Mr. Sunthorn. viewed SEATO as outmoded and as an obstacle to improving ties with the new Communist states of Indochina, which saw it as a military threat. "The wars and the enemy we are fighting are different from the type SEATO was set up to fight," Malaysia's Interior Minister, Sri Ghazali Shafie, said last month, in stressing the role of ASEAN. "These are internal wars now, domestic insurgencies, guerrilla fighting on our own terrain, that we are best able to handle. The major powers can help by seeing that we are strong economically so that our people are happy and will not turn to the Communists."

July 1, 1977

INDOCHINA: VIETNAMESE HEGEMONY

Vietnam Peace Hope Dim As the Last G.I.'s Leave

By SYLVAN FOX
Special to The New York Times

SAIGON, South Vietnam, March 28—The 60-day first phase of the Vietnam ceasefire came to an end today with fighting continuing, peace-keeping machinery in a state of disarray and the prospects for real peace in South Vietnam apparently remote.

The end of this phase is being marked by a momentous turning point in Vietnam's history: the complete withdrawal of American troops after more than eight years of intense involvement.

In the view of many Western and Vietnamese officials, this turning point does not mean that peace has come.

"The cease-fire isn't working," said one highly placed Western diplomat in summing up the critical two months since the Paris peace accord was signed. "It hasn't been implemented as it should have been."

"There certainly has been no cease-fire," said a high-ranking American official who only a few weeks ago predicted that the fighting would soon end. "The best we have is a significantly reduced level of fighting — but we have had these lulls before."

"The thing is," still another well-informed Western official commented, "there's a war on."

The situation has recently deteriorated so seriously, in the view of these and other Western and Vietnamese sources, that the expectation now is an upsurge rather than a decline in the fighting and a seemingly endless prolongation of the war.

At the heart of the new concern and fear is the evidence that the United States says it has collected showing that a heavy infiltration of weapons and supplies by the North Vietnamese is taking place along the Ho Chi Minh Trail net-

work into South Vietnam.

"My belief is that they would not send this stuff down if they didn't expect to use it." an American analyst said. "I think what they plan to do is have a limited offensive in the next few weeks."

"Rather than withering away," another official said wryly, referring to Henry A. Kissinger's comment about North Vietnamese troops in the South. "they are getting stronger."

Two months ago the United States, North Vietnam, South Vietnam and the Vietcong signed an agreement in Paris "on ending the war and restoring peace in Vietnam." President Nixon declared at the time that "peace with honor" had been achieved.

During the 60 days that followed, the United States was supposed to withdraw all its troops from Vietnam, and North Vietnam and the Vietcong were supposed to release all American prisoners of war. Those objectives are being achieved.

For Some It's Over

If, as some observers argue, the principal aim of the Paris agreement was to extricate the United States from the Vietnam war, it seems to be succeeding. For the United States and for North Vietnam—which is no longer the target of American air attacks—the war has ended.

But if the agreement also sought — as its articles and protocols state — to restore peace in Vietnam, then the record is a litany of almost uninterrupted failure:

¶The fighting in South Vietnam, which was supposed to be ended by the agreement, continues to flare—although at a relatively low level for the moment—long after American officials expressed certainty that it would come to a virtual halt. Saigon and the Communists accuse each other of violating the cease-fire without regard for either the letter or the spirit of the agreement.

¶Potentially even more threatening to future prospects for peace in Vietnam, the North Vietnamese have allegedly sent 40,000 fresh troops, 300 tanks and hundreds of artillery pieces into South Vietnam since the signing of the agreement, which expressly forbids such shipments. The Communists deny these allegations, charging that they are "a ruse by the United States to cover up" its own illegal shipments of arms to South Vietnam.

¶The peace-keeping machinery created by the Paris agreement has proved to be helpless—it has neither stopped the fighting nor established blame for its continuation. The Four-Party Joint Military Commission, which bore the primary responsibility under the agreement for bringing about a real cease-fire in the first 60 days after the accord was signed, never manned more than a fraction of its assigned sites around the country and now goes out of existence without functioning as the peace-keeping body it was designed to be. The International Commission of Control and Supervision has bogged down in ideological splits between Hungary and Poland on the one hand and Canada and Indonesia on the other and has had no significant impact on reducing the fighting.

Thus neither peace nor any real mechanism for bringing peace has been attained. However, the picture is not without bright spots.

A large-scale exchange of prisoners arranged between the Saigon Government and the Communists, involving some 27,000 men in Government captivity and almost 5,000 in Communist hands, has been completed.

As the Joint Military Commission goes out of existence at the end of this week, a Two-Party Joint Military Commission composed of Saigon and the Vietcong's Provisional Revolutionary Government appears ready to begin meeting, although no one is especially sanguine about its capacity for restoring peace in light of the record of the four-party commission.

In addition, representatives of Saigon and the Vietcong have opened talks in Paris aimed at creating a National Council of National Reconciliation and Concord to supervise elections and resolve the political future of South Vietnam.

Some newsmen and opposition politicians attach great importance to these talks, noting that they mark the first time the two South Vietnamese sides have actually sat down to discuss political differences. However, others, including some South Vietnamese, express strong doubt that the Paris talks will produce concrete results.

Hatreds Run Deep

"The differences between the two sides are so great and the hatreds run so deep," a South Vietnamese source explained, "that I believe the talks will ultimately break down."

Regardless of how the talks fare, the tentative first steps in search of a political solution to South Vietnam's problems do not alter the reality of the last 60 days, which have been marked by continued conflict on the battlefield and in the conference rooms.

Taking the elements of the situation separately, they shape up this way:

In the fighting, according to Saigon's count, a total of more than 15,000 Communist troops have been killed since the cease-fire began. The Government says its casualties have been more than 3,000 men killed and more than 15,000 wounded. In addition, it says, more than 400 civilians have been killed and 1,300 wounded.

Saigon charges that the Communists have committed more than 8,500 violations of the cease-fire. The Communists say Saigon has been guilty of thousands of "nibbling operations." Regardless of the truth of either side's claims, the fighting continues. And it is no longer diminishing, as it was a few weeks ago.

In the first six weeks after the cease-fire went into effect Jan 28, there was a series of increases and decreases in the level of military activity. American analysts repeatedly asserted that these peaks and valleys were following a generally downward trend that would, within a short time, virtually end the fighting. They now concede they were wrong. As one official put it, the fighting is "on a plateau right now,

I'm afraid." Another American analyst went even further; he expects an increase in the fighting.

"I think we are going to see another significant escalation some time in April," he said.

This official asserted that the North Vietnamese had more and better equipment in South Vietnam today than they had a year ago, when they launched their spring offensive.

Big Guns in South

He said the equipment the North Vietnamese now had in the South included large numbers of 130-mm. and 122-mm. artillery pieces and 57-mm. antiaircraft guns. He added that the 130-mm. guns, with a range of 17 miles, could cause Saigon's troops "great grief."

Where North Vietnam is weaker than it was a year ago, he said, is in the number of combat-ready troops it has available in the South. "I don't think they have the strength for a sustained offensive," he went on "but they do have the capability for major attacks that could take over individual places easily."

The purpose of such action, in the view of this analyst, would be to establish "a plausible base" for the Provisional Revolutionary Government, which, in his opinion, is now "without much real substance."

Isolated Shelling Attacks

As for the current fighting, much of it consists of isolated shelling attacks. There are some assaults on Government outposts by the Communists and attacks by Government troops on Communist positions. There is some skirmishing for hamlets and some attempts by the Communists to cut roads or by the Government to open them.

More significant than the fighting itself at the moment is the failure of any peace-keeping machinery to stop it.

One of the many specific instances in which the peace-keeping machinery broke down was the case of the alleged installation of missiles by the Communists at Khe Sanh.

According to the United States and Saigon, the Communists installed three missile sites at the former American Marine base in the extreme northwest corner of South Vietnam. The Communists denied the allegation and the United States asked the control commission to investigate. However, the Hungarians and the Poles refused to approve the investigation and the commission, which requires unanimous decision to act, was paralyzed.

On March 1 the Communists, under extreme pressure from the United States, reportedly withdrew the missiles. But on

March 21, according to the United States, the missiles were back in almost the same spot, bringing another stern warning from the United States that it would take "necessary action" if they were not removed.

Throughout this dispute the peace-keeping machinery remained essentially irrelevant. It was similarly irrelevant when the South Vietnamese charged that two of their small outposts were under siege and called upon the Joint Military Commission to halt the fighting in the two areas.

The commission took no action because its Communist members denied any violation at the two outposts, Rach Bap, about 22 miles north of Saigon, and Tong Le Chan, about 50 miles north of the capital.

Commission Moves Fast

Saigon then asked the International Control Commission to step in and investigate the situations at the two outposts. With surprising dispatch it agreed — but equally swiftly, the Hungarians and Poles refused to participate in any investigation until the fighting had stopped and it was safe to do so. They said the Communists had refused to guarantee the safety of the investigators.

With the peace-keeping machinery again paralyzed, Saigon announced that it had sent a regiment of men supported by tanks and aircraft to lift the siege of Rach Bap. Its forces encountered no resistance and the siege was ended. But as one Western diplomat pointed out, the only reason the incident did not erupt into major fighting was that in this instance the Communists chose to withdraw when faced with the prospect of a large-scale attack.

"That kind of solution," one diplomat said, "is war, not peace."

Sporadic shelling of the other besieged base at Tong Le Chan is reported continuing.

If the International Control Commission has been unable to play any direct role in reducing the fighting, as one official put it, it at least "went through the motions" of deploying its teams around the country as mandated by the Paris agreement. In one case, however, at Tri Ton, the Hungarian and Polish representatives left when the site came under Communist shelling.

The Joint Military Commission never even got that far. It was supposed to deploy peace-keeping teams to seven regional sites and 26 subregional sites in order to halt fighting and to monitor the cease-fire.

In the end, the military commission had not fully deployed except at four regional sites. The United States and the South Vietnamese sent their commission delegates to all seven regional sites and to all 26 local sites, but the North Vietnamese manned only five regional sites and four subregional ones. The Provisional Revolutionary Government never manned any subregional sites and had representatives at only four of the regional bases.

By the time the 60-day term of the Joint Military Commission had ended, neither the North Vietnamese nor the Vietcong were at any subregional sites. The North Vietnamese had withdrawn from the site at Ban Me Thuot after their delegation was attacked by a rock-throwing mob and, after similar incidents at Hue and DaNang, the Communists withdrew their staff from three other subregional sites.

Result Is Complete Failure

The result has been the complete failure of the Joint Military Commission to function as a peace-keeping body.

The Four-Party Military Commission held what was described as its final meeting today, according to an American spokesman, although speculation has persisted that its life might be extended. It was understood that the United States had been seeking such an extension, but South Vietnam has strenuously opposed the idea publicly and North Vietnam and Vietcong reportedly have opposed it in private. At today's meeting the commission was unable to agree on a communiqué summarizing its two months of activity.

The commission's only significant contribution to the cause of peace in Vietnam, except for

working out the release of the prisoners and the withdrawal of American troops, has been the issuance of an appeal early in the cease-fire for the immediate end of hostilities. The appeal had no discernible effect.

What does it all add up to?

In the opinion of a high-ranking Western official—not an American—"the war will go on and on and on."

"The only way I can see peace coming," this experienced diplomat said, "would be a surrender by the South."

"I have no evidence that the North has given up its design to reunify the country," he said, "and there is no indication that they are prepared to delay this to do it by peaceful means."

Like many other officials

interviewed, this diplomat said he expected continued low-level fighting for an indeterminate period, followed by a major offensive by one side or the other.

One well-informed official was more cautious about the outlook.

"I think in the next six months or a year," he said, "a decision will be made. Either the Communists will opt for a major military solution or they will decide to seek a political solution. But I don't think they've really made that decision yet."

March 29, 1973

BIG BOMBING TOLL IN CAMBODIA SEEN

Heavy Civilian Losses Laid to Raids, Said to Be Based on Inadequate Intelligence

By JOSEPH B. TREASTER
Special to The New York Times

PHNOM PENH, Cambodia, April 15—Knowledgeable Western diplomats here say that they believe that the heavy United

States bombing campaign in Cambodia is being carried out on the basis of inadequate intelligence data and often with imprecise control, causing high civilian casualties.

"The Americans are throwing air support around like a mad woman," one diplomat said. "They don't know what effect it's having."

United States officials refuse to discuss any aspect of the bombing, which is directed from the embassy here. Instead, they refer all queries to the United States Pacific Command in Honolulu, which has consistently refused to go beyond its

terse daily statement saying that the bombing is continuing at the request of the Cambodian Government.

Informed Western sources say, however, that American fighter-bomber pilots based in Thailand are flying an average of 250 strikes a day—almost as many as in South Vietnam, which is much larger, during the heavy fighting there last year.

In addition, the sources say, Cambodia is being pounded by an average of 60 B-52's a day, each carrying up to 30 tons of bombs. One day recently, they say, the United States mounted an attack by 120 of the huge bombers.

Military experts say that the bombing has slowed the Cambodian insurgents but not stopped them. The experts add, however, that the bombing has probably prevented the collapse of the Cambodian Army and, in turn, the fall of the Government of Marshal Lon Nol.

It is rare to find a high Government official critical of the bombing. One official said: "We know that some villagers have been hit by the bombs, but the other side has done worse. In a war like this some side effects are expected. So we consider it a side effect when bombs hit innocent civilians."

April 16, 1973

U.S. CONFIRMS PRE-1970 RAIDS ON CAMBODIA

Bombing Protected G.I.'s, Says the New Defense Secretary

By SEYMOUR M. HERSH
Special to The New York Times

WASHINGTON, July 16 — Secretary of Defense James R. Schlesinger acknowledged today

that Air Force B-52 bombers were secretly attacking Cambodia in 1969 and 1970 while

the United States was publicly professing its respect for that nation's neutrality in the Vietnam war.

In a letter sent to Senator Stuart Symington, acting chairman of the Senate Armed Services Committee, Dr. Schlesinger defended the unannounced and unreported raids—that ceased with the invasion of Cambodia in May, 1970—as "fully authorized" and necessary for the protection of American servicemen.

The Defense Secretary also said that "because of the sensitive operational and diplomatic situation, special security precautions were taken to insure that the operations would not be compromised," referring to operations inside Cambodia.

Tells of Fake Reports

Some of those "precautions" were described to the committee today by a former Air Force major, Hal M. Knight of Memphis, who served as operations officer for a secret Strategic Air Command radar site in South Vietnam that was responsible for electronically guiding the B-52's to their targets.

Mr. Knight, who left the Air Force this spring after he was twice passed over for promotion, told the Senators that he and others had deliberately falsified highly classified reports made after missions to prevent any official recording of the Cambodian bombings.

July 17, 1973

BOMBING OF CAMBODIA STOPPED, MARKING THE OFFICIAL U.S. END OF COMBAT IN SOUTHEAST ASIA

SUPPORT PLEDGED

American Planes Will Remain on Station in Guam and Thailand

By BERNARD GWERTZMAN
Special to The New York Times

WASHINGTON, Wednesday, Aug. 15—American bombing in Cambodia officially ended last midnight with the Nixon Administration still pledging to do everything possible within the law to support the Government of President Lon Nol.

The cessation of all bombing activity, voted by Congress on June 30, and accepted by President Nixon with "grave personal reservations," marks the official end to America's dozen years of combat activity in Southeast Asia. Some 46,000 American lives have been lost—most of them in South Vietnam — since the first American casualties in 1961.

The Vietnam cease-fire agreement, signed on Jan. 27 in Paris, ended the American combat role in North and South Vietnam, and the Laotian agreement a month later ended the American role there.

Fighting Goes On

The Cambodian fighting, however, has not stopped, and it is unclear what the effect the end of American bombing will have on the Cambodian belligerents.

But even as B-52 strategic bombers and F-4 fighter-bombers carried out their last missions, the Pentagon stressed that American planes would remain on station in Thailand and in Guam, prepared to resume their raids if Congress authorized them—something viewed as unlikely unless North Vietnam launched a vast invasion of South Vietnam.

Although the end to American

The New York Times/Denis Cameron

Refugees in motorcycle-drawn carts pass a bomb crater along Route 1 in Cambodia

bombing was a historic landmark in the long, controversial Indochina war, the Administration chose virtually to ignore it. Neither the White House, nor the Pentagon nor the State Department volunteered any statement on the occasion.

On the final day of United States bombing, 60 persons, in-

cluding the antiwar activists Daniel J. Berrigan and his brother Jerome were arrested as they knelt and prayed at the White House in a protest against the raids. [Page 14.]

At the Defense Department, officials said the end of the bombing was being treated routinely.

The Pentagon, in answer to questions, supplied statistics on the latest Cambodian phase of the bombing, between Jan 28, the day following the Vietnam cease-fire agreement, and Aug. 11, the last day for which figures were available. During that period, 35,410 sorties, or flights, were carried out, costing a total of $422.8-million.

There were no firm answers to a question being widely posed: What will happen to the Lon Nol Government without American air support?

Several officials at the Defense Department and the State Department said that they were hesitant to make any predictions.

They said that there were conflicting reports from the field about the military situation around Phnom Penh, the Cambodian capital, and there were different assessments about the possibility that some kind of cease-fire would be worked out by the Lon Nol Government and the insurgents opposing it.

Fear of Collapse

The prevailing sentiment, however, was that the Phnom Penh Government would do well if it could avoid a complete military collapse.

An Administration official said that it was impossible to talk about negotiations until the new military situation in Cambodia became clear.

He said that the bombing had been an important lever in the Administration's effort to persuade China and North Vietnam to prod the Cambodian insurgents into accepting a cease-fire. By forcing the end to the bombing, he said, Congress took away any incentive to negotiate.

A senior State Department official said recently that it "probably doesn't matter" what happens in Phnom Penh from a strategic point of view. But, he said, South Vietnam and Thailand may become gravely concerned about a Communist Government in Cambodia, and this could lead to a further disintegration of the Vietnam cease-fire agreement if Saigon feels so threatened that it sends forces into Cambodia.

Intervention Held Unlikely

For the moment, State Department officials said, it was unlikely that Saigon would intervene in Cambodia. South Vietnam was aware, they said, that Congress might respond by cutting off its economic aid.

Gerald L. Warren, the deputy White House press secretary, in answer to questions, repeated the standard Administration pledge that it "will do everything within the law to support the Government of Cambodia." He also said again that no combat activity would be undertaken without "proper authority" from Congress.

The law permits the United States to keep sending military and economic aid to Cambodia, but for this aid to be used, the Cambodian Government must keep its transportation arteries open. In coming weeks, some officials said, the insurgents will probably make a determined effort to cut off the major population areas from supplies.

Combat Activity Barred

The Congress on June 30, in attaching a rider to a crucial appropriations measure to keep the Government going, ruled out all combat activity in Indochina after Aug. 15.

Mr. Nixon, in a letter to Congressional leaders on Aug. 3, said the Administration would obey the law, but added:

"I cannot do so, however, without stating my grave personal reservations concerning the dangerous potential consequences of this measure. I would be remiss in my Constitutional responsibilities if I did not warn of the hazards that lie in the path chosen by Congress."

He said that the Aug. 15 cut-off had undermined negotiating efforts to get a settlement in Cambodia, and he warned that "this abandonment of a friend" could have a profound impact in other countries such as Thailand, "which have relied on the constancy and determination of the United States."

Some Flights Allowed

The bombing ban will not bar unarmed reconnaissance flights over Cambodia and Laos, the Pentagon said, but the planes involved will be prohibited from calling for armed support if fired upon.

Pentagon officials said that up to 400 fighter-bombers and 175 B-52s would remain on call in Thailand, Guam and aboard carriers. These will probably be withdrawn gradually to the United States, officials said.

Since Jan. 28, the Pentagon said, 27,626 fighter-bomber sorties were carried out in Cambodia, at a cost of $182.3-million. A total of 7,784 B-52 sorties were flown, it said, costing $240.5-million. Nine aircraft were lost, with six men killed and four missing.

August 15, 1973

Hanoi Bulldozers Drive Road Network Into South

By JAMES M. MARKHAM
Special to The New York Times

PLEIKU, South Vietnam, Jan. 5—North Vietnamese bulldozers and South Vietnamese fighter-bombers are fighting a duel in the forested expanses of the Central Highlands. The bulldozers are winning.

As South Vietnamese commanders watch apprehensively, North Vietnamese engineers are swiftly expanding and improving a skein of roads, lumbering trails that wind down the country's western flank, poking eastward at strategic junctures.

In addition to the much publicized north-south axis of 375 miles known as Corridor 613, the Communists have developed west-east systems that, however thinly, bring to life a nightmare that haunted American commanders in Vietnam: cutting South Vietnam in two.

"South Vietnam has been cut in two," commented one American here in the highlands. "But nobody has bothered to notice."

The rugged west-east trails

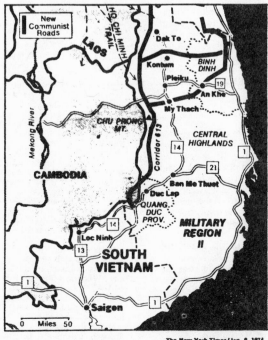

The New York Times/Jan. 8, 1974

— "they cannot be dignified as roads," one analyst said — appear to unsettle the South Vietnamese far more than does Corridor 613, because they jut ominously into disputed and Government-held areas.

The Communists have reportedly not begun to move large quantities of men and weaponry on the main west-east trail that loops over Kontum city and down to northern Binh Dinh Province on the coast.

But South Vietnamese propeller-driven Skyraiders and A-37 jet fighter-bombers, which are flying up to 80 missions a day in the highlands, have in recent weeks reported knocking out tanks, bulldozers and five-ton Russian-built Molotova trucks north and northwest of Kontum.

To the south of Pleiku, pilots said on Thursday that they had

January 8, 1974

279

Land Reform in Vietnam Reversed in Some Areas

By DAVID K. SHIPLER
Special to The New York Times

SAIGON, South Vietnam, Jan. 13—The Government has begun to slip back after having reached the brink of success in dissolving large land holdings, distributing them to poor tenant farmers and thus eliminating one of the Vietcong's most potent political issues.

Here and there in secure areas around the country, Vietnamese plantation owners are coming back to reclaim land they abandoned because of the war. Some local officials are demanding that peasants relinquish land titles they were given just a few years ago.

The recent developments have partly eroded what had been one of the most ambitious land-reform programs in Asia, financed largely by American aid and undertaken in 1970 as a frankly political effort to woo peasants from allegiance to the Vietcong.

In its three and a half years the program has clearly diminished grievances over land ownership by transferring 2.5 million acres to farmers, relieving them of onerous rents that frequently ran to a third of the crop or more.

The main target of the reform and the main area of its success was the rice-rich Mekong Delta, where tenancy has been virtually eliminated. The current backsliding — affecting provinces adjacent to Saigon and parts of the Central Highlands — does not yet appear to have revived the land issue for the Communists, but some legislators and Government officials are worried that it will.

January 14, 1974

PAROLE OF CALLEY GRANTED BY ARMY EFFECTIVE NOV. 19

He Is Completing a Third of His 10-Year Term—May Be Freed on Bail Today

By R. W. APPLE Jr.
Special to The New York Times

WASHINGTON, Nov. 8 — Former Lieut. William L. Calley Jr., who was convicted of murdering 22 South Vietnamese civilians at Mylai in 1968, will be paroled later this month, the Army announced tonight.

Howard H. Callaway, the Secretary of the Army, said that Mr. Calley would be freed on Nov. 19, when he will have completed one-third of his 10-year prison sentence.

Mr. Callaway made his announcement several hours after the United States Court of Appeals in New Orleans ordered that the 31-year-old former infantry officer be promptly freed on bail. That release may take place tomorrow.

An Army statement said that the Secretary had acted following "a thorough review of Calley's application for parole and the recommendation of officials at the United States Army disciplinary barracks and the Army and Air Force Clemency Board."

14 U.S. Judges Act

The day's fast-breaking developments in the Calley case began in New Orleans. Fourteen of the 15 judges of the United States Court of Appeals for the Fifth Circuit were secretly called together to decide whether Mr. Calley should be freed on bail pending review of a lower court's decision freeing him completely.

The deliberations ended in a 10-to-4 affirmative vote. The 15th judge, Thomas Gibbs Gee, excused himself because of his military background.

After exhausting his military appeals, Mr. Calley, who was convicted in a court martial in March, 1971, turned to the civil courts for relief. He was originally sentenced to life imprisonment, but that was cut to 10 years.

On Sept. 25, United States District Judge J. Robert Elliott in Columbus, Ga., where Mr. Calley had once been confined under house arrest, threw out the conviction, largely on the ground of prejudicial pretrial publicity.

Order Signed Oct. 30

That decision was appealed to the Fifth Circuit by the Army. Pending its review, the Circuit Court directed the Army to take Mr. Calley from Fort Leavenworth, Kan., where he has been incarcerated, to Columbus, Ga., tomorrow "for the purpose of releasing him on bail."

According to The Associated Press, Mr. Calley's lawyer, J. Houston Gordon, said after the decision that he expected his client to be released by Monday. He described Mr. Calley as "elated, excited and pleased."

The news of the decision prompted Mr. Callaway to disclose that he had signed a parole order on Oct. 30 to become effective Nov. 19. There was no explanation as to why the order had not been made public earlier.

Mr. Callaway said that the Army would take Mr. Calley to Columbus as directed and would not ask "any terms or conditions in connection with Calley's bail" because of the parole. But he said that the Army would press its appeal "because of the important legal issues raised in this case."

Regardless of the fate of that appeal, it will not affect Mr. Calley's freedom. After more than three years in custody, he has won his battle.

Mr. Callaway's order was based on his authority to review all court martials. He was once a Republican member of Congress representing the district that includes Columbus and Fort Benning, Ga., where Mr. Calley was tried.

Of a total of 25 Army officers and enlisted men who were charged with various offenses growing out of the slayings of at least 100 Vietnamese villagers at the undefended hamlet of Mylai 4 on March 16, 1968, only First Lieut. William L. Calley Jr. was convicted.

The public was not told about the slayings until 20 months later. The silence led to charges of suppression of information against former Maj. Gen. Samuel W. Koster, the commander of the Americal Division; his deputy, Brig. Gen. George H. Young, and 12 other officers.

Although the official and secret Army investigation of the mass killings, led by Lieut. Gen. William R. Peers, concluded that those two generals had committed 43 acts of misconduct or omission in their field inquiry of the atrocity, criminal charges against them were dropped. Ultimately, they were

stripped of their Distinguished Service Medals and censured.

Charges of either murder or suppression of information against 10 other officers and seven enlisted men were also dismissed.

Only six men were court martialed, and five were acquitted. Those included Col. Oran K. Henderson, Lieutenant Calley's brigade commander, and Capt. Ernest L. Medina, his company commander.

With his conviction for murdering no fewer than 22 civilians, Lieutenant Calley became for some Americans a symbol of the nation's moral confusion over the war. Others considered him a cold-blooded murderer. And many others, polls have shown, thought of him as the Army's scapegoat.

Three days after the lieutenant was placed in a stockade in 1971, former President Nixon intervened and ordered him under house arrest pending appeals. Until last February, when

he was freed on a bond, he was confined to a two-bedroom bachelor's apartment at Fort Benning. He spent much of his time watching television, building model airplanes, learning gourmet cooking, entertaining his girl friend, Anne Moore, and taking courses in accounting.

In late June, the bail was revoked, and he was taken to the stockade at Fort Leavenworth, where he worked as a clerk typist until his conviction was overturned in September.

Following is a statement issued by the Defense Department announcing Secretary Callaway's decision:

The Secretary of the Army, Howard H. Callaway, today announced that in accordance with instructions received from the United States District Court for the Middle District of Georgia, the Army will deliver William L. Calley Jr. before the court on Saturday, November 9, at 11

A.M. for the purpose of releasing on bail.

The United States Court of Appeals for the Fifth Circuit earlier today issued an opinion ordering him admitted to bail on reasonable terms and conditions to be fixed initially by the District Court. The order admitting Calley to bail

was issued pending a decision of the Court of Appeals on the merits of the Army's decision on Calley's appeal for a petition of habeas corpus.

Secretary Callaway states: that the Army would not request any terms or conditions in connection with Calley's bail, since on Oct. 30 he had

signed an order granting Calley parole effective Nov. 19, his parole eligibility date. He had made that decision based on a thorough review of Calley's application for parole and the recommendation of officials at the United States Army disciplinary barracks and the Army and Air Force Clemency Board.

The Secretary indicated that the Army intends to pursue vigorously its appeal of the District Court's decision granting Calley's petition of habeas corpus because of the important legal issues raised in this case.

November 9, 1974

Heroin Addiction Growing in South Vietnam, Especially at Remote Army Posts

PLEIKU, South Vietnam, Feb. 17—In the dingy, dimly lit back room of a house near the Roman Catholic cathedral here, two soldiers lay sprawled on a bed, their eyes closed.

Another soldier, in the mottled green camouflage uniform of a South Vietnamese ranger, entered the room and approached a tired-looking old man squatting in the corner over a water pipe. "Dad, may I borrow the bowl and sword," he asked. These were the code words used to ask for a heroin injection.

This was an example of a growing heroin addiction problem throughout the South Vietnamese armed forces and among some well-to-do young people, especially in Saigon.

According to military investigators in this dusty Central Highlands garrison city, about 30 per cent of the airmen and combat soldiers stationed here now use heroin in some form. At least part of this heroin is said to be sold by South Vietnamese officers.

There have been no known instances of plane crashes or avoidance of combat because of

this use of narcotics. But there have been several cases reported here recently of deaths among pilots and soldiers because of overdoses.

The drug problem began, Vietnamese familiar with it say, with the national mood of despair that accompanied the Communists' offensive in 1972 and then the ineffective Paris peace agreement in 1973. The problem is most acute in isolated garrisons such as Pleiku where there has been little actual fighting recently and boredom is almost as big an enemy as the North Vietnamese.

In the view of investigators, the heroin problem is also a direct legacy of the American presence in Vietnam.

"We always had some opium smoking, but we didn't know what heroin was until the G.I.'s brought it," a South Vietnamese official remarked. He was referring to the epidemic of heroin use that spread rapidly among American soldiers here in 1970 and 1971 as United States participation in the war was phased out.

The most commonly used Vietnamese term for heroin, "si ke," does in fact suggest an American origin. It is a corrup-

tion of the G.I. slang word "scag."

Moreover, narcotics specialists believe, much of the heroin being sold in Vietnam now is left over from the large stockpiles accumulated in those earlier years to supply American servicemen.

"The smugglers hadn't anticipated a drop in the market so soon," a Western specialist suggested. As evidence of his theory, he added that no heroin was now known to be moving into South Vietnam from Thailand, the usual source.

The wholesale drug business in Vietnam is thought to be carried on by Chinese networks operating from Cholon, the large Chinese section of Saigon.

But just who markets it to the troops is murky.

The ranger who bought a dose in the house near the cathedral here said that his former commander, a major, had once sold heroin at their border outpost in Kontum.

Pushers in Area Headquarters

Other knowledgeable Vietnamese and foreigners say they can point out pushers among low-ranking officers in the headquarters of Military Region II in Pleiku.

Lieut. Col. Nguyen Ngoc Tho-

ai, the chief of police in Pleiku, is well aware of the problem.

"As you can see, Pleiku is a city of soldiers," he said, sitting in a small coffee shop. "It is the soldiers who use the drugs, and they themselves protect the pushers. Then what can I do?"

There have been some police efforts at arresting suspected dealers in Pleiku. But heroin can still be purchased easily down dozens of back alleys and in some coffee shops for prices ranging from the equivalent of about 70 cents for the smallest cellophane packet to $10 for a plastic vial.

Because the heroin is of extremely high purity—from 90 to 97 per cent—it is dangerous to inject it directly and most users mix it with tobacco for smoking. Street heroin in New York often is of as low purity as 2 to 3 per cent.

The South Vietnamese Army has established several rehabilitation centers and hospital wards, including one at the Cong Hoa Military Hospital in Saigon, which has treated more than 1,000 patients in two years. But the methods are primitive and the rate of relapse is said to be high.

February 23, 1975

SOUTH VIETNAM REPORTED YIELDING MOST OF CENTRAL HIGHLANDS AREA; MAIN EVACUATION ROUTES CUT OFF

By JAMES M. MARKHAM
Special to The New York Times

SAIGON, South Vietnam, Tuesday, March 18—The Saigon Government has decided to abandon most of the Central Highlands of South Vietnam because the area has become militarily indefensible, well-placed

Western sources said today.

The decision, one of the most momentous of the long Vietnam war, was made after 14 days of sharp military reverses in the vast, rolling highlands. It was certain to have important political reverberations.

The area to be abandoned was reported to include the pivotal border provinces of Darlac, Pleiku and Kontum. South Vietnam has 44 provinces but these three are among the largest. They were the cradle of American involvement in the war and cover most — but

not all—of the high, mountainstudded plains that are commonly regarded as making up the Central Highlands.

Defensibility Considered

These provinces are divided along administrative lines, however, while the Saigon mili-

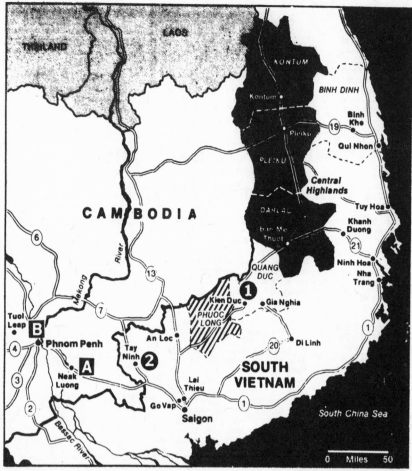

Saigon decided to abandon a roughly three-province area (shown in black). Phuoc Long Province (diagonally shaded) was previously lost. Kien Duc (1) was target of Communist drive, and heavy fighting was reported near Tay Ninh (2). In Cambodia, airstrip of Neak Luong (A) was attacked by rebels. Pressure was kept on capital (B).

tary command's decision could be expected to follow lines of military defensibility, perhaps leaving parts of the three provinces still within its new line of defense and consigning parts of adjoining highlands provinces to the other side.

The Government might try to hold certain sections of the highlands either as staging areas for further withdrawal or as staging points for future actions. One informant indicated that the Government might even attempt to retake the city of Ban Me Thuot, giving itself an anchor in the southern highlands, but the sources doubted that such an attempt would be made.

It could not be learned how swiftly the movement of Government forces from the highlands—and particularly the important cities of Pleiku and Kontum—was unfolding.

According to some accounts, Government units were trek-

king down little used paths and provincial roads because the two main routes leading out of the region, 19 and 21, are cut.

Speedy Action Taken

"I think it can be said that the Vietnamese moved very quickly," one Western analyst said this morning, "and that once the decision was made it was carried out with considerable speed."

The well-placed Western sources said that, with the civilian populations alerted to the pullout, airports had become a difficult withdrawal route and that most of the troops—and civilians who wanted to leave—might have to fight their way out.

The decision to abandon the area was reportedly made sometimes after Friday when President Nguyen Van Thieu flew to the coastal city of Nha Trang to confer with Maj. Gen. Pham Van Phu, commander of Military Region II, which

includes a stretch of the central coast as well.

Starting late last week, after the North Vietnamese seized the important highlands town of Ban Me Thuot and began rocket attacks on the corps headquarters and airfield at Pleiku, General Phu quietly began moving his staff to Nha Trang. The western defenses of Pleiku itself were threatened with tank-led attacks reported around the key district seat of Thanh An.

Reported to have weighed heavily in the decision to abandon the region were the vastness of the highlands, the enhanced North Vietnamese logistics and road systems, on which they have been feverishly working since the signing of the Paris peace agreements in January, 1973, and the increasing number of Communist troops in the area.

Also, with Routes 19 and 21 cut since the Communists began their highlands offensive on March 4, the South Vietnamese Air Force, already restricted by cuts in American assistance,

faced the prospect of a long, costly airlift to the embattled area, with little likelihood of its paying off in the long run.

Decision Ratified

On Saturday, according to one account, the National Security Council in Saigon ratified the decision that Mr. Thieu and General Phu sketched out in Nha Trang. It could not be learned what kind of consensus Mr. Thieu had built up for the move, which is expected to be a stunning blow to the morale of the nation. But there were no visible signs of dissent.

Military analysts have long considered the withdrawal an eventual necessity. General Phu had only two regular infantry divisions, the 22d and 23d, to defend his vast corps command. The bulk of the 22d had been committed to the defense of Binh Dinh Province, which rises from the ricelands of the coast to the highlands.

The 23d Division was believed to have been battered in the fight for Ban Me Thuot, which the North Vietnamese attacked early on March 10.

In addition, the II Corps area had roughly the equivalent of a division, about 10,000 men, in rangers and perhaps another division of regional forces.

Hanoi Force Put at 45,000

The exact strength of the North Vietnamese forces in the area is a matter of guesswork, though last month one reliable Western estimate put the total at 45,000.

But since then there have been reports of heavy infiltrations of North Vietnamese into the area. The Saigon command charged last week that elements of the 316th Division, a famous one that fought at Dien Bien Phu, had been seen in the highlands.

In addition, the North Vietnamese 320th and 10th Divisions are believed to be operating in the Darlac-Quang Duc area of the southern highlands, the 968th around Pleiku and the 3d at Binh Dinh.

The Communists also have regional forces and autonomous regiments—those not attached to a division—in the highlands.

Darlac, Kontum and Pleiku Provinces represent about 16 per cent of South Vietnam's land surface and their population of a half million compares with a nationwide population of 19.5 million.

One Western military analyst said that the pullout decision was "not all black" in that it would permit the South Vietnamese forces to regroup in the more defensible coastal areas, where their lines of communication are shorter and those of their foes extended.

A measure of the success of the regrouping operation, which is unparalleled in the recent history of the war, will be the number of troops and civilians who manage to walk, ride, fly or fight their way to the coast.

One knowledgeable informant said that a possible escape route was the little used provincial route leading out of Phu Bon Province to the town of Tuy Hoa on the coast.

It seemed possible that some military or civilian refugees might manage to move down Route 21 from Ban Me Thuot to Ninh Hoa on the coast. That highway is cut near the town of Khanh Duong, but Route 19 is cut in many places.

Also, army engineers have been improving an old French colonial road descending from the Quang Duc Province capital of Gia Nghia to Di Linh on Route 20.

One of the last correspondents known to be in Pleiku, Nguyen Tu, who works for the respected daily Chinh Luan, described the town on Sunday as a nightmarish place. He said people were running around the streets "as if they were caught in a trap," clinging to their most precious possessions. He said every imaginable kind of vehicle was being used in efforts to get out of the city, but that there was no real exit.

In yesterday's fighting, North Vietnamese tanks and troops mounted heavy assaults in remote, mountainous Quang Duc Province and stepped up attacks around Saigon, the military command said.

The regional thrusts, which the command called a nationwide Communist offensive, are now viewed with increased anxiety by Western military analysts. "It's grim and it's going to get grimmer," said one knowledgeable Western military source. "Every military region is in trouble now."

Losses Recounted

In recent weeks, the South Vietnamese have lost a vital province capital, Ban Me Thuot, retained only a tenuous grip on the key city of Tay Ninh, 65 miles northwest of Saigon, shifted the II Corps headquarters to Nha Trang, lost a half dozen district capitals in the highlands and other areas and witnessed a series of increased attacks around Saigon.

The Saigon command's spokesman, Lieut. Col Le Trung Hien, said in response to a question on Monday that the North Vietnamese attacks are "more serious" than the 1968 Tet offensive and the spring offensive of 1972. "The situation will be very critical if the enemy can cut the vital routes permanently," he said.

Although most Western military analysts would disagree with the official South Vietnamese assessment, there is a feeling among them that the momentum of the attacks is increasing and that Saigon's forces are hard-pressed.

Perhaps the command's most significant announcement was that North Vietnamese troops and tanks had mounted a series of assaults against the Kien Duc district headquarters and at the Nhon Ca airfield in Quang Duc Province. The attacks, according to military sources, are aimed at Gia Nghia, the province capital.

The district of Kien Duc, 120 miles north-east of Saigon, was the scene in December, 1973, of the first frontal assault by the Communists on a district capital since the cease-fire agreement. The North Vietnamese seized the district capital, held it for several days and were finally repulsed by heavy South Vietnamese tank and fighter bomber attacks.

At a press briefing this morning, Colonel Hien asserted that "there are movements of troops in the highlands but these movements of troops were made for tactical reasons." He added that "no such withdrawal decision has been posed for the South Vietnamese forces in the highlands yet."

The command reported heavy fighting at an important district town, Dinh Quan, 55 miles northwest of Saigon. Colonel Hien said that the attack completed the cutting of all but one of the country's principal roads leading out of the highlands to the coast. Dinh Quan lies on Route 20, which runs from the area north of Saigon to the hill resort of Dalat.

The command also reported heavy shelling and ground attacks around Binh Khe, a district town on Route 19 in the highlands.

March 18, 1975

HUE LOST, DA NANG MAY GO; U.S. ORDERS AN AID REVIEW AND BIG REFUGEE AIRLIFT

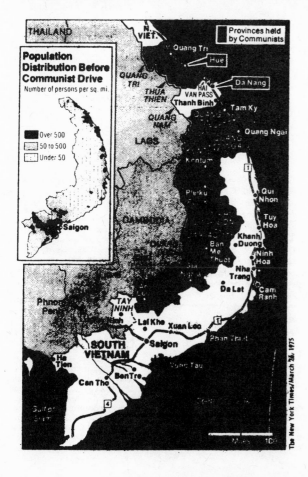

EVACUATION SPED

Saigon Forming New Line of Defense for Enclave in North

By MALCOLM W. BROWNE
Special to The New York Times

SAIGON, South Vietnam, Wednesday, March 26 — The northern city of Hue, the cultural heart of South Vietnam, was abandoned by the Saigon Government's forces yesterday.

Da Nang, the nation's second largest city 50 miles to the southeast, appeared imperiled. With refugees continuing to pour in from abandoned areas both north and south of the city, reports from Da Nang said it was expected to fall soon.

A Saigon Government spokesman said that 14 heavy 122-mm. rockets were fired in the outskirts of Da Nang this morning, apparently marking the beginning of a Communist operation in the area. Six civil-

ians were reported killed and 34 wounded.

A new line of defense has been organized to protect what has become the enclave of Da Nang, with Communist-held provinces to both the north and south.

Evacuation Accelerated

Meanwhile, the evacuation of South Vietnamese civilians and others from the city has been accelerated. An airlift was under way, and ships were reportedly available to take more people out. Most of the foreigners in Da Nang, including Americans, were being flown out.

An aviation official said pilots were worried that North Vietnamese MIG fighter planes would appear over Da Nang soon.

With new reverses reported for Government forces in many parts of the country, President Nguyen Van Thieu announced last night that a "war cabinet" would be formed to stiffen national resistance to the Communists.

Job for New Cabinet

A statement from the President's office, broadcast by the Saigon radio, said that Mr.

Thieu had instructed Premier Tran Thien Khiem to form a new Cabinet "to meet the urgent requirements of national defense, of relief and resettlement of war victims, to stabilize the economy in the rear areas, to increase production to support the front lines, to mobilize the anti-Communist spirit and to defeat the Communist aggressors."

There was no indication who would be invited to serve or when the President expected the Cabinet reshuffle. Nor were there any indications whether present plans envisaged the sweeping improvement in leadership that many diplomatic observers consider necessary if the rest of South Vietnam is not to fall swiftly.

Government reverses during the day, military sources reported, included the fall of a district capital in the southernmost part of the country. The informants said Ha Tien, on the Gulf of Siam near the Cambodian border, was overrun by Communist troops and tanks.

Most of Ha Tien was overrun as well during the Communist offensive of 1972 but was subsequently retaken by Government troops. The loss now was considered significant because the presence of Communist tanks in the area, 115 miles southwest of Saigon, appeared to presage a major push.

According to the official Saigon Government spokesman, 12 tanks were destroyed in an engagement Monday even closer to Saigon. That was in Vinh Long Province, 65 miles southwest of the capital.

The end of Saigon's control over Hue reportedly came after the last installations there were blown up yesterday and troops embarked on ships off the coast. Reached by telephone in Da Nang last night, a military source was asked whether the North Vietnamese army had yet moved in.

"We presume so," he replied.

Approximately one-third of the 200,000 people who lived in Hue were said to be left in the city, most of those remaining having elected to stay under Communist control.

Refugees from Hue arrived in Da Nang yesterday by boat, and other boatloads from southern provinces were also landing.

Hue became isolated from the rest of the country on Saturday, when Route 1 leading southeast to Da Nang was cut. Shelling thereafter effectively prevented air evacuation except for helicopter flights into the old part of the city on the northeast bank of the Huong River.

Finally, access to Hue was reduced to a fleet of sampans, landing craft and other vessels handicapped by staggering loads and heavy seas.

The loss of Hue will be an incalculable blow to the morale of the South Vietnamese people. While the city was not one of the country's most populous and its strategic significance is limited, its importance as the old capital, cultural center and an almost mystical place are great.

The Hanoi radio quoted foreign press reports as saying that American helicopter carriers were moving toward South Vietnam to evacuate Americans from Da Nang. The broadcast urged all Saigon troops, police officers and administration personnel in central Vietnam to switch sides quickly.

There are several hundred Americans in Da Nang, including about 40 officials of the consulate and associated agencies, businessmen, dependents, representatives of charitable organizations, and missionaries.

Communist pressure in other parts of the country continued to mount during the day, and it was expected that the next major enemy push would be against Tay Ninh, which has been increasingly threatened.

Tay Ninh, near the Cambodian border, is of great importance because of its dominance over the highway leading into Saigon.

March 26, 1975

Lon Nol Takes Off From Phnom Penh Into Probable Exile

By JOSEPH LELYVELD
Special to The New York Times

PHNOM PENH, Cambodia, Tuesday, April 1 — President Lon Nol boarded a military helicopter inside his palace compound early this afternoon and took off on a journey that was expected to carry him into permanent exile.

Clinging to the trappings of his office until his last moment on Cambodian soil, the head of state—who has been partly paralyzed since 1971—walked slowly in review past an honor guard and military band, followed by all the top ministers and generals in his Government.

The helicopter carried him to Pochentong Airport, which has been under daily rocket attack for almost three months. There, he boarded a waiting plane that was to carry him on the first leg of a trip to Indonesia.

A faint pulse of hope stirred in the besieged and war-weary capital as word spread that the President was finally leaving.

Sources at the presidential palace said that Marshal Lon Nol had been too overwrought yesterday to record a planned farewell address to the nation, which has learned of his plans only from foreign broadcasts.

Instead, it was said, a statement by Premier Long Boret was to be broadcast after Marshal Lon Nol's departure for Bangkok, Thailand, where he was to change to a plane for Jakarta, Indonesia.

The Premier was said to be planning to accompany the President as far as Indonesia and to return after a few days. His place will be filled by Hang Thun Hak, a former Premier who was restored to the Government 10 days ago as a First Deputy Premier.

When Marshal Lon Nol is out of the country the President of the Senate, Saukham Khoy, will be sworn in as Acting President. Such power as can be found in the enfeebled Government will presumably be shared by the civilian leadership with the military, represented by the new Minister of Defense, Lieut. Gen. Saksut Sakhan.

A Deputy Premier, Pan Sothi, said that he was one of about a dozen ministers and generals who signed a statement presented to the President on March 22 that called on him to stand aside for the good of the country.

Mr. Pan Sothi said he hoped that the Communist-led insurgents, who have cut all of Phnom Penh's supply links to the outside world except the airport, might be persuaded to negotiate after a few months if the United States Congress approved further aid for Cambodia.

A number of United States Senators, including Mike Mansfield and Hugh Scott, the Democratic and Republican leaders, have indicated that President Lon Nol's removal from the scene might improve the prospects of the $222-million in supplementary Cambodian aid.

Congress has approved a foreign aid bill without it.

Members of the shrunken diplomatic community are virtually unanimous in the belief that it is too late to negotiate on any subject but an orderly surrender of the capital to the insurgents without further bloodletting.

An Asian diplomat who was active in the efforts to persuade the President to go said the Government was unlikely to face the fundamental hopelessness of its situation until the fate of the aid was resolved.

"They only start to think when the need comes," the diplomat said. "They are just now starting to think."

Indonesia, which will be playing host to the Cambodian leader for two weeks before he flies on to Hawaii, closed her embassy here a week ago. In an interview in Jakarta last week the Foreign Minister, Adam Malik, said he thought that further aid would be useless. The only question, he said, is "how to prevent more killing."

Aside from aid the Government was said to be hoping for a revival of morale in the armed forces and of popular support as it seeks to convey the idea that it is re-forming itself in the hope of evolving a leadership that would be acceptable as a bargaining partner to the insurgents, who have shown no disposition to negotiate. Premier Long Boret, who was said to be a prime mover in the reform effort, is himself included on a list of seven so-called traitors whose removal the insurgents have demanded.

The popular reaction to the President's departure appeared to have been conditioned by his place at the head of the insurgents' list. Noting that they said that they would never negotiate with him, a sidewalk hawker said, "If he leaves it means the war will end soon."

Meanwhile, the fighting was less than five miles away. in action north of the airport the Government forces managed to hold a perimeter by sending two battalions of reinforcements and a squadron of armored personnel carriers to plug a hole in their defenses that the insurgents discovered over the weekend.

April 1, 1975

OVER 100 VIETNAM ORPHANS KILLED WITH 25 ADULTS IN SAIGON CRASH;

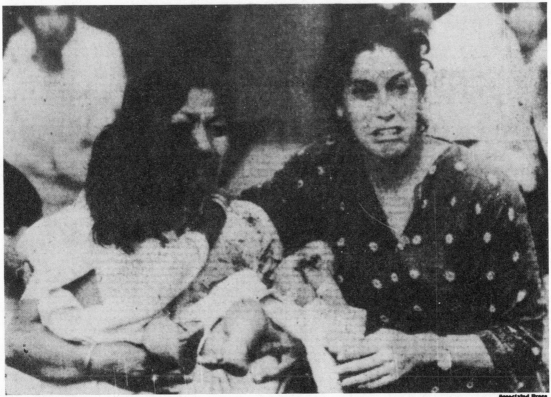

Associated Press

Grief-stricken women taking tiny survivors of the crash of a C-5A plane to a hospital in Saigon yesterday

305 ABOARD PLANE

By FOX BUTTERFIELD
Special to The New York Times

SAIGON, South Vietnam, Saturday, April 5—An American Air Force transport taking 243 Vietnamese orphans to refuge in the United States crashed and burned shortly after take-off here, yesterday. More than 100 of the children and at least 25 of the adults accompanying them were believed to have been killed.

Rescue work was still going on in the mud of rice paddies about five miles northeast of Tan Son Nhut air base. Bodies of the children, some of whom were as young as 8 months, were buried in the mud. Debris —a baby bottle, blankets, a Donald Duck comic book—was scattered over the scene.

The rescue effort for the orphans of the war was the first of an airlift series announced by the United States Government Wednesday to take about 2,000 children to safe homes away from the fighting.

More Than 100 Survive

There were 305 people aboard the Galaxy C-5A jet—the 243 orphans, 44 women volunteers acting as escorts, 16 crewmen and two flight nurses. About

100 of the children and 15 to 20 adults were known to have survived.

According to a preliminary report by the pilot, Capt. Dennis Traynor, the accident began when a sudden depressurization in the four-engine jet, the world's biggest, blew out the rear door "and struck the tail."

After that, Captain Traynor reported, he was able only to "maintain limited control," and tried to bring the plane back to Tan Son Nhut. Mr. Traynor's report was made public by the United States Embassy this morning.

The crash flattened the cargo hold, where about 50 children had been strapped in. "Some of us got through a chute from the top of the plane, but the children at the bottom of the plane didn't have a chance," one survivor said.

The orphans were to be taken to Travis Air Force Base in California. They were to be adopted by American families in what President Ford described as a "humanitarian effort."

"This is the least we can do, and we will do much, much more," the President said of the airlift Thursday in San Diego. The $2-million it will cost to transport the 2,000 came from a special foreign aid fund for children.

April 5, 1975

PHNOM PENH SURRENDERS AFTER OFFER OF A CEASE-FIRE IS REJECTED

REPORT IS ON RADIO

Government Soldiers Are Directed to Cease Combat

By United Press International

The Cambodian Government surrendered to insurgent forces today, the Cambodian radio announced. The Phnom Penh Government ordered all its troops to stop firing and lay down their arms.

Brig. Gen. Mey Sichan, chief of operations for the Cambodian Government Army, went on the radio and said soldiers and functionaries should cease all combat and invite the rebels to take power. This announcement was monitored in Saigon.

After his speech a "representative of the liberation forces" told all Government officers to report to the Information Ministry, site of the radio station, under a white flag of surrender.

"We enter Phnom Penh as conquerors," the insurgents' representative said. "We order the surrender of all officers and officials of the Phnom puppet regime under a white flag."

The rebels' representative said the final victory for the insurgents had come at 9 A.M. (10 P.M., Wednesday, New York time) when insurgent troops seized the Information Ministry. The ministry and its third-story broadcasting studio are in the center of Phnom Penh, about 200 yards from the Phnom Hotel.

There was no initial word on the fate of the foreigners sequestered at the hotel. These

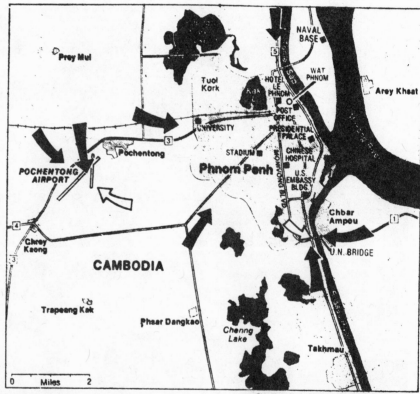

The New York Times/Louis Craca/April 17, 1975

Insurgents reportedly entered Phnom Penh, and the Government tried to set up defense line to the south. Rebels struck toward capital from all sides.

included newsmen, a few diplomats and representatives of the International Red Cross and the United Nations.

Truce Was Sought

By SYDNEY H. SCHANBERG
Special to The New York Times

PHNOM PENH, Cambodia, Thursday, April 17 — The Cambodian military Government asked yesterday for an immediate cease-fire from the Cambodian insurgents, who were attacking Phnom Penh from all sides. The Government said it would turn over power to them.

Several hours later, reports from Peking said that Prince Norodom Sihanouk, the nominal leader of the insurgents who is in exile there, had rejected the cease-fire proposal as unacceptable.

The Phnom Penh Government's proposal, which might be described as conditional surrender, had called for a complete transfer of power to the insurgent side under the supervision of the United Nations and representatives of the International Committee of the Red Cross who are now in Phnom Penh.

A second major point among the five in the proposal was a demand for assurances that there would be no reprisals against persons or organizations for their activities during the five-year war.

The cease-fire proposal, which was transmitted through the Red Cross delegation here, came as this suffering city of more than two million, relatively calm until now, began to show signs of collapse.

Throughout the day, the Communist-led insurgents had pressed closer and closer on all sides, inflicting enormous casualties and sending scores of thousands of refugees pouring frightened into the city from the near outskirts. Exhausted soldiers who had had enough joined the refugees. Many of the refugees came into the very center of this cosmopolitan city with bullock carts and squealing pigs looking for a place to rest and a bit to eat.

Shells Land Regularly

In the hospitals there were wounded two and three to a bed, floors slippery with blood and children's shrieks of pain that tore any visitor's heart out.

Insurgent shells began landing last night at regular intervals in the northern part of the city. The airport, west of the city, was said to be falling.

Fear was spreading. French residents of Phnom Penh started putting up French flags on their gates and walls to identify their nationality, since France has recognized the insurgent government.

Premier Long Boret, speaking in a telephone interview before the Sihanouk rejection had been reported, cited the United States decision to evacuate its embassy last Saturday and end its material support as the key factor in his Government's decision to ask for a cease-fire.

"We feel completely abandoned," he said in a voice whose weariness was discernible even over the telephone.

The 42-year-old Premier said the decision was made at about 11 A.M. yesterday at a meeting of the seven-member military-dominated Supreme Committee, which has been running the country since the Americans left last Saturday.

He said the decision was unanimous. Asked if there were any dissenting voices anywhere in the Government, such as some of the generals, he said, "No, we are realistic."

Mr. Long Boret, who with other Cambodian leaders has been marked for execution by the insurgents, said the military situation had become impossible, and added, "We have no more material means." As he spoke, rockets were exploding only about 200 yards from the telegraph office from which this correspondent was telephoning.

The Premier said that after the morning meeting, held at the headquarters of the military high command, the proposal was taken to the head of the Red Cross delegation here, André Pasquier, who was asked as a neutral intermediary to pass it to Prince Sihanouk. The Prince, the former Cambodian chief of state, was ousted by the Phnom Penh Government in 1970.

Mr. Long Boret, who declared "our first objective is to end the suffering of the people," said Mr. Pasquier informed him later that he had transmitted the message to Red Cross headquarters in Geneva at 3 P.M. Cambodian time (4 A.M., New York time) and that Geneva had quickly passed it to Prince Sihanouk in Peking.

Hotel a Neutral Zone

Mr. Pasquier sent the message over his shortwave radio from the Hotel Le Phnom, which was today turned into a Red-Cross-protected neutral zone for the treatment of the sick and the wounded. Huge Red Cross flags were hung around the building and atop it.

As dusk came, refugees and soldiers who had fled the fighting fronts wandered forlornly through the darkening streets looking for shelter and food. The setting sun was clouded by billows of black smoke from fires all around the city.

Last night, reports from refugees indicated that the airport, five miles to the west, was falling and might have already gone. It had been the Government's last supply link with the outside world. Insurgents were said to be inside the airfield. Government T-28 fighter-bombers were reported dropping napalm on them to try to halt their advance, apparently to little effect. The control tower was said to be in insurgent hands. Retreating Government troops were reported trying to pull together a defense line south of the airport.

Beyond the airport, the Government ammunition dumps, where everything including bombs is stored, are now cut off from the city. One of them may have fallen to the insurgents yesterday.

On the south, northwest and west, the insurgents were at the capital's edges. In the north, refugees who reached Phnom Penh said the rebels were only a little more than a mile from the city limits and advancing steadily down Route 5.

It was on this front that perhaps the greatest Government casualties were suffered today. Many were civilians caught in crossfire or hit by blindly fired insurgent rockets as they ran from the fighting.

Another battle raged along the city's southern border, centering on the United Nations Bridge, which spans the Bassac River. Though newsmen could not get very close, the fighting seemed to be intense only a few hundred yards to the east of the bridge, in a neighborhood called Chbar Ampou.

On Tuesday night, much of that neighborhood burned down as fierce fighting swirled in and around it. Hundreds of houses were reported destroyed in the blaze, which lit the sky.

Government reinforcements were being rushed to the bridge area yesterday. These soldiers looked somber as their trucks raced through the streets of the capital in the morning.

All Hope Gone

Insurgent shells, some of them deadly accurate 105-mm. rounds, were exploding sporadically in the southern districts of Phnom Penh.

A curfew was in effect from noon yesterday "until further notice."

Nowhere was there the slightest sign of hope for the Phnom Penh Government. The main military hospital, which normally gets an average of about 200 wounded a day, had received more than 500 by 6 P.M. yesterday and the ambulances were still coming in every five minutes.

Inside the emergency reception center, a converted basketball court, people were bleeding, moaning, whimpering and dying.

A 12-year-old boy died of heads wounds on a bed. Someone covered most of his body with a blue scarf. Then a soldier came in carrying his wife, bleeding from the head. There were no empty beds, so he pushed the dead boy to one side and placed his wife there as well.

Rivulets of blood flowed across the floor. A 13-year-old girl named Chan Ny, whose body was torn by shrapnel, lay on the floor yelling: "Help me! Help me! The pain is awful!"

Many in this hospital were wounded children whose parents had been killed alongside them. The chief doctor tried, by questioning the children, to find out where the bodies had fallen so he could have the parents cremated.

Behind the receiving center are the operating rooms, where surgery must be quick. An 80-year-old woman whose right leg had just been amputated lay groaning on a wheeled bed outside the operating room.

The Phnom Penh Government has made a number of suggestions in the past as its military fortunes have deteriorated that a cease-fire be declared and negotiations be started, but these have all been spurned by the insurgents.

Last July, for example, Marshall Lon Nol, then the President, proposed in a broadcast that talks be held without "prerequisite or condition."

Last Sunday, Premier Long Boret said at a news conference that while continuing the struggle the Government would make every effort to persuade the other side to "accept our offer of a cease-fire followed by negotiations and national reconciliation."

The Government's formal, five-point proposal followed yesterday.

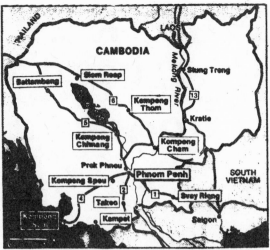

The New York Times/April 17, 1975

With insurgents advancing, Phnom Penh Government had only a number of enclaves left (indicated by panels).

April 17, 1975

THIEU RESIGNS, CALLS U.S. UNTRUSTWORTHY; APPOINTS SUCCESSOR TO SEEK NEGOTIATIONS

10-YEAR RULE ENDS

Vice President Huong, 71 Years Old, Takes Office in Saigon

By MALCOLM W. BROWNE
Special to The New York Times

SAIGON, South Vietnam, April 21—President Nguyen Van Thieu, denouncing the United States as untrustworthy, resigned tonight after 10 years in office.

He immediately appointed his Vice President, the 71-year-old Tran Van Huong, to replace him.

He said that President Huong would immediately press the enemy to cease all acts of war and enter into peace negotiations. The Vietcong have said repeatedly that they would not negotiate while Mr. Thieu held office.

[A spokesman for the Vietcong delegation in Saigon said Tuesday the resignation of President Thieu "decidedly cannot change the situation," Reuters reported.]

Accuses the U.S.

In an impassioned address to the nation, President Thieu defended his character and the accomplishments of his regime while chronicling its collapse. He called for peace, but also said the successor government would fight on.

Speaking before assembled members of his Government and National Assembly at the Presidential Palace, President Thieu accused the United States of breaking its promises to support an anti-Communist Government in Saigon.

Mr. Thieu said that he had objected in October, 1972, to Secretary of State Kissinger's "acceptance of the continued presence of North Vietnamese troops in South Vietnam."

Pledge by Nixon

Mr. Thieu added that South Vietnam would fight on to defend the territory left to it. The armed forces chief of staff, Gen. Cao Van Vien, also spoke briefly, to say that his troops would continue fighting to "defend the homeland against the communist aggressors."

"I resign but I do not desert," President Thieu said in concluding his one-and-a-half-hour address. "From this minute I will put myself at the disposal of the President and people. I will continue to stay close to you all in the coming task of national defense. Good-by to you all."

His voice taut with emotion, President Thieu devoted most of his speech to a scathing criticism of the United States, saying:

"The United States has not respected its promises. It is unfair. It is inhumane. It is not trustworthy. It is irresponsible."

Mr. Thieu said that former President Richard M. Nixon had described all accords, including the Paris peace agreement, as "pieces of paper" unless they were implemented, and had therefore promised Saigon not only military and economic aid, but also "direct and strong United States military intervention" in the event the Communists broke the accord.

But then, Mr. Thieu said, Watergate undid American resolve in aiding Vietnam, and Washington deserted its ally. By the time former Vice President Spiro T. Agnew visited Saigon later, he said, Mr. Agnew spoke "coldly," referring only to "Vietnamization" of the war and continuing military and economic aid, but not of President Nixon's promise before the Paris accord to send American troops and B-52's if needed.

The State Department has said that there was no specific commitment by the United States to intervene militarily. And the White House noted earlier this month that any private assurance given by Mr. Nixon was no longer valid because of the Congressional ban on American combat activity in Indochina imposed in August, 1973.

"Let me say that we need at least $722-million, plus the B-52's" Mr. Thieu said today. "Let me say that we need immediate — I say immediate — shipment of arms and equipment to the South Vietnam battlefield.

"I would challenge the United States army to do better than the South Vietnamese army without B-52's," the President said.

April 22, 1975

MINH SURRENDERS, VIETCONG IN SAIGON;

By The Associated Press
SAIGON, South Vietnam, Wednesday, April 30—President Duong Van Minh announced today the unconditional surrender of the Saigon Government and its military forces to the Vietcong.

Columns of South Vietnamese troops pulled out of their defensive positions in the capital and marched to central points to turn in their weapons.

[In Washington, the White House said that President Ford had "no comment" on the surrender of Saigon, but a White House spokesman said the surrender was considered "inevitable."

Troops Move In

Within two hours, Communist forces began moving into Saigon, and a jeep flying the

Vietcong flag and carrying eight cheering men in civilian clothes armed with an assortment of weapons could be seen driving near the United States Embassy compound.

The Vietcong flag was raised over the presidential palace at 12:15 P.M. (12:15 A.M. Wednesday, New York time), and soon after a detachment of Communist troops in a jeep arrived at the palace and asked General Minh to accompany them. He drove off with them, but their destination was not immediately disclosed.

Vietcong flags materialized on other buildings as well, and Vietcong soldiers soon walked along the main streets shaking hands with Saigon residents. The red, yellow-starred flag of North Vietnam could also be seen on trucks carrying soldiers in green helmets and uniforms.

Bursts of Fire

Sporadic bursts of firing could be heard, but the only resistance to the Communist take-over was reported to be from marines stationed at the zoo and public gardens.

The take-over followed by hours the ending of the American involvement in Vietnam through the evacuation of most of the approximately 1,000 Americans still here yesterday.

The surrender announcement, made in a broadcast to the nation, signaled the end of three decades of fighting. It came 21 years after the 1954 Geneva accords divided Vietnam into North and South and a little more than two years after the Vietnam cease-fire agreement was signed in Paris on Jan. 27, 1973. The last American troops left the country in March of that year.

President Minh, who took office on Monday to lead South Vietnam into peace negotiations,

said in his brief radio address:

"I believe firmly in reconciliation among Vietnamese to avoid unnecessary shedding of the blood of Vietnamese. For this reason, I ask the soldiers of the Republic of Vietnam to cease hostilities in calm and to stay where they are."

The President also asked the "brother soldiers" of the Vietcong to cease hostilities and added:

"We wait here to meet the Provisional Revolutionary Government of South Vietnam to discuss together a ceremony of orderly transfer of power so as to avoid any unnecessary bloodshed in the population."

There was no mention in his address of North Vietnam or of the North Vietnamese armies that had provided the bulk of the military force that defeated South Vietnam.

Gen. Nguyen Vuu Hanh, deputy chief of staff, then went on the air to order all South Vietnamese troops to carry out the orders of General Minh, who is known to foreigners as Big Minh.

"The military command," he said, "is ready to enter into contact with the military command of the army of the Provisional Revolutionary Government of South Vietnam in order to effect a cease-fire without bloodshed."

With the surrender announcement, made by President Minh at 10:24 A.M. (10:24 P.M. Tuesday, New York time), shellfire subsided along the northern rim of the city where the Vietcong had been bombarding the airport.

In the hours before the surrender statement, Communist troops had been pressing closer to Saigon. The Vietcong announced the fall of the Government's huge air base at Bien Hoa, 15 miles northeast of the capital, and there were reports that Vung Tau, the port city to the southeast, had also been captured during the day.

The end came as more than a dozen Communist divisions were ringing the city, which reportedly was defended by less

than one division of demoralized troops. Some South Vietnamese officers complained that the evacuation of the Americans had caused panic in the miiltary with many top army officers and most of the air force fleeing.

For two years after the 1973 cease-fire accords, both Government and Communist forces attacked each other without any major change in territory. The South Vietnamese then suffered their first major setback on Jan. 9 with the fall of Phuoc Binh, capital of Phuoc Long Province, due north of Saigon.

On March 13, Ban Me Thuot, capital of Darlac Province in the Central Highlands, was captured, and this reverse prompted Nguyen Van Thieu, then President, to decide on a withdrawal from the Central Highlands cities of Pleiku and Kontum as well.

A precipitous rout followed, with South Vietnamese forces withdrawing from Hue, the country's cultural heart, from Da Nang, the nation's second largest city, and then swiftly from coastal regions all the way to the approaches of Saigon.

Saigon's forces turned to fight at Xuan Loc, capital of Long Khanh Province, which was invaded by North Vietnamese troops on April 9. For two weeks the opposing sides battled there, turning the city into rubble. It was abandoned April 22.

As most of the country fell into Communist hands, demands were voiced in Saigon —by political figures, religious leaders and others—for the resignation of President Thieu. The Government said two coup attempts had been uncovered and foiled.

Mr. Thieu went on radio and television April 21 to make an emotional announcement that he was resigning. He blamed the United States cuts in aid for the debacle of his forces.

Mr. Thieu's Vice President, Tran Van Huong, took over and on Monday, with the concurrence of the National Assembly, named General Minh to become the president to end the war.

In an address on taking office, General Minh appealed to "our friends of the other side, the Provisional Revolutionary Government of South Vietnam," to join in a cease-fire and in negotiations for a solution to the long conflict.

Yesterday, the Minh Government renewed the appeal as it sought ways to enter into talks with the Vietcong.

The calls for a truce were made on radio and television by Vice President Nguyen Van Huyen. He said later in an interview that a Government delegation met twice during the day with a Vietcong delegation at Tan Son Nhut air base, at the edge of Saigon. But the Vietcong representatives there, he said, pronounced themselves as not qualified to make political decisions.

The Vice President noted that one of the Vietcong demands—that all Americans leave South Vietnam—was already being met. He added that additional Vietcong demands for the dissolution of the Saigon Government and its army were being considered.

The Vietcong delegation with which the Government representatives met during the day has been at Tan Son Nhut since the first days after the Paris accords were signed.

As the Vietcong flags were raised over Saigon, no Government soldiers were to be seen on the streets. The people, however, appeared to be moving about normally.

At the Defense Ministry building, about a dozen North Vietnamese soldiers talked with a South Vietnamese army colonel and several junior officers.

There was not interference with Western newsmen taking pictures. North Vietnamese machine gunners sitting in two trucks outside the Defense Ministry posed and smiled proudly.

One man riding in a jeep flying a Vietcong flag beckoned to an American reporter and said in English:

"Go home. Go home."

April 30, 1975

Evacuation From Saigon Tumultuous at the End

By GEORGE ESPER
The Associated Press

SAIGON, South Vietnam, Wednesday, April 30—With American fighter planes flying cover and marines standing guard on the ground, Americans left Saigon yesterday by helicopter after fighting off throngs of Vietnamese civilians who tried to go along.

Eighty-one helicopters from carriers in the South China Sea landed at Tan Son Nhut airport and on roofs at the United States Embassy compound to pick up most of the approximately 1,000 remaining Americans and several thousand Vietnamese.

But large groups of other Vietnamese clawed their way up the 10-foot wall of the embassy compound in desperate attempts to escape approaching Communist troops. United States marines and civilians used pistol and rifle butts to dislodge them.

At the airport, angry Vietnamese guards fired in the air and in the direction of evacuees on buses, shouting, "We want to go too."

The final stage of the evacuation, which stretched over 19 hours, brought to an end an American involvement in Vietnam that cost more than 50,000 lives and $150-billion. Four marines died during the final evacuation—two early yesterday as a result of a bombardment of Tan Son Nhut airport, two later when their helicopter plunged into the South China Sea.

While most Americans were pulling out, some newsmen and missionaries chose to remain.

Communist forces, meanwhile, pressed closer to Saigon. The Vietcong said they had captured the large Bien Hoa air base, 15 miles northeast of the capital. [A broadcast from

Peking monitored in Tokyo said the Communists had also seized Vung Tau, a port city southeast of Saigon.].

Earlier, fighting had been reported less than 10 miles west of Saigon along Route 1.

As the American airlift came to an end at 7:52 A.M. [7:52 P.M., Tuesday, New York Time], Vietcong gunners sent rockets hurtling into Tan Son Nhut air base. The last Americans to be flown out of Saigon were 11 of the 800 marines who had guarded the evacuation operation.

The 11, who served as the rear guard, fired a red smoke grenade to guide the CH-46 helicopted in. As it touched down on the roof of the Embassy, they scrambled aboard and were airbound within four minutes.

One of the last civilians to leave was Ambassador Graham Martin, who boarded the final regular lift of 19 helicopters that had flown out about two hours earlier.

After the last marines had left, hundreds of civilians swarmed into the compound and onto the roof. On the roof of a nearby building that had also served as an emergency helipad, several hundred civilians huddled together, hoping there would be more helicopters to carry them away.

Despite a 24-hour curfew, there was moderate traffic in the city's streets early today. there were also abandoned United States Embassy behicles that had been taken over by Vietnamese and driven around until they ran out of gasoline.

The American involvement ended in tumultuous scenes at both airport and embassy. Marines in battle gear pushed all the people they could reach off the wall, but the crush of people was so great that scores got over.

Some tried to jump the wall and landed on barbed wire strung along the top. A middle-

aged man and a woman were lying on the wire, bleeding. People held up their children, asking Americans to take them over the fence.

During the airport evacuation, two Vietcong rockets whistled overhead and exploded behind the United States defense attaché's compound, sending marines and evacuees diving for the pavement. The two marine guards had been killed at the compound by an earlier attack.

Across the street from the embassy, soldiers, police and youths stripped and stol. scores of abandoned embassy cars. Thousands of other Vietnamese stripped apartment buildings in which Americans had lived, collecting bathroom fixtures, books, furniture and food. They sat on sidewalks with their booty, waiting for friends in cars to pick them up.

American newsmen who had been taken to Tan Son Nhut airport earlier in buses could not be evacuated from there because Vietnamese guards would not let the buses into the air base.

The buses returned to the embassy, and the newsmen climbed over the wall themselves, beating off Vietnamese who tried to cling to them.

Among the newsmen remaining in Saigon were Peter Arnett, Matt Franjola and this correspondent, of The Associated Press.

Among the missionaries was Max Ediser, 28 years old, of Turpin Okla., who works with the Mennonite Central Committee.

"We have talked about this for years," he said. "We could never come up with a definite answer. Now we realize that having talked of love to our Vietnamese people, and told them not to yield to fear or ignorance, we cannot leave them in this hour of need. So we are staying."

Others remaining with Mr. Ediser included James Klassen, from Kansas, and Luke Marin,

from Pennsylvania, both Mennonites, and Claudia Krich and her husband, Keith Brinton, of the American Friends Service Committee.

The final evacuation followed the heavy shelling of Tan Son Nhut airbase yesterday morning and an order by President Duong Van Minh for the American defense attaché and his staff to leave. The general issued his order as he and his Government sought ways to open peace talks with the Vietcong.

As word of the evacuation spread, some Government officials telephoned the office of The Associated Press and asked if they could also be taken out.

Many South Vietnamese officers and officials were reported fleeing as rumors spread that Communist-led forces would soon march on the city.

Four buses drove around Saigon picking up American, European and Vietnamese evacuees. As the first bus arrived at the gates of Tan Son Nhut air base, Vietnamese guards fired at it.

Hundreds of South Vietnamese soldiers carrying weapons converged on the base, also seeking to leave the country.

Armed United States marines pushed and struck Vietnamese trying to get inside the United States defense attaché's compound where those being airlifted waited for helicopters coming from carriers offshore.

U.S. Planes in Action

SINGAPORE, Wednesday, April 30 (Reuters) — United States Navy fighter planes went into action over South Vietnam yesterday to protect fleeing refugees from marauding helicopters, according to military and civilian communications reports monitored here.

The fighters were said to have been called in when two boats on the Mekong River car-

The New York Times/April 30, 1975

Fall of Bien Hoa (1) and Vung Tau (2) was reported. U.S. planes covered flight of Americans from Can Tho (3).

rying the American consul general from the delta city of Can Tho reported that two helicopters with South Vietnamese markings were firing at his party. This consisted of 100 Vietnamese, six United States marines and 16 other Americans, according to the messages.

Later, the consul general was said to be stranded somewhere in the South China Sea.

Early in the day, United States naval authorities aboard ships about 40 miles offshore from Vung Tau, southeast of Saigon, could be heard promising air support for another group of refugees coming down the Saigon River from the South Vietnamese capital.

The messages monitored here indicated that 50,000 people fled through Vung Tau during the day. This evacuation was said to have occurred under intense shell fire.

The port's cable station, which handles much of South Vietnam's communications with the outside world, asked for United States air support early in the day when it was struck by mortar fire.

April 30, 1975

SAIGON SAYS HANOI BEGINS REBUILDING OF SOUTH VIETNAM

Broadcast Announces Vast Plan to Provide Jobs and Reverse War Devastation

The Saigon radio announced yesterday that North Vietnam had undertaken a vast recon-

struction program in South Vietnam to provide jobs and to begin reversing the devastation of 30 years of war.

The broadcasts, monitored in Bangkok, Thailand, said that people would have to work more hours each day. But they also held out the vision of new roads linking the cities of North and South Vietnam and of free-flowing travel and new accommodations.

Customary channels of communications with Saigon have been cut since Wednesday, when a new Communist regime seized the city and assumed power. Saigon broadcasts are providing what little news

there is under the aegis of the new Government.

Reorganization Under Way

The radio suggested that a wholesale reorganization of the country was under way. The regime, which previously announced the nationalization of all farms, factories and businesses, and ordered the suspension of unauthorized publications, took over the labor movement on Friday and began organizing "Revolutionary People's Committees" yesterday.

The committees were being formed throughout the country, ostensibly to protect government property. The Saigon ra-

dio said that 5,000 people in the Saigon area had signed up for duty.

All members of the defeated South Vietnamese military forces were ordered to register with the new regime or face punishment. The radio said that 1,000 officers and men of the former government's navy had surrendered, bringing with them their vessels from an offshore island.

Meantime, a new program was launched to register all ships, and a maritime transport office was set up. Shipowners were ordered to register ocean-going vessels and river craft of 16 tons and over.

The new Saigon government continued to consolidate its administration with the appointment of an 11-member committee for the military management of the capital. Gen. Tran Van Tra, former head of the South Vietnamese Communist delegation to the military talks with the previous government, was named chairman of the committee, the radio reported.

While normal communications were cut for the fourth day in a row, the French Government said in Paris that its embassy in Saigon had reported in a radio transmission that foreign residents were in good health and being well treated. It also said that life in Saigon appeared to be returning to normal.

Hsinhua, the Chinese press agency, said in another dispatch from Hanoi, that South Vietnamese workers in Saigon, Da Nang, Hue and other cities were returning to their jobs and that factories were resuming production.

The agency also said that electricity plants and water-supply companies in Ban Me Thuot, Pleiku, Kontum, Hue, Da Nang and Nha Trang had resumed operations interrupted by recent fighting.

Apparently, one of the new Government's principal problems will be the provision of jobs for hundreds of thousands of former soldiers. The Saigon radio gave few details about Hanoi's reconstruction program.

But it said that roads were to be built linking the South with northern cities. And it said the North Vietnamese Government was building more hotels to accommodate people in the South who wish to visit Hanoi and other northern cities.

In Jakarta, Indonesia, Chau Phong, the acting head of the South Vietnamese National Liberation Front, discounted rumors of a federation of the Indochina states as "nonsense." He also said there was no chance that war could spread to other countries of Southeast Asia.

Mr. Chau said that his Government was following a "good-neighbor policy" and was prepared to have diplomatic relations with the United States if Washington was willing to respect South Vietnam's sovereignty.

Meantime, however, the Saigon radio said that the new Government had condemned the United States for "stealing" aircraft, vessels and other equipment from South Vietnam. It said the Government was urging the United States to return the matériel immediately from the Philippines, Thailand, Malaysia, Singapore and Taiwan. This was an allusion to equipment used in the evacuation of tens of thousands of South Vietnamese.

May 4, 1975

Cambodia Reds Are Uprooting Millions As They Impose a 'Peasant Revolution'

Old and Sick Included; Economy Is at Standstill

By SYDNEY H. SCHANBERG

Special to The New York Times

BANGKOK, Thailand, May 8 — The victorious Cambodian Communists, who marched into Phnom Penh on April 17 and ended five years of war in Cambodia, are carrying out a peasant revolution that has thrown the entire country into upheaval.

Perhaps as many as three or four million people, most of them on foot, have been forced out of the cities and sent on a mammoth and grueling exodus into areas deep in the countryside where, the Communists say, they will have to become peasants and till the soil.

No One Excluded

No one has been excluded—even the very old, the very young, the sick and the wounded have been forced out onto the roads—and some will clearly not be strong enough to survive.

The old economy of the cities has been abandoned, and for the moment money means nothing and cannot be spent. Barter has replaced it.

All shops have either been looted by Communist soldiers for such things as watches and transistor radios, or their goods have been taken away in an organized manner to be stored as communal property.

Even the roads that radiate out of the capital and that carried the nation's commerce have been virtually abandoned, and the population living along the roads, as well as that in all cities and towns that remained under the control of the American-backed Government, has been pushed into the interior. Apparently the areas into which the evacuees are being herded are at least 65 miles from Phnom Penh.

In sum the new rulers—before their overwhelming victory they were known as the Khmer Rouge—appear to be remaking Cambodian society in the peasant image, casting aside everything that belonged to the old system, which was generally dominated by the cities and towns and by the élite and merchants who lived there.

Foreigners and foreign aid are not wanted—at least not for now. It is even unclear how much influence the Chinese and North Vietnamese will have, despite their considerable aid to the Cambodian insurgents against the Government of Marshal Lon Nol. The new authorities seem determined to do things themselves in their own way. Despite the propaganda terminology and other trappings, such as Mao caps and Ho Chi Minh rubber-tire sandals, which remind one of Peking and Hanoi, the Communists seem fiercely independent and very Cambodian.

Isolation From World Seen

Judging from their present actions, it seems possible that they may largely isolate their country of perhaps seven million people from the rest of the world for a considerable time—at least until the period of upheaval is over, the agrarian revolution takes concrete shape and they are ready to show their accomplishments to foreigners.

Some of the party officials in Phnom Penh also talked about changing the capital to a more traditional and rural town like Siem Reap, in the northwest.

For those foreigners, including this correspondent, who stayed behind to observe the take-over, the events were an astonishing spectacle.

In Phnom Penh two million people suddenly moved out of the city en masse in stunned silence — walking, bicycling, pushing cars that had run out of fuel, covering the roads like a human carpet, bent under sacks of belongings hastily thrown together when the heavily armed peasant soldiers came and told them to leave immediately, everyone dispirited and frightened by the unknown that awaited them and many plainly terrified because they were soft city people and were sure the trip would kill them.

Hospitals jammed with wounded were emptied, right down to the last patient. They went — limping, crawling, on crutches, carried on relatives' backs, wheeled on their hospital beds.

The Communists have few doctors and meager medical supplies, so many of these patients had little chance of surviving. On April 17, the day this happened, Phnom Penh's biggest hospital had over 2,000 patients and there were several thousand more in other hos-

Communists entering Phnom Penh from the north on Monivong Boulevard on morning of April 17. To the left, one uses portable communications set.

pitals; many of the wounded were dying for lack of care.

A once-throbbing city became an echo chamber of silent streets lined with abandoned cars and gaping, empty shops. Streetlights burned eerily for a population that was no longer there.

The end of the old and the start of the new began early in the morning of the 17th. At the cable office the line went dead for mechanical reasons at 6 A.M. On the previous day, amid heavy fighting, the Communist-led forces had taken the airport a few miles west of the city, and during the night they had pressed to the capital's edges, throwing in rockets and shells at will.

Thousands of new refugees and fleeing soldiers were filling the heart of the capital, wandering aimlessly, looking for shelter, as they awaited the city's imminent collapse.

Everyone—Cambodians and foreigners alike—thought this had to be Phnom Penh's most miserable hour after long days of fear and privation as the Communist forces drew closer. They looked ahead with hopeful relief to the collapse of the city, for they felt that when the Communists came and the war finally ended, at least the suffering would largely be over. All of us were wrong.

That view of the future of Cambodia—as a possibly flexible place even under Communism, where changes would not be extreme and ordinary folk

would be left alone—turned out to be a myth.

Inadequate Descriptions

American officials had described the Communists as indecisive and often ill-coordinated, but they turned out to be firm, determined, well-trained, tough and disciplined. The Americans had also said that the rebel army was badly riddled by casualties, forced to fill its ranks by hastily impressing young recruits from the countryside and throwing them into the front lines with only a few days' training. The thousands of troops we saw both in the countryside and in Phnom Penh, while they included women soldiers and boy militia, some of whom seemed no more than 10 years old, looked healthy, well organized, heavily armed and well trained.

Another prediction made by the Americans was that the Communists would carry out a bloodbath once they took over—massacring as many as 20,000 high officials and intellectuals. There have been unconfirmed reports of executions of senior military and civilian officials, and no one who witnessed the take-over doubts that top people of the old regime will be or have been punished and perhaps killed or that a large number of people will die of the hardships on the march into the countryside. But none of this will apparently bear any resemblance to the mass executions that had been

predicted by Westerners.

[In a news conference Tuesday President Ford reiterated reports—he termed them "hard intelligence"—that 80 to 90 Cambodian officials and their wives had been executed.]

Refugees Poured In

On the first day, as the sun was rising, a short swing by automobile to the northern edge of the city showed soldiers and refugees pouring in. The northern defense line had obviously collapsed.

By the time I reached the Hotel Le Phnom and climbed the two flights of stairs to my room, the retreat could be clearly seen from my window and small-arms fire could be heard in the city. At 6:30 A.M. I wrote in my notebook: "The city is falling."

Over the next couple of hours there were periodic exchanges of fire as the Communists encountered pockets of resistance. But most Government soldiers were busy preparing to surrender and welcome the Communists, as were civilians. White flags suddenly sprouted from housetops and from armored personnel carriers, which resemble tanks.

Some soldiers were taking the clips out of their rifles; others were changing into civilian clothes. Some Government office workers were hastily donning the black pajama-like clothes worn by Indochinese Communists.

Shortly before 9 A.M. the first rebel troops approached the hotel, coming from the north down Monivong Boulevard. A crowd of soldiers and civilians, including newsmen, churned forth to greet them—cheering and applauding and embracing and linking arms to form a phalanx as they came along.

The next few hours saw quite a bit of this celebrating, though shooting continued here and there, some of it only a few hundred yards from the hotel. Civilians and Buddhist monks and troops on both sides rode around town—in jeeps, atop personnel carriers and in cars—shouting happily.

Most civilians stayed nervously indoors, however, not yet sure what was going on or who was who. What was the fighting inside the city all about? they wondered; was it between diehard Government troops and the Communists or between rival Communist factions fighting over the spoils? Or was it mostly exuberance?

Some of these questions, including the nature of the factionalism, have still not been answered satisfactorily, but on that first day such mysteries quickly became academic, for within a few hours, the mood changed.

The cheerful and pleasant troops we first encountered—we came to call them the soft troops, and we learned later that they were discredited and

AS THE CITY OF PHNOM PENH FELL: Early on April 17, five years of war in Cambodia ended as rebel troops entered a capital where white flags had suddenly appeared, some Government soldiers had unloaded their weapons, while some had changed to civilian clothes. The black pajama-like garb of Indochinese Communists had been donned by some of the Government office workers. At first the mood was jubilant, with the rebels being welcomed. But later, the early arrivals were replaced by well disciplined, heavily armed soldiers, including young boys and women.

disarmed, with their leader declared a traitor; they may not even have been authentic —were swiftly displaced by battle-hardened soldiers.

While some of these were occasionally friendly, or at least not hostile, they were also all business. Dripping with arms like overladen fruit trees—grenades, pistols, rifles, rockets—they immediately began clearing the city of civilians.

People Driven Out

Using loudspeakers, or simply shouting and brandishing weapons, they swept through the streets, ordering people out of their houses. At first we thought the order applied only to the rich in villas, but we quickly saw that it was for everyone as the streets became clogged with a sorrowful exodus.

Cars stalled or their tires went flat, and they were abandoned. People lost their sandals in the jostling and pushing, so they lay as a reminder of the throng that had passed.

In the days to follow, during the foreign colony's confinement in the French Embassy compound, we heard reports on international news broadcasts that the Communists had evacuated the city by telling people the United States was about to bomb it. However, all the departing civilians I talked with said they had been given no reason except that the city had to be reorganized. They were told they had to go far from Phnom Penh.

In almost every situation we encountered during the more than two weeks we were under Communist control, there was a sense of split vision—whether to look at events through Western eyes or through what we thought might be Cambodian revolutionary eyes.

Brutality or Necessity?

Was this just cold brutality, a cruel and sadistic imposition of the law of the jungle, in which only the fittest will survive? Or is it possible that, seen through the eyes of the peasant soldiers and revolutionaries, the forced evacuation of the cities is a harsh necessity? Perhaps they are convinced that there is no way to build a new society for the benefit of the ordinary man, hitherto exploited, without literally starting from the beginning; in such an unbending view people who represent the old ways and those considered weak or unfit would be expendable and would be weeded out. Or was the policy both cruel and ideological?

A foreign doctor offered this explanation for the expulsion of the sick and wounded from the hospital: "They could not cope with all the patients—they do not have the doctors—so they apparently decided to throw them all out and blame any deaths on the old regime. That way they could start from scratch medically."

Some Western observers con-

sidered that the exodus approached genocide. One of them, watching from his refuge in the French Embassy compound, said: "They are crazy! This is pure and simple genocide. They will kill more people this way than if there had been hand-to-hand fighting in the city."

Another foreign doctor, who had been forced at gunpoint to abandon a seriously wounded patient in midoperation, added in a dark voice: "They have not got a humanitarian thought in their heads!"

Whatever the Communists' purpose, the exodus did not grow heavy until dusk, and even then onlookers were slow to realize that the people were being forcibly evacuated.

For my own part, I had a problem that preoccupied me that afternoon: I, with others, was held captive and threatened with execution.

After our release, we went to the Information Ministry, because we had heard about a broadcast directing high officials of the old regime to report there. When we arrived, about 50 prisoners were standing outside the building, among them Lon Non, the younger brother of President Lon Nol, who went into exile on April 1, and Brig. Gen. Chim Chhuon, who was close to the former President. Other generals and Cabinet ministers were also there—very nervous but trying to appear untroubled.

Premier Long Boret, who the day before had made an offer of surrender with certain conditions only to have it immediately rejected, arrived at the ministry an hour later. He is one of the seven "traitors" the Communists had marked for execution. The others had fled except for Lieut. Gen. Sisowath Sirik Matak, a former Premier, who some days later was removed from the French Embassy, where he had taken refuge.

Mr. Long Boret's eyes were puffy and red, almost down to slits. He had probably been up all night and perhaps he had been weeping. His wife and two children were also still in the country; later they sought refuge at the French Embassy.

only to be rejected as persons who might "compromise" the rest of the refugees.

Mr. Long Boret, who had talked volubly and articulately on the telephone the night before, had difficulty speaking coherently. He could only mumble yes, no and thank you, so conversation was impossible.

There is still no hard information on what has happened to him. Most people who have talked with the Communists believe it a certainty that he will be executed, if indeed the execution has not already taken place.

Soothing General

One of the Communist leaders at the Information Ministry

that day—probably a general, though his uniform bore no markings and he declined to give his name—talked soothingly to the 50 prisoners. He assured them that there were only seven traitors and that other officials of the old regime would be dealt with equitably. "There will be no reprisals," he said. Their strained faces suggested that they would like to believe him but did not.

As he talked, a squad crouched in combat-ready positions around him, almost as if it was guarding him against harm.

The officer, who appeared no more than age 35, agreed to chat with foreign newsmen. His tone was polite and sometimes he smiled, but everything he said suggested that we, as foreigners, meant nothing to him and that our interests were alien to his.

Asked about the fate of the 20 or so foreign journalists missing in Cambodia since the early days of the war, he said he had heard nothing. Asked if we would be permitted to file from the cable office, he smiled sympathetically and said, "We will resolve all problems in their proper order."

Clearly an educated man, he almost certainly speaks French, the language of the nation that ruled Cambodia for nearly a century until the nineteen-fifties, but he gave no hint of this colonial vestige, speaking only in Khmer through an interpreter.

In the middle of the conversation he volunteered quite unexpectedly: "We would like you to give our thanks to the American people who have helped us and supported us from the beginning, and to all people of the world who love peace and justice. Please give this message to the world."

Noting that Congress had halted aid to the Phnom Penh Government, he said, "The purpose was to stop the war," but he quickly added: "Our struggle would not have stopped even if they had given more aid."

Attempts to find out more about who he was and about political and military organization led only to imprecision. The officer said: "I represent the armed forces. There are many divisions. I am one of the many."

Is Asked About Factions

Asked if there were factions, he said there was only one political organization and one government. Some top political and governmental leaders are not far from the city, he added, but they let the military enter first, "to organize things."

Most military units, he said, are called "rumdos," which means "liberation forces." Neither this commander nor any of the soldiers we talked with ever called themselves Communists or Khmer Rouge (Red Cambodians). They al-

ways said they were liberation troops or nationalist troops and called one another brother or the Khmer equivalent of comrade.

The nomenclature at least is confusing, for Western intelligence had described the Khmer Rumdos as a faction loyal to Prince Norodom Sihanouk that was being downgraded by Hanoi-trained Cambodians and losing power.

The Communists named the Cambodian leader, who was deposed by Marshal Lon Nol in 1970 and has been living in exile in Peking, as their figurehead chief of state, but none of the soldiers we talked with brought up his name.

One over-all impression emerged from our talk with the commander at the Information Ministry: The military will be largely in charge of the early stages of the upheaval, carrying out the evacuation, organizing the new agrarian program, searching for hidden arms and resisters, repairing damaged bridges.

The politicians—or so it seemed from all the evidence during our stay—have for the moment taken a rear seat. No significant political or administrative apparatus was yet visible; it did not seem to be a government yet, but an army.

The radio announced April 28 that a special national congress attended by over 300 delegates was held in Phnom Penh from April 25 to 27. It was said to have been chaired by the Deputy Premier and military commander, Khieu Samphan, who has emerged—at least in public announcements—as the top leader. Despite that meeting the military still seemed to be running things as we emerged from Cambodia on Saturday.

One apparent reason is that politicians and bureaucrats are not equipped to do the dirty work and arduous tasks of the early phases of reorganization. Another is that the military, as indicated in conversations with Khmer-speaking foreigners they trusted somewhat, seemed worried that politicians or soft-living outsiders in their movement might steal the victory and dilute it. There could be severe power struggles ahead.

After leaving the prisoners and the military commander at the ministry, we headed for the Hotel Le Phnom, where another surprise was waiting. The day before, the Red Cross turned the hotel into a protected international zone and draped it with huge Red Cross flags. But the Communists were not interested.

Order Hotel Emptied

At 4:55 P.M. troops waving guns and rockets had forced their way into the grounds and ordered the hotel emptied within 30 minutes. By the time we arrived 25 minutes had elapsed. The fastest packing job in history ensued. I even had time to "liberate" a typewriter someone had abandoned since the troops had "liberated" mine earlier.

We were the last ones out. running. The Red Cross had abandoned several vehicles in the yard after removing the keys, so several of us threw our gear on the back of a Red Cross Honda pickup truck and started pushing it up the boulevard toward the French Embassy.

Several days before, word was passed to those foreigners who stayed behind when the Americans pulled out on April 12 that, as a last resort, one could take refuge at the embassy. France had recognized the new government, and it was thought that the new Cambodian leaders would respect the embassy compound as a sanctuary.

As we plodded up the road, big fires were burning on the city's outskirts, sending smoke clouds into the evening sky like a giant funeral wreath encircling the capital.

The embassy was only several hundred yards away, but what was happening on the road made it seem much farther. All around us people were fleeing, for there was no refuge for them. And coming into the city from the other direction was a fresh battalion marching in single file. They looked curiously at us; we looked nervously at them.

In the 13 days of confinement that followed, until our evacuation by military truck to the Thai border, we had only a peephole onto what was going on outside, but there were still many things that could be seen and many clues to the revolution that was going on.

We could hear shooting, sometimes nearby but mostly in other parts of the city. Often

it sounded like shooting in the air, but at other times it seemed like small battles. As on the day of the city's fall we were never able to piece together a satisfactory explanation of the shooting, which died down after about a week.

We could see smoke from the huge fires from time to time, and there were reports from foreigners who trickled into the embassy that certain quarters were badly burned and that the water-purification plant was heavily damaged.

The foreigners who for various reasons came in later carried stories, some of them eyewitness accounts, of such things as civilian bodies along the roads leading out of the city — people who had apparently died of illness or exhaustion on the march. But each witness got only a glimpse, and no reliable estimate of the toll was possible.

Reports from roads to the south and southeast of Phnom Penh said the Communists were breaking up families by dividing the refugees by sex and age. Such practices were not reported from other roads on which the refugees flooded out of the capital.

Executions Reported

Reports also told of executions, but none were eyewitness accounts. One such report said high military officers were executed at a rubber plantation a couple of miles north of the city.

In the French Embassy compound foreign doctors and relief agency officials were pessimistic about the survival chances of many of the refugees. "There's no food in the countryside at this time of year," an

international official said. "What will they eat from now until the rice harvest in November?"

The new Communist officials, in conversations with United Nations and other foreign representatives during our confinement and in statements since, have rejected the idea of foreign aid, "whether it is military, political, economic, social, diplomatic, or whether it takes on a so-called humanitarian form." Some foreign observers wondered whether this included China, for they speculated that the Communists would at least need seed to plant for the next harvest.

Whether the looting we observed before we entered the French compound continued is difficult to say. In any case, it is essential to understand who the Communist soldiers are to understand the behavior of some of them in disciplinary matters, particularly looting.

They are peasant boys, pure and simple — darker skinned than their city brethren, with gold in their front teeth. To them the city is a curiosity, an oddity, a carnival, where you visit but do not live. The city means next to nothing in their scheme of things.

One Kept, the Rest Given

When they looted jewelry shops, they kept only one watch for themselves and gave the rest to their colleagues or passers-by. Transistor radios, cameras and cars held the same toy-like fascination—something to play with, as children might, but not essential.

From my airline bag on the day I was seized and threatened with execution they took only some cigarettes, a pair of

boxer underwear shorts and a handkerchief. They passed up a blue shirt and $9,000 in cash in a money belt.

The looting did not really contradict the Communist image of rigid discipline, for commanders apparently gave no orders against the sacking of shops, feeling, perhaps, that this was the least due their men after five years of jungle fighting.

Often they would climb into abandoned cars and find that they would not run, so they would bang on them with their rifles like frustrated children, or they would simply toot the horns for hours on end or keep turning the headlights on and off until the batteries died.

One night at the French Embassy, I chose to sleep on the grass outside; I was suddenly awakened by what sounded like a platoon trying to smash down the front gates with a battering ram that had bright lights and a loud claxon. It was only a bunch of soldiers playing with and smashing up the cars that had been left outside the gates.

Though these country soldiers broke into villas all over the city and took the curious things they wanted—one walked past the embassy beaming proudly in a crimson-colored wool overcoat that hung down to his Ho Chi Minh sandals—they never stayed in the villas. With big, soft beds empty, they slept in the courtyards or the streets.

Almost without exception foot soldiers I talked with, when asked what they wanted to do, replied that they only wanted to go home.

May 9, 1975

A Chronology of the Mayaguez Episode

Special to The New York Times

WASHINGTON, May 15—
Following is a chronology of the events involving the seizure and subsequent freeing of the Mayagüez. The hours are given in Eastern daylight time; Cambodian time is 11 hours later.

MONDAY, MAY 12

5:03 A.M.—State Department gets a message from the ship, received in Indonesia in the offices of the Delta Exploration Company, relayed to the United States Embassy in Jakarta and then to Washington: "Have been fired upon and boarded by Cambodian armed forces. Ship being towed to unknown Cambodian port." She was then in the Gulf of Siam.

7:40 A.M.—Maj. Gen. Brent Scowcroft, deputy director of

the National Security Council, informs President Ford in the Oval Office.

Noon — President meets with the National Security Council.

2 P.M. — Press Secretary Ron Nessen announces the incident, and quotes the President as having described it as "an act of piracy."

Afternoon — The United States begins working through third countries, primarily China, to try to effect the release of the container ship and its 39-member crew.

TUESDAY, MAY 13

Morning—American reconnaissance planes locate the Mayagüez near Tang Island, 34 miles off the Cambodian coast, under the surveillance of two Cambodian patrol boats.

Kukrit Pramoi. the Thai Premier, warns that he will not permit the use of Thai air bases for American operations against Cambodia.

Secretary of State Kissinger, in Missouri, says that the United States will "wait a bit" before acting with force.

Afternoon — Mr. Ford meets with the National Security Council for 56 minutes, then orders that about 1,100 marines be flown from Okinawa to U Taphao air base in Thailand and that the aircraft carrier Coral Sea and destroyers head for the Gulf of Siam. These movements are not publicly announced.

United States planes flying reconnaissance missions over the Mayagüez are hit by gunfire.

8:30 P.M. — The White

House reports that the Cambodians are apparently attempting to move the crewmen to the mainland.

10:20 P.M.—The National Security Council meets again, this time for about two hours.

WEDNESDAY, MAY 14

1 A.M.—American warplanes sink three Cambodian gunboats, which. Defense Department officials said, were to be used to move the crew members. This attack is not announced in Washington for 11 hours.

Late morning—the destroyer escort Holt reaches the scene, the first American naval vessel to do so.

Afternoon — the United States asks the United Nations to help obtain the release of the Mayagüez. and Secretary General Waldheim asks the United States and Cambodia "to refrain from further acts of force."

3:52 P.M.—The National

Security Council meets again with the President. Orders for the beginning of the military operation off Cambodia are issued, according to the White House, at 4:45 P.M. and the meeting lasted until 5:40 P.M.

5:14 P.M.—Assault forces begin moving out.

6:40 P.M.—The President begins a meeting with the bipartisan Congressional leadership in the Cabinet room.

7:07 P.M.—Phnom Penh radio begins broadcast offering to release the Mayagüez.

7:20 P.M. (according to the Pentagon, the White House puts the time at 7:09 P.M.)—

Assault force lands under fire at Tang Island in the Gulf of Siam, near the Mayagüez.

8:15 P.M.—Foreign broadcast information service report of Cambodia broadcast is received by Secretary Kissinger, who then informs President.

8:30 P.M.—Marines board the Mayagüez from the Holt and find no one there. Later they hoist an American flag.

9:15 P.M.—Mr. Nessen issues text of American statement demanding release of the crew and promising to cease military operations as soon as the crew has been freed.

10:45 P.M.—Destroyer Wilson reports small boat approaching, flying white flag.

10:53 P.M.—Wilson flashes word to Pentagon that at least 30 Caucasians — the crewmen — are aboard the boat.

10:57 P.M. (or, according to a slightly different account also given at the Pentagon, 11:09 P.M.) — first strike by carrier planes based on the Coral Sea begins at Ream, an airfield near the port of Sihanoukville on the mainland.

11:14 P.M.—Defense Secretary James R. Schlesinger informs President that the Wilson has found the crewmen.

11:16 P.M.—President gives order to cease all offensive operations and to begin to withdraw from Tang Island.

THURSDAY, MAY 15

12:31 A.M.—President appears on television to announce that rescue is complete and that disengagement will begin soon. He praises valor of military forces involved.

7:13 A.M.—First lift of marines from Tang Island begins, again under fire.

9:20 A.M.—Last helicopter reaches the Coral Sea.

May 16, 1975

Saigon Tries Persuasion In Restoring Rural Life

SAIGON, South Vietnam, May 22 (AP)—The direction of the policy of South Vietnam's new leaders is becoming visible, one aspect of it being to persuade some of the people in overcrowded cities to return to the countryside.

For many the prospect of going back to the soil will not be too unpleasant. Because the closing of banks has virtually halted the flow of money, because unemployment is at an all-time high in the cities, some have already left them.

Communist cadres are sending out the word through block committees in the cities that families will be welcomed in their ancestral villages. This approach, a Vietnamese here said, is "more subtle" than that of the victorious Cambodian Communists, "who cleared Phnom Penh by telling the population the United States would bomb the city."

Families Sending Scouts

Many families are sending one member to test the rural climate. A Vietnamese journalist said that his brother went to the family's village, and was greeted by a Communist official who told him: "Hey, ranger! You're welcome to come back and farm the land again."

"So his whole family headed out of Saigon," the journalist said.

A few weeks ago, a general who had commanded combat troops of the fallen Government was seen riding a bicycle in Saigon. The price of gasoline here is now the equivalent of $8 a gallon.

Former President Tran Van Huong, 71, preferred to walk to his destination last Monday. He was seen hobbling past the Saigon basilica through Peace Square, the new name for John F. Kennedy Square, shaking hands with passers-by who recognized him.

The Communist authorities, moving cautiously toward a transformation of urban to rural society, are effecting these changes through communiqués issued by the Provisional Revolutionary Government's Military Administrative Committee, still in complete control of Saigon three weeks after the fall.

If diminished traffic in Saigon and other major centers is any indication, hundreds of thousands of people must have left for the countryside. Under the old Government, Saigon's population was about 3.5 million.

As in North Vietnam in the middle nineteen-fifties, after the war against the French, Communist authorities in South Vietnam are seeking total population control, most obviously by mixing soldiers with the population of the cities.

In hundreds of Saigon homes, regular soldiers either occupy one or two rooms, or take over completely the residences of Vietnamese who fled to the United States in the last days of the war. All homes so left have been confiscated by the state.

Precinct committees have been formed to indoctrinate Saigonese. Rallies, on vacant lots, in parks and back yards, are now common in Saigon. The people participate without complaint, if not with initial enthusiasm.

Other changes are more subtle. Military forces are still predominant in South Vietnam. The Saigon area is under the Military Administrative Committee headed by Lieut. Gen. Tran Van Tra, who commanded Communist forces in the Tet offensive of 1968.

These forces occupy all strategic bases and camps. The gun barrels of Soviet-built T-54 tanks poke through the trees of parks and over barbed-wire fences. The presence of this overwhelming force of tanks, troops and artillery probably allows local authorities to grant wide latitude to the South Vietnamese, most of whom were under government control long before the Communist victory of April 30.

The apparent benignity of the victors has astounded officials and military officers of the fallen administration, who, at most, have been undergoing moderate indoctrination.

Some unhappiness is expressed by moderate politicians and their supporters, who expected a transitional political regime that would include them. This now appears unlikely.

What is going on now may be only a transition to an eventual referendum that will decide irrevocably for reunification of the Vietnams.

May 23, 1975

5 IN LAOS CABINET REPORTEDLY QUIT

Resignations Could Cripple Rightists' Faction—U.S. Embassy Is Stoned

By The Associated Press

VIENTIANE, Laos, May 9— Five pro-American Cabinet ministers were reported to have resigned from Laos's coalition Government today.

The resignations were reported by highly placed sources amid mounting protests against United States policies, and following a demonstration by about 3,000 Laotian students and teachers protesting rising prices and foreign economic influences. Some of them threw stones at the United States Embassy.

There was no official confirmation of the resignations, but, according to the high sources, the five ministers included the powerful Defense Minister, Sisouk na Champassak, and Finance Minister Ngon Sananikone; Khamphai Abphay, Minister of Public Health; Tianethone Chantharasy, Deputy Foreign Minister, and Houmphanh Saignasith, Deputy Minister of Public Works.

Threat to Rightist Faction

Their withdrawal from the coalition would virtually eliminate the rightist faction, which, along with neutralists and the Pathet Lao, makes up the Government under Premier Souvanna Phouma.

The reports of the resignations came after the demonstration by the students and teachers. Some students tried to haul down the embassy's American flag, but a marine guard seized the standard and Government policemen drove the students out of the compound.

The demonstration by the 3,000 began at the Victory Monument, a few blocks from the embassy. Students carrying placards reading: "Yankee Go Home" and "Cut the Throats of the Rightists" paraded around the monument, chanting "C.I.A. go home."

On their way to a rally at the national stadium the demonstrators detoured to pass the embassy compound. However, Laotian and American guards could not get the gates shut, and several students climbed the fence.

A few stones were thrown and the attempt was made to lower the flag. But a student leader sitting on the fence, and Pathet Lao policemen, armed with rifles, shouted to the demonstrators to move on. They obeyed.

Laos has long been torn by conflict between the Communist-led Pathet Lao and the rightist faction. A cease-fire a year ago permitted formation of the coalition.

Many of Rich Are Gone

Scattered outbreaks of fighting have disrupted the cease-fire since, but Western military sources unanimously reject reports that the clashes are part of a Pathet Lao military offensive. The latest agreement to stop fighting was announced on Wednesday.

An order by Prince Souvanna Phouma forbidding rightist forces to fight Pathet Lao forces has led many Laotians to fear that their country is about to fall to Communism, as South Vietnam and Cambodia have.

Many wealthy Laotian, Chinese and Vietnamese have already left the country and others are following. Scores of automobiles have been lined up at a ferry here, waiting to cross the Mekong River to Thailand; planes leaving Vientiane have been booked solid for days in advance.

Laotians applying for visas crowded the Thai, American and French embassies. Many shops in Vientiane's once-flourishing business district were shuttered.

Still, there was no apparent parallel with the panicked flight out of Saigon before its fall, and the United States Embassy denied that it was evacuating Americans from Laos. The embassy listed 895 Americans in Laos, all but 75 of whom were attached to the embassy, the others being businessmen and unemployed young people.

An embassy spokesman said that the number of Americans had dropped in recent months and would continue to decline, under a long-range cutback.

May 10, 1975

Pathet Lao Announce Vientiane Take-Over

By DAVID A. ANDELMAN
Special to The New York Times

BANGKOK, Thailand, Aug. 23 —The Communist-led Pathet Lao took over Laos today, marking the last chapter in the rise to power of Communist-led movements in Indochina.

Some 300,000 people gathered on a parade ground in the capital, Vientiane, today to "welcome the people's revolutionary administration," according to broadcasts of the Vientiane radio and the Pathet Lao news agency, monitored here and in Hong Kong.

The rally marked the end of a process that began formally in Laos three months and two days ago, a process that has, so far, been generally peaceful.

According to the Pathet Lao news agency, the crowd at the rally was addressed by Thao Moun, identified only as chairman of the "uprising committee," who said that the advent of the new administration marked a major turning point in the development and growth of Vientiane Province.

The status of Premier Souvanna Phouma and King Savang Vatthana was not clear. Both had planned visits outside the country this month that were abruptly canceled last week, apparently because of the imminence of today's ceremonies and the spreading reports that if they left they would not return.

The Pathet Lao has said it continues to respect and recognize both Prince Souvanna Phouma as the head of the Government and the King as the head of state.

Vientiane Province was the last of the country's provinces to be "liberated," a process that has meant the arrival of Pathet Lao troops in strength, backed by tanks but accompanied too by cheers from much of the population.

Tonight, the time allotted for the regular nightly broadcast in French by the Vientiane radio was pre-empted by a broadcast in the Lao language accompanied by background sounds of throngs cheering and singing as the announcement of the Pathet Lao take-over was made.

Earlier today, the Vientiane radio announced the take-over of Laos's royal capital, Luang Prabang, 130 miles northwest of Vientiane, in a similar celebration earlier this week.

In that broadcast, the radio repeatedly referred to the "liberation" as a victory over "the United States imperialists and their henchmen."

'New Period of Struggle'

"This seizure of power" by the Pathet Lao "is of great importance," the broadcast said. "It is encouraging the Lao people in the new period of their struggle. Under foreign rule, especially since the United States invaded Laos, the centuries-old royal capital has been turned into a training center for the mercenary army to carry out air and ground attacks against the liberated zone of Laos."

The take-over of Vientiane Province, which had been expected for weeks, was heralded last night when the Laotian authorities sealed the country's borders, cut all international telecommunications, and closed airports for 24 hours.

Thailand, which has a long border with Laos, went further. Kampol Klinsukol, the Governor of Nong Khai Province, ordered the entire frontier sealed for at least what was expected to be a five-day celebration in Vientiane. The Laotian capital is just across the Mekong River from Thailand.

There have been a growing number of border incidents along this frontier, most of them involving river patrol craft, and diplomats of the two countries have been expelled in recent weeks as the bitterness has grown.

There have been, however, no reports of any incidents along the border while the celebrations were going on in Vientiane.

Today's "liberation" was the last of a series of such celebrations that began May 20 when Pathet Lao troops and tanks rolled through Savannakhet, a major southern provincial capital. Student demonstrators had prepared the groundwork there by ousting the right-wing administration, which had been linked with Vientiane, in a week-long demonstration that included the house arrest of 12 American aid officials.

The pattern was repeated in province after province, spreading in May from the southern panhandle area northward into all the area originally controlled by the right-wing Vientiane side of what had been the year-old provisional Government of national union.

After the take-overs started, the Laotian Premier, Prince Souvanna Phouma, a neutralist, said he had ordered that there be no resistance to any of the Pathet Lao actions in an effort to "avoid any bloodshed."

It was at the end of a long war that the coalition Government was established in April, 1974, with the aim of sharing responsibility equally between members of the old right-wing Vientiane side, the Pathet Lao and a group of avowed neutralists.

Under those terms, each party was to administer the territory it controlled at the time of the cease-fire.

The takeover of Savannakhet and neighboring Pakse, apparently marked the end of this arrangement, although the Pathet Lao and Prince Souvanna Phouma continued, almost to the end, to preserve the fiction of a coalition arrangement.

However, as so-called people's courts spread through the ministries, anti-American and pro-Communist demonstrators began to take to the streets and most of the strong figures behind the right-wing element of the coalition fled abroad.

Control Tightened

Gradually, the Pathet Lao tightened its administrative control, closing bars and night-clubs, imposing restrictions on travel and sending hundreds of government and military officials off to "re-education courses" in which they were encouraged to confess "reactionary" leanings.

August 24, 1975

Take-Over Ends Strife in Laos That Outsiders Had Intensified

By WOLFGANG SAXON

"A state by diplomatic courtesy" was the label pinned on Laos by Arthur M. Schlesinger Jr., who was an assistant to President John F. Kennedy when the United States was well on its way to becoming inexorably embroiled in the Indochina quagmire.

President Dwight D. Eisenhower, Professor Schlesinger related, had told his successor that Laos was the key to Southeast Asia—so important, in fact, that he would be willing to have the United States, as a last resort, intervene on its own to keep the country from Communist control.

The recent torment of Laos, which was taken over by the Pathet Lao yesterday, follows six centuries of feudal rivalries and brief spells of glory, disintegration, tutelage by more potent neighbors—whose goodwill the splintered kingdom needed to survive — and finally French imperialism, which at least gave it a measure of national identity again, along with its present borders and an area of 91,000 square miles (Oregon is 97,000).

Not that any of it mattered much to the vast bulk of the ethnically diverse Laotian population, much of which was engaged in subsistence agriculture and clustered in remote villages in the hills, with few roads or other means of communication. The people lived barely on the fringe of the cash economy and of national political processes, while a small educated élite in a few little towns and the two capitals, Vientiane and Luang Prabang, ran things—usually rather badly.

Independent Again in '53

Full independence, regained in 1953, only triggered new intrigue, resulting in kaleidoscopic changes in the "leadership" and fratricidal strife that was increased to tragic proportions by warring outsiders.

Some 350,000 men, women and children have been killed, it is estimated, and a tenth of the population of three million uprooted.

The Japanese, who dominated Indochina during World War II, had encouraged Laotion nationalism as a foil against France. At their behest the Laotian king proclaimed independence.

Three Princes—the then Premier, Phetsarat, his brother, Souvanna Phouma, and his half-brother, Souphanouvong—set up a Free Laos party to maintain that independence,

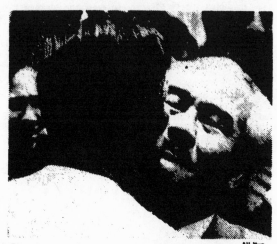

Returning to Vientiane, Laos, after an absence of 10 years, Prince Souphanouvong, at right, embraced his half-brother, Prince Souvanna Phouma, on April 3, 1974.

but they were forced to flee after Japan's defeat and to press their cause from exile in Bangkok.

With the French return, nationalist stirrings in Laos subsided. A Constitution was proclaimed that narrowed the traditional royal privileges. The king's main function was the appointment of a prime minister. Two years later, in 1949, the kingdom became a putatively sovereign entity within the French Union.

Most of the Free Laos notables returned to the fold, but Prince Souphanouvong was ousted from his position of leadership because of his close relations with the radical Vietminh of Vietnam.

Prince Souphanouvong emerged as the head of a new Communist-led movement, the Pathet Lao—Land of the Lao—and established a resistance "government" on Laotian soil in the northeastern hills, which by then had fallen under Vietminh sway.

There followed a period of guerrilla operations by the Pathet Lao against the national Government until 1953, when the hostilities between the Vietminh and the French rushed toward a climax. Vietminh units drove deep into Laos, bolstering Souphanouvong's position as they set the stage for the French defeat at Dien Bien Phu.

The 1954 Geneva conference left Laos with an ineffective International Control Commission and enough ambiguities for the Pathet Lao to retain its stronghold, from which it could build an organization and prepare for entry into national politics.

Prince Souvanna Phouma, a neutralist and conciliator, served as Premier from 1951 to 1954. Resuming the helm in 1956, he was able to negotiate an agreement with Souphanouvong to set up a coalition Government in which the Pathet Lao took part.

Washington had viewed the Pathet Lao-Vietminh entrenchment in northern Laos with alarm and Secretary of State John Foster Dulles opposed the idea of a coalition in Vientiane when the Laotian factions discussed it in 1954. Instead, the United States decided to rush in aid bolstering the Laotian anti-communists by building and maintaining a 25,000-man army at their disposal. Too many dollars poured in too fast, the economy went wild and corruption abounded.

Old Elite Consolidated

In an election in 1958 the Pathet Lao's political arm won a majority of the seats at stake, causing the traditional élite to consolidate. A rightwinger, Phoui Sananikone, was installed as Premier, and leftists saw their parliamentary activities curtailed.

In 1960 a coup led by a neutralist and mildly xenophobic paratroop captain, Kong Le, restored Prince Souvanna Phouma to the Premiership with the hope of saving Lao's neutrality.

An army strongman, Gen. Phoumi Nosavan, promptly marshaled rightist forces in southern Laos and retook Vientiane after a battle that was unusually bloody by Laotian standards. His proclaimed anti-Communism won him military aid from the Eisenhower Administration and the Thai Government.

Prince Souvanna Phouma, who had tried to save his neutralist government with Soviet assistance, fled to Cambodia and renewed his association with Prince Souphanouvong. Captain Kong Le allied his neutralist contingents with the Pathet Lao, which had managed to take further territory in the north during the confusion.

Aside from General Phoumi Nosavan, the man in charge in Vientiane was the new Premier, Prince Boun Oum of Champassak, a feudal southern ruler who had organized guerrilla actions against the Japanese with the aid of French officers. His forces were soon hard-pressed by Captain Kong Le's neutralists and the Pathet Lao.

The arrival of the Kennedy Administration in early 1961 brought a change of attitude in Washington to the extent that it would not be willing to accept a neutralized Laos. At the same time President Kennedy demanded a stop to the "armed attacks by externally supported Communists."

To back up his call, the President proceeded to set up a Military Advisory Assistance Group to strengthen Vientiane's army, and Americans began to train Meo tribesmen for the war against the Pathet Lao and North Vietnamese.

Efforts by Britain and the Soviet Union led to a new Geneva conference in 1961-62 at which the three Laotian factions were represented. As the talks dragged on into May, 1962, President Kennedy began to send 5,000 American troops to Thailand.

The next month, with fighting continuing in Laos despite yet another cease-fire agreement, the Laotians settled for yet another tripartite coalition, consisting of Prince Souvanna Phouma as Premier and Prince Souphanouvong and General Phoumi Nosavan as his deputies.

It was a ramshackle structure from the start and fighting resumed despite urgent French efforts to keep the peace.

There were political assassinations, Captain Kong Le and General Phoumi Nosavan went into exile and the neutralist units were reintegrated into the royal army, Prince Souvanna Phouma gained American support and consolidated his political hold as Premier, and the Pathet Lao ruled most of the country.

When the Vietnam war gathered force in the mid-nineteen-sixties the North Vietnamese made increasing use of their supply trails through Laos. American bombers started a campaign to halt the traffic, and American military aid flowed in larger quantities to further the Royal Laotian Government's campaigns against the Pathet Lao.

Prince Souvanna Phouma, confirmed in office by elections in 1967, reopened negotiations for a political settlement in

1971, but they remained inconclusive. Only after the Paris negotiations to end the Vietnam war could the Royal Laotian Government and the Pathet Lao put their signatures to a provisional agreement in February, 1973.

The settlement started taking effect toward the end of 1973, and once again a coalition was installed, with Prince Souvanna Phouma remaining as Premier and Prince Souphanouvong installed as his deputy. Ministerial portfolios were equally divided between right-wingers and Pathet Lao adherents.

After that the rightists began to lose what political support they had, their misfortunes being compounded by charges of corruption and ineptitude.

The Pathet Lao, though it: direct control extended over the smaller part of the population moved into a position from which it might seize both the Government and the rest of the country at will.

August 18, 1975

Laos, Stressing Self-Reliance, Is Finding the Road to Socialism Rough

By DAVID A. ANDELMAN
Special to The New York Times

VIENTIANE, Laos, Sept. 1—The Communist Pathet Lao, who for nine months have been firmly in control of the Government and people of Laos, are attempting to rebuild the tiny landlocked country into a self-sufficient socialist state.

The result to date has been mixed. The country is still reeling from the effects of a severe food shortage that is just easing, and it faces the prospect of a potentially serious drought in its most fertile rice-growing regions.

In wide areas of the countryside, particularly in the south and northeast, it is still dangerous for Pathet Lao troops or administrators to venture outside the town after nightfall as anti-Government insurgents are still active.

In Vientiane, the capital, little has changed outwardly, though the din of automobiles has largely given way to the soft swish of bicycle pedals as a result of a fuel shortage. But the strict measures that the Government has taken to insure conformity with its plans and philosophy have made the capital a far more intense city.

The tone is set by the presence everywhere of the ai nong—the Pathet Lao personnel who, in their baggy green fatigues, automatic rifles slung over their shoulders, swagger everywhere through the streets of Vientiane.

'The People Must Understand'

The Government itself dismisses the disillusionment, frequently with the often-heard phrase, "The people must understand." It is used to explain the hardships and complaints that officials believe merely reflect the growing pains involved in building a new spirit of self-reliance and a new and "purely Lao" state, society and economy.

"If what they say comes true in one year, perhaps two, then maybe the theory is correct," said a young Lao woman who works in a small hotel coffee shop. "There are some things they say that I particularly like—Laos is rich in natural resources and we should develop them, and before, under the old regime, we were not working hard enough, we just asked people for help."

These are the cornerstones of the Pathet Lao philosophy—hard work, self-reliance, national pride and the rich natural endowments of this country.

Yet this young woman learned her Pathet Lao catechism during 40 days of hard labor at a remote island penal colony,

a "re-education camp"—a fact that, she said, she doubts she will ever be able to forget. And she could tell her story to a foreign visitor only in an automobile being driven through the streets of Vientiane.

She was one of the few to be released from these re-education centers—thousands are still at their study and work programs. By the most conservative estimates, at least 20,000 people have been sent to re-education centers deep in the jungles or mountains.

Many sent to the camps were members of the old rightist regime that was deposed gradually, quietly in a revolution that is called "typically Lao" and that culminated last Dec. 2 in the final abolition of the monarchy and creation of a people's democratic socialist republic. But there were as well many "reactionaries and their lackeys," including prostitutes and bar girls as well as those who were caught walking the streets with long hair or immodest clothes, who were sent off to be re-educated.

Some, such as former Prime Minister Souvanna Phouma, the elder statesman of conciliation and accommodation, have been allowed to continue living in their homes in Vientiane. But Prince Souvanna who is said to be ill and whose title is Counselor to the Government, has been stripped of his power and reportedly spends most days with little to do.

Others, even harmless old men, former Information Minister Ouday Souvannouvong, former Minister of Posts and Telegraphs Touby Lyfong and thousands more, have been spirited out of their homes in and around the capital and sent off to the viengsay—a word that for many Laotians has begun to take on threatening proportions far beyond any evidence of torture or severe physical coercion that they believe could be taking place there.

Few have returned. And most of those who have come back have joined an estimated 200,000 or more other Laotians in fleeing across the Mekong River to Thailand.

Those who most ardently support the Pathet Lao's revolution point particularly to this new national pride, the work ethic.

In June, in a major address to the Supreme People's Council, Prime Minister Kaysone Phomvihan, who as secretary general of the Lao People's Revolutionary Party is clearly the leading figure in the country, outlined these priorities and ac-

knowledged major problem areas. And last week, in an interview here, Information Minister Sisana Sisane repeated the list, indicating that few if any of these difficulties have yet been resolved.

Problem of Security Is Stressed

Mr. Kaysone's list included the following:

¶In the area of security, "commando remnants have built commando strongholds to create disturbances in certain areas with the hope of creating further strongholds, hoping to overthrow our administrative power in various local areas so as to create chaos in the rural areas and unrest in towns with the view to undermining the efficiency of our administration."

¶Under the former regime, "the amount of rice and other food imported from foreign countries kept increasing every year. It was even more dependent on foreign countries in acquiring other necessities. The level of self-sufficiency in the country is extremely low."

¶The major flight of refugees from Laos has robbed the country of most of its skilled technocrats, agriculture specialists, economists and businessmen. Mr. Kaysone observed: "The enemy cajoled tens of thousands of Lao citizens, including intellectuals, engineers and skilled workers, to flee with him to Thailand. The enemy also took with him Lao property, factory machines and transport vehicles. In addition, he also abruptly and drastically cut his assistance to Laos, set up an economic blockage against our country by unilaterally closing the border and ceased to guarantee the Vientiane kip." The kip is the basic unit of currency, which has taken a severe beating on the open market in recent months.

Their Darkest Hour

At the time Mr. Kaysone was delivering his speech, the situations he was discussing—the economy and security, in particular—were reaching their darkest hour.

By early July, under severe restrictions imposed by the Government against any movement out of local areas in the countryside that the Government was seeking to make economically self-sufficient, Vientiane itself, which has never produced enough food to feed its more than 100,000 people, was being strangled.

Black-marketeers were braving the travel restrictions, moving off into the countryside seeking to barter goods from the capital for the scarce meat, fish, and poultry that had virtually disappeared from the small local markets that had been set up to decentralize the large morning market in downtown Vientiane.

Prices were far outstripping the remotest means of the average Lao, who was being paid little more than $6 to $10 a month at the black-market exchange rate, or $30 to $40 a month at the official, highly unrealistic rate.

The Government finally stepped in during July, lifting the travel ban and allowing goods to begin flowing again toward the city.

Prices are still high, but at least there is food again in the markets.

The security situation also began to improve gradually. The number and intensity of incidents have, by most reports, begun to drop, but bands of marauders still make travel dangerous on the road from Savannakhet to Pakse.

As a result of the security situation, or for a host of other reasons more closely connected with the origins of the Pathet Lao movement in the remote jungle provinces of northeastern Laos, the Government still operates behind a veil of the utmost secrecy.

Rarely Seen in Public

Rarely do the top Government ministers —Mr. Kaysone in particular—venture into public, leading to intense speculation in Vientiane over how the Government is run, who makes the decisions and whether the trend is toward liberalization or harshness.

The Minister of the Interior, a shadowy figure named Somsume Khamphithoune, has never been seen publicly in Vientiane. Yet his organization, which oversees the police and internal security, is reliably reported to be the toughest and most radical, probably the most powerful, in the Government.

Seven members of the party's Politburo have been identified, as have 15 members of the Central Committee, but the precise size of these bodies is also a mystery.

Most foreign observers believe that the sudden shift from severe restrictions before the shortages to more freedom of movement in July was a result of a decision to change course.

But for the people, particularly in the capital, it takes a long time for the decisions at the top of the slow-moving bureaucracy to filter to the bottom and out into the streets.

"Nevertheless," Prime Minister Kaysone said in June, "they are all ready to face all these difficulties for the sake of the independence and freedom of the country, and prefer to live a miserable life as the masters of their own country and destinies so as to build and develop the country than to live a happy life enslaved by foreigners. They prefer to live a temporarily miserable life for the sake of lasting happiness in the future."

September 7, 1976

40,000 REPORTED HELD IN HARSH LAOS CAMPS

Witnesses Talk of Food Shortages, Forced Labor and Many Deaths

By BERNARD GWERTZMAN
Special to The New York Times

WASHINGTON, Nov. 10—Thousands of former rightist and neutralist Laotians are confined in harsh and repressive internment camps scattered throughout Laos, according to accounts being received here.

The reports, provided mainly in interviews from escaped or released prisoners and from letters from within the camps sent to relatives in Laos, said that the camps differed widely in their levels of severity.

Some of them on islands near the capital, Vientiane, are apparently short-term "re-education" facilities to provide such former "undesirables" as prostitutes and wayward teen-agers with Communist indoctrination. These camps have been visited by foreign diplomats and journalists.

But 40,000 to 50,000 former members of the anti-Communist army units in Laos are said to be confined to what amount to forced labor camps, living on minimal food and medicine rations. These former soldiers are reportedly used at such heavy-labor tasks as cutting lumber and building canals, and the death rate is said to be high. These labor camps were set up following the takeover last December by the pro-Communist Pathet Lao and the collapse of the neutralist government, which was supported by rightists and was led by Prime Minister Souvanna Phouma. The former Prime Ministre, who is not in good health, lives eem or ably in Vientiane but has no influence on the Government headed by President Souvanouphong and Prime Minister Yaysone Phomvihan, the Pathet Lao's secretary general.

American officials said that in September Mr. Souvanna Phouma received medical treatment in Paris, where he also visited one of his sons who had fled the country, then returned to Laos.

The most repressive conditions, according to the reports, are at Phongsali, Samneua and Attapu, all long-time Pathet Lao strongholds used for internment of those high-ranking civil servants and military men of the former government who had not succeeded in escaping before the Communist takeover.

Escape Attempts Punished

Conditions are also described as "brutal" and overcrowded for political prisoners at Samkhe, in Vientiane Province, where 750 to 1,000 are reported incarcerated. The reports state that those attempting to escape either from the camps or prisons are subject to execution.

The United States Government has received many of these reports but is reluctant to discuss conditions in the camps publicly for fear that the Laotian authorities may retaliate against the staff of 25 still at the American Embassy in Vientiane, which serves as a listening point on Communist activities in Indochina. There no American missions in Vietnam or Cambodia.

There have been only fragmentary newspaper accounts of the camps in Laos. Many articles have been written on the fairly mild "re-education" camps near Vientiane, but virtually nothing about the more repressive camps. One report did receive wide circulation earlier in the year when about 500 prisoners were said to have escaped from Samkhe prison.

'Re-education' in Vietnam

Earlier there were reports of a network of "re-education" camps in Vietnam. There, following the takeover of the South by the North Vietnamese in April 1975, almost every soldier or civil servant or prominent personality of the former government was said to have spent some time in such a camp.

Sources here estimate that 100,000 to 300,000 Vietnamese are still in the camps, which are generally off-limits to foreigners. Conditions at the worst of those camps are believed to be somewhat harsher than the worst in Laos.

The death rate is reportedly high because of the poor diet and lack of medical attention. The worst aspect is said to be the psychological, with many people uncertain how long they will have to spend in the camps.

In both Laos and Vietnam, inmates are required to engage in heavy labor, with the food ration about one bowl of rice a day. Malaria and dysentery are said to be endemic. Prisoners are reportedly required to listen to hours of political indoctrination at night, for the most part attacks against the "imperialists," mainly the United States, and, in some areas, Thailand and France.

3-Year Terms in Vietnam

The Vietnamese have officially said the "re-education camp" term lasts only three years and it is expected that certain skilled people such as doctors and engineers may be released earlier.

The Laotians have not publicized their camps as have the Vietnamese and there is less information, although the amount and reliability has apparently increased in recent months.

Conditions in Cambodia were said to be the worst in Indochina after the Communist takeover in 1975, but apparently there has been a gradual improvement there as food has become more available. But the death toll caused by the forced evacuation of Phnom Penh and marches to rural areas was believed very high. As far as is known, all former members of the anti-Communist government who remained in Cambodia have been killed.

November 11, 1976

PHNOM PENH SAYS SINANOUK RESIGNS

Reports Ex-Chief of State Will Stay in Cambodia and Get a Pension

BANGKOK, Thailand, Monday, April 5 (UPI)—A Phnom Penh radio broadcast said today that Prince Norodom Sihanouk of Cambodia had resigned as chief of state and would be pensioned at $8,000 a year.

Prime Minister Khieu Samphan, in a lengthy speech to the nation, said that the prince would live in Cambodia. He added that a large statue of Prince Sihanouk would be erected, presumably in Phnom Penh.

Until the broadcast, which was monitored in Bangkok, the prince had been the nominal chief of state of the Communist country and had been living in the former royal palace. Under the Cambodian Constitution, the National Assembly will choose an executive committee to replace him.

In a speech to the 250-member National Assembly, Prince Sihanouk said: "For 30 years I have been guiding the country, and I request the representatives of the people to allow me to retire—while remaining to the end of my life an ardent supporter of the Khmer revolution, the democratic people, the Presidium and the Government."

'Forever Grateful'

On March 18, 1970, Lon Nol in mounting his coup d'état dragged me through the mud and sullied my name and my family," he said, referring to former President Lon Nol, whose government collapsed last year.

"In accepting me you have rehabilitated me in my human dignity. I will forever be grateful to you."

Theer had been reports last spring that Prince Sihanouk was dissatisfied with the new government. He returned to Phnom Penh from exile in Peking after the Communist victory last April 17. Later he made a world tour before returning to Phnom Penh last fall to live.

April 5, 1976

SAIGON AIDE SEES ECONOMY KEEPING A PRIVATE SECTOR

Mrs. Binh Says Vietnam Is Struggling Against Legacy of Wartime Disruption

INTERVIEWED IN MOSCOW

Foreign Minister Predicts Differences in Two Zones Even After Unification

By DAVID K. SHIPLER
Special to The New York Times

MOSCOW, March 6—South Vietnam, still struggling against a severe wartime legacy of economic and human disruption, has developed a longrange plan for a more privately oriented economy than North Vietnam, according to Saigon's Foreign Minister.

In an interview here yesterday Nguyen Thi Binh, a key figure in Saigon's Provisional Revolutionary Government, explained that even after the reunification of North and South Vietnam, the southern economy would be arranged in a five-tier system allowing considerable private enterprise to exist alongside a form of limited socialism.

Uniformity Ruled Out

Mrs. Binh's remarks were among the clearest indications so far that reunification would not mean the homogenization of the two Vietnams, at least in the near future. Among the Foreign Minister's other points were these:

¶Ten months after the fall of Saigon and the end of the war, South Vietnamese society remains burdened by extensive unemployment, including joblessness among one million former soldiers. Food shortages are still exploited by speculators, and the relatively small-scale return of population to the countryside has not yet relieved the acute crowding of the cities.

¶The main problems are economic, and to solve them the country needs large doses of international aid, including substantial help from the United States, which Mrs. Binh said had an obligation to assist in Vietnam's recovery from the war. American-made factory machinery, left behind after the collapse of the Washington-backed government headed by Nguyen Van Thieu, cannot be used without spare parts from the United States, she noted.

¶The Government regards its power as secure throughout South Vietnam, although a small number of opponents have engaged in sabotage. Mrs. Binh asserted that evidence has been obtained showing that those who are resisting have had contact with the Central Intelligence Agency.

¶The Revolutionary Government is working to change the educational content in the schools "to make it a national, progressive education." It has established new orphanages, centers for the rehabilitation of prostitutes, centers for the care of beggars and facilities to treat drug addicts.

"If you came back to Saigon now, you would realize that the atmosphere has completely changed," Mrs. Binh observed. "But if you go deeper, a lot of things still have to be done to change the life of the people there—to make radical change."

"There has been a total collapse in the economy," she said. "We have been trying by all means to make up for it, we have been trying by

—Associated Press

Nguyen Thi Binh

every means to restore and promote production in industry and agriculture. The greatest difficulty comes from unemployment — huge unemployment."

She put the number of jobless throughout South Vietnam at three million. The country's total population, including children, is only some 18 to 19 million. She said that about 300,000 people had been moved from Saigon back onto rural farmland.

Mrs. Binh's remarks clearly implied that the false urbanization caused by the war had not been eliminated. The cities were swollen by millions who fled the fighting in the countryside and were drawn to urban areas by the chance for lucrative work at American military bases. When the Americans withdrew, the refugees were left without jobs.

Mrs. Binh said that overcoming economic difficulties was now the main goal of the Government, but that too little aid had been received from United Nations agencies and other foreign sources.

U.S. Responsibility Seen

"We wish to emphasize the responsibility of the United States to contribute to the reconstruction of Vietnam after the war," she said, "because in South Vietnam now, in spite of the fact that the war has stopped, that there is no more American presence, that there are no more U.S. bombs, the sequels of the war are felt daily, hourly, and they are weighing heavily on our country. And the situation will last for a long time."

Mrs. Binh spoke softly. She did not seem like a victor, but like someone sobered by long battle, confronted now by a further, different struggle.

She wore a gold-colored ao dai, the graceful tunic traditionally part of women's dress in Vietnam. She spoke sometimes in French, sometimes in Vietnamese, which was translated into English by her interpreter.

The interview was conducted in the South Vietnamese embassy at the end of her official, two-week visit to Moscow to attend the 25th Soviet Party Congress.

In describing the five-tier economic system to be established in South Vietnam, Mrs. Binh explained that farmland would remain in private hands.

The government will ultimately buy all the rice produced by individual farmers and resell it, she said. This is aimed at eliminating the hoarding and speculation that still drives prices up.

"There are many people in Saigon living on that kind of job—speculation in goods," she said. "We will not tolerate speculation in rice, which is a staple food. The control of rice is beginning now; we are tackling that problem, although the fight against speculation is a very hard struggle."

Five Sectors Listed

Mrs. Binh listed the five economic sectors that would be permitted as follows:

1. Private sector, including factories operated "with the capital of the national bourgeoisie at home and foreign investments." Such enterprises would be taxed, but "of course we would allow them an adequate amount of profit so they would be encouraged to continue," she explained.

2. Joint private-state sector, where state and private resources would pool capital or management control.

3. State sector, including the rice-buying mechanism and key industries. She did not make clear whether the state would also buy other agricultural

goods, such as fruits and vegetables, or whether they would be sold on the free market.

4. Collective sector, described as mutual-aid projects in the countryside. "We will put it in practice by and by on the basis of self-willingness of the population," she said.

5. Individual sector permitting individual enterpreneurs, such as shopkeepers, to operate privately. "It is sure that it will last a long time," Mrs. Bing said. "It exists in North Vietnam itself."

Mrs. Binh said the five-sector scheme was "to give full play to all possibilities for the population to heal the wounds of war rapidly and to restore the economy." Asked whether it was seen as a permanent system or merely a transition step to fuller socialism, she replied, "We hold this policy as a long-range one."

At another point, she declared: "We'll build socialism in the whole country, but we will build socialism while taking into account the special characteristics of each zone."

March 7, 1976

2 Parts of Vietnam Officially Reunited; Leadership Chosen

By The Associated Press

BANGKOK, Thailand, July 2—North and South Vietnam were officially reunited today after more than 20 years of war, and Hanoi was declared the capital. The Hanoi radio said that leaders of the new Socialist Republic of Vietnam had been elected in the National Assembly by secret ballot.

The radio, monitored here, said that an "explosion of applause" had greeted the unification announcement in the 492-member Assembly.

The former North Vietnamese flag, anthem and emblem were approved as symbols of the country.

"A new page of Vietnamese history has been turned," the

The New York Times/July 3, 1976
Hanoi became capital of reunified Vietnam.

broadcast said. "At this moment, 8:30 A.M. [9:30 P.M. Thursday New York time] on July 2, 1976, the Vietnamese nation is officially considered

as a unified country from Cao Lang to Cau Mau."

Cao Lang is the northernmost point of what was North Vietnam, and Cau Mau is the southernmost peninsula of the former South Vietnam.

Vietnam was divided by the 1954 Geneva Agreement that followed the French defeat at Dien Bien Phu. The last Americans were withdrawn from the South on April 30, 1975, following the Communist victory over the Saigon forces supported by the United States.

The Hanoi broadcast did not say how the decision on reunification had actually been made.

The formal reunification announcement was something of an anticlimax, since Hanoi and Saigon have during the last year described Vietnam as one country. But the two halves maintained separate government machineries and leaders until today.

July 3, 1976

U.S. VETOES HANOI BID FOR U.N. MEMBERSHIP

Scranton Demands Information on Americans Missing in War

By KATHLEEN TELTSCH
Special to The New York Times

UNITED NATIONS, N.Y., Nov. 15—The United States today vetoed the admission of Vietnam to the United Nations on the ground that Hanoi had failed so far to give an accounting of the 800 American servicemen who are still officially listed as missing in action in the Vietnam war.

The vote in the Security Council was 14 to 1, with the United States using the veto for the 18th time. William W. Scranton, the chief United States delegate, de-nounced the Vietnamese for failing to hand over information he said they pos-sessed, saying:

"We cannot help but conclude from the Vietnamese refusal to provide a fuller accounting that the Socialist Republic of Vietnam persists in its attempts to play upon the deep anguish and the uncertain-ty of the families of these men in order to obtain economic and political advan-tage."

U.S. Hints at Reconsidering

Mr. Scranton was apparently alluding to the Vietnamese stand reiterated last Friday in Paris — that the United States had an obligation to help repair the dam-ages of the war. The United States dele-gate insisted that Hanoi's denial of infor-mation reflected unwillingness to abide by the United Nations Charter's require-ments for membership, which include ob-servance of human rights.

November 16, 1976

Vietnam, 2 Years After War's End, Faces Painful Problems of Peace

By FOX BUTTERFIELD
Special to The New York Times

HONG KONG—In the two years since the final collapse of the Saigon Govern-ment the problems of peace have proved almost as painful and intractable as the problems of war, according to diplomats, refugees and letters from Vietnam.

Some progress has been made by the new Communist leaders in improving the lot of the 50 million Vietnamese, northern and southern. While avoiding the brutal excesses that have followed the Commu-nist triumph in neighboring Cambodia, Hanoi has formally reunited North and South for the first time in three decades and has embarked on an ambitious pro-gram to reconstruct and reshape the war-shattered economy. Substantial tracts of land made fallow by the war have been reopened and a start has been made on eradicating illiteracy and prostitution in Saigon.

At the same time, however, life for many people in the southern region of the country is worse than during the war. Large numbers of soldiers, policemen and civilian servants who served under the South Vietnamese Government—per-haps 100,000 people—still remain con-fined in so-called re-education camps, with little indication when they will be released. In the last few months an in-creasing number have reportedly been transported north to camps near Hanoi, evidently as a further security measure.

Life in the camps is harsh, according to the scanty information available, with only enough food to subsist on, hard physical labor, long political indoctrina-tion sessions and frequent beatings. A woman who recently visited her husband, a 36-year-old former army captain held in a camp near Saigon, wrote a relative in the United States: "He is now a silver-haired old man. He has no hope."

In the period since the Communist victory, on April 30, 1975, it also appears that the northern Vietnamese have tended to treat the formerly more prosperous South like conquered territory. Northern soldiers and officials in Saigon have bought up or confiscated vast amounts of desirable goods and shipped them home—everything from cameras and wristwatches to cars, hospital equipment and hotel bathroom fixtures. A Scandina-vian diplomat arriving at the airport in Hanoi last month was surprised to see a small Soviet-built plane taxi up and unload its cargo—six Honda motorbikes from Saigon.

At the national level leaders from the North Vietnamese Communist Party and the Government have been given a virtual monopoly on key policy-making posts in the unified Government, with only a few less important positions going to leaders from the National Liberation Front in the South

Last year the governing Workers Party changed its name to Vietnam Communist Party and the country was renamed the Socialist Republic of Vietnam. The party, headed by Secretary General Le Duan and a 14-member Politburo, exercises control over the Government in Hanoi, which was designated as the national capital last year.

Big Migration of Civil Servants

In addition tens of thousands of North-erners, including teachers, tax collectors, customs agents, village leaders and provincial security chiefs, have been transferred to the South. An article last December by a member of the State Plan-ning Commission in the party newspaper, Nhan Dan, suggested that eventually a third of all northern officials would be sent south. "We are like aliens in our own country," another refugee arriving here remarked.

Of all the changes of the last two years, what may ultimately be the most sweep-ing is the program to resettle large num-bers of urban residents in the countryside to expand agriculture, relieve population pressure on the cities and neutralize such discontented groups as the middle class and the Saigon "cowboys." Already, ac-cording to Communist figures, 700,000 people from Saigon, many born there, have been moved to "new economic zones" to clear scrub jungle or unculti-vated land.

Eventually, Hanoi has said, 10 million, some of the Northerners who live in densely populated rural areas, will be transferred. In addition 1.5 million mon-tagnards, ethnic minority groups that live a nomadic existence in the highlands, will be resettled in permanent areas.

Vietnam, a thin, elongated country with a jungle-covered mountainous spine, stretches a thousand miles from the Chinese border in the north to the South China Sea in the south. Its popu-lation, 80 percent of them farmers, is concentrated along a narrow coastal strip. What little heavy industry Vietnam had before the war was in the North,

Women working on reconstruction of Highway 1 near Vinh in northern part of Vietnam. The major route between Hanoi and Saigon, road was heavily damaged by American bombers. Billboard showing Ho Chi Minh is in background.

with only a small amount of light industry in the South.

Rigors Described in Letter

There is little verifiable information on the new economic zones—no full-time American correspondents have been admitted since the war—but they are evidently not popular. A young woman from Saigon, a former teller in a bank that was closed by the Communists, wrote to relatives in Hong Kong that the area where she was sent had only unfinished bamboo huts for housing, little water and largely inedible food. She complained of stomach pains and was allowed to return to Saigon temporarily for medical treatment. A Saigon high school teacher who lost his job because he had once been in the South Vietnamese Army wrote to friends in the United States that he was just waiting for his call to go. "We are now fish in their basket," he said. "They take care of the big fish first, then the smaller ones sooner or later."

The Communists have defended the population transfers as natural and necessary since Saigon and other southern cities, in their view, were always artificial products of American military spending and aid. "Saigon was a consumer society grafted on an underdeveloped economy," said Van Dai, a deputy chairman of the People's Committee of Ho Chi Minh City, as the Communists call Saigon in memory of the founder of their movement. Mr. Dai, who was interviewed by the official Vietnam News Agency, estimated that during the war Saigon spent four or five times more than it produced. Almost everyone in the city, he said, was in an unproductive service industry.

High Unemployment, Low Salaries

On a similar basis the Communists defend the sharp drop in Saigon's standard of living as a progressive development, bringing its residents back to earth after a decadent flirtation with the luxuries of American consumer society. Another article cited the example of one Professor T, who rides a bicycle to work in Saigon though he has two Japanese cars in his garage. "More and more bicycles have appeared on Saigon's streets in the past two years, replacing the cars and motorcycles that used to choke the city with their fumes," the article said. "Is this a step forward or backward?" it asked rhetorically.

Whatever the answer, there is no doubt that many Southerners feel a sense of hardship. With the disbanding of the southern Government and the departure of the Americans, three million Southerners were unemployed, Communist data show, and the salaries of most of those who kept their jobs were cut, on average, to $22 to $27. Moreover, as the new authorities gradually took over the marketing of rice and other staples and imposed rationing, inflation soared last year by almost 50 percent, according to French people allowed to remain in Saigon. As a result the price of a bowl of noodles is about 2 dong, or almost $1, a chicken 20, which is half a month's wages, a shirt 60 and a bicycle over 400.

The combined effect of this deterioration in living standards and of the resettlement in the countryside has been to dispossess Saigon's substantial middle class. Some of this is probably intentional for, after all, Saigonese, with a few exceptions, did not support the Communist during the long war.

And a Little Child Sings

Take the example of the Truong family (the name is not their real one). The father, a former army colonel, is believed to be in a re-education camp near Hanoi; that is what his last letter said. One son, a former doctor, works for his in-laws as a rice farmer in the Mekong delta since the village chief, a Communist from the North, advised him to burn his past: he had once served in the army medical corps as major. Another son, a lawyer, has been without a job since the Communists abolished the legal profession and he has sold the family's possessions to earn a living. Still another son who was also in the army remains in a camp.

The eldest daughter, a low-ranking employee in the Ministry of the Interior, was discharged, and her husband, a wounded veteran, lost his disability allowance; they have nine children to support. A younger daughter, a graduate of Saigon University, has been sent to a new economic zone. A cousin died in childbirth because no medicine was available though she was in one of Saigon's best hospitals, a recent letter said.

As a counterpoint to the family's woes, one of the children, a 6-year-old, came home from school and sang a song the class had been taught: "Last night I saw the great Uncle Ho in a dream."

Some friends of the family consider themselves lucky. A young woman who majored in mathematics at Saigon University has gotten a job as a laborer in a tile factory in nearby Bien Hoa. Unaccustomed to the heavy work, she has to lie down frequently to keep from fainting, but it is better than being sent to the countryside, she says.

As for the broader economic picture, the Communists, conscious of their problems, have adopted a pragmatic five-year plan for 1976-80 that drops the stress on heavy industry and gives precedence to agriculture and light industry. It calls for doubling cultivated acreage, achieving self-sufficiency in food and increasing exports by 40 percent a year. As a measure of Vietnam's problems, it ran a trade deficit of $570 million last year and gross national product was $6.5 billion, an estimate made by V. K. Ranganathan, a Citibank economist in Hong Kong.

In an effort to speed development Hanoi has adopted what seems in some ways to be a surprisingly open attitude toward the outside world, appealing for aid from the non-Communist nations, assuming the ousted Government's debts to insure loans by the Asian Development Bank and putting out liberal guidelines for private foreign investment, which would allow up to 49 percent foreign ownership of joint ventures and repatriation of profits.

There has been speculation that the Vietnamese, who will open talks with the United States on normalization of relations in Paris May 3, are eager for President Carter to lift the embargo on American trade. If they can get back the American oil companies that had been exploring off the Mekong delta, petroleum would provide critically needed foreign exchange.

Question of Willingness, Ability

Businessmen and diplomats who have dealt with Hanoi express skepticism over how quickly the Communists would be willing or able to absorb foreign trade and investment. They note that there still seems to be some dissension among policy makers over whether to accept foreign investment, and they point to serious problems of bureaucratic inefficiency and corruption. "They won the war but they are going to lose the peace," a French businessmen who has been to Hanoi several times remarked.

May 1, 1977

Communist Changes in Laos Upset Easygoing Way of Life

By NORMAN PEAGAM
Special to The New York Times

VIENTIANE, Laos—Shortly after dawn, loudspeakers around this capital begin broadcasting revolutionary music and people leave for work. Most city people are employed by the Government nowadays, and in the hot season working hours are from 7 to 11 A.M. and from 2 to 5 P.M.

With the Laotian revolution making way for the traditional siesta, little of the surface of life seems to have changed in Vientiane two years after the Communists' gradual and bloodless seizure of power. Although the city's economy is badly run down, partly as a result of the halt in United States aid in 1975 and the blockade imposed by neighboring Thailand, French restaurants still serve good food and wine to foreigners, the movie theaters still show romantic films and thrillers along with Soviet and North Korean productions, and a few nightclubs remain open, though dancing is forbidden and only revolutionary songs are played.

But a closer look reveals that there have been some major changes. Crime, drug addiction and prostitution have been largely suppressed. Everyone is expected to work hard and take part in communal rice and vegetable projects in the evening and on weekends. Most people have lost weight because of the high prices and shortages of food. People are tired after all the work and the long political seminars everyone must attend, so the city streets are almost deserted by 9 P.M.

With rare exceptions foreigners are confined to the capital, where the economic changes have been greatest, and are therefore in danger of forming a distorted picture of the situation in the country as a whole. Information about conditions in the hinterlands comes mainly from Laotian travelers, though the diplomatic corps was recently taken to the former Communist stronghold of Vieng Say, in the northeast, and from time to time United Nations and Shell Oil personnel are allowed to travel to carry out their work.

Since the Communist takeover more than 100,000 people, including most of the professional and commercial élite, have fled. According to one official estimate, about 1,000 people a month are still crossing the long Mekong River frontier into Thailand, among them even farmers and urban workers. Border guards sometimes shoot at them, and bodies have washed up on the bank. Those who succeed in crossing face a long and uncertain stay in refugee camps, where Thai officials are said to cheat and rob them. But still they go, often leaving behind their families, their friends, their possessions and the only life they know.

Popular Support Squandered

According to a story circulating here that is almost certainly apocryphal, a leader of the governing Lao People's Revolutionary Party called at a recent top-level meeting for a change in Government policies to stem the exodus of the discontented. The Prime Minister and party chief, Kaysone Phomvihane, is described as having rejected the proposal, saying: "Let them go! We will continue on our present course." To which one of his colleagues reportedly replied: "But if everyone leaves, there will be no one left for us to govern!"

The story illustrates one of the main problems facing the Laotian Communists: Having won the war, with Vietnamese help, they have squandered much of their initial popular support through economic mismanagement, maladroitness and the enforcement of often harsh and arbitrary controls.

The Western visitor meets many who want to leave but lack the money, the connections or the courage. There is the young man who approaches a foreigner in the street and offers to sell his watch to help raise the $150 fare for an illicit boat ride across the river. There are the two 17-year-old students from formerly well-off families who want to go to France and say of the Communists that they are always forcing them to do things they do not want to do."

"They never try to understand us," one said. "If we do not go to dig fishponds on Saturdays they say wee are reactionaries. One of my cousins was arrested and taken away at 4 o'clock in the morning for going to the movies too often. All my friends want to leave, but we cannot swim and cannot afford the boat fare."

There are many others who support the new Government or at least accept it despite all the difficulties.

Prince Souvanna Phouma, the 76-year-old former Prime Minister, who headed the right-wing Government backed by the United States, still lives quietly in his old residence, occasionally attending diplomatic dinners. He has decided to stay despite pressure from his family to join them in exile in France. Treated with deference by the Government, he has been named a special adviser and attends the monthly Cabinet meetings and other important functions.

Students Return From Abroad

This year over 200 students returned from France, and smaller numbers have returned from other Western countries. A young civil servant who came back last November after six years at school in London said: "If everyone got together and really carried out the Government's policies, things would be great because their ideas are very good. But it's like building a new house. It takes time and there are bound to be problems and difficulties."

Laotian women cutting bamboo at a "re-education camp," where labor and political indoctrination are combined

Western diplomats agree that many of the Government's programs are well-conceived but say that practice often falls far short of theory. They list firm political will, honesty, patriotism and discipline as the new rulers' main strengths. But, they maintain, the priority of ideological over technical considerations, the Communists' deep suspicion of Westerners and intolerance of dissent and their poor managerial skills seriously hamper efforts to develop the country. An international aid official commented: "Time is not important to them. They have told me it will take a generation to straighten things out and admit they have a lot to learn about running the country."

It seems likely that the Communists have a solid political base in the two-thirds of Laos that they effectively controlled during the recurrent conflicts that began in the 1950's. In the fertile, populated Mekong Valley, where they are still relative newcomers, their power is largely maintained through apathy and the threat of armed force.

Reluctance to Ask Questions

In the so-called seminars that everyone must attend regularly, people appear afraid to ask questions although they are supposed to have the right to do so. In the weekly self-criticism sessions in government offices, where any member of the group can criticize anyone elsee for any shortcoming, even of a personal nature, people seem fearful of being denounced. In the wake of the arrest and

imprisonment without trial of numerous people, usually on charges of working for "the reactionaries" or the United States Central Intelligence Agency, people are afraid that their actions may be misinterpreted.

"The old regime was also arbitrary in its arrests but most people knew how to stay out of trouble," a Laotian explained. "Under this Government no one knows the rules of the game."

It is little consolation that the Communists deal severely with party members who commit mistakes. Recently a senior official in the Agriculture Ministry was arrested in his office and jailed without public trial on charges of corruption and nepotism. The former Minister of Economy and Planning, Soth Petrasi, who was officially said to have left the capital two years ago for a rest, is believed to have been undergoing re-education because he bought expensive jewelry for his wife and went to a nightclub during an official visit to Europe.

It seems that almost everyone in Vientiane knows someone who has been taken away for re-education, and many are afraid that they may be next.

30,000 Believed to Be Detained

According to Sisanane, chieef edeitor of the national press agency, tens of thousands are in re-education centers throughout the country, including most senior officials and police and military officers of the previous Government who did not flee. Western diplomats estimate the number of detainees at 30,000. They are being kept in centers ranging from picturesque islands for juvenile delinquents,

drug addicts and prostitutes to remote labor camps barred to outsiders from which only a handful of people have so far returned.

Officials are reluctant to talk about the program, but according to relatives of detainees there seems to be a hierarchy of camps with lower-ranking people kept near Vientiane and allowed to return home periodically while former senior officials are detained under more difficult conditions far from any towns, with the most important being held in several camps around Vieng Say.

According to the little information available, the detainees were told from the outset that they would have to depend on themselves, without regard for former rank or position. They have had to build their own wooden housing with primitive tools and grow or find their own food; the Government provides only a small ration of rice and salt. They are also believed to work on the construction of roads, schools and hospitals in remote areas.

In the censored letters they are allowed to send to their families, common requests are for medicines, clothes and blankets. Some families have been informed that their menfolk have died in the camps.

'New Role in the Revolution'

According to the officials here, re-education is not regarded as a form of punishment or disgrace. Mr. Sisanane said of the detainees: "They are being taught to understand their new role in the revolution. We need capable people to build up the country in the future."

Other officials maintain that conditions in the camps are not as harsh as those endured by the Communists during the war, when they lived in mountain caves to escape American bombing. The officials also refer obliquely to what has happened in Cambodia by saying that unlike some countries, they do not execute their former enemies.

Nevertheless, the way in which the detainees were taken away, without being told in advance or being allowed to reach their families, and the hardship caused to wives and children, who receive small allowances, have caused considerable distress. Many relatives of the detained men believe they will nevere see theem again. Earlier this year, however, families were told they could join the men, and a husband wrote to his wife, "Think very carefully before making up your mind," which led her to believe that if she went it would be a permanent move.

Popular discontent has been intensified by the difficult economic situation that has followed the ending of the capital's wartime boom. Derelict cars and trucks lie rusting all over the city, victims of an acute shortage of spare parts. For those cars and motorcycles still in circulation, gasoline supplied by Shell is rationed. Many shops are closed and shuttered, their owners having fled the country, while the few that remain open have little to sell and most people have no money to spend on anything but essentials. A driver for the United Nations who supports his wife and nine children on the standard wage of $12 a month had

to dispose of his furniture to make ends meet; he ended up selling his light bulbs.

Although there is sufficient food in the markets, especially fruit and vegetables, the Government has been unable to control prices, which have soared far beyond the modest salary levels, so that meat and fish have become luxury items. A black market in foreign currency and commodities flourishes. This form of corruption is apparently sanctioned by the authorities, a Western source commented, but it "creates cynicism and double standards and eats away at public morale." Government and party officials and soldiers, in effect a new elite, enjoy numerous privileges not available to others, including access to stores where Government-controlled low-price goods can be bought.

Tax on Harvest Resenteed

Partly to feed this unproductive class the Government imposed a tax on harvests last year that was extremely unpopular and was resisted in some places. Some officials reportedly refused to collect the tax, while some farmers are said to have burned their surplus crops rather than pay it. There is speculation that it will be repealed or greatly modified before this year's harvest in November to avoid alienating the farmers further and to restore some incentive for increased production.

The 1976 rice harvest was 15 percent below average, according to informed estimates, in large part because of bad weather and pests. Self-sufficiency

food remains a priority, along with road construction, but such goals are expected to take several years to achieve.

One factor hampering development has been the activities of rebels who have ambushed trucks and attacked troops in various parts of the country. Last year a Soviet helicopter was shot down by dissident Meo hill tribesmen in the mountains of the northeast, killing the Soviet crew. There have also been persistent reports of rebel activity in the northwest and the south.

The Government accuses the United States and Thailand of aiding the rebels, who are said to number 2,000, and it seems apparent that Thai officials give them support, but they have no charismatic leader and are poorly armed and supplied, and diplomats say they do not pose a serious threat.

At a private lunch a senior official spoke frankly about the problems of rebel activity, popular discontent and the flight of people abroad: "We socialists believe that change and progress only come through the conflict of opposites, in which one side loses and is discarded. This is inevitable. Although there are many difficulties, the situation is gradually getting better and more stable. Slowly we are building the basis for future development. Everything is still new to us. We are correcting our mistakes and getting rid of our old ideas. We ourselves are still learning."

May 3, 1977

CAMBODIANS BATTLE THAIS ALONG BORDER

Armor and Planes Used—Bangkok Puts Loss at 17, Enemy's at 50

By DAVID A. ANDELMAN
Special to The New York Times

BANGKOK, Thailand, July 21—Heavily armed Thai and Cambodian troops fought a battle across their border today, the first since the Communists assumed power in Cambodia more than two years ago.

The clash, involving Thai tanks and armored personnel carriers supported by air strikes by Thai fighters and helicopter gunships, left 17 Thai soldiers dead and 18 wounded, with the estimate of Cambodian troops killed put at 50, according to a spokesman for the Thai Supreme Command here.

The engagement, which was being described as a sharp escalation of the frequent skirmishes that have marked daily life at the frontier, erupted yesterday afternoon and continued sporadically through the night. Contact was broken at 3:30 P.M. today, and military officials at Aranyaprathet, the main regional

The New York Times/July 22, 1977
Thais and Cambodians battled in the Aranyaprathet area.

town, said that reinforcements moved in by Thailand were being pulled back.

Foraging Communist Soldiers

Bands of Communist soldiers, apparently foraging for food and supplies that are in increasingly short supply in Cambodia, have repeatedly entered Thai villages, looting them and on occasion killing their inhabitants.

Thai Supreme Command officials said the fighting broke out about two miles north of Aranyaprathet in the area of Ban Noi Parai, a village. The Thais said a small patrol moving about 500 yards

within the Thai border was ambushed by a Cambodian unit. The patrol was said to have radioed for assistance and an armored unit and several platoons of troops were dispatched. Before dusk yesterday air strikes were called in on the Cambodian positions.

Long a Volatile Region

The battle broke off at sundown but resumed shortly after 2 A.M. By nightfall at least a battalion (300 to 500 men) had been thrown in on each side of the border. Thai troops have standing orders not to pursue Cambodian soldiers into Cambodia.

Tonight a Thai brigade commander, reached by telephone, said that at its peak fighting penetrated up to "one kilometer inside Thailand" and involved mortars, rocket-propelled grenades and automatic weapons. "Everything is under control," he added. "There is nothing to worry about."

The border area north and south of Aranyaprathet has long been volatile, with both sides of the frontier heavily patrolled. It was only seven months ago that Communist troops began crossing into Thailand with some regularity.

The most serious such incident took place on Jan. 27 in the village where the current fighting took place and, in two nearby villages. On that occasion 200 Cambodians swept through, killing 11 women, 11 children and 8 men, and Cambodia later termed it "normalizing Cambodian internal relationships."

There was no comment from the Cambodian radio after the current incidents.

July 22, 1977

Cambodia Cuts Ties With Vietnam

By HENRY KAMM
Special to The New York Times

BANGKOK, Thailand, Saturday, Dec. 31 —Cambodia broke diplomatic relations with Vietnam today, accusing its fellow Communist country of "ferocious and barbarous aggression."

President Khieu Samphan, reading a 45-minute Government statement over the Phnom Penh radio, charged that since last September, Vietnamese armed forces had been waging "an undeclared and premeditated war in the same or even worse manner than Thieu-Ky and South Korean mercenary troops of the past."

The Cambodian leader was referring to Nguyen Van Thieu and Nguyen Cao Ky, former chiefs of the South Vietnamese Government, and the South Korean troops paid by the United States to participate in the war. The Koreans were widely feared for alleged cruelty.

Widespread Attacks Charged

The Cambodian President declared: "Aggressor Vietnamese armed forces destroyed rubber plantations, burned down forests, strafed the people—children and old people alike—burned houses, seized cattle, poultry, and property of the people, raped and killed our women."

The President went on to charge that foreigners were helping Vietnam in its aggression. In a reference evidently intended toward the Soviet Union, which has a multitude of experts and advisers in Vietnam, the chief of state said:

"If the foreigners act as advisers, experts and direct commanders in joining in the direct attack of Democratic Cambodia, the Government of Democratic Cambodia holds that these people and their government have directly committed aggression against Democratic Cambodia and the Cambodian people.

"The Government of Democratic Cambodia strongly warns that these foreigners and their Government must put an immediate end to their interference and aggression against Democratic Cambodia. Otherwise, you will bear full responsibility for this."

The Phnom Penh regime recently withdrew its diplomatic staff from Moscow without explanation. In its present highly isolationist mood, the Cambodia Government maintains significant relations only with China.

Border fighting between the two former allies reached a peak earlier this month, when Vietnamese armed forces were reported to have occupied a significant portion of a Cambodian salient jutting into Vietnam that is known as the Parrot's Beak.

The Vietnamese incursion followed a major Cambodian raid last month into Vietnam's Tay Ninh Province. According to diplomatic reports reaching here from Hanoi, Vietnamese casualties were estimated at 2,000 dead and wounded, both soldiers and civilians.

Cambodia announced its break in a Foreign Ministry statement read over the Phnom Penh radio. The diplomatic action took the novel form of a "temporary" rupture in relations, "until the aggressive forces of the Socialist Republic of Vietnam withdraw from the sacred territory of Democratic Cambodia and until the friendly atmosphere between the countries is restored."

Diplomats Ordered Out

In a Foreign Ministry declaration that preceded the Khieu Samphan speech, Cambodia demanded that Vietnamese diplomats in Phnom Penh leave before Jan. 7. In a separate statement, Cambodia also announced the suspension of the air link between the two countries.

The brief statement, in addition to charging Vietnamese aggression, also accused Hanoi of taking "an unfriendly attitude," as evidenced by the withdrawal of its ambassador from Phnom Penh.

In the secrecy that surrounds the relations between the two countries, neither the withdrawal of the Vietnamese ambassador nor the existence of an air link had previously been known.

The Cambodian President asserted that the Vietnamese attacks were being carried out by several divisions of ground forces, hundreds of tanks, hundreds of artillery teams and warplanes.

First Communist Break

The Cambodian action marks the first time that a formal diplomatic break has occurred between Communist nations. Even the enmity between the Soviet Union and China has not led to such a move.

The Communist Government in Phnom Penh owes its existence to a war that in its early period was fought for the Cambodian Communists by their Vietnamese allies. Cambodian Communist forces were not in the field until the North Vietnamese Army created them, and in the first years of the Cambodian war, which began in March 1970, most of the fighting was done by North Vietnam.

Even when the Cambodian Communists were fighting their own battles, all their military supplies, except for the considerable quantities that they captured from the American-supported army of former President Lon Nol, came from Vietnam.

The wartime alliance did not survive long after its victory in the spring of 1975. Historical enmity between the two countries quickly expressed itself in border incidents, although the Vietnamese Communist troops, who had throughout the war occupied most of the border areas on the Cambodian side to assure their supply system, had quickly withdrawn to their side of the frontier.

But Cambodia, under all its governments, has maintained that much of southern Vietnam was conquered Khmer territory.

December 31, 1977

PHNOM PENH CHARGES BIG GAINS BY VIETNAM

Says 6 District Capitals Have Fallen to Hanoi's Troops

BANGKOK, Thailand, Friday, Jan. 6 (UPI)—Cambodia charged today that invading Vietnamese troops had pushed to within 50 miles of the capital and had installed puppet administrations in the captured territories.

The Phnom Penh radio, giving the first details of the border war between the two Communist nations that broke out in November, said Vietnam had occupied at least six district capitals and were within six miles of a key provincial capital.

It indicated that heavy fighting was underway on several fronts and said Cambodian troops will "exterminate to the last man the aggressor Vietnamese force."

The radio said the fighting centered in three areas: The Parrot's Beak region that juts into Vietnam 40 miles west of Saigon; the Fishhook region to the north; and Kampot and Takeo provinces to the south.

The Cambodian broadcast said the Vietnamese invaders had "destroyed the apparatus of the Cambodian people's administrative power at all levels" in the occupied areas and installed puppet administrations.

If true, this would throw doubt on Hanoi's claims that its attacks on Cambodia are only a limited military reprisal against raids in the area.

In the Parrot's Beak, Vietnamese troops are said to have captured two key district towns on Highway 1, the Cambodian Army's main supply route, and were reported to be within six miles of Saairieng, a provincial capital 45 miles east of Phnom Penh.

In the Fishhook area, the radio said the invaders had occupied the district towns of Memot and Krek and controlled an area 20 miles inside the border and 12 miles on either side of the key Route 13.

In the southern provinces of Takeo and Kampot, Vietnamese forces have taken two district towns and laid siege to two others, the broadcast said.

But in southernmost Kampot " the aggressor Vietnamese forces were surrounded and badly mauled," the radio said. "They have all been crushed and forced to shamefully flee in disorder back to Vietnam."

At Soairieng, the Vietnamese "are now being surrounded. They are being attacked from the front, cut off from the rear and encircled in the middle, they cannot advance or retreat," the broadcast said.

The radio said the "Vietnamese aggressor forces are being cut to pieces by the Cambodian army and people who will completely crush them on the spot without allowing them to withdraw."

January 6, 1978

Associated Press

Caption of picture released by China's press agency said this Chinese family, expelled from Vietnam recently, had been robbed of possessions.

Chinese Fleeing Vietnam Report Harassment and Forced Moves

By FOX BUTTERFIELD
Special to The New York Times

HONG KONG, May 28—Accounts by Chinese refugees fleeing their homes in Vietnam tend to substantiate charges by Peking that Hanoi has harassed them, confiscated their property and forced many of them to "volunteer" to move to harsh, uninhabited areas in the countryside.

But at the same time, interviews with ethnic Chinese reaching Hong Kong, Taiwan and refugee camps in Thailand in the last few weeks from their homes in Vietnam also suggest that part of the trouble is simply that the Chinese got caught in Hanoi's drastic effort to abolish private business and move middle-class residents out of the country's cities. Many native Vietnamese have also been swept up in this campaign, which began suddenly in March, the refugees indicate.

Judging from the refugees' stories, what has happened is that some Vietnamese officials, soldiers and policemen have taken advantage of the new campaign to vent old animosities, singling out Chinese residents for special persecution.

90,000 Said to Flee

In the resulting atmosphere of racial hatred, fear and anxiety, 90,000 ethnic Chinese have fled across the border into southern China in the last two months,

Peking said today. Most of them appear to be residents of the mountainous frontier region or members of the Chinese community of 200,000 people in the northern half of the country. Other groups of Chinese from Ho Chi Minh City, formerly Saigon, which has been estimated to have 800,000 people of Chinese descent, have fled by boat or refugee plane flights to other places in Southeast Asia.

Peking, which announced Saturday that it intended to send ships to Vietnam to evacuate refugees, proposed in a note to Vietnam's deputy foreign minister today that the ships be allowed to dock at Haiphong and Ho Chi Minh City.

"The Vietnamese don't like Chinese—there is no future for us in Vietnam," said a 30-year-old woman of Chinese extraction who arrived in Thailand last week.

The woman, a former shop clerk, said that when Hanoi cracked down on private commerce in March, northern officials and soldiers came to her family store, ordered it closed and took away all the goods and even some personal clothing and food. "We had nothing left to earn our living with," she related.

The officials also told her that her family would have to sign papers "volunteering" to move to one of the so-called

New Economic Zones in the countryside within a month. Members of the family have been urban residents for three generations, the woman said, and have no experience in farming. To insure that they left Saigon, the officials told her they would take away the family house when the deadline arrived.

The woman said she had not heard of any Chinese in Ho Chi Minh City who had been beaten or shot, as Peking has charged. But she said there was widespread fear that some young Chinese being sent to the New Economic Zones were being settled in areas along the Cambodian border.

China has supported Cambodia, with some reservations, in its bloody border war with Vietnam, increasing traditional Vietnamese resentment against the Chinese. Historically, the two countries have been bitter enemies, with China exercising various degrees of control or influence over Vietnam for periods in the last 2,000 years.

However, most of the Chinese who now live in Vietnam are descended from those who migrated from poor parts of South China over the last two centuries. While many of them became successful shopkeepers, others were factory workers, teachers and even some peasants.

Power of Chinese Feared

What has particularly disturbed Hanoi, as it has previous Vietnamese regimes, is that the Chinese in Cholon, the Chinese quarter of Ho Chi Minh City, formed virtually a state unto themselves. They controlled the rice trade, much of the black market, foreign currency exchanges and the import-export business. Reportedly, even the first three years of Communist rule after the end of the war in 1975 did not basically alter this situation.

Evidently, Hanoi thinks the Chinese merchants were one of the major causes of the continued decline in the Vietnamese economy since the war. Articles in the Communist press have blamed big businessmen for high prices and a lack of consumer goods and rice.

Western visitors to Vietnam have reported that the Communists' own mismanagement and the prevalence of corruption have been at the heart of the economy's slide. But, analysts note, given Hanoi's rigid adherence to Communist dogma, closing all private stores may seem like a necessary step to improve the situation.

Story of Bribery

The woman shopkeeper's account of the situation was substantially corroborated by other Chinese refugees. A former schoolteacher from Ho Chi Minh City, who managed to get on a refugee flight to Taiwan because he held a Chinese Nationalist passport, said he had been forced to pay for his airplane ticket although it had already been paid for and mailed to him by a relative abroad.

"The officials told me if I wanted to use the ticket I would have to buy it myself," he recalled. "They told me I had to pay in U.S. dollars. Then, when I did pay in dollars, they fined me for still having dollars in my possession."

To get his exit visa, he had to bribe a northern official with seven ounces of gold, worth about $1,200 at today's prices, he reported. "Their attitude was, 'You Chinese are rich, you can afford to pay.' But when I left Saigon, all I had was the clothes on my back and 2,000 years.

May 29, 1978

Vietnam Plans Resettlement Of 10 Million Over 20 Years

By FOX BUTTERFIELD
Special to The New York Times

HONG KONG, May 30—Vietnam's recent directive ordering many Chinese residents of Ho Chi Minh City, formerly Saigon, to move to uninhabited areas in the countryside is part of an ambitious program to resettle 10 million people, one-fifth of the nation's population, in the next 20 years.

In its scope and severity, Hanoi's plan dwarfs the forced evacuation of refugees during the Vietnam War and could prove to be one of the most significant developments of the 20th century in Vietnam.

In the last two years, 1.33 million people have been relocated, according to official Vietnamese figures. But in the last few months, the program reportedly has run into serious resistance in the south and has come to a virtual halt. Analysts believe it was in part because of this slowdown that Hanoi decided in March to abolish private business and order many middle-class urban residents in the south to the so-called New Economic Zones in the countryside.

This crackdown, in turn, appears to have frightened and angered many of Vietnam's 1.2 million ethnic Chinese, who were seriously affected by the measures, and has led to the controversy between Hanoi and Peking over Vietnam's treatment of the Chinese.

The Program's Purposes

The resettlement program has a number of purposes: To relieve the major unemployment problem in parts of the south, to overcome chronic food shortages in the north by opening new farmland and to improve police control of the population by moving malcontent members of the bourgeoisie out of the cities.

Pronouncements by Hanoi indicate that the relocation program is also intended to improve the nation's defense by moving settlers to the sparsely inhabited area near Cambodia and to some coastal islands.

Vietnamese newspaper articles suggest that Hanoi sees the program as an opportunity to reshape Vietnamese society and make more rational use of the nation's

The New York Times/May 31, 1978

Hanoi's order that many Chinese be moved from Ho Chi Minh City has angered Peking.

manpower. "Generally speaking, our social labor force is not yet being used satisfactorily; the labor potentials are still considerable," said a deputy chairman of the State Planning Commission, Che Viet Tan, in a recent article.

The Cambodian Communists carried out an even more drastic plan to change their demographic map, emptying Cambodia's cities of their entire populations in the space of a few days after the end of the war n 1975. And in 1954, after the first Indochina war with France when Vietnam was divided, a million Vietnamese Catholcs moved to the south to get away from the Communists.

Under Vietnam's current redistribution plan, people are being moved from a variety of areas. Several hundred thousand peasants in the densely populated Red River delta near Hanoi have already been sent to the Central Highlands and the fertile Mekong delta in the south. Some

were encouraged to move with the once-in-a-lifetime opportunity to ride on a plane.

The Government says 700,000 people have also been moved out of Ho Chi Minh City to New Economic Zones in the scrub north and west of the city. Some of them are reported to have made their way back to the city after finding life in the countryside too harsh or after Cambodian attacks on settler camps near the frontier.

Montagnards Restricted

"The Government promised to give us rice for the first two months after we got to the zone, tools to clear the land and material to build a house," recalled Chan Yi-min, an ethnic Chinese who was a bank clerk in Ho Chi Minh City until she was sent to the countryside last year. But, said Miss Chan, who escaped back to the city and later fled by boat to Thailand, "actually they gave us almost nothing. We were hungry all the time and so weak we couldn't work. There was no water."

The Communists say they have also forced 260,000 Montagnards, the nomadic hill tribesmen in the south, to settle down in the last three years. Similar efforts by South Vietnamese regimes before 1975 drew angry protests from Americans opposed to the war.

In addition, Hanoi has transferred "tens of thousands" of low-level Government and Communist Party officials from the north to the south to do everything from working in Government offices to running factories, staffing airport customs posts and staffing the ubiquitous local street committees in Ho Chi Minh City.

Effect on Agriculture

Among the reasons for the large number of northerners sent south, analysts surmise, is the traditional Vietnamese antipathy between northerners and southerners. Hanoi simply doesn't trust people in the south. Also, there were only about 100,000 Communist Party members in the south at the end of the war, compared with 1.5 million in the north, reported a group of Yugoslav journalists who recently toured Vietnam.

According to Hanoi's plan, the relocation of the 10 million people, 4 million of them by 1980, will increase Vietnam's cultivated land area from 13.6 million acres to 25 million acres. At present, only 15 percent of the country is farmed.

The effect of the resettlement program may be greatest in sparsely populated parts of the country like the Central Highlands. Already Darlac Province, whose capital, Ban Me Thuot, was the scene of the opening battle in South Vietnam's collapse in 1975, has received 100,000 new settlers. Its previous population was about 300,000, most of them Montagnards.

May 31, 1978

Shortages, Misrule and Corruption Said to Plague Vietnam's Economy

By FOX BUTTERFIELD
Special to The New York Times

HONG KONG, June 8 — Vietnam's economy, which lay in ruins at the end of the war three years ago, is plagued by serious agricultural shortages, chronic mismanagement, corruption, demoralization and a decrepit transportation system, according to Western businessmen and diplomats in Hanoi.

There is also an unpopular war against a small but intractable enemy, Cambodia, and a new confrontation with a giant neighbor, China.

"You get the feeling of a people who are very tired, exhausted, as if something had broken after the end of the war," said a French businessman who travels frequently to Hanoi. "Sometimes they can still mobilize tens of thousands of people to build a road with their bare hands," added the Frenchman, who was born in Vietnam. "But that's all they can do, like being able to prepare one dish but not the whole meal."

Industrial production has risen 10 to 12 percent in each of the past two years, but from a very low base, largely reflecting recovery from war damage rather than new growth, analysts here believe. Exports jumped 41 percent last year, to about $300 million, but still pay for only a fifth of imports.

Hanoi, which has been candid about its difficulties, has revised the annual state plan to give greater priority to agriculture—a realistic move, the analysts believe. Investment in the agricultural sector is to be increased 65 percent in 1978, with proportionate cuts in spending and imports for industry.

In a dramatic example of the troubles and of the new concern with agriculture, Vietnam has abandoned an ambitious plan for a $200 million steel mill, which was to have been built by a French company with French aid. It was unable to meet its commitment to prepare a site and build a railway and other transportation facilities.

The Vietnamese harvest last year was considered a disaster—11.3 million tons of rice, almost 18 percent short of the target, forcing the importation of large and expensive quantities of wheat. Recent broadcasts from Vietnam indicate that as a result of bad weather, insects and peasant discontent this year's crop may be worse.

Under the 1976-1980 five-year plan, grain production was supposed to increase by 8 to 10 percent annually, with self-sufficiency in food by 1980. Recent vistors say officials have told them that self-sufficiency will not be reached until at least 1985, deferring hopes of utilizing agricultural surpluses to pay for industrial expansion.

The daily ration of rice, the staple food for Vietnamese, averages less than a pound a day, ranging from 20 to 35 pounds a month, diplomats say. According to a Yugoslav journalist who visited the country earlier this year, a chicken

costs the equivalent of half a month's pay for the manager of a cooperative farm in the North.

Though there is no available evidence of malnutrition, foreign technicians working on aid projects say some workers appear to tire easily.

In the Hong Kai coal mines, the backbone of the small industrial sector, popular disaffection has led to periodic strikes, a French engineer reported. The unrest has not been because of the miners' wages—they are said to be among Vietnam's best paid workers — but because they have nothing to spend their money on and are compelled to save.

In the South the abolition of private business in March and the accompanying confiscation of large amounts of personal property and forced conversion of currency have made food and consumer goods even more scarce, refugees assert. A letter reaching Hong Kong from an unemployed businessman in Saigon said he had had to wait three weeks after the currency exchange before officials gave him enough new money to purchase a stamp to mail the letter. "The Communists have not redistributed the wealth, as they promised, only poverty, making us all poor," said a Chinese resident of Saigon who arrived here this week.

Compounding the Problem

To a certain extent the South, which benefited from years of United States aid and military spending, had developed an artificially high standard of living that, as the Communists often assert, was bound to deteriorate once the Americans left, but accounts from Ho Chi Minh City, as Saigon is now known, suggest that mistakes and corruption have compounded the problem.

Refugees repeatedly complain that in order to sustain themselves they were forced to sell possessions—everything from television sets, refrigerators and motorbikes to wristwatches and clothes —-to officials and soldiers from the North. The Secretary General of the Communist Party, Le Duan, said not long ago that "a lot of property belonging to the revolution in the newly liberated areas was under loose management."

The Communists have sometimes attributed the corruption to the loose and decadent ways introduced into the South

by the Americans, as if it was a kind of infection, but it seems to exist in Hanoi, too. A West German chemical salesman who recently made his first visit to Hanoi was surprised to be asked by Vietnamese officials for pens, watches and cartons of cigarettes. "After we finished our negotiations they would say, 'If you want to take a picnic to the countryside on Sunday, it will cost you so many cartons of cigarettes.' They even had their favorite brands—Marlboro and Salem."

Adding to such troubles, visitors report, the highways are littered with Soviet and Chinese trucks abandoned for lack of maintenance or spare parts. A recent article in the Communist Party newspaper, Nhan Dan, estimated that machines throughout the country were operating for 55 percent of the prescribed time and that in some construction units only a quarter of vehicles and machinery were in working order.

At Haiphong, the major port in the North, ships must often wait two months or longer to be unloaded because of inefficiency or lack of machinery. This and other obstacles have delayed construction of a large paper mill donated by Sweden, pushing it two years behind schedule and raising its cost from $180 million to $320 million. Swedish sources say that when trucks were provided to get machinery to the factory site in the North, many were commandeered. Vietnam was supposed to supply 6,000 workers for the project, the sources report, but there are only 1,000, and technicians whom the Swedes have made efforts to train do not show up.

Foreigners have wondered how long the economy can deteriorate before something cracks. As an Asian agrarian society, Vietnam has the ability to withstand deprivation; furthermore, authoritarian regimes do not depend on popularity. Nevertheless, some of the analysts believe, the situation may get worse.

Hanoi has moved slowly to collective agriculture in the South, introducing only easy forms of cooperative organization, like joint marketing and work sharing. The rich peasants in the Mekong Delta have not been forced to surrender their land; when they are, output may decline further.

June 9, 1978

Vietnamese Reported Attacking Cambodia

SINGAPORE, June 28 (Reuters)—Vietnam has begun a military operation against its Communist neighbor Cambodia, thrusting troops well inside Cambodian territory with heavy bombing and artillery support despite the risk of further angering China, diplomatic sources said here today.

The Vietnamese were reported to have advanced in some places up to 30 miles into Cambodia, posing an increasing threat to the capital, Phnom Penh, the sources said. But diplomatic sources in Bangkok said the bulk of the fighting was north of the so-called Parrot's Beak salient, about three to six miles inside Cambodia, where the Vietnamese have controlled enclaves for some time.

These sources said that fighting had been going on in Cambodia for almost two weeks in this latest phase of the border war.

The preponderant view of United States and other Western diplomats in Singapore was that Vietnam was probably embarked on another punitive action designed to push the Cambodians back from the border. The Voice of America quoted United States officials as saying the objective appeared to be the destruction of Cambodia's ability to attack Vietnam.

WASHINGTON, June 28 (UPI)—United States officials said today that there were indications that border skirmishing was taking place between Vietnamese and Cambodian forces, but that there were no signs of a large-scale invasion from the Vietnamese side.

June 29, 1978

Hanoi Reports Creation of 'Front' Seeking to Oust Cambodia Regime

By HENRY KAMM
Special to The New York Times

BANGKOK, Thailand, Dec. 3 — The Hanoi radio announced this evening the formation of a Kampuchean United Front for National Salvation in what it termed the "liberated zone" of Cambodia and reported that the front had called on the entire people of Cambodia "to rise up for the struggle to overthrow the Pol Pot and Ieng Sary clique."

Prime Minister Pol Pot and Deputy Prime Minister Ieng Sary are the principal leaders of the Phnom Penh Government and "clique" is the term habitually used by Hanoi to refer to the Cambodian leadership.

The announcement was received here by diplomats who analyze Indochinese affairs as a decisive step in Vietnam's war against its western neighbor. It portends, in their view, a full-scale Vietnamese military and political campaign to overthrow the Pol Pot regime and replace it with a pro-Hanoi government, and provides a Cambodian "cover" for the operation.

Similar Step Taken in 1970

The Hanoi regime conducted a similar operation in the name of Cambodian Communist forces, then known as the United National Khmer Front — now the rulers of Cambodia — from 1970 to 1972, when a sufficiently trained and equipped Cambodian force was in the field against the army of Marshal Lon Nol's regime and the United States Air Force.

Diplomatic analysts believe that the announcement removed any doubt over Vietnam's determination to achieve Mr. Pol Pot's overthrow, in defiance of Chinese support of the Phnom Penh regime. China is Cambodia's sole source of arms and military equipment and is believed to have a considerable number of military experts among the many advisers it has sent to Cambodia.

Military Action Said to Intensify

With the waning of the monsoon season in recent weeks, Vietnamese armed forces are reported to have stepped up action in the salients they have wrested from Cambodia in the rubber plantation region northeast of Phnom Penh. This area, the scene of heavy fighting from 1970 to 1975, is assumed to be the principal "liberated zone."

The Hanoi broadcast did not say when or where the new front had been formed. It said that more than 200 Cambodians from all walks of life had attended the founding conference and assessed the Cambodian situation "under the Pol Pot and Ieng Sary militarist and dictatorial regime." They were said to have adopted an 11-point statement of "tasks and goals," the text of which was not broadcast.

The conference was said to have called "on all peoples, governments and democratic organizations fighting for peace, national independence and social progress to support the just struggle of the Kampuchean people."

Cambodian Communists have discarded the French spelling of their country's name and reverted to the earlier "Kampuchea," which is pronounced "Kom-POO-cha," with the stress on the second syllable.

Hanoi reported that those attending the conference had elected a 14-member central committee of the front and named Hen Somrim as its leader. Diplomatic sources reported that this name had only once before been mentioned in Vietnamese Government propaganda but not as leader of the pro-Vietnamese Cambodians.

Mr. Hen Somrim was described in the broadcast as a former member of the "eastern region party organization" and political commissar and commander of an army division.

The front also set up a news agency and a radio station called the "Voice of the Kampuchean People," Hanoi reported.

In a ceremony marking the election of the central committee, the radio said, Mr. Hen Somrim handed over the front's banner to the organization's military units, which were referred to as the Kampuchean Revolutionary Armed Forces. The Phnom Penh regime's army is called the Revolutionary Army of Kampuchea. The new banner was described as red with five yellow towers. The Phnom Penh flag shows a three-towered yellow image reminiscent of the famous temple of Angkor, on a red background.

These similarities, as well as a declaration attributed to 2,000 people said to have attended the inauguration of the central committee pledging themselves "to bring the Kampuchean revolution to a total success," strongly suggest that the Vietnamese-sponsored group will lay claim to be the legitimate representatives of those who won the war against the American-backed regime and describe the Pol Pot Government as Chinese-supported usurpers.

The Hanoi radio withheld any comment on the formation of the anti-Pol Pot organization. But in its daily official commentary, the Government station denounced the Phnom Penh regime in particularly violent terms and concluded:

"Pol Pot and Ieng Sary have put their heads in a noose. They are now in a predicament and on the verge of collapse."

December 4, 1978

HANOI REPORTS CAMBODIAN CAPITAL CONQUERED BY 'INSURGENT' FORCES; LONG GUERRILLA CONFLICT FEARED

VIETNAM IN KEY ROLE

By HENRY KAMM
Special to The New York Times

BANGKOK, Thailand, Jan. 7 — The Cambodian capital, Phnom Penh, was captured today, Vietnam and the insurgent front it is backing in Cambodia announced tonight.

"The regime of dictatorial, militarist domination of the Pol Pot-Ieng Sary clique has completely collapsed," the radio announcement declared. Nothing was said about the whereabouts of Prime Minister Pol Pot and Deputy Prime Minister Ieng Sary.

The Hanoi broadcasts also reported the conquest of Kompong Som, Cambodia's only major seaport and the point of entry for almost all the war material China has sent to Cambodian forces to allow them to continue fighting. Two airports that can be used by large transport planes — in Siem Reap and Kompong Chhnang — apparently remained in Government hands.

Vietnamese Said to Play Chief Role

The broadcasts credited the "revolutionary armed forces" of the Cambodian National United Front for National Salvation with the "liberation" of Phnom Penh and other regions.

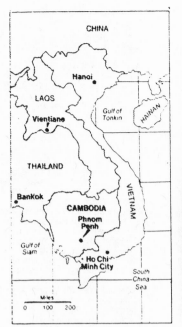

The New York Times/Jan. 8, 1979

Vietnamese-backed Cambodian rebels were said by Hanoi to have captured the port of Kompong Som and five more provinces, Kampot, Takeo, Prey Veng, Kompong | Cham and Kandal, as well as the capital, Phnom Penh. The insurgents were also said to control "vast regions" in other parts of Cambodia, as indicated by shading on map.

But political, diplomatic, military and intelligence analysts here and elsewhere have said that the war in Cambodia was being fought by as many as 13 regular Vietnamese divisions and supporting troops, numbering about 100,000 men.

Most of the analysts here see a strong possibility that Hanoi's announcement of the collapse of the Pol Pot regime may be premature and that Cambodia may be facing a long period of guerrilla war. Such fighting would severely test both Vietnam's ability to maintain its official position that its troops are not involved and the Pol Pot forces' capacity to continue fighting without the supplies they have up to now been receiving from China.

[The United States said that in the wake of the reports of the Cambodian capital's fall priority should be given to the withdrawal of Vietnamese forces from Cambodia and the avoidance of direct Soviet and Chinese involvement. Page A10.]

[A Soviet press commentary indicated that the "liberation" of Phnom Penh had the support of the Kremlin and was welcomed by it.

Fighting Started in Late 1977

Analysts in Bangkok who follow developments in Indochina feel that the goal of Vietnam in the fighting, which erupted in late 1977, is to bring down the Government 'of Mr. Pol Pot, which came to power in 1975 after having captured Phnom Penh from the right-wing Government of President Lon Nol with the aid of the Vietnamese.

After gaining power, however, the Cambodian Government rejected Hanoi's leadership, aligned itself with China — the power that Hanoi most fears — and engaged in raids along the Vietnamese border. Cambodia contends that parts of the Mekong delta that are ruled by Vietnam rightfully belong to Cambodia.

Analysts with access to monitoring of battlefield communications have said they have seen no evidence of any significant presence of Cambodian insurgents on the principal fighting fronts, which now appear to cover almost all of Cambodia.

In addition to the capture of Phnom Penh and Kompong Som, the broadcasts also announced that the "revolutionary armed forces and people completely liberated" the provinces of Kampot, Takeo, Prey Veng, Kompong Cham and Kandal.

Vast Area in Vietnamese Hands

Together with five other provinces known to have been seized over the last 10 days, this would mean the Vietnamese had gained control of all of Cambodia east of a diagonal line reaching from the northeastern point where the Mekong River crosses from Laos into Cambodia to the country's southwesternmost corner.

Furthermore, the broadcasts stated that "revolutionary armed forces" had gained control of "vast regions" in seven other provinces. Only two of Cambodia's 19 provinces, farthest from Vietnam, went unmentioned in the reports.

In view of reports by informed sources that the Vietnamese forces have largely confined their columns to the main roads and of the near emptiness of Cambodia's cities and towns as a result of the expulsion of their populations after the Communist victory in 1975, analysts find it difficult to determine how effective Vietnamese control of the conquered areas is.

The lightning advance of the Vietnamese troops since the present offensive got fully rolling in the last days of December is assumed to have bypassed heavily populated communes and significant Government military units. Mr. Pol Pot two days ago issued a call to his troops that was interpreted here as an order to prepare for a large-scale guerrilla war against the invaders. The Cambodian Government's army is believed to number 60,000 at most.

Lon Nol Regime Fell in 1975

The "liberation" of Phnom Penh came almost 45 months after the last remnants of the American-backed Lon Nol regime surrendered to the Communist forces under control of Mr. Pol Pot. The Lon Nol Government surrendered on April 17, 1975. According to the Hanoi broadcasts, Phnom Penh was captured at 12:30 P.M. today, 12:30 A.M. in New York.

The announcement by the Cambodian insurgent radio said:

"After annihilating and disintegrating the regular-force divisions of the Pol Pot-Ieng Sary army, and after destroying the external defense line, the revolutionary army, acting in coordination with the people, has entered Phnom Penh from all directions.

"The revolutionary forces occupied the vital positions of the enemy inside the city and the key organs of the reactionary Pol Pot-Ieng Sary administration. Today at 12:30 the capital of Phnom Penh was completely liberated. The regime of dictatorial, militarist domination of the Pol Pot-Ieng Sary clique has completely collapsed.

"The red flag, with five towers at the center, of the Kampuchean National United Front for National Salvation is fluttering on the tops of all buildings in Phnom Penh."

Kampuchea is the traditional name for Cambodia, adopted by the Communist regime after its takeover in 1975.

Government Radio Is Silent

The Cambodian Government radio broadcast its last program from 11:30 A.M. until noon, a half-hour before the city's reported fall, without mentioning the critical nature of the situation. Suspicions among observers here were first aroused when monitors noted that the stations did not come back for the scheduled 5:30 P.M. broadcast. The announcement of the fall was first broadcast by the insurgent radio at 9:37 P.M., followed 13 minutes later by the Hanoi radio.

In the absence of news of the whereabouts of Mr. Pol Pot and his associates, speculation here centered on possibilities that they may have been evacuated to China by air or have fled into the countryside, either to save their lives or to continue to lead a resistance movement. When the Communist-led forces seized the capital in 1975, the vast waves of killing that have marked their regime began with the execution without trial of all leaders of previous governments.

In a broadcast by the rebel radio less than three hours before its announcement of the conquest of Phnom Penh, Heng Samrin, the leader of the Salvation Front, called on troops of the Pol Pot army to turn their weapons against their officers. "The revolution will forgive and admire anyone who has done good for the nation," he said.

In a long statement broadcast last night, the front promised to abolish in its "liberated zone" many of the excesses of the Pol Pot regime, which organized the

Associated Press
Pol Pot

entire nation of perhaps seven million into communes, separated families, emptied the towns and destroyed the Buddhist religion and most of the traditional culture.

The front pledged to let families reunite freely and return to their regions of origin. Former city dwellers, however, were told that they could return "when the situation in the whole country permits." The front promised freedom of religion and the building or repair of destroyed temples.

The insurgent group said it would abolish the governmental and administrative bodies of the Pol Pot regime and replace them with elected "people's self-management committees." These committees, it said, will consist of people who suffered at the hands of the Pol Pot regime, persons of "meritorious service to the people" and respected elders.

The front promised also to provide general health care, which has been virtually nonexistent since 1975, and to build schools for all children 7 to 10 years old. Schools also virtually vanished under the Pol Pot regime.

Appeal Made to Defectors

The Salvation Front said it would welcome defectors from the Pol Pot Government and army and ruled out reprisals against prisoners of war. It said, however, that defectors would have to be examined for their past actions before being granted full rights of citizenship.

In a statement bound to infuriate China, which is believed to have thousands of advisers in Cambodia, the Salvation Front invited those people also to defect in return for good treatment. And it warned that advisers "who oppose the revolution will be duly punished." The whereabouts of the Chinese advisers and their status if they fall into Vietnamese hands is one of the most critical questions remaining unanswered.

Little is known here about the fate of members of the small diplomatic corps in Phnom Penh, though most of the Chinese Embassy staff was believed to have returned to China.

January 8, 1979

Laos Resists Newest Overlord, Hanoi

By HENRY KAMM
Special to The New York Times

BANGKOK, Thailand, Feb. 11 — Vietnam's military campaign to establish dominance over Cambodia is giving Hanoi responsibility over a second dependent country. It already wields almost total control over another neighbor, Laos.

As the United States learned in the decade and a half during which it dominated and supported Laos, the inherent weakness of the country made such an overlord role difficult.

Laos, an artificial national creation of colonial France, is an underpopulated nation, with perhaps three million people of varied ethnic origins, cultures and languages scattered through its mountainous and landlocked terrain.

Laos lacks roads capable of linking all parts of the country to each other in all seasons. The country has no industry, no railroad and almost no distribution system. The people eat what little they grow; to prevent starvation, Laos imports the rest of its diet, largely at the expense of the Soviet Union and Vietnam since 1975.

Replacement of Overlords

No correspondent of The New York Times has been permitted to visit Laos since 1976, but diplomats accredited to Vientiane, the capital, and other visitors have described Laos as a country in which relatively rich and liberal overlord forces, France and the United States, have been replaced by a dominant force, Vietnam, that is much less wealthy and more restrictive.

The political restrictions that Vietnam has introduced, in a country that raised tolerance and gentle laissez-faire to a level that often undermined the stern discipline and sense of purpose espoused by its French and American taskmasters, have caused armed resistance, the detention of thousands of educated Laotians and a refugee exodus that is the largest per capita in Southeast Asia, the diplomats said.

Vietnam has stationed at least 30,000 troops in Laos and has begun road-building, fuel pipeline and other development projects. But despite Vietnam's dominant role, until recently Laos had preserved a slight hope of nonsatellite status by striking a balance between China and the Soviet bloc, the diplomats said.

However, diplomatic observers in Asia now fear that the Vietnamese invasion of Cambodia, and China's strong support for the routed Government of Prime Minister Pol Pot of Cambodia, have so hardened divisions among Communist nations that Laos has lost its thin margin of independence and been pushed firmly into the Hanoi-Moscow camp.

Burdens Might Outweigh Gains

Because of the weakness of the economies, the administrations and the armed forces of Laos and Cambodia, many dip-

Associated Press
President Souphanouvong of Laos has counseled against showing hostility toward China.

lomats and others said the burdens that Vietnam's two satellites had imposed might outweigh the political advantages of Hanoi's regional dominance.

Vietnam has pressing domestic problems. Vietnam's reconstruction program was weakened when Hanoi sent its invasion force of at least 100,000 soldiers into Cambodia, to fight a war that is continuing. The population of Vietnam's south has been reluctant to allow itself to be integrated economically and politically into the northern-run national structure.

China has massed troops on Vietnam's border. Vietnam has had to live under wartime pressures for more than three decades.

While China has stressed in its propaganda the theme of Vietnam's weakness and dependence on the Soviet Union, a Chinese diplomat affirmed in a conversation here that Laos was more firmly under Vietnamese domination than ever, and that in China's view that domination put Laos in the Soviet camp.

The Chinese diplomat said that the satellite status of Laos would not cause China to aid the Meo mountain nomads in their continuing resistance to an enforced integration into the sedentary and centrally planned way of life of the Laotian Communists in the plains.

China's Temptation

However, non-Communist diplomats here were skeptical that China would resist the temptation to support the Meo and thus cause difficulties for Vietnam.

China has dominated a large area of Laos north and west of the former royal capital of Luang Prabang since 1962. No Vietnamese or Soviet experts have been allowed in the area, and some observers reported that even Laotian Government officials rarely venture into the region. China could easily supply the Meo from this region.

A number of diplomatic observers concluded long ago that the heavy Vietnamese presence in Laos since 1975 meant that Vientiane was no more than a puppet of Hanoi, and a willing one at that.

But other observers said that even now the leaders of Laos wish to retain a measure of independence. They said that at least two senior leaders, President Souphanouvong and Phoumi Vongvichit, a Deputy Prime Minister and the Education Minister, and have spoken in the Laotian Communist Party politburo against carrying support for Vietnam as far as open hostility toward China.

Minimal Denunciations

These diplomats pointed out that Vientiane has limited itself to only the minimal denunciations of China required by Communist ritual, and that Prince Souphanouvong and Mr. Phoumi Vongvichit remained respected leaders despite their moderation.

Diplomatic and other observers who said that Laos wants to retain some independence also pointed to expanding Laotian links with Thailand. Laotian-Thai trade has greatly expanded during the last year.

But other observers said that Laos had no choice but to trade with Thailand because only the non-Communist Thais were able to provide the food, fuel and consumer goods that have been sent daily across the Mekong River to Vientiane.

A frequent diplomatic visitor with access to the top of the Laotian Government structure described Laos today as a nation weaker than ever, beset with insurrections, "fragile" economic planning and administrative capacity and a "nonexistent" distribution system, in which traditional commercial channels have been dismantled and nothing has replaced them.

Quarter-Million Have Fled

The visitor said that the principal reason for the Laotian decline was human. Up to a quarter of a million people have fled to Thailand, and onward from there. The flow of refugees has included a heavy percentage of educated and skilled workers and professionals.

Tribesmen have continued to flee in long and often fatal treks. These refugees have been hunted by Government and Vietnamese soldiers through forbidding terrain. Those who escaped have related tales of starvation, brutal repression and the use of noxious, possibly poisonous, gas in air raids on their mountain redoubts.

At the same time, various dissident groups, apparently without central leadership but sometimes supported by refugees in Thai camps, have conducted ambushes and raids on small Laotian or Vietnamese military positions, particularly in the Laotian southern panhandle.

Communist and other diplomats said that the Vietnamese army was the principal guarantor of the Loatian Government's security and its hold over the main communications lines.

Much Regional Autonomy

Because of the traditionally poor communications system, the ambushes and a lack of qualified officials in the capital,

The New York Times / Feb. 12, 1979

Laos has had a degree of regional autonomy that some competent observers have said was extraordinary in the highly centralized Communist world. Provincial officials have made decisions that are usually determined in Communist capitals. The Laotians "have made a virtue of necessity," a diplomat reported.

However, as a result of the inadequate national distribution system, many regions have had rice. shortages even though the people in the rice-producing south have had rations higher than in Vietnam or Cambodia.

Reports have been spotty from regions outside Vientiane, where a small and highly restricted diplomatic community, including an American Embassy, has continued to function. Virtually no information has come out of the areas that have not been under Chinese control.

The best-informed neutral observers of Laos were pessimistic about the nation's future. Dr. Didier Sicard, a French physician who left Laos last year after four years at a hospital and the university's medical school, said this month in a leftist French magazine:

"The country is drained of its force. At the hospital, more and more, I diagnosed psychosomatic illnesses, ulcers — in short, the typical pathology of a state of being under constraint. Around us, all who had kept some courage were fleeing. The young ones above all, the vital force. In the void, the Vietnamese are settling, almost without conflict. Some years yet, and Laos will be a Vietnamese province."

February 12, 1979

CHINESE TROOPS AND PLANES ATTACK VIETNAM

By FOX BUTTERFIELD
Special to The New York Times

HONG KONG, Sunday, Feb. 18 — The Chinese Government announced last night that its troops had struck against Vietnam along much of their 480-mile border.

The Vietnam News Agency reported yesterday evening that Chinese troops, supported by aircraft and artillery, had attacked four Vietnamese border provinces earlier in the day from Quang Ninh in the east to Hoang Lien Son in the west.

There was no immediate word from either Peking or Hanoi on how far the Chinese had pushed into Vietnam. But Hsinhua, the Chinese press agency, called the action counterattacks. In a dispatch with the dateline "Kwangsi and Yunnan Border Fronts," the agency said "fighting is still going on" at the time of the transmission.

China Disavows Territorial Aims

Hsinhua asserted that Peking did "not want a single inch of Vietnamese ter ito-

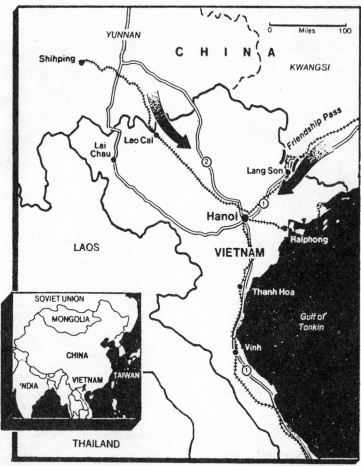

The New York Times / Feb. 18, 1979

Chinese forces reportedly attacked across most of the length of the Vietnam border. Arrows indicate movements thought to be the main thrusts.

ry" and that "after counterattacking the Vietnamese aggressors as they deserve, the Chinese frontier troops will strictly keep to defending the border of their own country."

The Chinese attack began at 4 A.M. yesterday Peking time (3 P.M. Friday, New York time). It followed by six weeks the Vietnamese invasion of Cambodia and seizure of its capital, Phnom Penh, and by 15 weeks the Vietnamese signing of a treaty of peace and cooperation with the Soviet Union.

China is still supporting Cambodian forces loyal to Prime Minister Pol Pot, whose regime was routed by the Vietnamese.

Vietnamese Ask Soviet Help

The Vietnamese news agency said last night that "the people and Government of Vietnam "urgently call on the Soviet Union, the fraternal socialist countries" and other friendly countries throughout the world to "support and defend Vietnam." A spokesman for the Vietnamese Foreign Ministry said a letter had been sent to the United Nations Security Council calling on China to cease its "invasion."

[At the United Nations, Vietnam accused China of launching a "war of ag-

gression" and asked the United Nations to take "appropriate measures" to force Peking's troops to withdraw from Vietnam. Page 11.]

China appeared to be trying to limit the repercussions of its actions to prevent a long fight with Vietnam or retaliation by the Soviet Union.

Hsinhua said the Chinese Government proposed that "the two sides speedily hold negotiations at any mutually agreed place" to discuss "the restoration of peace and tranquillity along the border."

The Chinese attack, if Peking cannot bring a quick end to the fighting, could seriously damage China's ambitious drive for economic modernization, diverting scarce resources and frightening off foreign businessmen. It could also impair Peking's new relations with the United States, raising fears that China might also invade Taiwan rather than seek to reunify the Nationalist-held island with the mainland peacefully.

Until 1975 when the Indochina war ended, China supported Vietnam against the United States, sending $10 billion worth of aid to the Vietnamese, much of it over the railroad that runs from the Chinese border to Hanoi in the area where the Chinese attacked today. If the Chinese push far along the western part of

the front, they will soon come to Dien Bien Phu, the scene of France's climactic defeat in the first Indochina war in 1954.

That the Chinese chose to attack Vietnam despite these considerations suggests that Peking felt very deeply it had to respond to what it saw as a joint Soviet-Vietnamese strategy to encircle and humiliate it.

Peking's anxieties were greatly heightened when Moscow and Hanoi signed an alliance accord last November, with provision for mutual defense, and then Vietnam invaded Cambodia in December.

Hsinhua said today that China acted only after Vietnam had "ignored China's repeated warnings" and "continually sent armed forces to encroach on Chinese territory and attack Chinese frontier guards and inhabitants."

"The Chinese frontier troops are fully justified to rise in counterattack when they are driven beyond forebearance," the dispatch asserted.

The press agency said that its announcement, released shortly after midnight Peking time, had been authorized by the Chinese Government.

Vietnamese Mission in Cambodia

The timing of the Chinese attack may be connected to the arrival in Cambodia Friday of a large segment of Vietnam's leadership. The Vietnamese delegation, headed by Prime Minister Pham Van Dong and the Army Chief of Staff, Gen. Van Tien Dung, reportedly was scheduled to sign an alliance with the new regime of President Heng Samrin, which Vietnamese forces installed in Phnom Penh last month.

The Chinese were deeply angered by the swift Vietnamese takeover of Cambodia, seeing it not only as an effort by a traditional enemy, Vietnam, to become a major regional power, but also as part of a maneuver sponsored by the Soviet Union to demonstrate China's inability to defend its friends.

The Chinese Communists have been very sensitive about threats to their borders, particularly when their warning signals have been ignored. In two earlier cases, when United States forces approached the Yalu River in the Korean War in 1950 and again in a dispute over frontier territory with India in 1962, Peking reacted by attacks.

Over the last few weeks China has reportedly evacuated a large number of civilians who live near the Soviet border in Sinkiang Province in the northwest. Analysts here say that the Russians have increased patrols by their warplanes in the area, where the Chinese have relatively fewer troops than along their northeast border, close to one of their major industrial centers.

Since Vietnam's takeover of Cambodia, China had reportedly moved about 100,000 troops, supported by tanks, artillery and up to one-third of its fighter planes, to the border with Vietnam. The Vietnamese are said to have about 60,000 to 80,000 troops in the frontier region, in well-fortified positions and heavily defended by Soviet-built surface-to-air missiles and the country's small but modern air force.

Ally of Teng Reported in Command

The Chinese forces are believed to be commanded by Hsu Shih-yu, a member of the Communist Politburo and close ally of Mr. Teng, and Yang Teh-chih, a former deputy commander of the Chinese troops during the Korean War. Mr. Hsu, a blunt man who was born a peasant, is head of the Canton military region, and Mr. Yang was transferred to command the Kunming military region along the border in Yunnan only last month.

Like most senior Chinese officials, they are both elderly. Mr. Hsu is 73 years old, Mr. Yang 69.

Although the attack began early Saturday morning, neither Peking nor Hanoi disclosed it until late last night.

Hsinhua, in its announcement, charged that over the last six months the Vietnamese had made over 700 armed "provocations" along the border and "killed or wounded more than 300 Chinese frontier guards and inhabitants."

The press agency said that "by such rampant acts of aggression the Vietnamese authorities have meant to provoke military conflicts."

"It is the consistent position of the Chinese Government and people that 'we will not attack until we are attacked — if attacked we will certainly counterattack,'" it said.

Analysts here are uncertain which side was actually responsible for most of the border incidents, though some diplomats feel there is evidence the Vietnamese had recently been acting provocatively, confident of Russian backing. In the past few weeks, for example, Vietnamese gunboats are said to have run in close to shore on China's Hainan Island, well across the Gulf of Tonkin from Vietnam, without the Chinese firing at them.

Hsinhua said last night that the Chinese Government was ready to hold talks with Vietnam at "an appropriate level" to discuss both the fighting and a full settlement of the border issue.

February 18, 1979

China Quitting Vietnam, Leaving a Trail of Debris

By HENRY KAMM
Special to The New York Times

BANGKOK, Thailand, March 8 — Chinese troops are withdrawing from Vietnam and are destroying bridges, rail and road facilities and other installations as they move toward the border, Western intelligence analysts said today.

It was the first confirmation that the Chinese had begun the withdrawal they had announced last weekend.

The analysts' reports were supported by broadcasts from Hanoi that continued to accuse China of acts of war, the burning and looting of property and the destruction of some houses and a hospital.

The analysts said that Vietnamese troops were not interfering with the retreat. In the analysts' view, Vietnam's forces and supplies have been depleted beyond the point where Hanoi can offer significant resistance or even pursue the retreating Chinese.

However, the analysts reported that a major movement of troops, equipment and supplies was under way from the south by road, rail, air and sea.

The analysts believe that the provincial Vietnamese troops, who bore the brunt of the fighting that began Feb. 17, have suffered such heavy casualties and have become so disorganized as a result of the invasion that they had to be replaced with regular troops, even if the border war is drawing to an end.

During the height of the battle for the provincial capital of Lang Son, captured by Chinese troops last weekend, Vietnam threw one regular division, as well as armor and artillery support units, into the struggle. But they had no more success than the provincial irregulars in keeping the Chinese from taking the town.

Message About Ability and Will

It was after their victory at Lang Son, never conceded by Hanoi, that the Chinese announced their intention to withdraw. Analysts interpreted this as a message to Vietnam that China had the ability to seize any military target in Vietnam.

In view of Vietnam's intensive resupplying and remanning of the border zone, the analysts said that, whatever the outcome of the fighting, China had achieved a long-term diversion of Vietnamese manpower, supplies, attention and energy to the border region.

In the view of most diplomats and analysts of Indochinese events here, China's long-term strategy is to stretch Vietnamese resources — both economic and military — to the utmost. These observers believe that China's analysis of Vietnam's liabilities coincides with theirs.

The liabilities are Hanoi's difficulties in integrating the former South Vietnam with the North, the enormous economic problems and shortages brought on by two years of disastrous weather, the burden of administering Laos and dominating Cambodia, and now the border conflict with China.

Analysts report that Vietnam's military problems in Cambodia, which Vietnam invaded, have continued, with forces loyal to the fallen regime of Prime Minister Pol Pot harassing Vietnamese troops throughout the country. Ambushes and minings are continuing on the roads that carry heavy Vietnamese military traffic.

The analysts noted the apparent paradox that the heaviest resistance to the Vietnamese occupation is along the Vietnamese border in southeast Cambodia, not in the regions farthest from Vietnam.

Along the Thai border in western Cambodia, Vietnamese troops accompanied by Cambodian forces loyal to the Vietnamese-imposed regime of President Heng Samrin, succeeded last weekend in dislodging Pol Pot forces from the border town of Poipet.

Analysts reported that Vietnamese troops are driving on the provincial capital of Pailin, the only provincial center held by Pol Pot forces. Indications are that the Pol Pot troops have already abandoned the town ahead of the invaders and will put up no resistance for it.

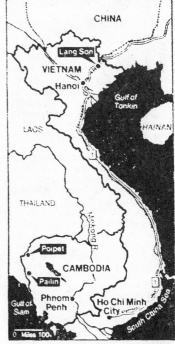

The New York Times / March 9, 1979

Chinese were reported withdrawing from Lang Son and other border areas. In Cambodia, Vietnamese troops were said to have captured Poipet and to be approaching Pailin, still held by Pol Pot forces.

March 9, 1979

Sihanouk Renews Plea For Parley on Indochina

PEKING, March 19 (Reuters) — Prince Norodom Sihanouk, saying that he was now refusing to represent the ousted regime of Prime Minister Pol Pot of Cambodia, tonight repeated his call for a new Geneva conference on Indochina and an international force to supervise a cease-fire in his country.

He estimated, however, that the Pol Pot Government still had 40,000 to 50,000 guerrillas receiving Chinese aid through Thailand and acknowledged that peace in Cambodia was unlikely.

The Prince, speaking at a dinner he gave for foreign correspondents here, cleared up a lingering mystery about his country by confirming that Pol Pot was the assumed name of the shadowy Cambodian leader Saloth Sar, who had been secretary general of the Communist Party and army chief of staff.

The Prince, who was chief of state until his ouster in 1970, now lives at a guest house in Peking with his wife, Princess Monique, and a 26-year-old son. He said his only desire was to see Cambodia turned into a truly neutral "Switzerland of the East."

While asserting that he had no personal ambition for power, he said he would be willing to run in free elections in Cambodia and assume a governmental role "if my people want me."

March 20, 1979

200 VIETNAMESE DIE OFF MALAYSIA COAST

A Refugee Boat Capsizes After It Is Towed Offshore by Police

By HENRY KAMM
Special to The New York Times

KUALA LUMPUR, Malaysia, Nov. 22 — About 200 refugees from Vietnam drowned today when the fishing boat on which they had escaped capsized after it had been towed from the Malaysian shore by the police. More than 50 refugees on board survived.

An official of the office of the United Nations High Commissioner for Refugees in Kuala Trengganu, scene of the disaster, witnessed the events, 180 miles northeast of Kuala Lumpur.

Meanwhile, the freighter Hai Hong, carrying more than 2,500 Vietnamese refugees, remains off Port Klang, on Malaysia's west coast, while negotiations continue on the details of where they will be resettled.

The fishing boat arrived this morning in the small port of the capital of Trengganu, the state where most Vietnamese refugees reach shore. According to a survivor, some local people greeted it by throwing stones.

A police launch attached a line to the boat and towed it into the river mouth, on which the town is situated. Local boatmen fear the river mouth because of its treacherous currents and sandbanks. Few of the refugee boats from Vietnam are manned by experienced seamen.

This morning the fishing boat was set loose in the river mouth. It could not be learned whether the police instructed the refugees to proceed to Pulau Bidong, an island refugee camp about 30 miles out in the South China Sea, or merely chased it off.

The boat ran onto a sandbank and capsized soon after the police launch had turned back. Tonight the overturned wreckage of the boat was still visible, mired in the sandbank. Many victims are believed to be trapped in its hold. Only about a dozen bodies had been recovered, including those of at least two children. About a third of those fleeing from Vietnam are children.

Today's tragedy occurred as the Malaysian Government, amid growing concern over the record number of refugees from Vietnam reaching its waters, announced the formation of a task force to stop the flow. Malaysia, while granting temporary asylum to more "boat people" than any other country, considers them illegal immigrants.

A highly placed official said privately, however, that for the time being the Government contemplated no change in its policy of accepting those refugees who make it ashore.

Informed sources suggested that internal political reasons might have provoked the formation of the task force. The official said that the creation of the new group, headed by Maj. Gen. Ghazali Che Mat, might have a positive effect for the refugees in making the issue a federal rather than a state matter. He said that states had refused land for the opening of new refugee camps, causing large-scale overcrowding and lamentable hygienic conditions in such camps as Pulau Bidong, where nearly 20,000 refugees are crammed on a beach.

The creation of the task force was announced in Parliament by Home Affairs Minister Muhammad Ghazali bin Shafie, who is in charge of all security matters. In private conversations, he has stressed Malaysia's continuing humanitarian concern for the refugees. But he said that the mounting flow was making the granting of asylum increasingly difficult.

November 23, 1978

Asian Neighbors Cold-Shoulder the Boat People

By HENRY KAMM

BANGKOK, Thailand — Twenty Vietnamese refugees arrived in Los Angeles last week, after three months spent aboard the freighter Hai Hong, wandering from port to port in Southeast Asia in search of a nation that would allow them to come ashore. They were the lucky ones. Thousands of others uprooted in the continuing mass exodus from Vietnam, Laos and Cambodia have still to find refuge. Officials involved in helping them believe the problem can be solved only if individual governments can be persuaded to accept a much greater number of refugees. But increasingly, governments have debated side issues instead of solutions.

Since late 1978, when the first freighters loaded with refugees from Vietnam appeared in the South China Sea seeking sanctuary, there has been much debate about a refugee "racket," how it is organized, who profits from it and whether people who escape in an organized operation should be considered genuine refugees or illegal immigrants. When the Hai Hong arrived off the Malaysian coast last November, the fate of the more than 2,500 passengers in its overcrowded holds and decks faded into obscurity as officials and diplomats in Kuala Lumpur focussed their atten-

Where Indochinese refugees have gone (from Aug 1975 to Dec. 31, 1978)

United States	59,760	Denmark	404
France	45,699	Netherlands	328
Australia	15,912	Italy	250
Canada	10,326	Austria	235
West Germany	2,319	Hong Kong	179
Malaysia	1,584	Philippines	126
Belgium	1,183	Israel	66
Switzerland	1,121	Japan	51
Britain	853	Iran	47
New Zealand	682	New Caledonia	38
Norway	601	Other	550

*U.S. also accepted approximately 150,000 refugees in April 1975. Source: U.N. High Commission for Refugees

Associated Press

Vietnamese refugees aboard the freighter Hai Hong anchored off Malaysia.

tion not on the refugees' lives or deaths, but on whether they had been transported by Hong Kong racketeers in collusion with the Vietnamese Government. There was similar controversy over 3,300 refugees who spent four weeks on the freighter Huey Fong in Hong Kong harbor before being allowed ashore for temporary shelter last weekend. The Tung An, with 2,300 aboard, still languishes at anchor off Manila.

In Malaysia, the representative of the United Nations High Commissioner for Refugees declared that the manner in which a refugee leaves his country has no bearing on his refugee status, but the High Commissioner has no enforcement powers — no power to find permanent homes for anyone, or to oblige any country to take one person rather than another, or to take the n today rather than tomorrow. Like the refugees themselves, he has no legal standing with sovereign nations except what they choose to confer on him.

The High Commissioner's office has three principal tasks: to protect the refugees' basic rights in countries of first asylum — above all, the right to be admitted rather than pushed back across the border or out to sea — to meet their primary needs for food, shelter, clothing and medical care, and to interest governments in giving them permanent asylum. United Nations officials have had little success in any of the three. No tradition of political asylum exists in Asia so, although some countries participated in the Vietnam war and many profited from it, no Asian country has been moved to take in Indochinese refugees as legal residents, aside from two small groups accepted by Singapore and Malaysia. The United States has taken in 190,000 so far, and 80,000 more have found homes in other Western countries, but it has been extraordinarily difficult to persuade Asian governments to provide even temporary asylum. Japan and Singapore insist on guarantees that any refugees given temporary shelter will later be permanently resettled elsewhere. While this may be understandable in the case of tiny Singapore, those concerned with humanitarian issues find it harder to justify in a major power like Japan.

Thailand — next door to Laos and Cambodia and accessible from Vietnam — and Malaysia perforce bear most of the refugee burden — more than 200,000 at the moment. They provide land for the refugees to camp on, fenced by barbed-wire, with armed guards to ensure that the refugees do not leave, except to emigrate. They do not provide food. The United Nations supplies subsistence rations, which are supplemented only by what the refugees themselves can afford to buy. Though hampered by those local officials who profit by cheating on the rations, and by difficulty in gaining access to refugees in Malaysia (where most internment camps are on offshore islands), the High Commissioner's staff is credited with supplying food and basic needs.

But when it comes to protecting their basic human rights, they are handicapped by lack of enforcement powers. Though aware of mistreatment by private citizens and local officials, sometimes with the connivance of high officials, they do not always protest, because they fear that governments which don't really want to take in refugees might respond to such protests by refusing to accept any more. However, some outsiders concerned with the question say that the United Nations might help prevent violations of human dignity by maintaining a constant presence, flying its blue-and-white flag in all refugee camps and receiving areas, where abuses are common. Such a reinforced presence, they suggest, would also help ease the bewilderment and ignorance with which refugees face their future.

But, confronted by governmental indifference or opposition, the High Commissioner can do little beyond alleviating the initial pain of exile. At a United Nations-sponsored conference in Geneva last month, the United States, which feels a special residual responsibility because of its role in Indochina, tried to "internationalize" the issue. Despite speeches deploring and sympathizing with the plight of the refugees, other countries offered only a few thousand new places, leaving the solution largely up to the Americans.

Unlike the refugees it welcomed from Hungary, Czechoslovakia, Cuba or the Soviet Union, the United States for the first time finds itself facing a major refugee flow in whose making it had a hand, coming from a culture with few past ties to the American people. It has taken in some but thousands remain, and they keep coming. The question for the foreseeable future appears to be how much more the United States can — and will — do.

January 28, 1979

Illegal Refugee Exodus Increasing, but Hanoi Denies Encouraging It

By HENRY KAMM
Special to The New York Times

SONGKLA, Thailand, May 1 — Refugees from Vietnam are arriving on Southeast Asian shores in record numbers. Ethnic Chinese are estimated to make up two-thirds to three-quarters of the total despite repeated denials by the Hanoi Government that it is abetting their departure.

And this is happening despite Vietnam's agreement last month, in talks with the United Nations High Commissioner for Refugees, to facilitate legal emigration to stop the illegal flow.

This illegal flow endangers the lives of the "boat people," creates mounting political problems for Asia's non-Communist countries and strains their relations with Western nations to whom they look for relief from their refugee burden.

Preliminary statistics indicate there were far more refugees in April than expected. More than 2,000 Vietnamese boat people reached Thailand, the largest monthly total ever. In Malaysia, the principal first stop for Vietnamese, more than 10,000 arrived, reversing a three-month decline.

About 100,000 Vietnamese are now in limbo — on land and on ships that no one **will let dock. In addition, more than 150,000 Laotian and Cambodian refugees** have stolen into Thailand, and about 6,000 more arrive each month.

In addition to the exodus of Chinese, hundreds of thousands of ethnic Vietnamese have secretly left their country since the Communist victory in 1975 because of the continuing war with Cambodia, tension with China and other political, economic and ethnic pressures.

Later this month, representatives of the Southeast Asian nations that receive most of the refugee boats will meet in Jakarta, Indonesia, with the United Nations refugee agency and representatives of the United States and other countries to which Asia looks for a permanent solution.

If the refugees were white, Asians say, the West would have accepted them long ago. A diplomat noted that a ship carrying more than 500 Vietnamese was towed out of Thai waters last week and has not been heard from since. He said that if those aboard were white, they would have become the object of an international search.

Vietnam is also expected to attend the Jarkarta meeting. There are likely to be complaints that it is not living up to its promises to do all it can to reduce the refugee flow. Only last week in Hanoi, in the presence of Secretary General Kurt Waldheim of the United Nations, Prime Minister Pham Van Dong reiterated his promises not to burden Vietnam's neighbors with a heavy flow of refugees.

But the burden continues to increase. A camp for boat people near this town in southern Thailand was moved earlier this year to a larger site, but its inhabitants have already had to build new shanties. The barracks built when the population was little more than 1,000 are badly overcrowded now that the population is nearing 4,000.

The great majority of refugees from Vietnam head for Malaysia, where nearly 60,000 wait in badly overcrowded island camps for countries to offer them asylum. On the grapevine in Vietnam, which is fed by letters from refugees and

by foreign broadcasts, Malaysia is depicted as the best place to go. One reason is the mistaken assumption that departure for permanent asylum is quicker from Malaysia. A more justified reason is the prevalence of pirates in waters near Thailand.

Most of those who land here made an error in navigation, or had mechanical troubles, or were towed in this direction by pirates who robbed them and often raped the women.

Watches are rare among the refugees in Songkla, and jewelry on women is even rarer. The pirates also harvest most of the slim tablets of gold, each worth about $250, that constitute the traditional family savings in Vietnam. Most of the refugee boats have been robbed more than once as they approached Thailand.

The consensus of refugees here, who include a number of highly educated and politically sophisticated men and women, is that the refugee flow will continue at a high rate, that Hanoi will continue to abet the flow of ethnic Chinese and that ethnic Vietnamese will continue to make their escape only at great risk and in defiance of the Government.

One educated refugee from Ca Mau, in southernmost Vietnam, reported seeing 12 to 15 boats under construction near the market in his town. It is generally believed that they are being built specifically for Government-authorized refugees. They have portholes, indicating that they are meant for passengers rather than cargo. The man, who worked for American intelligence organizations for 10 years, said they would probably hold 200 to 300 people each.

The refugees said the ethnic Chinese do not leave in secret. The boats are openly loaded not only with supplies for the trip but also with goods that will be needed in Malaysia. Because in Vietnam it is said that salt and building tools are scarce in Malaysia, sacks of salt and many hammers, saws and nails are loaded.

Often, according to witnesses, relatives

of those departing are allowed at pierside with their farewell gifts.

The most politically sophisticated refugees say Vietnam helps the Chinese leave both to acquire their gold and foreign-currency holdings and to relieve the country of an economic class for which there is no further use.

All refugees forfeit their visible belongings, particularly houses and lands, to the state. But the Chinese, a largely landless merchant and artisan class, have put their savings in gold. Vietnam, which is short of convertible currencies, gives the Chinese the choice of leaving for a price or being sent to new economic zones that have infertile land.

The refugees say the richest Chinese have probably left by now because the price demanded by Government agents has been dropping. Depending on the region, prices have averaged about seven tablets of gold, sometimes less.

Police and Army Are Rivals

Vietnamese who did not have important positions in the old regime can sometimes buy Chinese identity cards for two tablets of gold, refugees here said. Other Vietnamese benefit from the Chinese exodus by paying relatively small bribes to the security police handling departures.

In addition to the "official" passage money, which is generally believed to go straight to the national treasury, minor officials profit from the trade whenever they can. As a result, according to well-placed sources here, rivalry between the police, who handle the transport, and the army, which has no share in it, is great.

A source said this rivalry has been worsened by the fact that the police also round up young men for the draft. Sometimes this rivalry has led to refugee boats being sent off by the police only to be returned by naval patrols and held up until higher authorities order their release.

May 3, 1979

Hanoi Regime Reported Resolved To Oust Nearly All Ethnic Chinese

Millions of Dollars Being Exacted From the Refugees Said to Be a Major Source of Government Revenue

By FOX BUTTERFIELD
Special to The New York Times

HONG KONG, June 11 — Vietnam appears determined to expel virtually all the members of its ethnic Chinese minority and is exacting hundreds of millions of dollars from them before their departure, much of it to repay Soviet aid and arms sales, according to refugees and intelligence sources here.

Despite denials by Vietnamese officials, there is growing evidence that the exodus is being organized by the Government. The regime regards the Chinese as of doubtful loyalty and as unproductive city dwellers who are an obstacle to plans for rural development.

A Vietnamese official who is in charge of emigration in Ho Chi Minh City re-

cently told the representative of a foreign relief agency that the Government wanted to expel the Chinese as quickly as possible and asked for his help. The Vietnamese official, Vu Hoang, the head of the consular department of the Foreign Ministry, said there were still 800,000 to 1.2 million Chinese in southern Vietnam following the departure of 300,000 Chinese during the last year.

Roughly 200,000 others have been expelled or have fled from northern Vietnam in the last 12 months, leaving 50,000 there, by the count of a Western diplomat in Hanoi. Since Vietnam's border war with China in February, the number of departures has speeded up, with 3,000 a

day leaving from north and south in the last few weeks, refugee officials say.

Subjected to Harassment

To encourage the Chinese to depart, they have been subjected to harassment, including loss of jobs, closure of schools, curfews, intimidation by the police and the creation of detention camps.

An International Red Cross official who has worked in Vietnam believes that, as more refugees are putting out to sea, the likelihood of their reaching a foreign shore has been declining. From talks with leaders of the Chinese community in Ho Chi Minh City, the official calculates that the proportion of those drowning or dying of exposure, hunger and thirst at sea has risen from 50 to 70 percent. The reason, he believes, is that fewer seaworthy boats are being used.

The traffic in human beings has a double advantage for the Vietnamese Government since the police have been collecting 10 taels of gold, or over $3,000, from each adult leaving southern Vietnam. The diplomat in Hanoi estimates that these funds make up the largest single export commodity of Vietnam's threadbare economy, replacing its traditional leading export, coal.

An intelligence report reaching here contends that the Vietnamese have used some of this gold to make a down payment of $100 million to the Soviet Union for its aid and arms sales. Soviet aid to Vietnam runs $1 million to $2 million a day this year, the diplomat says.

The gold collected from the refugees is melted down in the Bank of Vietnam in Ho Chi Minh City and shipped to the Bank of Foreign Trade in Hanoi before transport to Moscow, refugees report. Some gold still bearing faint Vietnamese Government markings has shown up in Soviet gold sales in Europe, according to the intelligence report.

In addition, international banking sources here say, overseas Chinese eager to help their relatives in Vietnam remitted $242 million to the Bank of Vietnam in Ho Chi Minh City in April, the last month for which figures are available. Most of the money is thought to be designed to pay for boat passages.

Such an amount, in one month, is more than half of Vietnam's total estimated exports for all of 1978, $416 million. This year, because of the disruption caused by Vietnam's incursion into Cambodia in support of the new government there and because of the border war with China, regular exports are expected to be lower.

Change in Composition of Exodus

The refugees leaving now differ from the earlier small groups of boat people who escaped after the Indochina war ended in 1975. The earlier refugees were largely ethnic Vietnamese leaving clandestinely. About 80 percent of the present flow consists of ethnic Chinese and is arranged by the Vietnamese Government.

According to refugees arriving here, the Government is so eager to keep control of the flow, and evidently wring all possible profit from it, that some refugees planning to leave surreptitiously are being approached by police officials and are urged to arrange their departure openly through them.

In another case, according to refugees who arrived here on the freighter Sen On, Vietnamese security forces opened fire last Christmas on a boatload of 220 people who tried to leave without clearance. Only 18 people were said to have survived.

The descriptions by refugees of their experiences differ only in slight detail whether they are from north or south.

Tran Van Hong is a 44-year-old former printer from Haiphong, the port city. Last winter he was dismissed from his job without cause, he said in an interview here. He said he was repeatedly detained and interrogated by the security police and threatened with death if he did not either leave the country or report to one of the new rural resettlement zones.

Then his two children's Chinese school was closed and they were forbidden to attend regular Vietnamese schools, he said. His wife lost her job in a garage, and a curfew during hours of darkness was imposed an entire Chinese neighborhood. Vietnamese friends came to say that they could no longer remain in contact. The rice ration, a little over two pounds a month, was cut off, Mr. Hong said.

Finally, a policeman put him in touch with the captain of a fishing boat that was to leave for Hong Kong. For the equivalent of $650 a person, which he paid to the policeman, passage was arranged. "We had to sell all our furniture and our clothes," Mr. Hong said. "When we got aboard the boat, the police searched us and took the little jewelry we had hidden."

To insure that the emigration plan works, the Vietnamese have reportedly set up two camps in the north for Chinese who balk at the choice of risking their lives at sea or of moving to a resettlement zone. The camps, described by refugees as concentration camps, are at Vinh Bao, near Haiphong, and at Nghe An.

In the south, the authorities have set up two transit camps near the port of Vung Tau to process the refugees, according to some people who arrived on the Sen On. The refugees are brought to the camps by bus from Ho Chi Minh City and are then taken to their boats on other buses.

Chinese Connections Are Crucial

Evidently few people with Chinese connections are exempt. Nguyen Van Minh, 31 years old, was a Soviet-trained civil engineer from Hanoi and a party member. Two months ago, he says, he was called in by the police and questioned.

"You have always been a loyal Communist, but isn't your grandmother a Chinese?" the police were said to have asked. When Mr. Minh said she was, he was given the choice of a boat or a resettlement area.

In like fashion, Nguyen Van Tri, a 30-year-old postal clerk from Haiphong, was called in by the police. He is an ethnic Vietnamese, and his wife is Chinese. "Either you divorce her or you leave with her," he was told.

Even a former Vietcong provincial propaganda official from the Mekong Delta found himself condemned because one of his ancestors was Chinese. "I expected more, after 11 years of fighting for the motherland," he remarked in his new refugee camp home. He declined to give his name, having left his family behind.

Other refugees reported a new development in the Vietnamese Government's involvement. They said that after the police had put them aboard their boat and confiscated their belongings, they were ordered to sign the following declaration:

"I am very happy to give all this property to the Vietnamese Government. This government is very good to give us the opportunity to see our families again."

June 12, 1979

With War, a New Threat Of Famine

By HENRY KAMM

BANGKOK, Thailand — Cambodians are once more addressing a mute question to the world, and the answer, for now, is silence. The question: Who will feed a nation whose food has been largely destroyed by war and whose future food supply can hardly be planted while fighting continues?

The Cambodians have not been in control of such life-and-death matters since the Indochinese war engulfed their country a decade ago. First Vietnamese Communists implanted themselves in border regions, to be followed in 1969 by the full might of the United States Air Force and for two months in 1970, United States ground forces. Neither side bothered to ask Cambodian permission for the use of Cambodia as an extension of the Vietnamese battlefield. The regime of Pol Pot installed itself after defeating the American-backed regime of Lon Nol, whose fall was sealed when, again without Cambodian consent, the United States withdrew its support. For two and a half years the Cambodian people did not learn about Mr. Pol Pot's existence or that of the Communist Party he led. Until then, they had known only that their Government was called Angka, or the Authority, and sometimes Angka Loeu, or High Authority.

By mid-1977, when large-scale border skirmishing with Vietnam began, Cambodians along the frontier learned that the Vietnamese, whom they had been taught to love as neighbors and senior comrades-at-arms, were no longer to be loved. By the end of that year, the enmity was nationwide and open, but for many months Cambodians far from the border were unaware of it; their leaders had not told them.

Now that Vietnam has captured most of strategic Cambodia, the country is embroiled in a guerrilla war that in many ways resembles the conflict of 1970 to 1975. Today, Vietnam plays the role played then by the army of Lon Nol, controlling towns and main roads. But now as then, the roads are subject to frequent ambushes. Pol Pot loyalists play the role that was theirs in the past: They fight for control of the population in the countryside, applying the same punishment to those suspected of cooperating with the "enemy" that they did throughout their reign — death.

In the last two weeks, at various places along the Thai-Cambodian border, the harsh Pol Pot control over the population has been acted out for the first time for outsiders to see. Pol Pot soldiers have marched long columns of men, women and children escaping from the Vietnamese along the Thai side of the border, forcing them to re-enter Cambodia at places not occupied by the Vietnamese despite the civilians' obvious desire to stay in Thailand.

Reports of the fighting have been dominated by the leaders, the Heng Samrin regime installed by Hanoi and the Pol Pot regime broadcasting from China, and by their respective supporters — the Soviet Union and its allies speak-

Kraipit / Sipa Press–Black Star
Young Khmer Rouge fighters.

ing on behalf of Mr. Heng Samrin, China lending its voice to the Pol Pot loyalists, if not to Mr. Pol Pot himself, whom Peking apparently considers to have outlived his usefulness. The leaders denounce each other predictably in ideological terms. But judging from refugee accounts, the concerns of Cambodians are more vital than ideological.

Instead of fighting or keeping out of war's way, they should be preparing their fields for sowing in June and July. But all accounts from the isolated country suggest that farmers enjoy no security in the fields, that there is little seed, no fertilizer or pesticide and no transport even if these essentials were available. Under such conditions, diplomats who follow Indochinese events and the small number of refugees who have escaped the war fear that Cambodians will soon run out of rice. Many may already be starving, since much of the previous rice crop has been destroyed or carried away by Pol Pot troops.

Cambodia had about 8 million people, who were self-sufficient in food, when war began to disrupt their lives 9 years ago. How many survived the war, the despotism of the Pol Pot years and the present fighting, no one knows. Governments that follow events in Indochina know that the survi-

vors will need food from the outside to continue surviving, but no government has said so. International organizations that specialize in world food problems also have shown no public sign of awareness of the crisis though some belated contingency planning is said to have gotten under way.

The political decisions that will have to be made to mount a rescue action are difficult. The countries involved will have to loosen positions that have become rigid with time. Vietnam might have to concede that its troops, not its Cambodian surrogate's, are in charge in Cambodia and could distribute food if it were supplied. If the United States chose to supply food, it would have to deal with Hanoi, with which it has no diplomatic relations. Other potential food suppliers might have to overcome doubts founded on Vietnam's record of diverting aid given for one purpose to another. The United Nations might have to surmount its inability to act on behalf of a country whose government has not requested the action. Those who have followed Cambodian events are not optimistic about government actions when the issue at stake is Cambodian lives.

May 6, 1979

Vietnam Says Cambodia Denies It Is Hindering Aid

BANGKOK, Thailand, Dec. 2 (Reuters) — The Vietnamese-backed Government in Cambodia denied it was hindering Western aid shipments, The Vietnam News Agency said today.

The agency, in a dispatch monitored here, quoted a Cambodian Foreign Ministry statement as saying international aid "has been distributed to all parts of Kampuchea under the supervision and with the collaboration of the representatives of organizations." Cambodia is also known as Kampuchea.

"The more important aid from Vietnam, the Soviet Union and other friendly countries, which continues to arrive, has been effectively distributed long before the arrival of aid from Western countries," it added.

Controversy has surrounded the relief efforts since some diplomatic and refugee sources said last week that Vietnam was not cooperating.

Aid Believed Diverted to Vietnam

A group of French legislators said at a news conference in Paris upon returning from Phnom Penh that they believed a large quantity of international aid was being siphoned off to Vietnam instead.

Relief agency sources in Bangkok and some officials in Washington said they believed that much of the aid sent to Cambodia in the last two months still was stored in warehouses in Phnom Penh and Kompong Som, Cambodia's only deepwater port. Opportunities for international officials to monitor the distribution were very limited, they added.

This contrasted with a statement made in Singapore yesterday by the person coordinating Western relief efforts, Malcolm Harper of the British charity Oxfam. Mr. Harper said that, while there was widespread malnutrition, there was nothing to support assertions that the Cambodian Government was refusing to distribute aid. He said he and his assistants had no difficulty in moving around in areas under the Government's control and monitoring distribution.

But refugees among those arriving in large numbers at Thailand's eastern border with Cambodia alleged that Vietnamese-led Cambodian troops deliberately denied food to the starving people and mined ricefields to keep people away from ripening crops.

The Cambodian troops are fighting forces still loyal to the Pol Pot Government, which was overthrown by Vietnamese troops in January.

There have been allegations, most recently by the Thai minister for refugee affairs, that the Phnom Penh administration was using food as a weapon in its fight against the Pol Pot forces.

The Cambodian statement reported by the Vietnamese news agency denounced "the vile maneuvers of those who seek to dramatize the shortage of food in Kampuchea and who use humanitarian aid with political aims in an attempt to impede the irreversible evolution of the Kampuchean people's revolution."

The statement said allegations that the food aid was not being distributed properly were "naive and despicable slanderous charges not worth denying."

December 3, 1979

Cambodia Regime, After First Year, Still Faces Resistance

By HENRY KAMM
Special to The New York Times

BANGKOK, Thailand, Jan. 7 — Phnom Penh celebrated the first anniversary today of Vietnam's overthrow of the regime of Prime Minister Pol Pot with a parade and tokens of support from Vietnam, the Soviet Union and its allies.

But a year after Vietnamese troops stormed into the Cambodian capital, no other governments recognize the regime of President Heng Samrin put into power by Hanoi, and about 200,000 Vietnamese troops remain heavily engaged in putting down Cambodian resistance.

The resistance is strongest in western Cambodia, along the Thai border, but clashes are not limited to that region. Most of the armed opposition to Vietnamese occupation comes from forces of the former regime, but non-Communist resistance groups are also active.

Today's speeches in Phnom Penh stressed the irreversibility of the new Cambodia of Vietnamese design. And in a message of congratulations from Hanoi, the Vietnamese Communist Party Secretary, Le Duan, also called the situation irreversible. The Foreign Ministers of Cambodia, Laos and Vietnam met in the Cambodian capital and issued a communique saying they wanted to establish "long-term relations of friendship and cooperation with the countries of Southeast Asia with respect for the independence, sovereignty, territorial integrity and political regime of each country."

Opposition From Other Nations

However, Hanoi and Phnom Penh still face opposition from nations that are not ready to accept Vietnam's elimination of a hostile regime through invasion and military occupation.

China remains adamant in its opposition to Vietnam's dominance. While other opponents say their opposition to the Vietnamese occupation does not constitute support for Mr. Pol Pot's harsh regime, Peking continues to offer the fallen leader his principal propaganda platform through a radio station in China.

The non-Communist countries of this region, united in the Association of Southeast Asian Nations, continually reject the Vietnamese invasion. They follow the lead of Thailand, which shares a long border with Cambodia and whose national security is most immediately threatened.

The other members are Malaysia, Singapore, Indonesia and the Philippines. No Western nation has recognized the new regime.

Thailand Accused in Speech

In his anniversary speech in Phnom Penh today, Mr. Heng Samrin attempted to reassure Bangkok, but he also accused Thailand of provoking troubles by allowing its territory to be used for military operations by forces opposing the new regime. Both Pol Pot and anti-Communist troops are active in the border zone and live on food supplied via Thailand to Cambodians along the border by international relief organizations. Thailand and the organizations assert that they do not intend to feed combatants but have no way of controlling the supplies once inside Cambodia.

The Phnom Penh President reiterated warnings that no food should be distributed to foes of his regime across the Thai border. He acknowledged Western relief efforts in the areas of Cambodia under his control but said that the aid supplied by Communist countries was far more important in quantity.

About 600,000 Cambodians have fled from regions under Mr. Heng Samrin's dominance to the Thai border area and receive Western food. Supplies provided at the border points are also carried deeper inside Cambodia, where many tens of thousands insufficiently fed by Mr. Heng Samrin and its Vietnamese allies depend on Western sources for survival. About 130,000 others have crossed into Thailand and entered three "holding centers" established since the Vietnamese invasion.

The westward flow of Cambodians continues. The Heng Samrin regime says that about four million of the more than seven million Cambodians survived the 1970-75 war and the mass killings of the Pol Pot regime. The numbers along the Thai border may constitute as much as one-fifth of the entire populaton.

Entering its second year, the Heng

Samrin Administration according to refugees along the border and visitors from Communist and Western countries, remains desperately short of all that is required to govern a country and almost wholly dependent on Vietnam.

Its people live on hunger rations largely of foreign origin, and this year's rice harvest is deemed by visiting experts to be enough to feed the country for six months at most. Cambodia's physical installations — towns, villages, roads, irrigation works, river ports, processing plants — lie devastated from 10 years of war, mismanagement and neglect. The country's trained manpower has been decimated, and those who have fled to the

Thai border contain a far higher proportion of people of education than the national average.

Although Mr. Heng Samrin asserted in his speech that the Cambodian army was growing, he also said that the Vietnamese Army was staying on indefinitely.

The Vietnamese troops are opposed largely by remnants of Mr. Pol Pot's forces, estimated at 30,000. Their principal area of strength are the mountains of Cambodia's southwest, along the Thai border.

Western and Asian diplomats believe that China is directing an endeavor, backed by Thailand, to put pressure on

anti-Communist resistance groups to join in a united front with the Pol Pot forces.

Diplomats and Asian specialists in Indochinese affairs are divided on whether Vietnam's action can be reversed but agree that no end to the strife, both military and political, is in sight.

"The essential facts are that China has a population of one billion and Vietnam 50 million," said a European ambassador of long Asian experience. "It may last a long time, but it cannot last."

January 8, 1980

In Cambodia, A Holocaust. Clearly.

World Vision International

By Peter J. Donaldson

CHAPEL HILL, N.C. — When the Khmer Rouge marched into Phnom Penh on April 17, 1975, Cambodia had a population of seven million to nine million people — the exact number is not certain. Today, the country, according to an estimate by the United States Census Bureau, has 4.8 million. Thus, the Cambodian population declined by at least 30 percent over the last five years, and too few people have understood what this means.

To understand the magnitude of what has happened in Cambodia, we must remember that contemporary developing countries, which contain largely agricultural societies and have

few cities and hardly any industry, are characterized by high rates of population growth.

From the end of World War II to 1975 or so, Cambodia's population, like the rest of Southeast Asia's, probably grew at an average annual rate of nearly 3 percent. Ordinarily, the Cambodian population would have been expected to increase by about 15 percent between 1975 and 1980. Indeed, an estimate made at the University of Illinois in the early 1970's projected a 1980 population of almost 10 million.

Draconian measures are required to reduce a population by 30 percent or more in five years, especially if the population was growing as rapidly as Cambodia's.

If Cambodian women had slightly fewer than two children on average and, at the same time, mortality was as high as Europe's 200 years ago, the population would stop growing but would not be reduced to anything close to its estimated four to five million. Even if these outlandish demographic rates operated for five years, the 1980 population would be only 500,000 or so less than the 1975 population. In other words, with parents not even replacing themselves and almost a third of all children dying within the first year of life — a combination of circumstances that the world has never known — Cambodia's population would still be more than seven million.

What does it take to go from a population of no fewer than seven million people in 1975 to one with no more than five million in 1980?

We know that children were born during the horrible years between 1975 and 1980, so let's assume that the crude birth rate in Cambodia was 10 births per 1,000 total population, a third or less of what it was during the 1960's and early 1970's. This rate would yield roughly 70,000 births a year. If there were that many births and no deaths in each of the five years between 1975 and 1980, the total population in 1980 would be at least 7.35 million (7 million in 1975 plus 350,000 children born between 1975 and 1980).

Since our Census Bureau estimates that the 1980 population is only 4.8 million, 2.55 million people must have died during the five years. This represents over 500,000 deaths per year, or a crude death rate of more than 60 per 1,000.

This is higher than the death rate in England and Wales during the late 1550's when crops failed and many people starved. The Cambodian horror comes close to having the impact of the Black Death, in the 14th century, which reduced European populations by up to a third in a single year.

The refugees in Thailand make very little difference in these sad calculations. The maximum number of refugees is probably 300,000, and estimates run as low as half that. Three hundred thousand saved from death over five years would lower the death rate, but not by a demographically significant amount.

Is Cambodia another Holocaust? Approximately 65 percent of all European Jews died in the Holocaust, while no more than 50 percent of all Cambodians died between 1975 and 1980. The proportion of Jews who went to their deaths in the "Final Solution" varied among different countries. However, well over half of the Jewish population was killed in most countries.

Still, the end is not in sight for the Cambodians and the situation may get worse. Moreover, the Cambodians have suffered in the same brutal fashion the Jews did. Families have been separated, people have been starved, there has been untold mental and physical brutality.

Throughout Asia, people think Westerners don't care about Cambodia because Cambodians are not white. True, we don't care enough, but I'm not sure why. For Jews, the Holocaust is a tragedy that cannot be shared — it may be unrealistic or unreasonable or inappropriate to ask Jews to share the term "Holocaust." But it is even more unreasonable and inappropriate not to find a new name for what has taken place in Cambodia. We need a name that will inspire us to do something about what has been happening there because the only modern parallel to the events in Cambodia, from a demographic point of view, is the Holocaust.

April 22, 1980

THAILAND AND THE INDOCHINESE

THAIS ABANDONING HARD LINE ON REDS

Still Seeking Safe Borders, They Less Often Assert Support of U.S. Policy

---

By HENRY KAMM
Special to The New York Times

BANGKOK, Thailand, Feb. 15 — The American-supported South Vietnamese incursion into Laos has been met here with official silence that is a measure of how far Thailand has come from the time when she was one of the most vocal supporters of a hard line against Communism in Asia.

In private conversation, officials express their full approval of the attack on the Ho Chi Minh Trail network, but at the same time, they find the latest breach of Laotian neutrality a good occasion for applying a policy that a well-placed Foreign Ministry official called "de-emphasis on military cooperation with the United States."

Thais have continued and in some ways stepped up their participation in the war against the Communists in Indochina. But officials here have come to feel that since 1969 — when President Nixon declared America's intention of significantly decreasing its role on this continent—Thailand's national interest is best served by a minimum of statements identifying Thai interests with those of the United States.

A Foreign Ministry official went so far as to question the wisdom of Britain's declaration defending the incursion into Laos. Not long ago this statement would have been acclaimed here as a normal statement from a member of the "free world."

The official said he thought it prejudiced Britain's credibility with the Communists in her capacity of co-chairman of the Geneva conference for the neutralization of Laos in 1962.

But the official did not deny recurrent reports that Thai soldiers have been participating in the fighting in Laos and Thai planes in the air war over northwestern Cambodia. He said that no "regular" Thai forces were engaged but that the Government had no way of preventing individuals who wnted to fight in Laos from doing so.

Knowledgeable observers see no contradiction in the continuing Thai military engagement across Thailand's borders accompanied by diplomatic policy designed to dissociate Thailand from the Indochinese war.

Borders Are the Goal

They believe that the Thai military effort supports the goal of keeping the border region free of Communist troops. The long-term diplomatic effort, guided by Foreign Minister Thanat Khoman, pursues the goal of achieving for Thailand a wider field of international maneuver than was possible throughout the nineteen-fifties and es, when her identificatio   th the United States was nearly complete.

Responsible Thai officials are angered by charges from American Senators, news media and academics that Thais are opportunists who change sides when it is to their advantage. They contend that it is the United States that has changed its policies, in response to what the officials consider pressure on the Government from badly informed sectors of public opinion.

"The Nixon Doctrine is the opposite of what American policy was under Lyndon Johnson," an official said.

Soviet Is Encouraged

Since Mr. Nixon proclaimed his new policy for Asia — encouraging nations there to take a greater role in their defense — Thailand has not only given gentle encouragement to overtures from the Soviet Union and other European Communists powers but, more important, has also lifted the anathema on Communist China and has opened an avenue of communications with North Vietnam.

February 16, 1971

Thai Parliament Is Ended; Leaders Seize Full Power

Citing 'Dangers' to Country, Thanom and Aides Abolish Constitution—Pledge to Maintain Foreign Policies

Special to The New York Times

BANGKOK, Thailand, Thursday, Nov. 18—A group of military and other leaders headed by Premier Thanom Kittikachorn seized full powers yesterday to deal with "the dangers that have been threatening Thailand."

Organizing themselves as a "revolutionary" council, they announced in a nationwide broadcast that they had abolished the Constitution, dissolved Parliament, disbanded the Cabinet and established martial law.

They pledged to continue Thailand's foreign policy, which has been strongly anti-Communist and pro-American and which has included the sending of a contingent of troops to South Vietnam. Thus the change in regime would apparently not affect the United States air bases in Thailand, which have been used to support operations in Indochina.

[In Washington, United States officials said they were confident that the change would not imperil American interests in Thailand.]

The coup, which ousted Foreign Minister Thanat Khoman and other officials but kept many key leaders in power, came suddenly and without violence.

A few tanks appeared here, and some paratroops arrived to aid regular police patrols, but the capital appeared calm.

Bangkok residents learned from their radios that constitutional rule was over. To many, however, it did not seem that any great change had taken place, since in practice power had long resided in the leaders who have now announced a take-over as members of the revolutionary council. The council, which is composed of military, police and some civilian elements, said in an announcement issued in the name of the Premier that internal strife and a threatening world situation had made it necessary to seize control.

The announcement cited Communist insurrection in northern Thailand, student demonstrations, obstruction by members of Parliament, strikes, terrorism and subversion. It said there had been a clear danger that "the system of national administration" might be changed to one that would be hated by King Phumiphol Aduldet and by the people.

Therefore, the announcement concluded, effective action had to be taken to protect the King and the people.

November 18, 1971

New Thai Premier Named As Students Battle Troops

By Reuters

BANGKOK, Thailand, Monday, Oct. 15—A new Premier of Thailand was appointed yesterday after a series of violent clashes between troops and students in which up to 300 people were reported killed and hundreds wounded.

The appointment of Dr. Sanya Thammasak, dean of Thammasat University, which has been the center of student protests for the last week against the military-dominated Government of Premier Thanom Kittikachorn, was announced by King Phumiphol Aduldet.

Field Marshal Thanom had submitted his resignation earlier. However, he retains the post of Supreme Commander of the Armed Forces, a position that gives him considerable power.

Dr. Sanya, a former Chief Justice, who has been a close adviser to the King, said in a television speech tonight that he would try to form a new government as soon as possible. He declared that he hoped to introduce a new constitution within six months and hold general elections. The previous Government's delay in drawing up a new constitution to move the country toward democratic administration was one of the main complaints prompting the student demonstrations.

In a nationwide broadcast, the King appealed to the people of Thailand to support the new Premier to end the current conflict. He described today's violence as one of the most sorrowful events in the country's history.

The New York Times
King Phumiphol Aduldet

Violence erupted when troops backed by tanks opened fire on thousands of students attempting to take over a Government office. It quickly spread to other parts of the city and at least four large buildings were reported on fire. Many students were reported to have been killed and hundreds injured.

Soldiers opened fire again an hour after the King's announcement when students tried to crash a driverless bus into a police station. Witnesses said at least one person was killed in this incident.

A seven-hour curfew beginning at 10 P.M. was imposed, but the troops and police apparently made no concerted effort to move students from the streets. The crackle of automatic weapons was heard sporadically after the curfew went into effect.

Several Government buildings and cars were still burning early today in Ratdamnoen Road, in the center of the city near the palace, the military headquarters and Thammasat University.

Some students said that they had heard of the King's announcement but did not believe the Government had really changed. They said they would continue demonstrating until it was clear that Marshal Thanom and Deputy Premier Praphas Charusathien no longer had any power.

Protests by Students

The fighting came after a week of student protests against the arrest of 13 students and university lecturers who were accused of distributing leaflets calling for a permanent Thai constitution to replace the present temporary charter.

Officials said that Communist documents had been found showing that the 13 were planning to incite public unrest in an attempt to overthrow the Government.

Marshal Thanom, who became Premier in 1969, was the leader of a group of military men who abolished the constitution two years ago, dissolved Parliament and established a National Executive Council with power to rule by decree.

Last December, Thailand began a new experiment in constitutional government under the interim constitution, with the appointment of a 299-member National Assembly, drawn mainly from the military but including civilian representatives.

Marshal Thanom said then that the interim arrangements should not last more than three years, raising public hopes of a permanent constitution and an elected lower house within that period.

Restoration of Peace Asked

In a broadcast speech last night, Marshal Thanom said he had resigned because students and the public were dissatisfied with his administration. He appealed to the students to restore peace and order.

An official announcement broadcast early today said that the demonstrators had been trying to capture Government offices, including a police headquarters, and had shot at the military headquarters after raiding gun shops.

As supreme commander, Marshal Thanom had ordered military and police officials to save the freedom of the nation, the announcement said.

The violence followed protest marches yesterday by more than 200,000 students demanding the release of the 13 alleged leftists.

Marshal Thanom said in a broadcast before his resignation that he had ordered the temporary closing of all educational institutions in Bangkok and three nearby provinces.

Yesterday's violence broke out shortly before noon, despite a Government promise Saturday night to bow to the students' demands and release the 13 detained persons. The Government also promised that it would inaugurate a new constitution within a year.

Despite the Government's concessions, about 40,000 students camped out at various administrative buildings during the night. In the morning several thousand tried to take over the offices of the Government's Public Relations Department and broadcast from its radio.

Soldiers backed by tanks lobbed tear-gas grenades and fired over the heads of the crowd, and violence swept along the main avenue that leads to the country's Democracy Monument.

As dusk fell, troops in the area began to withdraw, firing over the heads of the demonstrators as they went, leaving only a thin line of marines to guard the Government buildings in the area.

Students then began burning coaches and cars and showed no signs of dispersing.

The new Premier, Dr. Sanya Thammasak, a well-known lawyer and jurist, is the first civilian head of government since Pote Sarasin presided over a caretaker regime for four months in 1957 after a military coup d'état.

October 15, 1973

MODERATES LEAD IN THAILAND VOTE

Turnout is Low in Free Election—First Since End of Military Regime

By FOX BUTTERFIELD
Special to The New York Times

BANGKOK, Thailand, Monday, Jan. 27 — The people of Thailand voted yesterday in an election unusually free not only for Thailand but for much of the rest of Asia.

Early returns showed the middle-of-the road Democrats won 23 out of 26 seats in Bangkok for the new House of Representatives and were scoring unexpectedly strong gains in the provinces.

In major upsets, the leader of the conservative Social Justice party, Dewitt Klinprathum, and the deputy leader of the conservative Thai Nation party, former General Siri Sirivothin, were defeated. Mr. Dewitt had been considered a possible choice for premier, since his party was expected to win the largest number of seats.

2,193 Candidates

Voter turnout in Bangkok was low, though many voters stayed by the open-sided sidewalk polling booths last night to watch while the ballots were being counted aloud.

A total of 2,193 candidates from 42 parties were vying for 269 seats in the new House of Representatives. It will select a new premier.

The outgoing Premier, Sanya Dharmasakti, yesterday named 100 members to the largely powerless Senate.

The election is to replace Mr. Sanya's interim Government, which was appointed by King Phumiphol Aduldet after student demonstrators toppled the old military Government in October, 1973. Before then Thai politics had been dominated by the military since the end of absolute monarchy in 1932.

Despite this background of military rule and the trend elsewhere in Asia toward authoritarian regimes of the left or right, Mr. Sanya's Government has sought only to get itself out of power. It confined itself to publicizing the election and helping set up the voting booths. Mr. Sanya's self-imposed restrictions are all the more surprising because under his leadership the outgoing National Assembly has enacted significant if limited progressive legislation. The measures include a land-reform act, a big increase in the minimum wage and a law to make holding civil service jobs contingent on merit.

Moreover, Mr. Sanya's Government has tolerated continuing protests, often violent, from farmers, workers and students. Many Thais who still have a traditional hierarchical view of society fear that these protests amount to virtual anarchy.

In the last week alone, rioting vocational school students here shot the Bangkok police commissioner, killed a newsman and bombed a series of buses, while angry farmers in the south burned down the house of a provincial governor. Two candidates were killed during the election campaign.

The Government has been reluctant to intervene because of the strong Thai prohibition, derived from Buddhism, against bloodshed. In addition, many Thais still harbor memories of the error made by the former government of Field Marshal Thanom Kittikachorn when it ordered its troops to fire on students in October, 1973, leaving 70 dead and enraging the populace.

Since those days, however, the students have become dispirited and disorganized, and their influence has waned.

In fact, the biggest gainers in the election are expected to be the four major conservative parties representing the old business, military and bureaucratic élite. These parties—the Social Justice party, the Thai Nation party, the Social Nationalists and the Social Agrarians—are largely made up of those who belonged to the old front group of the military government, the United Thai People's party. They are heavily financed, and most of their candidates have long ties with the villages where they are running.

Because of the multiplicity of parties, no single party or even two parties are expected to win a majority of seats in the lower house. But the conservatives are believed ready to put together a coalition.

Another possible coalition might be formed by the three moderate parties of the center, the Democrats, the Social Action party and the New Force, which tend to appeal to urban and educated voters.

The small left-wing parties, which are largely new, have been given little chance to win more than 20 seats. But public-opinion polls are new in Thailand, and no one is really sure of the outcome.

Even if the conservatives do win, most Thais regard the election as a watershed in their history and as a definite advance.

"It is a start—you have to begin somewhere," said Narong Ketudat, the editor and publisher of the respected left-wing daily Prachathipatai. "It is the first time in Thailand that a government has really been elected by the people."

At a polling station in front of a girls' school on the northern outskirts of Bangkok, a secretary in a miniskirt, Sumalee Puripat, expressed concern after emerging from the voting booth when she discovered she had accidentally voted for the wrong candidate.

Because of the number of illiterate voters and the many candidates, the Government used a ballot listing only the number of each candidate. A voter had to memorize the assigned number of his choice before entering the booth.

The military itself has remained officially neutral in the election, under orders from the commander of the armed forces, Gen. Kris Srivara. Many soldiers, however, appeared to be voting for the Thai National party, which is headed by three former generals.

January 27, 1975

U.S. WITHDRAWAL SOUGHT BY THAIS

Premier Proposes Pullout of Troops in a Year in Bid for Leftist Support

By The Associated Press

BANGKOK, Thailand, March 17 — Premier Kukrit Pramoj said in a policy statement today that his coalition would seek the complete withdrawal of the 25,000 American troops and 350 aircraft from Thailand within a year.

The statement, issued after his seven-party civilian coalition was confirmed by King Phumiphol Aduldet, also said the Government would seek to establish diplomatic relations with China and would try to open talks with North Vietnam. The new Cabinet faces a confidence vote in the lower house of Parliament Wednesday.

The previous cabinet, headed by Mr. Kukrit's brother, Seni Pramoj, was confirmed Feb. 22 and resigned eight days later when it lost a confidence vote.

Short of Majority

Mr. Kukrit's coalition has 124 of the 269 seats in the house, 11 short of a majority. His policy statement was aimed at winning the support of left-wing parties that have demanded the American withdrawal.

He said, however, that the withdrawal must be completed within a year only if "the political and military situation in this region permits." His brother had called for withdrawal in 18 months and failed to win the leftists' support.

"Withdrawing the American forces doesn't mean that we don't like America," Mr. Kukrit told reporters today. "Our good relations must continue."

The United States carried out bombing missions in Indochina from air bases in Thailand for eight years.

March 18, 1975

U.S. Pullout of G.I.'s In Thailand Complete

By DAVID A. ANDELMAN
Special to The New York Times

BANGKOK, Thailand, July 20 —The United States completed its military withdrawal from Thailand today, ending a 26-year military presence here.

The "designated" last American combat soldier in mainland Southeast Asia, George Leroy Davis, a 40-year-old Air Force master sergeant from Cincinnati, boarded a Cathay Pacific flight to Hong Kong at 10:30 A.M. with his wife and two children.

At the same time, the Military Assistance Command Thailand, established by an agreement on Oct. 17, 1950, ceased to exist.

According to American military estimates, the United States left behind nearly $400 million in fixed emplacements, ranging from the U Taphao Air Base and Sattahip Naval Station of the Gulf of Siam to radio and communications equipment that will be operated by the Thai military.

Tomorrow, Gen. Harry C. Aderholt, who headed both the Military Assistance Command and the advisory forces, will also leave. But the general, who retires next month, plans to return this fall. He has reportedly accepted a vice presidency with a Thai charter airline, Air Siam.

250 Americans Stay

About 250 American military advisers, operating under the continuing military-aid agreement, remained in Thailand today, the deadline set three months ago by the Thai Government for the American withdrawal.

American officials said that the number of Americans who administer military assistance would remain somewhat below the Thai-imposed ceiling of 270. At Thailand's request the last combat troops left last fall.

July 21, 1976

THAI MILITARY TAKES POWER AFTER POLICE BATTLE PROTESTERS

30 Believed Dead and 1,700 Seized —Constitution Is Suspended and Publications Banned

By DAVID A. ANDELMAN
Special to The New York Times

BANGKOK, Thailand, Thursday, Oct. 7 — Thailand's military seized power last night within hours after policemen and university students fought violent battles in which 30 persons were believed killed and hundreds wounded. More than 1,700 students were arrested.

The Defense Minister, Adm. Sa-ngad Chaloryu, said over television and radio that Thailand's 42 million people would henceforth be ruled by an Administrative Reform Committee headed by himself. He announced that the 1974 Constitution had been abolished, that all newspapers and periodicals had been banned and that a curfew would be enforced from midnight to 5 A.M.

The takeover followed several months of indications that right-wing military leaders were taking a more active role in Thailand's politics.

Protests Against Thanom

The Defense Minister, who is noted for his opposition to Communism, said that the military had to step in because the six-month-old Government of Prime Minister Seni Pramoj had proved unable to cope with the protests of the students, who, the minister said, were backed by Communist elements. The students were demanding the renewed exiling of the former Thai military dictator, Field Marshal Thanom Kittikachorn, who returned to Thailand nearly three weeks ago and is now in a Buddhist pagoda.

"The stability of the country is at stake." the Defense Minister said.

October 7, 1976

4,000 THAIS ARRESTED SINCE MILITARY COUP

Two-Thirds Still Held on Suspicion of Subversion, Junta Says

By DAVID A. ANDELMAN
Special to The New York Times

BANGKOK, Thailand, Oct. 20—Thailand's military rulers disclosed today that more than 4,000 people had been arrested since the coup of Oct. 6 on suspicion of being Communist subversives. Nearly two-thirds of them are still in custody, a spokesman for the junta said.

Meanwhile, the junta continued to tighten curbs on civil liberties throughout the country.

Among its recent actions, disclosed in a series of edicts and public statements by senior members of the junta, was an extension of the period of detention without trial and without charges from one month to six months.

List of Journalists Published

Areas called "Communist-infested zones" were created in which all civil liberties may be suspended and which may be declared out of bounds for residence. In addition the teaching of any political theory "including democratic concepts" was banned in the nation's schools.

At the same time, two right-wing newspapers believed close to the junta published a list of 57 editors, columnists and reporters, among them some of Thailand's most prominent journalists, who reportedly were going to be arrested. The newspapers said at least 70 percent of them were Communists.

October 21, 1976

Campaign Grows Against Vietnamese in Thailand Region

By DAVID A. ANDELMAN
Special to The New York Times

SAKON NAKHON, Thailand — Portraits of the royal family grace the facades of most of the shops along the main street of this tiny northeast Thailand provincial capital. Thai flags hang from the balustrades of the wooden houses, in honor of the King and Queen who have been in residence here recently at their new Buphan Palace.

But it is clear that the hearts of most of the shopkeepers and homeowners are hundreds of miles to the east—in Hanoi and other parts of Vietnam, from where most emigrated more than 30 years ago and where, politics and geography willing, most would like to return.

The fact, however, is that they cannot return, at least not for the present. And lately they have become the objects of calumny, persecution and racial antagonism from the Thais among whom they live, who deeply resent the strange language, alien faces and economic dominance the Vietnamese have managed to achieve in northeast Thailand by their frugal and industrious ways.

Thailand's Minister of the Interior, Samak Sundaravej, claimed the other day that he had "solid evidence" of a plot in which Vietnamese refugees would incite rioting in northeast Thailand, providing Vietnam with an excuse to invade Thailand through Laos and Burma on Feb. 15.

Up to 60,000 in Region

This allegation of a plot by Mr. Samak was, however, only the latest in a series of actions directed against the Vietnamese community here.

There have been many mysterious fires in Vietnamese-owned shops in recent months, widespread arrests since the coup that brought a military-backed Government to power here in October, and a feeling by most Government leaders that, in the words of the provincial governor, Somporn Klinpongsa, "they are all 100 percent Communists."

There are as many as 60,000 ethnic Vietnamese scattered throughout areas of northeast Thailand—some 5,000 here in Sakon Nakhon. They arrived here for the most part during and after World War II, many of them driven by the fighting between the French and the Vietminh.

Dao Duc Ho, 42 years old, arrived in Sakon Nakhon with his parents when he was about 10 years old. He grew up here, went to school, learned the Thai language, married and fathered four sons. They all work now in the fabric shop he owns on a small side street.

"It is terrible, terrible being a foreigner for 32 years," he told a visitor. He has an uncle and some other family in Hanoi, he continued, but no hope of seeing them for a long time.

He cannot even go to Udon Thani, 90 miles away, without permission, he said, "and they never allow me to go."

He does, he said, respect and admire Ho Chi Minh, the late president of North Vietnam, not because he was a Communist, but "because he was a great man, because he unified my country and because he brought peace there."

'My Heart Is in Hanoi'

But, he said, no one in Sakon Nakhon outside the Vietnamese community understands that, and he despairs of ever trying to make them understand. "They are not nice to us here, and I understand that, it is not my country," he said.

He began to cry softly, clutched his hand to his chest and whispered, "My heart is in Hanoi."

Mr. Ho and others in the Vietnamese community have tried to adopt. Most have learned the Thai language and, apart from the Red Cross refugee center, there are no signs here in Vietnamese.

But some 70 percent of the small shops that are the backbone of commerce and trade here are owned by Vietnamese, 20 percent by Chinese and a mere 10 percent by Thais, most of whom, though they form the bulk of the population, eke out a bare subsistence living on the dusty, barren soil in this, Thailand's poorest region.

In the last two months, however, there have been some new elements injected into the normally strained situation between the races here.

Hundreds of Vietnamese have been arrested, allegedly for Communist sympathies or for outright assistance to Communist insurgents operating in the jungles.

Vietnam has retaliated, charging, apparently inaccurately, that thousands of Vietnamese here have been herded into "concentration camps" and hinting of dire consequences should such "persecution" continue.

Yet it is clearly Vietnam that is partially responsible for the situation—

The New York Times/Dec. 12, 1976

refusing to accept back any of the Vietnamese refugees although large numbers would, given the opportunity, gladly give up all their accumulated wealth and, with the blessings of the Thai authorities, return.

But Vietnam apparently fears the presence of Thai agents among any returnees, just as Thailand fears the presence of Hanoi operatives among those who remain in Thailand.

"I doubt that many of them are Communists," said Lieut. Gen. Prem Tinsulanonda, the eminently realistic commander of the Second Army, which

329

oversees security throughout northeast Thailand. "But they want to go back to their homeland and they should be allowed to do so. Frankly, I'd be glad to seem them go."

Recently, the psychological war against the Vietnamese in Sakon Nakhon escalated still further.

Many Vietnamese in and around Sakon Nakhon operate restaurants that cater not only to their own countrymen but to many Thais as well.

A rumor began spreading recently—that the Vietnamese were putting a chemical into the food that caused impotence. Within hours there were long lines of men at the local hospitals worried that they had been affected. Medical experts were dispatched

from Bangkok when the national newspapers began displaying the story with huge headlines.

Restaurants Closed Down

Throughout northeast Thailand, Vietnamese restaurants closed down, though officials at the Ministry of Public Health vigorously denied that there was any truth to the rumors or that any such chemical even existed.

Nevertheless, the rumors persisted and intelligent, educated men and women were still relating it recently to visitors as gospel truth.

"Mama-san's" is the best restaurant in Sakon Nakhon. For years, the owner cared for American servicemen stationed at nearby airbases at Nakhon Phanom or Udon Thani or at the for-

ward command of Thailand's Second Army.

Mama-san herself, a large, friendly woman with clearly Vietnamese features, never bothered until last month to deny her Vietnamese parentage, which was generally accepted as fact and as a reason for her fine culinary abilities.

This week she was denying it. "I am half Vietnamese, half Lao," she smiled as several listeners, all college students who had been solemnly describing the symptoms of the "disease" elbowed each other in the ribs.

"But it's the Lao half that runs this restaurant," she added.

December 12, 1976

Thailand Finds Indochinese Refugees a Growing Problem

80,000 Wait in Camps for Permanent Resettlement but Few Find Homes

By HENRY KAMM
Special to The New York Times

BANGKOK, Thailand, June 30—More than 80,000 Indochinese refugees are killing time in camps throughout Thailand waiting for other countries to open their doors to them or Thailand to resettle them in this country. More arrive from Laos, Cambodia and Vietnam every day than leave for new homes.

Because of its long borders with Laos and Cambodia and its long coastline along which refugee vessels from Vietnam seek shelter, Thailand has been the most hospitable country in Asia for refugees from Indochina. As a result, it is the only Asian country in which the number of refugees is large enough to constitute a real problem for the host Government.

"Hospitable" in the context of the reception that awaits Indochinese refugees in Asian countries is a relative term. It is largely because Japan, Singapore, Malaysia, Indonesia and the Philippines show such little readiness to accept the refugees even temporarily that the word can be applied to Thailand. "We are unlucky to have the three countries close to us," said Interior Minister Samak Sundaravej, the official in charge of the problem, illustrating Thailand's unhappiness over its role as host.

People familiar with the situation say that, depending on their nationality, the refugees are at best treated with neglect by the Thai authorities and at worst are regarded as possible subversives and mercilessly exploited by petty officials and employers.

Vietnamese Are Worst Off

The Vietnamese, the smallest group, are in the worst situation. "We have some feeling for the Lao and Cambodians," said the Interior Minister, implicitly stressing the absence of sympathetic feelings for the Vietnamese.

"They think they are very smart," he said disparagingly.

Mr. Samak said he suspected the Vietnamese, particularly those who are arriving from Laos, where there is a large Vietnamese community, of subversive activities in connection with the Thai Communist insurgency.

The official antagonism sets the tone for the treatment of the 3,400 Vietnamese refugees, who complain of extortion and mistreatment in their camps. One Vietnamese was killed earlier this year in a riot in Si Khiu camp, where the inmates are mainly from Laos.

In the camps where refugees from Vietnam who arrive in fishing boats are sent, complaints of extortion or theft of the property they arrive with are widespread and believed to be true by outsiders.

Bribes Required

In the detention facilities maintained by the Bangkok immigration authorities, where refugees cleared for departure to other countries spend days or weeks awaiting final clearance, Vietnamese have to pay minor bribes to their guards to be allowed out for shopping. Laotians and Cambodians do not.

The most favored group are about 10,000 Laotians of Lao ethnic origin in the large camp at Nong Khai, across the Mekong River from the Laotian capital of Vientiane. Close to Thais in ethnic character and language, they enjoy correct treatment and relatively easy movement out of the camp.

The largest group of refugees are the more than 50,000 Laotian hill tribesmen, most of whom fled more than two years ago because of their close association with the American-sponsored army that did the bulk of the fighting against the Communists. They and the nearly 11,000 Cambodians enjoy less favorable treatment than the ethnic Laos but greater tolerance than the Vietnamese.

The refugees continue arriving: each month more than 1,000 Laotians, more than 100 Cambodians and, while the good weather at sea lasts, several hundred Vietnamese reach Thailand.

They arrive faster than they depart, and the Thai Government is painfully

conscious that groups of Laotian and Cambodian refugees that no other nation seems to want are building up. In a major reversal of Thailand's earlier attitude, the Interior Minister said in an interview that the Government will have to consider eventual resettlement in Thailand of some of the Laotian and Cambodian refugees.

But Mr. Samak said this could not be announced, citing probable negative reactions from Thais who would feel foreigners were being better treated than themselves.

In fact, it is the office of the United Nations High Commissioner for Refugees and not the Thai Government which bears the expenses of the refugees' upkeep.

A project that Mr. Samak is considering is the creation of border villages with mixed populations of Thais and Laotians or Cambodians. This, he explained, would not endanger Thai security by creating entirely foreign populations in border areas. But interviews with both Laotian and Cambodian refugees indicated that while they would favor settlement in Thailand, they feared being too near the border of their former homelands.

Vietnamese Excluded

But the minister said resettlement of the Vietnamese would not be considered. "They must have first priority for taking to other countries," he said. Only France is regularly taking sizable numbers of Indochinese from Thailand. A total of 771, mainly Laotians, left for France in May. Only 80 went to the United States. The only other departures for the same month were three each to West Germany and Norway and two to Britain.

Mr. Samak said that if other countries did not accept the Vietnamese, "we might one day have to make a deal with the Vietnamese Government to take them back."

Despite this ominous remark, the minister said that in accepting the United Nations high commissioner's help for the maintenance of the refugees, Thailand committed itself to the principle that refugees could be repatriated only with their consent.

July 1, 1977

Thai Junta Ousts Civilian Regime

Camera Press

Adm. Sa-ngad Chaloryu

The New York Times

Thanin Kraivichien

By HENRY KAMM
Special to The New York Times

BANGKOK, Thailand, Oct. 21—Thailand's military junta, in a coup that met no resistance, last night deposed the civilian Government it installed after a coup a year ago.

Defense Minister Sa-ngad Chaloryu, who was referred to in official announcements of the coup as head of what was called the revolutionary party, said in a televised address that the leadership group would aim for elections next year. The 12-year program for the re-establishment of democracy advocated by the deposed Prime Minister, Thanin Kraivichien, was longer than necessary, Mr. Sa-ngad said.

Mr. Sa-ngad retired last year as commander of the navy. The new junta, in its announcements throughout the night, described itself as being composed of military and civilian members. Mr. Sa-ngad was flanked by the supreme commander of the armed forces, Gen. Kriangsak Chamanand, and by the chiefs of the branches of the armed services and the police as he addressed this nation of 42 million people.

For the first time in Thailand's history of frequent military coups, a civilian Government has been deposed by the military leadership because the military felt it was too conservative. All of Thailand's elite, civilian and military, would be considered conservative in Western terms.

Political Life Stalemated

Mr. Thanin, a former member of the country's Supreme Court, had not only alienated the military that put him in power by ignoring its wishes, but had also stalemated all political life, banned most labor unions, put the press under strict censorship and imposed stern controls on university campuses, the principal centers of liberal and leftist opposition.

October 21, 1977

Thais on Refugees: West Must Take Them

By HENRY KAMM
Special to The New York Times

BANGKOK, Thailand, June 18 — The forcible expulsion of more than 50,000 Cambodian refugees from Thailand so far has provoked no public expressions of disapproval here.

From Japan in the north to Indonesia on the Equator, Asian nations have a common attitude toward the outpouring of refugees from Indochina: that the West must absorb them. Exceptions have been ethnic Chinese from Vietnam taken by China, 2,000 Cambodian Moslems taken by Malaysia and 100 ethnic Chinese from Vietnam taken by Singapore in 1975.

While diplomats and international officials in constant contact with the Thai Government, including Prime Minister Kriangsak Chamanand, have been unable to learn how the decision to eject the Cambodians at gunpoint was reached, it is known that the well-planned operation was devised by the Supreme Command of the armed forces, whose chief, Gen. Serm Na Nakorn, reports directly to the Prime Minister.

No domestic opposition to the decision has appeared, even in private conversation. This does not surprise ambassadors and other foreign officials because no important Thai political figure is suspected of being friendly to the refugees. Since the flow began in 1975, concerned Western officials here have found that benign indifference is the best they can hope for in the Government and the military.

'Front Line' Against Communism

Since the Communist victories in Indochina, Thailand thinks of itself as a "front line" state threatened by Communism. That attitude intensified when it

Asians Have Same Attitude From Japan to Indonesia With Few Exceptions

became evident that Laos, with which Thailand shares a long border, had become not only Communist but also dominated by Vietnam. The attitude became progressively what many here view as an obsession when Vietnamese designs on Cambodia evolved last year and Vietnamese troops reached the Thai-Cambodian border, where they remain, this year.

Explaining the decision on the Cambodians, one of the military planners of the operation said that the basic objective of the expulsion, which he said would continue as long as Cambodians entered Thailand, was to protect the security of the 45 million Thais. "It came from the head, not from the heart," he added.

He said that any "spillover" of the Vietnamese-Cambodian conflict onto Thai territory raised the danger of Vietnamese aggression against Thailand. In a view often expressed by Thai officials, he accused Vietnam of gradually "colonizing" Cambodia with Vietnamese at the expense of the Cambodian population. He said that Thailand's national interest was best served by the existence of an independent Cambodia, but that an underpopulated Cambodia could not fulfill its role as a buffer state.

This reasoning, he went on, gave additional impetus to forcing Cambodian refugees back into their country. "We do not want a Cambodia that has become a Lebensraum for Vietnam," he said, using the German geopolitical term denoting vital national space.

Another element that contributes strongly to shaping that opinion is an impression fostered by daily statements from political leaders, including the Prime Minister, that the presence of 160,000 refugees in camps supported by the United Nations High Commissioner for Refugees is imposing a heavy economic burden on Thailand.

Western diplomats and United Nations officials are uncertain and distrustful about this. Thailand pays only for the time spent by public servants concerned with the refugee problem and for the maintenance of those refugees that, for political reasons, it refuses to put under United Nations care. The latter category includes all Cambodians who have fled since the Vietnamese seized Phnom Penh, the Cambodian capital, last January.

The United Nations agency provides everything that the refugees receive — minimal food, housing and medical care, at the cost of about 25 cents a person a day. By the end of this year it will have spent $43 million, almost all expended for Thai goods and services.

In the case of the Cambodians now expelled, Thailand allowed the International Committee of the Red Cross to feed them until their departure. The Thai Government chose that organization because allowing the United Nations group to feed the refugees might have been interpreted as at least a moral commitment to abide by the international principle that they should not be forced back.

Any Improvement Prevented

United Nations officials said that they had often attempted to gain permission to improve the refugees' living conditions, which would increase the money expended here, but were told that to raise their standard of living would heighten the jealousy of people near the camps.

In addition to stressing an alleged economic burden caused by the refugee inflow, Thai leaders, particularly generals in key posts, emphasize that the Vietnamese refugees constitute a grave security risk. A frequently created impression is that the refugees are mainly Vietnamese, but at the end of last month 8,000 of the 160,000 refugees in United Nations-supported camps were Vietnamese.

Thai political sources and foreign diplomats believe that internal political factors played an important role in the decision to expel the Cambodians. General Kriangsak spent about a month in April and May on the difficult task of forming a coalition cabinet, and his hold on the various military and political elements vital for an effective government was shown to be shaky. The unpopularity of the Indochinese refugees was used by both the most security-minded generals and the most demagogic politicians as a weapon against the Prime Minister's policy of general tolerance toward refugees and against the Prime Minister himself.

The Thai and foreign sources believe that the decision to expel the Cambodians, despite frequent representations by Western diplomats and international officials, including Secretary General Kurt Waldheim of the United Nations, was motivated at least in part by General Kriangsak's desire to appease both the generals and the politicians.

June 20, 1979

MALAYSIA: THE FRUITS OF DEVELOPMENT

Malaysia to Spread Fruits of Economy Dominated by Energetic Urban Chinese

By SYDNEY H. SCHANBERG

Special to The New York Times

KUALA LUMPUR, Malaysia, Sept. 18—"In the entire region," a Western diplomat says, "this is the country that has the fewest problems. It's got good administration, natural resources, skilled technicians and money. The only fly in the ointment is race."

Unfortunately for Malaysia, it is a very big fly. It seems certain to remain so for a long time to come, as the rural Malays, who form the largest ethnic group and control the Government, push for a larger share of the economy, dominated until now by Malaysia's urbanized and hard-working ethnic Chinese.

By every yardstick other than race, Malaysia is making large strides forward. The per-capita income is about $500 a year, one of the highest rates in Asia.

The economy's growth rate has jumped to 10 or 12 per cent this year, compared with 6.5 per cent last year, as the demand and prices for Malaysia's natural resources—rubber, tin, palm oil and tropical hardwoods—have soared.

Urban construction is booming, particularly here in the capital. Hotels, factories and high-rise apartment and office buildings are going up at such a pace that a shortage of construction materials has developed.

On the international money markets, the Malaysian dollar remains firm.

But the race issue hangs as a specter over it all for Malaysia's 11.5 million people, 45 per cent of whom are Malays, 36 per cent ethnic Chinese and 9 per cent Indian, with the rest a mixture of Eurasians, Caucasians and people of tribal origins.

Despite the Government's talk of creating a "multiracial society," the people of Malaysia live in de facto ethnic separation. Neighborhoods are racially demarcated, although the Government of Prime Minister Abdul Razak is making attempts at mixing the races in its new low-rent apartment buildings.

Almost every step the Government takes involves two questions of which group will benefit the most and how the other groups will react.

This has been especially true since May, 1969, when race riots exploded in Kuala Lumpur, leaving hundreds — some say more than 1,000 — dead, most of them Chinese.

The spark was an election in which losses to a militant Chinese party temporarily threatened the hold of the governing multiracial Alliance party and spread fear and insecurity through the Malay community.

Hiring Practices Revised

After the riots, the Government immediately embarked on a crash program to uplift the Malays. All new businesses are now supposed to allot jobs at all levels according to the racial composition of the Malay-dominated population. Preference in university admission and hiring for the civil service also goes to Malays.

As for ownership, the pivotal issue, the Government's goal is to have at least 30 per cent of "all aspects" of the economy in Malay hands and under Malay management by 1991.

Government planners say privately that they are not likely to achieve this goal. But the hope is that enough progress will have been made by the target date to satisfy the Malays that the Government is doing its best for them.

At the same time, the planners stress, this program, which is described in official language as "restructuring the society," must be carefully guided so as not to cause unrest among the ethnic Chinese.

Animosities Persist

The success of the program is pegged to the belief that most of Malaysia's Chinese are moderates who realize that in the long run it is to their benefit to have an upgraded, satisfied Malay community rather than a bitter and riotous one.

On balance, it would appear that there has been progress toward racial harmony since the 1969 riots. But it is an exceedingly slow movement and animosities are still close to the surface.

The Malay Peninsula, the part of Malaysia where racial troubles are centered, known as West Malaysia, is a land of thick jungles and mangrove swamps, neat rubber plantations, tin mines, heavily laden fruit trees, frangipani blossoms, subsistence rice farms, sleeping towns now coming awake and the modern city of

The New York Times/Oct. 3, 1973

Rebels near Thai border (1) and in Sarawak (2) keep large numbers of troops tied down.

Kuala Lumpur, its population approaching a million.

The ethnic Chinese are mostly descended from migrants who poured down from South China in the last century, many of them as laborers who came to hack down jungle trees and work the tin mines. Industrious and always able to make accommodations with those in political power, the Chinese are now clustered in the cities and dominate most urban business, from huge banks to family-run grocery shops.

The Indians, originally brought in to work British-owned rubber estates, still predominate as plantation laborers. But they also have carved an in-between economic niche as small shopkeepers, clerks and professionals and, as such, also seem to do better than average Malays. Some Government agencies, notably Public

Works, have been traditionally staffed with Indians since colonial days.

When Malaya peacefully gained independence from Britain in 1957—the country did not become Malaysia until 1963 —ethnic Malays were guaranteed political dominance through an electoral system heavily weighted in their favor and a continued influential role for the hereditary Malay sultans. Malay was made the country's official language and Islam, the religion of the Malays, was made the state religion.

Political power, however, did not upgrade the Malays' low economic status. Wedded to the traditional Islamic biases against big business and modern education in the sciences, the Malays remained generally a rural, financially backward people.

But recent heavy migration to the cities opened Malay eyes to the fruits of the country's recent prosperity and raised their expectations — probably one of the underlying causes of the 1969 riots.

Complaints by Chinese

No one here denies that the Malays need special help to upgrade their status. But there are many complaints about how the special assistance is being provided.

There is, of course, the obvious complaint by the Chinese that they are in the position of Peter being robbed to pay Paul. The Government denies this and says the program is designed to increase the Malay part of the economy not by taking from those who already have but by "increasing the economic cake" — mostly through heavy Government investment and development.

"It is true the Chinese are still making money, but they have to work a damned sight harder," said Dr. Tan Cheekhoon, a physician who heads Pekemas, one of the small opposition parties.

"The Government uses the Chinese as a whipping boy," he asserts. He also says that the Government never mentions the large number of very poor Chinese.

Dr. Tan points out, using the Government's own figures, that more than 60 per cent of the share capital of the major industries and businesses in West Malaysia is held by foreign interests. More than 20 per cent is held by the ethnic Chinese and a meager 1.5 per cent by the Malays.

Dr. Tan's argument, shared by most Chinese, is that if the Government wants to upgrade the Malay share to 30 per cent by 1991, "it should take it from those who have the most—the foreign share."

The Government, however, has made it clear that it is not going to interfere with foreign capital at a time when it needs, and is trying to encourage, greater outside investment here.

Another criticism of the preferential program for Malays is that it has helped most those Malays who already have the most, the Malay élite who are usually educated in Britain. These would - be aristocrats have the best jobs in the civil service, are given most of the newly established Malay seats on the boards of directors of large companies and in general are able, through family and business connections, to amass personal fortunes.

Malaysia's foreign policy of nonalignment and "neutralization" of Southeast Asia is heading toward diplomatic relations with China, but is approaching this slowly because of Malay fears of a Chinese "fifth column" after recognition of Peking.

One of the obstacles to early recognition is the low-level Communist insurgencies that tie down large numbers of Government troops in both West Malaysia, near the northern border with Thailand, and in the East Malaysian state of Sarawak, on the island of Borneo 400 miles across the South China Sea. In Malaysia, Communism is Chinese, another factor complicating the racial problem.

To keep all the racial pressures under control, the Government uses a firm, though not an iron, hand.

It directs the press not to write anything that might arouse "communilism" — a word widely used in Asia to describe racial hostility. And sometimes it imposes news blackouts on local political infighting that might prove embarrassing to the Government.

But generally the climate of criticism is freer than in Malaysia's neighbor, the island state of Singapore at the southern tip of the Malay Peninsula, where meaningful dissent is forbidden and political life is rigidly controlled.

October 3, 1973

Critique of System Is Singapore Best Seller

By SYDNEY H. SCHANBERG
Special to The New York Times

SINGAPORE, June 6—A book that calls Prime Minister Lee Kuan Yew dictatorial and says his rule in Singapore is "reminiscent of Mussolini's Italy" has soared to the top of Singapore's best-seller list. The Prime Minister reportedly allowed the book into the country as a conscious attempt to rebut one of its theses—that freedom of expression has been stifled.

News Analysis

Whatever the motive for its clearance by the Controller of Undesirable Publications, the book is being bought up by a populace starved for the kind of critical comment about their government that they have not been allowed to read and are not allowed to make in public themselves.

"This is the first real criticism of Lee ever seen here," said one bookseller. "Even people who are satisfied with conditions are buying the book because it tells them things they never heard about before."

The 215-page book, called "Lee Kuan Yew's Singapore" and published by André Deutsch Ltd., of London, was written by T.K.S. George, an Indian journalist who until recently reported on Asia from Hong

United Press International
Lee Kuan Yew ·

Kong and is now working in New York.

Search for Tittle-Tattle

The book's significance does not lie so much in the fact that it is selling faster than any book in recent memory, except "Love Story," and has set the cocktail and intellectual circuits buzzing, for many people are reading it simply in a search for political tittle-tattle and it will cause no revolutions.

Its importance rests rather on the basic question it raises

about Asian, and perhaps all, societies: How authoritarian must a government be to produce efficiency and economic progress?

The book's basic theme is that in the nearly 15 years that Mr. Lee has been Prime Minister of the small island state of Singapore and its 2.3 million people, he has, in the name of progress, methodically quashed the political opposition, intimidated the press into total docility, suppressed the trade union movement and imposed government controls in the universities.

The book is punctuated with such phrases as "rigorous internal repression," "people pacification," "capitalist totalitarianism," "relentless drive to achieve monolithic authority," and "the characteristics of a police state."

At times, the author's language becomes shrill, indignant and emotional, detracting from his argument. Occasionally, he reads the Prime Minister's motives through the technique of psyco ~-history, contending, for examp , that the Mr. Lee, a 50-year-lawyer, is an "authoritarian by instinct" and an arrogant élitist by virtue of his breeding and his well-to-do background, including his Cambridge education.

Moreover, the author's in-

sider's view of Singapore as a virtual dictatorship would probably surprise casual visitors. For prosperous Singapore does not look like anyone's conventional notion of an authoritarian society.

This former British colony is "clean and green" (a government slogan), full of bustling shopping centers, freshly painted houses, neat lawns, flower-filled parks, new skyscrapers rising downtown, new factories rising in the industrial areas.

Slums and litter have virtually been eradicated, in vivid contrast to many hovel-ridden Asian capitals. The people are well-dressed and well-fed; they do not look or sound frightened, repressed or subjugated.

Satisfied With Life

Most Singaporeans, in fact, seem satisfied with their lives, and some express pride in their country's orderliness and economic success. The per capita income is about $1,600 compared with less than $100 in neighboring Indonesia.

Nevertheless, the book's historical facts are essentially accurate, and no independent observer would deny that this is a carefully controlled society. The universities are instruments of government policy.

the jury system has been abolished and the unions do what the Government tells them.

Major labor strikes do not happen and minor ones are quickly squelched. Last year, some of the laborers at a Gulf Oil plastics factory protested over an increase in their work load; the Government put an end to it by simply shipping home the protest leaders, who were immigrant workers from neighboring Malaysia.

At the universities, it is made clear to students that if they participate in a demonstration, no matter how peaceful, they will lose their scholarships and loans; as a result, demonstrations do not occur. Further, to

gain entrance to a university, a student must supply a suitability certificate from the Home Ministry, and this has been denied to students who have relatives considered politically undesirable.

Singapore has laws that permit the jailing of persons indefinitely without trial in cases where there is not enough evidence for a legal prosecution and the accused are nevertheless considered threats to society.

Public criticism is not tolerated. At least one newspaper and one student publication have been summarily shut down for having the boldness to criticize; now the newspapers report on fashions,

sports, the divorce courts and the latest automobile models.

Supporters of the government's methods point to countries like India where democracy is allowed to flourish with few restraints, and they contend that the lack of controls and discipline have contributed to chaos and poverty.

Critics of the Singapore system counter that there is no analogy between running an island of 225 square miles that is little more than a large city and running a sprawling nation of nearly 600 million people. The critics also say that Singapore's progress could have been accomplished in a more democratic manner.

Mr. Lee has said many times, in various ways, that Western-style democracy, with its principle of one man, one vote, does not suit Asian conditions.

"Government to be effective must at least give the impression of enduring," he said in a 1962 speech, "and a government that is open to the vagaries of the ballot box when the people who put their crosses on the ballot are not illiterate but semi-literate, which is worse, is a government that is already weakened before it starts to govern."

June 7, 1974

The New York Times/David A. Andelman

Yap Fong at her stall in the central market of Kuala Lumpur. The ginger root she holds sold for 20 cents five years ago. It now costs 80 cents and her profit is a few pennies. She is one of those that the generally successful five-year plan has passed by.

Malaysia Spurs Development Plans, But Poor People Get Little Benefit

By DAVID A. ANDELMAN
Special to The New York Times

KUALA LUMPUR, Malaysia —Malaysia is speeding headlong down the road of development at a pace that her supporters say will in five years

make her one of the most prosperous countries in Asia and that her critics say will blow her apart.

Within the next few months, the nation's second five-year plan will be coming to what,

by all economic indicators, is an overwhelmingly successful end. And sometime early next year the third five-year plan will launch the country into a new and ever-rising development spiral.

But for Yap Fong, who, selling vegetables in a squalid suburb of this rich capital, must make do on an income of less than 80 cents a day, the economic indicators mean little.

Yap Fong and tens of thousands of others — landless farmers, squatters, even some government workers — have simply been passed by under the "new economic policy."

Land Given to Landless

There are, of course, many who have benefited—including those fortunate enough to have been caught up in the Federal Land Development Program projects that have distributed rich, untouched land to the landless, allowing them for the first time to own their own houses, farm their own plots, even to buy motorcycles and television sets and to travel beyond a day's walking distance from where they were born.

But none of this exists in Jinjang, a Kuala Lumpur suburb. The largest and oldest of the so-called "new villages," it was established more than 25 years ago, when Malaysia was still under British rule, during the emergency period in which it was felt necessary to herd suburbanites into safe towns to protect them from Communist terrorists and at the same time keep watch on them.

Some 40,000 people have been crammed into this small town and 10,000 other squatters have made their way to open fields on the outskirts where their single-room dirt-floored shanties have housed many for an entire generation.

Only a quarter of Jinjang's roads have been paved. There are no telephones. The sewers are open slashes in the dusty ground and garbage is collected at most once a week. The first thing that a visitor notices is the odor.

'Everything Costs More'

Yap Fong, now 60 years old, has lived in Jinjang for 11 years, having moved there when government improvement projects demolished her old house in Kompong Siam, a nearby village.

"Everything costs more now —it is very hard to live," she said, standing by her tiny stall in the town's central market. She held up a ginger root that she would have sold for 20 cents five years ago. It now costs 80 cents and her profit on it has shrunk to only a few cents. She pays taxes now and license fees to sell her goods— funds that the Government says are essential for development.

"And it is dirty here," she said. She pointed to a street corner where a few unemptied trash baskets overflowed.

"Once a week they collect that, yet they do not let us put out any more rubbish baskets—that is what the Government does for us."

Yet village workers contended that Yap Fong was among the more fortunate. She lives with her daughter and son-in-law in a two-room wooden house that has electricity and running water.

Across the road, Lim Eng has lived in a squatter's hut for 10 years. Because it is not technically part of the "new town," however, the Government does not officially recognize that Lim Eng exists. So in his area there is no electricity, no run-

ning water, no sanitation, not even the weekly garbage pick-ups. His family of three children has grown up here, he said.

Spent Life as a Laborer

"I worked on government sanitation projects, digging drainage holes until I could work no more," he said. Now he sits in his one-room shack from morning to night listening to a transistor radio his children gave him. "We should have some of these things—our land, our house, water, electricity," he said.

What would he do if he had electricity, he was asked. "I would be able to have a light at night," he replied slowly.

"Malaysia and development work well until you look at an individual," said Dr. Tan Chee Khoon, an opposition Member of Parliament whose district includes Jinjang. "The distribution of wealth is all wrong, and most of the people in government just don't care."

Yet the Government of Prime Minister Abdul Razak delights in showing off its achievements. Its economists and planners are, by and large, trained in the top institutions of the West. Hundreds of millions of dollars of aid from the World Bank, the Asian Development

Bank and major private banking institutions in Asia, Europe and the United States are being poured into land reform, irrigation and industrial projects from one end of the country to the other.

Malaysia's economic growth rate has averaged nearly 6 per cent a year in the first half of the nineteen-seventies and per-capita annual income is now $570 — nearly 10 times that of Bangladesh.

Education More Widespread

"There is greater accessibility to health facilities, schools, electrification, than ever before," said Dr. C. L. Robless, an economist who is the chief architect of the five-year plans. "There are more growth centers in the hinterlands, more diversification in industrialization. And in our next five-year plan I foresee as much progress, if not more, than in our present one.

"I do not exclude the possibility that fairly soon we will be in a position even to begin helping our neighbors as well," he said.

Yet with all this progress, there are mammoth inequities. Despite the $570 annual per-capita income rate, 60 per cent of the population earns less than $200 a year.

New factories and new office buildings are going up everywhere, but particularly in Kuala Lumpur and scattered other areas.

Yet a major Government plan to spread industries into the less-developed areas, begun several years ago with a great flourish, has bogged down. Most foreign investors, while impressed with the highly favorable political and investment climate in Malaysia—perhaps the most favorable and stable in Southeast Asia — find little attraction in the jungle industrial zones the Government has designated.

"Why should we push out to the coast?" one British businessman asked. "There are practically no roads, no reliable electricity, and as for the workers, they're almost untrainable."

Yet the Malaysian Government has one of the best international credit ratings in the developing world.

"They've just discovered that they really can tap the foreign money markets to whatever extent they need to cover any shortfall they might experience, and they have begun doing it regularly," one Western financial analyst said.

September 9, 1975

Singapore Pushing a Stern Drive
To Silence Critics and Dissidents

By DAVID A. ANDELMAN
Special to The New York Times

SINGAPORE, April 8—Singapore's formidable Internal Security Department, under orders from Prime Minister Lee Kuan Yew, has begun a new campaign to repress dissent that has crippled his thin political opposition and a fledgling human rights movement.

A series of arrests in the three months since the governing People's Action Party swept every seat in a barely contested national parliamentary election has seen the detention or intimidation of political candidates, lawyers and journalists—all of whom, in one way or another, have been outspoken in their opposition to or criticism of government policies.

Public Confessions on TV

On several occasions, under apparent threat of indeterminate prison sentences, such critics have confessed publicly in television spectacles to a wide range of abuses, including adherence to the ideals of or membership in the Communist movement. The result has been to paralyze dissent.

For the 2.5 million people living in prosperity in this tiny island-nation at the southern tip of the Malay Peninsula, it has meant one more round of bombast and repression, designed, it would seem,

to soothe the Prime Minister's apparent fears that there are enemies all around and subversives within—a stance that is being used to preserve his own peculiar formula of dictatorship with a democratic facade.

In the months since the election, Mr. Lee, who has been in office since 1959, and the security department have moved on a broad front. People perceived as enemies have been arrested and some have been coerced into signing confessions and then appearing on television to recant. Though the number arrested is under a dozen, those affected are prominent and the intimidating effect has been devastating. Others have been targets of lawsuits growing out of alleged libels committed during the election campaign; these have led to stiff damage awards—$40,000, more than a lifetime's earnings, in one instance—that threaten to force many into bankruptcy.

Still others, among them professional men and a priest, have been implicated by innuendo, their names dropped in the course of public "confessions" by friends and associates who accuse them of being receptive to ideas that are defined as inimical to national security. The effect has been to isolate them though no formal charges have been brought and, indeed, may never be.

In Control From the Back Seat

All these people have been linked to one or more plots, conspiracies and left-wing ideologies that are said to include efforts to undermine relations between Singapore and Malaysia and the formation of such so-called Communist-front organizations as a human-rights committee.

Throughout all this Mr. Lee has taken a back seat, but that it is he who is in control is never questioned. In the televised confessions the moderator is James Fu, his press secretary and a close political adviser. In January, as the roundups and prosecutions were beginning, Mr. Lee, in an interview, said in reference to denunciation of the Government: "I think if we leave it alone, there may be foolish people who will continue to believe it and it will become worse in the next election."

The latest roundup began when a left-wing lawyer, Gopan Raman, was arrested and confessed to questionable activities, implicating a number of people who were being imprisoned or detained for questioning.

Two were prominent journalists—Arun Senkuttavan, one-time chief correspondent here for The Far Eastern Economic Review of Hong Kong and now part-time correspondent for The Economist and The Financial Times of London, and Ho Kwon Ping, his successor as Review correspondent and the son of one of Singapore's leading business figures. The circum-

335

stances surrounding their arrests and confessions provide a graphic picture of the way the Internal Security Department functions and the nature of the conspiracies that are being alleged.

Disclosing the Already Public

Mr. Ho was arrested first, shortly after the election, during which his coverage reportedly infuriated the Prime Minister. He was charged with endangering national security by disclosing arms production and sales by a small Singapore arms manufacturer—information it developed, that had been published elsewhere. Two weeks later, under heavy pressure resulting in part from the vulnerability of his brother, who is a member of the armed forces, he pleaded guilty, was fined $3,000 and was released.

Charges of criminal libel were then lodged against candidates of the opposition Workers Party and the Barisan Socialist Party. J. B. Jeyaretnam, leader of the Workers Party, was charged with civil libel and his case is pending. On Feb. 10 the Government moved against Mr. Raman, the lawyer, and Mr. Senkuttuvan, both being held under the Internal Security Act, which allows indefinite detention without charges.

Within three weeks Mr. Raman began confessing to such activities as conspiring with so-called Eurocommunists to bring pressure on Mr. Lee to free scores of alleged Communists, many held without trial for years. Mr. Raman also named a number of people whom he said he had approached and who had indicated sympathy with such activities as formation of a human-rights committee, agitation against the Government and preparation of anti-Government news articles and commentary. The whole thing was officially described as "a diabolical international Communist plot."

Mr. Senkuttuvan and Mr. Raman went before nationwide television in a public confession and news conference. Mr. Senkuttuvan implicated The Fare Eastern Economic Review and its editor, Derek Davies, a Briton, in what he described as an intricate plot involving secret tapes that was designed to undermine relations between Singapore and its larger neighbor, Malaysia. The evidence was slim and, in any case, Mr. Davies issued an indignant denial.

At the same time security policemen arrested Mr. Ho again, taking him to his office in the hope of going through his papers and books in search of evidence on which to detain him. There they found J. D. F. Jones, managing editor of The Financial Times, who had flown from London to support Mr. Senkuttuvan, and Anthony Rowley, who had come to replace Mr. Ho on the Review. The policemen demanded to know who the two men were, ordered them to say nothing to Mr. Ho and rifled the office, seizing notebooks, a telephone-address book and various papers.

Nearly a month has passed since the arrest of Mr. Ho—who had contemplated leaving the country but decided he had no need for concern since he had paid his fine in the previous case—and no one has seen him except his mother, who was permitted a brief visit. Meanwhile, friends and associates, including his secretary, have been detained. One young woman, held for six hours and questioned repeatedly, said she had been placed in a cold room and allowed to shiver for more than an hour. When she complained, she related, she was told, "If you don't like this, there are other places we can take you."

Methods Is Termed Psychological

There is little evidence, however, that any brutality is used by the security police apart from this cold treatment, which a number of prisoners have reported. "It's all psychological," said a Western diplomat who has looked into the arrest and interrogation process. "They simply say: 'Look at these people who have been in here for 15 years. We are perfectly capable of keeping you, too, for 15 years if that is what you want and if you do not confess.' For someone like Ho, who is 24 and has a whole life ahead of him, or like Arun Senkuttuvan, who has a wife and children and no money, that's a powerful argument."

Mr. Senkuttuvan and Mr. Ho are unlikely to be held much longer. The Government has disclosed its intention to revoke Mr. Senkuttuvan's citizenship and expel him, making him a stateless person. Mr. Ho has reportedly signed a new confession, but what will happen to him on his release is less clear.

The effects of such actions have been profound. Although much of the population, particularly the educated English-speaking elite at whom a good part of the Government policy is aimed, appears anesthetized by the proliferation of televised confessions and recantations, the broader message has not been lost. "The effect has been to silence everyone," said Mr. Jeyaretnam, the Workers Party leader. "It will deter anyone from speaking out on anything. If I were to approach someone now and say, 'This is a key issue'—say human rights, for instance—'let's do something about it,' the answer I'd get is, 'No, no, it may be a Communist front.'"

Once-Vocal Priest Is Cautious

A year ago 145 Roman Catholic pirests signed an open letter to the Prime Minister, saying, "We fear that measures of an overpowerful and self-confident government would erode the very basis of our people's living—their value and dignity as persons." When a correspondent approached one of the more outspoken of the signers the other day, he said, "They don't like us to talk to the international press." He finally agreed to speak, very cautiously, about the arrests after opening the rectory door a crack to assure himself, he said later, that it was a foreigner knocking and not someone from the Internal Security Department.

The arrests will not affect his continuing comment on social issues from his pulpit, he said, but he conceded that he doubted whether there would be a human-rights movement in Singapore or any serious debate on social issues for some time, perhaps years. "I only hope that people will not stop thinking entirely," he added.

While the effects of the campaign of repression seem clear, its motivations are somewhat less so. Chinese political scientists—the Chinese are a big majority in Singapore—talk of the Prime Minister's continued need to assert his command of a situation in which he has always held command.

"The Government is seen to have fulfilled the basics of benevolent government—maintaining peace, prosperity and material development," wrote Dr. Chan Heng Chee, perhaps the leading independent political scientist in Singapore. "Whilst these conditions prevail, the population is not fundamentally opposed to the authoritarianism in the political system. In fact the entire Confucian tradition, laying great stress on the deference to authority and stressing filial piety, will probably stifle or curb the tendencies to display any aggressive opposition or the rejection of authority."

Others discern a continuing effort by Mr. Lee to prove that he is not simply cracking down indiscriminately on dissent but is reacting to a real threat of Communist subversion. "We are just a tiny place here," said Dr. Goh Keng Swee, Minister of Defense and one of the founding members of the governing party, in an interview. "If we do not look after our own security, if we do not stamp out Communism as it appears, who will do so for us?"

April 9, 1977

Malaysia's Ruling Coalition Wins, But Voting Shows Minority Unrest

Special to The New York Times

KUALA LUMPUR, Malaysia, July 9 — Malaysia's ruling National Front won a sweeping new five-year mandate in federal and state elections yesterday, but the opposition scored gains that appear to reflect the Chinese community's unhappiness over Government policies.

Yesterday's polling determined the composition of Malaysia's Parliament and 10 of its 13 state assemblies. As results trickled in today, the National Front seemed to be retaining control of all the states and leading by a wide margin in Parliament, capturing 98 of the 154 seats.

Acknowledging victory today, Prime Minister Datuk Hussein Onn, who dissloved Parliament more than a year before its term expired to seek a fresh mandate from the electorate, said the elections "prove Malaysia's commitment to democracy," he pledged to continue vigorous suppression of the country's small but persistent Communist insurgency, which he said was aiming "to destroy democracy."

The National Front, in addition to the seats it has already captured, was expected to keep most of the 36 parliamentary seats in East Malaysia, where final results from staggered elections will not be in until later this month.

Democratic Action Wins 15 Seats

In the results so far, the Democratic

Action Party, one of the two main opposition groups, won 15 seats, and the Islamic Party won 5. The two also captured a scattering of seats in state assemblies.

The Islamic Party, a right-wing organization, campaigning on a platform of Islamic fundamentalism and strident Malay nationalism, suffered at the polls, and its leader, Mohammed Asri, failed to win even one seat.

But the left-wing, Chinese-based Democratic Action Party, which advocates wide-ranging social and economic reforms, increased its strength in what observers here interpreted as a protest vote by the Chinese community.

The Chinese, who make up about 35 percent of Malaysia's multiracial population, are unhappy over the Government's long-term policy of transferring wealth, jobs and educational opportunity out of their hands to the ethnic Malays. But their electoral strength is limited because they are concentrated in a few urban areas.

Hundreds of voters throughout the capital and its suburbs lined up in the hot sun yesterday, waiting to cast their ballots in an impressive display of Southeast Asia's only functioning parliamentary democracy. The Government reported a turnout of more than 3.5 million, or over 70 percent of the eligible voters.

Police and security forces were placed on full alert in case of clashes between rival-party supporters or Communist attacks; but no incidents were reported. Voting was orderly, and was observed by the police, officials of the Election Commission and party representatives, but there seemed to be frequent cases in which voters' names failed to appear on the registers or were posted in the wrong district. Some opposition candidates charged that the Government had deliberately tampered with the electoral lists, but others believed inefficiency was to blame.

Western analysts described the balloting as fair and honest, but there was never any doubt about the National Front's ultimate victory.

The front, a coalition of parties representing the country's Malay, Chinese and Indian communities, which has governed Malaysia since it became independent from Britain in 1957, had access to unlimited funds and a well-run organizational apparatus far superior to the opposition.

July 10, 1978

Malaysia's Ethnic Fabric Is Beginning to Fray Again

By HENRY KAMM
Special to The New York Times

KUALA LUMPUR, Malaysia, March 14 — Strains are evident in Malaysia's delicately poised balance in which the Malays, who make up slightly less than half the population, hold political power, while the ethnic Chinese, nearly 40 percent of the people, remain economically dominant.

The strains have been there since this nation of 13 million gained independence from Britain in 1957 and then erupted into fighting in 1969. This led the Government to institute a 20-year program of affirmative action on behalf of the Malays.

But the present unease appears to be caused by growing Islamic militancy and by mounting frustration in the Chinese population over what Government officials call "positive discrimination" to raise the economic and educational level of the Malays.

The Government of Prime Minister Hussein Onn is responding by attempting to defuse Islamic extremism through measures emphasizing the status of Islam as "the religion of the Federation." In addition, the Government is using internal-security legislation to curb the spillover of fundamentalist religious agitation into politics.

New Economic Plan Is Pressed

Chinese dissatisfaction has been answered — or not answered — by stern Government insistence on applying its program to aid the Malays.

The key to the plan is the so-called New Economic Policy, enacted in 1970, that tries to give Malays 30 percent ownership of share equity in all Malaysian companies, heavy preference in public employment and puts pressure on private concerns to employ more Malays. The plan also includes a quota system for university entrance under which the present student population of Malaysia's six university-level institutions is 64 percent Malay.

The Government feels strongly that it can contain both pressures. "Say what you like, they won't get anywhere as long as we stay around," said Home Affairs Minister Muhammad Ghazali bin Shafie in an interview. "And we are going to stay around."

Mr. Ghazali is one of the principal architects of the New Economic Policy, whose purpose, he said, "is to blunt the edges of intercommunal relations."

"We did foresee that in implementing the policies there will be unhappiness," he continued. "If we are dextrous enough, it will pass over."

Chinese Got a Head Start

The Government's case for its "positive discrimination" is that independence found Malaysia with a population of Malays that was largely employed in subsistence agriculture and menial work, whereas the Chinese, an immigrant population of the late 19th and early 20th centuries, controlled most of the cash economy and urban employment.

Their head start in the modern sector of the economy and in education, in the Government's view, gave the Chinese a disproportionate advantage in the economic development that followed independence and led to the 1969 explosion.

The Government's view, which is not publicly expressed, is that the wave of Islamic revivalism poses a more immediate threat, presumably because its focus is the Malay establishment itself and its solid political control, exercised through the leading political party, the United Malay National Organization.

The Government also fears that fundamentalism would jeopardize its economic development efforts.

Security Act Is Extended

The Internal Security Act outlaws political activity that the Government consid-

337

ers subversive. The law was originally intended to combat the threat of the illegal, and largely Chinese, Communist Party of Malaya, which was defeated during years of jungle warfare from 1945 to 1960.

Now the law serves to restrict open Moslem pressure in the religious and educational fields. It also makes Moslem spokesmen extremely prudent on internal matters. "My movement is the Moslem youth movement of Malaysia," said Anwar Ibrahim, the principal leader of the Islamic revival. "We can't call it otherwise. But our members are not entirely youths. Some are in their 40's and 50's."

Mr. Anwar, who is 33 years old and who spent two years in detention under the Internal Security Act, has found a wide echo for his movement's charges of widespread corruption and exploitation of the poor of all ethnic groups. In addition to Malays and Chinese, Malaysia has sizable communities of Indians, aborigines and tribal people in the two Borneo states of Sarawak and Sabah.

Unable to press for an Islamic nation and the general application of Koranic law, Mr. Anwar limits himself in public to praise of the Iranian revolution and admiration of Ayatollah Ruhollah Khomeini. In an interview, he said that he approved of the seizing of the American Embassy, but when asked about the holding of the embassy staff as hostages, Mr. Anwar said, "I do not approve, but I'm not ready to condemn."

Criticism Is Restrained

The Government is also hampered in its public comments because of a fear that any criticism would be used against it as an expression of anti-Islamic sentiment. It limits itself to reminders that lack of economic progress and national disunity are threats not only to Malaysia but also to Islam.

"So do not impede progress if you wish Islam to be permanent," Malaysia's elected King said in a speech prepared for him by the Government.

In all political sectors — pro-Government and opposition Moslems and Chinese — there is agreement that the present strains represent no immediate danger in view of Malaysia's prosperity. As the world's leading producer of natural rubber and tin, as well as sizable exports of oil, palm oil and lumber, Malaysia benefits from high world prices for all its commodities.

Exports Aided by Oil Prices

Its rubber and tin exports are aided by the fact that high oil prices help both commodities. Oil is the principal ingredient in the chief competitors of rubber and tin — synthetic rubber and plastic, and aluminum, whose smelting requires large amounts of energy. Malaysia's per capita gross national product is $1,500, which puts it near Singapore, Taiwan and South Korea, the strongest economies among developing Asian countries.

The hopes of the Chinese community, despite deep resentment over the educational limitations for their young people, lie in what they often refer to as "a growing economic cake." Despite official favoritism in business and employment for Malays, they have more than held their own economically and are convinced they can continue to do so as long as the cake gets bigger.

March 20, 1980

BURMA EMERGES FROM ISOLATION

Buddhism Retaining Its Hold in Burma

By BERNARD WEINRAUB
Special to The New York Times

PAGAN, Burma, Sept. 12 —This city of ruins is where the Burmese empire flourished, where an 11th-century King brought Buddhist monks to the arid plain to convert the spirit worshipers and animists. It is the city where craftsmen, buoyed by religious fervor, built brick and stucco temples and pagodas and monasteries covering 16 square miles.

The empire is gone now, and the fervor of Burmese Socialist leaders is more political than religious. Though official encouragement is scant and there is hostility between the ruling Burmese Revolutionary Council and the Buddhist monks, the religion that embodies the timeless quest for truth and inner peace is quietly flourishing in this central Burmese city as well as its neighbor, Mandalay, a hundred miles to the northeast.

A Government spokesman in Rangoon said: "We are a secular state and we will keep it this way. Our policy about religion is to keep it separate from the state, not to mix it with politics. We had trouble before, under the old regime, because of this."

After Burma became independent of Britain in 1948 she was in the hands of Prime Minister Nu, whose popularity was attributed to the common belief that he was a good Buddhist.

Under U Nu the religion flourished. The care of pagodas improved. The Sixth Great Buddhist Council was held in Rangoon from 1954 to 1956. Burma was on the brink of becoming the acknowledged center of the Buddhist world. Mr. Nu, leaning heavily on Buddhism to bolster his leadership, sought to make it the state religion.

Although it may have pleased the majority — about 85 per cent of the country is Buddhist — many of the hill tribesmen are Christian or animist, and they saw the move as a step toward domination.

The military coup in 1962 by General Ne Win, himself a nominal Buddhist, and the emergence of a Marxist "revolutionary government" resulted in a strong effort to break the power and influence of the Buddhist monks.

Viewing them as a potential threat to his rule, General Ne Win rounded up more than 200 politically active ones, sought to discredit the clergy with charges of corruption and sexual immorality — some were allegedly found in brothels — and ordered all organizations, including religious ones, to register with the Government.

The tension that prevailed in 1965, when monks branded the Government as antireligious and urged its overthrow, eventually dissolved as the army smothered Buddhist opposition. An undisclosed number of monks remain in prison, but the hostility between the Government and the monks has waned.

Now, especially in the dusty ancient city of Pagan, beside the Irrawaddy River, as well as in Mandalay, the last capital of the Burmese kings, Buddhism remains a powerful, deeply embedded force. On holidays thousands of Burmese pour into Pagan and trudge to the crumbling stupas and pagodas, the remains of 5,000 of which can be traced.

Many of the monuments, initiated by King Anawratha,

The New York Times/Sept. 24, 1973

are in decay and there are snakes in some. But the Burmese slip into the pagodas and stare at the stucco images of Buddha and medi-

tate in silence and then walk away, inevitably dropping some money in collection boxes marked for donations for gilding, electricity, pavement and general use.

The Government's economic policies may eventually have more impact on the monks than General Ne Win's political programs. Because the economy is in disarray, monks near Mandalay are finding that the daily alms of fruits, vegetables and rice offered along the road are dwindling. The donated orange and yellow cloth for the monks' robes invariably comes from the black market.

In Mandalay, the center of Burma's main monastic order, the number of monks is believed to have dropped from

15,000 to 10,000, although some have settled in villages.

The aged in central Burma still sell their homes and move into monasteries for final solace. Nuns in orange robes and with shaved heads still sit inert on pagoda steps with tin cups and barely flicker their eyes as strangers give them coins. And boys of 10 and 11 still appear at monasteries for a two-to-three-week coming-of-age ceremony in which they wash the shrine of Buddha each morning and chant: "To refrain from all evil, to do what is good, to purify the mind—this is the teaching of the Buddhas."

September 24, 1973

U Thant As a Symbol

In the 10 years he was Secretary General of the United Nations, U Thant was a conciliator. But in death he has become a symbol in his homeland, Burma, of the political divisions there.

Because Mr. Thant had been an ally of former Premier U Nu, deposed in 1962 as he sought to make Buddhism Burma's state religion, the present Government led by President Ne Win had planned little ceremony when Mr. Thant's body was returned to Rangoon; Mr. Thant died of cancer in New York Nov. 25.

The public was barred from the airport and burial was planned for a public cemetery. His family had instead sought burial near Rangoon's holiest shrine, the golden-spired Shwe Dagon pagoda.

But the body was seized by part of a mob of between 30,000 to 50,000 students and Buddhist monks. They took it to Rangoon University and placed it in a hastily constructed mausoleum.

December 15, 1974

70,000 Burmese Moslems Said to Flee to Bangladesh

DACCA, Bangladesh, April 30 (Reuters) —Official sources said here today that about 70,000 fleeing Burmese Moslems had crossed the border into Bangladesh in the last three weeks.

More than 18,000 were estimated to have come across in the last 24 hours despite efforts by Bangladesh forces to seal the 150-mile border, the sources said, adding that soldiers had been given orders to turn back illegal immigrants.

Many more Moslems were reported to be hiding in the jungle on the Bur side of the frontier, waiting to cross the Naf River, which cuts across the northwest border of Burma, the sources said. They said people who were turned back when they tried to enter Bangladesh were returning saying that Burmese Army soldiers had fired at them.

The Moslem refugees brought tales of torture, rape and robbery at the hands of Burmese forces, who they alleged drove them from their homes at gunpoint. One refugee asserted that the army had launched an operation to clear the border area of the Moslem community that was not originally Burmese.

RANGOON, Burma, April 30 (Reuters)— The Burmese Government said today that all those fleeing were Bengalis who wanted to escape from officials investigating

The New York Times/April 30, 1978

Refugee account said many fled area of Buthidaung, in northwestern Burma, to Bangladeshi camp near Teknaf.

illegal immigration. The official Burmese press agency said the Bengalis had fled because they lacked proper entry or registration papers.

May 1, 1978

Burma, Long Isolationist, Is Looking Abroad for Aid

By JAMES P. STERBA
Special to The New York Times

RANGOON, Burma — Burma, like a turtle, poked a little farther out of its isolationist shell in recent weeks, taking a few more halting steps along the development path that neighboring Southeast Asian nations sprinted down years ago.

After nearly two decades of socialism

managed by the army and largely unblessed by progress, President Ne Win's Government committed itself in April to accept sharply increased foreign aid from capitalist nations. And after a 17-year break, it has again sought aid from the United States, which hopes to finance a modest program this fall.

Burma's moves, which diplomats here attribute more to economic desperation

than to a willingness to join the global economic community, have been augmented by a call for selected private foreign investment, long avoided except in exploration for offshore oil.

Apparently feeling secure politically, the 68-year-old President, who as a general seized power in 1962, has eased police-state restrictions on everyday associations with foreigners, although the sl...htest criticism of his rule can still ...use arrests in the night by the military police.

On Better Terms With Neighbors

The Government has continued to improve relations with its neighbors. In mid-May, it agreed to exchange intelligence with Thailand on opium and heroin trafficking; on a state visit to Dacca late in May, the President signed a border demarcation agreement with Bangladesh and reportedly agreed to sell it 100,000 tons of rice on credit.

Since Burma grabbed an aid lifeline offered by a World Bank consortium of donor nations three years ago, it has begun to halt its economic disintegration, although most of its 34 million people continue to live in harsh poverty. At less than $140 a year, Burma's gross national product per capita is among Asia's lowest.

"I would say the economy has now improved to the point of mere stagnation," said a European diplomat. "It's really quite a feat to have failed so miserably for so long with a nation so rich in resources and talent, and Ne Win deserves full credit. Now things are improving a bit, but I do not think it is possible to underestimate the pace of future improvements."

In its latest confidential report, the World Bank was more charitable. Gross national product, mostly from rice farming and raw materials, grew at nearly 5 percent annually in the last four years, compared to less than half that rate in the previous decade. Major changes will take a long time, the report said, adding, "Nevertheless, the economic deterioration has been arrested and the process to resuscitate the economy is now under way."

Diplomatic sources attribute much of the improvement to the Government's new willingness to take elementary economic advice from the World Bank and the Asian Development Bank and to follow guidelines imposed by the International Monetary Fund. Last year, for example, it agreed to stop giving interest-free funds to state corporations, which run all but the smallest businesses. Now, instead of this subsidy, they must borrow on commercial terms from a Government bank.

"It is too early to tell whether this reform will increase the efficiency of the state enterprises, but it will at least provide a yardstick for evaluating their operations," said the latest economic survey issued by the United States Embassy.

Burma has many highly qualified economists who could have made similar recommendations. But under the rule of President Ne Win and his aides, suggestions from the ranks have long been considered criticisms, and those making them have often found themselves instantly unemployed.

The aid consortium, made up of the World Bank, the Monetary Fund, the United Nations Development Program, Japan, West Germany, Australia, France, Britain, the United States and Canada, held its third meeting since 1976 in April in Tokyo. There, Burmese officials solicited about $400 million in loans and grants for development projects, which donor nations agreed to without making specific pledges.

Private Investment Invited

Burmese officials also stressed their interest in private investments, first proposed privately last year for projects involving "mutually beneficial economic cooperation," the Burmese expression

The New York Times / James P. Sterba

Ancient pagodas rise in the center of Rangoon, Burma's capital

for joint ventures.

Citing guarantees against nationalization and for repatriation of profits and contract renewals, Burma's Finance Minister said his Government was ready to entertain proposals from private companies in such areas as fishing and seafood processing, forestry, mining, wood pulp and paper making, and agriculture and food processing. Much of Burma's natural wealth is now being exploited by smugglers.

In the last year, Government officials have met privately with a few foreign companies, mostly from Japan but including one American food-processor. Unlike neighboring countries, however, Burma has so far made no effort to solicit investments directly from companies and previous unsolicited offers have languished.

The main problem, according to knowledgeable Burmese and foreigners, it that President Ne Win refuses to delegate authority for even the smallest decisions having to do with the outside world. Even members of foreign-aid teams involved in development projects have to wait for weeks for Cabinet-level approval of travel plans.

Still, some minor progress has been made. Burmese who left the country before President Ne Win seized power and were treated as traitors are now allowed to visit, although they continue to be barred from returning to Burma to live.

Cultural exchanges have increased. The Government, interested in introducing television, sent an official to the

United States to study the field. And a Burmese employee at the American Embassy was recently allowed to go to the United States for a brief orientation, the first such visit in 16 years.

Government officials and other Burmese citizens have become less fearful of associating with foreigners, although officials must still get permission to accept dinner invitations to foreigners' homes and must write reports afterward.

"Three years ago, I would invite 15 Burmese to dinner or a party and only four or five would show up," said a Western diplomat. "Now most of them come."

With foreign help, Burma also recently established a ground station to send and receive long-distance telephone calls by satellite.

The Government is also reportedly moving to increase tourism to earn badly needed foreign exchange. Tourists are allowed only a one-week visit. Officials are said to have agreed to allow two-week stays, but have not put the decision into effect.

Also reportedly approved but not carried out is a decision to allow direct international flights from Bangkok, Calcutta, and Kunming, China, to Pagan, site of the ruins of Burma's ancient royal city. Although Burma is woefully unequipped to handle large numbers of tourists, offers from private foreign companies to build hotels and train managers and workers have gone without response.

June 14, 1979

INDONESIA TURNS TO THE RIGHT

INDONESIA SAYS PLOT TO DEPOSE SUKARNO IS FOILED BY ARMY CHIEF; POWER FIGHT BELIEVED CONTINUING

REBEL CAPTURED

Radio Says Nasution Saved Regime—Some Clashes Reported

By SETH S. KING
Special to The New York Times.

KUALA LUMPUR, Malaysia, Oct. 1—An attempt to overthrow President Sukarno was foiled tonight by army units loyal to Gen. Abdul Haris Nasution, the Indonesian radio announced.

It said troops of the crack Siliwangi Division had captured Lieut. Col. Untang, a commander in Dr. Sukarno's palace guard.

[In Washington, a State Department spokesman said Friday the situation in Indonesia was "extremely fluid, even confused." Robert J. McCloskey told a news conference the State Department was getting reports from the American Embassy at Jakarta, but "it is not presently possible to attempt any evaluation, explanation or comment."]

Late yesterday, a mysterious group calling itself the 30th of September Movement seized control of Jakarta.

Colonel Untang, who had announced over the Indonesian radio that he was the leader of the movement, said the group had seized control of the Government to prevent a "counter-revolutionary" coup by a Generals' Council.

General Backs Sukarno

General Nasution was quoted by the radio tonight as having denied that there had ever been a plan by the armed forces to depose President Sukarno.

With all communications with Indonesia cut except for the national radio, it was difficult for observers here to be certain what had happened in the confused 24-hour period beginning yesterday.

Keystone, Associated Press

TURMOIL IN INDONESIA: Armed forces loyal to Gen. Abdul Haris Nasution, right, are reported to have overthrown leaders of a plot directed against President Sukarno, left.

The Indonesian radio said tonight that units of the crack Siliwangi Division, which had been moved into Jakarta earlier this week to participate in an Armed Forces Day parade, had fought Colonel Untang's forces for control of strategic points in the capital.

In a special bulletin broadcast at 11 P.M., the Malaysia radio reported that Lieut. Gen. Ahmad Yani, the Indonesian Chief of Staff, had been killed by coup forces and that General Nasution had been wounded. The radio did not give its sources for this.

Struggle for Control

While it appeared that anti-Communist leaders of the army had regained control of Jakarta and that Dr. Sukarno had survived another attempt to remove him, the struggle for control of the floundering Government appeared to be continuing.

The Jakarta radio said at midnight that the Communist coup leader had inserted many names in his Cabinet list without knowledge of the individuals named. The radio said a number of lower-ranked military officers listed in the

rebel Cabinet were actually loyal to the Nasution forces.

Radio monitors here later reported hearing a broadcast from Surabaya, the large seaport in East Java, which announced that a Col. Suhirman, commander of army units in Semarang, Central Java, was supporting Colonel Untang.

Reds' Role Uncertain

There was still no indication of the role Indonesia's powerful Communist party played in the attempt to overthrow Dr. Sukarno.

The only mention of Communist officials was in a broadcast earlier today by the Untang group in which several minor members of the party were named in a 45-man Cabinet appointed by the 30th of September group.

If the Communists had accepted these posts, it would appear that they had supported the Untang movement. But there was no report here on the stand of D.N. Aidit, leader of the three-million-member Communist party.

Observers here noted that Dr. Subandrio, Deputy Premier and Foreign Minister, was named as a member of the 30th of September Cabinet. If he is shown to have been with

the rebels it will mean a drastic split in Dr. Sukarno's inner circle.

The Indonesian President has sought to preserve unity among Indonesia's divergent political factions through a "Nasakom" Government. The word is a contraction of the symbols for 60 nationalist, religious and Communist elements.

General Nasution has always been identified as a devout Moslem and anti-Communist. He led the Indonesian forces that put a bloody end to the Communist rebelion at Madiun in 1948. General Nasution tried in 1952 to force Dr. Sukarno to dissolve Parliament and

ch ck the drift of the Government to the left.

Observers here had been puzzled by the Indonesia radio's statement earlier today that the generals who allegedly planned the coup against Dr. Sukarno believed that the Indonesian leader had been in poor health since the first week in August.

After charging that these generals were sponsored by the United States Central Intelligence Agency, the broadcast said they had believed Dr. Sukarno would soon die.

"Their reasoning on this was not startling." the broadcast declared.

Yet President Sukarno has made many public appearances since Aug. 1. There have been no reports here to suggest that his health was any more fragile now than it had been in the past, when he was treated for a kidney ailment.

Dr. Sukarno apparently had not been seen publicly in the past two days, But on Monday night, he appeared with Dr. Subandrio at a Peasants' Day rally. In a speech he conceded that the Government could not force a halt in spiraling food prices.

October 2, 1965

OFFICES OF REDS RAZED IN JAKARTA BY MOSLEM MOB

Youths Shout 'Long Live America' as They Burn One-Story Building

SOLDIERS ARE HAILED

Army Does Not Interfere as Demonstrators Move in Indonesian Capital

JAKARTA, Oct. 8 (UPI)— Thousands of Moslem youths shouting "Long live America" stormed the headquarters of Indonesia's powerful Communist party (P.K.I.) today and burned it to the ground.

Informed sources said the armed forces had begun a quiet but systematic purge of Communists in its own ranks.

with an unpublicized series of arrests and summary executions.

The Communists were being openly blamed for aiding in the attempted coup against President Sukarno last Friday. The murder of six generals and a lieutenant by the rebels provoked tension.

Sukarno Was Adamant

President Sukarno had refused to bow to rising demands that he ban the P.K.I. Its three million members make it the largest Communist party outside the Soviet Union.

Mr. Sukarno had forged close links with Peking and had done nothing when mobs of Communist youths stormed through the streets of Jarkata and other Indonesian cities burning and attacking American buildings and libraries.

Throughout the past week, anti-Communist feeling has risen in this Moslem state and there have been mass demonstrations in Jakarta and other cities.

The military put heavy pressure on President Sukarno to ban the P.K.I. but at a Cabinet meeting on Wednesday he sat with two Communist Cabinet members. Notably absent was Gen. Abdul Haris Nasution, the stanchly anti-Communist De-

fense Minister, who was wounded by the rebels in an assassination attempt.

Feelings Reach Climax

The anti-Communist feeling reached a climax when the mobs of youths attacked the one-story Communist party building.

The demonstrators stormed the building with shouts of "Kill Aidit" and "Dissolve the P.K.I." D.N. Aidit is leader of the party. His whereabouts were unknown.

After setting fire to the Communist headquarters, the youths paraded through the streets of Jakarta to the headquarters of the Government-sponsored National Front organizations. On the way, they stopped cars and plastered windshield with signs reading "Crush P.K.I."

Demonstrators waved and shook hands with soldiers who passed by in a truck.

It was the army that broke the back of the coup led by Lieut. Col. Untung, a palace guard officer who masterminded the "30th of September Movement" to overthrow President Sukarno and replace his Government with a leftist "Revolutionary Council. "

Army Accused Youths

The army command here accused the youth wing of the

P.K.I. of murdering the six generals and a lieutenant in the early stages of the coup attempt. The army has launched a massive anti-Communist campaign, rounding up scores of P.K.I. members and seizing large quantities of weapons, some bearing Communist Chinese markings.

Army troops did not interfere with the demonstrators today, but streets leading to P.K.I. headquarters were cordoned off. Three fire trucks at the scene poured water on the ashes after the fire had leveled the building.

Truckloads of demonstrators passed later in front of the United States Embassy on the same street shouting "Long live America."

It was a sharp contrast to previous demonstrations in this capital, all of which have been Communist-inspired and directed against the United States. The pro-American slogans were the first heard in Jakarta for many months.

Most of the demonstrators belonged to Anso, the youth wing of the Moslem political party. First demands for the dissolution of the P.K.I. were made here last Sunday by the Moslems.

October 9, 1965

Associated Press
Major General Suharto

JAKARTA LEFTIST OUT AS ARMY CHIEF

Sukarno Announces Choice of Anti-Red Commander, a Foe of Coup Leaders

Special to The New York Times
SINGAPORE, Oct. 14—Command of the Indonesian Army was withdrawn from a leftist general tonight and given to an anti-Communist, Major General Suharto, who crushed the at-

tempted coup d'état against President Sukarno on Oct. 1.

President Sukarno said over the Jakarta radio that General Suharto would replace Maj. Gen. Pranoto Reksosamudro, the leftist he appointed immediately after the abortive coup. General Pranoto's next assignment was not announced.

The President said General Suharto would be made a Cabinet minister in addition to succeeding the army chief, Lieut. Gen. Achmad Yani, one of six anti-Communist generals killed by the rebels.

General Suharto, 44-year-old former commander of the army's strategic reserve, has

been field commander of the army forces carrying out an anti-Communist drive under the Defense Minister, Gen. Abdul Haris Nasution.

In effect, General Suharto, a tough and able soldier, has led the army since the coup attempt, for General Pranoto has hardly been heard from. Western diplomatic sources in touch with Jakarta said General Nasution had given General Pranoto a back seat and had persuaded President Sukarno to name the new chief of staff.

October 15, 1965

INDONESIANS BURN A CHINESE SCHOOL

One Student Reported Killed and 200 Hurt in Battle at Jakarta University

Special to The New York Times

SINGAPORE, Oct. 15 — A Chinese university was burned and one student was reported killed and more than 200 injured in Jakarta yesterday.

It was the worst violence in a wave of anti-Peking sentiment sweeping Indonesia since an attempted coup d'état two weeks ago.

Republika University was destroyed in a two-hour melee marked by hand-to-hand fighting between Moslem youths and Chinese students, according to reports received here.

Scores of policemen were unable to stop the brawl. The police fired into the two-story building with machine guns for 20 minutes. They said that Chinese students inside the building had started the shooting.

Campus Like Battlefield

About 60 students and 600 attackers fought with broken furniture, bottles, sticks and knives until the campus resembled a battle scene, with the flaming university in the background. One of the students was reported beaten to death.

Earlier young Moslems gathered outside Communist China's Embassy in Jakarta and screamed "Crush China!"

Anti-Chinese feeling has risen steadily in the last few days as the army-controlled press and radio have vigorously accused Peking and the pro-Chinese Indonesian Communist party of a role in the attempt at a coup against President Sukarno.

Fights between Moslems and Chinese have been reported in several parts of Indonesia, Chinese shops have been ransacked in villages and a Jakarta shopping district with many Chinese merchants has been closed to vehicular traffic for fear of bombings.

October 16, 1965

Indonesians Strip Reds in Parliament Of Their Functions

By The Associated Press

JAKARTA, Indonesia, Nov. 5 —The People's Consultative Assembly, Indonesia's highest legislative body, has stripped Communist members of their parliamentary functions.

The Third Deputy Premier, Chairul Saleh, said tonight that this did not as yet constitute a formal ouster of the Communists from the Assembly because such a step could be taken only by President Sukarno.

The action included the Communist party chief, D. N. Aidit, a member of the Assembly.

The legislature's action was made known as the army-controlled newspaper Api said the Government was drafting a decree banning the Indonesian Communist party.

President Sukarno has been under increasing army pressure to ban the party, but so far has resisted it. The army has suspended the Communists' political activities but wants a formal ban.

The official news agency, Antara, also under army control, reported statements were coming in from organizations all over Indonesia demanding that the Communist party and its affiliates be dissolved.

November 6, 1965

SUKARNO YIELDS POWERS TO ARMY TO CURB UNREST; COMMUNIST PARTY BANNED

TROOPS ACCLAIMED

Jakarta Is Reported Calm—President to Retain His Title

By Reuters

JAKARTA, Indonesia, Saturday, March 12—Army leaders under Lieut. Gen. Suharto staged a peaceful take-over of power in Indonesia today after all-night talks with President Sukarno lasting into the early hours.

Crack troops and paracommandos moved into the city and took up positions under cover of the predawn darkness. The moves followed days of mounting unrest by students engaged in anti-Communist demonstrations.

Early this morning the Jakarta radio announced that President Sukarno had transferred his powers to General Suharto.

The army's orders were being issued in the name of President Sukarno and he was evidently keeping the formal title of the office.

Victory Parade Held

Heavy armor and armed troops of the Indonesian Army held a massive victory parade today, wildly cheered by hundreds of thousands of students and citizens.

While the parade was going on General Suharto issued in President Sukarno's name a decree banning the Indonesian Communist party.

The ban applied to the party and its affiliates.

General Suharto ordered "immediate, precise and correct" action against the Communists. He said this was necessary because remnants of the Sept. 30 Movement, which staged the abortive coup d'etat last fall, were still active.

The order said that the Communists were conducting underground activities, including slander, aggravation, threats, rumors and armed activity, which seriously threatened the peoples' peace and security.

Grave Threat Seen

General Suharto said the party's underground activities posed a grave threat to the Indonesian Revolution in general and prevented it from continuing its course, especially in the economic field and in crushing Malaysia.

A particular target of the sweeping moves by General Suharto and the army leadership has been Foreign Minister Subandrio, who has shown strong leanings toward Communist Chinese policies.

The political fate of the unpopular Ministers, Dr. Subandrio and the Minister of Basic Education, Dr. Sumardjo, was not yet known officially.

Unofficial reports said the pro-Communist Ministers were already in army custody.

General Suharto is expected to announce a new Cabinet shortly.

March 12, 1966

INDONESIANS STRIP SUKARNO OF TITLE AS LIFE PRESIDENT

Congress Also Forbids Him to Issue More Decrees— Suharto to Form Cabinet

Special to The New York Times

JAKARTA, Indonesia, July 5 — The People's Consultative Congress today stripped President Sukarno of his title of President for Life.

It also authorized Lieutenant General Suharto to form a new Cabinet by Aug. 17, 21 years after Mr. Sukarno declared Indonesia's independence from the Netherlands.

Those decisions highlighted a series of resolutions unanimously adopted by the Congress, Indonesia's highest policy-making body, after a week of closed-door debates on issues facing the country.

In a "political note" to Parliament, the Congress stated that Indonesia should return to the United Nations, which President Sukarno abandoned early last year.

Malaysian Accord Urged

The note stated that Indonesia could press for reform in the world organization "more effectively from within than from outside."

The Congress also welcomed "any steps" toward solving Indonesia's dispute with Malaysia, the object of President Sukarno's policy of military and political confrontation for nearly three years.

The note to Parliament stated that the dispute with Malaysia should be settled according to the Manila agreement of 1963 between Malaysia, Indonesia and the Philippines.

Tonight President Sukarno, smiling and genial, attended an Algerian Independence Day party given by the Algerian Ambassador and declared: "I am the happiest man in the world."

Freedom a 'Deathless Cause'

The President attributed his happiness to the fact that he was honoring a country whose struggle for independence he had both "supported and admired."

He did not comment on today's resolutions by the Congress but in a brief statement referred to his speech before it 13 days ago.

"As I told our super-Congress, the cause of freedom is a deathless cause," he said. "The Algerian people have sacrificed much to this cause."

Seated at the same table with the President during dinner were two of the men who have done the most to upset his policies—Adam Malik, Deputy Premier for Social and Political Affairs and Foreign Minister, and Sultan Hamengku Buwono, Deputy Premier for Economic Affairs.

During the dinner the President chatted smilingly with various student leaders who have advocated the withdrawal of his titles and the formation of a new Cabinet devoid of any of his old allies.

The Congress will formally present its findings tomorrow to President Sukarno, who had fought vigorously to maintain his waning power and prestige.

Relegating President Sukarno to a figurehead role, the Congress ruled that he could no longer issue decrees. It ordered a review of all his decrees and regulations since July 5, 1959, when he reinstated Indonesia's 1945 Constitution.

The Congress also ordered a review of all laws adopted by Parliament and authorized the establishment of a commission "to reconsider all teachings inconsistent with the Constitution."

The commission was expected to act directly against President Sukarno's concept of Nasakom, a blending of nationalism, religion and Communism.

In an attempt to stamp out the last remnants of Communist influence in Indonesian life, the Congress adopted a controversial resolution banning the spread of Communist ideology, Marxism or Leninism anywhere in Indonesia.

The Communist party of Indonesia, responsible for last October's attempted coup d'état in which six generals were killed, was outlawed last March 11. In the purge that followed as many as 300,000 Communists may have been killed.

The Congress strengthened the position of General Suharto, to whom President Sukarno was forced to transfer authority March 11, by authorizing him to serve as "acting President" in case Mr. Sukarno is ill or out of the country.

The Congress on June 21 unanimously voted to extend President Sukarno's March 11 decree until a general election for a new Congress and Parliament.

July 6, 1966

Slaughter of Reds Gives Indonesia a Grim Legacy

By SEYMOUR TOPPING
Special to The New York Times

JAKARTA, Indonesia—From the terraced rice fields of Central Java to the exquisite island of Bali, from the rubber plantations of Sumatra to the fishing villages of remote Timor, the Indonesian people are troubled by the heritage of violence bequeathed by the staggering mass slaughter of Communists.

The killings of uncounted thousands of Communists in an orgy of reprisals and blood lust have left subsurface tensions among Indonesians that may not be eased for generations. The number of Indonesians who wait silently to collect blood debts is incalculable.

No one will ever know how many thousands of members of the Indonesian Communist party, their sympathizers and families and falsely accused persons died in retaliation for the abortive Communist-supported bid for greater power in Jakarta Sept. 30. The best-informed sources estimate 150,000 to 400,000, but they concede that the total could be far more than half a million. The killings still go on in some places.

The jails are jammed with people charged by the army with association with the Communist party. Major General Sugiharto, the Attorney General, says he hopes to release about 120,000 detainees by the end of the year. No legal machinery has been set up to try the prisoners, many of whom are living in overcrowded cells on bare subsistence rations.

In Central Java, at Solo, a former Communist stronghold, Lieutenant Colonel Wibhawa, the deputy commander of the Fourth Brigade, illustrated the problem. He said that in his region alone 10,000 people had been arrested "who are guilty and will be turned over to justice when legal facilities become available." He added: "We are still mopping up."

At some centers, such as Salatiga, not far from Solo, the military execution without trial of selected Communists is continuing. Uncontrolled communal killing by the population persists in some rural areas.

There has been no international intervention on behalf of political prisoners apart from

The New York Times (by Seymour Topping)

Bridge over the Brantas River in Kediri was one of many execution spots. The prisoners were slashed and hurled into the river, where they were left to bleed to death.

some private soundings in Jakarta by special delegates of Amnesty International, a humanitarian organization of lawyers, and the International Red Cross.

Soviet-bloc diplomats have pointedly told Foreign Minister Adam Malik that an issue of human rights is involved and that he should keep that in mind as his Government seeks

Haj Markus Ali, a Moslem leader, outside the school in Kediri where he lives. Some of the youths with him participated in last year's mass extermination of Communists.

re-entry into the United Nations. Western diplomats, unwilling to be charged by the sensitive Indonesians with interference in their affairs, have discussed the humanitarian aspects privately with Government officials without making any formal representations.

The brutality began on the night of Sept. 30 with the murder and mutilation by Communist youth squads of six senior right-wing generals. When the Communist uprising in Jakarta was foiled, a nationwide retaliatory purge of Communists began. It has engendered habits of violence in the Indonesian countryside.

In the Banyumas region of South Central Java, political killings have evolved into guerrilla class warfare, with youth gangs attacking adults, debtors eliminating creditors, and tenants taking revenge on landlords.

Army leaders say that most of the killing of Communists was done by the aroused population. On a tour of the principal former centers of Communist political influence, this reporter found that the executions were usually carried out by the military in Central Java and that the people in East Java and in Bali were incited by the army and the police to kill.

The military executed Communists by shooting, but the population was left to behead the victims or disembowel them with knives, swords and bamboo spears, often with ritual forms of extreme cruelty.

Foreigners who have lived in Indonesia for decades and been charmed by the gentle manners of the people, especially the placid dwellers on Bali, are at a loss to explain the explosion of violence when the army and police let down the bars.

Some say that the population, inflamed by highly colored stories of sexual mutilation of the slain generals, displayed what is considered a Malay tendency toward orgiastic violence. "There is a devil in us and when it gets loose, we can run amok en masse," one of Indonesia's most distinguished writers said, recalling his own moments of blood-anger.

One American scholar has suggested a Malthusian motivation—that the population on Java had been impelled to kill because of economic pressures, especially the shortage of land, which generates growing competition for subsistence.

The big island of Java is picturesque with emerald-green rice paddies, stands of banyan trees and 700 volcanic mountains that are often shrouded in mist. But two-thirds of Indonesia's population of 107,000,000 live on the crowded island, which constitutes only 7 per cent of the country's territory.

Survival Called Motive

Many of the Indonesians who participated in the killings justify their acts by saying, "It was them or us."

In most Indonesian cities and big towns, one is told that mass graves were dug by the Communists before Sept. 30 to receive the victims of an impending coup d'état. It is said that lists were seized in Communist party files naming army officers, religious leaders, foreign missionaries and local officials who were to be executed. Boxes of eye pluckers to be used in the torture of prisoners are also said to have been found in the possession of the Communists.

Most experienced observers believe that the stories have been spun out of a need to rationalize the mass killings. There is no substantial evidence that the Communists had large supplies of weapons or were planning a mass nationwide uprising to seize total power in the near future.

It is only at the places of the killings that one begins to ascertain specific motivations for the execution of Communists and the murder of neighbors.

On the idyllic island of Bali, the smell of death is gone from the villages with the red stone Hindu shrines, and the people go out once again to fish in the sea where not long ago hundreds of bodies floated on the waters, torn at by the sea creatures.

The maiden dancers, their black tresses plaited with fragrant white blossoms, dance entrancingly to the drums and gongs of the gamelin orchestras, and throw petals of hibiscus to the occasional visitor. The Balinese smile gently and declare that the terrible happenings were a "family affair" and best forgotten, and that they hope the American tourists will come back again, now

that the Communists are no more.

Yet the wounds are there, concealed amid the beauty. The prisons in Denpasar still are crowded. It is easy to rent a house in Bali now, because many were used by the army as depots for the roundup and execution of Communists, and the people will not live in them because they fear unexorcised spirits. In Negara, there is one house where 300 Communists are said to have been shot. The well in the garden is still stuffed with the bodies of 15.

Many of the children whisper about the fate of their teachers. About 2,000 teachers are said to have died in the purge. Most of the island's teachers, unable to live for even two weeks on their monthly pay because of inflation, had joined Communist organizations to seek relief from poverty.

No one knows precisely how many men, women and children were slain on beautiful Bali. Estimates range from 20,000 to 100,000. Foreigners who live on the island are convinced that about 50,000 of the population of 2,000,000 were killed. The army began the roundup of Communist party members at the end of October. The mass killing began in mid-November and continued until mid-January.

Parwanto, the prosecuting attorney of the Bali government —the possession of a single name is common in Indonesia— was asked if there had been any legal basis for the killings. "It was a revolution," he replied. The army had required Communist party officials before Sept. 30 to hand over lists of members of the party and its affiliate organizations, and most of those on the lists were subsequently hunted to be killed.

Most of the killings were carried out by army-selected civilian executioners who were known as Tamins. They were young men who were given loose black shirts and black trousers to identify them. They operated in teams, usually by night, and apparently met little or no resistance from the terrorized villagers.

There were reports, which could not be confirmed, that whole villages were wiped out. A responsible Balinese told what had happened to his typical village of about 2,000 persons. Twenty-seven Communists died. The village headman, who was a member of the party, hanged himself, and others of the Communists, who were not executed, took poison. Some escaped.

That evidently was the pattern for most of the several thousand villages on Bali.

Center for Killings

The largest scale of killings on Bali occurred in the district of Dembrana, in the western part of the island, a center of Communist influence. There, the palace of the Rajah of Negara, one of the eight traditional kings of Bali, was destroyed because he had allowed the party to meet on his grounds.

Eyewitnesses said that retain-

The New York Times   Aug. 24, 1966

Some of the most extensive executions of Indonesian Communists took place at Negara (1) and at Kediri (2).

ers were being dragged from the palace to have their bowed heads crushed by rocks hurled by the mob. The Rajah, father of the pro-Communist Governor of Bali, who is in a jail in Jakarta, was killed or died of a heart attack during the sacking of the palace. Most of his family were slaughtered.

In East Java, where informed estimates of the killings vary from 100,000 to 300,000, the most concentrated execution of Communists took place in the district of Kediri. The district, which had been dominated politically by the Communists, has a population of 3,000,000 to 5,000,000. Its major city, also called Kediri, has about 180,000 residents.

Religion a Factor

Maj. Willi Sudyono, the military commander of Kediri, organized the systematic execution of Communists in the district. His brother, Lieutenant General Sutoyo, was one of the six generals slain in the Sept. 30 putsch in Jakarta.

There were religious as well as political motives for the population's participation in the killings in Kediri, which is the center of Moslem religious instruction in East Java. Even before Sept. 30, there had been clashes between Communist youth groups and Ansor, the youth organization of the Moslem Scholars party.

In the purge of the Communists, most of the killings were carried out by army-trained squads of Ansor, mainly youths in their teens and early twenties who were attending the Moslem university and religious schools in the Kediri district.

Haj Markus Ali, the 57-year-old religious leader of the Moslem youth in the Kediri district and a top leader of the Moslem Scholars party, said that Ansor had "fulfilled the command of the army" and that the "killings were the will of God."

He said that 20,000 Communists had been killed in the Kediri district. Asked if there had been any resistance in the villages, he said he knew of 15 members of Ansor and one army man who had been killed in the mop-up. He had two specific complaints against the Communists: that they had taken "one-sided action" in redistributing land and that they had offended Moslems.

Telling of the Ansor squads, one Christian said, "We always wondered if they would eventually turn on us." A Christian pastor told of listening in helpless agony to cries of help in the night as Ansor squads pursued fugitives through the streets, and of hearing the thud of great peasant scythes as the executioners slashed their victims to death.

Toward the end of the mass

killings, when whole families were sometimes put to death at one time, the Ansor executioners began to wear masks.

Some Die by Error

There were often instances where men were killed who were mistaken for Communists or denounced because of some personal grudge. Old scores were settled under political pretexts. On the first day of the mass killings, one army officer in civilian dress cheerfully left Kediri city, carrying a machine gun, to shoot squatters who had refused to get off his untilled land.

In Central Java, where estimates of executions vary from 50,000 to 300,000, members of the Nationalist and Moslem Scholars parties joined the army as executioners. There were some outbreaks in the villages against Communist party members who had supervised the enforcement of the land-distribution and crop-sharing laws.

In West Java, apart from the Jakarta area, there were no major Communist political centers, and there were no mass killings. Reports from Sumatra and other islands of the archipelago tell of purges that took many thousands of lives.

In North Sumatra, hundreds were massacred in the Medan region, including many Chinese merchants and their families. The Chinese Communist Consulate was attacked Dec. 10. The demonstrators swept into the Chinese quarter, looting and killing more than 100 residents. Antara, the official Indonesian news agency, reported on Dec. 20 that 10,000 people had been arrested by the army in North Sumatra. Many were later shot.

Among Indonesians who participated in the killings there are few visible signs of remorse.

On Bali, young black-clad executioners bow before chanting Hindu priests who cleanse them of the taint of the blood of tens of thousands slaughtered on the island paradise. Such gestures of contrition during religious festivals are meant to placate the gods; they are not expressions of conscience for the victims. The

executioners march proudly in parades and their black garments have become the vogue for many youngsters.

General Suharto, the army chief who assumed executive administrative control of the country on March 11, promulgated a ban on the Communist party the next day. By then the great bulk of the executions had been carried out. The delay in issuing the ban had been caused by the opposition of President Sukarno.

Although there had been political uncertainty in Jakarta in November as General Suharto and President Sukarno jockeyed for political power, the army was in effective control of most of the country when the large-scale executions began in November. Earlier, tough, well-trained commando units had knifed through the Communist strongholds in Central and East Java without meeting any significant armed Communist resistance.

Originally, decisions were left to regional commanders as to how the killings should be done, but evidently an order went out from the army command in Jakarta that there should be an effective purge.

Major General Sumitro, the tough military commander of East Java, said in an interview that General Suharto had issued a detailed order in mid-November that the Communist party should be destroyed "structurally and ideologically." He said staff officers had visited the area commanders in early December to see if instructions had been understood and executed.

General Sumitro added that "most local commanders did their utmost to kill as many cadres as possible" of the Communist party.

The general, recalling the 1948 Communist uprising at Madiun, which was also crushed by the army, repeated what this reporter had heard from army officers throughout Java:

"They tried it at Madiun, and again in Jakarta, and we are not going to let them try again."

August 24, 1966

Indonesians Hail Liberalization of Investment Law

By ALFRED FRIENDLY Jr.
Special to The New York Times

JAKARTA, Indonesia, Dec. 25 — Indonesian leaders and their economic advisers celebrated today two victories they regard as the culmination of a long drive to reform the country's battered economic structure.

The double triumph came on Christmas Eve with the unanimous approval in Parliament of a balanced budget and a liberal foreign investment law.

General Suharto, the chairman of the Cabinet Presidium, told the delegates that they had scored "a new victory" for reform. Several members of Parliament called it a "happy and historic day," and a jubilant civilian cabinet adviser, a Moslem, said, "The bills make perfect Christmas presents."

In passing the Foreign Investment Act, which guarantees outside capital against expropriation without compensation and institutes five-year tax holidays for investors, Parliament actually went further than the original Government proposal in extending the freedom investors will enjoy.

The amended law gives the administration greater flexibility in determining whether an investor whose main business activities are outside Indonesia must incorporate his enterprise here as well and run the risk of double taxation.

Another amendment, which is regarded by official spokesmen as "not substantial," provides that after 30 years a foreign investor must convert his business to a joint enterprise with Indonesian capital or terminate his activities.

A draft 1967 budget of the equivalent of $820-million was approved unanimously. Almost all decisions by Parliament are unanimous by tradition.

The vote on the budget was not quite as favorable to Government policy as that on the other measure. Although representatives agreed in principle to keep the budget in balance, they inserted into the law a provision that will enable a Parliament commission to review the implementation to the budget and reallocate funds from one ministry to another or go beyond budgeted spending limits if it wishes.

General Suharto put the best possible face on this novel procedure by calling it "remarkable progress" and hailing the idea that "deputies of the people" will participate in the allocation of Government revenues.

The budget bill also called for such austerity measures as a prohibition on the construction of new buildings next year and on the purchase of new automobiles for Government use.

The measure also provided for the dissolution within the year of all "extra-constitutional" institutions. These include the military Supreme Operations Command, formerly the Crush Malaysia Command; a national body to integrate Chinese residents into Indonesian culture and an institute that had been devoted to the issuance of propaganda glorifying President Sukarno.

December 26, 1966

Investor Guarantee Signed by Indonesia

Special to The New York Times

JAKARTA, Indonesia, Jan. 13 —The United States and Indonesia have signed an investment-guarantee agreement, designed to insure American investors against expropriation of their assets and to encourage them to take part in rebuilding this nation's shattered economy.

Indonesia's Foreign Minister, Adam Malik, and American officials here hailed the recent agreement as a hopeful advance in the Indonesian program of economic stabilization.

Similar to pacts the United States has negotiated with some 75 other countries, the agreement provides insurance for American investors against illegal actions by the host Government, Indonesia, or on its territory. The United States Government agrees to act as claimant for the return of assets privately invested.

January 14, 1967

Title of President Is Lost by Sukarno

By ALFRED FRIENDLY Jr.
Special to The New York Times

JAKARTA, Indonesia, March 12—President Sukarno of Indonesia was "replaced" today by General Suharto, who took the title Acting President and assumed all executive powers.

The General was sworn in as Acting President "to uphold the Constitution and implement all laws and regulations with complete honesty."

The action, approved unanimously by the Provisional People's Consultative Congress, ended a 45-year public career that had carried the 65-year-old Mr. Sukarno to the undisputed leadership of his nation of 107 million people.

March 13, 1967

Most Indonesians Welcome Stability Under Suharto

By PHILIP SHABECOFF
Special to The New York Times

JAKARTA, Indonesia, May 23 —Peace and stability have settled over this archipelago nation of some 120 million people.

To some critics of the army-dominated Government of President Suharto, the stability and peace are nothing more than stagnation—the economy is still in poor shape—but most Indonesians, including many of Jakarta's intellectuals, appear to welcome the calm of the Suharto Administration after the chaos and fury and devastating inflation of the Sukarno era.

Within this political climate, President Suharto has apparently been able to gather more direct power into his own hands than his demagogic predecessor ever enjoyed.

"The political life of Indo-

Indonesian soldiers and officers working side by side with political prisoners to build a macadam road in West Java

nesia has been killed," said a liberal newspaper editor more in resignation than in sorrow.

"When we fought for our rights under Sukarno, at least we had to fight one man and one party," he added. "But now we have to fight a dehumanized machine formed by the army's alliance with the bureaucracy. In the process we are all losing our individuality and becoming a nation of clerks."

'Had Enough of Politics'

"We had enough of politics," said a former student activist now a writer and lecturer. "Now we need a long period of quiet to restore our strength and build up the economy."

"It looks now as though the military will be in power in Indonesia for another 10 years," he went on. "We think we can live with that. In fact, we see no alternative at the moment."

Even critics of the Government concede that it is no simple military dictatorship of the kind found in Latin America or Greece. General Suharto, they explain, is a Javan and believes in old Javanese ways of doing things. One such way is called musjawarah, a kind of mystic process of national consultation to reach consensus.

"Unlike Sukarno, who arbitrarily ordered people thrown in jail, the Suharto Government is attempting to stay within the law," a well-informed diplomat asserted. "Suharto always demands proof when the army asks him to put somebody in prison—except, of course, if they are Communists."

When the armed forces beat back the Communist uprising in 1965-66, Indonesia's political parties were drained of power. The Communist party was crushed and its remnants were driven underground. Mr. Sukarno's Nationalist party of Indonesia was splintered and rendered ineffective. The other parties were equally discredited.

No political group has been able to offer serious opposition to military rule and there are few important Communists left to hunt.

General Suharto and the army have taken steps to see that this condition does not change. When the Moslem party elected officers who belonged to a former party of Moslem extremists, the Government voided the elections.

Some Indonesians assert that the deepest internal cleavage is between the military nationalists and the orthodox Moslems,

who want to establish the sovereignty of Islam.

Recently critics of the Government maintained that the army had blatantly intervened at the convention of the Nationalist party, still the country's largest political group, to insure the election of officers it considered secure.

In addition to keeping a tight rein on the parties, the Government has adopted a law that will effectively enable it to dictate the results of the parliamentary elections scheduled for July, 1971. Under the law, the military—that is to say, President Suharto, who is his own Minister of Defense—will select 100 members of the 460-member Parliament. Moreover, the Government has reserved the right to approve all candidates.

Tighter Grip on Military

The President recently solidified his political base by strengthening his grip on the armed forces, which put him in power in the first place and help keep him there. A reorganization of the 250,000-man armed forces unifies the army, navy and air force and places them directly under the Defense Ministry.

One reason for the reorganization was said to be the President's desire to reduce the power of the military commanders of the county's 23 military districts.

Even with that reduction, military rule holds sway throughout most of the nation of more than 3,000 islands strung along the Equator. Most of the civilian governors and district chiefs are army generals, colonels and captains temporarily wearing civilian clothes.

There are frequent reports of abuses of power by the military, including smuggling, extortion and the levying of illegal taxes. More often, army men irritate the civilian population by high-handed use of power, as in commandeering private vehicles for personal errands.

Army's Help Wins Praise

On the other hand, the army's direct contributions to public welfare and its role in nation-building have won it a certain amount of respect and even admiration.

Under the military's "civic mission" program, a large part of the armed forces is engaged in such programs as road and school building, rural development and agricultural improvement.

One day last week a group of soldiers—officers as well as enlisted men—was encountered hard at work under the fierce equatorial sun of Java, laboring side by side with political prisoners to build a macadam road.

The soldiers and the prisoners were doing the same work. The difference is that the soldiers are paid 250 rupiahs a day—about 60 cents—while the prisoners get 25.

A heavily muscled military policeman from the island of Ambon insisted that he was proud to do road work. "I do this for my people and my country," he said with a broad grin. "I am very happy to do it."

In the political area, the Government is allowing the press an increasing amount of latitude to criticize the army and the Government itself—within certain limits. Jakarta's newspapers have recently maintained a sustained offensive against widespread corruption of officials and generals, and the Government has appointed a commission to investigate.

One reason why General Suharto has been able to cool once-enflamed passions is that he has concentrated on economic recovery rather than on politics or international diplomacy. This has suited the mood of a people who were tired of Mr. Sukarno's promises of glory and who want more rice for themselves and their children.

Order has been restored to the chaotic economy left by Mr. Sukarno and inflation has been arrested. Despite the Government's best efforts, however, the Indonesian people, with a per capita income of less than $100 a year, remain desperately poor.

General Suharto still has time to produce, his critics say, but he does not have forever.

May 27, 1970

SUKARNO, 69, DIES; LED INDONESIANS

First President of Republic Yielded Power in '66 After Abortive Red Coup

By Reuters

JAKARTA, Indonesia, Sunday, June 21 — Former President Sukarno of Indonesia died early today at Jakarta's Central Army Hospital, an official medical bulletin said. He was 69 years old.

A three-sentence communiqué said he had fallen into a coma at 3:50 A.M. local time and died at 7 A.M. He was admitted to the hospital Tuesday suffering from high blood pressure and a kidney ailment.

A statesman with a flair for the dramatic, Sukarno, who yielded power as President in March of 1966, was one of the first and most outspoken advocates of a third bloc of uncommitted nations, a concept he first articulated in 1955 at the Bandung conference of African and Asian nations.

A powerful speaker, Sukarno wielded almost absolute power in Indonesia for 20 years. He escaped five assassination attempts but was toppled from power by the army after an unsuccessful Communist coup in 1965 in which an estimated 100,000 persons were killed.

Sukarno died less than 10 hours after his fourth wife, Ratna Sari Dewi flew here from Paris to see him for the first time since he was placed under house arrest in 1967. With her was the couple's 3-year-old daughter, Kartika, whom Sukarno had never seen.

A Shared Identity

By ALFRED FRIENDLY Jr.

A giant among Asian nationalists for 20 years after World War II, Mr. Sukarno ended his life in obscurity. Dreaming of hegemony over the Malay Archipelago and a leading role in world politics, the flamboyant Indonesian leader pursued grandiose goals that reduced his nation to economic shambles. Flirting with Peking and the Indonesian Communist party (P.K.I.), he gave at least tacit consent to a left-wing coup d'état designed to oust the right-wing army high command. It failed.

In the violent army-led counteraction, several hundred thousand suspected Communists, their supporters, and other left-wingers, members of their families and others caught up in an uncontrolled upheaval were slaughtered. The right-wing military leaders consolidated their power and dethroned Mr. Sukarno.

Before his downfall, however, he gave the 110 million inhabitants of Indonesia's 3,000 islands a common language, a sense of shared identity and a vision of exuberant destiny. With an eloquence that was undiminished by defeat, he built the ancient legend of a Javanese empire encompassing Malaya and the Philippines into a modern political myth that filled Indonesians' hopes while emptying their purses. On his maps the Indian Ocean became the "Indonesian Ocean" and, on the world map, the Netherlands East Indies from Sumatra to New Guinea became Indonesia.

No sooner had he added the western half of New Guinea (West Irian) to Indonesia in May, 1963, than he turned the weapons of guerrilla warfare and braggadocio diplomacy, which he had used successfully on the Dutch, against his Malay neighbors to the north. Mr. Sukarno's drive to destroy Malaysia, however, set in motion the forces that eventually destroyed him.

Large Army Created

To win his "confrontation" against Malaysia, formed by the federation of Malaya with Singapore and the North Borneo states of Sabah and Sarawak in September, 1963, Mr. Sukarno created an outsize army of some 350,000 men and turned Indonesia's economic resources to the unproductive business of war.

Seeking domestic support for his international adventurism, he moved closer and closer to the large, well organized P.K.I., encouraging its leaders and its programs as they egged him on to ever more daring political and rhetorical extravagances.

Inevitably, the army and the Communists clashed. To the surprise of many, the army won, demolishing a political organization that had boasted 20 million members or sympathizers a few months before its leaders and some discontented army officers staged an unsuccessful coup d'état in Jakarta on Sept. 30, 1965.

With the destruction of the P.K.I.—including the massacre of an estimated 300,000 to 400,000 of its suspected adherents—came a political reaction against Mr. Sukarno and what his opponents called his "Old Order." Cementing their hold on political power, army leaders arrested and tried Mr. Sukarno's chief deputies, while militant students staged mass demonstrations demanding the trial of the President himself.

Instead of trying him, however, his successors punished Mr. Sukarno with isolation and obscurity. Culminating a process that was slowed by his many still loyal supporters in Central and East Java, the military rulers stripped him by degrees of his titles and his authority and, 18 months after the abortive coup attempt, confined him to his weekend palace at Bogor in the hills 40 miles south of Jakarta. He was finally replaced as President by General Suharto.

To visit the capital itself, Mr. Sukarno had to receive permission from military officials. They granted it with decreasing frequency, limiting his trips to those they said were necessary for him to receive medical treatment. For many years he had suffered from kidney malfunctions, for which he had been treated in Europe and China. A visit by Chinese doctors to him shortly before the attempted coup generated rumors that he was dying and contributed to the speed with which the plotters moved to seize power.

"When I die," he told his countrymen many times, "do not write in golden letters on my tomb, 'Here lies His Excellency Doctor Engineer Sukarno, First President of the Republic of Indonesia.'

"Just write, 'Here lies Bung [Brother] Sukarno, Tongue of the Indonesian People!'"

Another description of himself, which he adopted from an American author, was used to open his autobiography: "The simplest way to describe Sukarno is to say that he is a great lover. He loves his country, he loves his people, he loves women, he loves art and, above all, he loves himself."

Only occasionally in his last days did his vast self-confidence falter. While students were demonstrating in the capital demanding his ouster, he turned to an old American friend at a party in his Bogor palace to ask, "Tell me, I am still the father of my people, aren't I?"

More customary was the stance he took before an American audience when he said:

"When you think of public opinion in Indonesia, you speak about me. I am public opinion."

Like many Indonesians, Mr. Sukarno (who preferred the Dutch spelling of his name; Soekarno) had only one name. Some sources listed his first name as Ahmed, a noble one in the Moslem world, but he never used it.

He was 5 feet 8 inches tall, making him taller than most other Indonesians, and he kept his weight at 150 or 160 pounds. With his erect walk and black, brimless velvet petji, the traditional Moslem hat of Southeast Asia, covering his baldness, he looked younger than his years.

Noted for Vanity

Mr. Sukarno was noted for his vanity and his attractiveness to women. He was once joking with a photographer for a French magazine that had referred to the President as "the great seducer." When the photographer said, "Thas is a compliment in Paris," Mr. Sukarno roared with laughter.

The Russians anticipated his interest once by supplying his Aeroflot plane with an attractive blond interpreter. When the visit was over, the blonde returned to Indonesia with Mr. Sukarno.

In Washington on another visit, Mr. Sukarno left his car and approached an older woman who was on the sidewalk. "Dear Mother, may I kiss you?" he asked. After kissing her heartily on the cheek, he said, "That was an Indonesian kiss." The woman replied, "It certainly wasn't a Washington kiss."

Although he had no military training, Mr. Sukarno usually dressed in well-tailored uniforms of gray or mustard brown that he designed himself and carried a swagger stick imbedded with pearls.

He wore dark-rimmed glasses for reading, and was usually seen in public with a broad, full-toothed smile on his handsome face. In his last years, however, that expressive face showed a puffiness of age, the strain of constant pressure and the effects of deteriorating health.

Mr. Sukarno personified the mixed national and religious strains of his country. He was born on June 6, 1901, in Surabaya on the island of Java. His father was a Moslem Javanese schoolmaster of aristocratic background but modest resources.

His mother was a high-caste Hindu beauty from Bali, the romantic island to the east where in 1906 many natives committed suicide to avoid complete subjugation by the Dutch. The European traders had been on the island from 1597 but did not obtain control until 1908.

Mr. Sukarno had his early schooling in Surabaya. At the age of 14, he was sent to live as a foster son in the home of

Eastfoto

Mr. Sukarno, on trip to Communist China in 1956, watching National Day parade in Peking with Mao Tse-tung.

Haji Umar Sayid Tjokroaminoto, a businessman and early nationalistic political and religious leader. Surabaya was a center of unrest in the Dutch colony and the Tjokroaminoto home was a study and discussion center for local young intellectuals.

Favorite Among Nationalists

Mr. Tjokroaminoto was the founder of the political organization Indonesian Islamic League and was of sufficient standing to get the young Sukarno admitted as one of the few native students in a Western-style, Dutch-language high school.

The lively, arrogant, precocious youth was a favorite among the young Javanese nationalists who gathered around Mr. Tjokroaminoto's home. In future years some of these young men became the leaders of their country's religious, Socialist and Communist parties.

Mr. Tjokroaminoto recognized his foster son's abilities and directed him toward a life of politics. He taught the young man oratory, nationalism and party organization and succeeded in entering him, at the age of 19, as one of the first 11 native students admitted to a new Dutch technical college at Bandung.

The ties between the men were made tighter when Mr. Sukarno, in a Moslem "suspended" ceremony, married his mentor's under-age daughter, Siti Utari. It was the first of seven marriages for Mr. Sukarno.

At college he was a good student. He studied architecture and received a civil engineering degree, but he associated with teachers and students interested in politics.

Although he was called "the most promising student we ever had" by his Dutch professors, he displayed little interest in a career in architecture. He turned down several good offers from Dutch companies but worked for a while for the state railways. He formed an engineers' and architects' bureau in Bandung and designed a few homes for Chinese merchants and a mosque. He soon turned, however, to a full-time political career.

Mr. Sukarno broke with his foster father in a violent scene, divorced his wife and promptly married another, Inggit Garnasih, a rich widow.

After an unsuccessful, Communist-sponsored uprising in 1926 and 1927, Mr. Sukarno formed a new political party, the Indonesian Nationalist party, and became its chairman. He also formed a new, more lasting friendship with an older, well-educated man, Dr. Mohammed Hatta, who had studied economics in the Netherlands.

The Dutch arrested Dr. Hatta for his nationalist activities, and Mr. Sukarno moved to unite the existing parties under his leadership. At 26 he became the best-known nationalist leader in the country and proclaimed a philosophy of socialist reform called Marhaenism, drawn from the word Marhaen, a common Indonesian peasant name.

By 1929 he was enough of a danger that the Dutch arrested him. After a four-month trial he was sentenced to four years in jail.

He used the courtroom for his best nationwide forum. He gave a passionate speech attacking the "vile evils of colonialism" and promising to serve his people as an instrument of "historic necessity."

The trial gave Mr. Sukarno world standing for the first time and brought criticism to the Dutch Government for the broad powers it gave the island governor to punish any offense "endangering law and order."

While he was in jail, the nationalist movement was strengthened, partly because it now had martyrs to identify with. The P.N.I. that Mr. Sukarno formed split with the formation of the new Indonesian party.

Although he was released from jail in 1931, long before his sentence ran out, he moved immediately again to attack the Dutch.

He was greeted at the prison gates by a welcoming crowd that cheered him and gave him flowers and gifts. "Give me 10 youths who are fired with zeal and with love for our native land and with them I shall shake the earth," he announced.

Arrested and Exiled

Mr. Sukarno also wrote nationalist pamphlets and, after remaining aloof from parties for a short time, joined the Indonesian party (Partindo). He became its chairman but was arrested again in 1932 and exiled.

"I entered prison a leader and I shall emerge a leader," he said.

He spent the next eight years, on Flores and Endeh in the eastern, outer islands, and at Bengulen in South Sumatra. He found time during this period to divorce his second wife for the announced reason of childlessness, and to marry a younger beauty, Fatmawati.

Mr. Sukarno met with other exiled nationalists during his period of exile and studied literature from Dutch, English, French and Indonesian sources. He learned languages so that he was able to speak Malay, English, Dutch, French, German, Italian and Russian.

It was also during this period of forced contemplation that Mr. Sukarno picked up the hodgepodge of philosophic thinking that characterized his writings and speeches later. He read widely—Lenin, Jefferson, John Dewey, Lincoln, Otto Bauer, John Reed, Marx, Ernest Ronan, Ataturk, Sun Yat-sen and Mohammed.

When the Japanese invaded, the Dutch moved Mr. Sukarno twice. He was freed by the Japanese at Padang in Central Sumatra in 1942. Controversy shrouds this part of Mr. Sukarno's life.

The official Government biography says that Mr. Sukarno met with Dr. Hatta and two other leaders, the Socialists Sjahrir and Sjarifuddin, at Jakarta to determine how to keep the cause of nationalism alive under the Japanese occupation.

In this version, it was agreed that Mr. Sukarno and Dr. Hatta should cooperate with the invaders while the other two leaders would go underground and keep the nationalist movement alive. This tactic, according to the official version, enabled many Indonesians to receive skilled training from the Japanese and to prepare for freedom at the end of the war.

Mr. Sukarno was invited to Tokyo in 1943, where he was decorated by Premier Tojo.

The harsher version of this period pictures Mr. Sukarno as a Japanese collaborator who believed the Axis powers would win the war. He helped supply Japan with workers and soldiers from the Indonesian population and gave speeches against the Allied cause.

"America we shall iron out and England we shall destroy," was the message he repeated throughout his country.

The fall of Japan caught Mr. Sukarno and Dr. Hatta, his chief ally, unprepared. Mr. Sukarno had been in Saigon, where the Japanese appointed him chairman of the Commission for the Preparation of Indonesian Independence.

When the Japanese surrendered in August, 1945, British troops were on their way to help take over control of Indonesia for the Allies. Mr. Sukarno hesitated about the next move but two days after the surrender, at the insistence of the younger nationalist leaders, who held him at pistol-point, he declared Indonesia a republic in a Proclamation of Independence signed by himself and Dr. Hatta.

Five Principles Cited

The new nation was to follow the five principles Mr. Sukarno had pronounced two months before—nationalism, internationalism, democracy, social justice and belief in God.

After the proclamation, Mr. Sukarno and Dr. Hatta had to build a native government and army. They used weapons left behind by the Japanese and took to the jungles to fight a four-year war with the Dutch.

Mr. Sukarno's great gift for rousing public support through the sheer force of his personality was instrumental in rallying the disparate tribes and peoples of Indonesia to the nationalist cause.

When the Communists tried to capture the nationalist movement, Mr. Sukarno smashed their efforts decisively. "Choose Communism or choose me," he told his people on a radio broadcast.

This stand also helped him to win worldwide support for the Indonesian revolt. Later in 1948, Dutch paratroopers landed suddenly at the nationalists' headquarters at the ancient Javanese capital of Jogjakarta. He was exiled again, this time to Prapat and Banka.

The world opinion Mr. Sukarno had mobilized resulted in a resolution approved by the United Nations Security Council urging freedom of the new country. The Dutch freed Mr. Sukarno in July, 1949, and in December turned over administration of the island nation to his government.

Name Changed to Republic

The new country was called the United States of Indonesia with a structure similar to the United States and with Mr. Sukarno as President. In August, 1950, the name was changed to the Republic of Indonesia.

To the people of the country, however, Mr. Sukarno was best known as Bung Karno, or Brother Karno, and as Bapak Negara, father of the nation.

Independence brought no peace to Mr. Sukarno. The problems of building the country were severe enough, but Mr. Sukarno moved early to play an important role in international politics.

Through the postwar period he alternately won aid from the Communist bloc and the Western allies, particularly the United States. Within Indonesia Mr. Sukarno put on another political juggling game.

From 1945 to 1958, 17 Cabinets were installed and collapsed. There were 28 political parties fighting for power with the Communists being one of the largest. An election in 1956 saw the Communists poll 6 million votes.

From 1950, when American aid started, and 1956, when the Soviet Union joined in, Mr. Sukarno was able to borrow more than two billion dollars in economic and military assistance to keep the economy going. His successors inherited this staggering debt and a potentially wealthy nation, burdened by a population growth rate of more than 3 per cent a year and a legacy of mismanagement.

Inflation combined with widespread corruption and expropriation of foreign capital kept the country from realizing its wealth. To divert his countrymen from the economic failure, however, Mr. Sukarno poured funds into "prestige projects" — broad boulevards, monuments, sports facilities and luxury hotels and stores in the capital.

His personal life was also a spectacle of luxury and disregard for the Moslem rules he and 90 per cent of Indonesia's masses profess to observe. In 1954, without the formality of a divorce, he married a fourth wife, Hartini, a 32-year-old divorcee. The marriage infuriated many Indonesian women, who picketed his Jakarta palace in protest against his endorsement of polygamous customs they were trying to discard.

Five years later he brought a Japanese bar hostess, Dewi, back to Indonesia with him, but it is believed that they did not marry until 1965. By then he had also married another Indonesian girl, Haryati, and subsequently, without divorcing any of his by then four wives, he married a young Indonesian actress named Jurike Sanger.

While he ruled unchallenged, from 1959 to 1965, few objected publicly to these excesses. His prowess with women, in fact, was believed to have helped cement his hold on the peasantry, who were used to legendary rulers who traditionally took many wives and concubines.

Similarly, his adventures in international politics increased his stature at home. His convoking of the first Afro-Asian conference in Bandung in 1955 brought him a leading position in the "third world" of the developing nations and increased his prestige in Indonesia.

He knew well his hold on the people. "The Indonesian people will eat stones if I tell them to," he once boasted to a critic. Using this popularity for all it was worth, he introduced a dictatorship under the name of "guided democracy" in 1959, and allowed Communists a freer, more influential role in policy-making and politics.

Colleague Alienated

His trend toward one-man rule had alienated Dr. Hatta even earlier, provoking his resignation as Vice President in December, 1956. The split between them never healed.

His policies also aroused civilian and military resistance culminating in an armed rebellion in Sumatra in 1958. The revolt was quelled by the army, and its leaders, along with many others who voiced public criticism of the "President-for-Life," were jailed.

Coining slogans with the enthusiastic support of the Communists, he urged Indonesians to "reach for the stars" in one speech, or to enter joyously into "the year of dangerous living" in another. "We must dare," he shouted to applauding crowds. "We must start from the bottom. In the next few years we may be short of clothing."

In fact, the battle against Malaysia brought the nation shortages of everything, including foreign aid from the West. "To hell with your aid," Mr. Sukarno announced when the United States cut back its programs in 1964. "We can do without aid. We'll never collapse."

Under his rule, Indonesia did not collapse. It just stopped growing and began retrogressing. Aside from the legacy he bequeathed to his four sons and four daughters, he left his country only debts. economic decay and a tradition of political emotionalism that he first used to bind Indonesians together and then misused to stunt their growth.

June 21, 1970

Violent Crowds in Jakarta Protest the Visit by Tanaka

Thousands Take Part in Outburst Held Directed at Japan's Business Methods in Indonesia—8 Reported Killed

By RICHARD HALLORAN
Special to The New York Times

JAKARTA, Indonesia, Wednesday, Jan. 16—Many thousands of Indonesians took to the streets of Jakarta yesterday in violent demonstrations against the visit of Premier Kakuei Tanaka of Japan and what they regard as Japanese economic imperialism.

In a preliminary report on the outburst, an Indonesian police official said that eight persons had been killed and 35 wounded. He said that 125 cars had been burned, 10 buildings set afire, and 50,000 stores damaged. All casualties, he said were Indonesians.

From late morning until late at night, despite a curfew declared by the Government, high-school and university students and others roamed large sections of this sprawling city burning automobiles, trucks and motor bikes that were made in Japan. They built bonfires and fed them with furniture tossed out of Japanese office buildings.

Buildings with Japanese signs were attacked, flags were ripped down and stores were looted during the demonstrations, which were more violent than the street protests against Mr. Tanaka's visit to Bangkok, Thailand, last week.

Clashes After Curfew

For the most part, Indonesian policemen and soldiers who were sent out to patrol the streets stood by watching, rarely making any move to stop the rioters. Late in the afternoon, however, warning shots were fired over the heads of the demonstrators to disperse them, and after dark, when the curfew was supposed to be in effect, the police began getting rougher.

Policemen clashed with young people near a downtown hotel and hauled about a dozen of the demonstrators into a nearby police station. One demonstrator was clubbed on the back of the head. Meanwhile, what sounded like shooting could be heard in the distance.

The rioting forced the cancellation of Premier Tanaka's program during the day yesterday. At a dinner in his honor last night, President Suharto was said to have expressed his regrets over the day's events.

According to Japanese officials, Mr. Tanaka told his host that he understood the problems and asked President Suharto not to worry about it.

As in the Philippines, Thailand, Singapore and Malaysia, where Mr. Tanaka stopped earlier in his current tour, anti-Japanese resentments appear to have been caused more by the way the Japanese carry out their economic dealings than by the economic ventures themselves. Japanese investment here accounts for 15 per cent of all foreign investment and is smaller than that of Americans.

Complaints that the Japanese are ruthless and unscrupulous in business, that they keep Indonesians out of important jobs and that they pay Indonesians less than Japanese for identical work increased so much last year that the Japanese Embassy twice sent letters of warning to the 3,000 businessmen and other Japanese living in Indonesia.

There have been protests because 70 per cent of Japanese investors have met the requirements for joint ventures by taking ethnic Chinese instead of Indonesians as their partners.

In addition, anti-Japanese feelings among some university students seemed to be based on Indonesia's dependence on Japan for key imports of machinery and processed industrial supplies, economic aid and technology.

According to diplomatic observers here, a strong feeling of frustration over the lack of speed in economic development here also contributed to yesterday's anti-Japanese outburst.

Part of that is owing to envy of Japan, the diplomats said, and part to dissatisfaction with President Suharto's Government. But, they added, it is easier to criticize the Japanese than President Suharto.

The students are particularly angry over what many of them charge are widespread Japanese payoffs to high Government officials.

Premier Tanaka was to have met with student representatives this morning, but he canceled the session at the request of the Indonesian Government. Japanese officials said the Indonesians suggested that the situation would not permit it.

Japanese Residents Warned

Japanese residents here stayed out of sight during the rioting in response to a warning from the Japanese Embassy. The manager of the President Hotel, where Japanese newsmen accompanying the Premier were staying, warned his guests last night to pack their bags and be ready to leave in an emergency.

Last night the Government reportedly ordered the closing of Jakarta international airport.

During the day, two senior Government members—General Sumitro, who is considered the second most powerful man in Indonesia after President Suharto, and Adam Malik, the Foreign Minister—appeared in the streets to appeal for order.

General Sumitro, who is chairman of National Security Agency, climbed out on his jeep and onto the hood, where he took a Japanese-made megaphone from a student leader and, according to an English-speaking Indonesian, told the crowd:

"We admire your ideals but there is no need to go about doing things this way. If you don't want to go home, please stay here with me. But don't burn cars. Our diplomatic missions abroad are afraid now of what you have done. Many say our Japan policy is bad, but many also say it is good. We will try to realize your wishes within this year."

With that, the general got back in his jeep and drove slowly away, to the cheers of the crowd. Sometime later, also near the Japanese Embassy, Foreign Minister Malik delivered the same message.

At one time during the afternoon, plumes of dense black smoke drifted under a leaden gray sky in at least three widely separated places. Last night a blaze could be seen raging several miles from downtown in a Japanese shopping center.

"We will burn all the Japanese products," said a sweating and panting Indonesian high-school teacher. Asked why they were destroying things that belonged to Indonesians, he said: "It doesn't matter, we will burn them." The crowd around him cheered.

The flag in front of the Japanese Embassy, which had 23 broken windows, was torn down but handed to an Indonesian soldier, who returned it to the Embassy.

The Japanese Embassy lodged a formal protest with the Indonesian Government over the flag incident there, and President Suharto apologized during the dinner.

The mood of the young people changed from time to time and place to place. In one instance, they seemed to be having a lark, laughing and chanting as they roamed through the streets. One small group was led by a young man playing a guitar and leading the singing of an anti-Japanese song.

But at other times rocks were aimed at soldiers and policemen instead of windows.

January 16, 1974

16-Day Siege in Amsterdam Ends Safely

AMSTERDAM, the Netherlands, Dec. 19 (AP) — Seven terrorist gunmen ended a 16-day siege at the Indonesian Consulate today, symbolically lowering the flag they had hoisted as representing their Pacific homeland of South Molucca and freeing 25 hostages.

Police officers said the captives, including 10 women, were in "fine condition" and that no concessions had been made to the gunmen.

Joyful crowds danced in the streets under fluttering Dutch flags at the sight of the hostages, including one for whom the South Moluccans had held a birthday party last night.

"It's marvelous," said an elderly woman living in the consulate's neighborhood; "now I can go shopping again."

Strategy Is Stressed

Justice Minister Andreas A.M. van Agt said at a news conference that the Government had granted no concessions, and had followed the strategy it had worked out in another, 12-day seige by South Moluccan islanders aboard a train they had hijacked 90 miles away. That siege ended Sunday in freedom for 23 hostages and the peaceful surrenders of their six young captors.

The train was hijacked and halted Dec. 2 near the farm community of Beilen, and early in that siege the terrorists shot to death the engineer and two male passengers. The consulate was invaded on Dec. 4, and in the first confusion and panic several people inside leaped from windows to the ground. On Dec. 10 an Indonesian consular official who had jumped from a window died of his injuries.

The rebels had demanded that the Netherlands help them in their campaign for an independent homeland in the South Moluccan islands of Indonesia. The islands east of Borneo and southeast of the Philippines, were incorporated into Indonesia when the Dutch ended colonial rule in the area 25 years ago.

Tens of thousands of Moluccans fled to the Netherlands in 1950 after an uprising that failed. The Dutch Government, which is sensitive to its relations with Indonesia, said from the start that there could be no question of meeting the South Moluccans demands.

Prime Minister Joop den Uyl appealed once more today for peaceful coexistence with the 40,000 Moluccans living in the Netherlands. But, he added, "The Moluccans must have no illusions that the Dutch Government will suport a free Moluccan state in Indonesia."

He offered, however, to confer with Moluccan community leaders before the end of January "to clarify certain points and, above all, prevent any escalation of violence and terror."

Two leaders of the Moluccan exile community here entered the Indonesian consulate, in an Amsterdam suburb, to arrange the release of the hostages and turn their captors over to the police.

The hostages, 22 Indonesians and three Netherlands nationals, were taken in a bus to a police administrative center for family reunions. Some of them later went to the residence of the Indonesian Consul General for a party.

The mediators, Johannes Manusama, president of what he and other exiles have proclaimed as the South Moluccan Republic, and the Rev. Semeul Metiari, are both moderates in the independence campaign.

Charges the Gunmen Face

AMSTERDAM, Dec. 19 (Reuters)—A police spokesman said today that the seven gunmen who had held the consulate would be charged with unlawful deprivation of liberty and would go before a magistrate on Tuesday. The six train hijackers have all been charged with murder.

Associated Press

Dutch security men taking a bearded terrorist to a car yesterday in Amsterdam after he and six others who had held the Indonesian Consulate for 16 days surrendered.

December 20, 1975

PRESSURE ON JAKARTA IN WAKE OF ELECTION

Government, Its Share of Vote Less Than Expected, Facing Opposition Demands for Shifts in Policy

By DAVID A. ANDELMAN
Special to The New York Times

JAKARTA, Indonesia—The military-based Government has moved to deal with pressures emerging from last month's elections, in which its candidates' share of the total vote, though more than 60 percent, fell short of pre-election forecasts.

The pressures took the form of demands made during the campaign by the opposition, particularly the United Development Party, a coalition of four Moslem groups known by the initials of its Indonesian name as P.P.P.

One, for a return of religion, particularly Islam, to a more prominent place in the national consciousness of this predominantly Moslem country, was reported by an Indonesian intelligence offical and foreign military observers to have sent spasms of fear through the military and governmental leadership. The reason, the sources said, was the continuing vivid memory of riots staged three years ago by Moslem students against the Japanese and Chinese minorities.

Soon after the election the Government ordered the arrest of nearly 800 young Moslems said to be connected with a fanatical group accused of terrorist attacks in villages that supported Golkar, the Government party, during the eight-week campaign.

Rewards Said to Be Promised

Later, leaders of the P.P.P. were reportedly called in by President Suharto and told, according to a Moslem party source: "Calm your followers and your party will be rewarded. Everyone can share in the glory of the new order." There was speculation that this might mean the awarding of the Ministry of Religions to a member of the Moslem coalition.

Other opposition pressures that apparently brought Government reactions included demands for the end of corruption and flagrant abuses of authority and for a better distribution of wealth, particularly in the larger cities, were the riches of military officers, civil servants and well-connected businessmen contrast sharply with the lot of the masses. This nation of 131 million people, the fifth most populous in the world, is one of the lowest in per capita income.

"There is no longer any rule of law in this country for the people," said Chalid Mawardi, deputy secretary general of the United Development Party. "There is only law for the rich man or the Government or official. This is what we are fighting for—not for an Islamic state but for a state where the people come first."

In the balloting the Government party, which had expected to poll up to 70 percent, drew 62, emerging with 232 of the 360 seats in Parliament, a loss of four over its showing in the elections of July 1971. For the first time it lost metropolitan Jakarta.

The coalition of Moslem groups gained five seats for a total of 99, and the Indonesian Democratic Party, consisting of five Christian and nationalist groups, won 29 seats, or one fewer than in the previous election.

'The Results Will Be Different'

Speaking of the Government party's losses, a member of its executive board said, 'We are already moving to emplant a party structure, as distinct from the Government structure, in every village in Indonesia, so that next time the results will be different.' This involves nearly 300,000 officials in 53,000 villages and 4,000 counties.

In moves cited here as aimed at easing the pressure of corruption charges, Budiadji, former chief of the Government rice program on East Kalimantan, was sentenced two weeks ago to an extraordinary term of life imprisonment by a district court, while two lesser officials were sentenced to terms of 17 and 30 years. The three had been charged with defrauding the rice program of tens of thousands of dollars.

In addition, Government officials are quietly saying that some former officials of the bankrupt sate oil company, Pertamina, are to be brought to trial on corruption charges in connection with its collapse two years ago. A number of these officials, including the former president, Gen. Ibnu Sutowo, have been detained or placed under house arrest. However, most of them have since been granted a degree of freedom; General Sutowo, for example, has been seen playing golf in Jakarta.

In view of the Government's election setbacks, particularly in Jakarta, officials appear anxious to get to work on a wide range of development programs that would provide some immediate evidence of a desire to move wealth into the villages or, of even greater importance, into the lower-income areas of the major cities. Slum areas along some of the most polluted canals are being cleared and their inhabitants moved out of the city, a program upgrading middle-income housing is being pressed with World Bank and other aid funds.

Next March the elected members of Parliament, together with 100 military members appointed by President Suharto and an equal number of nonelected members, also appointed by the President, are to meet to select a new President and vice president. There has never been any doubt that General Suharto and his Vice President, Sultan Hamengku Buwono, will be re-elected.

June 19, 1977

Indonesia's Oil Fails to Wash Away the Blight of Poverty

By HENRY KAMM
Special to The New York Times

JAKARTA, Indonesia—Concrete office towers and imposing Government buildings have sprung up in this boom-town capital and in other cities of Indonesia, Mercedes-Benz automobiles are commonplace, and the initials of Pierre Cardin are worn like a badge of new riches by sleek men and women in public places.

But Indonesia is again expected to fall short, this year by 2.7 million tons, in production of rice, the country's staff of life. This means it will have to spend about a quarter of its foreign earnings from petroleum, the principal export, to buy rice abroad. Indonesia is the world's leading rice importer.

A recent study by a group of health and population experts, an Indonesian and two Americans, estimated that infant mortality on the island of Java, where more than 80 million of Indonesia's 135 million people live, was between 130 and 144 per 1,000, which is 30 to 40 times higher than in the West. The scientists estimated that one-fifth of the children born in Java do not reach 5 years of age.

Dr. Sjachroel Malasan, nutrition director at the Health Ministry, has estimated that 60 percent of Indonesia's population is malnourished. The daily per-capita protein intake is estimated at less than the minimum 40 grams set by the United Nations Food and Agriculture Organization. Average daily protein consumption in the United States is about 100 grams.

Low Meat and Milk Intake

The average yearly meat consumption is 8.4 pounds, compared with 176 in the United States. An average Indonesian drinks about a pint of milk a year, roughly what an American drinks in a day, and eats only 11 eggs a year.

These statistics are known to few Indonesians. But in a nation where most people live at or below the poverty line, the gap between rich and poor is leading to increased questioning among intellectuals about the course of development. Many, perhaps the majority, have become disillusioned, and direct this feeling principally at the Government of President Suharto, who has been in power since 1966.

It goes beyond Mr. Suharto, a former general, however, to all of the military, who have held the keys to power during his tenure, and to the businessmen who have reaped the profits from the extraction of Indonesia's natural resources—minerals, timber, rubber and coffee, in addition to oil.

Attitude Shared by Intellectuals

The disenchantment also extends to the technocrats who devised the country's development policy and executed it in close cooperation with the military-dominated Government. And it has spread to include the great number of foreigners connected with this development—private businessmen, officials of international organizations and other experts and Government aid representatives.

The critical attitude comes across particularly strongly in the students, who began late last year to defy political repression and stage public protests against the re-election of President Suharto. But it appears to be shared by many intellectuals, including those in public service. The students have subsided since a Government crackdown preceding the elections last month, but still express skepticism in conversations.

Their immediate targets are the most visible ones: the authoritarian Government, corruption and the inequality of distribution of wealth. They say that since the regime has been installed for five more years, they accept it. But they add that they now expect it to redirect the allocation of resources to let development reach the majority.

The students' ideas tend to be idealistic in a conservative nation that remains traumatized from the vast bloodletting that followed the 1965 Communist coup attempt. Many students interviewed in the course of a 19-day visit advocated a Gandhian village-based development approach, with small-scale or cottage industries to create jobs. About one million young Indonesians come into the labor market each year.

Foreigners Are Suspect

The Government's emphasis, however, is on development, based on the extraction of Indonesia's vast resources, in the expectation that each extraction operation will serve as a center of local development as well as of foreign exchange. The critics do not consider this program socially oriented enough. They regard it as more conducive to profiteering than to increasing the well-being of the people in the area.

The students tend to suspect foreigners involved in development projects of serving their own national goals or those of multinational corporations rather than Indonesia. They suspect international development experts of protecting their own interests and fulfilling functions that, if useful at all, should be carried out by Indonesians. This feeling goes far beyond the students to officials and intellectuals; a Cabinet minister said that he had seen many foreign consultants' reports that proposed a greater role for foreign experts than seemed necessary to him.

Some older Indonesian intellectuals believe that the continued presence of foreign experts and technicians is creating attitudes toward Westerners among young Indonesians, who have never been exposed to colonialism, that they recall from their days in the anticolonial struggle.

A faculty dean at the university in Ujung Pandang, the principal city on the island of Sulawesi, told of two large economic teams, one Canadian and one Japa-

nese, that are preparing development programs for the island. He felt that at his university alone there were enough experts who could do the same job with equal skill, deeper knowledge of the land and people and a greater commitment.

'You Don't Have Troubles With Machines'

And a prominent intellectual in Jakarta said, "Foreign aid enfeebles our own will and determination to put order in our own house. We think when we're in trouble our friends abroad will jump in and bail us out."

Discussing development here in general, the intellectual, a noted writer, said: "What has been built serves mainly the needs of the foreign investor and the Government, not the people of Indonesia. With a million every year coming on the labor market, most of the foreign investment in capital is intensive, using machines and not labor. Of course, you don't have the troubles with machines that you might have with workers."

The intellectual, one of Indonesia's most eloquent, spoke bitterly of the technocrats, people he said he, like many others, had trusted. But after 12 years in ministerial seats of power, he said, they have become part of the structure of Mr. Suharto's power.

"They are not really committed to any ideal," he said. "They are not really interested in the well-being of the people. They are indifferent to human rights and the rule of law. They will work for anybody who puts them there."

April 27, 1978

Indonesia's Chinese: 'Real Rulers' or a Harried Minority?

By HENRY KAMM
Special to The New York Times

JAKARTA, Indonesia, May 25 — The Chinese minority in Indonesia, about four million strong, is subjected to a broad range of discriminatory measures by the military-dominated Government of President Suharto. At the same time, the Chinese are strongly disliked by the most outspoken opponents of the regime for collaborating with it and profiting from it.

As elsewhere in Southeast Asia, the Chinese in Indonesia are particularly active in business, and this has led to their depiction as profiteers and exploiters, and thus has served to reinforce existing ethnic prejudices.

Moreover, the high value that Chinese attach to the education of their children has, here as elsewhere in Southeast Asia, created a feeling that Chinese consider themselves superior to the majority among whom they live and harbor strivings for exclusivity and an elite status.

"They call us the Jews of the East," M. H. Husino, an elderly lawyer said with a wry smile.

Status of Chinese Varies

Of the ethnic Chinese, about three million have Indonesian citizenship, nearly one million are claimed by Peking as its citizens and perhaps 70,000 are stateless.

Following communal violence against Chinese after the bloody repression of the Communist coup in 1965, the Suharto Government adopted a program of forced assimilation to eradicate Chinese cultural differences. The purpose of the measures was to take the sting out of anti-Chinese violence, assuring the physical safety of the Chinese as well as the cooperation of their financial community with the Government in the intensive economic-development program set in motion after the fall of the regime of President Sukarno.

The goals are being achieved, with the result that Chinese feel culturally deprived and increasingly hated by the disaffected political and intellectual classes who oppose the Suharto regime because they consider it politically repressive and economically unjust to the great majority, a majority that does not share significantly in the proceeds of development.

Anti-Chinese feelings are most vehemently expressed in conversations with Government critics of the two principal groups — intellectuals and Moslem leaders.

'The Real Ruling Class'

"The Chinese are the real ruling class," said an editor of Prisma, a respected journal of social and economic affairs. "They control 70 percent of trade;

they get 70 percent of the credit from the state banks; they have cornered 70 percent of the modern sector of the economy. Most Chinese say they are not running for president but only to control the president. They do. In economic and political terms they are the real ruling class."

Another editor, like his colleague modest, soft-spoken and highly educated, who had been indicating his agreement, added: "The Chinese are so close together in their ethnic group that they form an economic unit that excludes all others. Even when they are fishermen or farmers, they are the ones with the most modern equipment and get the most benefit."

"The contempt of the people is growing," said the first editor. Asked what possible solutions he saw, he replied, "A comparison to the Vietnamese situation is fair."

Asked whether he meant that Indonesia should adopt the Vietnamese policy of forcing the Chinese minority out of the country by cramming them on any available boat and setting it adrift, the editor had an answer.

May Be 'Inevitable'

"It is not my solution," he said, "but a softer solution is difficult. If the people want it, it is inevitable. It is beyond our responsibility to find a solution."

Prisma is published by the Institute for Economic and Social Research, Education and Information, a group that draws some of its financing from the Friedrich Naumann Foundation, a development assistance group close to the West German Free Democratic Party, a member of the Government coalition. The group's funds come mainly from West German Government development assistance.

The institute is making a major effort to stimulate the training of ethnic Indonesians to equip them better for economic competition with Chinese. A similar effort, on a broader scale, is being made by Muhammadiyah, a mass organization for the advancement of Islam.

A member of its central board, Lukman Harun, said in an interview:

"Most Indonesian people are poor and Moslem. Who controls the economy? Ninety percent of our economy is controlled by Chinese. We are not racists, but most people are not so happy about this. Government corruption always goes through the Chinese."

General Cites Chinese Power

Gen. Abdul Haris Nasution, a leading political and military figure of the independence struggle and the Sukarno regime, now sidetracked because of political differences with Mr. Suharto, contended in an interview that Chinese influence had greatly grown in the Suharto period, economically and politically.

Chinese economic power, he charged, is concentrated around Mr. Suharto's family. Their political power, according to General Nasution, is focused in an American-style "think tank" called the Center for Strategic and International Studies. The center, housed in an impressive modern building in the heart of Jakarta, is a creation of Lieut. Gen. Ali Murtopo, who is Information Minister and is known as Mr. Suharto's principal intelligence and political adviser and trouble-shooter.

"Its people are all Chinese, even the receptionist," General Nasution said. "They are the biggest influence on politics."

This opinion is widely shared in political and diplomatic circles, and the Roman Catholic faith of some of the center's staff is often noted critically.

"The Chinese Catholic group from the early beginning had a phobia against the majority, a religious phobia against Moslems," General Nasution said. "They want a polarization of the army against Islam. Their objective is to say Indonesia is not yet ripe for real democracy."

Vast Registration Under Way

Discriminatory measures against ethnic Chinese, of Indonesian nationality or aliens, are deeply resented by the Chinese community. A nationwide process of registration of all people of Chinese origin is under way, with the proclaimed aim of establishing their identity and citizenship as part of the process of "unfreezing" diplomatic relations with Peking, inactive since the 1965 coup.

The procedure is being carried out by the local offices of the prosecutor general, "men used to interrogating criminals," a Chinese said bitterly. Registration consists of completing a 29-page questionnaire, which probes deeply into all aspects of the person's life and family.

The questionnaire itself has to be paid for by the person interrogated, and the cost of about $4 is a heavy burden in a country whose per capita yearly income is $300. In addition, answers have to be supported by a great number of documents that have to be photocopied — birth, death and marriage certificates,

United Press International

Ethnic Chinese boarding a ship in an Indonesian harbor in 1966 to leave the country after widespread repression of Communists. The Chinese minority, regarded with suspicion at that time, is still subject to discrimination.

identity cards, name-change documents and business licenses.

Chinese in a variety of professions and businesses alleged that extortion, both petty and large scale, was the price their community paid for being allowed to pursue normal activities. Indonesians of Chinese origin, even people settled here for many generations with Indonesianized names and unable to speak Chinese, find access to government employment or military careers virtually closed.

All large-scale Chinese organizations have been dissolved, leaving only temples and burial societies as focuses of Chinese life. There is only one Chinese-language newspaper, owned by the Government and edited by a general of military intelligence. No Chinese books or magazines are printed, and since this year imports of Chinese publications, mainly from Singapore or Hong Kong, have been forbidden.

A 10 Percent University Quota

Chinese schools have been closed, and even privately organized language classes are unlawful. Universities limit the entrance of ethnic Chinese students to 10 percent of total enrollment. The latest estimate of Indonesia's population is about 140 million, making the four million ethnic Chinese a bit less than 3 percent of the total.

A dean at Hasanuddin University in Sulawesi, the former Celebes, said he applied the quota even if the applicants did better in their entrance exams than Indonesian candidates. "It's not only that too many Chinese would enter," he said. "Remember that nine out of ten of the Chinese who start their university education get degrees. Maybe not even half of the Indonesians here graduate."

The generals of military intelligence ascribed the policy of avowed cultural repression to the needs of nation-building. "The objections of some hundreds of thousands cannot jeopardize the fate of millions," said a member of the Center for Strategic and International Studies, himself of Chinese origin.

An Unjust War in East Timor

Americans have only gradually become aware of the unjust war Indonesia has been waging in remote East Timor. The former Portuguese colony has suffered a ruthless military occupation since Indonesia invaded it in 1975 and proclaimed its annexation a year later. The fighting, disease and starvation may have claimed a third of East Timor's 600,000 inhabitants — no one can say for sure, because Indonesia has restricted access by the international relief agencies.

Although most of the weapons of suppression are American-made, Washington has muted its concern for the familiar pragmatic reasons. Indonesia, the most populous Moslem nation, is a major oil supplier; its military government is rightist and repressive. But American silence about East Timor contrasts oddly with the indignation over Cambodia; the suffering is great in both places.

In East Timor, as in Cambodia, an unoffending people is starving following invasion by an aggressive neighbor. Here, too, refugees with bloated bellies are being crammed into resettlement camps. Jakarta asserts control only by bombing the populated coastal areas, forcing Timorese into the mountains and devastating their rice economy.

When the Portuguese empire was crumbling in 1975, little attention was paid to the poor and primitive colony of East Timor. Indonesia already controlled the western half of the island and coveted the rest. Two independence movements vied for power in East Timor, one being the leftist Fretilin party, and that conflict served as the pretext for Indonesia's attack.

Though Washington says it "understands" the seizure, it disagrees with Indonesian claims that "self-determination" prompted it. The annexation has been repeatedly condemned by the United Nations and has found no legal support anywhere.

Portuguese priests who have fled East Timor say a third of the population has died. Indonesia disputes this number, but former Foreign Minister Adam Malik said in 1977 that the military casualties were 50,000, perhaps 80,000. By that reckoning, at least one of ten East Timorese is a casualty of "integration."

Members of Congress have finally begun to ask why Indonesia should be exempt from American censure. But these protests have elicited only mumbles from the Carter Administration; it still sells military hardware to Indonesia. The acquiescent silence of America is no more just than the war.

December 24, 1979

MARCOS AND THE PHILIPPINES

Stark Contrasts Persist in Philippines's 'New Society'

By JOSEPH LELYVELD
Special to The New York Times

MMANILA — There have been few places in Asia where high society has been higher or the lower depths have been lower than in the Philippines. Now, according to the ideology that President Ferdinand E. Marcos has fashioned for his "new society," the oligarchs are being put in their place and the poor are rising.

"The new society is, first of all, a community of equals," the President declares in his latest theoretical work, which was serialized simultaneously in three major newspapers here. "To be poor in this society is no longer to be underprivileged."

Even now, Mr. Marcos contends, "an emergent sense of solidarity" can be found in the worlds of the very rich and the very poor. What follow are some random glimpses into those worlds.

●

The First Lady, Mrs. Imelda Marcos, was on hand recently for the opening of an exhibition of the Philippine Institute of Interior Design, held in the sumptuous Cultural Center that stands next to the yacht club on Manila Bay.

The show is supposed to be an annual affair, but this was the first in four years. In 1970, when masses of students were taking to the streets to demonstrate against the lavish life-styles of the rich, the decorators thought a cancellation prudent. Now, with martial law in force, they felt emboldened to show their latest ideas.

These included a "classic Vienna hatrack executed in chrome instead of bentwood" for display in an "eclectic foyer"; a master bedroom with a huge bed whose white leather fittings had been laminated with headlines from Italian newspapers, and a "bachelor's pad" with animal skins on the floor and silver goblets on a table set for two.

Edith Oliveros, a decorator, said her profession was flourishing in the new society. The Government has restricted foreign travel for the rich, she explained, with the result that Filipinos who used to go to New York or the south of France every year are building luxury vacation houses.

"Lots of people," she said, "now have three houses—a house in their province, where they have their land, a vacation house, and, of course, a house in Manila."

●

Alberto Languido had just finished building his house when he heard that a typhoon was threatening to pass his way. The interior was bare —one room about six feet by eight containing only a cardboard box and a small cotton sack, in which were packed the worldly assets of

357

Mr. Languido and his wife, Aquilina.

They had managed to find most of the wood that went into the shack on garbage dumps, but the beams and the corrugated metal roof, which was now rattling in the wind, had cost 70 pesos, or nearly $11—the equivalent of two weeks' earnings.

To preserve that investment Mr. Languido was urgently nailing lengths of timber to the side of the house in the hope that they would brace it when the typhoon struck. Asked why he was determined to remain in his house during the storm, he laughed and replied, "I have no other house where I can go."

•

Most of the streets in the wealthiest suburban enclaves here, Forbes Park and Dasmarinas, take their names from trees: Tamarind and Acacia Roads, Flame Tree and Cypress Streets. In each case nature answers to the whim of the real-estate developer so that on Flame Tree Street, for instance, there are only flame trees.

The houses cost a minimum of 300,000 pesos and as much as 300,000,000; at the official exchange rate that works out to $50,000 to $500,-000. Given the lower cost of labor and materials in the Philippines, it would probably take $125,000 to reproduce the humblest of these homes in the United States.

Filipino families are large —eight or nine children are not uncommon — and the wealthier usually allot one room and one servant, called a yaya, to each child. The result is that some of the houses, with their four-car garages, look like luxury motels.

These days it is fashionable to find magnificent old doors, carved from the best Philippine woods, to hang at the threshold of new houses. Often they are taken from churches of the Spanish colonial era, so that now, it is said, it is necessary to go more than 100 miles from Manila to find an old church with its doors intact.

By tradition a special meal of noodles is served to the carpenters when the front door is installed. Coins and religious medals are buried in the foundation of the house and, finally, a priest is invited to say mass.

•

In the squatter colonies near the docks in the area known as Tondo, the shanties are packed so tightly together that there is often nothing but a fetid drain or, worse, a railway track to separate them.

The land on which the squatters live is mostly garbage fill and ground glass

Photographs for The New York Times by JOSEPH LELYVELD

A shack in the Slip Zero section of Manila, built on garbage fill and ground glass. What streets there are take their names from extraterrestrial inspiration—Mars and Venus.

In an expensive suburb of Manila, houses cost $50,000 to $500,000. Real estate interests have given the streets the names of tropical trees—the tamarind and the flame tree.

from a brewery bottling plant so, of course, there can be few trees. When the residents of a section called Bonifacio banded together to lay out streets of a decent width, they could find no terrestrial inspiration for names; in Bonifacio now Venus Street crosses Mars.

In Slip Zero—the small split of fill on which Mr. Languido put his shack—some of the residents scavange for their living, burrowing into the mounds of ground class to find shards big enough to sell

to cement factories. On a good day this trade in the broken glass, which they call bubog, can yield as much as 6 pesos, nearly a dollar.

Mr. Languido, who worked as a longshoreman in Cebu until a few years ago, said he was attracted to Manila by the "greater opportunities" here. Asked what they were, he mentioned the bubog, explaining that here, at least, he is able to scavange when he cannot find work on the docks.

No priests were summoned

when the Languidos moved into their home, but on either side of the narrow doorway, which is covered by a strip of sacking, two crucifixes have been carefully chalked. "To keep the children away from diseases," Mr. Languido said.

•

"Conspicuous consumption is frowned on in the new society," remarked Manuel Jiz de Ortega, an insurance agent, just as waiters started to serve the quenelles des fruits de mer au champagne on the opening night of the Christian Dior fashion show at the Manila Hilton.

No irony was intended. In the old days, he explained, every millionaire in Manila would have turned out for such an event. Now there were few millionaires and a disproportionate number of Government functionaries.

The austerity sensed by veterans of the old society registered slowly. By 10:30 the mannequins from Paris had paraded their last caftans and the bombe glacé Christian Dior had been consumed.

Mrs. Marcos and her party got up to leave and, within moments, the ballroom had emptied.

Under martial law a midnight curfew is still in force. Everyone says it is enforced on rich and poor alike.

On Sunday morning in Slip Zero some red-eyed card players were still at a game called lucky nine that had obviously started before curfew the night before.

"They are only playing to pass the time," it was quickly explained. "It's a vigil. Otherwise, it would not have been allowed." The explana-

tion proved correct — a 2-year-old had died of convulsions.

Elsewhere in Tondo small groups of men were standing together with roosters gently cradled in their arms, waiting for lookouts to signal when no constables were in sight so they could start their cockfights, which happen to be illegal in settled neighborhoods.

"Since martial law, the constables have been afraid to take bribes," a well-dressed man explained as a red rooster and a white one were primed by their handlers,

Suddenly there was a huge thrashing, a blur of feathers and then, in less than 30 seconds, a dead white bird in the roadway.

The money changed hands even faster. "These people have nothing to eat but they have to play this game," the well-dressed bystander commented, not with disapproval but with pride. "They have to make bets."

The bystander was asked what he did for a living. "I'm in the police," he said, "but I'm not on duty."

November 5, 1973

Vote Favoring Marcos —He Has One Setback

MANILA, Feb. 28 (AP)— Early official returns from the referendum on President Ferdinand E. Marcos' one-man rule have given him nearly 90 per cent approval, but he has suffered a minor setback in one province.

In Cebu province—former stronghold of the Osmena family, old political rivals of Mr. Marcos—the voters fa-

vored continuance of his martial-law rule. But they were voting against him on another question on the referendum: should he appoint local officials when their terms end Dec. 31—or should they be elected?

Labor Secretary Blas F. Ople said this was "the exception that proves the rule," meaning that the referendum was not rigged.

March 1, 1975

Amnesty Group Says Manila Uses Widespread Torture

MANILA, June 26 (AP)—Amnesty International said today that torture of martial-law prisoners in the Phillippines was widespread and part of a "general approach" to intimidate suspected political offenders.

In a report to the Philippine Government, investigators for the human rights organization said that authorities had beat suspects "freely and with extreme cruelty, often over long periods," had used electric

shock on their genitals, had threatened women with sexual assault, had made detainees put pistols to their own heads and pull the triggers in a "Russian roulette," and had alternately scalded and chilled the prisoners.

The investigators said that 68 of the 105 prisoners they interviewed, including one American, had said they had been tortured. Authorities have said that 4,000 people are being held in Philippine prisons without charges.

June 27, 1976

Marcos, Rebels Cease Firing

The Moslem rebels of the southern Philippines have reached a provisional accord with the Government of President Ferdinand E. Marcos, agreeing to end their four-year guerrilla campaign in return for a referendum on limited autonomy for the southwestern provinces of the island of Mindanao, where most of the 2.8 million Moslems in the predominantly Roman Catholic country live. The step, announced last week in Manila, was taken for both internal and external reasons: to end the fighting between the insurgents and Government troops that has killed more than 10,000 persons, and to improve Mr. Marcos's relations with the Arab nations, who have supported the rebels and on whose oil the Filipino economy depends.

The Moslems are the largest religious minority in the country of 42 million people, and form a majority in 5 of

Moslem Areas In The Philippines
(Black areas)

South China Sea

Manila

Pacific Ocean

PALAWAN

Sulu Sea

LANAO DEL NORTE

ZAMBOANGA DEL NORTE

ZAMBOANGA DEL SUR

BASILAN

LANAO DEL SUR

SULU

NORTH COTABATO

SOUTH COTABATO

DAVAO DEL SUR

TAWITAWI

13 provinces on Mindanao. Moslem Mindanao was ruled for centuries by sultans, resisting Spanish conquista-

dors, recognized as an independent power by American colonial authorities after the Spanish-American war and formally joining the rest of the country only in 1940. The other ethnic and religious minorities among the Philippines' 4 million non-Christians inhabit fringe areas on scattered islands and have few external contacts.

A Moslem secessionist movement was formed in 1969 to protest increasing southward migration by Christian Filipinos and what the Moslems felt was neglect by the Manila Government. Mr. Marcos declared martial law in 1972; guerrilla-led strikes followed, with occasional hijackings and kidnappings.

The Government began negotiations with the rebels through Arab intermediaries after the Arab oil embargo of 1973-74. The Philippines has no oil of its own and needs Middle Eastern fuel to carry out an ambitious development program.

January 2, 1977

The New York Times/Sept. 21, 1977
Fighting erupted in Basilan

Philippine Troops Raid a Rebel Area As Truce Falters

ISABELA, Philippines, Sept. 20 (AP)—Troops supported by aircraft attacked suspected rebel forces today in a breakdown of the eight-month truce between the Government and Moslem insurgents in the southern Philippines.

Col. Salvador Mison, an army brigade commander, said he had ordered the operation after leaders of the Moslem-controlled Moro National Liberation Front ignored an ultimatum to surrender terrorists accused of killing 23 civilians with a land mine.

A cease-fire last Christmas Eve halted fighting in a four-year Moslem rebellion against the Manila Government. Periodic violations of the truce have occurred, reportedly on both sides, but apparently nothing on the scale of today's action on the island of Basilan, 550 miles south of Manila.

"The artillery and air strike operations were launched this morning," Colonel Mison said. He said that at least two light planes, designed for low-level strafing and bombing missions, had been used.

Two Government officials who saw the fighting at Maluso, a fishing village about 16 miles west of Isabela, said they watched as the planes dived twice, strafing and bombing targets on the ground.

The land-mine explosion that brought today's attack by the Government destroyed a truck carrying 81 workers at a Government-owned experimental rubber plantation. Besides the 23 dead, 58 passengers were wounded, 35 of them seriously.

Rear Adm. Romulo Espaldon, military commander in the southern Philippines, threatened leaders of the Moro National Liberation Front with reprisals unless those who planted the mine were turned over to the military by this morning.

Under the terms of the cease-fire agreement, the Government would have been restricted to moving against only the rebels in the area of the land-mine explosion to restore order. Today's fighting was relatively far from there.

September 20, 1977

5-Year-Old Philippine Martial Law Builds Personal Power of Marcos

By FOX BUTTERFIELD
Special to The New York Times

Associated Press
President Ferdinand E. Marcos and his wife, Imelda, last August. They have continued public appearances after five years of martial-law rule.

MANILA, Jan. 8—When President Ferdinand E. Marcos presided over the annual Armed Forces Day celebration here recently, he and his wife, Imelda, sat in twin antique gold throne chairs. The high-backed chairs are with the presidential couple wherever they appear in the Philippines these days and have become a widely recognized symbol of the five years of martial law under Mr. Marcos.

Although he has sought to preserve some semblance of a once-raucous democracy through annual referendums and other devices, he has created a personal power structure, backed by a vastly enlarged military establishment that tolerates virtually no opposition.

In the latest referendum, held in mid-December, the 60-year-old President won 90.6 percent of the vote on the question of whether he should remain in office indefinitely as President-Prime Minister, a position he established in the Constitution of 1973 and in amendments adopted last year.

He has won at least 87 percent of the vote in each of the five referendums he has called since imposing martial law in September 1972—after having held the presidency since the 1965 election—though many people believe the figures are sharply inflated. It was a measure of his power that even if the reported tally had gone against him in the latest referendum, the question was so phrased that he would have remained at his posts.

Mr. Marcos likes to refer to his system of governing as constitutional authoritarianism rather than martial law. "The term martial law is an unfortunate one," he remarked in a recent interview, "implying the army is taking over."

In the interview, in the elegant old Spanish structure that functions as the presidential palace, Mr. Marcos said that the referendum's outcome "irrevocably

360

commits us" to ending martial law. But he said he must first create an interim national assembly—he abolished the Congress in 1972—and stop the costly secessionist war being waged by Moslem groups in southern Mindanao and the Sulu Archipelago. In one form or another that conflict has been going on almost since the Spanish colonized the Philippines four centuries ago, and few people think it will end soon.

There is little doubt that Mr. Marcos's five years of authoritarian control have brought progress to this island nation of over 44 million people. By forcibly collecting firearms he wiped out the many private armies and gangs that made the country a kind of Far Eastern Wild West. His Government has pushed land reform and the construction of roads, schools and irrigation facilities in the remote villages where the majority still live.

Mrs. Marcos, an energetic and forceful 48-year-old woman who was appointed Mayor of Manila by her husband, has cleaned up the capital's chaotic streets and has begun efforts to relocate the hundreds of thousands of squatters who have flocked in from the countryside.

In foreign policy the Marcoses, working together, have helped fashion a new international stature for their country, freeing it from much of its longtime dependence on the United States while aligning it more closely with the developing world and establishing relations with China and the Soviet Union.

Yet for each of these accomplishments, President Marcos's critics contend, there are drawbacks. Although he has distributed more land to the peasants than did any of his predecessors, only about a third of the landless farmers have benefited so far and he has excluded the poorest of all—those on sugar and coconut plantations.

Funds for Hotels but Not Housing

While the Government, acting on a presidential order, lent almost $500 million last year for the construction of 14 hotels in Manila, it spent only $13 million for badly needed public housing. The hotels are less than half full and none have been able to meet the interest payments on their loans; Mr. Marcos recently promised to reschedule their debts.

Not coincidentally, critics charge, Mrs. Marcos is chairman of the board of the Cultural Center of the Philippines, the group that owns the largest and most expensive new hotel, while several of her husband's friends, including Roberto

Benedicto, a fraternity mate, own others Indeed, the growing wealth of Mr. Marcos's relatives and colleagues has become so obvious that it has spawned a series of jokes. "Under martial law everything is relative," one says. "You have to be related."

Virtually all Manila television stations and newspapers have passed into the hands of relatives or associates of Mr. and Mrs. Marcos since martial law was declared. The President's golf partner, Herminio Disini, who is related by marriage to Mrs. Marcos, has gone from a job with a tobacco company five years ago to the ownership of a conglomerate with assets exceeding $500 million.

President Marcos's supporters often cite the economic growth of 5 to 6 percent a year since 1972 as evidence of his accomplishments. But the real wages of workers in Manila have declined almost 25 percent in the past five years, according to Government figures, and the gap between the rich and the poor, already one of the largest in Asia, has reportedly broadened. The top 20 percent of the country's income earners took in 53 percent of the total national income last year, while the bottom 40 percent got only 14.7 percent.

Little Real Challenge Permitted

On the political side, though martial law seems less oppressive in some ways than elsewhere in Asia—political prisoners, for example, are allowed connubial visits—Mr. Marcos permits little real challenge. Recently a judge, Benigno M. Puno, who countered Mr. Marcos's wishes in a land case, was notified that his letter of resignation had been accepted. He has petitioned the Supreme Court, which, under Philippine law, has the only power to remove judges, contending that he had written no such letter.

Furthermore, 246 Roman Catholic priests, nuns and lay workers, including two highly respected American priests, face trial before military tribunals on charges of using church newsletters and radio stations to try to overthrow Mr. Marcos. With most legal opposition prohibited, the Catholic Church, which says over 80 percent of the people are members, has become the main focus of organized criticism.

The small Communist New People's Army, with perhaps 2,000 armed adherents, has continued to cause trouble in some remote areas, though the army has captured most of its recognized leaders. Neither it nor any of the other scattered opposition groups really poses a threat to Mr. Marcos, but knowledgeable Filipinos believe he has begun to lose much of the genuine popularity he had at the

start of martial law. A customs inspector at the Manila airport surprised an arriving American when he volunteered the opinion that the President had become corrupt dictator who should be thrown out.

Mr. Marcos has usually been able to deflect such criticism with a constant and bewildering series of actions—the referendums, pledges to end martial law and popular extravaganzas such as the Miss Universe pageant and the Mohammad Ali - Joe Frazier heavyweight boxing match.

Washington's Attitude a Factor

Some political observers believe that the referendum last month was partly directed at Washington. The President is in the midst of protracted negotiations with the United States over continued use of two large American military installations, Clark Air Base and Subic Bay Naval Base. He has made three demands: sovereignty over the bases, which Washington has already assented to in principle, jurisdiction over American servicemen involved in violations of the law while off duty, which is under discussion, and sizable financial compensation. Last year the President rejected a $1 billion offer.

While both sides have refused to discuss details of the talks, Mr. Marcos indicated in the interview that he would like the compensation tied to a five-year modernization of the armed forces. However, he said President Carter had made him aware that any military aid in exchange for the bases would have to be approved by Congress and he realizes that there may be some questions about his conduct of government. Both Filipinos and diplomats believe Mr. Marcos's pledge to hold elections for a national assembly by next spring may be designed to abate such criticism.

Whatever the case, one lasting result of martial law seems to be that the President has created a much larger and more politically involved army. Before 1972 the armed forces numbering 55,000, were among the smallest and least political in Asia. Today the army has grown to over 160,000 and generals sit on the boards of many corporations.

The armed forces obviously would play a major role if anything should happen to Mr. Marcos. As matters stand there is no formal provision for the succession; he has said only that he has formed a special small group that is instructed on what to do.

January 9, 1978

MANILA INNER CIRCLE GAINS UNDER MARCOS

Leader's Friends and Relatives Said to Amass Wealth and Power

By FOX BUTTERFIELD
Special to The New York Times

MANILA, Jan. 14—When President Ferdinand E. Marcos declared martial law in 1972, he avowed that one of its

main purposes was to break up the wealthy families that had long controlled money and politics in the Philippines. But his critics charge that the only redistribution of wealth has been from one elite to another.

Mr. Marcos's supporters contend that much of this criticism stems from embittered members of the wealthy old families that once controlled the Philippines, families the President has displaced by redistributing the nation's wealth under martial law.

Among those who are said to have benefited most from the President's powers under martial law is Roberto Benedicto, a fraternity brother of Mr.

Marcos at the University of the Philippines. Mr. Benedicto now heads the newly created Sugar Commission, which Mr. Marcos has given a monopoly over the export of the large sugar crop.

Ownership Difficult to Prove

A former ambassador to Japan and head of the Government-owned Philippine National Bank, Mr. Benedicto also reportedly owns a bank, a shipping line, the largest television and radio network in the country, a newspaper, sugar lands and several new sugar mills. Since some of these enterprises are registered in the names of friends or associates, it is difficult to prove his ownership.

Mr. Marcos's brother-in-law, Benjamin

361

Romualdez, is governor of the province of Leyte. He is said to control The Times Journal, a major Manila newspaper, and he is generally believed to have benefited from the forced takeover of the Manila Electric Company from the Lopez family, once the wealthiest in the Philippines.

Mr. Romualdez, who until recently was ambassador to China, has reportedly been proposed as ambassador to Washington. In a recent interview his sister, Imelda Marcos, said she thought the choice would be "good for the United States."

The Secretary of Defense, Juan Ponce Enrile, who comes from Mr. Marcos's home region of Ilocos in northern Luzon, is chairman of the Philippine National Bank, the Philippine coconut authority, the United Coconut Planters Bank, and he sits on the board of half a dozen other businesses.

Mr. Marcos's sister is governor of Ilocos Norte. Two of the most powerful military commanders also come from the President's home area, Maj. Gen. Fabian Ver, chief of the presidential security guard, and Maj. Gen. Fidel V. Ramos, head of the Philippine Constabulary, the national police.

Mrs. Marcos's younger brother, Alfredo Romualdez, is said by knowledgeable Filipinos to be involved in a lucrative floating casino in Manila Bay and the jai-alai fronton.

Ricardo Silverio, a close friend of the Marcoses, has made a fortune through owning the exclusive Toyota distributorship for the Philippines. Another friend, Rodolfo Cuenca, is head of the country's biggest construction company, which is currently engaged in a $500 million project to reclaim 4,000 acres of Manila Harbor. His company will get half the land.

Control of Newspapers

Virtually all of Manila's major newspapers are owned by friends or relatives of the Marcoses, and Mr. Benedicto controls three of the city's five television channels.

President Marcos helped a close friend and in-law, Herminio Disini, build a vast business empire by a secret presidential decree that forced a major competitor out of business.

The decree imposed a 100 percent duty on the imported raw materials of Mr. Disini's American and British-owned competitor and continued the usual 10 percent tariff on those used by Mr. Disini's company. The two companies made filters for cigarettes.

Mr. Marcos issued the decree in July 1975 after the foreign company, Filtrona Philippines Inc., had turned down an offer from Mr. Disini to buy it out, according to a former executive of Filtrona. The decree forced Filtrona to close its operations in the Philippines and left Mr. Disini with a near monopoly on the lucrative filter business here, with an estimated profit of more than $1 million a month.

When the then United States Ambassador to the Philippines, William Sullivan, protested the decree to Mr. Marcos, the former Filtrona officer charged, the President attempted to blackmail Filtrona by suggesting it join Mr. Disini as a partner in building a $40 million factory to manufacture cellulose for filters.

The cigarette deal is only one of many lucrative transactions in which Mr. Disini's access to the President appears to have been decisive. Here are some other instances:

¶A subsidiary of Herdis, Mr. Disini's company, has been appointed as government agent for a proposed $800 million petrochemical complex. A senior executive of a major United States petrochemical company that expressed interest in investing in the complex was told it would have to pay Herdis a commission of 2 to 3 percent of its investment as an agent's fee. The fee, which could amount to over $10 million, "was the most blatant, rotten thing I've heard in all my years," the executive said.

¶Herdis has financed many of its rapid acquisitions of new companies and investments in new factories by taking more than $200 million in foreign loans, all guaranteed by government banks. In a number of these cases Herdis had to put up little or no security of its own, bankers here say, and needed only political approval to win the government guarantee.

¶Mr. Disini has been accused of being the key figure behind a major stock market manipulation here in 1976. Some brokers say he acquired as much as $9.5 million worth of shares in an oil exploration company for only $675,000 shortly before President Marcos went on national television to announce that oil had been found. When afterward the major shareholders suddenly dumped their shares and the price plummeted 65 percent, the Philippines Securities and Exchange Commission found no evidence of wrongdoing.

In an interview with The New York Times yesterday, President Marcos promised to conduct a broad investigation of Mr. Disini's acquisitions and to divest him of some of the important ones, particularly a 500,000-acre timber concession, and the subsidiary that had been acting as Government agent for the proposed chemical complex. He said the subsidiary would lose its standing as a Government agent. Mr. Marcos denied that Mr. Disini had built his empire on the basis of presidential favor.

The size of the Marcoses' personal fortune is a subject of endless gossip in Manila, but there is virtually no real evidence about it. One story among acquaintances of the President's family is that Mr. Marcos maintains a staff of 15 or 20 lawyers and accountants just to keep track of his money.

One businessman with good contacts with Mr. Marcos recalls a dinner party in 1968, three years after Mr. Marcos first became President and four years before he proclaimed martial law, at which a group of Cabinet members and confidantes jokingly decided to list all they knew about the President's money. The total came to $60 million.

In 1966 the Marcoses purchased a 17th-century Spanish villa in a large lot near the official presidential residence. The sale price is said to have been more than $125,000.

The interior of the villa was redesigned by Manila's leading architect, Leandro Locsin, and furnished with crystal chandeliers, French period furniture, Mrs. Marcos's collection of Chinese export porcelain, antique European rugs and tapestries and several paintings by Picasso and Renoir, visitors to the home say.

Mrs. Marcos has become known among jewelers as an avid purchaser. A representative in Hong Kong for Cartier, the Paris company, said he believed Mrs. Marcos had put together the world's largest private collection of gems.

Sometimes, however, she can be choosy. Recently she returned a 40-carat sapphire, priced at $200,000, to Lane Crawford, a department store, after having kept it for several months, a jeweler connected with the store reported.

January 15, 1978

U.S. and Philippines Reach Accord On Aid and Use of Military Bases

Special to The New York Times

WASHINGTON, Dec. 31 — The United States and the Philippines announced agreement today on a new arrangement that will provide the Philippines with as much as $500 million in military and economic aid over the next five years in return for the Manila Government's allowing the Americans continued "unhampered" use of military bases there.

After more than two years of negotiations, the two sides agreed on a series of amendments to the current military bases agreement, which runs until 1999.

The Philippines had sought changes in the present arrangement, particularly to more clearly assert Filipino sovereignty over the bases and to provide for more military and economic aid.

Under the new terms, each American base will officially be under the control of a Filipino, and the Philippines will be in charge of overall security for the installation.

In addition, the Carter Administration will pledge its best efforts to obtain Congressional approval of $450 million to $500 million in aid to the Philippines, starting in the next fiscal year. The total is to be broken down into $50 million in grant military aid, $250 million in military credits and $150 to $200 million in economic support.

Manila Already a Major Aid Recipient

The Philippines already is a major recipient of American aid, getting about $37 million yearly in military assistance and about $100 million in economic aid, mostly in projects and agricultural goods under the Food for Peace program. The increase provided in the new program will be to raise the military aid to about $60 million a year.

The agreement had been sought for a long time by the United States to end questions about the ability of the American military forces to retain key bases in the Pacific.

"The bases in the Philippines, Clark Air Base, and the Subic Bay Naval complex, are important to our ability to project United States military strength throughout the Pacific," Thomas Reston, a State Department spokesman, said today.

"The steps we will take to give clearer expression to Filipino sovereignty over the bases will assure the durability of our defense relationship and thereby serve to preserve peace and stability in the region," he said.

Joint Statement Issued

In a joint statement, the United States and the Philippines also said that the size of the American bases would be reduced but that the agreement assured the United States of "unhampered military operations" from them.

As it turned out, President Ferdinand E. Marcos of the Philippines agreed to a substantially smaller aid package than he had been offered by the previous Administration. In December 1976, Secretary of State Henry A. Kissinger offered a five-year, $1 billion package, half in military aid and half in economic assistance.

But at that time Mr. Marcos wanted the entire $1 billion in military aid and refused the offer. Since then, officials here have told Mr. Marcos it was unlikely Congress would approve such an increase in aid.

Another factor in Mr. Marcos's thinking, officials said, was pressure from other Southeast Asian countries that wanted an end to the uncertainty about the bases.

The rise in Vietnam's power and growing tensions involving China, Vietnam and Cambodia, with the Soviet Union siding with Vietnam, have led many Asian leaders to urge that Mr. Marcos not interfere with an American presence.

January 1, 1979

Suggested Reading

Aveling, Harry, ed. *The Development of Indonesian Society.* New York: St. Martin's Press, 1979.

Barnett, Anthony. *The Cambodian Revolutions.* New York: Schocken, 1979.

Crouch, Harold. *The Army and Politics in Indonesia.* Ithaca; Cornell University Press, 1978.

Elliot, David. *Thailand: Origins of Military Rule.* Boston: Porter Sargent, 1979.

Evers, Hans-Dieter, ed. *Modernization in Southeast Asia.* New York: Oxford University Press, 1973.

Fall, Bernard B. *Last Reflections on a War.* New York: Schocken, 1972.

Fitzgerald, Frances. *Fire in the Lake: The Vietnamese and the Americans in Vietnam.* Boston: Little, Brown, 1972.

Gurtov, Melvin. *China and Southeast Asia — The Politics of Survival.* Baltimore: Johns Hopkins University Press, 1975.

Halberstam, David. *The Best and the Brightest.* New York: Random House, 1972.

Hersh, Seymour M. *My Lai Four: A Report on the Massacre and its Aftermath.* New York: Random House, 1970.

Lyon, Peter. *War and Peace in Southeast Asia.* New York: Oxford University Press, 1969.

Kerkvleit, Benedict. *The Huk Rebellion: A Study of Peasant Revolt in the Philippines.* Berkeley, Calif.: University of California Press, 1977

Martin, Edwin. *Southeast Asia and China: The End of Containment.* Boulder, Col.: Westview Press, 1977.

Neill, Wilfred T. *Twentieth-Century Indonesia.* New York: Columbia University Press, 1973.

Paulker, Guy J., et al. *Diversity and Development in Southeast Asia.* New York: McGraw-Hill, 1977.

Pike, Douglas. *War, Peace and the Vietcong.* Cambridge, Mass.: MIT Press, 1969.

Porter, M. *Cambodia: Starvation and Revolution.* Boston: Porter Sargent, 1979.

Ryan, N.J. *A History of Malaysia and Singapore.* New York: Oxford University Press, 1977.

Silverstein, Josef. *Burma: Military Rule and the Politics of Stagnation.* Ithaca, N.Y.: Cornell University Press, 1977.

Welch, Richard E., Jr. *Response to Imperialism: The United States and the Philippine-American War, 1899-1902.* Chapel Hill, N.C.: University of North Carolina Press, 1979.

Williams, Lea E. *Southeast Asia: A History.* New York: Oxford University Press, 1976.

Index

Abdul Rahman, Sir, 86, 248, 250-51
Africa-Asia unity, 230-31
Aguinaldo, Emilio, 2-5, 7, 16
Amboinese, 75
Ananda Mahidol, 62-63
Annam, 16-17, 19; *see also* Vietnam
Anti-Imperialist League, 5
Asia, 172, 230-31
Asia-Pacific Council, 274
assassinations, 82, 97
Association of Southeast Asia Nations, 274
Attlee, Clement, 87
Aung San, U, 87, 88
Australia, 252

Bangladesh, 339
Bao Dai, 58, 105-6
Ba Swe, U, 254
Binh, Nguyen Thi, 301-2
Bohlen, Charles, 261
Borneo, 21, 78, 252
Bounooum, Prince, 113-14, 121
Britain and: Burma, 30-32, 86-88; Malaya, 78-86;
    Malaysia, 246-47; Siam, 26-27; WW II, 36
Buddhists, 123-24, 147, 338-39
Burma, 30-32, 86-90, 338-40; Army of, 255-57; and
    Communist China, 256; election in, 31-32;
    independence of, 87, 88; international relations,
    339-40; Karen rebellion in, 90; neutrality of, 253-60;
    rebellion in, 31-32; unrest in, 86-87, 89-90; and U.S.
    aid, 256, 259; and West, 257; workers in, 31; and
    WW II, 39-40, 44-46

Calley, William, 179, 182, 197-98, 280-81
Cambodia: aid to, 323; anti-Vietnamese feeling,
    186-88; Army, 213; bombing of 277-79; break with
    U.S., 126; and Communist China, 108, 126; and
    Communists, 108, 183-85; economy of, 194; famine
    in, 321-22; and French-Indochina War, 54; and
    French ties, 106; holocaust in, 324-25; and
    Indochina armistice, 61-62; Khmer Rouge in, 187;
    Lon Nol, 204, 284-85; malaise of, 208-9; peasant
    revolution in, 291-95; revolt in, 164; sanctuary role
    of, 168; surrender of, 286-87; Thai battle, 307; and
    U.S., 137, 143, 185, 188-90, 193-94; and Vietnam,
    308, 311-14, 323-24; *see also* Indochina; Sihanouk,
    Norodom
Cao Daism, 18-19
Chiang Kai-shek, 253, 254
China, Communist: and Burma, 253-60; and

Cambodia, 126; and Malaya, 80, 83; recognition by
    Cambodia, 108; and Singapore, 84; and Vietnam,
    314-17
China, Nationalist, 253
Chinese: and Indonesians, 238, 343, 355-56; and
    Malays, 249; in Malaysia, 332-33, 337-38; in
    Thailand, 227; Vietnamese, 309, 320-21
CIA, 202
Communists: in Burma, 88-89; in Cambodia, 108-10,
    183-85, 187, 291-95; in East Indies, 22; and Ho
    Chi Minh, 175-79; in Indochina, 20, 51-62, 103; in
    Indonesia, 229-30, 233, 236-38, 243-44, 341; in
    Laos, 108-10, 173-74, 297-301, 305-7; in Malaya,
    79-83, 246; *vs*Moslems on Java, 243; and
    Philippines, 97, 263, 268; in Singapore, 245; in S.
    Vietnam, 101, 115, 117; in Thailand, 222-23,
    226-28, 325, 331; *see also* China, Communist,
    Vietnam, North
Coolidge, Calvin, 10-13
Correa, Lt. Gen., 3
Cuba, 4

De Castries, Christian, 60
de Gaulle, Charles, 45-47
Dhanarajata, Srisdi, 222
Diem, Ngo Dinh, 60-61; and Army, 105; assassination
    attempt on, 107; and Bao Dai, 105-6;
    demonstrations *vs*, 123-24; election of, 116; ouster
    of, 125-26; reform by, 104; repression by, 111-12;
    U.S. support of, 119; and Vietnam conflict, 116-17
Dulles, John Foster, 103, 235
Dutch: East Indies, 21-23; empire of, 21-23, 66-68;
    and Indonesia, 66-68, 232, 235, 239, 241, 353;
    Morotai landing, 43; New Guinea, 76, 240-41;
    post-war reforms of, 38

East Indies, 21-23, 37-38, 40-41; *see also* Indonesia
Eden, Anthony, 58
Egypt, 232
Eisenhower, Dwight D., 56-59, 103

France: in Asia, 25-26; and Cambodia, 106; and
    Indochina, 16-21, 50-62; and Loatian Army, 110;
    and Siam, 26; and Thailand, 63-64; and Vietnam
    indpendence, 58; *see also* Vichy France
friars, 7-8
Fulbright, J.W., 116

Garcia, Carlos, 99, 260-61
gas warfare, 136

367

Pol Pot, 312-14, 321-22
Prajadhipokl, King, 27-30

Quezon, Manuel, 15, 16
Quirino Elpidio, 95, 96

Raman, Gopan, 335-36
Rama IX, King, 65
rebellion; Burmese, 31-32; East Indian, 22; in
    Philippines, 2-7; in Siam, 28-29; in Sumatra, 22;
resources, natural, 17-18, 23-24, 35
Roosevelt, Franklin, 15, 42-43
Roxas, Manuel, 91-93
rubber industry, 23-24
Russia, 52; *see also* Soviet Union

Sa-ngad Chaloryu, Admiral, 328, 331
Sanya Thammasak, 326, 327
Sarit Thanarat, Marshal, 223-26
Savang Vathana, 113-14
Saw, U, 88
SEATO, 224, 246-47, 274-75
Senkuttavan, Aru, 335-36
Siam, 25-30; constitution of, 29; and Europe, 26-27;
    King of, 27-30; revolt in, 28-29; *see also* Thailand
Sihanouk, Norodom, 54; foreign policy of, 126;
    neutrality of, 143, 168; ouster of, 183-85; plea for
    parley of, 318; recognition of Communist China by,
    108; resignation of, 301
Singapore, 24-25; commerce of, 83-84; Communist in,
    245; left wing in, 84; and Malaysia, 251; political
    repression in, 334-36; self-rule in, 85-86; surrender
    to Japan by, 38
Sjafruddin Prawiranegara, 236
Sjahriffoedin, Amir, 70
Souphanouvong, Prince, 121, 298
Souvanna Phouma, Premier, 113, 121, 122, 173-74,
    296-300
Soviet Union, 119, 122, 232; *see also* Russia
Spain, 2-4, 91
Stanton, Edwin, 253
Suekiman, Premier, 77
Suez Canal, 232
Suharto, Major General: demands on, 354; and
    economy, 354-55; as head of Army, 342-44; stability
    of, 347-49
Sukarno, 67, 70-72, 229-45; at Asian-African
    Conference, 230-31; assassination attempt on,
    234-35, 240; and communism, 243-44; death of,
    349-52; as dictator, 238-39; election of, 73-74; and
    Hatta, 234; hostility to U.S. of, 244-45; and leftists,
    77; and Malaysia, 248-50; and New Guinea, 76,
    240-41; new style rule of, 233; plot *vs,* 341-42;
    revolt *vs,* 75; and U.S., 235, 244-45; yielding of
    power by, 343-44, 347
Sumatra, 22; *see also* Indonesia
Sunarjo, Foreign Minister, 78

Taft, William, 7-8
Tanaka, Kakuei, 352-53
Thailand, 62-66, 222-29; -Cambodia battle, 307;
    Chinese in, 221-28; communism in, 325; coup,
    223-24, 326, 328-29, 331; death of King, 62-63,
    dispute with France, 63-64; election in, 224, 327;
    and Indochinese, 325-32; and Japan, 33-34; martial

law in, 228; new constitution in, 228-29; and
    refugees, 65, 330-32; unrest in, 326-27; and U.S.,
    65, 225, 328; and Vietnam, 65, 229, 329-30; *see also*
    Siam
Thakin Nu, 88
Thanat Khoman, 224, 226
Thang, Nguyen Duc, 167
Thanin Kraivichien, 331
Thanom Kittikachorn, 224, 225-27, 326-28
Thant, U, 247, 339
Thieu, Nguyen Van, 149-50, 156, 167, 171-72; election
    of, 202-3; and Laos invasion, 196; martial law by,
    208; and peace accords, 214-17; resignation of, 288
Thompson, Carmi A., 12-13
Truman, Harry, 91-92, 201
Tydings, Millard, 91-92

United Nations, 72, 243, 303, 346
United States: aid pact with Indonesia, 77; aid for
    S. Vietnam, 229; atrocities, 179-82, 186; bombing of
    Cambodia by, 277-79; and Burma, 253-60; and
    Cambodia, 126, 137, 185, 188-90, 192-94, 277-79;
    CIA Army in Laos, 202; and Cuba, 4; denunciation
    of, by Thieu, 288; ECA accord, 95; end of bombing
    by, 169; and French arms in Vietnam, 104; Gulf of
    Tonkin, 129-30; impact of, on Vietnam, 164-67; and
    Indochina, 103-222; jet watch over Laos by, 127-28,
    133; and Laos, 110, 121, 127-28, 133, 174, 202,
    296-97; and Philippines, 2-16, 90-99, 261-63, 362-63;
    and Sukarno, 235, 244-45; troops in Asia, 116; and
    Vietnam, 117-22, 191, 201-2, 229, 302-3; in Vietnam
    War, 134-222, 275-79; -Spanish War, 2-4; and
    Thailand, 65, 225, 328; in WW II, 36
Van Mook Hurbertus, 67, 69, 70
van Royen, Jan Herman, 72
Vichy France, 34
Vietcong. *See* Vietnam, North
Vietminh, 53-62
Vietnam: and Asia-Pacific Council, 274; and
    Cambodia, 308, 311-14, 323-24; and China, 314-17;
    and Chinese, 309; domination of Laos by, 314-15;
    independence from France, 58; postwar, 302-5,
    310-11; reunited, 302; split at 17th parallel, 61-62;
    and U.N., 303; U.S. involvement in, 201; *see also*
    Indochina
Vietnam, South: Bensuc, 152; brutality in, 195,
    211-12; Buddhists in, 123-25, 147; collapse of,
    209-10, 288-89; communists in, 109; corruption in,
    151-52; coup in, 127; election in, 149-50, 212;
    French arms in, 104; guerrilla war in, 115; heroin
    in, 281; and Ho Chi Minh, 103-4; hostility to U.S.
    in, 202; Innocent Civilian Center, 170; Ky in, 156;
    law in, 107; mass execution in, 210-11; new
    government in, 301-2; N. Vietnamese intrusion in,
    279, 281-84; peasants in, 111, 118, 120; rebellion in,
    123-26; reforms in, 104-5, 144-45, 280; restoration
    of, 290-91, 296; sabotage of North by, 129; Saigon
    evacuation, 285-86, 289-90; shifts in, 137-38; Thieu
    in, 156, 202-3, 288; U.S. aid to 117-21; U.S.
    atrocities in, 179-82; U.S. impact on, 164-67; U.S.
    soldiers in, 109; U.S. withdrawal from, 204, 275-77;
    war in, 123-24, 131-33; *see also* Diem, Ngo Dinh;
    Vietnamese; Vietnam War
Vietnam, North: reform in, 107; sabotage in, 129; an
    S. Vietnam, 279, 281-84, 288-91; subversion, 122;

U.S. air strikes in, 134-36, 150-51; *see also* Vietnam War

Vietnamese: boat people, 318-20; Cambodia *vs,* 186-88, Chinese, 320-31; refugees, 65, 149, 319-21; Thais *vs* 329-30

Vietnam War, 133-222; accord, 214-17; atrocities, 179-82, 186, 197-98; Bentre raid, 161-62; brutality in, 139-40; chronology of, 218-22; civilian losses in, 153, 155; Da Nang evacuation, 283-84; defoliation, 196; drive into Laos, 196; Hue destruction, 162-63, 283-84; new weapons in, 146-47; N. Vietnam morale, 157; N. Vietnam movement, 205; peace talks, 169-70; POW release, 206-7; Quangtri, 205; refugees, 149; rocket attacks, 170-71; Saigon during, 140; search and destroy, 167-68; surrender of S. Vietnam, 288-89; Tet offensive, 157-62; U.S. atrocities, 197-98; U.S. bombings, 138-39, 141-45, 148, 150-51, 153, 155, 169, 190-91, 195, 203-4; U.S. casualties, 156; U.S. mines, 206-8; U.S. tactics, 154-55; U.S. withdrawal, 204, 275-77

Wainwright, Jonathan, 40

war, 2-4, 33; *see also* Vietnamese War

weapons, 146-47

West, 331-32

Westmoreland, William, 142

Wilopo, Dr., 77

Wilson, Woodrow, 9

Wood, Leonard, 10, 13

World War II, 35-47